Principles of
Cost Accounting:
Managerial
Applications

The Willard J. Graham Series in Accounting

Principles of

Cost Accounting:

Managerial

Applications

Letricia Gayle Rayburn, Ph.D., CPA, CMA, CIA
Professor of Accountancy
Memphis State University

1983 • Revised Edition

Richard D. Irwin, Inc.
Homewood, Illinois 60430

ISBN 0-256-02800-1

Library of Congress Catalog Card No. 82–82883

Printed in the United States of America

1 2 3 4 5 6 7 8 9 0 K 0 9 8 7 6 5 4 3

To
Mike, Doug, and Beverly

Preface

This cost accounting textbook has been written to allow instructors flexibility in the chapter material presented. The first 11 chapters discuss cost accounting principles and concepts concerned with the collection of costs, which is an influencing factor in such managerial decisions as determining sales price. The last part of the book emphasizes the application of cost principles and quantitative tools to decision making.

Chapter 1 introduces the students to determining the need for and use of cost information. Chapter 2 discusses the basic cost concepts. An appendix illustrates factory ledger and home office ledger accounts. If students have not had a good foundation in inventory costing, Chapter 3 contains an appendix demonstrating these concepts; quantitative models for materials planning and control are contained in the Chapter 3 text. Labor accounting and learning curve theory is presented in Chapter 4. The third element of production cost, overhead, is presented in Chapters 5 and 6, with emphasis on understanding the behavior of overhead costs through regression analysis and other methods. If an instructor prefers, Chapters 15 and 16 can be presented before Chapters 5 and 6. Process costing is introduced in Chapter 7 in a unique way. Students are encouraged to think of a snowball gathering snow (cost) as it travels from one department to another. This analogy communicates the essence of the procedure of accumulating costs in a process system.

Standard costs for overhead analysis is uniquely presented so a closer relationship can be understood between the various methods of analysis. Standards provide a good introduction into Chapters 12 and 13 concerned with the budgeting process. Capital budgeting is present in Chapter 14 along with the other chapters devoted to planning and controlling cost.

Quantitative models including PERT analysis, decision tree analysis and linear programming are presented in Chapter 18 and 19. The last part of the text is devoted to performance evaluation and pricing analysis with separate chapters for behavioral factors in accounting control and marketing cost analysis. The use of costs in pricing decisions is presented in Chapter 22 followed by chapters discussing segment analysis and transfer pricing.

An appendix annotates the Cost Accounting Standards Board pronouncements; details of the standards are integrated into the relevant chapters.

To aid the student, each chapter begins with an outline of the chapter and a set of measurable objectives which focus attention on important areas of coverage. Each chapter also contains a listing of the important terms and concepts which can be helpful to students for review.

End-of-chapter material totals 422 discussion questions, 178 exercises, 217 problems, and 47 cases. Most of it is new or revised and has been thoroughly tested.

The supplementary materials accompanying the text include a detailed instructor's manual, which offers teaching suggestions and the solutions to all questions, exercises, problems, and cases. A Student Study Guide and Workbook for the student's assistance in obtaining an understanding of the material has been written by the author. The Study Guide is keyed to a chapter of the text and provides a detailed outline of each chapter, matching questions containing important new terms and concepts, true-false questions, completion questions, and exercises. Answers to all the questions are included in the Study Guide, providing verification of responses, as well as explanation as to why the statement is true or false. A list of key figures for each exercise and problem is available for students. Instructors may also obtain a booklet of supplementary test material including multiple-choice questions and short-answer problems, along with more comprehensive problems.

My first and most important acknowledgment goes to my husband, Mike, and children, Douglass and Beverly, who have supported my commitment to writing this book and its accompanying materials. I also acknowledge the helpful comments and support of the following: Charles Bailey, Florida State University; Arthur J. Brissette, Sacred Heart University; Samuel Chesler, University of Lowell; Cindy Heagy, Memphis State University; Richard S. Roberts, The University of Akron; Lamon P. Steedle, Lehigh University; Mary F. Strecker, Kansas State University; and James T. Thompson, Memphis State University.

In addition, many students have worked the problems to insure that they are as error-free as possible, and they have contributed ideas for more effectively presenting the concepts.

Appreciation also goes to the American Institute of Certified Public Accountants, the Institute of Management Accounting of the National Association of Accountants, and the Institute of Internal Auditors, Inc., for their permission to use problem materials from their past examinations. Problems from the

Uniform CPA Examination are designated (AICPA), problems from the Certificate in Management Accounting examinations are designated (CMA), and problems from the Certified Internal Auditing Examination are designated (CIA).

Suggestions and comments regarding the textbook and related materials are welcome.

Letricia Gayle Rayburn

Contents

Defective units. Spoiled goods. Inventory planning: *Stockouts, TOS, and B/O.*
ABC analysis and two-bin system: *Two-bin system. Automatic reorder system.*
Economic order quantity: *Effect of quantity discounts. Economic production
runs. Lead time.* Calculating safety stock and reorder points: *Reorder point.*
CAS 411. Appendix 3–A: Inventory costing methods. Appendix 3–B: Lower
of cost or market rule.

PART II

PRODUCT COST ACCUMULATION PROCEDURES

PART III

PLANNING AND CONTROL OF COSTS WITH STANDARDS AND BUDGETS

Direct-materials-purchases budget. Direct labor budget. Factory overhead budget. Cost of goods sold budget. Limitations of budgets: *Unrealistic budgets. Reporting shortcomings.* Participative budgeting process.

PART IV

COST ANALYSIS FOR DECISION MAKING

APPENDIXES

PART I

Basic cost accounting concepts

OUTLINE OF CHAPTER 1

Business goals

Organization chart

Relationship of cost accounting to other tasks

Comparison of cost accounting with financial accounting

Professional and government organizations

OBJECTIVES OF CHAPTER 1

1. To discuss business goals and organization structure.

2. To describe the nature of the production and service departments in the organization structure of a manufacturing firm.

3. To discuss the role of controllers in the organization structure and their relationship to cost accounting and other departments.

4. To contrast cost accounting, financial accounting, and managerial accounting.

5. To present the professional and government organizations that influence the cost accounting system.

1

The role of cost accounting in planning and control

Managers are faced daily with the problem of allocating resources to meet company objectives. Because these resources are limited, managers must decide which actions provide optimal returns to the company. An important aspect of managerial planning is coordinating the activities of individual segments to meet overall company objectives. To ensure that company goals are being met, management must rely on cost accountants to frequently provide operating information. Cost accounting not only aids managers in directing day-to-day operations but also provides feedback to evaluate and control performance.

BUSINESS GOALS

Before cost accountants can fill their role in planning and control, attention must be directed to setting company objectives. The primary goal of a business is to produce goods and/or services and sell them at a price which recovers all costs and yields an adequate return on invested capital. While most companies do not explicitly state this goal, it must be achieved if the company is to survive in the long run. Some authorities argue that a company is inhuman and that only humans can have goals. Although true in the narrow sense, the fact is that the company's stated goals are actually those of its dominant members, usually top management. However, no matter who has actually established the goals, a company must formalize them or it will be difficult for employees to know what is expected of them. Cost accountants provide financial data to assist others in establishing individual and departmental goals consistent with overall company goals. They then aid management by establishing cost controls and preparing timely reports on how these goals are being met.

Trade-offs

In trying to meet established goals, a number of cost trade-offs may be made. For example, while the company may wish to produce the highest quality product possible, it may find that the sales price required to cover all costs and yield an adequate return on capital would be higher than that for comparable products, so the product might not sell at an adequate volume. In this circumstance, the company trades off quality for price; that is, management reduces the quality and the cost of producing the product so the goods can be sold at a lower price and an adequate sales volume. Cost trade-offs also occur when an inventory level is chosen. Management may decide that it is desirable to carry a large inventory of finished goods to reduce the risk of running out of stock and losing customers. Maintaining a larger inventory means incurring additional warehousing, insurance, taxes, and other costs associated with carrying increased inventories. The costs of maintaining larger direct material inventory levels must be weighed against the cost of running out of these materials, and thus interrupting the production flow.

Goal congruence

The cost accounting system should encourage managers to achieve overall organization goals. To do this, company goals must be broken down into subgoals for individual managers. These subgoals should be consistent with the company's overall goals. Such *goal congruence* is an ideal that is difficult to achieve, for each manager has his or her own goals. An important personal goal of a manager is to earn enough money to meet the family's physical and social needs. This may conflict with the goals of the company, because a manager's higher salary means lower company profits. In addition, managers may be interested in obtaining power and prestige by increasing their functional responsibilities and the number of employees reporting to them, as well as engaging in creative endeavors. While recognizing that goal congruence is difficult to achieve, managers should carefully explain the company goals so employees can better understand their responsibility in achieving these goals. Managers should try to establish company goals so that employee goals are satisfied at the same time. The company's objectives should be stated in such a way that employee performance does not conflict with top management's goals.

ORGANIZATION CHART

An organization chart for a typical manufacturing firm is illustrated in Exhibit 1–1, which shows each organization unit or management position in a way that indicates authority and accountability relationships. In Exhibit 1–1, only the departments under the controller and the vice president of manufacturing are detailed. The responsibilities of the controller will be described in more detail in the section on Responsibility Accounting. The following departments report to the controller: cost accounting, taxes, systems analyst, programming, data processing, budgets and statistics, and general accounting. The general accounting department, in turn, consists of six groups: accounts payable, payroll, general ledger, accounts receivable, billing, and purchase and expense ledger. The managers of each of these groups report to the manager of the general accounting department. The vice president of manufacturing has authority over the following six departments: purchasing, storeroom, repairs and maintenance, inspection, production control, and production manager. In turn, three supervisors of production departments are shown reporting to the production manager; generally, there are many more production departments than are shown in Exhibit 1–1.

Formal and informal relationships. An organization chart shows formal management relationships and lines of authority and responsibility. An organization chart does *not* show the complex, informal relationships that exist in every company. The informal organization is a network of personal and social relations among the various employees. It arises from the social interaction of people and develops spontaneously as people associate with each other. Communication within the informal organization is rapid and is not usually written. By its nature, the informal organization is unstable and subjective. While the formal organization states positions in terms of authority and responsibility, the informal organization focuses attention on people and their relationships. Because an organization chart does not display informal relationships, it does not show precisely how the management process is actually accomplished.

Production and service departments

The organization chart shows both production and service departments. A production department is directly involved in processing materials into finished goods. Service departments provide "support" to production departments and are only indirectly involved in manufacturing items. Service department activities facilitate other departments' operations and contribute to their efficiency. Usually service department activities are specialized and centralized for economy and control. For example, by centralizing personnel skills and specialized equipment needed for repairs and maintenance, the quality of service is improved. For the service departments to operate economically, a volume of work justifying the employment of specialized skills and equipment is necessary. In Exhibit 1–1, three production departments, fabricating, assembly, and finishing, report to the production manager. The service departments illustrated in Exhibit 1–1 which are found in many manufacturing companies, include purchasing, storeroom, repairs and maintenance, inspection, and production control. The controller's group, including the cost accounting department, consists of service departments.

EXHIBIT 1–1

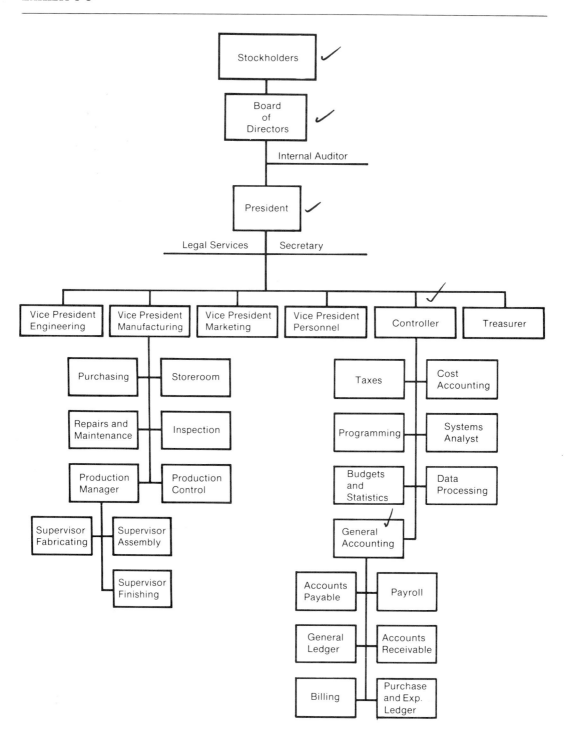

Service organizations.   While this discussion has centered around manufacturing activities, the production and service department concept is also applicable to nonmanufacturing organizations. For instance, the units which provide direct patient care in hospitals, such as surgery, are considered production departments while the administrative support departments, such as patient accounting and materials management, are referred to as service or ancillary departments.

Line and staff relationships

Some of the departments on the organization chart shown in Exhibit 1–1 are line departments and others are staff departments. Those holding line positions have the authority to make decisions and are responsible for the primary function, product, or service of the organization. Staff activities are those necessary to the organization but secondary or peripheral to the line functions. Those in staff positions give advice and service to other departments. The controller's organization is a staff department, and its members give advice and service to the production manager, supervisors, and others who report to the vice president of manufacturing. Controllers can only give specialized service and advice; they cannot compel departments to follow their recommendations. Controllers have staff authority because of their technical knowledge and the functions they perform. Generally controllers serve in a line capacity only with respect to the departments reporting to them (e.g., in Exhibit 1–1, the controller has line authority over taxes, cost accounting, programming, systems analyst, budgets and statistics, data processing and general accounting).

The creation of service departments is independent of line and staff relationships, although many service departments act in staff capacities. However, misunderstandings over delegated authority often develop when a service department acts in a staff capacity. For example, a production department may wish to move a machine to another plant location, but the repairs and maintenance department vetos the action because the move will create structural hazards. In this case, authority is delegated to the service department; it is not merely giving advice.

Functional authority.   Since a service department sometimes needs decision authority, it may be delegated functional authority. Functional authority is a hybrid relationship of staff and line and exists when an individual is permitted to act outside of the normal chain of command in certain specified activities. For example, often a service department will be given defined authority over certain activities of another department, or a controller will be given functional authority to instruct departments in compiling accounting information.

Responsibility accounting

In designing such an information system, the controller can use the responsibility accounting concept. The organization chart is the basis for a responsibility accounting system because it delineates areas of responsibility and indicates lines of authority. For example, in Exhibit 1–1, the president receives authority from the board of directors, who are elected by the stockholders. The president then delegates authority to the department managers who report to the president. These managers have authority over the units reporting to them. The accounting system can reflect this assignment of authority. With responsibility accounting, costs are reported to the person who has the decision-making authority for incurring the cost.

To be effective and able to hold one person accountable for results, management should assign task responsibility and the necessary authority to carry it out to the same person. Without clear responsibility delegation, control reports have little effect because no individual is responsible for taking corrective action. A responsibility accounting system is discussed in Chapter 20, Behavioral Factors in Accounting Control.

Controller is the common title given to the chief accounting officer in a company, but other titles may be used. The controller is the chief accounting executive and plays a significant role in planning and control activities. He or she is responsible for designing a cost accounting system so that all accounting functions, such as general accounting activities, as well as those relating to payroll, taxes, and financial reporting, can be performed effectively. The controller's functions also include establishing budgets and standard cost variance analysis. The controller may also prepare special managerial cost analyses, for example, comparing the cost of making parts with the cost of purchasing them.

The controller's duties differ significantly from those of the treasurer. The treasurer is concerned mainly with managing cash. A treasurer's duties include arranging short-term financing, maintaining banking and investor relationships, investing temporary excess funds, and supervising customer credit and collection activities. Each company separates the duties of the treasurer and controller differently. In fact, in many companies, both the controller and the treasurer report to the vice president of finance.

Role of controller and cost accountant. The controllership functions include assisting management in the decision-making process. The controller is responsible for establishing the cost accounting system that provides management with appropriate analytical data and operating results. The controller is concerned with internal reports to management and external reports to the public and government. As a member of the controller's department, the cost accountant is responsible for accumulating product costs and preparing accurate and timely reports to aid in evaluating and controlling company operations. The cost accountant has greater responsibilities in a manufacturing company than in a retail firm. In a manufacturing company, the accountant must accumulate information about the cost of a product from the time raw material is introduced until the manufacturing process is complete. Upon completion, the manufactured products are priced and are ready for sale. In a retail company, merchandise must only be purchased and priced before a sale can be made. The most significant difference between manufacturing cost accounting and retail cost accounting is that the manufacturing cost accountant must accumulate total product costs from many sources, while the retail accountant determines total product cost by referring to a vendor's invoice.

RELATIONSHIP OF COST ACCOUNTING TO OTHER TASKS

The cost accountant works closely with many people in other departments. Cost accounting reports are specifically designed to meet the needs of the user department. Consequently, the cost accountant must understand the user's information requirements and must also be able to communicate effectively with nonaccountants. The cost accountant frequently works with the following departments:

1. **Treasurer.** The treasurer uses budgets and related accounting reports to forecast cash and working capital requirements, and the cost accountant supplies this information. Cost accounting reports also assist the treasurer in investing temporary excess funds.

2. **Financial accounting.** The cost accountant also works closely with the financial accountants since cost information is generally integrated in the financial accounting system. This is discussed more fully in the next section. In determining the cost of inventory, the cost accountant provides input for income determination.

3. **Production.** Cost accountants work closely with production personnel to measure and report manufacturing costs. Cost accounting measures the efficiency with which the production department has scheduled and transformed material into finished units.

4. **Engineering.** The cost accountant may be asked to prepare cost estimates for a proposed product so management can decide whether to produce it. In establishing standards for the quality and quantity of material to be used in manufacturing and for the direct and indirect labor-hours required to produce each unit, the engineering staff must sample materials and conduct time and motion studies from which the standards are developed. Together, the cost accountant and the engineer translate these product specifications into estimated costs of material, labor, and overhead.

5. **Marketing.** Before the product's production schedule can be prepared, the marketing department must develop sales forecasts. Cost estimates supplied to marketing are used to establish selling prices and sales policies. While competition, supply, demand, and the state of technology principally determine the price to charge, manufacturing costs as well as marketing and administrative costs cannot be ignored.

   6. Personnel. Personnel must hire qualified people with the specific skills needed by the company. Personnel functions include interviewing job candidates, assessing their qualifications and skills in relation to the company's requirements, and hiring employees. Cost accounting uses the wage rates and pay methods supplied by personnel to the payroll department in calculating pay. Adequate labor records must be maintained for legal and cost analysis purposes.

   In meeting the information needs of other departments, cost accountants gather, report, and analyze cost data. Cost accounting is also concerned with accumulating all costs of making goods or rendering services. These cost data are necessary not only for income measurement and inventory valuation but also to help management plan and make operating decisions. As part of the job, the cost accountant interprets results, reports them to management, and provides analyses that facilitate decision making.

COMPARISON OF COST ACCOUNTING WITH FINANCIAL ACCOUNTING

   Financial accounting results in reports to *external* parties on the status of assets, liabilities, and equity; results of operations; changes in owners' equity; and changes in the source and use of funds for an accounting period. Creditors, present owners, potential owners, employees, and the public at large use financial accounting reports in decision making. On the other hand, cost data must be accumulated for *both* external financial accounting and internal management purposes. Cost accounting uses quantitative methods to accumulate, classify, and interpret information concerning the cost of materials and labor, and other costs of manufacturing and marketing. One objective of cost accounting is communicating financial information to management for planning, evaluating, and controlling resources. In fulfilling this objective, cost accountants develop data for determining the cost of inventory.

   One of the primary concerns of financial accounting is income determination; and in calculating income, financial accountants use the cost of inventory provided by the cost accountant. Consequently, cost accounting provides important input to financial accounting since it supplies the cost data for determining financial position and income. Ideally, cost accounting data are integrated into the financial accounting and reporting system. However, cost data may be compiled separately as statistical data.

   Cost accounting, then, is that part of accounting which identifies, defines, measures, reports, and analyzes the various elements of direct and indirect costs associated with manufacturing and providing a good and/or service. In the process of accumulating costs for inventory valuation and income determination, the needs of external users and management are fulfilled. Cost accounting also provides management with accurate, timely information for planning, controlling, and evaluating company operations.

Cost defined

Cost is a term used for the measure of the efforts associated with manufacturing a good or providing service. It represents the monetary measurement of material, labor, and overhead used. There is no one "true cost" of a good or service unless there is only one good being produced or service rendered. In that case, all costs will be allocated to this one good or service. Otherwise, costs incurred for all products or services must be allocated among these products and services. No two accountants may arrive at the same allocation when there is more than one product or service, even though both may be correct in their assumptions regarding the basis of allocation. As a result, the cost of a good or service may vary.

In a broad sense, "cost" refers to both assets and expenses and connotes a sacrifice made for the purpose of acquiring benefits. When benefits are to be received in the future, the incurred costs are initially recorded as an asset. When the asset benefits are received, the cost is matched against revenue and becomes an expense item when determining net income. For example, costs associated with the production of a good are reported as inventory (an asset) until the good is sold; at that time, inventory costs are transferred to cost of goods sold (an expense). Marketing and administrative costs are generally listed as expenses when incurred. Some costs, such as the acquisition of machinery, equipment, and plant facilities are capitalized as assets and charged to expenses through depreciation over their estimated useful lives since the services received from these assets extend over several accounting periods. Cost is generally used with other descriptive terms, such as historical, product, prime, labor, or material. Each of these terms defines some characteristic of the cost measurement process or an aspect of the object being measured.

Production, marketing, and administrative costs defined

All costs fall into three general classifications: *production, marketing, and administrative.* Production cost includes the direct material, direct labor, and factory overhead incurred to produce a good or service. Production activities also encompass product engineering and design. Marketing costs are incurred in selling and delivering products and include those costs incurred in promoting sales and retaining customers, as well as transportation, warehousing, and other distribution costs. Administrative costs are incurred in directing and controlling the company and for general activities such as personnel and legal functions. They include management and financial accounting salaries, clerical costs, telephone and telex costs, and rental fees. Administrative costs are incurred in assisting both production and marketing functions.

Since the access to cost data is not restricted to internal management, the cost accounting system must meet regulations which govern cost presentations in external reports. Internal Revenue Service regulations specify items to be included in taxable income and costs that may be deducted from income. The Financial Accounting Standards Board issues standards for external reporting.

The Cost Accounting Standards Board has standards that govern the measurement of costs in certain government contracts. Many cost reports for management are prepared for decision-making purposes (e.g., deciding what products to produce and the selling price). To the extent that these reports are used internally, there are few requirements imposed by regulatory bodies. Therefore, the cost accountant can use his or her initiative in applying cost accounting theory to the preparation of analyses and reports for management.

Planning and control activities

Cost accounting supplies information for management's planning and control activities. As an aid in planning, the cost accountant assembles, classifies, and summarizes financial and economic data on the production and pricing of goods or services and concisely presents the data to management. The cost accountant plays an important role in coordinating external and internal data so that management can better formulate plans. In the planning phases, cost accounting assists management by providing budgets reflecting estimates of material cost, labor cost, and other costs of manufacturing and marketing a product or providing a service. Cost accounting data also are used in product pricing, make-or-buy decisions, and capital budgeting. In planning and reviewing alternative courses of action, a company uses cost accounting reports to aid in selecting the best methods of attaining goals.

Control activities involve monitoring production processes and reporting variations from plans. In assisting in the control process, the cost accountant issues performance reports which provide a summary of activities. While planning activities look to the future, the control phase deals with the present. Actual results are compared with the budget to identify areas of deviation. Cost accounting then provides *feedback reports* for control activities and to ascertain whether established objectives are met. As related to the control process, *feedback* is information about current performance reported in such a way that future performance may be changed. Control reports can result in a change in performance only if management takes the initiative. A control report by itself cannot cause the change.

Even though cost information can be compiled outside the accounting system as statistical data, it is preferable to integrate cost data with the financial accounting system through accounting entries in journals and ledgers. Most cost accounting systems incorporate special factory journals to record and summarize cost data. Subsidiary ledgers record expense item details. In addition, special forms such as engineering bills of material, material requisitions, job time tickets, and job order sheets are designed and used for cost accounting purposes. Engineering bills of material indicate the type and quantity of material to be used in producing a specific part or job. Material issues to a production department are controlled using material requisitions. Job time tickets record the hours of labor applied to specific parts or jobs. Job order sheets accumulate the total cost for each production order. Under real-time systems, which are becoming more common, these forms are replaced by computer inputs. For example, employees may enter labor data directly into a computer terminal.

Cost analysis. Cost accountants obtain cost information from a variety of sources, and it is important that they organize all the facts obtained. Some of this information, such as vendor invoices, becomes the basis for journal entries, while engineering time and motion studies, timekeeper records, and planning schedules from production supervisors are used in cost analysis. Cost analysis first requires that the cost accountant identify and describe what is actually happening. Then, available alternatives must be identified before appropriate costing techniques are applied.

This book discusses several different types of analyses and control techniques which cost accountants can use in fulfilling their planning and control functions. These techniques include breakeven analysis, comparative cost analysis, capital expenditure analysis, and budgeting techniques. Each must be used appropriately. For example, while breakeven analysis indicates the capacity at which operations become profitable, it assumes a static condition in which sales price, expenses, and product mix are constant; however, a dynamic environment exists in the real world. Professional judgment must be used in applying and interpreting the results of such costing techniques.

In accounting there is a direct relationship between the time and the funds that management is willing to spend on cost analysis and the degree of reliability desired. If a company wants highly detailed records with a high degree of accuracy, it must provide additional time and money for compiling and maintaining such cost information. However, cost analysis and control techniques should not be used unless the anticipated benefits exceed the cost.

PROFESSIONAL AND GOVERNMENT ORGANIZATIONS

Several organizations have influenced the development of cost accounting theory. Some of these, such as the Financial Accounting Standards Board and the American Institute of Certified Public Accountants, are in the private sector, while other organizations, such as the Cost Accounting Standards Board, the Securities and Exchange Commission, and the Internal Revenue Service, are agencies of the federal government.

Financial Accounting Standards Board (FASB). Since 1973 when it replaced the Accounting Principles Board, the Financial Accounting Standards Board (FASB) has been the designated organization in the private sector for establishing standards for financial accounting and reporting. The seven members of the FASB serve full-time and must sever all connections with the firms or institutions they served prior to joining the board. The FASB issues *Statements of Financial Accounting Standards* which establish new standards or amend those previously issued. Some of these standards relate directly to the problems of measuring costs.

American Institute of Certified Public Accountants (AICPA).   The American Institute of Certified Public Accountants (AICPA) is a professional organization which publishes *The Journal of Accountancy*, a monthly publication that discusses recent developments in both financial and cost accounting. The AICPA also prepares, administers, and grades the Certified Public Accountant (CPA) examinations that are given each May and November. The CPA examination consists of five parts: commercial law, auditing, accounting theory, and two sections on accounting practice. Cost accounting is an important topic in the accounting practice sections. Candidates are tested not only on cost accounting procedures and techniques, but also on their ability to apply cost accounting principles to decision making. There are certain experience and education requirements involved.

American Accounting Association (AAA).   The American Accounting Association (AAA) is a professional organization of accounting educators and practicing accountants. The association establishes committees, some of which suggest cost standards. The AAA publishes the research reports of these committees as well as *The Accounting Review*, a quarterly journal of accounting theory.

National Association of Accountants (NAA).   Members of the National Association of Accountants (NAA) are interested in management accounting. Its Management Accounting Practices Committee has published several cost standards, although they are not binding. The NAA also publishes *Management Accounting*, a monthly journal concerned with current accounting practice. Several NAA research studies are published each year. The NAA established the Institute of Management Accounting which administers the Certificate in Management Accounting (CMA) program. The CMA program was created to recognize professional competence and educational attainment in the management accounting field. Candidates are required to pass a series of uniform national examinations that include five parts: economics and business finance; organization and behavior, including ethical considerations; public reporting standards, auditing, and taxes; periodic reporting for internal and external purposes; and decision analysis, including modeling and information systems. Cost accounting knowledge is tested in the last two parts. Candidates are also required to meet specific experience and education requirements.

The Institute of Internal Auditors (IIA).   The Institute of Internal Auditors (IIA) was organized in 1941 to develop the professional status of internal auditing. In the 1960s, the IIA's interest in a certification program grew, and the Certified Internal Auditing (CIA) program was developed. One of the requirements for attaining the CIA designation is successful completion of an exam which consists of the following four parts: principles of internal auditing, internal auditing techniques, principles of management, and disciplines related to internal auditing. Cost accounting is tested heavily in the last part. This certification program also has experience and education requirements.

Cost Accounting Standards Board (CASB). The U.S. Congress created the Cost Accounting Standards Board (CASB) in 1970 to promulgate cost accounting standards designed to achieve uniformity and consistency for government agencies in connection with cost-type negotiated contracts. The standards are to be used in pricing, administration, and settlement of negotiated defense contracts and subcontracts with relevant federal agencies. CASB standards become law 60 days after final publication in the *Federal Register* provided Congress does not enact a joint resolution in opposition. All negotiated *defense* contracts and subcontracts in excess of $100,000, except where exemptions and waivers are made, are subject to Cost Accounting Standards Board rules, regulations, and standards. CASB requirements are also adhered to in most *nondefense* cost-type contracts.

A contractor must indicate cost accounting practices in a *disclosure statement* usually filed before a contract is awarded. The practices used to develop contract proposal costs must be the same as those described in the disclosure statement. A summary of the cost accounting standards released is given in an appendix at the end of this text. In addition, certain standards are discussed in more detail in appropriate chapters.

As no funds were appropriated for the Cost Accounting Standards Board for fiscal 1981, the board went out of existence on September 30, 1980. The standards, rules and regulations of the board, however, remain in effect as the board was established by legislative mandate. Contracting agencies, principally the Defense Department and its auditors, continue to enforce the board's rules and regulations. New contracts are subject to the CAS clause requiring submission of a disclosure statement and compliance with the standards.

Internal Revenue Service (IRS). The Internal Revenue Service (IRS) is interested in cost accounting practices because of their impact on income determination for tax purposes. The IRS has issued a number of regulations regarding the costs that must be included in inventory. The IRS has also issued regulations on asset capitalization criteria, allowable depreciation methods and rates, indirect costs, and transfer pricing, among other topics.

Securities and Exchange Commission (SEC). The Securities Act of 1933 was designed to provide for full disclosure of relevant information and a record of representations involving the offering of securities for sale. Thus, any firm offering securities for public sale must file a registration statement and must also file financial statements and supporting schedules, most of which must be certified by an independent public accountant. The Securities Exchange Act of 1934 extended the disclosure principle to trading in already issued securities, and also established the Securities and Exchange Commission (SEC) to regulate the U.S. securities market. Since the SEC has statutory authority to regulate and prescribe the form, content, and compilation of financial statements, there has been close interaction between the SEC and the accounting profession in the development of financial accounting and reporting principles and practices.

Federal Trade Commission (FTC).   The Federal Trade Commission (FTC) administers the Robinson-Patman Amendment to the Clayton Anti-Trust Act. This law requires manufacturers to justify, on the basis of cost, discounts given to large-volume purchasers. Since complete cost information is necessary to defend charges under this law, it is an important motivating force for improved cost accounting.

Medicare.   The passage of the Medicare Bill of 1962 had a significant impact on the cost accounting systems used by health care institutions because it requires hospital management to submit cost information as a basis for reimbursement.

SUMMARY

Cost accounting is defined as that part of accounting which defines, identifies, measures, reports, and analyzes the costs of providing a good or service. This chapter explained the functions of the controller and of the cost accountant and their relationships with other departments in an organization. The cost accountant has flexibility in preparing cost accounting analyses and reports in a manner that best meets the company's needs. The needs of both external users and management are fulfilled by accumulating costs for inventory valuation and income determination. Cost accounting also provides information for management planning and control activities. Professional and government organizations that influence cost accounting systems were also discussed.

IMPORTANT TERMS AND CONCEPTS

Goal congruence	Feedback
Service departments	Financial Accounting Standards Board (FASB)
Production departments	American Institute of Certified Public
Line and staff departments	Accountants (AICPA)
Functional authority	CPA examination
Responsibility accounting	American Accounting Association (AAA)
Controller	National Association of Accountants (NAA)
Cost accounting	Certificate in Management Accounting (CMA)
Financial accounting	Certified Internal Auditor (CIA)
Cost	Cost Accounting Standards Board (CASB)
Production costs	Internal Revenue Service (IRS)
Marketing costs	Securities and Exchange Commission (SEC)
Administrative costs	Federal Trade Commission (FTC)

REVIEW QUESTIONS

1. Can a company have goals? If so, what are they?
2. What are the goals of managers? How can these be in conflict with the goals of the company?
3. (a) What is goal congruence? (b) Why is goal congruence difficult to achieve in a company? (c) What can be done to overcome this difficulty?
4. What does an organization chart show? Are some relationships not shown on the organization chart?
5. What production departments exist in a typical manufacturing company? Indicate the positions to which each department normally reports.
6. Discuss the level of authority inherent in line and staff departments.
7. What is functional authority? When may it be necessary for a controller to have functional authority?
8. What is the relationship between authority and responsibility?
9. Compare and contrast the duties of the controller, treasurer, and cost accountant.
10. Discuss the relationship of the cost accountant and other departments within the company.
11. Define cost accounting. How does it differ from financial accounting?
12. Define the term *cost* and compare it to *assets* and *expenses.*
13. What is the *true cost* of an asset or service rendered?
14. Describe the three classifications of costs.
15. Define the term *feedback.* What role does cost accounting play in providing feedback to management?
16. What is the function of the cost accountant and how does the cost accountant assist management?
17. Discuss the impact of professional organizations on the development of cost accounting theory.
18. What federal agencies influence accounting practices?

CASES

C1–1. Determining cost information needed

Joe Toone, a friend of your family, has just learned that you are now enrolled in a cost accounting course, so he seeks your advice. Joe has just finished high school, graduating in the top third of his class. However, his grades were not high enough to make him eligible for a scholarship. Joe's family has limited resources, and it will be a financial strain for Joe to major in accounting at the state college 100 miles from his home.

However, Joe has an opportunity to attend a vocational school in his hometown. He feels that with the accounting courses he takes at the vocational school he can become a cost clerk or bookkeeper with a local company.

Joe also has received an offer of a job as a machine operator from a local manufacturing company. He would receive on-the-job training at the same time that he earned a wage.

Required:

a.   In advising Joe, what cost information would be helpful?

b.   What factors are pertinent to the decision? Can they be quantified?

C1–2.   Evaluating cost accounting reporting system

You have recently been hired as a cost accountant for the Eliott Manufacturing Company. On your first day at work, the controller gives you a schedule for preparing cost reports that appears to be rather tight. The controller stresses that the cost statements and analyses must be on the president's desk by 9 A.M. on the specified day.

After the accounting period ends, you must work overtime to be certain that the statements are prepared on time. A fellow accountant tells you not to spend too much time on the reports, since there is never any feedback. He also comments, "Don't get any bright ideas and suggest to the controller that we start investigating any deviations from planned results, since our workload is heavy enough now."

Required:

Do you see anything wrong with the present cost accounting reporting system?

C1–3.   Line and functional authority

Portions of the organization chart for Love Company are given on page 19.

Required:

a.   If you were the supervisor of the preparation department, would the following persons have line or functional authority over you?
  (1)   Vice president-engineering
  (2)   Production control manager
  (3)   President
  (4)   Production manager
  (5)   Controller
  (6)   Director of purchasing
  (7)   Director of legal services
  (8)   General accounting manager

b.   If, instead, you were supervisor of the payroll department, would each of the persons indicated in *a* have line or functional authority over you?

c.   Indicate which production departments report to the vice president, manufacturing.

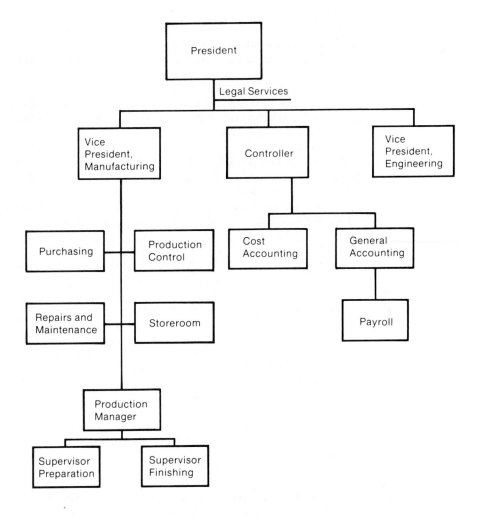

C1–4. Preparation of an organization chart

The Hall Company is being formed and solicits your help in preparing an organization chart. The following positions and departments, arranged in alphabetical order, are only a few of those the executive committee has approved:

Accounting systems design	President
Banking and financing	Production superintendent
Budgeting	Storeroom
Cash management	Tax administration
Controller	Treasurer
Cost accounting	Vice president—finance
General accounting	Vice president—engineering
Insurance management	Vice president—manufacturing
Investor relationships	

Required

Prepare an organization chart for the company.

C1–5. Evaluating a cost reduction plan

Under a continuing education program with a local university, all top and middle managers of the Tilly Company attend a managerial cost seminar. After hearing the session on cost reduction programs, one of the vice presidents actively begins to search for ways to cut costs in the company. He becomes alarmed when he finds that the company is furnishing employees styrofoam coffee cups costing $0.005 each. Department heads request these cups from purchasing. The cost is absorbed by the company, as each department is not billed individually.

Upon investigation, the vice president finds that each department has its own coffee pot. Employees drop in a dime for every cup of coffee they drink. This coffee fund is used to buy the department's coffee, cream, and sugar. The vice president decides that it is too expensive for the company to furnish the coffee cups and orders the purchasing department to inform the individual departments that they will be billed for the cost of the cups.

As a result, all departments become hostile and decide to take their coffee breaks in the company cafeteria. Previously they stayed in their departments, and if they were behind schedule, they drank their coffee at their desks. Due to the distance of many departments from the cafeteria, it takes some of the employees 20 to 30 minutes to get to the cafeteria, drink their coffee, and return to their desks.

Required:

Evaluate the effectiveness of the vice president's cost reduction plan.

C1–6. Planning and control activities: Production and service departments

As a cost accountant for the Chicago Manufacturing Company, Mary Miller has responsibility for supplying information for management's planning and control activities. Examples are given below.

1. Summarizing budgets reflecting estimates of material, labor, and overhead costs for the Mixing Department.
2. Preparing statements of income and balance sheets which provide a summary of performance activities.
3. Preparing a differential cost analysis reflecting estimates for buying plant equipment for the Fabricating Department as opposed to Chicago's production and engineering personnel building the equipment.
4. Comparing actual results of operation for the Maintenance Department to the department's budget.
5. Analyzing the impact on net income of a proposed new product using various contemplated prices and volumes.
6. Analyzing the costs of several different proposed combinations of skilled labor and automated equipment to process material in the Finishing Department.
7. Interpreting variances on a Mixing Department supervisor's performance report.
8. Making forecasts of future prices, tax rates, competitive strategies, and other economic factors.
9. Measuring the success of the Sewing and Treating Department by computing the ratio of earnings to investment of capital.
10. Preparing an analysis using various capital budgeting techniques to evaluate

purchase alternatives for a machine to be used in the Electronic Data Processing Department.

Required:

For each of the above items, identify whether the information being prepared will primarily serve management's planning or control needs. Also state, where possible, whether the departments mentioned are service or production departments.

C1–7.   Problems in information system

After looking at a pile of reports on his desk, the Vice President of Anthony McKinnon Manufacturers remarked to one of the supervisors reporting to him, "I take several reports home every night; I just don't have time at the office to read and study all the reports I receive. But I often can't even get through all the pages at home." The vice president then picked up a report on the top of the pile and said, "See this report? You should have also gotten a copy yesterday. It will take me two hours tonight to wade through all these data."

Further conversation revealed that with the introduction of the company's computer system two years ago, the amount of management data increased significantly. The vice president even remarked, "I almost wish for the 'good ole days' when one of the major problems was obtaining management control information."

When the computer system was installed, the old manual system was studied to determine how the conversion could best be accomplished. Since the majority of top managers were unfamiliar with computer design or occupied with pressing operational problems, they were not involved in designing the reports. The top managers contacted by the system designers generally gave the following comment, "Give me the computer run, and then I will figure out exactly how to use it." One top manager, who did supply the system designers with assistance, suggested that any actual cost that exceeded the budget adjusted for year to date by 10 percent be printed out on an exception report.

Required:

Discuss problems inherent in the information system.

C1–8.   Preparing present and future organization charts

Robert Banks was an engineer employed in research for a large manufacturing company before he left to form his own company which will be a single proprietorship engaged in the manufacture of pumps. He plans to divide the factory into three manufacturing departments—fabricating, assembly, and finishing—which will employ 150 people. Banks will be president and in charge of all engineering and research.

At present, he is trying to decide what key personnel are needed. He realizes that operations will be on a small scale in the beginning, but to attract these individuals into the company, he would like to show them not only their position on the organization chart now, but also their position and relationship when the company grows to its expected size, employing 1,500 factory workers.

Banks is limited financially to hiring no more than three people at a vice president level. One of these vice presidents could have an assistant. A supervisor will be hired for each of the three manufacturing departments.

Required:

a.   Prepare an organization chart for the newly formed company indicating a division of duties.

  b. Prepare a proposed organization chart for the company after it has grown and is hiring 1,500 people. Indicate the additional managerial positions you feel will be necessary for the production and accounting functions.
  c. Discuss the reasons for the division of duties you show in the organization chart prepared in *b.*

C1–9. Cost information needed

Having had experience in metal handling, Sam Miller decided to invest a part of his savings, form his own company, and "be his own boss." He realizes that his company will have to be small, especially at first, but he believes that his savings will be large enough to provide an initial down payment for equipment and supplies. He has talked with a local banker and received the bank's backing to borrow limited funds for working capital.

His analysis of the market reveals that the concern for energy will encourage consumers to install wood-burning fireplaces. He has designed self-contained units with enough flue pipe provided to reach an 8-foot ceiling. Some models will include a reducer and a grate along with brass ornaments, while other, lower-priced models will not include these items. The more expensive models will include glass paneled doors. The fireplaces will be priced from $500 to $800, depending on the model. Miller will employ two people who can install the fireplaces. Customers can either have the fireplaces delivered or pick them up at the factory.

After investigating the vacant buildings available, Miller secured a lease on a building which is adequate for initial production. The building was formerly used as a small factory for producing motors.

Miller plans to start operations with 5 employees and gradually hire another 5 so that at the end of the first year there will be 10 employees working one shift. His long-range plans include adding enough employees for a second shift in two to three years.

Miller and an engineer have drawn up plans for two standard styles of fireplace-heaters and plan to complete three more plans before operations begin next month. The engineer has not been hired on a full-time basis. Plans for custom-made fireplace-heaters will be prepared with the engineer being paid a fee.

Miller is undecided about the amount of advertising he will undertake; however, he realizes that there are several firms in his city performing similar work with which he will have to compete. He plans to advertise custom work in designing and installing fireplace-heaters for new homes and to emphasize the standard models for older homes that already have flues. He has talked with several local residential building contractors and is considering giving them a discount as a means of obtaining customers.

Miller realizes the importance of maintaining adequate accounting records, but he is reluctant to spend much of his time in detailed cost analysis since he is of the opinion that he can more profitably spend his time in production activities. He wonders if checkbook stubs and a few other records will be sufficient for tax return and management purposes.

Required:

What type of records does Miller need and why does he need the ones you suggest?

C1–10. Evaluating controls on telephone system

Lynn Grove Memorial Hospital is encountering some difficulties with its telephone system. At present, general accounting pays the telephone bill without checking the charges.

Your initial survey of the telephone situation reveals that there are several special styles of phones in the hospital other than the standard black model. In addition, there are phones of various colors in the hospital staff's offices. When you ask the assistant administrator the reason for this, you find that any time a hospital employee desires a special style or color, all that is necessary is to tell the chief telephone operator who sends the requisition to the Western Phone Company. The same procedure is also followed when an employee wants a phone moved.

Eleven months ago, Lynn Grove Memorial Hospital adopted a new phone system which allows calls from outside the hospital to be dialed directly to patients' rooms and staff offices. Management feels that this is an improvement over the switchboard system previously used. With the new phone system, Western Telephone provides a monthly computer printout of the telephones and equipment being charged to the hospital.

There are both public and semipublic pay phones in the hospital buildings. Public pay phones are located in the lobbies and high-traffic areas. These public pay phones do not cost the hospital anything as long as there are 30 calls a day. Semipublic pay telephones are not located in a lobby, but can be used by the general public. Because of their locations, fewer calls are made on semipublic phones than on public pay phones. As a result, a monthly charge is made to the hospital for these phones. The hospital staff feels that it is justified in asking Western Phone Company to install the semipublic phones; otherwise, there would be requests to place calls on nursing station phones. However, there is a question as to whether all semipublic phones are needed. Hospital management wants you to investigate this matter.

One of your first steps on the job is to locate all telephones and equipment using the computer printout supplied by the Western Phone Company. You find bills for 17 telephone lines at $15 per month that are no longer in existence, as well as various equipment totaling $250 per month that the hospital used in the past but no longer has.

You notice also that the hospital is incurring a large expense for long-distance calls each month. After tracing down these calls, you find that many arise when a collect long-distance call is made to a patient's room. The patient accepts the collect call, but in the majority of the cases, by the time the phone bill arrives the patient has left the hospital. Under the present billing system, the hospital is forced to absorb this expense. In addition, hospital employees making personal long-distance calls while at work are charging these calls to the hospital.

When you report your findings to the administrative staff, they contact Western Phone Company concerning the 17 nonexistent telephones and other equipment. This proves a very embarrassing situation to the sales representative serving the hospital's territory.

Required:

a. Determine the extra total expense the hospital has incurred for the nonexistent telephones and equipment as shown on the hospital records.

b. As their consultant, what would you advise them to do with regard to the expense of the nonexistent telephones and equipment? What factors should be considered in reaching a settlement with Western Phone Company?

c. What other changes would you advise the hospital to make in their telephone system?

C1-11. Flaws in the organization chart

Manual Company's organization chart is presented on the following page.

EXHIBIT C1–11

Flaws in an Organizational chart

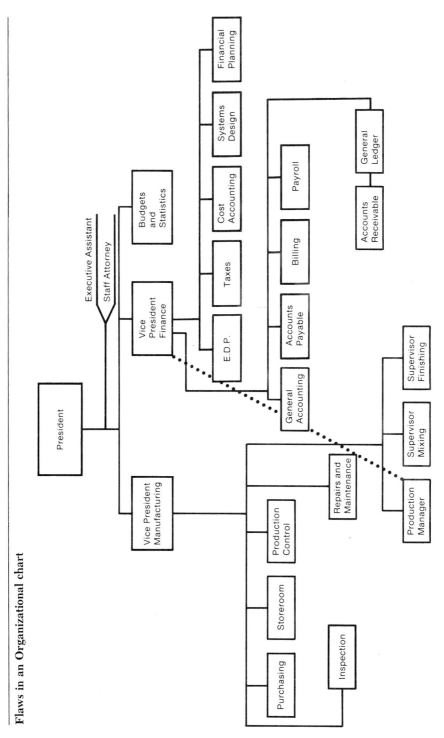

Each vice president is complaining about overlapping authority and responsibility. The vice president of finance argues that she needs indirect control over production areas; otherwise, she believes that the production personnel will not follow prescribed accounting policies. The vice president of manufacturing recognizes the dilemma but is finding that his production manager relies too much on what the vice president of finance says. The production manager points to a dotted line on the organization chart that extends from the vice president of finance to his box and asks to whom he is supposed to report. The production manager is also having problems with his two supervisors because they often fail to go through him; instead, they go directly to one of the vice presidents.

These are similar to the problems experienced by the general accounting supervisor. She is finding that her accounts payable and accounts receivable supervisors go directly to the vice president of finance. The budgets and statistics director contends that he must report to the president rather than to the vice president of finance because of the sensitivity of his areas. The vice president of finance finds this a most difficult arrangement since it precludes her receiving pertinent information.

The Manual Company seeks your advice regarding its organization chart.

Required:

a. Indicate any flaws you detect in the organization chart.
b. Draw an improved organization chart eliminating the flaws.

C1–12. Organization charts: Potential organizational problems

The Bevan O'Callaghan Company was organized by two engineers, an accountant, and an attorney. The principal business activity is the manufacture and assembly of telephone equipment. Basically, there are two product lines; one is a communication system designed for residential use while the second line is more elaborate and complex and is tailored for commercial installations. In addition, the company performs contract work for government units. Not only does the company have a healthy domestic market, but sales to European countries have also continued to grow.

Sales for the first year were $80,000 with a substantial deficit; however, the second year's sales increased to $700,000 with a sizable profit. Since then, both sales and earnings have increased yearly.

The following is the organization chart for the first year:

In the early stages, most of the accounting work was performed by O'Callaghan's external auditor who organized the books and set up the bookkeeping procedures. Very informal budgets employing approximations of factory overhead, marketing, and administrative expenses are still being used. The vice president of finance's main responsibility is preparing detailed cash flow projections since cash is a critical issue. A secretary keeps the cost records. Accounting information is used only to a limited extent; however, fairly adequate cost records are kept on the government contract work since it is required by government auditors.

The president assists the vice president of finance in closely checking the cash position and receivables. Quarterly income statements, which are prepared by the external auditors, are also examined closely since the company is strongly profit motivated. Projects engineers also play an important role in cost control, as each development program is budgeted or funded for a specific amount of money. Each project engineer has the responsibility for developing the product and, in turn, performing the designated task within the amount specified. If the engineers meet their

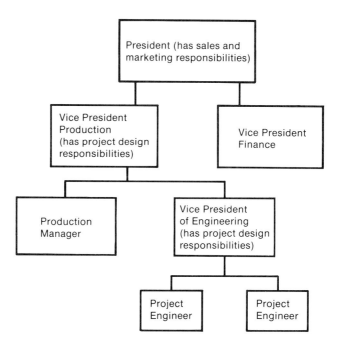

budgets, they are rewarded with bonuses; otherwise, they are penalized even to the extent of termination.

The project engineer's task is difficult because he or she is involved not only with many complex design problems but also with time and budget constraints. Many of the company's engineers have erred in designing technically perfect products that were so expensive to produce that sales prices were prohibitive. It is not surprising, then, that the average project engineer feels cost accounting data are a nuisance that impedes efforts to arrive at a superior design.

When the number of employees nears 100 and sales approach $3 million, management believes it will become necessary to substantially refine accounting and cost control procedures. A controller will be hired to establish a simple budgeting system and introduce a rudimentary standard cost system for production work. Management plans to employ an outside engineering firm to establish standards for material, labor, and overhead, which will be scientific goals or yardsticks by which the efficiency of factory employees will be measured.

At this time, it is anticipated that the basic organization of the company will be changed by dividing it into two separate, almost entirely autonomous, divisions— namely, the Residential Products Division and the Commercial Products Division. A sales manager reporting directly to the president will be hired for each division. The position of vice president of production will be split into two positions, one over each division. Each vice president will have a production manager and an engineering manager. Two project engineers will report to each engineering manager. The performance of each operating division will be measured on the basis of its profitability. Consequently, different criteria must be developed; it is anticipated that higher objectives and profit goals will be set for the commercial division.

It is also believed that management must continue to be extremely sensitive to company cash requirements. The vice president of finance or the controller will probably not have adequate time to devote to the preparation of detailed cash projections and the interaction necessary with company creditors.

Management predicts that major organizational changes will not be necessary until sales reach $19 million and employees total 550. Since management's philosophy of organization is that small units are more efficient than large ones, several profit centers will be added. A personnel director will also be hired for recruiting and handling employee transfers.

Several additions in the accounting organization will be necessary as the firm hires more employees and increases its number of creditors and customers. More sophisticated and rapid reporting will require the acquisition of a computer. Monthly and possibly biweekly income statements will be necessary.

Expansion will also be necessary in other areas as sales to the federal government and Europe increase. Managers overseeing these two areas will be needed. They, along with the sales manager of each division, will report to the newly created position of marketing manager. Profit centers for fixed channel equipment operations, synthesized equipment operations, and spare parts operations will be added under the vice president of commercial production. Each profit center will have its own production and engineering supervisors. A quality control manager will be needed in the residential division.

Required:

a. Prepare an organization chart to accommodate 100 to 550 employees.
b. Expand your organization chart for a period in which employees number 550 to 800.
c. Problems among the accounting, production, marketing, and engineering staffs are anticipated; mention five potential problems.
d. Give several factors in support of management's philosophy of small organizational units.

C1–13. Information needs for production and marketing

New York Manufacturing Company was organized 30 years ago. The President started with the company as a supervisor and has served in various managerial capacities. On the other hand, the vice president of marketing joined the company last year after serving as an administrator in another industry. A vice president of production and a vice president of accounting/finance have each been with the company 10 years.

The company has 1,000 employees producing and selling detergents and other household cleaning products in several neighboring states. All production is accomplished in one plant, but there are several marketing branches. Processing is accomplished with two labor shifts working six days a week. All research activities for new product development are performed in the plant facilities.

Required:

a. Contrast the information needs of the president and the vice president of marketing.
b. Discuss the important information needs of the production, marketing, and accounting/finance vice presidents in controlling operations.
c. Design a report format for the vice president of production and the vice president of marketing. Suggest possible items that should be included in each area.

C1–14. Determining information needed from an accounting system

Plywood Plastics Manufacturing Company was formed as a partnership 25 years ago by Buell Edmonds and Harold Douglass after Edmonds, a successful business executive in the floor-covering business, acquired a plastic franchise. His new product was to be bonded with plywood and used for sink tops, paneling, and tabletops. Edmonds and Douglass were long-time friends, and Edmonds considered Douglass to have the technical expertise necessary to successfully produce a product. For years, Douglass had been an industrial arts teacher in a large metropolitan school district.

Each partner placed $5,000 in the business, and the partnership leased space behind a garage. Edmonds worked for the business in an administrative capacity, while Douglass worked part-time, mainly at night and on Saturdays. After approximately two years, since the business was prospering, the company moved to a larger location at which time each partner invested additional money.

Originally, the company's business consisted of custom-made products for new and remodeled homes; however, it gradually expanded operations so that emphasis shifted from single custom orders to larger commercial orders. Eventually the bulk of its business came from several large national motel chains and one large, national mail-order house. Operations expanded to the extent that Plywood Plastics was producing custom counter tops for mail-order catalog sales for the entire United States and Canada. In addition, they were engaged in shipping vanity tops and bathroom sink tops all over the world for the motel chains. After the purchase of new, modern equipment, Plywood Plastics began producing rough-slab products for sale to several large makers of kitchen tables; these firms further processed the products.

By this time, Douglass had resigned from his teaching position and was working full-time with the company. Eventually, Plywood Plastics became a corporation with each partner receiving 50 percent of the stock and Douglass was named the general manager. Ten years ago, when Edmonds retired, Douglass purchased his holdings and became the sole owner. Five years later, Douglass sold all his holdings to a group of six investors; however, he remained a member of the board of directors since the investors owed him a portion of the sales price which was secured by collateral in the company.

Immediately after the sale, the assistant manager, who was also one of the six investors, became president and general manager. Within one year a very profitable business began to lose money, at which time the board fired the manager and rehired Douglass on a daily consulting-fee basis. Within six months, Plywood Plastics was once again experiencing sizable profits; however, since Douglass did not want to remain active, the board hired another full-time manager and president. Profits have decreased to the point where the company is breaking even.

At present, the company has a work force of 40 employees which represents a reduction from the 100 workers employed during peak production. Although the production work force has been cut, the administrative staff remains the same—a general manager, two bookkeepers, and two salespersons. The company remains approximately one month behind in filling orders which is presenting some problems since its competitors are able to fill orders much more quickly. Often it is unable to begin processing an order after it is received because the material necessary must be ordered first. The only finished goods inventory produced for stock are vanity tops processed for the mail-order company; all other items are manufactured only after an order is received.

Plywood and plastic constitute the two main raw material inputs. The manufacturing process operates on an assembly line with the following four main steps involved:

1. A section where the plywood and plastic are glued together.
2. A section where any necessary bending takes place.
3. A section where the slab is cut to specifications.
4. The final section where any molding or other refinements take place.

When Douglass was general manager, he would call the three factory supervisors into his office and give them their work orders for the day. When the regular assembly line employees reported each day, material necessary for production had already been obtained from the storeroom. Because of his long experience, Douglass was able to correctly estimate the labor-hours needed for each batch of products, and profits per square feet of production could be forecasted with a high degree of accuracy. During each workday, Douglass would check with the supervisors on the progress of each job.

The company does not have any type of cost accounting system nor does it maintain a perpetual inventory system. Even though the company is closing its books each month, a physical inventory is taken only once per quarter; management estimates inventory values for other months. Earnings are usually only determined for months in which management has estimated the inventory values. Finished goods are valued at 80 percent of sales price, and work in process at 70 percent of sales price. A local CPA firm prepares the year-end statements and tax returns.

Required:

What recommendations would you make for improving the company's profitability; include in your recommendations the type of information the company needs from its accounting system.

OBJECTIVES OF CHAPTER 2

1. To discuss and define the elements of manufacturing costs.
2. To identify, define, and discuss basic cost concepts and vocabulary.
3. To show the flow of manufacturing costs through the inventory accounts.
4. To introduce the cost of goods manufactured statement.
5. To emphasize the importance of cost behavior patterns.
6. To illustrate the basic journal entries associated with a job order cost accounting system.
7. To illustrate the use of reciprocal factory and home office ledger accounts.

2

Basic cost concepts and manufacturing statements

This chapter introduces and defines a limited number of basic ideas in order to develop a working knowledge of significant cost concepts. Additional concepts and terms will be discussed in subsequent chapters. Accumulating cost data to determine the cost of a product is emphasized. These product costs are shown on the cost of goods manufactured statement, which is discussed and illustrated. To compute the amounts appearing on this statement, the cost accountant must use ledger accounts which differ from those of the typical merchandising firm. These differences are illustrated in this chapter.

FINANCIAL STATEMENTS

A company's basic financial statements normally consist of the balance sheet and related statements of income, retained earnings, and changes in financial position. There is a significant difference in the inventory account titles used by a merchandising company, a manufacturing company, and a service organization. Retailers and other merchandising companies sell goods in substantially the same physical form that they purchased them in. A merchandiser generally has only one inventory account, called Merchandise Inventory, which shows finished goods available for sale. A manufacturing company converts materials into finished goods and generally has four inventory accounts, Direct Materials Inventory, Factory Supplies Inventory, Work in Process Inventory, and Finished Goods Inventory, showing materials available for processing, un-completed goods, and completed goods. A service organization furnishes intangible services rather than tangible goods and may have a Direct Materials Inventory. Professional service organizations may have unbilled work consisting of costs incurred for clients which corresponds to a manufacturer's work in process, but it does not have finished goods inventories. Exhibit 2–1 illustrates a balance sheet for a merchandising company, while Exhibit 2–2 contains a manufacturing company's balance sheet. Even though the four manufacturing inventory accounts generally are grouped into one inventory caption on a balance sheet, they are detailed for illustrative purposes in Exhibit 2–2.

Inventory accounts

In merchandising, the company buys a finished product, places a price tag on it, and displays it for sale. The merchandiser has an invoice from the

EXHIBIT 2–1

BROWN MERCHANDISING COMPANY
Balance Sheets
As of December 31, 19X1, and 19X0

Assets	19X1	19X0
Current assets:		
Cash	$ 20,000	$ 15,000
Accounts receivable	75,000	90,000
Merchandise inventory	183,000	240,000
Prepaid insurance	2,000	5,000
Total current assets	280,000	350,000
Property, plant, and equipment:		
Land	50,000	50,000
Building	100,000	100,000
Furniture and fixtures	150,000	155,000
Less: Accumulated depreciation	(80,000)	(55,000)
Total property, plant and equipment	220,000	250,000
Total assets	$500,000	$600,000
Liabilities and Stockholders' Investment		
Current liabilities:		
Accounts payable and accruals	$ 62,000	$150,000
Income taxes payable	8,000	10,000
Total current liabilities	70,000	160,000
Long-term liabilities—mortgage payable	110,000	140,000
Total liabilities	180,000	300,000
Stockholders' investment:		
Common stock, 20,000 shares authorized and issued,		
$10 par	200,000	200,000
Retained earnings	120,000	100,000
Total stockholders' investment	320,000	300,000
Total liabilities and stockholders' investment	$500,000	$600,000

supplier as evidence of what the product costs. Production accounting is more involved because the manufacturer must accumulate the costs of materials, labor, and overhead to determine the product costs. Exhibit 2–2 shows that a manufacturing company generally has four basic inventory accounts: Direct Materials, Factory Supplies, Work in Process, and Finished Goods. Through the application of labor, machinery, equipment, and other productive elements, the manufacturer converts raw materials into finished products.

Raw material on hand, which will become a part of the finished product, is reported in an asset account titled Direct Materials Inventory or Materials Inventory. Stores and Materials are also used as titles for this account; however, these titles inadequately describe the asset nature of the account.

EXHIBIT 2–2

WELLS MANUFACTURING COMPANY
Balance Sheets
As of December 31, 19X1, and 19X0

Assets	19X1	19X0
Current assets:		
Cash	$ 20,000	$ 15,000
Accounts receivable	75,000	90,000
Direct materials inventory	32,000	16,000
Factory overhead supplies	6,000	4,000
Work in process inventory	31,000	40,000
Finished goods inventory	114,000	180,000
Prepaid insurance	2,000	5,000
Total current assets	280,000	350,000
Property, plant, and equipment:		
Land	50,000	50,000
Building	100,000	100,000
Machinery and equipment	150,000	155,000
Less: Accumulated depreciation	(80,000)	(55,000)
Total property, plant and equipment	220,000	250,000
Total assets	$500,000	$600,000
Liabilities and Stockholders' Investment		
Current liabilities:		
Accounts payable and accruals	$ 62,000	$150,000
Income taxes payable	8,000	10,000
Total current liabilities	70,000	160,000
Long-term liabilities—mortgage payable	110,000	140,000
Total liabilities	180,000	300,000
Stockholders' investment:		
Common stock, 20,000 shares authorized and issued, $10 par	200,000	200,000
Retained earnings	120,000	100,000
Total stockholders' investment	320,000	300,000
Total liabilities and stockholders' investment	$500,000	$600,000

Supplies which will be used in factory maintenance, repair, and cleaning are classified as *Factory Supplies* Inventory.

The Work in Process Inventory account is used to accumulate costs incurred in manufacturing a finished product. At the end of a month or other accounting period, some units will be only partially completed. The production costs of these semifinished units at the end of a period are accumulated in the Work in Process Inventory account. This account may also be called Goods in Process Inventory. The finished product can be sold (1) to another manufacturer, who will further refine it or use it as a component of a product; (2) to a wholesaler or retailer for resale; or (3) directly to the final consumer. Cost of the finished product is ultimately accumulated in a Finished Goods Inventory account.

ELEMENTS OF PRODUCTION COSTS

Three types of factory costs are incurred in manufacturing an item: (1) direct material, (2) direct labor, and (3) factory overhead.

Direct material

Direct material is any raw material that becomes an identifiable component part of the finished product. For example, in manufacturing men's shirts, the fabric is direct material. Direct materials may be purchased in various forms. Some direct material is purchased in a finished state so the company only assembles the component parts into their final product. In the manufacture of radios and televisions, companies often purchase the finished tubes, cabinets, and other parts. These component parts are then assembled to become a finished appliance. Other companies purchase direct material in a raw state and apply labor, machinery, and equipment to change it into another form. In the processing of sugar, for instance, raw sugar cane is cut and cooked before becoming a finished product. In either case, direct material is debited to the Direct Materials Inventory account when the material is received. The offsetting credit is to Accounts Payable. When materials are purchased for a specific contract, they may be charged directly to the contract.

Direct labor

Direct labor cost is the amount of wages earned by workers who are actually engaged in transforming the material from its raw state to a finished product. For example, the amounts paid to workers in a shirt factory who cut fabric and those who sew the pieces are generally classified as direct labor, and their earnings would be treated as a direct labor cost. Only the wages earned by those workers who are actually involved in the physical manufacture of the product are treated as direct labor.

Prime cost.   Direct material and direct labor comprise the prime cost of a product. Usually these two cost elements can be measured quite easily and accurately. Neither of these costs is arbitrarily allocated to the product, since the amount of material and labor going into production can be determined and measured. Direct material costs are determined by maintaining accurate records which show the cost of material used in producing a specific product. The cost of direct labor can be determined by recording the time that each worker spends on a job, as indicated on clock cards or other time records, and multiplying the worker's basic wage rate by this amount.

Factory overhead

Factory overhead comprises the third cost element. It is sometimes referred to as factory burden, manufacturing overhead, or manufacturing burden. Factory overhead includes *all* production costs other than direct material and direct labor. The emphasis here is on the term *production* costs; marketing and administrative expenses are excluded. For example, a salesperson's salary is a marketing expense; salaries earned by top management, the controller, and the financial accountant are usually classified as administrative expenses. However, factory accounting salaries for recording factory payroll and cost data may be classified as factory overhead.

Indirect material.   All direct material items required to produce a product are recorded separately and costed. Small, insignificant items of material costs are accounted for as factory overhead. Since it may be difficult to determine the amount of thread used in the shirt and since the cost of the thread is relatively small in relation to the cost of all other raw materials in the shirt, it may be impractical to account for the cost of the thread as a direct material. Instead, such costs may be classified as *indirect material* and may become a part of factory overhead costs, which are allocated to all production during a particular cost accounting period. One of the considerations in classifying direct material is the ease of attaching the material cost to the finished product.

As previously discussed, it may not be feasible to maintain accurate records of the usage of all items that go into a finished product. If a manufacturer uses a small amount of an inexpensive glue to make desks, the cost accountant may decide to classify the glue as an indirect material and record this cost in the Factory Overhead account. There is a trade-off in accounting between how much it costs to collect information and the cost of the item. In the control of inexpensive items like glue, accountants do not want to spend many hours just accounting for it, because the accounting cost itself can make these materials expensive.

Other types of indirect material will be charged to factory overhead. For example, operating, repair, and janitorial supplies used in the factory are indirect material. They are used in production, but are not physically identified in the finished product and are therefore not direct material.

Indirect labor.   Direct labor includes the earnings of the workers who actually make the product. Plant superintendents do not actually work on the product, so their salary cannot be charged as a direct labor cost. Instead, the plant superintendent's salary is generally treated as a part of *indirect labor costs* which are charged to factory overhead. There are other skilled and unskilled workers involved in production, such as janitors, repairers, and supervisors. However, the results of their efforts are also not as easily traceable to the finished product. Consequently, they are usually classified as indirect labor, and their earnings become a part of factory overhead. Factory overhead costs are subsequently allocated to all products as indirect costs.

Other factory overhead.   In addition to indirect material and indirect labor, costs such as rent, taxes, insurance, and depreciation on manufacturing facilities are included in factory overhead. Other occupancy costs such as light, heat, and power used in manufacturing facilities are also included in factory overhead. In addition, the wage and salary payments classified as direct labor costs usually do not include employee benefits. Employers must pay not only the gross wages an employee earns but also additional costs for employee benefits, such as social security, unemployment compensation, vacation and holiday pay, sick pay, and life and hospitalization insurance. These expenditures for employee benefits have become an increasingly significant part of total payroll costs. While employee benefit costs that relate to direct labor workers are properly classified as direct labor costs, many companies have found it easier to treat all employee benefit costs as indirect costs that are subsequently allocated to all products. In some companies, retirement benefits, such as pension and profit-sharing costs, may be charged to expense as period costs and not allocated to the cost of the product, even though conceptually they are part of labor cost.

In summary, the factory overhead classification encompasses all factory costs other than direct material and direct labor.

Conversion costs.   In the processing of foods, chemicals, and certain other products, direct labor and factory overhead costs are sometimes referred to as *conversion costs* or processing costs. Both direct labor and factory overhead costs are incurred when raw material is converted into a finished product.

MANUFACTURING INVENTORY FLOWS

Exhibit 2–3 illustrates the flow of costs through the four inventory accounts, Factory Supplies, Direct Materials, Work in Process, and Finished Goods. After direct materials are issued from the storeroom to a production department, they are charged to Work in Process.

Supplies and insignificant materials, however, are charged to Factory Overhead Control as indirect material. The Factory Overhead Control account

EXHIBIT 2–3
Physical flow versus inventory account flow

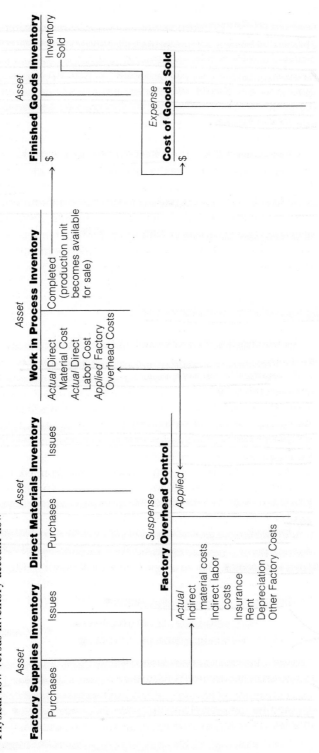

is a general ledger cost control account. Actual factory costs such as indirect material, indirect labor, insurance, and depreciation are charged as debits to this account and become part of total actual factory overhead. Only factory related costs are accumulated in this account. Depreciation, insurance, and rent on the office building and office equipment are not part of factory overhead. Instead, these costs are accumulated in an Administrative Expense Control account.

Control account. The Factory Overhead Control account is the same as any control account, such as the Accounts Receivable Control account used in financial accounting. Factory Overhead Control is a general ledger account supported by a subsidiary ledger that details various factory overhead costs. The subsidiary ledger listing of the separate costs items is necessary for management planning and control purposes. Management would not be able to analyze the details of factory overhead cost without in-depth accounting for each cost.

APPLICATIONS OF FACTORY OVERHEAD

When a product is completed, the accumulated costs in Work in Process are transferred to the Finished Goods Inventory account. The amount transferred is the sum of the three factory cost elements: direct material, direct labor, and factory overhead. Actual direct material and direct labor costs are obtained by adding the direct material and the labor costs charged. Determination of factory overhead costs is more complicated because the cost accountant cannot determine total actual factory overhead costs for an accounting period until after the period has ended. This means that the total cost of a product finished on the fifth day of a month cannot be determined until after the monthly accounting period has ended. If cost is based on actual factory overhead, this delay can cause many problems; thus, a more timely method is commonly used.

In practice, all factory overhead costs are estimated for budgetary purposes. The cost accountant also utilizes these data in determining a factory overhead application rate. For example, if management budgets $36,000 in factory overhead costs for the year and estimates that total direct labor will be $60,000, the factory overhead application rate is determined as follows:

$$\frac{\$36,000 \text{ budgeted factory overhead costs}}{\$60,000 \text{ budgeted direct labor dollars}} = \$0.60 \text{ per direct labor dollar}$$

For every direct labor dollar charged to a product or job, factory overhead costs will be applied at a rate of $0.60 per direct labor dollar. Direct labor cost is one basis for applying factory overhead; direct labor-hours, units of production, and machine-hours are three other commonly used bases. Each department may have its own factory overhead application rate, or a plantwide rate may be used.

Indirect costs included in factory overhead must be applied to the product at various stages of production to reflect the full cost of production. A journal entry can be made for each overhead application. For example, when a product is finished on the fifth of the month, a journal entry could be recorded to apply $0.60 for every direct labor dollar charged to the product or job. However, this practice involves much time and effort and is not practical. A more feasible approach is to separately record the amount of overhead applied for each job on its cost sheet (which is illustrated in Chapter 3) and then to prepare a summary entry at the end of the accounting period for the total factory overhead applied to each job finished during the period. At the end of each accounting period, factory overhead must also be applied to the partially finished units remaining in Work in Process Inventory. All production during the period, whether or not completed at the end of the period, must receive an overhead application for the period.

The cost accountant must devote much time and thought to developing the overhead application base and rate. Estimated factory overhead is supported by detailed budgets for each expense item. The estimating process will be described in a later chapter. The important point to note at this time is that much professional judgment and care enter into the calculation of the factory overhead application rate; it is not simply a guess.

Entry to apply overhead. The entry to record applied overhead in an actual cost system involves a debit to Work in Process Inventory and a credit to Factory Overhead Control. Assume that $65,000 in direct labor cost has been incurred on all jobs and the factory overhead application rate is 60 percent of direct labor dollars. The following journal entry should be made:

```
Work in Process Inventory . . . . . . . . . . . . . . . . . . . . . . . . . . . . .   39,000
    Factory Overhead Control ($65,000 direct labor × 60%
      factory overhead application rate = 39,000) . . . . . . . . .              39,000
```

After posting this entry to the general ledger, the production accounts involved would appear as follows:

Work in Process Inventory

Actual direct material	xx,xxx	
Actual direct labor	65,000	
Applied factory overhead	39,000	

Factory Overhead Control

Actual—Indirect labor	xx,xxx	*Applied*	39,000
Depreciation	xx,xxx		
Manufacturing supplies	xx,xxx		
Other factory overhead	xx,xxx		

Factory overhead applied account

Some companies use a separate Factory Overhead Applied account to accumulate applied overhead. This is an acceptable procedure, but using a single Factory Overhead Control account is simpler. If a separate Factory Overhead Applied account is used, the transaction flow would appear as follows:

Suspense		Suspense	
Factory Overhead Control		**Factory Overhead Applied**	
Actual xx,xxx		Applied 39,000	

Asset	
Work in Process Inventory	
Actual direct material xx,xxx	
Actual direct labor 65,000	
Applied factory overhead 39,000	

The Factory Overhead Control account must be closed at the end of the accounting period. For example, suppose the Factory Overhead Control account appears as follows at the end of the accounting period:

Factory Overhead Control			
Actual 39,500	Applied 39,000		
	60% Application		
	rate × $65,000 actual		
	direct labor dollars)		

Actual factory overhead consisting of such cost items as rent, depreciation, indirect material, indirect labor, and so forth, amounted to $39,500 for the year. A total of $65,000 direct labor dollars was actually incurred during the year. Overhead was applied to job or work orders for a total of $39,000 using the applied overhead rate of 60 percent per direct labor dollar (60 percent × $65,000 = $39,000). Even though the Factory Overhead Control account shows only one credit entry for $39,000, overhead is applied to each product and the $39,000 is a total for the year. Subsidiary records are available to show details of the overhead application. These are illustrated at the end of the chapter.

Under- or overapplied overhead

The debit balance of $500 in the Factory Overhead Control account indicates that the actual overhead costs incurred exceeded the amount of overhead applied to production for the period. Overhead is underapplied or underabsorbed when this occurs. If the overhead applied to production is greater than total actual factory overhead costs incurred, the credit balance in the Factory Overhead Control account indicates that factory overhead has been overapplied or overabsorbed. Periodically, the cost accountant analyzes actual factory overhead costs to determine the reasons for the over- or underabsorption.

If the amount necessary to close the Factory Overhead Control account is not significant, the over- or underapplied amount should be closed into the Cost of Goods Sold account. If the amount is significant, the over- or underapplied overhead should be allocated between inventory and cost of sales based on the relative proportion of units sold and units remaining in inventory, provided an analysis of the reasons for over- or underabsorption indicate it is a cost that can be inventoried and not the result of excessive rework, breakdowns, and other inefficiencies which should be treated as a loss. If the underabsorption of overhead results from inefficiencies and is significant, the amount necessary to close the Factory Overhead Control account should be written off to Revenue and Expense Summary as it represents a loss.

COST OF GOODS MANUFACTURED STATEMENT

The cost accountant is primarily responsible for preparing the Cost of Goods Manufactured Statement, which is illustrated in Exhibit 2–4. This statement is also known as the Statement of Manufacturing Costs or, more briefly, the Manufacturing Statement. The purpose of the Cost of Goods Manufactured Statement is to summarize all production costs for a cost accounting period. These production costs consist primarily of the three elements discussed previously—direct material, direct labor, and factory overhead.

EXHIBIT 2–4

WELLS MANUFACTURING COMPANY
Cost of Goods Manufactured Statement
For the Year Ended December 31, 19X1

Direct materials inventory, January 1, 19X1	$16,000	
Add: Purchases (net of discount)	33,000	
Direct materials available for use	49,000	
Less: Direct materials inventory, December 31, 19X1	32,000	
Direct materials used		$ 17,000
Direct labor		65,000
Factory overhead costs:		
Factory supplies, January 1, 19X1	4,000	
Add: Purchases	7,000	
Supplies available for use	11,000	
Less: Factory supplies, December 31, 19X1	6,000	
Indirect materials used	5,000	
Indirect labor	10,000	
Depreciation	18,000	
Insurance	3,000	
Taxes	2,500	
Miscellaneous	1,000	
Total factory overhead costs		39,500
Total manufacturing costs		121,500
Add: Work in process inventory, January 1, 19X1		40,000
Total costs to account for		161,500
Less: Work in process inventory, December 31, 19X1		31,000
Cost of goods manufactured		$130,500

As shown in Exhibit 2–4, the beginning balance of direct materials inventory on January 1, 19X1, is $16,000. Material purchases, net of purchase discount, are added. The total of $49,000 represents the direct material available for use in production. Not all of the direct material was used, since there is an ending inventory on December 31, 19X1, of $32,000. Direct material used was $17,000. A similar analysis of inventory flow for factory supplies reveals that $5,000 of indirect materials were used and charged to overhead.

Direct labor of $65,000 is next entered on the cost of goods manufactured statement. Factory overhead follows. For illustrative purposes, only a few items of actual factory overhead are listed in Exhibit 2–4; factory overhead costs total $39,500. As illustrated earlier, throughout the period overhead was applied at the rate of 60 percent of direct labor cost, giving a total of $39,000 absorbed. Since *actual* factory overhead totaling $39,500 is shown in Exhibit 2–4, applied overhead is not also shown. However, if applied overhead, rather than actual overhead is shown on the Cost of Goods Manufactured Statement, the $500 underapplied overhead must also be shown, either by including the balance with cost of goods sold or prorating it between inventory and cost of sales.

The beginning balance of work in process is then added to the total manufacturing cost for the period. The ending balance in work in process inventory, which represents the cost of the units that are not completed at the end of the accounting period, is then deducted to arrive at the cost of goods manufactured.

Manufacturer's statement of income

The statement of income for a manufacturer is illustrated in Exhibit 2–5. The cost of goods manufactured shown in Exhibit 2–4 is carried to the income statement and is added to the beginning balance in finished goods inventory to arrive at the cost of goods available for sale. Not all units were sold, since there was an ending balance in the finished goods inventory. The finished goods inventory ending balance on December 31, 19X1, must be deducted from the cost of goods available for sale to determine the cost of goods sold. Gross margin is then determined by subtracting cost of goods sold from sales. Marketing and administrative expenses are deducted from the gross margin to arrive at income before taxes. Income taxes are then deducted to arrive at net income. The manufacturer's statements of income and cost of goods manufactured could be combined into one statement, but such a statement would be long and somewhat difficult to read. In practice, only the cost of goods sold usually appears on the statement of income and the total cost of goods manufactured is not reported.

Merchandiser's statement of income

The statement of income for a merchandiser appears in Exhibit 2–6. One difference between a manufacturer's income statement and a merchandiser's

EXHIBIT 2–5

WELLS MANUFACTURING COMPANY
Statement of Income
For the Years Ended December 31, 19X1, and 19X0

	19X1	19X0
Sales	$299,500	$280,000
Less: Cost of goods sold:		
Finished goods inventory, January 1, ...	180,000	210,000
Add: Cost of goods manufactured	130,500	170,000
Cost of goods available for sale.	310,500	380,000
Less: Finished goods inventory,		
December 31.	114,000	180,000
Cost of goods sold	196,500	200,000
Gross margin	103,000	80,000
Marketing and administrative expense:		
Less: Marketing expense	38,000	30,000
Administrative expense.	35,000	26,000
Total.	73,000	56,000
Income before taxes	30,000	24,000
Income taxes	10,000	8,000
Net income	$ 20,000	$ 16,000
Earnings per share (based on 20,000 average shares		
outstanding during the year)	$ 1.00	$ 0.80

EXHIBIT 2–6

BROWN MERCHANDISING COMPANY
Statement of Income
For the Years Ended December 31, 19X1, and 19X0

	19X1	19X0
Sales	$299,500	$280,000
Less: Cost of goods sold:		
Merchandise inventory, January 1	320,000	320,000
Add: Net purchases	100,000	200,000
Cost of goods available for sale.	420,000	520,000
Less: Merchandise inventory, December 31	223,500	320,000
Cost of goods sold	196,500	200,000
Gross margin	103,000	80,000
Marketing and administrative expenses:		
Less: Marketing expense.	38,000	30,000
Administrative expense.	35,000	26,000
Total	73,000	56,000
Income before taxes.	30,000	24,000
Income taxes	10,000	8,000
Net Income	$ 20,000	$ 16,000
Earnings per share (based on 20,000 average shares		
outstanding during the year)	$ 1.00	$ 0.80

income statement lies in the terminology used. Since retailers buy goods that are already finished, their inventory account is usually called a *Merchandise Inventory,* and the goods they buy are classified as *Purchases.*

Inventory physical flow

It is important to understand the similarity between the flow of costs through a retailer's merchandise inventory and a manufacturer's inventory accounts. Exhibit 2–7 illustrates the similarity in all inventory accounts. Since raw material (which includes direct materials and factory supplies) in a manufacturing company is not generally ready for sale, the total of beginning inventory and net purchases represents the amount available for use. Partially completed products in work in process inventory and finished goods inventory are generally not purchased from an outside supplier but are produced using direct material, direct labor, and overhead.

In all manufacturing exhibits in this chapter, cost of goods sold is obtained by adding the finished goods beginning inventory to the cost of goods manufactured and then subtracting the finished goods ending balance from the total goods available for sale. In practice, this is not generally considered to be an aspect of cost accounting because there is no element of measuring cost; this was done at earlier stages. In a cost accounting system, product costs are determined when the product is manufactured and transferred to finished goods inventory.

While production costs are generally treated as *product costs* and included in either work in process or finished goods inventories, marketing and administrative costs are generally treated as *period costs,* that is, costs that are charged against revenue in each accounting period. When a product is sold, it becomes *cost of sales* and is an expired product cost which is charged against revenue.

EXHIBIT 2–7

Merchandise accounting	*Manufacturing accounting*
Merchandise inventory:	Raw material inventory:
Beginning inventory	Beginning inventory:
Add: Net purchases	Add: Net material purchases
Equals: Available for sale	Equals: Available for use
Less: Ending inventory	Less: Ending inventory
Cost of goods sold	Raw material used
Manufacturing accounting	*Manufacturing accounting*
Work in process inventory:	Finished goods:
Beginning inventory	Beginning inventory:
Add: Cost of direct material, direct labor, and overhead	Add: Cost of goods manufactured
Equals: Manufacturing costs to account for	Equals: Available for sale
Less: Ending inventory	Less: Ending inventory
Cost of goods manufactured	Cost of goods sold

Some costs, which are theoretically assets, may nevertheless be charged to expense at the time of purchase. For example, it may be too costly to account for supplies as an asset, and the cost is treated as an expense at the time of purchase. However, assets cannot be handled in this manner unless the cost is very small. The cost of significant assets, such as property and equipment, must be treated in the accounting records as an asset, and only the depreciation associated with these plant assets becomes a period expense.

THREE BEHAVIOR PATTERNS: FIXED, VARIABLE, AND SEMIVARIABLE (MIXED) COSTS

An important function of the cost accountant is analyzing cost behavior patterns. Some costs vary directly with changes in volume of output; these are *variable costs*. Direct material and direct labor costs are examples. Other costs remain the same in total for a given time period and production level, regardless of output; these are *fixed costs*, insurance and rent are examples. Many costs behave as partly variable and partly fixed, that is, they vary, but less than proportionately. These costs are referred to as *semivariable (mixed) costs;* costs of indirect material, indirect labor, and utilities for which there is a fixed monthly power cost plus a per kwh. charge, may be semivariable. Accountants analyze semivariable costs to determine their fixed and variable components. Chapter 5 discusses the methods of making these analyses.

Relevant range. Fixed and variable costs are defined in relation to a specific period of time and a designated range of production volume or activity. If fixed costs are said to be $100 for a year or other period of time, a certain volume range is assumed; for example, 1,000 to 2,000 labor-hours. If management finds that an expansion of the production facilities is necessary, it may either move to a larger plant or use the present facilities for additional shifts. In either case, this change in the production facilities or number of work shifts can cause a change in the relevant range; this can affect *total* fixed costs. While some fixed costs, such as depreciation, will not change unless new equipment or a larger plant is acquired, there may be an increase in other fixed costs. For example, more plant supervisors may be hired.

Total fixed costs may also change because of inflation and other conditions experienced in a different accounting period. For example, even if the same number of shifts works next year or if the plant size stays the same, the salary level paid to the plant supervisors or rent on present plant facilities may increase so that *total* fixed costs are affected. Thus, total fixed costs remain the same only if the relevant range is assumed not to change and prices remain constant.

Unit fixed versus total fixed costs. Fixed and variable costs can be expressed either as unit costs or in total. Exhibit 2–8 illustrates these concepts.

EXHIBIT 2–8

Cost behavior patterns

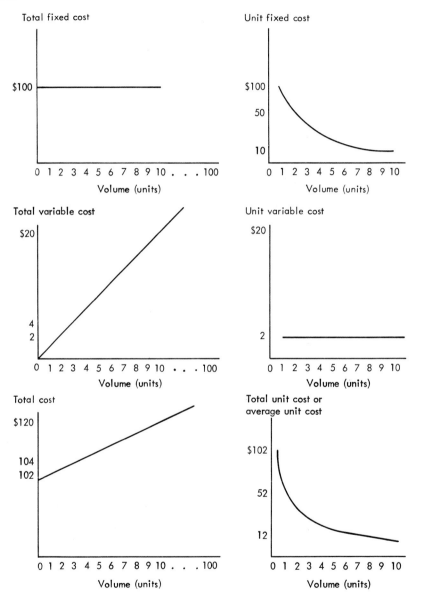

Total fixed cost is $100. This lump-sum fixed cost is divided by volume to give unit fixed cost. For example, if one unit is produced, *unit* fixed cost is $100; if two units are produced, the *unit* fixed cost is $50 ($100 total fixed cost ÷ 2 units); if 10 units are produced, the unit fixed cost is $10 ($100 total fixed cost ÷ 10 units); and so forth.

Unit variable versus total variable costs. Total variable costs and unit variable costs are also graphed in Exhibit 2–8. There is a direct relationship between total variable cost and volume; *total* variable costs increase in proportion to volume increases. However, unit variable cost remains constant. Assume that it takes two yards of material to make each shirt and that total material cost is $2 per shirt. As can be seen in Exhibit 2–8, if one shirt is produced, total variable costs will be $2. If 10 shirts are produced, total variable costs will be $20. The *unit* variable cost remains $2 per shirt.

Total cost per unit versus total cost. By adding the fixed and variable cost curves, total cost can be plotted. Total cost increases with output because of variable costs. Total cost per unit, sometimes referred to as average cost, is computed by dividing total cost by the units produced; for example, the total cost to produce two units is $104 ($100 fixed cost + $4 variable cost) or $52 total cost per unit ($104/2 units). Average unit cost decreases with output because the $100 fixed cost is being spread over more units.

Fixed costs can be either *committed costs* or *discretionary costs. Committed costs* are the result of previous managerial actions. Depreciation and property taxes on the manufacturing facilities are committed costs. After the asset is acquired, committed costs are not changed unless economic circumstances indicate a change in the depreciation method or useful life, or the asset is sold.

Other costs, such as factory supervision, are *discretionary costs* because management uses its professional judgment each period in deciding the amount of such costs. These costs are also called programmed or managed costs. Many marketing and administrative costs are discretionary costs. Changes in economic conditions and technology as well as plant layout and facilities location affect management's decision about the level of discretionary costs. For example, if a competitor's product is more technologically advanced, management may find it imperative to change the product design which involves an employee training program. Such costs arise from periodic appropriation decisions reflecting top management decisions; if unfavorable conditions develop for the company, these costs could be drastically reduced for a given year. Even though there is often no clear line between committed and discretionary costs, the distinction is helpful for planning and control decisions.

Effect on capacity. Since unit fixed costs decrease as volume increases, full plant utilization is an important goal of management. Managers worry greatly about failing to use available capacity because of the impact idle capacity has on product costs. In the above illustration, if the plant produces only one unit, the *unit* fixed cost is $100. After unit variable costs are added, the product costs might not be recovered at competitive prices. However, if 10 units are produced, the unit fixed cost is only $10. On the other hand, it may be more economical to build plant capacity beyond the requirements of the majority of the months so that peak demand may be satisfied by current production rather than having to stockpile inventories to meet peak demand, as would be necessary if plant capacity were set lower. Under these circumstances and when manufacturing facilities have been built to handle the company's expected needs but not all space is utilized at present, the company might consider leasing excess space to outside parties. Idle capacity should be avoided because it results in inefficient use of assets and increased unit costs. Management may decide not to make the product if sales demand doesn't allow a large enough production volume to permit reasonable unit cost.

Some companies have not realized the importance of using plant capacity. For example, they may expand by adding to manufacturing facilities instead of operating the present plant two or three shifts a day. It may make good sense from a cost standpoint to operate an additional shift rather than expand plant facilities because the increased usage will reduce the building's idle capacity. However, the decision to increase the number of shifts depends on many other factors. Even with a pay differential, the company may not find enough laborers to work on the midnight shift. In addition, it may be necessary to have the plant idle for certain periods for cleaning and maintenance.

Semivariable costs. Semivariable costs vary with changes in volume, but there is no proportional relationship, as there is for variable costs. Part of semivariable costs are costs that must be incurred regardless of the level of work performed, such as supervision, inspection, or wages of standby repairers. However, total cost will increase as higher activity levels are attained since more supervisors, inspectors, and repairers will be needed to support a higher production level. Semivariable costs are also referred to as semifixed costs or mixed costs.

Step-type semivariable costs. Semivariable costs can take several forms; one of these is shown in Exhibit 2–9. Assume that a person can inspect 100 units per month and earns $700 per month. When the volume increases beyond 100 units, a second inspector must be hired, and total inspection costs will then be $1,400. A third inspector must be hired when volume reaches 300 units, and so forth. The $700 earned by the first inspector represents the fixed portion of the semivariable cost, reflecting the minimum cost of supplying

EXHIBIT 2–9

Total semivariable costs—step-type

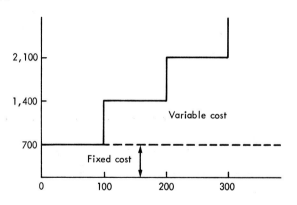

EXHIBIT 2–10

Total semivariable factory overhead—increasing at constant rate

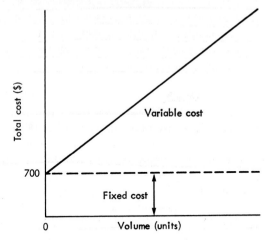

inspection service, and the difference between $700 and the amount paid is the variable portion, which is related to usage.

Another type of semivariable cost is graphed in Exhibit 2–10. Maintenance and repair of factory machinery and equipment may follow this semivariable pattern. Management may decide that it is a good preventive maintenance policy to keep one repairer at the plant at all times and pay the person $700 per month. As volume increases, more repairers and additional repair supplies may be needed. The $700 salary of the first repairer is the fixed component. The remainder of the semivariable costs is the variable portion, which may increase at a constant or increasing rate. The variable cost portion in Exhibit 2–10 is increasing at a constant rate.

Other semivariable costs such as heat, light, and power follow a pattern in which they increase at a decreasing rate. Utilities charge a fixed monthly fee for the service, and this base charge is constant for the period. But there is also a demand charge which varies with consumption. When more energy is consumed, the variable cost per unit may decrease.

Factory overhead is a mixture. Total factory overhead includes a mixture of cost types. Direct material and direct labor costs are usually variable costs. For example, if we assume that one pound of plastic at a cost of $2 is required to produce one unit, and two direct labor-hours at a cost of $5 per hour are required, we assume these per unit figures do not change when production changes. By contrast, the per unit factory overhead cost includes both fixed and variable costs. Total fixed costs such as rent and insurance will not increase if another unit is produced; but variable factory costs such as indirect material will increase directly with volume changes. Semivariable factory overhead costs such as inspection, repairs, and maintenance will vary but not in direct proportion to volume changes.

It is important to distinguish between short- and long-run time periods in relation to fixed and variable cost. In the long run, there are no committed costs because if management decides not to operate, they can usually cancel their lease agreement and avoid the rent payment. However, in the short run, management usually cannot inform the lessor that operations have ceased and they wish to terminate the lease immediately. When a cost is fixed, it is fixed for a certain short time period—a month or a year.

Standard costs. Chapters 10 and 11 introduce *standard costing*, which is a system of costing inventory on a predetermined basis. By using scientifically predetermined standard costs of production representing what costs should be incurred with attainable performance, the product can be costed when it is manufactured rather than waiting until actual costs are determined. As illustrated in Chapters 10 and 11, standard costs are also used to evaluate performance.

Whether a company employs standard or actual costs, two basic systems are used to assign costs to products or orders: job order costing and process costing. To calculate the unit cost of producing goods, a system for collecting costs and assigning them to products is necessary. The nature of manufacturing activities determines which of the two basic cost accumulation systems will be used.

JOB ORDER COSTING

With a job order cost system, costs are assigned to and accumulated for each job. A job may be an order, a contract, a unit of production, or a batch. In job order costing, the direct material and direct labor associated with each job are identified and accumulated. Since factory overhead cost cannot be traced to specific jobs, it is applied on some rational basis, such as direct labor dollars or direct labor-hours. Job order costing should be used if the production or service is being performed to meet customer specification. For example, when an automobile is to be repaired, the mechanic uses job order costing to accumulate the costs assigned to the repair job. The mechanic will collect the cost of repair parts and the direct labor-hours spent in repairing the car. Overhead cost will be applied using an overhead rate. Job order costing is also used in the construction of commercial and residential buildings, ships, and machines because the physical units can be identified. A printing company uses job order costing because each batch is usually produced to customer specifications. Job order costing may also be used if a company makes different components for inventory.

PROCESS COSTING

The second system is process costing. Under this approach, costs are accumulated for each department for a time period and allocated among all the products produced during the period. Process costing is used in chemical processing, petroleum refining, and in other industries where there is a continuous production process. Direct material, direct labor, and applied factory overhead are accumulated for each department for a time period, usually a month. At the end of the period, the number of units produced is divided into the departmental cost to obtain a cost per unit.

The production process dictates which cost accounting system must be used. Job order costing is described briefly in the next section and is discussed in detail in Chapters 4–6; process costing is introduced in Chapter 7.

Basic journal entries in job order costing

The following journal entries illustrate the basic transactions in a job order cost system. Each entry is made in a journal and is then posted to the general ledger accounts illustrated in Exhibit 2–11. In practice, special journals are normally used (i.e., normally the sales entry is recorded in a sales journal, and cash payments are recorded in a cash disbursements journal); only a general journal is illustrated here. A job order subsidiary ledger and a factory overhead subsidiary ledger are also illustrated. Subsidiary ledgers for direct material inventory and finished goods inventory are also normally used, but these ledgers are not illustrated.

Since subsidiary ledgers for work in process inventory and factory overhead control are usually more difficult to understand, these subsidiary ledgers are illustrated in Exhibit 2–11. The subsidiary ledger account titles are omitted from the journal entries illustrated to emphasize the general ledger accounts. To simplify the illustrations, the company is working on only three jobs.

Direct and indirect materials purchased. The entry to make when direct or indirect raw material is purchased on account is:

(a) Direct Materials Inventory	33,000	
Accounts Payable		33,000
INDIRECT MAT'L Factory Supplies Inventory	7,000	
Accounts Payable		7,000

Direct and indirect materials issued. Assume that $4,000 of direct material were issued for Job No. 101, $6,000 for Job No. 102, and $7,000 for Job No. 103. The total direct materials issued ($17,000) are transferred to Work In Process Inventory. Transfers detailing the costs of each job are also made to the job subsidiary ledger. The following entry also illustrates the issuance of indirect material of $5,000 from the factory supplies inventory which is charged to Factory Overhead Control. An entry is also made in the factory overhead subsidiary ledger to an indirect material account.

(b) Work in Process Inventory	17,000	
Job No. 101–4,000		
Job No. 102–6,000		
Job No. 103–7,000		
Factory Overhead Control—Indirect Material	5,000	
Direct Materials Inventory		17,000
Factory Supplies Inventory		5,000

Factory labor incurred.   The following entry to Work in Process Inventory is made to record the direct labor cost for the three jobs. Assume Job No. 101 incurred direct labor costs of $20,000, Job No. 102, $30,000, and Job No. 103, $15,000. Each amount is posted to the respective account in the subsidiary job ledger. Indirect labor of $10,000 is also recorded in the Factory Overhead Control account in the following entry; an entry is also required in the factory overhead subsidiary ledger. The credit of $75,000 to Payroll Payable represents the gross amount of wages payable. Additional entries are needed to record the taxes and other amounts withheld from the employees' wages and the employer's payroll taxes.

(c)	Work in Process Inventory	65,000	
	Job No. 101—20,000		
	Job No. 102—30,000		
	Job No. 103—15,000		
	Factory Overhead Control—Indirect Labor	10,000	
	Payroll Payable		75,000

Marketing and administrative salaries.   The following entry records the marketing and administrative salaries of $6,000. This entry could have been combined with entry (c) but is separated here to emphasize that only factory payroll is charged to Work in Process Inventory and Factory Overhead Control. Both the Marketing Expense Control and the Administrative Expense Control are detailed in subsidiary ledgers, but these are not shown in Exhibit 2–11.

(d)	Marketing Expense Control	6,000	
	Administrative Expense Control	5,000	
	Payroll Payable		11,000

Factory depreciation.   Assume that depreciation for the period amounts to $10,000 on the factory building and to $8,000 on the factory machinery and equipment. The Factory Overhead Control account in the general ledger and the depreciation account in the factory overhead control subsidiary ledger are charged for this period's depreciation. The credits are entered in the accumulated depreciation contra asset accounts.

(e)	Factory Overhead Control—Depreciation Expense	18,000	
	Accumulated Depreciation—Building		10,000
	Accumulated Depreciation—Machinery		
	and Equipment		8,000

Marketing and administrative depreciation.   A separate entry is made to record the depreciation on the office equipment used by sales and administrative personnel. This entry could also have been made at the time factory depreciation was recorded. All other marketing and administrative costs would be charged to these control accounts; only payroll and depreciation are illustrated here:

(f)	Marketing Expense Control	2,000	
	Administrative Expense Control	5,000	
	Accumulated Depreciation—Machinery		
	and Equipment		7,000

Factory insurance. The following entry records the expiration of $3,000 of prepaid insurance on the factory building and equipment. An entry was previously made to the Prepaid Insurance asset account when the policy premium was paid. An entry to the Factory Overhead Control account in the general ledger as well as to the insurance account in the factory overhead subsidiary ledger must be made to record this cost.

(g)	Factory Overhead Control—Insurance Expense	3,000	
	Prepaid Insurance		3,000

Property taxes. Estimates must be made for property taxes on the factory even though the exact amount to be paid may not be known. Both the tax rate and tax base require an estimate. Normally the liability for the taxes is accrued by using an estimate based on the rates and bases applicable in the preceding period adjusted for information available as to possible changes in the tax rates or assessed values. Estimated property taxes on the factory are recorded as a debit to Factory Overhead Control and as a credit to Taxes Payable. An additional debit entry is made to the taxes account in the factory overhead subsidiary ledger.

(h)	Factory Overhead Control—Property Tax Expense	2,500	
	Taxes Payable		2,500

When the taxes are paid, Taxes Payable is debited for the amount accrued and Prepaid Taxes is debited for the amount applicable to future periods; cash is credited. To simplify the illustration, there is no consideration of adjusting for the over- or underaccrual of taxes when they are paid.

Factory miscellaneous costs. Cash of $1,000 paid for miscellaneous factory costs is recorded as a debit to Factory Overhead Control in the general ledger and to the Miscellaneous Factory Cost account in the factory overhead subsidiary ledger. A credit is made to the Cash account in the general ledger. All other individual entries to the Cash account are omitted in this exhibit; other cash receipts totaled $191,000 and other cash disbursements totaled $185,000, including $73,000 for marketing and administrative expense and $30,000 for mortgage payments. The entry to record the payment for miscellaneous factory costs is as follows:

(i)	Factory Overhead Control—Miscellaneous Costs	1,000	
	Cash		1,000

Factory overhead applied. In the previous year, the factory overhead application rate was set at 60 percent of direct labor dollars. Overhead is applied to each job based on the direct labor costs incurred. Each job receives the following applied overhead:

Job No. 101	$12,000	(60% × $20,000 direct labor)
Job No. 102	18,000	(60% × $30,000 direct labor)
Job No. 103	9,000	(60% × $15,000 direct labor)

This entry is a summary entry recording the total overhead applied for this period. The $39,000 total overhead applied is transferred to Work in Process Inventory. A credit is made to the Factory Overhead Control account, as follows:

```
(j)   Work in Process Inventory . . . . . . . . . . . . . . . . . . . . . . .     39,000
            Job No. 101–12,000
            Job No. 102–18,000
            Job No. 103–9,000
            Factory Overhead Control . . . . . . . . . . . . . . . . . . . . .              39,000
```

Transfer to finished goods. The cost of finished jobs is transferred to the Finished Goods Inventory. Assume that during the period, Job No. 101 and Job No. 102 are transferred to Finished Goods Inventory. Job No. 101 had a beginning balance of $40,000; additions this period were direct material of $4,000, direct labor of $20,000, and factory overhead of $12,000. The total cost of Job No. 101 ($76,000) is transferred from both the job ledger and Work in Process Inventory by credits to these accounts. Job No. 102 was started and finished this period; the total cost is $54,000. Job No. 103, with costs of $31,000, remains unfinished in Work in Process Inventory at the end of the period.

```
(k)   Finished Goods Inventory. . . . . . . . . . . . . . . . . . . . . . .   130,000
            Work in Process Inventory . . . . . . . . . . . . . . . . . . . . .            130,000
                Job No. 101–76,000
                Job No. 102–54,000
```

Sale is made. The sales price of Job No. 101 is $100,000. The sale on account is recorded by debiting Accounts Receivable and crediting Sales. A charge is made to Cost of Goods Sold for the $76,000 cost of Job No. 101. The credit of $76,000 to Finished Goods Inventory removes the cost of Job No. 101 from this asset account. Additional sales on account totaling $199,500 are not illustrated in this journal entry. The cost of these sales is $120,000 and is debited to Cost of Goods Sold and credited to Finished Goods Inventory. A total of $314,500 is assumed to be received on account and credited to the accounts receivable ledger.

```
(l)   Accounts Receivable . . . . . . . . . . . . . . . . . . . . . . . . . .   100,000
            Sales . . . . . . . . . . . . . . . . . . . . . . . . . . . . . . .               100,000
        Cost of Goods Sold . . . . . . . . . . . . . . . . . . . . . . . . .    76,000
            Finished Goods Inventory . . . . . . . . . . . . . . . . . . . .               76,000
```

Underapplied factory overhead. The balance in the Factory Overhead Control account at the end of the period arises because actual factory overhead amounted to $39,500, while the overhead applied was only $39,000. The difference of $500 represents an underapplication of overhead. Because this balance reflects inefficiencies of the current month, it is closed as a debit to Cost of Goods Sold. After the credit of $500 is posted to Factory Overhead Control, the account is closed.

```
(m)   Cost of Goods Sold . . . . . . . . . . . . . . . . . . . . . . . . . . .    500
            Factory Overhead Control . . . . . . . . . . . . . . . . . . . . .               500
```

EXHIBIT 2–11

Cash

Beginning balance	15,000	(i)	Miscellaneous factory costs	1,000
Receipts	191,000		Disbursements	185,000
	206,000			186,000
Balance 20,000				

Accounts Receivable

Beginning balance	90,000	Received on account	314,500
(1) Sales	100,000		
Other Sales	199,500		
	389,500		
Balance 75,000			

Direct Materials Inventory

Beginning balance	16,000	(b)	Issues	17,000
(a) Purchases	33,000			
	49,000			
Balance 32,000				

Factory Supplies Inventory

Beginning balance	4,000	(b)	Issues	5,000
(a) Purchases	7,000			
	11,000			
Balance 6,000				

Work in Process Inventory

Beginning balance	40,000	(k)	Transfer to finished goods	130,000
(b) Direct material	17,000			
(c) Direct labor	65,000			
(j) Applied overhead	39,000			
	161,000			
Balance 31,000				

Finished Goods Inventory

Beginning balance	180,000	(1)	Transfers to cost of goods sold	76,000
(k) Transfers from work in process	130,000		Transferred to cost of goods sold for other jobs sold	120,000
	310,000			
Balance 114,000				

Prepaid Insurance

Beginning balance	5,000	(g)	Expired insurance	3,000
Balance 2,000				

Accumulated Depreciation—Building

		Beginning balance	40,000
		(e) Depreciation expense	10,000
		Balance	50,000

EXHIBIT 2–11 *(continued)*

Accumulated Depreciation—Machinery and Equipment

	Beginning balance	15,000
(e)	Depreciation expense	8,000
(f)	Depreciation expense	7,000
	Balance	30,000

Sales

(1)	Sale on account	100,000
	Other sales	199,500
		299,500

Cost of Goods Sold

(1)	Sale	76,000
	Other sales	120,000
(m)	Underapplied overhead	500
	Balance	196,500

Factory Overhead Control

(b)	Indirect material	5,000	(j)	Applied	39,000
(c)	Indirect labor	10,000	(m)	To close underapplied	500
(e)	Depreciation	18,000			39,500
(g)	Insurance	3,000			
(h)	Taxes	2,500			
(i)	Miscellaneous	1,000			
		39,500			

Marketing Expense Control

(d)	Payroll	6,000
(f)	Depreciation	2,000
	Cash disbursements for other expenses	30,000
	Balance	38,000

Administrative Expense Control

(d)	Payroll	5,000
(f)	Depreciation	5,000
	Cash disbursements for other expenses	25,000
	Balance	35,000

Work in Process Subsidiary Ledger Accounts
Job. No. 101

	Beginning balance	40,000	(k)	Transferred to finished goods	76,000
(b)	Direct material	4,000			
(c)	Direct labor	20,000			
(j)	Applied overhead	12,000			
		76,000			

EXHIBIT 2–11 (Continued)

Job No. 102

(b)	Direct material	6,000	(k) Transferred to finished	
(c)	Direct labor	30,000	goods	54,000
(j)	Applied overhead	18,000		
		54,000		

Job No. 103

(b)	Direct material	7,000
(c)	Direct labor	15,000
(j)	Applied overhead	9,000
Balance		31,000

Factory Overhead Subsidiary Ledger
Indirect Material

(b)	5,000

Indirect Labor

(c)	10,000

Depreciation

(e)	18,000

Insurance

(g)	3,000

Taxes

(h)	2,500

Miscellaneous Factory Costs

(i)	1,000

SUMMARY

This chapter introduced the basic terms used in cost accounting. The new vocabulary provides the reader with terminology to understand the cost flow described in a Cost of Goods Manufactured Statement. Manufacturers have three inventory accounts: direct materials, work in process, and finished goods to reflect the various stages of completion. Because retailers buy their products in a finished state, they record their goods for sale in only one account: merchandise inventory.

Direct material, direct labor, and factory overhead are the three factory cost elements incurred. Direct material is any raw material that becomes a component part of the product. The wages earned by the workers actually involved in changing the raw material into a finished product are classified as direct labor costs. Factory overhead costs comprise many different types of factory costs since this category includes all manufacturing costs other than direct material and direct labor costs.

It is important to understand the behavior of costs when volume changes. Within a relevant range, fixed costs remain unchanged despite fluctuations in activity. Variable costs vary directly with changes in volume. Semivariable costs have both fixed and variable components.

This chapter also illustrated the basic journal entries used in a job order cost system. Process costing, which is another approach to collecting product costs, will be introduced in Chapter 7.

IMPORTANT TERMS AND CONCEPTS

Direct Materials Inventory	Cost of Goods Manufactured Statement
Factory Supplies Inventory	Product Costs
Work in Process Inventory	Period Costs
Finished Goods Inventory	Fixed Costs
Direct Materials	Relevant Range
Direct Labor	Variable Costs
Prime Cost	Committed Costs
Factory Overhead	Discretionary Costs
Indirect Material	Semivariable (Mixed) Costs
Indirect Labor	Standard Cost
Conversion Costs	Job Order Costing
Applied Factory Overhead	Process Costing

APPENDIX: RECIPROCAL ACCOUNTS

Some companies have branch production plants in various locations. When this is the case, rather than establish a complete set of books at each branch factory, each branch may keep only the ledger accounts that apply directly to production. This system is appropriate if the company wishes to give each of its factories some managerial control, yet still have summarized managerial control data recorded at the general office. While the types of records maintained at the factory may not be uniform, at the minimum a factory journal and factory ledger with subsidiary ledgers for materials inventory, work in process, and factory overhead control should be kept.

The two reciprocal accounts most often used are a *home office ledger* account on the branch books and a *factory ledger* on the home office books. The title *general office ledger* may be used instead of home office ledger and the title *factory office* may be used instead of factory ledger.

Since these are reciprocal accounts, when the home office ledger account is debited by the factory, the factory ledger account is credited by the general office and vice versa. Exhibit 2–A1 gives several types of entries which illustrate the use of this system.

The number of accounts designated to the branch varies depending on the skill of the accounting personnel employed at the factory and on the size of the production plant. For example, entry (i) in Exhibit 2–A1 records the shipment of finished goods to the warehouse under the assumption that the Finished Goods Inventory account is maintained at the general office. In other companies, however, the finished goods account may be kept on the factory office books; under such circumstances, the entire entry is made on the factory office books. Similarly, some branch factories may keep their own plant assets and related accumulated depreciation accounts, while other companies centralize all asset accounts at the general office. There could also be some variation in recording factory payroll, since some branch factories maintain their own payroll records and payroll bank accounts. Entry (c) in Exhibit 2–A1 assumes that all payments for payroll are made by the general office.

REVIEW QUESTIONS

1. Discuss the three production inventory accounts. How do these accounts differ from retail inventory accounts?
2. Define the primary production cost elements.
3. Contrast direct and indirect material; direct and indirect labor.
4. What common element of total cost do prime cost and conversion cost share?
5. Why do many companies use applied rates for factory overhead as opposed to actual factory overhead rates?
6. Discuss the basic component parts of inventory flow. (Hint: A model may be helpful.)
7. What factors should be considered by a company to determine the number of units to be produced each period?
8. Which of the following are examples of period rather than product costs for a manufacturing company?
    a. Advertising campaign.
    b. Insurance on factory machines.
    c. Depreciation of factory building.
    d. Wages of salespersons.
    e. Factory machinery repairs.
    f. Wages of machine operators.
9. Are all variable costs direct and are all direct costs variable? Explain.
10. What effect does an increase in volume have on:
    a. Unit fixed costs?
    b. Unit variable costs?
    c. Total fixed costs?
    d. Total variable costs?
11. A company wants to realize a profit of $150,000. Its salespeople plan to sell 100,000

EXHIBIT 2–A1

Use of factory ledger and home office ledger accounts

	Transaction	*Entry if combined on one set of books*	
(a)	Factory purchases direct materials and factory supplies........	Direct Materials Inventory............... 12,000 Factory Supplies Inventory.............. 4,000 Accounts Payable..................	16,000
(b)	Direct materials requisitions...........	Work in Process Inventory .... 8,000 Direct Materials Inventory	8,000

(c)	Factory payroll..............	Work in Process Inventory 20,000
		Factory Overhead Control 8,000
		    FICA Taxes Payable (6.7% × $28,000)..
		    Income Taxes Withheld ....
		    Salaries Payable...................
			1,876
			9,000
			17,124

(d)	Employer's payroll taxes treated as........	Factory Overhead Control 2,632
		    FICA Taxes Payable (6.7% × $28,000)..
		    State Unemployment Taxes
		    Payable (2% × $28,000)............
		    Federal Unemployment Taxes
		    Payable (.7% × $28,000) ....
			1,876
			
			560
			
			196

(e)	Factory supplies used	Factory Overhead Control .... 2,180 Factory Supplies Inventory	2,180
(f)	Cash paid for factory overhead.............	Factory Overhead Control .... 500 Cash	500

(g)	Factory depreciation and expiration of factory insurance.......	Factory Overhead Control 2,000
		    Accumulated Depreciation...........
			1,500
			    Prepaid Insurance.................
				500

(h)	Factory overhead applied..............	Work in Process Inventory .... 15,000 Factory Overhead Control	15,000
(i)	Finished goods shipped to warehouse	Finished Goods Inventory .... 40,000 Work in Process Inventory	40,000

(j)	Goods shipped to customers............	Accounts Receivable................... 30,000
		    Sales ....
		Cost of Goods Sold................... 20,000
		    Finished Goods Inventory ....
			30,000
			
			20,000

(k)	Collections on accounts	Cash.............................. 30,000 Accounts Receivable...............	30,000

Factory Ledger

(a)	16,000	(i)	40,000
(c)	28,000		
(d)	2,632		
(f)	500		
(g)	2,000		
			To Balance 9,132

Balance   9,132

Home office journal				_Factory office journal_		
Factory Ledger. 16,000			Direct Materials Inventory 12,000			
Accounts Payable.	16,000		Factory Supplies Inventory	4,000		
			Home Office Ledger.		16,000	
No entry			Work in Process Inventory	8,000		
			Direct Materials Inventory		8,000	
Factory Ledger. 28,000			Work in Process Inventory 20,000			
FICA Taxes Payable	1,876		Factory Overhead Control	8,000		
Income Taxes Withheld	9,000		Home Office Ledger.		28,000	
Salaries Payable.	17,124					
Factory Ledger. 2,632			Factory Overhead Control	2,632		
FICA Taxes Payable	1,876		Home Office Ledger.		2,632	
State Unemployment Taxes						
Payable	560					
Federal Unemployment Taxes						
Payable	196					
No entry			Factory Overhead Control	2,180		
			Factory Supplies Inventory		2,180	
Factory Ledger.	500		Factory Overhead Control	500		
Cash		500	Home Office Ledger.		500	
Factory Ledger.	2,000		Factory Overhead Control	2,000		
Accumulated Depreciation	1,500		Home Office Ledger.		2,000	
Prepaid Insurance	500					
No entry			Work in Process Inventory 15,000			
			Factory Overhead Control.		15,000	
Finished Goods Inventory 40,000			Home Office Ledger 40,000			
Factory Ledger.	40,000		Work in Process Inventory.		40,000	
Accounts Receivable. 30,000			No entry			
Sales	30,000					
Cost of Goods Sold. 20,000			No entry			
Finished Goods Inventory	20,000					
Cash 30,000			No entry			
Accounts Receivable	30,000					

Home Office Ledger

(j)	40,000	(a)	16,000	
		(c)	28,000	
		(d)	2,632	
		(f)	500	
		(g)	2,000	
To Balance 9,132				

Balance	9,132

units of a product for $15 each; fixed costs are $250,000. To realize this desired profit, what would variable costs be?

12. Into which of the three behavior patterns, variable, fixed, or semivariable, does each of the following costs usually fall:
    a. Direct material.
    b. Direct labor.
    c. Factory overhead costs.

13. Is depreciation cost a fixed or variable cost? Indicate the factor determining whether the cost is fixed or variable.

14. Contrast job order and process costing systems. What factors dictate whether a job order or process cost system is more appropriate?

15. Classify the following costs as either production, marketing, or administrative costs:
    a. Materials used to make finished unit.
    b. Wages of production workers.
    c. Property taxes on factory building.
    d. Financial accounting salaries.
    e. Warehousing and handling costs.
    f. Factory rent.
    g. Depreciation on the sales executive's office.
    h. Insurance on factory machinery.
    i. Advertising.
    j. Production superintendent's wages.

EXERCISES

E2–1. Analyzing cost behavior

Follet Company provides you with a summary of its total budgeted production costs at three production levels:

	Volume in units		
	1,500	1,800	2,100
Cost A.	$1,625	$1,850	$2,075
Cost B.	2,400	2,800	3,360
Cost C	1,000	2,880	1,000
Cost D	1,200	1,200	1,800

Required:

a. Indicate the cost behavior for Costs A through D.
b. What would total budgeted costs be for Costs A through D if the company produces 1,880 units?
c. Give an example of a production cost that could have the same type of behavior as each of Costs A through D.

E2–2. Statement of cost of goods manufactured and partial income statement

The data appearing below were assembled from books and records of the King Manufacturing Company on December 31, 19X1:

	Debits (000)	Credits (000)
Purchases discounts..........................		$ 400
Sales		100,000
Direct materials inventory, January 1, 19X1	$15,000	
Work in process inventory, January 1, 19X1	15,300	
Finished goods inventory, January 1, 19X1	20,500	
Purchases—direct materials	30,000	
Direct labor	31,000	
Factory overhead—actual	15,180	
Sales discounts	500	
Direct materials inventory, December 31, 19X1......	18,100	
Work in process inventory, December 31, 19X1	14,200	
Finished goods inventory, December 31, 19X1......	16,200	

Required:

Prepare a combined Statement of Cost of Goods Manufactured and Income Statement through the calculation of gross margin.

E2–3. Determining costs put into process, goods manufactured and sold

The following account balances were on the books of McNutt Company on May 1 and May 31:

	May 1	May 31
Direct materials inventory	$42,000	$52,000
Work in process inventory........	68,000	80,000
Finished goods inventory	86,000	90,000

Direct material of $45,000 was purchased during the month, while 30,000 hours of direct labor were incurred in the Preparation Department and 52,000 direct labor-hours were incurred in the Fabricating Department. The labor rate for the Preparation Department was $4.25 and $4.50 for the Fabricating Department. Factory Overhead is applied at 60 percent of the direct labor cost in the Preparation Department and $2 per direct labor-hour in the Fabricating Department.

Required:

Without preparing a formal income statement, determine:
a. Total costs put into process.
b. Cost of goods manufactured.
c. Cost of goods sold.

E2–4. Cost of Goods Manufactured Statement and Income Statement

The following data are extracted from the records of the AYO Company:

Direct material used............................	$ 34,250
Gross margin..................................	69,600
Direct labor...................................	60,380
Sales..	221,400
Work in process, January 1, 19X1.................	8,060
Work in process, December 31, 19X1..............	12,070
Administrative expenses........................	23,700
Finished goods inventory, December 31, 19X1	31,500
Selling expenses	18,050
Finished goods inventory, January 1, 19X1	16,700

Required:

Prepare a Cost of Goods Manufactured Statement and an Income Statement for the AYO Company.

E2–5. Cost of goods manufactured and factory overhead application rate

Peyton Company applies factory overhead on the basis of a rate per direct labor-hour. The company provides you with the following data for the month of April, 19X1.

Selected inventories have the following balances:

	April 1	April 30
Work in process	$90,000	$110,000
Finished goods	70,000	55,000

Prime costs for the month were:

Direct material used	42,500
Direct labor (43,000 actual labor hours)	215,000

Sales have increased 30 percent over February's net sales of $400,000; as a result, gross margin for April is $160,000. Actual factory overhead was $110,000.

Required:

a. Prepare a Cost of Goods Manufactured Statement; only show applied factory overhead.

b. Determine the factory overhead application rate.

c. Determine the amount of over- or underapplied overhead.

E2–6. Cost of Goods Manufactured and Income Statements

Henry Company provides the following data for its year ended May 31, 19X2:

Administrative expense	$ 200,000
Direct labor cost (122,000 hours)	350,000
Gross margin	1,040,000
Marketing expenses	510,000
Sales	2,600,000

Factory overhead is applied at the rate of 150 percent of direct labor dollars. Selected inventory accounts have these beginning and ending balances:

	June 1, 19X1	May 31, 19X2
Work in process	$200,000	$178,000
Finished goods	450,000	480,000

Required:

Prepare a Costs of Goods Manufactured Statement and an Income Statement.

E2–7. Journal entries and cost of goods manufactured statement

Below are selected transactions for Glenn O'Neill Company that were completed during the month of April 19X1:

1. Direct materials costing $43,000 were purchased on account.
2. Direct materials costing $31,000 were issued into production.
3. Miscellaneous manufacturing costs of $2,700 were paid in cash.
4. The factory payroll was accrued and distributed as follows:

Direct Labor $29,000
Indirect Labor 3,500

5. The following adjusting entries were made on April 30:
   Depreciation on Factory Machinery and Equipment. $5,700
   Insurance Expired on Factory Machinery and Equipment. 950

6. Factory overhead is applied at 35 percent of direct labor cost.

7. The balance in Work in Process Inventory on April 1, 19X1, was $15,000; the balance on April 30, 19X1, was $13,000. Transfer the costs of goods finished to the finished goods storeroom.

8. Goods costing $61,900 were sold on account for $85,300.

9. Close the Factory Overhead Control by transferring any over- or underapplied overhead to cost of goods sold.

Required:

a. Prepare journal entries for these transactions using subsidiary ledger accounts for factory overhead.

b. Prepare a Cost of Goods Manufactured Statement for the month showing applied factory overhead instead of actual factory overhead.

E2–8. Manufacturing costs for specific jobs (AICPA adapted)

Tillman Corporation uses a job order cost system and has two production departments, M and A. Budgeted manufacturing costs for 19X1 are as follows:

	Department M	Department A
Direct materials	$700,000	$100,000
Direct labor	200,000	800,000
Manufacturing overhead	600,000	400,000

The actual material and labor costs charged to Job No. 432 during 19X1 were as follows:

Direct material—total	$ 25,000	
Direct labor:		
Department M	8,000	
Department A.		$ 12,000

Tillman applies manufacturing overhead to production orders on the basis of direct labor cost using departmental rates determined at the beginning of the year based on the annual budget.

Required:

Determine the total manufacturing cost associated with Job No. 432 for 19X1.

PROBLEMS

P2–1. Cost of Goods Manufactured Statement and Income Statement

Data from the records of the Janice Hartman Company show the following:

Factory supplies inventory, January 1, 19X1. . . . . $ 1,600
Direct materials inventory, January 1, 19X1 19,000

Purchase discount on direct materials	400
Accounts receivable	30,000
Direct labor	16,000
Administrative expense control	42,000
Purchases of factory supplies	2,200
Work in process inventory, January 1, 19X1	11,200
Sales	154,000
Direct materials inventory, December 31, 19X1	10,000
Indirect labor	1,560
Purchases of direct materials	31,000
Cash	400
Factory insurance	2,000
Depreciation on factory building	12,000
Factory miscellaneous expense	1,400
Work in process inventory, December 31, 19X1	20,240
Marketing expense control	36,000
Factory supplies inventory, December 31, 19X1	2,800

49.63

There were 1,300 units completed and transferred to the finished goods storeroom during the year. Finished goods inventory on January 1 contained 100 units at a value of $6,000. Sales during the year totaled 1,200 units. Inventory is costed out on a FIFO basis.

Required:

From the data given, prepare a Cost of Goods Manufactured Statement and an Income Statement for the Janice Hartman Company for the year 19X1. Round all unit costs to two decimal places.

P2–2. Journal entries for cost transactions

Webber Corporation has requested that the following data relating to manufacturing operations be recorded. Before operation began, management estimated direct labor costs for the year to be $575,000 and factory overhead costs to be $402,500.

1. Direct material costing $16,000 and factory supplies costing $10,000 were issued from the storeroom.
2. Cash in the amount of $1,700 was paid for miscellaneous factory expense.
3. Bimonthly direct labor wages were $25,000 and indirect labor wages were $5,000. (Ignore salary deductions.)
4. A job was finished and transferred to the warehouse on which $9,000 of direct labor was incurred. Apply factory overhead; $9,000 of labor costs were included in the bimonthly wages. Direct material costing $5,000 had already been recorded for this job.
5. Insurance of $800 on the factory assets expired.
6. Another job, on which $12,000 direct labor had been recorded, was completed and sent to the finished goods storeroom; $3,000 of direct material had already been issued for this job. This job was then sold for $28,000 cash.
7. Depreciation of $4,200 on the factory building and $2,600 on the factory machinery was recorded.
8. Accrued taxes on the factory assets were estimated to be $1,980.
9. Labor time tickets showed $22,500 in direct labor cost and $6,500 in indirect labor costs for the last half of the month. Ignore salary deductions.

10. Apply factory overhead to the remaining jobs in work in process which are uncompleted at the end of the month. Direct labor on these jobs amounted to $26,500. Close the under- or overapplied amount to cost of goods sold.

Required: ~~Subsid Act~~

Prepare journal entries for the transactions.

P2–3. Forecasted income statement; percentage changes

The controller of American, Inc. presented the following summarized income statement for the year ended May 31, 19X1, to the board of directors:

AMERICAN INC.
Income Statement
For the Year Ended May 31, 19X1
($000)

Sales.		$550,000
Less: Cost of goods sold:		
Direct material.	$210,000	
Direct labor.	140,000	
Factory overhead ($80,000 fixed).	120,000	
Cost of goods sold		470,000
Gross margin.		80,000
Less: Marketing and administrative expenses:		
Marketing expense ($22,000 variable*).	55,000	
Administrative expense (fixed)	70,000	125,000
Operating loss.		$ 45,000

*Variable with sales dollars.

After reviewing operations, the board decides that action must be taken immediately before future financial losses occur. They hire additional accounting and marketing personnel who jointly present the following plan for 19X2: increase sales price by 40 percent; increase sales volume by 15 percent by engaging in an additional advertising campaign costing $50,000; all other fixed costs will remain the same. Inflation is expected to cause a 10 percent increase in direct material costs, a 20 percent increase in direct labor costs, and a 6 percent increase for variable factory overhead. Variable marketing expenses will continue to be the same percentage of sales dollars.

Required:

a. Prepare a forecasted income statement for the next year, incorporating all expected changes.

b. Compare the percentage of production, marketing, and administrative costs with sales for 19X1 and 19X2.

P2–4. Preparing journal entries and using a subsidiary ledger for work in process

Before operations begin for the year 19X2, the management of the Dollar Company predicts factory overhead to be $51,200 while estimated machine hours will be 6,400.

At the beginning of 19X2, the Work in Process Account and the job order ledger appear as follows:

Work in Process Inventory				Job No. 1		
Balance	4,025			Direct material	500	
				Direct labor	1,000	
				Applied factory		
				overhead	875	
					2,375	

Job No. 2				Job No. 3		
Direct material	250			Direct material	200	
Direct labor	375			Direct labor	300	
Applied factory				Applied factory		
overhead	300			overhead	225	
	925				725	

Required:

a. Record the following journal entries using general ledger accounts; in addition, use subsidiary ledger accounts for work in process assuming that a perpetual inventory system is employed.

Jan. 2   Purchased direct material of $2,000 and repair supplies of $1,000 for cash.
     4   Issued materials as follows:

Job No. 1	$125
Job No. 2	175
Job No. 3	600
Repair supplies	825

     10 Job No. 1 was finished and transferred to the storeroom. It was determined that during the month of January direct labor cost on this job was $250 while machine-hours totaled 150 for January.
     16 The following factory items were paid in cash:

Rent	$400
Utilities	300
Miscellaneous expense	150

     19 Additional material was issued from the storeroom:

To Job No. 2	$154
To Job No. 3	62
Repair supplies	60

     20 Job No. 1 was sold for $4,750 on account.
     24 Job No. 2 was finished and transferred to the storeroom. It was determined that, during the month of January, direct labor cost on this job was $173 while machine-hours totaled 100.
     31 Analysis of the time sheets showed the following unrecorded factory labor: Job No. 3, $112; Factory supervision, $100; and Maintenance employees, $75.
     31 Overhead was applied to the remaining jobs in process. Machine-hours on Job No. 3 during January amounted to 35 hours.
     31 Depreciation of $338 on the factory building was recorded.
     31 Close the over- or underapplied overhead to cost of goods sold.

b. Prove your balance in a Work in Process Inventory.

P2–5. Missing amounts, over/underapplied overhead

Dale Asay Company presents the following selected general ledger accounts showing balances on May 1 of the current calendar year:

Cash			Payroll Payable	
12,000				–0–

4 050

Work in Process Inventory		Prepaid Insurance	
39,000		2,000	

6000
45000

Direct Materials Inventory		Finished Goods Inventory	
33,000		149,000	

31000 · 153000

Accumulated Depreciation		Factory Overhead Control	
	67,000	65,000	58,000

Cost of Goods Sold		Vouchers Payable	
197,000			31,000

Sales	
	314,000

Correct balances on May 31 of the current year include:

Payroll Payable. . . . . $ 4,000 (Cr.)
Direct Materials Inventory . . . . . .   31,000 (Dr.)
Work in Process Inventory. . . . . .   45,000 (Dr.)
Finished Goods Inventory . . . . . . 153,000 (Dr.)

The May transactions of Dale Asay Company are summarized as follows:

(a) Cash sales $107,000
(b) Materials purchased on account 38,000
(c) Cash disbursements to creditors 35,100
(d) Direct materials used. . . . . _____ 40,000
(e) Factory payroll paid 24,000
(f) Direct factory labor incurred 18,000
(g) Indirect factory labor incurred . . . . _____ 10000
(h) Factory overhead applied: 125% of direct labor cost . . . . _____ 22500
(i) Factory insurance expired   400
(j) Factory depreciation 1,400
(k) Factory repair services purchased on account 4,000
(l) Vouchers payable paid 53,000
(m) Cost of goods manufactured (using applied factory overhead) . . . . . _____ 74500
(n) Cost of goods sold (before over/underapplied factory overhead). . . . _____ 70500

Required:

a. Calculate the dollar amounts to fill the five blanks in the above list of transactions (d, g, h, m, n).

b. Post the amounts for all May transactions to the general ledger accounts given, using each transaction letter to cross-reference your posted debits and credits.

c. Prepare the entry to close the over/underapplied factory overhead to cost of goods sold.

P2–6.   Journal entries and supporting inventory schedules

The following data for Sardis Company summarize the operations related to production for November, the first month of operations. A job order cost system is used.

1. Direct materials costing $22,000 and indirect materials of $2,300 were purchased on account.

2. Materials requisitioned and factory labor used:

	Materials	Factory labor
Job No. 1	$2,340	$1,090
Job No. 2	3,390	1,990
Job No. 3	2,980	1,440
Job No. 4	4,765	2,890
Job No. 5	2,240	940
Job No. 6	1,940	1,090
For general factory use	515	690

3. Factory overhead costs incurred on account, $3,265.
4. Factory machinery and equipment depreciation totaled $1,340.
5. Factory overhead is applied at 60 percent of direct labor cost.
6. Jobs completed: Nos. 1, 2, 4, and 5.
7. Jobs No. 1, 2, and 4 were shipped and customers were billed for $5,690, $9,490, and $13,290, respectively.

Required:

a. Prepare entries in general journal form to record the summarized operations.
b. Open T-accounts for the Work in Process Inventory and Finished Goods Inventory and post the appropriate entries using the identifying numbers as dates. Insert memorandum account balances as of the end of the month.
c. Support the balance in the Work in Process account with a schedule of unfinished jobs.
d. Support the balance in the Finished Goods account with a schedule of completed jobs on hand.

P2–7. Budgeted cost of goods manufactured statement and income statement using FIFO, LIFO, and weighted-average inventory costing

Tiger Company produces and sells only one product. For the next year ending May 31, 19X2, management expects to sell 90,000 units at a sales price of $75 per unit. There are 5,000 units remaining in finished goods inventory at the end of the current year at a cost of $190,500. Management wants to have 8,000 units in finished goods inventory at the end of the period. The company wishes to maintain the end-of-period level of partially completed units.

Each unit of finished product contains three gallons of direct material; only one type of direct material is used, which costs $8 per gallon. Each unit requires two hours of direct labor before completion; the cost of direct labor is $10 per hour. Factory overhead is applied on the basis of $6 per direct labor-hour. Marketing costs at this level are budgeted to be $900,000; administrative costs are expected to be $300,000.

Required:

a. Prepare a budgeted Cost of Goods Manufactured Statement and Statement of Income using FIFO costing.
b. Assume instead that the company uses LIFO costing; determine the ending finished goods inventory.
c. Assume that the company uses weighted-average costing; determine the ending finished goods inventory. Round to two decimal points.

P2–8. Budgeted income statement and cost of goods manufactured under certain assumptions

Copies of the Carper Company's Cost of Goods Manufactured and Income Statements for the year ended December 31, 19X1 are given below. Beside the cost figures is an indication of whether they are variable (V) or fixed (F). There were 75,000 units produced in 19X1. Assume that first-in, first-out inventory costing is used and that material prices were stable during 19X1.

CARPER COMPANY
Cost of Goods Manufactured
For the Year Ended December 31, 19X1

Direct materials		
Inventory, January 1, 19X1		–0–
Purchases of direct material		$ 75,375
Direct materials available		75,375
Inventory, December 31, 19X1		375
Direct materials used		75,000(V)
Direct labor.		52,500(V)
Factory overhead:		
Utilities	$ 3,750 (V)	
Supervision	28,500 [7,500 (V), 21,000 (F)]	
Miscellaneous overhead	66,000 [6,000 (V), 60,000 (F)]	98,250
Cost of goods manufactured		$225,750

CARPER COMPANY
Income Statement
For the Year Ended December 31, 19X1

Sales.		$614,250
Less: Cost of goods sold:		
Finished goods, January 1, 19X1.	–0–	
Cost of goods manufactured.	$225,750	
Cost of goods available for sale	225,750	
Finished goods, December 31, 19X1	20,318	
Cost of goods sold		205,432
Gross margin.		408,818
Less: Marketing and administrative expense:		
Marketing expense	37,500 [24,570 (V),* 12,930 (F)]	
Administrative expense	37,500 F	75,000
Income before income taxes.		$333,818

*Variable with sales dollars.

Required:

Using the above information, prepare a budgeted income statement, including a schedule of cost of goods manufactured, for Carper Company for 19X1 under the following assumptions. (carry units costs to three decimal places):

a. Unit sales price will remain the same.
b. Variable cost per unit will remain the same.
c. Fixed costs will remain the same.
d. Sales will increase to 94,500 units.
e. Ending finished goods inventory, December 31, 19X2, will be 4,500 units and is to be valued using first-in, first-out costing. (Label all calculations and supporting computations.)

P2–9. Preparing journal entries and a cost of goods manufactured statement

A partial list of the account balances on November 1, 19X1, for the Don Dozier Manufacturing Company were Direct Materials, $65,000; Indirect Materials, $8,000; Work in Process, $70,000; and Finished Goods, $88,000. Transactions for the month include the following:

1. Purchased direct materials costing $30,000 and indirect materials costing $10,000 on account.
2. Paid cash for the factory rent, $1,500.
3. Issued material costing $28,160 to three jobs for the processing of units.
4. Janitorial supplies costing $1,080 and repair supplies costing $5,780 were issued from the storeroom.
5. Analysis of the payroll records revealed that direct labor of $43,000, indirect labor of $26,000, marketing salaries of $5,000, and administrative salaries of $6,000 were to be recorded. (Ignore payroll deductions.)
6. Depreciation on the factory machinery amounted to $2,770, and on the factory building to $2,850.
7. Insurance of $500 expired on the factory building and machinery.
8. The cost accountant has budgeted factory overhead for the year to be $450,000 and machine-hours to be 90,000. Machine-hours for November were 8,000. (Record the application of overhead.)
9. Paid cash for miscellaneous factory overhead of $330.
10. There were 3,000 finished units costing $150,000 transferred into the warehouse.
11. During the month, 4,000 units costing $200,000 were sold on account for $300,000.
12. It was determined that the reason for the difference in actual and applied factory overhead was due to inefficiencies in the operating conditions. (Close the Factory Overhead account.)
13. Other marketing expenses of $3,000 and administrative expenses of $4,600 were paid.

Required:

a. Prepare journal entries to record the transactions for the month, using subsidiary ledger accounts for factory overhead.
b. Prepare a Cost of Goods Manufactured Statement using applied factory overhead costs and also prepare a Statement of Income for the month.

P 2–10. Journal entry preparation using factory overhead subsidiary ledger

Before operations began, Bergen, Inc. decided to apply factory overhead on direct labor-hours. Annual factory overhead was estimated to be $524,400 based on 114,000 budgeted direct labor-hours; a subsidiary ledger is used to record the details of factory overhead. At the beginning of the year, the balances in the following accounts were:

Direct Materials Inventory . . . . $ 3,600
Repair Supplies Inventory   9,000
Work in Process Inventory 12,000
Finished Goods Inventory 19,900

January operations consist of the following transactions.

1. Direct material of $13,450 was purchased on account.
2. Direct material of $9,800 was issued out of the storeroom for use in production; $1,600 in materials were also issued for repair work.
3. Analysis of the bimonthly payroll records reveals the following (payroll deductions are to be ignored):

	Hours	Payroll costs
Direct laborers	4,500	$36,000
Superintendents	410	6,000
Factory repairers	300	2,800
Factory janitorial staff	700	3,200

4. Four jobs were finished on which 2,000 hours of direct labor had been incurred. (The transfer of total costs to the Finished Goods Inventory will be recorded at end of the month in a summary entry. Only apply factory overhead; the 2,000 direct labor-hours were included in the 4,500 hours recorded in 3 above.)
5. Miscellaneous factory expenses of $800 were paid in cash.
6. Analysis of the monthly depreciation schedules reveals the following:

Factory building $2,800
Production equipment 3,000
Office building (one quarter of the building is occupied by
  the marketing manager and marketing salespersons) 1,200
Office equipment (one third of the equipment is used by
  the marketing staff) 1,500

7. Repair supplies totaling $3,100 were issued from the storeroom.
8. Analysis of the insurance register reveals that the following prepaid insurance expired this month:

Coverage

Factory building $700
Factory equipment 150
Office building 600
Office equipment 300

9. End-of-the-month payroll records reveal the following (ignore payroll deductions):

	Hours	Payroll costs
Direct laborers	3,000	$25,000
Superintendents	400	5,400
Factory repairers	210	1,900
Factory janitorial staff	650	2,900
Marketing staff (monthly salary)		4,000
Administrative staff (monthly salary)		5,000

10. Factory overhead is applied to the six jobs remaining in process at the end of the

month; direct labor costs on these six jobs total $49,500 for 5,500 hours. (Assume that the entry to record direct labor has already been made.)

11. A physical count was made of the inventories on hand at January 31. The balances were as follows: direct material, $7,250; work in process, $61,500; and finished goods, $23,600. The difference reflects the costs transferred. The difference in the Finished Goods Inventory reflects goods that were sold on account at a markup on costs of 40 percent. (This markup was calculated before over- or underapplied overhead is closed.)

12. Close all revenue and expense accounts.

Required:

Prepare the general journal entries to record the monthly operations; use a factory overhead subsidiary ledger.

P2–11. Pro forma income statement based on projections given

The James Davis Manufacturing Company engages in the production of one model of a copy machine. The company has experimented with broadening its product line, but has found that it can maintain higher profits by concentrating its resources on one particular model that sells for $2,000. Davis has ascertained its per unit costs to be as follows:

Direct materials.	$600
Direct labor	450
Variable factory overhead	150
Fixed factory overhead	200
Marketing expense	150 (20% variable)
Administrative expense	100 (5% variable)

The company sold 8,000 units last year, but wants a 25 percent increase in sales this year. It has decided to reduce the sales price 15 percent to achieve the increased sales. The additional units can be produced with no alterations to or expansions of the existing plant facilities. It is estimated that direct material will decrease by $50 per unit by taking advantage of quantity discounts, and that direct labor will increase by $20 per unit.

Required:

a. Prepare a pro forma Statement of Income for this year taking into account the company's projections. Instead of preparing a separate Cost of Goods Manufactured Statement, detail the cost of sales on the Statement of Income.

b. Prepare a Statement of Income for last year so you can compare income before taxes on this statement to that prepared in (a) and advise the company regarding its decision to reduce the price.

P2–12. Cost of goods manufactured statement

Master Equipment Company accounts for costs incurred in the manufacture of its single product using a job order cost system. A review of the Cost of Goods Manufactured Statement for the fiscal year ended June 30, 19X1 discloses the following information and relationships:

1. Total manufacturing costs were $650,000 based on actual direct material used, actual direct labor, and applied factory overhead as a percentage of actual direct labor dollars.

2. Cost of goods manufactured was $618,500, also based on actual direct material, actual direct labor, and applied factory overhead.
3. Factory overhead was applied to work in process at 65 percent of direct labor dollars. Applied factory overhead for the year was 25 percent of the total manufacturing costs.
4. Beginning work in process inventory was 65 percent of ending work in process inventory.

Required:

Reconstruct the Cost of Goods Manufactured Statement for the year ended June 30, 19X1, in good form. Show supporting computations.

P2–13.   Cost of goods manufactured statement (AICPA adapted)

Rebecca Corporation is a manufacturer of special machines made to customer specifications. All production costs are accumulated by means of a job order costing system. The following information is available at the beginning of the month of October 19–.

> Direct Materials Inventory, October 1 . . . . $16,200
> Work in Process Inventory, October 1   3,600

A review of the job order cost sheets revealed the composition of the Work in Process Inventory on October 1, as follows:

> Direct materials. $1,320
> Direct labor (300 hours).   1,500
> Factory overhead applied   780
> $3,600

Activity during the month of October was as follows:

1. Direct materials costing $20,000 were purchased.
2. Direct labor for job orders totaled 3,300 hours at $5 per hour.
3. Factory overhead was applied to production at the rate of $2.60 per direct labor-hour.

On October 31, inventories consisted of the following components:

> Direct materials inventory $17,000
>
> Work in process inventory:
>   Direct materials . . . . $ 4,320
>   Direct labor (500 hours)   2,500
>   Factory overhead applied   1,300
>   Total. $ 8,120

Required:

Prepare in good form a detailed Cost of Goods Manufactured Statement for the month of October.

P2–14.   Theory of factory overhead (AICPA adapted)

Indirect manufacturing costs (factory overhead) include indirect materials, indirect labor, and other indirect costs.

Required:

a. Describe indirect materials and give an appropriate example.
b. Describe indirect labor and give an appropriate example.
c. Describe fixed indirect manufacturing costs (factory overhead).
d. Describe variable indirect manufacturing costs (factory overhead).
e. Describe semivariable indirect manufacturing costs (factory overhead).

APPENDIX PROBLEMS

P2–15. Home office ledger—factory ledger journal entries

Linda Black Company uses a home office ledger and a factory ledger. All asset accounts except the Direct Materials Inventory, Factory Supplies Inventory, Work in Process Inventory, and Finished Goods Inventory are maintained at the home office. All liabilities are also kept on the home office books. The following transactions occurred:

Jan. 5 Cash was paid for factory overhead of $8,100.
   6 Direct material costing $15,000 and factory supplies costing $9,000 were purchased on account for the factory.
   8 Requisitions of $9,500 of direct materials and $1,850 for factory supplies were filled from the storeroom.
   9 A weekly factory payroll of $15,000 was paid by the home office consisting of $9,000 for factory direct labor and $6,000 for repair employees. F.I.C.A taxes of $1,005 and income taxes of $1,200 were withheld. Employer's payroll tax is recorded at the end of the month.
  31 Depreciation on factory building and equipment was recorded in the amount of $4,800.
  31 Factory overhead was applied at $2.50 per machine-hour. Machine-hours for the month totaled 15,200.
  31 Goods costing $21,000 were completed and transferred to the finished goods storeroom.
  31 Goods costing $16,400 were sold on account for $20,000.

Required:

Prepare journal entries on the factory books and the home office books.

P2–16. Home office—factory journal entries

The home office of John Nixon Company is located in Michigan, but a major plant is located in San Antonio, Texas. The San Antonio office keeps a set of records separate from those of the home office. The factory trial balance on January 1 shows the following:

Accounts	Debit	Credit
Direct materials inventory	$18,900	
Factory supplies	3,000	
Repair supplies inventory	4,000	
Work in process inventory	9,500	
Finished goods inventory	16,200	
Home office ledger		51,600
	$51,600	$51,600

The following transactions occurred during January:

1. Direct materials purchased on account, $40,000.

2. Plant supervisor requisitioned direct materials of $22,000 along with repair materials of $2,500 and supplies of $900.

3. Cash in the amount of $26,700 was paid to vendors on account.

4. San Antonio payroll for the month consisted of: $56,000, direct labor; $20,100, indirect labor; $6,500, marketing salaries; $7,000, office salaries. In preparing the checks, the home office deducted 6.7 percent for F.I.C.A. tax and $15,800 for federal income tax. The liability for employer payroll tax is kept on the home office books. The state unemployment tax rate is 2 percent; the federal unemployment tax rate is 0.7 percent. Only expense controls for direct and indirect labor are maintained at the factory. Payroll taxes are treated as indirect costs.

5. The home office paid $10,000 cash for factory overhead and recorded $5,000 factory depreciation and $3,900 depreciation on office furniture and fixtures.

6. Direct materials costing $2,600 were defective and were returned to the vendor for credit.

7. Factory overhead is applied at a rate of 80 percent of direct labor cost.

8. Analysis of the inventory showed goods costing $15,700 remained partially complete at the end of the month. The remainder represented goods completed and transferred.

9. Goods were sold for $150,000, which represented a 40 percent markup on sales.

10. Close the factory overhead control account; any over- or underapplied balance is closed to the cost of goods sold account.

Required:

Prepare journal entries on the books of the home office and the factory to record the above transactions.

P2–17. Home office and factory office journal entries

Charles Mott Company uses both a factory ledger, which includes all transactions up to cost of sales, and a general ledger. All liabilities are maintained at the home office. The following transactions occurred during the month:

1. Direct materials purchased on account, $15,500.

2. Direct materials requisitions totaling $5,800 were filled from the storeroom.

3. Payroll for a month consisted of $14,000, direct labor; $18,800, indirect labor; $7,500, marketing salaries; and $12,000, office salaries. In preparing the checks, the home office deducted 6.7 percent for F.I.C.A. tax and $9,200 for federal income tax. The liability for employer payroll tax is kept on the home office books. The state unemployment tax rate is 2 percent; the federal unemployment tax rate is 0.7 percent. Payroll taxes are treated as direct costs. All wages are subject to the payroll taxes. Only expense controls for direct and indirect labor are maintained at the factory office.

4. Depreciation on factory machinery of $11,300 and $3,100 in expired prepaid insurance was recorded.

5. Cash of $600 for miscellaneous factory expense and $1,780 factory taxes were paid.

6. Factory overhead was applied at 260 percent of direct labor costs.

7. Goods costing $12,000 were completed in the factory.

8. Goods costing $7,000 were sold on account at $10,300.

9. Close the over- or underapplied factory overhead to cost of goods sold.

Required:

Record the above transactions using both home office and factory office books.

OBJECTIVES OF CHAPTER 3

1. To discuss what costs should be classified as material costs and to define the practical limitations of treating them as direct material costs.

2. To provide the theory behind and to illustrate the different methods of accounting for scrap material, spoilage, and defective units.

3. To present the selective control features of the ABC inventory method.

4. To illustrate the use of the tabular, graphic, and formula methods of computing economic order quantity (EOQ) and to show the effect of quantity discounts in selecting the most economical order size.

5. To discuss the impact of lead time and safety stock on inventory management.

6. To provide an overview of acceptable inventory valuation methods.

7. To illustrate the lower of cost or market rule for inventory valuation.

3

Costing materials and quantitative models for materials planning and control

Accumulating product cost for material is one of the responsibilities of cost accountants. In the process, they must decide how to treat material acquisition and handling costs for purchasing, storing, and receiving. While accounting theory indicates that all materials acquisition and handling costs, including invoice price, should be inventoried, practical limitations often exclude certain costs from total material cost. Quantitative models for material control also assume a significant role because, unless there are plans made for the purchasing, scheduling, and routing of material, some production departments may be idle while other departments are overworked. Without planning and control techniques, the effect would be inefficiency since inventory would be overstocked at some times and there would be shortages at others.

APPLICATION RATES FOR MATERIAL ACQUISITION AND HANDLING COSTS

In costing materials used in production, accounting for materials acquisition and handling costs may involve so much clerical expense that the benefits derived may not be worth the effort. However, if extra material handling costs are incurred because of the nature of an order, then a strong argument can be made for including these costs as a direct materials cost or increasing the factory overhead application rate on such orders requiring extra handling. Application rates can be developed for material acquisition and handling functions such as purchasing, receiving, and storing. For instance, the following formula could be used to determine an application rate for the purchasing department:

$$\frac{\text{Estimated purchasing department cost for a period}}{\text{No. of purchase orders or dollar value of purchases}} = \frac{\text{Rate per order}}{\text{or rate per purchase order}}$$

If purchasing department costs are estimated at $70,000 and the dollar value of direct material purchased is estimated at $1,000,000 for the next accounting period, the application rate is 7 percent, as computed below:

$$\frac{\$70,000 \text{ estimated purchasing department cost}}{\$1,000,000 \text{ estimated purchases}} = 7 \text{ percent}$$

The following formula could be used for applying receiving costs:

$$\frac{\text{Estimated receiving cost for a period}}{\substack{\text{Estimated number of items to be} \\ \text{received or dollar value received}}} = \substack{\text{Rate per item or} \\ \text{rate per dollar value}}$$

Using the following estimates, a 5 percent application rate is developed:

$$\frac{\$45,000 \text{ estimated receiving department cost}}{\$900,000 \text{ estimated dollar value received}} = 5 \text{ percent}$$

The following estimates could be used to determine the warehousing costs application rate:

$$\frac{\text{Materials–warehousing costs for period}}{\substack{\text{Number of items, square footage per} \\ \text{period, dollar value, or warehousing days}}} = \substack{\text{Rate per item,} \\ \text{square foot,} \\ \text{dollar value, or day}}$$

If warehousing department costs are estimated at $150,000 and the square footage is estimated to be 100,000, a $1.50 rate per square foot is computed as follows:

$$\frac{\$150,000 \text{ estimated warehousing costs}}{100,000 \text{ square feet estimated per period}} = \$1.50$$

Freight-in could also be handled in the manner illustrated above for other material handling costs. For example, assume the estimates for freight-in and material costs are as follows:

$$\frac{\$90,000 \text{ estimated freight-in}}{\$1,000,000 \text{ estimated purchases}} = 9 \text{ percent application rate}$$

Application of materials acquisition and handling costs illustrated

Assume that during the accounting period, direct material purchases of $60,000 are made, the dollar value of goods received is $58,000, and the square footage used is 3,000. The following journal entries would then be made to record the application of materials acquisition costs:

Direct Materials Inventory	17,000	
Purchasing Department Expense Control ($60,000 × 7%)		4,200
Receiving Department Expense Control ($58,000 × 5%)		2,900
Materials—Warehousing Department Expense Control (3,000		
square feet × $1.50)		4,500
Freight-In ($60,000 × 9%)		5,400

The actual cost is accumulated as a debit in the applicable expense control account. The applied amount is a credit. For example, if actual purchasing department costs total $4,500, there is a $300 underapplied balance in the Purchasing Department Expense Control account as seen below:

Purchasing Department Expense Control

Actual expenses	4,500	Applied expense based on rate per purchase dollar	4,200

The balance of the over- or underapplied material acquisition expenses is closed either to Cost of Goods Sold or directly to the temporary ledger account used for closing revenues and expenses, the Revenue and Expense Summary. Note the similarity between the treatment for applying material acquisition costs and that for applying factory overhead to units being manufactured; in both cases, actual costs are debits while the applied costs are credits to the ledger account. In both cases, the most significant aspect of the application process is computing rates using estimated costs and bases representative of departmental activity.

Conflict of theory and expediency.   Even though material acquisition and warehousing costs should be treated as direct costs, in practice they are all generally treated as indirect costs because such treatment is less costly and substantially the same results are achieved. Distributing material acquisition costs to the various material subsidiary ledger accounts affected can be time-consuming. Many companies argue that material acquisition and ware-housing costs are not related to volume and are really period costs. If material costs are not significantly misstated, there is no serious objection to treating material acquisition costs as either a part of administrative costs or as a part of factory overhead costs. Factory overhead costs are, in turn, allocated to all production in work in process inventory.

MATERIAL REQUISITIONS AND ISSUES

After materials are received, they may be classified as direct material because they become a component part of the finished product, or indirect material used in the manufacturing process. To record the material flow, a material requisition is presented to the storeroom. The *material (stores) requisition form* is a basic source document which informs the cost accounting department that material has been issued. No material should be issued from the storeroom if a material requisition isn't processed. This is a key internal control procedure. Cost accountants assign a cost to the department or job receiving the material. Exhibit 3–1 illustrates a typical manufacturing material requisition form which indicates that three pounds of thread and 15,000 yards of cloth are needed for Job No. 1212 in the sewing department. It is assumed that Material Requisition No. 914 (not illustrated) is issued to the treating department on January 18, 19X1, for 6 bags of calcium chloride. The material requisition not only fixes responsibility for the requisition of goods but also provides information for future reference. Requests for unusual material not normally carried in stock are made by the department requesting the material and are sent to the purchasing department.

Issuance of direct material.   Material requisitions facilitate assigning material cost to a job or department. Since the material requisition indicates the department requesting the material, it becomes the source document for recording the transfer of costs from Direct Materials Inventory to Work in Process Inventory or Factory Overhead. Most companies accumulate material requisitions for a week or month and make one entry to record the raw material used; otherwise, a company would have numerous entries per month. However, for illustrative purposes, the general journal entry to record the direct materials listed on the material requisition shown in Exhibit 3–1 is:

```
Work in Process Inventory—Job No. 1212 . . . . . . . . . . . . . . .    6,455.55
    Direct Materials Inventory . . . . . . . . . . . . . . . . . . . . . . . .                6,455.55
```

EXHIBIT 3–1

MATERIAL REQUISITION				
Department to be charged _Sewing Department_ Job no: _1212_ Date: _1/12/19X1_ Deliver to _Sewing Department_ Date wanted _1/15/19X1_				
Quantity	Unit of measure	Description of item	Unit price	Extension
3	Pound	Cotton-polyester thread	$1.85/lb.	$ 5.55
15,000	Yard	72″ 14 oz. cloth	$0.43/yd.	$6,450.00
Bill Cox Requested by			_Mary Miller_ Issued by	

Job order sheet

Direct material as well as other costs are accumulated for each batch or lot in a job order accounting system. With this system, a job order sheet must be prepared indicating the direct material and direct labor incurred on the job, as well as the amount of overhead applied. The job order cost sheet may be prepared and printed by a computer. The heading on the job order cost sheet illustrated in Exhibit 3–2 contains such information as the job number, customer, and date required. The subsidiary ledger for Work in Process Inventory may be an accumulation of the file of incomplete job order sheets. The material costs of $6,455.55 used in the Sewing Department and $37.50 used in the Treating Department are illustrated in Exhibit 3–2.

Material credit slips.   Material credit slips are issued when a department *returns* material to the storeroom. They can also be used to correct errors in material issuance. The credit slip transfers the material accountability from the production department back to the storekeeper. Material credit slips are the source document used by the accounting department to give credit to the department returning the material. In effect, they offset material requisitions. Normally an entry is made recording a batch of material credit slips; however, for illustrative purposes, the following entry is made to record the issuance of a material credit slip:

```
Direct Materials Inventory . . . . . . . . . . . . . . . . . . . . . . . . . . . . . . . .    XXX
      Work in Process Inventory—Job No. 1212. . . . . . . . . . . . . . . . . .          XXX
```

Only if the material can be reused in processing should material credit slips be used; if materials are changed or damaged, they are classified as scrap. In some operations in which materials such as fabric and wood are used, the material not needed is referred to as scrap and returned to the storeroom; this is really excess material and does not fall into the definition of scrap.

THE EFFECT OF PRODUCT WASTE

Waste control is one of the most important elements of inventory planning. The company should be keenly interested in the control of scrap, spoilage, and defective units because of the impact not only on costs, but also on the reputation of the company. Thus, rather than risk selling imperfect goods, a company may decide that increased quality control techniques and additional inspection points are profitable in the long run. A company also has several means for controlling excessive production costs. For example, some control can be accomplished through more effective supervision of the manufacturing facilities. Also, the use of scrap and spoiled goods reports that show the dollars lost because of imperfect goods may make management more aware of the importance of avoiding unnecessary spoilage costs.

EXHIBIT 3–2

JOB ORDER COST SHEET

JONES MANUFACTURING COMPANY

Customer: Job No. 1212

Douglass Warehouse, Inc.   Product 144″ # 8 Cloth (144 rolls)

309 North 12th Street   Date required 1/23/19X1

Murray, Kentucky 42071   Date started 1/16/19X1

                                                         Date completed 1/20/19X1

For stock

SEWING DEPARTMENT

Direct materials			Direct labor		Factory overhead		
Date	Requisition number	Amount	Date	Amount	Date	Basis	Amount
1/16/19X1	911	$6,455.55					

TREATING DEPARTMENT

Direct materials			Direct labor		Factory overhead		
Date	Requisition number	Amount	Date	Amount	Date	Basis	Amount
1/18/19X1	914	$37.50					

SUMMARY

	Sewing department	Treating department	Total	
Selling price				$XXX
Direct materials costs.	XX	XX	XX	
Direct labor costs.	XX	XX	XX	
Factory overhead applied.	XX	XX	XX	XXX
Gross margin.				$XXX

Scrap is defined as <u>materials that cannot be reused in the manufacturing process without additional refining;</u> this scrap <u>may or may not have a market value.</u> In fact, the company may have to pay to have the scrap which cannot be sold hauled away; conversely, other scrap, such as gold and other precious metals, is very valuable. Still other types of scrap may have limited dollar value.

Even though each unit of scrap has limited dollar value, the total value of scrap for any period may amount to a significant amount of money. For this reason, controls are needed to protect the scrap so that the company is able to sell all that is marketable. Otherwise, if workers see that the company is not properly accounting for scrap, they may be tempted to steal it, since they may feel that this would never be discovered.

Scrap report

If there is scrap, individual *scrap tickets* should be prepared. Periodically, a summary of these scrap tickets should be prepared in triplicate with the original given to the person responsible for maintaining the materials records, the second copy distributed to the accounting department for recording purposes, and the third copy retained in the department responsible for the scrap. Exhibit 3–3 illustrates a summary *scrap report* which shows not only the quantity of each item or part scrapped, but also the cost and reason for the scrap. The scrap report can also provide space for comparing the actual scrap against the scrap expected on that particular job. Often, an allowance for scrap is built into the material issued; for example, the material cost may include a 5 percent factor for cutting waste. Since scrap is sometimes inherent in the production process, the real concern is whether the actual scrap loss stays within the norms established. Exhibit 3–3 shows that there is a fairly large variance for Material Part No. 39C. After it is determined that the cause of the 39C scrap is defective molds, attention should be directed to correcting the molds. If the cause of the scrap variance is not expected to occur again, management may decide not to spend much time and effort in trying to correct the cause. The defective material causing the scrap in part No. 20A would be returned to the vendor for credit. If the sales value of the scrap is known, this can be inserted on Exhibit 3–3. Often the sales value is not known until the scrap is sold to the customer or scrap dealer.

ACCOUNTING FOR THE VARIOUS TYPES OF MATERIAL WASTE

The methods used in accounting for scrap depend on whether or not the sales value of the scrap is known when the scrapping of material occurs.

Sales value of scrap is not known

Time scrap occurs.   No journal entry is made, but the quantity of scrap material is itemized on the material ledger card.

Time of sale.   Cash or Accounts Receivable is debited with three possible accounts to be credited.

1.   Credit the job or department in which the scrap occurs:

EXHIBIT 3–3

SUMMARY SCRAP REPORT

Job	2509					Supervisor	Kent Miller
Department	Fabricating					Period	April 19X1

Material part no.	Description	Quantity scrapped	Unit cost	Total cost	Expected scrap	Variances	Sales value	Causes of actual scrap
20A	Supports	15	$1.25	$ 18.75	13	$ 2.50	$ 6.00	Defective material
39B	Copper pipe	5	4.80	24.00	1	19.20	Not known	Machine malfunction
39C	Plastic	11	8.70	95.70	5	52.20	$21.18	Defective molds
41E	Oak lumber	4	1.08	4.32	2	2.16	Not known	Operator inefficiency
41K	Tubing	12	.60	7.20	8	2.40	$ 4.10	Machine malfunction
		47		$149.97	29	$78.46		

```
Cash or Accounts Receivable . . . . . . . . . . . . . . . . . . . . . . . . . . . . . .  XXX
    Work in Process Inventory . . . . . . . . . . . . . . . . . . . . . . . . . . . .         XXX
```

While accounting theory indicates that this approach is the most correct method to use since it leaves the net cost in the job or department, it may present some practical problems. If the scrap is not significant for each job, it may not be feasible to associate scrap with a particular job. However, with difficult manufacturing jobs in which significant scrap is expected, the company may have agreed to credit customers for any revenues from scrap on their job.

2.   Credit the factory overhead control:

```
Cash or Accounts Receivable . . . . . . . . . . . . . . . . . . . . . . . . . . . . . .  XXX
    Factory Overhead Control—Recovery of Scrap . . . . . . . . . . . . . .         XXX
```

Here, the subsidiary ledger account, Recovery of Scrap, is credited for the sales price of the scrap. This method does not have as strong a theoretical justification as does the method crediting the sales value to Work in Process Inventory because it does not directly subtract the scrap sale from the cost of the job or department. Using this approach, scrap is not directly associated with any job or department; all products bear a portion of the scrap loss under this practical approach. At the time factory overhead application rates are being established, an estimate for scrap is made and deducted from the budgeted factory overhead costs. This procedure results in a lower factory overhead rate being applied to all products because of the value of scrap. This approach does have the advantage of being easier since the scrap sales are not traced to individual jobs or departments.

3.   Credit another income account:

```
Cash or Accounts Receivable . . . . . . . . . . . . . . . . . . . . . . . . . . . . . .  XXX
    Income from Sale of Scrap . . . . . . . . . . . . . . . . . . . . . . . . . . . . .         XXX
```

This approach is used frequently because it is easy to apply.

Sales value of scrap can be reliably estimated

Time scrap occurs.   Both the quantity of scrap and the dollar value are recorded when the scrap is sent to the storeroom. An asset account titled Scrap Inventory is set up with three possible accounts to be credited.

1.   Work in Process Inventory.

2.   Factory Overhead Control—Recovery of Scrap.

3.   Income from Sale of Scrap.

The advantages and disadvantages to consider in deciding which one of the three accounts to credit are the same as those mentioned above when one of these accounts is credited at the time of sale. However, in the situation we have here where the sales value can be estimated and scrap is recorded when it occured, alternative 3 has some inherent problems. With this approach, income is recognized before sales are made and variations in inventory cause an increase in income. But, as long as the income from scrap is not significant, the product or process cost is not materially misstated if this approach is followed.

Time of Sale.

At the time of sale, scrap inventory is credited as shown in this entry:

```
Cash or Accounts Receivable . . . . . . . . . . . . . . . . . . . . . . . . . . . . . . . . .   XX
      Scrap Inventory . . . . . . . . . . . . . . . . . . . . . . . . . . . . . . . . . . .          XX
```

Even though the exact sales price of the scrap may not be known at the time scrap occurs, if the dollar value of scrap is material and a time lag is expected before the scrap is sold, the company's assets are improperly recorded if no value is assigned to the scrap inventory. To avoid the understatement of assets, the best approach is to estimate and assign the expected market value of the scrap to Scrap Inventory.

Accounting for scrap illustrated

The following example describes the various methods used to account for scrap. Assume that in processing Job No. 42 it is determined that 10 parts have to be scrapped. Two different alternatives for scrap accounting are illustrated:

Assume that at the time the scrap is reported, the sales value of scrap cannot be determined. Later the scrap is sold for $30 cash.

Time Scrap Occurs   *NO JOURNAL*

Ten parts scrapped on Job No. 42 (memo entry only).
(A material ledger card is set up showing quantity.)

Time of Sale

```
1. Cash . . . . . . . . . . . . . . . . . . . . . . . . . . . . . . . . . . . . 30
      Work in Process Inventory—Job No. 42 . . . . . . . .           30
                              Or
2. Cash . . . . . . . . . . . . . . . . . . . . . . . . . . . . . . . . . . . . 30
      Factory Overhead Control—Recovery of Scrap . . .           30
                              Or
3. Cash . . . . . . . . . . . . . . . . . . . . . . . . . . . . . . . . . . . . 30
      Income from Sale of Scrap . . . . . . . . . . . . . . . .           30
```

Assume instead that at the time the scrap occurs, the company is able to reliably estimate that the scrap can be sold for $30. Later the scrap was in fact sold for $30. Using the three methods available, the entry is as follows:

Time Scrap Occurs

ESTIMATED VALUE

```
1. Scrap Inventory . . . . . . . . . . . . . . . . . . . . . . . . . . . . . 30
      Work in Process Inventory—Job No. 42 . . . . . . . .           30
                              Or
2. Scrap Inventory . . . . . . . . . . . . . . . . . . . . . . . . . . . . . 30
      Factory Overhead Control—Recovery of Scrap . . .           30
                              Or
3. Scrap Inventory . . . . . . . . . . . . . . . . . . . . . . . . . . . . . 30
      Income from Sale of Scrap . . . . . . . . . . . . . . . .           30
```

Time of Sale

Cash 30
    Scrap Inventory   30

Any difference between the amount recognized in the scrap inventory account and the sale price actually received is treated as a debit or credit adjustment to the Work in Process account, Factory Overhead Control account, or Scrap Income account consistent with the account credited at the time scrap occurred.

Cause of material scrap.   When parts with a high unit cost are scrapped, management should, besides keeping account of the scrap, determine the cause so that corrective action can be taken. For example, 11 39C plastic material parts in Exhibit 3–3 having a total cost of $95.70 were scrapped, and, while some scrap was expected, the actual quantity exceeds the norm. The company should, at this point, study the reasons for this scrap. While it may be possible to eliminate much of the scrapping of material, it may not always be economical to do so. The value of the scrap lost should be compared to the cost of controlling the scrap before a company establishes controls. Cost-benefit analysis enables management to determine what corrective action is economical.

Defective units

Another form of product waste is *defective units*. Defective units, as opposed to scrap, are those units that require extra work before they can be sold as first quality products. Two methods can be used to account for the added costs incurred to correct defective units:

1.   If the defective units result from unusual job requirements, the additional rework costs should be treated as direct costs of that job order. For example, if a customer requests an order on a rush basis, the cost of defective units should be charged to the job to the extent that time pressure has caused the defective units.

2.   If the defective units occur irregularly and are not the result of specific job requirements, the costs should probably be treated as departmental overhead costs. The rework costs should thus be charged to Factory Overhead Control and to a subsidiary ledger account called *rework costs*. When the factory overhead application rate is determined at the beginning of the year, an estimate for rework costs should therefore be included as additional factory overhead costs.

Accounting for rework costs.   For example, assume that after $500 direct material costs, $120 direct labor costs, and $150 factory overhead costs have all been accumulated for a job, it is determined that four units are defective and require additional direct material costing $65 and additional direct labor of $40. Since factory overhead is applied at 125 percent of direct labor cost, an additional $50 factory overhead is applied to account for the additional direct labor costs for reworking. The entries to record the cost of this job follow:

Original accumulation of costs

Work in Process Inventory	770	
Direct Materials Inventory		500
Wages Payable		120
Factory Overhead Control—Overhead Applied		150

Rework costs assigned to job

If the cost is to be assigned to the job, the following entry is needed:

Work in Process Inventory	155	
Direct Materials Inventory		65
Wages Payable		40
Factory Overhead Control—Overhead Applied		50

Transferred to finished goods

After the job is finished, the units are transferred to the finished goods storeroom. The following entry is needed to record this transfer:

Finished Goods Inventory	925	
Work in Process Inventory		925

Because of the rework costs, the costs of all units in the job have increased. Without the rework costs, the job would have cost $770. If an estimate for rework costs was included in arriving at the factory overhead application rate, a minor overcharge of factory overhead results when rework costs are charged directly to the job. To remedy this overcharge, an independent factory overhead application rate can be used or separate costs can be accumulated for this special job.

Costs assigned to overhead.   If the defective units were not the result of the job specifications, the following approach should probably be used to charge rework costs to factory overhead:

Original accumulation of costs

Work in Process Inventory	770	
Direct Materials Inventory		500
Wages Payable		120
Factory Overhead Control—Overhead Applied		150

Rework costs assigned to factory overhead

Factory Overhead Control—Rework Costs	155	
Direct Materials Inventory		65
Wages Payable		40
Factory Overhead Control—Overhead Applied		50

Transferred to finished goods

Finished Goods Inventory	770	
Work in Process Inventory		770

All the rework costs are transferred to Factory Overhead Control—Rework Costs; the job does not bear any rework costs.

Before reworking defective units, a company must determine that it is economical to perform such work. Sometimes, rather than spend substantial funds to correct defective units so that they can be sold as first quality, a company may find it more profitable to sell them in their current stage as scrap or spoiled goods. Operating procedures should prescribe when defective units should be reworked. Defective units should be reworked only after the production manager has authorized the rework or when company operating procedures indicate that it is economical.

Spoiled goods

While defective goods can be economically reworked so that they can be sold as first-quality finished goods, it is usually not profitable to correct spoiled goods enough to be sold as first quality. *Spoiled goods* are products which contain such significant imperfections that even with additional expenditures for material, labor, and overhead, they cannot be made into perfect finished products. It is generally felt that spoilage can be more effectively controlled if a distinction is made between spoilage due to the nature of the job versus spoilage that occurs because of a number of other factors, some of which are inherent in the manufacturing process. Some spoilage is considered to result from human error which cannot practically be avoided. Workers, after all, become fatigued and are not able to perform at peak efficiency during the entire workday; as a result, they may make errors in cutting fabric or wood or in mixing the needed ingredients.

Treatment of spoilage costs. Even though this chapter focuses only on job order costing, the procedures for process costing which are illustrated in Chapter 8 will follow approximately the same treatment of spoilage costs. Basically two ways of treating spoilage costs are used:

1. If spoilage is expected to occur regularly, the difference between the sales price of the spoiled goods and their total production costs should be accumulated in Factory Overhead Control.
2. If the spoilage is clearly traceable to a job because of its special requirements, the difference between the sales price of the spoilage and its costs is added to the cost of the good units only in that job.

The following example illustrates both methods of accounting for spoilage using a separate work in process account to accumulate each cost element. Assume a firm manufactures men's suits with the following cost per unit:

Materials	$30
Labor.	15
Factory Overhead	20 (using the applied rate)

If a lot contains 100 suits, the entry to record the costs in production is as follows:

Work in Process—Materials	3,000	
Work in Process—Labor	1,500	
Work in Process—Factory Overhead	2,000	
Direct Materials Inventory		3,000
Wages Payable		1,500
Factory Overhead Control		2,000

If 10 suits do not meet specifications and must be sold as "irregulars" for $260 and the spoilage is considered to be caused by a number of unpredictable factors, the spoilage cost is charged to Factory Overhead Control. The entire cost of the spoiled units is removed from the three work in process accounts. The sales value of the spoiled goods enters a special inventory account labeled Spoiled Goods Inventory. Factory Overhead Control with its subsidiary ledger account, Loss on Spoiled Goods, absorbs the difference. When factory overhead application rates are established, an estimate for the loss on spoiled goods should be included in budgeted factory overhead costs. In the example at hand, the 90 good units are transferred into finished goods inventory at a cost of $65 per unit (material, $30; labor, $15; and overhead, $20). This is illustrated below:

Spoilage charged to total production

Spoiled Goods Inventory	260	
Factory Overhead Control—Loss on Spoiled Goods	390	
Work in Process—Materials		300
Work in Process—Labor		150
Work in Process—Overhead		200
Finished Goods	5,850	
Work in Process—Materials		2,700
Work in Process—Labor		1,350
Work in Process—Overhead		1,800

Spoilage charged to job. If the spoiled units result because the job requires a special fabric or difficult pattern details, the 90 good units should bear the cost of all 100 suits, including the 10 spoiled units. The entry to record the original costs under these circumstances is the same as shown above:

Work in Process—Material	3,000	
Work in Process—Labor	1,500	
Work In Process—Factory Overhead	2,000	
Direct Materials Inventory		3,000
Wages Payable		1,500
Factory Overhead Control		2,000

Instead of crediting the three work in process accounts for the full cost of the spoiled units, only a portion of the cost is removed. The portion removed is determined as follows:

$$\frac{\$260 \text{ sales recovery of 10 units}}{\$650 \text{ total cost of 10 units}} = 40 \text{ percent sales recovery}$$

```
40% × $300 material cost of 10 units .........................    $120
40% × $150 labor cost of 10 units ...........................      60
40% × $200 overhead cost of 10 units .......................      80
                                                                 ─────
                                                                 $260
                                                                 ═════

Spoiled Goods Inventory ...................................    260
    Work in Process—Material ..............................          120
    Work in Process—Labor .................................           60
    Work in Process—Overhead ..............................           80
```

Similar computations can be determined using the following approach, which includes:

$$\frac{\$3{,}000 \text{ material cost of 100 units}}{\$6{,}500 \text{ total 100-unit job cost}} \times \$260 \text{ sales value} = \$120$$

$$\frac{\$1{,}500 \text{ labor cost of 100 units}}{\$6{,}500 \text{ total 100-unit job cost}} \times \$260 \text{ sales value} = \$60$$

$$\frac{\$2{,}000 \text{ overhead cost of 100 units}}{\$6{,}500 \text{ total 100-unit job cost}} \times \$260 \text{ sales value} = \$80$$

The cost of the remaining 90 good units has increased from $65 per unit to $69.33 computed as follows:

```
$6,500  total job cost
 −260   sales recovery value of spoilage
─────────
$6,240
  ÷ 90  good units = $69.33
```

The 90 good units are transferred to finished goods at the $69.33 unit cost as follows:

```
Finished Goods Inventory ..................................   6,240
    Work in Process—Materials .............................          2,880
    Work in Process—Labor ..................................         1,440
    Work in Process—Overhead ..............................          1,920
```

Defective and spoilage report. A report similar to the one illustrated in Exhibit 3–3 for scrap can be prepared for defective units and spoilage or all loss from scrap, defective units, and spoilage may be combined on one summary report. These reports should include (*a*) number of units defective or spoiled, (*b*) cost involved, and (*c*) cause of the spoilage if it can be determined. It is often difficult to determine who is responsible for the mistake causing the scrap, defective units, or spoilage. The person responsible for the mistake is not likely to admit it; as a result, such losses often go unreported. Requiring the supervisor to prepare such reports benefits the company only if they are used to aid in controlling scrap, defective units, and spoilage. Only if management is willing to spend time in studying the causes of material waste can they feel they have this aspect of material costs under control.

INVENTORY PLANNING

Inventory planning and control involves much more than minimizing the loss from scrap, spoilage, and defective units. For one thing, plans must be made for the scheduling of purchasing; otherwise the company will be overstocked during some periods and out of stock during others. The concern of management is that the investment in inventory represents an optimum balance between the two extremes of having inadequate or excessive inventories. Between these two extremes is a desirable inventory level; the objective is to find this level. Just as the financial manager wants to avoid idle cash on which no return can be earned, the controller wants to maintain the optimum inventory investment. After all, the cost of carrying unnecessary inventory stock reduces the profitability of the firm.

Stockouts, TOS, and B/O

When the company runs out of inventory, this is referred to as *stockouts, temporarily out of stock (TOS)*, and *back orders (B/O)*. The inadequate inventory does not allow the company to provide the level of service that its customers demand, and at the same time may destroy goodwill toward the firm. The type of product being sold influences this risk; for example, if a stockout occurs for a convenience item, the customer will usually switch brands. Repeat sales may therefore be lost when such shortages occur. If a shortage of raw material occurs, there is a possibility that the production cycle must stop or slow down. Stockouts of either raw materials or finished goods can cause the company's facilities to remain idle or be underutilized in some periods while being overtaxed at other times.

The degree of service reliability that the firm wishes to offer its customers is another factor to consider when determining inventory size. The willingness of the customers to tolerate a delayed delivery influences the size of inventory that must be carried. Clearly, the higher the degree of service reliability offered, the larger an investment in inventory that must be carried.

Despite all this, a large inventory investment is not advised for materials that are used in the manufacture of products that are subject to short and intense sales periods, such as novelties or high-fashion products. The company involved in such sales should try to match its purchases with sales and to avoid extra inventory buildups. Often this goal is not met, however, because the sales forecast is incorrect. Fortunately, less risk is involved in carrying larger stocks of materials used in manufacturing products which have a long sales life and are not subject to rapid market changes, technological obsolescence, or physical deterioration.

Costs of the two extremes.   In selecting the inventory level that minimizes costs in the long run, the company should evaluate the costs of carrying too much inventory and of not carrying enough. Many of these costs do not actually appear in accounting records but are used for planning purposes only. For example, the loss of sales or customer goodwill is never recorded in a formal accounting record; however, these costs are, of course, important in determining the optimum inventory level. In any case, there will always be a trade-off between carrying too much inventory and not carrying enough.

The costs of not carrying enough inventory are as follows:

Raw material inventory	Finished goods inventory
1. Additional costs due to interruptions of production.	1. Loss of customer goodwill.
2. Lost quantity discounts.	2. Contribution margin on lost sales.
3. Additional purchasing costs (due to rush).	3. Additional transportation costs.

The costs of carrying both excessive raw material and excessive finished goods inventories are as follows:

1.   Increased cost of the storage space.

2.   Increased insurance and property taxes.

3.   Increased cost of handling and transferring inventory.

4.   Increased risk of theft, technological obsolescence, and physical deterioration.

5.   Increased clerical costs in maintaining records.

6.   Loss of desired return on investments in inventory and storage space.

To meet the objective of minimizing costs in the long run, the company should decide which inventory items warrant the highest degree of control. Unless the company has unlimited funds to install all the control features the cost accountant wishes, decisions must be made as to what control methods are feasible for the type of inventories carried.

ABC ANALYSIS AND TWO-BIN SYSTEM

One such method is ABC analysis, a commonsense approach to deciding which inventories should receive tighter control. Other names such as 80/20 (i.e, 80 percent of the dollar cost of material used is in 20 percent of the inventory items) are given to this selective approach; however, the ABC method is the name most commonly used. The method operates on the exception principle, because it is neither feasible nor possible to give the same amount of attention to all inventory stock. Those inventories that are important either because they are critical to production or have a large dollar value deserve frequent reviews and tight control. A ranking of inventory, comparing the cost of running out of stock with carrying costs, can also be used in determining which inventories should be tightly controlled.

EXHIBIT 3–4

ABC analysis of inventory

Material part no.	Budgeted unit usage	Unit price	Total cost
X1.	3,300	$ 4.00	$ 13,200
X2.	11,900	0.54	6,426
X3.	15,750	0.26	4,095
X4.	3,600	13.15	47,340
X5.	990	26.70	26,433
X6.	9,980	0.90	8,982
	45,520		$106,476

EXHIBIT 3–5

Item	Budgeted unit usage	Total cost
X4.	3,600	$ 47,340
X5.	990	26,433
X1.	3,300	13,200
X6.	9,980	8,982
X2.	11,900	6,426
X3.	15,750	4,095
	45,520	$106,476

A few inventory items in Exhibit 3–4 illustrate the ABC system. In this system, management must first determine the future usage of each material item for a designated period. Then the unit price of each material is also estimated so that the total consumption cost can be determined. Some ABC systems are based solely on unit cost, while others use only turnover in identifying the controls necessary. One approach is to base the inventory controls on both usage and unit costs; this is the approach presented here.

The items from Exhibit 3–4 are listed in descending order of total consumption cost in Exhibit 3–5.

The items are next divided into classes based on their total cost. Arbitrary criteria are chosen by management to reflect both the number and the break between classes. Class divisions depend on the storage facilities, personnel, and other resources available.

ABC classes.   There are three classes established with Class A containing Items X4 and X5; Class B, Items X1 and X6; and Class C, Items X2 and X3. In most cases, management finds that, as here, a relatively large percentage of its inventory costs is tied up in a small percentage of the material items carried in stock. Exhibit 3–6 shows that only 10 percent of the total units account for 69 percent of the cost. Because so much cost is tied up in Class A, the greatest degree of control should be applied here. Frequent reviews of the stock in Class A should be made so that small inventory levels can safely be carried. Less control will be applied to items in Class B, and even less control for items in Class C. It is not necessary for elaborate controls to be used for the Class C, low-value items. Since the cost of each item in Class C is proportionately small, carrying more stock in Class C inventory than is needed for the period's production is less cause for concern.

The selective control features of the ABC method provide guidelines for the review procedures and types of controls to apply to the different inventory classes. The frequency of these reviews and the tightness of the controls are also dependent on the material inventory class. In addition, a trade-off between the cost of inventory control features and the cost of the material item controlled always exists.

Material parts in Class A of the ABC method that are of high value or of a critical nature to the production process should be reviewed frequently, perhaps even daily. Other Class A items not falling into this critical category can be reviewed less frequently. The quantity of stock on hand may be examined at regular intervals; for example, every 30, 60 or 90 days the stock status may be determined so that necessary purchase orders can be placed. In addition to setting time intervals for examining stock levels, desired inventory levels may also be established in advance.

EXHIBIT 3–6

Class	Unit usage	Percent of total units	Total cost	Percent of total cost
A.	4,590	10	$ 73,773	69
B.	13,280	29	22,182	21
C.	27,650	61	10,521	10
	45,520	100	$106,476	100

Two-bin system

For their low-value, noncritical items, some companies use a simple *two-bin system*. Two bins, piles, or other measures are used, with the first bin containing enough material to meet manufacturing needs between the time one order is received and another is placed. The reserve bin contains enough stock to satisfy production requirements for the time between placing an order and receiving the goods. When the first bin is empty and the reserve bin tapped, a purchase requisition for additional stock must be prepared immediately. If a purchase order is not placed when units are first withdrawn from the reserve stock, the company may use all its inventory stock and a stockout occurs. Perpetual inventory records are not maintained for material items under the two-bin system, because the expense of maintaining these records may outweigh the cost of the material being controlled. Because the two-bin system is an inexpensive means of material control, it is generally appropriate only for Class C, low-value material items.

Various other simple methods may also be used for indicating a reorder point. A line or some other mark may be placed on the storage bins, indicating the point at which a purchase order should be placed. This mark represents the minimum level the stock can reach before reorders are made. Because most companies have both limited storage space and inventory investments, maximum quantity and dollar limits for each inventory should be established. If the maximum quantity of each inventory that should be on hand at all times is adhered to, there is less chance of overstocking.

Automatic reorder system

Both manual and mechanical inventory systems can have an automatic reorder procedure built in so that a purchase order is typed out whenever the balance on hand drops to a designated level. This is easily done if the company has access to electronic data processing equipment. The quantity can be built into the computer so that the amount to be ordered is indicated when the machine generates the purchase order. More elaborate inventory techniques can be used depending on the capabilities of the electronic data processing equipment.

ECONOMIC ORDER QUANTITY

A more sophisticated approach to inventory management involves calculation of an economic order quantity (EOQ). EOQ is the order size that minimizes both the costs of ordering and the costs of carrying inventory in stock over a period of time, given a stable level of demand that is known with certainty. The ordering costs include the costs of preparing and processing an order and receiving the materials. Carrying costs include insurance, depreciation, taxes, rent on storage facilities, and the cost of money. Carrying cost may be expressed as a percent of the unit's purchase cost. Economic order quantity can be calculated in a table, graph, or using a formula. An example follows.

Assume the following facts for a company:

Annual requirements.	1,000 units
Ordering cost per purchase order (includes postage, telephone, clerical costs)	$15 per order
Carrying costs per unit for a year (taxes, depreciation, rent, insurance, and desired return on inventory investment) . .	$0.75 per unit

Tabular determination of EOQ. An approximate value for EOQ can be determined using a *tabular* analysis like that shown in Exhibit 3–7. Varying order sizes are arbitrarily used to satisfy the annual requirements of 1,000 units. Since it is assumed that the inventory level is zero when each purchase order is received, and the inventory level increases to the order size upon the order's arrival, the average inventory is computed as one half the order size.

EXHIBIT 3–7

Tabular determination of economic order quantity

Order size (selected arbitrarily)	100	200	400	600	800	1,000
Average inventory (order size/2)	50	100	200	300	400	500
Number of orders $\dfrac{\text{Annual requirements}}{\text{Order size}}$	10	5	2.5	1.6	1.25	1
Total ordering cost (no. of orders @ $15)	$150	$ 75	$ 38	$ 24	$ 19	$ 15
Total carrying cost (average inventory @ $0.75)	38	75	150	225	300	375
Total costs of carrying and ordering inventory	$188	$150	$188	$249	$319	$390

As units are used, the stock decreases so that just before another order is received, the stock is zero. As the order size increases, the number of orders necessary to meet yearly total needs decreases. Conversely, total ordering costs decrease when fewer orders are made, but the carrying costs increase because more space is required to hold the larger orders. Carrying costs and ordering costs move in opposite directions; at some point there is an order size at which total costs are minimized. Since the total annual costs for carrying and ordering are lowest at 200 units, this order size reflects the EOQ given the indicated order size.

Graphic Determination of EOQ. Rather than calculating the EOQ using a tabular analysis, a company can prepare *graphs*. Exhibit 3–8 illustrates the graphic method of determining EOQ. The ordering cost curve shows that total order costs decrease as the order size increases. Carrying costs move in the opposite direction; they increase as the order size increases because there is more inventory on hand. The curve representing the total costs of carrying and ordering begins to flatten between 200- and 400-units. After this range is found, an order size is chosen in this area at the lowest point. In Exhibit 3–8, the low point is 200 units, which is considered to be the EOQ.

EOQ formula. A method of determining EOQ which is even more accurate and timesaving than either the tabular or graphic approaches is the

EXHIBIT 3–8

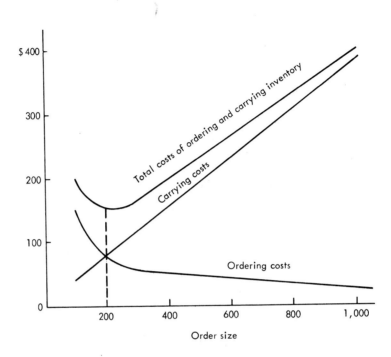

formula method. The EOQ formula is widely used and can be expressed in several ways using a variety of symbols. One simple variation of the formula is as follows:

$$EOQ = \sqrt{\frac{2QO}{C}}$$

where

Q = Annual quantity required in units.
O = Cost of placing an order.
C = Annual cost of carrying a unit in stock.

Using the data presented earlier with Q = 1,000, O = $15, and C = $0.75, the EOQ is determined as 200 below:

$$\sqrt{\frac{2(1,000)\,(\$15)}{\$0.75}} = 200$$

Not all calculations of EOQ result in such a neat answer as 200 units; depending upon annual requirements, ordering costs, and carrying costs, the answer could have been 218 or some other odd figure.

The EOQ determined by all three methods is the same only because the order sizes in Exhibits 3–7 and 3–8 were selected to correspond to the EOQ using the formula. If, for instance, the EOQ calculated by the formula were 415 using other data, it would be very unlikely that an order size of 415 was arbitrarily chosen for the tabular analysis or the graphic approach. The tabular or graphic approaches are, after all, not as exact as the EOQ formula. This is why the answer obtained through the tabular or graphic approach is only an approximate value. The formula method is generally preferred because of ease of application. However, even if the formula method is used, the graphical analysis provides a useful visual representation of the relationship between carrying and ordering costs and gives some appreciation of the consequences of ordering some amount greater or less than optimal. In addition, the tabular presentation can be used as a convenient form for communicating such relationships to some party not involved in the analysis.

Regardless of the method used to compute EOQ, the total cost of buying and carrying the units ordered can easily be determined through use of the following formula:

$$\frac{\text{EOQ}}{2} \text{ (Carrying cost per unit)} + \frac{\text{Annual requirements}}{\text{EOQ}} \text{ (Ordering cost per order)}$$

Using an EOQ of 200 units, $0.75 carrying cost per unit, 1,000 units annual requirements, and $15 ordering cost per order, the buying and carrying costs become the following:

$$\frac{200}{2} (\$0.75) + \frac{1,000}{200} (\$15) = \$150$$

EOQ is only one factor. Although the answer determined using EOQ analysis is mathematically correct, a company may still buy a quantity other than the EOQ. For while economic order quantity does represent a trade-off between carrying and ordering costs which move in opposite directions, it should be recognized that the EOQ model may not contain all relevant costs. Therefore, additional costs may have to be considered formally in a more complicated model or informally through some judgmental process external to the model. Carrying and ordering costs are only two factors in determining the actual order quantity a company uses. For example, a company may buy 50 or 100 units at a time rather than the 200 EOQ determined earlier in the illustrations because it cannot pay for the larger order even though it is more economical. In addition, a company may wish to maintain a larger stock of inventory than indicated by EOQ analysis so a high level of customer service is provided.

In addition to recognizing that EOQ is only one factor in determining order size, there are also several basic assumptions of EOQ that can be questioned. For example, a constant usage assumption is implicit in the simplified EOQ model presented here; yet inventory is not always used at a constant rate.

However, for this model, an activity volume at a stable demand level must be estimated before purchase price, carrying costs, and ordering costs per unit are determined. Therefore, these costs and annual sales are approximations. Also, the simplified EOQ models presented do not contain all relevant costs affecting the order size decision. For example, since the basic EOQ formula ignores the purchase price of the inventory, the formula does not consider the reduction in material costs of taking quantity discounts. However, there are a large number of alternative, more complex models which involve variable usage rates and variable lead times in addition to other relevant costs.

Effect of quantity discounts

The effect of quantity discounts, however, *can* be used with the tabular approach to determine EOQ. Exhibit 3–9 employs the same data presented in Exhibits 3–7 and 3–8 except that a quantity discount factor is included in the calculation of total annual costs. Such an economic order table may be prepared for each class of material. The data assumptions are as follows:

Annual quantity required.	1,000 units
Costs of ordering per purchase order	$ 15.00
Carrying costs per unit.	0.75 per unit
Material cost ($10 per unit at list price)	$10,000

The following discount is offered by the supplier:

Order size in units	Quantity discount (percent)	Price per unit
0–99	0	$10.00
100–199.	1	9.90
200–399.	2	9.80
400–599.	4	9.60
600–799.	5	9.50
800–999.	5	9.50
Over 1,000.	5.5	9.45

EXHIBIT 3–9

Economic order table with quantity discount effect

Order size (arbitrarily selected)	100	200	400	600	800	1,000
Average inventory	50	100	200	300	400	500
Number of orders.	10	5	2.5	1.6	1.25	1
Quantity discount.	1%	2%	4%	5%	5%	5.5%
Total ordering costs . . . . $	150	$ 75	$ 38	$ 24	$ 19	$ 15
Total carrying costs.	38	75	150	225	300	375
Net cost of materials.	9,900	9,800	9,600	9,500	9,500	9,450
Total annual cost. . . . . $	$10,088	$9,950	$9,788	$9,749	$9,819	$9,840

The most economical order, as shown in Exhibit 3–9 on the opposite page, is 600 units (increased from 200 units in Exhibit 3–7) because of the effect of quantity discounts. (Note that a neat answer of 600 is determined only because its cost is lower than any of the other five order sizes arbitrarily selected. Also, just as is the case above, the company may not purchase 600 units because of an inadequate cash flow.)

Economic production runs

By substituting the setup cost for a new production run in place of the unit ordering cost, the economic order quantity concept can be used to determine economic production runs. The setup cost includes the labor and other costs involved in preparing facilities for a run of a different production item. As seen in the following example, the problem of deciding when to start and stop production runs can be solved by this concept.

Management has determined the following costs are associated with one of its product lines:

Q = 60,000 units produced each year.
S = \$200 setup cost to change a production run.
C = \$4 carrying cost per unit.

The optimal production run size can be determined by using this variation of the formula used in computing economic order quantity:

$$\text{Optimal production run} = \sqrt{\frac{2 \times (60,000) \times \$200}{\$4}}$$

$$= \sqrt{\frac{\$24,000,000}{\$4}} = 2,450$$

The relatively high setup cost requires large production runs; as a result, overall cost is minimized if production runs of approximately 2,450 units are used.

Lead time

Through the use of EOQ analysis, the optimal order size can be determined; now the question is when to order. Several factors affect this decision; one is *lead time*—the time it takes to receive an order after it is placed. If the supplier is reliable, the time needed for delivery, or lead time, can be predicted with a high degree of certainty. However, for most products, it is not possible to predict lead time because of uncertainties in delivery schedules. In addition, it may be difficult to estimate the amount of material that will be used during the lead time. If material usage is not steady, there is a danger that stockouts will occur or that new customers' orders will arrive before the stock ordered is received.

CALCULATING SAFETY STOCK AND REORDER POINTS

Since it is difficult to forecast lead time and inventory usage with a high degree of certainty, an inventory buffer, or *safety stock,* is needed to protect the company from stockouts. There is often a temptation to be conservative and maintain a large stock; however, this can be costly and may result in excessive inventory carrying cost. If an inadequate safety stock is maintained, on the other hand, interruptions and inconveniences can result and stockouts may become frequent. The ideal safety stock level minimizes the possibility of stockouts and the cost of carrying inventory. The intangible costs of stockouts are difficult to measure because the loss of both a customer's goodwill and possible repeat sales cannot easily be quantified.

Several means are available to estimate safety stock. According to one method, management arbitrarily decides to use a certain number of average days' usage as its safety stock. Another method allows for the fluctuations between maximum daily usage and average daily usage. To illustrate, the following data refer to one material item used by a company:

Maximum daily usage . . . . 40 units
Average daily usage . . . . 30 units
Minimum daily usage . . . . 15 units
Lead time . . . . 18 days

The safety stock is computed as follows:

10 units (40 maximum daily usage −30 average daily usage)
×18 days *Lead time*
180 units of safety stock

Another method is to calculate the probability of running out of stock at various levels of safety stock and determine an annual expected stockout cost. To this cost is added the annual cost of carrying safety stock in inventory. Total annual carrying cost increases with the level of safety stock maintained, but stockout cost decreases as the level of stock increases. The goal is to determine the number of units of safety stock which results in the lowest annual cost. Assume the following options are available for a product:

Units of safety stock	Probability of running out of safety stock (percent)
20	50
40	30
60	25
Stockout cost	$100 per occurrence
Carrying cost . . . . of safety stock	$4 per unit per year
Number of purchase orders	8 per year

Exhibit 3–10 contains an analysis of these costs; the lowest cost results with 40 units of safety stock.

EXHIBIT 3–10

| | Safety stock costs | | | | Stockout costs | | | | |
Units of safety stock	×	Unit carrying cost per year	=	Total annual carrying cost	Cost per stockout	×	Probability of stockout	×	Annual Purchase orders	=	Expected Annual stockout cost	Expected total cost
20	×	$4	=	$80	$100		.50	×	8	=	$400	$480
40	×	4	=	160	100		.30	×	8	=	240	400*
60	×	4	=	240	100		.25	×	8	=	200	440

*Lowest costs.

Reorder point

After the safety stock is determined, it is possible to determine a *reorder point*, which is the inventory level at which it is necessary to place an order. The reorder point is computed as follows:

$$\begin{array}{l} 180 \text{ safety stock} \\ +540 \text{ (18 days lead time} \times 30 \text{ average daily usage)} \\ \hline 720 \text{ reorder point in units} \end{array}$$

The reorder point is computed by adding the safety stock to the average usage during the lead time. Safety stock can be built into the computation by multiplying the maximum daily usage by the lead time as follows:

$$\begin{array}{l} 40 \text{ maximum daily usage} \\ \times 18 \text{ days lead time} \\ \hline 720 \text{ reorder point in units} \end{array}$$

This computation may need to be expanded if lead time is long and/or the order quantity is small. Under these circumstances, there may be one or more orders placed but not received that must be included in the computation determining when to reorder. Using the above example, the company would reorder when units on hand plus orders in transit equal 720.

Reorder point with certainty. The above computation was based on realistic assumptions because an allowance was made for variations in lead time and in daily usage. Safety stock provided a cushion against stockouts and, in turn, this increased the reorder point. However, if usage is even throughout the year and lead time is always reliable, safety stock can be omitted from the reorder point computation. The reorder point then becomes the average usage during the lead time or 540 (18 days' lead time × 30 average daily usage) for the above example.

CAS 411

In 1975, the Cost Accounting Standards Board (CASB) promulgated Cost Accounting Standard 411—*Accounting for Acquisition Costs of Material*. The purpose of the standard is to provide for better allocation and measurement of material costs as they relate to specific contracts. The standard includes provisions on the use of inventory costing methods. It states that the accounting practices used for this purpose should be justified on the basis of their effectiveness for such allocation and measurement and should not be justified solely because they are acceptable for tax and financial reporting purposes. CAS 411 further states that generally accepted accounting principles do not specify the details of cost allocation to particular contracts but are concerned with reporting the financial results of operations of the company as a whole.

CAS 411 requirements.   CAS 411 requires that each contractor have and consistently apply written statements of accounting policies and practices for accumulating the costs of material and for allocating costs of material to cost objectives. A cost objective is defined as a function, organizational subdivision, contract, or other work unit for which cost data are desired and for which provision is made to accumulate and measure the cost of processes, products, jobs, capitalized projects, and so forth. CAS 411 further allows the costs of units of a category of material to be allocated directly to a cost objective provided the cost objective is specifically identified at the time of purchase or production of the units. This regulation states that the cost of material used solely in performing indirect functions or that is not a significant element of production cost may be allocated to an indirect cost pool. If such material was significant, the cost of such indirect material that is not consumed in a cost accounting period is established as an asset at the end of the period.

SUMMARY

The chapter dealt with application rates for distributing carrying costs to inventory. The most significant aspect of the application process is computing rates using estimated costs and bases representative of departmental activity. However, the distribution of material acquisition costs to the various material subsidiary ledgers can be complex and time-consuming. As a result, in practice, material acquisition and carrying costs are generally treated as indirect costs.

In many plants, some level of product waste is considered normal because of the inherent nature of the material or manufacturing process involved. While in some instances it may be technically possible to eliminate defective units and spoiled goods, it may not be economical on a cost/benefit basis because the costs of lowering product waste exceeds the cost of the current spoilage. Above all, accounting controls should ensure that product waste is minimized.

The ABC system of inventory control recognizes that there is always a trade-off between the cost of the control tool being used and the cost of the material being controlled. By analyzing where the bulk of the inventory cost lies, management can select its controls sensibly. The company should use frequent reviews and tight controls for material parts that are of high value or are critical to the manufacturing process.

While it is recognized that some of the control tools introduced in this chapter, such as safety stock and EOQ, are approximations at best, they do allow management to find the range from which to choose the quantity ordered. The simplified EOQ model presented gives accurate answers if usage or demand is stable; unfortunately, many companies experience erratic patterns. However, through the use of the tabular, graphic, or formula methods of determining EOQ which were presented, management gains insight into the relevant range of inventory levels. If a more exact answer is desired, which considers variable usage rates and variable lead times as well as costs other than ordering and carrying costs, more complex models are available.

The EOQ model presented can be supplemented to take into account the effect of quantity discounts on order size. Even though the answer obtained may be mathematically correct, the company may actually order other quantities because it may not be able to pay for the larger order even though it is more economical; or the company may feel that a high level of customer service warrants carrying a larger stock of inventory than that indicated by EOQ analysis.

Most companies find that they must provide for an inventory buffer, or safety stock, since accurately estimating lead time and inventory usage is difficult. The reorder point can be determined by multiplying maximum daily usage by lead time; this approach builds safety stock into the computation. Applications of reorder point and safety stock are quite common in practice.

IMPORTANT TERMS AND CONCEPTS

Applied material acquisition and handling costs

Materials requisition

Job order sheet

Materials credit slips

Scrap materials

Defective units

Spoiled goods

Optimum inventory level

Stockouts, TOS, B/O

ABC inventory system

Two-bin inventory system

Economic order quantity (EOQ)

Economic production runs

Lead time

Safety stock

Reorder point

CAS 411

APPENDIX 3–A: INVENTORY COSTING METHODS

A decision must be made regarding the inventory costing method to use. Costing material differs somewhat from costing labor and overhead because the accountant is faced with choosing which material cost to use in determining product cost. The primary objective is to achieve a proper matching of costs and revenues with some consideration given to the residual inventory values on the balance sheet. Several actual inventory costing methods are briefly described here.

FIFO inventory method

The first-in, first-out (FIFO) method assumes that the first costs incurred are the first costs selected, regardless of the physical flow. Material issues are costed at the unit cost of the oldest supply on hand. The ending inventory is composed of the most recent costs of material or production of goods. Exhibit 3A–1 illustrates a material ledger card using FIFO under a perpetual inventory system in which a record is made of each transaction so that a book balance of the quantity of material on hand is available at any time.

A disadvantage of using the FIFO inventory costing method is that a rise in material price matched by a corresponding increase in sales price tends to inflate income, while a decline in material price and sale price deflates income. This occurs because in periods of increasing costs and sales prices, the costs charged against revenue come from the older, lower priced inventory on hand, while the ending inventory is made up of the newer, higher priced stock. The lower cost is charged to cost of sales and the new higher cost remains in inventory. Income taxes are levied and paid on the artificially inflated profits which result. The advantage of FIFO is that it produces an ending inventory valuation which approximates current replacement costs, although most companies currently rely on the income statement rather than the balance sheet for performance evaluation.

LIFO inventory method

Using the last-in, first-out (LIFO) method of inventory valuation, the cost of the latest items purchased or produced is assumed to be the first to be assigned to units issued or sold. The materials in ending inventory are costed at prices in existence at a much earlier date since they represent the cost of the oldest stock on hand.

Exhibit 3A–2 illustrates the use of LIFO with a perpetual inventory method.

The LIFO inventory method has the advantage of matching current inventory costs with current revenues; this provides a more proper matching on the income statement. In a period of increasing prices, the cost of goods

EXHIBIT 3A–1

MATERIAL LEDGER CARD—FIFO—PERPETUAL INVENTORY

Item: Material A

Reorder point 40 Reorder quantity 60

ITEM DESCRIPTION

	Receipts			Issued					Balance		
Date	Quantity	Amount	Unit cost	Date	Req. no.	Job no.	Quantity	Amount	Quantity	Amount	Unit cost
Jan. 1	Balance								40	$ 88.00	$2.20
Jan. 7	60	$150.00	$2.50						60	150.00	2.50
				Jan. 9	112	84	64	$148.00	36	90.00	2.50
Jan. 18	60	152.40	2.54						60	152.40	2.54
				Jan. 22	113	86	75	189.06	21	53.34	2.54
Jan. 24	60	156.00	2.60						60	156.00	2.60

EXHIBIT 3A–2

MATERIAL LEDGER CARD—LIFO—PERPETUAL INVENTORY

Item: Material A

Reorder point 40 Reorder quantity 60

ITEM DESCRIPTION

	Receipts			Issued					Balance		
Date	Quantity	Amount	Unit cost	Date	Req. no.	Job no.	Quantity	Amount	Quantity	Amount	Unit cost
Jan. 1	Balance								40	$ 88.00	$2.20
Jan. 7	60	$150.00	$2.50						60	150.00	2.50
				Jan. 9	112	84	64	$158.80	36	79.20	2.20
Jan. 18	60	152.40	2.54						60	152.40	2.54
				Jan. 22	113	86	75	185.40	21	46.20	2.20
Jan. 24	60	156.00	2.60						60	156.00	2.60

January 9 issues:
60 units @ $2.50 = $150.00
4 units @ 2.20 = 8.80
$158.80

January 22 issues:
60 units @ $2.54 = $152.40
15 units @ 2.20 = 33.00
$185.40

used or sold is priced out with the higher material costs of the latest stock of inventory on hand, resulting in a tax savings. When prices are rising, the ending inventory valuation is made up of the lower priced, oldest inventory on hand, which does not reflect a current valuation. If the company experiences a decline in material prices, the reverse is true because the material used is costed out at the latest, lower priced inventory. Ending inventory, on the other hand, is valued at the oldest, higher priced inventory in a deflationary period.

Average costing methods

Instead of using the FIFO or LIFO costing methods, a number of variations of the average costing inventory method are available. Some of these are most appropriate for perpetual inventory systems, while others can be used with the periodic system in which the quantity of each material item is updated only when a physical inventory is taken.

These methods assume that the cost of materials on hand at the end of an accounting period is the average of the cost of the inventory on hand at the beginning of the period and the cost of the materials purchased during the period. The average methods are often used by companies which hold goods for a long period of time because they tend to "even out" the effects of net increases and decreases in costs. The abnormally low and abnormally high material prices are balanced under the average cost methods, giving stable cost figures. Although several methods are available, we will only discuss the moving-average cost method with a perpetual inventory procedure.

Moving-Average Method.   The moving-average method allows the issues to be costed out currently at the average unit cost of the goods on hand as of the withdrawal date. A new unit cost is calculated after each purchase. However, some companies follow the practice of making moving-average computations monthly. The established unit costs move upward or downward as new purchases of materials are made at higher or lower prices. A material ledger card is illustrated in Exhibit 3A–3 for Material A using the moving-average method. For example, the cost of the January 18 purchase, $152.40, is added to the balance on hand, $85.68, to arrive at a $2.480 unit cost as follows:

$$\frac{\$152.40 + \$85.68}{96} = \frac{\$238.08}{96} = \$2.480$$

APPENDIX 3–B: LOWER OF COST OR MARKET RULE

There is an accounting presumption that inventory should be stated at cost where cost is defined as acquisition and production cost for inventory. But accountants have traditionally argued that the proper basis for inventory valuation is the lower of cost or market. If a sales price declines, either because

EXHIBIT 3A–3

MATERIAL LEDGER CARD—MOVING AVERAGE

Item: Material A   Reorder point 40   Reorder quantity 60

ITEM DESCRIPTION

Receipts				Issued					Balance		
Date	Quantity	Amount	Unit cost	Date	Req. no.	Job no.	Quantity	Amount	Quantity	Amount	Unit cost
Jan. 1	Balance								40	$ 88.00	$2.200
Jan. 7	60	$150.00	$2.50						100	238.00	2.380
				Jan. 9	112	84	64	$152.32	36	85.68	2.380
Jan. 18	60	152.40	2.54						96	238.08	2.480
				Jan. 22	113	86	75	186.00	21	52.08	2.480
Jan. 24	60	156.00	2.60						81	208.08	2.569

of physical or technological obsolescence or competitive conditions, the residual inventory cannot be valued at an amount in excess of net realizable value. Net realizable value is defined as the estimated selling price in the ordinary course of business less reasonably predictable costs of completion and disposal. Under this procedure, after the cost of inventory is determined using any of the inventory costing methods discussed in Appendix 3–A (i.e., FIFO, LIFO, etc.), the inventory cost figure is compared with the market value to determine which is lower. The lower figure is the appropriate inventory valuation.

Market rule

A departure from cost is necessary when it becomes evident that the net realizable value of an inventory item is no longer as great as its cost. This decline should be recognized as a loss of the current period. This measurement of the loss is generally achieved by applying the lower of cost or market rule. Generally accepted accounting principles specify what figure should be compared against cost in valuing inventory where cost cannot be recovered:

> As used in the phrase lower of cost or market, the term market means current replacement cost (by purchase or by production, as the case may be), except that:
>
> (1) Market should not exceed the net realizable value (i.e., estimated selling price in the ordinary course of business less reasonably predictable costs of completion and disposal); and
>
> (2) Market should not be less than net realizable value reduced by an allowance for an approximately normal profit margin.[1]

The net realizable value is commonly referred to as the ceiling, while the net realizable value less normal profit is referred to as the floor. If replacement cost falls between the ceiling and floor, it is compared with cost. If, instead, replacement cost is greater than the ceiling, the ceiling is compared to cost to arrive at the lower of cost or market. Finally, if replacement cost is less than the floor, the floor is compared to cost in determining which is lower.

To illustrate the application of these limitations, three examples are shown in Exhibit 3B–1.

It may be easier to understand the limitations imposed by the ceiling and floor if charts similar to the ones prepared below for Item A and Item B are drawn.

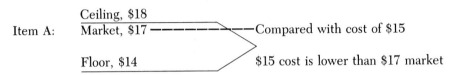

Item A: Ceiling, $18
         Market, $17 ——————————→——Compared with cost of $15
         Floor, $14 $15 cost is lower than $17 market

---

[1]AICPA, Committee on Accounting Procedures, *Accounting Research Bulletin No. 43*, Statement 6, p. 31.

EXHIBIT 3B–1

Item	Cost	Replace-ment cost (market)	Net realizable value (ceiling)	Net realizable value less normal profit (floor)	Inventory valuation
A...........	$15	$17	$18	$14	$15
B...........	20	21	18	14	18
C...........	20	12	18	14	14

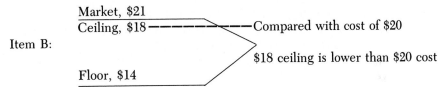

Item B:

Market, $21
Ceiling, $18 ————————— Compared with cost of $20
$18 ceiling is lower than $20 cost
Floor, $14

For Item A, since the $17 market figure falls between the $18 ceiling and $14 floor, it is compared with the cost of $15 to arrive at the inventory valuation of $15. For Item B, the $21 market is above the ceiling of $18, so $18 is compared with the cost of $20 to arrive at the $18 inventory valuation. For Item C, the $12 market is below the $14 lower limit, so $14 is compared with $20 cost to obtain the lower value of these two figures.

Entry to Record Inventory Price Decline.   Exhibit 3B–2 shows the rule of the lower of cost or market applied to each inventory item. After the lower of cost or market calculation is performed for all inventory items, an entry is required to reflect the price decline. But it is not practical to adjust all material ledger cards because the task would be overwhelming. For example, rather

EXHIBIT 3B–2

Inventory item	Cost	Market	Inventory valuation
Brattice cloth..............	$15,000	$14,500	$14,500
Jute cloth	28,000	29,000	28,000
Cloth bags................	3,700	3,500	3,500
Hemp thread.............	1,800	1,500	1,500
Cotton thread............	1,200	1,470	1,200
	$49,700	$49,970	
Inventory valuation..........			$48,700

than adjust the material ledger card for the brattice cloth listed in Exhibit 3B–2 for $500 ($15,000 cost less $14,500 inventory valuation), a summary entry should be made showing a price decline for all inventory items. This approach keeps the cost undisturbed in the material ledger cards. The price decline for all materials shown in Exhibit 3B–2 amounts to $1,000 ($500 for brattice cloth, $200 for cloth bags, and $300 for hemp thread). The following entry would be made:

Factory Overhead Control—Price Decline in Materials.   1,000

Or

Cost of Goods Sold . . . .
    Allowance for Inventory Price Decline   1,000

The Price Decline in Materials is a subsidiary ledger account of the Factory Overhead Control and can be used to record price declines; however, the more common approach in practice is to charge the price decline to the Cost of Goods Sold account. The allowance account can be presented on the balance sheet as a contra account to materials, as follows:

Materials, at cost $49,700
    Less: Allowance for price decline   1,000
Materials (at lower of cost or market). $48,700

The materials can also be shown at the net value on the balance sheet.

REVIEW QUESTIONS

1. What is the theoretical justification for applied rates for material acquisition and warehousing costs? Why aren't material acquisition and warehousing costs commonly applied in practice?

2. Under what conditions would there be a material misstatement of inventory costs if material acquisition and warehousing costs are not allocated?

3. In what ways can scrap be recorded on the books? Discuss the theoretical basis and practical limitations of each.

4. Define scrap, defective units, and spoiled goods.

5. How would you decide whether reworking defective units would be profitable?

6. To what account should the cost of reworking defective goods be charged if defective units are normal in the manufacture of a product?

7. What are stockouts, TOS, and B/O? What risks does the company run when these conditions occur?

8. What effect does the company's degree of service reliability have on the inventory level carried?

9. Identify and discuss the associated costs involved in computing the optimum investment in inventory.

10. Under what conditions would a company find the ABC method impractical? What alternatives are available in this case?

11. Discuss the two-bin system of inventory control and how it works. For what type of inventory do you think the two-bin system would be appropriate?

12. Define and discuss the terms safety stock, economic order quantity, and lead time.

13. Contrast the three EOQ computational methods presented. What are the inherent limitations of each? Why is it important to recognize these weaknesses?

14. Why is EOQ only one factor in determining order quantity? What additional qualitative and quantitative factors should be considered in selecting economic order quantity?

15. How can the effect of quantity discounts be added to the tabular approach of determining EOQ?

16. Discuss three ways of estimating safety stock.

EXERCISES

E3–1.   Computing safety stock and reorder point

Herald Company provides you with the following data concerning two inventory items:

	Metal disks	Pumps
Maximum daily usage	120 units	750 units
Average daily usage	100 units -	690 units
Minimum daily usage.	80 units	510 units
Lead time	20 days	15 days

Required:

a. Compute the safety stock allowing for the fluctuations between maximum daily usage and average daily usage.

b. Determine the reorder point in units using the safety stock computed in *a*.

E3–2.   Determining EOQ and number of orders

In the production of pumps, the Inout Company uses two different types of valves. One valve costs $15 and the other costs $3. The ordering cost is $4.50 per order while the carrying cost per annum is 10 percent of the cost of the valve. In controlling the inventory of 200,000 of each type of valve used annually, management applies the ABC Analysis of Inventory to determine order quantities. Management wants to compare the results obtained using the economic order quantity formula with their present method of purchasing.

Required:

a. Determine the economic order quantity for each valve.

b. Identify the number of orders needed per year for each valve.

E3–3.   Alternative approachs for recording scrap

Job No. 42, which is being processed by the Karen Costley Company, is expected to yield some amount of scrap. On November 22, 19X1, 10 items had to be scrapped.

Required:

a. (1) When the items were scrapped, their sales value could not be determined. Record any necessary entries.

   (2) On December 10, 19X1, the scrap was sold for $160. Record the sale using three alternative methods.

b. (1) When the items were scrapped, the sales value was estimated at $140. Make appropriate entries using three alternative approaches.

   (2) On December 10, 19X1, the scrap was sold for $160. Record the sale using three alternative methods.

E3–4.   Economical production runs

Management of Hyde Manufacturing has been quite concerned over the optimum production run. The company produces special pumps for a customer who orders 80,000 Type A pumps and 65,000 Type B pumps each year. Rather than manufacture these pumps as the orders are received monthly from the customer, management feels assured enough that the customer will continue these purchases to manufacture in larger lots. The setup cost is $800 for Type A pumps and $650 for Type B pumps. Carrying costs are estimated to be 10 percent of unit production cost per year. The production cost is $20 for the Type A pump and $15 for the Type B pump.

Required:

Compute the most economical production run size for each type of pump. Also indicate the number of production runs per year for each type of pump.

E3–5.   Recording scrap using alternative assumptions

In processing Job No. 515 for the Dave Company, it was determined that 50 No. 10 brass parts had to be scrapped. At the time the scrap was reported, the sales value of scrap could not be determined.

Required:

a. (1) What journal entry is needed at the time the scrap was reported?

   (2) Later the scrap was sold for $48 cash. Make the journal entry to record the sale using each of the three methods available.

b. (1) Assume instead that at the time the scrap occurred, the company was able to accurately estimate the sales value of the scrap to be $48. Using each of the methods available, make the necessary journal entry.

   (2) Later the scrap was actually sold for $48. Make the necessary journal entry.

E3–6.   Tabular analysis approach to EOQ

Ezell Company estimates that its annual requirements for the next year will be 25,000 units of 6-inch copper tubing. Ordering and carrying costs are as follows:

Cost of ordering per purchase order $25
Cost of carrying per unit   5

Required:

a. Compute the EOQ using tabular analysis. Use the following order sizes: 250; 500; 1,000; 2,500; 6,250; and 25,000 units.

b.   Using the above information, compute the EOQ using the formula.

c.   Why are your answers in *a* and *b* different?

E3–7.   Comparing the EOQ formula with ABC Analysis of Inventory

In the manufacture of hot-water tanks, the Ted Oury Company uses two different types of valves. Since one valve is more complex and sensitive, it costs $15, while the other valve costs only $3. The ordering cost is $8 per order, while the carrying cost is 18 percent per annum. In controlling the 2,500 units of each valve used each year, management applies the ABC Analysis of Inventory in determining the order quantities. Based on this approach, orders are made very two weeks for the $15 valve and bimonthly for the $3 valve. Management would like to compare the results obtained using the economic order quantity formula with their present system of purchasing.

Required:

a.   Determine the economic order quantity for each valve.

b.   Identify the number of orders needed per year for each valve using the EOQ computed in *a*.

c.   Compare the results obtained in *b* with the present purchasing system employing the ABC Analysis of Inventory.

E3–8.   Determining EOQ and annual savings

Arnold Company has been purchasing valves in lots of 6,000 units, which represent four-months' supply. The ordering cost is $15 per order and the carrying cost is 25 percent per annum. Valves cost $0.96 each.

Required:

a.   Determine the economic order quantity.

b.   Identify the number of orders needed per year.

c.   Determine the annual savings from buying in economical quantities.

E3–9.   Net market value of spoilage

The Inspection Manager of Chett Manufacturing Company informs you that 5,000 of the 8,000 units in Job No. 818 have been rejected. Even though these spoiled units had an assigned cost of $0.50 per unit in work in process inventory, they now can be sold for only $0.30 per unit. The cost of disposing of these spoiled units is estimated to be $500.

Required:

a.   Prepare the necessary journal entries to transfer the job out of production and to account for the 5,000 units if spoilage is the result of a defective pattern design. Explain the reason for the treatment in your entry.

b.   If, instead, the defects occur randomly throughout all manufacturing and this rate of rejection is not abnormal, prepare the journal entries to account for these units and the finished job. Explain the reason for your treatment under these circumstances.

E3–10.   Savings from EOQ (CMA adapted)

Hermit Company manufactures a line of walnut office products. Hermit executives estimate the demand for the double walnut letter tray, one of the company's products, at

6,000 units. The letter tray sells for $80 per unit. The costs relating to the letter tray are estimated to be as follows:

1. Standard manufacturing cost per letter tray unit—$50.
2. Costs to initiate a production run—$300.
3. Annual cost of carrying the letter tray in inventory—20 percent of standard manufacturing cost.

In previous years, Hermit Company has scheduled production of the letter tray in two equal runs. The company is aware that the economic order quantity (EOQ) model can be employed to determine optimum size for production runs. The EOQ formula as it applies to inventories for determining the optimum order quantity is shown below.

$$\text{EOQ} = \sqrt{\frac{2\,(\text{Annual demand})\,(\text{Cost per order})}{(\text{Cost per unit})\,(\text{Carrying cost})}}$$

Required:

Calculate the annual cost savings Hermit Company could expect if it employed the economic order quantity model to determine the number of production runs that should be initiated during the year for the manufacture of the letter trays.

PROBLEMS

P3–1. Summary of scrap report

On Job No. 25 in the finishing department, Joe Smith, the supervisor for the Estes Company, provides you with the following data concerning scrap for May, 19X1.

Material part no.	Description	Quantity scrapped	Unit cost	Expected scrap
28C	Plastic cups	20	$12.10	12
42X	Metal shields	100	15.00	109
60J	Electric motors	25	30.00	20
38M	Metal wheels	20	20.00	15

The actual quantity scrapped of Part No. 28C has a sales value of $20; it is not known what the sales value of Part No. 42X is. The other scrap has no value. It is discovered that the cause of the scrap for Part No. 28C is defective molds; for 42X, operator inefficiency; for 60J, defective material; and for 38M, machine malfunction.

Required:

Prepare a summary scrap report indicating the variances from expected scrap.

P3–2. ABC analysis of inventory control

Wayne, Inc. uses the following types of inventory listed by part number. Annual usage and unit price are as follows:

Inventory number	Unit usage	Unit price
X1	200	$1.10
X2	500	5.00
X3	1,800	2.10
X4	680	.80
X5	700	.65
X6	900	.90
X7	800	1.05

Required:

a. Advise management of the inventory controls that should be used based on the ABC Analysis of Inventory.

b. List three other factors that should be considered before making your final decision with regard to inventory control.

P3-3. Journal entries recording actual material costs and applied material costs

Turner applies material acquisition costs because many of their orders of material require extra care and inspection. The following estimates are provided:

Annual estimated warehousing department costs. . . . $ 112,000
Annual estimated purchasing department costs. 120,000
Annual estimated freight-in 140,000
Annual estimated direct materials purchased. 2,800,000
Annual estimated number of purchase orders 15,000

Actual data for the month are:

Direct materials purchased . . . . $ 300,000
Warehousing Department costs. 12,350
Purchasing Department costs 11,800
Freight-in costs incurred 14,300
Number of purchase orders 1,500

Required:

a. Determine application rates, applying freight-in cost, and warehousing department costs on the basis of material cost purchased, and purchasing department costs on the basis of purchase orders.

b. Prepare the journal entries to record both the actual costs incurred and the application of material acquisition costs. Close the balance of the material acquisition ledger accounts to Cost of Goods Sold.

P3-4. Economic order table with quantity discount effect

Ward, Inc. can order 10-ounce, 48-inch jute for its lamination operation in bales of 1,000 yards each. It projects annual usage to be 2 million yards and material list price to be $0.48 per yard. The cost of placing an order is estimated to be $20, while the annual carrying cost per bale is estimated at $32. Management does not believe it feasible to order more than one year's usage at a time. The supplier offers the following discount:

Order size (bales)	Quantity discount (percent)
0–100 ....:....	2
101–300	4
301–500	5
501–1,000.........	6
1,001–2,000.........	7

Required:

Determine the most economical order quantity.

P3–5. Tabular and formula approaches to determining EOQ

The annual requirements for Material XR2 used by the Marr Company is 4,800 units. Material XR2 costs $40 per unit, subject to quantity discounts of 5 percent for order sizes over 200, and 7 percent for order sizes of 400 units and over.

The annual cost of storage, including rent, insurance, taxes, and return on investment has been estimated at $2 per unit per year. Ordering costs are $3 for each order handled.

Required:

a. Prepare estimates of the total annual cost of material XR2 for each of the following order sizes: 60 units, 240 units, and 400 units. Assume usage is fairly uniform.
b. Using the formula, determine the economic order quantity.
c. Account for the difference in your answers to *a* and *b*.

P3–6. Alternative treatment of rework costs with defective units

Reba Wallace Company produces various types of lawn and garden tools. With one of its new product lines, lawn vacuum/shredders, it encountered some difficulty. The vacuums are produced in 500-unit lots with total costs per lot as follows:

Materials ....·	$60,000
Labor	40,000
Factory overhead (applied on the basis of machine-hours)...............................	30,000

Machine-hours average four hours per vacuum. When inspection was made at the end of the processing, it was discovered that 60 units were defective and must be reworked. The total costs for reworking were as follows:

Materials...................	$7,500
Labor.....................	2,200

The rework operations required two machine-hours per defective vacuum. The company uses a separate ledger account for each cost component of work in process inventory.

Required:

Assuming no entries have been made in connection with the order, record all journal entries to complete the order, to transfer it to the warehouse, and to sell 100 vacuums at $300 cash each when

a. The cost of the rework is to be charged to the production of the period.
b. The cost of the rework is to be charged to the job.

P3-7. Trade-off of costs

Householder, Inc. produces fancy glass flower vases, which sell for $5 each. Demand is so high that Householder, Inc. is unable to produce all that they could sell. Machine No. 212 in the firing operation is very critical to production and must be maintained in proper adjustment; otherwise, the vases will not pass inspection. Past data reveal that of the 1,000 vases produced daily, the number rejected is equal to 25 divided by the number of adjustments made. Each vase costs $3, and the rejected vases are worthless. The supervisor adjusts the machine before operations begin each day. Any additional adjustments are made at the supervisor's discretion. Each adjustment costs $5, but no vases are lost during the adjustment phase.

Required:

Determine the total optimal number of adjustments, including the initial adjustment, that should be made daily.

P3-8. Evaluating various methods of applying material handling costs

As a cost accountant recently hired by Johnson Company, a manufacturer of baseballs, you feel that a better procedure for treating material handling costs should be utilized. At present, material handling costs are treated as a part of factory overhead, which is allocated on a direct labor-hour basis. It is your contention that these costs should be an addition to material costs. Because a study you conducted indicates that some of the material, such as leather, involves extensive handling costs, while other materials, such as thread, cork, and rubber, involve fewer handling costs, you believe that applied rates for each of the following three material types should be used:

Type I—Material, such as thread, that is relatively inexpensive to handle.

Type II—Material, such as cork and rubber, that is three times as expensive to handle per unit as Type I.

Type III—Material, such as leather, that is twice as expensive to handle per unit as Type II.

When you present your suggestions, the controller agrees that these handling costs should be treated as additional material costs, but does not believe it is necessary to divide the material into three types. To prove your point, you extract the following data from company records:

		Total costs
Direct material:		
Type I .... (15,000 units)		$15,000
Type II. .... (18,000 units)		18,000
Type III .... (13,500 units)		64,800
Total direct material costs		$97,800
Direct labor (6,000 hours)		$30,000
Factory overhead (Including $6,000 of material handling costs)		$27,000

Material and labor costs for two of the five orders completed during the period were the following:

	Order no. 201	Order no. 202
Material:		
Type I.	$ 3,000	$ 2,250
Type II	9,000	4,500
Type III.	9,000	24,000
Total material	$21,000	$30,750
Direct labor	$ 6,000 (1,200 hours)	$ 6,750 (1,350 hours)

Required:

a. Determine the following application rates:
  1. Factory overhead rate presently used.
  2. Factory overhead rate if material handling costs are excluded and direct labor-hours are continued as the basis. Material handling costs are handled using the method you, the cost accountant, proposed in which there are separate rates for each type of material using weighted units as the basis for allocating a prorata share of handling costs to each material as a percentage of its purchase cost.
  3. Factory overhead rate is computed as in 2 above and material handling costs are dealt with using the method preferred by the controller using a blanket rate for all materials. The controller contends that the rate should be based on the total dollar value of material purchased.
b. Determine the total cost of each of the two orders using each of the three approaches in *a*.
c. Determine the total cost using each of the three approaches in *a* if, instead, the following orders are representative of all jobs processed (round to whole dollars.):

	Order no. 203	Order no. 204
Material:		
Type I.	—	$ 9,500
Type II	$26,500	24,250
Type III.	1,250	—
Total material	$27,750	$33,750
Direct labor	$ 6,000 (1,200 hours)	$ 6,000 (1,200 hours)

d. What factors would you consider in choosing the method to adopt?

P3–9. Cost-plus contracts

A company is so anxious for Karol, Inc. to make it a special order of athletic uniforms that it is willing to let Karol's cost accountant decide the costing procedure to use in submitting a bid. The company agreed to pay Karol $19,570 for the 500 uniforms of special design, or they will pay cost plus 15 percent. While the cost accountant intends to act ethically and according to good accounting principles, the price most financially favorable to Karol, Inc. is desired. It is recognized that if a cost-plus contract is chosen, the cost accountant will be required to provide the supplier with source documents and other records in support of the cost figures.

In evaluating the alternatives, the following is determined:

Cost per uniform

Material................... $7
Labor .... 2 hours @ $10 per hour
Factory overhead .... $4 per direct labor-hour

Scrap from cutting out the uniforms will result; its exact sales value is not known at the time scrapping occurs. The production supervisor believes the scrap can be sold for $600, but the production manager doubts that the scrap will be worth anything. Both agree that it depends on the size of the scrap pieces, which cannot be determined at this time. Also, sale of this scrap is partially dependent on Karol's obtaining another order requiring material like that used in the uniforms. If both orders are received, Karol will have enough scrap to attract further scrap sales.

A quick examination of the details of the uniform requested by the potential customer indicates that rework is likely. To sew in the zipper, the sewers must be well trained; otherwise, units will be defective. Several of the workers now employed have completed other jobs requiring such detail, so they can be expected to create little rework. Workers who have less on-the-job training are expected to find the sewing more challenging. The production supervisor expects 25 of the uniforms to require reworking. A new zipper costing $0.20 each, including thread, will be required for each defective uniform. It is expected that it will require one-half hour of a direct laborer's time to remove the old zipper and correct the uniform.

In addition to the 25 uniforms that are expected to be defective, the production supervisor expects the zippers in an additional 5 uniforms to be so badly sewn that it will be impossible to rework these and sell them as first-quality uniforms. Some of this error will be due to worker fatigue because careful attention must be paid to sew in these zippers. Management believes that it can remove the supplier's name from these five uniforms and sell them for $15 each. Inspection will occur only at the end of production, at which time spoiled and defective units will be identified.

Required:

a. If you were Karol's cost accountant, what approach would you choose regarding:
    1. Scrap.
    2. Defective units.
    3. Spoiled goods.
b. Determine the cost of the order using the approach chosen in *a.*
c. Indicate the price you would choose: $19,570 or a cost-plus contract.

P3–10. Minimizing total safety stock and stockout costs (AICPA adapted)

The Polly Company wishes to determine the amount of safety stock that it should maintain for Product D resulting in the lowest cost. The following information is available:

```
Stockout cost . . . . . . . . . . . . . . . $80 per occurrence
Carrying cost of safety stock . . . . . $ 2 per unit
Number of purchase orders . . . . . .    5 per year
```

The options available to Polly are as follows:

Units of safety stock	Probability of running out of safety stock (percent)
10	50
20	40
30	30
40	20
50	10
55	5

Required:

Determine the number of units of safety stock resulting in the lowest annual cost.

P3–11.   Values used in EOQ (CMA adapted)

SaPane Company is a regional distributor of automobile window glass. Management recognizes a need to determine the total inventory cost associated with maintaining an optimal supply of replacement windshields for the new subcompact cars introduced by each of the three major manufacturers. SaPane is expecting a daily demand for 36 windshields. The purchase price of each windshield is $50.

Other costs associated with ordering and maintaining an inventory of these windshields are as follows:

The historical ordering costs incurred in the purchase order department for placing and processing orders is shown below:

Year	Orders placed and processed	Total ordering costs
19X1	20	$12,300
19X2	55	12,475
19X3	100	12,700

Management expects the ordering costs to increase 16 percent above the amounts and rates experienced over the last three years.

The windshield manufacturer charges SaPane a $75 shipping fee per order.

A clerk in the receiving department receives, inspects, and secures the windshields as they arrive from the manufacturer. This activity requires eight hours per order received. This clerk has no other responsibilities and is paid at the rate of $9 per hour. Related variable overhead costs in this department are applied at the rate of $2.50 per hour.

Additional warehouse space will have to be rented to store the new windshields. Space can be rented as needed in a public warehouse at an estimated cost of $2,500 per year plus $5.35 per windshield.

Breakage cost is estimated to be 6 percent of the average inventory value.

Taxes and fire insurance on the inventory are $1.15 per windshield.

The desired rate of return on the investment in inventory is 21 percent of the purchase price.

Six working days are required from the time the order is placed with the manufacturer until it is received. SaPane uses a 300-day work year when making economic order quantity computations. The economic order quantity formula is:

$$EOQ = \sqrt{\frac{2 \text{ (Annual demand) (Ordering cost)}}{\text{Storage cost}}}$$

Required:

a. Calculate the following values for SaPane Company:
    1. The value for ordering cost that should be used in the EOQ formula.
    2. The value for storage cost that should be used in the EOQ formula.
    3. The economic order quantity.
    4. The minimum annual relevant cost at the economic order quantity point.
    5. The reorder point in units.
b. Without prejudice to your answer to *a*, assume the economic order quantity is 400 units, the storage cost is $28 per unit, and the stockout cost is $12 per unit. SaPane wants to determine the proper level of safety stock to minimize its relevant costs. Using the following probability schedule for excess demand during the reorder period, determine the proper amount of safety stock.

Number of units short due to excess demand during reorder period	Probability of occurrence (percent)
60	12
120	5
180	2

APPENDIX 3–A

PROBLEMS

P3–12.   Theory of inventory costing methods (AICPA adapted)

Cost for inventory purposes should be determined by the inventory cost flow method most clearly reflecting periodic income.

Required:

a. Describe the fundamental assumptions of the average cost, FIFO, and LIFO inventory cost flow methods.
b. Discuss the reasons for using LIFO in an inflationary economy.
c. Where there is evidence that the utility of goods, in their disposal in the ordinary course of business, will be less than cost, what is the proper accounting treatment and under what concept is that treatment justified?

P3–13. **Determining cost of material issued and inventory valuation using various inventory costing methods**

George Minmier Company had 49 units of direct material 2A costing $5.45 on hand on January 1. During January, the following Material 2A transactions occurred:

Jan. 2 Received 100 units @ $7.15 per unit; total cost, $715.
      8 Issued 60 units.
     10 Received 40 units @ $6.80 per unit; total cost, $272.
     18 Issued 70 units.
     23 Received 80 units @$7 per unit; total cost, $560.
     25 Issued 100 units.
     26 Received 20 units @ $6.90 per unit; total cost, $138.

Required:

Determine the cost of the material issued and the final inventory using the following inventory methods:

a. Perpetual LIFO.
b. Perpetual FIFO.
c. Moving average.

P3–14. **Perpetual inventory: Lower of cost or market**

A ledger card for a crucial item of material is shown for the Seaton Company:

	Receipts		Issues	
	Units	Unit cost	May	Units
May 1 . . . . Balance	300	$3.60	5	65
10 . . . . Purchase	150	3.75	15	300
20 . . . . Purchase	200	4.00	25	180

Required:

a. Determine the ending inventory cost, assuming a perpetual inventory system is used with FIFO costing.
b. Using the FIFO cost value determined in *a* and a replacement cost of $352, determine the value to be reported on the balance sheet if the lower of cost or market inventory valuation is used when the estimated unit sales price is $3.60, the estimated unit cost of disposal is $0.04, and the normal profit is 5 percent of the sales price.
c. Prepare the journal entry necessary to reflect the decline in inventory value determined in *b* assuming this cost is considered to be a normal cost of the manufacturing operation.

APPENDIX 3–B

PROBLEMS

P3–15. Lower of cost or market according to Bulletin No. 43

The following facts about four items included in the materials inventory of Smith Manufacturing Corporation are given:

	Case			
Item	1	2	3	4
Original cost	92	55	100	62
Replacement cost	80	52	105	48
Sales price less selling and completion expense	84	50	110	59
Sales price less selling and completion expense and normal profit	76	35	90	51

Required:

a. Indicate which figure would be used in pricing the ending inventory in accordance with the AICPA rule stated in *Accounting Research Bulletin No. 43.*

b. Make one journal entry to record any decline in cost. Assume there is just one unit of each item in cases 1 to 4.

P3–16. Lower of cost or market according to Bulletin No. 43

For December 31, the inventory data for the Marce Company are given below:

Inventory item	Unit sales price	Unit replacement cost	Unit historical cost	Unit cost of completion and disposal	Unit normal profit
A	$18	$18	$15	$2	$3
B	26	19	20	7	5
C	39	27	30	6	4
D	12	8	6	3	2
E	10	5	5	2	2
F	8	8	6	1	2
G	14	10	11	3	2
H	15	7	8	4	1

Required:

Compute the inventory valuation using cost or market according to *Accounting Research Bulletin No. 43* of the AICPA, applying the lower of cost or market rule to each individual item.

P3–17. **Computing inventory valuation using lower of cost or market, journal entries, and balance sheet presentation**

Thomas Hogancamp Dress Manufacturing Company experiences price declines in its high-fashion styles. As a result, there is a credit balance of $1,500 in the Allowance for Inventory Price Declines general ledger account.

As of December 31, 19X1, the direct material inventory data are given below:

Items	Quantity	Unit histori-cal cost	Total inven-tory valua-tion at cost	Unit replace-ment cost	Unit sales price	Unit cost to complete and sell	Normal profit (percent of sales price)
Sequins	400 packages	$4.00	$ 1,600.00	$6.00	$8.00	$1.15	15
Jeweled buttons	1,000 packages	1.00	1,000.00	0.90	1.20	0.35	10
Belts............	550 packages	2.60	1,430.00	2.50	4.00	0.70	30
Cotton fabric	2,000 yards	3.00	6,000.00	3.90	5.00	1.10	25
Silk fabric	1,410 yards	7.00	9,870.00	6.00	7.75	2.10	20
Wool fabric	580 yards	4.50	2,610.00	4.00	7.50	1.80	26
Lace............	975 yards	0.70	682.50	0.80	1.50	0.25	50
			$23,192.50				

Required:

a. Compute the inventory valuation item by item, using cost or market according to *Accounting Research Bulletin No. 43* of the AICPA. Show both unit and total inventory valuation.

b. Prepare any necessary journal entries.

c. Then prepare a partial balance sheet showing the inventory and related accounts.

P3–18. **Computing inventory valuation using lower of cost or market, journal entries, and balance sheet presentation**

William Bunetta Sporting Goods Company manufactures specialities in sporting equipment. Because the company experiences price declines, the Allowance for Inventory Price Declines general ledger account has a balance on June 30, 19X1, of $2,000.

On June 30, 19X1, the direct material inventory data are as shown at the top of the following page.

(Relates to P3–18)

Items	Quantity	Unit histori- cal cost	Total inventory valuation at cost	Unit replace- ment cost	Unit sales price	Unit cost to complete and sell	Unit normal profit
Golf gloves, fabric............	400 yards	$20.00	$ 8,000	$22.00	$40.00	$10.00	$6.00
Golf balls, mixture	580 cases	22.00	12,760	19.00	31.00	8.00	2.00
Golf clubs, metal............	200 pounds	45.00	9,000	48.00	65.00	11.00	4.00
Fishing reels, plastic	1,180 gallons	47.00	55,460	45.00	60.00	12.00	2.00
Fishing reels, metal............	1,300 pounds	71.00	92,300	70.00	82.00	10.00	8.00
Tennis racket thread	580 yards	7.80	4,524	7.85	9.00	1.30	0.50
Wood for tennis rackets..........	700 feet	8.40	5,880	8.38	9.30	0.50	0.20
			$187,924				

Required:

a. Compute the inventory valuation item by item, using cost or market according to *Accounting Research Bulletin No. 43* of the AICPA.

b. Prepare any necessary journal entries.

c. Then prepare a partial balance sheet showing the inventory and related accounts.

4

Learning curve theory and labor accounting

The wages and salaries earned by employees in return for labor expended in the production process constitute a large part of the cost of doing business. Although there is a divergence in goals—labor seeking the highest possible wage, and the employer attempting to keep cost of production at a minimum—management must adopt an enlightened compensation administration plan. The best method of serving the interests of both labor and owners is for management to increase the efficiency of labor through improvements in productivity.

Accurate, understandable methods for calculating payroll are necessary, since probably no other area in accounting has such an impact on the morale of employees than do employee wage and benefit policies. If employees feel that they are not being paid fairly, employee-employer relations soon deteriorate and a labor union may be voted in or the existing union may become stronger. Even if only a few employees are unsure about how their gross and net wages are being calculated or believe that there are errors involved, they will breed discontent in their peer group. Nothing strikes closer to the sentiments and heart of the employee than his or her payroll check. For this reason, the accountant must be certain that the wage payment and employee benefit plans are adequately explained to all employees.

Variety of labor systems

Explaining the wage payment and employee benefit plan is also important because of the variety of methods used to record labor cost. The method used depends upon such factors as the skills of accounting personnel, size of the company, and frequency of payment. For example, if a bookkeeper is hired at a branch office, the bookkeeper's sole payroll duty may be to total and forward the time cards and time sheets to a central location where gross pay, withholdings, and net pay are calculated. Other branch offices, however, may prepare their own payroll checks, record payroll deductions, and prepare employees' checks drawn on the branch office payroll bank account. In this case, the branch office periodically remits the payroll deductions made. Rather than classify payroll costs at each pay period, some companies wait until the end of the month and then assign the payroll to direct labor, indirect labor, marketing, or administrative costs in a summary entry. Other companies record the expense distribution and payment at the same time. However, after the basic concepts of labor accounting presented in this chapter are understood, there should be little difficulty in adapting them to a company's particular payroll system.

Labor costs include more than the basic earnings computed for each employee on an hourly or piecework basis, and thus represent a significant amount of money. There are, after all, many labor-related costs, from payroll taxes, bonuses, holiday and vacation pay, and free uniforms to hospitalization insurance and retirement pensions, among others. Studies have shown that the cost of these employee benefits add at least an additional 35 percent to the basic labor cost of the average employee. Costs of fringes vary considerably by industry and somewhat by size of company and region. Companies with 5,000 or more employees generally pay a higher percent in benefits, while those with fewer than 500 employees pay a smaller percentage of payroll. On the average, companies located in the Northeast pay a higher benefit package than those in the South.

To account for these labor costs, the financial accountant and the payroll or cost accountant must work closely together. The payroll accountant's prime concern is maintaining records of labor cost by job or department. The financial accountant meanwhile is concerned that payroll records are kept that not only conform with government regulations, but also provide the supporting data necessary to calculate each employee's gross pay, withholdings, and net pay.

For effective control over labor cost, accurate, timely information should be forwarded to management. Performance reports should be prepared for each department reflecting the level of efficiency of the workers. For this reason, departments other than cost accounting also have an impact on labor accounting; these include the personnel department, timekeeping department, and payroll department. A personnel department's function is maintaining a sufficient labor force for the company's operations; the timekeeping department is responsible for recording the total time worked on each job or product, or in each department. And the payroll department determines and records the employees' gross and net earnings. Earning records for each employee are also maintained by the payroll department.

TYPES OF PAYROLL-RELATED COSTS

Payment to employees for labor expended takes many forms. In accounting, the crucial problem is to match these expenditures with the period in which (or production on which) the labor was expended. However, before we discuss the intricacies of accounting for employee compensation, we will discuss the general types of compensation.

1. Direct benefits

We will define direct benefits as *payments to employees at or near the time the payments are earned.* Straight wages, salaries, overtime and shift premiums, and bonus payments fall into this category.

a. Wages and salaries.   The term *wages* is used to designate hourly or piece rates payment and as such, they are a variable cost. The term *salaries* describes a fixed periodic payment, such as a weekly or monthly payment. Ignoring voluntary and involuntary deductions, these payments are made at constant periodic intervals to the employees.

b. Incentive compensation plans.   Management is concerned with maximizing the productivity of labor; one of the tools to achieve this goal is some form of *incentive compensation* plan. This provides additional compensation to employees whose performance exceeds a predetermined goal or standard. Incentive plans may be adopted for these reasons.

1.   To give employees an opportunity to earn additional pay by performing at a more efficient level.

2.   To reduce the cost per unit of finished products. While wages may increase with an incentive compensation plan, factory overhead is not expected to increase significantly. The conversion cost per unit is expected to decrease after the increased direct labor cost and lower per unit factory overhead cost are spread over additional finished units. For example, the data in Exhibit 4–1 are computed under the assumption that 600 units were produced prior to introduction of an incentive plan and that 750 units are produced after the plan is initiated. While direct labor cost increased from $180 to $240, it is assumed that there was no change in factory overhead. The labor cost per unit has increased from $0.30 to $0.32, but the decrease in overhead costs per unit has been large enough to produce a lower total cost per unit.

The example in Exhibit 4–1 indicates that productivity, measured by labor cost per unit, has increased; however, incentive systems cannot guarantee higher production and greater efficiency. A number of incentive plans are

EXHIBIT 4–1

Effect on unit conversion cost after wage incentive plan is introduced

	Units produced	Direct labor cost per time period	Overhead cost per time period	Labor cost per unit	Total overhead cost per unit	Conversion cost per unit
Prior to initiation of incentive plan...............	600	$180	$120	$0.30	$0.20	$0.50
After initiation of incentive plan..........	750	240	120	0.32	0.16	0.48

available, including the straight piecework plan, 100 Percent Bonus Plan, and versions of Taylor Differential Piece Rate, Gantt Task, and the Emerson Efficiency System. As an example, under the straight piecework plan, the production standard is computed in minutes per piece and then transformed into money per piece. For example, if time studies showed that one unit requires two minutes of time, the standard becomes 30 units per hour. If the worker's base rate is $9 per hour, the piece rate is $0.30. If the worker completes 260 units in an eight-hour day, the pay is $78 (260 units × $.30) Generally, workers are guaranteed a base pay rate even if they do not meet the standard.

Some incentive plans express standards in terms of units per hour rather than in terms of money. For example, the following computations illustrate an incentive plan in which employees receive a guaranteed rate of $6 per hour and a premium of 70 percent of the time saved on production in excess of the standard of 50 units per hour. If an employee has produced 450 units on Monday and 525 units on Tuesday for the eight hours worked each day, daily earnings are:

Monday

$$\frac{50}{50} \text{ units } = \quad 1 \text{ hr. saved} \times \$6 \times 70\% = \$ \ 4.20 \text{ premium}$$
$$\underline{48.00} \ (8 \text{ hr.} \times \$6)$$
$$\$52.20$$

Tuesday

$$\frac{125}{50} \text{ units } = \quad 2.5 \text{ hours} \times \$6 = \$15 \times 70\% = \$10.50 \text{ premium}$$
$$\underline{48.00}$$
$$\$58.50$$

The important thing to consider in evaluating a plan is what effect it has on reducing the cost per unit of finished products while providing the employees an opportunity to earn additional wages. As with all wage payment plans, the mechanics of the system should be clearly explained to production employees so they can compute their incentive payments, even though some incentive plans employed in practice are so complex that this is not always possible.

Group incentive plans

Some production processes make it impossible to determine the individual production of each employee because the manufacturing operations require the joint effort of a group of employees. If teamwork is required, one individual cannot increase output without increasing productivity of the entire crew. Under these conditions, individual incentive plans are impossible to implement, and group incentive plans have been devised.

Bonus computations under a group incentive plan are illustrated in Exhibit 4–2. Each worker receives a guaranteed minimum hourly wage; in addition, each receives a bonus equal to 1 percent of the worker's hourly guaranteed minimum for each unit produced over standard. Standard production is 50 units per hour or 400 units per eight-hour day. Actual production for the group is 450 units.

There are several advantages to group incentive plans. For one, the amount of clerical effort required to compute the bonus is reduced. For another, because each employee's bonus depends upon the group's output, employees have a stronger incentive to work together as a team and may be more cooperative. Also, the group may apply pressure on the slower workers because the bonus calculated depends upon the group's efforts.

But there is also a danger in group incentive plans in that they may encourage too much competition between individual departments and thereby threaten goal congruence. *Suboptimization* may occur if each manager is so concerned about improving the profit performance of his or her own department, that what is best for the overall company is ignored. Suboptimization is a condition in which individual managers disregard major company goals and

EXHIBIT 4–2

Daily earnings summary—eight-hour day*

	Guaranteed hourly minimum wage	Regular wage	Bonus	Total
Employee A.	$8.00	$64.00	$4.00 (50 units × $0.08)	$68.00
Employee B.	6.00	48.00	3.00 (50 units × $0.06)	51.00
Employee C	7.00	56.00	3.50 (50 units × $0.07)	59.50

*Standard production, 400 units; actual production, 450 units.

interrelationships and focus their attention solely on their own division's activities. Often incentive plans force employees to look only at the short-run benefits for themselves rather than at the long-run benefits for both themselves and the company. In addition, incentive plans can lead to much quarreling within the team because individual members may feel they are doing more than their share of the group's tasks.

Controls on incentive plans.   Regardless of the type of incentive plan used, controls must be established to ensure that the plan is working properly. A common incentive plan includes a guaranteed minimum rate plus a piece rate for work completed. The guaranteed wage is provided regardless of the worker's output. In this case, controls are needed to prevent employees from improperly recording direct versus indirect time. Some employees may also cheat by hiding excess production in their work area or locker so that they will receive only the guaranteed wage that day; then, the next day the employee may turn in the overproduction with the day's production and receive an excessive bonus. Exhibit 4–3 illustrates one way Employee A has misused the incentive plan. Assume that the guaranteed daily wage is $48. For all production over 20 units, each worker receives a $1 per unit bonus in addition. As can be seen in Exhibit 4–3, Employee A has increased earnings on Tuesday and Thursday by including excess production from the previous day in the units turned in. Supervisors and timekeepers should be aware of the possibility of this happening and check variations in the production reported by individual employees.

In addition to the piecework incentive plans, many firms have adopted incentive plans based on the amount by which a company, division, or plant exceeds a specified target income. Most bonus plans are directed towards salaried rather than wage earners, as piecework measurement is not possible for most salaried workers. For example, the manager of Plant A may be given a bonus of 1 percent of all net income after bonus and taxes that exceeds $2

EXHIBIT 4–3

Weekly earnings summary

Employee A	Actual production	Turns in	Secret reserve balance	Daily earnings
Monday	18	16	2	$48
Tuesday	22	24	0	52*
Wednesday	20	17	3	48
Thursday	23	26	0	54†
Etc.				

*$48 guaranteed minimum + $1 × 4 units = $52.
† $48 guaranteed minimum + $1 × 6 units = $54.

million for the year. In these instances, it is important that the specifics of the bonus plan be clearly spelled out so that it is an incentive to increase net income and misunderstanding does not create hard feelings. Bonus payments based on income will not be known until some time after the end of the fiscal period and, therefore, must be estimated and accrued throughout the accounting period.

LEARNING CURVE THEORY

Often incentive wage plans do not motivate employees enough to reduce the cost per unit of finished product. The *learning curve theory,* also called the *improvement curve theory,* can improve incentive wage plans so higher productivity rates are achieved. The learning curve theory is based on the proposition that as workers gain experience in a task, less time is needed to complete the job and productivity increases. Cases during World War II showed that the time needed to complete an operation becomes progressively smaller at a constant percentage. Since this rate of improvement has a regular pattern, learning curves can be drawn which can be used to estimate the labor-hours required as workers become more familiar with the process. This pattern can be stated as follows: as cumulative quantities double, average time per unit falls by a certain percent of the previous time. For example, if it is assumed that this reduction is 20 percent, and it took two hours to produce the first unit, the accumulated average rate to double the present output from one to two units, is two hours × 0.80 = 1.6 hours. Since this is the *average* time per unit, the total time to produce two units is 1.6 × 2 = 3.2 hours. To again double production from two to four units, the average per unit time decreases to 80 percent of the previous average, 1.6 hours × 0.80 = 1.3. This makes the total time to produce four units equal to 5.2 hours. This progression is used to obtain the values in the table below. The reduction in time varies between 40 and 10 percent depending upon the repetitiveness of labor operations, with 20 percent being the most common reduction. The slope of the curve for operations that are complex and require much technical skill will be steeper than that for routine, repetitive operations.

Cumulative quantity	Cumulative average worker-hours per unit	Predicted total hours to perform task
1	2.0	2.0
2	1.6 (2.0 hours × 80%)	3.2 (2 × 1.6 hours)
4	1.3 (1.6 hours × 80%)	5.2 (4 × 1.3 hours)
8	1.0 (1.3 hours × 80%)	8.0 (8 × 1.0 hours)
16	0.8 (1.0 hours × 80%)	12.8 (16 × 0.8 hours)
32	0.6 (0.8 hours × 80%)	19.2 (32 × 0.6 hours)
64	0.5 (0.6 hours × 80%)	32.0 (64 × 0.5 hours)

EXHIBIT 4–4

Learning Curve

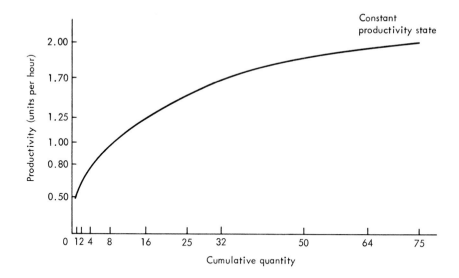

The table demonstrates the computations for an 80 percent learning curve, which is shown in Exhibit 4–4. These curves are plotted on log-log graph paper in practice. Points on the graph are determined by dividing the cumulative quantity at each point by the predicted total hours to perform the task. For example: 1 unit ÷ 2 hours = 0.50, 2 units ÷ 3.2 hours = 0.63, 4 units ÷ 5.2 hours = 0.76, 8 units ÷ 8 hours = 1.0, and so forth.

The table indicates that the reduction rate of 20 percent is constant at each doubling of the number of tasks performed. As shown in the last column, 32 hours are required to perform the task the first 64 times. Eventually, the skill is learned and further reductions in time become negligible. A constant productivity state sets in as indicated in Exhibit 4–4.

It is easily recognized that the second column in the table is simply the learning rate raised to a power corresponding to the number of times production is doubled. We can see this relationship conveniently for illustrative purposes, but it becomes cumbersome for practical applications. A mathematical expression of the relationship between production times and quantities is more useful. Tables have been developed which give the factor for each unit and for various improvement ratios. These tables eliminate the need for the unwieldy calculations with the formulas and provide greater precision than can be obtained with a graph.

Learning curves provide an insight into the ability of the worker to learn new skills. This information can assist management in establishing an incentive wage system because bonus pay usually should not be provided while the worker is in a learning stage. After the skill is learned, standards may be established so that the employee may earn bonus pay for performing operations in less than standard time. Certainly if standards are needed before the constant productivity state becomes apparent, the learning curve effect should be considered.

Managers can also use learning curves to estimate labor requirements and prepare cost estimates. In competitive bidding, the effect of learning on costs can be estimated if repeat orders are expected. Certainly, expected volume will have an impact on unit costs, especially when the pace is not set by an assembly line or if machines do not limit the worker's speed. Progress reports comparing actual results with estimated accomplishments as depicted by the learning curve can be used to evaluate performance.

2. Indirect or "fringe" benefits

The second large category of employee compensation includes payments which employees do not receive directly or immediately, but which do benefit the employee and are related to their employment. A brief description of some of these major items follows:

Holidays. Most firms have certain days of the year on which employees are not required to work but for which they receive their regular pay.

Vacations. Most firms have a policy of granting vacations with pay to their employees, and the amount of vacation is usually related to tenure with the company. For example, a company may grant two-week vacations per year for employees with five years or less of service and three-week vacations per year for service in excess of five years.

Insurance. Many firms pay all or part of an employee's premium for medical, dental, or life insurance. These are definite benefits to the employee.

Pensions. Pensions are an employee benefit that most firms provide but which the employee may not receive for many years after the benefit has been actually earned. The basic concept behind a pension is that the employee is earning the benefit each year he or she is employed, but defers the receipt of cash payments until leaving the firm. It is not possible to generalize about pension plans; the actual specifics are determined by agreement between the employees and management. Inadequately funded or poorly administered pension plans have in the past led to many employees receiving less than expected or no pension benefits. These pension plan failures led to the passage of the Employment Retirement Income Security Act (ERISA) in 1974 which established federal standards regulating private pension plans.

Stock and thrift plans. A number of companies have *thrift* plans which usually allow the employee to borrow on a thrift fund or purchase company stock. Another common compensation plan, primarily for salaried persons, is stock options; basically such plans consist of granting the employee an option (right) to purchase a certain number of shares of company stock at a specified price within a certain time period. The employee's compensation is the difference between the option price and the price of the stock on the date the option is exercised.

3. **Employer payroll tax**

   Voluntary withholding.   The employer in the role of payroll preparer is also forced to act as a "collector." There are various payments that employees voluntarily agree will be deducted from their pay by the employer and the employer will then make the payments to the proper institution in the employee's name.
   Examples of these are the following:

   1. Union dues—to be paid to the union.
   2. Pension funds—when the pensions are administered directly by the union.
   3. Medical and life insurance premiums—when the employee pays part or all of the insurance premium.
   4. Withholding for purchase of savings bonds.

   Involuntary withholding.   Various laws require that the employer withhold from the pay of employees certain taxes and remit these amounts periodically to the proper authorities. These tax withholdings are as follows:

   1. *Income tax*. This could include federal, state, and city income taxes. The amount to be withheld is determined by tables furnished by the authorities.
   2. *Social security taxes (F.I.C.A.)*. The law provides that as of 1983 the employee will pay 6.7 percent on the first $35,700 of earnings.

   Payroll taxes levied on the employer for the benefit of the employees.   The primary taxes levied directly on the employer are social security (F.I.C.A.), unemployment taxes, and state workmen's compensation insurance.
   1. F.I.C.A.   All employers not in excluded classes of employment such as agriculture, domestic service, nonprofit organizations, and federal, state, and municipal employment must withhold from employees and contribute an equal amount to the F.I.C.A. taxes withheld from their employees, up to a maximum per employee, per year as determined by current F.I.C.A. regulations. Therefore, if the employee is paying 6.7 percent of $35,700 (or $2,391.90) per year, the employer must pay a like $2,391.90 to the social security fund. As the social security rates and base increase, there are built-in increases in the employer's cost structure.
   2. Unemployment taxes. Under the Federal Unemployment Tax Act, employers of one or more workers in covered employment must also pay an unemployment insurance tax. The annual earnings base on which this tax is computed is specified by law. No employee contributions to federal unemployment tax are required. Various states also require employers to submit

labor reports and to contribute to a state unemployment compensation plan. In some states, employees are also taxed, but not necessarily at the same rate as the employer. Certain credits are allowed for employers with small numbers of employees collecting unemployment compensation.

3. *State workmen's compensation insurance.* Workmen's compensation insurance compensates workers or their survivors for losses caused by employment-related accidents or occupational diseases. The insurance or tax is levied only on employers, with the rate varying according to degree of occupational risk. This tax is determined by state law, with the benefits and premiums differing among states.

4. *Other legislation.* In addition to the foregoing payroll taxes, government regulations cover other various aspects of employment such as minimum wages, union negotiations, job hazards, and so forth. These regulations normally fall within the scope of a personnel department, but their administration is a definite cost to the firm. For example, the Fair Labor Standards Act of 1938, referred to as the Wages and Hours Law, established a minimum wage per hour with time and a half for any hours worked in excess of 40 in one week. However, certain types of workers and organizations are exempt from the act's provisions. In 1964, an amendment to the Civil Rights Act, Title VII, was passed by Congress which specifically prohibited discrimination for reasons of race, creed, color, national origin, age, physical disability, political affiliation, and sex. Title VII established the Equal Employment Opportunity Commission (EEOC) to administer the law and to receive, investigate, and reconcile employment discrimination charges under Title VII. The commission's responsibility is to ensure that all Americans will be considered for hiring and promotion on the basis of their ability and qualifications, without regard to race, color, religion, sex, or national origin. Another government regulation that affects employment is the Occupational Safety and Health Act (OSHA) which has the objective of protecting the worker and the environment. The act has had a costly impact on many companies, as they have been required to invest millions of dollars in changing production methods to conform to OSHA regulations.

PAYROLL ACCOUNTING

Following this discussion of the major elements of employee compensation and payroll taxes, we turn our attentions to the accounting and record-keeping functions.

Forms W–4 and W–2. Before starting work, employees must complete a withholding certificate (form W–4) in which they indicate the income tax exemptions they are claiming. The federal income deduction from an employee's gross wages depends on the amount of the employee's earnings and the exemptions claimed on form W–4. Employers are also required to furnish each employee with a Wage and Tax Statement (form W–2) on or before January 31 of the year following the one in which wages were earned. If employment ends before December 31, a W–2 form must be provided within 30 days of the last payday. Form W–2 indicates wages earned and taxes withheld.

Timekeeping records

From the employees' standpoint, paying the correct amounts, on time, is crucial for morale, while management is very interested in protecting against overpayments. Thus, a well-documented time record is necessary. For hourly employees, some form of time card is required to ensure that the employee was on the job for the specified hours. In addition, hourly employees are given premiums when working night shifts, working overtime (usually work over 8 hours a day or 40 hours a week is paid at one and one-half times normal earnings), and working on holidays (usually paid at twice the normal rate). Because of these premiums, the time of day, the particular days worked, and total hours per day and week are required from the timekeeping system. In addition, vacation days, sick days, and other absences must be reported and maintained for correct calculation of pay.

Time card.   An accurate record of the amount of time employees work is kept in several ways. Exhibit 4–5 illustrates a clock card or time card which provides evidence of when the employee was on the work site. Clock or time cards can be filled out manually or by a clock punch. Each employee has his or her own time card or sheet which shows the dates worked and the time the employee entered and left each day.

Job time tickets.   Since the time card only indicates the total time, a *job time ticket* is also needed to show the time each employee spent on individual jobs during the day. Exhibit 4–6 illustrates an individual job time ticket reflecting where the employee worked during the day, the name of the employee working on a particular job, the time the employee started and stopped, and the rate of pay. Employees can prepare their own forms if the forms are readily available and a minimum of time is required to complete them; in other instances, supervisors or dispatch clerks complete the forms when employees report to them for a new assignment. Sometimes work-ticket forms are computer punch cards that become input into an electronic data processing system.

Daily time ticket.   Instead of having an employee prepare a new ticket for each job worked during the day, a daily job time ticket can be used to summarize all jobs the worker performed. The *daily job time ticket*, as illustrated in Exhibit 4–7 on page 144, eliminates having more than one ticket per employee each day. Space is provided for the starting and stopping time for each job worked on. A tabulation at the bottom of the daily time ticket allows for the accumulation of hours worked on each assignment before the hours are

EXHIBIT 4–5

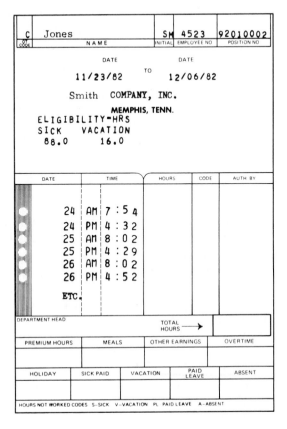

posted to a job order cost sheet. Total regular and overtime hours are also shown on Exhibit 4–7. Time cards and job tickets should be reviewed and approved by the supervisor.

Each day, the timekeeper collects the previous day's job time tickets and

EXHIBIT 4–6

Individual job time ticket

Date _____   Employee name (or no.) _____

Time started _____   Job. no. _____

Time stopped _____   Department _____

Hours worked _____   Pieces completed _____

Rate _____   Amount _____

                                Approved _____

EXHIBIT 4–7

Daily job time ticket

Date _____			Employee name (or no.) _____	
Started	Stopped	Hours	Job no.	Department
Job no.	Hours	Other work	Hours	Total hours
				Regular overtime

time cards. The time reported on these is compared; any differences should be investigated. If the difference is small, it may be considered idle time and charged to Factory Overhead. This often represents the time required for the worker to transfer from one job to another. If the job time ticket shows more hours than the time card, the cause should be determined by consulting the employee and his or her supervisor. After completion, time cards and job time tickets are sent to the payroll department for use in calculating and preparing the payroll check and accounting distributions.

Job order cost sheet.   After job charges have been computed from the job time ticket, the cost is entered on the *job order cost sheet* illustrated in Exhibit 4–8. This is the same form shown in Exhibit 3–2 to illustrate direct material charges.

TWO BASIC LABOR ENTRIES

Despite the variations found in practice, labor accounting entries are of two basic types that can be combined in one entry: (1) recording labor distribution, together with the liabilities from employee withholdings and net earnings; and (2) recording the employer's payroll taxes. An understanding of these two basic labor entries will allow the accountant to adjust to any payroll system found in practice. The payroll distribution requires entries to record the direct labor costs to Work in Process Inventory; indirect labor costs to Factory Overhead Control; and marketing and administrative wages and salaries to their respective control accounts. In this process, the amount of employee withholdings from gross pay and the net earnings are recorded in a liability account titled Payroll Payable, Accrued Salaries, or Salaries Payable. (Subsidiary ledger accounts are omitted in the illustration below.) Employee withholdings are not costs to the employees' gross pay. Exhibit 4–8 illustrates a job order sheet

EXHIBIT 4–8

JOB ORDER COST SHEET

JONES MANUFACTURING COMPANY

Customer:

Douglass Warehouse, Inc.

309 North 12th Street

Murray, Kentucky 42071

For stock _____

Job no. 1212

Product   144″ # 8 Cloth (144 rolls)

Date required   1/23/19X1

Date started   1/16/19X1

Date completed   1/20/19X1

SEWING DEPARTMENT

Direct materials			Direct labor		Factory overhead		
Date	Requisition number	Amount	Date	Amount	Date	Basis	Amount
1/16/19X1	911	$6,455.55	1/18/19X1	$1,300.00			

TREATING DEPARTMENT

Direct materials			Direct labor		Factory overhead		
Date	Requisition number	Amount	Date	Amount	Date	Basis	Amount
1/18/19X1	914	$37.50	1/19/19X1	$1,000.00			

SUMMARY

	Sewing department	Treating department	Total	
Selling price.				$XXX
Direct materials costs.	XX	XX	XXX	
Direct labor costs.	XX	XX	XXX	
Factory overhead applied.	XX	XX	XXX	XXX
Gross margin.				$XXX

---

where the direct labor cost distributed to the job order is recorded as $1,300 from the Sewing Department and $1,000 from the Treating Department.

Labor distribution.   The general ledger entry to record and pay this particular payroll of $3,910 according to work tickets would be as follows:

Work in Process Inventory	2,300.00	
Factory Overhead Control	710.00	
Marketing Expense Control	400.00	
Administrative Expense Control	500.00	
F.I.C.A. Taxes Withheld or Payable (required liability)		261.97
Federal Income Tax Withheld (required liability)		899.50
State Income Tax Withheld (required liability)		203.00
Union Dues Collected (liability)		125.00
Hospitalization Insurance Payable (liability)		180.00
Payroll Payable (liability)		2,240.53
Payroll Payable	2,240.53	
Cash		2,240.53

The above entry shows the total effect on the general ledger accounts. However, it may not be possible to record the total effect at one time, since at the time wages are paid, the data may not be available to record the labor distribution. In that case, a temporary ledger account called *Payroll* may be established for deferred recording purposes. Entries using a deferred payroll distribution are demonstrated below.

At the end of each pay period, the financial accountant records the following:

Payroll	3,910.00	
F.I.C.A. Taxes Payable		261.97
Federal Income Tax Withheld		899.50
State Income Tax Withheld		203.00
Union Dues Collected		125.00
Hospitalization Insurance Payable		180.00
Payroll Payable		2,240.53
Payroll Payable	2,240.53	
Cash		2,240.53

At the end of each month or some other period, the cost accountant analyzes the balance in the Payroll Summary account. Assume that there were several additional pay periods in the month and the Payroll account has a balance of $6,010. The cost accountant determines that direct labor costs account for $2,810 (including $2,300 incurred in the first pay period); indirect labor of $1,270 (including $710 incurred in the first pay period); marketing salaries of $1,015 (including $400 incurred in the first pay period); and $915 of administrative wages and salaries (including $500 incurred in the first pay period).

In this case, the labor distribution entry would be as follows:

Work in Process Inventory	2,810.00	
Factory Overhead Control	1,270.00	
Marketing Expense Control	1,015.00	
Administrative Expense Control	915.00	
Payroll		6,010.00

Payroll tax. Recording the employer's payroll taxes is the second type of labor entry, and two approaches can be used to record these taxes. Theoretically, payroll taxes on direct labor are an additional cost of direct labor and should be accumulated in the Work in Process Inventory account. While many employers recognize that this is the correct approach, they do not feel that the extra effort involved is worth the refinement. Instead, they accumulate the employer's taxes on all factory personnel in the Factory Overhead Control account. Payroll taxes on marketing and administrative personnel are generally charged to the respective control accounts, regardless of the treatment of the payroll tax on direct labor. Even though this indirect approach is found in practice, it is a poor cost accounting treatment of payroll taxes and definitely not recommended. The data from the example illustrating the labor distribution and withholdings from gross pay are used to illustrate the correct recording of the employer's payroll tax. Only three payroll taxes are used, under the assumption that all wages are subject to these taxes: a 6.7 percent F.I.C.A. tax, a 2.7 percent state unemployment tax, and a 0.2 percent federal unemployment tax. A comparison of the approaches is given below:

Employer's payroll tax treated as direct cost

Work in Process Inventory (9.6 percent total tax on $2,300 direct factory labor)	220.80	
Factory Overhead Control (9.6 percent total tax on $710 indirect factory labor)	68.16	
Marketing Expense Control (9.6 percent total tax on $400 marketing labor)	38.40	
Administrative Expense Control (9.6 percent total tax on $500 administrative labor)	48.00	
F.I.C.A. Taxes Payable (6.7 percent × $3,910)		261.97
State Unemployment Taxes Payable (2.7 percent × $3,910)		105.57
Federal Unemployment Taxes Payable (0.2 percent × $3,910)		7.82

Employer's payroll tax treated as indirect cost

Factory Overhead Control (9.6 percent total tax on $2,300 direct and $710 indirect factory labor)	288.96	
Marketing Expense Control (tax on marketing labor as above)	38.40	
Administrative Expense Control (tax on administrative labor as above)	48.00	
F.I.C.A. Taxes Payable		261.97
State Unemployment Taxes Payable		105.57
Federal Unemployment Taxes Payable		7.82

The illustration used above combines the employees' and employer's contribution to F.I.C.A. into one account titled F.I.C.A. Taxes Payable. However, an account titled F.I.C.A. Taxes Withheld could be used to record the employees' deductions, while another liability account titled F.I.C.A. Taxes Payable may be used to record the employer's tax. However, most companies record both contributions in one liability account. The entry to record the payment of the $261.97 F.I.C.A. tax that was withheld from the employees' gross wages and the $261.97 F.I.C.A. tax reflecting the employer's contribution is as follows:

F.I.C.A. Taxes Payable ($261.97 employees' withholdings + $261.97 employer's contribution)	523.94	
Cash		523.94

Employers are required to deposit the federal income tax and F.I.C.A.

withheld together with the employer's F.I.C.A. tax to either an authorized commercial bank depository or a Federal Reserve Bank by a designated time. In addition, the employer is required to submit payment for state and federal unemployment taxes. The following summary indicates the journal entry that is made when these taxes are paid. In all cases, the liability account is debited while Cash is credited.

Federal Income Tax Withheld.	XX	
State Income Tax Withheld	XX	
F.I.C.A. Taxes Payable	XX	
State Unemployment Taxes Payable	XX	
Federal Unemployment Taxes Payable.	XX	
Cash		XX

Adjusting and reversing labor entries

In addition to the two basic labor entries just illustrated, the company may utilize adjusting and reversing labor entries. Adjusting entries record accrued payroll costs which properly match the period in which the employee's compensation is earned. If adjusting entries are not made to record accrued payroll costs, both labor costs and liabilities will be misstated. Reversing entries are used to reverse the adjusting entry that was made at the end of the preceding period. Reversing entries are dated the first day of the next period. Reversing entries for labor are optional, as the same result can be achieved regardless of whether reversing entries are used. Most companies have a timing problem—the payroll cannot be paid up to the day of earnings, so employees are often paid late. Some companies stagger payment throughout the week or month; for example, Departments 1 to 20 are paid on Monday, Departments 21 to 40 on Tuesday, and so forth. Under this plan, all payments are made 3 to 10 days after the end of the payroll period.

Assume that total earnings are $2,000 per day for direct labor workers, $1,000 for indirect labor, $500 for marketing personnel, and $750 for administrative personnel. Assume further that all employees working a five-day week are paid every Friday for the previous week. If the company's accounting system is on a calendar year and December 31 is a Tuesday, the following journal entry should be dated as of December 31:

Work in Process Inventory ($2,000 × 2 days)	4,000	
Factory Overhead Control ($1,000 × 2 days).	2,000	
Marketing Expense Control ($500 × 2 days)	1,000	
Administrative Expense control ($750 × 2 days)	1,500	
Payroll Payable		8,500

The timing of the liability for payroll taxes differs. Some companies record the payroll tax as a liability when the wages are *earned*, while other employers wait until the wages are paid because the legal liability is not incurred until then. However, since payroll taxes are basically related to incurring labor cost—not to its payment—the preferred treatment is to accrue payroll tax liability at the time labor cost is recognized. The practice of waiting until payroll is paid to recognize the liability can be considered acceptable if the amounts are not material and if this practice is followed consistently.

Reversing labor entry. A reversing entry can be dated as of the first working day of the next period, as the balances in the three expense control accounts would be closed out through a closing entry at year-end. The entire gross wages and payroll tax for the first pay period in the new year can be distributed to the Work in Process Inventory and the three expense controls. The credits in the expense control accounts resulting from the reversing entry offset the gross wage and payroll tax expenses recorded for the first pay period. The net amount remaining in the expense control accounts represents the total wage costs incurred in the new accounting period. The following reversing entries could be dated on the first working day of the next accounting period.

Payroll Payable	8,500	
Work in Process Inventory		4,000
Factory Overhead Control		2,000
Marketing Expense Control		1,000
Administrative Expense Control		1,500

Holidays, vacations, and bonus pay

Another frequent year-end labor cost entry is for employee bonuses and vacations. Bonuses are calculated as agreed to by employer and employee; many are determined at the end of the fiscal year. Even though bonuses are calculated at a specified point and holidays and vacations are taken at irregular times throughout the year, both of these employee benefits are earned throughout the year and represent an expense of the entire year, rather than the period in which the benefit is paid.

According to *Statement of Financial Accounting Standard No. 43, Accounting for Compensated Absences*, issued by the Financial Accounting Standards Board, an employer is required to accrue a liability for employees' rights to receive compensation for future absences when certain conditions are met. Compensated absences are defined by this statement as employee absences, such as vacation, illness, and holidays, for which it is expected that employees will be paid. *Statement No. 43* does not apply to deferred compensation or stock options; in addition, the allocation of costs of compensated absences to interim periods is not addressed by this statement.

Statement No. 43 indicates that an employer shall accrue a liability for employees' compensation for future absences if all of the following conditions are met: (An exception is that an employer is not required to accrue a liability for compensation for an employee's absence due to illness—paragraph 6.)

a. The employer's obligation relating to employees' rights to receive compensation for future absences is attributable to employees' services already rendered.

b.   The obligation relates to rights that vest and accumulate and do not depend upon continued performance of services.

c.   Payment of the compensation is probable.

d.   The amount can be reasonably estimated.

In summary, a liability shall be accrued for vacation benefits that employees have earned but have not yet taken; however, a liability is generally not required to be accrued for future sick pay benefits, holidays, and similar compensated absences until employees are actually absent.[1]

Therefore, vacation, holiday, and bonus payments earned by direct labor workers are an additional labor cost that should be accumulated in Work in Process Inventory. However, this approach is rarely used in practice because it is difficult to apply. The more common procedure is to classify vacation and bonus payments to direct labor workers as indirect costs chargeable to the Factory Overhead Control account together with the payments made to indirect labor workers. Vacation, holiday, and bonus payments made to the marketing and administrative staff should be charged to their respective control accounts.

Even though most companies do not attempt to classify vacations, holiday pay, and bonus pay as a direct labor cost but instead use the simpler approach of accumulating these costs in the Factory Overhead Control, the problem still exists of charging the costs of these employee benefits to the accounting period in which the benefits are earned. Basically, the cost of these employee benefits should be spread over the entire year by including an estimate for vacation, holiday, and bonus pay in the predetermined factory overhead rate. There are several ways to develop an estimate of the cost of holidays, vacations, and bonuses to charge to each accounting period. For one, the total amounts may be estimated for each employee or homogenous group of employees.

Accruing vacations, holiday pay, and bonus pay.   To illustrate the accrual of these benefits, we will assume that an employee earns $30 per day and the union contract, company policy, or employment agreement specifies the employee is to receive 10 working days of vacation and 5 working days of holidays. In addition, at fiscal year-end, the employee is to receive a bonus of 0.1 percent of company income; total net income for the company is expected to be $100,000. Benefit payments are estimated as follows:

Vacations (10 days × $30 per day)	$300	
Holidays (5 days × $30 per day).	150	$450
Bonus (0.1% of $100,000 expected net income)		100

The cost of these employee benefits is spread over the productive labor time of each employee. Assume that the employee is paid weekly and that these

[1]Material in this section was adapted from the Financial Accounting Standards Board, *Statement of Financial Accounting Standards No. 43, Accounting for Compensated Absences.* Copyright © by Financial Accounting Standards Board, High Ridge Park, Stamford, Connecticut, 06905, U.S.A. Reprinted with permission. Copies of the complete document are available from the FASB.

employee benefit costs are spread over 49 weeks [52 weeks − (2 weeks of vacation + 1 week of holidays)] as follows:

$$\frac{\$450}{49 \text{ weeks}} = \$9.18 \text{ per week for vacations and holiday pay}$$

TOTAL COST
TOTAL WEEKS

$$\frac{\$100}{49 \text{ weeks}} = \$2.04 \text{ per week for bonus pay}$$

The following entry would be made to record five days of productive labor for the employee:

Work in Process (5 days × $30 per day)	150.00	
Factory Overhead Control ($9.18 + $2.04)	11.22	
Payroll		150.00
Accrued Vacation and Holiday Pay		9.18
Accrued Bonus Pay		2.04

Rather than illustrate the withholding for taxes in the above journal entry, the Payroll summary account is used. When one holiday occurs in the week, the weekly costs for vacations, holidays, and bonuses would be multiplied by four fifths; if two holidays occur, by three fifths, and so forth. A similar computation could be used in calculating employee benefit pay per productive hour or month.

Payment for holidays and vacations. Withholdings from the employee's gross pay are recorded at the time employees are paid for holidays and vacations. When the employee in the previous example receives vacation pay, the following journal entry should be made:

Accrued Vacation and Holiday Pay	300.00	
Federal Income Tax Withheld		80.00
State Income Tax Withheld		25.00
F.I.C.A. Taxes Payable (6.7% × $300)		20.10
Payroll Payable		174.90
Payroll Payable	174.90	
Cash		174.90

An entry similar to the one above for vacation and holiday pay is also made for bonus payments. Rather than calculate the cost of these employee benefits each pay period, a percentage of cost or time may be used. For example, assume in the above illustration for vacations and holidays that the employee works 1,960 productive hours during the year. Since vacation and holidays are expected to total 15 days or 120 hours (15 days × 8 hours assuming an 8-hour workday), a liability equal to 6.122 percent of wages can be accrued at every pay period.

$$\frac{120 \text{ nonproductive hours}}{1,960 \text{ productive hours}} = 6.122 \text{ percent}$$

Administrative and other personnel who receive a fixed salary, regardless of the hours worked, are also entitled to holidays, vacations, and bonuses. The cost of these employee benefits can be treated in the manner illustrated for direct labor workers so that a proper matching of costs and benefits can be achieved. However, some companies consider vacation pay and holiday pay as a cost of the period in which the benefit is received. Usually no other persons are temporarily employed to assume the duties of administrators. While they are taking holidays or vacations, their work load accumulates.

Overtime premium pay

Another added employee benefit is overtime pay. The Fair Labor Standards Act (1938) established a minimum wage for most nonfarm workers engaged in interstate commerce, prohibited child labor, and required time-and-a-half pay for hours in excess of 40 per week. For example, assume an individual is paid $6 per hour. If the individual works 44 hours in a week, weekly earnings are computed as follows:

Regular earnings (40 hours × $6)		$240
Overtime pay:		
At regular rate (4 hours × $6).	$24	
Overtime premium (4 hours × $3).	12	36
Total weekly gross earnings		$276

All hours at the regular pay for direct labor workers are debited to Work in Process, as shown in the following entry:

FOH CONTROL	12.00	
Work in Process Inventory (44 hours × $6)	264.00	
F.I.C.A. Taxes Payable		17.69
Federal Income Taxes Withheld		66.00
Payroll Payable		180.31 192.31

While the Fair Labor Standards Act requires time-and-a-half pay for hours in excess of 40 per week, a union contract may specify additional premium pay, such as double pay for Sunday work and time-and-a-half pay for hours in excess of eight per day. Such overtime earnings should be segregated into the base pay component and the premium pay component for planning, control, and reporting purposes. The overtime premium pay should be accumulated as a cost of the job or department in a Work in Process Inventory account if the demands of the job or process cause the overtime hours. For example, if an order is accepted on Monday with a promised delivery date of Wednesday and the workers are required to work overtime to complete the order, the premium pay should be charged to this job in addition to the regular direct labor charge for total hours computed at the regular rate. If, on the other hand, the employees work overtime because the workload is generally heavier than normal and overtime cannot be attributed to a specific job, only the total hours at the regular rate should be treated as a direct labor cost to be accumulated in the Work in Process Inventory account, while the overtime premium pay should generally be charged to the Factory Overhead Control account. In determining the overhead application rate, an estimate for overtime premium pay should be included if overtime is expected.

Shift premium

Shift premiums, like overtime pay, affect labor costs. Either because of union contract agreements or because of company policy, many employees working on an evening or night shift receive a higher wage rate to compensate for the less desirable schedule. Because it does not seem logical to charge a larger direct labor cost for a finished unit simply because it was manufactured on an evening or night shift, the preferred treatment is to accumulate the shift premium amount in the Factory Overhead Control account rather than charge the entire wage (the regular pay and the shift premium) to the Work in Process Inventory. Clearly, in determining the factory overhead application rate, an estimate of the shift premium should be included in total indirect expenses. For example, assume that an employee on the night shift receives $6.20 per hour rather than the regular day-shift rate of $6.00 per hour. The entry to distribute the weekly wage for this night shift employee would be as follows:

```
Work in Process Inventory (40 hours × $6) . . . . . . . . . . . . . . . . . . . . . . .    240
Factory Overhead Control—Shift Premium (40 hours × $0.20) . . . . . . . .      8
    Payroll . . . . . . . . . . . . . . . . . . . . . . . . . . . . . . . . . . . . . . . . . . . .           248
```

This approach facilitates the comparison of payroll costs for different work shifts.

Optional payroll deductions

While employers are required by law to withhold certain taxes from employees' wages, employees may also agree to have amounts for union dues, charity, savings plans, and health and life insurance deducted from their gross wages. The company may also provide a plan for systematic savings through a company sponsored credit union or by agreeing to withhold amounts for the purchase of savings bonds. Similarly, the employee can request deductions for united charity funds. For any such amount withheld, the company must establish a separate liability account and must periodically remit the deductions to the proper entity. The applicable payroll tax or other liability account is reduced when the payment is made. For example, if the company has agreed to withhold union dues from employees' wages, a liability account called Union Dues Collected is established at the time deductions are made. At specified intervals, the union dues are forwarded to the union treasurer; then the liability account is debited and Cash is credited. Hospitalization and life insurance plans are likewise often established with the employee and employer sharing the costs, and the amounts withheld from employees represent liabilities until they are paid to the insurer.

Another form of payroll deduction results from the payment of payroll advances. Due to the nature of their job and its travel requirements, salespersons and other such employees often request payroll advances. Employees may also ask for advances for personal reasons. Prior authorization from the employee's supervisor, from a person in a higher management level, or from the treasurer's department is necessary, since control over these advances is very important. When such advances are made, an asset account called Payroll Advances, Salespersons' Advances, or Employee Advances is debited and Cash is credited. At the time the advance is approved and made, the repayment terms should be recorded. When the advance is deducted from the employee's payroll check, the Payroll Advance account is credited.

Before agreeing to handle optional payroll deductions, the company must recognize the additional accounting costs involved and should establish a policy regarding the type of deductions the company will make. Otherwise, some employees may injudiciously request payroll advances and miscellaneous deductions. However, the company may not always have a choice, as the union contract may require that such deductions as union dues and hospital insurance be made as part of the employee benefit plan program.

ACCOUNTING FOR HUMAN RESOURCES

In most companies, employee compensation represents a large percentage of total manufacturing costs. Because of this, companies realize that changes in their human resources are as important as the status of their physical and financial assets. Therefore, other personnel-related expenditures for recruiting, training, and conferences, as well as an allocation of salaries for periods of training, are considered by most companies to be investments in human resources, the most important asset of a firm.

Human resource accounting has been proposed as providing management with more complete information on the resources managed. Data on human resources are important in dealing with labor turnover analysis, return on investment from training expenditures, and cost-benefit analysis of activities related to the human assets. Human resource accounting emphasizes the impact of training, recruiting, and development work on the company's operations.

Managers often hesitate to incur expenses for building human assets (recruiting, training, etc.) because these expenditures are treated as period costs and are charged against revenue in the year incurred. As these costs are beneficial over more than one period, there is an improper matching of revenues and expenses, especially in years when the firm is investing more heavily in creating new human capabilities. If assessments of human resources within companies were included in the accountant's evaluation, managers would be encouraged to give more serious consideration to human resource investment decisions because it would be easier to understand the large sum of money committed to these assets. In accounting for human resources, the measurement difficulties, cultural constraints against valuing an individual in monetary terms, and capitalizing employees that are not legally owned by a company present problems in treating them as "assets." There are also special problems involved in distinguishing between the future benefits of human resource investments and the portion currently consumed. As a result, conventional accounting practice reflects human resource expenditures as immediate charges without considering the timing of expected benefits.

The conventional approach of expensing all human resource investments impedes management attempts to control expenditures in this area. The fact is that human resource information will enable management to accurately identify criteria for the optimum magnitude and mix of human capital expenditures. Normal capital budgeting procedures can be applied to human capital investments. By emphasizing the payoff of human resource investment expenditures, management can become more selective in making investments in human resources. For example, though continuing training of employees is generally a sound investment, an employee may not be responsive to efforts at increasing his or her capabilities, or there may be no evidence of any increased value after the individual has been trained. It would thus be apparent that the investment is not paying off and that management should take remedial action. These data on human resources can redirect management's thinking and action toward a broader and more realistic concept of the contribution being made by *all* elements of the firm. However, too often, managers' decisions on cost, revenue, or income goals are not based on good data about the changing conditions of human resources.

Serious problems with human resource accounting. The primary difficulties in human resource accounting are as follows: (1) The difficulty of trying to measure the value of a person. The value of an individual, for instance, probably should not be limited strictly to the training the company provides. Even assuming that some fairly accurate estimate can be made of a person's worth, should this information be released to the individual worker? The effect on a person who learns of his or her dollar value to the company may be damaging. (2) Another problem area involves the write-off of human resource value. How does the value of an employee decline through the years so that when a person retires, his or her worth to the company is zero? (Does it decline?) That in itself may be very difficult for the worker to accept. At the same time that the human resource value is changing, the employee's salary is usually increasing, so the employee may get the idea that he or she is being paid merely to occupy the position. Also, while advocates argue that human resource accounting is helpful in decision making, in some cases it may actually cause a manager to make the wrong decision. For example, before replacing an employee, the company may look at the dollars already invested in the employee's training and experience and hesitate to replace the employee, even if that would be best for the company. Clearly, then, measurement must be improved before many companies include human resource data in their published financial statements. However, more managers are becoming aware of the economic importance of their labor in the process of analyzing their human resource investment.

CASB AND COMPENSATION ACCOUNTING

The *Cost Accounting Standard Board* (CASB) has issued four standards, 408, 412, 413, and 415 relating to employee compensation. Generally, these four standards involve the concepts covered in this chapter relating to a proper matching of employee compensation and the production or period in which the compensation is earned rather than to the period in which it is paid. A brief summary of CASB Standards 408, 412, 413, and 415 is presented below.

CAS 408

CASB issued Part 408 concerned with accounting for costs of compensated personal absence. The purpose of this standard is to improve and provide uniformity in the measurement of costs of vacation, sick leave, holiday, and other compensated personal absence for a cost accounting period, thereby increasing the probability that the measured costs are allocated to the proper cost objectives. CAS 408 requires that the costs of compensated personal absence are assigned to the cost accounting period or periods in which the entitlement was earned. In addition, the costs of compensated personal absence for an entire cost accounting period are allocated pro rata on an annual basis among the final cost objectives of that period. Compensated personal absence is defined in the standards as any absence from work for reasons such as illness, vacation, holidays, jury duty, or military training, or personal activities, for which an employer pays compensation directly to an employee in accordance with a plan or custom of the employer.

CAS 412

In 1975, Part 412, *Cost Accounting Standard on the Composition and Measurement of Pension Cost*, was promulgated. The purpose of this standard is to provide guidance in determining and measuring the components of pension costs; the basis on which pension costs are assigned to cost accounting periods is also established by the standard. It is felt that the provisions of CAS 412 should enhance uniformity and consistency in accounting for pension costs and increase the probability that those costs are properly allocated to cost objectives. CAS 412 describes a defined-benefit pension plan as one in which the benefits to be paid or the basis for determining such benefits are established in advance and the contributions are intended to provide the stated benefits. For defined-benefit pension plans, the components of pension cost for a cost accounting period are (i) the normal cost of the period, (ii) a part of any unfunded actuarial liability, (iii) an interest equivalent on the unamortized portion of any unfunded actuarial liability, and (iv) an adjustment for any actuarial gains and losses. For defined-contribution pension plans in which the contributions are established in advance and the benefits are determined thereby, the pension cost for a cost accounting period is the net contribution that must be made for that period, after taking into account dividends and other credits, where applicable.

CAS 413

In 1977, Part 413, *Adjustment and Allocation of Pension Cost*, was issued which indicates that actuarial gains and losses should be calculated annually. Part 413 further gives criteria for assigning pension expense to cost accounting periods, as well as for valuing and allocating pension fund assets to business segments. CAS 413 indicates that the amortization period for gains and losses should be 15 years for plans for which costs are measured by an immediate-gain method, and the remaining average working years of the work force for plans using a spread-gain method. Usually one of the more significant actuarial gains or losses arises from differences between assumed and actual investment return. In measuring the gain or loss, any recognized actuarial asset valuation method may be used, the standard says, but if the result does not fall within 80 to 120 percent of the assets' market value, it must be adjusted to the nearest limit. Generally, pension costs may be computed collectively for participants in two or more segments, then allocated among the segments using a formula representative of the factors on which benefits are based. However, if this method materially affects a segment's allocation, separate calculations must be made.

CAS 415

In 1976, Part 415, *Accounting for the Cost of Deferred Compensation*, was issued which provides criteria for the measurement of the cost of deferred compensation and the assignment of such to cost accounting periods. Deferred compensation is defined as an award made by an employer to compensate an employee in a future cost accounting period or periods for services rendered in one or more cost accounting periods prior to the date of the receipt of compensation by the employee. CAS 415 requires that the cost of deferred compensation be assigned to the cost accounting period in which the contractor incurs an obligation to compensate the employee. In the event no obligation is incurred prior to payment, the cost of deferred compensation is the amount paid and is assigned to the cost accounting period in which the payment is made. An additional requirement is that measurement of the amount of the cost of deferred compensation is the present value of the future benefits. The cost of each award of deferred compensation is considered separately for purposes of measurement and assignment of such costs to cost accounting periods. However, if the cost of deferred compensation for the employees covered by a deferred compensation plan can be measured with reasonable accuracy on a group basis, separate computations for each employee are not required.

SUMMARY

The importance of maintaining employee morale through prompt and correct payment of wages, and the magnitude of employer expenditures for the services of labor, emphasize the importance of timely and proper accounting in the area of personnel services. However, given the various labor-related costs, labor accounting involves a number of complexities.

Incentive wage systems, one factor in labor costs, are often introduced to lower the unit conversion cost while at the same time giving workers an opportunity to earn additional wages. Group incentive plans are used when the work flow requires team effort and it is not possible to determine the number of units each individual employee produces. Group incentive wage systems may introduce some behavior problems since each worker may feel that he or she is carrying a heavier share of the workload than are other employees in the group. Regardless of the wage system used, it is imperative that workers understand how gross pay is calculated.

The potential for human resource accounting, one more key element of labor accounting, is significant as information about human resources can improve the quality of managerial decisions. Because labor cost represents a significant portion of product costs, managers recognize that information concerning the status of human assets is needed for labor turnover analysis and cost-benefit analysis of labor-related activities. But while the implications of human resource accounting for internal purposes is significant, serious measurement problems must be overcome before many companies will include human resource investments in their published financial statements.

IMPORTANT TERMS AND CONCEPTS

Wages

Salaries

Learning curve theory or improvement curve theory

Employee Retirement Income Security Act of 1974 (ERISA)

Form W–4, Employee's Withholding Exemption Certificate

Form W–2, Wage and Tax Statement

Time or clock cards

Job time ticket

Job order cost sheet

Overtime premium pay

Shift premium pay

Human resource accounting

CAS 408, CAS 412, CAS 413, and CAS 415

REVIEW QUESTIONS

1. Discuss several factors which cause complexities in labor accounting.
2. As far as employee behavior is concerned, why is it important to have accurate, understandable methods for calculating payroll?

3. Discuss the variety of labor-related costs that an employer can incur for each worker.
4. Explain the significance of learning curve theory and the role it plays in cost accounting.
5. Discuss the relationship of the payroll accountant to the financial accountant.
6. Why might you advise companies to stagger payrolls throughout the week or month?
7. Explain the theory behind, and the accounting for, withholdings from employees' checks.
8. Indicate whether the employer or the employee pays the following taxes:
   a. Federal unemployment tax.
   b. Federal income tax.
   c. F.I.C.A. tax.
   d. State unemployment tax.
   e. State income tax.
   f. Workmen's compensation insurance.
9. What is the source document for the distribution of direct labor costs to Work in Process Inventory and indirect labor costs to Factory Overhead Control?
10. What could cause a difference between the time reported on a time card and that shown on a job time ticket? How should this difference be reported?
11. What account is usually charged for vacation, holiday, and bonus payments made to direct labor workers? Why?
12. As a member of the management team, what factor would you consider most important when evaluating an incentive plan?
13. Discuss the advantages and the disadvantages of group incentive payroll plans.
14. Discuss the ways human resource data can be used for internal purposes.
15. Briefly discuss the requirements of CAS 408, CAS 412, CAS 413, and CAS 415.

EXERCISES

E4–1. Learning curve application

Howershell, Inc. manufactures complex units for submarines. A high degree of technical skill is required, and there is an opportunity for employees to learn. In estimating direct labor-hours, a 75 percent learning curve can be used. To complete one unit, 1,500 direct labor-hours are required at a cost of $12,000.

Required:

a. Determine the cumulative average worker-hours per unit for a *total* of: two units, four units, and eight units.
b. If, after completing one unit, an order for seven additional units is received, what is the estimated direct labor cost for the order?

E4–2. Incentive wage plan

Flynn Company has installed an incentive wage system in which workers receive their guaranteed wage per hour and a premium of 70 percent of the time saved on production in excess of the standard of 50 units per hour.

The production and guaranteed wage for an eight-hour day for two employees is given below:

	Hourly guaranteed rate	Production Monday	Production Tuesday
Abe Appleton.	$3.75	380	475
Ben Brown.	3.00	450	525

Required:

Calculate the daily wages for the two employees.

E4–3.   Treatment of overtime premium pay

An employee at the Jay Taylor Company is paid $3.50 per hour for a regular week of 40 hours. The employee worked 52 hours on Job No. 4168 and earned time-and-a-half for overtime hours for the week ending November 12. A job order subsidiary ledger is used for work in process.

Required:

a.   Prepare the entry to distribute the labor cost if the overtime premium is charged to factory overhead costs.

b.   Prepare the entry to distribute the labor cost if the overtime premium is charged to the production worked on during the overtime hours.

E4–4.   Accounting for vacation, holiday, and bonus pay

A union agreement was recently entered into by the management of Greg Jones Company granting employees 10 working days of vacation and 5 working days of holidays. In addition, at fiscal year-end, each employee is to receive a bonus of 0.03 percent of net company income. Total net income is expected to be $500,000.

Required:

a.   Prepare the journal entry to record the total weekly labor cost for one employee who earns $45 for one day of productive labor. Assume a payroll summary account has previously been used and you are to distribute only the labor cost.

b.   Prepare the journal entry when the employee in *a* receives his entire vacation pay. Assume that amounts withheld are $90 federal income tax, $32 state income tax, and 6.7 percent F.I.C.A. tax.

c.   Compute the cost of holidays and vacations accruing to each pay period as a percentage of cost for this employee, assuming a 40-hour week.

E4–5.   Computing daily earnings under an incentive plan

Dobbs Company uses an incentive plan in which employees receive a guaranteed rate of $8 per hour and a premium of 60 percent of the time saved on production in excess of the standard of 80 units per hour. You have pulled the production records and find an employee has produced the following: Monday—700 units; Tuesday—720 units.

Required:

Compute the daily earnings for these two days.

E4-6. Use of learning curve theory in bidding

Miller Manufacturers has just completed the production and sale of a complex electronic unit. Management believes an opportunity exists to apply a 70 percent learning curve. In determining the cost of the first unit manufactured, the following data were obtained:

Material (60 pounds @ $4 per pound)	$ 240
Direct Labor (80 hours @ 10 per hour)	800
Factory Overhead ($2 per direct labor-hour)	160
	$1,200

A potential customer approaches management wanting to buy three units for a total price of $2,500.

Required:

Provide supporting data indicating the estimated profit or loss if the bid is accepted. Assume no quantity discount exists for materials.

E4-7. Journal entries for payroll, labor distribution, and payroll tax

Tripett Corporation has a payroll as follows for the week just ended:

	Gross wages	Wages subject to F.I.C.A.
Direct labor	$5,500	$5,500
Indirect labor	1,500	1,500
Marketing salaries	2,000	1,600
Administrative salaries	3,500	0
	12500	

Income tax withheld totals $2,000. Applicable tax rates are:

	Earned per person
F.I.C.A.	6.7% on first $35,700
State unemployment	2.0% on first $ 6,000
Federal unemployment	0.7% on first $ 6,000

All employees have earned over $6,000 except for one direct labor worker whose prior cumulative earnings are $5,000. This worker earned $1,200 this pay period.

Required:

a. Using a temporary payroll account, make the payroll entry. Then make the labor distribution entry and the subsequent wage payment entry.

b. Record the payroll taxes using the direct cost method.

PROBLEMS

P4-1. Journal entries for labor costs and payment of payroll and payroll taxes

The employees of the John Lewis Company are paid at the end of each month. During the month of October, the workload was heavier than usual and caused a group of direct labor workers to work overtime. The overtime is not attributable to any one job. The records of the company show the following information for October:

	Regular earnings	Overtime premium	Total gross earnings
Gross earnings of employees:			
Direct labor	$18,000	$750	$18,750
Indirect labor	8,000		8,000
Marketing expense	4,000		4,000
Administrative expense	3,000		3,000
Total	$33,000	$750	$33,750
F.I.C.A. tax*			6.7%
Federal unemployment tax*			.7%
State unemployment tax*			2.0%
Holiday and vacation pay (only on regular pay of direct and indirect labor)			2.5%
Total			11.9%
Union dues withheld	$ 650		
Employees' income taxes withheld	$4,000		

*All earnings are subject to these rates.

Required:

a. Prepare the journal entry(s) to record the incurrence of all labor costs for October. Include the employer's payroll tax and holiday and vacation pay, treating them as direct costs.

b. Prepare the journal entries to record payment of wages to employees as well as payment of the employer's payroll taxes and income and payroll taxes withheld from employees' earnings.

P4–2. Daily earnings and effective hourly rate using proposed incentive plans

Standard production in the Emma Knight Company is 40 units per hour. For the first week in April, a worker's record shows the following:

Monday	330 units	8 hours
Tuesday	350 units	8 hours
Wednesday	310 units	8 hours
Thursday	320 units	8 hours
Friday	340 units	8 hours

Management is considering the adoption of one of two different incentive plans and wants to use this representative worker's record to study earnings using each proposed incentive plan.

With incentive Plan A, workers are guaranteed a rate of $2.40 per hour and a premium of 70 percent of the time saved on production in excess of standard.

With incentive Plan B, workers are paid $0.07 per unit when daily output is below standard, $0.09 per unit when daily output is at standard and up to 5 percent above standard, $0.10 per unit for all production when the daily output exceeds 5 percent above standard.

Required:

Compute daily earnings and the effective rate per hour for each day using each of the incentive plans proposed.

P4–3.   Distributing labor costs and alternative treatment of payroll tax

Brock, Inc. is subject to the following tax rates:

	Paid to each employee
F.I.C.A.	6.7% on first $35,700
State unemployment	2.0% on first $ 6,000
Federal unemployment	0.7% on first $ 6,000

The company pays its employees biweekly and shows the following information for four employees:

1. Cab, President, has earned $36,000 this year. The gross salary now due him for the current pay period is $1,900, from which $570 federal income tax is withheld.
2. Ted, sales representative, has earned $35,300 this year. The gross salary now due him for the current pay period is $1,700, from which $300 federal income tax is withheld.
3. Hal, machine operator, has earned $9,000 this year and is now due $500 for the current pay period, from which $80 is withheld.
4. Dan, janitor, has earned $5,400 this year and is now due $300 for the current pay period, from which $30 is withheld.

Required:

a.   Record the distribution of labor cost for the current pay period and its subsequent payment.
b.   Record the payroll taxes, treating them as indirect costs.
c.   Record the payroll taxes, treating them as direct costs.

P4–4.   Impact of incentive plan on conversion cost

The management of Lucille Austin Company has recently adopted an incentive plan for its employees. Standards for each employee are expressed in time per unit of output. A performance efficiency ratio is computed for each employee by comparing actual output with standard output. This ratio is then applied against each employee's base rate. All employees are guaranteed $10.80 per hour if they do not meet standard production. The labor time sheets for the week ended June 15 are as follows:

Employee	Hours worked	Hourly rate for standard production	Actual output	Standard units per hour
H. J. Adams	40	$13.00	690	15
A. R. Baker	40	12.25	944	20
L. T. Smith	35	11.90	425	13
B. J. Wallace	38	11.50	855	18

Required:

a.   Compute the gross wages for each employee.
b.   Prior to the enactment of the incentive plan, the weekly output of the four employees was 2,500 units for the same number of hours worked. Total weekly

labor costs were $1,650. Total factory overhead averaged $550 per week prior to the incentive plan, but it was $551.29 after the plan was enacted. Calculate the conversion cost per unit prior to and after enactment of the incentive plan.

P4–5. Payment of payroll. Recording and paying payroll taxes

The following liability accounts of the FTA Company contained these credit balances on November 30:

Federal income tax withheld	$3,025.00
Federal unemployment taxes payable	12.50
F.I.C.A. taxes payable	⁻145.00
State unemployment taxes payable	85.00

For the December payroll, direct labor totaled $6,175; indirect labor, $1,425; marketing expense control, $1,425; and administrative expense control, $475. Income taxes of $2,250 were withheld. Only $1,500 of the payroll was subject to the 6.7 percent F.I.C.A. tax rate, while $1,000 of the payroll was subject to the 2 percent state unemployment tax rate and the 0.7 percent federal unemployment tax rate. Of the payroll and payroll taxes, 65 percent apply to direct labor, 15 percent to indirect labor, 15 percent to marketing personnel, and 5 percent to administration.

Required:

a. Prepare the entry to record, distribute, and pay the payroll for December.
b. Prepare the entry recording the employer's payroll taxes for December. Treat payroll taxes as direct costs.
c. Prepare the entry to pay all taxes due government agencies for the period ending December 31.

P4–6. Effect of incentive plan on unit product cost

The management of Vita, Inc. wants to maximize the productivity of its labor. In pursuing this objective, it is investigating the pros and cons of a wage incentive plan. The company has analyzed past results and arrived at the following data which are representative of an actual average month:

	Average month
Actual production	20,000 units
Direct material used	$49,000
Direct labor costs	63,000
Variable factory overhead	10,000
Fixed factory overhead	36,000

After conducting tests, management is satisfied that units produced will increase by 25 percent per month if it adopts the proposed incentive plan. It is anticipated that, after the incentive plan is initiated, total labor cost will be $80,000. Other factory costs behave as they have in the past.

Required:

Should management adopt the incentive plan? Base your recommendations solely on the effect that the incentive plan has on unit product cost. What other factors should Vita, Inc. consider before adopting the incentive plan?

P4–7. Evaluating alternative incentive plans

Blake McConnell, a management consultant, has designed two different incentive plans for a client. Plan A does not provide a guaranteed wage. Instead, workers are paid at a piece rate of $0.12 a unit. A bonus of 25 percent of the regular piece rate is paid for each unit over standard. The standard is 25 units per hour.

Plan B, a group incentive plan, includes an extra 4 percent on a guaranteed minimum wage for each 100 units over the group's weekly standard. The weekly standard for the group is 3,000 units. Data for all the employees in the group for a 40-hour week are given below. The bonus will be calculated for every hour worked.

Employee	Units produced	Guaranteed hourly minimum (for Plan B)
C. Xedus	900	$4.35
F. York	1,100	3.55
R. Zillis	1,200	3.65

Required:

a. Compute the gross earnings for each employee first under Plan A and then under Plan B.

b. Evaluate the plans and indicate which you feel is more appropriate in these circumstances.

P4–8. Controls for piecework

Payroll, Inc., has adopted an incentive plan. Employees earn 10 percent of their hourly minimum wage for each unit that they produce above standard. Because the nature of their jobs varies, a standard and hourly minimum is established for each job. An employee receives the guaranteed minimum wage if he or she does not meet the standard for a day. Employees work eight hours per day.

	Actual output	Standard per day	Minimum Hourly wage
Employee Able:		50	$2.75
Monday	48		
Tuesday	56		
Wednesday	58		
Thursday	52		
Friday	54		
Employee Benton:		60	3.10
Monday	45		
Tuesday	65		
Wednesday	40		
Thursday	80		
Friday	64		

Required:

a. Calculate each employee's daily wages.

b. Does a review of these employees' output lead you to believe that a control feature is needed?

P4–9.   Reversing entries for labor costs

The employees of Richard Tee Company are paid every other Friday. Since the last pay period of 19X2 ended on December 24, the company made the following adjusting entry on December 31 so that its financial statements would be correctly stated.

Work in Process Inventory.	2,000	
Factory Overhead Control.	6,000	
Marketing Expense Control.	1,500	
Administrative Expense Control.	900	
Payroll Payable		10,400

Gross regular earnings for the first payroll ending on January 7, 19X3, were direct labor, $4,000; indirect labor, $12,000; sales and distribution personnel, $3,000; administrative costs, $1,800. Because Job No. 49 had a time deadline, the company incurred overtime premium pay totaling $820. Authorizations from employees to withhold contributions to the United Neighbors charitable fund of $850 and union dues of $750 were received. Federal income taxes of $5,250 were withheld. The following taxes were imposed on 100 percent of wages at the rates indicated: F.I.C.A. at 6.7 percent each for employer and employee; federal unemployment tax at 0.7 percent; and state unemployment tax at 2 percent.

Required:

a.   Record the reversing entry for wages on January 1.
b.   Assuming a reversing entry was made, prepare the entries on January 7 to record the labor cost and its subsequent payment.
c.   Prepare the entries on January 7 assuming *no* reversing entry was made.
d.   Prepare the entry to record payroll taxes on the January 7 payroll, treating them as direct costs.
e.   Prepare the entry to record the payment of all taxes that have accrued.

P4–10.   Learning curve (CMA adapted)

The Kelly Company plans to manufacture a product called Electrocal which requires a substantial amount of direct labor on each unit. Based on the company's experience with other products which required similar amounts of direct labor, management believes that there is a learning factor in the production process used to manufacture Electrocal.

Each unit of Electrocal requires 50 square feet of direct material at a cost of $30 per square foot for a total material cost of $1,500. The standard direct labor rate is $25 per direct labor-hour. Variable manufacturing overhead is assigned to products at a rate of $40 per direct labor-hour. The company adds a markup of 30 percent on variable manufacturing cost in determining an initial bid price for all products.

Data on the production of the first two lots (16 units) of Electrocal are as follows:

The first lot of eight units required a total of 3,200 direct labor-hours.

The second lot of eight units required a total of 2,240 direct labor-hours.

Based on prior production experience, Kelly anticipates that there will be no significant improvement in production time after the first 32 units. Therefore, a standard for direct labor-hours will be established based on the average hours per unit for units 17 to 32.

Required:

a.   What is the basic premise of the learning curve?

b. Based upon the data presented for the first 16 units, what learning rate appears to be applicable to the direct labor required to produce Electrocal? Support your answer with appropriate calculations.

c. Calculate the standard for direct labor-hours which Kelly Company should establish for each unit of Electrocal.

d. After the first 32 were manufactured, Kelly Company was asked to submit a bid on an additional 96 units. What price should Kelly bid on this order of 96 units? Explain your answer.

e. Knowledge of the learning curve phenomenon can be a valuable management tool. Explain how management can apply the learning curve in planning and controlling business operations.

CASES

C4–1. Internal control over payroll procedures

Stella Paquette Manufacturing Company employs approximately 600 production workers and has the following payroll procedures. All hiring is performed by the factory supervisors, who make their decision after interviewing applicants. After the interview, the applicant is either hired or rejected. If the applicant is hired, a W–4 form is prepared indicating the number of exemptions claimed. This Employee's Withholding Exemption Certificate serves as a notice to the payroll clerk that the employee has been hired; the hiring factory supervisor writes the hourly rate on the form and forwards it to the Payroll Department. The factory supervisors verbally inform the payroll clerks of any rate adjustments for employees under their supervision.

Near the entrance to the factory is a box containing blank time cards. At the beginning of the week, each production worker removes a blank card and fills in his or her name in pencil. Arrival and departure time are recorded daily.

At the end of the pay period, payroll clerks replace the completed time cards with blank cards. If a worker does not have a time card, it is assumed that he or she is no longer employed, and his or her name is removed from the payroll. The chief payroll accountant manually signs payroll checks. Payroll checks for the majority of employees are distributed at the payroll department. During the days on which payroll is paid, employees go to the Payroll Department to pick up their checks. Unfortunately, some employees wait in line 45 minutes or more to receive them. Not only does this represent lost production time, but it also presents a traffic problem because space is limited outside the Payroll Department window.

Payroll checks for employees working in critical assembly lines are given to the factory supervisors for distribution. These supervisors arrange for the delivery of checks for workers who are absent.

The payroll bank account is reconciled by the chief payroll accountant, who also prepares state and federal payroll tax reports.

Required:

Make suggestions for improving control over hiring practices and payroll procedures.

C4–2. Improvement of productivity (CMA adapted)

Improved productivity is considered an important way to reduce or control expenditures during periods of inflation. This can be done in a variety of ways, including making additional capital investment and improving employee performance. The three cases presented below focus on attempts to increase employee productivity without added capital investment.

Case 1.   The customer complaints department is in charge of receiving, investigating, and responding to customer claims of poor service. The volume of paperwork is very large and growing because each complaint requires the processing of several forms and letters. A large staff is needed to handle this processing. There is a wide span of control, with 15 to 20 staff members reporting to each supervisor. The number of complaints processed per worker has shown a noticeable decline in recent months.

The department manager recommends that supervisors require increased performance. They should do this by setting performance objectives, making their presence more obvious, monitoring breaks and lunch hours, and seeing to it that talking among staff members is strictly curtailed. The supervisors should also make the staff aware that failure to achieve performance objectives will result in a negative evaluation of performance.

Case 2.   A department of an insurance company in charge of processing medical-related claims has had its budget reduced even though the number of claims has been increasing. This reduction comes after very small annual appropriation increases in previous years. Given the recent rate of inflation, the actual resources available to do the work have decreased.

Top management recently specified that certain claims be processed within 48 hours of receipt, a requirement that leads to special handling of such claims. Consequently, the budget reduction causes the processing of other claims to be delayed even further. The department manager complains that the budget cuts and the priority treatment of certain claims will reduce the department's overall productivity.

This manager recommends that top management allow all managers to participate more actively in budget development and budget adjustment during the year. Further, once the general objectives for a department are established, the department manager should be allowed to set the priorities for the work to be accomplished.

Case 3.   Investigative auditors within a welfare agency are responsible for detecting cases of welfare fraud. Because of the latest recession, the number of welfare fraud cases was expected to increase significantly. However, the number of cases discovered has not increased. This may be due to the fact that investigators are becoming discouraged because of the lack of follow-up action taken on their findings. Cases are backed up in legal processing. Even when the individuals are found guilty, the penalties are often very light. The investigators wonder whether all their time and effort uncovering the fraudulent claims are justified.

The manager of the investigative audit department has recommended an annual performance incentive program for the investigators which is related only to the number of cases of fraud detected. The annual performance evaluation report would be filed in each investigator's personnel record and each investigator's annual salary adjustment would be based primarily upon the number of fraud cases detected. Currently, evaluations relate to the number of cases closed with conviction.

Required:

For each of the three cases presented, discuss whether or not the proposal of the department manager will improve productivity within the department. Explain, in detail, the reasons for your conclusion in each case.

OUTLINE OF CHAPTER 5

Cost, profit, and investment centers

Cost behavior

Cost and engineering studies

Regression analysis

Fixed (static) and variable (flexible) budgeting

OBJECTIVES OF CHAPTER 5

1. To stress the important contribution of the cost accountant in advising management by predicting cost behavior.

2. To illustrate various approaches, including regression analysis, used to segregate the behavior patterns of costs into fixed and variable components.

3. To contrast the differences between the variances obtained using a fixed budget and those obtained using a variable budget; to stress the validity of variable budgeting.

4. To introduce variable budgeting prior to discussing overhead rates in Chapter 6.

5

Behavior of overhead costs and regression analysis

Chapter 2 introduced and discussed the fixed, variable, and semivariable (mixed) behavior patterns of costs. This chapter extends that discussion to show why cost behavior requires careful analysis in the budgeting process. There is usually little difficulty in determining whether a direct material or direct labor cost is fixed or variable; generally, these costs *are* variable. Overhead cost behavior, on the other hand, offers more challenge to the cost accountant, since some overhead costs vary erratically with production. For example, overhead costs increase in importance and amounts as factories become more automated. Before overhead costs can be effectively controlled, their cost behavior should be analyzed.

The budgeting process is discussed in detail in Chapters 12 and 13. It is, however, important to introduce the concepts of variable budgeting in this chapter as a lead-in to overhead rates, which are discussed in Chapter 6. With this concept, a variable budget formula is prepared in advance for each department or cost center, indicating both fixed costs and the variable cost rates per unit. These budgeted costs can then be applied to various levels of activity. Variable budgets are valuable tools for judging the efficiency of operations by comparing actual costs to the variable budget adjusted for the actual level of activity.

COST, PROFIT, AND INVESTMENT CENTERS

Cost centers

Before studying cost behavior patterns or developing variable budgets, costs should be classified according to *cost centers,* also known as *responsibility centers.* Since each company has a unique separation of authority and responsibility, cost centers can be known by a variety of names. At the lowest levels, a cost center may be a department or a grouping within a department. At a somewhat higher level, the branch or territory manager's cost center is the entire segment for which he or she is responsible. The chief operating executive's cost center is the entire company, because he or she is obligated to perform certain duties for the overall company. Thus, every operating cost is traceable to a responsibility center, whether that center is actually engaged in making the product or not.

One of the cost accountant's objectives is to measure and estimate the costs of each cost center. Chapter 6 introduces the methods of allocating the costs of nonmanufacturing or service centers to production cost centers engaged in direct work on the product.

The classification of costs by cost centers should follow a company's responsibility accounting system. Since costs should be accumulated following lines of responsibility and authority within an organization, accountants must use the organization chart and chart of accounts as the basic framework of the responsibility accounting system. Functional responsibility for each manager is defined in the organization chart. Similarly, the chart of accounts, which is a listing of a company's ledger accounts, facilitates budgetary control if areas of responsibility are shown on the organization chart. The chart of accounts should be designed to reflect cost centers so that proper accountability for costs can be established. After costs have been assigned to cost centers, the amount to budget at each output level should be studied.

Profit and investment centers

Some companies find that merely setting up cost centers does not provide their managers with enough incentive to perform effectively. They have found that changing cost centers to *profit centers* makes managers more concerned with finding ways to increase the center's revenue by increasing production or improving distribution methods. A *cost center* is a segment responsible only for costs, whereas a *profit center* is accountable for both revenues and costs. A profit center, however, must have the authority to earn revenue and incur costs. Some companies go one step further and establish *investment centers* in which the center's manager is responsible for the expenses, the profits, and the assets of the center. In evaluating the performance of an investment center, the accountant relates income to the invested capital in each segment to determine the return on investment.

One important concern of cost center managers, whatever their responsibilities, is factory overhead. Factory overhead costs are defined as all factory costs, except direct material and direct labor, and include many different types of costs from a variety of sources. Different factory overhead costs are also recorded in various ways. For example, certain costs such as electricity, fuel, and water are paid for each month, while other manufacturing costs, such as insurance, vacations, and holidays, are accrued and arise from adjusting journal entries made at the end of the relevant period. The source documents for some factory overhead costs, such as indirect material (material requisitions) and indirect labor (job time tickets), are generated *internally,* while other overhead costs arise from source documents prepared *outside* the company. The main source documents for fire insurance, property taxes, and utility expenses are vendor invoices. The coding of the source documents to the proper factory overhead account and cost center is vital to the success of the budgetary system.

Subsidiary factory overhead accounts

Chapter 2 illustrates the use of the Factory Overhead Control account in the general ledger and the necessity for using subsidiary ledger accounts to detail actual factory overhead costs. For most companies, the number of factory overhead costs is too great to set up individual accounts in the general ledger, so individual overhead accounts are instead established in a subsidiary ledger. The total balance of all accounts in the factory overhead subsidiary ledger should equal the balance in the Factory Overhead Control account in the general ledger. The association between the Factory Overhead Control account and its subsidiary ledger is similar to that for accounts receivable and accounts payable general ledger accounts and their respective subsidiary ledgers. Individual subsidiary ledger accounts for each expense item can be set up by department or by cost center. Codes used in the chart of accounts can facilitate the distribution of actual factory overhead to specific expense accounts and also to departments and other cost centers. For example, Account No. 5141 can indicate that indirect material (code 514) is charged to Cost Center No. 1. Instead of using account code numbers, detail for departments may be calculated in other ways. For example, analysis sheets for each department may be prepared for accumulating the actual factory overhead items incurred. Chapter 6 emphasizes the necessity of detailing actual factory overhead by department so that departmental factory overhead applied rates can be developed.

COST BEHAVIOR

In addition to selecting the subsidiary factory overhead accounts to use, a company must also consider such factors as relationship of expenses to activity level or volume before installing a budgetary system. As discussed in Chapter 6, volume can be measured in many ways, such as direct labor costs or machine-hours. This is especially crucial to a variable budgeting system, because such a system's success depends on a careful study of the relationship of expenses to volume. However, even if a fixed budget approach is used, costs must still be segregated into fixed and variable components. As you recall,

Chapter 2 introduced the three behavior patterns of costs: fixed, variable, and semivariable. Total fixed costs remain the same regardless of output, while total variable costs vary directly with changes in volume. Some fixed costs result from prior commitments to provide a certain capacity of operations; these are referred to as *committed costs*. While some variable overhead costs may vary closely with direct labor costs, others may vary closely with machine-hours. Useful cost analysis may require segregating such different costs into homogenous pools so that a better application of overhead is provided. Many costs contain both fixed and variable components and are referred to as semivariable costs. The fixed portion of semivariable costs is associated with providing the minimum service necessary for operations, while the variable portion reflects volume changes.

Fixed, variable, and semivariable (mixed) costs

Direct material, direct labor, and other costs that are expected to increase or decrease proportionately with corresponding changes in activity fall into the variable expense category. Fixed costs, such as depreciation, rent, and insurance, on the other hand, generally remain the same within a relevant range of volume changes. It is difficult in practice to find a truly fixed or truly variable expense; many expenses fall into a semivariable group that displays both fixed and variable characteristics. Semivariable (mixed) costs vary with volume changes, but the proportional relationship found in variable costs is missing. Before semivariable costs can be studied, they must be segregated into their fixed and variable components; methods for making this distinction are discussed later in this chapter.

Variable costs in the short run.   While direct material and direct labor are generally considered variable costs, their behavior is often semivariable. However, direct material is variable more often than direct labor because direct material can be placed in materials inventory until it is used or can be acquired as needed. The company will not have to use direct material if it decides not to produce one day. However, direct labor is variable with capacity only if the labor-hours can be accurately and rapidly adjusted to the activity level. As a result, most of the various types of labor—even direct labor, which is generally considered a strictly variable cost—behave in some semivariable fashion in practice. Usually, though, the fixed portion of direct labor is so small in relation to total labor costs that the total is simply designated a variable cost. If these complexities are ignored, direct labor costs can be assumed to be stopped relatively quickly and easily in the short run if management decides not to produce. As a result, direct labor costs tend to be strictly variable when measured over a longer period than one day, for example a month or year, and within a relevant range. The fixed cost inherent in supervisory wages, however, may be significant enough that attention should be devoted to separating the fixed and variable elements.

Fixed costs in the short run. Management cannot eliminate fixed costs easily in the short run. If a company decides to go into manufacturing, for example, it will have to buy or rent a building and will have either depreciation or rent expense on the building. The company will also have such fixed costs as insurance on plant facilities and wages for a plant superintendent. Then, even if management decides to stop production, the plant superintendent will have to receive due notice and probably some termination pay, and the company will have to sublease or sell their plant, machinery, and equipment. Therefore, it will take some time before all fixed costs can be eliminated.

Several methods are available to measure the variability of costs when volume changes. Some of these methods rely on historical data in determining the fixed and variable elements; such methods include the high-low method, the scattergraph method, and the method of least squares. Statistical analysis is emphasized in some of these approaches, while others stress engineering studies. Since each method has its advantages and disadvantages, no one method should be used to the exclusion of others.

Analyzing ledger accounts

However, regardless of the approach used, the first step in determining if the costs are fixed, variable, or semivariable is to study the general ledger accounts. Inspecting the ledger accounts is referred to as the "accountant's approach" because the accountant uses his or her professional judgment to distinguish fixed and variable costs. The degree to which the chart of accounts is analyzed varies from a superficial inspection of the cost accounts to a detailed analysis of cost behavior over time. In any case, this analysis should determine whether there are factors other than output that are influencing costs. Such factors might include seasonal changes, the introduction of new products or manufacturing processes, and other abnormal conditions. For example, if the economy faces a recession and the company establishes an austerity program, costs will be so tightly controlled that cost behavior at this point will differ considerably from what it would be under more relaxed conditions.

COST AND ENGINEERING STUDIES

While it is relatively inexpensive to analyze the ledger accounts for fixed and variable costs, additional cost studies may be needed to distinguish the fixed and variable components of semivariable costs. These studies may be more costly since some of them require fairly sophisticated accounting techniques. For example, while the high-low method can be inexpensively applied, the least squares method is more costly to use. In addition, the industrial engineering staff can be called on to assist in cost behavior studies determining how much material, labor, utilities, equipment, and other production items are needed. The experience and knowledge of management supervisors can also be utilized. Historical data can be compared to the results of the engineering study.

High-low method

Generally, an analysis of the chart of accounts is inadequate for separating semivariable costs into their fixed and variable components, so further analysis is needed. One of the simpler methods used for this purpose is the high-low method. In applying the high-low method, the accountant chooses two periods which should represent circumstances at two different levels of activity. However, these levels should be within the relevant range since fixed and variable costs should be defined in relation to a specific period of time and a designated range of volume or activity. The costs used should be representative of the normal costs incurred at these levels; all excessive costs resulting from abnormal conditions should be removed.

Mathematical high-low technique. Either a mathematical or graphical technique for the high-low method can be used. Exhibit 5–1 shows how the mathematical technique separates the fixed and variable elements of electricity costs. The activity base used for applying overhead is direct labor-hours because there is usually a correlation between electricity costs and direct labor-hours. However, in some departments, machine-hours, or some other base, may be more appropriate.

Variable budget formula. The variable budget formula for electricity is $500 per month, plus $0.32 per direct labor-hour. The change in the semivariable cost of $480 is divided by the change of 1,500 hours to give a variable cost rate of $0.32 per direct labor-hour. The increase in costs when the

EXHIBIT 5–1

High-low method of separating fixed and variable costs

	Activity level	Direct labor-hours	Cost of electricity
High capacity	85%	2,700	$1,364
Low capacity	35	1,200	884
Change in hours and semivariable costs	50%	1,500	$ 480

$$\text{Variable rate} = \frac{\text{Change in semivariable costs}}{\text{Change in direct labor-hours}} = \frac{\$480}{1,500} = \$0.32 \text{ per direct labor-hour}$$

	Low	High
Total expense	$884	$1,364
Variable expense		
($0.32 per direct labor-hours)	384	864
Fixed expense	$500	$ 500

volume changed from 1,200 hours to 2,700 hours results from variable costs only. The variable cost per unit remains the same the total variable cost increases. Total fixed costs remain the same at the high and low capacity levels.

Graphical high-low technique. The high-low method may instead be graphic, as shown in Exhibit 5–2. The high and low points of 2,700 and 1,200 direct labor-hours are plotted with their respective total costs. The fixed element is the intersection of the cost line with the vertical axis. This technique assumes that the costs for all volumes between these two points fall along a straight line and thus that a cost line can be drawn between these two activity levels. This assumption is questionable, however, since the high and low points may not be representative of all operations within the relevant range.

The use of statistical techniques to analyze cost behavior provides a more scientific analysis. While some of the statistical methods for separating fixed and variable costs elements are beyond the scope of this book, the scattergraph and the least squares method, sometimes called simple regression analysis, are two relatively simple, effective approaches.

EXHIBIT 5–2

High-low graphic technique

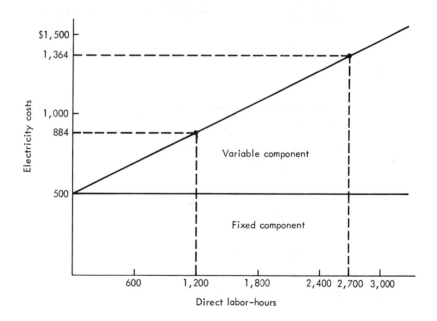

Scattergraph

The scattergraph is a simple analysis method that employs only two variables, such as cost and labor-hours. The data for 12 observations of a semivariable cost such as power are shown in Exhibit 5–3. After such data are

EXHIBIT 5–3

Month	Volume (direct labor-hours)	Power cost
January.	35,000	$ 650
February	28,000	598
March	34,000	641
April	42,000	678
May	37,000	700
June	30,000	613
July.	25,000	578
August	22,000	556
September	20,000	542
October.	37,000	710
November	45,000	720
December.	41,000	650
Total.	396,000	$7,636

gathered, the first step is to plot the costs on the vertical, or Y, axis of a graph and the variable measuring activity level, perhaps direct labor-hours or machine-hours, on the horizontal, or X, axis. Exhibit 5–4 illustrates the statistical scattergraph for these figures. Each point on the graph represents one of the 12 cost observations. For example, the data for June are plotted on the horizontal axis (30,000 direct labor-hours) and on the vertical axis ($613 cost).

Trend line.   The *trend line* (line of best fit) may be fitted mathematically or visually; it was plotted by visual inspection in Exhibit 5–4. It should be fitted so that there is an equal distance between the plotted points above and below the trend line. The fixed component of $400 in Exhibit 5–4 is determined where the trend line intersects the vertical axis. If the plotted points of the two variables on the scattergraph follow a generally straight line, a linear relationship between the two variables is assumed to exist. If the two variables show a linear relationship, they are correlated with each other.

From these figures, a quick estimate of variable costs per hour can be made for the power cost in Exhibit 5–3, assuming fixed costs of $400 per month:

	$7,636	total annual costs
Less	4,800	total annual fixed costs ($400 monthly fixed costs × 12)
	$2,836	total annual variable costs

$$\frac{\$2,836 \text{ total annual variable costs}}{396,000 \text{ direct labor-hours}} = \$0.0072 \text{ variable cost per direct labor-hour}$$

EXHIBIT 5–4

Statistical scattergraph

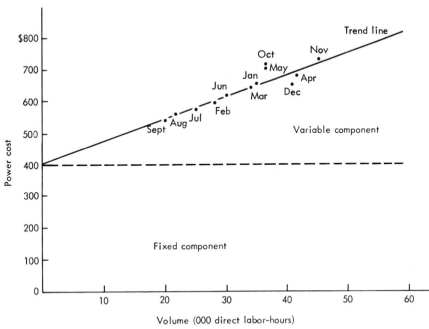

Volume (000 direct labor-hours)

Merely plotting points on a graph and visually fitting a trend line may not be adequate to give a clear indication of cost behavior. While the scattergraph is simple to apply and understand, it is not objective. Two accountants might easily fit two very different lines to the same set of data, each believing his or hers "fits" the data better. In addition, there may, in fact, be no correlation between the variables. This should be readily apparent when the points are plotted on the scattergraph; but sometimes when the trend line is fitted by visual inspection, personal bias may distort the true picture. Since misleading generalizations regarding cost behavior can result, a more accurate study of cost behavior than the scattergraph should be undertaken.

REGRESSION ANALYSIS

Regression analysis can be used to measure the average amount of change in a dependent variable, such as utilities, that is associated with unit increases in the amounts of one or more independent variables, such as machine-hours. The method of least squares is the most widely used regression analysis; this analysis can be easily performed using standardized computer programs which are available.

Least squares method

The least squares method is a mathematical approach based on the straight-line equation $(y = a + bx)$ with y representing the costs; a, the fixed component; b, the variable element; and x, the volume. This method is most appropriate when data have a uniform variance of deviations along the trend line.

Using the cost data from Exhibit 5–3, computations for the least squares method are shown in Exhibit 5–5. Column (1) represents direct labor-hours for each observation. The total of 396,000 for Column (1) is divided by the 12 observations to give an average of 33,000 hours. Column (3) represents total costs; the annual cost of $7,636 is divided by 12 observations to give an average of $636.33. The differences from the average are entered in Columns (2) and (4). The differences in Column (2) are squared, and the square is entered in Column (5) and totaled. Column (6) represents the extension of the data in Columns (2) and (4) with the results added.

Evaluation of least squares method.   The results computed using the least squares method differ slightly from those determined by the scattergraph. The least squares method is more objective because personal bias does not enter into fitting the trend line. However, the data should be plotted first on a scattergraph to be certain that there is a reasonable degree of correlation.

In the above illustration, cost behavior is shown as dependent on a single measure of direct labor-hours; however, more than one factor may cause a cost to vary. Simple regression analysis considers only one independent variable, while multiple regression analysis is a further expansion of the least squares method allowing the consideration of more than one independent variable. The straight-line equation $(y = a + bx)$ with y representing costs, a representing the fixed component, b representing the variable element, and x representing the volume used in simple regression can be expanded to include more than one independent variable. By including two independent variables, the equation becomes $y = a + bx + cz$ with c the rate of cost variability for z, an additional independent variable. The least squares method is time-consuming to apply manually, especially when more than one independent variable is considered, but a computer can make the computations quickly.

Establishing correlation.   Verified visually with a reasonable degree of correlation was the scattergraph in Exhibit 5–4. If perfect correlation existed, all plotted points would fall on the regression line. Several statistics can be used to measure the relationship between x (direct labor-hours) and y (power cost). The correlation coefficient (r) is the most commonly used statistic, as the square of this coefficient expresses the extent to which the variation in y is explained by changes in x. The closer the r value is to either $+1$ or -1, the stronger the statistical relationship between the two variables. As r approaches -1, a negative, or inverse, relationship is implied, meaning the dependent variable (y) decreases as the independent variable (x) increases. On the other hand, as r

EXHIBIT 5–5

Least squares method

Month	(1) Direct labor-hours (x)	(2) Difference from average of 33,000 hours (X)	(3) Total power costs (y)	(4) Difference from average of $636.33 (Y)	(5) Column (2) squared (X²)	(6) Column (2) × Column (4) (XY)
January	35,000	2,000	$ 650	13.67	4,000,000	$ 27,340
February	28,000	− 5,000	598	−38.33	25,000,000	191,650
March	34,000	1,000	641	4.67	1,000,000	4,670
April	42,000	9,000	678	41.67	81,000,000	375,030
May	37,000	4,000	700	63.66	16,000,000	254,640
June	30,000	− 3,000	613	−23.33	9,000,000	69,990
July	25,000	− 8,000	578	−58.33	64,000,000	466,640
August	22,000	−11,000	556	−80.33	121,000,000	883,630
September	20,000	−13,000	542	−94.33	169,000,000	1,226,290
October	37,000	4,000	710	73.66	16,000,000	294,640
November	45,000	12,000	720	83.66	144,000,000	1,003,920
December	41,000	8,000	650	13.66	64,000,000	109,280
Total	396,000	—0—	$ 7,636	—0—	714,000,000	$4,907,720
Average	33,000		$636.33			

a = Fixed component
b = Variable component
x = Volume
X = Deviations from average of x
y = Costs
Y = Deviations from average of y

Using the straight-line equation, the computation is

$$y = a + bx$$

where $b = \dfrac{\Sigma XY}{\Sigma X^2}$ $\dfrac{\$4,907,720}{714,000,000} = 0.00687$

$$y = a + bx$$
$$\$636.33 = a + (0.00687 \times 33,000)$$
$$\$636.33 = a + \$226.71$$
$$\$636.33 - \$226.71 = a$$
$$a = \$409.62 \text{ (the fixed cost)}$$

approaches $+1$, a positive relationship is implied, meaning the dependent variable (y) increases as the independent variable increases.

The coefficient of determination (r^2) is found by squaring the correlation coefficient. In Exhibit 5–6 the data in Exhibit 5–3 are used to provide the figures needed in the correlation analysis formula.

EXHIBIT 5–6

Month	(1) Direct labor-hours (x)	(2) Power cost (y)	(3) xy	(4) x²	(5) y²
January.....	35,000	$ 650	22,750,000	1,225,000,000	422,500
February....	28,000	598	16,744,000	784,000,000	357,604
March......	34,000	641	21,794,000	1,156,000,000	410,881
April	42,000	678	28,476,000	1,764,000,000	459,684
May........	37,000	700	25,900,000	1,369,000,000	490,000
June	30,000	613	18,390,000	900,000,000	375,769
July........	25,000	578	14,450,000	625,000,000	334,084
August......	22,000	556	12,232,000	484,000,000	309,136
September...	20,000	542	10,840,000	400,000,000	293,764
October.....	37,000	710	26,270,000	1,369,000,000	504,100
November ...	45,000	720	32,400,000	2,025,000,000	518,400
December ...	41,000	650	26,650,000	1,681,000,000	422,500
Total. . .	396,000	$7,636	256,896,000	13,782,000,000	4,898,422

In Column (3), each independent variable (x) is multiplied by its corresponding dependent variable (y). Each x value and each y value are squared and entered in Columns (4) and (5), respectively. After all columns are totaled, the figures are entered in the following formula. The number of observations (the 12 months in Exhibit 5–6) are designated as n and also used.

$$r = \frac{n\Sigma xy - (\Sigma x)(\Sigma y)}{\sqrt{[n\Sigma x^2 - (\Sigma x)^2][n\Sigma y^2 - (\Sigma y)^2]}}$$

$$= \frac{(12)(256,896,000) - (396,000)(7,636)}{\sqrt{[(12)(13,782,000,000) - (396,000)(396,000)][(12)(4,898,422) - (7,636)(7,636)]}}$$

$$= \frac{3,082,752,000 - 3,023,856,000}{\sqrt{(165,384,000,000 - 156,816,000,000)(58,781,064 - 58,308,496)}}$$

$$= \frac{58,896,000}{\sqrt{(8,568,000,000)(472,568)}} = \frac{58,896,000}{\sqrt{4,048,962,624,000}}$$

$$= \frac{58,896,000}{63,631,459} = +0.9256$$

$$r^2 = 0.8567$$

Application of the correlation analysis technique to the above data reveals a coefficient of determination of 0.8567. This means that more than 85 percent of the change in power cost is related to the change in direct labor-hours. The conclusion is that since a high correlation exists between power cost and direct labor-hours, this relationship can be used to calculate the power overhead rate and the construction of the variable budget.

The results of cost behavior studies like those discussed above may differ significantly from prestudy predictions. The cost accountant therefore should not presume to estimate the relationship of cost changes to volume variations without conducting such studies of cost behavior patterns.

FIXED (STATIC) AND VARIABLE (FLEXIBLE) BUDGETING

After cost behavior studies have separated costs into their fixed and variable components and the cost or profit centers are determined, the next step is for management to decide whether to use a fixed or variable budgeting approach. Under the fixed or static approach, a budget is prepared for a single estimated activity volume and is not adjusted when actual volume differs. Actual results are later compared with budgeted results. Fixed budgeting is appropriate only if a company's operating volume can be estimated within close limits and if the costs and expenses are behaving predictably. However, few companies are fortunate enough to fall into this category. Most companies experience drastically changeable market conditions and few completely predictable situations. As a result of these factors, a fixed budget is generally not adequate.

Flexible is not a good term.   The alternative to the fixed budget is the variable budget. While fixed, or static, budgets are established for a single activity level, flexible, or variable, budgets can be adjusted to the volume actually experienced. While "flexible" budgeting is the same as variable budgeting, the former term does not properly describe this approach. The term "flexible" merely indicates that the budget is subject to revision if the basic assumptions change (i.e., a major customer or market segment is lost or dropped). The term variable, on the other hand, emphasizes that the budget incorporates changes in volume to provide a valid basis of comparison with actual costs.

Comparison of fixed and variable budgets

Exhibits 5–7 through 5–9 illustrate the problems that can arise from using a fixed or static budget. Exhibit 5–7 shows the fixed budget for one cost center for January. It is expected that 1,000 units will be produced, each requiring two hours of direct labor, so costs are estimated at that level. At the end of the month, the company finds that because of a materials shortage, only 900 units were produced. In Exhibit 5–7 the costs incurred to produce 900 units are

EXHIBIT 5–7

Cost Center A
Performance Report
Fixed Budget
Factory Overhead
January 19–

	Budget	Actual	Variance
Direct-labor hours	2,000	1,800	200
Variable costs:			
Indirect materials	$ 4,000	$ 3,900	$100 favorable
Indirect labor	3,500	3,300	200 favorable
Supplies	6,000	5,600	400 favorable
Total variable overhead	13,500	12,800	700 favorable
Fixed costs:			
Depreciation—Buildings and			
equipment	1,000	1,050	50 unfavorable
Insurance	500	480	20 favorable
Total fixed overhead	1,500	1,530	30 unfavorable
Total factory overhead	$15,000	$14,330	$670 favorable

compared to the fixed budget for 1,000 units. In this case, management may incorrectly believe that costs are under control, since all variable costs have favorable variances. However, the variable costs to produce 900 units should be less than that to produce 1,000 units. Another problem is that while fixed costs may be easier to estimate in the short run, actual fixed costs may vary from budgeted fixed costs. As can be seen in Exhibit 5–7, the two fixed costs vary from the budgeted amounts.

Cost of idle capacity

The fixed budget results are therefore misleading. In fact, management should know that the cost center did not produce the planned volume and that actual production was 100 units less than that estimated for January. This is important from a product costing viewpoint since fixed cost must now be borne by only 1800 direct labor-hours rather than the estimated 2,000 hours. In addition, Cost Center A incurred idle capacity costs because it was not able to fully utilize the budgeted capacity level. Exhibits 5–8 and 5–9 depict a *variable* budget, which more accurately describes the cost situation.

Exhibit 5–8 gives the budget formula for fixed and variable cost behavior that can be used to compute budgeted costs at any capacity level. The basic budget formula for overhead is $6.75 per direct labor-hour and $1,500 per month. A series of three possible volumes—1,500, 2,000 and 2,500 hours, all within the relevant range of this cost center— are shown for illustration purposes. There is

EXHIBIT 5–8

Cost Center A
Variable Budget
Factory Overhead
January 19–

	Various levels of activity			*Budget formula*
Direct labor-hours	1,500	2,000	2,500	
		(budgeted)		
Variable costs:				
Indirect materials	$ 3,000	$ 4,000	$ 5,000	$2.00 per hour
Indirect labor	2,625	3,500	4,375	1.75 per hour
Supplies	4,500	6,000	7,500	3.00 per hour
Total variable costs	10,125	13,500	16,875	6.75 per hour
Fixed costs:				
Depreciation—buildings				
and equipment	1,000	1,000	1,000	1,000 per month
Insurance	500	500	500	500 per month
Total fixed overhead. . . .	1,500	1,500	1,500	1,500 per month
Total overhead	$11,625	$15,000	$18,375	$6.75 per hour and $1,500 per month

EXHIBIT 5–9

COST CENTER A
Performance Report
Variable Budget
Factory Overhead
For the Month Ended January 19–

	Budget adjusted to actual volume	*Actual*	*Variance*
Direct labor-hours	1,800	1,800	0
Variable costs:			
Indirect materials	$ 3,600	$ 3,900	$300 unfavorable
Indirect labor	3,150	3,300	150 unfavorable
Supplies	5,400	5,600	200 unfavorable
Total variable overhead	12,150	12,800	650 unfavorable
Fixed Costs:			
Depreciation—buildings and			
equipment	1,000	1,050	50 unfavorable
Insurance	500	480	20 favorable
Total fixed overhead	1,500	1,530	30 unfavorable
Total factory overhead	$13,650	$14,330	$680 unfavorable

some danger in illustrating more than one budget, since some students mistakenly believe that many budgets must be prepared when a variable budgeting approach is used. This is not correct. As shown in Exhibits 5–7 and 5–8, the actual volume obtained of 1,800 direct labor-hours is not reflected in advance in a preestablished budget. Indeed, the chances of preparing a budget in advance with a volume that coincides exactly with actual volume are very small. Using a variable budgeting approach, all the company must know is what total costs are expected to be at the volume level they forecast. Then, if actual volume differs from expected volume, the budget may be adjusted to actual volume at the end of the period. By having a variable budget formula available, a budget adjusted to actual volume is easy to compute at the end of the accounting period.

Exhibit 5–9 shows the variances obtained with a variable budget prepared using the data in Exhibit 5–7. Instead of the favorable variances shown in the fixed budget in Exhibit 5–7, all variances are now unfavorable. Comparing the costs of operations at 1,800 direct labor-hours against a budget prepared for this volume judges the efficiency of the cost center more accurately.

Variable budgeting may be expanded to include all costs including direct material and direct labor, as well as factory overhead. And in addition to incorporating all manufacturing costs, a variable budget may also include marketing and administrative expenses. In any case, adjusting all costs to the actual volume is appropriate regardless of whether the costs arise from factory-related transactions or from other phases of the company's operations.

SUMMARY

Before any sophisticated cost analysis can be performed, the behavior of individual costs must be studied. There are few costs found in practice that are truly variable or truly fixed because innumerable factors affect cost behavior. Costs which appear on the surface to be variable may in fact be semivariable. For example, direct labor is generally considered to be a variable cost; however, upon inspection of the policies followed in practice, it is normally a semivariable cost since a temporary decrease in product demand normally does not result in extensive production worker layoffs. Instead, the workers may be provided with employment even though there is not enough work available to keep the full work force busy.

In addition, direct labor is truly a variable cost only if the workers are paid on a piecework basis and if there is tight control over labor costs. Indirect labor costs often fall into the semivariable category because some indirect labor employees are needed for standby services. Direct material is often variable because it can be stored until used and is only acquired as needed.

While a number of techniques such as the high-low, scattergraph, and least squares methods can be used to segregate costs into fixed and variable components, the task in practice is more involved. Costs may vary due to several factors besides volume changes. The challenge facing the cost account-ant is to study these variables in hopes of getting a better "feel" for the causal factors. The methods available to the cost accountant may sometimes be inadequate to obtain more than a hint of the true cost behavior pattern; however, this is much better than carelessly lumping costs into variable and fixed categories without any analysis.

The company's cost, profit, and investment centers should also be estab-lished before the accountant initiates a variable budgeting system. Also, a careful study of the behavior of costs must be made before variable budgets can be considered good tools for analyzing efficiency. Variable budgets are useful for determining the efficiency of operations because the actual costs at any output level can be compared against a budget adjusted to the actual activity level. Distortions due to volume variations are eliminated with a variable budgeting approach.

IMPORTANT TERMS AND CONCEPTS

Cost or responsibility centers

Profit centers

Investment centers

Fixed costs

Variable costs

Semivariable costs

Mathematical high-low technique

Variable budget formula

Graphical high-low technique

Scattergraph regression analysis

Trend line

Least squares method

Correlation coefficient

Coefficient of determination

Fixed or static budget

Variable or flexible budget

REVIEW QUESTIONS

1. If the budget for mixed factory overhead is $19,500 for 45,000 direct labor-hours and is $24,500 for 65,000 direct labor-hours, what is the variable cost rate per month and the monthly fixed cost?

2. What is the difference between a cost center, a profit center, and an investment center?

3. What factors cause costs to vary?

4. Are direct material and direct labor *variable* costs? Explain.

5. If total costs for Ban Company are $280,000 for 600,000 machine-hours and $310,000 for 700,000 machine-hours, what are the budgeted fixed costs for the year?

6. Discuss three methods of segregating a semivariable cost into fixed and variable components.

7. Determine the budgeted fixed overhead and the variable overhead rate for indirect labor if the two budgets are:
    1,000 units—$4,000; 3,000 units—$8,000.

8. Can you compute the fixed overhead rate for the company described in Question 7?

9. Discuss the criteria that should be used in selecting the two activity periods for the high-low method.

10. How is the trend line fitted on a statistical scattergraph?

11. Discuss the limitations of a statistical scattergraph.

12. When is the least squares method most appropriate?

13. Contrast the results obtained using the least squares method with those obtained using a statistical scattergraph.

14. When is a fixed budgeting approach appropriate?

15. To gain better insight into budgeting methods used in practice, you interview a number of business executives. You ask if they have a flexible budgeting approach and are surprised to find that they all reply, "Yes." What is amazing is that you know an accountant from one of the firms, and the accountant has told you that the company uses fixed budgeting. Why do you think they all gave you a positive answer?

16. As a newly hired cost accountant for a manufacturing firm, you find that a fixed budgeting system is being used. You immediately suggest a variable budgeting approach. Your supervisor's reply is, "You haven't been here long enough to know how many hours it takes to set up only one budget! How on earth could we ever have the time to prepare four or five detailed budgets on a series of volumes?" What is your reply to your supervisor?

17. Why is it important to have available the budget formula for a company's fixed and variable cost behavior?

EXERCISES

E5–1. High-low method

Edward Bartell, Inc. wishes to determine the fixed portion of its semivariable expense, electricity, as measured against direct labor-hours for the first three months of the year. Information for this period is as follows:

	Direct labor-hours	Electricity expense
January	3,000	$600
February	3,400	635
March	3,000	600

Required:

What is the company's fixed portion of electricity expense rounded to the nearest dollar?

E5–2.   **Regression diagram**

The controller for Stern, Inc. prepared the regression diagram shown, drawing the line of best fit (trend line) for factory overhead and wages. The line of best fit in this diagram is described by the formula $y = a + bx$.

Required:

a.   Determine the slope of the line of best fit in numerical terms.
b.   If wages amount to $750,000, how much is the estimated overhead?

E5–3.   **High-low method**

Rosalie Holford, Inc. has provided the following actual costs data for your use in determining variable factory overhead costs and fixed factory overhead costs for budgeting purpose.

	Six months ago	Three months ago	Last month
Machine-hours	450,000	425,000	500,000
Direct material	$ 382,000	$ 345,600	$ 417,240
Direct labor	196,200	184,280	235,000
Factory insurance.	86,800	80,000	98,650
Indirect labor	104,300	100,000	108,800
Factory inspection costs.	69,300	66,000	71,000
Indirect material.	65,200	60,000	69,700
Factory utilities.	94,600	92,000	98,600
Salespersons' salaries	115,000	114,000	119,800
Advertising	96,000	92,000	108,100
Executive salaries.	80,000	80,000	80,000
Total	$1,289,400	$1,213,880	$1,406,890

Required:

Determine an overall variable factory overhead rate per machine-hour and total fixed factory using the high-low method, assuming management believes there are no other major factors that affect cost behavior.

E5–4.   **Variable budget formula**

Burton Company presents you with the following monthly factory overhead budgets that were prepared at the beginning of the year. Budgeted capacity was set at 60,000 hours.

Machine hours.	50,000	60,000
Supplies	$120,000	$144,000
Indirect labor.	67,500	81,000
Utilities	162,500	195,000
Supervision salaries.	10,000	10,000
Depreciation	9,000	9,000
Insurance	8,000	8,000
Property taxes.	15,000	15,000
Total.	$392,000	$462,000

At the end of the month, analysis of the cost records reveal that the following factory overhead was incurred in operating at 58,000 machine-hours.

Supplies	$136,000
Indirect labor	80,000
Utilities	190,000
Supervision salaries	10,200
Depreciation	8,880
Insurance	7,600
Property taxes	14,700
Total	$447,380

Required:

a.   Compute the variable budget formula.
b.   Determine the factory overhead application rate.
c.   Determine variances for each of the factory overhead items, indicating whether they are favorable or unfavorable.

E5–5.   **Cost behavior and variable budget formula**

David Littlehale Company provides you with a summary of the total budgeted factory overhead at four different volumes of operations.

Volume in direct labor-hours	4,000	5,000	6,000	7,000
		(normal capacity)		
Indirect labor.	$2,000	$2,300	$2,600	$2,900
Insurance	400	400	400	400
Depreciation	800	1,000	1,200	1,400
Power	1,800	2,200	2,600	3,000
Total.	$5,000	$5,900	$6,800	$7,700

At the end of the year, it is determined that the following factory overhead was incurred for production at 5,200 direct labor-hours.

	Actual costs
Indirect labor	$2,625
Insurance.	380
Depreciation	1,085
Power	2,318
Total.	$6,408

Required:

a. Indicate the cost behavior for each of the four overhead costs budgeted (i.e., whether fixed, variable, or semivariable).
b. Determine the variable budget formula for each of the four factory overhead costs using the high-low method.
c. Determine the variance for each of the four costs using a variable budget. Indicate whether they are favorable or unfavorable.

E5–6. High-low mathematical and graphical approaches

The total monthly overhead budget for RST Corporation is given for two volume levels:

2,000 machine-hours	$6,000
5,000 machine-hours	8,400

Required:

a. Management asks you to give them an approximate fundamental measure of fixed and variable cost behavior using both the mathematical and graphical techniques for the high-low method.
b. After the month ends, you find that 4,600 hours were actually worked and total overhead costs incurred amounted to $8,500. Prepare a simple variable budget and indicate whether the total overhead variance is favorable or unfavorable.

E5–7. High-low method, least squares, and coefficient of correlation

In manufacturing high-precision medical instruments, Dunn Company employs extensive technology as well as elaborate inspection tests. Each instrument requires five hours of machine time. Production volume is not steady because orders are received in irregular patterns. As a result, several inspectors must be available at all times, while others are transferred over as needed. The cost-accounting department has prepared the following data for the first six months of the year for use in analyzing inspection cost:

	Machine-hours (000)	Inspection cost (000)
January	200	$500
February	250	618
March	300	670
April	360	840
May	315	790
June	225	560

Required:

a. Use the high-low approach to determine the fixed and variable cost elements included in the inspection cost.
b. Use the least squares method to determine the fixed and variable cost elements.
c. Determine the coefficient of correlation (r) and the coefficient of determination (r^2).

E5–8. Variable budget formula and preparation of variable budget

Next year's monthly forecast for the Long Company indicates that the company will sell 10,000 units at a $25 per unit sales price. No change in inventory level is planned. Each unit will require three hours of direct labor. Based on this volume, monthly manufacturing overhead budget is:

Variable overhead:
    Supplies . . . . $ 94,500
    Inspection   82,500
    Repairs   33,000
Fixed overhead:
    Supervision   12,000
    Depreciation   32,000
    Insurance   8,000
                                                 $262,000

At the end of the month it was determined that 28,500 labor-hours were used to produce 9,500 units. Actual manufacturing overhead costs were:

Variable overhead:
    Supplies . . . . $ 90,000
    Inspection   78,100
    Repairs   32,000
Fixed overhead:
    Supervision   12,100
    Depreciation   31,800
    Insurance   8,300
                                               $252,300

Required:

a. What is the variable budget formula? Express the formula in direct labor-hours.
b. Prepare a variable budget for actual volume and determine the variances by detailed expense. Indicate whether the variances are favorable or unfavorable.

PROBLEMS

P5–1.   Cost-volume relationships illustrated in graphs: Unit cost

In the graphs shown, assume that *unit* costs for Butcher Company are measured on the vertical axis while the horizontal axis measures production volume.

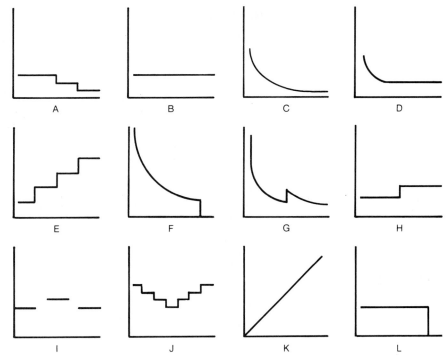

Required:

Indicate the graph that best describes the cost-volume relationship in the following situations (a graph may be used more than once):

a. Depreciation is calculated on a units-of-production basis.
b. For a fixed fee, a service maintenance company will provide a specific number of hours of repair work. When more hours of repair work are needed, Butcher has agreed to pay a stated fee per hour.
c. One component of each finished unit requires two hours of direct labor costing $10 per hour.
d. Depreciation is calculated on a straight-line basis.
e. Salaries of inspection personnel: earnings of $1,000 per period when the span of control is 100 units per inspector.
f. Discounts are not available on material purchased unless the company purchases 1,000 gallons or more per period; increasing discounts are available for each additional 500 gallons purchased.
g. Butcher has a limited number of department B workers so that when production exceeds a specified number of units per period, these laborers must work in excess of 40 hours per week and be paid time and one half.
h. In its effort to stimulate employment in the region, the Chamber of Commerce has leased the building under the following conditions: a $12,000 minimum rent covering production up to 2,000 labor-hours; if production exceeds that level per period, there is no rent charge.
i. The present supplier of disposable molds has limited capacity such that when production capacity exceeds a specified number of units, a more expensive mold supplier must be used.

j. Butcher has agreed to pay a certain fee for each plastic container used for each finished product. After a specified number of products are manufactured each period, there will be no charge for the container since the supplier believes that advertising for the containers will be sufficient to warrant this arrangement.

k. Containers in which the product is packaged can be purchased according to the following price schedule:

Packages	Per unit cost
1–100	$3.00
101–200	2.75
201–300	2.50
301–400	2.25
401–500	2.50
501–600	2.75
601–700	3.00

P5–2. Cost-volume relationships illustrated in graphs: Total cost

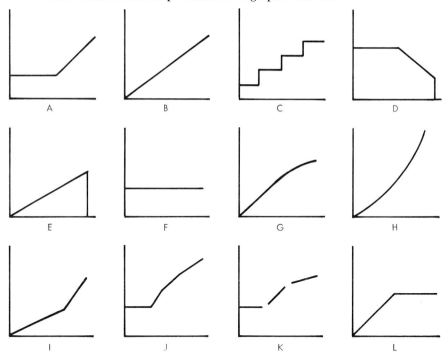

In the graphs shown, assume that *total* costs for the Greer Company are measured on the vertical axis while the horizontal axis measures the volume or activity level.

Required:

Indicate the graph that best describes the cost-volume relationship in the following situations (a graph may be used more than once):

a. The purchasing department is unable to obtain a discount on the direct material used until production increases to the point where they can buy in large quantities.

b. Depreciation on the building is calculated using a straight-line method.

c. The company has an agreement with an outside repair organization. They have agreed to provide a certain number of hours of repair work for a fixed fee. Greer has agreed to pay a fee per hour of repair work when more hours are required.

d. Depreciation on the factory equipment is calculated on a machine-hours basis.

e. The salaries of manufacturing supervisors when the span of control of each supervisor is overseeing the production of 1,000 units.

f. The company has agreed to pay a certain fee for each mold used in making Product A. After they manufacture and sell a specified quantity of Product A, the company will not be required to pay the fee. The supplier paid for the use of the mold believes that if enough Product A is introduced into the market, it will stimulate other customers.

g. A supplier of a direct material item has agreed to furnish the material at $1.10 per pound. However, since this supplier has limited capacity, another supplier, whose price is $1.50 per pound, must be used when demand exceeds the first supplier's ability to furnish materials.

h. The electricity bill is determined as follows:

0–500 Kilowatt-hours	$1.00 per Kilowatt-hour used
501–600 Kilowatt-hours	1.15 per Kilowatt-hour used
601–700 Kilowatt-hours	1.30 per Kilowatt-hour used
701–800 Kilowatt-hours	1.45 per Kilowatt-hour used
And so forth	

i. The Chamber of Commerce in its effort to attract industry furnished the organization with a building on which there is a rent of $500,000 less $1 for each direct labor-hour worked in excess of 100,000 hours. The agreement also specifies that after the organization works 300,000 hours, there will be no rent.

j. The lease agreement on the equipment is as follows:

Minimum $600 per month (this covers up to 500 machine-hours)	
Next 200 machine-hours	$3 per hour
Next 200 machine-hours	2 per hour
Above 900 machine-hours	1 per hour

k. An agreement with an advertising agency specifies that $0.15 per unit sold will be charged with a maximum payment of $10,000 for their work in developing an advertising campaign.

l. The cost of direct material and direct labor used in production.

P5–3. Determining variable budget

A variable budgeting approach is used by the Martha Sue Ryan Company for its producing departments. Capacity is based on direct labor-hours, with 25,000 direct labor-hours as normal capacity.

In the month of May, the finishing department operated 22,250 hours. The following budgets had been established previously for the finishing department:

Direct labor-hours.	19,500	23,000
Factory supplies.	$30,350	$34,900
Indirect labor	31,350	35,550
Maintenance supplies.	18,720	22,080
Depreciation	2,200	2,200
Property taxes	1,950	1,950
Insurance.	2,340	2,760
Total	$86,910	$99,440

Required:

a.   Prepare a variable budget for the actual volume level; indicate the cost behavior of each cost element.

b.   Express the variable budget formula.

c.   Indicate whether the variances would be favorable or unfavorable if the actual costs were: factory supplies—$34,600; indirect labor—$34,900; maintenance supplies—$22,100; depreciation—$2,400; property taxes—$1,890; and insurance—$2,800.

d.   Explain why actual depreciation and property taxes could differ from budgeted expenses.

P5–4.   Variable budget preparation with price increases

Each unit produced by Paige, Inc. requires 0.4 hours of direct labor. Last year, when the company operated at 80 percent of capacity, 120,000 units were produced. The following percentages indicate the makeup of fixed and variable costs:

Fixed Costs	*Percent*	*Variable costs*	*Percent*
Depreciation	35	Factory supplies	20
Rent	20	Utilities	40
Factory supervisor's salary	15	Indirect materials	30
Insurance	30	Indirect labor	8
	100	Miscellaneous	2
			100

Management expects to increase next year's volume to 95 percent of capacity. Total factory overhead is expected to be $360,000 at this level, using a ratio of variable cost to fixed cost of 2:1, with variable costs based on direct labor-hours. Not included in the $360,000 is a recent notice of a 20 percent price increase from the utility company. This utilities price rise is expected regardless of any capacity changes.

Required:

a.   Prepare a variable budget for next year using 80 percent, 95 percent, 100 percent, and 120 percent capacity levels; for each capacity level, determine the factory overhead rate per hour of production. Round to whole dollars for total costs, but carry variable cost per unit to five decimal places.

b.   Explain why the total factory overhead rate per hour has an inverse relationship to capacity.

P5–5.   Budget formula and variable budget preparation

Stephen Patterson, Inc. plans to produce 1,000 desks next accounting period. Time and motion studies reveal that it takes five direct labor-hours to manufacture each desk. The established monthly manufacturing overhead budget is as follows:

Fuel	$15,000
Repairs	7,500
Supplies	8,500
Depreciation	5,000
Rent	3,000
	$39,000

Assume depreciation is calculated on a straight-line basis and rent is paid monthly. At the end of the month, it is determined that 4,500 actual hours were incurred to make 900 desks and actual manufacturing costs were as follows:

Fuel	$12,000
Repairs.	6,000
Supplies	7,800
Depreciation	5,050
Rent	3,100
	$33,950

Required:

a. Prepare a fixed budget and an analysis of variances from budget.
b. What is the variable budget formula for the fixed and variable cost behavior per direct labor-hour? Express formula in direct labor-hours.
c. Prepare a variable budget for a production level of 4,500 direct labor-hours and analyze the variances from budget for each detailed expense.
d. What factors could cause the actual fixed costs to differ from budgeted fixed costs?

P5–6. Variable budget preparation at various volumes

Newsome Company asks that you assist them in analyzing the output of their variable budgeting system. They give you the following data for May 19X1 in which 50,000 units were produced and sold. The company plans to maintain the present level of inventories.

Direct material	$ 59,800
Direct labor	117,000
Factory overhead	120,000
Marketing expenses	17,500
Administrative expenses	30,000

After studying the above data, you find that the industry experienced a shortage of material in May; as a result, prices were 15 percent higher than normal. The monthly labor costs were 10 percent lower than normal. Total factory overhead was 20 percent lower than what is considered normal; 35 percent of the factory overhead for a normal month is fixed. Salespersons are paid a commission equal to $0.25 per unit; the remainder of the marketing expense is fixed. Of the administrative expense, 75 percent represents fixed costs. Of the fixed costs, salaries account for $8,200. Administrative personnel receiving a fixed salary got an 8 percent raise effective June 1.

Required:

Prepare variable budgets at volumes of 40,000, 45,000, and 55,000 units for June operations. Determine the cost per unit for each volume level for both fixed and variable costs.

P5–7. Variances using fixed and variable budgeting approaches

Green, Inc. is a manufacturer of Christmas decorations. The company uses greater capacity in the summer months, up to 90 percent of total. In the winter months, capacity often declines to 75 percent. Management believes that 80 percent capacity, or 8,000 hours, represent normal capacity and this is the basis used for budgeting.

The January 19– budget for one of the manufacturing departments is as follows:

GREEN INC.
Fixed Budget
For the Month Beginning January 19–

	Budget: 8,000 hours 80 percent capacity
Variable costs:	
Repairs.............	$16,000
Indirect material	12,000
Utilities.............	6,400
Total variable costs........	34,400
Fixed costs:	
Supervisors' salaries	6,000
Depreciation...........	7,000
Insurance.............	5,500
Rent................	8,400
Total fixed costs..........	26,900
Total costs........	$61,300

Due to an overstock in inventory, the company operated at only 70 percent of capacity in January. At the end of January, the controller determines that the following actual costs were incurred.

Variable costs:	
Repairs.............	$14,800
Indirect material	11,200
Utilities.............	6,000
Total variable costs........	32,000
Fixed costs:	
Supervisor's salaries	6,180
Depreciation...........	7,230
Insurance.............	5,450
Rent................	8,300
Total fixed costs..........	27,160
Total costs........	$59,160

Required:

a. Compute the variances by line items for the manufacturing department for the month of January using a fixed budget.

b. Assuming you convince the company that they should adopt a variable budgeting approach, construct a budget for 70 percent and 85 percent and give the budget formula by line item.

c. Using the information you computed in *b*, perform variance analysis for each expense item using the appropriate variable budget. Indicate whether they are favorable or unfavorable.

P5–8. Statistical scattergraph and least squares method

The data for six bimonthly cost observations of the Steve Douglass Company are given below:

	Direct labor-hours	Costs
January–February	100,000	$14,000
March–April	75,000	8,000
May–June	130,000	17,000
July–August	45,000	7,000
September–October	60,000	11,000
November–December	70,000	15,000

Required:

a. Plot a statistical scattergraph from the data to obtain the fixed and variable cost elements.

b. Use the least squares method to determine the fixed and variable cost elements.

P5–9. Appropriateness and preparation of variable budgets

McIntosh operates a production which has cyclical operations. Management has been using fixed budgeting and is displeased with the results. You have just been hired as their cost accountant and propose to change their procedure to a variable budget approach. You obtain the following data for use in budgeting:

	6,500 units or 9,750 hours
Budgeted monthly normal capacity	
Material (3 gallons @ $2)	$ 6 per unit
Direct labor (1.5 hours @ $8 per hour)	12 per unit
Variable overhead at normal monthly capacity:	
Inspection	$ 9,100
Indirect material	1,300
Repairs	1,950
Fixed monthly budgeted overhead:	
Depreciation	4,100
Insurance	2,500

While 6,000 units were planned for production in January, a breakdown in machinery caused only 5,400 units to be produced; actual direct labor-hours totaled 8,900. Actual cost incurred during the month was:

Material	$ 33,000
Direct labor	65,600
Inspection	7,200
Indirect material	1,224
Repairs	1,600
Depreciation	4,200
Insurance	2,200
Total	$115,024

Required:

a. Explain why you do or do not believe variable budgeting would be appropriate for this company.

b. Prepare a budget for January based on projected volume.

c. Using a variable budget, compare actual and budgeted costs for January.

P5–10.   Application of high-low and least squares methods and coefficient of determination

The manager of the Shelby Motel asks your assistance in analyzing his housekeeping costs so that variable budgeting can be adopted. You obtain the following costs data for the first four months for a section of his motel that he considers representative:

Month	Rooms occupied	Cost of housekeeping
January	460	$2,864
February	540	3,144
March	720	4,034
April	640	3,734

Required:

a.   Management asks you to give them an approximate fundamental measure of their fixed and variable cost behavior using the high-low mathematical approach.
b.   Use the least squares method to determine the fixed and variable cost elements.
c.   Determine the coefficient of correlation (r) and the coefficient of determination (r^2).
d.   What does the coefficient of determination you computed reveal?

P5–11.   High-low and least squares methods

Ewing Company provides you with the following overhead costs for the past year:

Month	Volume of production (direct labor-hours)	Overhead costs
January	13,875	$24,052
February	12,075	23,925
March	10,417	22,387
April	8,085	20,625
May.	7,500	19,500
June	9,525	21,450
July.	10,425	21,975
August	11,250	22,425
September.	12,825	23,250
October.	14,250	24,750
November	16,125	25,875
December	16,500	26,250

Required:

a.   Compute the budget formula for the fixed and variable amounts using the high-low method of determining the fixed and variable costs.
b.   Prepare monthly budgets of fixed and variable overhead for the first quarter based on:

	Estimated direct labor-hours
January	14,775
February	12,667
March	11,025

c.   Use the least squares method to determine the fixed and variable cost elements.
d.   Account for any difference between the answers determined in *a* and those determined in *c*.

P5–12. High-low, scattergraph, and least squares methods and coefficient of correlation (CMA adapted)

Ramon Company manufactures a wide range of products at several different plant locations. The Franklin Plant, which manufactures electrical components, has been experiencing some difficulties with fluctuating monthly overhead costs. The fluctuations have made it difficult to estimate the level of overhead that will be incurred for any one month.

Management wants to be able to estimate overhead costs accurately to better plan for its operation and financial needs. A trade association publication to which Ramon Company subscribes indicates that, for companies manufacturing electrical components, overhead tends to vary with direct labor-hours.

One member of the accounting staff has proposed that the cost behavior pattern of the overhead costs be determined. Then overhead costs could be predicted from the budgeted direct labor-hours.

Another member of the accounting staff suggested that a good starting place for determining the cost behavior pattern included the high-low method, the scattergraph method, simple linear regression, and multiple regression. Of these methods, Ramon Company decided to employ the high-low method, the scattergraph method, and simple linear regression. Data on direct labor-hours and the respective overhead costs incurred were collected for the past two years. The raw data are as follows:

	Direct labor-hours	Overhead costs
19X1:		
January	20,000	$84,000
February	25,000	99,000
March	22,000	89,500
April	23,000	90,000
May.	20,000	81,500
June	19,000	75,500
July	14,000	70,500
August.	10,000	64,500
September.	12,000	69,000
October.	17,000	75,000
November	16,000	71,500
December	19,000	78,000
19X2:		
January	21,000	86,000
February	24,000	93,000
March	23,000	93,000
April	22,000	87,000
May.	20,000	80,000
June	18,000	76,500
July	12,000	67,500
August.	13,000	71,000
September.	15,000	73,500
October.	17,000	72,500
November	15,000	71,000
December	18,000	75,000

Required:

Determine the following using the raw data for the past two years combined:

a. Using the high-low method, determine the cost behavior pattern of the overhead costs for the Franklin Plant.

b.   Prepare a scattergraph showing the relationship between overhead costs and production levels.
c.   Use simple linear regression (least squares method) to prepare a fixed-variable expense analysis. Use thousands of direct labor-hours to simplify computations.
d.   Determine the coefficient of correlation (r) and the coefficient of determination (r^2).
e.   Discuss the appropriateness of the three proposed methods (high-low, scatter-graph, linear regression) and indicate which one Ramon Company should employ to determine the historical cost behavior pattern of Franklin Plant's overhead cost.

P5–13.   Linear regression analysis (CMA adapted)

The Lockit Company manufactures doorknobs for homes and apartments. Lockit is considering the use of simple and multiple linear regression analysis to forecast annual sales because previous forecasts have been inaccurate. The sales forecast will be used to initiate the budgeting process and to better identify the underlying process that generates sales.

Larry Husky, the controller of Lockit, has considered many possible independent variables and equations to predict sales and has narrowed his choices to four equations. Husky used annual observations from 20 prior years to estimate each of the four equations.

Following is a definition of the variables used in the four equations and a statistical summary of these equations:

S_t = Forecasted sales (in dollars) for Lockit in time period t.
S_{t-1} = Actual sales (in dollars) for Lockit in time period $t-1$.
G_t = Forecasted United States gross national product in time period t.
G_{t-1} = Actual United States gross national product in time period $t-1$.
N_{t-1} = Lockit's net income in time period $t-1$.

Statistical summary of four equations (P5–13):

Equation	Dependent variable	Independent variable (s)	Coefficients Dependent variable (intercept) (000)	Independent variable (rate)	Standard error of the estimate	Coefficient of correlation	t-value
1	S_t	S_{t-1}	$ 500,	1.10	$500,000	.97	5.5
2	S_t	G_t	$1,000	.00001	$510,000	.95	10.0
3	S_t	G_{t-1}	$ 900	$ .000012	$520,000	.90	5.0
	$\{S_t$		$ 600		$490,000	.98	
4		N_{T-1}		$10.00			4.0
		G_t		$ .000002			1.5
		G_{t-1}		$ .000003			3.0

Required:

a.   Write Equations 2 and 4 in the form $y = a + bx$.
b.   If actual sales are $1,500,000 in 19X1, what would the forecasted sales for Lockit be in 19X2?
c.   Explain the meaning and significance of the coefficient of correlation.
d.   Why might Larry Husky prefer Equation 3 to Equation 2?
e.   Explain the advantages and disadvantages of using Equation 4 to forecast annual sales.

OBJECTIVES OF CHAPTER 6

1. To emphasize the concepts of traceability and attachability that distinguish direct costs from indirect costs.

2. To discuss the methods available for applying factory overhead costs so a sound basis will be selected for an accurate distribution of such costs.

3. To illustrate the determination and use of departmental factory overhead rates.

4. To present the various methods of allocating service department overhead to producing departments.

5. To introduce overhead variances for an actual cost system and graphically demonstrate that they represent over- or underapplied overhead.

6

Allocating overhead costs and variance analysis

Since factory overhead costs differ from direct material and direct labor costs in that total overhead costs may not be known until the end of the cost accounting period, an estimate of factory overhead costs must be used in determining product costs during the operating cycle. In addition, actual factory overhead costs may vary considerably from month to month; consequently, if actual costs were used, the value assigned to inventory could fluctuate considerably. To provide timely product costing data and to minimize fluctuations in overhead costs assigned to inventory, the company should estimate its overhead costs based on some attainable volume to arrive at a factory overhead application rate. This rate is then used to assign manufacturing overhead to the different departments and jobs.

This chapter also introduces the various methods of allocating costs from service departments to other cost centers. This procedure, known by such names as cost allocations, cost distributions, cost assignments, or cost apportionments, presents a number of problems because there is often an element of subjectivity in selecting the allocation basis. Such cost allocations are encountered in nearly all industries. For example, in manufacturing, the cost of service departments such as factory office, maintenance, and materials storeroom must be allocated to production departments so that total factory overhead costs can be allocated to the units being produced. Similarly, for cost reimbursement purposes, hospitals must allocate personnel and equipment costs to patient care centers, while colleges and universities must likewise allocate administrative costs to graduate and undergraduate programs to determine a cost per enrolled student.

PLANT CAPACITY CONCEPTS

Chapter 2 introduced overhead application rates; however, the question of what capacity should be used to establish the estimated factory overhead rate was ignored in that chapter. This chapter advocates selecting one specific activity level to be used for estimating costs and for establishing the factory overhead application rate. The costs and the volume level can be changed later if conditions vary; this will result in a change in the overhead application rate. A useful approach is to budget costs in relation to either sales or production volume, depending upon the capacity level to which each cost is more related. Reference was also made in Chapter 2 to the impact of volume changes on fixed and variable costs. Since an understanding of this is an important foundation for variable budgeting and the application of overhead costs, the topic is again discussed in this chapter. Several approaches can be used to select the plant capacity level. The approach chosen depends upon whether a short-range or long-range viewpoint is used and how much allowance management wants to make for possible volume interruptions. Four capacity approaches will be discussed: theoretical, practical, normal, and expected actual capacity.

Theoretical capacity

Theoretical capacity assumes all personnel and equipment will operate at peak efficiency and that 100 percent of plant capacity will be used. The theoretical activity level is also referred to as the maximum or ideal capacity. If the theoretical capacity is adopted, the company assumes that it will operate at full speed without even normal interruptions such as machine breakdowns or maintenance. Since theoretical capacity does not allow for unavoidable or normal interruptions, it is not usually considered a feasible basis for determining cost allocation rates.

Practical capacity

Practical capacity is more realistic than theoretical capacity since it allows for unavoidable delays due to holidays, vacations, time off for weekends, and machine breakdowns. Practical capacity does not consider idle time due to inadequate sales demand; instead, it involves the production volume that would be achieved if demand for the company's products allowed the plant to operate continuously at some hypothetical level determined by the engineering staff. Practical capacity represents the maximum level at which departments or divisions can operate efficiently. While this level varies from company to company, practical capacity is usually considered to be approximately 75 to 85 percent of full capacity.

Normal capacity

Normal capacity includes consideration of both idle time due to limited sales orders and human and equipment inefficiencies. While normal capacity may be the same as practical capacity, it usually is less, depending upon the sales volume forecasted. In budgeting the manufacturing volume to be used as normal capacity, forecasted demand data for a sufficient number of years must be used to account for cyclical changes in sales.

Expected actual capacity

Expected actual capacity is the production volume that is necessary to meet sales demand for the next year. This is a short-range concept, since it does not attempt to even out the cyclical changes in sales demand. Many accountants reject normal capacity because they believe that each year should be considered individually and that the overhead costs incurred each year should be allocated to the units produced that year. In allocating this overhead, these accountants disregard the relationship of each year's activity and average long-range activity.

Comparison of capacity levels

After a company decides on a specific capacity level, it should then estimate its fixed costs for the period. The budget formula for doing this was introduced in Chapter 5. For example, in Exhibit 5–7 the monthly fixed costs were estimated at $1,500 for Cost Center A. In this example, variable costs were stated as a cost per direct labor-hour, but fixed costs were expressed only as a total. This approach, however, is not adequate for applying factory overhead because fixed overhead must also be broken down into a cost per unit produced, per machine-hour, or on some other basis. Exhibit 6–1 does this to show the effect on the estimated fixed factory overhead rate of adopting several capacity levels. While few companies would ever consider using 100 percent of their plant capacity as the basis for applying factory overhead, theoretical capacity is included here for illustration purposes. Practical capacity at 80 percent of full capacity represents a production volume at which there is sufficient demand for the products to allow the company to operate at this high level. Normal capacity includes an allowance for idle time due to human and equipment inefficiencies. If company management believes that production for the next period will be depressed, expected actual activity at 60 percent of theoretical capacity could be used.

EXHIBIT 6–1

Capacity level effect on estimated fixed factory overhead

	Theoretical capacity	Practical capacity	Normal capacity	Expected actual
Capacity level	100%	80%	70%	60%
Machine-hours	20,000	16,000	14,000	12,000
Estimated factory overhead: Variable overhead @ $1 per machine- hour	$20,000	$16,000	$14,000	$12,000
Fixed overhead	60,000	60,000	60,000	60,000
Total overhead.	$80,000	$76,000	$74,000	$72,000
Factory overhead rate per machine-hour: Fixed overhead	$3.00	$3.75	$4.29*	$5.00
Variable overhead	1.00	1.00	1.00	1.00
Total overhead.	$4.00	$4.75	$5.29	$6.00

*Rounded to nearest two decimals.

Effect on unit fixed costs

In the Exhibit 6–1, total fixed costs remain at $60,000 within the relevant range of the various capacity volumes listed. If higher capacity levels are used, the fixed factory overhead rate per machine-hour is lower than it would be if the normal or expected actual capacity is used, because fixed overhead is spread over a greater number of machine-hours. For example, if 12,000 machine-hours were used, the fixed factory overhead rate would be $5 per machine-hour ($60,000/12,000 hours); if 20,000 machine-hours were used, the rate would be $3 per machine-hour ($60,000/20,000 hours). The variable factory overhead rate remains a constant $1 per machine-hour at all capacity levels. These illustrations emphasize the effect of using various activity levels to compute unit fixed costs.

Exhibit 6–1 illustrates the significant variation in the fixed overhead rate per hour using different capacity concepts; the choice of a capacity concept is a major decision that should be made by top management. In evaluating the four activity levels—theoretical, practical, normal, and expected actual—one finds it difficult to identify one capacity level to use in all circumstances. Several factors deserve management's attention in selecting the capacity to use in calculating overhead application rates. Most importantly, the feasibility of attaining a capacity level should be considered, because if an unrealistically high level is chosen, a large unfavorable volume (idle capacity) variance will result that will have limited meaning and usefulness.

Evaluating capacity levels

The choice of any one capacity level will have advantages and disadvantages. In turn, the choice of capacity level affects the factory overhead costs applied to the product. If product costs strongly influence the pricing policies or if cost-plus contracts are used extensively, as in government contracting, there is a danger to using the expected actual activity level in a seasonal or cyclical business; fixed unit costs would be less in peak production periods if this volume is used as the basis for applying factory overhead, and under these conditions, the sales price for these units would be less in a cost-plus contract than if the units were produced in a slack period. In fact, normal capacity would be a more appropriate basis for applying overhead under these circumstances, since normal capacity evens out the cyclical changes.

In addition, expected actual capacity may allow forecasts of sales demand to be accepted as the basis for applying factory overhead without management considering available plant capacity. While units sold and units produced are not always equal because the management strategy may be to build up or reduce inventory, inadequate attention may be given to marketing efforts designed to improve sales so that a higher level of manufacturing capacity can be utilized. However, expected actual capacity may be more appropriate than other capacity levels for appraising current performance. On the other hand, theoretical capacity is often not useful, since it is usually unrealistic, although it can be used to help measure efficiency of operations by providing "ideal" figures for comparison.

Merits of practical capacity. Since the two extremes of capacity level choice—theoretical and expected actual—are often unrealistic, a company must usually choose between normal capacity and practical capacity. Practical capacity is determined by deducting anticipated losses due to weekends and holidays and unavoidable repairs, breakdowns, and shortages of material and labor from theoretical capacity. Thus, practical capacity represents the level of activity at which a plant can operate realistically if it does not lack production orders.

Merits of normal capacity. Normal capacity, on the other hand, represents a modification of practical capacity for lack of production orders over a period long enough to include seasonal and cyclical fluctuations. It represents an average sales demand which is expected to exist over a long enough period that peak demand and slack demand are leveled out. Overhead rates based on normal capacity represent an attempt to apply fixed overhead by using a long-run average expected activity. By using normal capacity as the base, conceptually the overapplication of overhead in some years will be offset by the underapplication of overhead in other years. Normal capacity is generally the basis for long-range planning, standards, and the allocation of overhead costs.

Regardless of the capacity level chosen, making the decision can be complex because many factors must be considered. Generally, the approach used is to determine normal capacity for the company as a whole and then break it down for individual departments or segments. This analysis often reveals that a smooth flow of production is difficult unless problems in overloaded departments are eliminated. Also, departments with excess capacity can be encouraged to search for new orders to utilize unneeded capacity.

Idle capacity versus excess capacity

In determining factory overhead application rates, an accountant must also keep in mind the difference between *idle capacity* and *excess capacity. Idle capacity* is the temporary nonuse of facilities resulting from a decrease in demand for the company's products or services, while *excess capacity* refers to facilities that are simply not necessary. Just because the plant facilities are unused does not mean that there is idle capacity; there may be excess capacity. Management may have acquired larger manufacturing facilities than needed because it was more economical in the long run to provide for expected future needs at the time the facilities were acquired; this would explain the excess capacity. Idle capacity depends upon what volume is chosen as a budget basis. For instance, idle capacity under the practical capacity concept is considered a marketing expense, since it results from the inability to generate a sufficiently high volume of sales to keep the plant operating at a high production level. In an actual cost system, idle capacity is the difference between the actual hours and the budgeted hours determined under the capacity concept used. Under a standard cost system, idle capacity is the difference in the standard hours allowed for the output and budgeted hours. (This will be discussed more fully in Chapter 11.)

ACTIVITY MEASURES

The activity measure chosen should meet several criteria. First, the allocation base must be easy to compute. Direct labor dollars and direct material costs meet this criterion, because the data are already available for each job and there is little or no additional clerical cost incurred in gathering the information necessary to apply overhead. In practice, however, material cost is seldom used because there is usually little relationship between the occurrence of direct material costs and the incurrence of factory overhead. The computation using direct labor-hours or machine-hours, on the other hand, requires greater clerical effort, since direct labor-hours or machine-hours must be determined for each job or department, and management may not need these data for any other purpose. Consequently, the company should avoid the effort and costs of computing direct labor-hours or machine-hours only for factory overhead application purposes if the data for some other appropriate allocation base are already available. If the results do not differ significantly, the easier method should be used. However, whatever base is chosen, the data should be broken down by departments or jobs. Exhibit 6–2 illustrates the use of each of these bases and presents a comparison of the different rates.

After the capacity level is chosen, the activity volume may be expressed using any of the following terms:

1. Units of production.
2. Direct labor dollars or cost.
3. Direct labor-hours.
4. Machine-hours.
5. Materials cost.

To ensure that a proper allocation of costs is obtained, the components of factory overhead should be analyzed. If many of the factory overhead costs are related to labor, the most accurate allocation base is probably either direct labor-hours or direct labor dollars; however, if many overhead costs are related to time, direct labor-hours or machine-hours could be used as the allocation.

EXHIBIT 6–2

Determination of factory overhead rates

Estimated total factory overhead	$525,000
Estimated number of units to be produced in the period	140,000 units
Estimated direct labor costs for period	$500,000
Estimated direct labor-hours for period.	125,000 hours
Estimated machine-hours for period	375,000 hours
Estimated material costs for period.	$700,000

Unit of production base

If only one product is manufactured or a simple production process is involved, the unit of production base may be appropriate. However, if more than one product is manufactured, another base should probably be used because this base is valid only if the units produced receive equal manufacturing effort. Rather than allocate strictly on the unit of production basis, a company may assign points to the units produced to obtain a better apportionment of overhead. For example, a company may assign two points to each Product A estimated to be produced while only one point is assigned to Product B because Product A requires more manufacturing effort.

The formula for determining the factory overhead rate using the units of production data in Exhibit 6–2 is as follows:

$$\frac{\$525,000 \text{ estimated factory overhead}}{140,000 \text{ estimated number of units}} = \$3.75 \text{ per unit}$$

We are discussing actual cost systems in this chapter; systems utilizing standards or performance yardsticks are not introduced until Chapters 10 and

11. While the unit of production base may be appropriate with an actual cost system, this base should not be used with a standard cost system and variance analysis. The reason for this will become apparent in Chapter 11.

The unit of production base is generally not applicable to a non-manufacturing company. Instead, a variation may be used; for example, a health care institution could use the number of beds, a marketing company might use the number of sales calls or miles traveled by salespersons, and colleges and universities might use the number of students enrolled in different programs.

Direct labor cost or dollars

When direct labor cost or dollars, rather than units of production, are used as a base for applying factory overhead, it is assumed that higher paid workers are incurring a larger share of factory overhead than are lower paid workers. This may be true if the more highly paid, better trained workers are required to operate the more expensive and more sophisticated machinery and plant facilities. A case can also be made for using direct labor costs if the overhead costs include many employee benefits that are based on a percentage of employee base compensation.

Time-related factory overhead.   Some factory overhead costs such as heat, light, power, insurance, rent, and taxes represent amounts of resources consumed over a period of time. Thus, the use of direct labor costs as an allocation base has some weakness. Because most companies do not pay the same rate per hour to all direct labor workers, more factory overhead is allocated to the cost centers using higher paid workers, when, in fact, much of the factory overhead results merely from the use of the facilities. Departmental rates based on direct labor dollars do overcome part of this weakness as long as workers within each department receive an hourly rate that is in the same range.

Another weakness in applying factory overhead on the basis of actual direct labor dollars is that an inefficient use of direct labor will, in turn, cause an excessive amount of factory overhead to be applied. This is because fluctuations in the rate estimated when the factory overhead application rate was established are compounded when factory overhead is applied. For example, assume that when the direct labor costs from Exhibit 6–2 were estimated, the wage rate was $4 per hour. The allocation rate using direct labor costs as the allocation base is as follows:

$$\frac{\$525,000 \text{ estimated factory overhead}}{\substack{\$500,000 \text{ estimated direct labor costs} \\ (125,000 \text{ hours} \times \$4 \text{ per hour})}} = 105 \text{ percent of direct labor costs}$$

Assume that actual wages paid amounted to $4.25 per hour and that actual hours were 125,000 as budgeted. Total factory overhead applied would be

$4.25 \times 125,000$ hours $= \$531,250 \times 105$ percent $= \$557,812.50$ factory overhead applied. This means that the cost center applies more dollars of overhead by paying a higher labor rate than planned. In turn, this larger amount of applied factory overhead is compared to actual factory overhead, which would result in factory overhead being overapplied if actual factory overhead followed the expected behavior pattern. Rather than actual direct labor dollars, a standard or budgeted direct labor rate can be used. This concept will be discussed in Chapter 11 when standard overhead cost is introduced.

Direct labor-hours

The use of direct labor-*hours*, as opposed to direct labor dollars, as an allocation base follows the same principle as the unit of production approach, because both units of production and direct labor-hours cause costs to increase or decrease. When the direct labor-hours base is chosen as a means of expressing volume, important consideration is given to the fact that many factory overhead costs are related to the use of labor-hours. In addition, many factory overhead costs measure the amounts of resources consumed over a period of time. However, the use of direct labor-hours may require additional computations, since these hours must be computed for each job using information obtained from labor time tickets. Using the data from Exhibit 6–2, the computation of the allocation rate using direct labor-hours as the allocation base is as follows:

$$\frac{\$525,000 \text{ estimated factory overhead}}{125,000 \text{ estimated direct labor-hours}} = \$4.20 \text{ per direct labor-hour}$$

One inherent weakness in using actual direct labor-hours is that it is a measure of input. A better basis for applying factory overhead is some measure of output, such as units of production or standard hours allowed for the output. For example, assume that 10 hours of direct labor are budgeted to finish each product unit. If the workers took 12 hours to produce each unit, the number of finished units times a standard of 10 direct labor-hours would be a better basis for applying factory overhead than would applying overhead on the additional inefficient 2 hours of labor. Chapter 11 illustrates in detail why expressing output in terms of standard direct labor-hours is usually a better measure of efficiency than are actual hours.

Machine-hours

If the factory is highly automated, *machine*-hours, not labor-hours, may be the most accurate overhead allocation basis, since many of the factory overhead items, such as repairs and maintenance, depreciation, insurance, and property taxes, are related to the utilization of machinery. Yet, despite the strong theoretical justification for using machine-hours, there may be additional clerical effort in calculating these hours by job or by department. The calculation using machine-hours as a base for applying factory overhead is as follows, given the data from Exhibit 6–2:

$$\frac{\$525{,}000 \text{ estimated factory overhead}}{375{,}000 \text{ estimated machine-hours}} = \$1.40 \text{ per machine-hour}$$

Some companies have a fixed relationship between direct labor- and machine-hours; for instance, one direct labor worker is stationed at each machine. If this is true, the company can use either direct labor-hours or direct labor costs (if all workers in the department receive approximately the same wage per hour) rather than machine-hours as the allocation base, since wage and labor-hour data are already computed.

Direct materials cost

Still another alternative on which to base overhead is direct materials costs. Generally, however, direct materials cost is not a valid basis because there is normally no logical relationship between direct materials usage and overhead costs incurred. Only if each product involves approximately the same material costs or if the same amount of material is applied per hour (i.e., when material is controlled by an automatic machine), should direct material cost be used. That is, if material costs *are* controlled by a machine, the material cost *is* consumed on a time basis and consequently there *is* a relationship between material costs and overhead costs, the majority of which are also consumed on a time basis. Also, if many of the overhead costs result from material handling, direct material can more validly be considered a basis for allocation. The formula for computing the overhead application rate with direct material cost as the allocation base, using the data from Exhibit 6–2, is as follows:

$$\frac{\$525{,}000 \text{ estimated factory overhead}}{\$700{,}000 \text{ estimated material costs}} = 75 \text{ percent of material cost}$$

Prime cost

The list (page 211) of five different activity measures which can be used as a basis for applying factory overhead omitted prime cost, even though a few companies do use this as an allocation base. Prime cost is comprised of direct material and direct labor costs. But prime cost has the same weaknesses previously cited for direct material costs or direct labor costs as an allocation base. Since it has such a limited theoretical basis, the calculation of factory overhead rates is not illustrated.

Production and service departments

After the volume basis on which capacity will be expressed has been determined, costs must be accumulated for production and service departments. Production departments are those actually engaged in manufacturing activities such as fabricating, assembly, and finishing. Service departments, on the other hand, provide services to other departments and perform no production work. All factory costs, whether direct or indirect, must finally be charged to production departments or other cost centers so that overhead rates can be determined to apply overhead to the product.

Direct and indirect costs

When figuring overhead application rates, the accountant must distinguish between direct and indirect costs. This distinction depends on the *attachability* or *traceability* of the cost element. *Direct costs* do not have to be allocated to the costing center because they arise within the department or job and can be clearly traced to this cost center. (In Chapter 2, direct material and direct labor costs were contrasted to indirect material and indirect labor costs, respectively.) Indirect material and indirect labor, however, must be allocated on some basis. Indirect costs are also referred to as *common costs* because they serve two or more costing centers. For example, electric power and other utilities are indirect costs if each department is not individually metered. The term *indirect costs* thus refers to cost elements that cannot be traced to one costing center.

Because *traceability* is the key distinction between direct and indirect costs, the *object* of *costing* (costing center) must first be defined before we can say whether a cost is direct or indirect. For example, the plant superintendent's salary is an indirect cost for all service and production departments because this cost cannot be traced to only one department; however, when the object of costing is the overall company, the plant superintendent's salary is a direct cost of production.

ALLOCATION METHODS FOR SERVICE COSTS

Allocating service department costs is a particularly complex indirect costing procedure since while service departments such as janitorial service and materials storeroom are not directly involved in manufacturing products, all costs of service departments must be allocated to production departments. There are several methods for allocating these costs:

1. *Direct method.* Overhead of service departments is allocated to the production departments only.
2. *Step, sequential, or step-down method.* Service department costs are allocated to other service departments and to production departments which have received their services.
3. *Linear algebra, reciprocal, or matrix method.* This method uses simultaneous equations to take into account that service departments render reciprocal services.

Whatever method of service department cost allocation is used, the first step in the procedure should be to estimate the overhead costs for the entire plant. No allocations are necessary for direct costs, since they can be traced to the object of costing. However, some basis for making the *indirect* cost allocations must be determined. The information on which to allocate the indirect costs must be obtained from a survey of the plant. Exhibit 6–3 contains information, such as the number of employees, plant square footage, and so on, that can be used to allocate the indirect costs of service departments to the production departments.

EXHIBIT 6–3

Heagy Company plant survey

	No. of employees	Square footage	Kilowatt-hours	100 cubic feet	Estimated cost of materials requisitioned	Estimated labor-hours of repair service used
Materials handling.	5	15,000	80,000	40,000	—	—
Repair and maintenance	3	10,000	70,000	75,000	$ 30,000	—
Building and grounds	2	25,000	100,000	25,000	25,500	5,009
Producing department—sewing	10	40,000	450,000	400,000	33,000	1,100
Producing department—treating	15	30,000	300,000	500,000	42,000	2,300
Totals	35	120,000	1,000,000	1,040,000	$130,500	8,409

Note: Bases used for applying factory overhead to products: Sewing department—$157,500 direct labor costs; Treating department—45,000 direct labor-hours.

Cost allocation basis. The basis used to allocate indirect costs must bear a relationship to the kind of services being rendered. For example, if the purchasing department's costs are to be allocated, the allocation base could be the number of purchase orders processed or costs of materials used by each department; an appropriate allocation base for the personnel department, on the other hand, may be the number of employees or labor-hours in each department. Similarly, the costs of the materials handling function could be allocated using the number of requisitions, and the costs of the repair and maintenance department could be allocated using service-hours rendered. The most appropriate basis for allocating building occupancy costs may be occupied floor space, although this allocation base may be somewhat controversial. There may be some conflict if plant square footage is used, because this assumes all space is equally desirable, regardless of the number of windows or where the space is located. While it is recognized that cost accountants sometimes must resort to a somewhat arbitrary basis because there is no clear cause-and-effect relationship between the basis and the cost, there is a danger in relying on a basis such as sales dollars, gross margin, or some other ability-to-bear basis. In such cases, an inaccurate cost allocation will likely result. Instead, the cost accountant should determine the basis that most accurately reflects services or benefits received. These data may be used later for allocating service department costs to the other service departments and/or production departments. The bases for allocating the indirect costs are indicated in Exhibits 6–4 and 6–5 and are based on the data from the plant survey in Exhibit 6–3. For example, the indirect cost of superintendence is allocated to both service and producing departments based on the number of employees within each department. The material handling department receives:

$$\frac{5 \text{ material handling employees}}{35 \text{ total employees}} \times \$70{,}000 \text{ (total superintendence cost)} = \$10{,}000$$

The bases for allocating the other three indirect costs—factory rent, electricity, and water— are indicated.

ALLOCATING INDIRECT COSTS VERSUS ALLOCATING SERVICE DEPARTMENT COSTS

Note that tracing each department's direct costs and the allocation of indirect costs to each department is independent of the method of allocation (direct, step, or linear algebra) discussed below. For example, in Exhibits 6–4, 6–5, and 6–6, each service and production department has the same direct and indirect costs (e.g. materials handling has a total cost of $43,500). However, the exhibits differ in the method of allocation of each service department's direct and indirect costs.

Direct method

After the direct and indirect costs for each department are determined, the costs of all service departments are allocated. Exhibit 6–4 illustrates the direct method in which service department costs are allocated only to production departments. For example,

$$\frac{\$33{,}000 \text{ (sewing material requisitions)}}{\$75{,}000 \text{ (total sewing and treating material requisitions}} \times \$17{,}240 \text{ (variable material handling department cost)}$$

$$= \frac{\$7{,}586 \text{ variable cost}}{\text{allocations to sewing}} + \frac{\$33{,}000}{\$75{,}000} \times \$26{,}260 \text{ (fixed material handling department cost)}$$

$$= \frac{\$11{,}554 \text{ fixed cost}}{\text{allocations to sewing}}$$

yielding a total of $19,140 allocated to the sewing department with the

EXHIBIT 6–4

HEAGY COMPANY
Estimated Departmental Factory Overhead—Direct Method of Allocation
For Year 19—

	Service departments			Production departments		
	Materials handling	Repairs and maintenance	Building and grounds	Sewing	Treat- ing	Total
Direct costs:						
Indirect labor (variable)	$ 8,000	$ 6,500	$ 3,500	$ 2,500	$ 1,100	$ 21,600
Indirect labor (fixed).	7,000	7,000	4,500	1,500	1,000	21,000
Indirect materials (variable)	400	280	310	1,000	800	2,790
Indirect materials (fixed).	600	220	390	800	700	2,710
Depreciation of equipment (fixed)	700	800	400	800	1,200	3,900
Total departmental direct costs	16,700	14,800	9,100	6,600	4,800	52,000
Indirect costs and allocation base:						
Superintendence (no. of employees)(fixed)	10,000	6,000	4,000	20,000	30,000	70,000
Factory rent (square footage)(fixed)	6,000	4,000	10,000	16,000	12,000	48,000
Electricity (KWHR)(variable)	7,040	6,160	8,800	39,600	26,400	88,000
Electricity (KWHR)(fixed)	1,760	1,540	2,200	9,900	6,600	22,000
Water (100 cu ft)(variable)	1,800	3,375	1,125	18,000	22,500	46,800
Water (100 cu. ft)(fixed)	200	375	125	2,000	2,500	5,200
Total departmental indirect costs	26,800	21,450	26,250	105,500	100,000	280,000
Total factory overhead costs.	$43,500	$36,250	$35,350	$112,100	$104,800	$332,000
Total variable departmental costs	$17,240	$16,315	$13,735	$ 61,100	$ 50,800	$159,190
Total fixed departmental costs	26,260	19,935	21,615	51,000	54,000	172,810
Total departmental factory overhead before distribution of service departments . .	43,500	36,250	35,350	112,100	104,800	332,000
Distribution of service department costs:						
Materials handling (estimated cost of materials requisitioned: sewing, $33,000; treating, $42,000):						
Variable	(17,240)			7,586	9,654	
Fixed	(26,260)			11,554	14,706	
Repairs and maintenance (estimated labor-hours of service used: sewing, 1,100; treating, 2,300):						
Variable		(16,315)		5,278	11,037	
Fixed		(19,935)		6,450	13,485	
Building and grounds (square footage: sewing, 40,000; treating, 30,000):						
Variable			(13,735)	7,849	5,886	
Fixed			(21,615)	12,351	9,264	
Total variable overhead				81,813	77,377	
Total fixed overhead				81,355	91,455	
Total variable and fixed overhead				$163,168	$168,832	$332,000
Allocation bases to apply overhead to production:						
Direct labor cost				$157,500		
Direct labor-hours					45,000	
Variable factory overhead rates				52%	$1.72	
Fixed factory overhead rates				52	2.03	
Total factory overhead rates.				104% of direct labor cost	$3.75 per direct labor-hour	

EXHIBIT 6–5

HEAGY COMPANY
Estimated Departmental Factory Overhead—Step Method of Allocation
For Year 19—

	Service departments			Production departments		
	Materials handling	Repairs and maintenance	Building and grounds	Sewing	Treating	Total
Direct costs:						
Indirect labor (variable)	$ 8,000	$ 6,500	$ 3,500	$ 2,500	$ 1,100	$ 21,600
Indirect labor (fixed)	7,000	7,000	4,500	1,500	1,000	21,000
Indirect materials (variable)	400	280	310	1,000	800	2,790
Indirect materials (fixed)	600	220	390	800	700	2,710
Depreciation of equipment (fixed)	700	800	400	800	1,200	3,900
Total departmental direct costs	16,700	14,800	9,100	6,600	4,800	52,000
Indirect costs and allocation base:						
Superintendence (no. of employees)(fixed)	10,000	6,000	4,000	20,000	30,000	70,000
Factory rent (square footage)(fixed)	6,000	4,000	10,000	16,000	12,000	48,000
Electricity (KWHR)(variable)	7,040	6,160	8,800	39,600	26,400	88,000
Electricity (KWHR)(fixed)	1,760	1,540	2,200	9,900	6,600	22,000
Water (100 cu ft)(variable)	1,800	3,375	1,125	18,000	22,500	46,800
Water (100 cu ft)(fixed)	200	375	125	2,000	2,500	5,200
Total departmental indirect costs	26,800	21,450	26,250	105,500	100,000	280,000
Total factory overhead costs	$43,500	$36,250	$35,350	$112,100	$104,800	$332,000
Total variable departmental costs	$17,240	$16,315	$13,735	$ 61,100	$ 50,800	$159,190
Total fixed departmental costs	26,260	19,935	21,615	51,000	54,000	172,810
Total departmental factory overhead before distribution of service departments	43,500	36,250	35,350	112,100	104,800	332,000
Distribution of service department costs:						
Materials handling (estimated cost of materials requisitioned: repairs, $30,000; building, $25,500; sewing, $33,000; treating, $42,000):						
Variable	(17,240)	3,965	3,369	4,359	5,547	
Fixed	(26,260)	6,035	5,131	6,641	8,453	
Variable repairs and maintenance		20,280				
Fixed repairs and maintenance		25,970				
Total repairs and maintenance		46,250				
Repairs and maintenance (estimated labor-hours of service used: building, 5,009; sewing, 1,100; treating, 2,300):						
Variable		(20,280)	12,080	2,653	5,547	
Fixed		(25,970)	15,470	3,397	7,103	
Variable building and grounds			29,184			
Fixed building and grounds			42,216			
Total building and grounds			71,400			
Building and grounds (square footage: sewing, 40,000; treating, 30,000):						
Variable			(29,184)	16,677	12,507	
Fixed			(42,216)	24,123	18,093	
Total variable overhead				84,789	74,401	
Total fixed overhead				85,161	87,649	
Total variable and fixed overhead				$169,950	$162,050	$332,000
Allocation bases to apply overhead to production:						
Direct labor cost				$157,500		
Direct labor-hours					45,000	
Variable factory overhead rates				54%	$1.65	
Fixed factory overhead rates				54	1.95	
Total factory overhead rates				108% of direct labor cost	$3.60 per direct labor-hour	

remaining material handling cost distributed only to the treating department. This method ignores allocating the costs of any materials handling services provided to other service departments. The direct method is simple because the order of allocating each service department costs does not matter.

Regardless of the allocation method used (direct, step, or linear algebra), after all service department costs are distributed to production departments, the overhead rates can be calculated for each production department. To do this, one of the five most common and acceptable bases—units of production, direct labor-hours, direct labor costs, machine-hours, or direct materials costs—must be used to compute a departmental overhead rate by dividing estimated departmental overhead cost by the estimated base. In Exhibit 6–4, direct labor costs are used as the allocation base for the sewing production department and direct labor-hours for the treating production department. In deciding whether to use different bases for different departments, the accountant must study the cause-and-effect relationship between the cost and the cost allocation basis. After the departmental rate is determined, the estimated overhead rate can be used to apply overhead to the units produced.

Step method

When using the step method of service cost allocation, the accountant must detail the sequence in which the costs of all service departments are distributed to other departments. Generally, the costs of the service department that renders services to the greatest number of other departments should be allocated first, the department servicing the next greatest number of departments should be allocated next, and so forth. The last service department to be allocated is normally the one serving the smallest number of other departments. In the step method illustrated in Exhibit 6–5, material handling costs are allocated to all other service departments and the producing departments; repairs and maintenance receives $3,965 ($30,000/$130,500 × $17,240) variable costs and $6,035 ($30,000/$130,500 × $26,260) fixed costs. Then the repair and maintenance department costs, including its share of the material handling cost allocation, are allocated to all other departments. For example, the $20,280 total variable repairs and maintenance which is allocated is composed of the following: $6,500 + $280 + $6,160 + $3,375 + $3,965 = $20,280. Finally, the building and grounds department costs, which includes the department's share of materials handling *and* repair and maintenance cost allocations, are distributed.

Normally, the step method is preferable to the direct method, since it takes into account the benefits rendered by one service department to other service departments. However, the step method fails to recognize that, for example, the building and grounds department may have rendered some reciprocal service to the materials handling and repairs and maintenance departments. Since the costs of these departments were previously allocated, no building and grounds department costs were allocated to these departments. The method of allocations using linear algebra takes into account these reciprocal services.

Linear algebra or reciprocal method

Exhibit 6–6 illustrates the reciprocal method using linear algebra or simultaneous equations. This method achieves greater exactness than does the step method because it recognizes reciprocity between service departments. However, this greater exactness can be achieved only if the estimated level of service that departments render to each other is valid. For complex decisions regarding product pricing or make or buy, the linear algebra method should be used to obtain a more precise allocation of costs. But since linear algebra is more time-consuming and more costly to implement, it should be used only if the step method does not provide the allocation refinements and precision needed. Since three service departments are illustrated in Exhibit 6–6, three simultaneous equations are necessary. If additional service departments are used, more simultaneous equations may be required, in which case matrix algebra can be used to handle the series of equations. Because of the time involved in solving the equations, total factory overhead costs for each service department, instead of separate variable and fixed costs, are allocated and, consequently, only a total overhead rate is computed. However, fixed and variable overhead rates are needed at the end of the period for the accountant to compute the spending and volume variances, which are discussed later in this chapter.

As you recall, in Exhibits 6–4 and 6–5, direct costs and indirect costs were itemized as either fixed or variable. To allocate service costs, an accountant could use separate rates for fixed costs and variable costs, especially if the company uses a variable budgeting approach. For simplicity, Exhibits 6–4, 6–5, and 6–6 use full allocation rates, which include both fixed and variable costs. However, rather than allocate full costs, an accountant may use only variable costs when allocating service costs. This approach makes users of the service responsible only for variable costs. In addition, even though both fixed and variable costs may be allocated, user departments may be held responsible for only the variable costs.

Comparison of direct, step, and linear algebra methods. The overhead rates determined in Exhibit 6–4 using the direct method, Exhibit 6–5 using the step method, and Exhibit 6–6 using the linear algebra method vary slightly. For the sewing department, the basis is 104 percent of direct labor costs using the direct method, 108 percent of direct labor costs using the step method, and 106 percent of direct labor costs using the linear algebra method. For the treating department, the basis is $3.75 per direct labor-hour using the direct method, $3.60 using the step method, and $3.65 using the linear algebra method. The fact that these results are so close should not lead to the conclusion that the

EXHIBIT 6–6

HEAGY COMPANY
Estimated Departmental Factory Overhead
Linear Algebra Method of Allocation
For Year 19–

	Service departments			Production departments		
	Materials handling	Repairs and maintenance	Building and grounds	Sewing	Treating	Total
Department rendering service:						
Materials handling	—	23%	20%	25%	32%	100%
Repairs and maintenance	—	—	60%	13%	27%	100%
Building and grounds	16%	10%	—	42%	32%	100%
Departmental overhead before allocation						
of service departments	$43,500	$36,250	$35,350	$112,100	$104,800	$332,000
Materials handling department allocation . .	(56,468)	12,988	11,293	14,117	18,070	
Repairs and maintenance department						
allocation	—	(57,343)	34,406	7,455	15,482	
Building and grounds department						
allocation	12,968	8,105	(81,049)	34,040	25,936	
Total overhead	–0–	–0–	–0–	$167,712	$164,288	$332,000
Allocation bases to apply						
overhead to production						
Direct labor cost				$157,500		
Direct labor-hours					45,000	
Total overhead rates				106% of direct labor cost	$3.65 per direct labor-hour	

The three simultaneous equations to solve for the three unknowns are:
   Let M = Total costs of materials handling department
      R = Total costs of repairs and maintenance department
      B = Total costs of building and grounds department
  (1) M = $\$43,500 + .16B$
  (2) R = $\$36,250 + .23M + .10B$
  (3) B = $\$35,350 + .20M + .60R$
Substituting in (1)
    M = $\$43,500 + .16\ (\$35,350 + .20M + .60R)$
    M = $\$43,500 + \$5,656 + .032M + .096R$
  $.968\ M$ = $\$49,156 + .096R$
    M = $\$50,780.99 + .0991736R$
Substituting in (2)
  R = $\$36,250 + .23(\$50,780.99 + .0991736R) + .10\ [\$35,350 + .20\ (\$50,780.99 + .0991736R) + .60R]$
  R = $\$36,250 + \$11,679.63 + .02281R + .10\ (35,350 + 10,156.20 + .019835R + .60R)$
  R = $\$36,250 + \$11,679.63 + .02281R + .10\ (45,506.20 + .619835R)$
  R = $\$36,250 + \$11,679.63 + .02281R + 4,550.62 + .0619835R$
  R = $\$52,480.25 + .0847935R$
 $.9152065R$ = $\$52,480.25$
  R = $\$57,342.52$ or rounded to $\$57,343$
Substituting in (3)
  B = $\$35,350 + .20[\$50,780.99 + .0991736(\$57,342.52)] + .60\ (\$57,342.52)$
  B = $\$35,350 + .20(50,780.99 + 5,686.86) + 34,405.51$
  B = $\$35,350 + .20(56,467.85) + 34,405.51$
  B = $\$35,350 + 11,293.57 + 34,405.51$
  B = $\$81,049$
Substituting in (1)
  M = $\$43,500 + .16(\$81,049)$
  M = $\$43,500 + 12,968$
  M = $\$56,468$

allocation method chosen makes little difference in other situations. The three exhibits were purposely kept simple using a limited number of departments with small expenses.

ISSUES SURROUNDING ALLOCATIONS

Absorption and variable costing

Under *conventional, full,* or *absorption costing,* both fixed and variable overhead costs are applied to production. Under the method of *variable costing,* which is also referred to as *direct costing,* only variable overhead is included as a product cost because fixed costs are expensed in the period in which they are incurred. The two methods result in assigning different costs to inventory. Chapter 16 describes variable costing concepts in detail. Full-cost allocations have one advantage in that even though the user department lacks control over fixed costs, management does become more aware of the costs incurred for the benefits received from the service departments.

Allocating actual costs. Whether absorption or variable costing is used, there is a danger in allocating the service department's *actual* costs to user departments each month. In allocating actual service department cost, actual service-hours are divided into the service department's total actual costs to arrive at one rate. This allocation merely passes any cost inefficiencies of the service department to user departments. In addition, because unit fixed costs vary inversely with hours incurred, the allocation rate depends upon how many hours other departments used the center. An additional weakness is that the service department rate is not known in advance and is not subject to control by the department managers requesting the services. To correct for this, the accountant should use estimated rates based on variable budgets for charging departments for service rendered. Budgeted costs rather than actual costs should be used to determine the allocation rate; this way, cost inefficiencies will be properly borne by the service department.

Allocating standard costs. Direct costs of service and production departments can also be controlled at the service department level through use of budgets and standard costs. The advantage of allocating the costs of one department to others is that it causes department heads to question whether they really need the service before requesting it. If the department manager knows he or she will not be charged for the service requested, the manager may request an excessive amount of service, since there is little incentive to control costs. After it is agreed, therefore, that a service department's costs should be allocated to users, the next question is what type of costs should be allocated. Obviously, one department manager should not be held responsible for other departments' inefficiencies; consequently, the standard or budgeted costs should be allocated. By knowing the service department rate in advance, department managers can better assess their requests.

Behavioral aspects of allocation.   Unfortunately, if cost center managers have the responsibility for choosing a service, establishing a service department rate may cause them to refrain from using the service when needed. For example, if department managers realize that they will be charged for asking the systems designers to evaluate and improve their information flow, they may avoid this expense and thereby retain an outdated and inefficient system. If management wants to encourage the use of such services, it may not allocate service department cost to the user. If, on the other hand, management feels that there is a danger that departments may excessively use some service, the service department charges should be known in advance, and service department costs should be allocated to user departments. For example, some companies have found that when a new computer is installed, many department managers create new reports which they believe the computer can quickly prepare. To ensure that the reports are actually needed, many companies establish a rate per computer hour. Cost-benefit analyses must be performed to ensure proper utilization of computer time.

Plantwide versus departmental rates

The exhibits thus far have calculated departmental overhead rates. In a small plant with production moving through all departments, however, a single plantwide rate may be appropriate. Another consideration in selecting a plantwide rate or departmental rates is whether all departments use similar operating processes, direct labor, and machines. If all products do not go through the same departments, different rates must be calculated for each department. The procedure for applying factory overhead is the same whether single or multiple departmental rates are used.

As can be seen in Exhibit 6–7, if one order receives more services from one department than from another, the use of the plantwide rate will result in an inaccurate allocation of costs to the jobs. Order No. 1 required only two hours of machine work from the mixing department, which incurs less budgeted factory overhead, while it was a heavy user of the machines in the fabricating department. The plantwide rate resulted in $291 overhead being applied; if, instead, the departmental rates had been used, a total of $373.20 overhead would have been applied. The use of the departmental rates reflects the difference in time spent in each department, since Order No. 1 utilized two hours of mixing department machines and eight hours of fabricating department machines. As illustrated above, departmental rates are usually needed so the different jobs bear their share of factory overhead; otherwise, the application of overhead using a plantwide rate may be incorrect.

EXHIBIT 6–7

JENKINS MANUFACTURING COMPANY
Departmental Overhead Rates Contrasted to a
Single Plantwide Overhead Rate

| | Departmental rates | | Plantwide rate |
	Mixing	Fabricating	
Budgeted overhead:			
Indirect material	$ 400	$ 600	$ 1,000
Indirect labor	2,000	7,000	9,000
Depreciation.	1,000	5,000	6,000
Rent.	4,000	8,000	12,000
Insurance.	300	800	1,100
Total budgeted overhead	$7,700	$21,400	$29,100
Machine-hours	500	500	1,000
Rate per machine-hour	$15.40	$ 42.80	$ 29.10
Overhead application:			
To Order No. 1:			
Mixing (two machine-hours @ $15.40)			$ 30.80
Fabricating (eight machine-hours @ $42.80). . .			342.40
Total overhead applied using departmental rates			$373.20
Plantwide (10 hours @ $29.10).			291.00

Applying factory overhead.   After the departmental rate is determined, it can be used to apply overhead to each job, as shown in Exhibit 6–8. Factory overhead is applied to jobs and departments after the direct material and direct labor charges are recorded. The amount of overhead can then be entered on the job order cost sheet so the total cost of the job is known when the job is completed. The estimated factory overhead rate is applied to the allocation base, and the overhead applied is entered on the job order cost sheet. For example, the same job order cost sheet used for direct material (Exhibit 3–2) and direct labor (Exhibit 4–8) is shown in Exhibit 6–8.

Factory overhead is applied to Job No. 1212 using the following rates calculated in Exhibit 6–5: sewing department, 108 percent of direct labor costs; treating department, $3.60 per direct labor-hour. Factory overhead of $1,404 (108 percent × $1,300) is applied to the sewing department. It is assumed that 200 direct labor-hours were incurred in the treating department. Using the overhead application rate of $3.60 per direct labor-hour, the factory overhead applied in the treating department is $720 (200 hours × $3.60). The entry to record the overhead applied to Job No. 1212 is:

Work in Process Inventory—Job No. 1212 . . . .   2,124.00
    Factory Overhead Control. 2,124.00

As shown above, overhead is applied before the job is transferred to finished

EXHIBIT 6–8

JOB ORDER COST SHEET

JONES MANUFACTURING COMPANY

Customer: Job No. 1212

Douglass Warehouse, Inc.   Product   144″ # 8 cloth (144 rolls)

309 North 12th Street   Date required   1/23/19X1

Murray, Kentucky 42071   Date started   1/16/19X1

                                     Date completed   1/20/19X1

For stock

SEWING DEPARTMENT

Direct materials			Direct labor		Factory overhead		
Date	Requisition number	Amount	Date	Amount	Date	Basis	Amount
1/16/19X1	911	$6,455.55	1/18/19X1	$1,300.00	1/20/19X1	Direct labor cost	$1,404.00

TREATING DEPARTMENT

Direct materials			Direct labor		Factory overhead		
Date	Requisition number	Amount	Date	Amount	Date	Basis	Amount
1/18/19X1	914	$37.50	1/19/19X1	$1,000.00	1/20/19X1	Direct labor-hours	$720.00

SUMMARY

	Sewing department	Treating department	Total	
Selling price				$20,000.00
Direct materials costs.	$6,455.55	$ 37.50	$6,493.05	
Direct labor costs.	1,300.00	1,000.00	2,300.00	
Factory overhead applied.	1,404.00	720.00	2,124.00	10,917.05
Gross margin.				$ 9,082.95

goods inventory. However, a job does not have to be finished for overhead to be applied. To have proper matching of actual factory overhead and absorbed or applied overhead, factory overhead must be applied to all jobs (both completed and incompleted) worked on during the period.

After Job No. 1212 is finished and sold, the summary at the bottom of the job order cost sheet is completed. The entry to record the transfer of Job No. 1212 to Finished Goods Inventory is as follows:

Finished Goods Inventory 10,917.05
    Work in Process—Job No. 1212. . . . .   10,917.05

Since factory overhead application rates are generally established on a departmental basis to provide for better control of factory overhead costs, actual factory overhead must also be determined for each department or cost center. Since the subsidiary factory overhead ledger accounts are usually set up by individual expense item, a work sheet similar in format to one of those shown in Exhibits 6–4, or 6–5, or 6–6 should be used to determine actual departmental costs. Because estimated factory overhead rates are not usually established for service departments, actual service department costs should be allocated to the producing departments. After this is done, the actual factory overhead for each department can be compared to the factory overhead applied by each department. The difference between actual and applied overhead represents the over- or underapplied factory overhead.

SPENDING AND VOLUME VARIANCES

Overhead standards are introduced in Chapter 11. However, overhead variances can be computed even if standards are not used, as long as overhead application rates are employed. Two variances—spending and volume—represent the over- or underapplied amount. Remember from Chapter 2, if there is a debit balance in the Factory Overhead Control account the overhead has been underapplied; if there is a credit balance, overhead has been overapplied.

The calculations for the spending and volume variances are made for Cost Center A using the data from Exhibits 5–8 and 5–9. The data are repeated below:

$$\text{Budget formula} = \$6.75 \text{ per hour} + \$1,500 \text{ per month}$$
$$\text{Budgeted capacity} = 2,000 \text{ hours}$$
$$\text{Fixed overhead rate per hour} = \frac{\$1,500 \text{ budgeted fixed overhead}}{2,000 \text{ budgeted hours}}$$
$$= \$0.75 \text{ per hour}$$
$$\text{Total overhead rate per hour} = \$7.50 \ (\$6.75 \text{ variable} + \$0.75 \text{ fixed})$$
$$\text{Actual direct labor-hours} = 1,800 \text{ hours}$$

Actual total overhead costs:	
Indirect material	$ 3,900
Indirect labor	3,300
Repair supplies.	5,600
Insurance expired	1,050
Depreciation.	480
Total	$14,330

Exhibit 6–9 contains the computation of the spending and volume variances and indicates that the total of the spending variance and the volume variance equals the over- or underapplied overhead. Note that the total overhead spending variance is the same as determined in Exhibit 5–9 when the

EXHIBIT 6–9

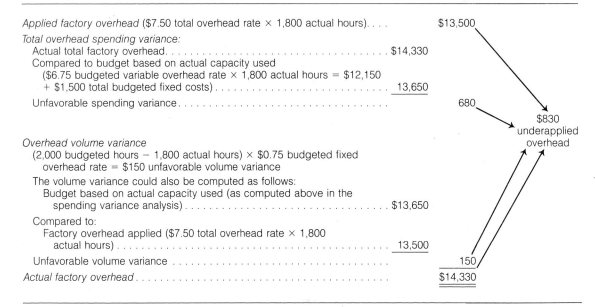

Applied factory overhead ($7.50 total overhead rate × 1,800 actual hours). . . .	$13,500

Total overhead spending variance:
  Actual total factory overhead. $14,330
  Compared to budget based on actual capacity used
    ($6.75 budgeted variable overhead rate × 1,800 actual hours = $12,150
    + $1,500 total budgeted fixed costs). 13,650
  Unfavorable spending variance.   680

$830
underapplied
overhead

Overhead volume variance
  (2,000 budgeted hours − 1,800 actual hours) × $0.75 budgeted fixed
  overhead rate = $150 unfavorable volume variance
The volume variance could also be computed as follows:
  Budget based on actual capacity used (as computed above in the
  spending variance analysis). $13,650
Compared to:
  Factory overhead applied ($7.50 total overhead rate × 1,800
  actual hours). 13,500
Unfavorable volume variance   150
Actual factory overhead. $14,330

---

individual expense items were compared to the variable budget adjusted to actual capacity. The spending variance is also called the budget variance and is due to incurring higher or lower costs on overhead items than originally estimated. Any time actual overhead is less than budgeted overhead adjusted to actual capacity, the spending variance is favorable. Conversely, an unfavorable spending variance results when the actual overhead exceeds the budgeted overhead for the actual capacity attained.

The volume variance is also called the idle capacity variance and is due to activity or volume factors. If actual production-hours exceed the planned or budgeted hours or units, the volume variance is favorable. On the other hand, if there are idle capacity hours (an unfavorable volume variance), less volume was used than planned. After the variances are computed, a study should be made to determine the cause of any significant variance.

The spending and volume variance may be set up in a ledger account as follows:

Total Overhead Spending Variance.   680
Overhead Volume Variance   150
    Factory Overhead Control   830

An alternative treatment is not to establish ledger accounts for the variances and still receive the same benefit from the analysis as to their cause. This is the important factor—not whether they are journalized. This closes out the Factory Overhead Control account balance which must be done at the end of the accounting period. Recall from Chapter 2 that the debit side of the Factory Overhead Control account shows actual costs incurred and the credit side shows the amount of overhead applied, with the balance representing the amount of over- or underapplied overhead. This, in turn, equals the spending and volume variances.

Disposition of over- or underapplied overhead

This over- or underapplied overhead amount may have been transferred into spending and volume variance (in a journal entry similar to the one above). It may be:

1. Treated as a period cost and charged to Cost of Goods Sold or directly to Revenue and Expense Summary.
2. Prorated to Work in Process Inventory, Finished Goods Inventory, and Cost of Goods Sold.

If spending and volume variances have been recorded in a ledger account and are not material, the entry would be the following using the data previously illustrated.

```
Cost of Goods Sold . . . . . . . . . . . . . . . . . . . . . . . . . . . . . . . . . . . . . . . .   830
    Total Overhead Spending Variance . . . . . . . . . . . . . . . . . . . . . . .          680
    Overhead Volume Variance . . . . . . . . . . . . . . . . . . . . . . . . . . . . . .          150
```

If, instead, the variances are not recorded, the entry becomes the following:

```
Cost of Goods Sold . . . . . . . . . . . . . . . . . . . . . . . . . . . . . . . . . . . . . . . .   830
    Factory Overhead Control . . . . . . . . . . . . . . . . . . . . . . . . . . . . . . . .          830
```

The Factory Overhead Control ledger account is now closed out. Theoretically, the overhead previously applied to the jobs worked on during this period should be corrected if there is a significant over- or underapplied variance, since the estimated overhead rate was not as large as (if there is underapplied overhead) or was larger than (if there is overapplied overhead) the actual rate which was determined at the end of the year. If this reasoning is followed, the over- or underapplied overhead is allocated to Work in Process Inventory, Finished Goods Inventory, and Cost of Goods Sold based on the proportional relationship of unadjusted factory overhead in these accounts.

Assume that the following accounts have these end-of-period balances of unadjusted factory overhead: Work in Process Inventory, $2,800; Finished Goods Inventory, $3,500; and Cost of Goods Sold, $7,200. With these balances, the $830 underapplied factory overhead would be significant and should be allocated as follows on the basis of $13,500 total unadjusted factory overhead balances ($2,800 Work in Process + $3,500 Finished Goods + $7,200 Cost of Goods Sold):

Work in Process Inventory $\left(\dfrac{\$2,800}{\$13,500} \times \$830\right)$ 172

Finished Goods Inventory $\left(\dfrac{\$3,500}{\$13,500} \times \$830\right)$ 215

Cost of Goods Sold $\left(\dfrac{\$7,200}{\$13,500} \times \$830\right)$ 443

Factory Overhead Control   830

(A further discussion of this topic appears in Chapter 11.)

If the annual overhead variance is significant, current Internal Revenue Service (IRS) regulations require that inventories include an allocated portion. If the overhead variance is not significant, an allocation is not required unless such allocation is necessary for financial accounting purposes. Volume variances can be expensed according to IRS regulations.

As previously indicated, the reliability of the factory overhead rate depends upon the accuracy of the estimates used for factory overhead costs and the allocation base. During the period, if it becomes evident that conditions have changed and the estimates are grossly in error, management must decide whether to change the factory overhead application rate or retain the incorrect rate and report a large over- or underapplied variance. In deciding whether to change the overhead rate, the company should investigate the number of jobs completed and the amount of clerical effort involved in revising the calculations for overhead previously applied. The company may decide, instead, to apply the revised overhead rate on a prospective basis to jobs subsequently finished.

COST ACCOUNTING STANDARDS

In addition to the aspects of overhead cost accounting discussed in this chapter and the previous one, accountants may be required to meet the regulations established by the Cost Accounting Standards Board (CASB).

CAS 402

One of the first standards issued by the Cost Accounting Standards Board (CASB) was Part 402 titled *Consistency in Allocating Costs Incurred for the Same Purpose.* The intent of this standard is to require that each type of cost is allocated only once and on only one basis to any contract or other cost objective. The criteria for determining the allocation of costs to a product, contract, or other cost objective should be the same for all similar objectives. Adherence to these cost-accounting concepts is necessary to guard against the overcharging of some cost objectives and to prevent double counting. According to CAS 402, double counting occurs most commonly when cost items are allocated directly to a cost objective without eliminating like cost items from indirect cost pools allocated to that cost objective. CAS 402 requires that all costs incurred for the same purpose, in like circumstances, are either direct costs only or indirect costs only with respect to final cost objectives. No final cost objective shall have allocated to it as an indirect cost any cost, if other costs incurred for the same purpose, in like circumstances, have been included as a direct cost of that or any other final cost objective.

CAS 410

Later, CASB issued Part 410, *Allocation of Business Unit General and Administrative Expenses to Final Cost Objectives,* with the purpose of providing criteria for the allocation of business-unit general and administrative expenses to business-unit final cost objectives based on their beneficial or causal relationship. As stated in CAS 410, these expenses represent the cost of the management and administration of the business unit as a whole. Criteria are also provided for the allocation of home office expenses of a segment to the cost objectives of that segment. It is felt that the standard increases the likelihood of achieving objectivity in the allocation of expenses to final cost objectives and comparability of cost data among contractors in similar circumstances. CAS 410 requires that business unit general and administrative expenses be grouped in a separate indirect cost pool which is allocated only to final cost objectives. In addition, the general and administrative expense pool of a business unit for a cost accounting period is allocated to final cost objectives of that cost accounting period by means of a cost input base representing the total activity of the business unit. An exception is made when the allocation of the expense pool to any particular final cost objectives involves benefits significantly different from the benefits accruing to other final cost objectives which are determined by special allocation. The cost input base selected is the one which best represents the total activity of a typical cost accounting period.

CAS 416

In September 1978, the Cost Accounting Board issued CAS 416, *Accounting for Insurance Costs.* The purpose of this standard is to provide criteria for the measurement of insurance costs, the assignment of such costs to cost accounting periods, and their allocation to cost objectives. According to the standard, the amount of insurance cost assigned to a cost accounting period is the projected average loss for that period plus insurance administration expenses in that period. The allocation of insurance costs to cost objectives is based on the beneficial or causal relationship between the insurance costs and the benefiting or causing cost objectives.

CAS 418

In May 1980, the Cost Accounting Standards Board issued CAS 418, *Allocation of Direct and Indirect Costs,* intended to provide for consistent determination of direct and indirect costs and to provide criteria for the accumulation of indirect costs, including service center and overhead costs, in indirect costs pools. A further purpose is to provide guidance in the selection of allocation measures based on the beneficial or causal relationship between an indirect cost pool and cost objectives. According to the standard, a business unit should have a written statement of accounting policies and practices for classifying costs as direct or indirect that is consistently applied. Further, indirect costs are accumulated in indirect costs pools which are homogenous. In addition, pooled costs are allocated to cost objectives in reasonable proportion to the beneficial or causal relationship of the pooled costs to cost objectives, as specified in the standard.

CAS 420

In September 1979, the board issued CAS 420 intended to provide criteria for the accumulation of independent research and development costs and bid and proposal costs, and for the allocation of such costs to cost objectives based on the beneficial or causal relationship between such costs and cost objectives. The standard requires that the basic unit for the identification and accumulation of independent research and development costs and bid and proposal cost is the individual project. These independent research and development and bid and proposal projects consist of all allocable costs, except business-unit general and administrative expenses. The standard further requires that bid and proposal costs incurred in a cost accounting period not be assigned to any other cost accounting period. In addition, independent research and development costs incurred in a cost accounting period are not assigned to any other cost accounting period, except as permitted under the provisions of existing laws, regulations, and other controlling factors. According to the standard, independent research and development and bid and proposal project costs should include costs which, if incurred in like circumstances for a final cost objective, would be treated as direct costs of the final cost objective and the overhead costs of productive activities and other indirect costs related to the project based on the contractor's cost accounting practice or applicable cost accounting standards for allocation of indirect costs. The cost pools for a segment consist of the project costs plus allocable home office independent research and development and bid and proposal costs.

SUMMARY

Before calculating factory overhead application rates, several important decisions must be made. First, management must decide which capacity level to adopt by weighing the practicability of the approach against setting a high level so that the fixed overhead per product unit is reduced. Theoretical capacity is usually not used, since it makes no allowance for production interruptions. Often, expected actual capacity is such a short-range approach that it is not considered feasible either. Usually the choice of capacity level is between the practical capacity and normal capacity. Because of its impact on the company, the decision concerning which capacity approach to adopt is major and should be made jointly by top management.

Because the product unit is routed only through production departments, estimated factory overhead rates are often established only for production departments. The overhead costs of service departments, in which no direct production work is performed, are allocated to production departments. In these allocations, the direct costs of the service and production departments are traced to their respective cost centers. The indirect costs must then be allocated based on causal or on cause-and-benefit relationships. After the costs of the service and production departments are determined, the service departments' direct and indirect costs are allocated. Three methods were illustrated in this chapter: the direct, the step, and the linear algebra (reciproal) methods. While the direct method is the simplest, it ignores allocating costs for services rendered to other service departments. Even though the step method takes into account that a service department may render services to both production and service departments, it does not consider the reciprocal benefits and cost allocations between service departments. The linear algebra method considers these reciprocal services and makes cost allocations between service departments. Despite the detailed computations involved in many cost allocations, precision is sometimes lacking because it is difficult to find a completely valid cause-and-effect relationship between the allocation base and overhead costs incurred.

After all factory costs have been allocated to the production departments, the factory overhead application rate can be determined. Five bases were suggested for allocating factory overhead costs: units of production, direct labor-hours, direct labor costs, machine-hours, and direct materials costs. The reliability of the factory overhead rate depends upon the accuracy of the factory overhead costs estimated as well as on the accuracy of the allocation base.

The overhead application rate is used throughout the period to apply factory overhead. At the end of the period, the difference between actual factory overhead and applied factory overhead reflects the over- or underapplied amount, which can be further analyzed as spending and volume variances. This variance analysis provides a springboard for further analysis of the causes of the variances to achieve better control over factory overhead costs.

IMPORTANT TERMS AND CONCEPTS

Cost allocations, distributions, assignments, and apportionments

Theoretical (maximum or ideal) capacity

Practical capacity

Normal capacity

Expected actual capacity

Idle capacity

Excess capacity

Unit of production basis

Direct labor cost or dollars basis

Direct labor-hours basis

Machine-hours basis

Material costs basis

Prime cost basis

Production departments

Service departments

Direct costs

Attachability and traceability

Indirect or common costs

Direct method of allocation

Step method of allocation

Linear algebra (reciprocal) allocation method

Full, conventional, or absorption costing

Variable costing or direct costing

Over- or underapplied factory overhead

Spending variance

Volume variance

CAS 402, 410, 416, 418, 420

PROBLEM FOR SELF-STUDY

Lottie Key Company's chief accountant has accumulated the following annual estimated departmental overhead data:

Service departments:	
General factory	$ 40,000
Storeroom	26,000
Repair shop.	20,000
Producing departments:	
Mixing	50,000
Finishing	80,000
	$216,000

Below is the information needed to make reapportionments. General factory is closed out first on the basis of square feet occupied. Storeroom expenses are prorated next, based on estimated requisitions to be handled for the departments. Repair shop expenses are closed out last, based on the number of estimated maintenance hours to be spent in departments.

Departments	Square feet	Material requisitions	Maintenance hours	Direct labor-hours
General factory	6,000	1,000	500	
Storeroom.	1,000	2,000	1,100	
Repair shop	3,000	2,000	600	
Mixing	7,000	2,000	6,000	50,000
Finishing.	9,000	3,000	4,000	30,000
	26,000	10,000	12,200	80,000

Required:

a. Use the direct method and allocate service department costs. Develop overhead rates as a rate per direct labor-hour for the mixing and finishing departments.
b. Use the step method and prepare the same analysis required in (a) above.

Solution

LOTTIE KEY COMPANY

	General factory	Storeroom	Repair shop	Mixing	Finishing
a. *Direct method*					
Departmental overhead.	$40,000	$26,000	$20,000	$50,000	$ 80,000
General factory $\frac{40,000}{16,000}$ = $2.50.	(40,000)			17,500	22,500
Storeroom $\frac{\$26,000}{5,000}$ = $5.20.		(26,000)		10,400	15,600
Repair shop $\frac{\$20,000}{10,000}$ = $2.00			(20,000)	12,000	8,000
Total production department costs				$89,900	$126,100
Divided by direct labor-hours.				50,000	30,000
Overhead rate per direct labor-hour. . . .				$1.798	$4.203

	General factory	Storeroom	Repair shop	Mixing	Finishing
b. *Step method:*					
Departmental overhead............	$40,000	$26,000	$20,000	$ 50,000	$ 80,000
General factory $\dfrac{\$40,000}{20,000} = \$2$	(40,000)	2,000	6,000	14,000	18,000
		$28,000			
Storeroom $\dfrac{\$28,000}{7,000} = \$4$		(28,000)	8,000	8,000	12,000
			$34,000		
Repair shop $\dfrac{\$34,000}{10,000} = \$3.40$			(34,000)	20,400	13,600
Total production department costs				$92,400	$123,600
Divided by direct labor-hours.........				50,000	30,000
Overhead rate per direct labor-hour....				$1.848	$4.12

Note that in the direct method only data for the two producing departments, mixing and finishing, are used as a denominator for applying the service department costs. This is because in the direct method, service department costs are allocated directly to production departments.

Also note in the step method that after a service department is closed, its data are omitted from the denominator in arriving at other service department costs rates. In addition, the data for the service department being closed is also omitted in arriving at the service department rate.

REVIEW QUESTIONS

1. Is there any difference in allocating indirect costs to departments and allocating service department costs to producing departments?

2. Discuss four different capacity concepts that can be used in budgeting activity. What factors would you study before choosing one of these levels?

3. If the company uses cost-plus contracts extensively in a business that is seasonal or cyclical, what capacity level would be most appropriate? Why is it necessary to specify the activity level at which management budgets operations?

4. Contrast idle capacity and excess capacity.

5. List five bases for expressing the capacity level.

6. When would it be most appropriate to use the direct labor cost basis as the means of applying factory overhead?

7. Why are direct material costs generally not a valid base for applying factory overhead? Under what conditions would it be appropriate to use direct material costs as an allocation base?

8. Distinguish between production and service departments. Give examples of each type.

9. Distinguish between direct and indirect costs. Give examples of each.

10. Give three methods for allocating service department costs.

11. Can overhead variances only be computed in a standard cost system? Explain your answer.

12. What factors would you consider in determining whether to adopt department rates for applying factory overhead rather than using a single plantwide rate?

13. Define spending and volume variances. How is each computed?

14. What factors could cause a company to have both unfavorable spending and volume variances?

15. In interviewing several manufacturing firms operating in the same industry, you find that Company A's factory overhead application rate is $2 per direct labor-hour while Company B's rate is $2.50 per direct labor-hour. Can you conclude that Company A is more efficient? Why or why not?

16. During interviews you determine that Company C has a favorable volume variance, while Company D, which is of like size and operations, has an unfavorable volume variance. In stating the cause of the idle capacity variance, can you conclude that Company C is more efficient? Why or why not?

EXERCISES

E6–1. Spending and volume variances

Brown Company's budget formula is $93,000 fixed overhead + a variable rate of $5 per machine-hour, yielding a total application rate of $8. Actual machine-hours for the period were 31,800; actual factory overhead of $254,800 was reported.

Required:

Determine the spending and volume variances.

E6–2. Actual and applied overhead relationship (AICPA adapted)

Dickey Company had total underapplied overhead of $15,000. Additional information is as follows:

Variable overhead:	
Applied based on standard direct labor-hours allowed	$42,000
Budgeted based on standard direct labor-hours	38,000
Fixed overhead:	
Applied based on standard direct labor-hours allowed	30,000
Budgeted based on standard direct labor-hours	27,000

Required:

What is the actual total overhead?

E6–3. Spending and volume variances

Oliver Ryder, Inc. estimates overhead for the year as follows:

	Unit cost per machine-hour	Total cost
Variable factory overhead	$6	$570,000
Fixed factory overhead	8	760,000

While production for the period reached 85 percent of the budget, actual factory overhead totaled $1,125,600.

Required:

a.   Determine over- or underapplied factory overhead.
b.   Calculate spending and volume variances.

E6–4.   Volume and spending variances

A cost accountant estimates that next year's normal capacity for the Susan Douglass Company will be 40,000 machine-hours. At this level, fixed costs are estimated at $140,000 with variable costs of $90,000. There were 41,000 actual machine-hours for the year ended February 28, 19X1, and total costs were $232,500.

Required:

a.   What is the fixed overhead rate at normal capacity?
b.   What is the total overhead rate used to apply factory overhead during the year?
c.   What is the amount of over- or underapplied factory overhead?
d.   Compute the volume variance and the spending variance for the year. Are they favorable or unfavorable? Prove your answer.

E6–5.   Departmental and plantwide overhead rates

Since the management of Penny Company is undecided whether to adopt departmental factory overhead application rates for its mixing and finishing departments or whether a plantwide rate would be adequate, they ask your advice. You obtain the following budgeted overhead for each department and data for one job so both approaches can be evaluated.

	Department	
	Mixing	Finishing
Supplies	$ 800	$1,100
Superintendent's salaries	1,200	1,400
Indirect labor	1,300	2,100
Depreciation	400	1,000
Repairs.	800	890
Insurance	180	260
	$4,680	$6,750
Total direct labor-hours	600	250
Direct labor-hours on Job No. 528	20	3

Required:

a.   Prepare departmental and plantwide overhead rates. Then apply overhead to Job No. 528 using both approaches.
b.   Evaluate the approaches indicating which you prefer.

E6–6.   Determining overhead application rates on various bases

The following information is taken from next year's budget of the Schultz Company:

Direct materials	$160,000
Direct labor (25,000 hours).	120,000
Marketing managers' salaries	32,000
Factory supplies	22,000
Office supplies	16,000
Factory inspection	20,000
Administrative wages	45,000
Factory utilities	15,000
Rent—Factory machinery	9,000
Rent—Office machinery	6,000
Depreciation—Factory furniture and fixtures	14,000
Depreciation—Office furniture and fixtures	5,000
	$464,000

Machine-hours are budgeted at 20,000.

Required:

a. Rounding rates to two decimal places, determine factory overhead application rates on the following bases:
    (1) Machine-hours.
    (2) Direct materials cost.
    (3) Direct labor-hours.
    (4) Direct labor cost.
b. Determine the amount of overhead applied to Job No. 431 having direct material costing $7,500, direct labor (1,200 hours) costing $4,600, and 1,200 machine-hours using each of the four rates computed in *a.*

E6–7.   Developing application rates using the linear algebra (reciprocal) method

Cindy Butcher Company has prepared overhead budgets for the production and service departments (before allocation) as follows:

Employee relations	$ 15,000
General factory administration	50,000
Fabricating	275,000
Finishing	180,000
	$520,000

The data below are needed to determine the percentage of service received from each service department. The company uses number of employees for allocating employee relations department costs and square footage for general factory administration.

Departments	No. of employees	Square footage	Direct labor dollars
Employee relations	8	9,000	
General factory administration	30	2,000	
Fabricating	150	33,000	$ 700,395
Finishing	120	18,000	512,055
Total	308	62,000	$1,212,450

Required:

Using linear algebra, determine the overhead application rates for the production departments per direct labor dollar. Round to whole dollars.

E6–8. Error in application rate

You have been asked to review the cost records of Saber, Inc. and to make any changes needed to correct errors in the financial statements of March 31, 19X1. Saber, Inc. started operations on March 1, 19X1, with no beginning inventories. Factory overhead costs are applied at 95 percent of direct labor cost. The determination was:

$$\frac{\$1,472,500 \text{ factory overhead costs budgeted}}{\$1,550,000 \text{ direct labor cost budgeted}} = 95 \text{ percent}$$

Work in process inventory of March 31 was fully complete for materials and one-third complete for conversion costs. Costs recorded for March were:

Direct material	$84,000
Direct labor	93,500

When the departmental budgets were prepared for the year 19X1, the following were classified as administrative expenses.

Factory accountants' salaries	$ 72,500
Payroll taxes applicable to factory.	135,000
Depreciation on building and equipment	300,000

Factory operations utilize 60 percent of the building and its equipment. Financial statements prepared on March 31 showed the following:

Work in process inventory, March 31 (15,000 units)	$ 52,500
Finished goods inventory, March 31 (7,500 units)	45,000
Cost of sales for March (30,000 units)	180,000

Required:

Determine the corrected balances on March 31 for:

a. Work in process inventory.
b. Finished goods inventory.
c. Cost of goods sold.

E6–9. Journal entries to record spending and volume variances

Hutson Manufacturing Company provides you with the following data concerning their operations for the year ended December 31, 19–.

Predetermined variable overhead rate per machine-hour.	$3.00
Predetermined total overhead rate per direct labor-hour.	$5.10
Budgeted capacity	20,000 direct labor-hours
Actual capacity during year	19,650 direct labor-hours
Actual factory overhead costs	$99,700

Required:

a. Compute the amount of overhead applied during the year and prepare a summary journal entry to record this.
b. Determine the amount of over- or underapplied overhead.
c. Compute the factory overhead spending and volume variance.

d. Prepare the journal entries required to record the variances and to close the Factory Overhead Control account; close variances to the Cost of Goods Sold account.

E6–10. Direct and step method for developing overhead rates

Calvery Company has prepared overhead budgets for the production and service departments (before allocation) as follows:

Utilities.	$ 19,220
Employee relations.	6,842
General factory administration.	59,060
Materials storeroom	1,185
Repairs and maintenance.	71,238
Fabricating.	133,100
Finishing	141,000
	$431,645

Below is the information needed to make the reapportionments:

Departments	Kilo-watt-hours	No. of em-ployees	Square footage	Material requi-sitions	Labor repair-hours	Direct labor cost
Utilities.	250	10	200	60	1,500	
Employee relations	200	5	500	20	300	
General factory administration. . . .	300	50	300	10	100	
Material storeroom	500	25	1,000	—	200	
Repairs and maintenance	400	10	1,500	80	—	
Fabricating.	1,200	175	20,000	200	8,000	$272,940
Finishing	3,600	150	30,000	300	7,000	283,675
	6,450	425	53,500	670	17,100	$556,615

Required:

a. Use the direct method and allocate service department costs. Develop overhead rates as a percentage of direct labor costs for the fabricating and finishing departments.
b. Use the step method and prepare the same analysis required in *a* above. Allocate service department costs in the following sequence and on the following bases:
   (1) Utilities—kilowatt-hours.
   (2) Employee relations—number of employees.
   (3) General factory administration—square footage.
   (4) Materials storeroom—material requisitions.
   (5) Repairs and maintenance—labor repair hours.

E6–11. High-low, application rates, and variances

Jasper, Inc. uses machine-hours to apply factory overhead with an operating range between 1,000 and 6,000 hours per month. A normal capacity of 4,000 hours will be used for applying factory overhead. Fixed costs per month amount to $24,000 while the strictly variable factory overhead costs total $3 per hour. In addition, semivariable factory overhead costs for 6,000 machine-hours total $32,000, while those for 1,000 hours are budgeted to be $20,000.

Required:

a. Separate the semivariable costs into their fixed and variable components using the high-low method.
b. Compute the fixed and variable factory overhead application rates.
c. Determine spending and volume variances for a month in which 5,000 hours were worked and actual factory overhead totaled $70,400. Prove your answer.
d. Calculate a bid price for a customer who approached you during the month when machine-hour capacity was 5,000. How much should be allowed for factory overhead if this special order requires 250 machine-hours?

E6–12. Objectives in selecting the overhead rate base (AICPA adapted)

Stein Company is going to use a predetermined annual factory overhead rate to charge factory overhead to products. In conjunction with this, Stein Company must decide whether to use direct labor-hours or machine-hours as the overhead rate base.

Required:

Discuss the objectives and criteria that Stein Company should use in selecting the base for its predetermined annual factory overhead rate.

PROBLEMS

P6–1. Applying overhead using various capacity concepts

Edith Garrant budgets its fixed factory overhead at $49,000; however, actual fixed factory overhead was $54,000. Management provides you with the following capacity volumes for a year.

	Direct labor-hours
Actual capacity	8,000
Practical capacity.	10,000
Normal capacity.	8,167
Expected actual capacity	7,000

Required:

a. If practical capacity is used as the basis for applying overhead, determine:
   (1) Applied rate per hour for fixed overhead.
   (2) Total fixed overhead applied.
   (3) Under- or overapplied fixed overhead.
b. If, instead, normal activity is used as the basis, determine (1) through (3) above.
c. If, instead, expected actual capacity is used as the basis, determine (1) through (3) above.
d. Discuss the effect of the capacity volume used on unit fixed and variable costs applied.
e. List at least four important factors to consider in choosing the capacity level for overhead application purposes.

P6–2. Determining application rates using the linear algebra (reciprocal) method

The controller for Michael Newman Company estimates that factory overhead will be as follows for its two producing departments and three service departments:

Mixing department $165,000
Finishing department 135,000
Repair department   35,000
Storeroom   35,000
Factory office   65,000

The controller also provides the following tabulation of the interdependence of departments:

| | Services provided by | | |
Services rendered to	Repair (percent)	Storeroom (percent)	Factory office (percent)
Mixing department.	42	52	64
Finishing department	30	30	36
Repair department.	—	8	—
Storeroom	18	—	—
Factory office	10	10	—

Required:

Round all answers to nearest dollar:

a. Determine the total estimated overhead for each of the three service departments after reciprocal transfer costs have been calculated algebraically.
b. Determine the total overhead of each producing department.
c. Determine factory overhead rates for the production departments assuming that budgeted direct labor-hours are 5,944 for mixing and 5,149 for finishing.

P6–3. Changes in application rate

Bobbie Hopkins Company uses a variable budget system and prepared the following information for 19X1:

Percent of capacity   75   88
Direct labor-hours   25,500   30,000
Variable factory overhead $114,750 $135,000
Fixed factory overhead . . . . . . $ 51,000 $ 51,000

Required:

a. If 25,500 hours are used as the budgeted normal capacity, what would the application rate be for factory overhead?
b. If, instead, 30,000 hours are used as the budgeted normal capacity, what would the application rate be for factory overhead?
c. Account for the difference in factory overhead application rates at the two capacity levels.
d. Assume that factory overhead was applied based on the 75 percent capacity level and that 24,000 hours were used for the period:
    (1) What is the budgeted factory overhead for actual capacity?
    (2) If actual factory overhead costs equal budgeted overhead for actual capacity, what is the total overhead variance and what kind of variance is it?
e. If, instead, both actual and budgeted hours were 25,500 and actual overhead was $168,000, what is the total overhead variance and what kind of variance is it?

P6–4. Basis for allocating costs of service departments (CIA adapted)

The Barnes Company has three production departments, each producing a separate product, and two service departments. For a number of years, Barnes has allocated the costs of the service departments to the production departments on the basis of annual sales revenue. In a recent audit report, the internal auditor stated that the distribution of service department costs on this basis would lead to serious inequities. It was recommended that maintenance and engineering service hours would be a better basis. For illustrative purposes, the following information was appended to the audit report.

	Service departments		Production departments		
	Maintenance	Engineering	Product A	Product B	Product C
Maintenance hours.....	—	400	800	200	200
Engineering hours	400	—	800	400	400
Department direct cost..	$12,000	$54,000	$80,000	$90,000	$50,000

Required:

a. Give *two* reasons to justify the internal auditor's criticism of using sales revenue as the basis for allocating costs of the service departments to the production departments.

b. Because the service departments perform work for each other, it is necessary to use simultaneous equations when hours are a basis for determining allocable service department costs. Calculate the engineering department's total cost after the allocation of interservice department costs but before allocation to the maintenance and production departments. Show the components of your calculations.

c. Cite a condition under which sales dollars might represent a satisfactory basis for allocating service department costs to the production departments.

P6–5. Effect of volume on unit cost

Bill Jones, supervisor of the mixing department, came screaming into the cost-accounting department when he received his monthly report. After demanding to talk with the "head bookkeeper," he was ushered into the office of Amy Well, Controller. Bill's contention was that his report should have been favorable but that something "went wrong with the accounting system and the computer must have spit out garbage this time." Before Amy could interrupt him to determine the exact problem, Bill continued by stating that he knew his per unit cost had dropped from the budgeted $5 to $4.80 per unit and that certainly looked favorable to him. Yet the plant superintendent had already scheduled a meeting with him to discuss cost overruns.

Amy was able to convince Bill that the accounting system was designed to fairly present information and that there was no computer error involved. She then obtained the following data for use in explaining the variances to Bill. Normal capacity for the department is 20,000 units per month. At this capacity, monthly fixed costs are $60,000. Bill was correct that since sales demand was above normal, the mixing department had manufactured 23,000 units last month. Assume that this increased volume was within the same relevant range and that actual fixed costs did not vary from budgeted.

Required:

Prepare a report showing the factors causing a change in cost per unit.

P6–6. Plant capacity concepts

Olive Branch Manufacturing Company produces a ball valve which is used in water systems. The company has selected normal capacity for estimating costs and for establishing the factory overhead application rate. For the December 31, 19X3, year just ended, the plant operated at only 90 percent of normal capacity. As a result, there is underapplied overhead for the year.

Olive Branch typically sells its valve for $160. However, at the beginning of 19X4, an order was received conditional on a sales price of $120. The controller is advocating that management accept the order. He mentions two factors that influence his recommendation. First, the total manufacturing cost of $130 is composed of $100 variable costs and $30 fixed costs. Second, the additional units can be manufactured within the company's practical capacity.

Required:

a.   Discuss the following capacity concepts:
     (1)   Theoretical capacity.
     (2)   Practical capacity.
     (3)   Normal capacity.
     (4)   Expected actual capacity.
b.   Discuss the financial aspects that should be analyzed before deciding whether or not to accept the order.
c.   Discuss the reason that the Factory Overhead Control account will probably reflect overapplied overhead for 19X4. Explain the disposition of any overapplied overhead.

P6–7. Calculating volume variances using practical, normal, and expected actual basis

The president of Oliphant Company has approached you for assistance in developing factory overhead application rates. Oliphant Company has been distributing actual factory overhead at the end of each month on the basis of direct labor-hours.

As a result, the hourly rate varies considerably and is of limited use in estimating prices for bidding purposes. Management believes that it is especially important to change methods before introducing a new product line.

Management and the cost accountant cannot agree on what capacity should be selected for applying factory overhead. However, they do all agree that machine-hours would be a better basis than direct labor-hours since 10 new machines have recently been purchased which will highly automate the factory. Each machine cost $40,000 and is expected to produce 12 completed units per hour. Because of rapid technology in the field, the machines have an expected life of eight years at which time their salvage value is forecasted to equal the dismantling cost. Depreciation will be computed using the straight-line method. Based on engineering studies, practical capacity for each machine for each year is 2,200 hours.

The marketing department does not believe that it can sell enough the first year to allow each machine to operate at 2,200 hours. They believe that only 216,000 units can be sold the first years, with an average of 252,000 units in later years. The cost accountant believes that this average of 252,000 units should be used as normal capacity; however, the marketing manager disagrees, believing expected actual capacity of 216,000 units should be used instead. On the other hand, the president believes practical capacity should be the basis.

Factory overhead is estimated as follows: variable $5 @ machine-hour; fixed costs excluding depreciation—$64,300 per year.

Required:

a. Calculate fixed and variable factory overhead rates per machine-hour on a practical, normal, and expected actual basis. Round to two decimal places.

b. Assuming that 216,000 units are produced next year and each machine produces 12 units per hour, determine the factory overhead applied and the volume variance under each of the three bases used in *a*.

c. Based on your findings, which basis would you advise the company to use? Explain your answer by discussing the advantages and disadvantages of the methods available.

P6–8.   Step and direct methods for developing overhead rates

The producing departments at Lisa Lewis Company are parts fabrication and assembly. The three service departments are building, administration, and engineering. Building maintains the plant facilities and the grounds. Administration is responsible for the scheduling, control, and accounting functions, while engineering plans and designs parts and procedures. Below are the annual budgets of direct charges and the budgeted operating data for all the departments.

	Building	Administration	Engineering	Parts fabrication	Assembly	Total
Indirect labor.	$400	$600	$280	$1,000	$ 800	$3,080
Indirect materials	60	130	100	400	250	940
Insurance	70	40	20	200	125	455
Depreciation	250	85	50	140	100	625
Totals	$780	$855	$450	$1,740	$1,275	$5,100
Floor space (sq. ft.).	150	200	100	600	400	1,450
No. of employees.	15	25	10	200	115	365
Engineering-hours	15	10	5	100	80	210

Required:

a. Allocate the costs of the service departments using the step method. First, allocate building based on floor space; next, administration based on number of employees; finally, engineering based on engineering-hours. Calculate factory overhead allocation rates using 800 estimated direct labor-hours for parts fabrication and 600 estimated direct labor-hours for assembly.

b. Compute an overhead allocation rate per service unit using the direct method with which no service department is charged for services provided by other service departments. Calculate factory overhead allocation rates using the same direct labor-hours as in *a*.

P6–9.   Evaluating bases to use for applying overhead

Previously, the Bretz Company has been distributing actual factory overhead to jobs at the end of each period, but found that this is not satisfactory. Since management is undecided as to which basis to adopt, they believe a study is necessary.

As a result, top management instructs the cost-accounting department to provide data so the most appropriate factory overhead rate can be developed. After studying the following annual data broken down on a monthly basis, direct labor dollars was chosen.

	Data for average month
Estimated variable factory overhead..........	$5,000
Estimated fixed factory overhead	2,500
Estimated total factory overhead	$7,500
Estimated number of units to be produced	800 units
Estimated direct labor dollars...............	$2,500
Estimated direct labor-hours................	500 hours
Estimated machine-hours...................	1,000 hours
Estimated material costs	$2,000

At the end of the first month, the job order sheets show the following:

	Job No. A1	Job No. B2	Job No. C3	Job No. D4
Beginning inventory:				
Material...........	$200	$ 700	Begun	Begun
Labor	500	900	in	in
Overhead	600	1,000	January	January
January cost:				
Material...........	$400	—	$840	$650
Labor	580	300	450	950
Overhead	?	?	?	?
Units...............	400	250	700	80
Stage of completion. . .	100%	100%	40%	80%
Machine-hours	500	200	120	340
Direct labor-hours	120	80	108	206

Job No. A1 and Job No. B2 were 20 percent complete at the beginning of the month. Actual total factory overhead for January was $7,020.

Required:

a. Using direct labor dollars as the basis, determine for January:
   (1) The factory overhead applied to each job during January.
   (2) Amount of over- or underapplied factory overhead.
   (3) Spending and volume variances.
b. The president is having second thoughts concerning the choice of direct labor dollars as the basis and asks that you prepare the analyses in *a* if instead the following were used as the basis:
   (1) Units produced.
   (2) Direct labor-hours.
   (3) Machine-hours.
   (4) Material cost.
c. Would you advise the president to change to another basis? Why or why not?

P6–10.   Complete cycle of developing rates, distributing actual service department expense, and calculating spending and volume variances

The following indirect factory overhead costs were budgeted for the Ethel Elizabeth Company for the year ended December 31, 19X1. The F or V notation indicates whether each cost is fixed or variable. The allocation bases are also given.

Indirect costs	Amount	Fixed or variable	Allocation base
Depreciation of factory building....	$10,000	F	Floor space
Factory superintendent's salary....	20,000	F	Number of employees
Insurance on machinery.........	1,600	F	Investment in machinery
Power costs.................	40,000	V	Kilowatt-hours

In addition to these indirect costs, direct costs were budgeted for the three service departments (factory office, maintenance, and materials storeroom) and the three production departments (mixing, assembly, and finishing) as shown in Exhibit P 6–10.

EXHIBIT P 6–10

ETHEL ELIZABETH COMPANY

Direct costs	Factory office	Mainte- nance	Materials storeroom	Mixing	Assembly	Finishing	Total	F/V
Fuel, heat, and light......	$ 645	$1,763	$1,000	$ 480	$ 690	$ 570	$ 5,148	V
Water.................	140	220	175	285	475	705	2,000	V
Indirect material.........	215	180	190	1,200	1,600	1,115	4,500	V
Indirect materials........	195	40	125	200	350	415	1,325	F
Indirect labor...........	500	600	800	200	600	1,000	3,700	V
Indirect labor...........	175	80	340	320	540	545	2,000	F
Total direct costs	$1,870	$2,883	$2,630	$2,685	$4,255	$4,350	$18,673	
Total variable direct costs..	$1,500	$2,763	$2,165	$2,165	$3,365	$3,390	$15,348	V
Total fixed direct costs....	370	120	465	520	890	960	3,325	F
Total direct costs..	$1,870	$2,883	$2,630	$2,685	$4,255	$4,350	$18,673	

A plant survey was taken and the following budgeted data were estimated:

Department	Square feet	No. of employees	Investment in machinery	Kilowatt- hours	Cost of materials used
Factory office...........	1,600	100	$ 500	800	$ 600
Maintenance............	2,500	150	1,000	600	100
Materials storeroom.......	7,000	300	700	500	—
Mixing................	10,000	550	15,000	47,000	5,000
Assembly.............	15,000	400	10,000	20,050	3,000
Finishing..............	13,900	500	12,800	11,050	2,000
Total............	50,000	2,000	$40,000	80,000	$10,700

Actual factory overhead costs were as follows:

Direct costs	Factory office	Mainte-nance	Materials store-room	Mixing	Assembly	Finishing	Total	F/V
Fuel, heat, and light	$ 663	$ 830	$1,100	$ 400	$ 790	$ 800	$ 4,583	V
Water.	160	150	200	275	500	900	2,185	V
Indirect materials	220	156	195	1,350	1,575	1,180	4,676	V
Indirect materials	230	155	130	285	400	415	1,615	F
Indirect labor	525	610	810	205	625	1,010	3,785	V
Indirect labor	275	90	348	330	540	550	2,133	F
Total direct costs. .	$2,073	$1,991	$2,783	$2,845	$4,430	$4,855	$18,977	
Total variable direct costs	$1,568	$1,746	$2,305	$2,230	$3,490	$3,890	$15,229	V
Total fixed direct costs	505	245	478	615	940	965	3,748	F
	$2,073	$1,991	$2,783	$2,845	$4,430	$4,855	$18,977	

The actual indirect costs were as follows:

	Amount	F/V
Depreciation of factory building	$10,000	F
Factory superintendent's salary	23,640	F
Insurance on machinery	1,800	F
Power costs	45,000	V

Actual data for the period were as follows:

Department	Square feet	No. of employees	Investment in machinery	Kilowatt-hours	Cost of materials used
Factory office	1,600	90	$ 500	1,000	$ 500
Maintenance.	2,500	160	1,000	2,600	200
Materials storeroom	7,000	325	700	700	—
Mixing	10,000	530	15,000	53,000	6,000
Assembly	15,000	350	8,000	27,800	3,140
Finishing	13,900	515	10,800	14,900	2,000
Total	50,000	1,970	$36,000	100,000	$11,840

Required:

a. Using the step method, calculate the predetermined variable and fixed factory overhead rates for the three producing departments. The estimated allocation bases are mixing, 81,778 direct labor-hours; assembly, $134,275 direct labor dollars; and finishing, 90,116 machine-hours. Allocate service departments in this order: factory office (on basis of employees), maintenance (on basis of square feet), and materials storeroom (on basis of material cost). Round to nearest dollar in allocating costs. (In allocating the indirect and service department costs, it will be helpful to distinguish between fixed and variable costs.)

b. Assume that the factory overhead allocation rates you determined above were used throughout the period. Actual direct labor-hours in mixing were 82,000 and direct labor dollars were $136,000 in assembly; actual finishing machine-hours were

85,000 hours. Assign to departments all factory overhead costs and allocate them to the three production departments. (It is not necessary to distinguish between fixed and variable costs.)

c. Calculate the over- or underapplied factory overhead for each department.

d. Calculate spending and volume variances for each of the production departments.

P6–11.   Direct and reciprocal allocation methods (CMA adapted)

Barrylou Corporation is developing departmental overhead rates based upon direct labor-hours for its two production departments—molding and assembly. The molding department employs 20 people and the assembly department employs 80. Each person in these two departments works 2,000 hours per year. The production-related overhead costs for the molding department are budgeted at $200,000 and for the assembly department at $320,000. Two service departments—repair and power—directly support the two production departments and have budgeted costs of $48,000 and $250,000, respectively. The production departments' overhead rates cannot be determined until the service departments' costs are properly allocated. The following schedule reflects the use of the repair and power departments' output by the various departments.

	Department			
	Repair	Power	Molding	Assembly
Repair hours	—	1,000	1,000	8,000
Kilowatt-hour	240,000	—	840,000	120,000

Required:

a. Calculate the overhead rates per direct labor-hour for the molding department and the assembly department using the direct allocation method to charge the production departments for service department cost.

b. Calculate the overhead rates per direct labor-hour for the molding department and the assembly department using the reciprocal distribution method (sometimes called the algebraic method) to charge service department costs to each other and to the production department.

c. Explain the difference between the methods and indicate the arguments which are generally presented to support the reciprocal method over the direct allocation method.

PART II

Product cost accumulation procedures

Contrast between job order and process costing

Cost of production report

Accounting for opening inventory

Completed and on-hand inventory

OBJECTIVES OF CHAPTER 7

1. To present the difference between process costing and job order costing in assigning costs to products.

2. To discuss the characteristics of manufacturing procedures which make the use of process costing appropriate.

3. To illustrate departmental cost of production reports so that total and unit costs can be determined and summarized.

4. To show, through the use of exhibits, the weighted-average and FIFO methods of treating opening inventory costs using process costing.

7

Process costing—weighted-average and FIFO costing

Costs can be assigned to products through two different accumulation procedures: job order costing or process costing. The preceding chapters have illustrated the use of job order costing. With a job order costing system, costs are accumulated by jobs or orders. Since each individual batch or job receives varying amounts of skill or attention, the unit cost per order differs from job to job. Accumulating costs by individual jobs is eliminated, however, by the process costing approach, which analyzes costs by operating centers or departments.

CONTRAST BETWEEN JOB ORDER AND PROCESS COSTING

Process costing is most appropriate for firms that employ a mass-production, assembly-line approach in which there is a continuous flow of goods. That is, units leave the manufacturing departments to be transferred to the finished goods warehouse; they are not produced for a specific individual customer. All units in the specific product line are identical. This is in contrast to job order manufacturing in which production is performed to customers' specifications; normally, manufacturing is not started until a customer places an order. With job order costing, the total cost is determined at the time that the order is finished; with process costing, the total cost is determined at the end of the costing period. With process costing, costs are accumulated for a given time period, whether it be a day, week, or month.

Departmentalization of work in process inventory

Process costing assumes a sequential flow from one department to other departments as units travel through the production process. Since each department performs a specific task, the costs of processing are added to the unit's cost as it moves from department to department. An easy way to visualize this flow is to think of a snowball gathering snow (costs) as it travels from one department to another. Process costing assumes that all units travel from the first department to subsequent departments and do not skip departments. That is, the units leave the first department and take their costs with them to the second department, and so on to all departments. If, for instance, Department 1 transfers part of its finished goods to Department 2 and another part to Department 3, this will be stated. A flowchart outlining the units' course of action is helpful if there is much variation in the pattern. Since the costs must be summarized by departments, the work in process inventory ledger accounts must be broken down by department.

Equivalent units

In a typical manufacturing operation, some units will remain unfinished at the end of the month. These units in the ending inventory must be assigned some costs. The total cost must be divided by not only the units finished in a period, but also by the partially completed units in ending inventory. This is achieved by converting the units in ending inventory into *equivalent finished units*. For example, if 100 units are three-fourths complete in terms of direct labor, then 75 equivalent units of direct labor exist. Through the use of equivalent units, costs can be assigned to the department's ending inventory. Equivalent units are also referred to as equivalent production.

Before computing equivalent units, the accountant must determine the stage of completion for each batch of work in process. In some industries, it may be quite easy to determine how much more material, labor, and factory overhead must be added before the product is completed. The amount of material and the number of hours of labor required to finish the units may be easily predetermined so that the percentage of completion can be calculated. In other industries, however, it may be difficult to determine how much material, labor, and overhead must be added, so an estimate must be made. The stage of completion in the exhibits and problems illustrated in Chapters 7 and 8 are more exact than is usually practical in actual manufacturing operations. The more exact stage, such as $2/7$, is used to better illustrate the costing procedure. For example, if inventory is said to be at the one-half stage of completion, a beginning student might obtain the correct answer using the wrong procedure, because in this case inventory is not only one-half complete, but it also needs the remaining one half of the production process added to it.

The calculation of equivalent units is illustrated by the following:

Beginning inventory	0
Units started in process	990
Units to account for	990
Units completed and transferred	890
Units in ending inventory.	100 (¼ complete)
Units accounted for	990
Total costs to account for	$1,830

Before a unit is transferred to the next department, it must have completed the entire operating cycle of the department. It is then referred to as being finished as far as that department is concerned, even though the unit may still not be in a finished state ready for sale to a customer. Only if the unit is leaving the company's final department is it ready for disposition to a customer or user. In the example above, there are 890 units transferred to the next department during the month.

Accounting for total costs

In the above example, it is assumed that material, labor, and overhead are added uniformly in the production process so that the ending inventory of 100 units is one-fourth complete as far as all three cost elements are concerned. There is a total cost of $1,830, representing material, labor, and factory overhead, that is to be assigned to the units transferred as well as to the partially completed units in ending inventory. To make this assignment, equivalent units (EU) are determined as follows:

EU = 890 units transferred + 25 units (100 units in ending
   inventory × ¼) = 915
Unit cost, per equivalent unit ($1,830 ÷ 915 units) = $2.00
Costs accounted for as follows:
   Costs transferred (890 units × $2) $1,780
   Cost in ending inventory (100 units × ¼ × $2)   50
                                                              $1,830

The unit cost is determined on the basis of equivalent units rather than on the total physical units of 990. This is because the 100 units in ending inventory have received only one fourth of the effort and application that the finished units have received. To determine the unit costs, these 100 partially completed units are converted into 25 equivalent finished units. This is computed strictly for unit costing purposes; in fact, of course, there are still 100 units that are not completely finished.

COST OF PRODUCTION REPORT

Total and unit costs are determined and summarized on a cost of production report. Either each cost center or department makes such a report, or the individual reports of several departments are summarized. Cost of production reports are illustrated later in the chapter. There are a number of useful formats. To be consistent, however, only one format is illustrated in this book. Regardless of the format used, the important thing to emphasize is that process costing requires an orderly approach to assigning costs to products. The following steps provide a uniform approach to preparing the cost of production report.

Five steps to preparing a cost of production report

Step 1.   Quantity schedule.   Not only must there be an accounting for the costs assigned to each department, but all units started in the department must be accounted for. The vehicle for showing the units for which the department is responsible is the quantity schedule. The disposition of these units must also be shown—that is, whether they are transferred to the next department, lost, or remain in ending inventory. This part of the cost of production report is often referred to as the physical flow section; it is concerned only with whole units, regardless of their stage of completion.

The units shown in the quantity schedule are expressed in terms of the department's finished products, and any appropriate measurement, such as feet, gallons, or pounds can be used. The important thing is that the units are all expressed in the same measure. Assume, for example, that a department produces shirts and each shirt requires two yards of fabric. If the department begins cutting and sewing 2,000 yards of fabric, the quantity schedule would show that 1,000 units (2,000 yards/2 yards per shirt) are started in process, since the units transferred out will be expressed in terms of finished shirts.

Step 2.   Determine the costs to account for.   The costs that a department are responsible for may come from several sources. For one thing, there may be some units in beginning inventory that are partially complete; and the costs of material, labor, and factory overhead that were assigned to these units last period become the cost of the beginning inventory and must be accounted for. Also, if the department is not the first cost center in the production process, it will receive costs from other departments when the units from these departments are received in its operations. In addition, each department will incur materials and/or labor and factory overhead in its own processing. The total of these costs must be determined so that they can be accounted for.

Step 3.   Calculate equivalent units and unit costs.   Costs are determined not only for each finished unit but also for each of the three cost elements: materials, labor, and factory overhead. To arrive at the unit costs, equivalent units must also be calculated. Obviously, if the equivalent units are calculated in error, the cost of production report will be incorrect.

Step 4.   Account for all costs.   After the costs for which the department is responsible are determined, an accounting for the disposition of these costs must be made. Some of the costs are assigned to cost centers receiving units transferred out of the department. The remaining costs are assigned to the units staying in the department and to any units that are lost. Assignment of costs of lost units is discussed in Chapter 8. While the unit cost is carried out to four or five decimal places in the exhibits and problems illustrated in Chapters 7 and 8, usually total cost is rounded to whole dollars.

Step 5.   Prove that all costs are accounted for.   The cost section of the cost of production report is composed of two parts. One part determines the total costs that must be accounted for, while the other section shows the disposition of these costs. There must be agreement between these two sections; otherwise, there is an error. The above steps are noted parenthetically by number in all exhibits in this chapter.

The mechanics of preparing a cost of production report are illustrated by presenting the reports of a company which manufactures a product in in two departments. To keep these introductory cost of production reports as simple as possible, the departments are merely referred to as Department 1 and Department 2. Exhibit 7–1 shows only the cost of production report for Department 1. This report is combined with the cost of production report for Department 2 in Exhibit 7–2 to illustrate the flow of costs from one department to another. Each section of the cost of production report will be discussed.

Department 1's quantity schedule.   The quantity section of the cost of production report shows that Department 1 placed 9,500 units into the production process and that it had no beginning inventory. Of the 9,500 units, 8,500 units were transferred to Department 2, while 1,000 units were partially complete in ending inventory. Because the quantity schedule is concerned with the physical flow of goods, the stage of completion is not needed. However, for ease in computing the equivalent units, the stage of completion is indicated next to the units in the quantity schedule.

At this introductory stage, it may appear that the quantity schedule is a waste of time and effort. However, with more complicated process costing operations in which units are added or lost, preparation of the quantity schedule provides assurance that all units are accounted for.

Department 1's costs to account for.   Since there was no beginning inventory and no costs received from a previous department, the total costs to account for originate in Department 1. During the current period, Department 1 incurred direct material cost of $19,000, direct labor cost of $13,125, and

EXHIBIT 7–1

DOUGLASS COMPANY
Cost of Production Report
For Month Ending January 31, 19–

	Department 1

Quantity schedule (Step 1):

Units in beginning inventory	-0-	
Units started in process	9,500	9,500
Units transferred.	8,500	
Units in ending inventory (all material, ¼ labor, ⅕ overhead)	1,000	9,500

	Total costs	Unit costs

Costs to account for (Steps 2 and 3):

Material	$19,000	$ 2.00
Labor.	13,125	1.50
Overhead.	26,100	3.00
Total costs to account for.	$58,225	$ 6.50

Costs accounted for (Step 4):

Costs transferred (8,500 units × $6.50)		$55,250
Ending inventory:		
Material (1,000 units × $2)	$ 2,000	
Labor (¼ × 1,000 units × $1.50).	375	
Overhead (⅕ × 1,000 units × $3)	600	2,975
Total costs accounted for (Step 5)		$58,225

Additional Computations (Step 3):

	Transferred		Ending inventory	
Equivalent units, material	8,500	+	1,000 (1,000 × 100%)	= 9,500

$$\frac{\$19,000}{9,500} = \$2 \text{ unit material cost}$$

Equivalent units, labor	8,500	+	250 (1,000 × ¼)	= 8,750

$$\frac{\$13,125}{8,750} = \$1.50 \text{ unit labor cost}$$

Equivalent units, overhead	8,500	+	200 (1,000 × ⅕)	= 8,700

$$\frac{\$26,100}{8,700} = \$3 \text{ unit overhead cost}$$

---

factory overhead of $26,100. After these costs are determined, the unit cost per cost component can be calculated through the use of equivalent units.

Department 1's equivalent units and unit costs. The computations for equivalent units and the unit costs are illustrated at the bottom of the cost of production report. Using this production process, material is introduced at the beginning of the operations, while labor and overhead are added throughout the process. This explains why, in the computation for equivalent units for *materials*, the units in ending inventory are multiplied by 100 percent. They have all the material they need for completion. Before any unit is transferred, it must have gone through the entire cycle of the department's operations. In computing the equivalent units for labor and factory overhead, the ending inventory is multiplied by its stage of completion. The units have only one fourth of the labor they need for completion; an additional three fourths must be added in subsequent periods before they can be transferred to Department 2. The units have even less of their factory overhead, only one fifth of the overhead needed for completion. A supervisor determines the stage of completion, either through inspection of the ending inventory or using specified formulas.

After the equivalent units for each of the cost components are determined, the equivalent unit figure is divided into the costs to arrive at the unit cost. The total material cost of $19,000 is sufficient to complete 9,500 units (8,500 units transferred and 1,000 in ending inventory). The unit material cost becomes $2 ($19,000/9,500 EU). A similar computation is made for labor and factory overhead, as shown in Step 3 in Exhibit 7–1, so that the unit labor cost becomes $1.50 ($13,125/8,750 EU), and the unit factory overhead cost becomes $3 ($26,100/8,700 EU). Each unit cost is inserted in the "Costs to account for" section of the cost of production report to arrive at a total departmental unit cost of $6.50 (the total of the calculated equivalent unit costs). The total cost to account for of $58,225 cannot be divided by any one equivalent unit figure to arrive at the unit cost of $6.50 because each of the three cost components (material, labor, and factory overhead) involves a different stage of completion.

The total cost transferred to the next department is determined by multiplying the 8,500 units transferred by the $6.50 departmental unit costs to arrive at $55,250. The costs do not need to be itemized by the three components of material, labor, and factory overhead; only the total unit cost of $6.50 is used. Because the 1,000 units in ending inventory have all their material, they are each assigned the $2 unit material cost. However, these units have only one fourth of their labor; therefore, the labor cost of the ending inventory of semifinished units is $375 [(¼ × 1,000 units = 250 units) × $1.50]. The overhead cost of the semifinished units is determined through a similar computation to arrive at a cost of $600 [(⅕ × 1,000 units = 200 units) × $3]. The $2,975 value of the ending inventory becomes the beginning inventory for the next period in Department 1.

The final step in the cost of production report is ascertaining that the total costs accounted for ($58,225) equal the total costs that the department is responsible for, which were computed in Step 2. After it is determined that these two figures are equal, the cost of production report is completed.

Second department is illustrated

Exhibit 7–1 is repeated in Exhibit 7–2; in addition, the data for a subsequent department are added so that the transfer of unit costs can be illustrated. The quantity schedule of Department 2 indicates that there were no units in beginning inventory when operations began. Department 1 transferred 8,500 units to Department 2 for further processing. In all cases, unless stated otherwise, units from the preceding department are assumed to be introduced at the beginning of operation in subsequent departments. Material, labor, and factory overhead are added in Department 2 before the units become finished products ready for sale to a consumer. Of these 8,500 units, 8,300 units were finished and transferred to finished goods. The other 200 units are semifinished and remain in ending inventory. Their stage of completion is indicated in the quantity schedule. Material is treated differently in Department 2, so that the ending inventory has only $\frac{1}{10}$ of its materials needed for completion.

Department 2's costs to account for. Since Department 2 received 8,500 units from Department 1, it must account for the preceding department costs of these units, which total $55,250. This $55,250 cost from the preceding department includes material, labor, and overhead. Arrows are drawn in Exhibit 7–2 to illustrate both the transfer of units and the transfer of costs. In addition to the $55,250 cost received from the preceding department, Department 2 has incurred material cost of $4,160, labor of $33,520, and factory overhead of $42,250.

Department 2's EU and unit costs. For brevity, only Department 2's computations for equivalent units and costs are shown in Exhibit 7–2. Equivalent units for the preceding department must now be calculated to arrive at a unit cost of $6.50. Since this is a simple introductory illustration, the computations for the preceding departmental costs are the same as the unit cost of $6.50 determined for Department 1. However, there is a danger in assuming that this will always be the case; several factors introduced in the more complex process costing operations can cause this cost to differ.

The 200 units in ending inventory have only $\frac{1}{10}$ of their material needed for completion, which represents 20 equivalent units. Unit cost for material is determined to be $0.50 ($4,160/8,320 units). Equivalent units for labor are 8,380, giving a unit cost of $4 ($33,520/8,380 EU). Since the ending inventory has only three fourths of its factory overhead, the equivalent units become 8,450 [8,300 + 150 (200 × ¾)]; the unit cost is $5 ($42,250/8,450 EU).

Disposition of Department 2 costs. With the preceding department cost of $6.50 and the Department 2 cost of material, $0.50; labor, $4; and factory overhead, $5, the total unit cost is $16. The 8,300 units transferred to finished goods are each assigned a $16 cost to give a total of $132,800 costs transferred.

EXHIBIT 7-2

DOUGLASS COMPANY
Cost of Production Report
For Month Ending January 31, 19–

	Department 1			Department 2	
Quantity schedule (Step 1):					
Units in beginning inventory	–0–			–0–	
Units started in process.	9,500	9,500		→8,500	8,500
Units transferred	8,500			8,300	
Units in ending inventory (all material, ¼ labor, ⅕ overhead	1,000	9,500	(¹⁄₁₀ M, ⅖ L, ¾ OH)	200	8,500

	Total costs	Unit costs		Total costs	Unit costs
Costs to account for (Steps 2 and 3):					
Costs received from preceding department				→$ 55,250	$ 6.50
Material	$19,000	$2.00		4,160	0.50
Labor	13,125	1.50		33,520	4.00
Overhead	26,100	3.00		42,250	5.00
Total costs to account for .	$58,225	$6.50		$135,180	$16.00
Costs accounted for (Step 4):					
Costs transferred (8,500 units × $6.50)		$55,250		(8,300 × $16)	$132,800
Ending inventory:					
Cost from preceding department			(200 × $6.50)	$1,300	
Material.	$ 2,000		(200 × ¹⁄₁₀ × $0.50)	10	
Labor	375		(200 × ⅖ × $4.00)	320	
Overhead	600	2,975	(200 × ¾ × $5.00)	750	2,380
Total costs accounted for (Step 5)		$58,225			$135,180

Additional Computations (Step 3):

	Transferred		Ending inventory		
Department 2:					
Equivalent units, preceding department	8,300	+	200	=	8,500
$\frac{\$55,250}{8,500 \text{ units}} = \$6.50$					
Equivalent units, material.	8,300	+	20	=	8,320
$\frac{\$4,160}{8,320 \text{ units}} = \$0.50$ unit material cost			(200 × ¹⁄₁₀)		
Equivalent units, labor.	8,300	+	80	=	8,380
$\frac{\$33,520}{8,380 \text{ units}} = \$4.00$ unit labor cost			(200 × ⅖)		
Equivalent units, overhead	8,300	+	150	=	8,450
$\frac{\$42,250}{8,450 \text{ units}} = \$5.00$ unit overhead cost			(200 × ¾)		

Since the ending inventory in Department 2 could never have entered Department 2 without completing Department 1 operations, the $6.50 cost from the preceding department must be added along with the Department 2 costs. The 200 units in ending inventory are multiplied by $6.50 to give $1,300, which represents the Department 1 costs. The material, labor, and factory overhead assigned to the ending inventory are computed by multiplying the 200 units by their respective stage of completion to give the representative equivalent units for each cost component. The unit cost for each element is then multiplied by its equivalent units to give a total inventory valuation of $2,380. The final step is proving that the $135,180 cost is accounted for.

Determining only the total costs for each processing department is not adequate for control purposes. Instead, the three cost components—direct material, direct labor, and factory overhead— are summarized by department on the cost of production report so that unit costs for each of the three elements can be determined. Since factory overhead is often applied on the basis of direct labor dollars or direct labor-hours, some cost of production reports combine factory overhead and labor under the classification of conversion costs. The cost of production report can detail each item of factory overhead so that a unit cost for each individual cost element can be calculated. However, for brevity, the cost of production reports illustrated in this book do not calculate unit costs for each item of factory overhead; instead, unit costs are calculated for total material, labor, and factory overhead.

Issuance of material

When preparing cost of production reports, one must remember that because production processes differ, material is entered into the process at various stages. Accountants should therefore make no assumptions regarding the stage at which material is introduced; instead, they must obtain accurate information regarding the point in the processing operation at which material is issued. For example, in manufacturing shirts, the fabric is introduced at the beginning of operations so that cutting and sewing operations may begin. In other types of operation, such as the chemical industry, material may be added in a continuous flow or at specific points in the manufacturing process. In still other operations, some of the direct material may be added at the end of the operations in a department.

Journal entries using process costing

In process costing, direct material, along with direct labor and factory overhead, is accumulated through entries similar to that for job order costing. However, instead of costs being traced to specific jobs or batches, costs are accumulated for departments or cost centers. The journal entries for each cost component are illustrated below using the data from Exhibit 7–2.

Material journal entries using process costing. Material requisitions used in job order costing were described in Chapter 3. In process costing, the material requisition indicates the department which is to be charged rather than the job order number. The entry charging Departments 1 and 2 for the material used during the period is as follows:

```
Work in Process—Department 1 . . . . . . . . . . . . . . . . . 19,000
Work in Process—Department 2 . . . . . . . . . . . . . . . .  4,160
    Direct Materials Inventory . . . . . . . . . . . . . . . . . .        23,160
```

Labor journal entries using process costing. The detailed work of accumulating labor by jobs is eliminated with process costing. Job time tickets are not needed in a process cost system; instead, daily or weekly time tickets or clock cards become the basis of distributing payroll charges. Since payroll deductions were discussed in Chapter 4, the following entry uses only a payroll summary account to distribute the payroll. A typical entry allocating the direct labor charges is as follows for Exhibit 7–2.

```
Work in Process—Department 1 . . . . . . . . . . . . . . . . . 13,125
Work in Process—Department 2 . . . . . . . . . . . . . . . . . 33,520
    Payroll . . . . . . . . . . . . . . . . . . . . . . . . . . . . . . . . . . .        46,645
```

Factory overhead using process costing. In a job order costing system, factory overhead application rates facilitate the costing of products. Rather than wait until the end of operations to distribute actual factory overhead, the accountant uses estimated factory overhead rates in job order costing. In certain *process* cost systems, on the other hand, actual factory overhead rather than applied factory overhead costs can be used since costs are not accumulated until the end of operations. If production is stable from one period to another and total fixed cost does not vary considerably, it is not necessary to use estimated factory overhead rates; instead, the fixed cost per unit charged to the product represents that calculated under normal conditions. A case can also be made for using only the actual cost if the processing department's fixed costs are a small percentage of the total departmental costs.

However, if production is not stable and if the actual fixed costs per unit therefore fluctuate considerably, applied factory overhead rates must be used. For example, if the work is of a seasonal nature, production varies so much between peak and slack periods that the costs would fluctuate considerably unless estimated factory overhead rates were used. The procedure for determining the factory overhead application rate is similar to that shown under job order costing. Total variable and fixed overhead is estimated for the period, and a base such as estimated direct labor-hours or machine-hours is chosen to compute the factory overhead application rate. Even though actual factory overhead may eventually be charged to the departments, the costs are first accumulated in the Factory Overhead Control account. Subsidiary ledger accounts detailing the factory overhead are also maintained. A typical entry for Departments 1 and 2 is as follows:

```
Factory Overhead Control. . . . . . . 68,350
    Prepaid Insurance. . . . . . . . . .        XX
    Accounts Payable. . . . . . . . . .        XX        Total
                                                            of
    Materials Inventory . . . . . . . . .      XX            68,350
    Accumulated Depreciation . . . .          XX
    And so forth.
```

Regardless of whether or not applied factory overhead rates are used, the actual factory overhead costs must be assigned to departments. If estimated factory overhead application rates are not used, assignment of actual factory overhead is necessary so that the cost of overhead for each product can be calculated. Even if applied factory overhead rates are used to cost the product, a comparison must be made of actual and applied factory overhead so that the spending and volume variances illustrated in Chapter 6 can be determined.

To assign overhead to departments, the factory overhead subsidiary ledger accounts or a separate departmental expense analysis is used to summarize the actual costs by departments. If actual factory overhead rather than an estimated overhead rate is used to cost the products, the following entry is made to distribute actual factory overhead:

```
Work in Process—Department 1 . . . . . . . . . . . . . . . . 26,100
Work in Process—Department 2 . . . . . . . . . . . . . . . . 42,250
    Factory Overhead Control. . . . . . . . . . . . . . . . . .          68,350
```

This becomes the source for the overhead charged to the departments, as shown on the cost of production report. The difference between actual and applied overhead remains in the Factory Overhead Control account. If estimated factory overhead rates are used instead, the same accounts are debited and credited as above.

Transfer of costs between departments.   In addition to assigning factory overhead, the process costing accountant must also record the transfer of costs between departments. When units are transmitted from one department to another, a journal entry must be made to record this. The entry to record the transfer of costs from Department 1 to Department 2 is the following:

```
Work in Process—Department 2. . . . . . . . . . . . . . . 55,250
    Work in Process—Department 1 . . . . . . . . . . . .          55,250
```

The entry to transfer the finished units from Department 2 to the Finished Goods Inventory is the following:

```
Finished Goods Inventory . . . . . . . . . . . . . . . . . . . 132,800
    Work in Process—Department 2 . . . . . . . . . . . .          132,800
```

ACCOUNTING FOR OPENING INVENTORY

Another factor in process costing is the opening inventories of the various departments. The departments illustrated in Exhibits 7–1 and 7–2 had no units in beginning inventory when operations began. In these introductory exhibits, it is felt that the basic concepts of process costing should be introduced before the accounting for opening inventory cost is illustrated. In practice, however, opening inventories are rarely, if ever, at zero. The ending inventories illustrated in Exhibit 7–2, for example, become the beginning inventories for Department 1 and Department 2 for the next period, which is the month of February in this example. The ending inventory valuations for Department 1 and 2 from Exhibit 7–2 are used in Exhibits 7–3 (pages 266–67), and 7–4 (pages 268–69).

Weighted average and FIFO

There are two methods used to account for the opening inventory costs:

1. *Weighted average:* The cost of the beginning inventory is averaged with the current period's costs so that all units that are finished bear the same unit cost. The units in beginning inventory receive the same treatment as the units started and finished during the period. The costs of getting the beginning inventory to a semifinished state are combined with current costs to arrive at a cost per unit. The weighted-average method is often simply referred to as the average method.

2. *First-in, first-out (FIFO).* With the FIFO method, the cost of the units that are finished from beginning inventory is kept separate from the cost of the units that are started and finished during the period. The cost of the goods transferred is composed of the cost of the goods finished that were in beginning inventory and the cost of the goods started and finished during the current period. Ending work in process inventory is valued at the unit cost of current production for the period. The unit cost of current production is determined by dividing equivalent units into the production costs incurred in the current period only.

Difference in equivalent units. Equivalent units calculated using first-in, first-out costing differ from those using weighted-average costing because of the difference in the way the beginning inventory is handled. The formulas for determining equivalent units under the FIFO and weighted-average approaches are given below. The discussion concerning the costs assigned to units that are lost in processing is not introduced until Chapter 8; however, to make the formulas complete, lost units are included here in the equivalent unit (EU) formulas. They are as follows:

$$
\text{EU, average} =
\begin{array}{l}
\text{Units} \\
\text{completed} \\
\text{and} \\
\text{transferred} \\
\times\ 100\% \\
\overline{}
\end{array}
+
\begin{array}{l}
\text{Units} \\
\text{completed} \\
\text{and on} \\
\text{hand in} \\
\text{ending} \\
\text{inventory} \\
\times\ 100\%
\end{array}
+
\begin{array}{l}
\text{Partially} \\
\text{completed} \\
\text{ending} \\
\text{inventory} \\
\times\ \text{stage of} \\
\text{completion} \\
\overline{}
\end{array}
+
\begin{array}{l}
\text{Units} \\
\text{lost} \\
\times\ \text{stage of} \\
\text{completion} \\
\text{at the} \\
\text{time the} \\
\text{loss is} \\
\text{determined}
\end{array}
$$

EXHIBIT 7–3

DOUGLASS COMPANY
Cost of Production Report—Weighted Average
For Month Ending February 28, 19–

	Department 1			Department 2	
Quantity schedule (Step 1):					
Beginning inventory					
(all material, ¼ labor, ⅕ overhead)	1,000		(⅒ M, ⅖ L, ¾ OH)	200	
Units started in process	9,000	10,000		8,500	8,700
Units transferred to next department	8,500			8,100	
Ending inventory					
(all material, ⅓ labor, ⅒ overhead)	1,500	10,000	(⅙ M, ⅓ L, ¼ OH)	600	8,700

	Total costs	Unit costs		Total costs	Unit costs
Costs to account for (Steps 2 and 3):					
Work in process—beginning inventory:					
Costs from preceding department	–0–			$ 1,300	
Material	$ 2,000			10	
Labor	375			320	
Overhead	600			750	
Total beginning inventory	$ 2,975			$ 2,380	
Costs received from preceding department				56,100	$ 6.5977
Current costs in department:					
Material	19,000	$2.10		3,680	0.4500
Labor	14,925	1.70		32,050	3.9000
Overhead	23,620	2.80		42,150	5.2000
Total costs to account for	$60,520	$6.60		$136,360	$16.1477
Costs accounted for as follows (Step 4):					
Costs transferred to next department					
(8,500 × $6.60)		$56,100	(8,100 × $16.1477)		$130,796
Work in process—ending inventory:					
Costs from preceding department			(600 × $6.5977)	$ 3,959	
Material (1,500 × $2.10)	$ 3,150		(600 × ⅙ × $0.45)	45	
Labor (1,500 × ⅓ × $1.70)	850		(600 × ⅓ × $3.90)	780	
Overhead (1,500 × ⅒ × $2.80)	420	4,420	(600 × ¼ × $5.20)	780	5,564
Total costs accounted for (Step 5) . .		$60,520			$136,360

EU, FIFO	= Units completed and transferred × 100%	+ Units completed and on hand in ending inventory × 100%	+ Partially completed ending inventory × Stage of completion	+ Units lost × Stage of completion at the time the loss is determined	– Beginning inventory × Stage of completion

For example, assume the quantity schedule appears as below:

EXHIBIT 7–3 *(concluded)*

Additional Computations (Step 3):

	Transferred		Ending inventory		
EU, Department 1, material	8,500	+	1,500	=	10,000
$\dfrac{\$2,000 + \$19,000}{10,000} = \dfrac{\$21,000}{10,000} = \$2.10$			(1,500 × 100%)		
EU, Department 1, labor	8,500	+	500	=	9,000
$\dfrac{\$375 + \$14,925}{9,000} = \dfrac{\$15,300}{9,000} = \$1.70$			(1,500 × ⅓)		
EU, Department 1, overhead	8,500	+	150	=	8,650
$\dfrac{\$600 + \$23,620}{8,650} = \dfrac{\$24,220}{8,650} = \$2.80$			(1,500 × 1/10)		
EU, preceding department costs	8,100	+	600	=	8,700
$\dfrac{\$1,300 + \$56,100}{8,700} = \dfrac{\$57,400}{8,700} = \$6.5977$			(600 × 100%)		
EU, Department 2, material	8,100	+	100	=	8,200
$\dfrac{\$10 + \$3,680}{8,200} = \dfrac{\$3,690}{8,200} = \$0.45$			(600 × ⅙)		
EU, Department 2, labor	8,100	+	200	=	8,300
$\dfrac{\$320 + \$32,050}{8,300} = \dfrac{\$32,370}{8,300} = \$3.90$			(600 × ⅓)		
EU, Department 2, overhead	8,100	+	150	=	8,250
$\dfrac{\$750 + \$42,150}{8,250} = \dfrac{\$42,900}{8,250} = \$5.20$			(600 × ¼)		

Beginning inventory (40% complete for all cost elements)	800	
Started in process	1,200	2,000
Units transferred.	1,800	
Ending inventory (20% complete for all cost elements).	200	2,000

Using average costing, the equivalent units (EU) are as follows:

EU, average = 1,800 units transferred + 40 ending inventory = 1,840
(200 units × 20%)

The EU calculated using FIFO costing differs as follows:

EU, FIFO = 1,800 units transferred + 40 ending inventory,
(200 units × 20%)
− 320 beginning inventory = 1,520
(800 units × 40%)

The reason for the difference in computation becomes apparent when the costing procedures for each method are presented.

Sources of units transferred

Regardless of whether FIFO or average costing is used, the total units transferred to the next department come from the two sources listed below:

EXHIBIT 7–4

DOUGLASS COMPANY
Cost of Production Report—FIFO
For Month Ending February 28, 19–

	Department 1			Department 2	
Quantity schedule (Step 1):					
Beginning inventory					
(all material, ¼ labor, ⅕ overhead)	1,000		(¹⁄₁₀ M, ⅖ L, ¾ OH)	200	
Units started in process	9,000	10,000		8,500	8,700
Units transferred to next department	8,500			8,100	
Ending inventory					
(all material, ⅓ labor, ¹⁄₁₀ overhead)	1,500	10,000	(⅙ M, ⅓ L, ¼ OH)	600	8,700

	Total costs	Unit costs		Total costs	Unit costs
Costs to account for (Steps 2 and 3):					
Work in process—beginning inventory:					
Costs from preceding department	–0–			$ 1,300	
Material	$ 2,000			10	
Labor	375			320	
Overhead	600			750	
Total beginning inventory	$ 2,975			$ 2,380	
Costs received from					
preceding department				56,081	$ 6.5978
Current costs in department:					
Material	19,000	$2.1111		3,680	0.4499
Labor	14,925	1.7057		32,050	3.8990
Overhead	23,620	2.7953		42,150	5.2037
Total costs to account for	$60,520	$6.6121		$136,341	$16.1504
Costs accounted for as follows (Step 4):					
Costs transferred to next department:					
From beginning inventory:					
Value of beginning inventory	$ 2,975			$ 2,380	
Material added	—		(200 × ⁹⁄₁₀ × $0.4499)	81	
Labor added					
(1,000 × ¾ × $1.7057)	1,279		(200 × ⅗ × $3.8990)	468	
Overhead added					
(1,000 × ⅘ × $2.7953)	2,236	$ 6,490	(200 × ¼ × $5.2037)	260	$ 3,189
From current production					
(7,500 × $6.6121)		49,591	(7,900 × $16.1504)		127,588
Total cost transferred		$56,081			$130,777
Work in process—ending inventory:					
Costs from preceding department	—		(600 × $6.5978)	$ 3,958	
Material (1,500 × $2.1111)	$ 3,167		(600 × ⅙ × $0.4499)	45	
Labor (1,500 × ⅓ × $1.7057)	853		(600 × ⅓ × $3.8990)	780	
Overhead (1,500 × ¹⁄₁₀ × $2.7953)	419	4,439	(600 × ¼ × $5.2037)	781	5,564
Total costs accounted for (Step 5) . .		$60,520			$136,341

↘ 1.   Beginning inventory.
↘ 2.   Current production—units started and finished during the period.

Even though it is always assumed that beginning inventory is finished before
the units that are started during the period, in average costing the source of the
units transferred does not matter since all units transferred during the period

EXHIBIT 7–4 *(concluded)*

Additional Computations (Step 3):

	Transferred		Ending inventory		Beginning inventory		
EU, Department 1, material......	8,500	+	1,500 (1,500 × 100%)	−	1,000 (1,000 × 100%)	=	9,000
$\dfrac{\$19{,}000}{9{,}000} = \$2.111$							
EU, Department 1, labor........	8,500	+	500 (1,500 × ⅓)	−	250 (1,000 × ¼)	=	8,750
$\dfrac{\$14{,}925}{8{,}750} = \$1.7057$							
EU, Department 1, overhead.....	8,500	+	150 (1,500 × ⅒)	−	200 (1,000 × ⅕)	=	8,450
$\dfrac{\$23{,}620}{8{,}450} = \$2.7953$							
EU, preceding department costs..	8,100	+	600 (600 × 100%)	−	200 (200 × 100%)	=	8,500
$\dfrac{\$56{,}081}{8{,}500} = \$6.5978$							
EU, Department 2, material......	8,100	+	100 (600 × ⅙)	−	20 (200 × ⅒)	=	8,180
$\dfrac{\$3{,}680}{8{,}180} = \$0.4499$							
EU, Department 2, labor........	8,100	+	200 (600 × ⅓)	−	80 (200 × ⅖)	=	8,220
$\dfrac{\$32{,}050}{8{,}220} = \$3.8990$							
EU, Department 2, overhead.....	8,100	+	150 (600 × ¼)	−	150 (200 × ¾)	=	8,100
$\dfrac{\$42{,}150}{8{,}100} = \$5.2037$							

are costed out at an average. However, using FIFO, the accountant keeps the costs of the units from these two different sources separate. In the above example illustrating equivalent unit computations, of the 1,800 units transferred, 800 come from beginning inventory and 1,000 from current production.

Weighted-average costing illustrated

Use of the weighted-average cost method of treating beginning inventory is illustrated in Exhibit 7–3 (pages 266–67). The ending inventory valuation for Departments 1 and 2 becomes the beginning inventory for the month of February. Department 1 has 1,000 units in beginning inventory that have received costs of $2,975 to get them to a semifinished state. After all units have been accounted for in the quantity schedule, the next step is to determine the total costs to be accounted for. Using average costing, the accountant considers the beginning inventory part of current production regardless of the fact that there were costs assigned to the units last month. The costs incurred for beginning inventory to reach a semifinished stage are added to current costs. Beginning inventory must be broken down by individual cost elements so that the cost of material, labor, and overhead can be added to current costs *element by element.* The sum of the costs of material, labor, and factory overhead that were currently incurred and in the beginning inventory give the total costs to account for.

Computing EU and unit costs.   As indicated in Step 3 of Exhibit 7–3 (pages 266–67), the stage of completion of the ending inventory is then multiplied by the units in inventory; to this figure is added the total units transferred, regardless of whether they came from beginning inventory or from current production. After this, the cost of the individual elements in the beginning inventory is added with the current cost to arrive at the total cost. This total cost is then divided by the equivalent units to arrive at the unit costs. For example, in Department 1 the units receive all their material after they enter the production process so that even though the units in ending inventory are not complete, they have all their material. The $2,000 material cost of the semifinished goods in beginning inventory is added to the $19,000 current material costs to give a total of $21,000 material cost, which is divided by 10,000 equivalent units to give a $2.10 unit cost. Similar computations are made for Department 1 labor and factory overhead to arrive at a total unit cost of $6.60. The total 8,500 units transferred are multiplied by the $6.60 unit cost to give a total cost of $56,100 transferred. Since the 1,500 units in ending inventory have all their material, the entire units are multiplied by the $2.10 unit cost. Because the ending inventory is only partially complete as far as labor and overhead are concerned, the units are multiplied by their stage of completion before being finally multiplied by the labor and overhead unit cost of $1.70 and $2.80, respectively.

In Exhibit 7–3, Department 2 only has 200 units which are semifinished in beginning inventory. The $1,300 cost that was incurred for these 200 units for the completion of preceding department operations in a prior period is averaged with the current cost of $56,100 transferred from Department 1 to arrive at a unit cost of $6.5977. The temptation to carry the previous departmental unit cost, which is $6.60 in Exhibit 7–3, over to the next department should be avoided; in most cases, a new unit cost must be computed.

The averaging procedure used in Department 1 is also illustrated in Department 2 to arrive at the departmental unit cost. Material is added uniformly in Department 2 so that neither the beginning nor ending inventory has all its material. After the unit costs for Department 2 material, labor, and overhead are determined, they are added to the previous department costs to arrive at a total unit cost of $16.1477. The 8,100 units leaving Department 2 are each assigned a cost of $16.1477, giving a total of $130,796 transferred to finished goods. Because all of the 600 units in ending inventory have been through a previous department, they each receive the averaged preceding department cost of $6.5977. The remaining cost assigned to the ending inventory reflects the stage of completion of the units.

FIFO costing illustrated

To understand the difference between FIFO and weighted-average costing, Exhibit 7–4 uses the data shown in Exhibit 7–3 to illustrate the FIFO costing method. The quantity schedules are identical. Using FIFO, the accountant need not detail the cost of each of the components found in beginning inventory, since only the total inventory valuation is used. However, the individual costs of material, labor, and overhead are shown so that a comparison with Exhibit 7–2 can be made. As you recall, average costing requires this detail so that the beginning inventory costs can be averaged with current costs. The difference between FIFO and average costing becomes apparent when equivalent units are calculated in Exhibit 7–4 (pages 268–69). Calculated under FIFO, these represent current production only; since the units completed and transferred are included at 100 percent with other units started and finished, the stage of completion of the beginning inventory is deducted in computing equivalent units under FIFO. A slightly different formula from that illustrated in Exhibit 7–4 for computing equivalent units using FIFO can also be used as follows:

EU, FIFO = Units started and completed × 100% + Ending inventory × Stage of completion + Units completed and on hand × 100% + Units lost × stage of completion at the time the loss is determined + Beginning inventory × Stage of completion to be added

Using the above formula, the computation for labor in Department 1 in Exhibit 7–4 is as follows:

EU, FIFO = 7,500 Started and finished + 500 ending inventory (1,500 × ⅓) + 750 beginning inventory (1,000 × ¾) = 8,750

Units started and finished.   As can be seen above, there is a difference between units transferred and units started and finished, because the total units transferred come from both the units started and finished in current production as well as from beginning inventory. For example, there were 9,000 units started in process but because 1,500 units remained in ending inventory, only 7,500 units were started and finished. This is an important point to remember in choosing the formula that appears easier. The correct use of either formula gives the same results.

Additional differences between FIFO and average costing appear when the cost of the units transferred is determined. Department 1 has 1,000 units in beginning inventory which must receive additional labor and overhead before being finished. Since the 1,000 units reached a one-fourth stage of completion in regard to labor last period, they must be assigned an additional three-fourths equivalent units of labor before they are transferred to Department 2. It is for this reason that the 1,000 units are multiplied by three fourths before being finally multiplied by the $1.7057 labor unit cost. In addition, the units have received only one fifth of their overhead and the remaining four fifths must be added before the units are transferred out of Department 1. A total of 8,500 units are transferred to Department 2; however, 1,000 units come from beginning inventory. This leaves 7,500 units that were started and finished in current production; these are assigned the total departmental unit cost of $6.6121. The ending inventory in Department 1 is multiplied by its stage of completion and the unit costs.

Averaging within FIFO.   The total costs of $56,081 transferred to Department 2 represent two batches—1,000 units that were finished during the period and 7,500 units that were started and finished in current production. Even though the $56,081 represents two batches, the cost is averaged after the batches are received in the new department. This is the reason that the FIFO method is often referred to as the modified or departmental FIFO method. FIFO costing is strictly applied within each department, but when the costs are transferred out, an averaging technique is used in the next department so that all units received from a preceding department bear the same average unit cost. This slight modification is justified because of the clerical cost involved in keeping costs strictly attached to each batch. Otherwise, the FIFO method would never be feasible in process costing because of the burdensome task of accounting for the mass of figures. If the company prefers, strict FIFO could be used when the goods are transferred out of the last department into finished goods. In Exhibit 7–4, the total cost transferred of $56,081 is divided by 8,500 equivalent units to give a single averaged preceding departmental cost of $6.5978, which differs somewhat from the $6.6121 computed in Department 1.

Note that in Exhibit 7–4 using FIFO costing, Department 2's total cost to account for of $136,341 differs from the corresponding figure of $136,360 in Exhibit 7–3, but the two methods have identical total costs to account for of $60,520 in Department 1. This difference in Department 2 results because the costs transferred from Department 1 are not the same under the two methods. This difference could also arise if the beginning inventories using FIFO and average costing were not identical. In Exhibits 7–3 and 7–4, the cost of beginning inventory is identical.

COMPLETED AND ON-HAND INVENTORY

Using average costing.   In practice, not all products finished during a period are always transferred to the next department by the time costing for that period is done. Thus, an added calculation must be made. Exhibit 7–5 illustrates the weighted-average process costing approach when a department has completed units in inventory that were not transferred to the next department during the period in which they were finished. The mixing department in Exhibit 7–5 has 500 completed units and 2,400 semifinished units in beginning inventory. The assembly department also has both completed and semifinished units in beginning inventory. These departments may have completed the units on the last day of the previous month and did not have time to transfer them to the next department. The completed units are included in the ending inventory for the previous month.

In this case, the cost allocated to both the completed and semifinished units is included with the current cost to arrive at the unit cost. For example, in computing the mixing department material unit cost, the $1,000 material assigned to the completed units is added to the $1,600 assigned to the 2,400 units to reach a one-third stage of material processing along with the $23,845 current material cost. This total material cost of $26,445 is divided by the 12,900 material equivalent units to arrive at a $2.05 unit material cost in the mixing department. Since overhead is often applied on the basis of direct labor dollars or direct labor-hours and thus will be at the same stage of completion as direct labor, some companies combine their direct labor costs and factory overhead costs into a conversion cost category, as illustrated in Exhibit 7–5. A computation similar to the one for material is made for the conversion cost to arrive at $11.95 unit cost. All 11,000 units transferred (500 completed and on hand + 2,400 semifinished units + 8,100 units started and completed this period) are assigned a total unit cost of $14.

An additional computation must be made for the assembly department because the average unit cost from the preceding department must be determined. The $5,264 cost for the 400 completed units is added to the $3,951 cost for the 300 semifinished units along with the $154,000 current cost transferred for the 11,000 units received from the mixing department. Average unit cost for material and conversion cost are then computed, giving a $23.85 total unit cost. The 10,900 units completed and transferred to finished goods inventory are each assigned the $23.85 unit cost, even though 400 units were completed and 300 units were partially completed last period.

Using FIFO costing.   Exhibit 7–6 uses the data presented in Exhibit 7–5 to illustrate FIFO costing when completed units are in beginning inventory. In arriving at the unit cost, only current cost is divided by the equivalent units. The completed units are treated as a separate batch of inventory that is transferred to the next department. In both the mixing and assembly departments, the cost transferred comes from the following three sources: completed units on hand in beginning inventory, semifinished units from beginning inventory that are finished during the month, and units that are started and finished during the month.

SUMMARY

In deciding whether to adopt process costing or job order costing, the accountant should first study the nature of the company's manufacturing operations. Process costing accumulates costs for a given time period in each department. This approach differs from job order costing in which the job becomes the focal point for assigning costs. Process costing would, therefore, be adaptable for a company with assembly-line operations where there is a continuous flow of products. However, if the products differ considerably

EXHIBIT 7–5

MARK MANUFACTURING COMPANY
Cost of Production Report—Weighted Average
For Month Ending December 31, 19—

	Mixing department		Assembly department	
Quantity schedule (Step 1):				
Completed and on hand	500		400	
Semifinished inventory				
(⅓ material, ¼ conversion cost) [Mixing]	2,400			
(⅙ M, ⅖ CC) [Assembly]			300	
Units started in process	10,000		11,000	
	12,900		11,700	
Units transferred to next department	11,000		10,900	
Ending inventory				
(all materials, ⅖ conversion cost) [Mixing]	1,900			
(¼ M, ⅗ CC) [Assembly]			800	
	12,900		11,700	
	Total costs	*Unit costs*	*Total costs*	*Unit costs*
Costs to account for (Steps 2 and 3):				
Work in process—completed inventory:				
Costs from preceding department	–0–		$ 5,264	
Material	$ 1,000		405	
Conversion cost	5,750		3,400	
	$ 6,750		$ 9,069	
Work in process—semifinished inventory:				
Costs from preceding department	–0–		$ 3,951	
Material	$ 1,600		53	
Conversion cost	6,300		1,044	
Total semifinished inventory	$ 7,900		$ 5,048	
Costs received from preceding department			154,000	
Current costs in department:				
Material	23,845	$ 2.05	11,752	$ 13.95
Conversion cost	128,482	11.95	95,700	1.10
				8.80
Total costs to account for	$166,977	$ 14.00	$275,569	$ 23.85
Costs accounted for as follows (Step 4):				
Costs transferred to next department (11,000 × $14)	$154,000			
Costs transferred to next department (10,900 × $23.85)			$259,965	
Work in process—ending inventory:				
Costs from preceding department	–0–		$ 11,160	(800 × $13.95)
Material (1,900 × $2.05)	$ 3,895			
Material (800 × ¼ × $1.10)			220	(800 × ¼ × $1.10)
Conversion cost (1,900 × ⅖ × $11.95)	9,082			
Conversion cost (800 × ⅗ × $8.80)			4,224	(800 × ⅗ × $8.80)
	12,977		15,604	
Total costs accounted for (Step 5)	$166,977		$275,569	

Additional Computations (Step 3):

	Transferred	+	Ending inventory	=	
EU, mixing department, material $\dfrac{\$1{,}000 + \$1{,}600 + \$23{,}845}{12{,}900} = \dfrac{\$26{,}445}{12{,}900} = \$2.05$	11,000	+	1,900 (1,900 × 100%)	=	12,900
EU, mixing department, conversion cost $\dfrac{\$5{,}750 + \$6{,}300 + \$128{,}482}{11{,}760} = \dfrac{\$140{,}532}{11{,}760} = \$11.95$	11,000	+	760 (1,900 × $\frac{2}{5}$)	=	11,760
EU, costs from preceding department $\dfrac{\$5{,}264 + \$3{,}951 + \$154{,}000}{11{,}700} = \dfrac{\$163{,}215}{11{,}700} = \$13.95$	10,900	+	800 (800 × 100%)	=	11,700
EU, assembly department, material $\dfrac{\$405 + \$53 + \$11{,}752}{11{,}100} = \dfrac{\$12{,}210}{11{,}100} = \$1.10$	10,900	+	200 (800 × $\frac{1}{4}$)	=	11,100
EU, assembly department, conversion cost $\dfrac{\$3{,}400 + \$1{,}044 + \$95{,}700}{11{,}380} = \dfrac{\$100{,}144}{11{,}380} = \$8.80$	10,900	+	480 (800 × $\frac{3}{5}$)	=	11,380

Note: The cost transfer entries for this cost of production report are:

Work in process—Assembly Department	154,000	
Work in process—Mixing Department		154,000
Finished Goods Inventory	259,965	
Work in Process—Assembly Department		259,965

EXHIBIT 7–6

MARK MANUFACTURING COMPANY
Cost of Production Report—FIFO
For Month Ending December 31, 19—

	Mixing department		Assembly department	
	Total costs	Unit costs	Total costs	Unit costs
Quantity schedule (Step 1):				
Completed and on hand	500		400	
Semifinished inventory				
(⅓ material, ¼ conversion cost)	2,400			
(⅙ M, ⅖ CC)			300	
Units started in process	10,000		11,000	
	11,000		10,900	
Units transferred to next department			11,000	
Ending inventory				
(all material, ⅖ conversion cost)	1,900		800	
	12,900		11,700	
	12,900		11,700	
Costs to account for (Steps 2 and 3):				
Work in process—completed inventory:				
Costs from preceding department	–0–		$ 5,264	
Material	$ 1,000		405	
Conversion cost	5,750		3,400	
	$ 6,750		$ 9,069	
Work in process—semifinished inventory:				
Costs from preceding department	–0–		$ 3,951	
Material	$ 1,600		53	
Conversion cost	6,300		1,044	
Total semifinished inventory	$ 7,900		$ 5,048	
Costs received from preceding department			153,911	$13.9919
Current cost in department:				
Material	23,845	$ 2.0556	11,752	1.1035
Conversion cost	128,482	12.0527	95,700	8.8122
Total costs to account for	$166,977	$14.1083	$275,480	$23.9076
Cost accounted for as follows (Step 4):				
Costs transferred to next department:				
From completed inventory	$ 6,750		$ 9,069	
From semifinished inventory:				
Value of semifinished inventory	$ 7,900		$ 5,048	
Material added				
(2,400 × ⅔ × $2.0556)	3,289			
(300 × ⅚ × $1.1035)			276	
Conversion cost				
(2,400 × ¾ × $12.0527)	21,695			
(300 × ⅗ × $8.8122)			1,586	
	32,884		6,910	
From current production				
(8,100 × $14.1083)	114,277			
(10,200 × $23.9076)			243,857	
Total cost transferred	$153,911		$259,836	
Work in process—ending inventory:				
Costs from preceding department			$ 11,194	
Material (1,900 × 100% × $2.0556)	$ 3,906			
(800 × ¼ × $1.1035)			220	
Conversion cost (1,900 × ⅖ × $12.0527)	9,160			
(800 × ⅗ × $8.8122)			4,230	
	13,066		15,644	
Total costs accounted for (Step 5)	$166,977		$275,480	

Additional Computations (Step 3):

	Transferred	+	Ending inventory	–	Completed inventory	–	Semifinished inventory		
EU, mixing department, material.....	11,000	+	1,900 (1,900 × 100%)	–	500 (500 × 100%)	–	800 (2,400 × 1/3)	=	11,600
EU, mixing department, conversion cost.............	11,000	+	760 (1,900 × 2/5)	–	500 (500 × 100%)	–	600 (2,400 × 1/4)	=	10,660
EU, preceding department costs.....	10,900	+	800 (800 × 100%)	–	400 (400 × 100%)	–	300 (300 × 100%)	=	11,000
EU, assembly department, material..	10,900	+	200 (800 × 1/4)	–	400 (400 × 100%)	–	50 (300 × 1/6)	=	10,650
EU, assembly department, conversion cost..............	10,900	+	480 (800 × 3/5)	–	400 (400 × 100%)	–	120 (300 × 2/5)	=	10,860

$\dfrac{\$23,845}{11,600} = \$2.0556$

$\dfrac{\$128,482}{10,660} = \$12.0527$

$\dfrac{\$153,911}{11,000} = \$13.9919$

$\dfrac{\$11,752}{10,650} = \$1.1035$

$\dfrac{\$95,700}{10,860} = \$8.8122$

because they are being manufactured according to customer specifications, process costing would not be appropriate. If all units within the product line are alike so that the company is manufacturing to meet future sales needs, process costing could be used.

The weighted-average and FIFO costing methods are two approaches in process costing for handling opening inventory cost. FIFO costing keeps the costs of the units in beginning inventory separate from the cost assigned to the units started and finished during the period. The computation of equivalent units differs with these two methods because of the treatment of beginning inventory. Both methods have their advantages, but it is generally felt that the FIFO method of treating opening inventory is more complex, and, therefore, less desirable, especially if several different batches of beginning inventory are semifinished.

As can be seen in the exhibits in the chapter, the difference using average costing and FIFO costing is insignificant, especially if the raw material price does not fluctuate considerably between periods. In addition, because the production and inventory levels of most industries using process costing usually do not differ widely, labor and overhead costs per unit stay approximately the same. While FIFO is strictly applied within each department, there is averaging of the costs received from previous departments when the units enter a new department. Even though it is recognized that if this averaging procedure were not used, the FIFO method would be burdensome, it does cause the FIFO method to lose some of its value because the costs assigned to the different batches are averaged.

IMPORTANT TERMS AND CONCEPTS

Job order costing

Process costing

Equivalent units or equivalent production

Cost of production reports

Weighted-average process costing

FIFO process costing

Units started and finished

Units transferred

PROBLEM FOR SELF-STUDY

Ann Wells Company manufactures motors through two departments, mixing and finishing. Data for the month of January 19– are given below.

	Mixing	Finishing
Beginning inventory in process.	1,000 units	600 units
Preceding department cost.	0	$ 3,450
Materials added last period. . . . . $	325 (¼ complete)	110 (⅙ complete)
Labor added last period	1,140 (⅗ complete)	330 (⅓ complete)
Overhead added last period	1,440 (⅗ complete)	346 (⅓ complete)

	Mixing	Finishing
Started in process this month	7,000 units	6,000 units
Materials added this month	$ 8,925	$ 6,630
Labor added this month	11,600	11,100
Overhead added this month	14,500	10,200
Ending inventory in process	2,000 units	1,600 units
Stage of completion—material	$1/10$	$1/8$
Stage of completion—labor	$1/5$	$3/4$
Stage of completion—overhead	$1/5$	$3/4$

Required:

Prepare a cost of production report for each department using:

a. The FIFO method.

b. The weighted-average method.

Solution for Problem for Self-Study (p.278)

a. FIFO

ANN WELLS COMPANY
Cost of Production Report—FIFO
For the Month Ending January 31, 19–

	Mixing department		Finishing department		
Quantity schedule (Step 1):					
Beginning inventory					
($1/4$ material, $3/5$ labor & overhead)	1,000		($1/6$ M, $1/3$ L, OH)	600	
Units started in process	7,000	8,000		6,000	6,600
Units transferred to next department	6,000			5,000	
Ending inventory					
($1/10$ material, $1/5$ labor & overhead)	2,000	8,000	($1/8$ M, $3/4$ L, OH)	1,600	6,600
	Total costs	Unit costs		Total costs	Unit costs
Costs to account for (Steps 2 and 3):					
Work in process—beginning inventory:					
Costs from preceding department	–0–			$ 3,450	
Material	$ 325			110	
Labor	1,140			330	
Overhead	1,440			346	
Total beginning inventory	$ 2,905			$ 4,236	
Costs received from					
preceding department				35,830	$ 5.9717
Current costs in department:					
Material	8,925	$1.50		6,630	1.3000
Labor	11,600	2.00		11,100	1.8500
Overhead	14,500	2.50		10,200	1.7000
Total costs to account for	$37,930	$6.00		$67,996	$10.8217
Costs accounted for as follows (Step 4):					
Costs transferred to next department					
from beginning inventory					

a. FIFO *(concluded)*

	Mixing department		Finishing department	
Value of beginning inventory.	$ 2,905			$ 4,236
Material added (1,000 × ¾ × $1.50)	1,125	(600 × ⅚ × $1.30)	650	
Labor added (1,000 × ⅖ × $2)	800	(600 × ⅔ × $1.85)	740	
Overhead added (1,000 × ⅖ × $2.50). . .	1,000	$ 5,830	(600 × ⅔ × $1.70)	680	$ 6,306
From current production (5,000 × $6). . . .		30,000	(4,400 × $10.8217)		47,615
Total costs transferred		$35,830			$53,921
Work in process—ending inventory:					
Costs from preceding department	–0–		(1,600 × $5.9717)	$ 9,555	
Material (2,000 × 1/10 × $1.50)	$ 300		(1,600 × ⅛ × $1.30)	260	
Labor (2,000 × ⅕ × $2.00)	800		(1,600 × ¾ × $1.85)	2,220	
Overhead (2,000 × ⅕ × $2.50)	1,000	2,100	(1,600 × ¾ × $1.70)	2,040	14,075
Total costs accounted for (Step 5). .		$37,930			$67,996

Additional Computations (Step 3):

	Transferred	+	Ending inventory	−	Beginning inventory		
EU mixing, material	6,000	+	2,000(1/10)	−	1,000(¼)	=	5,950

$\dfrac{\$8,925}{5,950} = \$1.50$ unit material

EU, mixing, labor and overhead	6,000	+	2,000(⅕)	−	1,000(⅗)	=	5,800

$\dfrac{\$11,600}{5,800} = \$2$ unit labor

$\dfrac{\$14,500}{5,800} = \$2.50$ unit overhead

EU, cost from preceding department . . .	5,000	+	1,600	−	600	=	6,000

$\dfrac{\$35,830}{6,000} = \$5.9717$

EU, finishing, material.	5,000	+	1,600(⅛)	−	600(⅙)	=	5,100

$\dfrac{\$6,630}{5,100} = \$1.3000$ unit material

EU, finishing, labor and overhead	5,000	+	1,600 (¾)	−	600(⅓)	=	6,000

$\dfrac{\$11,100}{6,000} = \$1.8500$ unit labor

$\dfrac{\$10,200}{6,000} = \$1.7000$ unit overhead

Solution for Problem for Self-Study (p. 278)
b. Weighted average

ANN WELLS COMPANY
Cost of Production Report—Weighted Average
For the Month Ending January 31, 19–

	Mixing department		Finishing department	
Quantity schedule (Step 1):				
Beginning inventory (¼ material, ⅗ labor & overhead).	1,000		(⅙ M, ⅓ L, OH)	600	
Units started in process	7,000	8,000		6,000	6,600
Units transferred to next department	6,000			5,000	

b. Weighted average *(concluded)*

	Mixing department			Finishing department	
	Total costs	Unit costs		Total costs	Unit costs
Ending inventory ($\frac{1}{10}$ material, $\frac{1}{5}$ labor & overhead).	2,000	8,000	($\frac{1}{8}$ M, $\frac{3}{4}$ L, OH)	1,600	6,600
Costs to account for (Steps 2 and 3):					
Work in process—beginning inventory:					
Costs from preceding department.	–0–			$ 3,450	
Material	$ 325			110	
Labor.	1,140			330	
Overhead.	1,440			346	
Total beginning inventory	$ 2,905			$ 4,236	
Costs received from preceding department				35,839	$ 5.9529
Current costs in department:					
Material	8,925	$1.4919		6,630	1.2962
Labor.	11,600	1.9906		11,100	1.8435
Overhead.	14,500	2.4906		10,200	1.7010
Total costs to account for	$37,930	$5.9731		$68,005	$10.7936
Costs accounted for as follows (Step 4):					
Costs transferred to next department (6,000 × $5.9731)	$35,839		(5,000 × $10.7936)		$53,968
Work in process—ending inventory:					
Costs from preceding department.			(1,600 × $5.9529)	$ 9,525	
Material (2,000 × $\frac{1}{10}$ × $1.4919).	$ 299		(1,600 × $\frac{1}{8}$ × $1.2962)	259	
Labor (2,000 × $\frac{1}{5}$ × $1.9906).	796		(1,600 × $\frac{3}{4}$ × $1.8435)	2,212	
Overhead (2,000 × $\frac{1}{5}$ × $2.4906).	996	2,091	(1,600 × $\frac{3}{4}$ × $1.7010)	2,041	14,037
Total costs accounted for (Step 5). .		$37,930			$68,005

Additional Computations (Step 3):

	Transferred	+	Ending inventory		
EU, mixing material	6,000	+	2,000 ($\frac{1}{10}$)	=	6,200

$$\frac{\$325 + \$8,925}{6,200} = \frac{\$9,250}{6,200} = \$1.4919 \text{ unit material}$$

| EU, mixing, labor, and overhead. . . . . | 6,000 | + | 2,000 ($\frac{1}{5}$) | = | 6,400 |

$$\frac{\$1,140 + \$11,600}{6,400} = \frac{\$12,740}{6,400} = \$1.9906 \text{ unit labor}$$

$$\frac{\$1,440 + \$14,500}{6,400} = \frac{\$15,940}{6,400} = \$2.4906 \text{ unit overhead}$$

| EU, cost from preceding department . . . . | 5,000 | + | 1,600 | = | 6,600 |

$$\frac{\$3,450 + \$35,839}{6,600} = \frac{\$39,289}{6,600} = \$5.9529 \text{ unit cost from preceding department}$$

| EU, finishing, material . . . . | 5,000 | + | 1,600 ($\frac{1}{8}$) | = | 5,200 |

$$\frac{\$110 + \$6,630}{5,200} = \frac{\$6,740}{5,200} = \$1.2962 \text{ unit material}$$

| EU, finishing, labor and overhead. . . . . | 5,000 | + | 1,600 ($\frac{3}{4}$) | = | 6,200 |

$$\frac{\$330 + \$11,100}{6,200} = \frac{\$11,430}{6,200} = \$1.8435 \text{ unit labor}$$

$$\frac{\$346 + \$10,200}{6,200} = \frac{\$10,546}{6,200} = \$1.7010 \text{ unit overhead}$$

REVIEW QUESTIONS

1. Discuss the characteristics of the production process which determine whether job order costing or process costing is used.
2. What factors help determine whether process or job order costing is used?
3. On what basis are costs accumulated using process costing?
4. Why is it suggested that the product unit under process costing may be visualized as a snowball as it travels from one department to another?
5. Define equivalent units.
6. Why is it necessary to compute equivalent units and how are they used?
7. On the quantity schedule for a department, 1,000 units are indicated as finished and transferred; does this necessarily mean that the unit is in a finished stage ready for sale to a customer?
8. What is the purpose of the quantity schedule on the cost of production report?
9. Why is it necessary to express the units in the quantity schedule on the cost of production report in terms of the department's finished product?
10. Indicate the steps in preparing a cost of production report.
11. How does the cost of production report provide proof as to the correctness of the disposition of costs?
12. What cost components does the preceding department cost represent?
13. Why is it necessary to summarize material, labor, and factory overhead by departments rather than merely to determine total cost for the finished product?
14. Why should the accountant be concerned about determining when material is issued into the production process?
15. Why is it not imperative that predetermined factory overhead rates be used in some process costing systems?
16. When would you advise using estimated factory overhead application rates in a process costing system?
17. Indicate the journal entry to transfer costs *(a)* from one processing department to another department; and *(b)* upon completion from the last processing department.
18. Contrast how the costs of beginning inventory are treated in the weighted-average and FIFO costing approaches used in process costing.
19. Indicate the equivalent unit formulas for average costing and for FIFO costing in a process cost system.
20. What is the difference between units transferred and units started and finished during current production?
21. What information regarding beginning inventory is needed for FIFO costing that is not needed to compute the unit costs under average costing?
22. Why is the FIFO method of accounting for beginning inventory costs sometimes referred to as the modified or departmental FIFO method? Why not use strict FIFO costing?
23. Why would a processing department have in its inventory units that were already complete?

24. With average costing, in which there are completed and incompleted units in inventory, what costs are added together to arrive at the equivalent unit cost?

EXERCISES

E7–1. Equivalent units, average costing, FIFO

Analysis of the records of the Burnett Company revealed the following:

Beginning inventory	3,000 units
⅕ of inventory is ⅓ complete	
⅘ of inventory is ¼ complete	
Transferred.	30,000 units
Started.	32,000 units
Ending inventory	
⅕ inventory is ¹⁄₁₀ complete	
⅘ of inventory is ¾ complete	

Required:

a. Calculate equivalent units for FIFO costing.
b. Calculate equivalent units for weighted-average costing.

E7–2. Cost of production report

ROBERT CURBO COMPANY
Department 2
Cost of Production Report
For the Month Ending February 19X1

Quantity schedule:			
Beginning inventory	100	(¼ M, ⅕ L, ¹⁄₁₀ OH)	
Received from prior department	900		1,000
Transferred.	800		
Ending inventory	200	(⅕ M, ½ L, ¼ OH)	1,000
Value of beginning inventory:			
Prior department costs	$100		
Material	55		
Labor.	48		
Overhead.	34		
Total value of beginning inventory		$ 237	
Current costs:			
Costs received from prior department		990	
Material		2,119	
Labor.		1,728	
Overhead.		2,520	
Total costs to account for		$7,594	

Required:

Using the above partial cost of production report, determine the following:

a. What does prior department cost represent (indicate in terms of cost elements)?
b. In what department was the $100 prior department cost incurred? To how many units was the $100 applied?

c. What figure represents the costs of the 900 units received?
d. What figure represents the cost incurred for the beginning inventory to reach a one-fourth stage of material content? In what department was it incurred? When was the cost incurred?
e. When was the $48 labor cost incurred and in what department?
f. Calculate the equivalent units and unit cost using FIFO costing for material.
g. Calculate the equivalent units and unit cost using FIFO costing for labor.
h. Calculate the equivalent units and unit cost using FIFO costing for overhead.
i. Calculate the equivalent units and unit cost using FIFO costing for prior department cost.
j. Calculate the equivalent units and unit cost using average costing for material.
k. Calculate the equivalent units and unit cost using average costing for labor.
l. Calculate the equivalent units and unit cost using average costing for overhead.
m. Calculate the equivalent units and unit cost using average costing for prior department cost.

E7–3. Equivalent units, FIFO, average costing

Marge Company has the following production cost data:

	Units
Beginning inventory	1,600
1/4 is 1/5 finished	
1/8 is 1/4 finished	
5/8 is 3/5 finished	
Started into process	8,000
Transferred	7,100
Ending inventory	2,500
2/5 is 3/4 finished	
1/10 is 1/5 finished	
1/2 is 2/5 finished	

Required:

a. Calculate equivalent production units using weighted-average costing.
b. Calculate equivalent production units using FIFO costing.

E7–4. FIFO process costing: Cost accounted for section

As another member of the Trident Company's cost accounting department leaves for a committee meeting, she hands you a cost of production report to complete. You notice that she has already determined that equivalent units for material are 2,860 and 2,885 for conversion cost.

A total of 2,785 units were transferred to the next department; ending inventory consisted of 300 units, two-thirds complete as to material and three-fourths complete as to conversion cost. The following data are available for your use:

Beginning inventory (500 units, 1/4 complete):	
Material	$ 375
Conversion cost	350
Current cost:	
Material	9,009
Conversion cost	8,078
Cost to account for	$17,812

Required:

Using FIFO costing, determine the cost transferred and the value of ending inventory.

E7–5. EU and EU cost calculations

The departmental Work in Process account for Watters Company is presented below. All direct materials are placed in process at the beginning of production.

Work in Process Department A

700 units, 40% completed	4,500	To Department B,	
Direct materials (1,850 @ $9)	16,650	2,550 units	34,185
Direct labor	7,900		
Factory overhead	5,135		
	34,185		34,185

Determine the following, presenting your computations:

Required:

a. Equivalent units of production for conversion costs.
b. Conversion costs per equivalent unit of production.
c. Total and unit cost of products started in previous period and completed in the current period.
d. Total and unit cost of current production (round computations to three decimals).
e. Indicate factors that could cause the unit costs computed in c and d to vary.
f. Are there units left in ending inventory? Explain your answer.

E7–6. FIFO process costing: Determining current cost

Because you are such an industrious cost accountant, you decide to return to the office tonight and finish the cost of production report you started during regular working hours. However, to your dismay, you find that the safe is locked up and you forgot to bring your keys. After extracting the work sheet from your drawer, you are delighted to find that the following figures have already been recorded on it:

BOWDEN COMPANY

Value of beginning inventory (880 units):
Material (¼ stage of completion) $242
Conversion cost (⅖ of completion). 704
Units transferred: 4,000
Ending inventory: 750 units having ⅓ material and
⅕ conversion cost

You remember that management was quite concerned that material cost had increased $0.05 per unit and conversion cost had an increase of $0.10 per unit from last period.

Required:

Prepare a cost of production report using FIFO costing.

E7–7. Average costing: Determining units transferred

By mistake, the cost of production report that you have been working on for the Hazel branch was thrown in the paper shredder. From your notes, you can determine that material unit cost was $4.20 and that conversion cost was $5.05 for this month. Reference to your records reveals that equivalent units were 2,100 for material and 1,950 for conversion cost. A total of 600 units having all of their material and three-fourths of their labor was in ending inventory. Last month's ending inventory showed that $560 of material and $380 of conversion cost had been added to these units.

Required:

Prepare cost to account for and costs accounted for sections of a production report using average costing.

E7–8.   Average and FIFO costing items

The production and cost data of Touch Company for June are as follows:

Production:
In process, June 1 (material fully issued; ¼ complete for labor and overhead)	16,400 units
Started in process during June.	120,000
Completed and transferred to next department	130,900
In process June 30 (material fully issued; ⅖ complete for labor and overhead)	5,500

Costs:
Work in process inventory, June 1:		
Materials.	$9,512	
Labor and overhead	1,844	$ 11,356
Materials issued during month		73,692
Labor and overhead.		62,044
Total		$147,092

Required:

a. Determine the following using average costing:
   (1)   The equivalent units for material.
   (2)   The material cost per unit.
   (3)   The equivalent units for labor and overhead.
   (4)   The labor and conversion cost per unit.
   (5)   The total cost transferred to the next department.
   (6)   The value of work in process, June 30.
b. Repeat the requirements in *a* using FIFO costing.

E7–9.   Theory of equivalent units (AICPA adapted)

An important concept in process costing is that of equivalent units.

Required:

a. Describe the difference between units placed in process for a period and equivalent units for a period when there is no beginning work in process inventory and the ending work in process inventory is 50 percent complete.
b. Describe the difference between units completed for a period and equivalent units for a period when there is no beginning work in process inventory and the ending work in process inventory is 50 percent complete.
c. Describe how equivalent units for a period are used to compute the cost of the ending work in process inventory.

PROBLEMS

P7–1. FIFO process costing: Determining current cost

The following limited data are available for Herbert Licon, Inc. for February:

Value of Beginning Inventory (2,400 units):
Material (⅓ stage of completion)	$320
Conversion Cost (¾ stage of completion)	$810
Units transferred	10,500

The ending inventory is 700 units having one-half material and three-sevenths conversion cost.

Material cost increased $0.10 per unit and conversion cost increased $0.15 per unit from January.

Required:

Prepare a cost of production report using FIFO costing.

P7–2. Process costing: One department, average costing

Fieldstone Manufacturing Company utilizes a process cost system for their factory departments. After leaving the Fabricating Department, one third of the goods finished are transferred to finished goods and sold immediately. The remainder is transferred to the next department.

You obtain the following data from the department's records for the month ending January 31, 19–:

	Fabricating department
Beginning inventory	200 units
Stage of completion	⅕ material
	¼ conversion costs
Started in process	8,230 units
Ending inventory	600
Stage of completion	⅖ material
	⅙ conversion costs
Value of beginning inventory:	
Material	$ 126
Conversion costs	250
Current material cost	24,891
Current conversion costs	37,814

Required:

a. Prepare a cost of production report using average costing.
b. If FIFO costing were used instead, determine:
   (1) Equivalent units for material in the Fabricating Department.
   (2) Equivalent units for conversion costs in the Fabricating Department.

P7–3. Equivalent units (AICPA)

The Felix Manufacturing Company uses a process cost system to account for cost of its only product, known as "Nino." Production begins in the fabrication department where units of raw material are molded into various connecting parts. After fabrication is complete, the units are transferred to the assembly department. There is no material added in this department. After assembly is complete, the units are transferred to the packaging department where they are packaged for shipment. At the completion of this process, the units are complete and transferred to the shipping department.

At year end, December 31, 19–, the following inventory of "Ninos" is on hand:

No unused raw material or packing material.

Fabrication department: 6,000 units, 25 percent complete as to raw material and 40 percent complete as to direct labor.

Assembly department: 10,000 units, 75 percent complete as to direct labor.

Packaging department: 3,000 units, 60 percent complete as to packing material and 75 percent complete as to direct labor.

Shipping department: 8,000 units.

Required:

Prepare in proper form schedules showing the following as of December 31, 19–.

a. The number of equivalent units of raw material in all inventories.
b. The number of equivalent units of fabrication department direct labor in all inventories.
c. The number of equivalent units of packaging department material and direct labor in the packaging department inventory.

P7–4. Process costing: FIFO and average costing, second department

The following information is given for Department 2 of the Tennyson Company, for the month of June, 19X1. The company uses a process cost system.

Beginning inventory.	600 units (⅓ material,
	⅙ conversion costs)
Prior department costs.	$925
Material.	$280
Conversion costs	$270
Started into process	5,000 units
Current costs:	
Material.	$ 7,245
Conversion costs	$13,832
Costs received from prior	
department	$ 7,750
Transferred	5,300 units
Ending inventory	300 units (¼ material,
	⅖ conversion costs)

Required:

a. Prepare a production cost report using FIFO.
b. Prepare a production cost report using the weighted-average method.

P7–5. Process costing: Completed and semifinished units in beginning inventory (weighted-average and FIFO costing)

Paden Reeves Company uses a process costing system in the grinding department and the assembly department. There were several batches of units finished and on hand when operations began for the month of February. Data from the records are as follows:

	Grinding department	Assembly department
Started in process	3,900 units	?
Completed and on hand	200 units	500 units
Value of completed units:		
Costs from preceding department. . . .		$ 2,365
Material . . . . $	460	400
Labor.	240	825
Overhead.	100	1,650
Semifinished units on hand.	1,800 units	600 units
Value of semifinished units and stage of completion:		
Costs from preceding department. . . .		$ 2,300
Material . . . . $	1,125 (1/6)	450 (1/3)
Labor.	531 (1/4)	192 (1/5)
Overhead.	336 (1/3)	495 (1/4)
Current costs:		
Material	10,588	2,975
Labor.	5,695	7,728
Overhead.	2,420	15,119
Ending inventory	900 units	1,200 units
Stage of completion:	(1/5 M, 1/3 L, 1/9 OH)	(1/6 M, 1/3 L, 1/4 OH)

There were no units completed and on hand at the end of the month.

Required:

a. Prepare a cost of production report using weighted-average costing.

b. Prepare a cost of production report using FIFO costing.

P7–6. FIFO costing: Two departments, two batches in inventory

Cherokee Manufacturing Company produces pumps in two departments, mixing and finishing. Each pump requires 3 pounds of material. After the mixing department has finished its operations, the pumps are sent to the finishing department in lots of 40. Data for the month of May follows:

Material is introduced at the beginning of operations in the mixing department; 3,000 pounds were introduced during the month. Material is added at the end of finishing department operations. There were two batches of beginning inventory in each department.

	Mixing department		Finishing department	
	Batch No. 1	Batch No. 2	Batch No. 1	Batch No. 2
Number of units	90 pumps	120 pumps	4 lots	2 lots
Stage of completion	2/5 conversion costs	2/3 conversion costs	3/4 conversion costs	1/2 conversion costs
Costs from preceding department:			$880	$478
Material cost. $362		$475		
Conversion costs . . . . . $ 70		$ 83	$ 42	$ 16
Current costs:				
Material cost.	$4,000		$ 315	
Conversion cost	$2,052		$2,640	

There were also two batches of ending inventory within each department:

	Mixing department		Finishing department	
	Batch A	Batch B	Batch A	Batch B
Number of units	30 pumps	60 pumps	5 lots	8 lots
Stage of completion	⅓ conversion costs	⅕ conversion costs	⅗ conversion costs	¼ conversion costs

Required:

a. Prepare a cost of production report using FIFO costing.
b. Without preparing a cost of production report, determine the following using average costing:
   (1) EU of material for the mixing department.
   (2) Equivalent unit cost of material for the mixing department.

P7–7. Average costing, FIFO for two months

Rosser Production Company employs a process cost system in the manufacture of industrial chemicals. Three departments are involved in the process: mixing, refining, and finishing. No units are lost in the refining department. Data for January and February operations in the refining department are extracted from their records as follows:

	January	February
Beginning inventory	600	?
Stage of completion	¾ material	?
	⅖ conversion costs	?
Received from preceding department	1,500	2,000
Ending inventory	330	500
Stage of completion	⅔ material	⅘ material
	⅙ conversion costs	¹⁄₁₀ conversion costs
Value of beginning inventory:		
Costs from preceding department	$1,170	?
Material cost	308	?
Conversion cost	132	?
Costs received from preceding department	3,000	$3,900
Current material cost	3,234	4,422
Current conversion cost	951	1,168

Required:

a. Prepare a cost of production report using FIFO costing.
b. Prepare a cost of production report using average costing.

P7–8. Process costing, two departments: Average costing and FIFO

William Schoof Manufacturing Company utilizes a process cost system for the two factory departments. After leaving the fabricating department, one third of the goods finished are transferred to finished goods and sold immediately. The remainder is transferred to the finishing department.

You obtain the following data from their records for the month ending January 31, 19–.

	Fabricating department	Finishing department
Beginning inventory	100 units	500 units
Stage of completion	¼ material	⅕ material
	⅗ conversion costs	⅒ conversion costs
Started in process	7,560 units	?
Ending inventory	700	1,140
Stage of completion	⅕ material	⅗ material
	2/7 conversion costs	¾ conversion costs
Value of beginning inventory:		
Costs from preceding department		$4,157
Material	$ 65	30
Conversion cost	330	43
Current material cost	14,135	2,312
Current conversion cost	41,198	2,870

Required:

a. Prepare a cost of production report using average costing.

b. Prepare a cost of production report using FIFO costing. Assume the 100 units in beginning inventory are included in the units transferred to the finishing department.

P7–9. Process costing: Completed and semifinished units in beginning inventory

Union Company uses a process costing system in the mixing and finishing departments. There were several batches of units finished and on hand when operations began for the month of June. Data from the records are as follows for the mixing department:

	Mixing department
Started in process.	3,800 units
Completed and on hand	400 units
Value of completed units:	
Material.	$ 1,960
Conversion costs	$ 1,700
Semifinished units on hand	500 units
Value of semifinished units and stage of completion:	
Material.	$ 680 (⅖)
Conversion costs	$ 550 (¼)
Current costs:	
Material.	$19,860
Conversion costs	$15,685
Ending inventory	600 units
Stage of completion	(⅔ material, ⅕ conversion costs)

There were no units completed and on hand at the end of the month.

Required:

a. Prepare a production cost report using the weighted-average method.

b. Prepare a production cost report using FIFO.

P7–10.   FIFO and average process costing: Third department

Data for Department 3 of Maud Key, Inc. for the month of May are given below for use in a process cost system.

```
Started in process . . . . . . . . . . . .   5,000 units
Current material cost . . . . . . . . . . $  4,675
Current conversion cost . . . . . . . . $16,926
Costs from prior departments . . . . . $35,000
Transferred. . . . . . . . . . . . . . . . . .   4,500 units
Beginning inventory . . . . . . . . . . .     900 units
                                           (⅔ material,
                                            ⅚ conversion costs)

      Costs from
        prior departments . . . . . . . . . $  6,100
      Material . . . . . . . . . . . . . . . . . . $    600
      Conversion costs . . . . . . . . . . . $  3,075
      Ending inventory . . . . . . . . . . . .   1,400 units
                                           (¼ material,
                                            ⅕ conversion costs)
```

Required:

a.   Prepare a production cost report using the FIFO method
b.   Prepare a production cost report using the weighted-average method.

P7–11.   Process costing: Weighted average and FIFO costing

Drew Company manufactures products under a process costing system in Department 35 and Department 36. There were several batches of units on hand when operations began for the month of January. Data from the records are as follows:

	Department 35	Department 36
Started in process	2,800 units	?
Beginning inventory	100 units	500 units
Value of beginning inventory and stage of completion:		
Costs from preceding department. . . .		$8,640
Material . . . . $	76 (¼)	280 (⅕)
Labor.	375 (⅗)	53 (¹⁄₁₀)
Overhead.	175 (⅕)	96 (¼)
Current costs:		
Material	4,311	7,140
Labor.	14,795	3,060
Overhead.	9,520	1,660
Ending inventory:.	600 units	800 units
Stage of completion	⅕ material,	⅗ material,
	¾ labor,	¾ labor,
	⅙ overhead	¼ overhead

There were no units completed and on hand at the end of the month.

Required:

Prepare cost of production reports using weighted-average and FIFO costing.

P7–12.   Weighted-average process costing (AICPA adapted)

You are engaged in the audit of the December 31, 19X1, financial statements of Spirit Corporation, which manufactures digital watches. You are attempting to verify the costing of the ending inventory of work in process and finished goods which were recorded on Spirit's books as follows:

	Units	Cost
Work in process (50% complete as to labor and overhead	300,000	$ 660,960
Finished goods	200,000	1,009,800

Materials are added to production at the beginning of the manufacturing process and overhead is applied to each product at the rate of 60 percent of direct labor costs. There was no finished goods inventory on January 1, 19X1. A review of Spirit's inventory cost records disclosed the following information:

	Units	Materials	Labor
Work in process January 1, 19X1 (80% complete as to labor and overhead)	200,000	$ 200,000	$ 315,000
Units started in production	1,000,000		
Material costs		$1,300,000	
Labor costs			$1,995,000
Units completed	900,000		

Required:

a. Prepare schedules as of December 31, 19X1 to compute the following:
   (1) Equivalent units of production using the weighted-average method.
   (2) Unit costs of production of materials, labor, and overhead.
   (3) Costing of the finished goods inventory and work in process inventory.
b. Prepare the necessary journal entry to correctly state the inventory of finished goods and work in process, assuming the books have not been closed. (Ignore income tax considerations.)

P7–13. Weighted-average cost of production report (AICPA adapted)

Lakeview Corporation uses the weighted-average process cost method to account for costs of production. The firm manufactures a product that is produced in three separate departments: molding, assembling, and finishing. The following information was obtained for the assembling department for the month of June 19–:

Work in process, June 1—2,000 units composed of the following:

	Amount	Degree of completion (percent)
Transferred in from the molding department	$32,000	100
Costs added by the assembling department:		
Direct materials	20,000	100
Direct labor	7,200	60
Factory overhead applied	5,500	50
	32,700	
Work in process, June 1	$64,700	

The following occurred during the month of June: 10,000 units were transferred in from the molding department at a cost of $160,000; and $150,000 in costs were added by the assembling department:

Direct materials . . . . $ 96,000
Direct labor   36,000
Factory overhead applied.   18,000
                                             $150,000

Eight thousand units were completed and transferred to the finishing department.

On June 30, 4,000 units were still in work in process. The degree of completion was as follows:

	Percent
Direct materials	90
Direct labor	70
Factory overhead applied.	35

Required:

Prepare in good form a cost of production report for the assembling department for the month of June. Show supporting computations. The report should include:

a. Equivalent units of production.
b. Total manufacturing costs.
c. Cost per equivalent unit.
d. Dollar amount of ending work in process.
e. Dollar amount of inventory cost transferred out.

Addition of material

Increase in units under average costing

Increase in units under FIFO costing

Loss of units

Normal versus abnormal loss

Inspection at end of operations

Inspection at the beginning of operations

Allocation of normal loss

Inspection at midpoint of processing

OBJECTIVES OF CHAPTER 8

1. To discuss the effect on operations of additional material.

2. To illustrate the costing procedure used when the addition of material results in an increase in units to account for.

3. To distinguish between the costing procedures used for abnormal loss and those used for normal loss of units.

8

Process costing—addition of material and lost units

The preceding chapter introduced the basic steps involved in preparing a cost of production report for a firm using a process costing approach. The FIFO and weighted-average methods of treating opening inventory costs were presented. However, many of the complexities that can be encountered in process costing are not discussed in Chapter 7. For one thing, product unit costs must be computed for inventory valuation, and this computation becomes more difficult if the material added to production increases the units to account for or if units are lost in the manufacturing operations. This chapter illustrates the costing procedures used to handle these complexities.

ADDITION OF MATERIAL

The addition of material may either increase the number of units that must be accounted for or increase only the unit costs of the product. For example, in manufacturing shirts, the fabric is issued at the beginning of manufacturing operations. Additional material is later introduced in the finishing department when buttons are sewed on. This material in the form of buttons does not increase the number of shirts; the only effect is an increase in the unit cost. A similar situation occurs when parts are added to toasters that are being assembled, as there is no increase in the units to account for; only the nature or character of the product is changed. The costing procedure used to account for material introduced in departments subsequent to the first was introduced in Exhibits 7–2 through 7–6. This approach is much simpler than if the material added increases the number of units in the department.

INCREASE IN UNITS UNDER AVERAGE COSTING

For manufacturing processes in which the addition of material may increase the number of units to be accounted for, the following procedures are employed. Assume that a 100-gallon chemical mixture received from a preceding department is now diluted by adding 50 gallons of water or other fluid. This increases the units to be accounted for to 150 gallons. Since the liquids will be mixed and cannot be distinguished, the cost from the preceding department must be spread over the entire 150 gallons.

Exhibit 8–1 illustrates the procedure using weighted-average costing when the introduction of material results in a larger number of units to account for. Department 1 is purposely kept simple so that emphasis can be placed on Department 2. In addition, labor and factory overhead costs are combined in the one category of conversion cost in Exhibit 8–1. Material is introduced throughout the process in Department 1, the only effect being that each product completed must absorb a $2 unit material cost. Since there is no beginning inventory in Department 1, all 6,500 units transferred to the next department come from current production. Each of the 6,500 units carries a $5 preceding departmental cost when transferred to Department 2. The journal entry recording this transfer of cost is:

```
Work in Process—Department 2. . . . . . . . . . . . . . . . . . . . 32,500
        Work in Process—Department 1 . . . . . . . . . . . . . . . . .          32,500
```

The ending inventory in Department 1 has only received one fifth of its material and two sevenths of its conversion cost. The units are multiplied by the stage of completion and finally by the unit cost to arrive at an ending inventory valuation.

Preceding department costs

After the 6,500 units arrive in Department 2, material costing $6,380 is introduced into operations, which results in an additional 1,000 units to account for. The units are not identified in Exhibit 8–1, but assume that there are 6,500 gallons of paint mixture received from Department 1. When the 6,500 gallons of paint mixture are received in Department 2, 1,000 gallons of oil are added before the paint mixture is processed in Department 2. Since the oil and paint mixture are combined, the cost from the preceding department must be spread over all the units. This can be accomplished by using the equivalent unit computation for average costing that was introduced in Chapter 7 as follows:

EU, preceding department costs = 7,400 transferred + 600 ending = 8,000

$$\text{inventory}$$
$$(600 \times 100\%)$$

$$\frac{\$2,000 + \$32,500}{8,000} = \frac{\$34,500}{8,000} = \$4.313$$

The 7,400 units transferred come from a mixture of the units in beginning inventory, the units received from the preceding department, and the units added in Department 2.

Change in per unit cost.   The $2,000 cost from the preceding department that the 500 units in beginning inventory received was affected last month by the addition of material. This $2,000 is averaged with the current costs received of $32,500 to arrive at a unit cost of $4.313. This is in contrast to the $5 per unit cost from Department 1. This difference partially arises because the costs received from the preceding department are spread over 1,000 additional units, which results in a lower cost per unit. This illustrates that the unit cost changes from one department to another with regard to output. In this case, the additional units contribute to the decrease in per unit cost; in addition, the 500 units in beginning inventory have a preceding department unit cost of $0.40 ($2,000 costs from preceding department ÷ 500 units) which reduces the averaged preceding department per unit cost. Other factors can cause the per unit cost from a preceding department to differ from the completed per unit cost calculated in the previous department. Normal loss of units and averaging with FIFO, which are discussed in this chapter, can also account for the unit cost from a department to change when units enter the subsequent department. These two factors are illustrated in Exhibit 8–5.

The computations for material and conversion cost are illustrated at the bottom of Exhibit 8–1. No difference exists between these computations and the ones presented for average costing in Chapter 7. Since the 600 units in ending inventory have each been through the preceding department, the adjusted unit cost of $4.313 is assigned to all 600 units. After the units in ending inventory are multiplied by their stage of completion and the cost per unit, an inventory valuation of $3,154 is determined. Because the unit costs are only carried out to three decimal places and only whole dollars are illustrated, a decimal discrepancy results. When the 7,400 units transferred are multiplied by $6.043 unit cost in Department 2, the result is $44,718.20. However, if this figure is added to the $3,154 ending inventory valuation, the total does not equal the costs to account for. Because the difference is so small and it is known to be caused by the use of whole dollars and three-digit unit costs, the costs are transferred out at a total of $44,714 ($47,868 costs to account for −$3,154 ending inventory).

It is necessary to arrive at a unit cost for each of the three following components: preceding department costs, Department 2 material, and Department 2 conversion cost. The material cost of $6,380 should not be averaged in with the $2,000 and $32,500 preceding department costs, even though this material did result in 1,000 more units to account for. Instead, a separate unit cost for material should be computed. In this example, material is added throughout the process, causing the material equivalent units to differ from the equivalent units for the preceding department.

EXHIBIT 8–1

WELLS MANUFACTURING COMPANY
Cost of Production Report—Average Costing—Addition of Material
For the Month Ending January 31, 19—

	Department 1			Department 2		
Quantity schedule:						
Beginning inventory.	–0–		(⅕ M, ⅒ CC)		500	
Received from						
preceding department	–0–				6,500	
Increase in units	–0–				1,000	
Started in process.	7,200					
Total units to account for		7,200				8,000
Transferred to next department	6,500				7,400	
Ending inventory						
(⅕ material, 2/7 conversion cost)	700		(⅓ M, ¾ CC)		600	
Total units accounted for		7,200				8,000

	Total costs	Unit costs		Total costs	Unit costs
Costs to acount for:					
Work in process—beginning inventory:					
Costs from preceding department.				$ 2,000	
Material				80	
Conversion cost				43	
Total value of beginning inventory. .				$ 2,123	
Costs from preceding department				32,500	$ 4.313
Current costs:					
Material.	$13,280	$ 2.00		6,380	0.850
Conversion cost.	20,100	3.00		6,865	0.880
Total costs to account for	$33,380	$ 5.00		$47,868	$ 6.043

		Total costs	Unit costs		Total costs	Unit costs
Costs accounted for as follows:						
Costs transferred to next						
department (6,500 × $5)			$32,500	(7,400 × $6.043)		$44,714*
Work in process—ending inventory:						
Costs from preceding department.				(600 × $4.313)	$ 2,588	
Material (700 × ⅕ × $2)	$ 280			(600 × ⅓ × $0.85)	170	
Conversion cost (700 × 2/7 × $3)	600		880	(600 × ¾ × $0.88)	396	3,154
Total costs accounted for			$33,380			$47,868

INCREASE IN UNITS UNDER FIFO COSTING

The data from Exhibit 8–1 are used in Exhibit 8–2 to illustrate the procedure for handling the increase in units using FIFO costing. Since there is no beginning inventory in Department 1, the equivalent units and unit costs are identical to those shown for the first department in Exhibit 8–1. However, differences arise in Department 2 because of the 500 units in beginning inventory. Using FIFO costing, the accountant subtracts the 500 units in

EXHIBIT 8–1 *(concluded)*

Additional computations:

	Transferred	+	Ending inventory		
EU, Department 1, material	6,500	+	140 (700 × ⅕)	=	6,640
$\dfrac{\$13,280}{6,640} = \$2$					
EU, Department 1, conversion cost	6,500	+	200 (700 × 2/7)	=	6,700
$\dfrac{\$20,100}{6,700} = \$3$					
EU, preceding department costs	7,400	+	600 (600 × 100%)	=	8,000
$\dfrac{\$2,000 + \$32,500}{8,000} = \dfrac{\$34,500}{8,000} = \$4.313$					
EU, Department 2, material	7,400	+	200 (600 × ⅓)	=	7,600
$\dfrac{\$80 + \$6,380}{7,600} = \dfrac{\$6,460}{7,600} = \$0.850$					
EU, Department 2, conversion cost	7,400	+	450 (600 × ¾)	=	7,850
$\dfrac{\$43 + \$6,865}{7,850} = \dfrac{\$6,908}{7,850} = \$0.880$					

*7,400 units × $6.043 = $44,718.20. To avoid decimal discrepancy the cost transferred is computed as follows: $47,868 − 3,154 = $44,714.

beginning inventory in the equivalent units calculation for preceding department costs. Only the $32,500 cost transferred from Department 1 is divided by the FIFO equivalent units to arrive at a unit cost of $4.333. As in the average costing method illustrated in Exhibit 8–1, the preceding department unit cost has decreased because the base unit count has increased by 1,000 units. Since the increase in units comes from 1,000 gallons of oil being added before the paint mixture is processed in Department 2, Exhibit 8–2 assumes that the larger base unit count relates only to *new* production. However, if the increase in units develops because materials are added continuously throughout the production process, the larger base unit count would relate to *both* new production and beginning inventory.

Since FIFO costing is being used, the equivalent units in beginning inventory are subtracted to arrive at the unit material and conversion cost for Department 2. The $2,123 value of beginning inventory is not averaged in with current cost. Material cost of $341 and conversion cost of $396 are applied to the 500 units in beginning inventory before they are transferred out of Department 2. Of the 7,400 total units transferred, 6,900 units were started and finished during January. The $44,702 cost transferred represents two batches of production—500 units from beginning inventory and 6,900 units from current production. The 600 units in ending inventory each receive the adjusted preceding department unit cost of $4.333. The cost of one third of the material and three fourths of the conversion cost necessary for completion is then applied to the ending inventory. The final step of proving that the costs of $47,868 are accounted for completes the cost of production report.

EXHIBIT 8–2

WELLS MANUFACTURING COMPANY
Cost of Production Report—FIFO—Addition of Material
For the Month Ending January 31, 19—

	Department 1			Department 2	
Quantity schedule:					
Beginning inventory	–0–		(⅕ M, ¹/₁₀ CC)	500	
Received from					
preceding department	–0–			6,500	
Additional units put in process	–0–			1,000	
Started in process	7,200				
Total units to account for		7,200			8,000
Transferred to next department	6,500			7,400	
Ending inventory					
(⅕ material, ²/₇ conversion cost)	700		(⅓ M, ¾ CC)	600	
Total units accounted for		7,200			8,000

	Total costs	Unit costs		Total costs	Unit costs
Costs to acount for:					
Work in process—beginning inventory:					
Costs from preceding department				$ 2,000	
Material				80	
Conversion cost				43	
Total value of beginning inventory . .				$ 2,123	
Costs from preceding department				32,500	$ 4.333
Current costs in department:					
Material	$13,280	$ 2.00		6,380	0.851
Conversion cost	20,100	3.00		6,865	0.880
Total costs to account for	$33,380	$ 5.00		$47,868	$ 6.064
Costs accounted for as follows:					
╲Costs transferred to next department:					
From beginning inventory:					
Value of beginning inventory				$ 2,123	
Material added			(500 × ⅘ × $0.851)	341*	
Conversion cost added			(500 × ⁹/₁₀ × $0.880)	396	$ 2,860
From current production (6,500 × $5) . .		$32,500	(6,900 × $6.064)		41,842
Total cost transferred		$32,500			$44,702
Work in process—ending inventory:					
Costs from preceding department			(600 × $4.333)	$ 2,600	
Material (700 × ⅕ × $2)	$ 280		(600 × ⅓ × $0.851)	170	
Conversion costs (700 × ²/₇ × $3)	600	880	(600 × ¾ × $0.880)	396	3,166*
Total costs accounted for		$33,380			$47,868

LOSS OF UNITS

In practice, units are frequently *lost*, as well as added, in the manufacturing process. Units can be lost, for example, through spoilage, evaporation, and shrinkage; and even though the company wishes to avoid all possible losses,

EXHIBIT 8–2 *(concluded)*

Additional computations:

	Transferred	+	Ending inventory	−	Beginning inventory		
EU, Department 1, material.	6,500	+	140 (700 × ⅕)			=	6,640
$\dfrac{\$13,280}{6,640} = \$2$							
EU, Department 1, conversion cost.	6,500	+	200 (700 × 2/7)			=	6,700
$\dfrac{\$20,100}{6,700} = \$3$							
EU, preceding department costs	7,400	+	600 (600 × 100%)	−	500 (500 × 100%)	=	7,500
$\dfrac{\$32,500}{7,500} = \$4.333$							
EU, Department 2, material.	7,400	+	200 (600 × ⅓)	−	100 (500 × ⅕)	=	7,500
$\dfrac{\$6,380}{7,500} = \$0.851$							
EU, Department 2, conversion cost.	7,400	+	450 (600 × ¾)	−	50 (500 × 1/10)	=	7,800
$\dfrac{\$6,865}{7,800} = \$0.880$							

*Rounded up $1 due to decimal discrepancy.

some spoilage and evaporation may have to be accepted as an inherent part of the production process. For example, part of the fabric designated for shirt manufacturing ends up in the rag barrel, and some lumber that was purchased to become furniture ends up as sawdust and splintered wood. Obviously, lost units increase the unit costs of the product being manufactured because the remaining (good) units must absorb the costs that had been applied to the units that are lost.

NORMAL VERSUS ABNORMAL LOSS

While it is recognized that in some industries the loss of units is an unavoidable aspect of the specific manufacturing operations, each company should set normal tolerance limits for such losses. A loss within these limits is called a *normal loss*. Loss of units outside of these limits is referred to as an *abnormal* or *avoidable loss*. Limits are usually set to allow for estimates of the number of units that will be lost. The nature of the loss and the point in the processing operations at which the loss takes place also help determine whether it is classified as normal or abnormal.

Normal tolerance limits

To arrive at this distinction between normal and abnormal loss of goods, the accountant must establish tolerance limits. The normal tolerance limits can be expressed as a percentage of the good units that pass the inspection point of the operations. For example, if in the past when inspection was made at the end of processing, a total of 1,000 units introduced into operations yielded an average of 48 bad units, the normal loss percentage would be $^{48}\!/_{952}$ or 5 percent of good production. This percentage would be accepted as the limit only if management's analysis verified that this loss was uncontrollable and an inherent part of operations. Suppose that in a given period, 1,500 units were completed and passed inspection at the end of the operations; it was then discovered that 100 units were lost through spoilage. The normal loss associated with the good units finished would be 75 (5 percent × 1,500 good units), with the remaining 25 units classified as abnormal loss. Cost is then separately determined for the normal and abnormal loss. This enables management to more easily recognize the investment lost through unavoidable and avoidable circumstances.

The loss of units may *occur* at the beginning, during, or at the end of operations within a department; lost units are *discovered*, however, when inspection is made. Typically, the loss is therefore assumed to take place at the end of the department's process because that is usually when inspection occurs and the loss is recognized. However, management may find that it is less costly to make more frequent inspections than to run the risk of applying cost to a unit that has already been spoiled. There is always a trade-off between the expense of additional inspection and the risk of incurring material and conversion cost for a unit that unknowingly has become spoiled.

INSPECTION AT END OF OPERATIONS

Exhibit 8–3 illustrates a cost of production report in which lost units are detected at the end of operations in a department. If final inspection is made at the end of processing, none of the spoiled units come from the current ending work in process inventory and no cost is allocated to the units still in process in ending inventory. The cost of the normal loss is charged only to the completed units. With these inspection arrangements, the units found to be spoiled have been completed. For this reason, completed units must be charged with the full cost of operations.

In Exhibit 8–3 there are 100 units lost through normal causes while 50 units are lost due to abnormal conditions. Because inspection is not made until the end of operations, all spoiled units have been through the assembly department's entire operations. For this reason, the units are added in the equivalent unit (EU) computations that follow:

$$\begin{array}{lccccc} \text{EU,} & = 4,500 & + 50 & + 100 & + 50 & = 4,700 \\ \text{material} & \text{transferred} & (350 \times \tfrac{1}{7}) & \text{normal} & \text{abnormal} & \\ & & \text{ending} & \text{loss} & \text{loss} & \\ & & \text{inventory} & & & \end{array}$$

$$\frac{\$47 + \$9,353}{4,700} = \frac{\$9,400}{4,700} = \$2$$

EXHIBIT 8–3

KNIGHT COMPANY—ASSEMBLY DEPARTMENT
Cost of Production Report
Average Costing, Lost Units
Inspection at End of Processing
For the Month of January 19—

Quantity schedule:

Units in beginning inventory	100	(¼ M, ⅕ CC)
Units started in process	4,900	
Total units to account for	5,000	
Units transferred	4,500	
Units in ending inventory	350	(½ M, ⅒ CC)
Normal loss of units	100	
Abnormal loss of units	50	
Total units accounted for	5,000	

	Total costs	Unit costs
Costs to account for:		
Value of beginning inventory:		
Material	$ 47	
Conversion cost	109	
Total value of beginning inventory	$ 156	
Current costs:		
Material:	9,353	$2
Conversion cost	13,946	3
Total costs to account for	$23,455	$5
Costs accounted for as follows:		
Costs of abnormal loss (50 × $5)		$ 250
Costs transferred before normal loss (4,500 × $5)	$22,500	
Costs of normal loss (100 × $5)	500	23,000
Ending inventory:		
Material (½ × 350 × $2)	$ 100	
Conversion cost (⅒ × 350 × $3)	105	205
Total costs accounted for		$23,455

Additional computations:

	Trans-ferred	+	Ending inventory	+	Normal loss	+	Abnormal loss	
EU, material	4,500	+	50 (350 × ½)	+	100	+	50	= 4,700

$$\frac{\$47 + \$9,353}{4,700} = \frac{\$9,400}{4,700} = \$2$$

	Trans-ferred	+	Ending inventory	+	Normal loss	+	Abnormal loss	
EU, conversion cost	4,500	+	35 (350 × ⅒)	+	100	+	50	= 4,685

$$\frac{\$109 + \$13,946}{4,685} = \frac{\$14,055}{4,685} = \$3$$

$$\begin{array}{cccccc} \text{EU,} & = 4{,}500 & + 35 & + 100 & + 50 & = 4{,}685 \\ \text{conversion} & \text{transferred} & (350 \times \frac{1}{10}) & \text{normal} & \text{abnormal} & \\ \text{cost} & & \text{ending} & \text{loss} & \text{loss} & \\ & & \text{inventory} & & & \end{array}$$

$$\frac{\$109 + \$13{,}946}{4{,}685} = \frac{\$14{,}055}{4{,}685} = \$3$$

Alternate ways of handling lost units. The illustration above includes lost units in the equivalent units calculation. Another approach suggested by accounting authorities, however, involves omitting the lost units in the equivalent unit computations and adjusting the costs from the preceding department for the lost units. This may appear to be a shortcut in that it automatically allocates the cost of the normal loss of units over the good units. However, this results in inaccurate costing if material, labor, and factory overhead costs are not incurred uniformly throughout the department's production process and if there are beginning and ending work in process balances. Since most manufacturing operations are continuous and have beginning and ending work in process balances, these restrictions are difficult to avoid. As a result, only the approach used in Exhibit 8–3 is illustrated in this book.

Cost of abnormal and normal loss. After equivalent units are calculated for material and conversion costs, the $5 total unit cost is assigned to the 4,500 units transferred out of the department to arrive at a total of $22,500 (4,500 units × $5). The $5 unit cost is also used to arrive at the cost of the abnormal loss and the normal loss. The cost of the abnormal loss of units is $250 (50 units × $5), while the cost of the normal loss of units is $500 (100 units × $5). The $500 cost charged to the units lost due to normal conditions is then added to the cost of the good units completed and transferred to arrive at a total cost transferred of $23,000 ($22,500 + $500). The 4,500 units enter the next department with a total cost of $23,000. Since only one department is illustrated in Exhibit 8–3, the next department is presumed to be finished goods. A separate journal entry is not needed to record the normal loss of units; the $500 cost is added to the $22,500 cost of the good units to arrive at the following:

Finished Goods Inventory.	23,000	
Work in Process—Assembly Department		23,000

The journal entry above assumes that the 100 units lost because of normal conditions have no sales value; this is obviously the case if the normal loss were due to evaporation. If we instead assume that the spoiled units could be sold as irregulars or scrap material for $100, the spoilage should be assigned net sales value and set up in an inventory account. The Work in Process—Assembly Department's account is credited for the sales value of the spoilage. The good units completed now bear only a $400 cost ($500 cost of normal loss − $100 sales value of normal loss) due to the normal loss of units. The journal entry is as follows:

Spoiled Goods or Scrap Material Inventory	100	
Work in Process—Assembly Department.		100
Finished Goods Inventory ($22,500 + $500 − $100)	22,900	
Work in Process—Assembly Department.		22,900

This is the approach suggested in Chapter 3 for accounting for scrap and spoiled goods.

When the units lost through normal conditions are sold, the entry is as follows:

Cash or Accounts Receivable	100	
Spoiled Goods or Scrap Material Inventory		100

Journal entry to record abnormal loss. A separate entry must be made to record the abnormal loss of units. If we assume first that the units lost through abnormal conditions have no salable value, the entry for the department in Exhibit 8–3 is:

Factory Overhead Control—Loss on Spoiled Goods	250	
Work in Process—Assembly Department		250

Now assume that the 50 spoiled units can be sold for $1 each. The entry to set up the inventory value of the units and to remove the cost of the abnormal loss from the department is as follows:

Spoiled Goods or Scrap Material Inventory	50	
Factory Overhead Control—Loss on Spoiled Goods	200	
Work in Process—Assembly Department		250

The same type of entry is made as illustrated earlier to record the sale of these spoiled goods or scrap material:

Cash or Accounts Receivable	50	
Spoiled Goods or Scrap Material Inventory		50

INSPECTION AT THE BEGINNING OF OPERATIONS

Exhibit 8–4 illustrates a correct approach for handling lost units if inspection is made at the beginning of operations. Since it is not logical for this to be done at the beginning of operations in the first department, inspection occurs at the beginning of operations in the second department. While it may not be logical for inspection to occur at the beginning of operations, certainly losses can occur there which can be observed, such as spillage in a mixing process. Because the average costing method of handling opening inventory cost is used, the stages of completion for beginning inventory are not needed and are omitted from the cost of production report. Labor and overhead costs are combined in one category as conversion costs. Since there were no units lost in the grinding

EXHIBIT 8–4

McHOOD MANUFACTURING CO., INC.
Cost of Production Report—Average Costing
Inspection at Beginning of Operations—Normal Loss Allocated
For the Month of January 19—

	Grinding department		Fabricating department	
Quantity schedule:				
Beginning inventory	3,000		2,000	
Units started in process	12,000	15,000	13,500	15,500
Units transferred.	13,500		12,500	
Units in ending inventory				
(⅕ material, ⅓ conversion cost).	1,500		(all M, ¼ CC) 2,000	
Normal loss of units	—		800	
Abnormal loss of units	—	15,000	200	15,500
	Total costs	Unit costs	Total costs	Unit costs
Costs to account for:				
Value of beginning inventory:				
Costs from preceding department	—		$ 7,210	
Material	$ 300		1,000	
Conversion cost	900		500	
Total value of beginning inventory	$ 1,200		$ 8,710	
Costs from preceding department.			46,575	$ 3.47
Current costs:				
Material	15,846	$ 1.17	7,265	0.57
Conversion cost	31,020	2.28	15,490	1.23
Total costs to account for	$48,066	$ 3.45	$78,040	$ 5.27
Costs accounted for as follows:				
Costs of abnormal loss			(200 × $3.47)	$ 694
Costs transferred before loss allocation . . .	(13,500 × $3.45)	$46,575	(12,500 × $5.27)	$65,875
Allocation of normal loss			$\left[\dfrac{12,500}{14,500} \times \$2,776^*\right]$	2,393
Costs transferred after loss allocation				68,268
Ending inventory:				
Preceding department costs				
before loss allocation.			(2,000 × $3.47)	6,940
Allocation of normal loss			$\left[\dfrac{2,000}{14,500} \times \$2,776^*\right]$	383
Adjusted preceding departmental costs. .				$ 7,323
Materials (1,500 × ⅕ × $1.17)	$ 351		(2,000 × $.57)	1,140
Conversion cost (1500 × ⅓ × $2.28). . . .	1,140	1,491	(2,000 × ¼ × $1.23)	615	9,078
Total costs accounted for.		$48,066		$78,040

department, the 13,500 units transferred to the next department are costed out at an average of $3.45 each. The entry is as follows:

Work in Process—Fabricating Department.   46,575
    Work in Process—Grinding Department   46,575

After the 13,500 units are received in the fabricating department, they are

EXHIBIT 8–4 (concluded)

Additional computations:

	Trans-ferred	+	Ending inventory	+	Ab-nor-mal loss	+	Nor-mal loss		
EU, grinding department, material	13,500	+	300	+	0	+	0	=	13,800
$\dfrac{\$300 + \$15,846}{13,800} = \dfrac{\$16,146}{13,800} = \$1.17$			(⅕ × 1,500)						
EU, grinding department, conversion cost	13,500	+	500	+	0	+	0	=	14,000
$\dfrac{\$900 + \$31,020}{14,000} = \dfrac{\$31,920}{14,000} = \$2.28$			(⅓ × 1,500)						
EU, preceding department costs	12,500	+	2,000	+	200	+	800	=	15,500
$\dfrac{\$7,210 + \$46,575}{15,500} = \dfrac{\$53,785}{15,500} = \$3.47$					(200 × 100%)		(800 × 100%)		
EU, fabricating department, material	12,500	+	2,000	+	0	+	0	=	14,500
$\dfrac{\$1,000 + \$7,265}{14,500} = \dfrac{\$8,265}{14,500} = \$0.57$			(2,000 × 100%)						
EU, fabricating department, conversion cost	12,500	+	500	+	0	+	0	=	13,000
$\dfrac{\$500 + \$15,490}{13,000} = \dfrac{\$15,990}{13,000} = \$1.23$			(2,000 × ¼)						

*Normal loss = 800 units × $3.47 = $2,776.

inspected and 1,000 units are found to be spoiled. Of these spoiled units, 800 are due to unavoidable conditions inherent in the production process. The 200 units remaining are lost because of carelessness, the incorrect quality of material purchased, or some other abnormal condition. The 1,000 units are added in the equivalent unit (EU) calculation for the determination of the preceding departmental unit cost as follows:

EU, preceding = 12,500   + 2,000   + 200   + 800   = 15,500
   department   transferred   ending   abnormal   normal
                           inventory   loss   loss

$$\$7,210 + \$46,575 = \frac{\$53,785}{15,500} = \$3.47$$

Units never put in process

The lost units are not added in the equivalent unit calculation for material and conversion cost in the fabricating department. For example, the equivalent unit for the fabricating department material is calculated as follows:

EU, fabricating = 12,500   + 2,000   + 0   + 0   = 14,500
   material   transferred   ending   abnormal   normal
                           inventory   loss   loss

It is assumed that units which are lost at the beginning of a process were never put into operations. The units are then only assigned a cost of $3.47 each, which represents the cost from the preceding department. If we average the preceding department cost found in beginning inventory with current cost, the unit preceding departmental cost can be seen to have increased from $3.45 to $3.47. Actual cost last month in the grinding department is higher than that incurred in the current month. This gives a $694 cost of abnormal loss (200 units × $3.47) and a $2,776 cost of normal loss (800 units × $3.47).

ALLOCATION OF NORMAL LOSS

The cost of units lost due to normal conditions is spread over the units completed and still in process. There are 2,000 units in ending inventory and 12,500 units transferred, giving a total of 14,500 units over which the cost of the normal loss is allocated. The allocation of the normal loss to the cost of the units transferred is shown in Exhibit 8–4 as:

$$\frac{12,500 \text{ units transferred}}{14,500 \text{ total units}} \times \$2,776 \text{ normal loss} = \$2,393$$

The allocation of normal loss to the ending inventory is shown in Exhibit 8–4 as:

$$\frac{2,000 \text{ units in ending inventory}}{14,500 \text{ total units}} \times \$2,776 \text{ normal loss} = \$383$$

The $2,393 is added to the cost of the good units transferred, while the $383 is added to the preceding department cost of the ending inventory to arrive at a total of $7,323, which represents the adjusted preceding department cost. The 200 units that were lost through inefficiencies and other abnormalties are assigned a total cost of $694 and shown separately on the cost of production report. The remaining steps in completing the cost of production report illustrated in Exhibit 8–4 are identical to those for other reports prepared using the average cost approach.

INSPECTION AT MIDPOINT OF PROCESSING

A final cost of production report is illustrated in Exhibit 8–5. This shows FIFO costing in which inspection is at the midpoint of both department's processing operations. Costs are rounded to whole dollars in both departments. Since material is included at the beginning of operations in both departments, the lost units are included in the equivalent unit (EU) calculation for material in both departments as follows:

| EU, mixing, material | = 5,300 transferred | + 1,800 ending inventory | + 400 normal loss | + 100 abnormal loss | − 1,000 beginning inventory | = 6,600 |

$$\begin{array}{ccccccc}
\text{EU, finishing} = & 4{,}600 & + 400 & + 320 & + 100 & - 120 \\
\text{material} & \text{transferred} & \text{ending} & \text{normal} & \text{abnormal} & \text{beginning} \\
& & \text{inventory} & \text{loss} & \text{loss} &
\end{array}$$

$$\text{inventory} = 5{,}300$$

However, since the spoiled units are detected at the midpoint of operations, they receive only one half of their labor and overhead in each department. For example, the equivalent units for labor in the mixing department are computed as follows:

$$\begin{array}{ccccc}
\text{EU, mixing,} = & 5{,}300 & + 600 & + 200 & + 50 \\
\text{labor} & \text{transferred} & \text{ending} & \text{normal} & \text{abnormal} \\
& & \text{inventory} & \text{loss} & \text{loss} \\
& & (1{,}800 \times \frac{1}{3}) & (400 \times \frac{1}{2}) & (100 \times \frac{1}{2}) \\
& & & & - 250 \\
& & & & \text{beginning} \\
& & & & \text{inventory} \\
& & & & (1{,}000 \times \frac{1}{4}) = 5{,}900
\end{array}$$

To determine the cost of abnormal and normal loss, all units are multiplied by the unit material cost; to repeat, the units only receive one half of the labor and factory overhead cost. It should also be remembered that the cost applied to the lost units in the finishing department represents work that has been performed in the mixing department as well as in the finishing department. For example, to determine the cost of normal loss in the finishing department, the following computations are shown on the cost of production report; they take into account that the 320 units lost because of normal causes have all been through the mixing department and have received an adjusted cost of $6.755.

Costs of normal loss:

Costs from preceding department (320 × $6.755)	$2,162
Materials (320 × $1.40)	448
Labor (320 × ½ × $1.80)	288
Overhead (320 × ½ × $1.70)	272
Total cost of normal loss	$3,170

Assigning current costs to units spoiled. In this case, the cost of the normal loss of units is not allocated to the units in ending inventory because they have not yet reached the inspection point in the production cycle; instead, the loss is allocated strictly to the units that have passed inspection. If, however, the ending inventory were more than one-half complete as far as the production cycle was concerned in both departments, the normal-loss cost would be allocated to both completed units and ending inventory. Because it is usually not possible to determine whether the lost units came from beginning work in process or from current production, the cost of the normal loss of units should be allocated to the total units transferred. An additional issue with FIFO costing is whether lost units should be costed at the current period's cost (as shown in all examples in this book) or at costs partly influenced by the cost of beginning work in process. Conceptually, if the units in beginning work in

EXHIBIT 8–5

MILLER PRODUCTION COMPANY
Cost of Production Report, FIFO-Inspection at Midpoint of Processing
For the Month Ending January 31, 19—

	Mixing department			Finishing department		
Quantity schedule:						
Beginning inventory						
(all material, ¼ labor, ³⁄₁₀ overhead)....	1,000		(all M, ⅓ L, ¼ OH)	120		
Units started in process..............	6,600	7,600		5,300	5,420	
Units transferred to next department.....	5,300			4,600		
Ending inventory						
(all material, ⅓ labor, ⅕ overhead)	1,800		(all M, ¼ L, ⅕ OH)	400		
Normal loss of units................	400			320		
Abnormal loss of units	100	7,600		100	5,420	

	Total costs	Unit costs			Total costs	Unit costs
Costs to account for:						
Work in process—beginning inventory:						
Costs from preceding department.....	–0–				$ 680	
Material .... $	1,500				160	
Labor.........................	450				70	
Overhead......................	890				48	
Total value of beginning inventory.. $	2,840				$ 958	
Costs received from preceding department					35,803	$ 6.755
Current costs in department:						
Material	10,890	$ 1.65			7,420	1.400
Labor.........................	10,797	1.83			8,766	1.800
Overhead......................	16,830	3.00			8,262	1.700
Total costs to account for	$41,357	$ 6.48			$61,209	$11.655
Costs accounted for as follows:						
Costs transferred to next department:						
From beginning inventory:						
Value of beginning inventory......... $	2,840				$ 958	
Labor added (1,000 × ¾ × $1.83)....	1,373		(120 × ⅔ × $1.80)		144	
Overhead added (1,000 × ⁷⁄₁₀ × $3)...	2,100	$ 6,313	(120 × ¾ × $1.70)		153	$ 1,255
From current production						
(4,300 × $6.48)		27,864	(4,480 × $11.655)			52,215
Total costs transferred before spoilage		$34,177				$53,470
Costs of normal loss:						
Costs from preceding department.....			(320 × $6.755)		$ 2,162	
Material (400 × $1.65) .... $	660		(320 × $1.40)		448	
Labor (400 × ½ × $1.83).........	366		(320 × ½ × 1.80)		288	
Overhead (400 × ½ × $3)	600	1,626	(320 × ½ × $1.70)		272	3,170
Total costs transferred........		$35,803				$56,640
Work in process—ending inventory:						
Costs from preceding department.....			(400 × $6.755)		$ 2,702	
Material (1,800 × $1.65)............. $	2,970		(400 × $1.40)		560	
Labor (1,800 × ⅓ × $1.83)	1,098		(400 × ¼ × $1.80)		180	
Overhead (1,800 × ⅕ × $3).........	1,080	5,148	(400 × ⅕ × $1.70)		136	3,578
Costs of abnormal loss:						
Costs from preceding department.....			(100 × $6.755)		$ 676	
Material (100 × $1.65) .... $	165		(100 × $1.40)		140	
Labor (100 × ½ × $1.83)...........	91		(100 × ½ × $1.80)		90	
Overhead (100 × ½ × $3)	150	406	(100 × ½ × $1.70)		85	991
Total costs accounted for		$41,357				$61,209

EXHIBIT 8–5 *(concluded)*

Additional computations:

	Transferred	+	Ending inventory	+	Normal loss	+	Abnormal loss	−	Beginning inventory		
EU, mixing, material.....	5,300	+	1,800	+	400	+	100	−	1,000	=	6,600
$\dfrac{\$10,890}{6,600} = \$1.65$											
EU, mixing, labor.......	5,300	+	600	+	200	+	50	−	250	=	5,900
$\dfrac{\$10,797}{5,900} = \$1.83$			(1,800 × ⅓)		(400 × ½)		(100 × ½)		(1,000 × ¼)		
EU, mixing, overhead....	5,300	+	360	+	200	+	50	−	300	=	5,610
$\dfrac{\$16,830}{5,610} = \$3$			(1,800 × ⅕)		(400 × ½)		(100 × ½)		(1,000 × ³⁄₁₀)		
EU, preceding department costs.....	4,600	+	400	+	320	+	100	−	120	=	5,300
$\dfrac{\$35,803}{5,300} = \$6.755$											
EU, finishing, material ...	4,600	+	400	+	320	+	100	−	120	=	5,300
$\dfrac{\$7,420}{5,300} = \$1.40$											
EU, finishing, labor	4,600	+	100	+	160	+	50	−	40	=	4,870
$\dfrac{\$8,766}{4,870} = \$1.80$			(400 × ¼)		(320 × ½)		(100 × ½)		(120 × ⅓)		
EU, finishing, overhead ..	4,600	+	80	+	160	+	50	−	30	=	4,860
$\dfrac{\$8,262}{4,860} = \$1.70$			(400 × ⅕)		(320 × ½)		(100 × ½)		(120 × ¼)		

process have not passed the inspection stage, some will likely be spoiled in processing. However, for the cost assigned to lost units to be influenced by beginning work in process costs, the number of lost units in beginning inventory found to be spoiled and the number of units started in the period and spoiled must be estimated. Thus, the expedient procedure is to assume all losses are from current production and assign current costs to lost units as illustrated.

Change in per unit cost. Units spoiled under normal conditions affect the unit cost of all units transferred. Note that the current unit cost in the mixing department shown in Exhibit 8–5 is $6.48; however, the cost increases to $6.755 in the finishing department because of the 400 lost units and averaging with FIFO. Averaging with FIFO occurs when the various batches of units transferred are received in the next department. In Exhibit 8–5, a 1,000 unit batch and a 4,300 unit batch are transferred from the mixing department to the finishing department; combining the cost of the two batches affects the per unit cost in the subsequent department. The ending inventory and the lost units of the finishing department receive this higher $6.755 preceding department cost.

Assuming that none of the units lost has any salable value, the following journal entries are necessary to recognize the abnormal loss and to transfer the units from one department to another:

```
Factory Overhead—Loss of Spoiled Goods (406 + 991) . . . . . . . . .   1,397
        Work in Process—Mixing Department . . . . . . . . . . . . . . . . . . . .              406
        Work in Process—Finishing Department . . . . . . . . . . . . . . . . . .              991

Work in Process—Finishing Department . . . . . . . . . . . . . . . . . . . . . 35,803
        Work in Process—Mixing Department . . . . . . . . . . . . . . . . . . . .           35,803

Finished Goods Inventory . . . . . . . . . . . . . . . . . . . . . . . . . . . . . . 56,640
        Work in Process—Finishing Department . . . . . . . . . . . . . . . . . .           56,640
```

SUMMARY

As goods pass through manufacturing operations, product unit costs must be computed for inventory valuations to be determined. There are different variables which complicate the determination of product cost in this process. The addition of material, for example, can cause an increase in unit cost or in units to account for. It is much simpler if the material added does not increase the units involved; this was illustrated in Chapter 7. The increase in the number of units to be accounted for resulting from the addition of material requires that the preceding department unit cost be calculated again so that the cost is spread over the increased number of units.

Units can also be lost in processing because of, for example, spoilage, shrinkage, or evaporation. Management should determine normal tolerance limits for the loss expected. Any loss exceeding these limits is an abnormal loss. Lost units are included in equivalent unit calculations so that a cost can be placed on the units spoiled. The cost of abnormal loss of units is charged to factory overhead as a current cost. The point at which inspection occurs and lost units are detected determines whether the cost of the normal loss of units is allocated to both ending inventory *and* units transferred or solely to units transferred. This method of indicating the cost of lost units provides an incentive for management to become more conscious of ways to prevent losses.

IMPORTANT TERMS AND CONCEPTS

Addition of material where unit
    cost is increased

Addition of material where a larger
    base unit count occurs

Normal loss or spoilage

Abnormal loss or spoilage

Tolerance limits for normal loss
    or spoilage

Allocation of normal loss

PROBLEM FOR SELF-STUDY

Addition of material which increases base unit count

Swann, Inc., manufactures a product known as CXI. For the month of March 19X1 they have incurred the following costs:

	Department A	Department B
Current costs:		
Materials	$35,451.00	$15,620.00
Labor.	25,680.00	30,091.28
Overhead.	21,838.00	12,744.00
Beginning inventory:		
Prior department costs		1,170.00
Materials	3,600.00	198.00
Labor.	810.00	72.00
Overhead.	540.00	55.00

The material introduced in Department B increases the number of units produced. The beginning inventory in Department A was composed of 1,200 units having one-third labor and one-fourth overhead. There were 11,700 units started in process in Department A. There were 12,000 units transferred; 600 units were in ending inventory involving one sixth of their labor and one third of their overhead. Of the remaining units, one sixth were lost because a new worker failed to close a valve at the end of the process in Department A; the others represent a loss inherent in the production process. Inspection is made at the end of the process in Department A.

In Department B, 2,200 units of water were added to dilute the mixture received at the beginning of processing from Department A. There were 180 units in beginning inventory that were one-fifth complete for labor and one-third for overhead. There were 14,000 units transferred; 200 units were in ending inventory at a one-fourth stage of completion for labor and one-fifth for overhead. Of the remaining units, one third were lost due to abnormal conditions, and two thirds were lost due to normal production conditions.

Required:

a. Prepare a cost of production report using the FIFO method. (Solution appears on pp. 316–17.)

b. Prepare a cost of production report using the weighted-average costing method. (Solution appears on pp. 318–19.)

PROBLEM FOR SELF-STUDY

FIFO—normal loss allocated

Joseph Martin, Inc. uses the FIFO method to account for its product. Operations take place in the mixing department. Since loss is inherent in the production process, management allocates this to its finished goods transferred and ending inventory. Inspection is made when the units are one-third complete in the department. Assume that at the inspection point, material and conversion costs are at the same stage of completion. A summary of the costs incurred is as follows:

Work in process beginning inventory
(400 units, ¼ material, ⅖ conversion costs)..... $ 400
Material................................ 11,360
Conversion costs...................... 29,064

There were 15,000 units started in production in the mixing department, while 12,500 units were transferred to the finishing department; 2,000 units were incomplete at the end of the month having three fourths of their material and three fifths conversion costs.

Required:

Prepare a cost of production report using FIFO costing. (Solution appears on pp. 320.)

Solution for Problem for Self-Study (p.315)

a. FIFO

SWANN, INC.
Cost of Production Report—FIFO
For the Month Ending March 30, 19X1

	Department A			Department B	
Quantity schedule:					
Beginning inventory...............	1,200 (all M, ⅓ L, ¼ OH)			180 (all M, ⅕ L, ⅓ OH)	
Put into production..............	11,700				
Received from Department A				12,000	
Increase in units				2,200	
Total units to account for.......		12,900			14,380
Transferred....................	12,000			14,000	
Ending inventory	600 (all M, ⅙ L, ⅓ OH)			200 (all M, ¼ L, ⅕ OH)	
Normal loss of units	250			120	
Abnormal loss of units	50			60	
		12,900			14,380

	Total costs	Unit costs		Total costs	Unit costs
Costs charged to department:					
Beginning inventory...............	$ 4,950.00			$ 1,495.00	
Transferred in during month				85,181.00	$ 6.00
Added by department:					
Material......................	35,451.00	$3.03		15,620.00	1.10
Labor.........................	25,680.00	2.14		30,091.28	2.12
Factory overhead...............	21,838.00	1.79		12,744.00	0.90
Total costs to be accounted for..	$87,919.00	$6.96		$145,131.28	$10.12
Costs accounted for as follows:					
Transferred:					
From beginning inventory	$ 4,950.00			$ 1,495.00	
Labor added (⅔ × 1,200 × $2.14) ..	1,712.00		(⅘ × 180 × $2.12)	305.28	
OH added (¾ × 1,200 × $1.79)....	1,611.00		(⅔ × 180 × $0.90)	108.00	
Transferred from beginning inventory ..	$ 8,273.00			$ 1,908.28	
Transferred from current production					
(10,800 × $6.96)	75,168.00		(13,820 × $10.12)	139,858.40	
Total cost transferred before loss ..	$83,441.00			$141,766.68	
Normal loss (250 × $6.96).........	1,740.00		(120 × $10.12)	1,214.40	
Total costs transferred............		$85,181.00			$142,981.08
Abnormal loss (50 × $6.96)		348.00			588.20*

a. FIFO (concluded)

	Department A		Department B	
Work in process—ending				
Costs in Department A			(200 × $6.00) $1,200.00	
Material (600 × $3.03)	$1,818.00		(200 × $1.10) 220.00	
Labor (100 × $2.14)	214.00		(50 × $2.12) 106.00	
Factory overhead (200 × $1.79)	358.00	2,390.00	(40 × $0.90) 36.00	1,562.00
Total costs accounted for		$87,919.00		$145,131.28

Department A:

$$\text{EU, material} = 12{,}000 + 600 + 250 + 50 - 1{,}200 = 11{,}700; \frac{\$35{,}451}{11{,}700} = \$3.03$$

$$\text{EU, labor} = 12{,}000 + 100 + 250 + 50 - 400 = 12{,}000; \frac{\$25{,}680}{12{,}000} = \$2.14$$

$$\text{EU, OH} = 12{,}000 + 200 + 250 + 50 - 300 = 12{,}200; \frac{\$21{,}838}{12{,}200} = \$1.79$$

Department B:

Prior department costs:

Units transferred in 12,000

$$\frac{\$85{,}181}{14{,}200} = \$6.00 \text{ adjusted unit cost for prior department}$$

Additional units put into process . . . $\dfrac{2{,}200}{14{,}200}$

or EU, prior department costs = 14,000 + 200 + 120 + 60 − 180 = 14,200

$$\text{EU, material} = 14{,}000 + 200 + 120 + 60 - 180 = 14{,}200; \frac{\$15{,}620}{14{,}200} = \$1.10$$

$$\text{EU, labor} = 14{,}000 + 50 + 120 + 60 - 36 = 14{,}194; \frac{\$30{,}091.28}{14{,}194} = \$2.12$$

$$\text{EU, OH} = 14{,}000 + 40 + 120 + 60 - 60 = 14{,}160; \frac{\$12{,}744.00}{14{,}160} = \$0.90$$

*To avoid decimal discrepancy, abnormal loss is computed as follows: $145,131.28 − ($142,981.08 + 1,562.00) = $588.20.

Solution for Problem for Self-Study (p.315)

SWANN, INC.
Cost of Production Report—Weighted Average
For the Month Ending March 30, 19X1

	Department A		Department B	
	Total costs	Unit costs	Total costs	Unit costs
Quantity schedule:				
Beginning inventory	1,200 (all M, ⅓ L, ¼ OH)		180 (all M, ⅕ L, ⅓ OH)	
Put into production	11,700			
Received from Department A			12,000	
Increase in units			2,200	
Total units to account for	12,900		14,380	
Transferred	12,000		14,000	
Ending inventory	600 (all M, ⅙ L, ⅓ OH)		200 (all M, ¼ L, ⅕ OH)	
Normal loss of units	250		120	
Abnormal loss of units	50		60	
Total units to account for	12,900		14,380	
Costs charged to department:				
Beginning inventory:				
Prior department costs			$ 1,170.00	
Material	$ 3,600.00		198.00	
Labor	810.00		72.00	
Overhead	540.00		55.00	
Value of beginning inventory	$ 4,950.00		$ 1,495.00	
Costs received from preceding department:				
Transferred in during month			85,183.00	$ 6.00507
Added by department:				
Material	35,451.00	$3.02721	15,620.00	1.10000
Labor	25,680.00	2.13629	30,091.28	2.11970
Factory overhead	21,838.00	1.79024	12,744.00	.90007
Total costs to be accounted for	$87,919.00	$6.95374	$145,133.28	$10.12484

Costs accounted for as follows:

Transferred before loss
  (12,000 × $6.95374) $83,445.00
Normal loss (250 × $6.95374) 1,738.00

Total costs transferred $85,183.00
Abnormal loss (50 × $6.95374) 348.00

Work in process:
  Prior department costs ....
  Material (600 × $3.02721) .... $ 1,816.00
  Labor (100 × $2.13629) 214.00
  Factory overhead (200 × $1.79024) ... 358.00
                                       2,388.00

Total costs accounted for $87,919.00

  (14,000 × $10.12484) $141,747.76
  (120 × $10.12484) 1,214.98
                                                  $142,962.74
                                                  607.55*

  (200 × $6.00507) .... $ 1,201.01
  (200 × $1.10) 220.00
  (50 × 2.11970) 105.98
  (40 × $0.90007) 36.00
                                     1,562.99
                                     $145,133.28

Department A:

EU, material = 12,000 + 600 + 250 + 50 = 12,900; $\dfrac{\$35,451 + \$3,600}{12,900} = \$3.02721$

EU, labor = 12,000 + 100 + 250 + 50 = 12,400; $\dfrac{\$25,680 + \$810}{12,400} = \$2.13629$

EU, OH = 12,000 + 200 + 250 + 50 = 12,500; $\dfrac{\$21,838 + \$540}{12,500} = \$1.79024$

Department B:

EU, prior department costs = 14,000 + 200 + 120 + 60 = 14,380; $\dfrac{\$1,170.00 + \$85,183.00}{14,380} = \$6.00507$

EU, material = 14,000 + 200 + 120 + 60 = 14,380; $\dfrac{\$15,620.00 + \$198.00}{14,380} = \$1.10000$

EU, labor = 14,000 + 50 + 120 + 60 = 14,230; $\dfrac{\$30,091.28 + \$72.00}{14,230} = \$2.11970$

EU, OH = 14,000 + 40 + 120 + 60 = 14,220; $\dfrac{\$12,744.00 + \$55.00}{14,220} = \$0.90007$

*To avoid decimal discrepancy, abnormal loss is computed as follows: $145,133.28 − ($142,962.74 + 1,562.99) = $607.55.

Solution for Problem for Self-Study (p. 315)

Solution for Problem for Self-Study (p. 315)

JOSEPH MARTIN, INC.
Cost of Production Report—FIFO
For Period Ending —

	Department	
Quantity schedule:		
Beginning inventory.	400	(¼ M, ⅖ L & OH)
Started in production.	15,000	15,400
Transferred	12,500	
Still in process	2,000	(¾ M, ⅗ L & OH)
Lost in process	900	15,400

	Total cost	Unit cost
Cost charged to department:		
Work in process—beginning	$ 400	
Current costs		
Material.	11,360	$ .80
Conversion costs.	29,064	2.10
Total costs to account for.	$40,824	$ 2.90
Costs accounted for as follows:		
Transferred from beginning inventory:		
Value of beginning inventory.	$ 400	
Material added (400 × ¾ × $.80).	240	
Conversion costs (400 × ⅗ × $2.10)	504	
Total value of beginning inventory		
finished before loss allocation.	$ 1,144	
Transferred from current production		
(12,100 × $2.90)	35,090	
Costs transferred before loss		
allocation.		$36,234
Loss allocation (12,500/14,500 × $870)*		750
Total costs transferred.			$36,984
Work in process—ending		
Materials (2,000 × ¾ × $.80)	$1,200	
Conversion costs (2,000 × ⅗ × $2.10)	2,520	
Value of ending inventory before		
loss allocation.		$ 3,720
Loss allocation (2,000/14,500 × $870)*		120	$ 3,840
Total costs accounted for.			$40,824

EU, Material = 12,500 + 1,500 + 300 − 100 = 14,200 $\dfrac{\$11,360}{14,200} = \$ \ .80$

EU, Conversion costs = 12,500 + 1,200 + 300 − 160 = 13,840 $\dfrac{\$29,064}{13,840} = \$2.10$

*Loss allocation:
Loss = 900 × ⅓ × $2.90 = $ 870

REVIEW QUESTIONS

1. Assuming the company has units in beginning and ending inventory, indicate the equivalent unit computation for the preceding department cost when the units received from the preceding department are mixed with additional material using (*a*) weighted-average costing, and (*b*) FIFO costing.

2. What effect on preceding department unit cost does the condition described in Question 1 above have?

3. What two different effects can the addition of material have in a production process?

4. What is the entry if Department A
   a. Transfers 1,000 units costing $2,200 including a cost of $200 resulting from the normal loss of 42 units to Department B?
   b. If, instead, the 42 units can be sold for $1 each as spoiled units?

5. Distinguish between normal and abnormal loss of units.

6. What is the FIFO equivalent unit calculation for material, labor, and overhead if material is added in processing at the beginning of operations and 12,800 units were started in production. Beginning inventory consisted of 2,600 units, one-fourth complete for labor and overhead, and ending inventory consisted of 1,500 units, three-fourths complete for labor and overhead. Inspection is at the two-thirds stage of production, and 600 units were found to be spoiled.

7. What factors would you consider in deciding at what points in the manufacturing operations to make inspections? Why is there a trade-off in selecting more frequent inspection points?

8. Why are the units lost through either normal or abnormal spoilage included in the composition of equivalent units?

9. What determines the treatment that should be used to assign the cost of normal loss?

10. What are the equivalent units for material, labor, and overhead using the weighted-average method of product costing if: 1,200 units were started in process, 200 units were lost, and ending inventory consisted of 500 units, having one-fifth material, three-fifths labor, and four-fifths overhead. Inspection is at the end of the process.

11. Assuming that inspection is at the beginning of a department's operations, how would you allocate the cost of normal loss of units?

12. Assuming that inspections are made at the midpoint of the department's processing and that ending inventory is two-thirds complete, how would you allocate the cost of the normal loss of units?

13. Why does this chapter advocate assigning a cost to the units lost under normal conditions and abnormal conditions before the cost is assigned to other units or transferred out to an expense?

14. If inspection is made at the beginning of operations in processing departments except the first department, what cost is assigned to the lost units?

15. Assume inspection is made at the midpoint of operations in a department subsequent to the first department and material is introduced at the beginning of operations. What cost is assigned to any lost units?

16.   What journal entry is made to record the abnormal loss of units when:
  a.   The spoiled units have no salable value?
  b.   The spoiled units have some salable value?

EXERCISES

E8–1.   EU calculations

The mixing department of McAlprin Company had 900 pounds of minerals that were two-fifths complete in beginning inventory. When the 8,500 pounds received from the preceding department entered mixing operations, 2,000 pounds of thinner were added to dilute the solution. At the end of operations, 144 pounds of mixture were in ending inventory, one-fourth complete.

Required:

a.   Indicate the equivalent unit calculation for the preceding department cost using:
  (1)   FIFO costing.
  (2)   Weighted-average costing.
b.   Indicate the equivalent unit calculation for the Mixing Department material and conversion cost using:
  (1)   FIFO costing.
  (2)   Weighted-average costing.

E8–2.   Costs to account for and costs accounted for sections

Analysis of the Ron Regis, Inc. records reveals the following limited data. The equivalent units for material are 6,400 and unit cost is $5.10, while conversion costs equivalent units are 6,200 with a unit cost of $1.80. A total of 4,800 units were transferred, 600 equivalent units of material remained in ending inventory, and 1,000 units were lost due to normal causes. There were 400 equivalent units of labor in ending inventory.

Required:

Prepare "costs to account for" and "costs accounted for" sections of a production report using average costing.

E8–3.   Material EU using various processing assumptions

Vince Company provides the following data for the month of May:

Units received from preceding department.   45,000
Units transferred   38,000
Units in process, May 31 (80% complete except for material)   6,500
Units lost when processing was at ⅕ stage of completion.   500

Required:

What are the equivalent units for material under each of the following independent assumptions?

a.   Materials are issued at the end of processing.
b.   Materials are issued at the beginning of processing.
c.   Materials are issued as follows: one fifth when production is started; one fifth when

production is 40 percent complete; one fifth when production is 80 percent complete; and two fifths at the end of processing.

E8–4. FIFO process costing

Given for a process costing operation of the Priscilla Company:

Beginning work in process, ¼ completed	300 units
Received from preceding department	3,600 units
Good units transferred out	2,780 units
Ending work in process, ⅔ completed.	900 units
Material costs in beginning inventory.	$ 258.75
Current material costs.	$12,183.50

One fourth of the units lost were due to abnormal conditions. Inspection is at the four-fifth state of operations.

Required:

Find by the FIFO method:

a. Units lost due to abnormal conditions.
b. Equivalent units for material costs.
c. Unit material costs.
d. Total material costs transferred out to the next process.
e. Total material costs of abnormal spoilage.
f. Total material costs in ending inventory.

E8–5. Equivalent units, FIFO and weighted average

Data for the Lowen Company are given below:

	Units	State of completion
Beginning inventory	600	(⅙ material, ⅔ labor, ⅕ overhead
Started in process	1,800	
Units lost (⅓ are from abnormal loss)	300	
Ending inventory	400	(¼ material, ⅗ labor, ⅛ overhead

(handwritten: 100, 400, 120)
(handwritten: 200 NORMAL)
(handwritten: 100, 240, 50)

Assume inspection is at the end of the production process.

Required:

a. Calculate equivalent units for material, labor, and overhead using the FIFO method of product costing.
b. Calculate equivalent units for material, labor, and overhead using the weighted-average method of product costing.

E8–6. Equivalent units—loss of units

Walton Company experiences spoilage in the manufacture of chemical BB20. Inspection is at the three-fourths stage of production. Labor and overhead costs are added evenly up to the inspection point. Material is added at the beginning of operations. Beginning inventory consisted of 1,800 gallons, one-sixth complete for processing. Ending inventory consisted of 2,200 gallons, seven-eighths complete for processing; 500 gallons were found to be spoiled. There were 15,800 gallons of materials transferred to the next department.

Required:

a.   Prepare a quantity schedule.
b.   Determine equivalent units for material, labor, and overhead using FIFO costing.
c.   Determine equivalent units for material, labor and overhead using weighted-average costing.

E8–7.   Journal entries for spoiled units

A total of 6,000 units which passed inspection are transferred by the milling department of James Company to the finishing department. The cost per unit is $7.20 before any adjustment is made for the 300 units found to be spoiled.

Required:

a.   Record the entry for the transfer, assuming the 300 units were spoiled under normal conditions.
b.   Assuming the same conditions except that the 300 units can be sold for $4 each. What would the journal entry(s) be to record the inventory valuation of the spoiled goods and the transfer of cost to the finishing department?
c.   Assume, instead, that the loss of 300 units was due to abnormal operating conditions and that the spoiled units could be sold for $4 each.

E8–8.   Equivalent units when units are added and loss is incurred

Department 2 of Ingrid, Inc. received 1,000 gallons of product from the preceding department. Immediately upon receipt, the mixture was diluted with 500 gallons of water. Department 2 also added material to the product at the end of processing which did not increase the units to account for.

Inspection occurred at the one-fifth stage of processing in Department 2. Of those entering inspection, 90 percent of the units met the quality control standards; 1,200 units were transferred to the next department, while 150 units remained in ending inventory at a 60 percent stage of processing. Of those lost, one-third were due to abnormal causes, while the remainder were due to conditions inherent in the production process.

Required:

a.   Prepare a quantity schedule.
b.   Calculate equivalent units for preceding department, material, and conversion costs.

E8–9.   Weighted-average process costing

Given for a process costing operation of the Gregory Patterson Company:

Beginning work in process (⅕ completed)	540 units
Received from preceding department	8,480 units
Good units transferred out.	7,860 units
Ending work in process (⅗ completed)	800 units
Labor costs in beginning inventory.	$ 1,649
Current labor costs	$19,372

One quarter of the units lost were due to abnormal conditions. Inspection is at two thirds of operations.

Required:

Find by the weighted-average method:

a. Units lost due to normal conditions.
b. Equivalent units for labor costs.
c. Unit labor costs.
d. Total labor costs transferred out to the next process.
e. Total labor costs of abnormal spoilage.
f. Total labor costs in ending inventory.

E8–10. Equivalent units—increase in units, preceding department: material and conversion costs

Department 2 of the Bartil Company has 630 gallons (one-third complete) in beginning inventory and 400 gallons (two-fifths complete) in ending inventory. Immediately before processing, the 7,800 gallons of paint pigment received from the previous department are mixed with 900 gallons of oil.

Required:

a. Indicate the equivalent unit calculation for the preceding department costs using:
   (1) Weighted-average costing.
   (2) FIFO costing.
b. Indicate the equivalent unit calculation for Department 2 material and conversion costs using:
   (1) Weighted-average costing.
   (2) FIFO costing.

E8–11. Weighted-average process costing

Given for a process costing operation of the Potter Fain Company:

Beginning work in process (¼ completed)	500 units
Received from preceding department	2,500 units
Good units transferred out	1,800 units
Ending work in process (⅖ completed)	600 units
Labor costs in beginning inventory.	$ 320
Current labor costs	$5,881

One third of the units lost were due to abnormal conditions. Inspection is at the midpoint of operations.

Required:

Find by the weighted-average method:

a. Units lost due to normal conditions.
b. Equivalent units for labor costs.
c. Unit labor costs.
d. Total labor costs transferred out to next process.
e. Total labor costs of abnormal spoilage.
f. Total labor costs in ending inventory.

PROBLEMS

P8–1. FIFO—addition of material which increases base unit count; journal entries

Grove, Inc. manufactures a product in Departments 1 and 2. The FIFO method of process costing is used.

Material increasing the number of units produced is introduced in both departments. In Department 1, the beginning inventory consisted of 300 units having one-fifth material and one-sixth labor and overhead added; the costs incurred are $135. There were 10,300 units started in process, while 10,000 units were transferred to Department 2. There was no loss in either department. Ending inventory had three-quarters material and one-fifth labor and overhead added.

In Department 2, a total of 4,000 units were purchased and added to the units in process at the beginning of operations in the department. There were 500 units in beginning inventory with three-fifths of their labor and overhead. The total value of beginning inventory is $1,740. There were 200 units in ending inventory having one-fourth of their labor and overhead. All Department 2 material is added at the beginning of operations.

Costs incurred in each department this month are as follows:

	Department 1	Department 2
Material	$8,312.00	$ 9,100.00
Labor	5,035.00	11,240.00
Factory overhead	9,566.50	8,430.00

Required:

a. Prepare a cost of production report using the FIFO method.
b. Record all the journal entries required for Department 1 for the month.

P8–2. Weighted average—addition of material which increases base unit count

Pickett Manufacturing Company produces a chemical in Departments 82 and 83. For the month ending January 31, 19—, they had 500 gallons having one fourth of material and three fifths of conversion cost in beginning inventory in Department 82 and 200 gallons in Department 83 having three fourths of material and one tenth of conversion cost. A total of 6,200 gallons of unprocessed chemicals were entered into production in Department 82 and 6,500 gallons of chemical mixture were transferred to Department 83. Upon arrival in Department 83, 800 gallons of alcohol were added to the chemical mixture; 6,700 gallons of processed chemicals were transferred to finished goods. The ending inventory in Department 82 had one fifth of material and one half of its conversion cost; the ending inventory in Department 83 had one eighth of material and three fifths of conversion cost. There were no units lost in either department.

Cost data for the month are as follows:

	Department 82	Department 83
Work in process, January 1, 19–:		
Costs from preceding department		$ 350
Material.	$ 95	20
Conversion costs.	310	55
Current costs:		
Material.	5,137	1,000
Conversion costs.	7,610	2,099

Required:

Prepare a cost of production report for both departments using the weighted-average method of process costing.

P8–3.   Weighted-average and FIFO costing

A successful diversified manufacturing concern, John Schmidt, Inc. is considering changing from the weighted-average method of process costing to FIFO. Two departments (463 and 464) have been selected for study. The president wants to know the difference in the amount of costs transferred between the two departments using the different methods.

You are provided with the following information: Departments 463, 464, and 465 produce a floor cleaner. The product originates in Department 463 where various solids are dissolved in a liquid base; the liquid is then transferred to 464. No materials are added in 464 until the halfway point when 1 liter of material is added for each liter reaching the midpoint of the conversion process. After the materials are added, the liquid is mixed for four hours and then piped to Department 465. No liters are lost in or between the three departments.

Inventory records for November show that Department 463 had a beginning inventory of 1,500 liters, 20 percent complete as to material and 30 percent as to conversion costs, and that 10,900 liters were started in process. The ending inventory was 60 percent complete as to materials, and 80 percent as to conversion costs; 10,400 liters were transferred to Department 464.

Department 464 put into process its beginning inventory of 400 liters which were 40 percent complete as to conversion costs, as well as all the liters transferred to it. The 600 liters in ending inventory were 70 percent complete as to conversion costs. Cost data are as follows:

Work in process, November 1:	Department 463	Department 464
Cost from preceding department		$ 528
Material.	$ 427	236
Conversion costs	1,344	443
Current costs:		
Material.	$ 7,345	$97,612
Conversion costs	12,936	54,178

Required:

a.   Prepare a production report for November using the weighted-average method. (Round to the nearest cent.)

b.   If FIFO costing is used instead, prepare a cost of production report for Department 463 only.

P8–4.   FIFO—addition of material which increases base unit count; journal entries

Dick Heagy, Inc. uses the FIFO method of process costing in accounting for its product. The product is manufactured in Departments 1 and 2. On June 1, the inventory in Department 1 consisted of 500 units having one-fourth material and three-fifths labor and overhead added; costs incurred last month for these units were $200. There were 12,500 units started in process, while 12,000 units were transferred to Department 2. There was no loss in either department. Ending inventory had three-fourths material and three-fifths labor and overhead added.

In Department 2, material is added which increases the number of units manufactured. In June, a total of 3,600 units were purchased and added to the units in process at the beginning of operations in the department. There were 800 units in beginning inventory having three fifths of their labor and overhead. The total value of beginning inventory was $2,080. There were 200 units in ending inventory having one fourth of their labor and overhead. All Department 2 material is added at the beginning of operations.

Costs incurred in each department this month are as follows:

	Department 1	Department 2
Material	$5,050	$10,140
Labor	4,182	7,885
Factory overhead	2,706	9,462

Required:

a. Prepare a cost of production report using the FIFO method.
b. Record all the journal entries required for Department 1 for the month.

P8–5.   Normal loss of units; FIFO

Tiff Company records the following data for the month of March. Any units that are not accounted for are to be considered lost through the normal process. Inspection occurs at the end of the process.

	Department 1
Beginning inventory	8,000 (100% material, 40% labor & overhead)
Units entered into process this month	34,000
Units transferred	32,000
Ending inventory	9,000 (100% material, 30% labor & overhead)

Beginning inventory cost:
Prior department cost	-0-
Materials	$4,000
Labor and overhead	7,000

Current cost:
Material	21,200
Labor and overhead	67,970

Required:

Prepare a production cost report using the FIFO method.

P8–6.   Effect of lost goods on unit cost

Products alpha and beta are manufactured by the Merritt Company. Product alpha is of higher quality and goes through two cycles of the baking process, while product beta goes through the baking cycle only one time. Past records show that products lost during baking as a percentage of good output from each baking cycle amount to 10 percent. There is a $2 cost per unit for each baking cycle. Prior to the baking process, product alpha has accumulated an $8 cost per unit and product beta has accumulated a $5 cost. A total of 242 units of each product goes into the baking process daily, and no products remain in baking at the end of the day. Inspection is at the end of the baking process, and products that do not pass inspection have no sales value.

Required:

a. Assuming that lost units are treated as a normal cost of production, prepare the journal entry removing all direct costs from the baking process and transferring completed products alpha and beta into finished goods inventories at the end of a normal day.

b. Determine the finished unit cost of each product for the conditions in *a*.

c. If, on a particular day, the baking process machinery goes out of adjustment and only 160 units of product alpha and 150 of product beta pass inspection at the end of the first baking process and 110 of product alpha are accepted after the second cycle, prepare the journal entry removing all direct costs from the baking process and transferring completed products alpha and beta to their respective finished goods inventory at the end of this day.

d. Determine the finished unit cost of each product for the conditions in *c*.

P8–7. Specific FIFO and weighted-average costs questions

Molt Company has three processing departments, L, M, N. Department M reveals the following information:

Work in process, April 1: 1,500 pounds

Department L: Cost (100%)	$ 4,710
Department M: Material (80%)	1,710
Department M: Conversion costs (70%)	1,365
	$ 7,785

During April, 6,000 pounds from Department L plus 3,000 pounds in Department M, were put into process:

Department L: Cost added in April	$28,125
Department M: Material cost added in April	13,320
Department M: Conversion costs added in April	9,990
Total costs to account for	$59,220
Completed in April and transferred to	
Department N.	7,500 pounds
Lost in April*	750 pounds
Work in process, April 30	2,250 pounds
Department L: Cost	100%
Department M: Material.	60%
Department M: Conversion costs.	40%

*525 pounds is considered a normal loss.

Losses are discovered when the process reaches the 90 percent stage of completion for Department M material and Department M conversion costs.

Required:

a. Assume that Molt Company uses the weighted-average method of determining cost. Calculate each of the following, rounded to five decimal places.

(1) Total cost of the 7,500 good pounds completed and transferred to Department N.

(2) The total cost of the 225 pounds of abnormal loss.

(3) The total cost of the 2,250 pounds in the ending inventory.

b. Instead, assume the Molt Company uses the FIFO method of determining cost. Make the same three calculations as in *a.*

√P8–8. **Normal loss of units; average costing and FIFO**

Morgan Company reports the following data for the month of March. Any units that are not accounted for are to be considered lost through the normal process. Inspection occurs at the end of the process.

	Department 1
Beginning inventory	2,000 (100% material, 60% labor & overhead)
Units entered into process this month	18,000
Units transferred.	16,000
Ending inventory	2,500 (100% material, 20% labor & overhead)
Beginning inventory cost:	
Prior department cost	-0-
Materials.	$ 1,700
Labor and overhead	3,200
Current cost:	
Material	$15,480
Labor and overhead	43,680

Required:

a. Prepare a cost of production report using FIFO costing.
b. Prepare a production cost report using the weighted-average method.

P8–9. **Two departments—spoiled units**

Frodo Company manufactures a single product. The cutting and assembling departments are the only departments involved in the continuous process of production. Materials are added to the product in each department without increasing the number of units produced.

The company records indicate the following production statistics for each department for the month of June 19–.

	Cutting department	*Assembling department*
Units in process, June 1, 19–.	-0-	-0-
Units transferred from preceding department	-0-	70,000
Units started in production.	100,000	-0-
Units completed and transferred	70,000	50,000
Units in process, June 1, 19–*	30,000	15,000
Spoiled units	-0-	5,000
Status of units in process at June 1, 19– as to completeness:		
Materials.	100%	100%
Labor	60	65
Overhead	30	65

The spoiled units had no value as scrap and were 50 percent complete as to material, labor, and overhead. The following charges were made during June:

	Cutting department	Assembling department
Materials.	$350,000	$ 97,875
Labor	198,000	168,075
Overhead	86,900	32,370

Required:

Prepare a cost of production report for both departments for June.

P8–10. Tolerance limits: FIFO, and weighted-average

Richard Borto Company uses a process costing system for its processing and assembling departments. Due to the nature of the product, spoilage occurs. In the processing department for the month of May 19X1, there were 200 units lost; management considers four fifths of this due to normal causes. A normal tolerance limit of 10 percent of the good units finished and transferred has been established for the assembling department; any units lost over this limit is considered due to abnormal causes. Inspection is at the end of the operations in both departments.

The following data are obtained from each department's records:

	Processing department	Assembling department
Beginning inventory	1,700 units	2,540 units
Stage of completion.	(¼ material, ⅗ conversion cost)	(All material, ⅘ conversion cost)
Ending inventory.	2,340 units	3,030 units
Stage of completion.	(⅔ material, ⅔ conversion cost)	(All material, ⅔ conversion cost)
Started in process	6,300	5,460
Transferred to next department	?	4,500
Costs of beginning inventory:		
Prior department costs		$8,490
Material.	$ 489	3,048
Conversion cost	2,040	1,717
Current costs:		
Materials.	6,927	6,712
Conversion cost	14,566	4,574

Required:

Prepare a cost of production report using:

a. FIFO costing.
b. Weighted-average costing.

P8–11. Average costing, FIFO: two months

Amy Wells Production Company employs a process cost system in the manufacture of industrial chemicals. Three departments are involved in the process: blending, fabricating, and finishing. No units are lost in the fabricating department. Data for January and February operations in the fabricating department are extracted from the records as follows:

	January	February
Beginning inventory	1,200	?
Stage of completion	⅗ material, ⅓ conversion cost	?
Received from preceding department. . . .	3,000	2,500
Ending inventory	800	900
Stage of completion	½ material, ¼ conversion cost	⅓ material, ⅙ conversion cost
Value of beginning inventory:		
Costs from preceding department	$4,110	?
Material	1,350	?
Conversion cost	720	?
Cost received from preceding		
department	2,820	$3,225
Current material cost	4,928	3,910
Current conversion cost	864	1,128

Required:

a. Prepare a cost of production report using FIFO costing.
b. Prepare a cost of production report using average costing.

P8–12. Cost of production report and variable budgeting (CMA adapted)

West Corporation is a divisionalized manufacturing company. A product called Aggregate is manufactured in one department of the California division. Aggregate is transferred upon completion to the Utah division at a predetermined price; there, it is used in the manufacture of other products.

The raw material is added at the beginning of the process. Labor and overhead are added continuously throughout the process. Shrinkage of 10 to 14 percent, all occurring at the beginning of the process, is considered normal. In the California division, all departmental overhead is charged to the departments and divisional overhead is allocated to the departments on the basis of direct labor-hours. The divisional overhead rate for 19– is $2 per direct labor-hour.

The following information relates to production during November 19–.

Work in process, November 1:.	4,000 pounds—75% complete
Raw material	$22,800
Direct labor (@$5.00 per hour).	$24,650
Departmental overhead	$12,000
Divisional overhead	$ 9,860
Raw material:	
Inventory, Nov. 1, 2,000 lbs.	$10,000
Purchases, Nov. 3, 10,000 lbs.	$51,000
Purchases, Nov. 18, 10,000 lbs.	$51,500
Released to production during November	16,000 lbs.
Direct labor costs (@$5.00 per hour)	$103,350
Direct departmental overhead costs	$52,000
Transferred to Utah division	15,000 pounds
Work in process,	
Nov. 30.	3,000 pounds—33⅓% complete.

The FIFO method is used for materials inventory valuation and the weighted-average method is used for work in process inventories.

Required:

a. Prepare a cost of production report for the department of California division producing Aggregate for November 19– which presents:

   (1) The equivalent units of production by cost factor of Aggregate (e.g., raw material, direct labor, and overhead).

   (2) The calculation of equivalent unit costs for each cost factor of Aggregate.

   (3) The cost of Aggregate transferred to the Utah division.

   (4) The cost of abnormal shrinkage, if any.

   (5) The cost of the work in process inventory on November 30, 19–.

b. The California division intends to implement a variable budgeting system to improve cost control over direct labor and departmental overhead. The basis of the variable budget will be the production that occurs in the budget period. For the department producing Aggregate, what amount reflects the best measure of production activity for the November 19– variable budget? Explain your answer.

OBJECTIVES OF CHAPTER 9

1. To define joint products and by-products.

2. To provide the basic framework for determining whether a value should be assigned to by-products before they are sold.

3. To present the various methods for distributing joint costs to by-products and joint products so that the most appropriate inventory valuation can be chosen.

4. To emphasize the limitation of joint cost allocations for future planning and control.

9

Joint product and by-product costing

In many manufacturing operations, management has no choice but to produce several products simultaneously. Even though the products may be manufactured in different proportions or quantities, no one product can be produced without the other. For example, in the meat-packing industry, the production of hams leads to the concurrent production of pork chops and pigs' feet. Whether such products are called "joint products" or "by-products" depends on their relative importance. For example, ham, pork chops, and the other *important* cuts of pork are classified as joint products, while such relatively insignificant products as the skin and feet are called by-products. Obviously, by-products and joint products are found in many other manufacturing operations as well, including petroleum and chemical processing and lumbering.

JOINT PRODUCTS AND BY-PRODUCTS DEFINED

In those manufacturing operations in which two or more products of significant sales value are produced simultaneously, they are referred to as *joint products*. Thus, the distinction between joint products and by-products is largely dependent upon the market value of the products. Joint products are produced in larger quantities than are by-products and make a more meaningful contribution to revenue. Joint products can also be referred to as *main products*.

By-products, on the other hand, are merely incidental products resulting from the processing of joint products. They have a small market value in comparison with the main or joint products. The distinction between by-products and joint products is also based on the quantity of each produced. Since the quantity and market value are small, by-products are considered a minor result of processing operations. However, it must be remembered that while a single by-product may make only a small contribution to revenue, in the aggregate, the company's by-products may make a significant contribution.

Because the dividing line between joint products and by-products is not rigid and is subject to change, professional judgment is needed to make the distinction, and management should be constantly alert for developments that could change a by-product into a more profitable product. For example, a product previously classified as a by-product may suddenly be able to command a higher sales price and become a joint product. Likewise, the market for a joint product may diminish to the point that the product will be more accurately classified as a by-product.

Compared with scrap

There is no clear distinction between by-products and scrap. Scrap was defined in Chapter 3 as salable materials that result from the manufacturing process and have limited dollar value. For example, in manufacturing shirts, when the pattern is laid and cut, any excess fabric between the pattern pieces is labeled scrap. It may have a minimal market value or it may be merely thrown in the waste bin. It is true that such scrap is produced at the same time as the shirts and could possibly be called a joint product or a by-product. However, it has so little value that it is questionable whether this scrap should be referred to as a product at all. Nevertheless, the various methods illustrated in Chapter 3 for the treatment of scrap do not differ significantly from the accounting methods shown for by-products. The correct way to treat both scrap and by-products is as a deduction from the cost of the main products.

Common costs and joint costs

To analyze production costs for joint products and by-products, one must distinguish between common costs and joint costs. While the object of assigning production costs to a costing center is the same for common costs and joint costs, this text does not use these terms interchangeably. The term *joint cost* is more restrictive; it is limited to those costs incurred to simultaneously produce two or more products of significant market value. *Common costs*, on the other hand, are associated with the sharing of facilities in which products may or may not actually be manufactured.

Common costs differ from joint costs in that the common cost products or services could have been obtained separately. Joint costs are indivisible and must be assigned to products; they represent the production costs incurred up to the point at which the products can be separately identified. For example, common costs would include such service department costs as building repair and maintenance, cafeteria, and utilities. While each production department could have its *own* service department, common costs are usually incurred to effect cost savings, since it is normally less expensive for production departments to share such facilities. The service departments' costs are allocated on the basis of usage; for example, building occupancy costs may be allocated based on square footage. As you recall, Chapter 6 illustrated some of the problems associated with allocating indirect or common costs to departments.

Inventory valuations

Different problems face the accountant who must allocate *joint* costs. The major problem is how to objectively choose the best approach. The crux of the difficulty is that each product's amount of shared facilities, materials, and labor is inseparable from that of every other product. Yet the assignment of joint cost is essential, for assigning values to joint products and by-products remaining on hand is a necessity, and these inventory valuations must be acceptable according to accounting standards for financial reporting.

SPLIT-OFF POINT AND SEPARABLE COSTS

To make reasonable cost allocations for joint products and by-products, one must first determine the *split-off point*. This is the point at which joint products and by-products are separately identifiable. The split-off point, also called *the point of separation*, may not be the same for all products, since it can occur at different stages in operations. To assign costs, the accountant must accumulate the costs incurred for the entire batch of products up to the split-off point and then distribute those costs among the units produced. Since it is impossible to directly trace these costs to the specific products, a consistent method for allocating the costs must be discovered.

After the split-off point, the products can be identified, and thereafter the costs are more easily traceable. The costs of material, labor, and overhead used in this later processing of the distinguishable products are referred to as *separable costs*. The total inventory valuation of each joint product is therefore its allocation of joint cost, plus the separable costs necessary to put it in a condition for sale.

ACCOUNTING FOR BY-PRODUCTS

While there are numerous ways that by-products can be accounted for, basically all approaches are a variation of the following two methods:

1. By-products are assigned an inventory cost equal to their net market value at the time they are *produced*, and this amount is deducted from the cost of

production. The maximum amount that should be assigned to by-products is their net market value. The market value of the by-products produced less (*a*) the cost of material, labor, and overhead used in further processing; (*b*) marketing costs; and (*c*) administrative costs is referred to in this book as the *net market value*.

2. By-products are assigned no inventory value. At the *time of sale*, the net market value is shown in any one of the following four ways on the income statement (listed in order of preference):

    a.   Income from by-products *sold* is deducted from the cost of production.

    b.   Income from by-products *sold* is deducted from the cost of sales.

    c.   Income from by-products *sold* is shown as other income.

    d.   Income from by-products *sold* is shown as additional sales revenue.

Assigning inventory value to by-products produced

A big distinction among the different methods presented involves whether any value should be assigned to by-products before they are sold. The advantage of assigning an estimated value to by-products produced is that recognizing their value is a method that most nearly resembles those employed in *joint* product costing. At the same time, giving net production cost value to the by-products is more accurate than waiting until they are sold; unfortunately, it is also more costly. This method can also be used if management wishes to make a desired percentage profit on by-products produced. In this case, the net market value is reduced by the amount of the desired profit, and joint costs bear more of the production costs.

If any inventory value is assigned to by-products, the market value is first estimated; in addition, the cost of further processing, marketing, and administration must also be estimated. If the by-products can be sold in their original form at the split-off point, there are no additional processing costs; in this case, only the marketing and administrative costs associated with placing the by-products on the market are deducted from the market value. (A percentage of the selling price may be used to estimate marketing and administrative costs.)

Income from by-products sold

The other basic approach to by-product accounting assigns no value to the inventory when the by-products are first produced. Instead, a memorandum entry is made to record only the physical amount of by-products manufactured. The income from the by-products sold is treated in one of the following four ways on an income statement: (*a*) as a deduction from cost of production, (*b*) as a deduction from cost of sales, (*c*) as other income, and (*d*) as additional sales revenue. Since the intention was not to produce by-products (they just result when the joint products are produced), the argument can be made that no part of the joint cost was incurred in their production. Costs incurred after the separation point, however, must be traced to the by-products, in any case. When the sale is made, the expenses associated with the by-products are deducted, and only the net is set up in a ledger account.

The following data will be used in Exhibit 9–1 to illustrate the two basic approaches to by-product costing; all four variations of reporting income from the by-products *sold* are shown.

	Joint products (pounds)	By-products (pounds)
Production.	50,000	20,000
Sales.	48,000	19,000
Ending inventory	2,000	1,000
Sales value	$10 per pound	$1.10 per pound
Costs of further processing of by-products only:		
Materials		$0.03 per pound
Labor.		0.02 per pound
Factory overhead applied		0.01 per pound
Marketing costs applied		0.015 per pound
Administrative costs applied		0.025 per pound
		$0.10 per pound
Production costs:		
Material	$ 50,000	
Labor.	150,000	
Factory overhead	100,000	
	$300,000	
Marketing and administrative costs	$ 40,000	

Income from by-products:
19,000 pounds sold × $1.00 ($1.10 − $0.10) = $19,000

Net market value, by-products:
20,000 pounds produced × $1.00 ($1.10 − $0.10) = $20,000

Joint product—Value of ending inventory
Method 1:
$$\frac{2{,}000 \text{ pounds}}{50{,}000 \text{ pounds}} \times \$280{,}000 \text{ ($300,000 production cost}$$
− $20,000 by-products' net market value) = $11,200

Method 2:
$$\frac{2{,}000 \text{ pounds}}{50{,}000 \text{ pounds}} \times \$300{,}000 = \$12{,}000$$

The first method illustrated in Exhibit 9–1 uses the net market value to account for by-products. The $0.10 per pound cost of further processing is deducted from $1.10 by-product sales value to give a net market value for the by-products. The $20,000 total net market value for the by-products is then subtracted from the $300,000 total production cost yielding a net production cost for the joint product of $280,000. The 2,000 pounds of joint product left in ending inventory are assigned a value equal to their net production cost (2,000 pounds/50,000 pounds × $280,000 = $11,200).

Exhibit 9–1 also illustrates the other basic method of accounting for

EXHIBIT 9–1

Two basic methods of accounting for by-products

Income Statement

	Method 1 Net market value of by-products produced assigned to inventory	Method 2 No value assigned to by-products inventory; Only revenue from by-products sold reported			
		Deduction from cost of production	Deduction from cost of sales	Other income	Additional sales revenue
Sales, joint products	$480,000	$480,000	$480,000	$480,000	$480,000
Sales, by-products					19,000
Total sales	$480,000	$480,000	$480,000	$480,000	$499,000
Cost of sales:					
Gross production costs . . .	$300,000	$300,000	$300,000	$300,000	$300,000
Less net market value					
of by-products					
produced	20,000				
Less sales, by-					
products		19,000			
Net production costs	$280,000	$281,000	$300,000	$300,000	$300,000
Ending inventory	11,200	12,000	12,000	12,000	12,000
Cost of sales (gross)	$268,800	$269,000	$288,000	$288,000	$288,000
Less sales, by-					
products			19,000		
Cost of sales (net)	$268,800	$269,000	$269,000	$288,000	$288,000
Gross margin	$211,200	$211,000	$211,000	$192,000	$211,000
Marketing and adminis-					
trative expense	40,000	40,000	40,000	40,000	40,000
Operating income	$171,200	$171,000	$171,000	$152,000	$171,000
Other income:					
Revenue from by-					
products sold				19,000	
Income before taxes	$171,200	$171,000	$171,000	$171,000	$171,000

by-products. No value is assigned to the 20,000 pounds of by-product at the time of production. Instead, the $1 per pound ($1.10 sales values less $0.10 cost of further processing and marketing and administrative costs) for the 19,000 pounds of by-products sold can be reported in one of four ways.

Difference between actual and estimated values. If the net market value of the by-products is deducted from the cost of production (the first method illustrated in Exhibit 9–1), the By-products Inventory ledger account is assigned the value credited to the cost of production. Clearly, since the $1 net market value in Exhibit 9–1 is estimated, a difference between the actual and estimated value of the by-products could arise; but if the market value of the by-products is fairly stable, this difference should be small. It certainly does not warrant restating the By-products Inventory account and/or adjusting income from prior periods. The difference can be shown as income or loss from by-product sales or as any of the other three methods for recognizing income in Exhibit 9–1. If the difference is material, the product involved may more properly be classified as a joint product, not a by-product.

As the actual processing costs of the by-products are incurred, material, labor, and overhead are charged to the By-products Inventory account. Marketing and administrative costs can also be applied to the By-products Inventory account. Together, these form the inventory valuation for the by-products. Using the data given in Exhibit 9–1, the entries to record the value assigned to the By-products Inventory are given below.

Journal entries for by-products

The estimated net market value of $1 per pound is charged to the account as follows:

By-products Inventory......................	20,000	
Work in Process Inventory		20,000

As additional processing is done, actual costs are charged to the By-products Inventory account:

By-products Inventory	1,200	
Material.............................		600
Payroll...............................		400
Factory Overhead Costs		200

The application of marketing and administrative costs would be as follows:

By-products Inventory......................	800	
Marketing Expense Control...............		300
Administrative Expense Control...........		500

For simplicity, this assumes that all administrative and marketing expense is applied to the 20,000 pounds produced, even though 1,000 pounds remain unsold. Assuming the 19,000 pounds of by-products are sold for cash at $1.10 per pound, the entry would be as follows:

Cash	20,900	
By-products Inventory		20,900

The By-products Inventory ledger account would appear as follows:

By-products Inventory

20,000	20,900
1,200	
800	
————	
22,000	
Balance 1,100	

The $1,100 balance in the By-products Inventory ledger account is shown as an asset, along with the other inventory accounts, on the balance sheet.

Practical, as well as theoretical factors help determine which method of handling by-products should be chosen. The importance of the by-products involved helps determine which method is most appropriate. Deducting the net market value of the by-products manufactured from production costs has theoretical merit, but this approach may not be practical; there may be no assurance, after all, that the by-products can be sold or that the market value at which they can be sold will remain stable. Certainly, the stability of the market and the reliability of the market value for the by-products help determine whether value is assigned before the sale is actually made. The practical response to market instability is to only recognize the sale of by-products as income and assign no value to the by-products inventory. Even though this approach fails to properly match cost with revenue, the by-product's value may not merit assigning a value to the ending inventory of by-products and setting them up in a separate ledger account. If approximately the same amount of by-products are produced every period, there will be no material difference between the methods chosen. In addition, since by-products by definition have a small market value, the choice of the method may not significantly affect operating results.

ASSIGNMENT OF COSTS TO JOINT PRODUCTS

After the method of by-product costing has been determined, production costs can be allocated to the joint products. The physical measure and the market or sales value methods are the two basic costing procedures for doing this. The following variations of these two methods will be illustrated:

1. Physical measures.   2.   Market or sales value.
    a.   Quantity method.   *a.*   Gross market value.
    b.   Average unit cost.   *b.*   Net market value.
    c.   Weighted factor.

Regardless of the method chosen to distribute joint costs, some arbitrary decisions may be made merely because no alternatives appear preferable. For this reason, it should be emphasized that these methods are used for inventory valuation only and that the allocation method may have limited usefulness for control and planning.

Diagram processing operations

Exhibit 9–2 portrays the manufacturing operations that will be used to illustrate various joint cost allocations. The importance of diagramming the production process will become evident later in the chapter when multiple

EXHIBIT 9–2

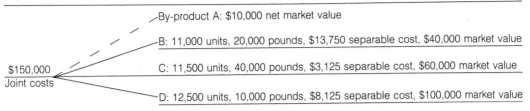

By-product A: $10,000 net market value

B: 11,000 units, 20,000 pounds, $13,750 separable cost, $40,000 market value

C: 11,500 units, 40,000 pounds, $3,125 separable cost, $60,000 market value

$150,000
Joint costs

D: 12,500 units, 10,000 pounds, $8,125 separable cost, $100,000 market value

split-off points are discussed. It is assumed that the net market value of the by-products produced is $10,000, which is deducted from the joint cost of $150,000 to arrive at $140,000 net production cost to be assigned to joint products. This is the by-product costing approach illustrated in the first column in Exhibit 9–1.

Quantity method

Proponents of the quantity method argue that since all the joint products come from the original joint material, labor, and factory overhead, all products should receive a share of the joint costs based on a physical measure. This requires that all products be converted to the same physical measure, whether that is tons, gallons, or pounds. Exhibit 9–3 illustrates the assignment of net production cost to the three joint products on the basis of pounds. For example, since there were 20,000 pounds of Product B manufactured out of a total of 70,000 pounds of joint products for this batch, Joint Product B receives $40,000 of the joint costs (20,000/70,000 × $140,000). This procedure simply assumes it cost the same ($2 per pound in Exhibit 9–3) to produce a pound of output regardless of whether it is B, C, or D. For example, if this were a meat-packing operation, each pound of steak would be assumed to cost as much to process as a pound of hamburger. Clearly, this method completely ignores the market value of the products involved.

Once the net costs of production are allocated to the joint products under the quantity method, the actual costs incurred after the split-off point (separable costs) are added to arrive at the inventory valuation. This is shown at the bottom of Exhibit 9–3.

Average unit cost approach

A variation of the physical measure approach to joint product costing is to assign production costs on the basis of units, ignoring the weight or sales value of the products involved. The total number of units is divided into the net production costs to arrive at a joint cost per unit. Exhibit 9–4 illustrates this method. As long as the units do not differ greatly, the weaknesses of this simple method are not too great.

EXHIBIT 9–3

Use of quantity method in allocating joint cost

Joint products	pounds	Distribution of net cost of production
B	20,000	$ 40,000 $\left(\dfrac{20,000}{70,000} \times \$140,000\right)$
C	40,000	80,000 $\left(\dfrac{40,000}{70,000} \times \$140,000\right)$
D	10,000	20,000 $\left(\dfrac{10,000}{70,000} \times \$140,000\right)$
	70,000	$140,000

A slightly different approach would be to first obtain the net cost of production per pound. This cost would then be multiplied by the number of pounds in each joint product to obtain the distribution of the net cost of production. This approach is illustrated below:

$$\frac{\$140,000 \text{ net production cost}}{70,000 \text{ pounds}} = \$2 \text{ net production cost per pound}$$

Joint products	Distribution of net cost of production
B	$ 40,000 (20,000 pounds × $2)
C	80,000 (40,000 pounds × $2)
D	20,000 (10,000 pounds × $2)
	$140,000

After the net costs of production are assigned, the inventory valuations can be determined as follows:

Joint products	Net cost of production	Separable cost	Inventory valuation
B.	$ 40,000	$13,750	$ 53,750
C	80,000	3,125	83,125
D	20,000	8,125	28,125
	$140,000	$25,000	$165,000

EXHIBIT 9–4

Use of average unit cost method in allocating joint costs

Joint products	Units	Distribution of net cost of production
B	11,000	$ 44,000 $\left(\dfrac{11,000}{35,000} \times \$140,000\right)$
C	11,500	46,000 $\left(\dfrac{11,500}{35,000} \times \$140,000\right)$
D	12,500	50,000 $\left(\dfrac{12,500}{35,000} \times \$140,000\right)$
	35,000	$140,000

Weighted factors

Rather than use the number of units, pounds, or other physical measure produced as the basis for allocation, the accountant may assign factors to each product. These weighted factors can reflect the varying amounts of time required to process the units, the difficulty of the processing procedures, the amount of material or labor used, and other factors which management considers significant. Exhibit 9–5 illustrates the use of this weighted factor method, with the joint products being assigned the following points: Joint Product B, 10 points; C, 5 points; and D, 9 points.

EXHIBIT 9–5

Use of weighted factor method in allocating joint costs

Joint products	Units	Points per unit	Weighted unit	Distribution of net cost of production	
B.........	11,000	10	110,000	$ 55,000	$\left(\dfrac{110,000}{280,000} \times \$140,000\right)$
C.........	11,500	5	57,500	28,750	$\left(\dfrac{57,500}{280,000} \times \$140,000\right)$
D.........	12,500	9	112,500	56,250	$\left(\dfrac{112,500}{280,000} \times \$140,000\right)$
	35,000		280,000	$140,000	

Market or sales value

Still another approach to joint product costing is the market or sales value method. There are several variations of this method in which the selling prices of the joint products are used as the basis for allocation. The market value approximation is based on the thesis that if a product has a higher sales price, then it costs more to produce. Without such costs, there could be no sales. Therefore, joint costs are prorated on the basis of the market value of the products manufactured. A weighted market value is used to take into account the various quantities of each product produced.

Gross market value. Exhibit 9–6 illustrates the use of the gross market value method. Gross market value is appropriate only if the joint products can be sold at the split-off point without further processing. Since, in this case, there would be no separable costs, the inventory valuation of the joint products would be the joint cost assigned. Also, the gross margin percentage (gross margin/sales) would be identical for all three products because there are no costs after the split-off point. Assuming the sales prices shown in Exhibit 9–6 and assuming no further processing cost, the gross margin of Joint Product B is $12,000 ($40,000 gross market value − $28,000 joint cost assigned) resulting in a gross margin percentage of 30 percent:

EXHIBIT 9–6

Gross market value method

Joint products	Number of units produced	Market value per unit	Total gross market value	Distribution of net cost of production
B........	40,000	$1	$ 40,000	$ 28,000 $\left(\dfrac{\$\ 40,000}{\$200,000} \times \$140,000\right)$
C	30,000	$2	60,000	42,000 $\left(\dfrac{60,000}{200,000} \times \$140,000\right)$
D	25,000	$4	100,000	70,000 $\left(\dfrac{100,000}{200,000} \times \$140,000\right)$
			$200,000	$140,000

$$\left(\frac{\$12,000}{\$40,000}\right)$$

An identical gross margin percentage is calculated for Product C of

$$30 \text{ percent } \left[\left(\frac{\$60,000 - \$42,000}{\$60,000}\right) = \frac{\$18,000}{\$60,000}\right]$$

and for Product D

$$\left(\frac{\$100,000 - \$70,000}{\$100,000} = \frac{\$30,000}{\$100,000} = 30 \text{ percent}\right)$$

This reinforces the statement made earlier that allocation of joint costs has limited usefulness in decision making.

If market prices at the split-off point are known or can be determined, they should be used as the basis for assigning joint costs. Many products, however, cannot be sold at the split-off point; instead, they must be processed further. Since no market value can be obtained for these products at the split-off point, an alternative approach must be used to arrive at a product cost. For example, each cut of meat requires varying amounts of processing before it can be sold. To repeat, those costs incurred for each product after the split-off point are referred to as separable costs. If these separable costs are significant or vary considerably among products, they must be considered in allocating the joint costs to the products.

Net market value.   If the products have no market value at split-off, then the most appropriate alternative is to arrive at an approximate market value at split-off by deducting the separable costs from the market value at the first possible point of sale. Whether there are additional sales points after processing and the sales point actually realized do not matter; the *first* sales point is presumed to give the best approximation of sales value at split-off. Exhibit 9–7 illustrates the procedures involved. If the separable costs for each product vary

EXHIBIT 9–7

Net market method of allocating net costs of production

Joint products	Total gross market value	Separable cost	Net market value	Distribution of net costs of production
B	$ 40,000	$13,750	$ 26,250	$ 21,000 $\left(\dfrac{\$\ 26{,}250}{\$175{,}000} \times \$140{,}000\right)$
C	60,000	3,125	56,875	45,500 $\left(\dfrac{\$\ 56{,}875}{\$175{,}000} \times \$140{,}000\right)$
D	100,000	8,125	91,875	73,500 $\left(\dfrac{\$\ 91{,}875}{\$175{,}000} \times \$140{,}000\right)$
	$200,000	$25,000	$175,000	$140,000

A different approach is to obtain the percentage of cost to market value. This percentage is then multiplied by each joint product's market value as follows:

$$\frac{\$140{,}000 \text{ net cost of production}}{\$175{,}000 \text{ net market value}} = 80 \text{ percent}$$

Joint products	Net market value	Distribution of net cost of production
B	$ 26,250	$ 21,000 (80% × $26,250)
C	56,875	45,500 (80% × $56,875)
D	91,875	73,500 (80% × $91,875)
	$175,000	$140,000

Based upon the net market method of allocating the net cost of production, the following inventory valuations would result:

Joint products	Net cost of production	Separable cost	Inventory valuation
B	$ 21,000	$13,750	$ 34,750
C	45,500	3,125	48,625
D	73,500	8,125	81,625
	$140,000	$25,000	$165,000

and separable costs are not proportional to gross sales value, as in Exhibit 9–7, the joint products will not be equally profitable. After allocating the cost of production, the separable costs are added to arrive at the inventory valuation. This is illustrated at the bottom of Exhibit 9–7.

The production process used to illustrate the joint cost allocation methods in Exhibits 9–3 through 9–7 involved only one split-off point to simplify the discussion. However, many manufacturing operations contain multiple split-off points with separable costs for each stage. For example, suppose a company manufactures three joint products—E, F, and G—having sales prices per pound of $9, $12, and $11 respectively. In Department 1, 100,000 pounds of raw material are processed at a total cost of $250,000; 65 percent of the units are transferred to Department 2, where the material is further processed at a total

EXHIBIT 9–8

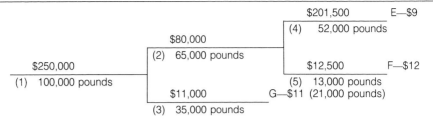

The approximate net market value at the split-off point is determined for use in allocating joint cost.

Products E and F:
Market value—E (52,000 pounds × $9) $468,000		
Less: Processing—Department 4 201,500	$266,500	
Market value—F (13,000 pounds × $12) $156,000		
Less: Processing—Department 5 12,500	143,500	
Total market value	$410,000	
Less: Processing—Department 2	80,000	
Net market value—E and F	$330,000	

Product G:
Market value—G (21,000 pounds × $11) $231,000		
Less: Processing—Department 3 11,000	220,000	
Total approximate market value at split-off point	$550,000	

The joint costs of Department 1 are allocated on the basis of approximate market value at the split-off point as follows:

Allocated joint costs

$$\text{Products E and F} \ldots \ldots \ldots \$150,000 \left(\frac{\$330,000}{\$550,000} \times \$250,000 \right)$$

$$\text{Product G} \ldots \ldots \ldots \ldots \underline{100,000} \left(\frac{\$220,000}{\$550,000} \times \$250,000 \right)$$
$$\underline{\underline{\$250,000}}$$

Next, the $150,000 allocated joint cost from Department 1 is added to the $80,000 Department 2 joint costs and distributed to Products E and F as follows:

Allocated joint costs

$$\text{Product E} \ldots \ldots \ldots \$149,500 \left(\frac{\$266,500}{\$410,000} \times \$230,000 \right)$$

$$\text{Product F} \ldots \ldots \ldots \underline{80,500} \left(\frac{\$143,500}{\$410,000} \times \$230,000 \right)$$
$$\underline{\underline{\$230,000}}$$

The inventory valuation will be as follows:

Products	Allocated joint costs	+	Separable costs	=	Inventory valuation
E	$149,500		$201,500		$351,000
F	80,500		12,500		93,000
G	100,000		11,000		111,000
					$555,000

additional cost of $80,000. The other 35 percent of the units leaving Department 1 are processed in Department 3 at a total additional cost of $11,000. Evaporation occurs in the processing, so that only 21,000 pounds emerge as Product G.

Eighty percent of the units processed in Department 2 are transferred to Department 4 and emerge as Product E after further processing which costs $201,500. The other 20 percent leaving Department 2 is processed in Department 5 at a cost of $12,500 and emerges as Product F. This is illustrated in Exhibit 9–8.

Inventories at sales price

It must be admitted that there are many weaknesses in each of the joint cost allocation methods presented. Because of the difficulty in finding an approach which satisfies all of management's criticisms, some companies avoid the joint costing issue completely by assigning sales value or sales value net of separable costs to products resulting from joint production. Joint costs are ignored completely, since only the realizable value or net market value is assigned to the inventory. However, carrying inventories at sales price or net of separable cost recognizes profits before sales are made. Either approach is opposed to generally accepted inventory costing methods as variations in inventory can affect profit. For example, an increase in inventory can cause an increase in a company's income.

If, on the other hand, the joint costs are for perishable items so that there is a rapid turnover, the use of sales prices as a basis for inventory valuation is less subject to criticism. In addition,.if the normal profit percentage is small so that there is little difference between cost and selling price, the approach is more defensible. Perhaps the most sensible variation of this method is to deduct a normal profit percentage from the sales price net of separable cost. This avoids the criticism that a profit is recognized before the sale is made.

While joint cost allocations are required for inventory valuation, they provide no guidelines for planning and control. In fact, they can mislead the reader of a financial statement if he or she fails to consider the limitations involved. Joint cost procedures have little or no purpose in decisions over whether a product should be processed further or sold as is; this is illustrated later in the chapter. The "sell or process further" decision must rest on a different type of cost-income analysis which is discussed in detail in Chapter 17. It is mentioned briefly here to emphasize the limitation of joint product cost allocation procedures in decision making.

DIFFERENTIAL COST AND REVENUE

Differential costs, not joint product costs, are the only relevant costs which should be considered in making decisions regarding the most profitable stage at

EXHIBIT 9–9

Comparison of joint cost allocation for decision making

	By net market			By quantity method	
Sales.		$52,000			$ 52,000
Joint cost					
(from Exhibit 9–7)	$21,000		(from Exhibit 9–3)	$40,000	
Added cost	28,750	49,750		28,750	68,750
Margin.		$ 2,250			$(16,750)

which to sell a product. *Differential cost* is the extra cost that is incurred for different alternatives. That is, when the company is considering further processing, the additional cost for extending operations is referred to as incremental or differential cost. The additional revenue is classified as *differential revenue*. This classification is reserved solely for those costs or revenues that will change depending on the decision made. A comparison between differential revenue and differential cost is used to arrive at the extra earnings or differential earnings that will result.

The following example briefly explains the analysis necessary to determine differential earnings. It was assumed in Exhibit 9–7 that Product B has no market value at the split-off point but that after it is processed and costs of $13,750 are incurred, the product can be sold for $40,000. Gross differential revenue in this case is $40,000; differential cost is $13,750; and the net differential revenue is $26,250. In effect, the company will lose $26,250 if it fails to further process Product B and merely dumps it in a waste bin.

Manufacturers are daily faced with such decisions regarding the most profitable stage at which they can sell their products. For example, suppose an opportunity arises for the company to further process Product B at an additional cost of $15,000 to become Super Product B, which can be sold for $52,000. If management bases its decision on either the net market value or quantity method of allocating the net cost of production, Exhibit 9–9 indicates the margin that results.

Conflict of analysis.   Product B now has separable costs totaling $28,750 ($13,750 to become Product B and $15,000 to become Super B). Since the net market value is normally determined by the first sales possible after split-off, further processing to become Super B does not change the joint cost allocation as determined in Exhibit 9–7. The possibility of further processing Product B also does not change the $40,000 joint cost allocation under the quantity method which was presented in Exhibit 9–3. The separable cost would simply be added to the joint cost allocation determined under each of the methods. The use of the net market value method indicates that further processing Product B would be profitable, even though it results in a margin smaller than the $5,250 [$40,000 sales − ($21,000 joint cost allocation + $13,750 separable cost)] determined without the additional processing. However, the quantity method indicates a loss of $16,750.

As can be seen in Exhibit 9–9, inconsistent results would be obtained if either of these approaches were used; in addition, neither method is relevant to the decision. Instead, in deciding whether the additional processing would be profitable, the company must compare the additional separable cost with the additional revenue that would be generated:

Additional revenue ($52,000 Super B − $40,000 Product B).....................	$12,000
Additional separable cost..................	15,000
Net differential cost	$ 3,000

If there are no factors other than costs that should be considered, the decision should be to sell the product as B rather than to process it further.

SUMMARY

The accountant is faced with two important problems involving by-products and joint products. One is that it is difficult to allocate joint costs for inventory valuation or product costing purposes. Another quite different problem concerns the use of differential costs in identifying the most profitable point in the manufacturing cycle at which the products should be sold.

The chapter presented two basic methods of accounting for by-products—a value can be assigned to the by-products at the time they are produced or the accountant can wait until the by-products are sold and record the income at that time. Variations of these two approaches were presented in the chapter. Two basic procedures are also used to assign production costs to joint costs—the physical measure and the market or sales value method. As illustrated with the two basic methods of accounting for by-products, there are varying approaches to these costing procedures. The physical measure can be based solely on the quantity of joint products manufactured or a weighted factor can be used to reflect the amount of time needed to process the unit, the difficulty of processing, and other factors management considers significant. Gross market value can be used as the basis for allocating joint cost, but it is appropriate only if the joint products can be sold in their state at the split-off point without further processing. If the joint product requires additional processing before it can be sold, the separable costs incurred must be subtracted from the market value and used as a basis for joint cost allocations.

There is a difficulty in deciding which is the most appropriate method of assigning joint cost because each of the allocation methods presented operates on different conditions and assumptions. A single cost allocation method that solves all by-product and joint product problems has not been discovered. Completely satisfactory solutions cannot be determined with the joint costing allocation methods now developed. However, the accountant must understand the by-product and joint costing allocation methods available, since they are needed for financial reporting.

IMPORTANT TERMS AND CONCEPTS

Joint products

By-products

Scrap

Common costs

Joint costs

Split-off point or point of separation

Separable costs

Net market value of by-products produced

Market or sales value methods of joint cost
  allocations

Physical measures of joint cost allocations

Quantity method of joint cost allocation

Average unit cost method of joint cost allocation

Weighted factor method of joint cost allocation

Gross market method of joint cost allocation

Net market method of joint cost allocation

Differential cost and revenue

Net differential revenue

REVIEW QUESTIONS

1. Why should management be alert for market developments affecting their by-products and joint products?

2. Under what conditions should a product be treated as a by-product rather than as a joint product?

3. Contrast scrap, by-products, and joint products.

4. Compare common costs with joint costs.

5. Since by-products by definition have limited market value, why is it important to account for by-product costs?

6. Discuss the basic difference between the method of accounting for by-products and that for joint products.

7. Define the relationship between the split-off point and separable costs.

8. Defend the practice of setting up joint product inventories at sale prices and ignoring joint costs completely. What variation of this method overcomes some of the criticisms?

9. Discuss the methods available for accounting for by-products and describe the advantages and weaknesses of each method.

10. Discuss the methods available for accounting for joint products and describe the advantages and weaknesses of each method.

11. If weight factors are used as the basis for allocation, what can these weight factors reflect?

12. Why is the assignment of joint costs often a result of approximations?

13. Since the choice of joint cost allocation method used is often arbitrary, why are these approximations necessary?

14. Why do the joint cost allocation methods illustrated in the chapter have limited usefulness in cost control and planning?

15. In reference to the above question, what type of cost analysis would yield results that management can use in deciding on the most profitable stage at which the joint products can be sold?

16. Define differential cost and differential revenue and indicate in what type of decisions they would be useful.

EXERCISES

E9-1. Gross market and net market value methods

Clifford Ward, Inc. produces a high-density liquid plastic used in the aerospace industry. The raw materials are mixed in 500-gallon batches. The following data pertain to one batch of raw material:

Chemical	Market price per gallon	Yield per batch (percent)
Q.	$150	20%
R.	400	25
S.	300	40
Waste	0	15

Direct material costs $50,000; conversion cost per batch is $30,000 at normal capacity.

Required:

Determine the cost per gallon for each product assuming:

NOT TRUE ABOUT NO FURTHER PROCESSING

a. Chemicals Q, R, and S are classified as joint products, and the gross market value method is used to allocate joint costs. *USE NET REAL. VAL. METHOD*

b. Treat Chemical Q as a by-product and deduct the net market value of the by-product processed from the production cost. Separable costs of Chemical Q are $5,000.

E9-2. Allocation of joint costs

Gail Clickner, Inc. manufactures three joint products, A, B, and C. The products are undistinguishable in the early stages of production before they are split off. The following data are known by the company.

Joint product	Total gross market value	Net market value
A	$ 70,000	$ 40,250
B	30,000	23,000
C	60,000	51,750
	$160,000	$115,000

Net cost of production is $90,000.

Required:

Using the net market method of allocating net costs of production, what is the correct inventory valuation for joint products A, B, and C?

E9–3.   Physical and net market value allocation methods

Freedman Corporation uses a joint process to manufacture Products A, B, and C. Each product may be sold at its split-off point or processed further. Additional processing costs are entirely variable and are traceable to the respective products produced. Joint production costs for 19X1 were $580,000. The following data are available:

Product	Units produced	Sales value after additional processing	Separable costs
A........	28,000	$200,000	$24,500
B........	32,000	$250,000	$20,500
C........	40,000	$280,000	$10,000

Required:

a. Determine the joint cost allocation and inventory value for each product, assuming all products are processed beyond the split-off point:
   (1) Using the physical method of allocation.
   (2) Using the net market value method of allocation.
b. If Product A can be sold at the split-off point for $185,000, what would you advise management to do?
c. If Product C can be sold at split-off point for $265,000, what would you advise management to do?

E9–4.   Further processing of products

James Carr, Inc. employs a joint production process in manufacturing Jee, Kee, and Lee. Each product can be sold at the split-off point or can be processed further. All separable costs are direct as to product line. Joint production costs total $300,000 and are allocated on the basis of the sales value at split-off point. The company has the following information on the production of Jee, Kee, and Lee:

Product	Sales value at split-off	Separable costs	Sales value
Jee	$100,000	$20,000	$116,000
Kee	175,000	12,500	195,000
Lee	125,000	7,500	142,500
	$400,000		

Required:

a. Determine the joint cost allocated to each product and the inventory valuation assuming the products are further processed.
b. For the company to maximize profits, which products should it process further?

E9–5.   Classification of products

At the Mitchell Company, chemicals are mixed in 4,000-gallon batches. The yield of one batch of raw material and the market price are:

Chemical	Market price per gallon	Yield per batch (percent)
A.	$50	20
B.	30	30
C.	20	35
Waste.	0	15

Direct material costs $21,600 per batch; conversion cost per batch is $20,000 at normal capacity.

Required:

Determine the cost per gallon for each product assuming:

a.   Chemicals A, B, and C are classified as joint products, and the gross market value method is used to allocate joint costs.

b.   Treat Chemical C as a by-product and deduct the net market value of the by-product processed from the production cost. Separable costs per gallon of Chemical C are $11.

E9–6.   Net market value of allocation

Charles Cattermole Company manufactures two products, XH1 and XH2. Initially, they are processed from the same raw material; after split-off, they are further processed separately. Additional information is as follows:

	XH1	XH2	Total
Final sales price	$27,900	$18,600	$46,500
Joint costs prior to			
split-off.	?	?	11,240
Costs beyond split-off	9,660	3,120	12,780

Required:

a.   Using the net market value approach, what are the assigned joint costs of XH1 and XH2 respectively?

b.   (1)   If instead, the gross market value approach was used, what would be the assigned joint costs of XH1 and XH2 respectively?

(2)   What weaknesses do you see in using the gross market value approach?

(3)   When would the gross market value approach be acceptable to use?

E9–7.   Physical basis and net market value

Germantown Company produces three main products: A, B, and C. It also has a by-product, DD, that requires additional material and processing before it can be sold. The company assigns joint production costs to Product DD that are equal to the product's market value less additional costs incurred after the split-off point.

The products are manufactured in batches, costing $3,600. A batch produces the following:

Product	Volume	Market value	Separable cost
A	40 gallons	$1,800	$40
B	50 gallons	1,790	115
C	60 gallons	2,100	135
DD	20 gallons	200	20

Required:

a. Using net market value, determine the production costs that should be allocated to all four products. Also indicate the inventory value for each product.

b. Using the physical basis, determine the production costs that should be allocated to all four products. Also indicate the inventory value for each product.

c. Indicate the ending inventory valuation using the physical basis and the net market value method if 5 gallons of Product A, 10 gallons of B, 12 gallons of C, and 4 gallons of DD are on hand at the end of the period.

E9–8. Sell-or-process further decision

Watts Company manufactures three products, A, B, and C from a particular joint process. Each product may be sold at split-off or may be processed further. All costs of additional processing are variable and are directly traceable to the products involved. Joint production costs for the period were $240,000.

The following data are extracted from company records:

Joint product	Units produced	Total sales value at split-off	Separable costs	Sales value after further processing
A	6,000	$30,000	$15,000	$ 48,000
B	18,000	60,000	9,000	80,000
C	8,000	90,000	16,000	100,500

Required:

a. Using the gross market value approach, determine the joint costs to allocate to each group of products.

b. For each product group, determine the unit production cost that is most relevant to a sell or process further decision.

c. Make a recommendation to management concerning which products should be subjected to additional processing to maximize net contribution to profits. Support your recommendation with a cost analysis.

PROBLEMS

P9–1. Net market value method of allocation

Cindy Heagy Refining Company produces three different chemicals. A batch costing $23,750 produces the following:

Chemicals	Gallons produced and sold	Unit sales price	Additional cost beyond split-off
W	12,500	$4.00	$10,000
Y	5,000	8.00	5,000
Z	10,000	3.50	15,000

Required:

a.   Using the net market value method for allocating joint costs, determine the joint cost to be assigned to each product and the gross margin for each chemical.

b.   The company is considering selling Chemical Y directly at the split-off point for $36,000. In the plant space used for the further processing of Chemical Y, Chemical Z can be processed even further to become Super Chemical Z which can be sold for $75,000. Additional costs of $38,000 would be incurred. What would you advise management to do? Support your answer with computations.

P9–2.   Physical basis of allocating joint cost

Ojay Perfume Company produces two product lines, cream oil and cologne. In addition, they are able to sell the oil extract from their mixture to another manufacturer for $58. The joint cost of processing one batch is $454. From one batch, the company is able to obtain 50 jars of cream oil, 45 bottles of cologne, and 200 ounces of oil extract. Ojay packages the cream oil in 4½-ounce jars and the cologne in 6-ounce bottles. Each jar of cream oil sells for $6 and each bottle of cologne for $10.50. The added processing costs are: cream oil, $60; and cologne, $52.50. There is no change in the weight of the products after the additional processing. The company deducts the net market value of the by-products produced from production costs.

Required:

a.   If the physical weight basis is used, what joint cost should be allocated to the products?

b.   With the method used in *a*, what is the inventory value of the products per ounce?

c.   Using the method preferred in the chapter, give the joint cost and inventory value of the products per ounce under this method.

P9–3.   Deciding whether additional refining is profitable

Bruce Manufacturing Company produces various chemicals from a joint mixture. At the split-off point, the chemicals are refined and become Amacol, Bencol, and Cencol. Production for July was as follows:

	Production (gallons)	Sales price per gallon
Amacol	2,000	$150
Bencol.	400	75
Cencol.	100	15

Costs during July were:

Joint costs of materials and processing	$238,775
Refining and packaging, Amacol	1,975
Packaging and labeling, Bencol.	525

Chemical wastes were sold for $75. The company treats Cencol as a by-product. The firm deducts the net market value of the by-products from production costs.

Required:

a.   Calculate the joint costs allocated to Amacol and Bencol. Use the net market value method of allocation.

b.   Assuming that July is a representative month, determine whether it would be profitable to hire some workers to refine Bencol so it can be sold as Amacol. The refining would occur before Bencol is refined and packaged. What is the maximum amount that can be paid per month for the workers and supplies to perform the refining before there is a change in income?

P9–4. Allocating according to physical and net market basis

Bill McDowell Manufacturing Company processes three products: JJ, KK, and LL. At the same time that these products are made, Product MM is obtained. Over the years, the company has tried to find a market for MM, but it has been unsuccessful and has had to properly dispose of the product at a cost of $60 per batch. This year, the marketing research department has found a customer who will pay $0.08 per gallon for Product MM if it is first distilled and bottled. The distilling and bottling operations are expected to cost $0.10 per gallon. The company has adequate personnel and facilities for these processes.

McDowell Manufacturing Company mixes the ingredients for the products in batches. The costs incurred for each batch are as follows:

> Direct material $1,176
> Direct labor 2,300
> Factory overhead 2,500

From each batch, the following products are obtained: 10,000 gallons of JJ; 5,250 gallons of KK; 6,500 gallons of LL; and 1,200 gallons of MM. These are the market values per gallon: $0.25 for JJ; $0.82 for KK; and $1.05 for LL. Product KK can be sold without further processing. However, each gallon of JJ requires additional processing of $0.022, and LL must be bottled and refined at a cost of $0.14 per gallon.

Required:

a. The company wants your advice concerning the most profitable alternative for Product MM.

b. Using the alternative you choose for MM, allocate the net joint production costs according to:

    (1) Physical basis, using weight factors of 2 per gallon for JJ, 4 per gallon for KK, and 6 per gallon for LL.

    (2) Net market value.

P9–5. Methods of accounting for by-products

Kay Company provides you with the following data regarding their processing operations.

	By-products	Joint products
Sales	9,500 lbs.	24,000 lbs.
Production.	10,000 lbs.	25,000 lbs.
Estimated sales value	$1.20 per lb.	$10 per lb.
Costs of further processing . . . . of by-products:		
Materials	$0.05 per lb.	
Labor.	$0.06 per lb.	
Factory overhead applied.	$0.03 per lb.	
Marketing costs applied	$0.04 per lb.	
Administrative costs applied	$0.02 per lb.	
Total production cost		$150,000
Marketing and administrative costs.		20,000

Required:

a. Prepare income statements using the two basic methods of accounting for by-products. One of these methods has four variations; include all of them.
b. Using the net market value method, prepare the journal entries to record the costs assigned to the by-products.
c. Prepare the journal entry to record the sale of 9,500 pounds of by-products at $1.10 per pound.

P9–6. Multiple split-off; inventory valuation

Susanne Forman, Inc. processes salmon meat and eggs into Products A, B, C, and D. The first three products, A, B, and C, are treated as joint products. Product D is considered a by-product. The production processes for a given accounting period are as follows:

In the cleaning department, 3,000,000 pounds of raw fish are processed at a cost of $600,000. After processing in the cleaning department, 2 percent of the fish processed is fish eggs, which are then transferred to the egg packing department (Product A). An additional cost of $100,000 is incurred, and Product A is then sold for $25 per pound.

Ninety-six percent of the processed fish is transferred to the fish processing department. The remainder (2 percent) is considered a by-product (Product D) and is sold at $0.50 per pound as animal food with no additional processing. Selling expense to dispose of Product D is $5,000. The company accounts for this by crediting the net market value of by-products produced to the production costs of the main products.

In the fish processing department, the meat is processed further at a cost of $800,000. In this department, the fish that is to become Product B is canned, and the fish that is to become Product C is bagged.

Seventy-five percent of the fish (Product B) is transferred to the cooking department at an additional cost of $700,000. After processing, B is sold at $2 per pound. The remaining fish (Product C) is transferred to the freezing department where additional costs of $300,000 are incurred. Product C is sold for $3 per pound.

Required:

a. Diagram the production process indicating the appropriate data associated with each product (i.e., quantities, separable cost, and gross market values).
b. Using the net market valuation method of allocating joint costs, determine the distribution of production costs and the total inventory valuations for each of the four products. (Round to the nearest dollar.)

P9–7. Joint products and by-products

Allen Manufacturing Company produces one by-product, Cy-O, and three joint products—Di-O, Ey-O, and Fe-O. Joint costs of production totaled $508,000 for May. Because the skills needed to process each product vary, the engineering staff has provided points per pound. Data for each product follow:

	Pounds produced	Points per pound	Gross total market value of production	Separable costs
Cy-O.	500	—	$ 7,250	$ 1,050
Di-O	2,000	2	415,000	60,000
Ey-O.	4,000	4	289,000	15,000
Fe-O.	6,000	3	188,000	45,000

The company uses the approach of deducting the net market value of the by-products produced from production costs.

Required:

a. (1) Using the weighted factor method in allocating joint costs, determine the distribution of production costs and total inventory valuation of each of the four products.

   (2) Would this method be acceptable for this set of circumstances?

b. Using the net market method in allocating joint costs, determine the distribution of production costs and total inventory valuation of each of the four products.

P9–8.   Multiple split-off points

Mike Dalton Corporation produces Products A, B, C, and D. A, B, and C are treated as joint products, while D is a by-product. The production processes for a given year are as follows:

In the mixing department, 500,000 pounds of raw meat are processed at a total cost of $283,000. After processing in the mixing department, 40 percent of the units are transferred to the fabricating department and 55 percent of the units (now C) are transferred to the finishing department. The remaining pounds emerge as D, the by-product, to be sold at $1 per pound. Selling expenses related to disposing of D amount to $2,000. The company accounts for by-product production by deducting the net market value of by-products produced from the production costs of the main products.

In the fabricating department, the material is further processed at a total cost of $180,000. Sixty percent of the units (now A) are transferred to the cleaning department, where they are further processed at a total additional cost of $89,625. After this processing, A is ready to be sold at $3 per pound. The remaining units (now B) are transferred to the polishing department, where costs of $69,875 are applied before Product B is ready to be sold at $2 per pound.

In the finishing department, C is processed at a total additional cost of $29,250. A normal loss of units of C, which equals 10 percent of the good output of C, occurs in this department. The remaining good output of C is then sold for $1.20 per pound.

Required:

a. Diagram the production process, indicating the quantities, separable costs, and gross market values associated with each product.

b. Using the net market method in allocating joint costs, determine the distribution of production costs and total inventory valuation of each of the four products.

P9–9.   Unit cost determination

Winter Fertilizer Company operates three departments. As a result of the unique process in each department, the company has a variety of products which it markets.

All products originate in Department A. Raw materials are converted at this phase into three products: Z1, Z2, and Z3. Z1 is sold at this stage, but Z2 must be processed further before it can be marketed. Z3 could be sold at this stage, but Winter has chosen to subject it to additional processing.

Z2 is transferred to Department B. Here it is converted into Z2B and is sold at this stage.

Z3 is transferred to Department C. Here another raw material is added and Z3 is converted into Z3C, which is sold at this stage. In processing Z3 into Z3C, an incidental product, Z4, results. Winter has a customer for all the Z4 it produces; there are no additional processing costs beyond this point, neither are there any marketing or administrative costs allocable to Z4.

Since inventory costs are determined on a FIFO basis, the unit costs of the most recently produced items must be determined. Winter accounts for the by-product Z4 by deducting its net market value from the cost of production.

An inspection of company records reveals the following information for the month of March:

Department A:
Raw materials . . . . $ 4,500
Conversion costs   45,000

Department B:
Conversion costs   6,120

Department C:
Raw materials   1,260
Conversion costs   30,000

Inventories:

	Pounds produced	Ending inventory Feb. 28	Ending inventory March 31	Sales price per pound
Z1.	4,000			$4.32
Z2.	3,200	320	120	
Z3.	6,000	400	580	4.80
Z2B	3,060			6.00
Z3C	7,000			9.00
Z4.	2,000			1.00

Required:

a. Compute for the month of March the cost per pound of Z1, Z2, and Z3 produced using the average unit cost method based on physical units.

b. Compute the costs as in *a* using the gross market value method.

c. Compute the cost per pound of Z3C produced in March. Assume for this computation that the cost per pound of Z3 produced is $3.90 in February and $4 in March.

P9–10.   Journal entries (AICPA adapted)

Lares Confectioners, Inc. makes a candy bar called Rey, which sells for $0.50 per pound. The manufacturing process also yields a product known as Nagu. Without further processing, Nagu sells for $0.10 per pound. With further processing, Nagu sells for $0.30 per pound. During the month of April, total joint manufacturing costs up to the split-off point consisted of the following charges to work in process:

Raw materials. $150,000
Direct labor 120,000
Factory overhead   30,000

Production for the month was 394,000 pounds of Rey and 30,000 pounds of Nagu. To complete Nagu during the month of April and obtain a selling price of $0.30 per pound, further processing during April would entail the following additional costs:

Raw materials. $2,000
Direct labor 1,500
Factory overhead   500

Required:

Prepare the April journal entries for Nagu, if Nagu is:

a.   Transferred as a by-product at sales value to the warehouse without further processing, with a corresponding reduction of Rey's manufacturing costs.

b.   Further processed as a by-product and transferred to the warehouse at net realizable value, with a corresponding reduction of Rey's manufacturing costs.

c.   Further processed and transferred to finished goods, with joint costs being allocated to Rey and Nagu based on relative sales value at the split-off point.

P9–11.   Process costing—joint products versus by-products

Peoples Company produces a chemical compound known as JP which sells for $6 per gallon. The following departments are involved in the manufacturing process:

1.   Blending department in which raw materials are tested for purity and blended.

2.   Cooking department in which raw materials are cooked. An 8 percent loss in material due to evaporation occurs here.

3.   Fermentation department in which raw materials must remain for several hours after cooking. The top 15 percent is siphoned off and sold in bulk as a by-product, BYP, for $1 per gallon. Handling costs are approximately $0.10 per gallon.

4.   Bottling department in which JP is placed in 1-gallon bottles costing $0.40 each and shipped to customers.

A new use for BYP has been discoverd requiring further processing in a new refining department. It would then be sold in bulk for $4 per gallon. Because of this new development, 30 percent of the mixture from the fermentation department would be siphoned off and pumped to the refining department. In the refining department, the following additional cost would be incurred per gallon of BYP:

```
Material . . . . . . . . . . . . . . . . . . . . . . . . . . . . . . . . . . . . . $0.40
Refining department variable conversion cost . . . . . . . . . . .   0.30
Refining department fixed conversion cost. . . . . . . . . . . . . .  600 per month
```

Actual costs incurred last month when BYP was sold at $1 per gallon were as follows:

```
                    Raw material . . . . . .    5,000 gallons @ $2
```

Processing costs per gallon of departmental input were as follows:

```
                        Blending department . . . . . . . . . . $0.20
                        Cooking department . . . . . . . . . . .   0.35
                        Fermentation department . . . . . . .   0.15
                        Bottling department . . . . . . . . . . .  0.30
```

Because great demand exists for the company's products, all products processed are sold on the same day processing is completed.

Required:

a.   Prepare a statement showing actual gross margin assuming BYP is treated as a by-product and the company assigns cost to it equal to its net market value and deducts this from joint production cost.

b.   Assuming BYP is further processed and treated as a joint product, determine the total manufacturing cost for each batch of JP and BYP. Use the net market value basis for allocating joint cost.

P9–12. Multiple split-off points

Cantt, Inc. manufactures products Alpha, Beta, and Gamma in a joint process. Alpha is manufactured in two phases; in the first phase, raw materials are processed to produce two intermediaries in fixed proportions. One of these intermediaries is processed to yield a product called Beta. The other intermediate product is converted into Alpha in a separate finishing operation which yields both finished Alpha and another product, Gamma. Gamma must be further processed before yielding a salable product. Production quantity, market price per gallon, and sales volume are as follows for a normal period:

Product	Gallons	Market price per gallon
Beta	105,000	$4
Gamma	57,000	$5
Alpha	69,600	$5

At these normal volumes, material and processing costs are expected to total as follows:

	Basic process	Beta process	Alpha-Gamma process	Gamma process
Material	$ 22,500	$18,000	$ 9,000	$ 6,210
Direct labor	7,500	30,000	2,700	9,000
Variable factory overhead	39,000	27,000	21,000	5,400
Fixed factory overhead	126,000	3,000	9,300	12,390
	$195,000	$78,000	$42,000	$33,000

Output can be increased by as much as 15 percent of normal volume without any increase in fixed costs. Marketing and administrative costs are fixed and are not traced to any products.

Required:

Using the net market method in allocating joint costs, determine the distribution of production costs and the inventory cost per gallon for each product.

P9–13. Evaluating profitability of joint products

A partial product line statement for Dobson, Inc.'s Product B is presented below:

Sales (2,000 units)		$26,000
Variable cost of goods sold:		
Material—Product A	$ 8,000	
Conversion cost	16,000	24,000
Contribution margin		$ 2,000

Product B is manufactured from Product A on a one-for-one ratio. Product A can be sold at split-off for $4; however, Dobson's competitors, nationally known companies, are charging $7 for similar products. Joint costs of $1 per unit are allocated to Product A on the basis of net market value. Dobson's present plant capacity allows the production of only 1,000 units of Product B each period; the remaining needed units are purchased.

Required:

a. Evaluate the product line statement.

b. Indicate any areas of concern.

c. At what Product A price would there be no advantage to further processing Product A?

d. Make any appropriate suggestions for increasing earnings.

P9–14.   Inventory values for joint products and by-products (CMA adapted)

Doe Corporation grows, processes, cans, and sells three main pineapple products—sliced pineapple, crushed pineapple, and pineapple juice. The outside skin is cut off in the cutting department and processed as animal feed. The skin is treated as a by-product. Doe's production process is as follows:

Pineapples first are processed in the cutting department. The pineapples are washed and the outside skin is cut away. Then the pineapples are cored and trimmed for slicing. The three main products (sliced, crushed, juice) and the by-product (animal feed) are recognizable after processing in the cutting department. Each product is then transferred to a separate department for final processing.

The trimmed pineapples are forwarded to the slicing department where the pineapples are sliced and canned. Any juice generated during the slicing operation is packed in the cans with the slices.

The pieces of pineapple trimmed from the fruit are diced and canned in the crushing department. Again, the juice generated during this operation is packed in the can with the crushed pineapple.

The core and surplus pineapple generated from the cutting department are pulverized into a liquid in the juicing department. There is an evaporation loss equal to 8 percent of the weight of the good output produced in this department which occurs as the juices are heated.

The outside skin is chopped into animal feed in the feed department.

The Doe Corporation uses the net market value method to assign costs of the joint process to its main products. The by-product is inventoried at its market value.

A total of 270,000 pounds were entered into the cutting department during May. The schedule presented shows the costs incurred in each department, the proportion by weight transferred to the four final processing departments, and the selling price of each end product.

P9–14.   Processing data and costs, May 19X1

Department	Costs incurred	Product by weight transferred to departments (percent)	Selling price per pound of final product
Cutting	$60,000	—	—
Slicing	4,700	35	$.60
Crushing	10,580	28	.55
Juicing	3,250	27	.30
Animal feed	700	10	.10
Total	$79,230	100%	

Required:

a. The Doe Corporation uses the net market value method to determine inventory values for its main products and by-products. Calculate:
   (1) The pounds of pineapple that result as output for pineapple slices, crushed pineapple, pineapple juice, and animal feed.
   (2) The net market value at the split-off point of the three main products.
   (3) The amount of the cost of the cutting department assigned to each of the three main products and to the by-product in accordance with corporate policy.
   (4) The gross margins for each of the three main products.
b. Comment on the significance to management of the gross margin information by main product.
c. In the production of joint products either a by-product or scrap could be generated.
   (1) Distinguish between a by-product and scrap.
   (2) Would the proper accounting treatment for scrap differ from that for by-products? Explain your answer.

P9–15. Process costing and by-product costing (AICPA adapted)

Adept Company is a manufacturer of two products known as Prep and Pride. Incidental to the manufacture of these two products, it produces a by-product known as Wilton. The manufacturing process covers two departments, grading and saturating.

The manufacturing process begins in the grading department when raw materials are started in process. Upon completion of processing in the grading department, the by-product Wilton is produced, which accounts for 20 percent of the material output. This by-product needs no further processing and is transferred to finished goods.

The net market value of the by-product Wilton is accounted for as a reduction of the cost of materials in the grading department. The current selling price of Wilton is $1 per pound and the estimated selling and delivery costs total $0.10 per pound.

The remaining output is transferred to the saturating department for the final phase of production. In the saturating department, water is added at the beginning of the production process which results in a 50-percent gain in weight of the materials in production.

The following information is available for the month of November 19–:

	November 1		November 30
Inventories	Quantity pounds	Amount	Quantity pounds
Work in process:			
Grading department	—	—	—
Saturating department	1,600	$17,600	2,000
Finished goods:			
Prep	600	14,520	1,600
Pride	2,400	37,110	800
Wilton	—	—	—

The work in process inventory (labor and overhead) in the saturating department is estimated to be 50 percent complete both at the beginning and end of November. Costs of production for November are as follows:

Cost of production	Materials used	Labor and overhead
Grading department	$265,680	$86,400
Saturating department	—	86,000

The material used in the Grading department weighed 36,000 pounds.

Adept uses the FIFO method of process costing.

Required:

Prepare a cost of production report for both the grading and saturating departments for the month of November. Show supporting computations in good form. The answer should include:

a.   Equivalent units of production (in pounds).
b.   Total manufacturing costs.
c.   Cost per equivalent unit (pounds).
d.   Dollar amount of ending work in process.
e.   Dollar amount of inventory cost transferred out.

CASES

C9–1.   Bases for allocating

Sellar Cheese Company manufactures a high-quality cheddar cheese using fresh, sweet milk which it pasteurizes. The milk flows from the pasteurizer into stainless steel vats that hold 10,000 pounds of milk each. Sellar Company has found it takes about 11 pounds of milk to make 1 pound of cheddar cheese.

In making cheese the curd, or solid parts, of milk must be separated from the whey, or liquid part. Sellar uses a starter culture of lactic acid bacteria, which is added to each vat to accomplish this separation. When the bacteria are distributed throughout the vat, the milk begins to ripen or ferment. Rennet extract, a substance from the lining of a calf's fourth stomach, is added to make the milk curdle. The milk then coagulates into a curd, or soft, semisolid mass.

Paddles are used to stir the curd and whey before the mixture is heated to about 102°F to remove any remaining whey and to develop the proper firmness and acidity. Cheese workers drain the whey from the vat and push the curd to the sides.

Curd processing.   After the whey is drained off, workers place the curd in a machine that cuts it into pieces about 10 cm. long and 13 ml. thick. They salt the cut curd and press it into molds. The molds are stacked in a press and kept under great pressure overnight. The next morning, the cheese is removed and placed in a curing room where it remains for 90 days.

Whey processing.   Whey is drained off into vats where a preservative agent is added, which allows a two-month storage. After a short mixing and cooking process, the whey is refrigerated for sale to cattle-feed producers. Within the last few years, a new process has been developed in which soybeans are mixed with whey for livestock food. If whey is not further processed, it has no value and is poured down the drain.

Because Sellar's cheddar cheese has such a fine reputation, the cheese is easy to sell at $4 per pound and is shipped as fast as it is cured. More effort is required to sell the whey, even though both are sold to the same food-producing companies by the same marketing force. Often, when the accumulation of whey becomes especially heavy and the date of spoilage is coming close, buyers are required to purchase some amount of whey to be able to buy the cheddar cheese. Sellar Company justifies this by arguing that they want to stimulate the use of whey in livestock food processing.

This is the reason that Sellar's marketing manager is excited when Beyer Foods, Inc. offers to buy 100,000 pounds of whey for $0.50 per pound. However, Sellar's production manager argues that the $0.50 per pound offer should not be accepted because the cost of production is at least $0.80 per pound and probably more. The marketing manager points out that the production manager's insistence on $0.80 has led to a heavy accumulation of whey in refrigeration.

The production manager counters the argument by saying, "Your salespersons are so incompetent and so lacking incentive that they would pour out the whey unless we had inventory controls."

Cost data.   Both managers realize they need assistance from the cost accountant and request the preparation of financial data for their use. After analysis of past results, the cost accountant indicates that Sellar Company processes 50,000 pounds of milk into cheese in the one eight-hour shift that operates daily.

Out of 10,000 pounds of milk processed, 1,400 pounds of output are saved—910 pounds of cheese and 490 pounds of whey that can be preserved. Raw milk costs $1,000 per 10,000 pounds, while lactic acid bacteria and rennet extract together average $150 per 10,000 pounds of milk. Labor and overhead costs average $800 per 10,000 pounds of milk processed through the stage where whey is drained off. Labor and overhead in curd processing average $500 per 910 pounds of cheese; salt averages $29 for a 910-pound batch.

In whey processing, the preservatives average $16 for a 490-pound batch. Labor and overhead per 490-pound batch average $25. Selling costs average $0.10 per finished pound each for the cheese and the whey.

Production manager's basis.   After studying the cost data, the production manager presents the following support for refusing the offer of $0.50 sales price per pound of whey:

$$\frac{\$1{,}000 \text{ milk} + \$150 \text{ bacteria and rennet extract}}{1{,}400 \text{ pounds of output}} = \$0.82$$

The production manager emphasizes that an $0.80 price per pound does not even cover the materials much less the labor and overhead.

Marketing manager's basis.   The marketing manager contends that the production manager's basis has no merit because it assumes that the company had just as soon make whey as cheese, and everyone knows that is a fallacy. Instead, the marketing manager presents the argument that the material for the cheese initially is worth more per pound than is the material for the whey. Based on this contention, he presents the following analysis:

	Output of 10,000 pounds of milk	Market price per pound	Total market value	Percent of total	Costs applicable to each	Cost per pound
Cheese . . .	910	$4.00	$3,640	93.7	$1,827*	$2.00
Whey.	490	.50	245	6.3	123	.25
			$3,885	100.0	$1,950	

*93.7% × ($1,000 + $150 + $800).

The production manager disagrees with the approach, arguing that the cost allocation should not be a function of their relative market prices. The marketing manager then asks, "Why not treat the whey as a by-product, because you'll agree that we prefer to process cheese all the time rather than whey if we could." Under this approach, the market value of the whey ($.50) is deducted from the cost of operations and all income or loss is carried by the cheese.

The production manager does not completely agree with this approach because the cost allocated is still a function of the market value of the whey. The belief that an accurate cost is needed to establish sales policy is still strong.

Because of the inability to solve the issue, the controller and president are consulted to determine whether a $0.50 per pound sales offer for the whey should be accepted.

Required:

a.   Evaluate the following bases proposed:
  (1)   The production manager's allocation of material resulting in an $0.82 cost per pound of total output.
  (2)   The marketing manager's allocation resulting in a $0.25 cost per pound of whey.
  (3)   The marketing manager's by-product allocation.
b.   Suggest other bases that you believe appropriate and determine the cost per pound of cheese and whey using these bases.
c.   Should the offer of $0.50 per pound of whey be accepted?

PART III

Planning and control of costs with standards and budgets

OBJECTIVES OF CHAPTER 10

1. To present the concepts of a standard cost system and the benefits gained from its application.
2. To discuss the procedures involved in establishing material and labor standards.
3. To provide the material and labor variance analysis that can aid in the evaluation of actual performance for use in either job order or process costing systems.
4. To illustrate the journal entries necessary for the incorporation of standards in the accounting system.

10

Standard costs for material
and labor

Control of costs cannot exist without some standard against which actual results can be compared. Thus, the costs incurred in a specific period have little significance unless these figures are compared with some base data. After all, top management is concerned not only with knowing what costs are but also with knowing just how satisfactory they are. If no measurement is furnished in the cost report, those receiving quantitative data supply their own yardstick; and since it is unlikely that any two will supply the same mental yardstick, no two will evaluate the report alike. To avoid such inconsistencies of interpretation, the accountant must provide some cost standards against which to measure actual cost results.

Comparing actual costs with those incurred in a previous period is one way to do this, but this method may be misleading, as the company may be working under conditions different from those prevailing during the earlier period. Thus, allowances must be made for the differences between past and present performance, and this situation can lead to arbitrary and false conclusions.

STANDARD COST DEFINED

Because historical data do not satisfy the need for determining the acceptability of performance, a system of costing on a predetermined basis—standard costing—has been developed. Cost standards are scientifically predetermined costs of production used as a basis for measurement and comparison. Standard costs represent what costs should be under attainable good performance;

standard costs do not necessarily represent what the cost would be if perfection in performance has actually been attained.

Standard costs may differ from *estimated costs* in that estimated costs are frequently less accurately determined. *Standard costs* are usually determined much more scientifically through the use of time studies and engineering estimates. However, this difference is not conclusive, for estimated costs may also be worked out on a scientific basis.

Budgets and standard costs

Standard costs become the unit building block for the company's budget. After standards are established for each unit produced, standard costs are multiplied by the total units to be produced or sold to determine budgeted costs. Chapter 11 will discuss this relationship in more detail; this will be further incorporated in the two budgeting chapters which follow (Chapters 12 and 13).

Standard costs are tools for estimating and comparing costs. However, they cannot stand alone without historical data. Instead, standard costs are compared to actual costs incurred. Standards are yardsticks by which achievement, or lack of achievement, can be measured. Cost trends are indicated by a comparison of actual costs and standard costs. These yardsticks are normally developed through engineering or time-study analysis and tend to reflect historical experience.

Advantages of a standard cost system

A standard cost system makes executives cost-conscious because it makes cost variances clearly observable by management. Standards establish desirable minimum costs, and if they are exceeded, the variances can be investigated. The variances between standard cost and actual cost can be studied and the physical causes of the variance determined. Thus, standards make available a measuring device which calls attention to cost variations. In turn, these standards serve as a compass that guides management toward improvements.

The process of setting standards can be of primary assistance in the management function of planning. Management must plan for efficient and economical operations for standard cost to be effective. This process involves thorough investigation and study of and research concerning all factors affecting costs.

Standard cost systems also integrate managerial, accounting, and engineering aspects. This encourages coordination, since all elements of the business organization are striving for the same goal. Setting standards especially involves defining goals and explaining to all concerned their role in the attainment of those goals. For example, workers will know what is expected of them when their standard is expressed as so many units per hour and they have helped establish this standard.

The establishment of correct standards for a company's manufacturing expense is of great importance and requires considerable insight into the complexities of business management, because the accuracy of the standards usually determines the success of the standard cost system. In determining the standards, each cost should be carefully analyzed to ensure that all factors have been considered.

In addition, the bases for the standards should be approved by the major executives in charge of the departments responsible for meeting the standards. Also, those responsible for meeting standards should have the opportunity of passing upon them before they are finally set. Supervisors should also have an honest desire to meet the standards. They should feel that the standard is accurate and is explained in terms that the employees under their supervision will understand. So while the accountant and the industrial engineer provide technical information regarding the tightness of standards, the final decision should reflect input from the production line manager and his or her immediate supervisor. The standard should only be set after there has been face-to-face communication, bargaining, and interaction between these two individuals. Finally, the basic plan should win the support of top management.

Levels of activity

Before proceeding to set standards, certain decisions must be made by management. First, the number of units of each product that the company plans to make and sell must be determined. The anticipated hours of operation needed to provide for this production level must also be determined. Before estimating the hours of operation, however, management must decide how demanding they wish their standards to be. The following capacity levels, introduced in Chapter 6, can be used for setting standards:

1. Theoretical and practical.
2. Normal.
3. Expected actual.

Theoretical and practical standards. Standards that are set on the basis of theoretical capacity are often referred to as ideal standards, since they reflect maximum efficiency. When this capacity concept is adopted, the company assumes it will operate at full speed without any interruptions—even such normal ones as machine breakdowns. While practical capacity is more realistic than theoretical capacity and makes allowance for unavoidable delays, practical capacity also makes no allowance for idle time resulting from a sales demand that is inadequate to keep the plant facilities and personnel working efficiently. Even though standards set on a practical or theoretical capacity are usually not attainable, they can be useful in motivating employees. However, standards are usually set on a less demanding level. Both normal and expected actual standards make allowance for machine breakdowns, normal material loss, and lost time that is expected, but no allowance is made for abnormal loss or waste.

Normal standards.   Standards can be set on a normal capacity basis, which is a long-range approach because data from several years are used to even out the cyclical swings in sales demand. Normal capacity represents a volume that averages out the company's peak and slack periods.

Expected actual standards.   Standards can also be set on an expected actual capacity, which is a short-range approach. Cyclical swings are not evened out; instead, expected actual capacity represents the volume presumed to be achieved in the next period.

Levels of efficiency

There are varying degrees of tightness in standards based on attainable performance. Many competent managers believe that to encourage high standards of performance, the standards must be tight. They believe this establishes a goal to strive for. However, this is often detrimental to employee morale, because it is nearly impossible to attain this goal. Such tight standards may discourage individuals whose efforts are being measured, and they may slow down their results. Some employees may even think the standards are ridiculous and have no place in the cost system. Finally, the cost figures derived from these unrealistic standards can give management a false sense of security.

Other managers believe in providing for contingencies in standards by making them fairly loose. They feel these contingencies are likely to arise in plant operations and should be provided for. However, we believe that no safety factors or arbitrary allowances should be included in cost standards. Standard costs based upon comparatively low efficiency tend to hide and to perpetuate waste that should be highlighted so management recognizes it as the result of inefficient use of material, labor, and equipment. Loose standards provide unreliable data for measuring cost because they underwrite in-efficiencies that should be reviewed and corrected. In sum, the inclusion of excessive contingencies will defeat the purpose of the standard cost system.

Rigid adherence to either extreme is usually unsound. Standards should be set on a reasonable basis that takes into consideration all known normal factors. There should be no provision for abnormal losses, but a reasonable provision for contingencies should be provided. Generally, management will find that standards attainable only with good performance and use of proper methods are most successful. Such standards involve expectation of more than a continuation of the past, but are not set on a perfect or ideal level, since they make fair allowances for waste, spoilage, and idle time; they are usually set tightly enough that the operating personnel will consider achievement possible.

Job order and process cost systems

Standards costs are general and can be applied in both job order and process costing systems. Standards are very effective in process costing because the conflicts and complexities of the FIFO and weighted average methods that were introduced in Chapters 7 and 8 are eliminated. The examples illustrated in this chapter first utilize standards in a job order costing system; they are followed by examples employing standards for process costing. Also, the self-study problem at the end of this chapter and of Chapter 11 illustrate the use of standards in a process cost system.

Incorporation in the accounting system

Standard costs may be used only for statistical purposes and not entered in the accounting system. Under these conditions, variances can be prepared and studied. However, the author believes that executives will take standard costs and variances more seriously and be more responsive to cost reduction if these costs and variances are entered in the ledger accounts. The incorporation of cost standards in the accounting system provides an orderly and somewhat compulsory plan for cost analysis. The approach illustrated in this chapter is to include standard costs and variances within the accounting system, whether a job order or a process costing system is used. However, the important thing is that actual costs are subjected to proper measurement and control.

SETTING MATERIAL STANDARDS

An accountant seeking to establish standard costs should first set material standards. Year-to-date totals of material quantity should be studied and used as guides in setting the physical quantity of materials needed. To do this, the accountant should enlist the aid of the industrial engineering department which will usually develop specifications for the kinds and quantities of material to be used in the production of the goods specified and budgeted on the operating forecast. The standard specification will be determined only after a study of factory operations has been conducted.

Material quantity standards

Often, however, it is not sufficient to base material quantity standards on engineering specifications. The accountant may need assistance from a manufacturing supervisor who is thoroughly familiar with the raw materials composing the finished article. Together, they can conduct tests under controlled conditions. A quantity of material is put into process, and the results are carefully analyzed. But there may be a tendency for the workers to produce with less scrap material under these test conditions, and the accountant must watch for this artificial element because, if it is not considered, the material quantity standard will be understated.

The operation schedule and bills of material established jointly by the engineering department, manufacturing supervisor, and accountant are forwarded to the purchasing department and used as a basis for the material price standard. On these operation schedules are listed the materials and quantities required for the expected volume of production. These physical standards should include factors for scrap, shrinkage, and waste. A waste allowance must be added when the material is purchased in bars or lengths and where definite sizes of parts are cut from sheet stock of material. The percentage for waste should be determined using a formula similar to the following:

$$\frac{\text{Waste expressed in pounds (or gallons, tons, etc.)}}{\text{Net pounds (or gallons, tons, etc.) in finished unit}} = \text{Percent waste to be added}$$

Shrinkage can be provided for in a similar manner by adding a percentage to the material required in the finished unit.

Material price standards

Since the purchasing agent is responsible for the material price variance, he or she should help set the price standards. The purchasing department places an expected material price on the material quantities specified, and this determines the material price standard. In arriving at the standard, the purchasing agent must predict the changes in price that are expected to occur. In addition, the entire operation associated with acquiring the goods should be considered. If bargaining and searching out the lowest price for the material will be exhaustive, the price standard should reflect this. The strictness of the company's policy regarding soliciting bids versus forwarding all business to a favorite supplier will also have an impact on the price standard.

A practical solution to the problem of setting price standards for material is to consider the economies that are available. Price standards should not be based on possible economies which may not be attainable, but on probable savings used. For example, if attention is given to ordering in the most economical order size, the price standard should reflect this.

The adequacy of the company's cash balance used in taking advantage of cash discounts should also be considered. Even where cash discounts are not taken, there is support for deducting these discounts from the material cost and placing discounts not taken in the expense section of the financial statement to reflect *standard* costs.

Applied rates for material handling.   If material handling costs are applied to the materials inventory accounts, as illustrated in Chapter 3, the price standard should also reflect this. Applied rates can be developed for freight-in, purchasing, receiving, and other costs associated with the material handling function. An alternative to using applied rates for freight charges on raw material is to use only FOB destination prices in establishing the standards.

The current standard concept calls for the purchasing department to forecast the expected actual material cost. The prices may be based upon existing purchase contracts, or statistical forecasting may be used to estimate the actual material cost for the coming period. After reference is made to the prices recorded on the latest purchase invoices, a weighted average may be drawn from these figures. Or, instead of setting a short-range material price standard, reference may be made to the prices for several years. Allowance is made for market fluctuations and seasonal trends.

SETTING LABOR STANDARDS

The fact that one is dealing with human beings makes it more difficult to set labor standards than to establish standard material costs. There are many elements, such as the state of a person's health and fatigue or eating habits, that can cause a variance in productivity. A person's attitudes toward a supervisor and manager, along with other psychological factors, also affect productive efficiency. These things, along with the age, skill, and seniority, must be considered in establishing the standard labor costs.

To determine labor standards, labor must first be classified as direct or indirect. Direct labor is treated as a separate item of cost in standard cost systems, while provision for indirect labor is made in manufacturing overhead costs. The cost accountant may classify such operations as setup time, lost time, and cleanup after jobs as part of labor cost. The standard labor cost must then be increased to include these operations.

Preliminary plant survey

Examination of past payroll and production records will reveal the worker-hours used on various jobs and can help determine standard performance. Such analysis may give an indication of the workers' potential performance; however, this provides no assurance that all unnecessary operations are eliminated. Historical records should never be accepted until they have been reviewed in light of existing procedures, but past performance averages can be useful in setting labor standards. If, on the other hand, the present plant layout is different from the plant used in the past, the records will not give reliable information on which to base the labor standard. A special investigation may be necessary to determine the probable effects of this change.

In industries where no data reflecting past performance are available, it may be necessary to obtain time reports from the workers for a limited period as a basis for the standards. These time reports should be kept as simple as possible. A minimum of information is required: usually, simply the job description, the time taken, and the input are reported. The main objection to this method is that the resulting labor standards are largely expressions of opinion. This method also does not reveal potential economies.

Often an experienced analyst can look at the work and plant layout and determine the labor requirements. However, there are dangers to this approach. An inexperienced analyst, for example, would not be able to combine all the details to form a satisfactory standard.

Time and motion study

In all possible instances, time study should be the basis for setting labor quantity standards. The object of such a study is to develop time standards and piece rates which the average operator can meet daily without affecting his or her well-being. The study may be based on time required to produce individual pieces or an assembly of parts. If improvements in the work method can be incorporated, the time standard analyst should refer the matter to the supervisor.

The operating cycle should be broken up into as many distinct elements as it is possible to observe. With these smaller work units, stalling attempts and irregularities can be detected earlier. The rating of the operation should be placed on time-study sheets and should include both the skill and effort of the employees. Rating calls for expert knowledge and skill, as an incorrect estimate of the operator's skill or speed will distort the setting of rates.

The selection of the worker representative to be studied is very important. It is best for the plant supervisor to observe the worker's manner of performance before selection. The workers assigned should not be abnormally fast or slow but rather seasoned workers who perform at a steady pace. The character and honesty of the worker are also important, as is the worker's willingness to participate in the study. There should be no evidence of an attempt to confuse the time and motion operator. Results may vary substantially between workers. The time-study analyst must exercise judgment in excluding those observations that reflect abnormal conditions.

Where the industry operates with a fixed labor force, labor standards can be computed on an estimated allowed hours per month. These hours should be broken down by department or area of supervisory responsibility. Obviously, provision must be made for the fact that months have varying numbers of days. A certain amount of monthly overtime must also be included in the standards.

Advance estimates may be used as the basis for setting labor standards if the operation has never been performed before. These are also used for operations of a special type that are not expected to be repeated and for bidding or quoting a price to a customer. The standards are then used in the process to ensure control of the actual operations thereby making sure that anticipated profit is realized.

Test runs

Another way to establish labor standards is to use test runs, which are a last resort if management does not think time studies or past-performance averages are feasible. A weakness in the test run approach is that conditions in the plant are never static and no two similar jobs take the same amount of time in manufacture; hence, an average situation is difficult to derive from a test run. Past performance, on the other hand, does give an average, while time and motion study gives an objective result. Management should consider using a combination of these methods to obtain more accurate labor standards.

Labor rate standards

After time standards are determined, rate standards are applied to obtain the total labor cost standard. Clearly, reference only to the rates paid previously may result in inaccurate rate standards, since labor rates are often determined by a competitive market in which supply and demand are active and constantly changing. The labor rate standard should therefore adhere closely to the actual labor rates that will be paid in the next period.

The procedure for determining rate standards will depend upon the method by which employees are paid. There are two general methods. A rate may be established for the job, and, no matter who performs the job, the rate stays the same. On the other hand, a rate may be established for the individual worker, and the worker receives this rate regardless of the work performed. There is a hybrid form in which a limited range of rates is set for each occupation. The individual's standing in this range depends upon skill and length of service.

The labor rates for a company may be set by the prevailing area rates. The cost accountant should investigate the specific plant conditions to see whether rates are of this type or whether rates are set up by a labor contract. Labor rate standards may be easily established under the latter condition. Since the wage is relatively fixed, it may be used as standard.

The nature of direct labor operations in each center determines whether separate rates for each labor operation should be used. If these operations are not uniform and require varying degrees of skill, each operation should have a separate standard hourly labor rate. If the operations are rather uniform, a standard labor rate can be used, which will result in less time spent in cost computation.

Where a continuous operation employing a conveyor system is used, the wage payment may be based on the speed of the conveyor belt. In this case, the accountant and management may forecast labor market conditions and set a standard rate per day. The speed of the conveyor belt can be set with reference to the estimated production.

When a new manufacturing process is introduced, it is not wise to establish a piece rate until the operators are trained. After the operators become experienced, a time study should be conducted. The cost accountant should make allowance for this factor. The weakness in this method is that if the base hourly rates are changed, all the piece rates will have to be recalculated. The result can be costly.

Group piece rates

A group piece rate plan can be adapted to departments where it is very difficult to apply a straight piecework plan. Departments in which a multiplicity of operations are performed use this plan under which payments are made on the completed job, not on the individual units. The total price of the completed job is determined by adding the unit rates. This price includes an allowance for repairing defective work, supervision, and breaking in new employees. Time lost due to the handling of parts is also allowed in group rates.

Many employers today recognize the importance of a good wage incentive program in which workers are given the opportunity to increase their earnings by producing a number of units greater than the standard or expected number and have added this into their payroll program. The hourly base rate for the standard or expected number can be obtained from time studies and job evaluations. The hourly rate shown on the job evaluation sheet used for pricing the allowed time on the job may also be used. This base rate also often becomes the guaranteed rate that is paid workers regardless of their output. Management may feel that a guaranteed wage rate should be established to be fair to the new, inexperienced worker who is unable to produce at a high level of output because of lack of training. In determining the guaranteed and incentive wage rates, management should make certain that the spread between the figure used as a base rate and the possible earnings is great enough to encourage the worker to greater productivity.

However, guaranteed wage plans also often result in idle labor time. For example, assume workers are guaranteed an 8-hour day, five days a week, and a machine is down for repairs for 10 hours leaving six workers idle a total of 60 worker-hours. The wages earned for these 60 idle hours should be charged to Factory Overhead Control rather than to the Work in Process Inventory account.

Salaried personnel

While the previous discussion reviewed the establishment of labor standards for wage earners paid a piece or time rate, consideration must also be given to the personnel employed on a salary basis. Some salaried personnel will be engaged in transforming material from its raw state to a finished product, and their wages will be classified as a direct labor cost. Other salaried personnel, such as plant supervisors, repairers, and inspectors, will be classified as indirect labor and become a part of factory overhead. The cost accountant should design a schedule showing the number of salaried people and their individual salaries. From this the average salary figure can be derived. The standard salary figures are applied to each department according to the number of salaried personnel employed in that department.

The average plant salary figure should also include the employee benefits of salaried personnel. In fact, allowance must be made for the cost of all employee benefits because these increase the labor cost considerably. For this reason, the cost accountant must study the union agreement to find the extra payments the company is required to make. Examples of such payments are vacation pay, jury allowance, free insurance, and pensions. Since state and federal legal requirements also play a role in labor costs, allowance must be made for payroll taxes such as unemployment tax, state disability tax, and old-age benefits. Moreover, local company practices must frequently be considered: floral donations, gifts, first aid, and recreation may thus be regarded as a form of labor cost. While the extra compensation received from shift bonuses or vacations with pay may be charged to departmental overhead, it may also be included as a part of the standard direct labor cost. Either method results in accurate figures if the overhead is applied on direct labor dollars or worker-hour rates, but management may consider these benefits part of direct labor cost and prefer to include them in the labor standard. In this event, the employee benefit costs should be estimated for the year and applied as a percentage of direct labor cost.

STANDARD SPECIFICATIONS

After material and labor quantity and price standards are determined, a standard specification for each product unit can be prepared. Even though the establishment of overhead standards will not be discussed until Chapter 11, the following standard specification for a unit includes overhead to be complete. The following quantity (physical) and price specifications are established for all three cost components.

	Cost per unit
Material (3 pounds @ $4 per pound)......	$12
Labor (2 hours @ $5 per hour)..........	10
Overhead (2 hours @ $10 per hour.......	20
Total standard cost per unit........	$42

In the above standard specification, it is assumed that overhead is applied on the basis of direct labor-hours. At the same time that the two hours of labor are used to make the product, overhead is being applied. The standard therefore specifies not a total of four hours, but two hours to finish the product.

After the quantity and price standards for material are calculated, the following material variances can be determined:

1. Material usage or quantity or efficiency variance: (Actual material quantity − Standard material quantity) × Standard material price.
2. Material price variance: (Actual material price − Standard material price) × Actual material quantity.

Material variances for job order costing

The following data are used to illustrate the calculation of material variances:

Standard cost per unit: 3 pounds @ $4 per pound = $12
Pounds purchased: 2,820 pounds @ $3.90 per pound
Pounds used in production: 2,750
Units finished: 900

Standard quantity allowed.   The standard must be applied against actual production of finished units. Since there were 900 units produced, the standard quantity allowed must be 2,700 pounds (900 units × 3 pounds). In computing the material usage variance, actual quantity used to produce the 900 units (2,750 pounds) is compared against the 2,700 standard pounds allowed. The difference in quantity used is multiplied by the standard material price to arrive at the material usage variance.

Material usage (quantity or efficiency) variance

(2,750 actual material quantity − 2,700 standard material quantity)
× $4 standard material price = $200 unfavorable *material quantity variance*

The material usage variance is unfavorable since 50 more pounds were used to make the 900 units than specified in the standard. Of course, one way to have favorable material quantity variances is to inject only a portion of the material required to make each finished unit. However, the final result of this will be a shoddy, imperfect product, and quality control established in the factory will prevent this from occurring. It is always assumed that the units produced are perfect units which have passed inspection.

Let us continue the illustration. The company purchased 2,820 pounds of material costing $3.90 per pound; however, only 2,750 pounds were used in production. The price variance can be computed either on the basis of material purchased or material used as follows:

Material purchase price variance

($3.90 actual material price − $4.00 standard material price)
× 2,820 pounds *purchased* = $282 favorable *material purchase price variance*

Material usage price variance

($3.90 actual material price − $4.00 standard material price)
× 2,750 pounds *used* = $275 favorable *material usage price variance*

Regardless of the approach used, the variance is favorable since the material was purchased at a saving of $0.10 per pound ($3.90 − $4). It is again assumed that the same grade of material specified is being purchased and that the savings does not result from a lower and cheaper grade of material being bought.

Material variances for process costing

The above example illustrates the use of standards in a job order cost system. The approach is slightly different, however, for a process costing system. The standard cost specifications in a process costing system, as in a job order cost system, are known in advance for all three cost components: material, labor, and overhead. However, the standard hours, gallons, pounds, or other measures allowed for the operations performed in a process costing system cannot be determined until the operations for the accounting period have ended. Then, if the standards are being applied for a process costing system, the standard quantity per unit is multiplied by the equivalent units for each cost element. For example, assume the same material standards were used in another company employing a process costing system, there was no beginning inventory, and the following goods were transferred or remain in ending inventory:

Units transferred . . . . 1,000 units
Ending inventory (⅕ material, ¾ labor). . . . .   100 units

The equivalent units (EU) for material would be as follows:

$$\text{EU, material} = 1,000 + 20 \ (100 \text{ units} \times \tfrac{1}{5}) = 1,020$$

The standard pounds allowed would be 3,060 (1,020 EU × 3 pounds)

If this process costing company used 3,000 pounds, the material quantity variance would be favorable, as follows:

(3,000 actual material quantity − 3,060 standard material quantity)
× $4 standard material price = $240 favorable *material quantity variance*

Assume further that 3,150 pounds of material costing $4.15 per pound were purchased. As in a job order costing system, the price variance can be computed in either of the following ways:

Material purchase price variance

($4.15 actual material price − $4.00 standard material price)
× 3,150 pounds *purchased* = $472.50 *unfavorable material purchase price variance*

Material usage price variance

($4.15 actual material price − $4.00 standard material price)
× 3,000 pounds *used* = $450 *unfavorable material usage price variance*

Journal entries for material

As illustrated above, the material price variance can be computed on the basis of either pounds used or pounds purchased. The approach chosen depends upon how the material standards are integrated in the accounting system, as there are three different methods of reflecting material price and quantity variances.

1. The price variance can be isolated at the time of purchase so the material inventory is kept at standard cost. This is the preferred method, it saves clerical costs because no actual inventory costing method (FIFO, LIFO, or average cost) need be used.
2. The price variance is not recorded until materials are issued from the storeroom into production. An alternative treatment for recording the usage price variance is to wait until all unused materials are returned to the storeroom and total usage on the job is determined. This means that the material inventory ledger account must be kept on some actual costing basis. An appendix to Chapter 3 discusses the FIFO, LIFO, and average costing methods of inventory costing. All of these are actual cost methods and require much clerical effort to account for inventories.
3. A material purchase price variance is recorded when the material is received from a supplier, allowing the material inventory account to be kept at standard. Then the price variance on the material used is transferred from the purchase price variance ledger account to the material usage price variance ledger account. The remaining balance in the purchase price variance is treated as a valuation account and is deducted from (if a favorable or credit balance) or is added to (if an unfavorable or debit balance) the standard cost of material to arrive at an adjusted actual cost of material.

The last is a combination of the two previous methods, since it determines both a material purchase price and a material usage price variance. If there is a large difference between the amount of material purchased and the amount of material used each accounting period, the additional effort required under this method is warranted. Each of these methods is illustrated below using the data presented earlier for a job order costing system.

Standard cost per unit: 3 pounds @ $4 per pound = $12
Pounds purchased: 2,820 pounds @ $3.90 per pound
Pounds used in production: 2,750
Units finished: 900
No beginning inventory in the Direct Materials Inventory account

Note that because the eventual output is rarely known at the time the materials are issued, the practical procedure is to charge the entire quantity to work in process and sort out the quantity variance, if any, after the job has been completed. Whenever lost or spoiled units are likely to result from the production process, or whenever the eventual yield is not known when the job is started, the prudent manager estimates how much material will be needed to complete the order and requisitions accordingly.

This does not mean, however, that no attempt is made to be aware of variances as production is progressing. In every process there are certain key points at which it is possible to monitor progress and estimated costs. If there are inspection points at which the ratio of bad units to good ones can be measured, certain machines or operators whose performance is typical of the process as a whole, or whatever, these points can serve as reliable indicators of the job as a whole and management can be appraised without awaiting variance analyses. The journal entries would be as follows:

Material price variance recognized at time of purchase (material inventory at standard)

Direct Materials Inventory (2,820 pounds × $4)	11,280	
Material Purchase Price Variance		
(2,820 pounds × $0.10 @ pound)		282
Accounts Payable (2,820 pounds × $3.90)		10,998
Work in Process Inventory (2,750 pounds × $4)	11,000	
Direct Materials Inventory (2,750 pounds × $4)		11,000

When the output of 900 units is known, the following entry is made:

Material Quantity Variance (50 pounds × $4)	200	
Work in Process Inventory		200

Material price variance recognized at time of usage (material inventory at actual)

Direct Materials Inventory (2,820 pounds × $3.90)	10,998	
Accounts Payable		10,998
Work in Process Inventory (2,750 pounds × $4)	11,000	
Direct Materials Inventory (2,750 pounds × $3.90), ...		10,725
Material Usage Price Variance (2,750 pounds × $0.10)		275

When output is known, the following entry is made:

Material Quantity Variance (50 pounds × $4)	200	
Work in Process Inventory.		200

Material purchase price and usage price variance

Direct Materials Inventory (2,820 lbs × $4).	11,280	
Material Purchase Price Variance (2,820 pounds × $0.10 per		
pound)		282
Accounts Payable (2,820 pounds × $3.90)		10,998
Work in Process Inventory (2,750 pounds × $4)	11,000	
Direct Materials Inventory (2,750 pounds × $4)		11,000
Material Purchase Price Variance.	275	
Material Usage Price Variance (2,750 pound × $0.10)		275
Material Quantity Variance (50 pounds × $4)	200	
Work in Process Inventory.		200

This leaves a balance of $7 in the Material Purchase Price Variance account which reflects the $0.10 variance per pound for the 70 pounds left unused in inventory.

Material Purchase Price Variance

(2,750 pounds used × $0.10 variance)	275	(2,820 pounds purchased × $0.10 variance) (70 pounds in inventory × $0.10 variance) Balance 7	282

This method would leave a balance sheet like this:

Direct materials inventory (at standard cost)	$280
Less material purchase price variance	7
Direct materials inventory (adjusted to actual)	$273

To simplify the example, the methods illustrated above assume that there is only one purchase made of a single material inventory item. In practice, however, in a typical manufacturing operation there will be many different items of material purchased and a varying number of orders placed each period. In addition, the examples assume that the variances were recorded at the time they occurred. Indeed, to have effective daily control, variances must be isolated quickly. However, in practice, a journal entry recording the variance may not be made at the time the variance first occurs; instead, a summary entry may be made at the end of the month to record in total the variances incurred each day.

There are other combinations of journal entries to record the material price and quantity variances, depending upon the sequence of events occurring. The important thing to remember is that the net amount debited as the cost of the job should reflect Standard quantity allowed × Standard price. It is not necessary to determine the standard cost of the job to compute the material variances. However, when the standards are entered into the journal, the standard cost of the job must be computed.

LABOR VARIANCES

Variances identical to those illustrated for material can be computed for labor, too, after the standards for labor are determined.

1. Labor time (quantity or efficiency) variance: (Actual labor-hours − Standard labor-hours) × Standard labor rate per hour.
2. Labor rate variance: (Actual labor rate − Standard labor rate) × Actual labor-hours.

To illustrate the computation of these variances, assume the following for a job order processing company:

Standard cost per unit: 2 hours @ $5 per hour = $10;
Labor: 2,000 hours @ $5.20 per hour
Units: 900 units finished

Standard hours allowed.   The standard hours allowed for actual production amount to 1,800 (2 hours × 900 units produced). As in the case of material, the standard quantity allowed for the actual units produced must be determined. After standard hours allowed are determined, the labor efficiency variance can be computed. This variance is also referred to as a *labor time* or *quantity variance.*

Labor time (quantity or efficiency) variance

(2,000 actual labor-hours − 1,800 standard labor-hours)
× $5 standard labor rate per hour
= $1,000 *unfavorable labor efficiency variance*

The labor efficiency variance is unfavorable because 200 more hours were used to manufacture the 900 units than specified in the standard. The 200 excess hours are multiplied by the standard labor rate so that only the effects of quantity are isolated.

Labor rate variance

($5.20 actual labor rate − $5 standard labor rate)
× 2,000 actual labor-hours
= $400 *unfavorable labor rate variance*

The labor rate variance is unfavorable because the workers were paid $0.20 more per actual hour worked than indicated in the standard specifications.

Labor variances for process costing

In computing labor variances in a process costing system, equivalent units (EU) must first be determined. The data presented earlier in which there was no beginning inventory, 1,000 units transferred, and 100 units in ending inventory, ¾ complete as to labor are used. The following labor variances are computed, assuming the process costing company used 1,900 hours of labor this period and paid $4.75 per hour:

EU, labor = 1,000 + 75 (100 units × ¾) = 1,075
The standard hours allowed would be 2,150 hours (1,075 EU × 2)

Labor efficiency variance

(1,900 actual labor-hours − 2,150 standard labor-hours) × $5 standard labor rate per hour = $1,250 *favorable labor efficiency variance*

Labor rate variance

($4.75 actual labor rate − $5.00 standard labor rate) × 1,900 actual labor-hours = $475 *favorable labor rate variance*

Journal entries for labor

There are a number of combinations of journal entries to record the labor variances. The following illustrates one combination that records only the rate variance while the job is in process. Neither the amount nor the direction (whether favorable or unfavorable) will be known until the job is completed. Work in Process should be adjusted at that time, not while the job is in process.

Work in Process Inventory (2,000 hours × $5 per hour)	10,000	
Labor Rate Variance ($0.20 × 2,000 hours)	400	
Wages Payable (2,000 hours × $5.20 per hour)		10,400

When the output of 900 units is determined, the Labor Efficiency Variance is recorded as follows:

Labor Efficiency Variance (200 hours × $5)	1,000	
Work in Process Inventory		1,000

The job will not be transferred into Finished Goods Inventory until its factory overhead has been applied. Chapter 11 discusses the standards for factory overhead costs.

Combined net variances. Rather than determine separate price and quantity variances for material and labor, some companies merely determine total variances for these factors. This approach is not recommended, since it provides no way to identify factors that cause the variance. Instead of combining all contributing factors, an approach should pinpoint each one.

MIX AND YIELD VARIANCES

In many production operations, especially those using process costing, a recipe or formula is used to indicate the specifications for each class of material used. Changes in the various material classes can then be made when a substitute material becomes less costly, although tolerance limits are established beyond which changes cannot be made. The quantity variance for material and labor can thus be broken down into mix and yield variances, and this detailed analysis can lead to better management control. Price or rate variances are calculated for *each* type of material or *each* category of labor in the usual manner; the overall price or rate variance is the sum or difference of the individual variances.

A *mix* variance is computed by comparing the standard formula to the standard cost of material actually used. The resulting variance results from mixing raw material or classes of labor in a ratio that differs from standard specifications. For example, in the textile or chemical industry, different combinations of raw material can be mixed and still yield a perfect product. A *yield* variance results because the yield obtained differs from the one expected on the basis of input. In making candy, for example, sugar, corn syrup, cocoa and milk are cooked to yield fudge. A certain quantity of these raw materials is expected to yield a specified number of pounds of fudge. A yield variance results if the actual output of fudge differs from that expected. Often an advantage created by a mix or yield variance is canceled out by the other. For example, the new mix may result in a favorable variance, but it is offset by an unfavorable yield variance. Likewise, the advantages gained from a favorable yield variance may result in an unfavorable mix variance. A *labor yield* variance is usually considered the result of the quantity and/or the quality of the material handled.

Standard product mix

The standard product mix for a certain type of sausage is as follows:

	Pounds	Standard price	Standard cost
Meat A.	250	$0.40	$100
Meat B.	600	0.25	150
Meat C.	50	0.88	44
Meal	200	0.18	36
Input	1,100		$330
Output.	1,000		

Standard cost per pound of input ($330/1,100 pounds). $0.30
Cost per pound of output ($330/1,000 pound) $0.33

At the end of the month, it was determined that the following actual pounds of meat were used to produce 40,000 pounds of sausage:

	Actual quantity	Total standard cost
Meat A	9,900	$ 3,960 (9,900 × $0.40)
Meat B	24,600	6,150 (24,600 × $0.25)
Meat C	2,400	2,112 (2,400 × $0.88)
Meal.	8,100	1,458 (8,100 × $0.18)
	45,000	$13,680

To compute the mix variance, one must realize that the actual quantities used did not conform to the standard formula. For example, 40,000 pounds of sausage were finished; if the standard formula was used, 10,000 pounds (250 pounds × 40 batches) of Meat A should have been used instead of 9,900 pounds actually used. In a mix variance the actual quantities used are multiplied by the standard price per pound and then compared against the actual quantities multiplied by the standard cost per pound of input. The mix and yield variances are illustrated below.

Material mix variance

Actual quantity at standard price:

Meat A (9,900 pounds @ $0.40) $3,960
Meat B (24,600 pounds @ $0.25) 6,150
Meat C (2,400 pounds @ $0.88) 2,112
Meal (8,100 pounds @ $0.18) 1,458 $13,680

Actual quantity at standard input cost
  (45,000 pounds × $0.30).   13,500
      Unfavorable material mix variance . . . . . $ 180

Material yield variance

The yield variance is computed as follows:

Actual input quantity at standard input cost
  (45,000 pounds × $0.30) $13,500
Actual output quantity at standard output cost
  (40,000 pounds × $0.33) 13,200
      Unfavorable material yield variance . . . . $ 300

An alternative approach to computing material yield variances is to compare the expected loss from processing with the actual loss as follows:

Expected loss from processing . . . .   100/1,100 = 9.09%
5,000 Actual loss . . . .   (45,000 − 40,000 pounds)
4,091 Expected loss . . . .   (9.09% × 45,000 pounds put into process)
  909 × $.33 cost per pound of output = $300 unfavorable yield variance.

Since direct materials inventory is kept at standard, a material price variance would be recorded for each of the four materials at the time the material was purchased, using the analysis presented earlier. The following journal entry would be made to record the material mix and yield variances:

Work in Process (40,000 pounds × $0.33)   13,200
Material Mix Variance   180
Material Yield Variance   300
    Direct Materials Inventory (kept at standard)   13,680

Just as the above example illustrates how to determine *material* mix and yield variances, the following example illustrates how to figure *labor* mix and yield variances.

Standard crew mix

Assume operations are performed by a crew of employees in three different pay grades. A standard crew hour consists of 20 worker-hours distributed among the pay grades as follows:

Pay grade	Hours	Standard rate	Standard cost
A2	6	$5	$ 30
C4	5	4	20
D5	9	6	54
	20		$104

Output: 400 gallons

Standard cost per hour: $\dfrac{\$104}{20 \text{ hours}} = \$5.20$

During the month, charges to the department included 570 hours of A2 at an actual rate of $5.10, 420 hours of C4 at an actual rate of $4.05, and 700 hours of D5 at an actual rate of $5.93, giving a total labor cost of $8,759. If there were 32,000 gallons of the product finished during the month, the labor mix and labor yield variances would be computed as shown in the tables that follow.

Labor mix variance

Actual hours at standard rate

	Actual hours	Standard rate	Total standard cost
A2.	570	$5	$2,850
C4.	420	4	1,680
D5.	700	6	4,200
	1,690		$8,730

Actual hours at standard cost:
  1,690 actual hour × $5.20 standard hourly
    rate 8,788
      Favorable labor mix variance . . . . $ 58

Labor yield variance

Actual hours at standard cost
  (1,690 hours × $5.20) $8,788
Output at standard cost expressed in standard hours:
  $\dfrac{32,000}{400}$ = 80 batches × 20 hours = 1,600 hours
1,600 hours × $5.20 standard hourly rate 8,320
Unfavorable labor yield variance . . . . $ 468

Labor rate variance
The following labor rate variance for each pay grade of labor is calculated as previously illustrated:

Pay grade	Actual rate	Standard rate	Rate variance	Total rate variance
A2	$5.10	$5	$0.10 U*	$57 U ($0.10 × 570 hours)
C4	4.05	4	0.05 U	21 U ($0.05 × 420 hours)
D5	5.93	6	0.07 F	49 F ($0.07 × 700 hours)
				$29 U

*U = unfavorable; F = favorable.

The following journal entry records the labor mix, labor yield, and labor price variance:

Work in Process Inventory.	8,320	
Labor Yield Variance	468	
Labor Rate Variance.	29	
Labor Mix Variance		58
Payroll.		8,759

CAS 407

Not only must accountants be certain that cost standards are fulfilling management's needs for internal analysis, but they must also be assured that these standards satisfy the requirements of the Cost Accounting Standards Board (CASB). In 1974, Part 407—*Use of Standard Costs for Direct Material and Direct Labor*—became effective. The purpose is to provide criteria under which standard costs may be used for estimating, accumulating, and reporting costs of direct material and direct labor, and to provide criteria relating to the establishment of standards, accumulation of standard costs, and accumulation and disposition of variances from standard costs.

According to CAS 407, standard costs may be used for estimating, accumulating, and reporting costs of direct material and direct labor only when all of the following criteria are met:

1.   Standard costs are entered into the books of account.
2.   Standard costs and related variances are appropriately accounted for at the level of the production unit.
3.   Practices with respect to the setting and revising of standards, use of standard costs, and disposition of variances are stated in writing and consistently followed.

CAS 407 requires that a contractor's written statement of practices with respect to standards shall include the bases and criteria (such as engineering studies, experience, or other supporting data) used in setting and revising standards; the period during which standards are to remain effective; the level (such as ideal or current) at which material quantity standards and labor time standards are set; and conditions (such as those expected to prevail at the beginning of a period) which material price and labor rate standards are designed to reflect. CAS 407 allows the use of material price standards and the recognition of their related variances either at the time purchases of material are entered into the books of account or at the time material cost is allocated to production units. CAS 407 also specifies the conditions under which a labor rate standard may be set to cover a group of direct labor workers and where only the material price or material quantity is set at standard, with the other component stated at actual.

The responsibility for variances as well as the possible causes for their occurrence will be discussed in more detail in Chapter 11. The following outline of the material and labor variances is given for review.

SUMMARY OF MATERIAL AND LABOR VARIANCES

Material usage (quantity or efficiency) variance

$$\text{(Actual material quantity } - \text{ Standard material quantity)} \times \text{Standard material price}$$

For control purposes this variance should be isolated as quickly as possible; however, it may be impossible to calculate until the work is completed.

Possible causes of unfavorable variances:

1. Waste and loss of material in handling and processing.
2. Spoilage or production of excess scrap.
3. Changes in product specifications that have not been incorporated in standards.
4. Substitution of nonstandard materials.
5. Variation in yields from material.

Responsibility. Line supervisors should be held responsible for material under their control.

Material price variance

$$\text{(Actual material price } - \text{ Standard material price)} \times \text{Actual material quantity}$$

Practice varies with respect to when and how such variance is computed and accounted for in cost and profit determination as a material *purchase* price and/or *usage* price variance can be computed. However, for purposes of control, the variance should be computed at the time of purchase; in this case, the difference between actual and standard material price is multiplied by the material quantity *purchased.* In computing a material *usage* price variance, this difference is multiplied by the material quantity *used.* To delay the computation until the time the quantity is issued usually destroys the usefulness of the information for control, because then corrective action is seldom possible. Since this treatment charges material inventory at standard, detailed record-keeping is simplified, for records can be kept in terms of quantities only. An objection to this procedure is that unless buying is closely allied to production and sales volume, variations in the volume of purchasing can cause a distortion in operating results.

Possible causes for unfavorable variance:

1. Fluctuations in material market prices.
2. Purchasing from unfavorably located suppliers, which results in additional transportation costs.
3. Failure to take cash discounts available.
4. Purchasing in nonstandard or uneconomical lots.
5. Purchasing from suppliers other than those offering the most favorable terms.

Responsibility.   The purchasing department should usually be held responsible. However, supervisory factory personnel should be held responsible when they specify certain brand-named materials or materials of certain grade or quality. If a price variance occurs because a request was made for a rush order, the production planning department could be responsible, as this may be the result of poor scheduling.

Labor time (quantity or efficiency) variance

$$\text{(Actual labor-hours} - \text{Standard labor-hours)} \times \text{Standard labor rate per hour}$$

Possible causes for unfavorable variances:

1. Inefficient labor.
2. Poorly trained labor.
3. Rerouted work.
4. Inefficient equipment.
5. Machine breakdowns.
6. Nonstandard material being used.

Responsibility.   Line supervisors should be held responsible for labor under their control. The production planning department or the purchasing department should be held responsible for any labor efficiency variance that results from the use of nonstandard material.

Labor rate variance

$$\text{(Actual labor rate} - \text{Standard labor rate)} \times \text{Actual labor-hours}$$

Possible causes for unfavorable variance:

1. Change in labor rate that has not been incorporated in standard rate.

2. Use of an employee having a wage classification other than that assumed when the standard for a job was set.
3. Use of a greater number of higher paid employees in the group than anticipated. (This applies when the standard rate is an average.)

Responsibility.   If line supervisors must match workers and machines to the tasks at hand by using the proper grade of labor, they should be responsible. Line supervisors should also be responsible if they control the wage rate of their labor force. If they do not, the personnel department may be responsible.

SUMMARY

Comparing present performance with past performance may or may not be useful, depending upon the quality of past performance. In any case, because production costs determined under an actual cost system come too late to be of much benefit in planning and control, and because by themselves actual costs provide no basis for measuring performance, actual costs become meaningful only when compared with other figures which are suitable bases of comparison. We call these figures standard costs. Under a standard cost system, actual costs can be compared against standard costs instead of against previous actual costs.

Standard costs are not replacements for historical costs; certainly, historical costs serve a useful purpose, as all companies should maintain a record of past events. Instead, standard costs separate historical costs into the portion that represents the standard allowance from the portion that represents the deviation from the standard. Analysis of variances between actual and standard costs is a very useful means of evaluating operations and finding areas which require correction.

Historical costs are of little assistance in determining future prices, particularly in periods of changing costs. These costs fail to provide a reliable guide for future performance, since it is not likely that conditions prevailing in one period will repeat themselves in another period. Historical costs are also deficient in that they provide no motivation for cost reduction, since they set no goals for employees. They are also ineffective in cost control because they are not available in time to correct inefficiencies which are causing excessive costs.

To have fair cost standards, a company should devote much time and effort to their development. Under no circumstances should these standards be set by unqualified or untrained people. This field is highly technical and requires a person who is well trained and experienced. Unless a skilled work-study engineer is in charge, the project will likely end in disorder and confusion. The engineer must, for instance, be alert to the shortcomings of the procedure of setting standards using work sampling and time and motion studies. In smaller companies where there is no time-study department, manufacturing management and top management will have the dual responsibility of determining the direct labor standards.

The most important principle to keep in mind in establishing price standards is that the standard should be based on the best information possible. A standard should take into consideration, for example, past prices, anticipated prices, and all foreseeable factors such as strikes, wide fluctuations in prices, weather conditions, and union agreements. For this reason, the purchasing department, which should have access to the latest price information, can render valuable aid in pricing material standards. Likewise, the manufacturing department will have available job rates and probable bonus data to help in the determination of direct labor standards. The process of setting standards also requires a review of the company's plant layout and work flow; this review provides management with a better understanding of possible cost savings.

IMPORTANT TERMS AND CONCEPTS

Standard costs

Estimated costs

Theoretical standards

Practical standards

Current standards

Pilot runs or test runs

Standard specifications

Standard quantity allowed

Material usage (quantity or efficiency) variance

Material purchase price variance

Material usage price variance

Labor time (quantity or efficiency) variance

Labor rate variance

Material and labor mix variance

Material and labor yield variance

CAS 407

PROBLEM FOR SELF-STUDY

Material and labor variances in a process costing system

Mary Miller, Inc. produces batches of a petroleum product on an assembly line. The standard costs per batch are as a follows:

	Total
Direct materials (80 gallons)	$ 40
Direct labor (60 hours).	216

A total of 480 batches were completed this period; ending inventory consists of 69 batches, one third complete. There was no beginning inventory. The following costs were incurred:

Direct materials used (40,743 gallons)	$ 17,519.49
Direct labor (29,677 hours)	108,321.05

Required:

A variance analysis for material and labor.

Solution:

$$EU = 480 + 23 = 503 \text{ batches}$$

Material quantity variance

503 batches $\times$ 80 gallons = 40,240 standard gallons
(40,743 actual gallons $-$ 40,240 standard gallons)
$\times$ \$0.50 standard rate = \$251.50 unfavorable

Material price variance

$$\frac{\$17,519.49 \text{ actual material cost}}{40,743 \text{ actual gallons}} = \$0.43 \text{ actual rate}$$

(\$0.43 actual rate $-$ \$0.50 standard rate) $\times$
40,743 = \$2,852.01 favorable

Labor quantity variance

503 batches $\times$ 60 hours = 30,180 standard hours

(29,677 actual hours $-$ 30,180 standard hours)
$\times$ \$3.60 standard rate = \$1,810.80 favorable

Labor rate variance

$$\frac{\$108,321.05}{29,677 \text{ hours}} = \$3.65 \text{ actual rate}$$

(\$3.65 actual rate $-$ \$3.60 standard rate) $\times$ 29,677 actual hours
= \$1,483.85 unfavorable

Proof of material variance

Actual material costs	\$17,519.49
Standard material costs	
(40,240 standard gallons $\times$ \$0.50)	20,120.00
Net favorable variance	\$ 2,600.51
Material price variance.	\$ 2,852.01(F)
Material quantity variance.	251.50(U)
	\$ 2,600.51

Proof of labor variance

Actual labor costs	\$108,321.05
Standard labor cost (30,180 standard hours	
$\times$ \$3.60 standard rate)	108,648.00
Net favorable variance	\$ 326.95
Labor quantity variance	\$ 1,810.80(F)
Labor rate variance	1,483.85(U)
	\$ 326.95

F = favorable; U = unfavorable.

REVIEW QUESTIONS

1. Two standards are normally developed for material and labor costs. Indicate and describe how these variances are calculated for:

   a. Material.
   b. Labor.

2. Why is it incorrect in a labor efficiency variance to compare actual hours and budgeted hours?

3. Which departments should be held responsible for an

   a. Unfavorable materials usage variance?
   b. Unfavorable material price variance?

4. Why are yardsticks for performance measurement needed? What limitations are inherent in any approach in which actual current costs are compared with historical cost data?

5. Would you advise recognizing material quantity variances at the time the materials are charged to production?

6. What is the relationship between budgets and standard costs?

7. Discuss the advantages of a standard cost system.

8. Why is it imperative that the standard cost system have the support of top management before initiation of the system?

9. What factors should a company consider in deciding how tight standards should be?

10. What are the advantages of integrating standards in the accounting system as opposed to only using them for statistical analysis?

11. Discuss the procedures that can be used to establish material quantity standards.

12. In making an allowance for waste and shrinkage in material quantity standards, what factors should a company consider?

13. Who should assist the cost accountant in setting material price standards?

14. Why is the worker representative important to the success of time and motion studies?

15. Discuss the disadvantages of using a test run as a basis for establishing labor quantity variances.

16. Discuss the methods available for developing labor rate standards.

17. When can the total standard quantity allowed be determined? How is it determined?

18. Which of the methods for entering material standards in the ledger accounts do you prefer? Why?

19. Can standard costing be incorporated in both a job order and a process costing system? Explain.

20. For what types of operations would material mix and labor yield variances be appropriate?

EXERCISES

E10–1.   Material variances

Gregory Bowman Company's direct material costs for the manufacture of a product are as follows for a month:

Actual unit purchase price.	$ 3.30
Standard quantity allowed for actual production	5,100
Quantity purchased and used for actual production.	5,500
Standard unit price	$ 3.00

Required:

a.   Determine the material price variance.

b.   Determine the material usage variance.

c.   Prove your answers.

E10–2.   Material and labor variances

Dalton Company adopted a standard cost system several years ago to account for its single product. The standard was set as follows:

Material A: 3 pounds @ $6 per pound
Direct labor: 4 hours @ $4.50 per hour

The following operating data were taken from the records for June:

In process (beginning inventory): 200 units, 20% complete as to labor.
In process (ending inventory): 600 units, 80% complete as to labor.
Completed during the month: 6,400 units.

20,900 pounds of material were used in production for a total cost of $123,310. Material is issued at the beginning of processing. Direct labor was $127,370, which was a rate of $4.70 per hour.

Required:

An analysis of variances for material and labor separating each into the factors that caused them; use FIFO costing.

E10–3.   Material and labor variances

Bolton Corporation engaged its engineers to analyze factory conditions and to determine material and labor standards. Their analysis generated the following standards:

	Per finished unit
Material (20 lb @ $4).	$80
Labor (4 hrs. @ $5).	20

Management had planned to produce 1,500 units, but due to favorable conditions, 1,550 units were produced. There were 30,400 pounds of material used at a cost of $118,560. There were 6,380 hours of labor employed at a cost of $32,410.40.

Required:

Calculate material and labor variances, indicating whether they are favorable or unfavorable.

E10–4.   Determining standard quantity (CMA adapted)

Danson Company is a chemical manufacturer which supplies industrial users. The company plans to introduce a new chemical solution and needs to develop a standard product cost for it.

The new chemical solution is made by combining a chemical compound (nyclyn) and a solution (salex), boiling the mixture, adding a second compound (protet), and bottling the resulting solution in 10 liter containers. The initial mix, which is 10 liters in volume, consists of 12 kg of nyclyn and 9.6 liters of salex. A 20 percent reduction in volume occurs during the boiling process. The solution is then cooled slightly before 5 kg of protet are added; the addition of protet does not affect the total liquid volume.

The purchase prices of the raw materials used in the manufacture of this new chemical solution are as follows.

Nyclyn.	$1.30 per kg
Salex.	1.80 per liter
Protet	2.40 per kg

Required:

Determine the standard quantity for each of the raw materials needed to produce a 10-liter container of Danson Company's new chemical solution and the standard materials cost of a 10-liter container of the new product.

E10–5.   Material and labor variances

Standards for the only product manufactured by Overman Company were established as follows:

Direct material A:	5 gallons @ $2 per gallon
Direct material B:	2 gallons @ $1.00 per gallon
Direct labor:	4 hours @ $4 per hour
Factory overhead:	Applied at $3 per direct labor-hour

A summary of the first year's costs and related data for the manufacturing process is given below.

1. Purchases of material were: 2,500 gallons of Material A for a total of $5,125; 900 gallons of Material B for a total of $882. (Direct Materials Inventory is recorded at standard.)
2. Four hundred units were finished and 100 units were at the one-fifth stage of completion. This required 2,150 gallons of Material A, 820 gallons of Material B, and 1,750 hours of direct labor costing $7,140.

Required:

a. Indicate the total credits to the direct materials account for the issuance of Material A for the year.
b. Determine:
    (1) The material quantity variance for Materials A and B.
    (2) The material purchase price variance for Materials A and B.

(3) The labor quantity variance.

(4) The labor rate variance.

E10–6. Unit standard and actual material cost

Jeanne Teutsch, Inc. records show the following data relating to direct materials cost for November:

Units of finished product manufactured.	8,500
Standard direct materials per unit of product	8 lbs.
Quantity of direct materials used	68,750 lbs.
Direct materials quantity variance (unfavorable)	$ 2,850
Direct materials price variance (favorable).	$13,750

There is no work in process either at the beginning or the end of the month.

Required:

a. Calculate the standard direct material cost per *unit* of finished product.

b. Derive the actual direct material cost per *unit* of finished product.

PROBLEMS

P10–1. Material price, mix and yield variances and journal entries

In processing a speciality type of sausage, the Tucker Company experiences some loss. The standard product mix for a 100-pound batch is as follows:

20 pounds of Meat A @ $.41 per pound
25 pounds of Meat B @ $.80 per pound
30 pounds of Meat C @ $.30 per pound
45 pounds of Meat D @ $.60 per pound

The company records the material price variance at the time of purchase. Materials were purchased as follows:

1,480 pounds of Meat A =	$	666.00
1,550 pounds of Meat B =		1,209.00
1,750 pounds of Meat C =		577.50
3,000 pounds of Meat D =		1,650.00
		$4,102.50

In producing the 60 batches during the month, the following actual material quantities were put into production:

1,280 pounds of Meat A
1,490 pounds of Meat B
1,740 pounds of Meat C
2,650 pounds of Meat D

Required:

a. Determine material purchase price and material mix and yield variances.

b. Prepare journal entries to record the variances determined in *a* and the disposition of variances assuming all completed units are sold.

P10–2.   Labor rate, mix and yield variances

Dunston Company's production process is performed by a crew of employees in different pay grades. A standard crew hour consists of 60 labor-hours distributed as follows:

Pay grade	Hours	Standard rate	Standard cost
A	25	$ 4	$100
B	12	6	72
C	18	5	90
D	5	10	50
	60		$312

Output—100 tons

During the month, charges to the department included 1,260 hours of A at a total cost of $5,166; 610 hours of B at a total cost of $3,538; 925 hours of C at a total cost of $4,810; and 265 hours of D at a total cost of $2,915. There were 5,000 tons of finished goods produced during the month.

Required:

a.   Compute a labor rate, a labor mix, and a labor yield variance.
b.   Prepare the journal entry to record these variances and the direct labor cost.

P10–3.   Material price, mix and yield variances, and journal entries in a process cost system

Spaghetti sauce is processed and canned by Dennis E. Linane Manufacturers in lots of 144 cans (a gross), each weighing 16 ounces. The standard mixture for a gross is as follows:

Tomato paste.	141.5 pounds @ $ 0.28 per pound
Mixed spices.	1.5 pounds @ $12.60 per pound
Chopped onions	5.0 pounds @ $ 0.50 per pound
Mushrooms	2.0 pounds @ $ 2.61 per pound

While the company desires to maintain a special flavor for their sauce, they are able to use varying combinations of the above materials within limits. The following materials were purchased during the month. Direct materials inventory is kept at standard.

Tomato paste (12,500 pounds).	$3,750.00
Mixed spices (130 pounds)	1,631.50
Chopped onions (450 pounds).	216.00
Mushrooms (180 pounds)	460.80
	$6,058.30

There were 80 gross of cans finished during the period. Beginning inventory of work in process consisted of 20 gross of sauce one-fourth completed, while ending inventory of work in process consisted of 15 gross, two-thirds completed. Assume all inventory is past the cooking stage in which evaporation occurs. The following actual material quantities were put into production:

	Pounds
Tomato paste.	12,007
Mixed spice	135
Chopped onions	474
Mushrooms	210

Required:

a.   Determine material purchase price, material mix and yield variances.
b.   Prepare journal entries to record these variances, including the disposition of variances, assuming they are treated as period costs.

P10–4.   Labor hours and material needed: Planned labor variance (CMA adapted)

The Lenco Company employs a standard cost system as part of its cost control program. The standard cost per unit is established at the beginning of each year. Standards are not revised during the year for any changes in material or labor inputs or in the manufacturing processes. Any revisions in standards are deferred until the beginning of the next fiscal year. However, to recognize such changes in the current year, the company includes planned variances in the monthly budgets, prepared after such changes have been introduced.

The following labor standard was set for one of Lenco's products, effective July 1, 19X1, the beginning of the fiscal year.

Class I labor (4 hrs. @ $ 6.00)...............	$24.00
Class II labor (3 hrs. @ 7.50)...............	22.50
Class V labor (1 hr. @ 11.50)...............	11.50
Standard labor cost per 100 units	$58.00

The standard was based upon the quality of material that had been used in prior years and what was expected to be available for the 19X1–19X2 fiscal year. The labor activity is performed by a team consisting of four persons with Class I skills, three persons with Class II skills, and one person with Class V skills. This is the most economical combination for the company's processing system.

The manufacturing operations went as expected during the first five months of the year. The standard costs contributed to effective cost control during this period. However, there were indications that changes in the operations would be required in the last half of the year. The company had received a significant increase in orders for delivery in the spring. There was an inadequate number of skilled workers available to meet the increased production. As a result, the production teams, beginning in January, would be made up of more Class I labor and less Class II labor than the standard required. The teams would consist of six Class I persons, two Class II persons, and one Class V person. This labor team would be less efficient than the normal team. The reorganized teams work more slowly, so that only 90 units are produced in the same time period in which 100 units would normally be produced. No raw materials will be lost as a result of the change in the labor mix. Completed units have never been rejected in the final inspection process as a consequence of faulty work; this is expected to continue.

In addition, Lenco was notified by its material supplier that a lower quality material would be supplied after January 1. One unit of raw material normally is required for each good unit produced. Lenco and its supplier estimated that 5 percent of the units manufactured would be rejected upon final inspection due to defective material. Normally, no units are lost due to defective material.

Required:

a.   How much of the lower quality material must be entered into production to produce 42,750 units of good production in January with the new labor teams? Show your calculations.

b. How many hours of each class of labor will be needed to produce 42,750 good units from the material input? Show your calculations.

c. What amount should be included in the January budget for the planned labor variance due to the labor team and material changes? What amount of this planned labor variance can be associated with the (1) material change; and (2) the team change? Show your calculations.

P10–5. Methods of recording materials using a standard cost system

Brian Murray, Inc. has asked their CPA to provide them with three different approaches for recording material price variations. In their first month of operation, they decided to adopt a standard cost system and have purchased enough raw materials for several months of operations using the following data:

Standard cost per unit	4 gallons @ $3.00 per gallon
Gallons purchased	40,000 for $90,000
Gallons used in production	13,200
Units finished	3,000

Required:

a. Using the three different methods illustrated in this chapter for recording materials in a standard cost system, prepare the journal entries.

b. Evaluate these methods using the data given.

P10–6. Different systems for recording material

Louis Wells, Inc. has 20 pounds of Direct Material A2 in its beginning inventory, the actual unit cost of which was $3.90. The company uses a LIFO perpetual inventory system. During the month of January, the following purchases of Direct Material A2 were made on account:

Jan. 2 . . . . 30 pounds @ $4.15 per pound
6 . . . . 50 pounds @ $4.22 per pound

The engineering staff has determined that for each finished unit, the standard should be 2 pounds at a standard price of $4 per pound.

On January 8, 70 pounds of direct material were requisitioned for a 30-unit order. After production of the 30 units, 4 unused pounds were returned to the material storeroom at the end of the month.

Required:

a. Prepare the journal entries necessary to record the material transactions under each of the following accounting systems:

(1) Actual cost system.

(2) Standard cost system with direct materials inventory kept at actual cost.

(3) Standard cost system with direct materials inventory kept at standard cost. (Record only one type of price variance.)

b. Account for the difference in the material price variance computed using (2) and (3) above. Show details of computation.

P10–7. Unit material yield, mix, and price variance

Cynthia Stomper Company has determined that after allowing for normal processing losses, the standard mix of material used in producing a finished product is as follows:

Material AX (3 gallons @ $4). $12
Material BR (8 gallons @ $1.50) 12
Material CT (9 gallons @ $2). 18
                                                            $42

During a given period, the actual cost per unit was as follows:

Material AX (4 gallons @ $4.10) $16.40
Material BR (7 gallons @ $1.40) 9.80
Material CT (8 gallons @ $1.85) 14.80
                                                           $41.00

Required:

Determine the following:

a. Material yield variance per finished unit.
b. Material mix variance per finished unit.
c. Material price variance per finished unit.
d. Prepare a journal entry to record the issuance of material and the material variances. The materials inventory is kept at actual cost.

P10–8. Material price, mix, and yield variances

Mary Blalock Soup Company has developed a secret recipe for vegetable soup. The standard input for material per batch is as follows:

	Pounds	Standard price per pound
Beef and beef broth	40	$1.00
Potatoes.	50	0.30
Cereal and flavoring	20	0.15
Tomatoes	30	0.40
Lima beans	50	0.35
Green beans	60	0.28
Input	250	
Output	225	

The soup is packed in 24-ounce cans. During the month, 15,000 cans were filled with the following materials put in process:

	Pounds	Total actual cost
Beef and beef broth	4,205	$ 4,541.40
Potatoes.	4,910	1,374.80
Cereal and flavoring	3,216	611.04
Tomatoes	2,800	1,260.00
Lima beans	5,118	1,586.58
Green beans	6,310	2,208.50
	26,559	$11,582.32

Required:

a. Compute a material price variance for each of the materials and a material mix and yield variance for the month. Indicate whether the variance is favorable or unfavorable.

b.   Prepare journal entries to record the issuance of material and the variances. The materials inventory is kept at actual cost.

P10–9.   Journal entries for material and labor variances

Charles Dorr Company has the following standards per finished batch of units:

Materials (6 lbs @ $2)	$12
Labor (4 hrs @ $15)	$60

Management planned to produce 20,000 units; however, only 17,600 units are actually produced because of a labor problem. Purchasing bought 110,000 pounds of material at $247,500. Actual pounds used were 108,610. Direct labor costs were $1,067,647 for 70,940 hours.

Required:

a.   Record journal entries for all material transactions for the variances, assuming that the price variance reflects usage; record only one type of price variance.
b.   Make journal entries for the material transaction, assuming the material price variances are isolated on purchase; record only one type of price variance.
c.   Record all journal entries for labor variances.

P10–10.   Material price, mix, and yield variances (CMA adapted)

The LAR Chemical Company manufactures a wide variety of chemical compounds and liquids for industrial uses. The standard mix for producing a single batch of 500 gallons of one liquid is as follows:

Liquid chemical	Quantity (gallons)	Cost per gallon	Total cost
Maxon	100	$2.00	$200
Salex	300	.75	225
Cralyn.	225	1.00	225
	625		$650

There is a 20 percent loss in liquid volume during processing due to evaporation. The finished liquid is put into 10-gallon bottles for sale. Thus, the standard material cost for a 10-gallon bottle is $13.

The actual quantities of direct materials and the respective cost of the materials placed in production during November were as follows:

Liquid chemical	Quantity (gallons)	Total cost
Maxon	8,480	$17,384
Salex	25,200	17,640
Cralyn	18,540	16,686
	52,220	$51,710

A total of 4,000 bottles (40,000 gallons) was produced during November.

Required:

a.   Calculate the total direct material variance for the liquid product for the month of November and then further analyze the total variance into a:

(1) Material price variance.
(2) Material mix variance.
(3) Material yield variance.
b. Explain how LAR Chemical Company could use each of the three material variances—price, mix, yield—to help control the cost of manufacturing this liquid compound.

P10–11. Tight and current standards

BMD Corporation has recently installed a standard cost system. Management adopted fairly tight standards which they felt could be achieved if the workers perform at an efficient level. The monthly labor budget established for 1,600 units called for 5,600 hours at a total cost of $23,800. The monthly direct material budget for 3,600 gallons was set as $10,800.

The vice president in charge of manufacturing believes that the quantity standards established are too tight and that an additional set of "expected standards" should be established. He believes that an extra hour of labor and three-fourths gallon of materials per unit should be added to the standards; he also believes, however, that the standard labor rate and the standard material prices correctly reflect currect conditions. His reasoning is that top management is not going to get upset if the employees take an extra hour to complete the units or use more material since they recognize that the standards are tight.

The cost clerk determines that 1,550 units were completed during the month. The summary of labor time tickets reveals that 5,813 direct labor-hours were used at a cost of $24,995.90. There were 4,650 gallons used at an actual cost of $14,415.

Required:

a. What would you advise the company to do in regard to establishing another set of standards?
b. What are the direct material variances and labor variances using the tight standards? Label each variance indicating whether it is favorable or unfavorable.
c. What would the direct material variances and labor variances be using the vice president's "expected standards"? Label each variance indicating whether it is favorable or unfavorable.

P10–12. Standard cost system (CMA adapted)

The Kristy Company has grown from a small operation of 50 people eleven years ago to its present staff of 200 employees in 19X1. Kristy designs, manufactures, and sells environmental support equipment. In the early years, each item of equipment had to be designed and manufactured to meet each customer's requirements. The work was challenging and interesting for the employees, as innovative techniques were often needed in the production process to complete an order according to customers' requirements. In recent years, the company has been able to develop several components and a few complete units which can be used to meet the requirements of several customers.

The early special design and manufacture work has given the Kristy Company a leadership position in its segment of the pollution-control market. Kristy takes great pride in the superior quality of its products and this quality has contributed to its dominant role in this market segment. To help ensure high-quality performance, Kristy hires the most skilled personnel available and pays them above the industry average.

EXHIBIT P10–12

							19X1				
	Jan.	Feb.	March	April	May	June	July	Aug.	Sept.	Oct.	Nov.
Absenteeism rate (percent)	1.0	1.0	1.0	1.0	.5	1.0	2.0	4.0	6.0	8.0	11.0
Turnover rate (percent)	.2	.5	.5	.5	.3	.8	.7	1.4	1.9	2.5	2.9
Direct labor efficiency variance (U)	—	—	—	—	—	$(10,000)	$(11,500)	$(14,000)	$(17,000)	$(20,500)	$(25,000)
Direct materials usage variance (U)	—	—	—	—	—	(4,000)	(5,000)	(6,500)	(8,200)	(11,000)	(14,000)

U = unfavorable

This policy has resulted in a labor force that is very efficient, stable, and positively motivated toward company objectives.

The recent increase in government regulations requiring private companies to comply with specific environmental standards has made Kristy's market very profitable. Consequently, several competitors have entered the market segment once controlled by Kristy. While Kristy still maintains a dominant position in its market, it has lost several contracts to competitors that offer similar equipment to customers at a lower price.

The Kristy manufacturing process is very labor intensive. The production employees played an important role in the early success of the company. As a result, management gave employees a great deal of freedom to schedule and manufacture customers' orders. For instance, when the company increased the number of orders accepted, more employees were hired rather than pressuring current employees to produce at a faster rate. In management's view, the intricacy of the work involved required that employees have ample time to ensure the work was done right.

Management introduced a standard cost system which they believed would be beneficial to the company. They thought it would assist in identifying the most economical way to manufacture much of the equipment, would give management a more accurate picture of the costs of the equipment, and be used in evaluating actual costs for cost control. Consequently, the company should become more price competitive. Although the introduction of standards would likely lead to some employee discontent, management was of the opinion that the overall result would be beneficial. The standards were introduced on June 1, 19X1.

During December, the production manager reported to the president that the new standards were creating problems in the plant. The employees had developed bad attitudes, absenteeism and turnover rates had increased, and standards were not being met. In the production manager's judgment, employee dissatisfaction outweighed any benefits management thought would be achieved with the standard cost system. The production manager supported this contention with the data in Exhibit P10–12 for 19X1, during which monthly production was at normal volume levels.

Required:

a. Explain the general features and characteristics associated with the introduction and operation of a standard cost system that makes it an effective cost control tool.

b. Discuss the apparent impact of Kristy Company's cost system on:
    (1) Cost control.
    (2) Employee motivation.

c. Discuss the probable causes for employee dissatisfaction with the new cost system.

CASES

C10–1.   The use of standards as a motivational device

The management of Pinkerton Manufacturing Company has become alarmed over a consistent increase in production costs. Most of the increase is attributed to direct labor. The company has been advised that a standard cost system will help control labor as well as other costs.

Since detailed production records have not been maintained, the company has hired Comer Consulting Engineers to establish labor standards. Upon conclusion of a thorough study of the manufacturing process, Comer recommended a labor standard of one unit of production every 15 minutes, or 32 units per day per worker. As a part of their report to management, the engineers informed Pinkerton that their wage rates were below the industry average of $4.50 per hour.

The production manager was somewhat concerned about Comer's labor standard. It was her position that the employees could not attain it because it is too tight. Based on firsthand experience, she considered one unit of production every 20 minutes, or 24 units per day, more reasonable.

Management recognized that the standard should be at a high level to motivate workers, but not so high that it fails to provide adequate information for control and cost comparison purposes. After giving the matter much thought, management agreed on a dual standard. The engineers' labor standard of one unit every 15 minutes was adopted by the plant as a motivational device, but a labor standard of one unit every 20 minutes was adopted for reporting purposes. The workers were not to be informed of the different labor reporting standard.

The production manager held a meeting with the workers to inform them that a standard cost system was being implemented and to educate them about how the system works.

The new cost system was put into effect on March 1 along with a wage increase to $4.50 per hour. Six months later, the following data, based on the standards recommended by Comer, were reviewed by management:

	March	April	May	June	July	August
Production in units.	10,000	9,800	9,200	9,000	8,600	8,800
Direct labor-hours	2,800	2,650	2,700	2,750	2,850	2,800
Variance from labor standard	$ 1,350 (U)	$ 900 (U)	$1,800 (U)	$2,250 (U)	$3,150 (U)	$2,700 (U)

U = Unfavorable.

Other factors of production had not changed materially during this six-month period.

Required:

a. Discuss the different types of standards and their influence on motivation. Include the effect on plant workers of Pinkerton's acceptance of the engineering firm's labor standard.

b. Discuss your reaction to the adoption of dual standards.

Determining standard overhead rates

Budgeted volume

Two-variance method

Three-variance method

Four-variance method

Disposition of variances

Variance analysis

Causes and responsibility for variances

1   To present factory overhead variance analyses that can be computed under a standard cost system.

2   To achieve an understanding of what the overhead variances are measuring.

3   To illustrate the close similarity between applied overhead rates in an actual cost system and overhead standards in a standard cost system.

4   To emphasize that the value of a standard cost system begins when the causes of the variances are analyzed.

11

Standard costs for factory overhead and variance analysis

After standards have been set for material and labor, the cost accountant must give attention to establishing rates for factory overhead costs. As you recall, manufacturing overhead consists of all factory charges that are not directly identified and charged to the product. These include the costs of those services that must become part of the product cost. Apportioning such costs is difficult because there are so many different elements involved.

The same care exercised in determining material and labor standards is required in setting factory overhead standards. Unfortunately, in this case, there are fewer opportunities for applying scientific measurement. The standard cost of material and labor for each unit of production is more definite because these costs do not vary greatly with the volume of production. Factory overhead costs, however, are greatly affected by volume changes and in addition do not vary in a definite pattern. As a result, the cost accountant must utilize various methods in setting factory overhead standards.

DETERMINING STANDARD OVERHEAD RATES

Factory overhead cost standards are a means of allocating factory overhead so that inventories can be costed. This provides management with a cost per unit which can be used in pricing the products. In addition to fulfilling these objectives, factory overhead standards and the subsequent calculation of variances provide a means of controlling expenses and evaluating the overhead costs incurred.

Four capacity levels

There is a close similarity between applying factory overhead in an actual cost system and determining standards for factory overhead under a standard cost system. Chapter 6 presented the four capacity levels that can be used to apply factory overhead under an actual cost system. Another brief discussion of these four capacity levels—theoretical, practical, normal, and expected actual —follows.

Theoretical capacity assumes that all personnel and equipment will operate at peak efficiency and that 100 percent of plant capacity will be used. Practical capacity is more realistic in that it takes into account unavoidable delays due to holidays, machine breakdowns, vacations, and time off for weekends. Practical capacity assumes that sales demand is adequate to keep plant facilities and personnel busy and makes no allowance for idle time resulting from this factor. Normal capacity considers idle time that is due to limited sales orders and human and equipment inefficiencies. In determining normal capacity, enough years are taken into account to even out the cyclical swings in sales demand. Expected actual capacity is a short-range approach based on the production volume that is necessary to meet sales demand for the next year. It does not attempt to even out the cyclical swings in sales demand.

In a standard cost system, one of these capacity levels is chosen as a basis. Because a standard cost system emphasizes the efficient use of resources, a higher capacity level may be selected than is chosen when application rates are being determined under an actual cost system. Despite this emphasis, standards should represent attainable performance. Since theoretical capacity does not represent an attainable level of performance, it is generally not chosen. Standards set on practical capacity are more likely to be attainable and are more realistic than theoretical standards. Current standards are established on either normal capacity or expected actual capacity. A disadvantage of using expected actual capacity is that frequent, costly revisions of the standards may be necessary.

BUDGETED VOLUME

The capacity level—theoretical, practical, normal, or expected actual— chosen for a standard cost system can be reflected in several units of measurement. The volume may be expressed in any of the following terms:

1. Units of production.
2. Direct labor costs.   4.   Machine-hours.
3. Direct labor-hours.   5.   Material costs.

The evaluation of these bases given in Chapter 6 also applies to a standard cost system; however, units of production is usually not an appropriate basis for a standard cost system, as was mentioned in Chapter 6. A later discussion in this chapter concerning the three volume level used explains the reasons for this.

Overall, direct labor-hours and machine-hours are the most commonly used basis in a standard cost system. After the volume is expressed in a unit of measurement (such as direct labor-hours or machine-hours), the factory overhead that will be incurred at this level is estimated. It may not be feasible for the cost accountant to develop a standard rate for each type of factory overhead, for example, a separate rate for indirect labor, indirect material, and rent. Instead, the overhead costs may be estimated in total and spread over production in the form of a total factory overhead rate per capacity hour.

Plantwide or departmental rates.   In some companies, a single plantwide rate for standard factory overhead is used; in others, a standard overhead rate is set for each cost center or department. Deciding on the number of standard overhead rates to use is dependent upon several factors. If a high degree of refinement in costing is desired, a rate should be established for each cost center. If the amount of overhead relative to other costs in one department is large when compared with that in another department, separate departmental rates should be established. The individual manufacturing process must also be considered; sometimes products may not pass through the same departments. Under these circumstances, standard overhead rates for each department must be determined.

At this point, it should be recalled that standard factory overhead rates which are used to cost inventory are determined for producing departments only. The process, illustrated in Chapter 6, of allocating budgeted indirect costs to production and service departments under an actual cost system and then distributing the budgeted costs for the service departments to production departments is also used in a standard cost system. This procedure is not illustrated again in this chapter; the only difference here is that under an actual cost system, less attention is usually given to estimating factory overhead costs because these are often established on the basis of historical cost rather than using scientific methods. The factory overhead application rates under an actual cost system do not reflect scientifically predetermined costs in most cases.

After deciding to use the normal capacity level as the budgeted volume, the accountant must estimate the standard variable and fixed factory overhead that will be incurred at this volume. Assume, for example, that the following capacity and standard factory overhead costs are used to determine the standard factory overhead rates:

Normal capacity or budgeted volume	
(1,000 units × 2 hours).	2,000 direct labor hours
Standard variable factory overhead	$ 4,000
Standard fixed factory overhead.	16,000
Standard total factory overhead	$20,000

Standard variable factory
overhead rate per direct labor-hour . . . . $\dfrac{\$\ 4{,}000}{2{,}000} = \$2$

Standard (budgeted) fixed factory
overhead rate per direct labor-hour . . . . $\dfrac{\$16{,}000}{2{,}000} = \$8$

Standard (budgeted) total factory
overhead rate per direct labor-hour . . . . $\dfrac{\$20{,}000}{2{,}000} = \$10$

The total factory overhead rate of $10 per standard direct labor-hour is applied to the product through a debit to Work in Process Inventory. Since this is known throughout the accounting period, it is applied to each job as it is finished and to the unfinished jobs remaining in work in process at the end of the period. Under a process costing system, the standard overhead rate is applied to the equivalent units calculated for overhead, as illustrated in the Problem for Self-Study at the end of the chapter. Clearly, the standard overhead cost applied under a standard cost system is similar to the factory overhead applied in an actual system using predetermined rates. The only difference is that the factory overhead applied in an actual cost system is determined by multiplying the factory overhead application rate by actual hours or some other basis. In a standard system, the total factory overhead rate is multiplied by the standard hours allowed for actual production.

No uniform set of overhead variances.   The net overhead variance is the difference between the actual overhead incurred and the overhead applied to the products using the standard factory overhead rate. Although the computation of material and labor variances is usually the same regardless of the standard cost system employed, the computation of overhead variances is not uniform in practice. Accountants have differing views concerning the best way to determine factory overhead variances. The variances illustrated in accounting literature are often given different titles and are sometimes combined. The greatest difference between systems lies in the number of detailed factory overhead variances desired. Because control and responsibility for fixed and variable overhead usually rests with different members of the management team, the four-variance method is preferred since it distinguishes between cost behavior better than do the two- or three-variance methods. For example, it would be unfair to hold a line supervisor responsible for the difference between actual fixed and budgeted fixed overhead because the line supervisor usually does not have the authority to decide what plant facilities will be used or which insurance policy will cover these facilities. As a result, fixed overhead variances should be isolated and top management should be held accountable. Certainly it must be recognized that the four-variance method is more costly and time-consuming to prepare; however, the additional variances computed give better insight into the reasons why actual overhead differed from that budgeted.

Differences also occur because, in some companies, variances are most usefully expressed in physical terms only—for instance, in direct labor-hours or machine-hours. There is also some difference in the timing of the isolation of variances in the ledger. Each company should choose the combination of factory overhead variances which it believes gives the most valuable information. In any case, the combination of factory overhead variances this author considers most helpful should distinguish between fixed and variable cost—this is the reason this author prefers the four-variance method.

Three different sets of factory overhead variances along with their computations will be presented. Analysis of the net overhead variance is illustrated as follows:

1. Two-variance method:
    a. Controllable variance.
    b. Volume variance.
2. Three-variance method:
    a. Total overhead spending variance.
    b. Variable overhead efficiency variance.
    c. Volume variance.
3. Four-variance method:
    a. Variable overhead spending variance.
    b. Fixed overhead spending variance.
    c. Variable overhead efficiency variance.
    d. Volume variance.

The volume variance is computed in the same manner in all three methods presented.

The three-variance method is very similar to the spending and volume variances employed in Chapter 6 with an actual costing system. However, no mention was made at that point of any difference between hours worked and the standard hours allowed for actual production which is reflected in the variable overhead efficiency variance.

TWO-VARIANCE METHOD

The following outline can be used to compute two variances for factory overhead:

Controllable variance
Actual total factory overhead
1. *Compared with:* Budget based on *standard* capacity used [(Standard variable factory overhead rate × Standard hours) + Total budgeted fixed factory overhead costs].

Volume variance (noncontrollable variance)
2. (Budgeted hours, such as normal capacity hours, used for determining standard overhead rates − Standard hours allowed for the output achieved) × Standard fixed factory overhead rate at budgeted capacity.

THREE-VARIANCE METHOD

The following outline can be used to compute three variances for factory overhead:

Controllable variances
1. Total overhead spending variance:
   Total actual factory overhead
   Compared with: Variable budget allowance adjusted to *actual* capacity used (Standard variable factory overhead rate × Actual hours) + Total budgeted fixed factory overhead costs.
   Note again that this is the same spending variance that is computed under an actual cost system using applied factory overhead rates.
2. Variable factory overhead efficiency variance:
   (Actual hours − Standard hours) × Standard variable factory overhead rate.

Noncontrollable variance
3. Volume variance:
   (Budgeted hours − Standard hours) × Standard fixed factory overhead rate at budgeted capacity.

FOUR-VARIANCE METHOD

Total overhead spending variance can be divided into a variable overhead spending variance and a fixed overhead spending variance, as shown below. The variable factory overhead efficiency variance and the volume variance are the same as shown for the three-variance method.

Controllable variances
1. Variable overhead spending variance:
   Actual variable factory overhead

Compared with: Budget allowance for variable costs adjusted to actual capacity used (Standard variable factory overhead rate × Actual hours).
2. Variable overhead efficiency variance:
(Actual hours − Standard hours) × Standard variable factory overhead rate.
3. Fixed overhead spending variance:
Budgeted fixed factory overhead
Compared with: Actual fixed factory overhead.

Noncontrollable variance
4. Volume variance:
(Budgeted hours − Standard hours) × Standard fixed factory overhead rate at budgeted capacity.

With the four-variance method, fixed overhead spending variance is classified as controllable. This is not universally accepted. However, the position in this book is that even though this variance may be beyond the control of low and possibly middle management, fixed costs can be controlled at top management levels. And while line supervisors may not be able to control committed costs, they can often control discretionary fixed factory overhead.

Data for overhead variance. The computations of the three different methods of factory overhead variances are presented in Exhibits 11–1, 2, and 3 based on the following data:

Standard variable overhead, 2 direct labor-hours @ $2 per hour	$ 4 per unit
Standard fixed overhead, 2 direct labor-hours @ $8 per hour	$16 per unit
Standard (budgeted) fixed factory overhead	$16,000
Budgeted volume (1,000 units × 2 hours) 2,000 direct labor-hours	
900 units of finished product were completed.	
Actual direct labor-hours	1,890 hours
Actual variable factory overhead	$ 4,500
Actual fixed factory overhead	15,500
Actual total factory overhead	$20,000

Three volume levels used

Before beginning the actual computation of factory overhead variances, one should identify the three volume levels used in overhead variance analysis. Note that the time period in which they are known is important. The volumes are indicated using the data presented above:

1. Known before operations begin:
Budgeted, normal, or predetermined capacity—2,000 direct labor-hours.

EXHIBIT 11–1

Two-variance method illustrated

Based on the data presented, the controllable and volume variance in the two-variance method are determined:

Controllable variance

$20,000 actual total overhead costs

Compared with: 19,600 ($2 variable overhead rate
_____ × 1,800 standard hours) + $16,000 budgeted fixed overhead
costs

$ 400 unfavorable

The controllable variance is unfavorable because $400 more overhead was incurred than indicated by the budget based on standard hours.

Volume variance

(2,000 budgeted hours − 1,800 standard hours)
× $8 fixed overhead rate = $1,600 unfavorable

2. Known after operations end:
    Standard volume allowed—900 units × 2

    hours = 1,800 direct labor-hours.
3. Known after operations end: Actual volume—1,890 direct labor-hours.

If units of production rather than direct labor-hours were used, it would not be possible to correctly compute the standard volume allowed.

The volume variance is unfavorable because there were 200 idle hours to which the lump-sum budgeted fixed factory overhead could not be applied. If standard hours had exceeded budgeted hours, the variance would have been favorable because it indicates the plant facilities were utilized more than was expected or estimated in the budget. The volume variance is often referred to as "idle" capacity variance. The volume variance for use in an actual cost system was presented in Chapter 6: actual hours are compared to budgeted hours and the difference is multiplied by the fixed factory overhead rate. In an actual cost system in which there are no standards, this is the only computation available since no standard hours are allowed for actual production. Using a standard cost system, some companies compute their volume variance by comparing actual hours (instead of standard hours allowed) to budgeted hours. The variance then indicates how much fixed factory overhead was over- or underapplied because actual hours were less or more than budgeted hours. We suggest, however, that a better measure of idle capacity can be determined by comparing budgeted hours to standard hours which represent efficient hours based on actual production.

Using the data given above, the three-variance method of analyzing factory overhead in a standard cost system is illustrated in Exhibit 11–2.

The total overhead spending variance found with the three-variance method

Exhibit 11–2

Three-variance method illustrated

Total overhead spending variance

$20,000 actual total overhead costs
Compared with: 19,780 ($2 variable overhead rate × 1,890 actual hours)
+ $16,000 budgeted fixed overhead
$ 220 unfavorable

The total overhead spending variance is unfavorable because $220 more overhead was incurred than indicated by the budget based on actual hours.

Variable overhead efficiency variance

(1,890 actual hours − 1,800 standard hours)
× $2 variable overhead rate = $180 unfavorable

(Note the similarity between this variance and the labor efficiency variance computed in Chapter 10.)

The variable overhead efficiency variance reflects the effect of labor efficiency on overhead when direct labor-hours or direct labor cost is the basis of application. If, instead, machine-hours were used as the application basis, the overhead efficiency variance would reflect their efficient or inefficient use.

Volume variance

The volume variance is as computed earlier:
(2,000 budgeted hours − 1,800 standard hours)
× $8 fixed overhead rate = $1,600 unfavorable

---

can be further analyzed into a variable overhead spending variance and a fixed overhead spending variance as shown in Exhibit 11–3 (see page 422).

Outline of interrelationship

Exhibit 11–4 contains an outline of the methods discussed showing their interrelationship. The four-variance method involves a more detailed breakdown of factors not directly related to volume than does the two-variance method.

Proof of method used

Regardless of the method used, the variances computed represent a breakdown of the total difference between actual and standard cost. This difference, which is referred to as the net factory overhead variance, can be used to prove the correctness of the variances computed regardless of the method used, as shown on Exhibit 11–4. Using the different methods, the net variance equals $2,000:

EXHIBIT 11–3

Four-variance method illustrated

Variable overhead spending variance

$4,500 actual variable overhead costs
Compared with: 3,780 budget allowance for variable overhead
           ($2 variable overhead rate × 1,890 actual hours.)
$ 720 unfavorable

The spending variance is unfavorable because $720 more factory overhead was incurred than indicated by the budget based on actual hours. If a spending variance is computed for each cost center or department, the variance becomes the responsibility of the supervisor of the center involved.

Fixed overhead spending variance

$16,000 budgeted fixed overhead
15,500 actual fixed overhead
$ 500 favorable

The fixed overhead spending variance is favorable because actual fixed factory overhead is less than budgeted fixed factory overhead. Even though this variance may be beyond the control of low and possibly middle management, it does reflect the impact of the actual price level on fixed factory overhead.

Variable overhead efficiency variance

The variable factory overhead efficiency variance is as computed using the three-variance method.
(1,890 actual hours − 1,800 standard hours)
× $2 variable overhead rate = $180 unfavorable.

Volume variance

The volume variance is as computed using any of the three methods presented:
(2,000 budgeted hours − 1,800 standard hours)
× $8 fixed overhead rate = $1,600 unfavorable

$20,000 actual total overhead
18,000 standard hours × $10 total standard overhead rate per hour
$ 2,000 unfavorable net factory overhead variance

Journal entries illustrated

The following journal entries would be made to summarize the actual factory overhead incurred and the variances computed using the four-variance method.

Factory Overhead Control ($4,500 + $15,500).   20,000
     Various Credits   20,000

This reflects a summary entry recording actual fixed and variable factory overhead incurred. Numerous credits—including supplies, inventory, payroll,

EXHIBIT 11–4

Overhead variance analysis

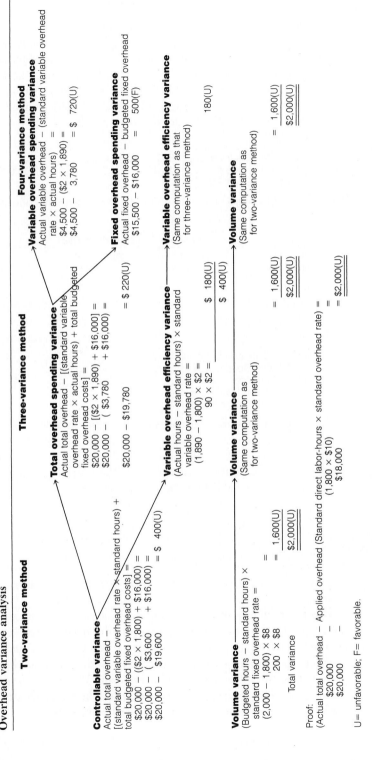

Two-variance method

Controllable variance

Actual total overhead −
[(standard variable overhead rate × standard hours) +
total budgeted fixed overhead costs] =
$20,000 − (($2 × 1,800) + $16,000) =
$20,000 − ($3,600 + $16,000) =
$20,000 − $19,600 = $ 400(U)

Volume variance
(Budgeted hours − standard hours) ×
standard fixed overhead rate =
(2,000 − 1,800) × $8 =
200 × $8 = 1,600(U)

Total variance $2,000(U)

Proof:
(Actual total overhead − Applied overhead (Standard direct labor-hours × standard overhead rate) =
$20,000 − (1,800 × $10) =
$20,000 − $18,000 = $2,000(U)

U= unfavorable; F= favorable.

Three-variance method

Total overhead spending variance

Actual total overhead − [(standard variable
overhead rate × actual hours) + total budgeted
fixed overhead costs] =
$20,000 − [($2 × 1,890) + $16,000] =
$20,000 − ($3,780 + $16,000) =
$20,000 − $19,780 = $ 220(U)

Variable overhead efficiency variance
(Actual hours − standard hours) × standard
variable overhead rate =
(1,890 − 1,800) × $2 =
90 × $2 = $ 180(U)
$ 400(U)

Volume variance
(Same computation as
for two-variance method)
= 1,600(U)
$2,000(U)

Four-variance method

Variable overhead spending variance

Actual variable overhead − (standard variable overhead
rate × actual hours) =
$4,500 − ($2 × 1,890) =
$4,500 − 3,780 = $ 720(U)

Fixed overhead spending variance

Actual fixed overhead − budgeted fixed overhead
$15,500 − $16,000 = 500(F)

Variable overhead efficiency variance
(Same computation as that
for three-variance method)

180(U)

Volume variance
(Same computation as
for two-variance method)
= 1,600(U)
$2,000(U)

accumulated depreciation, and prepaid insurance—would have been made during the accounting period at the time actual factory overhead was recorded. The entry for all these is combined and illustrated above to indicate what the debit balance would be in the Factory Overhead Control account. A separate ledger account could be used for fixed and variable overhead.

The entry below records the application of total overhead to the products included in the Work in Process Inventory based on the standard hours allowed.

Work in Process Inventory (1,800 standard hours ×
    $10 total standard overhead rate)   18,000
       Factory Overhead Control   18,000

The Factory Overhead Control account now appears as follows:

Factory Overhead Control

Actual	20,000	Applied at	18,000
Balance 2,000		Standard	

The underapplied factory overhead balance of $2,000 reflects the four overhead variances computed. The Factory Overhead Control account is closed by recording these overhead variances under the four-variance method:

Variable Overhead Spending Variance   720
Variable Overhead Efficiency Variance   180
Volume Variance 1,600
    Fixed Overhead Spending Variance   500
    Factory Overhead Control   2,000

The three unfavorable variances are recorded as debits, while the favorable fixed overhead spending variance is recorded as a credit. The impression must be avoided, however, that there will always be a special combination of unfavorable and favorable variances. Only the actual operating facts, in addition to the standards established, determine whether a variance is favorable or not.

DISPOSITION OF VARIANCES

There are two basic procedures used for the disposition of standard cost variances.

Chapter 6 gives a more complete explanation to the disposition of over- or underapplied overhead, which represents the net variance. One procedure is to consider these variances as a cost of inefficiency rather than as a cost of the product. The variances are then charged or credited against the revenues of the period. They are either closed to Revenue and Expense Summary or to Cost of Goods Sold. If this procedure is used, the following journal entry would be made to dispose of the overhead variances computed:

Fixed Overhead Spending Variance	500		
Revenue and Expense Summary (or Cost of Goods Sold)	2,000		
Variable Overhead Spending Variance		720	
Variable Overhead Efficiency Variance		180	
Volume Variance		1,600	

The other procedure is to consider variances as a cost of the product and allocate them to Work in Process, Finished Goods, and Cost of Goods Sold. Significant material purchase price variances would be allocated not only to these, but also to Direct Materials Inventory. When the variances arise because of some unforeseen condition, allocation is the more appropriate procedure. The advisable approach to follow is to judge each variance individually and to make a decision based on the nature of its cause.

IRS and standard costs. To comply with current Internal Revenue Service (IRS) regulations, inventories must include a portion of significant annual standard cost variances. If the amount of the variance is not large in relation to actual annual factory overhead, regulations do not require the allocation unless it must be made for financial accounting purposes. Favorable and unfavorable variances must be treated consistently for tax purposes. Variances due to idle capacity do not have to be inventoried, however. Significant standard cost variances must also be included to meet Cost Accounting Standards Board regulations.

VARIANCE ANALYSIS

The analysis of cost variances is the first step toward identifying factors that caused the difference between the standard and actual costs to eliminate inefficiencies. It is a waste of paper and time for the accountant simply to compute the variances and place them neatly on a page for distribution to management; certainly, computing variances is not as important as knowing what to do in the event of a *significant* variance. The benefit of a standard cost system comes from determining the cause of the variance and correcting the situation. While it is recognized that the accountant will not investigate every variance, he or she should follow up all *significant* variances, thus emphasizing the management by exception principle.

As we have emphasized, timing is very important in a standard cost system. To be useful in controlling costs, standard costs must be applied before or at the time the costs are incurred. To this end, the person responsible for a cost should know the standard in advance, and any variances should be reported to this person promptly. The more quickly a variance is isolated, the greater the chance that the cause of the variance can be detected and corrected before excessive cost is incurred.

The effectiveness of the control is often in direct proportion to the speed with which a change is recommended after an unsatisfactory operating condition is discovered. The quality and price of materials are best controlled prior to or at the time of purchase. Overhead cost should be analyzed as the decisions creating such cost elements are made. Many times, the accounting system fails in this respect, for variances are compiled in lengthy reports which arrive long after the cost was incurred; thus, the reports are of little value for cost control.

In cost control not only must management know the amount of the variances but also what caused them and who was responsible for them. Management should study significant variances which disclose problems needing attention. Analysis of significant deviations from standard cost indicates the need for managerial attention without laborious study of many detailed figures.

As a first step in the managerial interpretation of variances, it is necessary to identify who has primary responsibility for each of the variances. The individual who has authority to incur a cost should be held responsible for that cost. The cost factors which are directly controllable by operating supervision must be separated from those cost factors for which executive management is responsible.

Although methods of establishing standards and techniques of determining variances have been widely emphasized in accounting literature, methods of analyzing variances and the purposes served by such analysis have not been described with equal thoroughness. In fact, many accountants receive the impression from accounting literature that after the variances are determined, the work is completed. Clearly, they are mistaken.

Revision of standards

Management has an excellent opportunity to exercise preventive cost control through variance analysis. Obviously, cost control must be exercised before the fact, rather than after the fact, if it is to do any good. Preventive cost control therefore depends upon prompt action taken at the point where losses and waste can occur. This type of control involves current basic operating standards. To be effective measures of performance, the standards must be accurate, and this requires that management continuously review them and make any necessary revisions.

After standards are determined, however, they should not be too frequently adjusted in an attempt to keep them in line with actual results. This would destroy a valuable device for examining cost. Standards should be adjusted only when events such as labor rate changes, material price changes, changes in production flow, or technological advances warrant it. However, the revision of standards more often than once a year should be avoided. Not only may this destroy the control aspect of standards, but additional clerical detail will be necessary.

Budgets and standards

Besides being an aid in controlling costs, standard costs also serve as the building blocks with which budgets are constructed. Budgets are statements of expected costs and are used to forecast production requirements. Budgets attempt to set up a predetermined standard of operations for a period or project taken as a whole, while standards are concerned with cost per unit. Thus, when standard costs are employed, the budget is largely a summary of standards for all items of revenue and expense. Even though standards and budgets do differ in some aspects, they both aim toward the same goal of better managerial control. Both budgets and standard costs make available reports for executive guidance in comparing actual costs with predetermined costs.

CAUSES OF AND RESPONSIBILITY FOR VARIANCES

The following outline provides management with a basic understanding of possible causes of unfavorable controllable and noncontrollable variances. With this general knowledge, management gains an insight into what areas of operations should be investigated to determine more exact causes of the variances reported. In addition, the individual responsible for any deviation is identified.

Possible causes of unfavorable controllable variances
1. Unfavorable terms in buying supplies and services.
2. Waste of indirect material.
3. Avoidable machine breakdowns.
4. Using wrong grade of indirect material or indirect labor.
5. Poor indirect labor scheduling.
6. Lack of operators or tools.

Responsibility for controllable (spending) variances
Supervisors of cost centers are responsible since they have some degree of control over these budget or expense factors.

Responsibility for variable factory overhead efficiency variances
Line supervisors are responsible since this variance reflects the effects of labor efficiency on factory overhead when labor dollars or labor-hours are the basis for applying factory overhead. This variance shows how much of the factory's capacity has been consumed or released by off-standard labor performance. If machine-hours are the basis for applying factory overhead, the variance measures the efficiency of machine usage.

Possible causes for unfavorable noncontrollable variances
1.   Poor production scheduling.
2.   Unusual machine breakdowns.
3.   Storms or strikes.
4.   Fluctuations over time.
5.   Shortage of skilled workers.
6.   Excess plant capacity.
7.   Decrease in customer demand.

Responsibility for noncontrollable variances

The line supervisor can control fixed overhead to the extent that the items of cost are discretionary rather than committed.

Top sales executive may be held responsible if budgeted volume (i.e., theoretical, practical, or normal capacity) was geared to anticipated long-run sales.

Responsibility usually rests with top management, for the volume variance represents under- or overutilization of plant and equipment.

SUMMARY

Standard costs provide a framework for gauging performance, for building useful budgets, and for guiding pricing for meaningful product costing. To properly provide this guide, however, certain principles must be followed in setting the standards. The principle of maintaining lines of responsibility along with authority applies in completing the specifications necessary to establish standards. Those persons responsible for meeting the standards should participate in establishing these yardsticks. Management must also be confident that the standards in use are accurate and a good basis on which to make decisions.

Many people believe standard costs are complicated and difficult to understand. However, standards are based on simple and direct approaches to control. Management obtains much useful information from standard costs because a comparison of actual costs with standard costs enables management to see which cost elements are not in line and to be aware of the cost centers in which variations exist. Matters needing control are quickly pointed out using cost information in a standard cost system.

By studying costs for the purpose of establishing standard unit costs and analyzing the variance between standard and actual cost, a company may discover many opportunities for cost reduction and control. Often, the savings resulting from the information obtained through an analysis of variances pays for the expenses involved in selecting standard costs. Comparison of actual and standard cost also provides management with a sound basis upon which to plan future finances. Standards will frequently indicate solutions that will enable management to plan the way out of an unprofitable situation.

IMPORTANT TERMS AND CONCEPTS

Theoretical capacity

Practical capacity

Normal capacity

Expected actual capacity

Controllable variance

Volume variance

Total overhead spending variance

Variable overhead spending variance

Variable overhead efficiency variance

Fixed overhead spending variance

Management by exception

PROBLEM FOR SELF-STUDY

Material, labor, and overhead variances in a process costing system

Products at the Glen Jones Company are produced in batches using a standard cost system. Mangement budgets 750 of these batches per period. Fixed factory overhead at this level is $90,000. The standard costs per batch are as follows:

	Total
Direct material (80 gallons).................	$ 32
Direct labor (60 hours)	324
Total factory overhead (60 hours)	378
	$734

The following costs were incurred in finishing 700 batches during the period. In addition, 109 batches were one-half complete as to processing in ending inventory; there was no beginning inventory.

Direct material used (61,114.5 gallons)	$ 23,223.51
Direct labor (44,515.5 hours)................	244,835.25
Actual variable factory overhead..............	195,687.00
Actual fixed factory overhead	90,750.00

Required:

A variance analysis and proof of variances for:
a.   Material.
b.   Labor.
c.   Factory overhead: two-variance method.
d.   Factory overhead: three-variance method.
e.   Factory overhead: four-variance method.

Solution

$$EU = 700 + 54.5 = 754.5 \text{ batches}$$
$$(109 \times 0.5)$$

a. Material quantity variance

$$754.5 \text{ batches} \times 80 \text{ gallons} = 60,360 \text{ standard gallons}$$
$$[(61,114.5 \text{ actual gallons} - 60,360 \text{ standard gallons}) \times \$.40 \text{ standard rate}]$$
$$= \$301.80 \text{ unfavorable}$$

Material price variance

$$\frac{\$23,223.51 \text{ actual material cost}}{61,114.5 \text{ actual gallons}} = \$.38 \text{ actual rate}$$

$$[(\$.38 \text{ actual rate} - \$.40 \text{ standard rate}) \times 61,114.5 \text{ gallons}] = \$1,222.29 \text{ favorable}$$

Proof:

Actual material cost	$23,223.51
Standard material cost (60,360 × $.40)	24,144.00
Favorable	$ 920.49
Material price variance—favorable	$ 1,222.29
Material quantity variance—unfavorable	301.80
Net variance	$ 920.49

b. Labor quantity variance

$$754.5 \text{ batches} \times 60 \text{ hours} = 45,270 \text{ standard hours}$$
$$[(44,515.5 \text{ actual hours} - 45,270 \text{ standard hours}) \times \$5.40 \text{ standard rate}]$$
$$= \$4,074.30 \text{ favorable}$$

Labor rate variance

$$\frac{\$244,835.25}{44,515.5 \text{ hours}} = \$5.50 \text{ actual rate}$$

$$[(\$5.50 \text{ actual} - \$5.40 \text{ standard rate}) \times 44,515.5 \text{ actual hours}] = \$4,451.55 \text{ unfavorable}$$

Proof:

Actual labor cost	$244,835.25
Standard labor cost (45,270 × $5.40)	244,458.00
Unfavorable	$ 377.25
Labor rate variance—unfavorable	$ 4,451.55
Labor quantity variance—favorable	4,074.30
Net variance	$ 377.25

c. Overhead variances

$$750 \text{ batches} \times 60 \text{ hours} = 45,000 \text{ budgeted hours}$$

Total overhead rate	$6.30 per hour ($378/60 hours)
Less:	
$\dfrac{\$90,000 \text{ fixed overhead}}{45,000 \text{ budgeted hours}}$	$= \$2.00$ fixed factory overhead rate
Variable overhead rate	$4.30

Two variance method for factory overhead

1. Controllable

Actual overhead	$286,437
Variable budget	
(45,270 standard hours × $4.30 variable overhead rate	
= $194,661 variable + $90,000 budgeted fixed)	284,661
Unfavorable controllable variance	$ 1,776

2. Volume
(45,000 budgeted hours − 45,270 standard hours) × $2
fixed factory overhead . . . . $ 540 favorable

Proof:

Actual overhead ($195,687 + $90,750) $286,437
Standard overhead (45,270 × $6.30)   285,201
Unfavorable. . . . . $ 1,236

Controllable variance—unfavorable. . . . . $ 1,776
Volume variance—favorable   540
Net variance . . . . $ 1,236

d.   Three variance method for factory overhead
Controllable

1. Total overhead spending variance

Total actual overhead costs $286,437.00
Variable budget for actual hours
$90,000 budgeted overhead + ($4.30 variable
factory overhead × 44,515.5 actual hours)   281,416.65
                                                    $ 5,020.35 unfavorable

2. Variable overhead efficiency variance

(44,515.5 actual hours − 45,270.0 standard hours)
× $4.30 = $3,244.35 favorable
Noncontrollable
3. Volume variance

· (45,000 budgeted hours − 45,270 standard hours)
× $2 = $540.00 favorable

Proof:

Actual overhead $286,437
Standard overhead   285,201
Unfavorable. . . . . $ 1,236

Total overhead
spending variance—unfavorable $5,020.35
Variable overhead
efficiency variance—favorable. $3,244.35
Volume variance—favorable 540.00   3,784.35
Net variance $1,236.00

e.   Four variance method for factory overhead
Controllable

1. Variable overhead efficiency variance

[(44,515.5 actual hours − 45,270.0 standard hours) × $4.30] = $3,244.35 favorable
2. Variable overhead spending variance

Actual variable overhead $195,687.00
Budget for actual hours (44,515.5 actual hours
× $4.30) 191,416.65
                                                    $ 4,270.35 unfavorable

3. Fixed overhead spending variance

Actual fixed overhead $90,750.00
Budgeted fixed overhead. 90,000.00
                                                      750.00 unfavorable

Noncontrollable

4. Volume variance

(45,000 budgeted hours − 45,270 standard hours) × $2 = $540.00 favorable

Proof:

Actual overhead.		$286,437
Standard overhead		285,201
Unfavorable.		$ 1,236
Variable overhead spending		
variance—unfavorable	$4,270.35	
Fixed overhead spending variance—unfavorable	750.00	$5,020.35
Variable overhead efficiency variance—favorable. . .	$3,244.35	
Volume variance favorable	540.00	3,784.35
Net variance.		$1,236.00

REVIEW QUESTIONS

1. What is the difference between the controllable variance in the two-variance method and the total overhead spending variance in the three-variance method? What features do they share?

2. When would total standard hours for operations equal budgeted (normal capacity) hours?

3. Discuss the three different capacity levels that are used in overhead variance analysis. Indicate the point in the operating cycle at which information used to determine these capacity levels becomes available.

4. What capacity level is normally chosen as a basis for establishing standard factory overhead rates? In what terms is the capacity level chosen as the basis for standard overhead most often expressed?

5. With what conditions would it be appropriate to determine plantwide standard overhead rates?

6. Why is the determination of factory overhead standards often more difficult than determination of material and labor standards?

7. What similarities are there between factory overhead application rates in an actual cost system and those in standard factory overhead rates? Discuss the difference between applying factory overhead in an actual cost system and applying it in a standard cost system.

8. What are the objectives of establishing factory overhead standards?

9. Why are the standard factory overhead rates used to cost inventory determined for production departments only?

10. Discuss the similarities in and differences between budgets and standard cost.

11. Discuss some environmental conditions that have an effect on the standard cost system.

12. What does the volume variance measure? What conditions are necessary for it to be favorable?

13. What is the danger involved if a company automatically loosens a standard every

time an unfavorable variance occurs? Why is there a danger in frequently revising standards?

14. How often do you think standards should be reviewed for possible revisions?

EXERCISES

E11–1. Missing data

Hert Company has asked your assistance in preparing an overhead analysis. Management provides you with the following monthly information.

Total actual overhead	$35,100
Actual units produced.	475
Standard direct labor-hours per unit	5 hours
Actual direct labor-hours worked	2,440
Standard variable overhead rate per direct labor-hour	$5.75
Standard fixed overhead rate per direct labor-hour.	$8.00
Budgeted fixed overhead	$20,000

Required:

Calculate the overhead variances, using the three-variance method for overhead analysis. Indicate which variances are controllable and which noncontrollable.

E11–2. Time frame and the four-variance method

ADD Company has determined that its total standard overhead per direct labor-hour is $2; of this, 60 percent is variable. Management has planned to produce 200 units. Time and motion studies reveal that four hours should be considered as standard per unit.

Required:

a. (1) What time frame are you in now—that is, beginning of operations or end of operations?

(2) With the information you have, which capacity level can you compute? How many hours is this?

(3) What is total budgeted fixed cost and in what way is this used in variance analysis?

(4) What is total budgeted variable cost, and is this used directly in calculating any of the variances?

b. It is now determined that actual output for the period was 180 units; actual hours were 815. Total actual overhead was $1,750, of which 40 percent was fixed. Calculate the standard overhead variances using the four-variance method. Indicate which variances are controllable and noncontrollable and whether they are favorable or unfavorable.

E11–3. Labor efficiency and the two-variance method for analyzing overhead

As the controller for SPA Company, you extract the following data from the records:

Standard hours for finished output.	21,500 direct labor-hours
Budgeted hours	22,000 direct labor-hours

Actual hours used	21,000 direct labor-hours
Total overhead application rate per	
standard direct labor-hour...............	$7.25
Actual total overhead	$160,000
Direct labor rate variance—favorable..........	$3,150
Budgeted fixed costs	$88,000
Actual total direct labor...................	$87,150

The company uses a two-way analysis of overhead variances.

Required:

a. Determine the direct labor efficiency variance.
b. Determine the controllable and volume variances for overhead using two-variance analysis.

E11–4.   Assumptions of the two-variance method (CPA adapted)

Meyer Company's cost accounting department has prepared a factory overhead variance analysis report using the two-variance method. The plant manager of Meyer Company is interested in understanding the managerial usefulness of this report.

Required:

a. What are the purposes of a factory overhead variance analysis report?
b. Identify and explain the underlying assumptions associated with the two-variance method. Discuss the significance of each variance.

E11–5.   Missing data

A fire destroyed some of the records of Caroline Company. Only the following limited information is available:

Budgeted capacity.........................	50,000 direct labor-hours
Budgeted variable costs...................	$65,000
Budgeted fixed costs	$90,000

Debit balances in the following accounts exist:

Work in process—Labor.........................	$306,000
Work in process—Factory overhead...............	158,100
Factory overhead—Variable.....................	65,000
Factory overhead—Fixed........................	90,360

The payroll time cards showed that 49,900 direct labor-hours were worked at a cost of $294,410.

Required:

Calculate the labor and overhead variances using the four-variance method for overhead.

E11–6.   Four-variance method for analyzing overhead

The following information for Anne Nichol Company is obtained from company records:

| Standard hours allowed .... | 2,880 |
| Actual hours................................. | 3,200 |

Budgeted total overhead	$33,000
Actual labor cost	$16,800
Actual variable overhead	$12,000
Actual fixed overhead.	$21,700

Standard specification per unit of finished product:	*Total*
Direct labor (6 hours)	$30
Variable overhead.	24
Fixed overhead.	42

Required:

Compute labor and overhead variances. Use the four-variance method for overhead. Show proof of your figures for overhead variances.

E11–7.   Components of Standard cost

On June 1, 19X1, Martin Hanifin Company began manufacturing Fazar. The standard costs for a unit of Fazar are as follows:

Direct materials (12 pounds @ $2/pound)	$24.00
Direct labor (1 hour @ $8/hour).	8.00
Factory overhead ($0.75 for every direct labor dollar).	6.00
	$38.00

Hanifin's records revealed the following for June:

Actual production of Fazar	8,000 units
Units sold of Fazar	5,000 units

	Debit	Credit
Sales		$100,000
Purchases	$54,600	
Material price variance	2,600	
Material quantity variance	2,000	
Direct labor rate variance	780	
Direct labor efficiency variance		1,600
Manufacturing factory overhead total variance	1,000	

The amount shown above for material price variance is applicable to direct material purchased in June.

Required:

Compute each of the following items for Hanifin for June (show computation in good form):

a.   Standard quantity of direct materials (in pounds).
b.   Actual quantity of direct materials used (in pounds).
c.   Standard hours allowed.
d.   Actual hours worked.
e.   Actual direct labor rate.
f.   Actual total factory overhead.

E11–8.   Allocating labor variances (CMA adapted)

Nanron Company has a process standard cost system for all its products. All inventories are carried at standard during the year. The inventories and cost of goods sold are adjusted for all variances considered material in amount at the end of the fiscal year for financial statement purposes. All products are considered to flow through the manufacturing process to finished goods, and ultimate sale in a first-in, first-out pattern.

The standard cost of one of Nanron's products manufactured in the Dixon plant, unchanged from the previous year, is shown below:

Raw materials.	$2
Direct labor (.5 direct labor-hours @ $8)	4
Manufacturing overhead	3
Total standard cost	$9

There is no work in process inventory of this product due to the nature of the product and the manufacturing process.

The schedule below reports the manufacturing and sales activity measured at standard cost for the current fiscal year:

	Units	Dollars
Product manufactured	95,000	$855,000
Beginning finished goods inventory	15,000	135,000
Goods available for sale.	110,000	$990,000
Ending finished goods inventory.	19,000	171,000
Cost of goods sold	91,000	$819,000

Manufacturing performance relative to standard costs both this year and last year was not good. The balance of the finished goods inventory, $140,800, reported on the balance sheet at the beginning of the year included a $5,800 adjustment for variances from standard cost. The unfavorable standard cost variances for labor for the current fiscal year consisted of a wage rate variance of $32,000 and a labor efficiency variance of $20,000 (2,500 hours at $8). There were no other variances from standard cost for this year.

Required:

Assume that the unfavorable labor variances totaling $52,000 are considered material in amount by management and are to be allocated to finished goods inventory and to cost of goods sold. Determine the amount that will be shown on the year-end balance sheet for finished goods inventory and the amount which will be shown for cost of goods sold on the income statement prepared for the fiscal year.

PROBLEMS

P11–1.   Labor variances and the three-variance overhead analysis

Becky McConnell Company accounts for producing its single product under a standard cost accounting system. Management has agreed on a budgeted monthly production of 75 units a day for 22 workdays per month. Standard cost per unit for direct labor is eight hours at $3.75 per hour. The standard rate for overhead is determined as follows:

Fixed overhead per month	$ 9,900.00
Variable overhead per month	14,850.00
Total budgeted overhead	$24,750.00
Expected direct labor cost	$49,500.00
Overhead rate per dollar of labor	.50
Standard overhead rate per unit	$ 15.00

During the month of April, the plant operated only 20 days. Costs for 1,525 actual units produced are:

Direct labor (12,000 hours @ $3.80)		$45,600.00
Fixed overhead	$10,200.00	
Variable overhead	13,725.00	23,925.00

Required:

a. Compute the variance from standard in April for:
    (1) Direct labor costs.
    (2) Factory overhead costs.
b. Analyze the variations from standard into identifiable causes for:
    (1) Direct labor.
    (2) Fixed and variable overhead. (Use the three-variance method of analysis.)

P11–2.   Comparison of various variance analysis methods

The following monthly data were obtained from the records of the Taylor Company:

Actual variable factory overhead	$ 8,707
Actual fixed factory overhead	$13,353
Actual units produced	1,200 units
Actual machine-hours	4,010 hours
Standard machine-hours per unit	3 hours

Management has budgeted 1,300 units monthly. Budgeted variable cost at this level is $8,385, while fixed cost was budgeted to be $14,040.

Required:

Calculate overhead variances indicating whether they are controllable or noncontrollable using the:
a. Two-variance method.
b. Three-variance method.
c. Four-variance method.

P11–3.   Labor variances and the four-variance method for analyzing overhead

Lem Manufacturing Company estimates that it will incur the following labor and overhead costs:

Estimated variable overhead	$44,200
Estimated fixed overhead	50,050
Total estimated overhead	$94,250
Estimated direct labor costs	$65,000

The standard direct labor rate is $5 per hour; it is estimated that each unit will require 26 hours of labor. Management plans to produce 500 units next period.

At the end of that period, it is determined that 13,015 actual direct labor-hours were used to produce 510 units. Actual costs for variable overhead were $45,009; for fixed overhead, $50,125; and for direct labor costs, $66,116.20.

Required:

Prepare direct labor and factory overhead variances. Prove your answers. Use the four-variance method of analyzing overhead.

P11–4.   Determining specific standard cost data

Budgeted data at two volumes for the Speight Company are as follows:

Volume of activity in direct labor-hours per month	30,000 hours	40,000 hours
		(normal capacity)
Total budgeted monthly factory overhead costs.	$40,000	$46,000

At the end of operations the following data are determined:
Actual fixed overhead cost. $17,640
Standard direct labor-hours allowed for work
     done on product units manufactured . . . . 38,800 hours

The company uses the four-variance method for analyzing factory overhead.

Required:

Indicate whether favorable or unfavorable for all variances:

a.   The budgeted variable cost rate per direct labor-hour.
b.   The budgeted fixed cost per month.
c.   Standard rate for fixed overhead per hour.
d.   Applied fixed overhead.
e.   Volume variance.
f.   Fixed overhead spending variance.
g.   Make journal entries to record overhead incurrence and application.
h.   Record volume and fixed overhead spending variances and close the fixed factory overhead account.

P11–5.   Material, labor and factory overhead variances.

Roberts Corporation, which produces a single product, operates a standard cost system. The variable costs per product unit are as follows:

	Total
Materials (4 pieces)	$ 2
Labor (2 hours)	6
Factory overhead (variable)	3
	$11

Fixed factory expenses are budgeted at $4,000 per month, and production is budgeted at practical capacity of the factory, which is 2,000 units per month. Actual production for

January was 1,800 units. Material prices were 5 percent over standard, and labor rates were likewise 10 percent over standard. The supervisor spent 80 percent of the variable factory expense, which was budgeted for a full month's production, and actual fixed overhead was $100 over budgeted fixed overhead. The factory used 8 percent more pieces of material than were allowed for actual production; and likewise 6 percent more labor-hours.

Required:

Calculate variances between standard and actual cost of production for material, labor, and overhead. Label each variance controllable or noncontrollable and favorable or unfavorable. Use the four-variance method of analyzing overhead.

P11–6.   Comparison of various variance analysis methods

The following monthly data were obtained from the records of the Kelly Company:

Actual variable factory overhead	$11,360
Actual fixed factory overhead	$10,600
Actual units produced	550 units
Actual machine-hours	2,690 hours
Standard per unit:	
Variable factory overhead.	5 hours @ $6 per hour
Fixed factory overhead.	5 hours @ $3 per hour

Management has budgeted 600 units monthly.

Required:

a.   Calculate overhead variances indicating whether controllable or noncontrollable using the
   (1)   Two-variance method.
   (2)   Three-variance method.
   (3)   Four-variance method.
b.   Prepare journal entries to summarize actual factory overhead incurred and to apply overhead. Record overhead variances using the four-variance method. Dispose of the variances.

P11–7.   Material, labor and overhead (four-variance method) variances

The standard specification for each LP–402 motor produced by the Wright Company is as follows:

	Per unit
Direct material (2 pounds @ $5 per pound).	$10
Direct labor (4 hours @ $6 per hour).	24
Factory overhead—variable (4 hours @ $1 per hour). . . .	4
Factory overhead—fixed (4 hours @ $2.50 per hour). . . .	10
Total standard cost	$48

Factory overhead rates are based on a normal 70 percent capacity and use the following variable budgets:

	Normal 70 percent	85 percent	100 percent
Motors produced	2,000	2,500	3,000
Variable factory overhead	$ 8,000	$10,000	$12,000
Fixed factory overhead	20,000	20,000	20,000

The company produces 2,500 motors during the month and incurred the following costs:

Material (4,880 pounds)	$25,856
Labor (11,800 hours @ $6.15 per hour)	72,570
Fixed factory overhead	20,495
Variable factory overhead	9,810

Required:

Determine the material, labor, and factory overhead variances using a standard cost system. Use the four-variance method of analyzing factory overhead.

P11–8. Determining specific standard cost data

On April 1, 19X1, Cabriz Company began the manufacture of a new device known as "Whiz." The company installed a standard cost system in accounting for manufacturing costs. The standard costs for a unit of Whiz are as follows:

Direct materials	
(6 pounds at $1 @ pound)	$ 6
Direct labor	
(1 hour at $4 @ hour)	4
Overhead	
(75 percent of direct labor cost)	3
	$13

The following data were obtained from Cabriz's records for the month of April:

Actual production of Whiz	2,000
Units sold of Whiz	1,250

	Debit	Credit
Sales		$25,000
Purchases	$13,650	
Material price variance	650	
Material quantity variance	500	
Direct labor rate variance	380	
Direct labor efficiency variance		400
Manufacturing overhead total variance	250	

The amount shown above for the material price variance is applicable to direct material purchased during April.

Required:

Compute each of the following items for Cabriz for the month of April:
a. Standard quantity of direct materials allowed (in pounds).
b. Actual quantity of direct material used (in pounds).
c. Standard hours allowed.
d. Actual hours worked.
e. Actual direct labor rate.
f. Actual total overhead.

P11–9.   Variable budget and overhead analysis

The following factory overhead budget was established by the Mark Company for the year 19X1. The company planned to manufacture 160 product units. Time and motion studies show that the standard direct labor-hours per unit should be 50 hours.

Repair expense	$ 6,400	(¼ is considered variable)
Indirect labor.	12,000	(⅙ is considered variable)
Depreciation on factory building	4,000	(straight-line depreciation is used)
Depreciation on factory machines. . . .	1,200	(depreciation is calculated on the basis of units of production)
Utilities	17,600	(½ is considered fixed)
Insurance	1,440	(premium is paid in advance and is not subject to change)
Miscellaneous	1,280	(considered to vary with production)
	$43,920	

The company uses the four-variance method of analyzing overhead.

Required:

a. Prepare a variable budget per line item for 120 units, 140 units, and 175 units based on the above data.
b. What is the total factory overhead budget formula based on direct labor-hours?
c. Prepare an overhead variance analysis per line item for each variable expense item; assume the following actual results were achieved:

Actual units	150
Actual hours	7,600
Actual factory overhead:	
Repair expense ($1,610 of this amount is variable).	$ 6,390
Indirect labor ($2,199 of this amount is variable).	11,979
Depreciation on machinery	1,135
Depreciation on building	4,010
Utilities ($8,405 of this amount is variable)	17,255
Insurance.	1,480
Miscellaneous.	1,305
Total	$43,554

d. Prepare an overhead variance analysis in total for the fixed factory overhead.

P11–10.   Material, labor, and overhead variance using various methods of overhead analysis

Krelt is a product manufactured in a standard package of 500 units. Anthony Frankos, Inc. manufactures it using a standard cost system. Management had planned to produce 30 packages for the period. The following data were obtained from the accounting and production departments for a recent operating period:

Standard cost per 500-unit package:	
Direct material (1,750 gallons @ $.90 per gallon)	$ 1,575
Direct labor (375 hours @ $6.20 per hour)	2,325
Variable factory overhead (375 hours @ $4 per hour)	1,500
Fixed factory overhead (375 hours @ $2.60 per hour).	975

Actual results for 25 packages produced: *Total*

Direct material used (43,140 gallons). $40,551.60
Direct labor (9,400 hours) 57,810.00
Variable factory overhead incurred. 38,180.00
Fixed factory overhead incurred 23,590.00

Required:

a.   Calculate material and labor variances.
b.   Calculate overhead variances using:
     (1)   Two-variance method.
     (2)   Three-variance method.
     (3)   Four-variance method.

P11–11.   Standards and production and service departments

As cost accountant for the SJ Manufacturing Company, you have worked with the production supervisor as well as top and middle management in arriving at the standard overhead rates. Together all of you have derived the following variable and fixed standard overhead costs for the two service departments and two production departments.

	Service		Production	
	Repair	*Factory superintendence*	*Fabricating*	*Finishing*
Standard factory overhead:				
Variable department	$1,000	$3,000	$15,000	$30,000
Fixed department	500	600	7,375	5,025
	$1,500	$3,600	$22,375	$35,025
Budgeted data:				
Repair-hours requisitioned.			275	225
Number of employees.			700	500
Direct labor-hours			2,000	5,000
Machine-hour				5,000
Budgeted units of production. . .			500	1,000

After operations end, your cost clerk distributes the actual service cost to the production departments. The cost clerk then provides you with the total actual production department costs.

	Fabricating	*Finishing*
Actual variable overhead. . . .	$17,000	$32,000
Actual fixed overhead	$ 7,750	$ 5,800
Actual direct labor-hours	1,950	—
Actual machine-hours	—	5,040
Actual units produced	480	1,020

Required:

a.   Determine the standard variable and fixed overhead rates for the two production departments, using the direct method of allocating service department costs.
b.   Prepare complete overhead cost analysis for each department. Prove your answer. Use the four-variance method of analysis.

P11–12.   Recording and prorating material, labor, and overhead variances

Cantrell Company established a standard cost system several years ago; budgeted annual capacity is 2,000 units. The following information is available for the year ended December 31, 19X1:

Standards per unit:
Direct material
(6 pounds @ $3 per pound) $18
Direct labor
(4 hours @ $7 per hour) 28
Factory overhead:
Variable
(4 hours @ $5) 20
Fixed
(4 hours @ $4.50) . . . . __18__
$84

There were 12,825 pounds of direct material used in manufacturing; 13,200 pounds were purchased at a cost of $37,620. Fewer skilled workers were employed than planned, at a cost savings of $0.20 per hour less than standard. Actual labor hours totaled 8,375. Actual variable overhead and fixed overhead totaled $42,738.30 and $38,900, respectively. A total of 1,640 units were finished and transferred out of production; 1,300 of these were sold. Work in Process contained 1,640 units, one-fourth complete. Much time was spent in establishing standards for the first year of operations; however, due to unforeseen conditions, variances did arise.

Material variances are prorated at year-end on the basis of direct material balances in the appropriate accounts. Variances associated with direct labor and overhead are prorated based on the respective direct labor and overhead balances in the appropriate accounts.

Required:

a.   Determine material, labor, and overhead variances using the four-variance method for analyzing overhead.
b.   Prepare summary journal entries to record the variances. For this problem, assume no entries involving standard costs have been made. Record Direct Materials Inventory at standard cost.
c.   Prepare journal entries to allocate the variances.
d.   After all variances have been prorated, give the balances in Direct Materials Inventory, Work in Process, Finished Goods, and Cost of Goods Sold.

P11–13.   Material, labor, and the two-variance method of overhead analysis (AICPA adapted)

Armando Corporation manufactures a product with the following standard costs:

Direct materials (20 yards @ $1.35 per yard) $27
Direct labor (4 hours @ $9 per hour) 36
Factory overhead (applied at ⅚ of direct labor.
Ratio of variable costs to fixed costs: 2 to 1) . . . . __30__
Total standard cost per unit of output $93

Standards are based on normal monthly production involving 2,400 direct labor-hours (600 units of output). The following information pertains to the month of July:

Direct materials purchased (18,000 yards @ $1.38 per yard)	$24,840
Direct materials used (9,500 yards)	
Direct labor (2,100 hours @ $9.15 per hour).	19,215
Actual factory overhead	16,650

500 units of the product were actually produced in July.

Required:

a. Prepare the following schedules computing:
    (1) Variable factory overhead rate per direct labor-hour.
    (2) Total fixed factory overhead based on normal activity.
b. Prepare the following schedules for the month of July, indicating whether each variance is favorable or unfavorable:
    (1) Materials price variance (based on purchases).
    (2) Materials usage variance.
    (3) Labor rate variance.
    (4) Labor efficiency variance.
    (5) Controllable factory overhead variance.
    (6) Capacity (volume) factory overhead variance.

P11–14.   Standard cost variances using equivalent units (AICPA adapted)

Melody Corporation is a manufacturing company that produces a single product known as "Jupiter." Melody uses the first-in, first-out (FIFO) process costing method for both financial statements and internal management reporting. In analyzing production results, standard costs are used, whereas actual costs are used for financial statement reporting. The standards, which are based upon equivalent units of production, are as follows:

Direct material per unit.	1 pound ($10 per pound)
Direct labor per unit.	2 hours ($4 per hour)
Factory overhead per unit:	
Variable	2 hours ($1.00 per hour)
Fixed	($0.25 per hour)

Budgeted units for April were 12,000. Data for the month of April 19X1 are: beginning inventory consisted of 2,500 units which were 100 percent complete as to direct material and 40 percent complete as to direct labor and factory overhead; an additional 10,000 units were started during the month; ending inventory consisted of 2,000 units which were 100 percent complete as to direct material and 40 percent complete as to direct labor and factory overhead.

Costs applicable to April production are as follows:

	Actual cost	Standard cost
Direct material used (11,000 pounds).	$121,000	$100,000
Direct labor (25,000 hours actually worked)	105,575	82,400
Factory overhead	31,930	25,750

Required:

a. For each element of production for April (direct material, direct labor, and factory overhead) compute the following:

(1) Equivalent units of production.
(2) Cost per equivalent unit of production at actual and at standard. Show supporting computations in good form.

b. Prepare a schedule analyzing whether the following variances were favorable or unfavorable for April production.
(1) Total materials.
(2) Materials price.
(3) Materials usage.
(4) Total labor.
(5) Labor rate.
(6) Labor efficiency.
(7) Total factory overhead.
(8) Factory overhead volume.
(9) Controllable factory overhead.
Show supporting computation in good form.

P11–15.   Standard cost analysis for job order costing (AICPA adapted)

Vogue Fashions, Inc. manufactures ladies' blouses of one quality, produced in lots to fill each special order from its customers, comprised of department stores located in various cities. Vogue sews the particular stores' labels on the blouses. The standard costs for a dozen blouses are:

Direct materials (24 yards @ $1.10)	$26.40
Direct labor (3 hours $4.90)	14.70
Manufacturing overhead (3 hours @ $4)	12.00
Standard cost per dozen	$53.10

During June 19X1, Vogue worked on three orders, for which the month's job cost records disclose the following:

Lot No.	Units in lot (dozens)	Material used (yards)	Hours worked
22	1,000	24,100	2,980
23	1,700	40,440	5,130
24	1,200	28,825	2,890

The following information is also available:

1. Vogue purchased 95,000 yards of material during June at a cost of $106,400. The materials price variance is recorded when goods are purchased. All inventories are carried at standard cost.
2. Direct labor during June amounted to $55,000. According to payroll records, production employees were paid $5 per hour.
3. Manufacturing overhead during June amounted to $45,600.
4. A total of $576,000 was budgeted for manufacturing overhead for the year 19X1, based on estimated production at the plant's normal capacity of 48,000 dozen blouses annually. Manufacturing overhead at this level of production is 40 percent fixed and 60 percent variable. Manufacturing overhead is applied on the basis of direct labor-hours.
5. There was no work in process on June 1. During June, Lots 22 and 23 were completed. All materials were issued for Lot 24, which was 80 percent completed as to direct labor.

Required:

a.   Prepare a schedule showing the computation of the standard cost of Lots 22, 23, and 24 for June 19X1.

b.   Prepare a schedule showing the computation of the materials price variance for June 19X1. Indicate whether the variance is favorable or unfavorable.

c.   Prepare a schedule showing, for each lot produced during June 19X1, computations of the
   (1)   Materials quantity variance in yards.
   (2)   Labor efficiency variance in hours.
   (3)   Labor rate variance in dollars.
   Indicate whether each variance is favorable or unfavorable.

d.   Prepare a schedule showing computations of the total controllable and noncontrollable (volume) manufacturing overhead variances for June 19X1 using the three-variance method. Indicate whether the variances are favorable or unfavorable.

CASES

C11–1. Analysis of standard cost system (CMA adapted)

The Ashley Company manufactures and sells a household product marketed through direct mail and advertisements in home improvement and gardening magazines. Although similar products are available in hardware and department stores, none is as effective as Ashley's model.

The company uses a standard cost system in its manufacturing accounting. The standards have not undergone a thorough review in the past 18 months. The general manager has seen no need for such a review because:

1.   Material quality and unit costs were fixed by a three-year purchase commitment signed in July 19X1.
2.   A three-year labor contract had been signed in July 19X1.
3.   There have been no significant variations from standard costs for the past three quarters.

The standard cost for the product, as established in July 19X1, is presented below:

Material (.75 lb. @ $1 per pound).	$0.75
Direct labor (.3 hrs. @ $4 per hour)	1.20
Overhead (.3 hrs. @ $7 per hour).	2.10
Standard manufacturing cost per unit.	$4.05

The standard for overhead costs was developed from the following budgeted costs based upon an activity level of 1 million units (300,000 direct labor-hours).

Variable manufacturing overhead	$ 600,000
Fixed manufacturing overhead	1,500,000
Total manufacturing overhead	$2,100,000

The earnings statement and the factory costs for the first quarter are presented in Exhibits C11–1A and C11–1B. The first-quarter results indicate that Ashley probably will achieve its sales goal of 1.2 million units for the current year. A total of 320,000 units

EXHIBIT C11–1A

ASHLEY COMPANY
First Quarter Earnings
Period ended March 31, 19X3

Sales (300,000 units).		$2,700,000
Costs of goods sold:		
Standard cost of goods	$1,215,000	
Variation from standard		
costs	12,000	1,227,000
Gross profit.		$1,473,000
Operating expenses:		
Selling:		
Advertising	$ 200,000	
Mailing list costs	175,000	
Postage	225,000	
Salaries	60,000	
Administrative:		
Salaries	120,000	
Office rent	45,000	
Total operating expenses		825,000
Income before taxes		$ 648,000
Income taxes (45%)		291,600
Net income		$ 356,400

were manufactured during the first quarter to increase inventory levels to those needed to support the growing sales volume.

Action Hardware, a national chain, recently asked Ashley to manufacture and sell a slightly modified version of the product which Action would distribute through its stores.

Action has offered to buy a minimum quantity of 200,000 units each year over the next three years and has offered to pay $4.10 for each unit, FOB shipping point.

The Ashley management is interested in the proposal because it represents a new

EXHIBIT C11–1B

ASHLEY COMPANY
Factory Costs
For the Quarter Ended March 31, 19X3

Materials.	$ 266,000
Direct labor.	452,000
Variable manufacturing overhead.	211,000
Fixed manufacturing overhead.	379,000
Total manufacturing costs.	$1,308,000
Less:	
Standard cost of goods manufactured	1,296,000
Unfavorable variation from standard cost	$ 12,000

EXHIBIT C11–1C

ACTION HARDWARE
Sales Proposal
First 12 Months Results

Proposed sales (200,000 @ $4.10).	$820,000

Estimated costs and expenses:
 Manufacturing (200,000 @ $4.05). $810,000
 Sales salaries.   10,000
 Administrative salaries   20,000
   Total estimated costs $840,000
Net loss . . . . $ (20,000)

Note: None of our regular selling cost is included because this is a new market. However, a 16.6 percent increase in sales and administrative salaries have been incorporated because sales volume will increase by that amount.

market. The company has adequate capacity to meet the production requirements. However, in addition to the possible financial results of taking the order, Ashley must consider carefully the other consequences of this departure from its normal practices. The president asked an assistant to the general manager to make an estimate of the financial aspects of the proposal for the first 12 months. The assistant recommended that the order not be accepted and presented the analysis in Exhibit C 11–1C to support the recommendation.

Required:

a. Review the financial analysis of the Action Hardware proposal prepared by the general manager's assistant.

 (1) Criticize the first year's financial analysis.

 (2) Using only the data given, present a more suitable analysis for the first year of the order.

b. Identify the additional financial data Ashley Company would need to prepare a more comprehensive financial analysis of the Action proposal for the three-year period.

c. Discuss the nonfinancial issues Ashley management should address in considering the Action proposal.

OBJECTIVES OF CHAPTER 12

1. To present the advantages of budgets as a management tool.
2. To emphasize the important role of top management in the budgeting process.
3. To illustrate the preparation of several budgets in the master budget plan.
4. To discuss how the misuse of budgets leads to long-run problems.
5. To present the advantages and limitations of applying a participative budgeting approach.

12

The budgeting process

Many managers claim that budgets are impracticable because their companies experience so many uncertainties. However, it is very probable that their competitors are using budgets as indispensable tools, and these competitors are probably the industry leaders. Managers have to deal with uncertainties whether they have a budget or not. Budgets help managers in dealing with these uncertainties and make the decision-making process more effective. The objective of budgeting is to substitute deliberate, well-conceived business judgment for accidental success in enterprise management. Budgeting should not be regarded as an expression of wishful thinking but rather as a description of an attainable objective. Certainly it should be emphasized that budgets reflect plans and that planning should have taken place before budgets are prepared.

Cost accounting provides total and detailed costs of the products manufactured or the services rendered by a company. To measure the efficiency of these costs, they must be compared with a "yardstick" that was prepared in advance of production and that reflects a good level of performance. The most common method used to evaluate actual performance is through budget analysis. Of all management tools available, budgets are generally used most often and are of greatest importance. In addition, top management has been adequately exposed to the budgeting process so that the cost accountant generally does not have to spend much time convincing management of a budget's importance as a planning and control device.

However, the cost accountant may have to convince management that proper budgeting techniques should be applied. Fixed budgets should be replaced by variable ones so that actual costs can be compared with a budget prepared for the actual capacity volume achieved. The cost accountant should also encourage management to combine a standard cost system with budgets to better perform the tasks and achieve the goals assigned. Management should also be aware of the behavioral factors inherent in the budgeting process. As this chapter illustrates, honest attempts should be made to explain the budgeting process to employees and to involve as many of them in the process as feasible.

Unfortunately, in some companies, the budgeting process is first initiated not because management has recognized the need for budgets but because a request for outside funding must usually be supported by budgets for future operations. These budgets allow banks and other financial institutions to study projected operations before supplying the requested financial backing. Because management realizes that these budgets are studied by outside financial institutions, cost-consciousness and maximum utilization of available resources are encouraged. Budgets can thus also provide an incentive to perform more effectively.

Budgeting defined.   Budgeting is a means of coordinating the combined intelligence of an entire organization into a plan of action based on past performance and governed by a rational judgment of factors that will influence the course of business in the future. Without the coordination provided by budgeting, department heads may follow courses that are beneficial for their own department, but not from an overall company viewpoint. Budgeting control should thus be looked upon as a company operation with a complete plan of execution—a program which encompasses much more than monetary aspects.

While budgets usually express numerical data—dollars and cents, direct labor-hours, machine-hours, or units—they should not be considered merely as an abstract listing. Rather, budgets translate human endeavor into quantitative data. This translation shows how the company's objectives will be reached and what equipment, material, and personnel will be required.

PRINCIPLES OF BUDGETING

Regardless of the type of budget being prepared, certain general principles apply. First of all, top management support is crucial to the success of the budgetary program. Even though top management may not realize the important role they play in budgeting, their philosophy toward budgeting soon filters down in the company. If they view the budget as some mechanical process that must be done as quickly as possible, employees are less likely to give budget preparation much attention. The budgeting process also fails if management views budgets as a scapegoat on which all the company's problems can be blamed. On the other hand, if management considers the budget as an excellent means of planning and takes an active role in the execution of budgets, the company is more likely to gain all the benefits the budgeting process offers.

In the initial phase of the budgetary process, management members must deal with each other's problems. Otherwise, management may be unaware of the activities of each company segment and fail to provide for the necessary coordination among these segments. Since budgets force management to express objectives in written form, an exchange of views is usually made as management plans where it wants the company to be in the next 5 or 10 years. It is likely that there are many different views of future company plans, and the budget helps management arrive at a compromise. If this compromise is not made, each company segment may follow courses of action which benefit only itself rather than the entire company. If the budgeting process does not facilitate long-range planning, management is likely to be concerned with meeting only daily operational goals. Coordination is best achieved using a participative budgeting approach in which all managers provide input into the process of goal setting.

There is little purpose to setting goals if the individuals who must meet these goals are unaware of their existence. It is most unfair to hold a person responsible for a level of achievement that he or she does not know about. Just as unfair is the failure to communicate results to the involved parties. The more rapidly these results can be communicated, the greater the probability that a more efficient level of performance can be achieved.

Another principle of budgeting is that the process must allow for flexibility. Conditions both inside and outside the company can change which may require revision of the budget. For example, additional competitors may enter the market with a product that sells at a lower price and is a good substitute for the company's product. This may make meeting the budgeted market share and sales unlikely. If management recognizes that even with increased promotional expenditures, budgeted sales are not realistic, all budgets affected should be revised. These revisions are preferable to using unattainable budgets.

Advantages of budgets

Budgets can be prepared in numerous ways depending on the desired complexity. Even simple budgets offer a large number of advantages for external and internal reasons. The following are a few of the advantages a formalized system of budgeting or profit planning offers:

1. It obligates management to specify objectives for the short and long run.
2. It forces management to analyze future problems so that alternative plans are recognized.
3. It directs effort and funds toward the most profitable of all possible alternatives.
4. It emphasizes the need for coordination of all elements of a company since budgeting quickly reveals weaknesses in organization.
5. It serves as a means of communication.

6. It provides performance standards which serve as incentives to perform more effectively.
7. It indicates those areas lacking control by providing data used to analyze variances between actual and budgeted operations. These variances should provide the springboard for study of the source of the problem.

Budget committee

Line management has the ultimate responsibility for the preparation of individual budgets, but there is also a need for someone to provide technical, unbiased assistance. The president or chief executive normally establishes budgeting principles, while direction and execution of all budget procedures are generally delegated to the budget committee. The budget committee serves as a consulting body to the budget officer; members include the budget director and top executives representing all company segments.

Since the budget committee's functions include coordination of all planning, the committee should review and evaluate all reports prepared at the time the budgetary system is initiated. Duplication can be more easily eliminated if the budget committee prepares a list of the reports believed to supply the information needed, and then asks other managers within the company whether these reports are sufficient. Otherwise, given the normal resistance to change, most managers would continue to request reports, even if they are redundant.

Budget manual

The budget committee's functions also include reviewing and approving budget estimates and suggesting revisions. It should review segment budgets to determine whether they are excessively optimistic, conservative, or make provision for slack. The committee also has the responsibility of recommending action to improve efficiency where necessary. In addition, it is helpful for the budget committee to prepare a budget manual as a reference for implementation of a budget program. This manual has long-range usefulness, for it documents procedures that are otherwise carried around in the heads of individuals who will not have the same job forever.

Even after budgets are prepared, the budget committee should continue in an advisory capacity because it must approve possible changes in the budget as conditions change. For the same reason, the budget committee needs to review the budget periodically. Executives on the budget committee are usually provided information by the budget director, who also serves in an advisory staff capacity.

Budget directors.   The budget director, who serves in a staff capacity, is usually the controller or someone reporting to the controller. The budget director requests estimates of the cost of running each cost center from department heads and supervisors. Similarly, he or she requires sales estimates from sales executives. The budget director should also supply executives with information regarding past operations to guide in the preparation of new budgets. The success of the budget director in generating goodwill toward himself or herself and the budget department is crucial to the success of the budget program.

One of the budget director's most important qualifications is the ability to converse with executives with tact and dignity and to display a thorough knowledge of general accounting and cost accounting. The budget director must also have the ability to analyze organizations and define the duties of principal executives. Many accountants fail as budget directors, not because they lack accounting knowledge, but because they fail to recognize the administrative problems which evolve from budgeting. Budgets and standards are indispensable when they are administered skillfully. When they are not, they can do more harm than good.

Budgets should follow the framework of the organization chart. Clear lines of authority and responsibility should be indicated so that there is no question as to which individual is held accountable for each expenditure. Each employee whose operations justify a budget should be easily identified by reference to the organization chart.

Length of budget period

Generally, a company's budget corresponds to the fiscal period used in the accounting system. Budgets can be short or long range. While the long-range budget lacks the detail supplied by a short-range budget, it does provide broad guidelines. For example, a long-range budget covering as many as 10 or 15 years anticipates long-term needs and opportunities which may require that definite steps be taken in the short run. Because long-range budgets are subject to many changes, they may not be circulated among middle and lower management. Since short-term budgets are prepared for shorter periods, they have the advantage of being more accurate.

Some companies prepare an annual budget in detail using a *rolling* or *continuous* approach. For example, using a rolling approach, at the end of May of each year, the company adds a budget for May of the next year; as each month ends, a new 12th month is added. With this method, the company always has a 12-month detailed budget in advance. The advantage offered by rolling budgets is that changing economic conditions can be incorporated into the plans each time a new month is added. Budgeting thus becomes a continual process rather than a once-a-year task. Other companies prepare their annual budget in two phases, detailing the first half of the year while summarizing the remaining six months by quarters in less detail. A new, short-range, detailed budget is prepared every six months, partly on the basis of earlier summarized data and partly on the results of the previous six months.

Fixed versus variable budgets

As discussed in Chapter 5, variable (flexible) budgets make possible closer control of performance than do fixed budgets. This is because actual revenue and expense are compared with budgeted data based on the actual volume obtained. Variable budgets are prepared for a range of activity levels instead of for a single level, as in a fixed budget. Variable budgets consist of a budget formula which can be used for a series of possible volumes, all considered within the range of probability. A budget can then be prepared for any activity level as long as it is within the relevant range considered feasible. With variable budgets, items can be different in each month or in selected months according to seasonal variation and the activity of the cost center. Fixed budgets, on the other hand, are not adjusted to the actual volume attained; instead, the fixed budget is based on certain definite assumed conditions and actual results are compared with this point fixed in advance. Only when a company's activities can be estimated within close limits is a fixed budget satisfactory.

Standards and budgets

Standard costs are closely related to budgets because they serve as building blocks for the construction of the budget. As discussed in Chapters 10 and 11, once standard costs have been established, the production requirements needed to obtain stated company goals can be translated into total standard costs. Thus, the budget becomes a summary of standards for revenue and cost items. However, the scope of the budget is broader, for it serves to keep the company on a specified path. On the other hand, standards indicate what the costs will be if a predetermined level of performance is achieved, not what the costs are expected to be.

Financial forecasts

The accounting profession has been in the midst of a controversy concerning the publication of financial forecasts for external users. Investors and others suggest that not only should corporations include financial forecasts in their annual reports, but also that the CPA attest to those forecasts. A basic argument for the publication of financial forecasts is to provide the investor with additional information about the future activities of the company upon which to base investment decisions. A second argument is that some investors currently have access to forecast data; it would be more equitable if all investors had access to such information. In support of attestation of such data by the CPA is the argument that this would make the data more reliable and give the investor confidence in the forecast.

One argument raised against the publication of such forecasts is the expectation that management would present a conservative forecast to "look good" when actual results for the year are in. A second point often considered is the prospect that the forecast would provide competitors with confidential information, thus endangering business strategy and the performance of the firm. A third argument is that forecasts are narrow estimates, which makes them difficult to interpret given that the future is not a certainty; as a result, investors may be misled by them.

Attestation by CPAs also can be questioned. There may be a conflict of interest if the forecast in the current year's report and the actual results of the next year are both audited by the CPA. There would be concern that the reported results might be adjusted so that the forecast appears to be borne out by the actual results.

In view of the increased awareness of the importance of these forecasts, the American Institute of Certified Public Accountants (AICPA) issued a statement in 1975 establishing guidelines for published financial forecasts. The Securities and Exchange Commission encourages the inclusion of these forecasts and has guidelines which do not conflict with those of the AICPA.

Formal communication

Not only is the general operating budget or annual profit plan an important operating tool, but this plan also represents a formal communication channel within a company. A formal commitment on the part of management to take positive actions to make actual events correspond to the formal plan is involved. In addition, profit plans are usually reviewed and approved by a higher authority and are changed only in unusual specified circumstances after approval is granted. Profit plans also contain explicit statements concerning implementation of management objectives for a period of time; these are communicated to all parties with control responsibility. As discussed later in the chapter in detail, comparison of actual results with the profit plan forms the basis for management control, motivation, and performance evaluation.

Steps in developing a profit plan

The following steps are employed in the development of an annual profit plan when a company employs a bottom-up approach. The level of management involved and the nature and direction of the communication process is also indicated. Each of these steps will be discussed more thoroughly later in the chapter.

1. Identification of planning guidelines by top management. All levels of management are involved and communication is downward.
2. Preparation of the general operating budget or profit plan beginning with a sales budget. Lower levels of management receive sales targets which provide a basis for the preparation of production budgets and other components. Consultation with a higher (middle) management level may be needed to arrive at certain aspects of the specific manager's budget. The

communication process is primarily lateral with some upward communication possible.

3. Negotiation may be necessary to arrive at final plans; communication is upward.

4. Coordination and review of the profit plan; top level management makes recommendations and returns the various plans to middle level management. After middle management makes these changes, the plan is resubmitted for approval. Communication is generally downward; however, there may be some lateral communication during the adjustment phase.

5. Final approval and distribution of the formal plan is made. Top management gives final approval and communicates its decision downward.

MASTER BUDGET

The master budget in a manufacturing company covers various types of budgets, many of which are supported by additional budget schedules. However, only the following types of budgets are illustrated in this book:

1. Sales budget broken down by
    a. Territory and product.
    b. Territory, product, and customer grouping.
2. Production budget in units.
3. Direct materials purchases budget.
4. Direct labor budget.[1]
5. Factory overhead budget.[1]
6. Cost of goods sold budget.
7. Marketing and administrative budgets.
8. Budgeted income statement.
9. Budgeted statement of cash receipts and disbursements.
10. Budgeted balance sheet.
11. Capital expenditure budget.

Chapter 13 discusses and illustrates nonmanufacturing budgets, including the marketing and administrative budget, the budgeted income statement, the budgeted statement of cash receipts and disbursements, the budgeted balance sheet, and the capital expenditure budget. All other budgets are discussed and illustrated in this chapter.

Sales budget

Before any of the budgets listed above can be prepared, a forecast of sales for the budget period must be made. The chief marketing manager is responsible

---

[1]Can be combined with direct material in a manufacturing budget estimate.

for the preparation of the sales prediction, but a number of other individuals and factors must be considered. The sales forecast, in turn, usually determines the activity level on which all budgets are established. However, if a company can sell more than it can produce, the production constraint has to be considered first. For example, assume the company can sell 1,000 units because of increased market demand; however, if company manufacturing facilities can only produce 750 units, the activity level for all budgets is based on 750 units unless additional production facilities are acquired.

The marketing manager must also consider internal factors, such as historical sales pattern, desired profit, product characteristics (whether it is a new product or a seasonal one), and sales force estimates. Among other things, previous period sales should be analyzed for possible fluctuations caused by seasonal variations, economic cycles, and labor strikes. However, previous period demand may not be fully reflected in historical sales, since most companies have no record of unfilled orders. A figure closer to past demand is the sum of unfilled orders added to past sales. Since this information is not usually available, future demand estimates are normally based only on historical sales, which reflect only past demand that was satisfied.

Future sales are also affected by a large number of external factors. Understandably, management has much less control of these; however, if a causal relationship can be established, a more accurate estimate can be made. For example, historical data may show that there is a relationship between the company's sales and personal disposable income or gross national product. A company may also study the relationship of each of its products to the others.

Certainly, general economic and social conditions cannot be ignored in sales forecasts. An environment of high unemployment with little hope that conditions will improve in the future, for instance, indicates that a conservative sales forecast should be made. The purchasing power of the population, as well as population shifts and changes in buying habits, should be studied before sales forecasts are finalized. Any change in the number of competitors, as well as changes in the sales promotion program of present competitors, also play a significant role in forecasting sales. Even though government monetary and fiscal policies regarding taxation, international trade, and politics are not designed to influence one particular company but rather general economic conditions as a whole, their impact should be recognized by the forecaster.

Methods of estimating future sales. Various methods are available for estimating future sales. The uses of these methods vary widely depending on the products being sold as well as on the channel of distribution used. Regardless of the methods actually used, there are two basic approaches. With one approach, individuals within the company who are familiar with operations originate the sales forecast. With the other, market research techniques, such as trend analysis and correlation analysis, are used.

The company's sales force can obviously contribute useful information in the sales forecasting process. Among other things, each salesperson can supply his or her supervisor with an estimate of what the salesperson thinks can be sold in his or her territory during the next period. Not only is information gained from a firsthand source, but this can also stimulate the interest of the salesperson in the budgeting process. The district marketing manager should review each of these individual estimates because they are likely to be biased in one direction or another. Either the individual salesperson is usually optimistic and overestimates future sales, or he or she may build in some "slack" by underestimating future sales so that if sales are depressed, he or she will not have to justify a large variance. However, before adjusting any of the individual salesperson's budgets, the district sales manager owes them the courtesy of discussing with them the need for revisions. Such a method is often referred to as the *bottom-up* approach because the budgets are combined at successively higher levels of management.

The experienced judgment of key executives within the company should be used, as well. Their subjective estimates of future sales reflect many factors that are difficult to quantify, such as general economic and industry conditions, competition, and the quality of the sales force. The value of estimates based on management's intuition and evaluation of market conditions varies among companies. Often, executive input is used to refine the sales estimates determined through other sources, as in the bottom-up approach. At other times, companies begin their sales forecasting process with estimates from key executives. Sales forecasts in small, owner-managed companies are often based exclusively on executive judgment.

The disadvantage of using salespeople to prepare the sales forecast is that, while they are familiar with the current conditions in their territory, they are not well informed about broad economic developments. In addition, many salespeople have an aversion to analyzing figures and may resent the time spent in making such forecasts; the result may be a hastily prepared sales forecast which does not reflect all important factors. For example, they can usually estimate customer potential quite accurately, but are less likely to understand the effect of economic cycles on product sales. It is for this reason that most companies also utilize market research in making sales forecasts. The company's market research staff should supply district marketing managers with information that can be of use in estimating territorial sales.

Trend and correlation analysis. The other basic approach to sales forecasting utilizes the marketing research department, which develops and analyzes the sales forecast data centrally. Through the use of correlation analysis, cycle projection, and trend analysis, market researchers arrive at projected sales. The market research department may also use motivation research to measure consumer motivation. Subconscious motives of buyers are studied using word association, in-depth interviews, and other behavioral science techniques. However, such techniques may be of more use in making industry forecasts than in a sales forecast for a single company.

Market researchers may study actual sales for several years in the past as well as for the corresponding period in the previous year so that a trend can be projected. However, using only historical sales data in forecasting has some weaknesses, since some of the company's policies may have changed, which, in turn, affects future sales. For example, a product's quality may have improved so that there is a higher demand for the product, or more liberal credit terms may have been adopted. Even though the simplest way of using past data in forecasting is to average all available data for a specific number of past periods, the weakness of this approach is that the most recent historical data are given no more significance than data from accounting periods further in the past. This weakness is overcome, however, if moving averages are used since only recent data are then used in determining the average. Secular, or long-term, trends may be forecast by plotting sales for previous periods on a moving-average basis. Correlation analysis is an attempt to establish the relationship between the values of two attributes—that is, the relationship between an economic indicator (independent variable) and sales (dependent variable). For example, in predicting sales for baby bottles, the projected birth rate is the independent variable. The use of these statistical forecasting techniques is most effective for products having a stable market pattern. For products with markets that fluctuate considerably and which require extensive sales promotion, more subjective estimates must be used.

Regardless of the approach used in determining the sales forecast, the underlying assumptions used for each forecast should be documented. The forecast user can thus evaluate the significance of each assumption. The major sources of information used, as well as the techniques used to arrive at the final forecast, should also be included in the documentation. Documentation of the data provides a good source for reviewing the accuracy of the forecast and enables the forecaster to refine his or her assumptions so more accurate future estimates may be made.

Territorial sales budget.   As shown in Exhibit 12–1, the sales budget is prepared on a monthly basis and is classified as to type of product. A sales

EXHIBIT 12–1

HART COMPANY
Sales Budget
For the Year Ending December 31, 19X2

	Product A		Product B		Product C		Total
	Quantity	Sales	Quantity	Sales	Quantity	Sales	
January.........	100	$ 4,000	1,150	$ 69,000	800	$ 72,000	$ 145,000
February........	120	4,800	980	58,800	770	69,300	132,900
March..........	110	4,400	1,000	60,000	650	58,500	122,900
April...........	115	4,600	1,080	64,800	600	54,000	123,400
May	140	5,600	1,200	72,000	680	61,200	138,800
June...........	150	6,000	1,250	75,000	725	65,250	146,250
July............	145	5,800	1,375	82,500	780	70,200	158,500
August	155	6,200	1,400	84,000	820	73,800	164,000
September	160	6,400	1,500	90,000	850	76,500	172,900
October	150	6,000	1,600	96,000	900	81,000	183,000
November.......	145	5,800	1,770	106,200	925	83,250	195,250
December.......	130	5,200	1,800	108,000	975	87,750	200,950
Totals....	1,620	$64,800	16,105	$966,300	9,475	$852,750	$1,883,850

EXHIBIT 12–2

HART COMPANY
Sales Budget
For the Year Ending December 31, 19X2

	Units	Average sales price	Total sales
Product A.............	1,620	$40	$ 64,800
Product B.............	16,105	60	966,300
Product C.............	9,475	90	852,750
			$1,883,850

budget could also indicate whether the sale is to wholesalers, retailers, government agencies, foreign buyers, and so forth. With this customer breakdown, management can better determine the percentage of sales generated by each group. To simplify the budget presented in Exhibit 12–1, no customer groups are indicated.

The sales budget should also be broken down for each territory. However, rather than display all of the Hart Company's individual territorial budgets, only the combined data are used in the examples for the budgets illustrated in Exhibits 12–1 through 12–9. A simplified annual sales budget is shown in Exhibit 12–2, which combines the monthly data from Exhibit 12–1.

Production budget

After the sales budget is completed, a production budget stating the physical units to manufacture is prepared. The production budget is the sales budget adjusted for any changes in inventory, as follows:

Units to produce = Budgeted sales + Desired ending inventory
of finished goods − Beginning inventory of finished goods

While sales may be of a seasonal nature, many companies tend to stabilize their production through the use of inventory. That is, inventory is the buffer which absorbs extra production when demand is slack and from which units are drawn during the heavy demand periods. A production budget is illustrated in Exhibit 12–3 for finished goods inventory only. If work in process inventory constitutes a significant portion of the inventory or if the production cycle is extended, partially completed goods cannot be ignored. It is assumed that the beginning finished goods inventory is obtained from Hart Company's records, while the desired ending finished goods inventory is supplied by management.

Exhibit 12–3 is a summary of each product's production budget which is prepared for each month. The partial production budget shown in Exhibit 12–4 reflects production each month for one product.

The above production budgets are readily adaptable for a company manufac-

EXHIBIT 12–3

HART COMPANY
Total Production Budget
For Year Ending December 31, 19X2

	Products		
	A	B	C
Planned sales (from Exhibit 12–2)	1,620	16,105	9,475
Desired ending finished goods inventory	100	500	450
Total units to provide for	1,720	16,605	9,925
Less beginning finished goods inventory	70	475	525
Units to be produced	1,650	16,130	9,400

turing a standard product. However, for a company that manufactures only after receipt of a customer order, plans have to be less detailed. If standardized direct material parts are used in production, though, the company may be able to budget in a similar manner. The important factor in job order costing, in which manufacturing is performed according to customer specification, is to avoid delays and costly overtime by properly routing and scheduling work through the factory.

To provide as smooth a flow of production as possible, management should coordinate the sales and production budget. Often marketing personnel are not fully aware of the plant capacity available and may fail to consider what products can be produced and what products cannot be produced with the company's manufacturing facilities. Sales efforts may have to be shifted to avoid idle capacity and to fully utilize production facilities. Because the production budget determines the volume of manufacturing operations, it becomes the basis for the direct-materials-purchases budget, labor budget, and factory overhead budget.

EXHIBIT 12–4

HART COMPANY
Product A Production Budget
By Months for Year Ending December 31, 19X2

	January	February		December	Year, 19X2
Planned sales.	100	120		130	1,620
Desired ending finished goods inventory	60	65		100	100
Total units to provide for.	160	185		230	1,720
Less beginning finished goods inventory	70	60		85	70
Units to be produced	90	125		145	1,650

Direct-materials-purchases budget

After the number of units of each product that will be manufactured is determined, the material required for this level of operations can be calculated and combined in a direct-materials-purchases budget, as shown in Exhibit 12–5. Only two different material items are shown to keep the illustration simple. As provided for in the production budget, management must indicate the desired level of ending direct materials inventory it wishes to maintain. The beginning direct materials inventory balance is obtained from the inventory records. The budget is prepared in the unit of measure (pounds, gallons, etc.) used for the material.

While Exhibit 12–5 summarizes the annual direct material needs (with data obtained from the monthly budgets for each direct material), Exhibit 12–6 illustrates the production and inventory requirements for Direct Material AA2 broken down on a monthly basis. A similar budget can be prepared for each item of direct material, especially for the significant material items. Only direct material is shown in Exhibits 12–5 and 12–6, since indirect material and supplies are usually shown on the factory overhead budget.

EXHIBIT 12–5

HART COMPANY
Direct-Materials-Purchases Budget
For Year Ending December 31, 19X2

	Material AA2	Material BB3	Total
Units needed for production (from below)	54,360	81,540	
Desired ending direct materials inventory	2,500	4,500	
Total material units to provide for.	56,860	86,040	
Less: Beginning direct materials inventory	1,900	5,000	
Units to be purchased	54,960	81,040	
Unit purchase price	$ 1.10	$ 2.25	
Total purchase cost	$60,456	$182,340	$242,796

Direct material usage

	Production					
	Product A (1,650 units)	Product B (16,130 units)	Product C (9,400 units)	Total direct material usage	Material unit cost	Cost of material used
AA2 (2 units per finished product)	3,300	32,260	18,800	54,360	$1.10	$59,796
BB3 (3 units per finished product)	4,950	48,390	28,200	81,540	$2.25	183,465
						$243,261

EXHIBIT 12–6

HART COMPANY
Material AA2 Purchase Budget
By Month for Year Ending December 31, 19X2

Direct material AA2	January	February		December	Total
Units needed for production........	4,260	3,740	} }	2,905	54,360
Desired ending direct materials inventory.................	1,000	1,500	} }	2,500	2,500
Total material units to provide for	5,260	5,240	} }	5,405	56,860
Less: beginning direct materials inventory.................	1,900	1,000	} }	1,600	1,900
Units to be purchased	3,360	4,240	} }	3,805	54,960
Unit purchase price.............	$ 1.10	$ 1.10	} }	$ 1.10	$ 1.10
Total purchase cost........	$3,696	$4,664	} }	$4,185.50	$60,456

Direct labor budget

The direct labor budget ties in with the number of units to be produced according to the production budget. Generally, only direct labor is included, since indirect labor is part of the factory overhead budget. The information provided in the direct labor budget guides the personnel department in manning operations so that the required employee skills are available. Reference to the annual direct labor budget allows the personnel department time to make arrangements to either hire or lay off workers. After determining the number of direct labor-hours needed per time period, the hours are translated into dollars by applying appropriate labor rates. Exhibit 12–7 illustrates a summarized annual direct labor budget. More detailed budgets should be prepared for each department by month.

Factory overhead budget

While factory overhead expenses can be grouped in several ways, such as by function, cost behavior, or department, usually the natural expense classifica-

EXHIBIT 12–7

HART COMPANY
Direct Labor Budget
For the Year Ending December 31, 19X2

	Units produced	Direct labor-hours per unit	Total hours	Total budget @ $4 per hour
Product A..........	1,650	3	4,950	$ 19,800
Product B..........	16,130	5	80,650	322,600
Product C	9,400	10	94,000	376,000
			179,600	$718,400

tion is used. However, the natural expense classification, which involves such categories as utilities, indirect labor, and indirect material, has limited usefulness for budgeting purposes. Instead, factory overhead budgets should be prepared for each cost center so that the supervisor of the cost center can be held accountable and responsible for the expenses incurred. A distinction should be made for controllable and noncontrollable expenses so that the supervisor is held accountable for only those expenses over which he or she has control. Each departmental factory overhead budget is summarized in an annual factory overhead budget similar to the one shown in Exhibit 12–8. A limited number of expense items is shown.

Cost of goods sold budget

After the budgets for direct material, direct labor, and factory overhead are determined, the data are summarized in a cost of goods sold budget, as illustrated in Exhibit 12–9. The unit cost for each of the three products is shown so that a valuation can be placed on the ending balance of finished goods inventory. The beginning balance of finished goods inventory is obtained from the accounting records.

LIMITATIONS OF BUDGETS

While budgets are a useful management tool, they must be applied correctly for management to reap the greatest benefits. Certainly, budgets are not a substitute for skilled management, and it must be remembered that they depict only a series of estimates which appear to represent good means of measurement at the time the budget is established. If conditions change, management should not feel that the budget is a straitjacket and that it cannot be revised. All too often, the budget becomes an inhibiting factor, and management is afraid to take any risks for fear of not meeting the budget.

If the company is of any size, the accomplishment of the preliminary steps in implementing a budget takes more than a year. This time lag often causes the budgetary program to lose top management's support because the results are too long in materializing. Frequently, executives lose interest before the results are apparent. Departmental supervisors may also lose interest because, after hearing about the budget, they see nothing further for months. They may conclude that the matter has been dropped.

A budgetary program needs the cooperation and participation of all members of management. Faithful, but not mindless, adherence to and enthusiasm for the budget plan by top management is the basis for the success of budgets. Too often, a budgetary plan fails because top management has paid only lip service to its execution. Often no one but the person who made the budget knows much about it or has much interest in it. In addition, the accounting techniques of budgeting are often emphasized without giving much attention to

EXHIBIT 12–8

HART COMPANY
Factory Overhead Budget
For the Year Ending December 31, 19X2
(at budgeted capacity of 179,600 direct labor-hours)

Indirect material.	$ 94,000	
Indirect labor.	75,000	
Depreciation—variable portion	25,000	
Total variable overhead		$194,000
Insurance	$ 50,000	
Depreciation—fixed portion	125,000	
Supervision	80,000	
Total fixed overhead		255,000
Total factory overhead		$449,000

($449,000 ÷ 179,600 hours = $2.50 per direct labor-hour)

EXHIBIT 12–9

HART COMPANY
Cost of Goods Sold Budget
For the Year Ending December 31, 19X2

Direct materials used (from Exhibit 12–5)	$ 243,261.00
Direct labor (from Exhibit 12–7)	718,400.00
Factory overhead (from Exhibit 12–8)	449,000.00
Total manufacturing costs	$1,410,661.00
Add finished goods, January 1, 19X2 (per accounting records)	53,698.00
	$1,464,359.00
Less finished goods, December 19X2 (see below)	56,847.50
Cost of goods sold	$1,407,511.50

	Unit cost	Product A Units	Product A Amount	Product B Units	Product B Amount	Product C Units	Product C Amount
Direct Material AA2	$1.10	2	$ 2.20	2	$ 2.20	2	$ 2.20
Direct Material BB3	2.25	3	6.75	3	6.75	3	6.75
Direct labor	4.00	3	12.00	5	20.00	10	40.00
Factory overhead	2.50	3	7.50	5	12.50	10	25.00
			$28.45		$41.45		$73.95

	Units	Unit cost	Total amount
Ending balance:			
Product A	100	$28.45	$ 2,845.00
Product B	500	41.45	20,725.00
Product C	450	73.95	33,277.50
			$56,847.50

the human factors. For example, the task of educating personnel about the important benefits of the budgeting process is often ignored. In addition, management often fails to realize that, since the natural reaction to control and criticism is resistance and self-defense, the budget must be sold.

Because budgets set goals against which to measure people, they are naturally complained about. A budget is one of the few evaluation tools that is set in writing and is concrete. One cause of friction between budget and production personnel is the difference in outlook and background. Budgets emphasize past performance, and this is not usually the emphasis of production personnel who are concerned with the day-to-day situation, not the future or the past. If factory personnel are only interested in the short run, and the budget staff gives the impression that the short run is not crucial, then trouble naturally arises.

Narrow viewpoint.   In addition, the manner in which budget records are administered often fosters a narrow viewpoint. Management may decide to forward to each supervisor only the budget for his or her department. This encourages the philosophy that if every supervisor worries about his or her own department, there will be no trouble in the plant; further, each supervisor is held responsible only for his or her individual cost center. An important point is overlooked: a company is something different from the sum of its individual parts. The various segments of the company operate in a certain relationship to each other. These relationships are important and should not be overlooked.

Unrealistic budgets

Another frequent problem with budgeting is that top management often has the opinion that budgets can be used to increase production. Even if this assumption is not expressed overtly to the employees, it often filters down to them in very subtle ways—for example, when the budget is kept purposely tight so that it is almost impossible to meet. The unrealistic budget does not work and it breeds resentment. Supervisors resent this practice for it places both workers and supervisors in a situation in which they can never succeed. This practice also implies that the company does not believe the supervisor's own desire to do a good job is sufficient to meet a reasonable budget. Budget personnel often simplistically believe that employees are lazy and will do as little work as possible and that the production personnel are too liberal with the workers. Finance people need to realize that it is easier to solve problems with figures than it is to deal with individual employees.

Often when a budget *is* met, a new higher goal is set in the next budget. Such constantly increasing pressure for greater production often leads to long-run negative results. People living under conditions of tension tend to become suspicious of every new move management makes to increase production. People can stand just so much pressure; once that point is passed, it becomes intolerable. To combat such tensions, employees may establish informal groups antagonistic to management, and these groups may be difficult to disband even after the tension dissipates.

Supervisors also feel pressure, but they, in turn, cannot join a group against management because they are a part of it and such a move does not help their chances of promotion. Many supervisors avoid the use of the term "budget" with their employees because they believe the price of mentioning budgets is high; they may be faced with a resentful work group. Since budgets place employees under restrictions and control, the natural reaction is resistance and self-defense. The word "budget" often represents a penny-pinching, negative brand of managerial pressure. Budgets often arouse fear, resentment, hostility, and aggression among employees—all of which may lead to decreased production. Many supervisors try to combat such resentment and fear by translating budget results into informal shop language.

Even though front-line supervisors usually do not use budgets freely with their employees, top management usually use budgets frequently and strongly on the supervisors below them. This forces the supervisors into positions where they receive pressure from above but cannot pass it to the people below them. They thus often release much of this pressure by blaming unfavorable variances on the budget. They may spend more time thinking up good reasons for exceeding it than they do trying to keep within the budget. Under such circumstances, budgets and budgetary accountants are likely to be unpopular not only with supervisors but with all employees. On the other hand, employees may bottle up the pressure and make it a part of themselves. Constant tension leads to frustration; a frustrated person cannot operate as effectively as he or she would normally.

Management needs to guard against immediate increases in efficiency that hinder long-range growth in employee relations. Applying too much pressure to increase efficiency generates forces which, in the long run, decrease efficiency. The better approach is to involve the employees and thereby weaken the forces which tend to decrease efficiency.

Budget personnel think budgets are extremely important because they provide a goal, a motivating force, for production employees. Budgetary accountants often find it hard to understand why factory executives do not think highly of budgets, since they are designed to help individuals improve. The problem is that budget personnel are constantly encouraged to find things that are wrong; often the success of the budgetary accountant depends on finding errors and deficiencies in the plant and singling out the guilty party. Thus, the budget places the accounting staff in a position of achieving success only by finding fault with production personnel. Clearly, such constant faultfinding will alienate production personnel.

Reporting shortcomings

Another factor causing misunderstandings is the method used by budget personnel to report shortcomings. Budget personnel cannot take the shortest route and go directly to the supervisor involved. In fact, it may be a violation of policy for staff personnel to go directly to line personnel. Also, the budgetary accountant wants his or her immediate supervisor to know he or she found errors and is doing a good job. Thus, information about shortcomings is relayed up the line and down into the factory line structure. This places factory supervisors in an embarrassing position because they know that their superiors are aware of the error and also that they have placed their superiors in an undesirable position. This failure may also be published in budget reports and circulated through many top management channels. To compound the embarrassment, the reasons for the unfavorable variance are often not published along with the results. If any reason is given, it is the budget personnel's reason, not the line supervisor's. The budget staff may say the cause is excessive labor costs, but the supervisor also wants to explain why there were excessive labor costs and may feel frustrated that this cannot be done.

The effects of failure on people are significant. Some factory supervisors do not feel failure when singled out because of errors; these are employees who are not extremely concerned about doing a good job. Other supervisors highly interested in their work may suffer unduly when deficiencies in their departments are pointed out. These factory supervisors tend to lose interest in their work and confidence in themselves. They may refuse to try new methods if they fear failure. They may also develop a tendency to blame others and to be overcritical of the work of others. The method of reporting unfavorable variances needs to be examined because of its differing effects on supervisors.

PARTICIPATIVE BUDGETING PROCESS

Since a crucial problem in budget administration is acceptance of the budgets by employees, more companies should experiment with a participative budgeting process. Participative budgeting is the practice of allowing individuals who are accountable for activities and performance under a budget to participate in the decisions by which that budget is established. The people directly involved in certain functions will thus have more understanding of that particular function and its needs. In addition to the better operation of the company, a real value of participation at all management levels is psychological. Research in motivational theory has shown that it is in the organization's best interest to attempt to meet the esteem and self-actualization needs of participants by making tasks more challenging and giving individuals a greater sense of responsibility. There is evidence that participation in budget making in connection with the comparison and reviewing process may lead to increased goal acceptance. Participation in the budgetary control system is an attempt to get the participants ego involved, not just task involved.

Participative budgeting increases the probability that involved individuals will accept budget goals as their own and become personally committed to the control system. Resistance from employees can be reduced, since employees are more likely to believe that the budget is theirs and not just management's.

The budget's influence on motivation may be greater if the budget is not imposed but accepted. Many companies have found that the best way to gain acceptance is to have all supervisors participate in making the budgets that affect them. If goals are internalized by the individuals responsible for meeting them, the chances for success are higher. Thus, this budgeting technique provides the challenge and sense of responsibility needed to effectively motivate individuals. Participative budgeting encourages the accomplishment of objectives because the needs, goals, and attitudes of the individuals subject to the budget are considered. Improved morale and greater initiative are often the result of a high degree of participation.

Often management wants employees to believe that it solicits their suggestions when, in fact, it desires only false participation. Such insincere attitudes soon filter down the line to the employees; employees strongly resent being led to believe that they are assisting in the budgetary process when they really are not. This false participative approach is no better than imposing the budget. Management may realize that halfhearted acceptance is risky. To ensure its position, management may request the signatures of the acceptors so they cannot later deny that they accepted the budget, but this does little good.

While participative budgeting offers substantial improvement over more traditional and authoritarian practices, letting employees participate in the budgeting process may not be the best solution for all companies. Participation will not work in all budget situations because a number of psychological variables that can lead to decreased or increased performance enter in. While participation should be directed toward the achievement of organizationally desirable goals, the freedom of managers with participative budgeting in establishing their own budgets can have negative results for the organization. Often in budget development and other decisions, employees use their influence to arrive at a goal that is less demanding. Managers can use participation to build "organizational slack" into their budget by overestimating costs and underestimating revenues. *Slack* can be defined as the difference between the total resources available to the firm and the total resources necessary to maintain organizational activities. Involved individuals are motivated to build in slack because, by gaining extra resources in the budget, they have more flexibility in achieving such personal goals as relaxation, while at the same time meeting objectives. While some slack is seen as desirable by behavioral scientists since it allows the blending of personal and organizational goals, excessive slack is clearly detrimental to the best interests of an organization. The problem can be overcome if management establishes procedures for in-depth reviews during budget development.

Participative budgeting's influence on aspiration levels is another possible limitation. By participating, individuals accept budgeted objectives as their own aspiration levels or personal goals. The interaction between aspiration levels and actual performance can result in behavior that is either desirable or undesirable. This depends upon the difficulty of achieving budgeted performance, the nature of the task, and the personality of the individual. An atmosphere should be created in which individuals will be encouraged to continually set and meet high personal performance standards. Repeatedly achieving easy goals or continually failing to attain goals that are too high can adversely influence aspiration levels and performance.

Management must also ask itself whether the personality and history of the employees is conducive to participation. Participative budgeting is not an all or nothing proposition. Instead, companies can and do differ dramatically in both the amount and form of participation and influence they afford their operating managers in the budget- or target-setting process. Because the budgeting process differs so much from the tasks normally performed in manufacturing operations, line personnel often prefer to relinquish budget responsibilities to the budget staff. Their attitude is simply that they do not wish to be bothered with budgets.

Differences in managers' budget-oriented behavior also affect the outcome; if managers give the impression that they value the time spent in planning, subordinates will be more willing to prepare accurate forecasts.

The operation of a company's budgeting system provides the opportunity for much interaction between various management levels. Before a program of participative budgeting is started, top management must ask itself whether it is willing to be flexible and accept refined decisions jointly made by employees and low and middle level managers.

Basic constraints. By taking part in developing the budget, individuals become aware of the reasons for budget constraints. Another approach that may help overcome the inability of the budget staff to obtain line participation in developing budgets is to give employees a framework of basic constraints in which they are to work before preparation of the budget begins. Management objectives and goals should be explained, as should any important factors expected in the future to affect operations. The intelligence and human dignity of employees at lower organizational levels should never be discredited. If these employees do not understand and accept company objectives, they are less willing to attempt to meet organization goals.

SUMMARY

The true success of any budgetary system depends on its acceptance by all company members affected by the budget. If participation is conducted properly, it should build acceptance of the budget by those responsible for meeting the budget. Accountants should not view their function as primarily one of criticizing the actions of others; instead, they should demonstrate that they are willing to revise the budget whenever experience indicates that this is necessary. The accountant should try to separate the budget from the person involved and look for the cause of or reason for unfavorable performance. Certainly the administration of the budget must not be rigid, since changed conditions may require revisions in the budget.

For the budget to be effective, those individuals being measured by the budget should know beforehand the norm used for evaluation so that they have a guide when incurring expenditures. The budgeting process allows for thorough review of operations. However, there is little value in merely determining that a difference between actual and budgeted performance exists. Instead, the true value of a budgetary program comes from identifying the causes of the variances. When used properly, budgets pave the way to higher morale and a better working relationship among employees and management.

IMPORTANT TERMS AND CONCEPTS

Rolling (continuous) budgets
Fixed and variable (flexible) budgets
Trend analysis

Correlation analysis
Participative budgeting process
Slack

REVIEW QUESTIONS

1. Indicate some actions that management can take in overcoming human problems in budgeting.
2. Why is it important that top management become involved in the budgeting process?
3. Under what conditions do you think a fixed budget would be appropriate? What advantages does a variable budget offer that a fixed budget does not?
4. What abilities does the budget director need to perform effectively?
5. Discuss the rolling budget approach and indicate any advantages that you see.
6. Discuss the membership of the budget committee and their functions.
7. List the budgets a company should prepare as part of a master budget plan.
8. Indicate some internal and external factors that influence the sales forecast.
9. How is the number of units to produce determined? How is this shown on the production budget?
10. What information is needed to prepare a direct-materials-purchases budget and a direct labor budget?
11. What is the objective of budgeting? Justify the use of budgets in a period of uncertainty.
12. How can budgets be viewed as a means of coordination?
13. Discuss several advantages of budgets, both for internal and external purposes.
14. Discuss several limitations of budgets.
15. What dangers are inherent in unrealistic budgets?
16. How can the reporting of variances cause further breakdowns in the working relationship of employees and supervisors? Suggest a better approach for reporting variances.
17. Discuss the strengths as well as the weaknesses of participative budgeting.
18. Why do some managers believe that the purpose of budgetary control has already been accomplished after a new budget for the next period has been prepared?

19. Compute the number of units of finished goods management expects to have on March 1 if 75,000 units are to be manufactured in March, finished goods ending inventory of 16,000 units is desired, and sales are forecast to be 69,000 units in March.

EXERCISES

E12–1. Production requirements

Budgeted data for the Irma McHood Company indicate that 25,000 pounds must remain in the ending inventory of direct materials. Beginning direct materials inventory is expected to contain 31,000 pounds. The expected cost per unit of direct materials is $0.75 per pound. The expected total cost of direct materials purchases is $150,000.

Required:

From the information, compute the production requirements in terms of pounds of direct materials.

E12–2. Quantity to order

Management of the Mary Miller Company asks that you determine the number of gallons of Material RK2 to order for March delivery. According to the production schedule, 5,500 gallons of Material RK2 will be used in January; 6,150 gallons in February; and 6,580 gallons in March.

The material ledger card showed 3,500 gallons in inventory on January 1, 6,000 gallons on order for January delivery, and 6,750 on order for February delivery. Management wants to have an April 1 inventory equal to 90 percent of the January 1 inventory.

Required:

a. Determine the number of gallons to order for March delivery.
b. Determine the estimated number of gallons on hand on March 1.

E12–3. Budget preparation

Bristol, Inc. budgets sales for 1,000 units to be sold for $50 each. Direct material of ½ pound of B2 and 2 pounds of G8 will be required. Cost of direct material of B2 is expected to be $2 per pound, while G8 is expected to be $0.70 per pound. Direct labor of 2.5 hours is required per unit; the direct labor rate is expected to be $5. The factory overhead application rate is 80 percent of direct labor dollars. Management indicates that inventories are to be as follows:

	January 1, 19X1	January 31, 19X1
Finished goods	170 units ($4,250)	200 units
Direct material—B2	100 pounds ($200)	185 pounds
Direct material—G8	185 pounds ($129.50)	165 pounds

LIFO inventory costing is used.

Required:

Prepare the following:
a. Direct-materials-purchases budget.

b. Direct labor budget.
c. Cost of goods sold budget.

E12-4. Budget preparation

Bailey Company provides you with the following data to be used in preparing budgets for the next quarter ending September 30, 19X1:

		Inventory levels in units	
Products	Expected unit sales	Actual July 1	Desired September 30
D............	1,000	400	380
E............	580	165	170
F............	600	140	155

Each product requires the following units of material and labor:

Product	Material AX @ $2 per pound	Material B4 @ $3 per pound	Direct labor @ $5 per hour
D.............	3 pounds	8 pounds	2 hours
E.............	2 pounds	6 pounds	4 hours
F.............	4 pounds	10 pounds	3 hours

Inventories at the beginning of the quarter and desired quantities at the end of the quarter are as follows:

	July 1 (pounds)	(dollars)	September 30 (pounds)
Material AX	1,820	$ 3,640	2,000
Material B4	3,800	11,400	4,000

Required:

Prepare the following:
a. Production budget.
b. Direct-materials-purchases budget. (Also determine the cost of material used.)
c. Direct labor budget.

PROBLEMS

P12-1. Materials purchases budget

Lawrence Alexander, Inc. manufactures three products (X, Y, and Z). Each product requires different quantities of material input. Planned unit production of each product in 19X1 is 10,000 for X; 40,000 for Y; and 30,000 for Z. The direct material requirements for one unit of each product are summarized below:

	Unit material requirements			
Product	A	B	C	D
X.................	3	—	2	—
Y.................	1	1	—	4
Z.................	2	2	1	3

Beginning and desired ending inventory as well as unit costs are as follows for each direct material:

Inventory in units:
January 1, 19X1	20,000	5,000	3,000	10,000
December 31, 19X1	8,000	1,000	6,000	30,000
19X1 unit cost	$4.00	$7.00	$8.00	$2.00

Direct material unit prices as budgeted are the delivered unit costs experienced.

Required:

Prepare a direct-materials-purchases budget for 19X1.

P12–2.   Preparation of five production budgets

Grady Company manufactures and sells only one product, chemical B8. The finished goods inventory on May 1 costs $861,800 and contains 13,900 units. The finished goods inventory on May 31 is expected to contain 15,600 units. The company will sell its finished products for $80 per unit, and 85,000 units of finished goods are expected to be sold during the month. Only one kind of direct material is used to produce each finished good. Six gallons of direct material are needed to produce each unit of finished goods. Beginning direct material inventory on May 1 is expected to be 115,000 gallons, while ending direct material inventory is expected to be 113,800 gallons, and direct material is expected to continue costing $2.20 per gallon. FIFO inventory costing is used.

Two hours of direct labor are needed to produce each unit. Direct labor workers are paid $12 per hour.

Variable factory overhead at the budgeted level of operations is expected to amount to $1,184,840, while fixed factory overhead is expected to be $1 million. Factory overhead is applied to work in process on the basis of direct labor dollars.

Required:

Prepare the following:

a. Sales budget.
b. Production budget.
c. Direct-materials-purchases budget.
d. Direct labor budget.
e. Cost of goods sold budget.

P12–3.   Preparation of five production budgets

The budget committee of Econo Company provides the following information. The budget period is the year ending December 31, 19X4. The company manufactures only one chemical product, which it sells for $100 per gallon.

A total of 10,000 gallons of finished goods is expected to be sold during 19X4. Finished goods expected to be on hand on January 1, 19X4 total 2,500 gallons with 2,800 gallons on hand on December 31, 19X4. FIFO inventory costing is used.

Direct materials expected to be on hand on January 1, 19X4 total 1,000 gallons; direct materials expected to be on hand on December 31, 19X4 total 1,200 gallons. Only one kind of direct material is used to produce the product; 1.5 gallons of direct material are needed to produce each gallon of finished goods, due to evaporation. Direct materials are expected to continue to cost $20 per gallon during 19X4.

Five hours of direct labor are required to manufacture each product, and direct labor workers are paid $5.10 per hour.

Factory overhead is applied to work in process on the basis of direct labor-hours. Variable factory overhead at the expected level of operations is expected to amount to $150,075. Fixed overhead is expected to be $110,000.

The finished goods inventory on January 1, 19X4 amounts to $199,800.

Required:

Prepare the following budgets:

a. Sales budget.
b. Production budget.
c. Direct-materials-purchases budget.
d. Direct labor budget.
e. Cost of goods sold budget.

P12–4. Conflict of policy on production budget preparation

Gloria, Inc. produces shirts. When the plant is operating at 90 percent of capacity, it can produce 80,000 shirts in one month. At this level, which is considered full capacity, 45 hours are being used per workweek. The company tries to follow a policy of no personnel layoffs by adjusting the hours in the workweek to maintain a constant work force. When the workweek is reduced to 40 hours, 72,000 shirts are produced monthly; at 35 hours, only 64,000 shirts are produced.

Maximum storage capacity for finished goods inventory is 40,000 shirts. A policy of always having a minimum of 10,000 shirts on hand for special orders is followed.

The sales forecast for next year is as follows:

January	72,000	July	88,000
February	46,000	August	80,000
March	62,000	September	72,000
April	66,000	October	90,000
May	72,000	November	92,000
June	76,000	December	62,000

Beginning finished goods inventory for next year will consist of 10,000 shirts, and a supply of 20,000 shirts on hand at year-end is desired.

Required:

a. Complete a monthly unit production budget for next year indicating monthly beginning and ending inventory balances assuming that:
    (1) 72,000 shirts are produced monthly.
    (2) 80,000 shirts are produced monthly.
b. Using each of the production budgets prepared in a, indicate the months in which (1) management policy, (2) storage capacity, and (3) availability of product to meet sales demand are violated.
c. Prepare monthly production and sales budgets that do not violate any of the three factors mentioned in b. The workweek can be increased only in even increments of five hours from one month to the next because of layoff policies.

P12–5. Territorial sales and production budgets

Sam Wise Company plans expansion into the northern territory after experiencing success in the southern territory. The company forecasts northern territory sales based on southern territory forecasted sales data, as shown on page 478:

Forecasted sales data for the southern territory for the quarter ending March 31, 19X2

	Product 1		Product 2		Product 3	
	Quantity	Unit sales price	Quantity	Unit sales price	Quantity	Unit sales price
January	90	$55	1,140	$10	790	$7.00
February	110	56	970	9	760	6.00
March	100	52	990	9	640	6.50

Management plans to introduce only Product 1 and Product 2 in the northern territory. Forecasts of the sales quantities are based on a percentage of the southern market for each product, as shown:

	Product 1		Product 2	
	Percentage of southern (percent)	Unit sales price	Percentage of southern (percent)	Unit sales price
January	60%	$55	10%	$7
February.	50	57	15	7
March.	50	57	18	8

On January 1, 19X2, an inventory count revealed 32 finished units of Product 1; 475 units of Product 2; and 130 units of Product 3. Management desires an ending inventory on January 31, 19X2 of 40 units of Product 1; 315 units of Product 2; and 150 units of Product 3. Material and labor requirements for each of the products are as follows:

	Product 1	Product 2	Product 3
Material 128	2 pounds	4 pounds	6 pounds
Material 314	3 gallons	2 gallons	4 gallons
Direct labor.	2 hours	4 hours	3 hours

Material 128 costs $1.75 per pound, while Material 314 is expected to cost $2.10 per gallon. Direct labor workers are under a union contract which specifies that they receive $4 per hour. On January 1, 19X2, an inventory count showed that there were 1,000 pounds of Material 128 and 1,575 gallons of Material 314. Management desires an ending inventory of each of these materials, which represents 25 percent of the material needed for the next month's sales.

Required:

a. Prepare sales budgets for the first quarter for each territory. (Round to the nearest dollar.)
b. Prepare a production budget for January only for both territories combined.
c. Prepare a direct-materials-purchases budget for January only for both territories combined.
d. Prepare a direct labor budget for January only for both territories combined.

P12–6.   Preparation of various budgets (AICPA adapted)

Scarborough Corporation manufactures and sells two products. Thingone and Thingtwo. In July 19X1, Scarborough's budget department gathered the following data to project sales and budget requirements for 19X2:

	19X2 projected sales	
Product	Units	Price
Thingone.	60,000	$ 70
Thingtwo	40,000	$100

	19X2 inventories (units)	
Product	Expected January 1, 19X2	Desired December 31, 19X2
Thingone.	20,000	25,000
Thingtwo	8,000	9,000

To produce one unit of Thingone and Thingtwo, the following direct materials are used:

		Amount used per unit	
Direct material	Unit	Thingone	Thingtwo
A . . . . . pounds		4	5
B . . . . . pounds		2	3
C . . . . . each		—	1

Projected data for 19X2 with respect to direct materials are as follows:

Direct material	Anticipated purchase price	Expected inventories January 1, 19X2	Desired inventories December 31, 19X2
A	$8	32,000 pounds	36,000 pounds
B	$5	29,000 pounds	32,000 pounds
C	$3	6,000 each	7,000 each

Projected direct labor requirements for 19X2 and rates are as follows:

Product	Hours per unit	Rate per hour
Thingone	2	$3
Thingtwo	3	$4

Overhead is applied at the rate of $2 per direct labor-hour.

Required:

Based upon the above projections and budget requirements for 19X2 for Thingone and Thingtwo, prepare the following budgets for 19X2:

a. Sales budget (in dollars).
b. Production budget (in units).
c. Direct-materials-purchases budget (in quantities).
d. Direct materials purchases budget (in dollars).
e. Direct labor budget (in dollars).
f. Budgeted finished goods inventory on December 31, 19X2 (in dollars).

CASES

C12–1. Importance of planning and identification of problems (CMA adapted)

George Mai invented a special valve for application in the paper manufacturing industry. At the time of its development, he could not find any company willing to manufacture the valve. As a result, he formed the Maiton Company to manufacture and sell the valve.

The Maiton Company grew quite slowly. George Mai found it difficult to persuade paper companies to try this new valve designed and manufactured by an unknown company. However, the company has prospered and now has a number of smaller paper companies as regular customers. In fact, there is increasing interest of a number of large paper companies because of the very good results with the valve.

The size of the potential new customers and their probable needs over the next several years will dramatically increase the sales of the valve. George Mai was an engineer for a large company prior to starting his company. His business experience is limited to the activities of Maiton Company.

Required:

a. Explain why it is important for George Mai to introduce business planning and budgeting activities into his company at this time.

b. Identify three major problems that probably would be disclosed as the Maiton Company attempts to prepare a five-year plan. Explain why you selected the problems identified.

C12–2. Behavioral aspects of budgeting

Thelma Ezell, Inc. is a small, dynamic, and very successful electronics company. In its first year of operations, management decided the accounting system must keep pace with the rapid changes that were taking place in the firm; thus, the system has become complex. The original purpose of accounting was to provide profitability data for use by top management, since the major concerns of the company were survival and preparation for the future. If the company proved successful, the original members of the management team would receive sizable rewards in promotions and increases in stock ownership. As the company began to grow, however, the reporting system changed since there were fewer and fewer direct personal benefits from increases in corporate profits.

In the last few years, the focus has been on greater accomplishment. As a result, the accounting system has developed another set of reports which emphasize budget aspects rather than departmental profitability. These reports include the standard, or goal, to be used as a measuring stick of performance and the actual results of operation. Since management has found that standards are more acceptable when operating personnel participate in their establishment, the division manager being evaluated is allowed sufficient voice in setting the standards. Budgets are determined at the division manager level and are discussed and revised until each division manager is satisfied with the budget for his or her division. Then each division manager subdivides this budget among the various departments.

Division managers are concerned primarily with their overall performance because they are judged on whether they meet the aggregate goals. How these goals are achieved is the division manager's job. Generally, division managers believe that it is as bad to be under target as to be over target. If the division is under target, either the manager was too optimistic in the projection or the projection had "fat" in it; if over target, the project was either incorrect or new, unplanned costs have appeared.

An insight into this budgeting process can be gained by examining a specific division. Jay Hugg's report at midyear shows his departments' goals and expenditures have been:

Department	Goal	Expenditures	Variance
A	$100,000	$110,000	$10,000 unfavorable
B	100,000	90,000	10,000 favorable
C	100,000	100,000	—
	$300,000	$300,000	$ —

The original division budget was $600,000, equally divided among three departments. Jay is concerned that Department A has exceeded its goal, but Department B has offset this variance, and the division as a whole is on target. Jay is considering taking $10,000 out of B's budget and transferring it to A's.

Required:

a. Briefly, what are your reactions to this budgeting system?
b. Would you advise the division manager to make this trade-off of $10,000 between departments?
c. Assume that at midyear the entire division's budget must be cut.
   (1) How would you advise Jay to pass the cut along to subordinate departments?
   (2) To what extent should human factors be considered in this decision?
   (3) Discuss the order in which specific budget items should be cut.
   (4) What do you think of a "big meat-axe" approach that dictates an arbitrary cut of X percent across the board?

C12–3. Evaluating the budgeting process (CMA adapted)

Springfield Corporation operates on a calender-year basis. It begins the annual budgeting process in late August when the president establishes targets for total dollar sales and net income before taxes for the next year.

The sales target is given to the Marketing Department where the marketing manager formulates a sales budget by product line in both units and dollars. From this budget, sales quotas by product line in units and dollars are established for each of the corporation's sales districts.

The marketing manager also estimates the cost of the marketing activities required to support the target sales volume, and prepares a tentative marketing expense budget.

The executive vice president uses the sales and profit targets, the sales budget by product line, and the tentative marketing expense budget to determine the dollar amounts which can be devoted to manufacturing and corporate office expense. The executive vice president prepares the budget for corporate expenses and forwards to the Production Department the product line sales budget in units and the total dollar amount which can be devoted to manufacturing.

The production manager meets with the factory managers to develop a manufacturing plan which will produce the required units when needed within the cost constraints set by the executive vice president. The budgeting process usually comes to a halt at this point because the Production Department does not consider the financial resources allocated to be adequate.

When this standstill occurs, the vice president of finance, the executive vice president, the marketing manager, and the production manager meet to determine the final budgets for each of the areas. This normally results in a modest increase in the total amount available for manufacturing costs, while the marketing expense and corporate office expense budgets are cut. The total sales and net income figures proposed by the president are seldom changed. Although the participants are seldom pleased with the compromise, these budgets are final. Each executive then develops new, detailed budgets for the operations in his or her area.

None of the areas has achieved its budget in recent years. Sales often run below the target. When budgeted sales are not achieved, each area is expected to cut costs so that the president's profit target can still be met. However, the profit target is seldom met because costs are not cut enough. In fact, costs often run above the original budget in all functional areas. The president is disturbed that Springfield has not been able to meet the sales and profit targets. He hired a consultant with considerable experience with companies in Springfield's industry. The consultant reviewed the budgets for the past four years. He concluded that the product line sales budgets were reasonable, and that the cost and expense budgets were adequate for the budgeted sales and production levels.

Required:

a. Discuss how the budgeting process as employed by Springfield Corporation contributes to the failure to achieve the president's sales and profit targets.
b. Suggest how Springfield Corporation's budgeting process could be revised to correct the problems.
c. Should the functional areas be expected to cut their costs when sales volume falls below budget? Explain your answer.

C12–4.   Planning process (CMA adapted)

RV Industries manufactures and sells recreational vehicles. The company has eight divisions strategically located near major markets. Each division has a sales force and two to four manufacturing plants. These divisions operate as autonomous profit centers responsible for purchasing, operations, and sales.

John Collins, the Corporate Controller, described the divisional performance measurement system as follows. "We allow the divisions to control the entire operation from the purchase of raw materials to the sale of the product. We at corporate headquarters only get involved in strategic decisions, such as developing new product lines. Each division is responsible for meeting its market needs by providing the right products at a low cost on a timely basis. Frankly, the divisions need to focus on cost control, delivery, and services to customers to become more profitable.

"While we give the divisions considerable autonomy, we watch their monthly income statements very closely. Each month's actual performance is compared with the budget in considerable detail. If the actual sales or contribution margin is more than 4 or 5 percent below the budget, we jump on the division people immediately. I might add that we don't have much trouble getting their attention. All of the management people at the plant and division level can add appreciably to their annual salaries with bonuses if actual net income is considerably greater than budget."

The budgeting process begins in August when division sales managers, after consulting with their sales personnel, estimate sales for the next calendar year. These estimates are sent to plant managers who use the sales forecasts to prepare production estimates. At the plants, production statistics, including direct material quantities, are developed by operating personnel. Using the statistics prepared by the operating personnel, the plant accounting staff determines costs and prepares the plant's budgeted variable cost of goods sold and other plant expenses for each month of the coming calendar year.

In October, each division's accounting staff combines plant budgets with sales estimates and adds additional division expenses. "After the divisional management is satisfied with the budget," said Collins, "I visit each division to go over their budget and make sure it is in line with corporate strategy and projections. I really emphasize the sales forecasts because of the volatility in demand for our product. For many years, we lost sales to our competitors because we didn't project high enough production and sales, and we couldn't meet the market demand. More recently, we were caught with large excess inventory when the bottom dropped out of the market for recreational vehicles.

"I generally visit all eight divisions during the first two weeks in November. After that, the division budgets are combined and reconciled by my staff, and they are ready for approval by the Board of Directors in early December. The board seldom questions the budget.

"One complaint we've had from plant and division management is that they are penalized for circumstances beyond their control. For example, they failed to predict the recent sales decline. As a result, they didn't make their budget and, of course, they received no bonuses. However, I point out that they are well rewarded when they exceed their budget. Furthermore, they provide most of the information for the budget, so it's their own fault if the budget is too optimistic."

Required:

a. Identify and explain the biases the corporate management of RV Industries should expect in the communication of budget estimates by its division and plant personnel.

b. What sources of information can the top management of RV Industries use to monitor the budget estimates prepared by its divisions and plant?

c. What services could top management of RV Industries offer the divisions to help them in their budget development, without appearing to interfere with the division budget decisions?

d. Top management of RV Industries is attempting to decide whether it should get more involved in the budget process. Identify and explain the variables management needs to consider in reaching its decision.

C12–5. Participative budgeting

Realizing that in designing budgeting systems, cost accountants are often faced with the problem of deciding how much and what form of participation operating managers should be allowed in setting budgets, you are conducting a survey of various industries to gain an insight into budgeting procedures. After visiting four companies in the state of Maryland, you compile the following notes concerning their participative budgeting procedures.

In Company A, top management sets operating budgets using information generally available at the time. General managers of each operating division are usually not consulted when divisional earning targets are established because top management believes it has all the relevant data. Aggregate divisional sales forecasts are derived from the earnings targets. Division general managers and their marketing, finance, and production managers formulate their labor, material, and other production requirements and order forecasts from these estimates. These production budgets and forecasts are used to prepare each division's detailed operating plan. The president indicates that this procedure is best because fewer hours are spent in budgeting, and divisional managers are freed to spend their time in day-to-day operations.

In Company B, divisional general managers establish operating budgets for their divisions. However, before they set these budgets, the production manager for each division obtains detailed forecasts for usage of direct material, direct labor, and direct factory overhead by department from each department manager. Production managers review the forecasts submitted by department managers and adjust these where they deem appropriate. Adjusted forecasts are then submitted to the division's general manager for consideration and use in setting operation budgets for the division.

In Company C, a large manufacturing company, cost center managers work closely with department managers in preparing initial forecasts for their cost centers for the coming year. Then, department managers bring their cost center managers together for a series of group meetings to help set departmental goals. Each cost center manager presents an initial forecast for a joint evaluation by all of the cost center managers present and the department manager. Together, they make any necessary adjustments to meet overall company goals. Group target-setting meetings are also held at the various management levels. Finally, the budgets set in these meetings are compiled in an overall operating plan.

Management of Company D devotes much of its time in late October and November to preparing budget proposals. Weekends find many of the managers in group meetings trying to meet deadlines in the budgeting procedure. One division manager and his immediate subordinates refer to this season as "management's folly." Taking this as a cue, department managers in this division often refer to the efforts at forecasting dollar outlays in such terms as "playing with funny money." Budgets in this department are often unrelated to actual expenditures and serve no control purpose. Funds are transferred from one account to another when it appears that certain budgeted expenses are far less than actual results. Also, at year-end, expenses are charged off to other expense classifications to prevent significant unfavorable variances in certain categories.

Required:

a. Define the term "participative budgeting."
b. Discuss two advantages of participative budgeting.
c. Discuss the problems and limitations of participative budgeting.
d. Discuss the budgeting procedures used by each of the four companies.

C12–6.   Evaluation of budget procedure (CMA adapted)

Clarkson Company is a large multidivision firm with several plants in each division. A comprehensive budgeting system is used for planning operations and measuring performance. The annual budgeting process commences in August, five months prior to the beginning of the fiscal year. At this time, the division managers submit proposed budgets for sales, production and inventory levels, and expenses. Capital expenditure requests also are formalized at this time. The expense budgets include direct labor and all overhead items, which are separated into fixed and variable components. Direct materials are budgeted separately in developing the production and inventory schedules.

The expense budgets for each division are developed from its plant's results, as measured by the percent of variation from an adjusted budget in the first six months of the current year and from a target expense reduction percentage established by the corporation.

To determine plant percentages, the plant budget for the just completed half-year period is revised to take into account changes in operating procedures and costs outside the control of plant management (e.g., labor wage rate changes, product style changes, etc.). The difference between this revised budget and actual expenses is the controllable variance, and is expressed as a percentage of actual expenses. This percentage is added (if unfavorable) to the corporate target expense reduction percentage. A favorable plant variance percentage is subtracted from the corporate target. If a plant had a 2 percent unfavorable controllable variance and the corporate target reduction was 4 percent, for example, the plant's budget for next year should reflect costs approximately 6 percent below this year's actual costs.

Next year's final budgets for the corporation, the divisions, and the plants are adopted after corporate analysis of the proposed budgets and a careful review with each division manager of the changes made by corporate management. Division profit budgets include allocated corporate costs, and plant profit budgets include allocated division and corporate costs.

Return on assets is used to measure the performance of divisions and plants. The asset base for a division consists of all assets assigned to the division, including its working capital, and an allocated share of corporate assets. For plants, the asset base includes the assets assigned to the plant plus an allocated portion of the division and corporate assets. Recommendations for promotions and salary increases for the executives of the divisions and plants are influenced by how well the actual return on assets compares with the budgeted return on assets.

The plant managers exercise control only over the cost portion of the plant profit budget because the divisions are responsible for sales. Only limited control over plant assets is exercised at the plant level.

The manager of the Dexter plant, a major plant in the Huron division, carefully controls his costs during the first six months so that any improvement appears after the target reduction of expenses is established. He accomplishes this by careful planning and timing of his discretionary expenditures.

During 19X1, the property adjacent to the Dexter plant was purchased by Clarkson Company. This expenditure was not included in the 19X1 capital expenditure budget. Corporate management decided to divert funds from a project at another plant, since the property appeared to be a better long-term investment.

Also during 19X1, Clarkson Company experienced depressed sales. In an attempt to achieve budgeted profit, corporate management announced in August that all plants were to cut their annual expenses by 6 percent. To accomplish this expense reduction, the Dexter plant manager reduced preventive maintenance and postponed needed major repairs. Employees who quit were not replaced unless absolutely necessary. Employee training was postponed whenever possible. The raw materials, supplies, and finished goods inventories were reduced below normal levels.

Required:

a.   Evaluate the budget procedure of Clarkson Company with respect to its effectiveness for planning and controlling operations.

b.   Is the Clarkson Company's use of return on assets to evaluate the performance of the Dexter Plant appropriate? Explain your answer.

c.   Analyze and explain the Dexter Plant Manager's behavior during 19X1.

■ **OUTLINE OF CHAPTER 13** ■

Cash management

Marketing and administrative budgets

Budgeted income statement and balance sheet

Zero-base budgeting

Incremental budgeting

■ **OBJECTIVES OF CHAPTER 13** ■

1. To discuss the goals of cash management.

2. To illustrate the preparation of cash budgets, nonmanufacturing expense budgets, budgeted income statements, and budgeted balance sheets.

3. To compare an appropriation and a business budget.

4. To compare zero-base budgeting and incremental budgeting.

13

Nonmanufacturing budgets, cash management, and forecasted statements

The previous chapter discussed manufacturing budgets and the human factors involved in budgeting. This chapter discusses nonmanufacturing budgets, including the cash budgets, marketing and administrative budgets, capital expenditures budgets, and forecasted statements. As introduced in Chapter 12, budgets can be of utmost importance in internal control. If the budgetary process is properly constructed and followed, it can be the springboard for many other control techniques. Control is implemented if progress toward the company's ultimate goals is measured and compared with budgeted plans at designated intervals.

Budgets also aid in the coordination of the acquisition and use of a company's resources. Since objectives and constraints differ among companies, budgets should be tailor-made for the individual company. For example, some companies may find that zero-base budgeting best fits their needs, while other companies adopt other approaches. Just as the budgeting approach may differ among companies, so do the detail and number of specific budgets prepared. Because the effective management of cash plays such an important role in the survival of a company, much attention should be devoted to this phase of budgeting.

CASH MANAGEMENT

Cash management is very important in today's economy as evidenced by the fact that failure to provide cash resources adequate to meet liabilities as they come due has become one of the most common causes of business failure. Cash management developed originally from the custodial function of cash control and safekeeping; however, the role today has been expanded. Collecting accounts receivable and making cash disbursements have always been functions of cash management, but today cash utilization also involves evaluating the cost of money or its ability to earn a return. While the concepts of cash management are certainly not new in the business environment, important changes in the conduct of business within the last few years have had an impact on its development. Improvements in communications and transportation, for example, have facilitated the movement and clearing of funds, and the expansion of business firms with subsidiaries in foreign countries has increased the problems of controlling and funding corporate operations.

Because of the importance of cash, stockholders and corporate managers spend much time discussing their corporation's cash balance. However, many companies have reserves of cash and near-cash securities which are in excess of any immediate or expected future requirements. These balances exceed an adequate reserve to meet operating needs and emergency requirements. For example, many companies simply maintain a cash balance of, say, $10,000, which they feel to be satisfactory without ever studying their needs. As a result, management usually errs on the side of having too much cash in their bank account rather than too little if no analysis is made of how much cash is needed to support expected activity levels. Companies generally have three objectives in managing their cash, in descending order: security of principal, liquidity of principal, and yield.

Companies are often willing to accept low *yields*, or rates of return, to achieve security and liquidity of principal. Companies are concerned about the liquidity of their investment so that they are able to meet their maturing short-term obligations. *Security of principal* refers to the protection, or assurance, that the obligation will be fulfilled. This conservative policy can be justified if the cash balance is low and is necessary to meet operating needs and emergencies; however, when these cash funds have grown to the point where they are in excess of projected or probable expected uses, this policy should be discontinued.

Centralization of cash

Another cash management problem is that high interest rates cause some companies to reduce their cash balances or to take another look at the age of their receivables, but this is often done piecemeal by individual departments; only in rare instances is there a multidepartmental review of cash functions. This review is critical to better cash management since, in most cases, there are advantages to having cash-handling functions centralized. Centralized management of cash is accomplished by having receipts deposited in centrally controlled bank accounts and making branch disbursements from imprest funds or payroll accounts, which are replenished as needed by cash transfers from central bank accounts. In most cases, the decentralized functions should be limited to the payment of local operating expenses and receipt of payment from local customers. Authority over major capital expenditures should be centralized and so should functions which must be performed for the company as a whole, such as the sale of capital stock, payment of income tax, and payment of dividends. Centralization of cash also prevents the unauthorized expenditure of funds and helps control all bank signing and borrowing. In addition, it is often more *economical* to have accounting and other paperwork related to cash centralized at a single location.

With centralization of cash, a smaller balance is required to support a given level of operation, since it allows cash that would be tied up in numerous local bank balances to be released for investment. In most instances, another good reason for concentrating bank accounts in a few banks is that it enables a corporation to maximize its importance as a customer of a particular bank. It usually is also easier to obtain credit, often on short notice, and financial counsel when needed because the larger the account, the more incentive there is for the banker to be accommodating. Some companies, however, have a policy of maintaining deposit accounts in every bank in communities where they have a business office. They do this to maintain good public relations within the service area, but it is doubtful whether the additional cost of this policy is justified.

Earlier availability of receipts.   Cash management also requires improving cash collections. A review of credit, billing, discount, and collection procedures sometimes discloses opportunities to obtain prompt payments from customers. Slow-paying accounts should be reviewed, for example, to determine the extent to which cash is tied up because of disputes which could be avoided. A review of credit policies should also be made to determine whether the granting of credit is too strict and is cutting down the inflow of cash because sound sales are rejected. Conversely, the credit terms may be too liberal, increasing the number of slow-paying customers and bad-debt losses. Any delay in billing obviously results in delayed receipt of cash, as well; errors in bills mailed to customers also slow down cash receipts. Various techniques, such as highlighting on the invoice the amount of cash saved if the discount is taken, can induce customers to pay promptly. After cash is received by the company, it is available for use earlier if receipts are processed and deposited promptly.

Cash budgets

Management is beginning to realize that cash invested in manufacturing and marketing operations usually earns a markedly higher rate of return than does capital held in cash fund assets. A review of a company's cash management practices may reveal that essentially idle cash is held in bank accounts which are unnecessary. Forecasts of future cash receipts and disbursements, as shown in Exhibit 13–1, can help reduce the cash balance required. Management needs not only detailed short-range forecasts of cash positions but also a

EXHIBIT 13–1

HART COMPANY
Budgeted Statement of Cash Receipts and Disbursements
For Year Ending December 31, 19X2

	January	February	December	Total
Cash receipts from sales				
From November 19X1 sales:				
27% × $125,000	$ 33,750			
From December 19X1 sales:				
30% × $135,000	40,500			
27% × $135,000		$ 36,450		
From January 19X2 sales:				
40% × $145,000	58,000			
30% × $145,000		43,500		
From February 19X2 sales:				
40% × $132,900		53,160		
From October 19X2 sales:				
27% × $183,000			$ 49,410	
From November 19X2 sales:				
30% × $195,250			58,575	
From December 19X2 sales:				
40% × $200,950			80,380	
Total receipts.	$132,250	$133,110	$188,365	$1,860,000
Disbursements:				
Purchases—prior month.	$ 18,000	$ 19,000	$ 22,000	
Fixed costs	50,000	50,000	50,000	
Variable cost:				
January sales:				
5% × $145,000 = $7,250				
30% × $7,250	2,175			
70% × $7,250		5,075		
February sales:				
5% × $132,900 = $6,645				
30% × $6,645		1,994		
November sales:				
5% × $195,250 = $9,763				
70% × $9,763			6,834	
December sales:				
5% × $200,950 = $10,048				
30% × $10,048			3,014	
Property taxes.		60,000		
Dividend.			80,000	
Equipment purchases	50,000			
Total disbursements	$120,175	$136,069	$161,848	$1,827,983
Excess of receipts over disburse-				
ments	$ 12,075	$ (2,959)	$ 26,517	$ 32,017
Beginning cash balance	20,100	32,175	25,600	20,100
Ending cash balance	$ 32,175	$ 29,216	$ 52,117	$ 52,117

long-range cash projection. The long-range projection does not show detailed estimates of revenues and expenses; instead, its purpose is to show whether money can be generated through working capital growth and at what time funds are needed. The effects of corporate growth and long-term trends are portrayed in a long-range cash projection.

A budget showing expected cash receipts and disbursements indicates the months in which cash shortages and excesses are forecasted so that management can take proper action in advance. Cash budgets should usually be prepared for a year in the future, broken down by months. Exhibit 13–1 illustrates a cash budget for only three months. Actual cash receipts and disbursements should be compared with the budget so that necessary corrective action can be taken. The procedure used in Exhibit 13–1 is to estimate each expected source and disbursement of cash for the given time period. The only source of cash assumed in Exhibit 13–1 is from charge sales, with 97 percent of the charge sales collected. The following collection pattern and sales are assumed in the exhibit:

40% in the month of sale
30% in the month following sale
27% in the second month following sale
 3% uncollectible
___
100%

Actual sales for—
      November $125,000
      December 135,000

Budgeted sales for the year 19X2 are obtained from the sales budget, Exhibit 12–1 in Chapter 12.

Accounts payable are paid for in the month following the purchase, and no purchase discounts are available. The following purchases by month are given:

December 19X1. . . . . $18,000
January 19X2 19,000
February 19X2. 20,000
November 19X2. 22,000

Cash disbursements for fixed costs are expected to be $50,000 per month.

Cash disbursements for variable costs are expected to be 5 percent of monthly sales; 30 percent is paid in the month incurred and 70 percent in the following month.

Property taxes of $60,000 will be paid in February; dividends of $80,000 are expected to be paid in December. The cash balance on January 1 is $20,100 and on December 1, $25,600. Equipment purchases totaling $50,000 are expected to be paid for in January. The cash budget reflecting these forecasts for the first two months and December is given in Exhibit 13–1. Only total receipts and disbursements are added in the total budget column since, for simplicity, nine months are omitted from the cash budget.

MARKETING AND ADMINISTRATIVE BUDGETS

Marketing and administrative expenses may be more difficult to control and budget than production costs because conditions are not standardized. However, because of their significant impact on profits, management should apply budgeting techniques to this area, too. Exhibit 13–2 illustrates an annual

EXHIBIT 13–2

HART COMPANY
Marketing and Administrative Expense Budget
For Year Ending December 31, 19X2

Variable marketing expenses:		
Salaries and wages	$10,500	
Sales commissions.	10,000	
Advertising	10,000	
Traveling	18,000	
Total variable marketing expenses.		$ 48,500
Fixed marketing expenses:		
Warehousing	$20,000	
Advertising	10,000	
Marketing manager's salary	22,000	
Total fixed marketing expenses		52,000
Total marketing expenses		$100,500
Variable administrative expenses:		
Clerical wages.	$10,000	
Supplies	10,213	
Total variable administrative expenses.		$ 20,213
Fixed administrative expenses:		
Depreciation	$90,000	
Salaries.	40,000	
Total fixed administrative expenses		130,000
Total administrative expenses		$150,213
Total marketing and administrative expenses. . . .		$250,713

---

marketing and administrative expense budget classified as to fixed and variable expenses. (Separate budgets for each of these expenses could be prepared.) The annual budget should be broken down on a monthly basis so that actual expenses can be compared with the budget monthly.

A combined marketing and administrative budget similar to the one illustrated in Exhibit 13–2 would not be adequate for a large company; instead, such a company should prepare individual expense budgets for each function. This allows the marketing and administrative functions to be detailed so that factors affecting the expense can better be considered. For example, the advertising budget should take into account the amount to be spent, the projects on which it is to be spent, and the timing of the projects. A margin of safety should be built into the advertising budget since advertising can be quickly and greatly influenced by outside factors. Some sales promotion investments are for immediate response, while others are for delayed response. In addition, *institutional advertising* is meant to promote all aspects of the company, while other advertising promotes specific products.

Advertising budgets

The advertising budget is difficult to establish because so many factors influence the success of an advertising campaign. The fact that a sale is made may be due to reasons other than promotion of the product; for example, a consumer may be influenced by the availability of money or credit or the approach used by the salesperson. The influence of economic conditions may also be an important factor, given that all sales usually increase in periods of high employment. The time lag between the point at which advertising expenditures are incurred and the sale also increases the difficulty of setting the advertising budget, and measuring the effectiveness of different advertising media is also often complicated. Local advertising is more easily measured than national advertising, and media advertising which contains reply cards or coupons can be measured relatively easily.

Because the advertising budget is influenced by so many factors, many of which are difficult to measure, intuitive judgment is generally used more often in establishing this budget than in any other budget. Nevertheless, the advertising budget should be determined jointly by marketing, financial, and accounting personnel so that problems in each area can be considered as objectively as possible. Often companies use one of the following bases for establishing the advertising budget: a percentage of sales, an amount per unit of product in budgeted sales, competitors' actions, "all we can afford," market research, or the task method or sales objective.

Fixed percentage of sales.   While setting the advertising budget as a fixed percentage of sales is a popular approach, this method has great weaknesses, since sales are supposed to be the end result of advertising rather than vice versa. Even though many executives argue that this method is advantageous because it makes additional funds available for following a favorable market, it lacks flexibility. Certainly, if this approach is used, it is logical to correlate advertising appropriations with *forecasted* sales since the company is assuming that advertising precedes sales rather than the reverse.

Amount per unit.   Instead of setting the advertising budget as a percentage of sales, the advertising appropriation may be based on a unit cost per product grouping, customer, or other segment. This approach can be easily adapted with variable budgeting. For example, the advertising budget may be set up as a cost per promotion item mailed, cost per newspaper inch, or minute of radio or television time. This unit cost should be a scientifically estimated standard cost which is determined after a careful study of prevailing communication rates.

Competitors' actions.   Competitors' actions are important, especially with regard to the amount of advertising and activity of competitors' sales personnel. However, this method allows competitors to set the pace because advertising expenditures are established in relation to competitors' advertising budgets. Companies use this method in an attempt not to spend more than the competition. Yet, a company that just reacts ignores its own competitive strengths and does not take into account its real needs. Instead, competitors' actions and other factors including population characteristics should affect the specific type and kind of media used for advertising in each territory.

All we can afford.   This method disregards the relationship between advertising costs and advertising effects because advertising activities are funded only after all other expenses are budgeted. One form of this approach is to specify a fixed sum that will be spent for advertising without regard to other factors.

Market research.   Market research can determine the probable relationship between demographic characteristics of the population and advertising medium chosen. In determining advertising expenditures, the marketing manager must consider the density of the population, whether urban or rural, types of industry found in the market territory, and climate. Management can vary the amount spent on sales promotion in limited market areas to observe the returns from incremental increases in these costs. The results of these tests can be used to provide measurements.

Task method or sales objective.   Using this method, a definite advertising objective is established for each product, such as a desired level of customer acceptance. Then the amount of advertising considered necessary to meet this objective is determined. This method is cumulative as the sum of appropriations for individual products become the advertising budget.

Because advertising is considered a *discretionary cost* which arises from periodic appropriation decisions that reflect top management policies, the size of the advertising budget may merely be the amount of funds available. If there are excess funds, the advertising budget is increased. While there is no logic in this approach, the appropriation may reflect the business climate in which a company is operating. Because of the significance of the advertising expenditure, however, a more valid approach should be used. Most companies, in practice, use a combination of the approaches presented.

Direct selling expense budget

Another budget which is difficult to estimate is the direct selling budget, which is concerned with those order-getting costs resulting primarily from personal presentation of the service or product to prospective buyers. Before preparing a direct selling expense budget, management should establish its reimbursement policy. Generally a company considers out-of-town meals and lodging, transportation, tips, telephone, and telegraph as legitimate business expenses. Policies vary concerning reimbursement for gifts and entertainment, however. In any case, the method of reimbursing salespersons or advancing them funds should be simple and economical to administer, although salespeople should be required to support their expenses with paid receipts. To maintain harmony within the company, salespersons should fully understand the expense plan so that there is no question over which expenses will be reimbursed. Standards and budgets for direct selling activities are discussed in detail in Chapter 21.

Research and development budget

Research is a continuing function in many industries, and research program components, like other expenses, should be identified and their cost estimated. The budget is the most useful tool for both planning and controlling research and development expenses. Research and development budgets should be based on reasonably accurate estimates, coordinated with the general policies of the company, and made flexible because of their nature. To set up an effective budget, projects should be planned and evaluated and then grouped according to long- and short-term objectives. In the short run, management must be assured that research and development efforts are directed toward projects on which a satisfactory rate of return on the funds invested is expected. The long-run objective is to be assured that the experimental programs are in line with forecasted future market trends. The research and development budget can serve as a means of coordinating these objectives with the overall objectives of the company.

In arriving at the size of the budget for research and development, management must be concerned with whether or not the appropriation will produce enough income to justify the expense incurred. To answer this question, management may rely on a basis that has been used in the past, such as a certain sum per year or a specified percent of sales. Because research and development expenditures represent discretionary costs, many companies follow a flexible approach in regard to these activities. For example, if economic conditions are depressed and operating income is decreased, some research activities are postponed.

Budgets for research and development activities should be broken down by projects. Each project should then be broken down into phases, and the completion date for each phase forecasted. Separate departmental budgets should be established for each project if more than one department is involved. Exhibit 13–3 illustrates a detailed budget for the development of the new product Zerxx, broken down by expense items for the three phases of the project. Overhead is applied on the basis of $30 per labor-hour to complete the different phases.

Status reports. Periodically, a status report, as illustrated in Exhibit 13–4, should be prepared for all phases or departments involved in each project. In this report, the expenditures incurred to date and the commitments made are matched against the budget to determine the unexpended amounts. The project director can then study the unexpended amounts to determine whether they are sufficient to complete the phase. Revisions in the budget may need to be approved by top management if it is determined that planned results cannot be achieved with the remaining unexpended amount.

Periodically all research projects should be reviewed. Exhibit 13–5 illus-

EXHIBIT 13–3

BUDGET FOR NEW PRODUCT ZERXX

Project director: Mr. Harold Douglas
Project numbers: 2118

| Expenses | Phase of department | | | Total budget |
	Planning	Production	Promotion	
Direct materials	$ 4,000	$ 26,300	$ 2,700	$ 33,000
Labor cost	1,000	29,000	6,000	36,000
Consulting fees	10,000	3,000	5,000	18,000
Indirect labor	1,500	2,800	300	4,600
Supplies and other				
indirect material	1,500	6,800	2,900	11,200
Equipment	–0–	40,000	–0–	40,000
Overhead allocation	1,500	9,000	3,000	13,500
	$19,500	$116,900	$19,900	$156,300
Estimated labor-hours	50	300	100	450
Completion date	May 31, 19X1	January 31, 19X2	April 30, 19X2	

EXHIBIT 13–4

STATUS REPORT FOR NEW PRODUCT ZERXX—PROJECT NUMBER 2118
Production Department
December 31, 19X1

Expense	Budget	Expenditures to date	Commitments	Total expenditure and commitments	Unexpended
Direct materials	$ 26,300	$ 25,100	$ 100	$ 25,200	$ 1,100
Labor cost	29,000	20,000	1,000	21,000	8,000
Consulting fees	3,000	2,700	200	2,900	100
Indirect labor	2,800	2,300	700	3,000	(200)
Supplies and other					
indirect material	6,800	4,200	1,800	6,000	800
Equipment	40,000	40,000	–0–	40,000	–0–
Overhead allocation	9,000	6,800	1,800	8,600	400
	$116,900	$101,100	$5,600	$106,700	$10,200

EXHIBIT 13–5

RESEARCH AND DEVELOPMENT COST SUMMARY
December 31, 19X1

Project no.	Project description	Costs to January 1, 19X1	Year 19X1 costs	Future costs	Total costs	Annual forecasted income
2118	Product ZERXX	-0-	$101,100	$5,600	$106,700	$16,000
2119	Product YERXX	$5,000	4,000	3,000	12,000	4,000
2120	Improve Product AAX	1,000	15,000	2,000	18,000	5,000

trates a review of the three research projects that are being conducted. Costs incurred in previous periods are shown along with the current year's expenses; future costs are added to these two expenses to give the expected total cost of the project. Annual forecasted income can also be included to facilitate evaluation of the project's success.

Time budget analysis. Not only should research and development expenses be evaluated, but a comparison of the actual hours spent on a project with the hours budgeted should also be made. Exhibit 13–6 provides a form for doing this. As can be seen, 27 more hours were used in developing product Zerxx than forecasted.

Often the competition for market share makes time even more important than dollars. The differential or extra revenue to be gained by introducing a product several months earlier and beating competition should be compared with the differential cost of increasing production and market tests. This differential income should then be compared with the income estimated if the original time schedule is followed. These efforts to complete the project ahead of schedule are referred to as *crashing* and are part of Program Evaluation and Review Technique (PERT) analysis. PERT-Time and PERT-Cost analysis involving networks indicating paths to completion are discussed in detail in

EXHIBIT 13–6

TIME BUDGET ANALYSIS—PRODUCT ZERXX
May 30, 19X2

Phase	Hours budgeted	Actual hours	Variance
Planning:			
Product specification. . . .	20	24	4 unfavorable
Personnel involved	5	3	2 favorable
Research	6	8	2 unfavorable
Market analysis	10	7	3 favorable
Finance	9	14	5 unfavorable
	50	56	6 unfavorable
Production:			
Personnel training	25	26	1 unfavorable
Purchasing	15	20	5 unfavorable
Control functions	10	8	2 favorable
Test runs.	200	225	25 unfavorable
Product revisions.	50	40	10 favorable
	300	319	19 unfavorable
Promotion:			
Field testing	15	20	5 unfavorable
Advertising	85	82	3 favorable
	100	102	2 unfavorable
Total hours	450	477	27 unfavorable

Chapter 18. A detailed timetable is essential to any new product introduction, whether it involves a simple method of preparing calendars or a more sophisticated computerized PERT network.

BUDGETED INCOME STATEMENT AND BALANCE SHEET

After preparing the sales budget and all expense budgets, a budgeted income statement similar to that shown in Exhibit 13–7 can be prepared. As indicated, no new estimates are made; instead, figures are taken from budgets previously prepared. Exhibit 13–7 represents a simplified annual budget; in practice, a more detailed budgeted income statement should be prepared on a monthly basis. With monthly forecasted income statements, management can frequently analyze actual performance and investigate causes for variances. In addition, most companies round these figures to hundreds of dollars or thousands of dollars; however, in Exhibit 13–7 figures are rounded to the nearest dollar to facilitate the carryover from one budget to another.

Exhibit 13–8 illustrates a budgeted balance sheet which represents all expected changes in assets, liabilities, and stockholders' equity. Similar budgets can be prepared on a monthly basis. The means of calculating the ending balances are also shown on Exhibit 13–8; most of these data are taken from other budgets. As a result, a budgeted balance sheet is also used to prove the accuracy of all other budgets. For example, the ending cash balance reported on Exhibit 13–1 is shown on the budgeted balance sheet along with all other changes in assets, liabilities, and owners' equity. Ratio analysis can also be applied to the budgeted balance sheet so that unfavorable ratios expected to occur are discovered in time for corrective action to be taken. A return on investment ratio can also be prepared by relating expected net income to the capital employed. A lower return than desired by management may provide the stimulus to adjust management plans.

EXHIBIT 13–7

HART COMPANY
Budgeted Income Statement
For Year Ending December 31, 19X2

	From Exhibit—	
Sales	12–1	$1,883,850
Cost of goods sold	12–9	1,407,512
Gross margin		$ 476,338
Marketing and administrative expenses	13–2	250,713
Income before income taxes		$ 225,625
Income taxes assumed		107,625
Net income after income taxes		$ 118,000

EXHIBIT 13–8

HART COMPANY
Budgeted Balance Sheet
December 31, 19X2
Current assets

Cash (from Exhibit 13–1).	$ 52,117
Accounts receivable (beginning balance $30,250 +	
$1,883,850 sales − $1,860,000 receipts)	54,100
Direct materials inventory (from Exhibit 12–5).	12,875
Finished goods inventory (from Exhibit 12–9)	56,848
Total current assets.	$175,940

Plant assets

Land (from beginning balance)	$ 80,000
Building and equipment ($650,000 beginning balance +	
$50,000 purchases)	700,000
Less accumulated depreciation ($60,000 beginning balance +	
$150,000 from Exhibit 12–8 + $90,000 from Exhibit 13–2)	(300,000)
Total plant assets	$480,000
Total assets	$655,940

Current liabilities

Accounts payable (beginning balance + purchases of material,	
labor, overhead—disbursements of material, labor,	
overhead)	$ 60,000
Income taxes payable (from Exhibit 13–7).	107,625
Total current liabilities.	$167,625

Stockholders' equity

Common stock (from beginning balance sheet)	$200,500
Retained earnings (from beginning balance sheet + $118,000	
net income − $80,000 dividends from Exhibit 13–1).	287,815
Total stockholders' equity.	$488,315
Total liabilities and stockholders' equity	$655,940

Capital expenditures budget

Capital budgeting is of considerable importance because large sums of money and long periods of time are often involved. Capital budgeting, to be effective, should be based on dependable estimates from different departments concerning their required capital expenditures. These estimates should be incorporated into the budget only after proper authorization by top management, which should study the desirability of the expenditure in terms of planned availability of funds. Chapter 14 will deal with definite procedures and methods for evaluating each proposed project's merit. Control of capital expenditures is exercised in advance by requiring that each proposed project be evaluated using one or more of these methods. After alternative investment projects have been investigated and chosen, the investments that have been implemented should be reviewed.

Capital expenditure budgets should be prepared for both short- and long-range projects. Short-range projects should be detailed regarding costs and completion dates. Since long-range projects are not implemented in the current period, their budgets can be stated in general terms. Because timing is important and many capital expenditures involve significant dollar amounts, top management has the responsibility of translating long-range capital projects into budget commitments.

Government budgeting

The concept of budgeting can have different connotations depending on the use and profit status of the organization involved. For example, a fundamental difference between business and nonprofit budgets, such as government budgets, is the latter is an *appropriation budget*. That is, one that establishes fixed amounts which can be applied to achieve the objectives of the organizational unit for the period specified. Several factors exist in government that cause appropriation budgets to be used. The stewardship function, which is symbolized by spending limits, is very strong as the government is spending the taxpayers' funds. The revenue sources of governments are limited and fixed for selected time periods. Thus, many expenditures cannot be based on changing demands for services because the revenues do not vary with demand. In addition, specific revenues, such as taxes, are earmarked for specific activities by taxpayer vote or legislative action, and expenditures on such activities are limited by the available revenues.

The appropriation budget concept often leads managers to focus more toward spending resources than toward obtaining results. At year-end, government managers are tempted to spend the appropriation amounts, even if they are not needed. Unfortunately, this budgeting concept encourages managers to think in terms of incremental increases in budget amounts rather than to consider the services offered. Government managers behave in this manner because appropriation budgets direct attention to spending up to the limit of the appropriation. Financial performance evaluation is often based on the spending limit rather than on the cost/output relationship. Thus, managers are motivated to act in ways that result in favorable evaluations regarding the spending limit. Further, failure to spend to the allowable limit implies the amount is not needed, leading to reduced future limits.

A step toward improvement.   However, an important modification in government budgeting resulting in more effective management control is to relate costs to outputs or results. There are several methods which relate cost to output. A common form is *performance budgeting* whose focus is on the ends served by the government rather than on dollars spent. In formulating a performance budget, a precise definition of the work to be done and a careful estimate of what that work will cost is made. Work units and unit cost then become the basis for evaluating service levels. Performance budgets are prepared on the basis of functions and objectives of government agencies and departments. This budgeting approach is often considered an extreme form of *program budgeting* which involves attempts to describe program objectives and alternative methods of meeting them. Objectives are then matched with the costs of achieving them. A zero-base budgeting system, which calls for a reevaluation of all activities and their costs on a regular basis, could also be considered. The focus in zero-base budgeting, similar to program budgeting, is on the objectives of the organization. Zero-base budgeting applies to profit-making organizations as well, and an application of zero-base budgeting will be presented in the following section.

ZERO-BASE BUDGETING

Zero-base budgeting was introduced in the early 1970s in some business and government organizations because managers were dissatisfied with the results of the budgeting process. When the zero-base procedure is used, all programs are reviewed, which places on each manager the burden of justifying his or her entire budget, not just the changes proposed for the budget year. That is, the assumption is made that zero will be spent on each program or activity until greater expenditure is justified—thus, the term "zero base." The beginning point in the budgeting procedure is zero, rather than the amount already being spent.

Decision packages

Because in zero-base budgeting each manager must justify any expenditure, he or she must prepare and rank *decision packages.* This is the first step in the development of a zero-base budget. A decision package is a document which identifies and describes a specific activity for management to evaluate and rank against other activities competing for the available resources. So that a decision package can be compared and evaluated with other packages, each one should be developed at the same organizational level. This should be the lowest operational level at which meaningful cost data can be compiled. Allowing the people who are responsible for the activity to identify alternatives has the added advantage of generating interest.

Levels of effort

While decision packages vary in format depending on the organizational level involved, all decision packages include different methods of performing the same function as well as different levels of effort in performing the function. Thus, the best method can be chosen and rejection of alternative methods can be explained. The different levels of effort are defined by incremental packages. A minimum level of effort is established; then additional levels of effort are identified as separate decision packages. For example, a package can be developed for a current level of effort and another one for an improved level. Even though only three levels are illustrated later in the chapter, any number of levels of effort can be suggested. While the minimum level of effort does not usually fulfill the purpose of a function, it should identify and attack the most important elements. Generally, the minimum level of effort is below the current level of expenditures. To ensure approval, the minimum level of effort should be ranked higher than the additional packages. Since the minimum level of effort package requests only those funds required to perform the primary duties of a function, a second decision package is usually prepared requesting increased funds so the function can be performed at normal capacity. Other incremental packages may be prepared for the function to finance new duties. By developing different levels of effort as separate decision packages, the functional manager is implying that all levels of effort deserve consideration. Top management can then compare levels of effort within each function and decide on the best trade-offs among functions. In addition to the two types of alternatives discussed, decision packages generally involve a breakdown of requested funds by line items of expense and some quantitative measures of efficiency and effectiveness. However, for simplicity, only the total expenditures requested are shown in Exhibits 13–9 through 13–11. These exhibits illustrate a decision package series containing three levels of effort for advertising Product Alpha during 19X2. The total expenditure requested is supported by backup descriptions and expenditure requests by line item on additional forms so that the bulk of paperwork forwarded for review does not become cumbersome.

Minimum objective level. Exhibit 13–9 contains the minimum objective level, which requires less effort and expenditure ($380,000) than the $525,000 spent in 19X1 for the advertising of Product Alpha. But the chances of achieving the 19X1 sales of $4.5 million, much less the $5 million budgeted 19X2 sales, are slim. Certainly it is not reasonable to expect that an additional $500,000 sales can be generated if advertising is lower than it was in the preceding year. As explained in Exhibit 13–9, the minimum objective level excludes radio advertising and display advertising in Chamber of Commerce publications in large cities in the area. This minimum objective level requires six positions, while nine positions were utilized in 19X1; thus one clerk-receptionist, one copywriter, and one layout artist must be laid off if this package level is adopted.

Current objective level. Exhibit 13–10 illustrates an increased level of effort which has as its objective to reach 15 percent of the population in the market territory, while the minimum objective level's goal is 10 percent. This planned expansion of the marketing area requires an additional copywriter. The planned expenditures for the current objective level alone are $180,000; to this is added the $380,000 minimum objective level to give a $560,000 19X2

EXHIBIT 13–9

ZERO-BASE BUDGET REQUEST
Decision Package—Minimum Objective Level
For Year 19X2

Department: _Marketing_   Activity: _Advertising_   Program: _Product Alpha_

Describe the program in terms of its major objective:

To properly advertise Product Alpha so that $5 million 19X2 budgeted sales are met.

Describe the program in terms of the current objective in 19X1:

To advertise Product Alpha so that $4.5 million 19X1 budgeted sales are met.

Explain the minimum level limited objective this package provides:

Since 10 percent of the population in the market territory will be reached through newspaper advertising, $4.3 million sales are expected to be generated.

Explain the service now provided that this minimum objective level excludes:

Radio advertising and display advertising in Chamber of Commerce publications in large cities in the area are excluded. One clerk-receptionist, one copywriter, and one layout artist are deleted.

	19X1	19X2
Total expenditures.	$525,000	$380,000
Average cost per newspaper advertisement . . .	750	800
Average cost per display advertisement	250	—
Average cost per radio minute	90	—
Positions	9	6

Package name: Advertising Alpha   Package _1_ of _3_

Prepared by: Louis Wells   Activity rank _1_

---

cumulative amount. This represents an increase from the $525,000 spent in 19X1 for the current objective level. Four positions are planned for the current objective level, to give a total of 10 cumulative positions including the 6 positions in the minimum objective level.

Any number of improvement objective level decision packages may theoretically be prepared, although a predetermined upper limit of expenditures holds down the number. Each improvement-level decision package should request the _incremental_ funds needed to perform the service.

Improvement objective level. If an improved level of effort is chosen for advertising Product Alpha, an additional $340,000 must be budgeted, as shown

EXHIBIT 13–10

ZERO-BASE BUDGET REQUEST
Decision Package—Current Objective Level
For Year 19X2

Department: Marketing   *Activity:* Advertising   *Program:* Product Alpha

---

Describe the program in terms of its major objective:

To properly advertise Product Alpha so that $5 million 19X2
budgeted sales are met.

Describe the program in terms of the current objective in 19X1:

To advertise Product Alpha so that $4.5 million 19X1 budgeted
sales are met.

Explain the current level limited objective this package offers:

Since 15 percent of the population in the market territory will be
reached through newspapers, display advertising in Chamber of
Commerce publications, and radio advertising, $4.5 million sales
are expected to be generated.

Explain any cost change in the current level over the minimum level:

Add radio advertising and display advertising in Chamber of
Commerce publications. Add one clerk-receptionist, two copywriters, and one layout artist.

Explain any workload change in the current level over 19X1:

To expand the target marketing area outside the regional
territory. To do this, one copywriter must be added.

	19X1 program	*19X2 this package*	*19X2 cumulative amount*
Total expenditures	$525,000	$180,000	$560,000
Average cost per newspaper advertisement	750	—	800
Average cost per display advertisement. .	250	275	275
Average cost per radio minute	90	100	100
Positions	9	4	10

Package name: Advertising Alpha   *Package* 2 *of* 3

Prepared by: Louis Wells   *Activity rank* 4

---

in Exhibit 13–11. In addition, two more copywriters must be hired to reach 25
percent of the target population. The improvement objective level includes
television advertising that is not provided at the current objective level. If this
increased level of effort is adopted, the cumulative amount of total expenditure
is planned at $900,000.

EXHIBIT 13–11

ZERO-BASE BUDGET REQUEST
Decision Package—Improvement Objective Level
For Year 19X2

Department: _Marketing_　　　　Activity: _Advertising_　　　Program: _Product Alpha_

Describe the program in terms of its major objective:

To properly advertise Product Alpha so that $5 million 19X2
budgeted sales are met.

Describe the program in terms of the current objective in 19X1:

To advertise Product Alpha so that $4.5 million 19X1 budgeted
sales are met.

Explain the improvement level limited objective this package provides:

Since 25 percent of the target population in the market territory
will be reached through newspaper, display, radio, and television advertising, $5 million sales are expected to be generated.

Explain this package in terms of cost:

To reach an additional 10 percent of the target population will
require two more copywriters.

Explain the services provided that the current level excludes:

Television advertising is included in this package.

	19X1 program	19X2 this package	19X2 cumulative amount
Total expenditures	$525,000	$340,000	$900,000
Average cost per newspaper advertisement	750	—	800
Average cost per display advertisement. .	250	—	275
Average cost per radio minute.		5,000	5,000
Positions.	9	2	12

Package name:　Advertising Alpha　　Package _3_ of _3_

Prepared by:　　Louis Wells　　　　Activity rank _6_

Ranking decision packages

After the various objective levels are evaluated, they are compared and ranked with other decision packages. The ranking of decision packages allows management to decide which operations are most important in reaching the goals and objectives of the activity and also allows them to decide how much should be spent for each operation. Completed decision packages are ranked in order of decreasing benefit to the activity or company. Exhibit 13–12 shows

EXHIBIT 13–12

ZERO BUDGET REQUEST
Decision Package Ranking

Department: _Marketing_ Activity: _Advertising_

Rank	Package name	19X1 budgeted by program		19X2 requested by package		Cumulative requested		
		Expenditures	Positions	Funds	Position	Expenditures	Percent 19X2/19X1	Positions
1	Advertising Alpha Product (1 of 3)	$ 525,000	9	$ 380,000	6	$ 380,000	35	6
2	Institutional Advertising (1 of 2)	300,000	3	100,000	2	480,000	44	8
3	Advertising Delta Product (1 of 2)	260,000	7	120,000	4	600,000	55	12
4	Advertising Alpha Product (2 of 3)			180,000	4	780,000	72	16
5	Advertising Delta Product (2 of 2)			150,000	3	930,000	86	19
6	Advertising Alpha Product (3 of 3)			340,000	2	1,270,000	117	21
7	Institutional Advertising (2 of 2)			225,000	2	1,495,000	138	23
	Activity totals.	$1,085,000	19	$1,495,000	23	1,495,000	138	23

$$\frac{\$1,495,000}{\$1,085,000} = 138\%$$

J. M. R.
Approved by

Marketing Manager
Title

11/11/19X1
Date

Page 1 of 1

seven ranked advertising packages from the marketing department. These activity ranks are then inserted in the individual decision package; for example, the current or second level of effort for advertising Alpha received a ranking of 4 which is inserted in the appropriate space on Exhibit 13–10. A comparison of the 19X1 expenditures with those for 19X2 is also provided in Exhibit 13–12. The 19X2 cumulative requested is also computed as a percentage of the 19X1 expenditures; for example, after the second ranking is given, the $480,000 cumulative expenditure represents 44 percent ($480,000/$1,085,000) of the 19X1 expenditures.

This ranking process enables management to identify the benefits to be gained at each expenditure level and the consequences of not approving additional decision packages ranked below that level. The ranking process should begin at the lowest organizational level which has more than one function reporting to it. Each initial ranking of decision packages is then sent to a higher organization level, where it is evaluated and merged with rankings of other activities within the same organizational structure. Changes in the order of rankings are made at this stage to reflect the broader goals of the reviewing activity; during this consolidation, some decision packages are dropped from consideration. This process of reviewing and merging decision packages is repeated until all decision packages from a company are consolidated into a single ranking which represents the budget for the company.

The task of ranking decision packages becomes increasingly difficult as the procedure progresses upward through the organizational hierarchy. Even though at lower organizational levels a single individual may be able to rank decision packages, the expertise needed at higher levels is usually best achieved through a committee. The committee should consist of all managers whose packages are being ranked and a chairperson selected from the next higher organization level.

Little consideration should be given to those decision packages which are absolutely essential for the proper operation of the company; these packages should clearly be ranked high to ensure their approval. Most of the ranking effort should be directed toward packages which are essentially marginal in nature. Because these packages receive a lower ranking, the possibility of some being rejected becomes greater. The manager's evaluation of marginal decision packages strongly influences which are approved for next year's budget.

A *cutoff line*, the point of acceptance or rejection, may be employed to facilitate the ranking of decision packages. In determining the cutoff line, managers may use an arbitrary percentage of the previous year's budget. Generally, the greater the number of packages to be evaluated and ranked, the larger is the percentage employed in determining the cutoff line. As the rankings from the lower levels of the company are consolidated, the percentage of decision packages subject to close examination is decreased or the cutoff line is raised. Packages which are ranked above this line are not given a thorough examination, while packages below this line receive a more rigorous examination of their relative contributions in satisfying the objectives of the company.

A number of advantages accrue from zero-base budgeting, for it requires that planning take place before the actual budgeting process is begun. That lower and middle management participate in the budgeting process by ranking decision packages increases the quality and quantity of management information at all organizational levels. A zero-base budgeting system also furnishes the data necessary for measuring effectiveness in discretionary cost centers, because a more formalized structure for budgeting discretionary costs is provided. Correct application of zero-base budgeting techniques should therefore provide an efficient allocation of financial resources by directing resources more equitably to those divisions and departments making the largest contribution to the company's profit.

Limitations of the method.   Zero-base budgeting does have limitations, some of which can be used to conceal inefficiencies and slack. Since zero-base budgeting often generates a large volume of paperwork, some government and business officials have found that decision packages are unmanageable. Certainly the volume of paperwork usually increases geometrically with the size of the department. This has led many people to conclude that this budgeting process may be more useful to the managers who formulate the budget rather than to top managers or members of Congress who later examine the budget. There usually is not enough time for these people to analyze the merits of each decision package; yet if the task is delegated to others, the idea of comparing priorities is compromised. Even if the number of decision packages is reduced, there is not enough time for a thorough analysis during the period when the budget is set. Experience also shows that ranking decision packages can be complex and expensive; for example, government officials find it difficult to rank highway department programs against health department programs.

Federal employees and managers may also quickly learn the skill of preparing convincing decision packages for the purpose of protecting their projects. Members of Congress and managers have found that there has been little, if any, reallocation of resources as a result of implementing the zero-base budgeting system.

Despite these severe limitations, certain aspects of zero-base budgeting can be adapted to become an extremely valuable part of the control process. A review of each department's purpose, costs, and methods of operations may reveal areas needing improvements. Stating measurable results in the budget proposal, similar to those required in decision packages, can also be beneficial even though management may choose to avoid the volume of paperwork often required in zero-base budgeting. Since improvements in budgeting operations are needed, the adoption of certain zero-base techniques may achieve the results desired without an expensive, time-consuming budgeting process.

INCREMENTAL BUDGETING

Traditional budgeting, as opposed to zero-base budgeting, directs attention to changes or differences between existing budget appropriations and proposed expenditures. Since such a budgeting procedure accepts the existing base and examines only the increments involved, it can be referred to as *incremental budgeting.* The decision maker's attention is focused only on a small number of the total relevant factors involved since only those areas in which there are different alternatives are analyzed. Incremental budgeting is a simpler approach, and its proponents argue that movement toward objectives should take small steps because of management's limited ability to forecast the future.

Incremental budgeting is a conservative approach which has the weakness of often encouraging companies to retain functions and duties which have lost their usefulness. Because company goals in practice are constantly changing, new functions and duties should be added; but with the incremental budgeting procedure, it is often difficult to allocate resources away from outdated functions to new tasks. Since few companies experience the same kinds of problems, utilization of resources may be more efficient with zero-base budgeting because each request for funds is compared with and evaluated against all other claims to the company's limited financial resource base.

Budget revisions

Certainly, budgets should not be revised every time a budgeted goal is not met since this type of revising would completely defeat the control functions of budgets. However, budget revision is necessary in some situations. For example, an error in the actual compiling of budget data dictates a budget revision, as would the reorganization of a company. However, budgets are most frequently revised when factors external to the company change, and these factors have a major impact on the company; for example, a new company or product enters the market and is expected to increase competition. Budget revisions are usually made or approved by top management.

SUMMARY

As discussed in this chapter and the previous one, budgets can be extremely useful internal control tools, but they do have limitations in that they can lead to faultfinding and pressure. In addition, there is the danger that budget estimates and bases are not as accurate as possible. However, accuracy should not be interpreted as complexity; budgets should not be too complex for common usage. In addition, the budget should not be allowed to take the place of management nor should it be used as a device to hide the inefficiencies of a company. Budgets can serve as excellent planning and control tools only if attention is devoted to properly establishing them and explaining to employees how they function.

Companies simply cannot operate or grow without adequate working capital or cash resources. This makes it imperative that more timely, more detailed, and more reliable information about cash flows be available. Reliable forecasts of future cash receipts and disbursements are essential for more effective management of cash fund assets. The cash budgets presented in the chapter should be adapted to fit each company's needs so that the cash flow is better understood. Proper utilization of cash by management can bring additional savings to the company; every opportunity for improvements in this area should be taken.

The chapter also discussed the preparation of marketing and administrative budgets, including budgets for advertising and research expenditures. Since the nature of these activities may be less standardized and repetitive than production activities, the construction of these budgets may challenge the accountant. However, even though it is impossible to budget marketing and administrative activities as factually as production expenses, experience has shown that careful planning of expenditures and comparison of actual expenses with the budget avoid wasteful spending without impairing effectiveness.

While zero-base budgeting may be seen as a simple approach, it does require that managers justify everything they are doing or are about to do. Instead of merely setting forth proposed budget increases, the managers must start from zero every year and present alternatives involving any increases or decreases in department activities. Decision packages are prepared which provide a description of the activity, the consequences of failing to go ahead with it, alternative courses of action, and the estimated costs and benefits. The next step is developing the criteria for ranking the packages and then deciding which programs to accept and on what scale.

As indicated in this chapter, zero-base budgeting must be carefully tailored to each company's needs. Many companies use it on a selective basis to evaluate operations. Many managers have also found zero-base budgeting most useful for nonproduction, discretionary expenses. The constant pressure to reduce costs in manufacturing operations of highly competitive businesses forces management to make many changes during the year. Such changes rapidly outdate decision packages approved at the beginning of the year. In addition, the system is generally of use only to large companies because the formality of the process is usually feasible only where there is limited communications. Zero-base budgeting is not practical in small companies where principal managers can sit down and make decisions because the system requires more time than does the normal budgeting process.

IMPORTANT TERMS AND CONCEPTS

Yield

Security of principal

Institutional advertising

Discretionary cost

Crashing

Program evaluation
    and review technique (PERT)

Appropriation budgeting

Performance budgeting

Program budgeting

Zero-base budgeting

Decision packages

Levels of effort

Cutoff line

Incremental budgeting

PROBLEM FOR SELF-STUDY

Monthly cash forecast for a quarter

As a CPA employed by Beverly, Inc., a retail firm, you must prepare a cash forecast. You study the sales for the last year, which were as follows:

January	$ 410,000
February	390,000
March	275,180
April	405,600
May	325,000
June	315,180
July	290,800
August	285,175
September	305,190
October	318,750
November	335,600
December	350,700
	$4,007,175

In relation to the corresponding quarter of last year, you believe that sales for the first quarter will increase 25 percent, for the second quarter 15 percent, for the third quarter 10 percent, and for the last quarter 8 percent. You further believe that the existing collection pattern will continue as follows:

40 percent in the month of sale
25 percent in the first subsequent month
15 percent in the second subsequent month
10 percent in the third subsequent month

Accounts receivable are $441,883 and the cash balance is $15,168 on January 1. On that same day, there is a $280,000 merchandise inventory on hand. Gross margin represents 60 percent of estimated sales. Management has decided they want to maintain an inventory at the end of each month that represents sales forecast for the next two months. All purchases are paid for in the following month. Accounts payable for purchases from December total $115,905. Cash expenditures for recurring fixed cost of $115,000 are made each month. Fixed costs have remained the same since last November. Depreciation expense of $35,000 is also incurred each month. Variable costs amount to 5 percent of sales each month. The payment schedule for fixed and variable costs are as follows:

	During month incurred	Following month
Variable costs	40%	60%
Fixed costs	35	65

It is anticipated that property taxes of $175,000 will be paid in February. The company has followed a dividend policy of $10 per share per quarter, payment made on the 10th day of the third month in each quarter; 5,175 shares are outstanding.

Required:

Prepare a cash forecast for the first quarter by months. Round to whole dollars.

Solution

BEVERLY, INC.
Budgeted Statement of Cash Receipts and Disbursements
First Quarter

	January	February	March
Cash receipts from sales:			
From January sales			
$410,000 × 125% = $512,500			
$512,500 × 40%.....................	$205,000		
$512,500 × 25%.....................		$128,125	
$512,500 × 15%.....................			$ 76,875
From February Sales			
$390,000 × 125% = $487,500			
$487,500 × 40%.....................		195,000	
$487,500 × 25%.....................			121,875
From March sales			
$275,180 × 125% = $343,975			
$343,975 × 40%.....................			137,590
From December sales			
25% × $350,700.....................	87,675		
15% × $350,700.....................		52,605	
10% × $350,700.....................			35,070
From November sales			
15% × $335,600.....................	50,340		
10% × $335,600.....................		33,560	
From October sales			
10% × $318,750.....................	31,875		
Total receipts......................	$374,890	$409,290	$371,410
Disbursements:			
Purchases—prior month			
(see schedule)	$115,905	$257,590	$186,576
Fixed costs	115,000	115,000	115,000
Variable costs:			
5% × $512,500 January sales = $25,625			
$25,625 × 40%......................	10,250		
$25,625 × 60%		15,375	
5% × $350,700 December sales = $17,535			
$17,535 × 60%	10,521		
5% × $487,500 February sales = $24,375			
$24,375 × 40%......................		9,750	
$24,375 × 60%			14,625
5% × $343,975 March sales = $17,199			
$17,199 × 40%			6,880
Property taxes........................		175,000	
Dividend (5,175 shares × $10)...............			51,750
Total disbursements..................	$251,676	$572,715	$374,831
Excess of receipts			
over disbursements....................	$123,214	$(163,425)	$(3,421)
Beginning cash.........................	15,168	138,382	(25,043)
Ending cash	$138,382	($ 25,043)	($ 28,464)

BEVERLY, INC.
Purchases Disbursement Schedule

	January
February sales.	$487,500
March sales.	343,975
Total sales	$831,475
Required inventory	
on January 31: 40% × $831,475. . . .	$332,590
+ January sales requirements	
40% × $512,500	205,000
To account for	$537,590
− Beginning inventory	280,000
January purchases to be	
paid for in following	
month	$257,590

BEVERLY, INC.
Purchases Disbursement Schedule

	February
March sales	$343,975
April sales ($405,600 × 115%)	466,440
Total sales.	$810,415
Required inventory	
on February 28: 40% × $810,415. . . .	$324,166
+ February sales requirements	
40% × $487,500	195,000
To account for.	$519,166
− Beginning inventory.	332,590*
February purchases	
to be paid for	
in following month	$186,576

*Same as required inventory on January 31.

REVIEW QUESTIONS

1. Discuss the characteristics in the government sector that encourage the use of appropriation budgeting.
2. List several modifications of government budgeting that would allow more effective managerial control.
3. Discuss how the cash management function has expanded in recent years.
4. Explain why so many companies have a conservative policy of managing cash.
5. What do you see as the advantages of centralizing cash management? What cash management functions would you decentralize?
6. Discuss the relationship between the size of a company's cash balance in a bank and its importance as a bank customer. What advantages are there to maintaining a larger cash balance in fewer banks?

7.   Why may it be more important to allow for a margin of safety in advertising budgets than in other budgets?

8.   Give some advantages of preparing cash forecasts.

9.   Discuss four different approaches that can be used to establish an advertising budget.

10. Of what significance is a status report for research and development projects?

11. What aspects of capital projects not prevalent in other areas make capital budgeting important?

12. How could you use PERT in time budget analysis?

13. Discuss the preparation of decision packages. What is included in each decision package?

14. How are decision packages ranked? Where does the ranking process begin?

15. Indicate the advantages of employing zero-base budgeting.

16. Define incremental budgeting.

17. What advantages over zero-base budgeting do proponents of incremental budgeting stress?

EXERCISES

E13–1.   Credit sales collections with discounts

You have been asked to forecast the cash receipts from credit sales for the month of May for the Reid Company. The company is engaged in seasonal production, and May credit sales are estimated to be only $144,000. Discount terms of 2/10, n/30 are offered customers as an incentive to pay their bills early. The collection pattern is assumed to be 20 percent during the discount period and month of sale; 7 percent after the discount period has expired, but within the month of sale; 43 percent in the first month after sale; 28.5 percent in the second month after sale. The accounts receivable balance as of April 30 is $164,250; one third of the balance represents March sales and the remainder, April sales. All accounts receivable from months prior to March have been paid or written off.

Required:

Determine the May cash receipts from credit sales.

E13–2.   Cash receipts by month

Milton Vacon Company began operations on January 1. Judging by management's experience with similar organizations, the collection pattern for accounts receivable is forecast as follows: 20 percent of the credit sales are paid within 10 days of the end of the month; an additional 60 percent of credit sales are paid within 30 days of the month in which the sale is made; an additional 10 percent of credit sales are paid within 60 days of the month in which the sale is made.

Management has agreed to offer cash discounts for credit sales only on a term of 2/10 EOM, N/60 EOM. Cash and credit sales by month are forecast as follows:

	Cash sales	Credit sales
January	$10,000	$30,000
February	18,000	50,000
March	25,000	60,000

Required:

Prepare the cash receipts budget by month for the first quarter of the year.

E13–3. Monthly detailed cash budget

The management of Massey, Inc. requests that you prepare a cash budget for May. The cash balance is $42,800 on May 1.

Analysis of their collection pattern in the past shows that accounts receivable are paid as follows: 40 percent during the month of sale; 28 percent in the first month after the sale; 18 percent in the second month after the sale; 8 percent in the third month after the sale.

On May 1, accounts receivable are $300,000. Of this balance, $180,000 came from April sales; $50,000 from March sales; $55,000 from February sales; and $15,000 from January sales. No accounts receivable have been written off.

A 10 percent, $50,000 loan is due at the end of the month. A final monthly interest payment is due at the end of each month. Additional expenses for the month will be:

Wages and salaries.	$160,000
Materials and supplies	130,000
Depreciation.	20,000
Insurance.	10,000
Amortization of goodwill	45,000

Total sales for May are forecasted to be $500,000.

Required:

Prepare a detailed cash budget for May.

E13–4. Additional financing necessary

Osborne Inc. is a manufacturer of electrical motors. Actual sales for the first quarter of 19X2 and projected sales for April and May are as follows:

	Sales
January (actual)	$300,000
February (actual)	308,000
March (actual)	312,000
April (projected)	316,000
May (projected)	322,000

The average markup on cost for the company's merchandise is 40 percent. The company collects 60 percent of its sales during the month in which the sale is made; 25 percent is collected during the month following the sale, and 15 percent is collected in the second month following the sale.

Purchases of merchandise are paid for as follows: 40 percent paid during the month of purchase and 60 percent during the month following the purchase. Merchandise is purchased in the month preceding the sale. The company plans to maintain the current level of inventory.

To meet loan obligations, there must be a cash balance of $25,000 on hand at the end of the coming month of April. Other cash payments anticipated during the month of April are: salaries and wages, $58,000; other expenses, $12,000; equipment purchases, $15,000. The cash balance on April 1, 19X2 is $1,800.

Required:

Prepare a cash budget for April, 19X2. (Round to nearest whole dollar.) Will additional financing be necessary to have the required ending cash balance?

E13–5. Monthly cash budget

Bridges Corporation asks you to prepare its cash budget for May. Management expects sales for May to be $150,000, with a beginning cash balance for May of $45,000. Their collection pattern in the past, which you believe will continue in the future, has been 40 percent in the month of sale, 48 percent in the month after the sale, and 10 percent in the second month after the sale.

The accounts receivable as of May 1 are: $60,000 from April sales and $15,000 from March sales. No bad debts have been written off from the sales for these months.

The company has experienced a 30 percent gross profit on sales before considering the purchase discount. They have enough stock in inventory for lead time and safety stock and have been following a purchase pattern for the last three months of ordering only enough for current sales. Their payment pattern is 25 percent in the month in which the sale is made because their suppliers allow a cash discount of 3 percent. Remaining purchases are paid in the month after the sale is made. Payroll disbursements for May will be $25,800. Other disbursements will be:

Rent	$ 1,200
Loan repayment and interest	25,000
Miscellaneous cash expenses	4,800

Required:

Prepare a cash budget for May. Round to whole dollars.

E13–6. Estimated cash receipts and disbursements

The treasurer for Roderick Banister Corporation has estimated activity for December 19X1. She provides you with the following:

Sales	$200,000
Gross margin (based on sales)	25%
Increase in inventory during month	$ 3,000
Increase in trade accounts receivable during month	$ 6,000

Variable marketing and administrative expenses include a charge for uncollectible accounts of 1 percent of sales.

Total marketing and administrative expenses are $25,500 per month plus 16 percent of sales, which includes the 1 percent uncollectible accounts charge. Depreciation expenses of $10,000 per month are included in fixed marketing and administrative expenses. There was no change in accounts payable during the month.

Required:

a. Determine the estimated cash receipts from operations for December based on the above data.
b. Detemine the estimated cash disbursements from operations for December based on the above data.

E13–7. Estimated cash receipts and disbursements

Management of Wong Company provides you with the following selected data for a month:

Sales	$200,000
Gross profit (based on sales).	40%
Increase in trade accounts	
receivable during month.	$ 7,000
Change in accounts payable	
during month.	-0-
Increase in inventory during	
month	$ 6,000

Variable marketing and administration expenses include a charge for uncollectible accounts of 2 percent of sales. Total marketing and administrative expense is $40,000 per month plus 10 percent of sales. Depreciation expenses of $15,000 per month are included in fixed marketing and administrative expenses.

Required:

a. On the basis of the above data, what are the estimated cash receipts from operations for the month?
b. On the basis of the above data, what are the estimated cash disbursements from operations for the month?

E13–8. Budgeted collections and pro forma balances

The January 31, 19X1 balance sheet of Gary Brown Company for the first month of operations follows:

Cash.	$ 22,750
Accounts receivable (net of allowance for	
uncollectible accounts of $2,700)	33,300
Inventory.	41,700
Property, plant, and equipment	
(net of allowance for accumulated	
depreciation of $62,000).	54,600
	$152,350
Accounts payable	$ 89,600
Common stock	100,000
Retained earnings (deficit).	(37,250)
	$152,350
Budgeted sales:	
February	$140,000
March	$179,000

Collections on sales are expected to be 60 percent in the month of sale, 37 percent in the next month, and 3 percent uncollectible. The gross margin is 36 percent of sales. Purchases each month are for the next month's projected sales. The purchases are paid in full in the following month. Other expenses for each month, paid in cash, are expected to be $19,000. Depreciation each month is $5,200.

Required:

a. What are the budgeted cash collections for February 19X1?
b. What is the pro forma (loss) before income taxes for February 19X1?
c. What is the projected balance in accounts payable on February 28, 19X1?

E13–9. Cash collections and disbursements (AICPA adapted)

The following information was available from Montero Corporation's books:

19–	Purchases	Sales
January	$42,000	$72,000
February	48,000	66,000
March	36,000	60,000
April.	54,000	78,000

Collections from customers are normally 70 percent in the month of sale, 20 percent in the month following the sale, and 9 percent in the second month following the sale. The balance is expected to be uncollectible. Montero takes full advantage of the 2 percent discount allowed on purchases paid for by the 10th of the following month. Purchases for May are budgeted at $60,000, while sales for May are forecasted at $66,000. Cash disbursements for expenses are expected to be $14,400 for the month of May. Montero's cash balance at May 1 was $22,000.

Required:

Prepare the following schedules:

a. Expected cash collections during May.
b. Expected cash disbursements during May.
c. Expected cash balance at May 31.

PROBLEMS

P13–1. Quarterly cash requirements

For the first quarter of 19X2, Bluefield Company prepared the following estimates of unit sales:

	Product A (units)	Product B (units)
January	10,100	5,000
February	9,800	5,600
March	9,200	5,200
April.	9,400	5,480

The company must have a beginning inventory of each type of product that is equal to three quarters of the upcoming month's sales in units. During December 19X1, the company sold 9,900 units of Product A and 4,580 units of Product B.

The unit cost of the company's products amounted to $15 per unit for Product A and

$20 per unit for Product B during 19X1. During 19X2, the unit costs are expected to increase by 10 percent.

The company pays for all purchases during the month following the purchase.

Required:

Determine the cash requirements for each of the first three months of 19X2 for merchandise purchases. Assume December budgeted sales were the same as actual sales.

P13–2. Budgeted income statement (CMA adapted)

Rein Company, a compressor manufacturer, is developing a budgeted income statement for the calendar year 19X2. The president is generally satisfied with the projected net income for 19X1 of $700,000 resulting in an earnings per share figure of $2.80. However, next year he would like earnings per share to increase to at least $3.

Rein Company employs a standard absorption cost system. Inflation necessitates an annual revision in the standards as evidenced by an increase in production costs expected in 19X2. The total standard manufacturing cost for 19X1 is $72 per unit produced.

Rein expects to sell 100,000 compressors at $110 each in the current year (19X1). Forecasts from the sales department are favorable and Rein Company is projecting an annual increase of 10 percent in unit sales in 19X2 and 19X3. This increase in sales will occur even though a $15 increase in unit selling price will be implemented in 19X2. The selling price increase was absolutely essential to compensate for the increased production costs and operating expenses. However, management is concerned that any additional sales price increase would curtail the desired growth in volume.

Standard production costs are developed for the two primary metals used in the compressor (brass and a steel alloy), the direct labor, and manufacturing overhead. The following schedule represents the 19X2 standard quantities and rates for material and labor to produce one compressor.

Brass (4 pounds @ $5.35/pound)...................	$21.40
Steel alloy (5 pounds @ $3.16/pound)	15.80
Direct labor (4 hours @ $7.00/hour)	28.00
Total prime costs	$65.20

The material content of the compressor has been reduced slightly; it is hoped without a noticeable decrease in the quality of the finished product. Improved labor productivity and some increase in automation have resulted in a decrease in labor-hours per unit from 4.4 to 4. However, the significant increases in material prices and hourly labor rates more than offset any savings from reduced input quantities.

The manufacturing overhead cost per unit schedule has yet to be completed. Preliminary data are as follows:

	Activity level (units)		
Overhead items	100,000	110,000	120,000
Supplies	$ 475,000	$ 522,500	$ 570,000
Indirect labor.............	530,000	583,000	636,000
Utilities	170,000	187,000	204,000
Maintenance.............	363,000	377,500	392,000
Taxes and insurance	87,000	87,000	87,000
Depreciation.............	421,000	421,000	421,000
Total overhead........	$2,046,000	$2,178,000	$2,310,000

The standard overhead rate is based upon direct labor-hours and is developed by using the total overhead costs from the above schedule for the activity level closest to planned production. In developing the standards for the manufacturing costs, the following two assumptions were made:

The cost of brass is currently $5.65/pound. However, this price is historically high and the purchasing manager expects the price to drop to the predetermined standard early in 19X2.

Several new employees will be hired for the production line in 19X2. The employees will be generally unskilled. If basic training programs are not effective and labor productivity is not improved, then the production time per unit of product will increase by 15 minutes over the 19X2 standards.

Rein employs a LIFO inventory system for its finished goods. Rein's inventory policy for finished goods is to have 15 percent of the expected annual unit sales for the coming year in finished goods inventory at the end of the prior year. The finished goods inventory on December 31, 19X1, is expected to consist of 16,500 units at a total carrying cost of $1,006,500.

Operating expenses are classified as selling, which are variable, and administrative, which are all fixed. The budgeted selling expenses are expected to average 12 percent of sales revenue in 19X2 which is consistent with the performance in 19X1. The administrative expenses in 19X2 are expected to be 20 percent higher than the predicted 19X1 amount of $907,850.

Management accepts the cost standards developed by the production and accounting departments. However, they are concerned about the possible effect on net income if the price of brass does not decrease, and/or labor efficiency does not improve as expected. Therefore, management wants the budgeted income statement to be prepared using the standards as developed but to consider the worst possible situation for 19X2. Each resulting manufacturing variance should be separately identified and added to or subtracted from budgeted cost of goods sold at standard. Rein is subject to a 45 percent income tax rate.

Required:

a. Prepare the budgeted income statement for 19X2 for Rein Company as specified by management. (Round all calculations to the nearest dollar.)
b. Review the 19X2 budgeted income statement prepared for Rein Company and discuss whether the president's objectives can be achieved.

P13–3.   Cash budget (CMA adapted)

The Triple-F Health Club (Family, Fitness, and Fun) is a nonprofit, family-oriented health club. The club's board of directors is developing plans to acquire more equipment and expand the club facilities. The board plans to purchase about $25,000 of new equipment each year and wants to begin a fund to purchase the adjoining property in four or five years. The adjoining property has a market value of about $300,000.

The club manager, Jane Crowe, is concerned that the board has unrealistic goals in light of its recent financial performance. She has sought the help of a club member with an accounting background to assist her in preparing a report to the board supporting her concerns.

The club member reviewed the club's records, including the cash basis income statements presented below. The review and discussions with Jane Crowe disclosed the additional information which follows the statement.

TRIPLE-F HEALTH CLUB
Statement of Income (Cash Basis)
For Years Ended October 31
($000)

	19X2	19X1
Cash revenues:		
Annual membership fees	$355.0	$300.0
Lesson and class fees	234.0	180.0
Miscellaneous	2.0	1.5
Total cash received	$591.0	$481.5
Cash expenses:		
Manager's salary and benefits	$ 36.0	$ 36.0
Regular employees' wages and benefits	190.0	190.0
Lesson and class employee wages and benefits	195.0	150.0
Towels and supplies	16.0	15.5
Utilities (heat and light)	22.0	15.0
Mortgage interest	35.1	37.8
Miscellaneous	2.0	1.5
Total cash expenses	$496.1	$445.8
Cash income	$ 94.9	$ 35.7

1. Other financial information as of October 31, 19X2:
   a. Cash in checking account, $7,000.
   b. Petty cash, $300.
   c. Outstanding mortgage balance, $360,000.
   d. Accounts payable arising from invoices for supplies and utilities which are unpaid as of October 31, 19X2, $2,500.

2. No unpaid bills existed on October 31, 19X1.

3. The club purchased $25,000 worth of exercise equipment during the current fiscal year. Cash of $10,000 was paid on delivery and the balance was due on October 1, but has not been paid as of October 31, 19X2.

4. The club began operations six years ago in rental quarters. In October, four years ago it purchased its current property (land and building) for $600,000, paying $120,000 down and agreeing to pay $30,000 plus 9 percent interest annually on November 1 until the balance was paid off.

5. Membership rose 3 percent during 19X2. This is approximately the same annual rate the club has experienced since it opened.

6. Membership fees were increased by 15 percent in 19X2. The board has tentative plans to increase the fees by 10 percent in 19X3.

7. Lesson and class fees have not been increased for three years. The board policy is to encourage classes and lessons by keeping the fees low. The members have taken advantage of this policy and the number of classes and lessons has grown significantly each year. The club expects the percentage of growth experienced in 19X2 to be repeated in 19X3.

8. Miscellaneous revenues are expected to grow at the same percentage experienced in 19X2.

9. Operating expenses are expected to increase. Hourly wage rates and the manager's salary will need to be increased 15 percent because no increases were granted in

19X2. Towels and supplies, utilities, and miscellaneous expenses are expected to increase 25 percent.

Required:

a. Construct a cash budget for 19X3 for the Triple-F Health Club.
b. Identify any operating problem(s) that this budget discloses for the Triple-F Health Club. Explain your answer.
c. Is Jane Crowe's concern that the board's goals are unrealistic justified? Explain your answer.

P13–4. Quarterly cash budget

Earl Douglass Wholesalers ask your advice in preparing cash and other budget information for October, November, and December 19X1. The September 30, 19X1, balance sheet showed the following balances:

Cash	$ 20,100
Accounts receivable	995,816
Inventories	660,000
Accounts payable	289,915

Management supplies you with the following assumptions to use in budget preparation. All sales are credit sales and are billed on the last day of the month and customers are allowed a 3 percent discount if payments are made within 10 days after the billing date. Receivables are recorded at gross. The actual collection pattern is: 60 percent within the discount period; 25 percent in the month after billing; 9 percent in the second month after billing.

Fifty-four percent of all material purchases and marketing and administrative expenses are expected to be paid for in the month purchased and the remainder in the following month. Each month's units of ending inventory are equal to 120 percent of the next month's units of sale. Each unit of inventory costs $50. Marketing and administrative expenses, of which $3,500 is depreciation, are equal to 10 percent of the current month's sale. Actual and budgeted sales are as follows:

	Units	Dollars
August	10,000	$750,000
September	10,500	787,500
October	11,000	836,000
November	11,200	851,200
December	11,500	874,300
January 19X2	11,800	890,000

Equipment costing $200,000 is paid for in November. Dividends of $40,000 are paid in December.

Required:

Prepare a cash budget for the last quarter of 19X1. (Round to whole dollars.)

P13–5. Interim income statements (CMA adapted)

The Kalman Company, a subsidiary of the Camper Corporation, submits interim financial statements. Camper combines these statements with similar statements from other subsidiaries to prepare its quarterly statements. The following data are taken from the records and accounts of the Kalman Company.

Sales forecasts for the year are:

Quarter	Units	Percent
First.	450,000	30
Second	600,000	40
Third	150,000	10
Fourth	300,000	20
	1,500,000	100

Forecasted sales have been achieved in the first and second quarters of the current year.

Management is considering increasing the selling price from $30 to $34. However, management is concerned that this increase may reduce the already low sales volume forecasts for the third and fourth quarters.

The production schedule call for 1.5 million units this year. The manufacturing facilities can produce 1,720,000 units per year or 430,000 units per quarter during regular hours. The quarterly production schedule shown below was developed to meet the seasonal sales demand and is being followed as planned.

Quarter	Scheduled production (in units)	Percent
1	465,000	31%
2	450,000	30
3	225,000	15
4	360,000	24
	1,500,000	100%

The standard manufacturing cost of a unit, as established at the beginning of the current year, is as shown below. This standard cost does not incorporate any charges for overtime.

Material	$ 4
Labor.	9
Variable overhead.	2
Fixed overhead.	3
Standard cost per unit	$18

A significant and permanent price increase in the cost of direct material resulted in a material price variance of $270,000 for the materials used in the second quarter.

There was a $120,000 unfavorable direct labor variance in the second quarter due, in part, to overtime pay to meet the heavy production schedule. An overtime premium equal to .5 times the standard labor rate is paid whenever production requires working beyond regular hours. The remaining amount of the labor variance during the quarter occurred as a result of unexpected inefficiencies.

The second quarter unfavorable variable overhead variance of $36,000 was entirely related to the excess direct labor costs.

Total fixed overhead expected to be incurred and budgeted for the year is $4.5 million. Through the first two quarters, $2,745,000 of fixed overhead has been absorbed into the production process. Of this amount, $1,350,000 was absorbed in the second quarter. The high production activity resulted in a total fixed overhead volume variance of $495,000 for the first two quarters.

Selling expenses are 10 percent of sales and are expected to total $4,500,000 for the year.

Administrative expenses are $6,000,000 annually and are incurred uniformly throughout the period.

Inventory balances as of the end of the second quarter are as follows:

Direct material—at actual cost	$400,000
Work in process, 50 percent complete—	
at standard cost	72,000
Finished goods—at standard cost	900,000

The product line is expected to earn $7.5 million before taxes this year. The estimated state and federal income tax expenses for the year is $4,050,000.

Any unplanned variances which are significant and permanent in nature are prorated to the applicable accounts during the quarter in which they are incurred.

Required:

Prepare the second-quarter interim income statement for the Kalman subsidiary of Camper Corporation.

P13–6. Production budgets, projected income statements, and cash budgets

Laurena, Inc. sales were budgeted at 599,000 units for October 19X1; 600,000 units for November 19X1; and 610,000 units for December 19X1 and January 19X2. The selling price is $28 per unit. All sales are on credit and are billed on the 15th and last day of each month with terms of 2/10, net 30. Past experience indicates sales are even throughout the month and 30 percent of the collections are received within the discount period. The remaining collections are received by the end of 30 days; bad debts average 1 percent of gross sales. Laurena, Inc. deducts the estimated amounts of cash discounts on sales and the losses from bad debts from sales on its income statement.

The inventory of finished goods on October 1 was 90,000 units; the finished goods inventory at the end of the each month is to be maintained at 25 percent of sales anticipated for the following month. There is no work in process inventory. FIFO inventory costing is used.

Direct materials of one-half gallon of A432 and one and one-half gallons of B287 are required per finished unit. The inventory of direct materials on October 1 was 20,125 gallons of A432 and 80,375 gallons of B287. A432 costs $2.25 per gallon while B287 costs $0.80 per gallon. At the end of each month, the direct materials inventory is to be maintained at 10 percent of production requirements for the following month. Direct material purchases for each month are paid in the next succeeding month on terms of net 30 days.

Direct labor of one-half hour is required per unit; the direct labor rate is expected to be $8. All salaries are paid in the month earned. A factory overhead application rate of 60 percent of direct labor dollars is used; depreciation of $60,000 per month is included in the rate. Marketing and administrative expenses total $5 million per month, which include depreciation of $4,000 per month. All manufacturing overhead and marketing and administrative expenses are paid on the 10th of the month following the month in which they are incurred.

The cash balance on November 1 is expected to be only $10,000; a loan of $3,550,000 is due on November 10.

Required:

Prepare the following for Laurena, Inc.:

a. Direct-materials purchases budget by month for October and November.
b. Direct labor budgets for October and November.
c. Projected income statement for the month of November. Do not consider income taxes and ignore over- and underapplied overhead. (Round to the nearest whole dollar.)
d. A cash forecast for the month of November, showing the opening balance, receipts itemized by date of collection, disbursements, and balance at the end of month.

CASES

C13–1. Analysis of cash receipts (CMA adapted)

Metro Court Club (MCC) is a sports facility which offers racquetball courts and other physical fitness facilities to its members. There are four of these clubs in the metropolitan area. Each club has between 1,800 and 2,500 members.

Revenue is derived from membership fees and hourly court fees. The annual membership fees are as follows:

Individual	$40
Student	25
Family	95

The hourly court fees vary from $6 to $10 depending upon the season and the time of day (prime versus nonprime time).

The peak racquetball season is considered to run from September through April. During this period, court usage averages 90 to 100 percent of capacity during prime time (5:00–9:00 P.M.) and 50 to 60 percent of capacity during the remaining hours. Daily court usage during the off-season (i.e., summer) only averages 20 to 40 percent of capacity.

Most of MCC's memberships expire in September. A substantial amount of the cash receipts are collected during the early part of the racquetball season due to the renewal of the annual membership fees and heavy court usage. However, cash receipts are not as large in the spring and drop significantly in the summer months.

MCC is considering changing its membership and fee structure in an attempt to change its cash receipts. Under the new membership plan, only an annual membership fee would be charged rather than a membership fee plus hourly court fees. There would be two classes of membership with annual fees as follows:

Individual	$250
Family	400

The annual fee would be collected in advance at the time the membership application is completed and submitted to the club. Members would be allowed to use the racquetball courts as often as they wish during the year with the new plan.

All future memberships would be sold under these new terms. Current memberships would be honored on the old basis until they expire. However, a special promotional campaign would be instituted to attract new members and to encourage current members to convert to the new membership plan immediately.

The annual fees for individual and family memberships would be reduced to $200 and $300 respectively during the two-month promotional campaign. In addition, all memberships sold or renewed during this period would be for 15 months rather than the normal one-year period. Current members also would be given a credit toward the annual fee for the unexpired portion of their membership (on a pro rata basis) and for all prepaid hourly court fees for league play which have not yet been used.

MCC's management estimates that 60 to 70 percent of the present membership would continue with the club. The most active members (45 percent of the present membership) would convert immediately to the new plan while the remaining members who continue would wait until their current memberships expire. Those members who would not continue are not considered active, i.e., they play five or fewer times during the year. Management estimates that the loss of members would be offset fully by new members within six months of instituting the new plan. Furthermore, many of the new members would be individuals who would play during nonprime time. Management estimates that adequate court time will be available for all members under the new plan.

If the new membership plan is adopted, it would be instituted on February 1, 19–, well before the summer season. The special promotional campaign would be conducted during March and April. Once the plan is implemented, annual renewal of memberships and payment of fees would occur as each individual or family membership expires.

Required:

a.   Will Metro Club's new membership plan and fee structure improve its ability to plan its cash receipts? Explain your answer.

b.   Metro Court Club must evaluate the new membership plan and fee structure completely before it decides to adopt or reject it.
   (1)   Identify the key factors that MCC must consider in its evaluation.
   (2)   Explain what type of financial analyses MCC should prepare to make a complete evaluation.

c.   Explain how Metro Court Club's cash management would change if the new membership plan and fee structure were adopted.

C13–2.   Budgeting directive for research and development (CMA adapted)

Lymar Products is a corporation in the agribusiness industry with several divisions; corporate headquarters are in Philadelphia. The R&D Division is located in central Illinois and is responsible for all of the corporation's seed, fertilizer, and insecticide research and development. Research and development is conducted primarily for the benefit of Lymar's other operating divisions. The R&D Division conducts contract research for outside firms when this does not interfere with the division's regular work and is not directly competitive with Lymar's interests.

Lymar's annual budget preparation begins approximately five months before the beginning of the fiscal year. Each division manager is responsible for developing the budget for his or her division within the guidelines provided by corporate headquarters. Once the procedure is completed and the budget is accepted and approved, the division managers have complete authority to operate within the limits prescribed by the budget.

The budget procedures also apply to the R&D Division. However, because this division does work for other Lymar divisions and for the corporate office, the budget of the R&D Division must be carefully coordinated with the other units. Further, the costs associated with the contract research require special consideration by Lymar's management. In the past, cooperation has been good, which has resulted in sound budget preparation.

R&D's management has always presented well-documented budgets for both internal and contract research. When the submitted budget has been changed, the revisions are the result of review, discussion, and agreement between R&D's management and corporate management.

Staff travel is a major item in R&D's budget. Some 25 to 35 trips to corporate headquarters for meetings are made annually by R&D's employees. In addition, members of the division's technical staff make trips related to their research projects and are expected to attend professional meetings and seminars. These trips always have been detailed in a supporting schedule presented with the annual budget.

Lymar's performance for the current year is considered reasonable in light of current and expected future poor economic conditions, but corporate management has become extremely cost conscious to maintain corporate performance at the best possible level. Divisions have been directed to cut down on any unnecessary spending. A specific new directive has been issued stating that any travel in excess of $500 must now be approved in advance at corporate headquarters. In addition, once a division's total dollar amount budgeted for travel has been spent, no budget overruns will be allowed. This directive is effective immediately, and corporate management has indicated that it will continue to be in effect for at least the next two years.

The R&D Division Manager is concerned because this directive appears to represent a change in budget policy. Now, travel which was thought already approved because it was included in the annual budget must be reapproved before each trip. In addition, some scheduled trips previously approved may have to be cancelled because travel funds are likely to run out before the end of the year. R&D staff members already have had to make five special trips to corporate headquarters which were not included in the current year's budget.

The new directive probably will increase costs. The approval process may delay the purchase of airline tickets, thus reducing the opportunity to obtain the lowest fares. Further, there will be a major increase in paperwork for the R&D Division because virtually every trip exceeds the $500 limit.

Required:

a. The directive requiring "the reapproval of all travel in excess of $500" could have far-reaching effects for Lymar Products.
    (1) Explain how this directive could affect the entire budget process, especially the validity of the annual budget.
    (2) Explain what effect this directive is likely to have on the care with which divisions prepare their annual travel budgets in the future.
b. Explain what effect the directive on "reapproval of travel costs" is likely to have on the morale and motivation of the manager and research staff of the R&D Division.

C13–3. Zero-base budgeting

The following decision package series was developed for use in zero-base budgeting. It varies in format from the examples illustrated in the chapter.

Package series name: Ely Petrochemical Company public relations department.

Objective of the department: Build rapport with employees, stockholders, and the public by the periodic release of financial and nonfinancial data. Since top management would review all materials prepared by the public relations department, the chance of misinterpretations and misinformation would be reduced. This consistent policy and interpretation of management to the public would lead to the desired company image being projected.

Description of
activities:

Inform employees, stockholders, and the public of various external and internal factors affecting petrochemical industry, particularly the Ely Company, through such activities as the following:

1. Issue news releases.
2. Publish in-house newsletter for employees.
3. Publish magazines for stockholders, dealing with trends in technology and other general information. (No financial data would be included.)
4. Assist in format of financial data given to stockholders.

1. Different ways of performing same functions:

 a. Recommended method of performing the function: Use a centralized public relations department located at headquarters of Ely Company to perform all the functions of public relations including news releases, editorial services, photography, and printing material. Cost, $300,000. This expenditure would allow for regular news stories which are reviewed by top management prior to their release, for the issuance of an employee newsletter and financial data. By centralizing the public relations function, consistent information from one source which has been reviewed by management would be released.

 b. Alternatives not recommended:

  (1) Contracting with an outside agency to perform the functions of the public relations department, $92,000; cost of independent print-shop activities, $210,000.

  (2) Public relations function performed only at each of two regional locations: Additional first year setup cost and purchase of duplicating equipment at each location would cost $620,000, with a total cost of $390,000 in ensuing years. These separate public relations departments would be staffed with a minimum level of personnel and equipment.

  (3) Eliminate all functions of public relations department and force top management to do the company's public relations activities; however, present top management is overworked and it would be difficult for them to find time to adequately fulfill these duties.

   The recommended way of performing the public relations function of Ely Company was chosen because of control by upper management of news releases, allowing the external and internal information to be consistent with company objectives and philosophy. High-quality photographs and print material would be released.

2. Different levels of effort performing the function:

 a. Public relations department (1 of 3) cost, $174,000. Minimum package: release news stories regularly, publish quarterly in-house employee newsletter, an annual stockholders' magazine, and maintain print shop along with performing other functions of the public relations department. Assistance would also be provided in reviewing and preparing annual stockholders' report containing financial data. Six employees including a public relations director would be employed.

  Consequences of not performing the function:

   Eliminating the public relations department will eliminate the above-mentioned benefits and waste the money already spent in securing the firm's public relations facilities and director already hired.

   Services now provided that this minimum objective level excludes:

Reduce employee in-house newsletter from bimonthly to quarterly, reduce stockholders' report from semiannual to annual.

b. Public relations department (2 of 3) cost, $66,000; cumulative amount, $240,000. Publish in-house newsletter every two months; publish stockholders' report and magazine semiannually as well as maintaining print shop at a higher level of staffing. Total of seven employees, including assistant public relations director, would be hired. Add one assistant public relations director (current level of operations).

c. Public relations department (3 of 3) cost, $60,000; cumulative amount, $300,000. Publish in-house employee newsletter monthly as well as maintaining print shop at higher staffing level and additional equipment. Total of eight employees. Add one employee.

Required:

Study the above decision package series and answer these questions:

a. Under what conditions would you advise management to choose
 (1) Minimum objective level (1 of 3)?
 (2) Maintain current level of operations (2 of 3)?
 (3) Improve current level of operations (3 of 3)?
b. If management chose to adopt level (3 of 3) and improve operations, how much money would be budgeted for the public relations department?
c. Are you able to rank these levels? Why or why not?

C13–4.   Zero-base budgeting

As a well-respected consultant, you have been requested to assist William Barnes Company in applying zero-base budgeting to the activities of the marketing research department. Several weeks ago, you spent several hours explaining the theory and implementation of this technique to the managers involved. You assigned each of them the task of gathering specific data for the various activities they are proposing to implement in year 19X2. The plans are for you to then assist each manager in preparing zero-base budgeting requests for various levels of effort.

Harold Smith presented raw data concerned with obtaining dealers' and consumers' opinions of Product A. Management has expressed a continued desire for identifying the product and promotional features which should be improved to increase their market share. This was started last year, but only the dealers' attitudes were ascertained through mail questionnaires and telephone interviews. Barnes Company hopes to have enough funds this year to survey both dealers' and consumers' attitudes.

After studying the data gathered, the following three levels of effort will be used: (1) minimum objective level involving the study of dealers' and consumers' attitudes using mail questionnaires only, (2) current objective level involving mail questionnaires and telephone interviews, and (3) improvement objective level utilizing personal interviews in addition to mail questionnaires and telephone interviews.

Harold Smith and his staff feel that mail questionnaires would be less expensive than telephone or personal interviews because they will be surveying the more highly educated, upper-income brackets. Also, they feel that the number of returns received will be higher since most of the dealers are busy executives and they are more easily approached by mail questionnaire. Since a smaller field staff is required than is the case with interviews, it is felt that one clerk and one interviewer can be deleted from the seven positions filled last year if this minimum objective level is adopted.

The total expenditures in 19X1 were $615,000 which resulted in a $0.50 average cost per mail questionnaire and a $0.70 average cost per telephone interview. Smith has prepared line item budgets for the various proposed expenditures at this level. Because the postal rate has been increased, proposed expenditures total $700,000, resulting in a $0.60 cost per mail questionnaire. The next level of effort utilizes both mail questionnaires and telephone interviews. By increasing the study, one clerk and two interviewers will be required that were not needed at the minimum level. This represents one additional interviewer not used at the current level last year. Costs of using telephone interviews are budgeted to be $100,000 in 19X2 or $0.75 per call.

Management would prefer to have the assurance that the respondents are representative of the entire population by also including personal interviews in their study. This improvement level of effort is expected to require two more interviewers and a data analyst, resulting in proposed expenditures of $75,000. The average cost per personal interview in 19X2 is budgeted for $12. By including personal interviews in the survey, Smith feels more valid data concerning the causes and reasons for the respondent's actions or attitudes can be obtained.

All managers understand that after the budgeting requests are prepared for each activity proposed in the department, they will be ranked.

Required:

Prepare zero-base budgeting requests for this activity.

C13–5. Zero-base budgeting for a nonprofit organization

The business manager of United Church, which has 3,000 members, is interested in adopting zero-base budgeting to his institution. He believes that he can effectively combine this budgeting technique with a program budget approach. To test its adaptability, the manager plans to have two areas within his church prepare zero-base budgets initially: Evangelism and Music. The chairperson of each area understands zero-base budgeting concepts but requires your assistance in submitting the request forms. All committee members involved expect a 10 percent increase in costs, with the exception of ministers' salaries, to maintain the same level of service provided in 19X1.

The 19X1 budgets for the two areas are given below:

	Evangelism	Music
Salaries:		
Senior minister (including housing)....	$35,000	
Director........................		$18,000
Organist (part-time)..............		7,000
Car allowance	3,000	500
Robe maintenance and cleaning		400
Literature and supplies	1,500	2,000
Postage.........................	4,300	
Continuing education	800	200
Advertising in Yellow Pages...........	700	
Newspaper advertising..............	2,500	
Guest musicians and substitutes		850
	$47,800	$28,950

Evangelism Committee. In discussing the needs of the evangelism committee in critical areas, concern was expressed that the church has not had a special evangelistic crusade for three years. It is felt that a well-known speaker from out of town is an essential ingredient for the crusade's success. It is expected that the expense associated with the speaker will be $2,000. As part of the crusade, one committee member believes that the church should provide a friendship banquet on the last night for the entire congregation. The meal will be free, but church members and friends will be required to register in advance. Based on past attendance, the committee believes 500 people will attend at an average cost of $4 each. If a lighter meal is served and decorations and flowers are kept to a minimum, the expense can be reduced to $2.50 per person.

The entire congregation approved keeping the senior minister's salary the same as it was in 19X1. However, one member of the evangelism committee believes the minister's car allowance should be increased an extra 8 percent above the 10 percent general price rise to cover spiraling gasoline prices. Another committee member suggests that church members visit prospective members as well as current members who, according to the attendance pads, have not been to a church service in three months. The consensus of the committee is that this is a good idea, but that these individuals need some initial instruction and probably should meet together first, possibly for a meal, before going out in teams to visit. Approximately 40 carefully chosen members could visit monthly in groups of two. If dinner is prepared for them, the cost will be $2.25 each.

Team visiting led to a discussion regarding the use of church advertising, minister's calling cards, and a brochure describing the church's services and ministry. Several committee members believe that since the minister's supply of calling cards is not depleted, the annual expense of $200 is not imperative. They share the same view with regard to the brochure describing the church's activities. The fact that some of last year's brochures had to be thrown away because they became dusty while "sitting in the racks out front" is support for their view. The cost of the brochure was $150 in 19X1.

Presently, the church has a display ad in the Yellow Pages of the city's telephone directory and also places weekly display ads in the shoppers' news and local newspaper. One committee member expressed concern that several active church members had been dismayed by these advertisements because they believe such solicitation lacks dignity and should be discontinued.

Another member said, "Well, now that you are talking about cutting costs, how about dropping those monthly letters all church members receive from the church staff informing us of activities that have already been publicized in the weekly church bulletin? I'd rather see us keep our Yellow Pages display ad and change the monthly letters to quarterly ones." The cost of each monthly mailing is estimated to be $250.

Another member indicated that he had heard several church members grumbling about last year's continuing education expense for the ministerial staff, since some members perceive this as merely a paid vacation for the participants.

Dial-a-devotion telephone tape systems are available for $550 per year; the senior minister has expressed a desire to add this system.

Music committee.   One of the prime concerns expressed by the music committee is providing for 200 new hymnals. Not only are some pews lacking enough hymnals, but many of the books presently in use are torn. Several Sunday school classes have asked for these worn hymnals. Different types of binding are available, but the cost per hymnal of the type desired is expected to be $6.

Several committee members thought that not only should a car allowance be provided the director of music, but that the organist should also be given a $200 car allowance. If this is approved, the director's car allowance will be increased an additional 8 percent above the general price rise.

Other committee members felt that car allowances were "luxury items" and could be omitted if "times got tight." These members also believed that continuing education fell into the same category as car allowances and could be adjusted depending on the total budget. The organist has expressed a desire to attend a religious music workshop in Cincinnati next year; this will cost $400.

An increase in the music library for the choir and special groups, costing $600 above the present amount budgeted, is desired. Additional guest musicians are available for $50, which includes one rehearsal and performance; several music committee members think guest musicians should be hired on at least five more occasions during the church year.

Required:

Prepare zero-base budgeting requests for these activities and rank them.

OUTLINE OF CHAPTER 14

Tax impact on capital decisions

Evaluation techniques

Inflation in the capital budgeting process

Assets constructed for own use

CASB standards

OBJECTIVES OF CHAPTER 14

1. To explain the planning and control tools that should be applied to achieve more efficient utilization of plant assets.

2. To present several means of evaluating capital expenditure proposals so that the most appropriate ones may be applied.

3. To illustrate the incorporation of inflation into capital budgeting.

4. To present positions regarding the capitalization of general factory overhead when assets are constructed for own use.

14

Capital budgeting and cost analysis

Because capital expenditures involve significant resources that are committed for a long time in the future, much time and effort should go into the evaluation of plant assets' proposals. The length of time for which the resources are committed makes capital expenditures more risky than other investments. Capital expenditure analysis is also crucial because after the committment for the capital investment has been made, management may have difficulty in recovering the cost other than through the use of the capital asset. This chapter discusses the various means available for evaluating capital expenditures and the controls necessary to ensure their efficient utilization. The capital expenditure budget proper was introduced in Chapter 13.

Most companies do not have all the funds necessary to finance all proposed capital expenditure projects, and available funds can be put to different uses. As a result, before beginning a capital expenditure program that involves a large outlay of funds tied up for several years, management should seek assurance that it will receive an acceptable return on the investment. To quantitatively select projects, predicted cash flows must be compared with the investment required. Management should then determine whether the return generated by these projects exceeds what is considered acceptable. Determining what rate is acceptable is a difficult problem involving financial concepts more than accounting concepts.

Top management involvement. Top management should be involved in evaluating large capital expenditure proposals because the individual projects must be consistent with objectives established for the overall company.

However, some authority must also be delegated to middle managers who have the required competence to properly evaluate the proposal. Companies vary in decentralization of authority for capital expenditure approval. For example, some companies allow division managers much leeway in selecting the plant and equipment to use in the operation of their divisions. Other companies specify a small dollar amount as the limit for approval by division managers; only top management can approve capital expenditure proposals above this limit.

An important phase of a capital investment program is the analysis and evaluation of capital expenditures. Policies reflecting management's objectives should be established in advance so that evaluation can be objective and consistent. Detailed guidelines are especially necessary at lower management levels. Policy manuals which detail the procedures and document flow for administering capital expenditure proposals should be available. These manuals should be designed so that employees are encouraged to search for profitable investments within their own technical specialties. While a thorough review is important, management must guard against having such detailed, time-consuming procedures that employees hesitate to introduce new projects or rapid project development is impeded. Employees are also more stimulated to search for capital improvements if they feel assured that their proposals will be given a fair review.

Capital expenditure proposals involve not only additions of new plant assets but also expansion and improvement of existing investments and the replacement of capital assets. The basis of analyzing the improvement and replacement of capital assets involves comparing the costs of existing facilities with future cost savings. Differential cost studies are presented in Chapter 17 and can be used when the expansion of capital assets is proposed.

Sunk cost in replacement decisions. When management is faced with having to replace plant assets, only future cost savings and revenue changes should be considered. This type of analysis is difficult to prepare because the economic life of the new asset must be estimated in addition to the prospective purchase price less any salvage value that can be expected. The original cost less the accumulated depreciation taken on the equipment to be replaced, or the book value, is a *sunk cost*. Since the cost cannot be changed by any future decision, it is irrelevant to the decision regarding the replacement of the equipment. However, book values do affect income tax liability related to plant asset transactions because of Internal Revenue Service regulations regarding the recognition of gains and losses on exchanges of plant assets.

TAX IMPACT ON CAPITAL DECISIONS

Income tax laws that apply to capital budgeting situations are often complex. Because the main objective of this book is not to explain current tax law, we will use only a few pertinent provisions in our illustrations. However, income tax laws have a significant impact on capital expenditure analysis, and the illustrations and problems represent an attempt to follow the current tax rulings regarding depreciation and other aspects of capital budgeting.

Tax shield.   The purchase cost of capital assets is deductible as yearly depreciation. This deduction is called a *tax shield* because it protects an amount of income equal to the depreciation from taxation. As is illustrated in this chapter's exhibits, depreciation further affects capital decisions because it does not involve a yearly outflow of cash.

One act that wrought substantive changes in the tax provisions applicable to capital budgeting is The Economic Recovery Tax Act of 1981. Under its provisions, changes were made in capital cost recovery with the Accelerated Cost Recovery System (ACRS) which generally applies to assets placed in service after 1980.

Accelerated methods.   ACRS permits cost recovery to be accelerated over predetermined periods which are generally shorter than the "useful lives," of the items involved. The unadjusted basis (cost) of eligible "recovery property" is recovered over a 3-, 5-, 10-, or 15-year period, depending on the type of property. ACRS also disregards salvage value. The deductions approximate those made under accelerated depreciation and are specified in tables showing the percentage of the cost of recoverable property deductible during the recovery years for each class of property. Built into the tables is the "half-year convention" for the year of acquisition. For example, for 5-year property, 15 percent is deductible in year 1, 22 percent in year 2, and 21 percent in each of the three remaining years. The unadjusted basis of the property is simply multiplied by the statutory percentage.

Election to use straight-line method.   Specified optional recovery periods with straight-line rates may also be used. For example, the optional recovery period may be 5, 12, or 25 years for 5-year property. However, the half-year convention also applies to the straight-line method and has the effect of extending every recovery period by one year. There are additional provisions regarding the election for all property of that class placed in service for the year the election is made.

Investment credit.   To stimulate capital investment, Internal Revenue Service regulations permit companies to take an *investment credit* under certain specified conditions when certain types of depreciable assets are purchased. Under the new tax law for ACRS property, the investment credit is based on the asset's prescribed recovery period. For eligible 5-year and 10-year property and 15-year public utility property, a full 10 percent of the purchase price is allowed and can be subtracted directly from the amount of the tax bill in the year the asset is purchased. For three-year recovery property, 60 percent of the investment qualifies for the credit. Additional rules and limitations are involved, but are beyond the scope of this book.

EVALUATION TECHNIQUES

There are several techniques for evaluating capital expenditure proposals. These range from simple methods such as cash payback to more sophisticated methods which use the time value of money in computing an estimated return on investment. Three quantitative methods used in making capital budgeting decisions and their advantages and weaknesses will be discussed: (1) payback or payout, (2) unadjusted return on investment, and (3) discounted cash flow. Two variations of the discounted cash flow method are (a) net present value (sometimes referred to as excess present value) and (b) internal rate of return (often called time-adjusted rate of return). After studying each of these methods, the accountant is better able to determine which is most appropriate. In evaluating proposals involving large sums of money, the use of more than one approach may be advantageous. However, when a comparison is made of several proposals, the same evaluation techniques should be used consistently for each project by all segments of the company. For example, the calculations determined by the mixing department with the payback method should not be compared with results using the net present value method determined by the fabricating department. Because the detail and cost of applying each evaluation technique vary, the dollar amount of the prospective investment should be used as a criteria in justifying the evaluation technique used.

Capital expenditure proposal.   Management of the Krebs Company is considering the expansion of its producing facilities through the purchase of an asset costing $80,000. For tax purposes, this is five-year property, and its depreciation is calculated using ACRS guidelines; its economic life to the company is also five years. The cash flows associated with the proposal are

EXHIBIT 14–1

Aftertax cash flow for Equipment A—Carl Krebs Company

Year	(1) Pretax increase in cash inflow	(2) Depreciation*	(3) (1 − 2) Cash inflow subject to tax	(4) 3 × Rate federal and state income tax†	(5) (1 − 4) Net increase in aftertax cash flow
1........	$43,302	$12,000	$31,302	$13,302	$ 30,000
2........	47,076	17,600	29,476	15,076	32,000
3........	52,736	16,800	35,936	17,736	35,000
4........	58,396	16,800	41,596	20,396	38,000
5........	62,170	16,800	45,370	22,170	40,000
		$80,000			$175,000

*Computed using ACRS guidelines.
†Percentage varies each year.

shown in Exhibit 14–1 and will be used to illustrate the application of the four evaluation techniques discussed.

For ease of computation, the net increase in aftertax cash flow is expressed in even thousands of dollars; however, to reach these figures, uneven numbers for the pretax increase in cash inflow and a varying federal and state income tax rate are used. The effect of subtracting federal and state income tax from the pretax increase in cash flow is to add depreciation back in to measure the full amount of cash that flows into the business. It should be noted here that one of the most difficult and important stages in the capital budgeting process involves the definition and estimation of cash flows. This topic was introduced in Chapter 13 and further discussed in Chapter 17.

Payback or payout method

The payback or payout method is a simple approach measuring the length of time required to recover the initial outlay for a project. While this model lacks sophistication, it represents an improvement over merely basing the decision on management's intuition. The payback method can be more appropriately used if it is necessary to screen proposals rapidly and if decisions involve extremely risky proposals.

If the net increase in aftertax cash flow in Exhibit 14–1 were an even $35,000 ($175,000/5 years) each year, the $80,000 purchase price of the asset could be divided by the cash flow to give the payback of 2.29 ($80,000/$35,000). However, since the net increase in cash flow increases each year and is not uniform, a different calculation is required, as shown in Exhibit 14–2. Each year's net cash inflows are accumulated until the initial investment is recovered. With the net annual cash inflows as given, the amount of the investment is returned in 2.51 years.

Companies often hesitate to apply methods more sophisticated than the payback method because many investment decisions are automatic if the company wishes to maintain operations. In these cases, management relies on professional judgment coupled with the payback method. In other cases, management may feel that the proposals are unacceptable when first presented and use the payback method to screen them. The payback method does offer the advantage of being simple, and it gives a quick evaluation that does offer

EXHIBIT 14–2

Traditional payback for Equipment A

	Cash flow	Payback years
Year 1.	$30,000	1.00
Year 2.	32,000	1.00
Year 3.	18,000	0.51 $\left(\dfrac{\$18,000}{\$35,000}\right)$
Investment . . .	$80,000	2.51 years

some improvement over strictly intuitive judgment. However, there are serious inherent weaknesses in that the payback method ignores the time value of money and the salvage value of the investment. Income that is generated beyond the payback period is also given no consideration. Despite these disadvantages, the payback method is widely used as an initial screening for capital expenditure proposals.

Bailout payback method. This is a variation of the payback method; it focuses on measuring the risk involved in a capital expenditure. The traditional payback approach attempts to answer the question: "How soon will I recover my investment if operations proceed as planned?" The bailout payback method instead asks: "If things go wrong, which alternative offers the best bailout protection?" For example, if the capital item is of a special type, and its disposal value is less than that of standard equipment, the bailout payback reflects these disposal values. Suppose Equipment A under consideration in Exhibit 14–1 and 14–2 is being compared with Equipment B costing $60,000, which is expected to produce uniform annual cash savings of $15,000. Equipment A's disposal value is expected to be $30,000 at the end of year 1 and decline at the rate of $20,000 annually due to the special nature of its technology. Equipment B's disposal value is expected to be $45,000 at the end of year 1 and decline only $5,000 annually because of its general adaptability. Both are five-year property items. The bailout payback period is reached when the cumulative net increase in aftertax cash flow plus the disposal value equals the original cost. As seen in Exhibit 14–3, there is less risk with purchasing Equipment B because its bailout period is reached at the end of year 1. However, as Exhibit 14–3 shows, its traditional payback period is four years, which is longer than Equipment A's traditional payback period of 2.5 years. Exhibit 14–3 also indicates that different analyses of the payback method can yield different results.

EXHIBIT 14–3

Bailout payback

	At end of year	Cumulative cash	Disposal value	Cumulative total
Equipment A.	1	$30,000	$30,000	$60,000
	2	62,000	10,000	72,000
	3	97,000	—0—	97,000

Bailout payback is between years 2 and 3, depending on assumptions made regarding cash flow.

Equipment B.	1	$15,000	$45,000	$60,000

Bailout payback is at the end of year 1.
Traditional payback for Equipment B: $60,000/$15,000 = 4 years

Unadjusted return on investment

The unadjusted return on investment is also known as the book value rate of return, the accounting or financial statement method, or the approximate rate of return. The following equation is used to determine the unadjusted return on investment:

$$\frac{\text{Average annual net aftertax income}}{\text{Initial investment}}$$

Using the data from Exhibit 14–1, depreciation of \$80,000 is deducted from the \$175,000 net increase in aftertax cash and divided by five years to give a \$19,000

$$\frac{\$175,000 - \$80,000}{5 \text{ years}} = \$19,000$$

average annual income after taxes. The average annual income is then divided by the \$80,000 initial investment to give a 23.75 percent return as follows:

$$\frac{\$19,000 \text{ average annual net aftertax income}}{\$80,000 \text{ initial investment}} = 23.75 \text{ percent}$$

Instead of computing the return on initial investment, the return on average investment can be determined. Because straight-line depreciation is not used in this illustration, the original book value and the book values at the end of each year must be averaged to determine average investment as follows:

Year	Book value (end of year)
1	$ 68,000
2	50,400
3	33,600
4	16,800
5	–0–
Original investment	80,000
	$248,800

$248,800/6 years = $41,467 average investment

Using these data, the return on average investment becomes:

$$\frac{\$19,000 \text{ average annual net aftertax income}}{\$41,467 \text{ average investment}} = 45.8 \text{ percent}$$

If, instead, straight-line depreciation were used, the original investment would be divided by 2 to arrive at the average investment since this \$80,000 asset had no salvage value. If an asset has a scrap value at the end of its economic life, the scrap value would be added in to determine average investment regardless of the depreciation method used because the scrap value represents the investment at the end of its economic life.

While the unadjusted return on investment does improve on the weaknesses of the payback method because it takes into account profitability, it fails to consider the time value of money. Also, the unadjusted rate of return compares savings to be received in the future to an investment that requires a current outlay of funds. However, this method is familiar because it is based on the accrual method of preparing financial statements and is easy to apply. It also facilitates follow-up of expenditures, since the data are available in the accounting records. But despite its advantages, unadjusted return on investment is not appropriate if additional capital expenditures are made after the project has started.

Discounted cash flow methods

The *net present value method* and the *internal rate of return*, which are variations of the discounted cash flow method, do, however, consider the time value of money. The value of money today is called its present value. For example, the present value of one dollar today is $1, while the present value of $1 that will be available at some time in the future is less than $1, assuming no deflation. A process called *discounting* is used to convert the cash inflows for each year to their present value by multiplying each year's cash inflow by the appropriate factor from a present value table. Managers would rather have a dollar today than in the future because they can put today's dollar to work earning a return and have more than $1 in the future. This is the reason that present value decreases as the number of years in which payment is to be received increases. When present value is applied to a capital investment, the future return is in the form of cash generated by the asset acquired. This return is designated as cash inflow in Exhibit 14–1. Since an outflow of cash must be made in the present to purchase the plant asset, management is concerned over whether the cash inflow generated by this plant asset warrants making the investment.

Present value tables. Present value tables are included in an appendix at the end of the book to facilitate applying the discounted cash flow methods. The present value for a single amount to be received *n* years from now is given in Table A. Multiplying the appropriate present value factor from the table by an expected future cash flow, the accountant can determine the present value of the cash flow. Table B (also given in the appendix) can be used to find the present value of a stream of equal cash inflows received annually for any given number of years. Table B is technically known as a table of "Present value of an annuity of $1," and the numbers it contains are determined by adding together the amounts for the corresponding year and all preceding years in the same column of Table A. Tables A and B are both based on the assumption that cash inflows are received only once annually on the last day of the year. However, if the cash inflow is generated through increased revenues and lower costs which are received throughout the year, annual present value tables are not precise, but are sufficiently good approximations. Thus, annual tables are most often used in investment problems because they are easier to apply and are adequate in view of the necessary estimates involved in any capital investment proposal.

Net present value method.   A variation of the discounted cash flow method is called the net present value or excess present value method; it assumes some minimum desired rate of return. This desired rate of return is the rate at which the cash inflows are discounted to the present. A capital investment proposal is considered acceptable if the present value of its future expected net cash inflows equals or exceeds the amount of the initial investment. If more than one investment is being considered, the net present value of each alternative is compared with that of the others to choose the most profitable investment.

Examination of Tables A and B indicates that the higher the required rate of return, the lower the present value of the cash inflows. As a result, if a higher required rate of return is used, fewer capital expenditure proposals have cash inflows that exceed the initial outflow of the investment cost. This means that a company may have to adjust the rate of return it is applying if it feels that too many proposals are being rejected. Conversely, if it feels that more proposals are acceptable than management believes are warranted, it should consider raising the rate of return.

Weighted cost of capital.   In economic theory, the required rate of return can be based on the cost of capital used, which is the cost of debt capital added to the cost of equity capital, each weighted by its proportion of the company's total capital structure. For example, assume a company has the following debt and equity:

	Percent of total	Component cost	Weighted cost
Debt	20	4.0%	0.8%
Equity	80	14.0	11.2
	100		12.0%

The cost of capital is multiplied by the percent of debt and equity yielding a 12 percent weighted cost of capital, which can be used as the required rate of return. However, even though the rate that investors expect, referred to as the cost of capital in the above illustration, is given a component cost, it is difficult to arrive at this figure. The rate of return investors expect is reflected in the market price of the company's stock, but other factors, such as dividend policy, general economic conditions, and projected company earnings, also influence the market price. Because of the difficulty in estimating the cost of capital, this approach is not widely used in practice.

Management should use its judgment in arriving at the required rate of return. However, the rate is usually above the general level of interest rates at which banks and other institutions are lending money because there is greater risk with a capital investment than with a bank loan. This approach is generally used for investment proposals considered to involve average risk; for projects considered higher risk, the required rate of return should be raised for this uncertainty.

After a company's required rate of return is estimated, the present value method can be applied. Using the data from Exhibit 14–1, the net present value concept can be illustrated using a 12 percent estimated cost of capital. As discussed above, the discount rate may be set above the cost of capital to allow for risk or inflation. Computations from Exhibit 14–1 follow:

Year	Aftertax cash (outflow) or inflow	Present value of $1 at 12%	Net present value of flow
0	$(80,000)	1.000	$(80,000)
1	30,000	0.893	26,790
2	32,000	0.797	25,504
3	35,000	0.712	24,920
4	38,000	0.636	24,168
5	40,000	0.567	22,680
Net present value			$ 44,062

Since the above project has a positive net present value, the effective rate of return earned is above the 12 percent cost of capital used. When the cash flows vary as they do in this illustration, Table A showing the present value of $1 must be used for each period. However, if the cash flows had been uniform, a simpler approach using Table B, the present value of $1 received annually for N years, could have been used; the cumulative factor is multiplied by the cash flow of one period. For example, if the $175,000 annual net increase in aftertax cash flows had been earned uniformly, giving a $35,000 annual cash flow ($175,000/5 years), the following computation could be made using a cumulative factor of 3.605 from Table B for the annual cash flow:

Present value of annual cash flows . . . . $126,175 ($35,000 × 3.605)
Less initial investment   80,000
Net present value . . . . $ 46,175

Present value payback.   With the present value payback method, management knows the minimum necessary life over which a project will recover its initial investment and still earn the desired rate of return. The net present value of flow shows the present value payback years required, as in the following illustration:

Year	Cash flow	Payback years
1	$26,790	1.00
2	25,504	1.00
3	24,920	1.00
4	2,786	$0.12 \left(\dfrac{\$2,786}{\$24,168} \right)$
	$80,000	3.12 years

Based on the above calculation, 3.12 years are required to recover the $80,000 initial investment and earn the desired 12 percent rate of return on the annual unrecovered investment balance.

Weighted net present value or expected value. An allowance for risk and uncertainty can be made by determining the present value of the net cash flows for each alternative investment being considered according to various assumptions about future conditions. For example, the present value of the net cash flows should be determined for normal conditions, for pessimistic conditions, and for optimistic conditions. The probability of each of these conditions occurring is then applied to the present value of the net cash flows so that the weighted net present value, or expected value, can be calculated. This is very similar to the approach shown in Exhibit 17–8 in which probabilities are attached to the payoff of alternatives. The net present value calculated earlier is rounded to $44,000 and is assumed to represent the normal condition most likely to occur. The weighted net present value, or expected present value, for this investment is illustrated below:

	Net present value	×	Probability weights	=	Weighted net present value
Normal conditions.	$44,000		0.60		$26,400
Optimistic conditions.	66,000		0.25		16,500
Pessimistic conditions	30,000		0.15		4,500
Weighted net present value or expected present value					$47,400

The net present values given for the optimistic conditions and pessimistic conditions are determined using the present value method; however, the calculations are not shown. This method is employed to estimate the most likely amount of future cash receipts.

Internal rate of return. A second variation of the discounted cash flow method is the internal rate of return (often called the time-adjusted rate of return). Like the present value method, the internal rate of return approach measures project profitability. However, it differs from the net present value method in that no discount rate is known in advance with this approach. The computation shown below is determined by trial and error before a discounted rate is found that yields a zero net present value.

Year	Cash (outflow) or inflow	Present value of $1 (30 percent)	Net present value of flow	Present value of $1 (35 percent)	Net present value of flow
0	$(80,000)	1.000	$(80,000)	1.000	$(80,000)
1	30,000	0.769	23,070	0.741	22,230
2	32,000	0.592	18,944	0.549	17,568
3	35,000	0.455	15,925	0.406	14,210
4	38,000	0.350	13,300	0.301	11,438
5	40,000	0.269	10,760	0.223	8,920
			$ 1,999		$(5,634)

The discounted rate is greater than 30 percent because a positive net present value results, but it is less than 35 percent because a negative present value is determined at this level. The trial-and-error search should continue until adjacent rates in the table are found such that a positive net present value is achieved with the lower rate and a negative net present value with the higher rate. If a present value table no more detailed than Table A is used, an approximation of the percentage can be obtained by interpolation, as follows:

$$30\% + \left(5\% \times \frac{\$1,999}{\$7,633^*}\right) = 30\% + (5\% \times 0.262)$$
$$= 30\% + 1.31 = \underline{\underline{31.31\%}}$$
$$= 31\%$$

*$1,999 + $5,634.

Through the use of the internal rate of return, management can choose the proposal with the highest rate of return; this return should be higher than the company's cost of capital. The method used, present value or internal rate of return, does not normally affect the indicated desirability of investment proposals. However, the rankings of mutually exclusive investments determined using the internal rate of return are often different from those determined through using the net present value method. This can occur when the mutually exclusive proposals have unequal lives or when the size of the investment differs even though the lives are identical. The differences in these two variations of discounted cash flow result from the assumptions made regarding the reinvestment rate of return. With the internal rate of return, earnings are assumed to be reinvested at the same rate earned by the shorter lived project. However, many people argue that it is more reasonable to adopt the net present value method assumption that earnings are reinvested at the rate of discount, which is the company's minimum rate of return.

Exhibit 14–4 indicates the different rankings for mutually exclusive capital investment proposals obtained using the net present value and internal rate of return methods. With identical annual aftertax net cash inflow, but with

EXHIBIT 14-4

Comparison of rankings for mutually exclusive proposals

Capital investment proposal	Investment	Life (years)	Annual aftertax net cash inflow	Net present value method using 12 percent discount Amount of net present value	Rank	Internal rate of return Rate of return	Rank
A	$2,500	4	$1,000	$ 537	3	22%	1
B	5,000	12	1,000	1,194	2	17	2
C	6,000	18	1,000	1,250	1	15	3

varying investments and years of life, the rankings differ. (Since the computations are omitted in Exhibit 14-4, check your understanding of the methods by making the calculations using the present value tables.) There is a difference in results because the rate of return method assumes that the Proposal A amount at the end of the fourth year will be reinvested to earn a 22 percent rate of return. However, the net present value method assumes the Proposal A amount at the end of the fourth year will be reinvested to earn only a 12 percent return, which is presumed to be the minimum desired rate of return.

Thus, as long as the minimum desired rate of return is lower than the internal rate of return, projects with shorter lives will show a higher rank with the internal rate of return. If reinvestment at the minimum desired rate of return is expected, the net present value approach should be used because it better reflects the opportunity rate of return.

Opinions differ concerning comparison of the profitability of projects with different lives or significantly different cash inflow patterns. The rate of return earned on the reinvestment of funds recovered by the project with the shorter life span is thus an important factor. One way to handle this is to consider the shorter-lived investment's period only and include an estimate of the recoverable value of the longer-lived investment at the end of the shorter period. The analysis would cover only the shorter period, with the recoverable value of the longer-lived investment treated as a cash inflow at the end of the period.

Sensitivity analysis. Another approach for dealing with uncertainty is sensitivity analysis, which measures the effect on the estimate if changes in the critical data inputs vary. Sensitivity analysis can be used in capital budgeting to study the effect on net present value or rate of return if a project factor, such as cash flow or economic life, changes. The financial cost of possible errors in forecasting is measured by sensitivity analysis using either a table or a graph. Sensitivity analysis is helpful because it focuses the manager's attention on the more sensitive areas. This topic is further discussed in Chapter 19.

Computer studies. The vast capabilities of electronic data-processing equipment offer management additional means of evaluation that are not feasibly done manually. Various models simulating possibilities and probabilities of results can be created by the computer. More reliable information can be obtained from computer studies than from manual evaluation techniques.

Management should carefully examine projects with forecasted results very near the cutoff point because there is little room for error. For example, if an investment proposal is expected to yield an 11 percent return when the required rate of return is 10 percent, there is a smaller zone for error than there is for an investment forecasted to yield a 20 percent return. A higher degree of sophistication in evaluation is needed to better determine the profitability of the proposal. This additional cost is warranted if two alternative proposals yield approximately the same acceptable results, or if the evaluation indicates results that are near the rejection point.

Choice of a method.   Companies often hesitate to apply present value or internal rate of return and rely on nondiscounting criteria, such as professional judgment, the payback method, or the unadjusted rate of return. These managers do not use discounting techniques because they feel that cash flows and economic life must be estimated so roughly in many cases that the cost of applying such refined methods is not justified. Instead, they feel that the payback method or the unadjusted return is satisfactory. This is understandable if a company has no choice; for example, a safety device may be necessitated by law or employee welfare. Similarly, profitability is not the prime consideration when some capital expenditures, such as luxurious offices, are incurred because they are status symbols.

While management should apply one or more of the above evaluation techniques in making capital investment decisions, other factors, such as legal requirements and social responsibilities, cannot be ignored. The capital investment program must also allow for emergencies. For example, a machine that is expected to operate efficiently for several more years may break down. If this machine is crucial to production, management may have no choice but to incur major expenditures in repairing or replacing it. Provision must be made to handle proposals of this nature more rapidly than less critical projects.

INFLATION IN THE CAPITAL BUDGETING PROCESS

An important aspect of capital budgeting is the impact of inflation on budgeting techniques, particularly incorporating price level changes into the model. In a taxless world, inflation would affect cash flows and the applicable discount rate in a comparable manner. Therefore, the effect on present value calculations would be irrelevant. However, we do not live in such world, and the impact of tax must be considered in almost all business decisions. In addition, assuming the price level is constant is erroneous because the general price level changes over the life of the project. An increase in the general price level index increases the future revenues, wages, and material costs of the project.

Inflation's effect. The following illustrates capital investment selection when inflation is incorporated. Assume that in the current year 19X0, a company is considering the purchase of equipment which will be classified as five-year property for tax purposes. Its usefulness to the company also corresponds to this life. The controller indicates that the company's cost of capital unadjusted for inflation is 14 percent. Economic advisors determine that the general price level index should rise by 10 percent a year for the next five years. The company anticipates operations from the equipment to yield $55,000 in cash revenue and require $20,000 cash expenses, all in 19X0 prices. The requested 14 percent rate for the cost of capital (the discount rate) is adjusted for inflation as follows:

$$1.14 \times 1.10 = 1.254 = 25\%$$

Adding the cost of capital to the inflation rate is not appropriate; instead, these values should be multiplied to incorporate the compounding effect of inflation. As illustrated in Exhibit 14–5, both the discount rate and the predicted cash

EXHIBIT 14–5

The effects of inflation on capital budgeting procedures

Revenue	19X1	19X2	19X3	19X4	19X5	Total
Revenue.	$55,000	$55,000	$55,000	$55,000	$55,000	
Less: Cash						
expenses	20,000	20,000	20,000	20,000	20,000	
Pretax cash						
flow unadjusted						
for inflation	$35,000	$35,000	$35,000	$35,000	$35,000	
Inflation index	1.10	1.21	1.331	1.464	1.610	
Inflation						
adjusted pretax						
cash flow	$38,500	$42,350	$46,585	$51,240	$56,350	
Less: Depreciation.	15,000	22,000	21,000	21,000	21,000	
Inflation adjusted						
taxable income.	$23,500	$20,350	$25,585	$30,240	$35,350	
Less: Income tax (45%).	10,575	9,158	11,513	13,608	15,908	
Inflation adjusted						
aftertax income	$12,925	$11,192	$14,072	$16,632	$19,442	
Add: Noncash						
depreciation						
expense.	15,000	22,000	21,000	21,000	21,000	
Net aftertax						
cash flow						
adjusted						
for inflation	$27,925	$33,192	$35,072	$37,632	$40,442	
Present value						
factor.	0.800	0.640	0.512	0.410	0.328	
Present value	$22,340	$21,243	$17,957	$15,429	$13,265	$ 90,234
Less: investment						
in equipment						
(1.00 × $100,000)						$100,000
Net present value						$ (9,766)

inflows are adjusted for inflation. Each year is adjusted for an inflation increase of 10 percent for the next five years; for example, in year 2, 110 percent × 110 percent = 121 percent. Alternatively, the estimated specific year-end index value for each of the next five years could have been used. The present value factors obtained from Table A in the Appendix reflect the discount rate adjusted for inflation (25 percent in Exhibit 14–5). Note that depreciation and its tax shield are unaffected by inflation because the income tax deduction must be based on the original cost of the asset in 19X0 dollars. Depreciation is calculated using the percentage of the unadjusted basis that is to be deducted each year under the Accelerated Cost Recovery System. Finally, a tax rate of 45 percent is assumed.

As indicated in Exhibit 14–5, the project appears unacceptable because the real cash inflows from the equipment purchase are not adequate. To prevent the erroneous acceptance of capital investment projects and provide optimum resource allocation, the effects of inflation should be incorporated into the capital budgeting process during times of changing prices.

ASSETS CONSTRUCTED FOR OWN USE

A chapter on capital budgeting and cost analysis would not be complete without considering some of the measurement problems which arise in determining the asset cost to be capitalized when assets are constructed for a company's own use. While the material, labor, and factory overhead costs that can be directly identified with the assets that should be capitalized present little difficulty, it may be more complex to determine the amount of normal factory overhead to assign to the assets constructed for the company's own use.

In determining the amount of factory overhead to assign, the capacity level at which the plant is operating is an influencing factor. For example, if the plant is operating at planned capacity at the time the asset is constructed, manufacturing of some products must be postponed so plant space, machinery, and personnel are available to build the asset. Under these conditions, a fair share of general factory overhead should be allocated to the asset on the same basis as that applied to goods manufactured for sale. This allocated factory overhead is included with the direct material, direct labor, and additional factory overhead costs of the construction.

If the plant is operating with idle capacity and part of this capacity is used to manufacture the asset instead of its being purchased from an outsider, production of units may not be reduced. In this case, the question arises of whether any of the general factory overhead that is normally allocated to the units produced should be assigned to the constructed asset. No doubt exists concerning the capitalization of direct material, direct labor, and additional factory overhead caused by the construction; however, accountants have differing views concerning general factory overhead.

Capitalizing general factory overhead

Accountants who take the position that a portion of general factory overhead should be assigned feel that such assets should be treated in the same manner as regular products manufactured. Additionally, they feel that the full cost of constructed assets should include general factory overhead; otherwise, the cost of idle capacity is overstated. They argue that normal manufacturing operations should not be penalized by bearing all general factory overhead when other assets are using some of the facilities. They also argue that future periods will reap the benefit of constructed assets, and the costs should be deferred since no special status should be accorded these assets.

Other accountants believe that none of the general factory overhead should be assigned when idle plant capacity is utilized because none of this cost was considered in the differential cost analysis used in deciding to make the asset. They feel that the cost of this idle capacity would occur regardless of whether the construction was undertaken or not; thus, no general factory overhead should be assigned because the cost of producing units should not be affected. Admittedly, both positions have merit; however, this author feels that a fair portion of general factory overhead should be assigned in determining the cost of assets constructed for a company's own use. This approach conforms more closely to the cost principle that an allocation is necessary if the true cost of both the units produced and the asset constructed are to be used. It is felt that this position does not penalize either asset involved. This is also the position taken in Cost Accounting Standards Board (CASB) Regulation 404, which is discussed in more detail later in the chapter. CAS 404 indicates that tangible capital assets constructed by a contractor for its own use be capitalized at amounts which include all indirect costs allocable to such assets.

Capitalizing interest costs

FASB Statement No. 34, *Capitalization of Interest Cost*, requires capitalizing interest as part of the historical cost of acquiring certain assets. Assets qualifying for interest capitalization generally are those that require a period of time to get them ready for their intended use. Examples of qualifying assets are those constructed for an entity's own use (e.g., a manufacturing facility) or those intended for sale or lease that are constructed as discrete projects (e.g., ships or real estate projects). Interest should not be capitalized as part of the cost of inventories that are routinely manufactured or otherwise produced in large quantities on a repetitive basis, even if the inventories have long maturation periods, such as whiskey or tobacco.

Interest costs eligible for capitalization are limited to amounts incurred on borrowings and other obligations. The amount to be capitalized is determined by applying an interest rate to the average amount of accumulated expenditures for the asset during the construction or development period. If a specific borrowing can be associated with a qualifying asset, the rate on that borrowing should be applied to the appropriate portion of the average accumulated expenditures.

Excess construction cost

The position taken regarding allocation of general factory overhead and the capitalization of interest is only one measurement problem in the construction of assets for a company's own use. It is generally recognized that the full cost of the constructed asset should be capitalized because the cost of outside producers is not now available to use. However, if the constructed asset cost materially exceeds its fair value, the excess cost should be treated as a period cost. Under these conditions, a position must be taken that full construction cost does not represent a valid charge against future operations through capitalization. The company may have been less efficient than an outside producer, and this should be recognized in the current period.

After a project has been approved, control techniques must be applied to ensure that planned objectives are being followed. Periodically, actual costs incurred on the project should be compared with budgeted costs so that variances can be noted. If it appears that actual costs may exceed the original estimate, either additional appropriations of funds must be approved or plans revised. Even after the object of the capital expenditure is in operation, its performance should be compared with that expected to determine whether overly optimistic claims were made regarding its efficiency. Even though the investment now represents a sunk cost, this comparison is helpful for future decisions. In addition, if individuals realize that the company makes postmortem examinations of all capital expenditures, they are discouraged from making overly optimistic estimates and are more likely to support their claims with as much data as feasible.

CASB STANDARDS

There are several Cost Accounting Standards Board standards which relate to subjects discussed in this chapter.

CAS 404

In 1973, the Cost Accounting Standards Board (CASB) issued Regulation 404, which establishes criteria for the capitalization of tangible assets. According to the regulation, the acquisition cost of tangible capital assets is capitalized based on a written policy that is reasonable and consistently applied. CAS 404 further states that the contractor's policy should designate a minimum service life criterion which does not exceed two years, but may be shorter. Each contractor's policy should also designate a minimum acquisition cost criterion which does not exceed $1,000 but which may be less. For example, if the contractor's established policy is to capitalize assets which have a service life of more than one year and a cost of $250, a tangible asset with a life of 18 months and a cost of $300 that is acquired must be capitalized even though it is for a shorter period and a smaller dollar amount than that specified in the Standard. Under these circumstances, the contractor's written policy must be followed.

CAS 404 also indicates that tangible capital assets constructed or fabricated by a contractor for its own use are capitalized at amounts which include all indirect costs properly allocated to such assets. General and administrative expenses that are material and can be identified with the constructed asset are also to be allocated to the constructed tangible capital asset. CAS 404 further states that when the constructed assets are similar or identical to the contractor's regular product, such assets should be capitalized at amounts which include a full share of indirect costs.

CAS 409

In January 1975, CAS 409 was issued to provide criteria and guidance for assigning costs of tangible capital assets to cost accounting periods. The Standard recognizes that depreciation costs identified with cost accounting periods and benefiting cost objectives within periods should be a reasonable measure of the expiration of the service potential of the tangible assets subject to depreciation.

The Regulation states that an accelerated method of depreciation is appropriate when the expected consumption of services is significantly greater in the early years of asset life, while the straight-line method is appropriate when the expected consumption of asset services is reasonably level over the service life of the asset.

If the contractor must change the depreciation method, it must meet the criteria outlined in the regulation. The standard also provides a two-year period for contractors to develop analyses of historical asset lives which would be used as a basis for estimating useful lives and which could be adjusted for expected changes in physical or economic lives.

CAS 414

In 1976, CAS 414, *Cost of Money as an Element of the Cost of Facilities Capital*, was issued. The purpose of this Standard is to establish criteria for the measurement and allocation of the cost of capital committed to facilities as an element of contract cost. CAS 414 requires that a contractor's facilities capital be measured and allocated in accordance with the criteria set forth in the Standard. The allocated amount is used as a base to which a cost of money rate is applied. The cost of money rate is based on interest rates determined by the Secretary of the Treasury. The cost of capital committed to facilities is separately computed for each contract using facilities capital cost of money factors computed for each cost accounting period. The investment base used in computing the cost of money for facilities capital is computed from accounting data used for contract cost purposes. The cost of money rate for any cost accounting period is the arithmetic mean of the interest rates specified by the Secretary of the Treasury. According to the Standard, a facilities capital cost of money factor should be determined for each indirect cost pool to which a significant amount of facilities capital has been allocated and which is used to allocate indirect costs to final cost objectives. For each CAS-covered contract, the applicable cost of capital committed to facilities for a given cost accounting period is the sum of the products obtained by multiplying the amount of allocation base units (such as direct labor-hours or dollars of total cost input) identified with the contract for the cost accounting period, by the facilities capital cost of money factor for the corresponding indirect cost pool. In the case of process cost accounting systems, the contracting parties may agree to substitute an appropriate statistical measure for the allocation base units identified with the contract.

CAS 417

In July 1980, the Cost Accounting Standards Board issued CAS 417, *Cost of Money as an Element of the Cost of Capital Assets Under Construction*. The purpose of this Standard is to establish criteria for the measurement of the cost of money attributable to capital assets under construction, fabrication, or development as an element of the cost of those assets. According to the Standard, the cost of money for an asset is calculated as follows: *(a)* the cost of money rate used is based on interest rates determined by the Secretary of the Treasury, and *(b)* if substantially all the activities necessary to get the asset ready for its intended use are discontinued, the cost of money is not capitalized for the period of discontinuance. However, if such discontinuance arises out of causes beyond the control and without the fault or negligence of the contractor, cessation of cost of money capitalization is not required.

SUMMARY

Capital budgeting decisions are among the more difficult ones that management must make, primarily because large commitments are usually involved and the returns on these commitments are complex to forecast. The chapter presented the following techniques for evaluating capital expenditures: (1) payback or payout, (2) unadjusted return on investment, (3) present value, and (4) internal rate of return. The length of time a project requires to recover the initial outlay is simply determined using the payback or payout method. However, the time value of money and the salvage value of the investment are ignored. Profitability is considered in the unadjusted return on investment method by determining the relationship of average annual net aftertax income to the initial or average investment. While the unadjusted return on investment method is familiar because it is based on the accrual method of financial statement preparation, it fails to take into consideration the time value of money.

The other two evaluation techniques presented, present value and internal rate of return, do consider the time value of money, but they are more expensive to apply. The present value of expected future cash inflows can be determined by applying appropriate present value factors for the rate of return required. The required rate of return can be based on the cost of capital employed, or it can be a rate above the general level of interest rates at which institutions are lending money. The internal rate of return differs from the present value method because no discount rate is known in advance. Through trial and error, a discounted rate is found that yields a zero net present value.

Some managers argue that present value and internal rate of return are too complex and difficult to apply. Yet, the amount of money proposed to be invested often warrants more exact and sophisticated evaluation techniques that consider both the profitability of the project and the present value of money. An insight into the reasons that management is often hesitant about applying the more sophisticated techniques is given in the chapter. In many cases, a company has no choice but to replace a worn-out machine if it wants to continue operations. In other cases, the alternatives available may be so limited that one proposal is obviously the best selection. However, the amount of funds required by many capital expenditure projects warrants more exact and sophisticated evaluation techniques which take into consideration both the present value of money and profitability.

In choosing which evaluation technique to apply, the desirability of the project carries much weight because, in some cases, the extra effort and cost the more complex techniques involve are not justified. However, even if one of the more complex methods is used, management should give attention to other factors which often cannot be quantified. The evaluation techniques used should serve as an adjunct to consideration of legal requirements, social responsibilities, and emergencies. Certainly, overall company objectives should be studied to ensure that the investments selected are consistent with company goals.

IMPORTANT TERMS AND CONCEPTS

Sunk cost

Accelerated cost recovery system (ACRS)

Investment credit

Payback or payout method

Bailout payback method

Unadjusted return on investment

Discounted cash flow methods

Discounting

Net present value method

Present value payback

Weighted net present value or expected value

Internal rate of return or time-adjusted rate of return

Sensitivity analysis

Inflation impact on capital budgeting

FASB Statement No. 34

CAS 404

CAS 409

CAS 414

CAS 417

REVIEW QUESTIONS

1. Why should so much time and effort go into the evaluation of plant asset proposals?
2. To what extent should management be involved in evaluating large capital expenditure proposals?
3. Discuss the impact of inflation on capital budgeting.
4. How does the treatment of interest affect assets which are constructed for a firm's own use?
5. Define sunk cost and indicate the role this cost plays in replacement decisions.
6. In comparisons of plant asset proposals, what guidelines should be followed regarding the use of the various evaluation techniques?
7. Discuss the payback or payout method and state its advantages.
8. What information is gained from the present value payback method?
9. On what two different bases can the unadjusted return on investment be calculated?
10. What are the strengths and weaknesses of the unadjusted return on investment evaluation approach?
11. Discuss the concept underlying the present value method. What strengths does this evaluation method have over the payback method or the unadjusted rate of return?
12. What methods are used to arrive at the required rate of return in the present value method of evaluation?
13. Why is the required rate of return used in the present value method usually above the general level of interest rates at which banks and lending institutions are loaning money?
14. How can the probability of occurrence be given consideration in the net present value approach to evaluating plant asset proposals?
15. Discuss the strengths and weaknesses of the internal rate of return approach.
16. How can two projects with different lives be compared in a plant asset expenditure program?
17. How can sensitivity analysis be used in capital budgeting?
18. Which capital budgeting methods require use of a present value table?
19. What capital budgeting method assumes that funds are reinvested at the company's cost of capital?

EXERCISES

E14–1. Net present value and internal rate of return

Dixie Krebs Company is considering the purchase of Machine A or B. Machine A costs $35,000 and has a life of 12 years, while Machine B costs $60,000 and has a life of 18 years. The cost of removing either machine at the end of its life is expected to equal any salvage value. Annual aftertax cash inflow for Machine A is expected to be $5,000 and $7,000 for Machine B.

Required:

For both machines, prepare the following analysis:

a.   Internal rate of return.
b.   Net present value at 6 percent.

E14–2.   Determining capital expenditures cost

Management of Winters Company is planning to purchase a new tooling machine with a payback period estimated to be eight years. Straight-line depreciation of $2,500 will be expensed each year of the payback period. Cash flow from operations, net of income taxes, for years 1 to 3 will be $4,000 and will then decrease by $500 from the previous year for each of the remaining years.

Required:

Determine the cost of the tooling machine.

E14–3.   Difference in profits with machine acquisition (AICPA adapted)

Maxwell Company has an opportunity to acquire new equipment to replace one of its present machines. The new machine would cost $90,000, have a five-year life, and no estimated salvage value. Variable operating costs would be $100,000 per year.

The present machine has a book value of $50,000 and a remaining life of five years. Its disposal value now is $5,000, but it would be zero after five years. Variable operating costs would be $125,000 per year.

Required:

Ignore present value calculations and income taxes. Considering the five years in total, what would be the difference in profit before income taxes by acquiring the new machine as opposed to retaining the present one?

E14–4.   Maximum interest rate (AICPA)

Herman Company acquired an asset at a cost of $46,600. It had an estimated life of 10 years. Annual aftertax net cash benefits are estimated to be $10,000 at the end of each year. The following amounts appear in the interest table for the present value of an annuity of $1 at year-end for 10 years:

16%	4.83
18%	4.49
20%	4.19

Required:

What is the maximum interest rate that could be paid for the capital employed over the life of this asset without loss on this project?

E14–5.   Capital budgeting techniques

Whitehead Company is considering a machine involving an initial outlay of $75,000. Straight-line depreciation is to be used, with no estimated salvage value at the end of its useful life of five years. Net annual *aftertax* cash receipts are forecasted to be $18,000 for five years.

Required:

Determine the following:

a. Payback period.
b. Unadjusted rate of return on initial investment.
c. Unadjusted rate of return on average investment.
d. Net present value at 12 percent.
e. Internal rate of return.

E14–6.   Capital budgeting techniques

Keat Company is considering a machine involving an initial outlay of $43,000. Straight-line depreciation is to be used, with no salvage value at the end of its useful life of 10 years. Net annual *aftertax* cash inflow is forecasted to be $9,000 for ten years.

Required:

Determine the following:

a. Payback period.
b. Unadjusted rate of return on initial investment.
c. Unadjusted rate of return on average investment.
d. Net present value at 10 percent and present value payback period.
e. Internal rate of return.

E14–7.   Equipment costs to capitalize

Brodnax, Inc. received bids from several companies for a machine needed in production. Bids ranged from $100,000 to $125,000. Management decided to construct the machine using its own facilities. Costs incurred are as follows:

Materials.	$40,000	(2/10, n/30 discount not taken because of a cash shortage)
Direct labor.	30,000	
Variable overhead	34,000	
Fixed overhead	10,000	(allocated on basis of direct labor cost)
Installation.	1,000	
Operational test time	600	
and test material		

The company would bear the installation and the testing costs if the machine were purchased.

Required:

Ignore interest capitalization:

a. What costs should management consider in arriving at the decision to make or buy the machine?
b. What cost should be entered in the accounting records? Provide support for your answer.
c. Was management correct in deciding to construct the machine rather than to buy it?

E14–8.   Net present value, internal rate of return and bailout payback

Penton Company management is evaluating the purchase of either a machine built by the Addleton Company or a longer-lived machine built by the Beaton Company. The

Addleton machine costs $53,000 and has a useful life of 12 years, while the Beaton machine costs $55,000 with a useful life of 18 years. Neither machine is expected to have any salvage value at the end of its life. The annual aftertax net cash inflow for both machines is expected to be $14,000. The Addleton machine's disposal value is expected to be $30,000 at the end of the first year and decline at the rate of $4,000 annually. The Beaton machine's disposal value is expected to be $20,000 at the end of the first year and decline by $8,000 annually.

Required:

a. For both machines, prepare the following analyses:
    (1) Net present value at 8 percent.
    (2) Internal rate of return.
    (3) Bailout payback.
b. Which machine would you advise purchasing? Explain why.

E14–9. Payback period and internal rate of return

Cave Corporation is planning to sell a new mineral which it can extract in addition to its normal product line. New equipment costing $400,000 with a useful life of 10 years (salvage value is zero) will be required. Depreciation is computed on a straight-line basis.

The new equipment will be installed in an existing building which is fully depreciated and has been idle for several years. Sales of the new mineral are estimated at $1 million per year for the duration of the life of the equipment.

Annual cash flow costs are as follows: sales $770,000, marketing expenses $40,000. The income tax rate is 45 percent.

Required:

Ignoring the half-year convention for depreciation, determine the:

a. Payback period.
b. Internal rate of return to determine the discount rate.

PROBLEMS

P14–1. Aftertax benefits, present value, payback period

Hodges Company is planning to purchase a machine costing $117,000 to use in the mixing department. Management determined that this is 10-year property with a recovery allowance of 8 percent for year one and an estimated salvage value of $5,000. The annual cash savings from using this machine are estimated to be $22,000. The company's cost of capital has been determined to be 14 percent and its income tax rate, including state income tax, is 45 percent.

Required:

a. Calculate the annual aftertax net cash benefits of this machine for year one.
b. Calculate the net present value of this investment if the annual aftertax cash benefits of this machine were $20,000 each year for the machine's life.
c. Calculate the payback period assuming that the annual aftertax cash benefits of this machine were $20,000 each year for the machine's life.

P14–2.   Average rate of return, present value

K Company's capital expenditures budget committee is considering two projects. The estimated operating income and net cash flows from each project are presented below:

	Project X		Project Y	
Year	Operating income	Net cash flow	Operating income	Net cash flow
1	$ 8,000	$18,000	$ 4,000	$14,000
2	7,000	17,000	5,000	15,000
3	5,000	15,000	6,000	16,000
4	3,000	13,000	6,000	16,000
5	2,000	12,000	4,000	14,000
	$25,000	$75,000	$25,000	$75,000

Each project requires an investment of $40,000 with no residual value expected. The committee has selected a rate of 15 percent for purposes of discounted cash flow analysis.

Required:

a. Compute the following:
   (1) The average rate of return for each project, allowing for depreciation on the investment.
   (2) The excess or deficiency of present value over the amount to be invested as determined using the discounted cash flow method for each project.
b. Prepare a brief report for the budget committee, advising it on the relative merits of the two projects.

P14–3.   Net present value and expected value

Kingston Company is considering the purchase of equipment to use in their processing plant. Its cost is $80,000, and the equipment dealer requires a cash payment on delivery. Life of the machine is expected to be four years; salvage value at the end of the equipment's life is forecasted to be $5,000.

The following estimates of aftertax cash flow are based on three different market conditions. The probability of a poor market is 40 percent; of a normal market, 45 percent; and of an excellent market, 15 percent.

Year	Poor market	Normal market	Excellent market
1.	$10,000	$15,000	$18,000
2.	18,000	25,000	29,000
3.	25,000	32,000	36,000
4.	30,000	40,000	45,000

Required:

a. Using an interest rate of 10 percent, determine the net present value of the cash flow for each of the three market conditions assumed.
b. Assuming the net present value was $(12,000) for the poor market, $10,000 for the

normal market, and $22,000 for the excellent market, calculate the weighted net present value or expected value of the investment.

P14–4. Various capital budgeting methods (CMA adapted)

Hazman Company plans to replace an old piece of equipment which is obsolete and is expected to be unreliable under the stress of daily operations. The equipment is fully depreciated, and no salvage value can be realized upon its disposal.

One piece of equipment being considered would provide annual cash savings of $7,000 before income taxes. The equipment would cost $18,000 and have an estimated useful life of five years. No salvage value would be used for depreciation purposes because the equipment is expected to have no value at the end of five years.

Hazman uses the straight-line depreciation method on all equipment for both book and tax purposes. The company is subject to a 40 percent tax rate. Hazman has an aftertax cost of capital of 14 percent.

Required:

a. Calculate for Hazman Company's proposed investment in new equipment the aftertax:
   (1) Payback period.
   (2) Accounting rate of return.
   (3) Net present value.
   (4) Profitability (present value) index.
   (5) Internal rate of return.

Assume all operating revenues and expenses occur at the end of the year. Appropriate discount tables are given in the appendix at the end of the book.

b. Identify and discuss the issues Hazman Company should consider when deciding which of the five decision models in *a* it should employ to compare and evaluate alternative capital investment projects.

P14–5. Ranking proposals using net present value, internal rate, and bailout payback

Cody, Inc. is considering the purchase of Machine A, B, or C. The President believes the final decision should depend upon the ranking determined using the net present value method, while other members of the management team believe the internal rate of return is more appropriate. The predicted annual aftertax cash inflow is $1,000 for each machine, and no machine is expected to have any salvage value at the end of its life. Machine A's purchase price is $2,500 with a four-year life; Machine B's cost is $5,000 with a 12-year life; Machine C's cost is $6,000 with an 18-year life. The disposal value at the end of the first year is: $1,200—Machine A, $3,500—Machine B, and $4,000—Machine C. Machine A is expected to decline in disposal value by $400 annually after the first year and Machines B and C by $500 each annually.

Required:

For all three machines, prepare the ranking according to:

a. Net present value method at 12 percent.
b. Internal rate of return.
c. Bailout payback.

P14–6. Automatic versus manual operation

McBride Corporation has been manually placing the label on its bottles of perfume which are sold in designer containers. Part-time employees earning minimum wages have been used to put the labels on these perfume bottles. Direct costs of performing this task have been:

> Wages and payroll taxes $10,500
> Labels, glue, and other supplies   3,000

The company presently seals labels for its other cosmetic products using a machine since these containers are of standard design.

A salesperson for an equipment dealer has recently approached managment with an automatic machine which will seal labels on unique containers. The machine will cost $40,000 with $2,000 salvage value at the end of an eight-year life. Sales terms are cash on delivery. Since the machine is expected to become jammed periodically, 15 percent more labels and supplies will be used than were used with manual operations. In addition to labor required placing labels in the machine, some supervision will be required while the machine is in operation. Management proposes to utilize the services of an employee presently working in the manufacturing plant; he or she will also perform present duties. It is expected that this employee will devote one fifth of his or her time to the supervision of the new machine; the annual salary of this employee is $15,000, including payroll taxes.

Utilities are expected to increase $1,200 annually due to the operations of the proposed machine; however, all machinery repairs above $800 per year will be covered by the equipment company. The machine will occupy space presently being used for the manual operations.

The company presently has taxable income on its other operations and pays an average 42 percent rate of income tax.

Required:

a. Assuming an 18 percent cost of capital, use present value analysis to determine whether the new equipment should be purchased.
b. Determine the payback period.
c. What additional factors should be considered before a decision is made regarding the purchase?

P14–7. Aftertax cash flows: Net present value (CMA adapted)

Wyle Company is considering a proposal to acquire new manufacturing equipment. The new equipment has the same capacity as the current equipment, but will provide operating efficiencies in direct and indirect labor, direct material usage, indirect supplies, and power. Consequently, the savings in operating costs are estimated at $150,000 annually.

The new equipment will cost $300,000 and will be purchased at the beginning of the year when the project is started. The equipment dealer is certain that the equipment will be operational during the second quarter of the year it is installed. Therefore, 60 percent of the estimated annual savings can be obtained in the first year. Wyle will incur a one-time expense of $30,000 to transfer production activities from the old equipment to the new equipment. No loss of sales will occur, however, because the plant is large enough so that the new equipment can be installed without interfering with the operation of the current equipment. The equipment dealer states that most companies use a five-year life when depreciating this equipment.

The current equipment has been fully depreciated and is carried in the accounts at zero book value. Management has reviewed the condition of the current equipment and has concluded that it can be used an additional five years. Wyle Company would receive $5,000 net of removal costs if it elected to buy the new equipment and dispose of its current equipment at this time.

Wyle currently leases its manufacturing plant. The annual lease payments are $60,000. The lease, which will have four years remaining when the equipment installation begins, is not renewable. Wyle Company would be required to remove any equipment in the plant at the end of the lease. The cost of equipment removal is expected to equal the salvage value of either the old or new equipment at the time of removal.

The company uses the sum-of-the-years'-digits depreciation method for tax purposes. A full year's depreciation is taken in the first year the asset is put into use.

The company is subject to a 40 percent income tax rate and requires an aftertax return of at least 12 percent on any investment.

Required:

a. Calculate the annual incremental aftertax cash flows for Wyle Company's proposal to acquire the new manufacturing equipment.

b. Calculate the net present value of Wyle Company's proposal to acquire the new manufacturing equipment using the cash flows calculated in *a* and indicate what action Wyle's management should take. For ease in calculation, assume all recurring cash flows take place at the end of the year.

P14–8. Net present value and expected value

Wallis Key, Inc. is considering the purchase of a machine that will be used in manufacturing a new product developed by the firm's engineering department. The cost of the machine is $150,000, and the machine dealer requires a cash payment on delivery. Life of the machine is expected to be six years; salvage value at the end of the machine's life is forecasted to be $20,000.

Estimates for the success of this new product are difficult to determine; however, based on various market tests, management feels that the availability of personal disposable income will be a critical factor. The following estimates of aftertax cash flow are based on three different market conditions. The probability of a poor market is 30 percent; of a normal market, 55 percent; and the probability of an excellent market, 15 percent.

Year	Poor market	Normal market	Excellent market
1	$10,000	$20,000	$30,000
2	21,000	30,000	45,000
3	35,000	40,000	50,000
4	40,000	45,000	57,000
5	32,000	38,000	45,000
6	18,000	25,000	30,000

Required:

a. Using an interest rate of 8 percent, determine the net present value of the cash flow for each of the three market conditions assumed.

b. Using the information determined in *a*, calculate the weighted net present value or expected value of the investment.

P14–9. Nonquantitative factors in capital investment decisions (CMA adapted)

The WRL Company makes cookies for its chain of snack food stores. On January 2, 19X1, WRL purchased a special cookie-cutting machine; this machine has been utilized for three years. WRL Company is considering the purchase of a newer, more efficient machine. If purchased, the new machine would be acquired on January 2, 19X4. WRL expects to sell 300,000 dozen cookies in each of the next four years. The selling price of the cookies is expected to average $0.50 per dozen.

WRL Company has two options: (1) continue to operate the old machine, or (2) sell the old machine and purchase the new machine. No trade-in was offered by the seller of the new machine. The following information has been assembled to help decide which option is more desirable:

	Old machine	New machine
Original cost of machine at acquisition	$80,000	$120,000
Salvage value at the end of useful life for depreciation purposes	$10,000	$ 20,000
Useful life from date of acquisition	7 years	4 years
Expected annual cash operating expenses:		
Variable cost per dozen	$0.20	$0.14
Total fixed costs	$15,000	$ 14,000
Depreciation method used for tax purposes:	Straight-line	Sum-of-years-digits
Estimated cash value of machines:		
January 2, 19X4	$40,000	$120,000
December 31, 19X7	$ 7,000	$ 20,000

WRL Company is subject to an overall income tax rate of 40 percent. Assume that all operating revenues and expenses occur at the end of the year. Assume that any gain or loss on the sale of machinery is treated as an ordinary tax item and will affect the taxes paid by WRL Company at the end of the year in which it occurred.

Required:

a. Use the net present value method to determine whether WRL Company should retain the old machine or acquire the new machine. WRL requires an aftertax return of 16 percent.

b. Without prejudice to your answer to *a*, assume that the quantitative differences are so slight between the two alternatives that WRL Company is indifferent to the two proposals. Identify and discuss the nonquantitative factors important to this decision that WRL Company should consider.

c. Identify and discuss the advantages and disadvantages of using discounted cash flow techniques (e.g., the net present value method) for capital investment decisions.

P14–10. Numerous capital budgeting techniques

Management of Frank Barton Company is considering expanding its operations through the purchase of a blending machine costing $165,000. The tax and economic life of the asset is five years. The estimated salvage value at the end of its life is $45,000; the recovery allowances using ACRS are: 15 percent—year 1; 22 percent—year 2; 21 percent each in years 3 to 5. Based on engineering and accounting studies, management believes the pretax increase in cash inflow will be as follows: year 1, $65,000; year 2, $73,000; year 3, $85,000; year 4, $98,000; and year 5, $96,000. Federal and state income taxes have averaged 52 percent in the past and no change is expected.

Required:

Determine the following:

a. Payback period.
b. Unadjusted rate of return on investment based on initial investment and average investment (ignore salvage).
c. Net present value of the machine assuming the cost of capital is 14 percent.
d. Present value payback.
e. Internal rate of return approach to determine the discount rate.
f. Payback period assuming that the aftertax cash flow was even over the five years.

P14–11. Required investment, cash flows, net present value (CMA adapted)

Wisconsin Products Company manufactures several different products. One of the firm's principal products sells for $20 per unit. The sales manager of Wisconsin Products has stated repeatedly that more units of this product could be sold if they were available. In an attempt to substantiate the claim, the sales manager conducted a market research study last year at a cost of $44,000 to determine potential demand. The study indicated that Wisconsin Products could sell 18,000 units annually for the next five years.

The equipment currently in use has the capacity to produce 11,000 units annually. The variable production costs are $9 per unit. The equipment has a book value of $60,000 and a remaining useful life of five years. The salvage value of the equipment is negligible now and will be zero in five years.

A maximum of 20,000 units could be produced annually on new machinery which can be purchased. The new equipment costs $300,000 and has an estimated useful life of five years with no salvage value at the end of this time. Wisconsin Product's production manager has estimated that the new equipment would provide increased production efficiencies that would reduce the variable production costs to $7 per unit.

Wisconsin Products Company uses straight-line depreciation for tax purposes on all of its equipment. The firm is subject to a 40 percent tax rate, and its aftertax cost of capital is 15 percent.

The sales manager felt so strongly about the need for additional capacity that an economic justification was prepared for the equipment although this was not one of the manager's responsibilities. The analysis, presented below, disappointed the manager because it did not justify acquiring the equipment.

Required investment

Purchase price of new equipment . . .		$300,000
Disposal of existing equipment:		
Loss of disposal.	$60,000	
Less tax benefit (40%)	24,000	36,000
Cost of market research study		44,000
Total investment.		$380,000

Annual returns

Contribution margin from product:		
Using the new equipment		
[18,000 × ($20 − 7)]		$234,000
Using the existing equipment		
[11,000 × ($20 − 9)]		121,000
Increase in contribution margin.		$113,000
Less: Depreciation.		60,000
Increase in beforetax income		$ 53,000
Income tax (40%)		21,200
Increase in income		$ 31,800
Less: 15% cost of capital on the additional		
investment required (.15 × $380,000)		57,000
Net annual return of proposed		
investment in new equipment		$ (25,200)

Required:

a. The controller of Wisconsin Products Company plans to prepare a discounted cash flow analysis for this investment proposal. The controller has asked you to prepare corrected calculations of:

(1) The required investment in the new equipment.

(2) The recurring annual cash flows.

Explain the treatment of each item of your corrected calculations which is treated differently from the treatment in the original analysis prepared by the sales manager.

b. Calculate the net present value of the proposed investment in the new equipment.

P14–12. Discounting differential cost in a make-or-buy decision

Since Lamb Company's old equipment for making motor parts is no longer operable, the company principals are faced with the following alternatives:

1. Replace the old equipment with new equipment.

2. Buy motor parts from an outside supplier who quoted a unit price of $2 per part on an eight-year contract for a minimum of 70,000 units per year.

For the past three years, production has averaged 80,000 units in each year, and forecasts are that this level will remain unchanged for the next eight years. Records for the past three years reveal the following costs of manufacturing the motor parts on the old equipment.

Direct material . . . . $ .38
Direct labor 37
Variable factory overhead 17
Fixed factory overhead (including $0.30 depreciation
 and $0.15 for supervision and
 other direct departmental fixed overhead). 45
                  $1.37

The new equipment will cost $250,000 and will have a disposal value of $10,000 at the end of its eight-year life. Straight-line depreciation is to be used on the new equipment. Assume a tax rate of 40 percent.

The sales representative for the new equipment provides the following information regarding operations. The new machine will allow direct labor and variable overhead to be reduced by $0.16 per unit. Based on cost data supplied by a competitor using identical equipment and similar operating conditions, except that production generally averages 60,000 units per year, the unit costs are:

Direct material . . . . $ .45
Direct labor 30
Variable factory overhead 08
Fixed factory overhead,
 including $0.30 depreciation 50
                  $1.33

Required:

a. Determine which alternative is more attractive assuming the company desires a 12 percent return on investment. Support your decision with calculations.

b. What additional factors should be considered before a decision is made?

P14–13. Return on investment and discounted cash flow (CMA adapted)

Peterdonn Corporation made a capital investment of $100,000 in new equipment two years ago. The analysis made at that time indicated the equipment would save $36,400 in operating expenses per year over a five-year period, or a 24 percent return on capital before taxes per year based upon internal rate of return analysis.

The department manager believed that the equipment had "lived up" to its expectations. However, the departmental report showing the overall return on investment (ROI) rate for the first year in which this equipment was used did not reflect as much improvement as had been expected. The department manager asked the accounting section to break out the figures related to this investment to find out why it did not contribute more to the department's ROI.

The accounting section was able to identify the equipment and its contribution to the department's operations. The report presented to the department manager at the end of the first year is shown below.

Reduced operating expenses due
 to new equipment. . . . . $ 36,400
 Less: Depreciation—20% of cost. 20,000
Contribution before taxes . . . . $ 16,400
Investment—beginning of year. $100,000
Investment—end of year . . . . $ 80,000
Average investment for the year . . . . $ 90,000

$$\text{ROI} = \frac{\$16,400}{\$90,000} = 18.2\%$$

The department manager was surprised that the ROI was less than 24 percent because the new equipment performed as expected. The staff analyst in the accounting section replied that the company ROI for performance evaluation differed from that used for capital investment analysis. The analyst commented that the discrepancy could be solved if the company used the compound interest method of depreciation, which yields a constant return on investment throughout the life of an investment, for its performance evaluation reports.

Required:

a. Discuss the reasons the return on investment of 18.2 percent for the new equipment as calculated by the accounting section differs from the 24 percent internal rate of return calculated at the time the machine was approved for purchase.

b. Will the use of the compound interest method of depreciation resolve the discrepancy, as the analyst claims? Explain your answer.

c. Explain how Peterdonn Corporation might restructure the data from the discounted cash flow analysis so that the expected performance of the new equipment is consistent with the operating reports received by the department manager.

P14–14. Equipment replacement

Ray Conder Company had just purchased a new machine costing $57,000 to produce fad merchandise with a life cycle that can be expected to be five years. While the company's other product lines represent more stable merchandise, management believes that this product line is needed to add balance to its products. Immediately after the purchase, a salesperson approached management with a machine which is claimed to be specially designed to meet the company's needs. To support this claim, the salesperson provides data indicating that the machine can produce one and one-quarter times as many units per hour as the company's newly purchased machine. Further analysis reveals, however, that a more expensive quality of material must be used which can result in a material cost increase of 30 percent. The new machine will cost $75,000 and have zero salvage value at the end of the five years. Neither machine will have any use after the market potential is exhausted.

Regardless of which machine is used, production and sales are planned to be 50,000 units per year with a unit sales price of $10. The present equipment has a $15,000 sales value now and a value of $3,000 five years from now. Annual cost of operating the present equipment will be direct material, $100,000; direct labor, $180,000; and variable overhead, $135,000. Fixed production cost excluding depreciation is $42,000 annually; fixed marketing and administrative costs are $29,000 annually. Assume a 48 percent tax rate. (Ignore the half-year convention for depreciation.)

Required:

a. Assuming the company's cost of capital is 16 percent, use the net present value method to show whether the new machine should be purchased.

b. Determine the payback period for the new machine.

c. Determine the unadjusted rate of return on the initial investment for each machine.

P14–15. Comparing methods of accounting for inflation

In evaluating the purchase of finishing equipment, June Allen, Inc. estimates that two positions could be eliminated if the equipment were purchased. However, additional inspection would be required for optimal operations. In current 19X0 annual prices, the wages and benefits of the two positions eliminated total $50,000 while the inspection amounts to $8,000 annually.

The equipment can be purchased and installed at a cost of $75,000. The economic and tax life is three years. The statutory percentages for the ACRS deduction are: 25 percent, year 1; 38 percent, year 2; and 37 percent, year 3.

Management insists that a 15 percent rate for cost of capital be used. This rate does not include an allowance for inflation, which is expected to occur at an average annual rate of 10 percent over the next three years. The company adjusts for inflation in capital expenditure analyses by adding the anticipated inflation rate to the cost of capital and then using the inflation-adjusted cost of capital to discount the projected cash flows. The company pays an average income tax rate of 46 percent. Assume all operating revenues and expenditures occur at the end of the year.

Required:

a. Analyze the expenditure under consideration using the company's method.
b. A consulting firm proposes a different adjustment for inflation in capital expenditure analyses, adjusting the cash flows by an estimated price level index. The adjusted aftertax cash flows are then discounted using the appropriate discount rate. The estimated year-end index values for each of the next four years are as follows:

Year	Year-end price index
19X0 (current year)	1.00
19X1.	1.10
19X2.	1.16
19X3.	1.25

Prepare a schedule, using the price index values provided, showing the aftertax annual cash flows adjusted for inflation for the equipment under consideration.

c. Determine the net present value for the equipment using the method proposed by the consulting firm.
d. What advice would you give management regarding the purchase?
e. Compare the consulting firm's approach to the one presently used to compensate for inflation.

P14–16. Inflation impact in capital budgeting

The New York division of Sandra Rogers, Inc. is evaluating the purchase of an assembly and finishing machine for use in the production of its appliances. Estimates indicate that, if the machine is purchased, three positions could be eliminated; however, additional utilities and indirect material will be required to operate the machine. Analysis shows the following cost savings and additional costs in current 19X0 prices:

Wages and employee benefits of the three positions eliminated	$72,000
Cost of additional utilities.	12,000
Cost of additional indirect material	4,000

All equipment dealers contacted have promised delivery at the end of the current year. The machine will be purchased and installed at a cost of $100,000. This machine will be classified as five-year property for tax and economic purposes. The recovery percentages for depreciation under ACRS are: 15 percent in year 1; 22 percent in year 2; and 21 percent each in years 3 to 5.

Management's philosophy is to allow division management much freedom in decision making, believing this is good training for future corporate leaders. As a result, each division has the authority to make capital expenditures up to $250,000 without corporate headquarter's approval.

However, corporate management does insist that a 16 percent rate for cost of capital be used in all analysis. This rate does not include an allowance for inflation, which is expected to occur at an average annual rate of 12 percent over the next five years. The New York division accounts for inflation in capital expenditures analyses through adjusting the cash flows by an estimated price level index. The adjusted aftertax cash flows are then discounted using the appropriate discount rate. The estimated year-end index values for each of the next six years are as follows:

Year	Year-end price index
19X0 (current year)	1.00
19X1	1.08
19X2	1.18
19X3	1.27
19X4	1.37
19X5	1.46
19X6	1.54

Sandra Rogers, Inc. pays income taxes at a 38 percent rate. Assume all operating revenues and expenditures occur at the end of the year.

Required:

Round to whole dollars.

a. Prepare a schedule, using the price indexes provided, showing the aftertax annual cash flows adjusted for inflation for the machine under consideration by the New York division.

b. (1) Determine the net present value for the New York division's machine.
    (2) What advice would you give New York division management regarding the purchase?

c. An investment analyst informs New York division management that they are not properly recognizing inflation in the capital expenditure analysis. The analyst's approach compensates for inflation by adding the anticipated inflation rate to the cost of capital and then using the inflation-adjusted cost of capital to discount the projected cash flows. Use this approach to analyze the machine under consideration.

d. Compare the investment analyst's approach with the one presently used to compensate for inflation.

PART IV

Cost analysis for decision making

OBJECTIVES OF CHAPTER 15

1. To explain the importance of understanding the cost-volume-profit relationships that exist in a company.

2. To illustrate the computations and use of breakeven analysis.

3. To emphasize that even though breakeven analysis is based on rigid limitations, it can result in effective answers without costly analysis.

4. To present sales-quantity and sales-mix variances which measure the effect of changes in product line volumes.

15

Cost-volume-profit analysis

While previous chapters have emphasized product costing for inventory valuation and income determination, this chapter focuses on cost-volume-profit relationships and the impact of cost behavior patterns on decision making. An understanding of a company's cost behavior patterns is helpful in making management decisions on such matters as product pricing, accepting or rejecting sales orders, and promotion of more profitable product lines. Through the use of cost-volume-profit analysis, the sales volume necessary to achieve desired profit objectives can be determined. One of the more popular forms of cost-volume-profit analysis is the computation of a company's breakeven point.

BREAKEVEN ANALYSIS

The breakeven point is the volume of sales at which there is no profit or loss. Even though breakeven analysis is a static concept, it can be applied to a dynamic situation to aid management in planning and controlling operations. The focus of breakeven analysis is the impact of volume on costs and profits. Because operating at the breakeven point is not the goal of management, the benefit of breakeven analysis might be questioned. However, since breakeven analysis forces a study of the company's fixed and variable cost behavior, and since management often is not as interested in the actual breakeven point as in the effect of decisions upon costs and sales, the concept is important because it can be adapted to determine the necessary sales to earn a specific income.

Breakeven equation expressed in units. The breakeven point may be determined either using equations or graphic techniques and can be expressed in units or in sales dollars. The breakeven equation is derived from the following:

$$\text{Sales} = \text{Variable expense} + \text{Fixed expense} + \text{Income}$$

Remember in Chapter 2, *variable costs* were defined as those costs which vary directly with changes in the volume of output; direct material and direct labor costs are examples. *Fixed costs*, on the other hand, remain the same in total for a given time period and production level; insurance and rent are examples.

Assuming a $10 unit sales price, a $4 unit variable cost, and fixed costs of $36,000, the breakeven sales equation is as follows because there is no income at the breakeven point.

$$X = \text{Units to be sold at breakeven point}$$
$$S = \text{Variable costs} + \text{Fixed costs} + \text{Income}$$
$$\$10X = \$4X \quad\quad + \quad \$36,000 \quad + \quad 0$$
$$\$6X + \$36,000 + 0$$
$$X = \frac{\$36,000 + 0}{\$6}$$
$$X = 6{,}000 \text{ units to break even}$$

Total fixed costs are divided by the $6 unit contribution margin to arrive at breakeven units. The above equation indicates that if a company sold in the range of 6,000 units, it would break even. It should not be assumed, however, that when the company's volume is exactly 6,000 units, breakeven conditions automatically occur, because production volume must be estimated before variable and fixed costs are established. Breakeven may not occur because actual cost rates may vary from those forecasted. For example, the actual unit variable cost may not be $4, and actual total fixed costs may vary from $36,000.

Unit variable cost, rather than *total* variable cost, is used in breakeven analysis because total variable cost can be calculated only after the volume of activity is determined. In the above example, only after the breakeven point of 6,000 units is determined can total variable cost of $24,000 be calculated (6,000 units × $4 unit variable cost). It is therefore necessary for variable cost to be expressed on a per unit basis in breakeven analysis.

CONTRIBUTION MARGIN

Contribution margin is the portion of the sales dollars that is left after variable costs are deducted; contribution margin is the amount available to cover fixed costs and render an income. Contribution margin may be expressed as a total, as an amount per unit, or as a percentage. In the above illustration with a $10 sales price and $4 per unit variable cost, the contribution margin is as follows:

$10 unit sales price − $4 variable expense = $6 unit contribution margin.

Contribution margin can be used to compute the breakeven point expressed in units sold as follows:

$$\frac{\text{Fixed expenses} + \text{Desired net income}}{\text{Unit contribution margin}} = \frac{\$36,000 + 0}{\$6} = 6,000 \text{ units}$$

The contribution margin technique is merely a restatement of the breakeven equation presented earlier.

Breakeven equation expressed in sales dollars.   The above data could also be used to determine breakeven sales dollars. After arriving at the 6,000 units needed to sell to break even, these units could be multiplied by the unit sales price to arrive at breakeven sales of $60,000 (6,000 units × $10 sales price). Rather than use the breakeven equation to determine breakeven units, the equation could be used to determine breakeven sales dollars either by expressing unit variable cost as a percentage of sales dollars or determining the contribution margin ratio, which is the ratio of unit contribution margin to unit sales price.

Variable cost ratio

The variable cost ratio is defined as variable costs divided by sales. With the illustration used above, the variable cost ratio would be 40 percent ($4 unit variable cost/$10 unit sales price). The variable cost ratio can also be deter-mined by subtracting the contribution margin ratio from 100 percent. With a 60 percent contribution margin ratio, the result is a 40 percent variable cost ratio. By using the variable cost ratio in the breakeven equation, breakeven sales dollars are determined as follows:

$$
\begin{array}{lll}
100 \text{ percent} = & \$4/10 & + \$36,000 \\
\text{sales price} & \text{variable} & \text{fixed costs} \\
& \text{cost} & \\
& \text{percentage} & \\
100 \text{ percent} = & 40 \text{ percent} & + \$36,000 \\
60 \text{ percent} = & \$36,000 & \\
\dfrac{\$36,000}{60 \text{ percent}} = & \$60,000 \text{ breakeven sales} &
\end{array}
$$

In the above computation, total fixed cost is divided by the 60 percent *contribution margin ratio*. The contribution margin ratio ($6/$10 = 60 percent) can be used directly to obtain the breakeven point expressed in dollars as follows:

$$\frac{\text{Fixed expense} + \text{Desired net income}}{\text{Contribution margin ratio}} = \frac{\$36,000 + 0}{60 \text{ percent}} = \frac{\$60,000 \text{ Breakeven}}{\text{sales dollars}}$$

This is another restatement of the breakeven equation; personal preference usually determines which of the techniques is used. Since cost-volume-profit analysis often expresses the information in terms of dollars instead of units, the contribution margin ratio is useful.

Marginal income

The term contribution margin is sometimes used interchangeably with *marginal income*. However, accountants generally use the term "marginal" when referring to only one product unit; thus, when accountants refer to marginal income, they generally mean the contribution margin generated by the sale of one additional unit. Besides being known as the marginal income ratio, the contribution margin ratio is also known as the *profit-volume (P/V) ratio*.

Exhibit 15–1 illustrates the calculation of the P/V ratio. The contribution margin is $48,000; the profit-volume ratio is 60 percent.

EXHIBIT 15–1

Sales (8,000 × $10)	$80,000	100%
Variable costs (8,000 × $4)	32,000	40
Contribution margin	$48,000	60%
Fixed costs	36,000	45
Income before taxes	$12,000	15%

Margin of safety

Margin of safety, another key concept of breakeven analysis, is defined as the excess of actual or budgeted sales over the breakeven sales volume. This provides the buffer by which sales may decrease before a loss occurs. The margin of safety concept is a mechanical way of saying a company is (or is not) close to the breakeven point. With breakeven sales of $60,000 ($36,000 fixed costs ÷ 60 percent P/V ratio) and actual sales of $80,000, the margin of safety becomes:

Margin of safety = $80,000 actual sales − $60,000 breakeven sales = $20,000
Margin of safety ratio (M/S ratio) = $20,000/$80,000 actual sales = 25 percent

The margin of safety can be used with the contribution margin ratio (or P/V ratio) to determine the percentage of sales that income represents. Using the 25 percent margin of safety ratio and the 60 percent contribution margin ratio from Exhibit 15–1, income is 15 percent (25 percent × 60 percent) of sales. This income percentage can be applied against $80,000 sales to yield $12,000 (15 percent × $80,000) income before taxes.

The margin of safety concept assumes the cost relationship used in breakeven analysis. Margin of safety can be used to draw management's attention to the importance of efficient operating conditions. Since not all administrators have financial backgrounds, the margin of safety concept may impress upon them how close to breakeven the company's operations really are and how critical certain cost controls are.

When management finds its margin of safety is low, it should concentrate on examining the contribution margin and total fixed costs. If the contribution margin is high but fixed costs are also high, management should concentrate on reducing the fixed costs or increasing sales. If the margin of safety is accompanied by a low contribution margin ratio, effort should be made to increase the contribution margin ratio by either reducing variable costs or increasing sales price. While the above statements may represent oversimplifications of the real situation, certainly management should recognize improvements are needed and take action in that direction.

Cash flow breakeven point

In addition to calculating the breakeven point in sales, a cash flow breakeven point may be determined. Assume the fixed costs in Exhibit 15–1 were comprised of the following:

Superintendent's salary	$17,000
Rent—building	11,000
Insurance	2,000
Depreciation—equipment	6,000
	$36,000

Using a 48 percent income tax rate and the $6 per unit contribution margin, the cash flow breakeven point becomes the following:

Cash flow fixed costs:	
Superintendent's salary	$17,000
Rent	11,000
Insurance	2,000
	$30,000
Less tax shield on noncash expense:	
Fixed costs of depreciation (48% × $6,000)	2,880
	$27,120

$$\frac{\$27,120}{\$6} = 4,520 \text{ units for cash flow breakeven}$$

Although most expenses involve cash when they are incurred, such charges as depreciation and amortization are noncash reductions in income. Depreciation expense would be deducted along with other expenses in arriving at net taxable income, but since it did not require a cash expenditure, a *tax shield* in the amount of the tax rate multiplied by the depreciation charge is presented ($2,880 in the example above). It is called a tax shield because it protects that amount of income from taxation. Chapter 14 introduced this concept in capital expenditure analysis. All other fixed expenses in the above example—salaries, rent, and insurance—do require a cash outflow. An alternative approach to calculating cash flow breakeven would be to ignore the tax shield. If only 4,520 units were sold, the company would suffer a tax loss and there would be no tax shield at this level.

In addition, few companies operate on a "cash only" basis. Accruals of assets and liabilities and the change in inventories would affect the computation. The cash flow breakeven computation also ignores the timing of cash flow as many companies experience a slow cash inflow while the outflow is faster.

Despite these limitations, the cash flow breakeven point does give some insight into the number of units that must be sold so that cash outflow is covered. The breakeven point calculated would be more realistic if the computation was made for one segment only and it is assumed that the overall company would earn a taxable income.

Breakeven chart

A breakeven chart, which is a graphic display of the relationship of cost to volume and profits, can be prepared to illustrate the computations previously presented. A breakeven chart can also be used to determine profit or loss at any sales volume level. The advantage of a breakeven chart is that it is easy to read; it may thus better indicate cost-volume-profit relationships to line managers and nonaccountants than do numerical exhibits. It can forcefully show the impact of volume on costs and profits.

In a breakeven chart, dollars of revenue, costs, and expenses are expressed on the vertical scale. The horizontal scale is used to indicate the sales volume, which may be expressed in units of sales, direct labor-hours, machine-hours, percent of capacity, or other suitable indexes of volume. In Exhibit 15–2, three lines are drawn representing fixed expenses, total expenses, and sales revenue. Fixed expenses are drawn as a horizontal line at $36,000 because fixed expenses are the same regardless of the capacity volume. Even if there are no sales, fixed expenses for this relative range will remain at $36,000. Variable expenses are added to fixed expenses so that a total expense line can be drawn. Variable expenses are zero if there are no sales because of the direct relationship between sales and variable costs. As sales increase, the total expense line increases, reflecting the $4 per unit variable charge. The sales revenue line is drawn from the zero intersection of the horizontal and vertical sales to $100,000

EXHIBIT 15–2

Breakeven chart

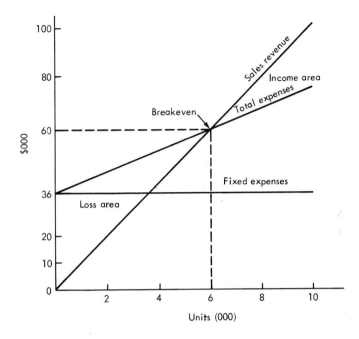

maximum sales for this relevant range.

The breakeven chart can be constructed in an alternate manner that readily shows the contribution margin at any sales volume. Using the facts given in the previous example, one can prepare the breakeven chart in Exhibit 15–3. Capacity percentages, rather than units sold, are illustrated on the horizontal axis.

Since it is felt that breakeven charts are best used as a simple means of illustrating various cost-volume-profit alternatives, no complex breakeven chart is illustrated. However, occasions may arise in which the probable effects of complex alternative proposals are best communicated through more elaborate breakeven charts. A curved sales line can be constructed to indicate that the sales line does not have to be constant at all capacity levels, or fixed and variable expenses may be divided according to production, administrative, and marketing expenses. Fixed expenses can also be drawn in a step fashion to indicate the increase expected at various capacity levels. While all of the breakeven charts illustrated in this chapter depict a constant unit variable cost, the slope of the variable cost line can also be altered at different capacity levels. Increases in variable costs and decline in sales are among other conditions which can be shown.

EXHIBIT 15–3

Breakeven chart Showing contribution margin

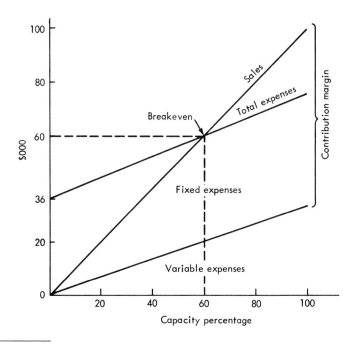

ASSUMPTIONS OF BREAKEVEN ANALYSIS

Breakeven analysis is easy to use and inexpensive to apply. However, several assumptions underlie cost-volume-profit analysis, among them the following:

1. That relevant range is specified so that fixed and variable costs can be defined in relation to a specific period of time and designated range of production level. The relevant range is usually a range of activities in which the company has operated. This volume of activity is expressed in common terms for sales and expense; direct labor or machine-hours, units produced, and sales value of production are often used.
2. That volume is assumed to be the only important factor affecting cost behavior. Other influencing factors such as unit prices, sales mix, labor strikes, and production method are ignored. A change in expected cost behavior will cause the breakeven point to be modified.
3. That all costs fall into either a fixed or variable cost classification.
4. That unit variable costs remain the same and there is a direct relationship between costs and volume. For example, no quantity discounts on materials or other possible savings in costs are assumed.

5. That unit sales price is assumed to remain the same. No quantity discounts are assumed to be available.
6. That inventory changes are so insignificant that they have no impact on the analysis.
7. That if breakeven analysis covers more than one product line, there is a specific sales mix assumed. Sales mix is the combination of quantities of product that a company sells. For example, in a tennis sporting shop, it may be six cans of tennis balls to one tennis dress to one tennis racket. Since the contribution margin earned on each of the products in the sales mix usually differs, the specific sales mix assumed has a significant impact upon breakeven analysis.
8. That fixed costs remain constant over the relevant range considered.
9. That there is no increase in efficiency in the period of activity studied, and that managerial policies and techniques will have no effect on costs.

Even though breakeven analysis assumes total fixed costs are constant over a relevant range, we, of course, know that fixed costs are not changeless period after period. Management may decide, for example, to purchase machinery to replace direct labor workers, which, in turn, may lower the unit variable costs but increase the total fixed costs through increased depreciation costs. Increases in the sales force or advertising will also alter fixed costs. When one of these events occurs, a new breakeven point and a new breakeven chart must be constructed.

While the limitations of breakeven analysis do not invalidate the concept, the assumptions are so restrictive that a breakeven calculation should be interpreted cautiously. The value of breakeven analysis is the insight it gives into cost behavior patterns and the cost-volume-profit relationship. It must be recognized that breakeven analysis is not always a cut-and-dried decision tool. There are other opportunity and relevant cost considerations; for example, maintaining good relations with current, large customers whose supplies are critical may override the decision computed through use of breakeven analysis.

Sales mix effect on breakeven

One of the assumptions surrounding breakeven analysis is that either one product is sold or, for a company selling more than one product, there is a specified *sales mix*. Although the example of a two-product company may not be realistic since many companies sell numerous product lines, the following illustration of sales mix limits the number of products to show how to calculate a breakeven point for the overall company. An assumption must be made regarding sales mix so that average revenues and average costs may be determined. Assume a $2 per unit contribution margin for Product A and a $5 per unit contribution margin for Product B is estimated. Total fixed costs are $30,000. If only Product A is sold, the breakeven point would be as follows:

$$\frac{\$30,000}{\$2} = 15,000 \text{ units of Product A to break even}$$

If only Product B is sold, the breakeven point is as follows:

$$\frac{\$30,000}{\$5} = 6,000 \text{ units of Product B to break even}$$

Assume management plans to sell a total of 9,000 units with a planned mix of 3 units of Product A (or 3,000) to 6 units of Product B (or 6,000), resulting in a contribution margin for the combined products of $6 (3 units ×$2) Product A contribution margin + $30 (6 units × $5) Product B contribution margin. The average budgeted contribution margin is $4 ($36/9 units of Products A and B). The breakeven point for the two products becomes

$$\frac{\$30,000}{\$4} = 7,500 \text{ units resulting in 2,500 of Product A and}$$
$$5,000 \text{ of Product B.}$$

The above calculation indicates that 7,500 units must be sold to break even; when the planned mix of 3:6 (3 units of Product A to 6 units of Product B) is applied, we see that there will be 2,500 units of Product A and 5,000 units of Product B at the planned breakeven point.

Suppose, instead, that 8,000 units composed of 1,600 units of Product A and 6,400 units of Product B are sold, resulting in an actual sales mix of 2 units of Product A to 8 units of Product B. Now the breakeven point for the two products becomes

$$\frac{\$30,000}{\$4.40} = 6,818 \text{ units resulting in 1,364 units of}$$
$$\text{Product A and 5,454 units of Product B}$$

The actual mix of 2:8 (2 units of Product A to 8 units of Product B) results in a lower breakeven point because more units of the higher contribution margin Product B are sold than was planned. Since breakeven analysis becomes less valid when more than one segment or division of a company is involved, the breakeven point should be determined for as small a segment as possible.

SALES-QUANTITY AND SALES-MIX VARIANCES

While breakeven analysis becomes less valid as more product lines are combined, accountants can compute *sales-volume variances* that compare budgeted and actual quantity and mix. Our focus will be on contribution margin only, but a separate computation for sales and variable costs could be made. Using the information presented above, these variances are:

Sales-quantity variance = (Actual volume in units − Fixed budget volume in units)
                            × Budgeted average unit contribution margin

For Product A:

  $(1,600 \text{ units} - 3,000 \text{ units}) \times \$4 \text{ budgeted contribution margin} = \$5,600U$

For Product B:

  $(6,400 \text{ units} - 6,000 \text{ units}) \times \$4 \text{ budgeted contribution margin} = \underline{\$1,600F}$

  $\underline{\$4,000U^*}$

U = unfavorable.
F = favorable.

  Sales-mix variance = (Actual volume in units − Fixed budget volume in units) ×
       (Budgeted individual unit contribution margin −
            Budgeted average unit contribution margin)

For Product A:

  $(1,600 \text{ units} - 3,000 \text{ units}) \times (\$2 - \$4) = \$2,800 \text{ favorable}$

For Product B:

  $(6,400 \text{ units} - 6,000 \text{ units}) \times (\$5 - \$4) = \underline{400} \text{ favorable}$

  $\underline{\$3,200} \text{ favorable}$

The net sales-volume variance becomes:

Sales-quantity variance, total	$4,000 unfavorable
Sales-mix variance, total	3,200 favorable
Net sales-volume variance	$ 800 unfavorable

This can be proved by:

Budgeted contribution margin:	
(9,000 units × $4)	$36,000
Actual contribution margin:	
Product A Product B	
(1,600 × $2) + (6,400 × $5)	35,200
Difference	$ 800

Note that the sales-quantity variance formula uses fixed budget volume; Chapter 5 introduced fixed and variable (flexible) budgeting concepts in which fixed or static budgets are not adjusted to the actual volume achieved. Because the physical volume used in variable budgeting equals actual physical volume (except, possibly, where the variable budget is prepared for standard capacity), the formula could have been expressed as: Variable budget volume − Fixed budget volume.

The *sales-quantity variance* weights all units at the budgeted average contribution margin, showing the impact on profits of a change in physical volume. The *sales-mix variance* measure the effect of changes from the budgeted average unit contribution margin combined with a change in the quantity of specific product lines. The overall sales mix variance computed above was favorable because: (1) more units of Product B, with a unit contribution margin higher than average ($5 actual versus $4 budgeted), were sold than planned; and (2) fewer units of Product A, with a unit contribution margin lower than average ($2 versus $4), were sold than budgeted.

Desired income level

The breakeven equation can be adapted to reveal more useful information indicating the sales necessary to yield a specified desired net income. For example, assuming a $10 unit sales price, $4 unit variable cost, $36,000 fixed costs, and a desired income before tax of $6,000, the number of units that must be sold is figured this way:

Let X = Number of units to be sold to yield a desired net income
Sales = Variable expenses + Fixed expenses + Desired income
$10X = $4X + $36,000 + $6,000
$6X = $42,000
X = 7,000 units

This calculation reveals that 7,000 units must be sold to earn a $6,000 beforetax income.

The same basic approach is used to compute the number of units to be sold if income is expressed as a percent of sales. Assume that with a $10 unit sales price, $4 unit variable cost, and $36,000 fixed costs, management wishes to earn a return on sales resulting in 15 percent before taxes. The calculation necessary to determine the sales level to earn this return is as follows:

Sales =	Variable expense	+	Fixed expense	+	Desired before-tax income
100%X =	40%X $\left(\frac{\$4}{\$10}\right)$	+	$36,000	+	15%X
45%X =	$36,000				
X =	$80,000 sales to earn 15 percent return on sales before tax				

The following simplified statement of income proves that the sales figure determined is correct.

Statement of Income

Sales		$80,000
Expenses:		
Variable expenses (40% × $80,000)	$32,000	
Fixed expenses	36,000	68,000
Income before taxes (15% × $80,000)		$12,000

Aftertax income.   Management may indicate that a specified return after taxes is desired. Using the above illustration, except that a 10 percent return on sales after taxes is desired and a 48 percent tax rate is assumed, the calculation becomes the following:

$$Sales = \frac{Variable}{expense} + \frac{Fixed}{expense} + \frac{Desired\ aftertax}{income}$$

$$100\%X = 40\%X + \$36,000 + \frac{10\%X}{100\% - 48\%}$$

$$100\%X = 40\%X + \$36,000 + 19.23\%X$$

$$100\%X - 59.23\%X = \$36,000$$

$$40.77\%X = \$36,000$$

$$X = \$88,300 \text{ sales to earn 10 percent aftertax income}$$

With a 10 percent aftertax return desired, the sales needed to fulfill this objective must not only consider variable and fixed expenses, but must also cover income taxes before yielding an aftertax income. Since income taxes will be calculated at 48 percent, the desired aftertax income represents 19.23 percent ($10\%X/52\%X$) of sales. This sales figure is proved by the following statement of income.

Statement of Income

Sales...		$88,300
Expenses:		
Variable expenses (40% × $88,300)	$35,320	
Fixed expenses.............................	36,000	71,320
Income before taxes........................		$16,980
Income taxes (48% × $16,980)...............		8,150
Net income after taxes (10% × $88,300)........		$ 8,830

If the company is manufacturing a product whose market is declining with volume, income, and profit margin all decreasing, it may not be feasible to establish a sales objective of $88,300. After using market research to determine what sales range is realistic, management may be forced to reassess its objectives or change the promotional expenditures planned.

EFFECT OF VOLUME CHANGE

Breakeven analysis can also be used to estimate the effect on earnings if sales volume is increased or decreased. In the example used earlier and displayed in Exhibit 15–2, 60 percent of theoretical capacity must be achieved to break even. If operations are estimated to reach 80 percent of capacity, breakeven analysis can be used to estimate income at $12,000 [$80,000 − ($36,000 + 40% × $80,000)]. This information can be used in estimating the most profitable alternative with regard to expansion of plant facilities and product lines, as well as financing and dividend policies.

Assume that in the above illustration, management has the opportunity to purchase an adjacent building and expand operations to a maximum sales volume of $125,000, but this expansion will increase fixed costs to $42,000. With variable costs remaining at 40 percent of sales, the following calculation can be made:

	With present facilities	With expanded facilities
Sales at breakeven	$100\%X = 0.40X + \$36,000$ $= \$60,000$	$100\%X = 0.40X + \$42,000$ $= \$70,000$
Income at $80,000 sales	$\$80,000 - [(40\% \times \$80,000)$ $+ \$36,000]$ $= \$12,000$	$\$80,000 - [(40\% \times \$80,000)$ $+ \$42,000]$ $= \$6,000$
Sales necessary to earn $20,000 income before taxes	$X = \$36,000 + 0.40X$ $+ \$20,000$ $= \$93,333$	$X = \$42,000 + 0.40X$ $+ \$20,000$ $= \$103,333$
Income at 90% capacity	$\$90,000 - [(40\% \times \$90,000)$ $+ \$36,000]$ $= \$18,000$	$\$112,500 - [(40\% \times \$112,500)$ $+ \$42,000]$ $= \$25,500$

The effect on the breakeven point of increasing fixed expense can be illustrated in a breakeven chart, as shown in Exhibit 15–4. The proposed total expense and fixed expense lines are indicated by broken dotted lines. As indicated on the chart, the proposed increase in fixed expenses has caused the breakeven point to be higher.

In deciding whether expansion is warranted, management should determine potential sales possibilities. A higher sales volume is required to break even if the plant is expanded. In addition, a higher sales volume is necessary to earn $20,000 in income using the expanded facilities. However, if a significant market for the product exists, the company has the possibility of earning a higher level of income through the use of expanded facilities operating at 90 percent capacity. (As previous chapters have emphasized, it is not realistic to assume maximum capacity can be obtained.)

Price and volume alternatives

Cost-volume-profit analysis is helpful in predicting the change in income that will occur if sales price or sales volume is altered. The accountant can prepare an analysis similar to that shown in Exhibit 15–5 which measures the effects of various sales prices and volumes. No change in unit variable cost or total fixed costs is assumed. It is assumed that management has budgeted to sell 7,000 units at a $10 per unit sales price, yielding $6,000 net income before taxes, as shown in Column (1). Because of the influence of supply and demand, Column (2) assumes that an increase in sales price will result in a lower volume sold. Column (3) illustrates the results obtained if there is a decrease in sales price and an increase in volume. Marketing research should assist in arriving at such probable sales price and volume combinations. Column (4) indicates the effect on the breakeven point and income when a 5 percent increase in sales

EXHIBIT 15–4

Breakeven chart with an increase in fixed costs

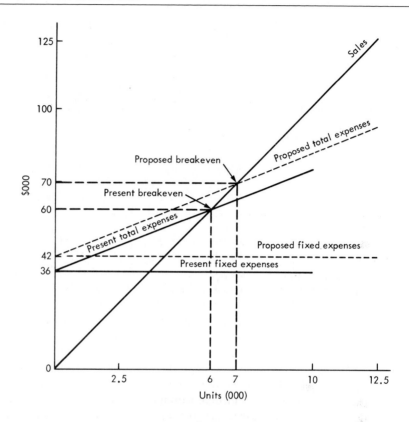

price occurs with no decrease in volume. Management may feel that demand for the product is high enough because of brand loyalty or product quality and that a sales price increase will have no effect on volume.

As shown in Exhibit 15–5, income is projected to be highest when there is a 10 percent increase in sales price with a 5 percent decrease in volume. Breakeven sales with these conditions are also lower than at budgeted volume. The least favorable alternative is to lower the sales price 15 percent with a resulting 20 percent increase in volume. Not only is income lowest with this alternative, but breakeven sales are also highest. If sales price is increased 5 percent with no corresponding decrease in volume, a marked increase over budgeted income will occur.

P/V chart

The impact of sales price and volume changes upon income and breakeven can also be illustrated through the use of a profit-volume graph (P/V chart). The

EXHIBIT 15–5

Effect of sales price and volume changes on income and breakeven

	(1) Budgeted 7,000 units @ $10	(2) 10% increase in sales price 5% decrease in volume	(3) 15% decrease in sales price 20% increase in volume	(4) 5% increase in sales price no change in volume
Sales:				
7,000 units @ $10	$70,000			
6,650 units @ $11		$73,150		
8,400 units @ $8.50.			$71,400	
7,000 units @ $10.50. . . .				$73,500
Variable costs:				
7,000 units @ $4	28,000			
6,650 units @ $4		26,600		
8,400 units @ $4			33,600	
7,000 units @ $4				28,000
Contribution margin.	$42,000	$46,550	$37,800	$45,500
Fixed costs.	36,000	36,000	36,000	36,000
Income before taxes	$ 6,000	$10,550	$ 1,800	$ 9,500
P/V ratio (contribution margin ÷ sales).	60%	63.6%	52.9%	61.9%
Breakeven sales (fixed costs ÷ P/V ratio).	$60,000	$56,604	$68,053	$58,158

first graph in Exhibit 15–6 illustrates such a chart using data from Exhibit 15–2 in which fixed costs are $36,000, unit variable cost is $4, and unit sale price is $10. The vertical axis represents net income in dollars, while the horizontal axis is volume, which may be expressed in units or sales dollars. If no units are produced, the net loss will be $36,000, the amount of the fixed costs. The net income line intersects the volume axis at the breakeven point of 6,000 units; net income at 10,000 units becomes $24,000.

The second graph in Exhibit 15–6 shows the impact on net income and the breakeven point if the unit variable cost increases to $4.50 while total fixed cost decreases to $27,500. The breakeven point falls from 6,000 units to 5,000 units, as follows:

$$\frac{\$27,500}{\$5.50 \text{ unit contribution margin}} = 5,000 \text{ units}$$

The new net income, a dashed line in the second graph, is steeper, which means that the net income will increase at a faster rate as volume increases.

Data presented in any cost-volume-profit analysis such as those illustrated in Exhibits 15–5 and 15–6 are of great importance in analyzing which available alternative is most profitable. However, the accountant will usually have to spend time studying the information because cost-volume-profit analysis requires the segregation of fixed and variable costs, and the data that appear on

EXHIBIT 15–6

P/V chart

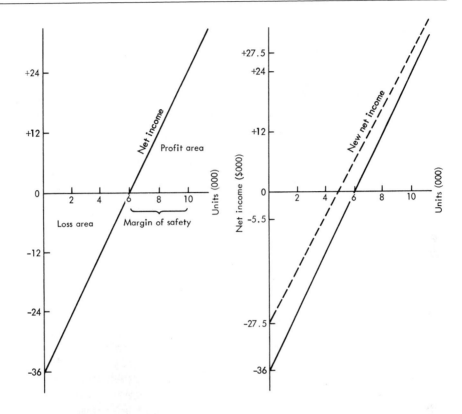

the conventional absorption statement of income cannot be used directly. Instead, semivariable expense must be broken down into variable and fixed components. For this purpose, the methods presented in Chapter 5 can be used, and the chart of accounts can be designed so that separate accounts can be used for fixed and variable costs. For example, two control accounts for Factory Overhead Control could be used: Factory Overhead Control—Variable Expenses and Factory Overhead Control—Fixed Expenses. In addition, the data used in any type of cost-volume-profit analysis should reflect current conditions, since the behavior of variable and fixed costs tends to change over time.

SUMMARY

While breakeven point analysis portrays only static cost-volume-profit relationships under limiting assumptions, it can offer insight into the effect upon profits when any of these components is changed. A breakeven chart may also more vividly show line management these relationships than would detailed numerical statements. Some of the decision-making analytical tools discussed, however, such as breakeven analysis, are based on rigid limitations which are designed to simplify real-world situations. Nevertheless, rather than introduce more complex realistic illustrations which require more costly analysis, an accountant can often use breakeven analysis to find answers which can be used just as effectively.

As discussed in the chapter, it is important for a company to know the contribution margin ratios for each of its products so that high contribution margin products can be promoted while reduced emphasis can be put on less profitable products. Contribution margin analysis is also helpful in certain types of pricing decisions which are discussed in detail in Chapter 22. For example, it lets management make an informed decision on whether to accept an extra order when capacity is below normal. Average cost information could give a distorted answer if it did not conform to the current actual contribution margin.

Certainly, the usefulness of cost-volume-profit data justifies the effort required in separating fixed and variable costs. The accountant also has the flexibility of presenting the data in various forms. Regardless of which specific cost-volume-profit analysis is used, it can provide useful information for such decisions as pricing, short-term bidding, and deleting or adding product lines.

IMPORTANT TERMS AND CONCEPTS

Breakeven analysis

Variable costs

Fixed costs

Contribution margin

Variable cost ratio

Marginal income

Contribution margin ratio, profit-volume ratio, or marginal income ratio

Margin of safety

Cash flow breakeven point

Tax shield

Breakeven chart

Assumptions of breakeven analysis

Relevant range

Sales mix

Sales-volume variances

Sales-quantity variance

Sales-mix variance

Profit-volume graph

REVIEW QUESTIONS

1. For what purpose is cost-volume-profit analysis used?
2. Explain the meaning of each of the following terms that are implicit in cost-volume-profit analysis:
    a. Breakeven point.
    b. Fixed costs.
    c. Variable costs.
    d. Sales mix.
    e. Relevant range.
    f. Margin of safety.

3. What assumptions are implicit in cost-volume-profit analysis?

4. University Company plans to sell 500,000 units of a product for $3 a unit. Management expects to break even at this level of sales. If the contribution margin is 40 percent, what are the fixed costs?

5. Define contribution margin and explain how contribution margin can be expressed.

6. Discuss the uses management can make of the contribution margin and contribution margin ratio.

7. Discuss the relationship between the contribution margin ratio and the variable cost ratio.

8. Define marginal income.

9. In breakeven point calculations, why is the unit variable cost rather than total variable cost used?

10. At a breakeven point of 1,000 units sold, variable costs were $1,500 and fixed costs were $750. What will the 1,001 unit sold contribute to profit before income tax?

11. Discuss the various complexities that can be illustrated on breakeven charts.

12. A company sells its product for $45 per unit. Fixed costs amount to $600,000 per year. Variable expenses amount to $1,120,000 if 40,000 units are sold. Management anticipates that variable expenses will increase 15 percent per unit during the coming year, as a result of direct materials price increases and a new labor contract. How many units of product must be sold if the firm is to make $40,000 in earnings before taxes?

13. The budget formula for the Brown Company is $200,000 plus $0.75 per machine-hour. It takes four hours to manufacture a unit before it can be sold for $7. Based on the overhead budget formula, how many units must be sold for the company to generate $60,000 more than total budgeted overhead costs?

14. Describe circumstances in which the overall sales-mix variance would be unfavorable.

15. Why is breakeven analysis more accurate for one segment rather than for the overall company?

16. What is the relationship between a company's product mix and its breakeven point? Does a change in the assumed product mix affect the breakeven point previously determined?

17. What should management do when a low margin of safety is accompanied by
a. A high contribution margin and high fixed costs?
b. A low contribution margin ratio?

18. Why should management study the potential sales possibilities of its products when considering the expansion of its facilities?

19. Assume the market saturation point for a product is almost met and management does not feel it can increase present sales volume; in fact, they would not be surprised if there is a decrease in volume. With these conditions, the company has the opportunity of replacing some of its equipment and machinery, which is being depreciated on a straight-line basis, with direct labor workers. Assume at present volume there is an equal exchange of total fixed costs for total variable costs. Ignoring other factors, what recommendations would you make?

EXERCISES

E15–1.   Units to sell to earn a specific profit percentage and determining the breakeven point

Gandulf, Inc. sells orcs for $5 per unit. Variable costs are 40 percent of selling price. Fixed costs are $10,000.

Required:

a.   How many orcs must be sold to realize a beforetax income of 10 percent of sales?
b.   What is the breakeven point in units?

E15–2.   Acceptance of short-run bid

An overseas typewriter manufacturing company has contacted Michelle McGee Products with an offer to purchase 40,000 platen cylinders at a price of $3.50 each. McGee's full cost of producing the cylinder is $4, of which $2.50 is variable. The regular selling price is $6. The typewriter manufacturer's offer is on an all or none basis. But because of capacity constraints, McGee has to reduce sales to its regular customers by 10,000 cylinders annually if it accepts the overseas manufacturer's offer.

Required:

Should McGee accept the offer in the short run?

E15–3.   Determining the breakeven point and breakeven chart

Management of the Culver Company wants to earn a 20 percent return on sales. The sales price is $15 per unit, and unit variable cost is $8. Fixed expenses amount to $12,000.

Required:

a.   How many units must be sold to earn the income desired?
b.   What is the breakeven point for the company? Express your answer in units.
c.   Assuming a maximum capacity of 4,000 units, construct a breakeven chart.

E15–4.   Breakeven units before and after plan

Knoxville Company projects that sales for next year will be 80,000 units if the sales price is $57. At this level, unit fixed costs will be $20, while total variable costs will be $2 million.

The marketing research department advises management to reduce the sales price to $52 and give salespeople a commission equal to $2 per unit.

Required:

a.   What is the breakeven point for the company in terms of units, before putting the marketing research department's plan into effect.
b.   What is the breakeven point in units after putting the plan in effect?
c.   The marketing research department believes that the plan will result in before-tax earnings of $50,000. How many units must be sold to reach this earnings level?

E15-5.   Sales price to achieve objectives

Gold Company has fixed expenses of $325,000, variable expenses of $5.60 per unit, and a selling price of $12 per unit. A 15 percent return on invested capital of $500,000 is desired.

Required:

a.   Estimate the dollar sales required to obtain the desired return on capital.
b.   Assume, instead, that the selling price per unit is unknown. Estimate the selling price per unit needed to earn a 15 percent return on the company's invested capital. Assume sales of 60,000 units.

E15-6.   Discontinue product line

The management of Brian Grove Electronics is holding a meeting in five days to discuss whether to discontinue its hand-held calculator product line. Each person attending the meeting is expected to express an opinion and to substantiate that opinion with a quantitative analysis. Management has been furnished the following product statement for the year just ended:

Revenue	$900,000
Cost of goods sold	850,000
Gross margin	$ 50,000
Marketing and administrative expenses.	70,000
Net loss	$ (20,000)

Cost of goods sold is 35 percent factory overhead, of which 15 percent is fixed.

Required:

What opinion and supporting data should you present if you were to attend this meeting?

E15-7.   Units to sell

A department of Rivendell Company provides the following information relating to the fourth quarter of 19X1:

Budget formula.	$120,000 plus $0.50 per hour
Volume variance.	2,400 (favorable)
Actual total overhead	
(fixed plus variable).	550,000
Spending variance	4,000 (unfavorable)
Total overhead	
application rate.	.70 per hour

Required:

Each unit takes six hours to manufacture, and the selling price is $5 per unit. Based on the overhead budget formula, how many units must be sold to generate $30,000 more than total budgeted overhead costs?

E15-8.   Breakeven units under forecasted conditions

Jesse Company produced and sold 2,000 units for the year ended July 31, 19X1. Their income statement appears as follows:

Sales.		$20,000
Direct material	$4,000	
Direct labor	6,000	
Variable overhead	1,000	
Fixed overhead	4,410	15,410
Income before taxes.		$ 4,590

Required:

a.   Compute the units the company must sell to break even.

b.   Compute the sales in dollars necessary to earn $6,840 income.

c.   Management expects direct material costs to increase 10 percent next year; in addition, analysis of the component parts of variable overhead reveal that a 5 percent decline is expected. Additional fixed costs of $693.50 will be incurred. Compute breakeven units under these forecasted conditions.

E15–9.   Sales to break even

Latimer Company is considering establishing a branch plant in Peru. Predicting sales of 50,000 units, they provide the following estimated expense:

	Total annual expenses	Percent of total annual cost that is variable
Material.	$30,000	80
Labor	28,000	75
Factory overhead	36,000	55
Marketing and administrative	20,000	40
	$114,000	

The units will be sold by a marketing firm in Peru which will receive a commission of 20 percent of the sales price. None of the home office expense will be allocated to the plant in Peru.

Required:

a.   Compute the sales price per unit that would cover all total annual expenses for the plant in Peru.

b.   If unit sales price is $3, compute the breakeven point in sales dollars for the plant in Peru.

E15–10.   Volume to warrant expansion

Michael Antonucci, Inc. owns a movie theater that has a seating capacity of 400. The price of one ticket is $3. The theater is open 52 weeks a year, and attendance averages 4,200 a week. Direct costs are $0.75 per person, and other annual costs are $131,040. Because consumer demand is for more than 400 seats for some movies, Antonucci is considering expanding the seating capacity to 600 for an annual cost of $29,160. Direct costs per person will remain constant.

Required:

How much does average attendance have to increase to warrant the expansion if management wishes to maintain the same profit margin on sales? Show your calculations.

E15–11.   Calculating income with contribution margin and margin of safety ratios given

Analysis of the budget for the Capri Company reveals that variable manufacturing costs are $25 per unit and variable marketing and administrative costs are $10 per unit. Budgeted fixed factory overhead is $500,000, while budgeted fixed marketing and administrative cost is $250,000. Normal capacity for the plant is 160,000 units per year. The unit sales price is $50.

Required:

a.   Calculate:
   (1)   The breakeven point expressed in dollars.
   (2)   The units that must be sold to earn a profit of 20 percent on sales.
b.   Actual operations for the year resulted in a margin of safety ratio of 30 percent and a contribution margin ratio of 25 percent. Determine actual income before taxes for the year assuming actual fixed costs were 5 percent more than those budgeted.

E15–12.   Breakeven units and units to earn profit percentage

Fritz McCameron Company has conducted cost studies and projected the following annual cost based on 60,000 units of production and sales:

	Total annual cost	Percent of fixed portion of total annual cost
Direct material	$ 90,000	0
Direct labor	45,000	20
Factory overhead	120,000	60
Marketing and administrative	100,000	76

Required:

a.   Determine the number of units that must be sold for the company to break even if the unit sales price is $7.
b.   Compute the company's unit sales price necessary to yield a return on sales of 10 percent before taxes if sales are 60,000 units.

PROBLEMS

P15–1.   Computation of breakeven

Jackson Company records for the year ended December 31, 19X3, include the following information. (Variable costs are designated V and fixed costs, F.)

Sales (25,000 units @ $15)		$375,000
Costs:		
Direct material.	$ 60,000 (100%V)	
Direct labor.	90,000 (100%V)	
Factory overhead	120,000 (80%F, 20%V)	
Marketing expenses.	40,000 (50%F, 50%V)	
Administrative expenses	30,000 (80%F, 20%V)	
Total costs		340,000
Income.		$ 35,000

Required:

Show all computations.

a. Compute the breakeven point in number of units and sales dollars.
b. Compute number of units required to generate a net profit of $70,000.
c. Compute the breakeven point in number of units if fixed costs were increased by $7,000.

P15–2. Computing sales with desired income and breakeven sales

Annual costs for Winkler Company based on a 48,000 unit volume of production and sales are as follows:

	Percent of fixed portion of total annual costs	Total annual costs
Direct material.	0	$514,360
Direct labor.	20	280,000
Factory overhead	65	360,000
Marketing	40	185,000
Administrative	100	195,680

Required:

a. Determine the unit sales price that will yield a projected 18 percent profit if sales are 48,000 units.
b. Using the above variable-fixed costs relationships, and a $40 unit sales price:
   (1) Determine breakeven units.
   (2) Determine the number of units that must be sold to yield a projected 18 percent profit on sales.

P15–3. Breakeven using different sales mixes: Sales-quantity and sales-mix variances

Even though Chris Krebs, Inc. recognizes the danger of computing a company-wide breakeven point, management feels this information will be helpful for planning purposes. Analysis of the budget reveals the following:

	Product lines		
Per unit	A	B	C
Sales price.	$ 100	$ 80	$ 60
Variable expenses	40	30	20
Budgeted volume	8,000	16,000	16,000
Total fixed expenses		$1,200,000	

Required:

a. Compute the breakeven point in units per product line for the entire company.
b. (1) Determine sales-quantity variances and sales-mix variances for each product line assuming that actual sales prices and variable costs were the same as budgeted and there was a sales mix of 6,000 units of Product A; 12,000 units of Product B; and 18,000 units of Product C.
   (2) Prove your answer in (1).
c. Assume the sales mix given in *b* but that actual variable expenses of Product A were 10 percent higher than budgeted, while the variable expenses of Products B and C were 15 percent lower. Actual fixed expenses were $1,249,500; however, actual

sales prices did not vary from those budgeted. Compute the new actual breakeven point in units per product line for the overall company.

P15–4. Constructing breakeven charts under varying conditions

A product line of the Gunn Company produced the following results during 19X1:

Sales (9,000 units).	$135,000
Total fixed expenses	24,000
Total variable expenses	108,000

During 19X2, company management plans to slightly modify the product by reducing the direct material cost per unit by $0.80. In addition, the sales price will be reduced by $1.80 per unit. An extensive advertising campaign will be started that will increase total fixed expenses by $1,000. Maximum capacity for the company is 15,000 units.

Required:

a. What is the breakeven point for the company in terms of dollars and units before taking account of the changes?
b. What is the margin of safety before allowing for the changes?
c. What is the breakeven point for the company in terms of dollars and units after accounting for the changes?
d. Draw a breakeven chart in terms of the original data, *not* involving the expected changes.
e. On the breakeven graph that you prepared for *d* above, draw in the following: (1) the 19X2 sales line, with the changes; (2) the 19X2 fixed expenses line; and (3) the 19X2 total cost line.

P15–5. Breakeven at various capacity levels

Tim Wilmot, Inc. produces quality clothing. Its monthly budgeted income statement at full capacity is as follows:

		000s omitted
Sales (500,000 units)		$6,000
Less variable costs:		
Direct material	$ 500	
Direct labor	2,500	
Variable overhead	1,500	4,500
Contribution margin		$1,500
Fixed expenses:		
Manufacturing	$ 460	
Marketing.	120	
Administrative	260	840
Income before taxes		$ 660

When operations are completely idle, total fixed costs amount to $480,000; at 50 percent of capacity and below, fixed costs are $660,000. Fixed costs at levels above 50 percent equal those at full capacity.

Required:

a. Compute the breakeven point in units.
b. At what sales level in dollars would it be more economical to close the factory rather than operate?

c. Prove your answer to *b*.

d. Management's concern that they are operating at only 50 percent of capacity prompted a market study. One alternative is to reduce the sales price to $11.25. At what percentage of capacity must the company operate to break even at the reduced sales price?

P15–6.   Cash flow breakeven point

Horrell Company provides you with the following budgeted income statement for one of its departments:

Units sold	1,000	1,200
Sales.	$20,000	$24,000
Less:		
Cost of material sold	$ 8,000	$ 9,600
Cost of direct labor sold.	6,000	7,200
Repairs	1,000	1,200
Supervisor's salary.	2,000	2,000
Rent	1,800	1,800
Depreciation	1,500	1,500
Amortization of patent	500	500
Total	$20,800	$23,800
Income before taxes	$ (800)	$ 200

Required:

a. Determine the breakeven point in number of units that must be sold.

b. Assuming a 48 percent tax rate, determine the cash flow breakeven point in number of units that must be sold. Management expects other departments within the company to be profitable so that payment of income taxes will be required.

P15–7.   Calculating aftertax income

Wurlitzer Company produces quality motors. The statement of income for the year ended December 31, 19X1 is as follows:

Statement of Income

Sales (5,000 units)		$300,000
Less variable expenses:		
Direct material.	$75,000	
Direct labor.	90,000	
Variable overhead	25,000	
Total variable expenses. . . .		190,000
Contribution margin		$110,000
Fixed expenses:		
Manufacturing.	$32,000	
Marketing	18,000	
Administrative	10,000	
Total fixed expenses		60,000
Income before taxes.		$ 50,000

Company management believes that 5,500 units can be sold in 19X2. Assume a tax rate of 48 percent.

Required:

a.   What is the forecasted aftertax income for 19X2, assuming the same cost behavior as in 19X1?

b.   Calculate the breakeven point for 19X2 in units.

c.   Management believes that forecasted 19X2 sales can be maintained even if a sales promotion costing $4,000 included in 19X1 expenses is eliminated. What will the breakeven volume in dollars be if this sales promotion is cancelled?

d.   If the $4,000 sales promotion is cancelled, what are the sales dollars required in 19X2 to maintain the aftertax net income in dollars for 19X2 determined in *a*?

P15–8.   Sales mix and breakeven: sales-quantity and sales-mix variances

Next year's budget for Pattie Moody, Inc. a multiproduct firm, is given below:

	Product lines			
	A	B	C	Total
Sales	$1,060,000	$800,000	$880,000	$2,740,000
Less: Variable costs.	580,000	600,000	740,000	1,920,000
Fixed costs allocated on square footage. . . .	140,000	150,000	91,300	381,300
Income before taxes	$ 340,000	$ 50,000	$ 48,700	$ 438,700
Units.	160,000	100,000	140,000	400,000

Required:

a.   Compute the budgeted breakeven point in units per product line for the overall company.

b.   At year end, you determine that sales price, total fixed costs, and unit variable costs were exactly as budgeted, but the following units per product line were sold:

Product line	Units
A	175,000
B	150,000
C	175,000
Total units	500,000

Determine the company's breakeven point in units using the actual sales mix.

c.   Compute sales-quantity variances and sales-mix variances for each product line.

d.   Prove your answer in *c*.

P15–9.   Breakeven units and dollar sales to earn income

Flinn Corporation's accountant gathered the following data concerning the fixed and variable cost structure of the company:

Selling price per unit of product.	$325
Variable cost per unit of product	285
Fixed costs per unit of product	60
(if the firm produces and sells 30,000 units)	

Required:

Compute the following, assuming each situation below is a *separate* case:

a.   Breakeven point in units and dollars.

b. Breakeven point in units if the variable costs per unit are expected to increase to $295.
c. Breakeven point in dollars, if the fixed costs are expected to increase by $80,000.
d. The number of units that must be sold if income before taxes is $132,000, and if the company variable expenses are to increase to $290 per unit.
e. The dollar sales necessary to produce an income before taxes of $150,000 if the selling price is reduced to $300 per unit.
f. The number of units that must be sold if income before taxes is $200,000 and fixed expenses are expected to increase by $60,000.

P15–10.   Breakeven charts

Elaine Company's income statement for the year ended December 31, 19X1, was as follows:

Sales ($8 per unit)		$100,000
Variable costs	$42,000	
Fixed costs	24,000	66,000
Income		$ 34,000

Required:

a. Calculate the present breakeven point in dollars and units.
b. The company is considering adopting a new production procedure that will result in an increase in contribution margin of 15 percent and an increase in fixed cost of $4,300.
  (1) Calculate the breakeven point in dollars and units under these conditions.
  (2) Graph present and forecasted total and unit fixed costs and total and unit variable costs. Label the forecasted costs TFC (total fixed costs), UFC (unit fixed costs), TVC (total variable costs), and UVC (unit variable costs). Graph paper is not necessary as only the change in cost behavior is to be shown.
c. The company is also considering an alternative marketing plan which would result in an increase in sales volume of 15 percent and a decrease in fixed costs of 10 percent.
  (1) Calculate the breakeven point in dollars and units under these conditions.
  (2) Graph present and forecasted total and unit fixed costs and total and unit variable costs. Label the forecasted costs TFC, UFC, TVC, and UVC. Graph paper is not necessary, as only the change in the cost behavior is to be shown.

P15–11.   Computing income, P/V ratio, and breakeven sales dollars

William Swyers Company asks that you prepare cost-volume-profit analysis for their use in predicting a change in income if they alter sales price or sales volume. Management has budgeted to annually sell 15,000 units at a $12 per unit sales price. Fixed costs are budgeted to be $50,000. Contribution margin per unit is $5.

The vice president of marketing believes that the following three alternative sales prices and expected volumes are feasible:

1. Increase sales price 15 percent with an expected 10 percent decrease in volume. Because of the decrease in volume, the company can lease part of its building. This would result in a $2,200 decrease in fixed costs.
2. Decrease sales price 10 percent with an expected 12 percent increase in volume. Because of the increase in volume, the company must also rent an adjacent building at an annual cost of $1,000.

3. Marketing research indicates that if the company placed their product in a more attractive reusable container, sales price could be increased 5 percent with no decrease in volume. The additional cost of this reusable container would be $0.50 per unit.

Required:

a. Compute income, P/V ratio (round to two decimal points), and breakeven sales dollars for the budgeted volume and each of the three alternatives proposed.

b. What course of action do you think the company should take?

P15–12. Breakeven analysis under various proposals

Towery Company presently has a highly automated production process. Management is concerned because annual budgeted fixed costs are $1.4 million for next year. The current sales price is $12 per unit, and unit variable cost is $5.

An outsider has approached the company wanting to buy some of its machinery, which Towery could sell at book value. Management has been considering replacing its machines with direct labor workers since the product could be produced as skillfully in this manner. This proposed change would lower fixed costs by $200,000, with a resulting increase of $2 per unit in variable costs.

Required:

a. Compute the budgeted breakeven point in units and sales dollars under present conditions.

b. Compute the breakeven point in units and sales dollars if the machines are replaced by direct labor workers.

c. Assume that market research indicates 300,000 units could be sold; prepare income statements and margin of safety ratios for each alternative using this sales volume. Indicate which alternative you recommend.

d. Prepare the same analysis as in c assuming that 420,000 units can be sold.

e. Prepare only income statements for the two alternatives assuming a depressed market will exist in the future in which 180,000 units will be sold. Indicate which alternative you recommend.

f. Based on your analyses in c through e, prepare a general recommendation statement.

P15–13. Calculating units to sell; choosing alternatives

Overton, Inc. is considering producing a new unit; forecasted costs associated with this production are as follows:

Material cost	$ 4 per unit
Packaging cost	$ 1 per unit
Salesperson's commission on retail sales only	8% of retail price
Machine setup time (40 hours @ $8/hour).	$320
Special packing machine designed for this project only.	$180
Marketing costs	$250

The unit retail selling price will be $10; 30 units will be sold directly to wholesalers at 30 percent off the retail price.

Required:

a. Calculate the number of units that must be sold to break even on the project.

b.   Calculate the number of units that must be sold to earn a beforetax profit of $6,000 on the project.
c.   Assume Overton, Inc. pays income taxes of 40 percent of net income. How many units must be sold to earn an aftertax income of $5,000?
d.   Would it be more profitable to sell 1,500 units to retailers with a retail price of $9 or 800 units to retailers with a retail price of $12? (Thirty additional units would still be sold to wholesalers at the 30 percent discount.) Discuss your answer.

P15–14.   Choosing the most profitable alternatives

Faber, Inc. produces fishing equipment. For one of its product lines, the 19X2 sales price will be $100 per unit with unit variable costs of $70; fixed costs are budgeted at $36,000. A tax rate of 40 percent is to be considered.

Required:

a.   If management desires an aftertax income of $42,000, how many units must be sold?
b.   What would breakeven units be for 19X2?
c.   Later in 19X2, management finds that sales are not meeting expectations because of a recession. After selling 1,000 units at the established sales price with variable costs as planned, at midyear management realizes it will never meet the desired aftertax income of $42,000 unless action is taken. The following three alternatives are proposed. Indicate the remaining number of units that must be sold to achieve management's desired aftertax income.
(1)   Reduce sales price by $10 based on the Marketing Department's forecast that 3,000 units will be sold during the last six months of 19X2. Total fixed and unit variable costs will remain the same as budgeted.
(2)   Reduce variable cost per unit by $5 with a substitution of a cheaper grade of material. Sales price will be reduced by $2; sales of 2,400 units are expected for the remainder of the year.
(3)   Slash fixed costs by $8,000 and cut sales price by 3 percent. Variable costs per unit will remain the same. Sales of 2,400 units are forecast.

P15–15.   Breakeven analysis: Changing costs

Operating results for the fiscal year just ended for Daniel Humphreys, Inc. are presented below:

Sales (3,500 units)		$70,000
Variable costs:		
Production	$31,500	
Marketing and administrative.	10,500	
Total variable costs.		42,000
Contribution margin		$28,000
Fixed costs:		
Production	$10,600	
Marketing and administrative.	7,000	
Total fixed costs		17,600
Income before income taxes.		$10,400
Income taxes (40%)		4,160
Net Income after income taxes		$ 6,240

Manufacturing capacity of the company's facilities is 5,000 units of product.

Required:

Consider each of the following items independently of the other items.

a. Compute the breakeven volume in units of product.

b. A potential foreign customer has offered to buy 1,700 units at $15 per unit. If all of Humphreys' costs and rates were to stay at last year's levels, what net income after taxes will Humphreys make if it takes this order and rejects some business from regular customers to prevent exceeding capacity?

c. If sales price is reduced by 20 percent, management expects to sell 4,100 units. What is the aftertax net income or loss that Humphreys can expect next year if costs and rates stay at the same levels?

d. Humphreys is considering replacing a highly labor intensive process with an automatic machine; this should result in an annual increase of $16,000 in production fixed costs. However, variable production costs will decrease $4 per unit. Compute the

(1) New breakeven volume in units.

(2) Sales volume in dollars that would be required to earn an aftertax net income of $8,340 next year if the automatic machine is purchased.

e. Humphreys has an opportunity to market the product in a new area. Using this strategy, an advertising and promotion program costing $8,400 annually must be undertaken for the next two or three years. A $2 per unit sales commission in addition to the current commission will be required for the sales force in the new territory. How many units will have to be sold in the new territory to maintain Humphrey's current aftertax income of $6,240? Show proof of your answer.

f. Management estimates that the per unit sales price should decline 15 percent next year. Production materials should increase $1 due to the scarcity of petroleum products, but fixed costs should not change. What sales volume in units will be required to earn an aftertax net income of $7,500 next year? Is this feasible?

CASES

C15–1.   Breakeven and cash flow breakeven for professional services

Dr. Douglass Edwards asks your financial advice regarding the establishment of an emergency center designed and staffed to care for minor emergencies and general medical visits. Market analysis reveals that an individual with unexpected illness or minor injury can presently receive medical treatment from two sources: a physician's office between prescheduled appointments or a hospital emergency room. Both sources are regarded as inconvenient and generally require waits of two to four hours. Emergency room visits cost three to four times more than an office visit and costs of most minor complaints are not reimbursed; physicians' offices are often not accessible to new patients. Dr. Edwards' emergency center will be designed to provide medical care at any time, for any reason, on a freely accessible basis and at a reasonable cost. He believes consumers will appreciate the quick purchase of medical care under pleasant circumstances voluntarily selected by the consumer.

The center would utilize a sophisticated marketing campaign to attract patients who routinely use hospital emergency rooms for their medical needs. Patients who do not have a physician or who have a physician but are unable to obtain unscheduled visits would find the clinic designed to meet their needs. The medical resource would be highly visible and provide excellent, convenient (no appointments) care. Expediency is another factor since the mean total visit time would be less than 60 minutes. The medical care would be relatively inexpensive with a mean visit charge of $40, which is less than the $65 charge for an emergency room visit.

The center would be designed to treat an average maximum of 100 patients per day. It will be housed in a 4,500 square-foot ground-floor space in an existing building remodeled to specifications at no cost to Dr. Edwards. The site is near a major retail center in a city of approximately 1 million. Parking space for 10 cars will be immediately adjacent, with a lighted sign visible from the street. The facility will be open 365 days a year, 16 hours each day from 7:00 A.M. to 11:00 P.M. using two 8-hour shifts. Minimum staff on duty per shift includes one physician, one licensed practical nurse, one clerk, one receptionist, and one off-duty fire department paramedic assisting in routine nursing and orderly duties.

Charges.   All charges will be payable at the time of service by cash, personal check, or major credit card. No personal credit will be extended, and no Medicare or Medicaid assignments will be accepted. Insurance assignments will be accepted only on a very limited basis for known policies and on known reimbursable charges, with the deductible payable at the time of treatment. Since Dr. Edwards is operating the center as a private physician's office, there is no legal or ethical requirement to accept indigent or nonpaying patients.

Marketing.   The community in general and the private medical practitioners' patients will constitute the two markets serviced. Advertising will be directed toward the middle-income, suburban population. A concentrated media effort will be used to launch the project, and subsequent advertising will be limited to Yellow Pages listings and Welcome Wagon literature. Word of mouth will be the most important long-term advertising.

Expenses.   Dr. Edwards supplies you with the following hourly salary expense per person: physician—$45; nurse—$10.50; clerk—$5; receptionist—$5; paramedic—$8. Fringe benefits and payroll taxes are expected to average 36 percent of the hourly salary expense. Since the facilities will be open daily, some workers will be required to work more than 40 hours a week. Included in the total hours of operations for the entire year are 160 hours of overtime for each class of worker. Assume personnel are paid time and one half for overtime hours, and base the overtime premium on an amount that includes the wage rate per hour as well as the fringe benefit and payroll tax rate per hour.

Desired space can be leased for $11 per square foot annually. Property insurance of $6,000 and malpractice insurance of $11,000 are expected per year. An average annual expenditure of $3,000 is planned for advertising. The fixed portion of utilities for the facilities is estimated to total $18,000. Each patient visit is expected to cause an increase of $4.50 in medical/office supplies and $0.50 in utilities because of the additional usage of the facilities.

Dr. Edwards is concerned about the large outlay of funds required for necessary equipment. His analysis indicates $10,000 of office equipment, $70,000 of minor medical equipment, and $38,000 of X-ray equipment will be needed initially. All equipment is assumed to have a five-year life.

Required:

a.   Determine the number of patient visits on an annual, daily, and hourly basis:
   (1)   To break even.
   (2)   For cash flow breakeven for the first year (ignore the tax shield on noncash fixed expenses).

b.   Suggest other factors that should be studied before plans are implemented.

OUTLINE OF CHAPTER 16

Variable costing (direct costing)

Comparison of variable and absorption costing

Advantages of variable costing

Dangers of variable costing

Opinions on variable costing

OBJECTIVES OF CHAPTER 16

1. To contrast the product costing concepts that variable costing and absorption costing involve.

2. To study the uses of variable costing so that the concept will not be discarded simply because it cannot be used for external reporting.

3. To present the dangers that can stem from the misapplication of the variable costing principle.

16

Variable costing

Previous chapters have been limited to discussing absorption costing in which both fixed and variable costs are treated as product costs. *Absorption costing* is also known as *conventional costing* or *full costing* and is generally accepted for external reporting. This chapter, however, discusses a different approach to product costing known as variable or direct costing, which employs another inventory valuation concept. While variable costing has a growing number of supporters, the accounting profession has not recognized the concept as a generally accepted inventory valuation method.

VARIABLE COSTING (DIRECT COSTING)

The *variable* or *direct costing* concept assumes that only those production costs which vary directly with volume should be considered as *product costs*, thus leaving all other manufacturing costs to be treated as *period costs*. Since direct material and direct labor are usually variable, variable costing treats these costs and variable overhead as product costs; all other costs are charged off as expenses in the period incurred. With variable costing, therefore, fixed costs are considered to be the costs of providing for a level of capacity and are charged in their entirety against the revenue of the period.

In referring to variable costing, this book does not use the term "direct costing," even though this terminology is popularly used in practice. It is felt that this term is by no means the best name for the concept, for it does not completely describe the underlying costing method, given that those costs which *are* identified with this method are the variable costs. The word "direct" implies a high degree of traceability, and this is not the distinction that should be emphasized as both variable and fixed costs can be direct costs which are traceable to a costing center. For example, in a department that makes only one product, direct product costs are all costs which can be traced to the department including supervision, depreciation, and all other fixed costs as well as variable costs. Variable costing is a more appropriate term because the concept makes a distinction between fixed and variable costs. Direct costing may also suggest that this is a concept that can be used only where there are cost accounting systems; however, variable costing can be very effectively used in small businesses where there are no such systems. Variable costing differs from prime costing in which only direct material and direct labor are inventoried. The prime cost method is based on a weak theoretical concept and is not acceptable for external reporting.

Absorption costing

Absorption costing, as discussed previously, distinguishes between production and nonproduction costs in determining which costs to capitalize as assets. Only production costs are inventoried, while marketing and administrative costs are usually expensed in the period incurred. The use of absorption costing provides that a part of both fixed and variable manufacturing cost is deferred in inventories until the product is sold. At that time, the cost is charged against revenue. With variable costs, in addition to making the same distinction among production, marketing, and administrative costs as does absorption costing, fixed and variable costs are distinguished.

Since both absorption and variable costing exclude marketing and administrative costs from inventory, these two methods differ only in this: variable costing excludes fixed production costs from the costs of goods manufactured, while absorption costing does not. This treatment of fixed factory overhead— whether it is charged off against income when the cost is incurred, or against income when the goods are sold—is the primary difference between variable and absorption costing.

Variable costing can be used either with a strictly actual cost system or in a standard cost system, discussed in previous chapters. With a standard costing system, scientific estimates of an efficient level of performance are established. By applying variable costing to standards, the company has an excellent tool for managerial decision making. If a variable costing system is combined with standard costs, estimates are established only for direct material, direct labor, and variable factory overhead, and no standard is set for fixed factory overhead.

Development of variable costing

Historically, variable costing is an outgrowth of management's increased need for quantitative data analyzing the effect on the company of cost-volume-profit relationships. Antecedents of variable costing may be traced to the development of the principle of overhead application around the turn of the 19th century. Because charging certain actual manufacturing expenses to production must be delayed until the end of the fiscal period, accountants developed the idea of estimating overhead in advance and creating a predetermined overhead rate. The overhead application concept takes into account not only that certain costs defy identification with certain output but, in addition, that some of these costs may have service potential extending beyond a single accounting period. Chapter 6 presents the various capacity concepts for applying factory overhead.

However, the creation of overhead pools, the methods of estimating volumes, and the final determination of overhead application rates are not without problems. As pointed out in Chapter 6, cost allocations are sometimes arbitrary. In addition, at the end of the fiscal period, the disposition of the over- or underabsorbed balance resulting from the differences between actual and applied expenses still presents a problem. Often, the variances are treated as period costs and are not allocated to inventories. This type of adjustment is generally most useful for annual statements rather than for shorter-period statements.

With automation on the increase in American industry, factory overhead has become an ever larger element in the cost of products. A large portion of this burden is fixed, not variable. The spread of guaranteed annual wage contracts also changes the portion of costs which are fixed to the company, since it causes more of the labor costs to be fixed. Such shifts in the cost characteristics of a company emphasize the importance of management understanding the impact of fixed cost: the company will have less flexibility in altering decisions, since more dollars will be invested in machinery and plant: and better information will be needed because management will have to deliberate more carefully over the expansion of labor force and production facilities.

Income distortion

With an increase in the portion of costs which are fixed, seasonal variations in production and sales tend to cause a distortion in income reported on the income statement. Since absorption costing assumes that existing facilities and management were set up to make and sell an average volume of goods over a period of years, it supplies a base for price determination and eliminates great fluctuations in inventory values, but income is still distorted. Exhibit 16–1 contains a simple example showing this. To simplify the illustration, no distinction is made between production, marketing, and administrative costs. Unit variable costs of $10 and total fixed costs of $50,000 are assumed each year, at a budgeted capacity of 10,000 units per year. With absorption costing, when production volume exceeds sales in the first year, fixed costs are built up in inventory and are not charged off until the inventory is sold. Thus, even though there is a lag in sales, absorption costing shows higher profits than does variable costing during this period of heavy production. The opposite is true during the reverse cycle, as can be seen for the second year in Exhibit 16–1. Absorption costing income is lower than variable costing income despite the large increase in sales.

EXHIBIT 16–1

	First year	Second year
Units produced	10,000	9,000
Units sold	6,000	13,000
Absorption costing:		
Sales @ $20	$120,000	$260,000
Less expenses:		
Variable expense @ $10	$ 60,000	$130,000
Fixed expenses @ $5*	30,000	65,000
Underapplied fixed expenses		5,000†
	$ 90,000	$200,000
Absorption costing income	$ 30,000	$ 60,000
Variable costing:		
Sales @ $20	$120,000	$260,000
Less variable expenses	60,000	130,000
Contribution margin	$ 60,000	$130,000
Less fixed expenses	50,000	50,000
Variable costing income	$ 10,000	$ 80,000

$*\dfrac{\$50,000}{10,000 \text{ units}} = \$5.$

†$5,000 underapplied (10,000 units − 9,000 units) × $5.

Even though sales volume has more than doubled from 6,000 units to 13,000 units, absorption costing income does not reflect this increase as dramatically as does variable costing. Since production was only 9,000 units in the second year, fixed expenses were underapplied by $5,000. Under the variable cost approach, fixed expenses are not applied to units of production; instead, the entire $50,000 fixed expense is charged off each year. Management could therefore be completely confused as income often seems to have no direct relationship to sales volume in absorption costing.

COMPARISON OF VARIABLE AND ABSORPTION COSTING

To assist management in evaluating the factors affecting income, short-period earning statements that do not consider the entire production and sales cycle are needed in addition to long-range statements that can employ the normal capacity concept. To satisfy this need, variable costing was introduced in the early 1950s as a new approach to overhead costing which could give management more understandable answers. Some regard this method as a consolidation of the desirable features of breakeven analysis, profit planning, and other developments involving the relationship between volume, costs and profits.

Exhibit 16–2 illustrates the absorption and variable costing concepts when standard costs are used. To simplify, no partially completed units are assumed to be in inventory. The top part of the income statement provides production and sales statistics. A $10 unit sales price is assumed. The following standards are assumed: direct material, $2; direct labor, $3; and variable factory overhead, $1. To simplify the illustration, no variances from standard costs are indicated. Actual and budgeted fixed factory overhead are assumed to be equal. Marketing and administrative expenses are treated as period costs in both the absorption and variable costing methods. However, the variable costing concept separates fixed and variable marketing and administrative expenses so that the contribution margin can be determined.

Volume variance

Factory overhead application rates are determined for both fixed and variable factory overhead in absorption costing. In Exhibit 16–2, the variable factory overhead rate is $1 and the fixed overhead rate is $2. However, in a variable costing approach, fixed costs are not inventoried; as a result, no application rate for fixed factory overhead is determined. With the absorption costing concept, a favorable or unfavorable volume variance will result when actual production differs from budgeted production used to compute the fixed overhead rate. The volume variance for the absorption costing method is shown at the bottom of Exhibit 16–2. For example, in the first year, 125,000 units were budgeted to be produced, but only 100,000 units were produced. This results in a $50,000 [(125,000 units − 100,000 units) × $2] underapplication of overhead. No volume variance is computed for the variable costing concept, since the total fixed factory overhead is closed directly to the temporary account, Revenue and Expense Summary. To simplify the illustration, Exhibit 16–2 indicates no variances between actual cost and standard cost. However, in a real-world situation, the spending and efficiency variances (if a three- or four-variance method is used) or a controllable variance (if a two-variance method is used) illustrated in Chapter 11 for a standard cost system would be determined with both the variable and absorption costing concepts. A fixed overhead spending variance (if using a four-variance method) would be computed only for absorption costing.

After studying Exhibit 16–2, which compares absorption and variable costing, one can make the following important observations:

1. In the statements of income prepared using absorption costing, no distinction is made between fixed and variable costs. As a result, cost-volume-profit relationships are not usually shown in absorption costing income statements as they are in statements of income prepared using variable costing.
2. Inventory values are smaller with variable costing because only the three variable costs totaling $6 (direct material, $2; direct labor, $3; and variable overhead, $1) are capitalized as assets. Inventory values using absorption costing have an additional $2 fixed factory overhead per unit.
3. Variable costing income in the first and second year is lower than that for absorption costing because production exceeds sales. With variable costing, the total fixed cost incurred is charged off against sales revenue in each

EXHIBIT 16–2

HICKS COMPANY
Income Statements on Absorption and Variable Costing Basis
For Years Indicated

	First year	Second year	Third year	Fourth year	Four years combined
Absorption costing:					
Finished goods inventory:					
Units in beginning inventory	—	10,000	20,000	10,000	—
Units produced	100,000	120,000	130,000	140,000	490,000
Units sold	90,000	110,000	140,000	145,000	485,000
Units in ending inventory	10,000	20,000	10,000	5,000	5,000
Sales @ $10	$900,000	$1,100,000	$1,400,000	$1,450,000	$4,850,000
Less: direct material @ $2	$200,000	$ 240,000	$ 260,000	$ 280,000	$ 980,000
Direct labor @ $3	300,000	360,000	390,000	420,000	1,470,000
Variable factory overhead @ $1	100,000	120,000	130,000	140,000	490,000
Fixed factory overhead @ $2	200,000	240,000	260,000	280,000	980,000
Cost of goods manufactured	$800,000	$ 960,000	$1,040,000	$1,120,000	$3,920,000
Add: beginning inventory @ $8	—	80,000	160,000	80,000	—
Available for sale	$800,000	$1,040,000	$1,200,000	$1,200,000	$3,920,000
Less: ending inventory @ $8	80,000	160,000	80,000	40,000	40,000
Cost of goods sold	$720,000	$ 880,000	$1,120,000	$1,160,000	$3,880,000
Volume variance*	50,000	10,000	(10,000)	(30,000)	20,000
Adjusted cost of goods sold	$770,000	$ 890,000	$1,110,000	$1,130,000	$3,900,000
Gross margin	$130,000	$ 210,000	$ 290,000	$ 320,000	$ 950,000
Marketing and administrative expense	80,000	89,000	100,000	98,000	367,000
Absorption costing income before taxes	$ 50,000	$ 121,000	$ 190,000	$ 222,000	$ 583,000
Variable costing:					
Sales @ $10	$900,000	$1,100,000	$1,400,000	$1,450,000	$4,850,000
Less: direct material @ $2	$200,000	$ 240,000	$ 260,000	$ 280,000	$ 980,000
Direct labor @ $3	300,000	360,000	390,000	420,000	1,470,000
Variable factory overhead @ $1	100,000	120,000	130,000	140,000	490,000
Total variable manufacturing cost	$600,000	$ 720,000	$ 780,000	$ 840,000	$2,940,000
Add: beginning inventory @ $6	—	60,000	120,000	60,000	–0–
Available for sale	$600,000	$ 780,000	$ 900,000	$ 900,000	$2,940,000
Less: Ending inventory @ $6	60,000	120,000	60,000	30,000	30,000
Costs of goods sold	$540,000	$ 660,000	$ 840,000	$ 870,000	$2,910,000
Manufacturing contribution margin	$360,000	$ 440,000	$ 560,000	$ 580,000	$1,940,000
Less: Variable marketing and administrative expense	30,000	39,000	50,000	48,000	167,000
Net contribution margin	$330,000	$ 401,000	$ 510,000	$ 532,000	$1,773,000
Less: Fixed factory overhead	250,000	250,000	250,000	250,000	1,000,000
Fixed marketing and administrative expense	50,000	50,000	50,000	50,000	200,000
Variable costing income before taxes	$ 30,000	$ 101,000	$ 210,000	$ 232,000	$ 573,000

*Volume variance based on normal capacity of 125,000 units $\frac{\$250,000 \text{ fixed overhead}}{125,000 \text{ units}} = \$2.$

First year . . . . $50,000 underapplied (125,000 − 100,000) × $2
Second year. . . . . . . 10,000 underapplied (125,000 − 120,000) × $2
Third year . . . . 10,000 overapplied (125,000 − 130,000) × $2
Fourth year . . . . 30,000 overapplied (125,000 − 140,000) × $2
Four years total . . . . $20,000 underapplied (500,000 − 490,000) × $2

of these years, while in absorption costing, part of it is applied to inventory and deferred until the product is sold. If there is an increase in inventories, variable costing income will be less than absorption costing income, as seen in the first two years.

4. In the third and fourth year, variable costing income is higher than absorption costing income because the units sold exceed the units produced. Variable costing income always moves in the same direction as sales volume. The cost of goods sold using variable costing includes only a $6 per unit variable cost, while the unit cost of goods sold is $8 with absorption costing.

5. Conventional absorption costing determines an intermediate income figure called *gross margin*, which reflects the difference between sales and the fixed and variable costs of sales. This figure normally varies significantly from the *manufacturing contribution margin* determined with variable costing, because only the variable expenses of the goods sold are subtracted from sales revenue in determining manufacturing contribution margin. *Net contribution margin* is determined by subtracting all production, marketing, and administrative variable expenses from sales.

6. The income for the four years combined using the two concepts differs by $10,000 ($583,000 absorption costing income − $573,000 variable costing income). This $10,000 difference in income results from the 5,000 units remaining in ending inventory which have $2 fixed overhead assigned to each under absorption costing. However, over the complete cycle of inventory buildup and liquidation, total income would be identical. It should be noted that the costs available for use cannot be added horizontally in Exhibit 16–2 because of the inclusion of inventory values more than once.

7. As discussed in Chapters 6 and 11, the volume variance computed for absorption costing should be prorated if it is a significant amount. However, to simplify the illustration, the volume variance is treated as a period cost in Exhibit 16–2.

Adjustment to include fixed costs

Since variable costing cannot be used for external reporting, an adjustment to an absorption costing basis must be made. This adjustment for periods in which the application rate remains unchanged is shown in Exhibit 16–3 and is determined by multiplying the change in the quantity of all inventory by the $2 fixed factory cost per unit. For example, in the first year, there was an increase of 10,000 units in finished goods inventory (from a zero beginning inventory to 10,000 units). This change of 10,000 units is multiplied by the $2 fixed factory overhead rate to arrive at an adjustment of $20,000. This adjustment is added to the variable costing income from Exhibit 16–2 to determine the income calculated under absorption costing. In the fourth year, there is a 5,000-unit decrease in inventory. This decrease is multiplied by a $2 fixed factory overhead cost per unit to arrive at the $10,000 adjustment, which is then

EXHIBIT 16–3

Adjustment of variable costing income to absorption costing basis

	First year	Second year	Third year	Fourth year	Four years combined
Variable costing income per Exhibit 16–2	$30,000	$101,000	$210,000	$232,000	$573,000
Variation for fixed cost influence of inventory (Units produced − Units sold) × Fixed factory overhead per unit at normal capacity.	20,000	20,000	(20,000)	(10,000)	10,000
Absorption costing income per Exhibit 16–2	$50,000	$121,000	$190,000	$222,000	$583,000

deducted from the variable costing income in calculating absorption costing income. In a period like the fourth year, in which the units sold exceed the units produced, the fixed factory overhead adjustment for the change in inventory must be deducted from variable costing income to determine absorption costing income.

Admittedly, Exhibit 16–3 represents an oversimplification of the reconciliation of absorption and variable costing, as it was assumed that the $2 fixed overhead application rate did not change over the four-year period. If beginning and ending inventories carry different fixed overhead rates, the reconciliation of absorption costing and variable costing income becomes more complex. Assuming first-in, first-out inventory costing, Exhibit 16–4 uses the data given in Exhibit 16–2 for the first two years, but the fixed overhead application rate increases to $2.20. This increase causes a decrease in absorption costing income to $100,000 and in variable costing income to $76,000 for the second year. Rather than use the formula multiplying the change in inventory by the fixed overhead application rate, the following analysis should be used. This analysis is appropriate for periods in which a rate change occurs as well as for periods in which the rate remains unchanged:

	First year	Second year
Variable costing income before taxes	$30,000	$ 76,000
Add: Fixed costs of period deferred in ending inventory.	20,000 ($80,000 − $60,000)	44,000 ($164,000 − $120,000)
	$50,000	$120,000
Less: Fixed costs of prior year absorbed in period through beginning inventory	–0–	20,000 ($80,000 − $60,000)
Absorption costing income before taxes	$50,000	$100,000

EXHIBIT 16–4

HICKS COMPANY
Income Statements on Absorption and Variable Costing Basis
With Change in Application Rate
For Years Indicated

	First year		Second year
Absorption costing:			
Finished goods inventory:			
Units in beginning inventory	—		10,000
Units produced	100,000		120,000
Units sold	90,000		110,000
Units in ending inventory	10,000		20,000
Sales @ $10	$900,000		$1,100,000
Less: direct material @ $2	$200,000		$ 240,000
Direct labor @ $3	300,000		360,000
Variable factory overhead @ $1	100,000		120,000
Fixed factory overhead @ $2	200,000	@ $2.20	264,000
Cost of goods manufactured	$800,000		$ 984,000
Add: Beginning inventory @ $8			80,000
Available for sale	$800,000		$1,064,000
Less: Ending inventory @ $8	80,000	@ $8.20	164,000
Cost of goods sold	$720,000		$ 900,000
Volume variance*	50,000		11,000
Adjusted cost of goods sold	$770,000		$ 911,000
Gross margin	$130,000		$ 189,000
Marketing and administrative expense	80,000		89,000
Absorption costing income before taxes	$ 50,000		$ 100,000
Variable costing:			
Sales @ $10	$900,000		$1,100,000
Less: direct material @ $2	$200,000		$ 240,000
Direct labor @ $3	300,000		360,000
Variable factory overhead @ $1	100,000		120,000
Total variable manufacturing cost	$600,000		$ 720,000
Add: Beginning inventory @ $6	—		60,000
Available for sale	$600,000		$ 780,000
Less: Ending inventory @ $6	60,000		120,000
Costs of goods sold	$540,000		$ 660,000
Gross contribution margin	$360,000		$ 440,000
Less: Variable marketing and administrative expense	30,000		39,000
Contribution margin	$330,000		$ 401,000
Less: Fixed factory overhead	250,000		275,000
Fixed marketing and administrative expense	50,000		50,000
Variable costing income before taxes	$ 30,000		$ 76,000

*Volume variance based on normal capacity of 125,000 units.

First year   Second year

$\dfrac{\$250,000 \text{ fixed overhead}}{125,000 \text{ units}} = \$2.00$ $\dfrac{\$275,000}{125,000} = \$2.20$

First year .... $50,000 underapplied (125,000 − 100,000) × $2.00
Second year .... 11,000 underapplied (125,000 − 120,000) × $2.20

ADVANTAGES OF VARIABLE COSTING

After the inadequacies of absorption costing are noted, the advantages of variable costing can be more easily understood. The greatest of these is that management can easily comprehend variable costing data. Accountants must provide information that is accurate, complete, and timely; but the information must also be understood. If management finds company reports are too complex, the result is that management has no faith in the figures and will not realize their importance. Variable costing overcomes this problem.

Variable costing particularly improves the collecting and presenting of information on the relationship between cost, pricing, profits, volume, and product mix. Managers can better understand financial reports prepared using variable costing because they show that profits move in the same direction as sales; this effect is more logical than that shown with absorption costing, where profit is affected by changes in inventory. Variable costing also eliminates the confusion often associated with the movement of profits in absorption costing statements of income; absorption costing takes into consideration both sales volume and production volume, while variable costing involves primarily only sales volume. For example, if sales volume exceeds production volume, variable costing will show a larger profit than will absorption costing, since fixed costs associated with the lower production volume are charged off as period costs, while the cost of goods sold associated with the higher sales volume does not include any fixed costs. Conversely, when production volume exceeds sales volume, a higher profit is shown with absorption costing because a portion of fixed costs are assigned to inventory and deferred. Profits determined with variable costing are not affected by changes in inventory as they are in absorption costing. If sales and production volume are equal, there is no difference in profits shown with absorption and variable costing. However, if sales volume is constant but production volume varies between periods, a difference in profits will be reported using the two concepts. Under these conditions, variable costing will show a constant profit while the absorption costing profit will fluctuate because of the change in inventory.

Cost-volume-profit relationships

Another advantage of variable costing is that it facilitates the analysis of cost-volume-profit relationships by separating fixed and variable costs on the statement of income. Management is therefore able to identify the cost-volume-profit ratio without working with two and sometimes several sets of data. In addition, variable costing emphasizes contribution margin, discussed in Chapter 15. This emphasis aids management in selecting product lines, in determining the optimal sales mix for pricing purposes, and in solving other problems involving choices. The data are especially important to companies that face make-or-buy decisions, since variable costing facilitates comparing company costs with the costs of buying from outsiders. The cost-volume-profit relationship also provides a valuable tool for other short-run planning activities; many of these are discussed in later chapters.

Marginal products

Variable costing is also of considerable use in the appraisal of *marginal products* or *marginal volume*, because variable cost, in effect, corresponds closely with current out-of-pocket expenditure for a product. The problem of product line simplification is not always easy; yet an important aspect of the appraisal is apparent using variable costing, which provides a sharper focus on the profitability of products, customers, and territories. The relative importance of a product's contribution can be disclosed by multiplying the volume of the item by the contribution margin per unit. Management can then study the contribution the product has made to fixed overhead and more easily identify the unprofitable items that should be eliminated. This is true because the data are not obscured by the allocation of fixed costs.

Because variable costing data can be presented in an uncomplicated manner, managers without strong accounting backgrounds can understand and use the information for profit planning. Often, the application of fixed overhead may be difficult for a nonaccountant to understand because budgeted costs and budgeted capacity must be estimated. The nonaccountant can better grasp the relationship of variable costs and profit planning. Costs and profit forecasting is easier if fixed factory overhead applications are not included.

Impact of fixed costs

Some managers argue that decisions can be more easily made if fixed expenses are separated and not buried in inventory or cost of sales. Since the total fixed expense for the period appears in the variable costing income statement, the impact of fixed expenses on profits is emphasized. Variable costing proponents contend that fixed costs represent *committed costs* arising from a basic organization of providing property, plant, equipment and other facilities to produce. They feel this justifies treating fixed costs as period costs because, they argue, product costs should reflect only those costs which will expire when the asset is sold. Thus, because most fixed costs are committed and cannot be avoided, those advocating variable costing feel that such costs should not be part of inventory.

Since variable costing advocates believe that variable costs are the crucial costs for decision making, they claim that one of the important purposes of variable costing is in helping management control operating costs. They contend that separating fixed and variable costs automatically focuses a manager's attention on cost reduction. Advocates of variable costing also believe that the concept is an accurate means for measuring responsibility for departmental supervisors. With a system of variable costing, responsibility accounting is easier than it is with conventional absorption costing because, since fixed costs are not allocated to products, tracing costs by lines of managerial responsibility is simplified.

This fixed-variable manufacturing cost breakdown aids in the preparation of budgets, too, as variable costing provides a simple budget based on estimated average monthly sales, at the beginning of the year. Each account is broken down into variable and fixed cost, and in any month the expected costs can be figured merely by multiplying the unit variable cost by actual sales and adding the fixed costs. Monthly comparison of budgeted costs and actual costs can then be made easily without adding to clerical expense, and the results are more meaningful, since a comparison between actual and budgeted costs can be made, even though the budget was prepared based on sales different from actual sales.

Pricing policies

Furthermore, variable costing advocates feel more relevant information concerning pricing policies is provided with variable costing than with absorption costing. Often, it is assumed that no product should be kept in a company's product line for any substantial length of time unless its price is higher than average full cost. However, even in the long run, it cannot be assumed that competitive conditions will remain the same for all products, since market conditions vary. Pricing to cover average full costs thus may not be advantageous for a company in specialized situations. In any pricing decision, the effect of prices on volume and the effects of volume on cost must be considered. With variable costing, management has the data to determine when it is advisable to accept orders if other than normal conditions exist. In this way, management can take advantage of sales which may contribute only partly to fixed expenses. A knowledge of contribution margin provides guidelines for the most profitable pricing policies. (This aspect of contribution margin will be discussed in Chapter 22.) However, opponents of variable costing argue that sales price is determined by more than reference to contribution margin.

Finally, variable costing highlights the serious results that often accompany price cutting. A common error is to cut prices by a certain percentage and try to increase volume by the same percentage under the assumption that the volume increase will compensate for the price reduction. To gain volume from a competitor, however, one should understand just how far a cut in price can go before it becomes unprofitable. After management understands how price cutting to gain volume seriously affects profits, they should be more cautious about cutting prices just for the purpose of underselling a competitor, since they may be cutting themselves out of business.

DANGERS OF VARIABLE COSTING

The simplicity of variable costing allows management to easily understand the resulting figures. However, the principle of variable costing may be misapplied. Many accountants contend that variable costing does not provide all the answers or necessarily the best answers in certain business situations.

Accounting figures are used by persons outside and inside the company, many of them not accountants. These people have become accustomed to the normal relationship of sales to total costs and to using gross margin and net income data. A change to another accounting method that will give a completely different picture under similar labels may confuse them. Although the purpose of the change in costing methods is to bring about better understanding, it may cause more confusion instead. More harm than good may result, even though better information may be available under variable costing.

Another danger is that variable costing income may be assigned a broader significance than it deserves. When sales substantially exceed current production, for instance, variable costing profits are higher than those under absorption costing, and management may take improper action based on these "increased" profits: marketing executives might be misled and ask for lower prices, or managers may demand higher employee benefits or sales bonuses when, in fact, there may be no justification for such actions. At the other extreme, variable costing results may mislead management during a business recession because, when sales lag behind production during the early recession stages, the variable costing profit will be minimized and the variable costing loss maximized. Management may miss future profit opportunities by thus misreading the severity of the recession.

Income figures determined using variable costing techniques may need to be adjusted when management decides to expand or contract activities connected with specific product lines or other specific business units. For example, most businesses which produce or sell several products that differ in ratios of variable costs to sales revenue and contribution rates can improve the total profit picture by eliminating the products contributing the smallest amount and by continuing to carry the products making large contributions to profits. On the other hand, this approach, too, can be misleading. If the items contributing small amounts of profits are dropped, the fixed unit cost that must be covered by other products will increase. As a result, profits will likely decrease if no other products are added to the company's line. Intangible factors must also be considered because a product with a low contribution margin ratio may be necessary for the convenience of customers. The loss in customer goodwill which might result from dropping this item could easily offset any gain from products with higher contribution margin ratios.

Long-range pricing policies

Since variable costing income is higher than absorption costing income when sales substantially exceed current production, opponents of variable costing also argue that if managers are given only variable costs, they will be tempted to cut prices to the degree that company profits will suffer. However, if the pricing system is adequate, this will be avoided because, for long-range policy decisions, especially those involving pricing, fixed overhead must be allocated on some volume base. Admittedly, allocations are somewhat arbitrary; however, cost allocation techniques are being improved as more companies have a better understanding of the nature of their business as well as access to computer facilities. Despite the many other advantages of the method for internal purposes, variable costing generates product figures providing little basis for long-range pricing policies.

Opponents of variable costing argue, in addition, that all costs are variable in the long run, and too great an emphasis on the arbitrary classification of costs into variable and fixed categories should be avoided. Strictly separating costs into two categories is impossible, as many costs have both fixed and variable components. It is not enough merely to define fixed and variable costs according to the rate of output, for whether a cost is fixed or variable usually depends on the terms in which output is measured, the time period allowed for adjustments, the degree of flexibility, and the extent to which certain costs are calculated in advance. Even strict fixed costs have some variable characteristics. Since the behavior of certain costs, especially overhead, is exceedingly complex, occasionally, the separation will be decided on the basis of practicality or expediency rather than on the basis of strict adherence to an established accounting principle. There may be strong temptation to include as product costs only those costs which are obviously variable, such as direct material and direct labor. In extreme cases, the *prime cost method* is used with which variable overhead is eliminated from product cost, thus producing misleading profit contribution data. Variable costing advocates, however, argue that while this separation of fixed and variable costs sometimes is arbitrary, the accountant can usually arrive at figures which are accurate enough. They feel that cost behavior is usually not so erratic that it cannot be predicted if proper controls are applied.

Another weakness of variable costing is that since fixed expenses are considered period costs, over- or underapplied factory overhead is minimized, and the volume variance can only be expressed in physical, not monetary, terms. This may appear to be an improvement to some accountants; however, in some situations, the measure may be more appropriately expressed in monetary terms.

Fixed costs must be covered.   Elimination of fixed overhead costs from inventories should not be overlooked because there has been an increasing trend toward automation in manufacturing which results in more overhead and less direct labor cost. It is possible to foresee a time when direct material would constitute the only variable item of manufacturing cost. Thus, the company with the largest fixed expenses would have the smallest unit inventory costs. This appears contrary to the fact that management must meet the objective of having expenses covered by sales—regardless of how inventory is valued. This looms as a serious threat to the usefulness of variable costing and is far from the accepted theories of inventory valuation. It is one reason that the FASB and the Internal Revenue Service have not recognized variable costing as an acceptable method of inventory costing.

OPINIONS ON VARIABLE COSTING

FASB position. Thus, while most accountants agree that variable costing provides valid information for internal decision making, there is no agreement concerning its appropriateness for external reporting. Variable costing has not been recognized as a generally accepted inventory valuation method by the FASB because it is felt that fixed production costs are as much a part of manufacturing the product as are variable costs.

IRS regulations. Likewise, the IRS does not recognize this as an acceptable inventory valuation method; a 1973 Amendment to Section 471 of the IRS Code expressly prohibits using the variable costing and the prime cost method, in which only direct material and direct labor are inventoried. Full absorption costing is required of all taxpayers engaged in production operations. The regulations establish the three following categories for use in deciding whether indirect production costs must be included in inventory:

Category (1) costs include repair expenses, maintenance, utilities, rent, indirect labor and materials, and so forth, to the extent that these costs are incident to and necessary for production or manufacturing. Costs in Category 1 always must be included in inventory.

Category (2) costs are marketing expenses; selling expenses; interest, research, and experimental expenses; losses; tax depreciation in excess of the amount used for financial reports; pension contributions representing past services cost; and the like. Category 2 costs need not be included in inventory.

Finally, Category (3) costs include taxes (other than income taxes), book depreciation, cost depletion, employee benefits, factory administrative expenses, and so forth. These costs can be included or not in accordance with the taxpayer's financial reporting treatment and generally accepted accounting principles.

SEC and variable costing. The Securities and Exchange Commission (SEC) also does not accept annual financial statements employing the variable costing method. Like the FASB, the SEC does not consider variable costing a generally accepted accounting procedure. The SEC's policy on consistency in reporting by companies is another reason for its stand against variable costing.

Variable costing evaluated

While reporting for external purposes is expected to conform to generally accepted accounting principles, financial data prepared for internal uses need not. Even though variable costing has not been accepted for external reporting purposes, the validity of variable costing for external reporting does not affect its importance and special usefulness as a tool of analysis for management. It must be conceded that the first objective of costing should be to meet internal requirements; management information must come first. Variable costing can contribute to this objective because it overcomes many of the weaknesses in reporting with conventional absorption cost accounting systems. Many companies have converted to variable costing to obtain certain advantages and have found many others not initially thought of. Certainly, the cost accounting staff can perform contribution margin and breakeven point analyses for each of the company's segments without preparing variable costing statements. However, other individuals in the company should be encouraged to use variable costing data.

In the past, much of the discussion concerning variable costing has centered around the importance of arriving at a variable costing income as opposed to the retention of absorption costing income. The pros and cons of both systems have been discussed at great length; however, variable costing and absorption costing do not have to be mutually exclusive. Very little attention has been given to the idea that variable costing is not intended to replace absorption costing. A well-informed management needs both contribution margin analysis and full cost data in budgeting and decision making. The accountant can take advantage of the variable costing concept to develop a clearer picture of these cost relationships.

Combined approach.   This chapter suggests that the income statement be arranged to show both an income under variable costing and the conventional net income. To do this, an increment measuring the effect of the change in the fixed cost components of inventory variation can be deducted from variable costing income so that the conventional concept of profits would not be changed. Income resulting only from sales can be distinguished from that resulting from inventory changes. One advantage of this approach is that in the income statement, costs which are variable are separated from costs which are fixed.

Having both sets of profit figures enables the executive to form judgments with much greater facility than would be the case if only one profit figure were available, and it also facilitates responsibility accounting by making it possible to have information by organizational level. This dual approach provides the additional information that management needs for making decisions and still complies with accepted accounting principles. The system combining variable costing and absorption costing with standard costs and variable (flexible) budgets provides for more effective cost control, since each tool can be used where it best serves.

SUMMARY

The advantages as well as the disadvantages of variable costing were presented in the chapter because it is difficult to state with full assurance which costing concept presents the best measure of unit cost. Thus, a combined approach is recommended. Since variable costing cannot be used for external reporting, inventories must be adjusted to include fixed costs on all external reports. However, this adjustment can be accomplished relatively easily. A variable costing income statement can be prepared in which variable costs are first subtracted from sales to give a net contribution to fixed costs and income, and then fixed costs are subtracted to give income before taxes.

Rather than reject variable costing because the concept cannot be used for external reporting, accountants should be aware of the advantages it offers to managers. For a business to reach its full potential in a mature business economy, management must have all the information necessary for the various decisions it must make. Managers therefore should not hesitate to use variable costing data for internal purposes if they find the information more useful than that determined with the absorption costing approach. For example, in evaluating the effectiveness of individual and departmental performance, the accountant needs to use variable costing as a tool. Solutions to such problems as how to determine the effect on overall profits of a new product would be impossible if absorption costing is used. In preparing cost control reports, there is little need to include such cost items as insurance and depreciation, over which the individuals to whom the report is addressed have no control; a departmental income statement prepared on the variable costing basis would be more useful here.

There is a danger, however, in adopting variable costing strictly to the exclusion of absorption costing. The mere fact that absorption costing is accepted for external reporting makes it a valuable tool. In the long run, all costs, both fixed and variable, must be covered if a company is to realize a profit. There is a danger in overlooking fixed costs, especially in price setting. Variable costing could endanger the company if only a profit allowance is added to a product's variable cost to determine the sales price. While variable costing may be superior to absorption costing in giving the short-range view of profits, the case is not so clear in long-range profit planning because period costs usually are committed for relatively long periods and are important in long-term, not day-to-day, decisions. As will be discussed in Chapter 22, average full cost is a better measure of the resources required for other than short-run decisions. It is felt that for long-range profit planning, fixed costs should be allocated to product groups.

This chapter does not claim that variable costing is a "cure-all" meeting all the needs of management. As long as management must operate in a world of uncertainty, there is little hope that any pure accounting principle can do much more than make a partial contribution to decision making. Yet, when variable costing is used with an awareness of its limitations and weaknesses, it can be one of the most useful tools of an accountant in aiding management.

IMPORTANT TERMS AND CONCEPTS

Absorption (conventional) costing

Variable (direct) costing

Product costs

Period costs

Volume variance

Gross margin

Manufacturing contribution margin

Net contribution margin

Marginal products or marginal volume

Committed costs

REVIEW QUESTIONS

1. What distinction in cost behavior is made with variable costing and how does this differ from the distinction made with absorption costing? What is the primary difference between variable costing and absorption costing?

2. Contrast and explain the difference in income using absorption and variable costing if:
   a. Production volume exceeds sales volume.
   b. Sales volume exceeds production volume.
   c. Sales volume equals production volume.
   d. Sales volume remains constant, while production volume fluctuates.

3. How is the difference between net income computed using absorption costing and using variable costing calculated?

4. Compare the difference between the absorption and variable costing incomes as the accounting periods get longer.

5. Indicate several questions or decisions for which the use of variable costing would be more appropriate than the use of absorption costing.

6. Discuss the positions taken by the FASB, IRS, and SEC in regard to variable costing. Do these positions destroy the validity of variable costing as a managerial tool?

7. What factor related to manufacturing costs causes the difference in net earnings computed using absorption costing and using variable costing?

8. What is the unit cost of a product if, during the month, the company produced 1,000 units having costs as follows: direct materials—$32,000; direct labor—$45,000; variable overhead—$62,000; and fixed overhead—$70,000?

9.   Why are inventory valuations smaller with variable costing than with absorption costing?

10.   Can variable costing be used in a strictly actual cost system as well as in a standard cost system? How can it be implemented?

11.   Discuss the development of variable costing and why there was a need for this concept.

12.   Why have many manufacturing companies experienced an increase in fixed costs in recent years?

13.   Should sales volume and/or production volume affect income?

14.   Why is the unit cost assigned to inventory using variable costing generally considered to be uniform?

15.   Why do variable costing advocates feel that it is a better index of profit performance?

16.   Why may a statement of income prepared using absorption costing continue to show a profit even if sales decline?

17.   Assuming you were using a four-variance method of analyzing overhead, what variances would you compute with a standard variable costing approach? How do these differ from those variances computed with a standard absorption costing approach?

EXERCISES

E16–1   Absorption costing and variable costing income

The following information is available for the Lipsey Company's first year of operations in which 35,000 units were produced:

Sales ($50 per unit)	$1,600,000
Total fixed production cost	700,000
Total variable production cost	595,000
Total variable marketing and administrative costs . . .	140,000
Total fixed marketing and administrative costs	130,000

Required:

Without preparing a formal income statement, determine income using:

a.   Variable costing.

b.   Absorption costing.

E16–2.   Standard absorption costing recast to variable costing

James Thompson Company uses a standard absorption costing system. The Engineering Department has determined that the standard variable production cost is $16 per unit, while standard fixed factory overhead is $4 ($200,000 ÷ 50,000 units of normal activity). Variable marketing and administrative costs are $2 per unit sold, while fixed marketing and administrative costs are $80,000. Variances from standard variable production costs during the year totaled $50,000 unfavorable. Sales during 19X1 were 45,000 units. Beginning inventory was 1,000 units; ending inventory was 6,000 units. Sales price per unit is $32.

Required:

a.   Prepare an absorption costing income statement for 19X1 assuming all variances are written off directly as an adjustment to the Cost of Goods Sold account at year-end.
b.   Recast the income statement as it would appear using variable costing.
c.   Explain the difference in income as calculated in *a* and *b*.

E16–3.   Adjustment to convert from variable costing to absorption costing.

Budgeted fixed factory overhead for the Carrell Company at normal capacity of 600,000 units is $3 million. The company uses variable costing for internal purposes and adjusts the income to an absorption costing basis at year-end. Analysis over the last three years shows the following:

	1st year	2d year	3d year
Units produced	602,000	598,000	595,000
Units sold	596,000	603,000	595,000
Variable costing income	$500,000	$521,000	$497,000

Required:

Determine the adjustment necessary each year to convert the variable costing income to an absorption costing basis. Indicate the absorption costing income for each year.

E16–4.   Adjustment to convert from variable costing to absorption costing with a rate change

The Cotton Company uses variable costing for internal purposes and adjusts the income to an absorption costing basis at year-end. FIFO inventory costing is used. Analysis over the first three years of operation shows the following:

	1st year	2d year	3d year
Units produced	800,000	850,000	870,000
Units sold	780,000	860,000	875,000
Variable costing income . . . . $	60,000	$ 70,000	$ 78,000
Budgeted capacity (units)	850,000	870,000	880,000
Budgeted fixed overhead	$1,700,000	$1,957,500	$2,112,000

Required:

Determine the adjustment necessary each year to convert the variable costing income to an absorption costing basis. Indicate the absorption costing income for each year.

E16–5.   Theory of variable costing (AICPA adapted)

Although variable (direct) costing is not currently a generally accepted method of costing inventory for external reporting, it is useful for internal purposes.

Required:

a.   Describe the difference between variable costing and the current generally accepted method of costing inventory for external reporting.
b.   Describe how a variable costing structure facilitates calculation of the contribution margin and the breakeven point.

E16–6.   Comparison of absorption and variable costing

The following information is available for Thomas Doran Company's new product line:

Variable production cost per unit	$ 24
Total annual fixed production cost (60,000 units budgeted capacity)	120,000
Total annual fixed marketing and administrative costs	72,000
Variable marketing and administrative cost per unit of sales.	12
Selling price per unit	60

There was no inventory at the beginning of the year. During the year, 60,000 units were produced and 54,000 units were sold.

Required:

a. Determine the cost of ending inventory assuming Doran uses absorption costing.
b. Determine the cost of ending inventory assuming Doran uses variable costing.
c. Determine the total variable costs charged to expense for the year assuming Doran uses variable costing.
d. Determine the total fixed costs charged against the current year's operations assuming Doran uses absorption costing.
e. Without preparing a formal income statement, determine income using variable costing.
f. Without preparing a formal income statement, determine income using absorption costing.
g. Account for the difference in income derived using the two concepts.

PROBLEMS

P16–1.   Use of high-low method of separating cost components and comparative statements.

Truel Hicks Company provides you with the following two condensed budgets for standard costs and expenses:

	14,000 units	16,000 units
Direct material	$ 32,200	$ 36,800
Direct labor	117,600	134,400
Factory overhead	82,100	87,400
Total	$231,900	$258,600

Marketing and administrative expense were budgeted as follows:

Marketing expense:		
Variable	$1.50 per unit sold	
Fixed		$25,000
Administrative expense:		
Variable	$2.40 per unit sold	
Fixed		$42,000

Overhead will be applied on the basis of a standard capacity of 15,000 units.

Required:

a. Using the high-low method of separating cost components, determine the standard cost per unit under absorption costing.

b. Assume that 14,500 units are manufactured and 13,800 are sold at a price of $38. Determine the income using:
   (1) Absorption costing.
   (2) Variable costing.

c. Account for the difference in absorption costing income and variable costing income.

P16–2.   Reconciling the difference between absorption costing and variable costing income

The June 1, 19X1, balance sheet for Clarence Dunn Company contained an inventory amounting to $280,000, which included fixed overhead costs of $40,000. The June 30, 19X1, balance sheet revealed an inventory amounting to $120,000, which included fixed overhead amounting to $18,000.

Operations for the month of June 19X1 resulted in the following:

Variable costs:

Direct materials used in production	$520,000
Direct labor used in production	318,000
Factory overhead	200,000
Marketing expenses.	35,000
Administrative expenses	90,000

Fixed costs:

Factory overhead	$ 15,570
Marketing expenses.	80,000
Administrative expenses	100,000

Net sales for June 19X1, were $1,600,000.

Required:

a. Prepare an income statement for the month using variable costing.

b. Prepare an income statement for the month using absorption costing.

c. Reconcile the difference in the income figures reported using each of these costing methods.

P16–3.   Comparison of variable and absorption costing (CMA adapted)

CLK Company is a manufacturer of electrical components. The company maintains a significant inventory of a broad range of finished goods because it has built its business upon prompt shipment of any stock item.

The company manufactured all items it sold until recently when it discontinued the manufacturing of five items. The items were dropped from the manufacturing process because the unit costs computed using the company's full cost system did not provide a sufficient margin to cover shipping and selling costs. The five items are now purchased from other manufacturers at a price which allows CLK to make a very small profit after shipping and selling costs. CLK keeps these items in its product line to offer a complete line of electrical components.

The president is disappointed at recent profitability performance. He thought that the switch from manufacture to purchase of the five items would improve profit performance. However, the reverse has occurred. All other factors affecting profits—

sales volume, sales prices, and incurred selling and manufacturing costs—were as expected so the profit problem can be traced to this decision. The president has asked the controller's department to reevaluate the financial effects of the decision.

The task was assigned to a recently hired assistant controller. She has reviewed the data used to reach the decision to purchase rather than manufacture. Her conclusion is that the company should have continued to manufacture the item. In her opinion the incorrect decision was made because full (absorption) cost data rather than direct (variable cost) data were used to make the decision.

Required:

a. Explain what features of direct (variable) costing as compared to full (absorption) costing make it possible for her conclusion to be correct.

b. For internal measurement purposes, compare the income, return on investment, and inventory values under full (absorption) costing and direct (variable) costing for periods in which:
   (1) Inventory quantities are rising.
   (2) Inventory quantities are declining.
   (3) Inventory quantities are stable.

c. What advantages are said to accrue to decision making if direct (variable) costing is used?

P16–4. Contribution margin under various assumptions (AICPA adapted)

Part 1. The Wing Manufacturing Corporation produces a chemical compound, Product X, which deteriorates and must be discarded if it is not sold by the end of the month during which it is produced. The total variable cost of the manufactured compound, Product X, is $50 per unit and its selling price is $80 per unit. Wing can purchase the same compound from a competing company at $80 per unit plus $10 freight per unit. Management has estimated that failure to fill orders would result in the loss of 80 percent of the customers placing orders for the compound. Wing has manufactured and sold Product X for the past 20 months. Demand for Product X has been irregular and, at present, the sales trend is not consistent. During this period, monthly sales have been as follows:

Units sold per month	Number of months
8,000.	5
9,000.	12
10,000.	3

Required:

a. Compute the probability of sales of Product X of 8,000, 9,000, or 10,000 units in any month.

b. Compute the contribution margin if 9,000 units of Product X were ordered and either 8,000, 9,000, or 10,000 units were manufactured in that same month (with additional units, if necessary, being purchased).

c. Compute the average monthly contribution margin that Wing can expect if 9,000 units of Product X are manufactured every month and all sales orders are filled.

Part 2. In the production of Product X, Wing uses a primary ingredient, K-1. This ingredient is purchased from an outside supplier at a cost of $24 per unit of compound. It is estimated that there is a 70 percent chance that the supplier of K-1 may be shut down by a strike for an indefinite period. A substitute ingredient, K-2, is available at $36 per unit of compound, but Wing must contact this alternative source immediately to secure sufficient quantities. A firm purchase contract for either material must now be made for production of the primary ingredient next month. If an order were placed for K-1 and a strike occurred, Wing would be released from the contract and management would purchase the chemical compound from the competitor. Assume that 9,000 units are to be manufactured and all sales orders are to be filled.

d.   Compute the monthly contribution margin from sales of 8,000, 9,000, and 10,000 units if the substitute ingredient, K-2, is ordered.

e.   Prepare a schedule computing the average monthly contribution margin that Wing should expect if the primary ingredient, K-1, is ordered with the existing probability of a strike against the supplier. Assume that the expected average monthly contribution margin from manufacturing will be $130,000 using the primary ingredient, and the expected average monthly loss due to purchasing product X from the competitor (in case of a strike) will be $45,000.

P16–5.   Absorption costing and variable costing income statements

The President of Britten Enterprises projects the following data for the month of November 19X1:

	Units
Beginning inventory.	6,000
Production	20,000
Available for sale.	26,000
Sales	23,000
Ending inventory	3,000

Management has established the following standard cost per unit for the one product the company manufactures:

	Standard cost per unit
Direct material (all variable)	$20.00
Direct labor (all variable).	15.00
Factory Overhead:	
Variable cost.	3.00
Fixed costs (based on 22,000 units per month)	2.00
Marketing and administrative:	
Variable cost (per unit sold).	1.80
Fixed costs (based on 22,000 units per month)	1.20

The sales price per unit is projected to be $50 per unit. The fixed costs remain static within the relevant range of 15,000 to 25,000 units of production.

Required:

a.   Prepare projected income statements for November 19X1, for management purposes using each of the following product costing methods:

(1)   Absorption costing with all variances charged to cost of goods sold each month.

(2)   Variable (direct) costing.

b.   Reconcile the difference in the income reported with the two methods.

P16–6. Decrease in earnings with increased sales

One of the objectives that top management of Hasin Company has established for next year is to produce earnings before taxes of $75,000. They are confident that this objective can be achieved, since sales revenues have been exceeding the budget by 8 percent. But now the accountant in charge of cost functions presents them with the following data:

HASIN COMPANY
Operating Forecast

	Budgeted forecast as of 1/1/19–	Adjusted forecast as of 10/31/19–
Sales	$300,000	$324,000
Cost of sales at standard	180,000	199,400*
Gross margin	$120,000	$124,600
Marketing expenses ($5,000 is		
fixed cost)	20,000	28,000
Administrative expenses (all		
fixed cost)	25,000	24,000
Total operating expenses	$ 45,000	$ 52,000
Earnings before taxes	$ 75,000	$ 72,600

*Standard cost of sales includes over- or underabsorbed fixed overhead.

The variable cost of sales remained the same percentage of sales as budgeted. Fixed production overhead was budgeted to be $50,000; there were 20,000 estimated production units. Due to a scarcity of skilled labor, only 18,000 units were produced. There was no change in sales mix or sales price. Top management cannot understand why earnings before taxes are below budgeted earnings, even though sales revenue has increased. Hasin's finished goods inventory was large enough to fill all sales orders received.

Required:

a.   Prepare a schedule explaining to management why there is a decrease in earnings before taxes in spite of increased sales.
b.   What suggestions can you make for the company to improve its performance?
c.   Illustrate an alternative internal cost reporting procedure which would better show the financial picture. Explain why you chose the approach you did.
d.   Account for any difference in income using the procedures in *c* with the $72,600 earnings before taxes as of 10/31/19–.

P16–7. Income statements using absorption costing and variable costing

McIntosh Company had the following units in inventory for the years 19X1 and 19X2. Production for the two years is also given below.

	19X1 (units)	19X2 (units)
Beginning inventory.	–0–	50,000
Production	310,000	280,000
Ending inventory	50,000	30,000

A standard cost system is used with unit standards as follows:

Direct material.	$2.00
Direct labor.	3.00
Variable factory overhead	1.00
Fixed factory overhead ($1,200,000 ÷ 300,000	
units at normal capacity)	4.00
Total production cost at standard.	$10.00

No variances from standard variable costs occurred. Under- or overapplied overhead is closed to Cost of Goods Sold. Unit sales price was $20 for both years. Variable marketing and administrative cost was $560,000 in 19X1 and $600,000 in 19X2, while fixed marketing and administrative cost was $800,000 in 19X1 and $850,000 in 19X2.

Required:

a.   Prepare statements of income using absorption and variable costing for both years.
b.   Account for the difference in income for each of the years.

P16–8.   Standard variable costing income statement

   Shain Company uses a variable costing system employing standard costs. Management expects to operate the plant at 25,000 machine-hours per month. The following data are obtained for the month of February 19X1:

Standard variable product cost per unit:	
Direct Material	$2.00
Direct labor	8.00
Variable factory overhead (4 machine-hours × $1).	4.00
Variable marketing expense (per unit sold).	3.00
Variable administrative expense (per unit sold).	2.50
Total variable cost per unit	$19.50

Production and sales data:	
Units started in operation	6,200
Units completed.	6,000
Units in ending work in process (all material, ¾	
labor and factory overhead)	200
Units sold ($40 sales price per unit)	5,500

Cost data for the month:	Actual	Budgeted at normal capacity
Direct material used	$12,772	
Direct labor cost	48,339	
Variable factory overhead	25,338	
Variable marketing expense	17,200	
Variable administrative expense	13,580	
Fixed factory overhead expense	51,400	$50,000
Fixed marketing expense.	7,600	6,000
Fixed administrative expense.	4,300	4,000

Required:

   Prepare an income statement using variable costing showing actual and standard costs with a variance for each item. Indicate whether each variance is favorable or unfavorable. After determining the variable costing income, adjust it to an absorption costing basis.

P16–9. Absorption and variable costing's influence on bonus

Management of the Sharon Russell Company is concerned since last year's operations resulted in the worst loss in the history of the company, as shown below:

Sales (50,000 units)		$500,000
Cost of goods sold:		
Beginning inventory (10,000 units)	$75,000	
Cost of goods manufactured		
(50,000 units)	375,000*	
Goods available for sale	$450,000	
Less: Ending inventory		
(10,000 units)	75,000	
Cost of goods sold		375,000
Gross margin		$125,000
Marketing and administrative		
expense		140,000
Loss		($15,000)

*Includes $125,000 fixed factory overhead; remaining costs are $5 variable per unit.

The board of directors replaced the president and hired an individual who agreed to assume the position if he would receive a bonus of 60 percent of profits generated. The new president agreed to reimburse the company for any losses incurred. Within a short period, the new president had the production facilities operating at full capacity of 75,000 units.

Despite no growth in sales, the next period's income statement showed a profit with no change in the cost behavior patterns. Immediately after the income statement was prepared, the new president accepted his bonus and resigned with no explanation. The boards of directors cannot understand the President's actions.

Required:

a. Explain why you know that the company's income statement for last year was prepared on a variable costing or an absorption costing basis.
b. Determine normal volume used for overhead application.
c. Prepare an income statement for the next year based on absorption costing assuming there was no change in sales or cost behavior patterns.
d. Using an alternative reporting procedure, prepare an income statement which would have contradicted the new president's stance.
e. Do you think the new President deserved the bonus? Why or why not?

P16–10. Variable costing and absorption costing income statements

The executives of James Evans Company have been pleased that their accounting staff is using variable costing for internal management purposes because they have obtained valuable information through its use. At year-end, the variable costing data is converted to absorption costing for external reporting.

Forecasts prepared at the end of 19X1 indicated that sales would increase 20 percent the following year. To meet this predicted sales increase, production was increased from 10,000 units to 12,000 units. However, there was no sales increase in 19X2.

The following data pertain to 19X1 and 19X2:

	19X1	19X2
Selling price per unit . . . . $	15	$ 15
Sales (units). . . . . '. . .	10,000	10,000
Beginning inventory (units)	1,000	1,000
Production (units).	10,000	12,000
Ending inventory (units)	1,000	3,000
Unfavorable labor, materials, and		
variable overhead variances (total) . . . . . . $ 2,500		$ 2,000

Standard variable costs per unit for 19X1 and 19X2 were

Labor.	$3.75
Materials	2.25
Variable overhead.	1.50
	$7.50

Budgeted and annual fixed costs for 19X1 and 19X2 are as follows

Production.	$30,000
Marketing and administrative	35,000
	$65,000

There was no variance between actual and budgeted fixed costs. The overhead rate under absorption costing is based on practical plant capacity, which is 15,000 units per year. All variances and under- or overabsorbed overhead are charged to Cost of Goods Sold.

Required:

Ignore all taxes:

a.   Present the income statement based on variable costing for 19X2.
b.   Present the income statement based on absorption costing for 19X2.
c.   Explain the difference, if any, between the net income figures. Give the entries needed to adjust the book figures to the financial statement figures, if any are necessary.
d.   What advantages and disadvantages are attributed to variable costing for internal purposes?

P16–11.   Variable costing where all costs are fixed

Several years ago, the city of Oxford approached the management of Mississippi Fertilizer Company concerning the possibility of using garbage obtained from the city's residents in manufacturing fertilizer. After conducting many engineering studies, the company built a completely automated processing plant which has its own source of utilities. Under the agreement with the city, garbage is delivered to the plant daily at no cost to the company. Because of the factory's unique features, volume can be easily adjusted. All operating costs are fixed, and employees are paid a fixed salary. Fertilizer is sold in bulk at $2 per pound to farmers who bring their trucks to the factory for filling. The following data relate to the first three years of operation:

	19X1	19X2	19X3
Pounds processed	10,000	6,000	12,000
Pounds sold	6,000	10,000	11,000
Fixed production costs	$15,000	$15,000	$15,000
Fixed marketing and administrative			
expense	$ 2,000	$ 2,000	$ 2,000

Required:

a. Using 10,000 pounds as normal capacity, prepare income statements using variable costing and absorption costing.

b. Indicate the inventory value shown on the balance sheet at year-end for each of the three years using each method.

c. If the company changes its manufacturing facilities, purchases utilities from the city, and pays its employees on an hourly basis, fixed costs will be reduced to $10,000 per year and variable cost per pound will become $0.60. Using the same data as above except for the change in cost behavior, prepare income statements using variable costing and absorption costing.

d. Account for the difference in income for 19X2 using conditions in which all costs are fixed as compared to having both fixed and variable costs.

P16–12. Variations in price, volume, and costs (CMA adapted)

JK Enterprises sold 550,000 units during the first quarter ended March 31, 19X1. These sales represented a 10 percent increase over the number of units budgeted for the quarter. In spite of the sales increase, profits were below budget, as shown in the condensed income statement presented below:

JK ENTERPRISES
Income Statement
For the First Quarter Ended March 31, 19X1
($000)

	Budget	Actual
Sales.	$2,500	$2,530
Variable expenses:		
Cost of goods sold	$1,475	$1,540
Selling	400	440
Total variable expenses	$1,875	$1,980
Contribution margin	$ 625	$ 550
Fixed expenses:		
Selling	$ 125	$ 150
Administration.	275	300
Total fixed expenses.	$ 400	$ 450
Income before taxes	$ 225	$ 100
Income taxes (40%)	90	40
Net income	$ 135	$ 60

The accounting department always prepares a brief analysis which explains the difference between budgeted net income and actual net income. This analysis, which has not yet been completed for the first quarter, is submitted to top management with the income statement.

Required:

Prepare an explanation of the $125,000 unfavorable variance between the first quarter budgeted and actual beforetax income for JK Enterprises by calculating a single amount for each of the following variations:

a.   Sales price difference.
b.   Variable unit cost difference.
c.   Volume difference.
d.   Fixed cost difference.

P16–13.   Reconciliation of variable and absorption costing methods (CMA adapted)

The Vice President for Sales of Huber Corporation has received the income statement for November 19–. The statement has been prepared on a variable cost basis and is reproduced below. The firm has just adopted a variable costing system for internal reporting purposes.

HUBER CORPORATION
Income Statement
For the Month of November 19—
($000)

Sales.		$2,400
Less: Variable standard cost of goods sold		1,200
Manufacturing margin.		$1,200
Less: Fixed manufacturing costs at budget	$600	
Fixed manufacturing cost spending variance.	–0–	$ 600
Gross margin.		$ 600
Less: Fixed selling and administrative costs		400
Net income before taxes.		$ 200

The controller attached the following notes to the statements: The unit sales price for November averaged $24; the standard unit manufacturing costs for the month were:

Variable cost	$12
Fixed cost	4
Total cost	$16

The unit rate for fixed manufacturing costs is a predetermined rate based upon a normal monthly production of 150,000 units. Production for November was 45,000 units in excess of sales. The inventory at November 30 consisted of 80,000 units.

Required:

a.   The Vice President for Sales is not comfortable with the variable costing basis and wonders what the net income would have been under the previous absorption cost basis.
    (1)   Present the November income statement on an absorption cost basis.
    (2)   Reconcile and explain the difference between the variable costing and the absorption costing net income figures.
b.   Explain the features associated with variable cost income measurement that should be attractive to the Vice President for Sales.

Constraints on decision making

Differential cost analysis

Opportunity cost analysis

Replacement cost analysis

OBJECTIVES OF CHAPTER 17

1. To present the factors affecting decision making and the constraints placed upon the decision maker.

2. To illustrate the various applications of differential costs which can influence a decision.

3. To emphasize the advantages of calculating the payoff and expected values of the alternatives being considered as opposed to a subjective evaluation of opportunity cost.

4. To discuss the relevance of replacement cost data to decision making.

17

Decision models and cost analysis

Merely collecting cost accounting data does not completely fulfill the accountant's responsibility, for recommending solutions to cost-profit problems commands much of the accountant's time. In fulfilling these duties, cost accountants are faced with the challenge of using their own initiative, professional knowledge, and personal judgment in assessing what data are most beneficial to management. The accountant works closely with economists, statisticians, marketing managers, and production managers in many of these decisions. Using each of these individual's special skills and experience, the accountant should arrive at the most appropriate analysis and recommendation.

This chapter is concerned with the use of decision models and cost analysis. Often, when management is faced with choosing between alternative courses of action and costs collected using conventional accounting procedures are inadequate, the accountant is asked to prepare special cost studies. This is not the same as costing for inventory valuation purposes. In fact, many of the costs discussed, such as differential costs, opportunity costs, and replacement costs, are never entered in formal accounting records; instead, they are gathered for internal use in decision making.

Decision making is the process of studying and evaluating two or more available alternatives leading to a final choice. This selection process is not automatic; rather, it is a conscious procedure. Decision making is intimately involved with planning for the future and is directed toward a specific objective or goal.

One factor which colors any decision is the environment. The environment affects the decision-making process by defining and limiting the full discretion of the decision maker. He or she is affected by such personal factors as family background, health, tension, and fatigue. In addition, decision making is based on certain assumptions, such as company and departmental goals, that are given by the environment. Company policy, for example, may be so inflexible that it is difficult to modify or change any established procedure. Or managers and employees may have developed patterns of thought and behavior that are hard to change; for example, the company may have such a tradition for operating flamboyantly that cost control programs are difficult to put into effect. In addition, the specific decision made varies directly with the individual person and environment involved. For example, if the decision maker has been given inadequate cost accounting data, he or she may not have all the facts necessary to make a wise decision.

CONSTRAINTS ON DECISION MAKING

Even if the decision maker has been provided with financial data concerning the alternatives available, he or she is faced with many constraints. For example, the decision maker must have the necessary authority to make and implement the decision. External factors also place definite limitations on the decision-making process. The decision maker must be concerned not only about the physical welfare of subordinates, superiors, and others, but also about their opinions. Additionally, the economic climate must be considered; if, for instance, the government has adopted a high tariff, this must be taken into account in planning. Trade associations, government agencies, and other external groups also have regulations which influence decisions; for example, the existence of a strong labor union may also restrict freedom in business planning.

After considering all this, the decision maker may choose a solution only to find that it is not economically feasible. Cost trade-offs occur in almost all decisions, and the company may find that the first decision is too expensive. So economics may also be a constraint on decision making. Similarly, technology may not be advanced enough to implement the decision. Even though technological changes may be rapid, at any given time, the available technology is relatively inflexible. The capital investment in machinery and equipment thus represents a sunk cost which cannot be changed in the future.

Time also influences decision making because the shorter the time planned for, the more accurate and detailed the analysis can be. The company should guard against planning for longer time periods than is economically justifiable; however, planning can be misleading if the planning period is too short. In addition, the more time devoted to planning, the better the plans may be; however, beyond a certain point, additional time devoted to the decision becomes too costly to be justified. As always the benefit of the data accumulated and analyzed must be balanced against the cost of obtaining the information. The time necessary to implement the alternatives available should also be considered. For example, in make-or-buy decisions discussed later in the chapter, the company may have to reject manufacturing its own machine or other products simply because it does not have time to design, test, and begin production while the market is favorable.

Relevant-irrelevant costs

Regardless of the alternatives studied, the decision maker must decide which costs are relevant. *Relevant costs* are those that are pertinent, or valid, and bear upon the decision to be made; all other costs become irrelevant and do not apply to that particular selection process. As illustrated later in this chapter, the ability to distinguish between costs that are critical to the decision and costs that have no significance is important in arriving at correct conclusions. By emphasizing the relevant costs, the accountant avoids diverting the manager's attention to irrelevances.

Often among such relevant costs are *out-of-pocket costs*. These are costs which involve either an immediate or near-future cash outlay. Often, variable and differential costs fall into this classification. Frequently, these costs are relevant costs for the decision at hand. For example, the direct material and direct labor needed to fill additional orders are both relevant *and* out-of-pocket costs; however, depreciation on the existing manufacturing facilities used does not fall into either classification. Out-of-pocket costs are important in decision making because management should determine whether the proposed project would, at the minimum, return the initial cash outlay.

Sunk costs, on the other hand, are historical expenditures for equipment or other productive resources which have no economic relevance to the present decision-making process. A decision was made in the past to incur these costs, and no present or future decision can change it; thus, the costs are irrevocable in a given situation. One of the most common examples of a sunk cost is plant asset investments, because after the physical facilities are installed, management can either use the asset and attempt to recover costs through the revenue generated by the asset or sell the plant asset, realizing market value. Decisions regarding the exchange of an old asset for a new one involve sunk cost because the undepreciated book balance of the old asset cannot be changed and is irrelevant to the decision-making process except in determining income tax liability. In deciding whether to continue or abandon operations, the book value of any equipment that will be discarded at no scrap value is ignored. If operations are continued, depreciation of the equipment is a production cost; however, the book value of the equipment is irrelevant in deciding to abandon operations.

DIFFERENTIAL COST ANALYSIS

Unlike sunk costs, differential costs are very useful in planning and decision making. *Differential costs*, or *incremental costs*, are the differences in the cost of two alternatives. As you may recall, differential cost was introduced in

Chapter 9 as being useful when management is faced with the decision of finding the most profitable stage of production at which to sell a product. Differential cost analysis also involves such choices as accepting or rejecting orders, make-or-buy decisions, and increasing or abandoning operations.

Differential and marginal costs are closely related because *marginal cost* refers to the change in total cost resulting from increasing the volume of activity by *one unit* per period. If fixed and semivariable costs do not increase due to the enlarged production, marginal cost is measured by the change in total variable cost. As long as total variable cost increases along a straight line, marginal cost is constant and equal to average variable cost.

Even though a differential cost is more likely to be variable or semivariable, fixed costs can be included among differential costs when a change in capacity is anticipated. For example, assume present plant facilities can manufacture between 80,000 and 90,000 units without adding plant space or machinery. The differential cost of these two capacity levels is strictly variable cost, as shown in Exhibit 17–1. However, if production is increased to 120,000 units, additional factory space, machinery and equipment, and factory supervisors costing a total of $56,000 are required. The variable cost of $2 per unit remains the same, yielding a total of $240,000 variable cost if 120,000 units are manufactured. The differential cost of increasing production from 80,000 units to 90,000 units is $20,000 ($2 variable cost × 10,000 units). The differential cost for the extra 30,000 units manufactured to yield a total production of 120,000 units is $116,000 [$60,000 variable cost ($2 variable cost × 30,000 units) + $56,000 additional fixed costs].

As shown in Exhibit 17–1, the average unit cost is lowered from $3.25 ($260,000/80,000) to $3.11 ($280,000/90,000) when production is expanded within the present facilities. The average unit cost is reduced because the $100,000 total fixed cost is absorbed by 10,000 more units. Fixed costs do not increase because idle capacity is used to produce the additional 10,000 units. Production at the 80,000-unit capacity absorbs all the fixed cost. However, when additional plant facilities are acquired, the average unit cost increases to $3.30 even though unit variable costs remains at $2.00—there is an additional

EXHIBIT 17–1

	80,000 units	Normal capacity 90,000 units	120,000 units
Variable costs: $2 per unit. . . .	$160,000	$180,000	$240,000
Fixed costs.	100,000	100,000	156,000
	$260,000	$280,000	$396,000
Average unit cost	$ 3.25	$ 3.11	$ 3.30
Total differential cost		20,000	116,000
Unit differential cost		2.00	3.87

EXHIBIT 17–2

Variable budgets employing differential cost analysis

	70 percent	Normal capacity 85 percent	125 percent
Volume	70 percent	85 percent	125 percent
Units of output.	7,000	8,500	12,500
Variable costs:			
Direct material	$ 56,000	$ 68,000	$100,000
Direct labor	105,000	127,500	187,500
Factory overhead.	42,000	51,000	75,000
Fixed factory overhead	85,000	85,000	100,000
Total cost.	$288,000	$331,500	$462,500
Average unit cost	$ 41.14	$ 39.00	$ 37.00
Total differential cost		43,500	131,000
Unit differential cost.		29.00	32.75

	Standard specification per unit
Direct material	$ 8.00
Direct labor	15.00
Variable factory overhead	6.00
Fixed factory overhead	10.00
Total cost	$39.00

$56,000 fixed cost which must be absorbed. This change in cost behavior is reflected in the unit differential cost computed and shown in Exhibit 17–1. The acquisition of additional plant facilities causes a significant increase in unit differential cost.

Variable budgets can be prepared at different levels of production to indicate the direct material, direct labor, and factory overhead at each level. From this information, the average unit cost, total differential cost, and unit differential cost can be computed. Exhibit 17–2 illustrates the application of variable budgeting to differential cost analysis. Normal capacity is budgeted at an 85 percent volume. If production volume is increased to 125 percent by adding an additional shift or through plant expansion, fixed factory overhead increases to $100,000. However, despite this increase in total fixed costs, the average unit cost has decreased from $39 to $37.

Accept-or-decline decisions

Exhibit 17–2 would be useful for decision making and profit planning results if the company is faced with an accept-or-decline decision. Differential cost of the additional 4,000 units should be compared with the revenue to be received in deciding whether manufacturing additional units is profitable. For example, assume the company is producing 8,500 units when it receives an offer to sell 4,000 units at a unit sales price of $36. The average unit cost as shown in Exhibit 17–2 indicates that this $36 sales price is below the $37 average unit full cost at the 125 percent capacity level. Management may not take advantage of the sales offer if it relies on the average cost per unit to make the decision. Instead, differential cost should be used in evaluating short-term projects when the objective is to make better use of existing facilities.

The revenue received from this extra production should be compared with the differential cost as follows to determine whether the increased production is profitable:

Differential revenue (4,000 units × $36) $144,000
Differential cost (4,000 × $32.75)   131,000
Differential profit . . . . $ 13,000

If the sales offer is accepted, a $13,000 contribution to the recovery of fixed costs is made and, after full recovery, to income. The sales price should be accepted even though it is lower than average unit cost. Even though the price is given in this example and setting a "minimum sales price" is not involved, new short-term business should be accepted as long as the variable cost is recovered—variable costs represent the minimum sales price under these conditions.

Net differential income. Assume, instead, that when the company is operating at 85 percent capacity, it receives an order for 5,000 units that are slightly different from their regular products. Because management feels that this is a one-time order, it does not wish to expand plant facilities. After evaluating the requirements of the new order, management finds that it must temporarily cut regular production by one third. Under these conditions, it is important to calculate the net change in income, or net differential income, that the company will experience. Assume simply that each of the 5,000 units in the order require $6 direct material, $8 direct labor, and $4 variable factory overhead. New tools, which will have no use after the order is completed and which cost $2,000, must be purchased for use in making the 5,000 units. Exhibit 17–3 illustrates the analysis needed to determine whether the order should be accepted. It is assumed that one third of the regular production can be sold for $92,750 and that the sales price of the order being considered is $130,000. As seen in Exhibit 17–3, the company will receive net differential income of $27,417 after the $38,000 differential income from the 5,000-unit order is compared with the $10,583 income from regular production that will not be earned. An analysis similar to that in Exhibit 17–3 comparing the $92,000 differential cost of 5,000-unit order with the $82,167 differential cost of one-third regular production could be made. The difference, which is referred to as net differential cost, is then compared to the difference in revenue to yield a $27,417 advantage of accepting the order. However, many qualitative factors

EXHIBIT 17–3

Net differential income

Differential revenue from 5,000-unit order.		$130,000	
The differential cost of the 5,000-unit order is:			
Costs incurred to fill the order:			
Direct materials (5,000 units× $6). $30,000			
Direct labor (5,000 units × $8) 40,000			
Variable factory overhead (5,000 units × $4). . . . 20,000			
Tools 2,000			
Differential cost of 5,000-unit order		92,000	
Differential income from 5,000-unit order			$38,000
Less: Differential income from regular production:			
Regular production sales		$ 92,750	
Costs reduced for regular production:			
Direct material (⅓ × $68,000). $22,667			
Direct labor (⅓ × $127,500). 42,500			
Variable factory overhead			
(⅓ × $51,000) 17,000		82,167	10,583
Net differential income—advantage of accepting 5,000-unit order			$27,417

must be considered, such as *(a)* the impact on future earnings of temporarily cutting regular production by one third, *(b)* the possibility of selling additional units beyond the 5,000-unit initial order, and *(c)* the reliability of the cost estimates associated with the order.

While contribution margin and differential cost analysis are useful for accept-or-decline decisions, they are not valid for use in long-term planning and pricing. Managers must use differential cost cautiously because all costs, both fixed and variable, must be covered in the long run before profits are earned. Basing the accept-or-decline decision on the differential profit generated is defensive planning and pricing; the objective is to best utilize existing plant facilities given the circumstances. By using differential cost analysis, management is accepting the fact that if profits cannot be obtained, a contribution to overhead will be accepted. However, this approach ignores long-run survival since a company cannot continue unless *all* costs are covered, and a normal rate of return on capital employed is produced.

Rather than merely accept any short-run project that generates a contribution to overhead, therefore, management should investigate the possibility of using any idle capacity for more profitable alternatives. Even though the company may be experiencing idle capacity, management should guard against placing no cost on these facilities. The accountant should help management search for profitable ways to eliminate idle existing facilities.

Robinson-Patman Amendment.   As will be discussed in Chapter 21, the Robinson-Patman Amendment may be a legal deterrent to accepting or rejecting orders based on differential profit analysis. According to this amendment, a company cannot quote different prices to different competing customers unless such price differentials represent cost savings passed on to the customer or unless the pricing strategy is used to meet competitors' price quotations. Courts have generally held that costs established with the exclusion of fixed costs cannot be accepted as a defense for price differentials. Thus, a company should be advised to consult legal counsel before engaging in a short-term pricing strategy.

Another danger inherent in such short-term pricing is that the price reductions may be carried over to sales of repeat orders and into future periods. Differential cost analysis can lead to effective decision making only if it is applied to nonrepeat orders which will not compete with the regular sale of products at the normal sales price. To protect the future sales price of recurring orders, management should limit such short-term pricing strategy to orders that are nonrepetitive or are subject to competitive bidding. An additional safeguard is to avoid such pricing techniques unless the orders are different in design or brand name from current product lines.

Make-or-buy decisions

Differential cost can also be appropriate to use in short-run make-or-buy decisions. In this context, a company does not have to be concerned over whether it is violating government regulations or affecting the future market of its repeat orders as it does with accept-or-decline decisions. Make-or-buy decisions involve internal considerations, such as the desire to control the quality of an asset, rather than external ones, which might include fear of violating customer relations or public policy. Nearly every manufacturing company must periodically undertake make-or-buy decisions for such assets as new machinery and equipment and new parts needed in the production of goods for sale.

As in accept-or-decline decisions, the objective is to profitably use the various levels of productive capacity available with the existing facilities. Differential cost analysis is especially valid if the company has idle capacity and idle workers that can be used to make the tools or parts.

For example, suppose a company has determined that the standard costs for two components parts it uses in processing are:

	Machine part X2	Machine part Y4
Variable materials, labor, and overhead.	$ 6	$ 7
Fixed factory overhead	3	4
Total	$ 9	$11
Machine-hours per unit	7	.5

The company has been producing the 10,000 units of X2 and the 9,000 of Y4

EXHIBIT 17–4

Make-or-buy analysis

	Machine part X2	Machine part Y4
Outside purchase price......................	$9.50	$12.50
Relevant unit production cost	6.00	7.00
Potential cost savings per unit.................	$3.50	$ 5.50
Machine hours per unit......................	÷ 7	÷ 5
Potential cost savings per machine hour	$0.50	$ 1.10

needed annually. However, a recent fire destroyed part of the building in which the parts were manufactured. As a result, only 87,000 hours of otherwise idle machine-hours can be devoted to the production of these two parts. An outside company has offered to supply a comparable quality of parts at $9.50 for X2 and $12.50 for Y4. Management wants to schedule the 87,000 available machine-hours so that the company realizes maximum potential cost savings.

In this make-or-buy decision, only the variable costs are relevant. To meet the company's current needs, the number of units of X2 and Y4 to be produced, assuming the allocation of machine time is based on potential cost savings per machine-hour, is illustrated in Exhibit 17–4.

Since the potential cost saving is greater for Y4, priority should be given to using as much capacity as possible to produce Y4. The remaining capacity should then be used to manufacture part X2, with the following purchases from the outside supplier:

Available idle machine-hours	87,000
Part Y4 annual usage (9,000 × 5 hours).......	45,000
Remaining machine-hours	42,000
Part X2 annual usage in units..............	10,000
Units to be manufactured	
$\dfrac{\text{42,000 remaining machine-hours}}{\text{7 machine-hours per unit}}$	6,000
Part X2 units to be purchased from outside suppliers	4,000

As pointed out above, plant assets or component parts of the finished product may be constructed on the company premises rather than acquired outside; thus, idle capacity and personnel are used and a cost saving realized. The construction may also be necessary because the asset cannot be purchased from an outsider in the required specifications or allotted time period. The decision to make the parts or plant asset may thus be based on the desire to control the quality of the asset involved.

It is difficult to make clear-cut rules for make-or-buy decisions because the individual circumstance may warrant additional considerations. The price quoted by an outside supplier to make the products should be competitive; the first quoted price may be high, so bargaining may be necessary. In comparing the cost-to-make with the purchase price, identical quantities and product quality level should obviously be used, and quantity discounts should be considered. Unfortunately, the company may have no experience to use as a general guide in finding a cost figure to compare with the outside bid, so the process of estimating costs in these circumstances may be loaded with difficulty.

The make-or-buy decision is often complex, involving not only present cost but also projections of future costs resulting from such factors as capacity, trade secrets, technological innovation, product quality, seasonal sales, and production fluctuations. For example, numerous alternatives may be available in designing the product, including various types of material. Top management should, therefore, provide basic policies governing the factors that should be taken into account in make-or-buy decisions and specify the division of responsibilities among the management team. In other words, make-or-buy decisions are not exclusively problems of top management; instead, as management makes these decisions, it must keep prevailing market forces and conditions in mind. The purchasing department and the production and industrial engineering departments thus often have more responsibility in such cost studies than does the cost accounting department. Before undertaking make-or-buy cost studies, management should analyze the capacity available because the number of shifts the facilities must operate to engage in both normal production and the manufacture of the asset in question may not be feasible.

Another factor to consider in make-or-buy decisions is the technical ability of the labor that will be utilized in making the product; this should be evaluated against any special training and skills needed. The company should have assurance that their workers' knowledge is adequate to produce a product of the quality desired. Likewise, it may also be necessary to acquire specialized plant facilities and equipment to manufacture the new product. In addition, new sources of material suppliers may be required; in fact, very often a change from buy to make increases the total number of suppliers involved.

Just as it is difficult to find a comparative cost figure for making the asset rather than buying it from an outside supplier, the accountant also encounters special cost measurement problems when the company contemplates the possibility of buying a commodity or service that it has been producing. One advantage that this contemplated shift may have is that the experience of the past may prove helpful. However, in all cases, the current and prospective level of costs, rather than historical costs, should be used in the estimation process. Regardless of how carefully compiled, historical cost data have serious limitations for planning and decision making because conditions may have changed. By using the costs that will be incurred if the company continues to perform the work rather than employ an outsider, the company can make a more valid decision.

Escapable costs

When a shift from making the product to buying it is contemplated, those costs that are eliminated if the activity is discontinued are referred to as *escapable costs*. Escapable costs are those costs so directly related to the activity that they are not incurred if the activity is suspended, while non-escapable costs are the costs which are not eliminated if the activity is discontinued but, instead, are reassigned to other segments. When a company is considering a shift from making a product or service to buying it from an outsider, only escapable costs are relevant. For example, if the company eliminates the manufacture of a part and purchases it already finished, the wages paid to the workers making the part as well as the material cost of the part are escapable costs. On the other hand, even if a product line or customer grouping is eliminated, factory rent or insurance may remain unchanged. The other product lines must then absorb these nonescapable costs, as shown in the following example: Suppose a company furnishes the following recent operating statement for its three product lines, A, B, and C:

	A	B	C	Total
Sales.	$200,000	$180,000	$150,000	$530,000
Variable costs and expenses	$140,000	$108,000	$120,000	$368,000
Fixed expenses:				
Salaries of product line supervisors	15,000	16,000	20,000	51,000
Marketing costs allocated to product lines on basis of sales	4,000	3,600	3,000	10,600
Administrative costs allocated equally	11,000	11,000	11,000	33,000
Total costs and expenses	$170,000	$138,600	$154,000	$462,600
Operating income (loss)	$ 30,000	$ 41,400	$ (4,000)	$ 67,400

Management is considering discontinuing Product C operations and expects Product A sales to increase 10 percent, while Product B sales will increase 15 percent if this happens. No increase in fixed costs is projected as a result of the increased sales of Product A; however, the salaries of Product B's product line supervisors will increase 10 percent due to the increased sales. No increase in total assets required is expected. Assets used in Product C operations can be sold at book value. Product C supervisors will be laid off with no termination pay.

Exhibit 17–5 illustrates the projected operating statement based on the assumption that Product C operations are discontinued. Notice that variable costs for Products A and B remain the same percentage of sales, but Product C's variable costs and expenses are escapable. However, fixed marketing and administrative expenses are nonescapable, and Product C's share must now be covered by Products A and B. As shown in Exhibit 17–5, net income is increased slightly from $67,400 to $72,600 with no increase in total assets required. However, other factors such as the future sales of Product C and whether the increased sales of Product A and B will continue should be considered before Product C operations are eliminated.

EXHIBIT 17–5

	Product lines		
	A	B	Total
Sales.	$220,000	$207,000	$427,000
Variable costs and expenses	$154,000 (70%)	$124,200 (60%)	$278,200
Fixed costs:			
Salaries of product			
line supervisors	15,000	17,600 (110%)	32,600
Marketing costs $\left(\frac{\$10,600}{\$427,000}\right)$ = 2.4824% of sales	5,461	5,139	10,600
Administrative costs	16,500	16,500	33,000
Total costs and expenses	$190,961	$163,439	$354,400
Operating income (loss)			
before taxes	$ 29,039	$ 43,561	$ 72,600

Consideration of escapable and nonescapable costs also arises in make-or-buy decisions, as shown in the following illustration. Assume a company has the following costs when it receives an offer from an outside company to supply the parts at $7 per unit.

	Per unit	Per 1,000 units
Direct material, direct labor,		
variable overhead.	$2	$2,000
Fixed overhead, direct.	3	3,000
Fixed overhead, indirect but allocated	4	4,000
	$9	$9,000

On first observation, this offer appears to be lower than the manufacturing cost of $9 per unit. However, a distinction must be made to determine what costs are relevant in the future. If the indirect fixed cost of $4,000 continues regardless of the decision, it is a nonescapable cost and irrelevant. If all of the direct fixed costs of $3,000 are avoided in the future if the decision is made to buy, they are escapable costs and relevant. In this case, the escapable costs of $5,000, or $5 per unit, is lower than the outside price of $7 per unit, indicating that the company should continue manufacturing the product itself.

OPPORTUNITY COST ANALYSIS

Other quantitative factors should be considered if the plant facilities can be used advantageously in some other production activity or if they can be leased to other parties. *Opportunity costs* are often defined as the profit that is lost by the diversion of an input factor from one use to another. Opportunity costs are not ordinarily incorporated in formal accounting systems, since they do not involve cash receipts or outlays. Accountants usually record only data concerning the alternative selected rather than alternatives rejected. However, these rejected alternatives do have significance in decision making. The merits of any particular course of action are relative merits since they involve the difference between this action and some other alternative.

Even though most managers are continually weighing alternatives, they may not actually use opportunity cost to their advantage. Instead, managers may resort to some rough, subjective evaluations of opportunity cost. These rough evaluations are dangerous because opportunity costs are significant for many decisions. For example, a single proprietor or partner has foregone the opportunity to earn a salary elsewhere by owning a company, and the opportunity cost of services in producing the product is the value of goods that would have been produced had the proprietor worked elsewhere in a similar capacity. In deciding to own a business, the proprietor weighs the salary that would have been earned if he or she worked elsewhere. Likewise, the opportunity cost of using a machine or laborer to manufacture a product is the sacrifice of the earnings that would have been derived from using the machine or laborer to make other products. In deciding which product to manufacture, the earnings that would be received from other products should be a major influencing factor. Company assets that are wholly owned also involve opportunity costs, because the funds used to purchase the asset could have been used elsewhere and earned a return.

Opportunity costs are also referred to as *alternative costs*. When resources are used by a firm in the production of a product, certain quantities of other products which those resources aid in producing must be foregone by society. This is true because supplies of economic resources in the economy are limited in relation to human wants.

In the above example illustrating escapable and nonescapable costs in which an offer to supply parts for $7,000 is received from an outside company, the escapable cost of $5,000 is lower. In addition, there is an opportunity cost of continuing to make the part—it is the earning if the capacity had been applied to some alternative use. Suppose the forecasts show that if the plant capacity were rented to another company, $500 rental income would be received. This opportunity cost becomes relevant to the decision, and the following factors should be considered:

	Make	Buy
Cost of obtaining parts	$5,000	$7,000
Opportunity cost, rental income lost	500	
	$5,500	$7,000

Even with opportunity cost included, it appears that the company should continue to manufacture the part.

Payoffs of alternative actions

As can be seen from the above illustrations, even though opportunity costs are not included in the statement of income, they are important factors in decision making. For example, when a company has a large sum of money to invest, management should identify the alternatives and determine the respective payoffs of each opportunity available. A payoff table is a means of displaying the results expected for each alternative being considered under possible states of the environment. The net benefit, which can be expressed in cash flow or income, is known as the *payoff*. One of the first steps in preparing a payoff table is the identification of the alternative actions management will analyze. As seen in Exhibit 17–6, management has established payoffs for the four alternatives considered feasible in view of the company's funds and objectives; two of these alternatives involve the introduction of new products, while the other two alternatives involve strategy changes for Product A presently being manufactured. Only four alternatives are given; obviously the funds could be invested in the stocks or bonds of other companies, but these alternatives are omitted to simplify the illustration. An important factor is the speed with which the data are gathered, for management must not take so much time in searching for alternatives that action is delayed.

The next step involves listing the environmental conditions which influence the payoff. These environmental conditions are listed across the top of the payoff table. Exhibit 17–6 considers three conditions: excellent, average, and poor. Each cell on the payoff table contains a unique combination of alternative action and environmental condition. The next step involves estimating the payoff for each alternative and environmental condition since the income generated is affected by conditions prevailing in the future. Each cell indicates the estimated payoff for the alternatives studied if the environmental condition at the head of the column prevails. For example, it is forecasted that improving Product A will result in $200,000 in income in an excellent environment, $80,000 in income in an average environment, and a $15,000 loss if a poor

EXHIBIT 17–6

Payoffs of alternative actions

Alternatives	Excellent environmental conditions	Average environmental conditions	Poor environmental conditions
Physical improvements to present Product A (now being produced).........	$200,000	$ 80,000	$ −15,000
Advertising campaign for present Product A	100,000	75,000	−10,000
Manufacture Product B..........	500,000	100,000	−100,000
Manufacture Product C..........	300,000	200,000	−80,000

market exists. Exhibit 17–6 indicates that manufacturing Product B is most profitable in an excellent market, while producing Product C is the most profitable alternative in an average market. However, the strategy of an advertising campaign for Product A involves less loss in a poor environment.

If the decision were based solely on the information in Exhibit 17–6, one market condition would be assumed to exist. As a result, the probability of each of the environmental conditions occurring is ignored. A more valid approach is to consider the likelihood of alternative market conditions. In addition, the payoff table in Exhibit 17–6 does not contain an alternative that is clearly dominant over all other alternatives. Certainly, a decision problem exists.

Quantified regrets table

Exhibit 17–7 is a chart showing the opportunity costs of alternative actions, or the return foregone; it can be referred to as a quantified regrets table. For example, if an excellent environment is assumed, Exhibit 17–6 indicates that the company would earn $500,000 if Product B were manufactured, while it would only earn $200,000 if physical improvements were made to the present product being manufactured; it would thus lose $300,000, the difference in projected incomes. To prepare a quantified regrets table, the accountant compares the highest payoffs under each of the forecasted market conditions; in this case, $500,000 is the highest payoff in an excellent market, $200,000 in an average market, and $10,000 loss in a poor market.

One way of choosing the most desirable alternative is to choose the alternative whose maximum opportunity cost is a minimum. The maximum opportunity cost for physical improvements to Product A is $300,000; $400,000 for an advertising campaign for Product A; $100,000 to manufacture Product B; and $200,000 to manufacture Product C. This analysis indicates that management should choose to manufacture Product B; however, no probability is attached to any of the future environments.

Management should not rely solely on the information in Exhibit 17–7 and

EXHIBIT 17–7

Opportunity costs of alternative actions

Alternatives	Excellent environmental conditions	Average environmental conditions	Poor environmental conditions
Physical improvements to present Product A	$300,000	$120,000	$ 5,000
Advertising campaign for present Product A	400,000	125,000	—
Manufacture Product B	—	100,000	90,000
Manufacture Product C	200,000	—	70,000

fail to consider the probabilities of the alternative market conditions. For example, Exhibit 17–6 indicates that manufacturing Product B provides an opportunity to generate the highest income; however, there may be only a small chance that this high income will result. By attaching a probability of each outcome occurring in each market condition, management has more data upon which to base the decision.

Management may know enough about the likelihood of each environment to attach probabilities of occurrence to each alternative. If so, management certainly wants to select the alternative that appears to produce the largest income, as long as that alternative does not expose the company to a high probability of a large loss. The payoffs using each alternative can be reduced to one figure; one way to do this is to weigh the possible payoffs according to the relative probabilities that the various conditions will occur.

Expected value

The probability distribution could be based on past evidence if it is felt that the same forces will continue to operate in the future. Otherwise, the decision maker has to assign probabilities that he or she thinks appropriate to the possible states of nature. The probabilities for the states of nature (market conditions) usually vary among the alternatives according to management's evaluation of market forecasts. The state of the economy also causes the probabilities to vary. To the extent possible, relevant and reliable evidence should be used by the decision maker to improve assignment of probabilities.

Assume the probabilities assigned are: 30 percent each for an excellent or average environment and 40 percent for a poor environment. The resultant weighed payoff is called the *expected value*, which is found by multiplying each possible payoff by its probability and adding the products, as shown in Exhibit 17–8. The higher the expected value, the more favorable the investment. The difference between the highest expected value and that of other alternatives represents an *opportunity gain* from investing in the most desirable alternative rather than the other alternatives. It appears from looking at the expected values that, to maximize profits, management should decide to manufacture Product B. If this approach is chosen, $118,000 is lost from the manufacture of Product C; $78,000 from the physical improvements to Product A; and $48,500 from the advertising campaign.

The risk that a company is willing to assume obviously influences the choice of an alternative. Management's preference for or aversion to risky alternatives may depend on how much the dollar amounts in Exhibit 17–8 are subjectively valued. For example, if in manufacturing Product B a loss of $100,000 could throw the company into bankruptcy or, less seriously, if it could cut working capital considerably, management should be cautious and weigh the possible loss by a factor much larger than its relative probability. Under these circumstances, management may want to use a criterion other than expected value.

EXHIBIT 17–8

Probability of the payoffs of alternative actions

Alternatives	Excellent environmental conditions (probability × payoff)	Average environmental conditions (probability × payoff)	Poor environmental conditions (probability × payoff)	Expected value
Physical improvements to Product A	0.3 × $200,000 = $ 60,000	0.3 × $ 80,000 = $24,000	0.4 × –$ 15,000 = –$ 6,000	$ 78,000
Advertising campaign for Product A	0.3 × $100,000 = $ 30,000	0.3 × $ 75,000 = $22,500	0.4 × –$ 10,000 = –$ 4,000	$ 48,500
Manufacture Product B	0.3 × $500,000 = $150,000	0.3 × $100,000 = $30,000	0.4 × –$100,000 = –$40,000	$140,000
Manufacture Product C	0.3 × $300,000 = $ 90,000	0.3 × $200,000 = $60,000	0.4 × –$ 80,000 = –$32,000	$118,000

On the other hand, if income of at least $300,000 is needed to satisfy a certain goal, such as paying off a pressing debt, the decision maker might consider the production of only Products B and C with the hope of operating in excellent environmental conditions. In this way, factors that affect the subjective worth of income or loss do influence the decision process.

Expected value of perfect information.   Even though the $140,000 expected value of manufacturing Product B is highest, management and/or owners may not be happy in playing the percentages involved in making a decision under risk. The only uncertainty is what environmental conditions will occur. The probabilities associated with each condition (for instance, a 40 percent probability of an excellent environment) are based on existing information. The worst payoff of a $40,000 loss results in manufacturing Product B under poor environmental conditions.

The company may be willing to hire a marketing consultant to obtain additional information on the environmental situation. The amount that the company is willing to pay for the marketing research team's errorless advice is called the *expected value of perfect information.* If it is assumed that the research team could indicate with certainty which condition would occur, the manager could make a decision with complete certainty. For example, if the research team tells management that an excellent environment will prevail, the company will manufacture Product B and obtain a $500,000 payoff.

Of course, "perfect" information isn't perfect in the sense of absolute predictions. Thus, the probabilities of each event or environment condition being determined are identified. Assume that these probabilities are: 30 percent each for an excellent or average environment and 40 percent for a poor environment. This then allows the computation of the expected value with perfect information using the highest payoff for each given environment. The expected value of the decision with perfect information is the sum of the optimum outcome for each event multiplied by its probability as follows:

$$.3 \times \$500,000 + .3 \times \$200,000 + .4 \times (-\$10,000) = \$206,000$$

The expected value with perfect information is then compared with the expected value with existing information to arrive at the expected value of perfect information as follows:

Expected value *with perfect information* $206,000
Expected value *with existing information* 140,000
Expected value *of perfect information* $66,000

In this example, $66,000 represents the upper limit that a decision maker would be willing to spend to reduce uncertainty. This amount is the maximum amount to spend for perfect information because in a real world, perfect forecasters are difficult to find.

REPLACEMENT COST ANALYSIS

Replacement cost is another concept that may not be entered in the company's accounting records but is of use in decision making. The concept was introduced in Appendix B to Chapter 3 when the lower of cost or market is applied to inventory. Replacement costs indicate what would be paid for assets if they were acquired at current prices. However, financial accounting in this country has traditionally employed historical cost. Historical costs show what was originally paid for the property, while replacement costs show what would be paid if the assets were acquired at present price levels. Many accountants feel that historical cost is significant primarily because this cost is the most dependable measure of the initial cost of goods and services. While the alleged major advantage of historical cost is that it is definite with regard to assets coming into the business, often replacement cost, which reflects the cash required to have assets available for use by the company, is more valuable for planning purposes.

By valuing assets at current replacement cost, the accountant determines the cost that is currently required to purchase assets with the same service potential as those now used. The replacement costs chosen may be based on prices in the current market or on an anticipated future market. For decision making, the lowest replacement cost found in the market in which the company trades should be used. An added advantage of using replacement cost is that it assumes survival is a basic need of the company and the net income reported should be positive only if there has been provision made for the survival of the company as a going concern. In other words, the company must have the capacity to replace the services used, which are expressed in current replacement cost terms.

Applications of replacement costs

Since replacement cost data are probably of greatest significance when decisions regarding depreciable assets must be made, the value of plant and equipment should be restated in terms of current replacement cost at periodic intervals. The impact of changing conditions on the specific properties a company owns and operates is important for make-or-buy decisions and for plans concerning plant and equipment improvements, additions, replacements, and retirements. Restating plant and equipment values on a replacement cost basis reveals which assets are most expensive to replace, which can be of assistance in capital investment planning and decisions concerning design capacity. Managers may be misled because asset turnover ratios based on historical costs are usually higher in the long run than those based on replacement costs.

Managers often argue that recording depreciation on a historical cost basis is inadequate. However, this point of view overemphasizes the relation of depreciation accounting to the financing of replacements. The purpose of depreciation is, after all, to record operating costs, not to provide funds. This is not to ignore the fact, however, that for internal decisions, depreciation may be restated on a replacement cost basis. Depreciation charges must then be recorded in terms of the prevailing level of the expected replacement. However, determining an appropriate economic life presents some challenges since the life used for depreciating historical cost is consistent with the special set of rules mandated in the Economic Recovery Tax Act of 1981 for computing a corporation's earnings and profits. Since computing depreciation on a replacement cost basis has as one of its objectives reflecting inflation, a realistic useful life should be used.

Even though replacement costs of plant assets may be helpful, plant and equipment are difficult to measure since there is a distinction between the physical object and the services it renders; the market for the services the plant asset renders is the future, while the physical asset itself has a present market. Another problem related to this restatement results because current technology may differ from that at the time existing facilities were acquired. Usually, current technology facilities require higher capital investment for each unit of productive capacity than do the existing facilities. Yet, a company may not be able to or want to replace its existing facility with current technology because of the cost and availability of capital, risks associated with higher fixed costs, and consideration for the present labor force. If management developed replacement cost data under the assumption that current technology was adopted, it could be interpreted as an intention to make drastic reductions in the labor force. Conversely, if management merely developed replacement cost data for existing facilities, that implies that management plans to reproduce present facilities as they are. Obviously, there is no easy solution to this problem.

Replacement cost of land

The measurement and replacement cost of land, as opposed to plant and equipment, depends in part on what use is made of it. While urban land, on the one hand, may not be subject to erosion or other physical factors, its value may increase or decrease due to the environment or other factors. For example, the value of urban land in a downtown section of a city experiencing decay and deterioration is expected to decrease in value. Conversely, land in the suburbs could increase in value as the city expands.

Restatement of inventories. Management may find it helpful to restate assets other than plant, equipment, and land on a replacement cost basis for internal purposes. For example, regardless of the actual inventory valuation method used, a manufacturer should use the replacement cost in estimating the cost of filling an order, even though the material may come from the stock on hand. Assume that the manufacturer's material inventory is costed at $20 using the LIFO valuation, but it costs $23 to replace the material; here, the relevant cost is the $23 replacement cost, not historical cost. On a replacement cost basis, inventories should be measured at net realizable value. This value is obtained by subtracting the costs of completion and disposal from the sales proceeds. By-product inventories can be measured on the same basis. The use of replacement cost as the basis for inventory valuation eliminates some assumptions, such as LIFO and FIFO, and the flow of actual goods is not considered.

Accountants should give serious thought to a substitute for historical cost-revenue realization. Even though replacement costs are not acceptable substitutes for historical costs in financial reporting, they may be more appropriate for certain decisions. A wise policy in regard to the internal use of replacement costs is to examine each particular situation on its own merit with reference to the sound requirements of good management.

SUMMARY

Not all of the costs that are needed in decision making are provided by accounting records and financial statements. This is true because normally accounting records show only costs which have or will require an outlay of cash or its equivalent at a future date. But some decision-making costs, such as opportunity costs, do not involve cash outlays. Costs prepared for financial statement purposes may thus be of limited use when management is faced with the problem of choosing between alternative courses of action. Costs must be tailored to fit the specific problem, and only relevant costs should be considered.

However, determining which costs are relevant is often debatable, and the result is, at best, an estimate. Relevant costs are generally those which will respond to managerial decision making, but they vary with individual projects and the length of the project planning period. With problems such as make-or-buy decisions, historical costs, for example, have such serious limitations that they cannot be used for short-run planning. Instead, differential costs, or those costs which change with alternatives, must be used as a basis for defensive decision making, the objective of which is to better utilize existing facilities to increase profits or reduce loss. However, a cost study prepared for a make-or-buy decision should merely indicate the direction of a decision. Other factors such as trade secrets, seasonal sales, production fluctuations, and the quality and design of the product must be considered, and the application of make-or-buy principles should not overshadow more complicated problems facing management.

Certainly, most managers are continually weighing alternatives. Decisions must be made not only when problems exist, but also when opportunities have arisen. Opportunities are, in a sense, problems which must be solved in regard to company objectives, environmental conditions, and outcomes. In decision making, many managers do attempt to incorporate a subjective evaluation of opportunity cost into the final decision. Many, however, fail to fully understand its significance and do not focus enough attention on the sacrifice of the profit which might have been made if an alternative decision were chosen.

The opportunity cost approach is primarily an economic concept which should be included only in internal cost analysis. Opportunity cost can be applied when management is attempting to evaluate the relative economies of different methods of production, make-or-buy decisions, or proposals for investment of assets. As a rule, a potential investment should not be accepted unless it appears that the rate of return will at least equal that which can be earned from other investment alternatives in the same risk category. Assembling the outcomes of each alternative on a payoff table directs attention to the profit lost from rejected alternatives.

Replacement costs are also useful in many cost studies. Unfortunately, the replacement cost concept, like the opportunity cost concept, is difficult to apply in routine cost accounting. As a result, in many systems, there is no attempt to use it. Replacement costs and opportunity costs are also highly subjective; for example, it is often difficult to determine a rate of return on an investment which involves risks comparable to those of the alternatives in question. However, this risk is part of the decision-making process, since decisions are made on the basis of possibilities, not facts. Determining the replacement cost of productive facilities also presents challenges in deciding whether to assume existing facilities are replaced as they are or whether new technology is employed. Certainly, the cost accountant faces the challenge of fulfilling management's needs for varying types of cost studies designed for the various kinds of problems which may arise.

IMPORTANT TERMS AND CONCEPTS

Relevant costs	Net differential costs
Irrelevant costs	Escapable costs
Out-of-pocket costs	Nonescapable costs
Sunk costs	Opportunity costs
Differential costs	Alternative costs
Incremental costs	Expected value
Marginal cost	Expected value of perfect information
Net differential income	Replacement costs

REVIEW QUESTIONS

1. Generally would you advise choosing an alternative if unit differential cost exceeded present average unit cost for a given choice? Why or why not?
2. Discuss the types of cost analysis that are important in internal decision making.

3. Does management have full discretion in making decisions? If not, why not?

4. Discuss three constraints upon decision making and how their impact may alter the course of action taken.

5. What is the relationship between time and planning?

6. What are relevant costs, and why is the ability to determine relevant costs necessary in decision making?

7. Define out-of-pocket costs and indicate their significance in decision making.

8. Why are sunk costs irrelevant in decision making? Give an example of a sunk cost.

9. Indicate the type of decisions in which differential cost analysis may be helpful.

10. Define the term "marginal costs."

11. Are differential costs composed only of variable costs?

12. Why do unit differential costs sometimes establish the minimum sales price in short-run pricing decisions?

13. When would net differential income be calculated and used in decision making?

14. If, to fill a sales order, a company purchases a machine or other asset which has no use beyond the order, how much of the asset cost should be included in determining the differential cost of the sales order?

15. Why is the use of differential cost analysis in short-term pricing considered a defensive planning technique?

16. What is the objective in evaluating short-term projects?

17. Why may differential cost analysis not be appropriate for determining the asset value of the component parts manufactured rather than purchased?

18. What is the danger in using historical cost when a shift from making to buying is contemplated? What costs should be used instead?

19. Distinguish between escapable and nonescapable costs.

20. Why are opportunity costs not incorporated in accounting records?

21. What is the importance of establishing payoff tables for all alternatives?

EXERCISES

E17–1. Make or buy

Wickers, Inc. has been purchasing a part for $30 per unit. The cost of producing this part based on absorption costing is $34 computed as follows:

Direct material.	$ 4
Direct labor.	15
Factory overhead (100% of direct labor cost)	15
	$34

Since Wickers is presently operating with excess capacity, there is enough capacity to provide facilities to make the part with no increase in the total amount of fixed factory overhead costs. Variable overhead costs are estimated at 80 percent of direct labor costs.

Required:

Determine whether the part should be manufactured.

E17–2.   Determining unit and differential costs for various capacity levels

The variable costs of Jordon Company, including direct material and direct labor, amount to $20 per unit. Fixed costs of operating the present facilities with a normal capacity of 60,000 units amount to $640,000. Management is considering renting for $500,000 per period an additional building, in which 25,000 units per period can be processed. Other fixed costs associated with the rented building total $332,500.

Required:

Determine average unit cost, total differential cost, and unit differential cost at these three capacity levels: 50,000 units, 60,000 units, and 75,000 units. (Compare them with the preceding lower volume.)

E17–3.   Make-or-buy, opportunity costs (CIA)

International Sports Supplies Company, Ltd. manufactures specialized sportswear and accessories such as bathing suits, tennis shorts, golf gloves, and tote bags, Recently, the company had difficulty in acquiring sufficient quantities of tanned leather to meet its production requirements and is considering the possibility of taking steps to vertically integrate into the raw leather field. Furthermore, there is adequate space in the main plant to accommodate a tanning operation since the company discontinued the manufacture of saddles several years ago. You are asked by management to study the process of tanning leather and to provide cost data on both a *make* and a *buy* basis. The results of your study are as follows for 5,000 units:

	5,000 units (annual consumption)	
	Make	Buy
Cost of purchasing		$105,000
Direct material	$ 40,000	
Direct labor	15,000	
Fixed overhead, direct	10,000	
Fixed overhead, allocated	25,000	
Variable overhead	20,000	
	$110,000	$105,000

Required:

a. Assume that the labor market is favorable and disregard opportunity costs. Use the results of your study to support a recommendation to make or buy.
b. Define opportunity costs.
c. State how opportunity costs might affect the recommendation.

E17–4.   Accept/decline order

Peter Schwartz Company is considering manufacturing a special order of 4,000 products for an agency of the government. Before receiving the special order, the company had planned to manufacture 50,000 units of the product for a total cost of $250,000. The production manager estimates that if the order from the governmental agency is accepted, the unit cost of all units produced will decrease from $5 to $4.75.

The 50,000 units of regular production will be sold for $6 each; however, the government agency is willing to pay the company only $3 per unit for the 4,000 units.

Required:

Prepare an analysis indicating the advantage or disadvantage if the company accepts the order from the government agency.

E17–5. Accepting a single order

Valley Production Company signs a four-year lease on a building in which to manufacture motors. At the beginning of the lease, management purchases a processing machine costing $7,000 which has a life of five years and can be economically removed from the building. Salvage value is expected to be $700 at the end of five years. Sum-of-the-year's-digits depreciation is used.

A casting machine is also purchased costing $23,200. Engineers estimate that the machine can cast 1,000 motors per year for six years. The casting machine cannot be removed from the manufacturing facilities without incurring more expense than the machine is worth. The productive output method of depreciation is used.

There were 700 motors produced during the first year of operations. Costs per motor, exclusive of depreciation, were as follows:

Direct material	$2.85
Direct labor	0.95
Variable factory overhead	0.18
Fixed factory overhead	0.34

There were 650 motors sold for a total sales revenue of $12,000.

Required:

a. Calculate the total cost per motor for the first year of operations.
b. Early in the second year of operations, a European buyer approaches the company wanting to buy a single order of 250 motors for a unit sales price of $15. The company estimates that it will cost $0.65 per motor to ship the order. The company believes that the annual domestic market for motors will become saturated above a 700-unit level. Management does not believe accepting this order will affect the domestic sales price, neither will they face difficulty in securing the material and labor necessary to fill the foreign order. What would you advise management to do?

E17–6. Relevant costs for make-or-buy decision

Carter Company has established the following standard cost for two component parts it uses in processing:

	Machine part A	Machine part B
Direct material	$3.00	$ 3.50
Direct labor	2.60	2.90
Factory overhead:		
Variable	1.80	1.50
Fixed	2.50	3.50
Total	$9.90	$11.40

The company has been producing the 5,000 units of A and the 8,000 of B needed annually. However, a recent hurricane destroyed part of the building in which the parts were manufactured. As a result, only 34,000 hours of otherwise idle machine-hours can be devoted to the production of these two parts. An outside company has offered to supply a comparable quality of parts at $13 for A and $12 for B. Management wants to schedule the 34,000 available machine-hours so that the company realizes maximum potential cost savings. Each unit of A requires five machine-hours, while B requires four and one-half machine-hours.

Required:

a. What costs are relevant to the make-or-buy decision? (Determine these on a unit cost basis)

b. To meet the company's current needs, determine the number of units of A and B to be produced, assuming the allocation of machine time is based on potential cost savings per machine-hour.

E17–7. Calculating unit and total differential cost

McDonald Manufacturing Company has established the following standard specification based on a normal capacity of 25,000 units.

*Standard specification
per unit*

Direct material	$ 4.00
Direct labor	5.50
Variable factory overhead. . . .	3.40
Fixed factory overhead.	6.00
	$18.90

Management feels that present manufacturing facilities are adequate to produce a maximum of 28,000 units. If additional units are produced, another factory must be rented at an annual cost of $20,000. Machinery costing $9,000 must be purchased to produce additional units above 25,000 units. Straight-line depreciation on a five-year basis will be used.

If the company produces in a volume larger than 25,000 units, it will have to change the mode of delivery, which will result in a 5 percent increase in all material purchased.

Management has hesitated to increase production above 25,000 units in the present factory because the additional direct labor workers required would be eligible for an 8 percent night-shift differential pay. Management plans to employ only one work shift, producing 2,000 units, in the new factory.

Required:

a. Prepare variable budgets for volume levels of 23,000, 25,000, 28,000, and 30,000 units.

b. Calculate the average unit cost.

c. Calculate the total differential cost, comparing it with preceding lower volume.

d. Calculate the unit differential cost.

PROBLEMS

P17–1. Capacity issues; Acceptance of order

Elizah Corporation's budget for the following year is shown below. Only one product is manufactured.

ELIZAH CORPORATION
Budgeted Income Statement
For the Year Ended December 31, 19X1

Sales (270,000 units of LX7 @ $67 per unit)		$18,090,000
Variable costs and expense:		
Direct material (LX material, 6 pounds per unit @ $1.25 per pound)	$2,025,000	
Direct labor (8 hours per unit @ $4.45 per hour)	9,612,000	
Manufacturing overhead (30% of direct labor cost)	2,883,600	
Marketing and administrative expense ($1.22 per unit)	329,400	14,850,000
Contribution margin		$ 3,240,000
Fixed expenses		1,049,000
Income before tax		$ 2,191,000

Required:

Consider each part independent of the others.

a. If actual sales in 19X1 are 10 percent below the budgeted figure, what income will result?

b. If actual sales in 19X1 are 15 percent above the budgeted figure, what income will result?

c. Assuming that existing capacity is sufficient to handle the transaction, what cost per unit will be incurred if additional sales are made beyond the budgeted figure?

d. The beginning inventory of LX7 is 45,000 units; the company wants to have an ending inventory of 50,000 units. How many LX7 units must be produced this year according to the budget? Based on this production level, how many pounds of material LX must be acquired, assuming management wants to have 15,000 pounds in ending inventory and beginning inventory of LX material is 12,000 pounds?

e. Elizah Corporation is operating at capacity when it sells 270,000 units of LX7. An additional order for 25,000 units of LX7 is received at a sales price of $59 per unit. If the order is accepted, an additional $91,000 of fixed expense will be incurred. Assuming the only criterion in this decision is the impact on income, should the order be accepted? Support your conclusion by showing the change in income.

P17–2. Incremental (differential) contribution margin (CMA adapted)

Helene's, a high-fashion women's dress manufacturer, is planning to market a new cocktail dress for the coming season. Helene's supplies retailers in the East and mid-Atlantic states.

Four yards of material are required to lay out the dress pattern. Some material remains after cutting which can be sold as remnants. The leftover material could also be used to manufacture a matching cape and handbag. However, if the leftover material is to be used for the cape and handbag, more care will be required in cutting, which will increase the cutting costs.

The company expected to sell 1,250 dresses if no matching cape or handbag were available. Helene's market research reveals that dress sales will be 20 percent higher if a matching cape and handbag are available. The market research indicates that the cape and/or handbag will not be sold individually but only as accessories with the dress. The various combinations of dresses, capes, and handbags which are expected to be sold by retailers are as follows:

	Percent of total
Complete sets of dress, cape, and handbag	70
Dress and cape.	6
Dress and handbag	15
Dress only	9
Total	100

The material used in the dress costs $12.50 a yard or $50 for each dress. The cost of cutting the dress if the cape and handbag are not manufactured is estimated at $20 a dress, and the resulting remnants can be sold for $5 for each dress cut out. If the cape and handbag are to be manufactured, the cutting costs will be increased by $9 per dress. There will be no salable remnants if the capes and handbags are manufactured in the quantities estimated.

The selling prices and the costs to complete the three items once they are cut are presented below:

	Selling price per unit	Unit cost to complete (excludes cost of material and cutting operation)
Dress	$200.00	$80.00
Cape	27.50	19.50
Handbag	9.50	6.50

Required:

a. Calculate Helene's incremental (differential) profit or loss from manufacturing the capes and handbags in conjunction with the dresses.

b. Identify any nonquantitative factors which could influence Helene's management in its decision to manufacture the capes and handbags which match the dress.

P17–3. Escapable/nonescapable costs

Ledbetter Company maintains its home office in Chicago and leases a plant and office facilities in each of its three territories. All plants manufacture the company's single product; however, there is some variation in the production process at each plant. Management supplies you with the following data concerning last year's operations:

	Western Territory	Northern Territory	Eastern Territory
Sales ($20 per unit)	$400,000	$360,000	$200,000
Variable costs:			
Material	$120,000	$126,000	$ 70,000
Labor	40,000	36,000	30,000
Factory overhead	10,000	10,800	60,000
Fixed costs:			
Factory overhead	60,000	80,000	20,000
Marketing	70,000	37,000	10,000
Administrative	40,000	30,000	12,000
Allocated home office expense	20,000	18,000	10,000
Total	$360,000	$337,800	$212,000
Income from operations	$ 40,000	$ 22,200	$ (12,000)

Home office expense is allocated on the basis of sales dollars. The company is undecided over whether certain territory operations should be expanded or reduced. Because of the unprofitable operations in the Eastern territory, management is considering closing the plant facilities there. There are two alternatives available to continue serving the Eastern territory customers. One is to enter into a contract with an outside plant which will pay Ledbetter Company a commission of 8 percent of sales price. The outside plant plans to increase the sales price to $22 even though their marketing research departments feels that the higher price will cause them to sell 20 percent fewer units. The other alternative is that the Western plant can be expanded to absorb the units presently produced by the Eastern facilities. An additional production supervisor earning $22,000 and a marketing manager earning $25,000 will be required. There will be additional shipping and selling costs of $4 per unit on the increased production.

Required:

Prepare a schedule showing the company's total income:

a.   If they enter into the commission agreement.
b.   If the Western plant is expanded.

P17–4.   Calculating unit and total differential cost

Sarah Dawkins Manufacturing Company has established the following standard specification based on a normal capacity of 10,000 units.

Standard specification per unit

Direct material	$ 3.10
Direct labor	3.60
Variable factory overhead	1.50
Fixed factory overhead	2.00
	$10.20

Management feels that present manufacturing facilities are adequate to produce a maximum of 11,000 units. If additional units are produced, another factory must be rented at an annual cost of $6,000. Machinery costing $9,000 must be purchased to produce additional units above 11,000 units. Straight-line depreciation on a three-year basis will be used.

If the company produces in a volume larger than 10,000 units, it will be able to take a 5 percent quantity discount on direct materials because of the increased purchases.

Management has hesitated to increase production above 10,000 units in the present factory because the additional direct labor workers required would be eligible for 5 percent night-shift differential pay. Management plans to employ only one work shift in the new factory producing 1,000 units.

Required:

a. Prepare variable budgets for volume levels of 9,000, 10,000, 11,000, and 12,000 units.
b. Calculate average unit costs.
c. Calculate total differential costs, comparing them with those for the preceding lower volume.
d. Calculate unit differential cost.
e. Which alternative would you advise management to choose?

P17–5. Escapable/nonescapable costs

An advertising agency recently approached the management of Clyde Hopkins Company with cost figures for specific types of promotion materials. The charge amounts to $5,000 a month; however, this does not include any direct mail promotions. The following annual costs are determined for each function.

Expenses	*Advertising*	*Warehousing*	*Direct selling*
Salaries	$53,000	$52,000	$40,000
Telephone and telegraph. . . .	2,100	1,800	1,500
Supplies.	5,800	1,000	3,000
Utilities.	4,380	4,200	6,300
Taxes and insurance	5,000	3,000	10,000
Administrative.	4,600	4,400	2,800
Travel.	–0–	–0–	8,000
Depreciation.	7,000	1,500	6,000
	$81,880	$67,900	$77,600

If the contract is signed with the outside advertising agency, the following changes are expected to occur:

1. An advertising supervisor earning $14,000 annually will be retained to coordinate work with the agency. The supervisor will report to the administration department. All advertising employees who are released will receive two-weeks' salary; this termination pay will not be allocated to any other year. Direct selling salaries will increase by $3,000 annually because personnel will assume some of the direct mail promotion activities.
2. Included in the telephone and telegraph costs are $900 for advertising and $600 for direct selling, which represents long-distance charges. The arrangement with the external agency will reduce this charge by one third; the remainder of the expense represents the organization's basic service charge, which has been allocated on the number of employees within each department. Advertising has been employing

four workers; administration—four workers; production—seven workers; ware-housing—two workers; and direct selling—three workers.

3. The only supplies affected by an external contract are advertising supplies, which will all be eliminated except for $200.

4. Each function has its own utility meter. In addition, the overall organization has a basic service charge of $17,280, which it allocates on the following ratios: Administration—6; production—18; advertising—6; warehousing—2; and direct selling—4. It is forecasted that the direct selling direct utility cost will increase by $1,400.

5. Taxes and insurance will not be affected by the move; however, management will be able to lease its present advertising office space for $400 per month.

6. The move will not cause a reduction in administrative staff. The amount allocated to each function is determined by top management on an arbitrary basis.

7. Because direct selling will be absorbing some of the duties of the advertising department if the outside agency is used, their travel expense is expected to increase $1,200 annually.

8. Additional equipment costing $6,000 will be required which will increase direct selling's annual depreciation by $500. The advertising equipment can be sold for its book value of $30,000 at no gain or loss. These funds in excess of the new equipment purchase and termination pay can be invested in secured bonds earning 14 percent interest. Annual depreciation on the building amounts to $32,000 and is allocated on the following ratios: Administration, direct selling, advertising—1 each; ware-housing—2; and production—3.

Required:

Prepare cost comparisons showing the net savings before taxes or extra cost of utilizing the advertising agency.

P17–6. Unit and total differential cost

As an accountant employed by the Phillip Hershfield Company, you have been asked by the President for advice concerning several alternatives.

The company presently rents a building to house the processing plant. The plant owner has indicated that the rent will not be raised from $2,000 per month. One work shift is being used in these facilities to manufacture 8,000 units monthly. The following sales price and unit cost have been determined based on an 8,000-unit normal monthly capacity.

	Per unit
Sales price	$45.00
Cost:	
Direct material	$12.00
Direct labor	10.00
Variable factory overhead	8.00
Fixed factory overhead	
(including rent)	5.50
	$35.50

The President is considering the following alternatives and wants you to provide cost studies for each.

1. Renew the lease on the present building but increase to two work shifts.

Management would produce 8,000 units on the day shift and 4,000 units on the night shift monthly. Night-shift workers would get a shift differential which would cause a $0.20 per unit cost increase for the units produced on that shift. Because a larger quantity of direct material will be purchased, the company can take a 10 percent quantity discount. However, to sell this larger volume, sales price must be lowered to $40. No additional machinery would be required. A factory supervisor earning $24,000 a year will be needed on the night shift.

2.   A smaller nearby building is available for a monthly rent of $900. However, Hershfield Company must purchase additional machinery costing $12,000 which will be depreciated over five years with no salvage value. Other fixed factory overhead should amount to $19,000 monthly. Unit variable factory overhead will be $8.40. Two shifts producing 5,000 units each will be used. The night shift differential, shift supervisor, material quantity discount, and lower sales price in alternative 1 will be in effect for this alternative also.

Management is confident that all units produced will be sold in the same period because of high market demand.

Required:

a.   For the alternatives and the current conditions presented, determine:
      (1)   Monthly income before taxes.
      (2)   Average unit cost.
b.   For the two new alternatives, determine:
      (1)   Total differential cost compared to present operations.
      (2)   Unit differential cost compared to present operations.
c.   Indicate which of the three alternatives is preferable.
d.   Discuss why the average unit cost under present conditions is significantly different than unit differential cost under either alternative 1 or 2.

P17–7.   Make-or-buy decision

Jeffrey Pflum Company, a manufacturer of mopeds, is trying to decide whether to continue manufacturing its own engine units or to purchase them from an outside supplier. Bids have been taken, and a unit that meets all specifications can be purchased for $35 each. Pflum needs 12,000 units a year.

The fabricating department makes all of the engine parts. The unit is completed by direct labor in the finishing department and is then installed in the moped by the assembly department.

The fabricating department is used 25 percent for the production of the engine parts; however, phasing out this segment will not affect the remaining operations. Last year's records show the following information for the fabricating department for 12,000 units:

	Total costs	Allocation to engine units
Direct materials	$1,200,000	$125,000
Direct labor	700,000	160,000
Indirect labor	90,000	30,000
Utilities	24,000	6,000
Depreciation	25,000	6,250
Property taxes and insurance	32,000	8,000
Miscellaneous supplies	18,000	2,000

The finishing department incurred $60,000 of direct labor costs on the engine units. The basis for overhead allocation in this department is 25 percent of direct labor cost.

If the engine units are not manufactured, the direct labor cost in the finishing department will be eliminated. Machinery can be sold at its book value of $50,000 and the proceeds invested to yield 10 percent. The machinery has a remaining useful life of eight years with no estimated salvage value. Sale of the machinery will reduce property taxes and insurance by $2,000 a year. Purchasing the units will result in shipping costs of $2 a unit, and receiving, handling, and inspection costs of $6,000 annually.

Required:

a. Compare the total annual cost of engine units if they are manufactured to their annual cost if purchased. Ignore income taxes.
b. Without regard to your answer in *a*, assume that the annual cost of engine units if manufactured or purchased was $425,000 each. Compute the annual net cash outflow (ignoring income taxes) if:
   (1) Engine units are manufactured.
   (2) Engine units are purchased.
c. Explain the working capital requirements that should be considered in deciding whether to make or buy.

P17–8. Payoff table and expected value of perfect information

The management of Elizabeth Sorenson Company is undecided about the most profitable means of investing a sum of money. After eliminating a few alternatives that would not fully meet company objectives, they feel the following actions are feasible:

1. Hire a public relations director to improve the image of the company. Management believes that the director's efforts could cause a $60,000 income increase if an excellent market prevails; a $40,000 income increase if there is an average market; and a $15,000 loss in a poor market.
2. Hire a team of inspectors who will initiate quality control procedures that will improve the reputation of the company's technology. If this is successful, a sales price will be warranted which will result in a $80,000 income increase in an excellent market; a $45,000 income increase in an average market; and a $25,000 loss in a poor market.
3. Manufacture a complementary product which it is felt will also increase sales for the present product. With these operations, income is expected to increase $90,000 in an excellent market and $70,000 in an average market, with a $30,000 loss resulting in a poor market.

The current assessment of the probabilities for each environmental condition are: excellent—30 percent; average—60 percent; and poor—10 percent.

Required:

a. Prepare a payoff table for each of the alternatives available.
b. Determine the opportunity cost of the alternatives available.
c. Determine the expected value of the alternative actions being considered.
d. Evaluate the alternatives, indicating the course of action you would advise the company to take.
e. A consultant can be hired to study the situation. How much should the company be willing to pay for perfect information?

P17–9.   Evaluating alternatives

Three different products, U–1, U–2, and U–3, are produced by the Kathy Freeman Company. All fixed costs are allocated as follows: fixed cost of units sold according to various allocation bases, such as square footage for factory rent and machine-hours for repairs; fixed general and administrative expenses based on a percentage of revenues.

Pro forma income statements by product line are presented for next year.

	U–1	U–2	U–3	Total
Sales (units)	20,000	400,000	200,000	620,000
Revenue	$1,000,000	$800,000	$650,000	$2,450,000
Variable cost of units sold	$ 200,000	$250,000	$175,000	$ 625,000
Fixed cost of units sold	350,000	325,000	200,000	875,000
Gross margin	$ 450,000	$225,000	$275,000	$ 950,000
Variable general and administrative expenses	175,000	200,000	52,500	427,500
Fixed general and administrative expenses	120,000	96,000	78,000	294,000
Income (loss) before taxes	$ 155,000	$ (71,000)	$144,500	$ 228,500

Because management is concerned about the loss for U–2, it has taken under advisement two alternative courses of action, either of which should remedy the situation.

First alternative—discontinue producting U–2. This will have several effects. Some of the machinery used in the production of U–2 can be sold at scrap value. The proceeds will just cover the removal costs. Without this machinery, however, fixed costs allocated to U–2 will be reduced by $55,000 a year. The remaining fixed costs allocated to U–2 include $130,000 annual rent expense. The space used for production of U–2 can be rented to another firm for $135,000 annually. The selling prices of U–1 and U–3 will remain constant. U–3 production and revenues should increase by 30 percent.

Second alternative—purchase some new machinery for the production of U–2. This will require an initial cash outlay of $500,000. The new machinery will reduce total variable costs (cost of units sold and general and administrative expenses) for U–2 to 50 percent of revenues. Total fixed costs allocated to U–2 will increase to $450,000. No additional fixed costs will be allocated to U–1 and U–3.

Required:

Analyze the effects of each alternative on total projected income before taxes.

P17–10.   Cost of alternatives

Top management of Walley Company is very interested in converting as many of the company's records to microfilm as possible. However, any additional cost or cost saving resulting from the adoption of microfilm must be identified before the project can be approved.

The general accounting supervisor has made a study which reveals that the microfilm application will require two independent microfilming systems. The first is a source document microfilming system in which documents such as vendor invoices, billing documents, and other accounting-related documents will be reduced to ¼₄ of the original size and stored on rolls of film in the department using the documents.

The second is a computer-output microfilm system in which computer-generated reports would be produced on 4 by 6 inch film, called microfiche, thus eliminating some of the bulky hard copy of the report.

The following equipment must be purchased for the microfilming systems; a life of six years is assumed. (The equipment can also be leased, but these data have not been obtained.)

	Purchase price	Maintenance contract per year
Source document system:		
One camera.	$ 3,438	$ 325
Two readers.	2,350	230
One reader/printer	2,140	220
Total	$ 7,928	$ 775
Computer-output system:		
Seven 75% viewers	$ 1,155	$ 100
Four 100% viewers.	960	50
Two 60% viewers	230	24
One viewer/printer	925	70
Total	$ 3,270	$ 244
Total equipment	$11,198	$1,019

Investigation by the accounting supervisor revealed the following comparison of monthly costs.

Computer subsystem	Number of reports	Present cost	Computer-output microfilm proposed cost	
			Hard copy	Microfilm
Master files	9	$ 57.42	$ 0.20	$ 41.84
Sales	15	194.12	77.84	153.63
Inventory.	8	27.00	4.31	235.56
Fixed assets	24	73.05	3.94	76.75
Accounts payable	6	42.72	3.87	63.20
General ledger	23	148.60	74.76	193.02
Billing	2	1,596.00	—	1,066.00
Total	87	$2,138.91	$164.92	$1,830.00

In addition, the supplies used in operating this system, including photocopies of the reports, are estimated to cost $360 per year. The source document system film and processing will require 402 rolls of film for microfilm storage. The film cost per roll is expected to be $8.37.

However, microfilming will result in the annual saving of 275 storage boxes that will not be needed; storage boxes cost $1.15 each. Each box requires 1.95 square feet; annual storage cost is estimated to be $3 per square foot.

Required:

a.   Determine the difference in annual costs if the microfilming system is adopted.

b.   What other factors should be considered?

c. List any additional analysis that top management may need to make a decision on the formal request for approval of the project.

d. What decision would you advise management to make regarding this project?

P17–11.   Differential and opportunity cost of taking additional order

Jean Company builds regular and deluxe truck oil filters. A customer has asked whether the company could produce 2,000 super filters. Since management feel that this may be a one-time order, they do not wish to expand plant facilities; instead, they have evaluated the requirements of the super filter and find that if they cut regular filter production by one fourth and deluxe filters by one third, the super filter order can be completed in one year.

The customer has agreed to pay $12 for each super filter at the end of the year when the entire order is completed. The engineering staff of Jean estimates that the direct material cost will be $5 per unit and the direct labor cost will be $3 per unit. In addition to using the machines presently located in the regular and deluxe facilities, super filter production will require a special machine costing $5,000. Management expects to be able to sell the machine after one year for $2,400. Cash will be required initially for the purchase. Jean management expects to sell an investment currently earning 10 percent interest to provide these funds. It is expected that the special machine purchased for super filter production will require $515 annual power expense in addition to the power required for the regular and deluxe filter machines that will be devoted to super filter production.

Rent and the other utilities, heating and lighting, are allocated on the basis of floor space. The accountant furnishes you with a portion of last year's financial statements, shown below:

	Regular	Deluxe
Sales.	$8,000	$6,000
Direct material	$2,400	$1,500
Direct labor	1,600	900
Factory overhead:		
Indirect labor	300	150
Depreciation.	500	450
Power	400	600
Rent.	200	60
Other utilities	552	90
Total expenses	$5,952	$3,750
Operating income	$2,048	$2,250

Required:

a. What is the net differential cost of the 2,000 super filter order?

b. What is the opportunity cost of taking the order?

c. What is the full cost of the super filter order?

d. Should Jean Company accept the order? Support your decision with quantitative as well as qualitative findings

P17–12.   Make-or-buy decision

The Marketing Research Department of the Chester Company has developed a unique idea which they feel will appeal to children. They are presently packaging their chewing gum in a simple paper wrapper in a stick form. They are considering processing the gum in individual balls and placing them in a decorated plastic bank. For the child to obtain a gum ball, a nickle must be deposited in the bank.

The company will be able to make the plastic banks in the present facilities. It presently owns a machine which can be converted to processing the banks. The machine cost $100,000 and is being depreciated on a straight-line basis over a five-year period. The only other fixed costs to be allocated to the production of chewing gum and banks will be $10,000, which represents a portion of the company's present fixed costs.

The cost accounting department estimates that 100,000 banks can be sold if they are able to place these on the market before the Christmas season begins. Estimates of the costs including chewing gum and the banks have been developed as follows:

Direct material. . . . . $1.25 per bank with gum inside
Direct labor. . . . . 0.80 per bank with gum inside
Total overhead . . . . _0.90_ per bank* with gum inside
$2.95 per bank with gum inside

*The overhead does include the machine's depreciation and allocated fixed costs.

A plastic specialties company has approached the Chester Company and offered to supply the banks for $0.40 per unit. Based on their study, Chester feels that if it buys the banks and merely puts gum balls in them, the firm can cut the above direct material cost by 6 percent, variable overhead by 15 percent, and direct labor by 25 percent.

Required:

a. Should the Chester Company purchase the plastic banks or manufacture them in the company's own facilities?

b. Assume that after the Marketing Department conducts more extensive tests, they feel that since they will be able to sell the banks through a variety of distribution channels, 150,000 banks can be sold. The company's present facilities will not be able to exceed the production of 100,000 banks. The company must rent a nearby empty building for $20,000 and equipment for $6,300 to handle the extra production. How would you advise management to obtain the plastic banks under these conditions?

c. What qualitative factors would you advise the company to consider before making a decision?

P17–13. Payoff table, expected value of alternatives, and perfect information

A large sum of money has recently been received by the Lawrence Curbo Company through the estate of a former stockholder. Management is undecided about the most profitable means of investing this money. The Accounting Department has worked with the Engineering and Production Departments, and the Market Research Department is evaluating the alternatives available. After eliminating a few alternatives that would not fully meet company objectives, they feel the following actions are feasible:

1. Hire sales training personnel who will upgrade the selling techniques of the marketing force. Management believes that income will increase $100,000 if an excellent market prevails and $90,000 in an average market, and there would be a $20,000 loss in a poor market.

2. Upgrade their present product by employing skilled engineers to improve the quality of the motors contained in the product. With these operations, a sales price will be warranted which is expected to result in a $200,000 income increase in an

excellent market, a $125,000 income increase in an average market, and a $140,000 loss in a poor market.

3. Manufacture a complementary product which it is felt will also increase sales for the present product. Forecasts indicate a $160,000 increase in income in an excellent market, a $120,000 income increase in an average market, and a $50,000 loss in a poor market.

An assessment of the probabilities for each environmental condition are: excellent—40 percent; average—15 percent; and poor—45 percent.

Required:

a. Prepare a payoff table for each of the alternatives available.
b. Determine the opportunity cost of the alternatives available.
c. Determine the expected value of the alternative actions being considered.
d. Evaluate the alternatives, indicating the course of action you would advise the company to take.
e. If perfect advance information can be obtained, how much should the company be willing to pay for it?

CASES

C17–1.   Differential margin under various volumes in a nonprofit organization

Harry Moss, administrator of Las Vegas General Hospital, requests your assistance in preparing a cost analysis for a proposed addition to the telemetry unit. The hospital presently has 10 telemetry units in operation on a 40-bed floor. A telemetry unit is used to monitor patients who have had heart attacks or cardiac problems. This unit allows a patient to move about freely in that particular hospital wing without being confined to a hospital bed. A radio-controlled device attached to the patient monitors the cardiac system. The present 10-unit telemetry monitoring system is located in the nursing station, which can accommodate the proposed 8 additional units without renovation.

Telemetry units represent a step down unit from cardiac intensive care rooms. Not only do telemetry units offer patients more freedom, but there is a considerable cost saving. Cardiac care rooms average $300 per day, while the telemetry unit charge is the regular room charge of $120 plus an additional $40 to $60 daily.

Expected revenue.   Hospital management is undecided whether to charge $40 or $60 differential a day for the proposed unit. Also, there is lack of consensus among the managers regarding the rate of utilization. The expected range is from 40 percent to 60 percent. A 10 percent allowance for bad debts and insurance discount is estimated.

Expected cost.   Space for the unit will be obtained by converting a wing of the hospital presently being used for medical-surgical patients; the regular room rate is charged for this wing. Equipment total cost is expected to be $44,570; the life is estimated to be only five years due to technological changes: Straight-line depreciation will be used.

The administrator indicates that you are to determine total cost for the five-year period for each cost element and then divide by five years to obtain an average for the five-year period.

Service contract costs for routine maintenance and service call costs for overtime, labor, and parts are expected to be $3,060 and $2,400 respectively in year 2, with an increase of 10 percent per year thereafter for inflation; no such costs are expected for year 1 since the equipment will be under warranty during this time. Costs of supplies will be $2,800 for the first year, with a 12 percent annual increase thereafter due to inflation and aging of the equipment. One registered nurse earning $14,000 annually, and two licensed practical nurses, each earning $8,000 annually, are needed for the eight-bed unit. Personnel cost in the hospital industry has increased 8 percent annually in the last few years.

Required:

a. Determine differential margin that will be received and the percentage return on equipment using a:
   (1) $40 charge per day and a 40 percent use rate.
   (2) $40 charge per day and a 50 percent use rate.
   (3) $40 charge per day and a 60 percent use rate.
   (4) $60 charge per day and a 40 percent use rate.
   (5) $60 charge per day and a 60 percent use rate.
b. Advise management as to the alternative to choose.
c. List other factors that should be considered before installation of the unit.

C17–2.   Manufacture in-house or use outside manufacturer (CMA adapted)

Ace Corporation has been a leading manufacturer of cash registers and accounting and proofing machines for almost 50 years. Much of Ace's success can be attributed to an extensive and excellent marketing organization and its reputation for reliable business machines within the retailing and banking industries.

Until the 1960s, Ace's equipment was primarily mechanical with few electronic components. However, many of the mechanical components in business machines were replaced by electronic units in the 1960s; these electronic components were cheaper, more efficient, and provided additional machine flexibility. Ace's management has been reluctant to switch from its old-line mechanical machines to new electronic systems because of the heavy investment in engineering development and manufacturing facilities for mechanical systems. Competitive pressures from new electronic machines have caused a rapid deterioration in Ace's market share and profit margins. Consequently, management has decided to initiate a program to introduce new lines of electronic business machines as replacements for its current mechanical models.

Although this new electronic equipment will be introduced several years after the competitors' electronic equipment, management believes that further deterioration in Ace's market position can be prevented by capitalizing on some of Ace's strong points. Ace has a superior sales force which has maintained good relations with the retail and banking industries. Traditionally, Ace's customers have replaced or upgraded their old equipment with Ace equipment. Ace's new line can incorporate unique features that the competition lacks, thereby making it more attractive to customers.

Developing new products at Ace has primarily been the responsibility of the Development and Engineering Research Department (DER) in conjunction with the Marketing and Manufacturing Departments. DER is primarily responsible for developing product specifications, building and field-testing prototype products, and evaluating any changes in manufacturing facilities which may be required. Once a product is approved for sale and production, it is released to the Manufacturing Department for production.

Numerous changes have to be made in all three departments. For example, DER needs additional strengths in electronics engineering. Marketing needs to reorient its sales force. Manufacturing needs to retool extensively and retrain its maintenance and service personnel. Much of the present manufacturing equipment and inventory of unfinished goods will become obsolete.

Another option available to Ace's management is to approach an outside equipment manufacturer to produce part or all of the new equipment. In this case, Ace would determine the specifications for the new equipment and then have it engineered and/or manufactured, wholly or in part, by outside firms. The equipment would be marketed under the Ace label.

Management has asked its staff to recommend a suitable strategy for transforming Ace Corporation from a supplier of primarily mechanical machines to a company offering electronic systems. The staff has specifically been asked to study the ramifications of Ace: (1) developing and manufacturing new equipment in-house, or (2) approaching an outside manufacturer to produce equipment which would then be marketed under the Ace label, according to Ace's specifications. Management has instructed its staff to consider the broad financial, technological, organizational, and market conditions and constraints in developing its strategy.

The current statement of financial position for Ace Corporation is presented below. Selected five-year averages for the most recent five years are as follows:

	Percent
Operating margin (before taxes)	12
Annual increase in net income	11
Return on sales	5
Return on investment	7
Return on equity.	16

ACE CORPORATION
Statement of Financial Position
May 31, 19–
($ millions)

Current assets:	
Cash and equivalents	$ 15
Accounts receivable (net)	148
Inventories:	
Materials and supplies.	25
Work in process.	14
Finished goods	56
Prepaid expenses and deposits.	10
Total current assets.	$268
Plant and equipment:	
Land.	$ 4
Buildings.	69
Machinery and equipment	140
Construction in progress	5
Accumulated depreciation	(101)
Equipment on rental (net)	8
Other assets (net).	18
Total assets	$411

Current liabilities:
Notes and loans payable. . . . . $ 15
Accounts payable.   42
Accrued payroll and other expenses   37
Current maturities of long-term debt.   3
Income taxes   14

    Total current liabilities $111
Long-term debt:
9¼% sinking fund debentures (due in 10 years) . . . . $ 25
8½% senior notes (due in 14 years)   60
Other long-term debt.   36
Deferred income taxes   15

    Total liabilities. $247

Stockholders' equity
Common stock (par value, $1.00) . . . . $ 9
Additional paid-in capital.   11
Retained earnings.   144

    Total stockholders' equity $164
Total liabilities and stockholders' equity $411

Required:

Identify and explain the important issues and questions which should be addressed and considered by the staff of Ace Corporation in recommending whether the company should develop and manufacture the new electronic equipment products in-house or approach an outside manufacturer. Structure your answer in terms of:

a. Financial considerations.
b. Technological considerations.
c. Organizational considerations.
d. Market considerations.

C17–3. Differential contribution with hospital capacity; payoff table

Last year, administrators of Memphis General Hospital converted an unused wing of the hospital to a 12-bed ambulatory surgery unit (ASU). An ASU is utilized by patients whose conditions require minor surgery; these patients enter the hospital early on the day of surgery and are usually discharged late that afternoon. It was hoped that this arrangement would relieve the delay for elective surgery experienced by some patients that was caused by the high occupancy of the medical-surgical floors. The creation of the ASU was also intended to result in a higher turnover of the surgery suites or operating rooms. Hospital administrators believed that there were sufficient surgery suites to handle an increased volume per day, but that a problem resulted from too few rooms for patients.

Administrators hoped that there would be not only higher utilization of the operating room facilities, but additional benefits to the patient as well. Patient costs should be reduced by the elimination of unnecessary days of hospitalization, even though there would be no reduction in the quality of care delivered in the ASU as compared to that delivered to other patients. This elimination of unnecessary hospitalization could be partially accomplished by preadmission testing. In addition, there would be a psychological benefit to the patient who was able to spend the pre- and postoperative period at home with minimal disruption of schedule and habits. Physicians would also save time because fewer hours would be spent on pre- and postoperative rounds.

Management's objective was to reduce the bed shortage through better utilization of hospital beds. Reducing the stay of ambulatory patients would free beds for the more acutely ill patients.

The ASU was opened for 5½ days per week, excluding holidays, resulting in 281 possible days of usage. Cost to the patient was reduced by an average one and one-half days of hospital stay, with the majority of the other charges remaining the same. Management was satisfied that the quality of care rendered to ambulatory surgery patients was the same as that given to other patients. However, even though 1,360 patients using this facility resulted in 1½ days saved, or a total of 2,040 days (1360 × 1½ days), better utilization of hospital beds was not achieved because of the low occupancy rate of the ASU. In addition, the objective of increasing utilization of the operating room facilities was only partially attained because of this low occupancy rate. Consequently, hospital administration is considering alternative courses of action for the wing. After much discussion, the following alternatives were deemed worthy of further analysis:

1. Retain the present 12-bed ASU as private rooms with the hope that, as physicians become more accustomed to this facility, utilization will increase. Management is uncertain that the excess space could be utilized in other ways.
2. Convert the wing to a combination of (a) a 16-bed medical-surgical floor consisting of 12 private rooms and one 4-bed ward, and (b) one 4-bed ward used as an ASU.
3. Convert the wing completely to a medical-surgical floor with 12 private rooms and two 4-bed wards.
4. Convert the wing to a psychiatric floor or a combination psychiatric and medical-surgical floor.

After the initial study, management determined that converting the wing to a psychiatric floor would not be feasible because of the potential increase in problems associated with another psychiatric floor and the restrictive admission laws. If the wing were converted to a combined psychiatric and medical-surgical floor, it would be difficult to admit medical-surgical or other categories of patients to the floor, considering the nature of the nursing personnel and routine on the floor.

Management asks that you ignore indirect expenses in your analysis, since they are convinced that inclusion of these expenses would not materially affect the results. Instead, they prefer the use of differential analysis. Your review of the records and interviews with hospital personnel yields the following for each alternative.

Retain ASU. Gross revenue from the ASU would be $111,276 at 100 percent occupancy; however, management does not believe it is realistic to prepare an analysis based on this level. Instead, they can foresee occupancy ranging from 30 to 80 percent of full capacity. Discussion with numerous hospital employees convinces you that the probability of 80 percent occupancy is 5 percent; of 70 percent occupancy, 10 percent; 60 percent occupancy, 20 percent; 50 percent and 40 percent occupancy, 30 percent each; and 30 percent occupancy 5 percent. Gross revenue is expected to have a direct relationship to occupancy.

Bad debts and courtesy discounts are expected to average 4 percent of gross revenue. Total salaries for 80 percent occupancy are forecasted to be $41,787; for 60 and 70 percent occupancy, $38,037 each; for less than 60 percent occupancy, $34,287. F.I.C.A. and pensions average 11.054 percent of total salaries. Since supplies and other expenses contain an element of fixed and semivariable expenses, they cannot be expressed as a percentage of gross revenue. After much analysis, you determine supplies and other expenses to be: 80 percent occupancy—$3,483; 70 percent occupancy—$3,209; 60 percent occupancy—$2,959; 50 percent occupancy—$2,709; 40 percent occupancy—$2,459; and 30 percent occupancy—$2,259.

Medical-Surgical and ASU Wing. For simplicity, management indicates that you are to assume a constant 75 percent occupancy of the 4-bed ASU ward, open 281 days a year, resulting in gross revenues of $27,819 regardless of the utilization rate of the medical-surgical beds. At 100 percent occupancy, assuming seven days a week utilization, gross revenue on the medical-surgical unit is estimated to be $346,020; a direct relationship between medical-surgical occupancy and revenue is assumed. The probability of 90 percent occupancy is 20 percent; of 85 percent occupancy, 50 percent; of 80 percent occupancy, 20 percent; and of 75 percent occupancy, 10 percent.

The bad debt and courtesy discount rate is higher on the medical-surgical floor than the 4 percent rate for the ASU unit because emergency patients are admitted who may not have insurance and may not be able to pay. ASU patients tend to undergo an elective form of surgical procedure, so the hospital's insurance department has more time to verify insurance coverage and establish realistic payment schedules for patients whose insurance is inadequate. Past records indicate that a 15 percent bad debt and discount rate can be expected for the medical-surgical unit.

Total salaries for this alternative (2 in the list above) at 100 percent capacity are expected to be $137,660; $100,000 of these salaries are fixed. F.I.C.A. and pensions average 10 percent of total salaries; this is slightly lower than for the ASU in alternative 1 because of the differences in salary ranges. For simplicity, assume supplies and other expenses will average 3 percent of gross revenue.

Medical-Surgical Wing. If conversion to a medical-surgical floor is made, $423,400 in gross revenue is expected if 100 percent occupancy is achieved. However, management does not anticipate such a high utilization rate. In fact, they estimate the probability of a 90 percent occupancy is 20 percent; 85 percent occupancy, 60 percent; and 80 percent occupancy and 75 percent occupancy, 10 percent each. Gross revenue is expected to have a direct relationship to occupancy.

Bad debts and courtesy discounts are expected to be 17 percent of gross revenue. Total salaries at 100 percent capacity are expected to be $150,000; $100,000 of these salaries are fixed. F.I.C.A. and pensions average 10 percent of total salaries. Assume supplies and other expenses are expected to average 3 percent of gross revenue.

Required:

(Round to whole dollars.)

a. Prepare estimated differential contribution if the ASU is retained; use occupancy ranges of 80, 70, 60, 50, 40, and 30 percent.
b. Prepare a payoff table using the capacity utilization probabilities given for retaining the ASU.
c. Prepare estimated differential contribution if conversion is made to a medical-surgery unit and four-bed ASU; use occupancy rates of 75 percent for the ASU ward and ranges of 90, 85, 80, and 75 percent for the medical-surgical unit.
d. Prepare a payoff table for the alternative analyzed in c.
e. Prepare an estimated differential contribution if conversion is made to a medical-surgical floor; use occupancy ranges of 90, 85, 80, and 75 percent.
f. Prepare a payoff table for the alternative analyzed in e.
g. Indicate which alternative you would advise management to choose.
h. Give some limitations of your analysis.

PART V

Quantitative models for planning and control

18

Gantt charts, PERT, and decision tree analysis

Increasingly, cost accountants are devoting more attention to furnishing management and other interested parties with data that can be used in cost control and planning rather than emphasizing cost accumulation and determination. Cost accounting now involves the predictive ability of data rather than emphasis solely on the past. Accounting control models are being integrated within the cost accounting system to monitor actual results against plans so that feedback for corrective action is provided. This involvement in managerial planning and control has led to the use of Gantt charts, Program Evaluation Review Technique (PERT), and decision tree analysis.

GANTT CHARTS

One aid to planning that is simple to prepare is a *Gantt chart*, which is a bar chart with time shown on the horizontal axis and the duration of the task represented as a bar running from the starting date to the ending date. Gantt charts are mainly used in industry as a method of recording progress toward goals. On a given date, a Gantt chart easily shows how expected performance of a specific task compares with actual performance, which tasks should be in progress on a specific date, and how close to completion a task should be on a given date.

Control device

Gantt charts are a control technique because they readily allow the comparison of scheduled production and actual production so that variations can be identified and corrective action initiated. As shown in Exhibit 18–1, a Gantt chart involves identifying and showing the sequence of activities and scheduling the work by periods. The Y-axis of a Gantt chart represents the tasks or activities to be performed, while the X-axis represents the time available for work. Work scheduled by periods within the departments is represented by the horizontal broken line. Work unfinished or carried over from previous periods is shown by the short vertical broken lines. The heavy solid bar line is a summation of the individual horizontal broken lines and represents cumulative work to be performed.

In Exhibit 18–1, time is divided into weeks for each month. Task A is scheduled for the first and third weeks of January, the middle of February, and the last week of March. This scheduled work is shown for Task A by the four horizontal lines. When added together, these lines represent four weeks of cumulative work, and this is indicated by the heavy horizontal line. Upon examination, ·the chart shows that additional jobs could be scheduled during the second and fourth weeks of January. There is no backlog of work to be completed on Task A, because there are no short vertical lines as there are for Task B.

EXHIBIT 18–1

Gantt chart—Each block represents one workweek beginning on Monday and ending on Friday

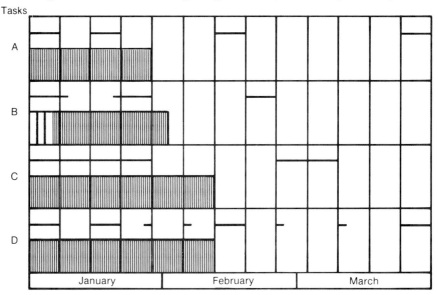

Advantages of Gantt charts

Gantt charts provide a visual display of planned utilization of facilities so that appropriate revisions can be made to obtain better use of facilities. After examining when work is scheduled and illustrated by the use of the horizontal broken lines, additional tasks can be planned for the time periods represented by breaks in the horizontal lines. The heavy bold line representing cumulative work assists managers in computing total work-hours required for each task as well as in scheduling repairs and maintenance. Gantt charts also alert managers to areas in which large variations in planned and actual performance exist so that resources can be reallocated.

NETWORK MODELS

While Gantt charts are simple systematic tools for planning, they fail to indicate which tasks must be completed before others begin, because all activities are arranged vertically on a Gantt chart. To provide for this aspect of planning, network models have been developed. One of the more sophisticated planning and control devices developed in this context is called Program Evaluation Review Technique (PERT).

Program Evaluation Review Technique

Program Evaluation Review Technique (PERT) is a systematic procedure for using network analysis to plan and measure actual progress toward scheduled events. PERT was developed by the military for the Polaris program to aid in controlling this large-scale project. Generally, PERT is used for exceptional projects in which managerial experience is limited. The *critical path method (CPM)* developed by industry is closely related to PERT.

As illustrated in Exhibit 18–2, PERT diagrams are free-form, network diagrams showing each activity as an arrow between events. A *network for PERT-Time analysis* contains a sequence of arrows showing interrelationships among activities with time being the fundamental element in these activities. An *event* is represented by a circle and indicates the beginning or completion of a task. Events are discrete points which consume no resources; they are numbered for identification. *Activities* are represented by arrows and are tasks to be accomplished to go from one event to the next. An activity consumes resources and has a duration over time starting at one event and ending with the occurrence of the next event. Activities are shown from left to right in the necessary order of their accomplishment. All the activities leading to an event must be completed before an event can occur. This is the reason that the event at the head of the arrow should have a higher number, if possible, than an event at the end of the arrow.

EXHIBIT 18–2

Network for PERT-Time

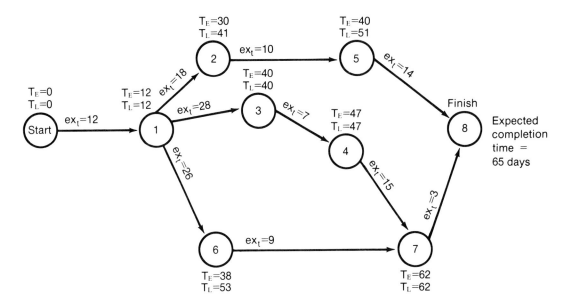

Expected activity time.   After drawing the network diagram, an estimate is made of the time needed to complete each activity. The expected activity time is based on the 1-4-1 three-estimate method, which is a weighted average of the shortest time, the average time, and the longest time. The shortest and the longest times are weighted one, and the average time is weighted 4. The formula for time estimations is:

$$ex_t = 1/6 \text{ (optimistic time + 4 most likely time + pessimistic time)}.$$

Only the expected time (ex_t) is shown in Exhibit 18–2; to illustrate, the expected time of the activity beginning at 6 and ending at 7 is computed as follows:

$$
\begin{aligned}
\text{optimistic estimate} &= 6 \text{ days} \\
\text{most likely estimate} &= 9 \text{ days} \\
\text{pessimistic estimate} &= 12 \text{ days} \\
\frac{6 + 4(9) + 12}{6} &= 9 \text{ days } ex_t
\end{aligned}
$$

The expected times for the other activities are computed in a similar manner and written on the upper sides of the arrows in Exhibit 18–2. Rather than expressing time in days, the time estimates could be expressed in one-week units.

Critical path.   With the use of a PERT network, the longest duration for completion of the entire project can be determined. This longest path is referred to as the *critical path*. The total time of the project can be shortened only by shortening the critical path. The reason this path is critical is that if any activity on the path takes longer than expected, the entire project will be delayed. Every network has at least one critical path. To find the critical path, the cumulative expected activity time along each of the paths is computed. In Exhibit 18–2, the cumulative paths are:

Paths	Cumulative expected activity time (in days)
0–1–2–5–8	12 + 18 + 10 + 14 = 54
0–1–3–4–7–8. . . .	12 + 28 + 7 + 15 + 3 = 65*
0–1–6–7–8	12 + 26 + 9 + 3 = 50

*Critical path with cumulative activity time of 65 days.

Slack.   Paths which are not critical have *slack time*, while activities along the critical path do not. The slack associated with an event is the amount of time the event can be delayed without affecting the completion of the project. The larger the amount of slack, the less critical the activity, and vice versa. Slack is the difference between the latest allowable time that an event may be completed and the earliest expected time. Exhibit 18–2 also indicates the *earliest completion time*. The earliest completion time (T_E) is the cumulative time of that event. In Exhibit 18–2, the T_E of event 6 is 38 days (12 + 26), the duration of activity 0–1 and 1–6. The T_E for activity 7 is more complex because it has two cumulative paths, one along path 0–1–3–4–7 (62 days) and the other along the path 0–1–6–7 (47 days). When an event has more than one cumulative path, the longest completion time of any path is the T_E for that event. This means the earliest completion time for event 7 is 62 days. The T_E for all other events is indicated in Exhibit 18–2.

After computing the earliest completion time for all events, the *latest completion time* (T_L) is determined. The T_L on the critical path equals the T_E because there is no slack on this path. The other events' latest completion times are computed by working backwards through the network. For instance, the T_L for event 5 is 51 days, the latest completion time for event 8, the event that follows it, and the 14 days of activity 5–8 (65 − 14 = 51 days). If an event has several activities flowing from it, there may be several latest completion times. However, the minimum of these times is the T_L for that event.

Slack now can be computed using the following formula:

$$S = T_L - T_E$$

The slack at event 2 is 11 days ($S = 41 - 30 = 11$ days). This allows management to delay event 2 up to 11 days without delaying the overall project's expected completion time of 65 days. However, if a noncritical activity uses more than its expected time, the slack time for subsequent events must be recomputed. For example, if activity 1–2 takes 20 days instead of the estimated 18 days, event 5's slack time has been reduced 2 days, for a total slack of 9 days.

Flexibility with slack.   Slack introduces flexibility into the network because it serves as a buffer for events not located on the critical path. When time lags appear on the critical path, materials, labor, and equipment that are transferable can be applied to the problem areas. However, managers must be alert to the effect of these transfers on other paths, because they have made little or no progress if transfers in turn create problems on other paths.

Crashing.   Not only does information about slack time allow management to continually monitor a project's status, but these data may serve as a guide in rescheduling tasks so that the overall project's completion time is shortened. In Exhibit 18–2, event 2 has 11 days of slack. If these days represent idle resources, it may be possible to utilize these resources in critical events and cut the 65-day completion time of the project. Of course, there are limits to transferring idle resources, depending on the task's specifications. Activity time may also be reduced by hiring more labor, overtime, or acquiring more equipment. These efforts designed to complete the project ahead of schedule are referred to as *crashing*. However, when crashing is used, the project's variable costs will increase. Crashing the network means finding the minimum cost for completing the project in minimum time so that an optimum trade-off between time and cost is achieved. Determining the appropriate trade-off is referred to as *PERT-Cost analysis.*

PERT-Cost analysis

PERT-Cost analysis of the trade-off between time and cost is essential in studying the cost effectiveness of crashing. The same type of network illustrated in Exhibit 18–2 for use in PERT-Time is employed in PERT-Cost. However, two estimated times, a crash time and a normal expected time, are included for each activity. In Exhibit 18–3, the expected time (ex_t) from Exhibit 18–2 is indicated along with the crash time (cr_t) for each activity. If the activity is as shown in 3–4 and 7–8 in Exhibit 18–3 and cannot be crashed, there is no difference in these times and the crash time can be omitted.

The costs of completing the activity under normal expected conditions and under crash conditions are estimated. A comparison of these two cost projections results in the determination of the *differential, or incremental, crash cost* for each activity that can be crashed. For example, the expected cost of activity 2–5 is $26,000 requiring 10 days; if, instead, the activity is completed in 8 days, the cost is projected to be $32,000, resulting in a $3,000 differential cost per day ($32,000 − $26,000/10 − 8 days). In Exhibit 18–3, differential crash cost per day is written below the arrow for each activity. Note that activity 3–4 and 7–8 have no differential crash cost because neither of these activities can be crashed.

In PERT-Cost analysis of the trade-off between time and cost, the current

EXHIBIT 18–3

Network for PERT-Cost

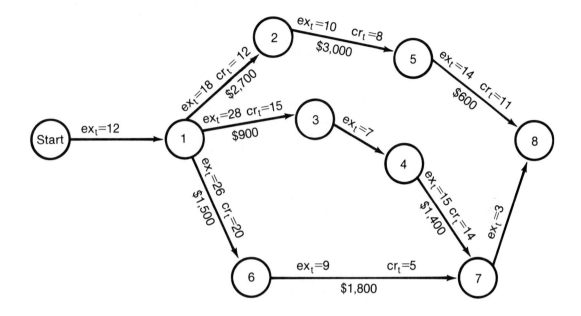

status of the project is studied. Assume that the project illustrated in Exhibits 18–2 and 18–3 has a normal cost of $200,000, as shown below, if no crashing occurs.

No activities crashed

Paths	Cumulative expected days
0–1–2–5–8	54
0–1–3–4–7–8	65*
0–1–6–7–8	50

*65 days for project completion
$200,000 project cost.

In studying trade-offs, the critical activity to be crashed is the one with the lowest differential cost. Even though activity 5–8 has the lowest differential cost ($600) in the network, it is not on the critical path and crashing it will not shorten the overall project's completion time until another activity is crashed first. Crashing activity 5–8 would only increase slack time from 11 to 14 days. Instead, activity 1–3, with a differential cost of $900, is the one to crash because its differential cost is lowest of those activities on the critical path. However, it can be shortened only 11 days before path 0–1–2–5–8 also becomes critical. This results in the following status analysis showing that project time has been reduced by 11 days, but cost has increased $9,900 (11 days × $900). Now we have two critical paths and the schedule can be shortened only by reducing the length of both of them.

First iteration

Activity 1–3 crashed

Paths	Cumulative expected days
0–1–2–5–8	54*
0–1–3–4–7–8	54*
0–1–6–7–8	50

*54 days for project completion
$200,000 + (11 × $900)
= $209,900 project cost.

Second iteration. The next iteration is to shorten activity 5–8, with the lowest differential cost on path 0–1–2–5–8, two days since this activity can be jointly shortened with activity 1–3 by two more days.

Activity 1–3 and 5–8
crashed two days each

Paths	Cumulative expected days
0–1–2–5–8	52*
0–1–3–4–7–8	52*
0–1–6–7–8	50

*52 days for project completion
$209,900 + 2($900) + 2($600)
= $212,900 project cost.

Third iteration. The next iteration involves shortening activities 5–8 and 4–7 each one day. By crashing these two activities, overall project cost has increased with an extra day saved, as illustrated below:

Activities 5–8 and 4–7
crashed one day each

Paths	Cumulative expected days
0–1–2–5–8	51*
0–1–3–4–7–8	51*
0–1–6–7–8	50

*51 days for project completion
$212,900 + $600 + $1,400
= $214,900 project cost.

Even though path 0–1–2–5–8 can be further crashed, overall project time cannot be reduced because there is no further reduction in path 0–1–3–4–7–8; the remaining activities along this path cannot be crashed. This results in a final trade-off of crashing three activities and finishing the project in 51 days, or 14 days earlier, at a minimum crash cost of $14,900, or total project cost of $214,900.

In deciding whether the company should proceed at the normal pace or attempt a crash program, the total differential cost of the crash program ($14,900 in our example) should be compared with the cost savings or benefits of the crash program. If the contribution margin earned is expected to be $1,200 a day, then the crash program should be undertaken because the $16,800 differential earnings ($1,200 × 14 days) exceed the $14,900 differential cost. If, however, the additional contribution to profits expected to be received by completing the project early does not exceed $14,900, the normal schedule should be followed.

Constant monitoring of progress. Expected and actual time and cost may be displayed on the PERT-Cost network so that immediate attention can be directed to slippage in time of the activities on the critical path. Comparison of actual with budgeted time and costs can help management decide which activities need investigation and corrective action. Time slippage in noncritical activities, however, may not warrant managerial study because of available slack.

DECISION TREE ANALYSIS

Another method which has tremendous potential as a decision-making tool is decision tree analysis because it provides a systematic framework for analyzing a sequence of interrelated decisions which may be made over time. This technique expresses decision making in terms of a sequence of acts, events, and consequences under the assumption that projects management considers today often have strong implications for future profitability. In turn, the relationship between the investment decision that must be made at present and the results of that decision in the future is complex. Stemming from the present investment decisions are alternative scenarios which depend on the occurrence of future events and the consequences of those events. Decision tree analysis encourages the study and understanding of these scenarios.

Advantages of decision tree analysis

The decision tree can clarify for management the choices, risks, monetary gains, objectives, and information needs involved in an investment problem. In comparison with other analytical tools, a decision tree may be a more lucid means of presenting the relevant information. Regardless of its size, a decision tree will always combine action choices with different possible events or results of action which are partially affected by chance or other uncontrollable circumstances.

It is generally agreed that today's decisions should be made in light of the anticipated effect these decisions and the outcome of uncertain events will have on future decisions and goals. Today's decisions affect tomorrow's decisions both directly and indirectly, and decision tree analysis allows management to focus on this relationship. Analytical techniques, such as discounted cash flow and present value methods, can be utilized to obtain a better picture of the impact of future events and decision alternatives. Use of a decision tree permits management to consider various alternatives with greater ease and clarity. The interactions among present decision alternatives and uncertain events and their possible payoffs become clearer. Decision trees do not show anything that management does not already know since no new financial data are presented. The advantage of this concept is that data are presented in a manner that enables systematic analysis and better decisions.

Weaknesses of decision tree analysis

A decision tree does not give management the answer to an investment problem. Instead, it helps management determine which alternative yields the greatest expected monetary gain at any particular choice point, given the information and the alternatives important to the decision. Not all possible events are identified; neither are all the decisions that must be made on a subject under analysis listed. The number of possible choices in the business world is usually not restricted to two or three. However, it is impossible to analyze all the implications of every act into the indefinite future and take them formally into account in selecting a decision strategy. Only those decisions and events or results that are important to management and have consequences they wish to compare are included. If more than a small number of choices is incorporated, decision tree analysis by hand becomes tedious and complicated. The use of computers is especially suitable when studying the effect of variations in figures and/or the events involved extend for some distance in time. The interactions of such decisions with the objectives of other parts of the business organization would be too complicated to compute manually.

Using the decision tree, uncertain alternatives are generally treated as if they were discrete, well-defined possibilities. For example, uncertain situations are often assumed to depend basically on a single variable, such as the level of demand or the success or failure of a development project. While cash flow may depend solely on demand in some situations, it may also be dependent on a number of independent or partially related variables subject to such chance influences as cost, demand, yield, and economic climate.

Requirements

Making a decision tree requires the following elements, which will be illustrated later in the chapter:

1. The points of decision and the alternatives available at each point must be identified.
2. The points of uncertainty and the type or range of alternative outcomes at each point must be determined.
3. Probabilities of different events or results of actions must be estimated.
4. The costs and gains of various events and actions must be estimated.
5. The alternative values must be analyzed in choosing a course of action.

Investment problems like those in the following example are appropriate for the application of the decision tree. Management of Tucker Industries must decide whether to build a small plant or a large one to manufacture a new product with a market life of 12 years. The company's managers are uncertain about what size the market for their product will be. The company grew rapidly between 1970 and 1980; however, the last few years have seen only small market gains.

If the market for this new product turns out to be large, present management will be able to push the company into a new period of profitable growth. Consequently, the research and development department, particularly the development project engineer, argues that building a large plant will enable the company to exploit the first major product development the department has produced in several years. However, if the company builds a big plant, it must live with it whatever the market demand. If demand is low in the first years, the fixed costs of operating a large plant will result in unprofitable operations. A large plant costs $4.8 million, while a small plant costs $3.2 million with expansion costing an additional $2.4 million later.

The marketing manager supports the large plant because of fear that competitors will enter the market with equivalent products if Tucker is unable to fill the demand for the new product. Further, this officer is confident that the company's sales personnel will be aggressive enough to promote the product sufficiently. Ideas for an exhaustive advertising campaign are already on the drawing board.

The controller is wary of large, unneeded plant capacity. This officer favors building a small plant that can be expanded in two years in the event that demand is high during the introductory period. However, the controller recognizes that later expansion to meet high volume demand will involve a total plant costing more than would a large plant built initially. In addition, a large plant is more efficient to operate than an expanded plant.

After consultation, top management arrives at the following marketing estimates:

	Initially	Long-term
Initially low demand and long-term high:.	20%	60%
Initially high demand and continued high:. . . .	40%	
Initially low demand and continued low:	10%	40%
Initially high demand and long-term low:.	30%	

Management estimates an initial high demand of 70 percent (40 + 30); if it is high initially, there is a 57 percent (40/70) conditional probability that demand will continue at a high level. Comparing 57 percent with 40 percent, it is apparent that a high initial sales level increases the estimated chance of high sales in subsequent periods. On the other hand, there is a 30 percent (20 + 10) chance that sales will be low initially; the chances are 33 percent (10/30) that initial low sales will lead to low sales in the subsequent period, and a 67 percent (20/30) chance that initial low sales will lead to high demand after the first two years. However, if an initial low demand is experienced with a small plant, management has agreed there will be no expansion. Based on these projections, management estimates a 60 percent chance of a large market in the long run and a 40 percent chance of a low demand in the long run.

The accounting staff arrives at the following estimated cash flows:

1. Small plant:
   a. With expansion after two years and continuous high demand, annual $600,000 cash flow for the first two years and annual cash flows of $1,000,000 thereafter would result.
   b. With expansion after two years and high demand not sustained, estimated annual cash flows of $280,000 from year three onward would result.
   c. With initially high and sustained demand and no expansion, $600,000 annual cash flows would be the yield for the first two years. Competition would cause this to drop to $480,000 in the long run when other companies are attracted by the high demand.
   d. With initially high demand and low long-term demand and no expansion, $600,000 annual cash flows for the first two years and $350,000 a year thereafter.
   e. With initially low demand and high long-term demand and no expansion, $350,000 annual cash flows for first two years increasing to $480,000 per year thereafter.
   f. With a continuous low demand, annual net cash flows of $350,000 would be the yield.
2. Large plant:
   a. With an initially low demand and long-term high demand, $200,000 cash flows each for the first two years and $1,200,000 annually thereafter since this large plant is more costly to operate than the small plant for the first 2 years, but more efficient to operate for the last 10 years than would be a small, expanded plant.
   b. With continuous high demand, $1,200,000 annual cash flows would be the yield.
   c. With continuous low demand, only $200,000 annual cash flows because of high fixed costs and inefficiencies.
   d. With initially high but long-term low demand, $600,000 cash flow for each of the first two years and $200,000 for each of the next years.

The decision tree shown in Exhibit 18–4 incorporates the foregoing data. In

697

EXHIBIT 18–4

Decision tree with financial data

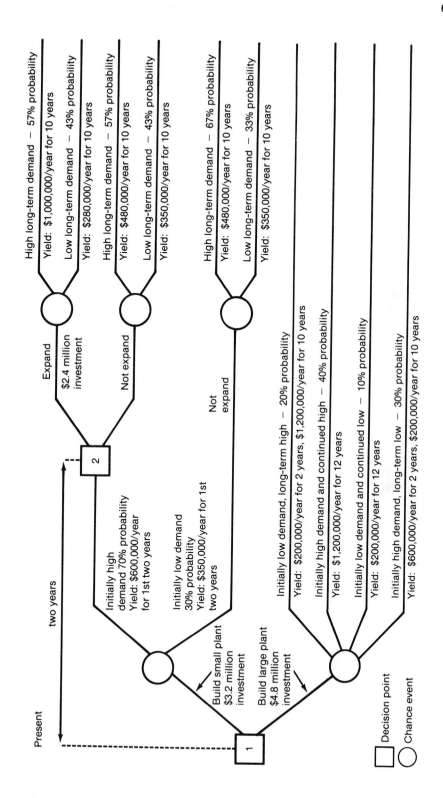

this decision tree, the *action (decision) points (forks)* are indicated by square nodes and the *chance event forks* by round ones. There is no single way to diagram a decision problem; rather than use squares and circles, the terms "act" and "event" may be placed above or below the appropriate fork. While there may be several variations of the shape of the tree, the order in which the acts and events are represented from left to right are rarely changed. While nothing shown in Exhibit 18–4 was not known by Tucker management before preparing the decision tree, using it, executives are able to engage in a more systematic analysis which leads to better decisions. The decision tree shows management what decision today will contribute most to its long-term goals.

ROLL-BACK CONCEPT

The next step in the analysis uses the *roll-back* concept. Briefly, the roll-back method involves (1) proceeding from right to left on each terminal point, (2) finding the total expected value at every chance event, and (3) choosing that course of action with the highest expected value. At the time of making Decision 1 regarding whether to build a large or small plant, management does not have to deal with Decision 2. Also, as in the case of initially building a large plant, it may not even have to make a second decision. Exhibit 18–5 illustrates this analysis. Using the maximum expected total cash flow as the criterion, and rolling back to Decision 2, it can be seen that the company would expand the plant *if* it had the option. The total expected value of the expansion alternative is $263,000 ($4,504,000 − $4,241,000) more than

EXHIBIT 18–5

Expected value of decision 2

Choice	Chance event	(1) Probability	(2) Total yield (10 years)		(1) × (2) Expected value
Expand.	High long-term demand	.57	$10,000,000		$5,700,000
	Low long-term demand	.43	2,800,000		1,204,000
				Total	$6,904,000
				Less expansion cost	2,400,000
				Net	$4,504,000
Not expand	High long-term demand	.57	$ 4,800,000		$2,736,000
	Low long-term demand	.43	3,500,000		1,505,000
				Total	$4,241,000
				No expansion cost	–0–
				Net	$4,241,000

EXHIBIT 18–6,

Cash flows for Decision 1

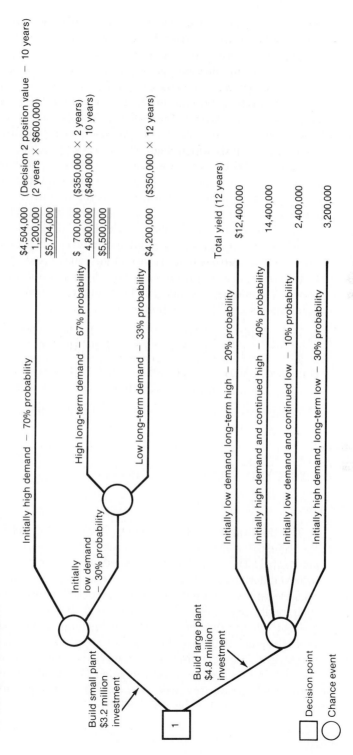

the no-expansion alternative over the 10-year life remaining. (Discounting future profits is ignored now; this is introduced later.)

Even though the present issue is how to make Decision 1, we start at Decision 2 using the roll-back concept. By putting a monetary value on Decision 2, management can compare the gain from building a small plant (the upper branch) to initially building a large plant (the lower branch). The $4,504,000 net expected value from expansion with Decision 2 can be referred to as its *position value*. In other words, if you repeated Decision 2 over and over again, you would expect annually to get a $1 million yield 57 percent of the time and a $280,000 yield 43 percent of the time. It is worth $4,504,000 for Tucker management to get to the position where it can make Decision 2. Given this value, management can ask, what is the best action at Decision 1?

The cash flows for Decision 1 are compiled in Exhibit 18–6. In the top half are the yields for a small plant, including the Decision 2 position value of $4,504,000 plus a $1.2 million yield for the two years prior to Decision 2. In the lower half are the yields for 12 years for various events if a large plant is built. These yields are the annual cash flow from Exhibit 18–4 multiplied by the appropriate number of years. The following comparison is obtained when these yields are reduced by their probabilities:

Build small plant: ($5,704,000 × .70) + ($5,500,000 × .20) + ($4,200,000 × .10) − $3,200,000 = $2,312,800

Build large plant: ($12,400,000 × .20) + ($14,400,000 × .40) + ($2,400,000 × .10) + ($3,200,000 × .30) − $4,800,000 = $4,640,000

The choice which maximizes expected total cash yield at Decision 1 is to build the large plant initially.

DISCOUNTED EXPECTED VALUE OF DECISIONS

Accounting for time

The time value of future earnings, however, has not been considered, and the time between successive decision stages on a decision tree may be substantial. The differences in immediate cost or revenue must be weighed against differences in value at the next stage. The two alternatives can be placed on a Decision 2 basis if the value assigned to the next stage is discounted by an appropriate percentage. This is similar to the use of a discount rate in the present value or discounted cash flow techniques and makes allowance for the cost of capital. Both cash flows and position value are discounted.

Using a 12 percent discount rate applied to the cash flows from Exhibit 18–4, the data in Exhibit 18–7 are obtained. When the time value of money is considered, the decision tree as in Exhibit 18–4 is first prepared; the next step is that shown in Exhibit 18–7. (There is no need to prepare the analysis

EXHIBIT 18–7

Decision 2 with discounting

	Yield	Present value
Expand—high demand	$1,000,000/year for 10 years	$5,650,000 ($1,000,000 × 5.65)
Expand—low demand	$ 280,000/year for 10 years	$1,582,000 ($280,000 × 5.65)
Not expand—high demand	$ 480,000/year for 10 years	$2,712,000 ($480,000 × 5.65)
Not expand—low demand	$ 350,000/year for 10 years	$1,977,500 ($350,000 × 5.65)

illustrated earlier in Exhibits 18–5 and 18–6.) The cash flow for all 10 years is discounted, including the first year's cash flow. The figures in the present value column represent the present value as of the time Decision 2 is made, not at the time Decision 1 is made. (Remember that if a large plant is built initially, there is no Decision 2.)

Exhibit 18–8 uses the same approach as previously illustrated in Exhibit 18–5; however, now discounted yield figures are used to arrive at a discounted expected value. Since the discounted expected value of the no-expansion alternative is higher, the $2,396,165 becomes the position value of Decision 2.

The same analytical procedure used previously for Decision 1 is repeated in Exhibit 18–9; however, discounting is now incorporated. The Decision 2 position value of $2,396,165 is treated at the time of Decision 1 as if it were a lump sum received at the end of the two years. Note that the discount rate of .797 comes from Table A, present value of $1, 2 years, at a 12 percent rate, shown in Appendix A to this book. Again, a 12 percent discount rate is assumed

EXHIBIT 18–8

Discounted expected value of Decision 2

Choice	Chance event	(1) Probability	(2) Present value yield		(1) × (2) Discounted expected value
Expand	High long-term demand	.57	$5,650,000		$3,220,500
	Low long-term demand	.43	1,582,000		680,260
				Total	$3,900,760
				Less expansion cost	2,400,000
				Net	$1,500,760
Not expand	High long-term demand	.57	$2,712,000		$1,545,840
	Low long-term demand	.43	1,977,500		850,325
				Total	$2,396,165
				No expansion cost	–0–
				Net	$2,396,165

702

EXHIBIT 18–9

Decision 1 analysis

Choice	Chance event	(1) Probability	Yield	(2) Discounted value of yield	(1) × (2) Discounted expected yield
Build small plant	Initially high demand	.70	$600,000/year, 2 years Decision 2 value: $2,396,165 at end of 2 years	$1,014,000 ($600,000 × 1.690) 1,909,744 ($2,396,165 × .797) $2,923,744	$2,046,621
	Initially low demand, high long-term	.20	$350,000/year, 2 years $480,000/year, 10 years	$ 591,500 ($350,000 × 1.690) 2,161,920 [$480,000 × (6.194−1.690)] $2,753,420	550,684
	Continuous low demand	.10	$350,000/year, 12 years	$2,167,900 ($350,000 × 6.194)	216,790
				Total	$2,814,095
				Less investment	3,200,000
				Net	$ (385,905)
Build large plant	Initially low demand, high long-term	.20	$200,000/year, 2 years $1,200,000/year, 10 years	$ 338,000 ($200,000 × 1.690) 5,404,800 [$1,200,000 × (6.194−1.690)] $5,742,800	$1,148,560
	Continuous high demand	.40	$1,200,000/year, 12 years	$7,432,800 ($1,200,000 × 6.194)	2,973,120
	Continuous low demand	.10	$200,000/year, 12 years	$1,238,800 ($200,000 × 6.194)	123,880
	Initially high demand low long-term	.30	$600,000/year, 2 years $200,000/year, 10 years	$1,014,000 ($600,000 × 1.690) $ 900,800 [$200,000 × (6.194−1.690)] $1,914,800	574,440
				Total	$4,820,000
				Less investment	4,800,000
				Net	$ 20,000

with the cash flow for all years discounted, including the first year's cash flow. Cash flows for years 3 through 12 are discounted to the present by a factor derived by subtracting 1.690, the factor for 12 percent, 2 years, in Table B in the Appendix A, from 6.194, the factor for 12 percent, 12 years, in Table B. The large-plant alternative is again the preferred decision based on the discounted expected cash flow. The margin of difference of $405,905 ($20,000 + $385,905) is smaller than the $2,327,200 ($4,640,000 − $2,312,800) obtained without discounting.

Other factors to consider

The expected monetary gains must be considered along with the risks, and managers have different viewpoints toward risk. Thus, they draw different conclusions about the various alternatives. The controller will likely see the uncertainty surrounding the decision in a much different light than will the marketing manager or the development project engineer. A major investment might also pose risk to an individual's job and career. While one individual may stand to gain much from a project's success and lose little from its failure, others in the company may be risking much if a project fails. The types of risks and how individuals regard them from a personal viewpoint affect not only the assumptions they make, but also the strategy they follow in dealing with the risks.

The political environment in which a decision concerning the scale of a plant is introduced should be evaluated jointly by top management. They should ask what risks and prospects are at stake. Is it a possible bankruptcy, job stability, an opportunity for large profit increases, or is it a major career opportunity? The individuals who bear the risks—whether employees, stockholders, managers, or the community—and the numbers affected, assume significance. In addition, the character of the risk that each person bears should be evaluated. How disastrous would a failure be to individuals as well as to the company and the community's economy? Whether the risk is once in a lifetime, insurable, or unique is important. The decision tree does not eliminate these risks; however, it shows management what decision makes the largest contribution to long-term goals.

SUMMARY

This chapter presents several techniques and analyses that prove helpful in planning complex projects and in investment analysis. Gantt charts are a simple control technique which can be used to compare scheduled and actual production. However, Gantt charts are generally considered inadequate for sophisticated projects which require an understanding of what tasks must be completed before others are begun. Network models, such as PERT, have been developed which show interrelationships among activities. With the use of a PERT network, the critical path can be determined so that attention can be focused on this schedule, preventing delay of the project's completion time. Paths that are not critical have slack and thus provide some flexibility for managers. Slack time also serves as a guide in rescheduling tasks so that the overall project's completion time is shortened. PERT-Cost analysis also can be used in deciding whether crashing the project is economically feasible.

Decision tree analysis clarifies choices and risks and the related profits of long-term investment alternatives. Because it presents financial data in a systematic manner, the relationships and consequences of present decision alternatives and uncertain events and their possible payoffs become clearer. Certainly, decision tree analysis does not provide the single, accurate solution to an investment decision; instead, the objective is to assist managers in assessing which alternative at any particular choice point yields the greatest expected monetary gain given the information available and alternatives to the decision. In using decision tree analysis, it is recognized that the expected monetary gains must be considered along with the risks and that members of the management team view these risks differently. Unless these differences are recognized and dealt with initially, those who must assist in making the decision by supplying data and analyses, and those who are operating the plant and promoting the product will view the decision in conflicting ways. The criteria for success may be vastly different.

IMPORTANT TERMS AND CONCEPTS

Gantt charts

PERT

Critical path method (CPM)

PERT-Time analysis

Event

Activities

Expected activity time (ex_t)

Critical path

Slack time

Earliest completion time (T_E)

Latest completion time (T_L)

Crashing

PERT-Cost analysis

Decision tree analysis

Action or decision points

Chance event fork

Roll-back concept

Position value

Discounted expected value

REVIEW QUESTIONS

1. Outline the characteristics of Gantt chart techniques.
2. Outline the characteristics of PERT.
3. Identify two ways that PERT is superior to Gantt chart techniques for complex projects.

4. Discuss how PERT can be used in planning a complex project.

5. Explain the difference between an activity and an event.

6. What is the expected time of an activity if its optimistic, most likely, and pessimistic time estimates are 4, 5, and 12?

7. Define the term critical path and explain why is it referred to as critical.

8. What is slack and how can management utilize it?

9. What is meant by crashing the network and what is the differential crash cost of an activity?

10. If an activity is expected to take 10 days and its normal cost is $80,000, but it can be crashed and finished in 7 days at $116,000, what is the unit differential crash cost?

11. What is the purpose of decision tree analysis?

12. List three advantages and three weaknesses of decision tree analysis.

13. Give the requirements for making a decision tree.

14. Define the roll-back concept; discuss how it is used in decision tree analysis.

15. Why should the time value of future earnings be considered in decisions?

16. How can the time value of future earnings be used in decision tree analysis?

17. Discuss some of the factors that must be considered in decision making that decision tree analysis does not incorporate.

EXERCISES

E18–1.   Determining critical path, slack time

Michael Desposito Construction, Inc. has contracted to complete a complex machine and has asked for assistance in analyzing the project. Using the Program Evaluation Review Technique, the following network has been developed:

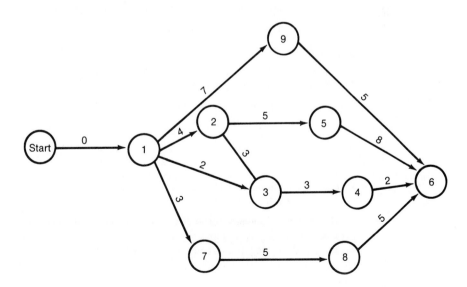

Required:

a.   Determine the critical path.
b.   Determine the latest time for reaching event 6 via path 1–9–6.
c.   What is the slack time on path 1–2–3–4–6?
d.   If all other paths operate on schedule but path segment 1–9 has an unfavorable time variance of 2, what is the effect on the critical path?
e.   What is the earliest time for reaching event 6 via path 1–7–8–6?

E18–2.   Gantt charts

Mary-Jo Kovach, Inc. received four orders for specially designed sport uniforms. Each uniform must go through two departments in sequence, design/cutting and sewing/finishings. The supervisors estimated the time required for each order. Expressed in days, these times are:

	Orders			
	1	*2*	*3*	*4*
Design/cutting.	9	5	6	7
Sewing/finishing	4	4	6	10

There is no backlog on orders in process in the departments. To minimize time in departments, select the shortest times for orders in both departments. Then schedule first the order requiring the least amount of design and cutting time. Schedule last the order requiring the least amount of sewing and finishing time. Repeat this until all orders are in sequence.

Required:

a.   Develop a Gantt Chart for the four orders. Move each order from one department to the next minimizing the total time required to complete all orders.
b.   Determine how long it will take to complete work on all four orders.

E18–3.   PERT-Time network and expected completion time

The following sequence of activities is needed for Mason, Inc.'s project:

0–1, 1–2, 1–3, 1–4, 2–5, 3–5, 4–7, 5–6, 5–8, 6–7, 7–8.

Required:

a.   Draw a PERT-Time network for these activities.
b.   Determine the expected completion time for a limited number of these events:

Event	Optimistic	Most likely	Pessimistic
1.	2	4	9
2.	1	3	5
3.	2	3	7
4.	4	6	11

E18–4.   Developing a PERT network and determining the critical path (CMA adapted)

The Dryfus Company specializes in large construction projects. The company management regularly employs the Program Evaluation Review Technique (PERT) in planning and coordinating its construction projects. The following schedule of separable activities and their expected completion times has been developed for an office building which is to be constructed by Dryfus Company.

Activity description	Predecessor activity	Expected activity completion time (in weeks)
a. Excavation.	—	2
b. Foundation	a	3
c. Underground utilities	a	7
d. Rough plumbing	b	4
e. Framing.	b	5
f. Roofing	e	3
g. Electrical work	f	3
h. Interior walls	d,g	4
i. Finish plumbing	h	2
j. Exterior finishing	f	6
k. Landscaping	c,i,j	2

Required:

a. Identify the critical path for this project and determine the expected project completion time in weeks.

b. Briefly discuss how the expected activity completion times are derived using PERT and what the derived value for the expected activity completion time means with PERT.

PROBLEMS

P18–1. Critical path and slack

Washington Company has contracted with a local business group to construct a large addition to a building. To help them organize and control this project, their accountant has developed the following PERT-Time network. The expected time of each activity (ex_t) is expressed in weeks.

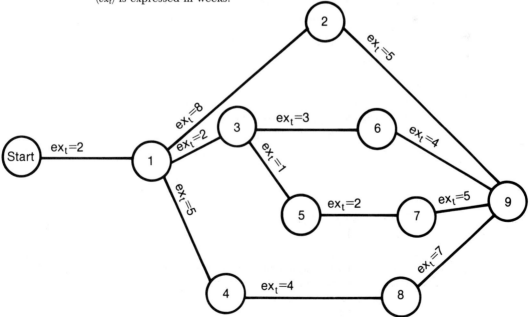

Required:

a. Determine the critical path.
b. Compute the slack at each event.

P18–2. Network preparation and crash time

Diane Hilgers, Inc. is in the process of constructing a building that will house manufacturing facilities for a new product line. Because market demand for the new product is expected to grow rapidly within the next few months, management is interested in having the building completed in optimum time. The contribution margin from the new product line is expected to be $3,000 per week. The cost accountant has suggested that network analysis be applied to the construction. The following schedule has been prepared for use in this analysis:

Activity	Expected normal time (in weeks)	Crash time (in weeks)	Cost (000) Normal conditions	Cost (000) Crash conditions
0–1	4	NC	$23	NC
1–2	6	4	8	$9
1–3	5	3	3	6
2–5	8	NC	6	NC
3–4	3	NC	2	NC
3–6	10	NC	12	NC
4–5	2	NC	1	NC
5–7	4	NC	2	NC
6–7	5	2	3	6

NC = No change in time or cost is possible.

Required:

a. Determine a network for PERT-Cost analysis.
b. Establish the critical path under normal conditions.
c. Identify the normal costs to be incurred in constructing the building.
d. Determine the minimum time in which the building could be constructed and the costs of achieving this earlier occupancy.
e. Advise Hilgers, Inc. as to whether the firm should attempt a crash program or a normal schedule.

P18–3. PERT network and critical path

In building a PERT-Time network, management of Melany Medloch, Inc. listed the events necessary to finish a project. They next arrived at the following activities leading to these events:

Activity	Time estimates in weeks Optimistic	Most likely	Pessimistic
0–1	2.0	2.5	3.0
1–2	1.0	2.0	3.0
1–3	1.5	2.0	2.5
1–4	0.6	2.0	4.0
2–5	0.6	3.5	7.0
3–6	2.0	2.8	6.0
4–8	0.8	1.9	2.4
5–8	1.0	4.5	5.0
6–8	0.6	0.9	1.8

Required:

a.   Construct the PERT network.
b.   Determine the expected completion times for all activities.
c.   Determine the critical path.

P18–4.   PERT network and slack time

In planning the activities necessary to construct a large building, Utah Company arrived at the following activities and their related expected completion times:

Activities	Expected completion time (in weeks)
0–1	1
1–2	2
1–3	2
1–4	7
2–3	1
3–5	8
3–6	12
4–5	10
5–7	13
6–7	6

Required:

a.   Develop a PERT network for the listed activities.
b.   Identify the critical path.
c.   Indicate on the PERT network the earliest completion time and the latest completion time.
d.   What is the slack time on:
   (1)   Path   0–1–3–6–7?
   (2)   Path   0–1–4–5–7?

P18–5.   PERT-Cost analysis (continuation of P18–4)

The management of Utah Company, mentioned in P18–4, has determined that some of the activities can be crashed. The crash time in weeks and the related total differential cost to achieve the crash program are indicated below. The cost of the project following the normal schedule is $600,000.

Activity	Crash time	Total differential cost
0–1	NC	—
1–2	1	$ 1,000
1–3	NC	—
1–4	1	24,000
2–3	NC	—
3–5	5	15,000
3–6	8	16,000
4–5	8	24,000
5–7	NC	—
6–7	2	1,000

NC = No change in time or cost is possible.

Required:

a.   Prepare a PERT network showing (or insert in the network prepared in P18–4) the expected and crash times and the differential cost per week.

b.   Indicate the minimum time in which the project could be completed and the costs incurred to achieve this earlier opening.

c.   What is the minimum additional contribution to profits needed to justify completing the project early?

P18–6.   Decision tree using discounted expected yield

After two years of study, Kingsberry Company's engineering staff presented a proposal for an expansion installation of their computer-based control system. The present system has been in operation for four years and cash savings are being achieved. The expected cost of the new system is $1.2 million. A reduction in labor costs and less material waste are the claimed advantages. The equipment needed for the expansion can be purchased and installed quickly because the supplier is anxious to further test the system in an actual application. The supplier's bid of $1.2 million represents a reduced price for this on-site testing; the price will be $1.4 million in one year. Possible technical malfunctions, as well as uncertain product demand, have convinced several Kingsberry vice presidents that additional engineering studies should be conducted. The vice president of production suggests that action be postponed until the Tire Industry Association completes both its one-year study of the technical capacities of the system and a forecast of market demand; cost of this survey will be $25,000. The marketing vice president argues that more reliance could be placed on analysis conducted by an independent research team than on that from industry studies; the cost of an independent research team's analysis will be $40,000. However, all vice presidents agree that cost studies and probabilities of various events should be carefully estimated since the investment is substantial. They are also in agreement that one of the three alternatives must be chosen. After many hours of study, the following data are obtained:

		Probability
Postpone expansion and use industry studies:		
Weak initial market, negative technical studies.	. . . .	30%
Strong initial market, positive technical studies	. . . .	70
Postpone expansion and hire independent research team:		
Weak initial market, negative technical studies.	. . . .	35
Strong initial market, positive technical studies	. . . .	65

If the expansion is made in year one, there is a 55 percent chance of an initial weak market and many technical problems and a 45 percent chance of an initial strong market and limited technical malfunctions. Using either the industry study or the independent research study, it will be one year before the results can be examined and the machine installed. The system's impact is expected to extend eight years from the present, regardless of the date of installation. Probabilities for long-term market demand are given below for the three different alternatives:

Market based on industry study or *for immediate expansion*	*Percent*
Weak long-term after a weak initial	70
Strong long-term after a weak initial	30
Weak long-term after strong initial.	20
Strong long-term after strong initial.	80

Market based on independent study	Percent
Weak long-term after weak initial	60
Strong long-term after weak initial	40
Weak long-term after strong initial	25
Strong long-term after strong initial	75

Market	Year 1		Years 2–8	
	Without expansion	*With expansion*	*Without expansion*	*With expansion*
Weak	$40,000	$200,000	$ 50,000	$240,000
Strong	$75,000	$450,000	$100,000	$580,000

Annual cash savings

Required:

a.   Using a 10 percent discount rate for the cash flow, prepare a decision tree; discount the cash flow for all years.

b.   Indicate the course of action you would advise.

P18–7.   PERT-Cost analysis (CMA adapted)

The Tipton Company acquires retail hardware stores that are having difficulties or have recently gone out of business. Generally, the interior of stores can be used with little additional cost or effort. Tipton usually stocks the stores with its own brands of merchandise, hires new employees, and modifies the building exterior to match the company's standard store exterior.

The company has experienced difficulty in getting the stores opened on schedule. The person responsible for store openings in the past had many years experience in the retail business and managed the opening process on an ad hoc basis. The new manager for store openings has less retail experience but has used network analysis to organize and control store openings for a previous employer.

The new manager for store openings has suggested that network analysis be applied to the opening of the new Fox Village store. A network diagram and accompanying schedule have been prepared for the Fox Village store, as shown below. The schedule

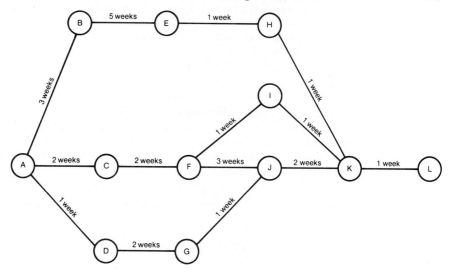

Activity	Description of activity	Normal time (in weeks)	Crash time (in weeks)	Normal cost	Total incremental cost to achieve crash time
A–B	Design exterior	3	1	$ 5,000	$4,500
A–C	Determine inventory needs	2	NC	500	–0–
A–D	Develop staffing plan	1	NC	500	–0–
B–E	Do exterior structural work	5	3	27,000	3,500
E–H	Paint exterior	1	NC	4,000	–0–
H–K	Install exterior signs	1	NC	15,000	–0–
C–F	Order inventory	2	NC	1,500	–0–
F–I	Develop special prices for opening	1	NC	2,000	–0–
I–K	Advertise opening and special prices	1	NC	8,000	–0–
F–J	Receive inventory	3	2	4,000	2,000
D–G	Acquire staff	2	1	3,000	1,000
G–J	Train staff	1	NC	5,000	–0–
J–K	Stock shelves	2	1	3,500	1,500
K–L	Final preparation for grand opening	1	NC	6,000	–0–

NC = no change in time is possible.

describes the activities, the estimated normal times for each activity, and the normal cost of each activity required to open the store. The schedule also presents the crash time for those activities which can be accomplished in a shorter time period and the related additional cost required to meet the crash time. The sales manager estimates that the Fox Village store should produce a contribution to corporate profits of about $2,000 per week.

Required:

a.   Determine the normal critical path for the opening of the Fox Village store and identify:
   (1)   Those activities on the critical path.
   (2)   The length in weeks required to open the store.
   (3)   The normal costs to be incurred in opening the store.
b.   What is the minimum time in which the Fox Village store could be opened and what costs are incurred to achieve this earlier opening? Support your answer with appropriate explanation and calculations.
c.   Should Tipton Company proceed with the normal schedule or should it attempt a crash program? Explain your answer.

P18–8.   Decision tree; expected value of perfect information

   Janet Humphreys, Inc. manufactures and sells nationally a carbonated soft drink. A strong market was developed but has recently been slacking off, and management credits this slump to the increasing popularity of diet sodas. Janet Humphreys, Inc. has not entered the diet drink market but is in the process of developing a low-calorie version of its cola.

   Marketing personnel have been considering potential strategies. If the diet cola is introduced nationally, a large amount of money and many hours of effort will be required for a full, nationwide advertising and distribution campaign. Since Janet Humphreys, Inc. will be entering the market later than its competitors, additional promotion will be required; in addition, there is some risk in a nationwide introduction because of Humphrey's late market entrance. After assessing the market, management arrives at two reasonable alternative strategies:

1. Immediately introduce the diet drink nationwide without a test campaign. A decision will be made on whether to stop production of the diet drink 18 months later. Management estimates there is a 40 percent chance of the strategy being successful. If $50 million in revenues are generated in the 18-month period, management will consider the national introduction a success. If revenues are $20 million for the period, management will consider the campaign unsuccessful. Variable costs are expected to be 70 percent of sales. Fixed costs are expected to total $8 million for the period regardless of the result of the campaign.

2. Limit the introduction to a 10-state area. Based on the result of this test campaign, Humphreys will decide whether to introduce the low-calorie drink nationally. There is the possibility that the test results will indicate that Janet Humphreys, Inc. should conduct a nationwide promotion and distribution campaign when, in fact, a nationwide campaign will be unsuccessful. Conversely, the test results may indicate that Humphreys should not conduct a nationwide promotion and distribution campaign when, in fact, a nationwide campaign will be successful.

Required:

a. Prepare a decision tree identifying all alternatives and possible outcomes.
b. Determine the expected monetary value of the first strategy.
c. Assuming the test campaign can perfectly predict whether or not a nationwide campaign will be successful, use expected monetary value as the decision criterion to calculate the maximum dollar amount Humphreys should be willing to pay for perfect information.
d. Identify and discuss at least three criticisms of using expected monetary value criterion for decision problems.

P18–9.   PERT diagram and crashing (CMA adapted)

Edward Jones is responsible for finding a suitable building and establishing a new convenience grocery store for Thrift-Mart, Inc. Jones enumerated the specific activities which had to be completed and the estimated time for each activity. In addition, he prepared a network diagram, which appears below, to aid in the coordination of the activities. The list of activities involved in locating a building and establishing a new store is as follows:

Activity number		Description of activity	Estimated time in weeks
1–2	. . . .	Find building	4
2–3	. . . .	Negotiate rental terms	2
3–4	. . . .	Draft lease	4
2–5	. . . .	Prepare store plans	4
5–6	. . . .	Select and order fixtures	1
6–4	. . . .	Delivery of fixtures	6
4–8	. . . .	Install fixtures	3
5–7	. . . .	Hire staff	5
7–8	. . . .	Train staff	4
8–9	. . . .	Receive inventory	2
9–10	. . . .	Stock shelves	1

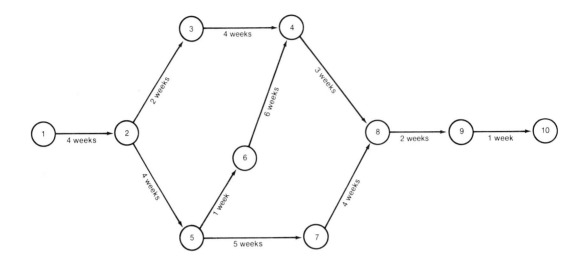

Required:

a. Identify the critical path for finding and establishing the new convenience store.

b. Edward Jones would like to finish the store two weeks earlier than indicated in the schedule; as a result, he is considering several alternatives. One is to convince the fixture manufacturer to deliver the fixtures in four weeks rather than six. Should Jones arrange for the manufacturer to deliver the fixtures in four weeks if the sole advantage of this schedule change is to open the store two weeks early? Justify your answer.

c. A program such as the one illustrated by the network diagram for the new convenience store, cannot be implemented unless the required resources are available at the required dates. What additional information does Jones need to properly administer the proposed project?

P18–10.   Short-run decision tree analysis

Wheat, Inc., a large chemical manufacturer, has been selling a plastic material known as Romac to industrial users for several years. Presently, Wheat has 35 percent of the market; two other large competitors have captured the remainder. Romac is basically a modification of another plastic material, Cocmel; however, Romac's characteristics make it superior in many respects, even though Romac's price averages $1.50 per pound higher. Wheat, Inc.'s initial tests of Romac showed that waste could be reduced significantly with the use of Romac rather than Cocmel. Recently, however, several university studies reveal that this claim is unfounded. In view of the publicity given these independent studies, Wheat management is concerned about whether its present $5 price per pound can be maintained. Marketing research indicates that an appropriate strategy is to attempt to capture more of the Cocmel market by emphasizing the flexibility of Romac and giving less attention to possible waste reduction. Attempts are also being made to find other plastic materials for which Romac can be used as a substitute. After careful study, four possible pricing alternatives are suggested:

1. Reduce price of Romac to $4 per pound.
2. Reduce price to $4.50.
3. Maintain price at $5; Wheat expects to sell 42,000 pounds of Romac at this level.

4. Raise price to $5.20 and attempt product differentiation; Wheat expects to sell 30,000 pounds of Romac at this level.

In view of the oligopoly market environment, it is believed that any reduction in price will be matched by competitors. However, if Wheat raises its price to $5.20 or maintains its present $5 price, its two competitors probably will not follow and Wheat will lose some of the Romac market unless it is able to establish more product differentiation.

If Wheat lowers Romac's price to $4, there is a 60 percent probability that competitors will charge $4; a 30 percent chance they will charge $4.50; and a 10 percent chance they will continue to charge $5.

If, instead, Wheat lowers Romac's price to $4.50, there is a 15 percent probability that competitors will charge $4; a 50 percent chance they will charge $4.50, and a 35 percent chance they will continue to charge $5. If Wheat lowers Romac's price to $4 or $4.50 and Romac competitors continue to charge $5, 70,000 pounds are expected to be sold per year.

Price retaliation by Cocmel producers is expected if Wheat and its Romac competitors reduce Romac's price. If Wheat charges $4 or $4.50 for Romac and its competitors charge $4, there is a 40 percent probability that Cocmel producers will charge $2.50. Wheat's sales of Romac are then expected to be 45,000 annually. A 35 percent probability exists that Cocmel producers will charge $3.25; at this level, Wheat expects Romac sales of 48,000. There is a 25 percent chance that a $3.50 price will continue to be charged by Cocmel producers. Wheat's annual sales are expected to be 58,000 at this level.

If Wheat charges $4 or $4.50 for Romac and its competitors charge $4.50 for Romac, there is a 20 percent probability Cocmel producers will charge $2.50 for Cocmel; Wheat's sales of Romac are expected to be 50,000 annually. A 50 percent probability exists that Cocmel producers will charge $3.25, and Wheat's annual sales of Romac will be 55,000 at this level. Finally, there is a 30 percent chance Cocmel producers will continue to charge $3.50; Wheat's annual sales of Romac are expected to be 60,000 pounds at this level.

For simplicity, assume a $3 variable cash cost per pound and cash annual fixed costs of $50,000 at all anticipated sales volume.

Regardless of the pricing arrangement chosen, the market for Romac is not expected to be stable beyond two years.

Required:

Prepare a decision tree using estimated cash flow for two years and indicate the preferred pricing strategy.

P18–11. Slack time and probability of implementing a system (CMA adapted)

Whitson Company has just ordered a new computer for its financial information system. The present computer is fully utilized and no longer adequate for all of the financial applications Whitson would like to implement. The present financial applications must be modified before they can be run on the new computer. Additionally, new applications which Whitson would like to have developed and implemented have been identified and ranked according to priority.

Sally Rose, Manager of Data Processing, is responsible for implementing the new computer system. Rose listed the specific activities which had to be completed and determined the estimated time to complete each activity. In addition, she prepared a network diagram to aid in the coordination of the activities, as shown.

716

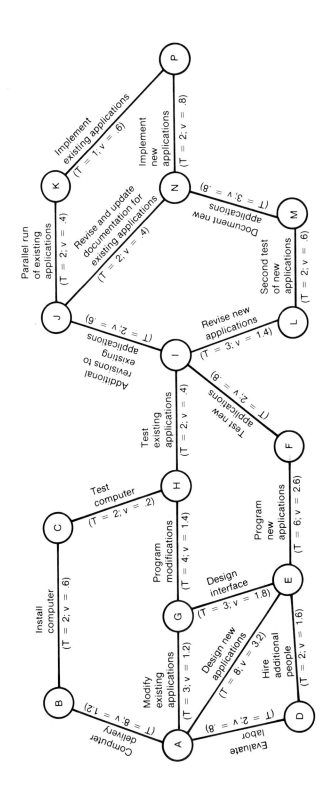

Key

T = Expected time in weeks to complete activity.

v = Variance in expected time in weeks.

Activity labels (as read from the network diagram):

- Install computer (T = 2; v = .6)
- Computer delivery (T = 8; v = 1.2)
- Modify existing applications (T = 3; v = 1.2)
- Evaluate labor (T = 2; v = .8)
- Design new applications (T = 8; v = 3.2)
- Hire additional people (T = 2; v = 1.6)
- Design interface (T = 3; v = 1.8)
- Program new applications (T = 6; v = 2.6)
- Program modifications (T = 4; v = 1.4)
- Test computer (T = 2; v = .2)
- Test existing applications (T = 2; v = .4)
- Test new applications (T = 2; v = .8)
- Additional revisions to existing applications (T = 2; v = .6)
- Revise new applications (T = 3; v = 1.4)
- Second test of new applications (T = 2; v = .6)
- Document new applications (T = 3; v = .8)
- Revise and update documentation for existing applications (T = 2; v = .4)
- Implement new applications (T = 2; v = .8)
- Implement existing applications (T = 1; v = .6)
- Parallel run of existing applications (T = 2; v = .4)

Activity	Description of activity	Expected time required to complete (in weeks)	Variance in expected time (in weeks)
A–B	Wait for delivery of computer from manufacturer	8	1.2
B–C	Install computer	2	.6
C–H	General test of computer	2	.2
A–D	Complete an evaluation of labor requirements	2	.8
D–E	Hire additional programmers and operators	2	1.6
A–G	Design modifications of existing applications	3	1.2
G–H	Program modifications of existing applications	4	1.4
H–I	Test modified applications on new computer	2	.4
I–I	Revise existing applications as needed	2	.6
J–N	Revise and update documentation for existing applications as modified	2	.4
J–K	Run existing applications in parallel on new and old computers	2	.4
K–P	Implement existing applications as modified on new computer	1	.6
A–E	Design new applications	8	3.2
G–E	Design interface between existing and new applications	3	1.8
E–F	Program new applications	6	2.6
F–I	Test new applications on new computer	2	.8
I–L	Revise new applications as needed	3	1.4
L–M	Conduct second test of new applications on new computer	2	.6
M–N	Prepare documentation for the new applications	3	.8
N–P	Implement new applications on the new computer	2	.8

Required:

a.   Determine the number of weeks required to fully implement Whitson Company's financial information system (i.e., both existing and new applications) on its new computer and identify the activities which are critical to completing the project.

b.   The term slack time is often used in conjunction with network analysis.
   (1)   Explain what is meant by slack time.
   (2)   Identify an activity which involves slack time and indicate the amount of slack time available for that activity.

c.   Whitson Company's top management would like to reduce the time necessary to begin operation of the entire system.
   (1)   Which activities should Sally Rose attempt to reduce to implement the system sooner? Explain your answer.
   (2)   Discuss how Sally Rose might proceed to reduce the time of these activities.

d.   The General Accounting Manager would like the existing financial system applications to be modified and operational in 22 weeks.
   (1)   Determine the number of weeks required to modify the existing financial information system applications and make them operational.
   (2)   What is the probability of implementing the existing financial system applications within 22 weeks? (Use table of areas under the normal curve given on page 718.)

Table of areas under the normal curve

Z	Area	Z	Area	Z	Area
0.1	.540	1.1	.864	2.1	.982
0.2	.579	1.2	.885	2.2	.986
0.3	.618	1.3	.903	2.3	.989
0.4	.655	1.4	.919	2.4	.992
0.5	.692	1.5	.933	2.5	.994
0.6	.726	1.6	.945	2.6	.995
0.7	.758	1.7	.955	2.7	.997
0.8	.788	1.8	.964	2.8	.997
0.9	.816	1.9	.971	2.9	.998
1.0	.841	2.0	.977	3.0	.999

P18–12.   Weaknesses of decision tree; adjusting cash flow for time value of money

As a consultant for Yale Company, you have been asked to assist in its decision regarding the optimal size of plant facilities expansion. In talking with you, members of top management, who are all in their 50s and 60s, are quick to emphasize that they want some conventional decision tools used to answer this investment problem rather than some "cute, way-out approach," such as decision tree analysis. Later, in talking with younger management personnel on lower levels, you begin to understand the significance of top management's remark regarding decision tree analysis. These younger managers had recently used it as a scientific tool to support the main argument another problem involved, only to be strongly rebuffed by top management.

Yale has recently developed a new product with an expected life of 10 years. Present manufacturing facilities are inadequate to produce the product, so a decision must be made regarding how much the present plant should be expanded. Market research believes it has reliable tests indicating that the domestic market alone is sufficient to require a 20,000-square-foot expansion. Data concerning an export market are less accurate; however, marketing personnel believe that if demand is high in the export market, a 40,000-square-foot expansion is warranted. Management is faced with the immediate decision of whether to expand by 20,000 square feet now with a possible later 20,000-square-foot expansion, or to expand 40,000 square feet initially. Management is in agreement that there is not enough space available at the present site to exceed a total 40,000-square-foot expansion.

Bids from local contractors have averaged $75 per square foot; however, if a second expansion of 20,000 square feet is undertaken, the price is expected to be $120 per square foot for this additional space. This price is estimated to reflect inflation as well as additional costs due to remodeling the first expansion. If the smaller expansion is undertaken, it will be four years before a second expansion is made, if at all.

Market research studies indicate there is a 60 percent chance that the initial demand will be high. Management agrees that if the initial demand is low, there is complete assurance that the long-term demand will also be low, and they will not expand. They believe there is a 50 percent chance that if initial demand is high it will continue, while only a 10 percent chance that a low long-term demand will follow a high-demand initial market. The projections of net annual cash flow are given on page 719.

You are convinced that decision tree analysis is appropriate and believe that you can demonstrate this to top management.

	Years 1–4	Demand level	Annual cash flow
1.	Small expansion	High	$300,000
2.	Small expansion	Low	200,000
3.	Large expansion	High	700,000
4.	Large expansion	Low	100,000

	Years 5–10		
1.	Small expansion with later additional expansion	High	600,000
2.	Small expansion with later additional expansion	Low	200,000
3.	Small expansion, no further expansion	High	400,000
4.	Small expansion, no further expansion	Low	250,000
5.	Large initial expansion	High	700,000
6.	Large initial expansion	Low	100,000

Required:

a. Discuss potential reasons for top management's resistance to decision tree analysis.

b. Give the weaknesses or limitations of decision tree analysis.

c. Draw a decision tree; adjust the cash flow for the time value of money using a discount rate of 14 percent. Discount the cash flow for all years.

d. Indicate the course of action you would advise.

e. Discuss other factors that could affect your decision.

P18–13.   Short-run decision tree analysis

Last week Kent Miller, president of Miller Chemicals, Inc., signed a contract with Everett Manufacturing Company to produce 200,000 gallons of HHX, an industrial lubricant, at a fixed price of $10. Delivery of the first 20,000 gallons is scheduled for 90 days with the remainder to be delivered in 15,000-gallon batches each month thereafter.

Although Miller feels sure that his company can meet the product specifications, he is concerned about available production capacity. Construction of a research laboratory has just been completed, and it is possible that HHX could be processed in this facility. Miller knows that the research director is anxious to experiment with a new mixing process, and this would give her that opportunity. The research director's initial tests show that the new mixing process can cut costs by 10 to 15 percent, to $5.50 per gallon; however, she has tried neither to process such a large quantity nor to process it under the time constraints of the Everett contract. If numerous failures occur, the cost would increase to as much as $8.80 per gallon. Management estimates the following: a 20 percent probability that the mixing process will require no rework, resulting in a cost of $5.50 per gallon; a 40 percent probability of limited rework, resulting in a $7.10 cost per gallon; a 30 percent probability of additional rework, resulting in an $8 per gallon cost; and finally, a 10 percent probability of many failures resulting in an $8.80 cost per gallon.

With proper planning, 200,000 gallons of HHX could be produced in the company's regular production operations. This would require additional labor shifts, but no undue problems are anticipated. The regular process cost is estimated to be $7 per gallon, but the company's labor union is negotiating for a wage increase which would result in a $0.25 increase in cost per gallon. There is a 30 percent chance that the labor union will receive its requested raise. However, if regular production facilities are used, it will mean that production on some existing orders may be delayed. Also, the company had planned to introduce a new product line with additional labor shifts using existing facilities. If, instead, HHX is produced with these facilities, the introduction of the new product will be delayed. The impact that this delay will have on demand has not been determined.

With these thoughts in mind, Miller contacted a local real estate agency concerning leasing a building next door. Machinery to process HHX could also be leased. Preliminary cost studies reveal that the cost will be $8.60 with a probability of 60 percent, $8.50 with a probability of 30 percent, and $8.30 with a probability of 10 percent.

Chemical companies were contacted to determine the availability of manufacturing capacity; only one of these companies was interested. Douglass Company indicated that they were presently experimenting with a new process with a success rate, under testing conditions of 40 percent. If success were achieved, their bid would be $5.80 per gallon. However, if they are not able to use this new process in the production of HHX, they must resort to a more elaborate process involving less automated techniques. If the new process fails and a more elaborate process is used, management is willing to submit only maximum and minimum prices of $7.40 and $5.90 per gallon, respectively, with equal chances that this will be the bid. Douglass company has a good reputation, so quality is not an issue.

In talking with Carr Chemicals' management last week, Miller was informed by Carr's president that they had experienced an unforeseen drop in customers' orders but were anxious to keep their present labor force employed by securing short-term orders until they could shift production from lubricants to other chemicals. In view of his pressing capacity problem, Miller asked whether they were willing to engage in subcontracting work. After much discussion, Carr management proposed purchasing the Everett Manufacturing Company contract from Miller for $600,000 and assuming all liabilities. Miller is not concerned about Carr's quality; however, he does have some reservations concerning the impact that a transfer would have on future business with Everett.

Required:

a. Discuss the advantages of a decision tree.
b. What are the requirements for making a decision tree?
c. Draw a decision tree incorporating the financial data given.
d. What course of action would you advise management to take? Support your answer.

Linear programming defined

Effect of constraints

Graphic method

Objective function lines

Simplex method

Sensitivity analysis

1. To introduce linear programming techniques that can be applied in cost accounting.

2. To focus attention on the interpretation of linear programming solutions, not on the procedures for obtaining the solution.

3. To provide an understanding of model formulation in linear programming so that cost accountants can apply these techniques in management decision making.

4. To provide background material needed to answer questions similar to those appearing on recent CPA, CMA, and CIA exams.

19

Linear programming and the cost accountant

As the problems of management become more complex, it becomes imperative to have more accurate information. For accountants to satisfy this need, they must have quantitative tools. One of the major benefits of using such tools is the low expense involved in calculating the impact of change on a proposed course of action. One of the best known operations research models used in the business environment is linear programming.

LINEAR PROGRAMMING DEFINED

Linear programming is a mathematical approach to maximizing profits or minimizing costs by finding a feasible combination of available resources that accomplish either objective. Linear programming recognizes that resources are not only limited, but also that they have alternative uses. Linear programming is a powerful planning tool, but it is complex and usually requires a computer to derive solutions.

Linear programming can be applied to the following types of business-related problems:

1. Allocating resources (e.g., assigning jobs to machines) so that profit is maximized.
2. Selecting product ingredients (e.g., blending chemical products) to minimize costs.
3. Assigning personnel, machines, and other business components (e.g., scheduling flight crews).

723

4. Scheduling output to balance demand, production, and inventory levels.
5. Determining transportation routes so distribution cost is minimized.

Accountants should possess basic knowledge of linear programming; i.e., they should recognize problems that can be analyzed using linear programming. Accountants should also be able to specify objectives and marketing and production constraints. While the ideal situation is for the accountant to understand the mathematics involved and be able to communicate with operations researchers and mathematicians, the position taken in this chapter is that the accountant should focus on drafting and formulating the models and then analyzing the solution obtained. This approach leaves the technical details to the operations researchers.

The emphasis of this chapter is not on the procedures used to obtain the solution; instead, the focus is on the interpretation of the solution. If a solid understanding of linear programming is desired, books on quantitative models should be consulted.

Lack of constraints

The focus in linear programming is on scarce resources. Managers face few challenges in decision making if there are unlimited resources, and selecting a course of action to achieve a specific objective in this situation is relatively easy. Assume, for example, that a company has unlimited resources and its aim is to maximize profits. Its manufacturing facilities can be used to produce either of two products, A or B. Assume further that the entire output of either product can be sold, and the contribution margin per machine-hour is as follows:

	Product	
	A	B
Unit sales price	$10.00	$4.50
Unit variable cost	8.00	3.00
Unit contribution margin	$ 2.00	$1.50
Machine-hours required per unit	1	4
Contribution margin per machine-hour	$ 2.00	$0.375

Since the company can sell all it manufactures, the obvious decision is to use all available capacity in manufacturing Product A, because it has the higher contribution per hour of capacity.

EFFECT OF CONSTRAINTS

Unfortunately, most business problems are not this simple because production and marketing constraints affect the choice of action. Assume, instead, that the manufacturer has a total of 1,000 machine-hours available per period (a production constraint) and that it can sell only 600 units of Product A and 500 units of Product B (a marketing constraint).

In this simple situation with few constraints, the decision is to produce as many units of the more profitable Product A as can be sold, and then use the remaining machine time to produce Product B. The maximum contribution to existing nonvariable cost is $1,350, producing 600 units of Product A and 100 units of Product B to fully utilize the 1,000 machine-hours.

Product A—600 units @ $2 contribution margin per unit $1,200
Product B—100 units @ $1.50 contribution margin per unit . . .   150
Maximum contribution margin. $1,350

Since fixed costs are assumed to be the same whether Product A or B is produced, they are not considered relevant and are ignored in the solution. In addition, it should be noted that even though Product A's $2 unit contribution margin is higher than Product B's $1.50 contribution margin, it is the contribution margin per hour that is important because machine-hours are limited to 1,000 hours and are considered a scarce resource.

Linear programming terms

In the above example, production and marketing constraints are introduced. However, because the data are limited, linear programming analysis is not needed. In many situations, the solution cannot be so readily attained, and linear programming is needed to find the optional combination of resources that maximizes profits or minimizes costs. The purpose of linear programming is to find a mix of the two products which yields the *objective function*, or the factor to be maximized or minimized. In this example, the objective function is to maximize total contribution margin which, in turn, maximizes profit. In other uses of linear programming, the objective function might be to minimize costs. The limitations on the feasible solution are determined by the *constraints*. Constraints are the conditions which restrict the optimal value of the objective function. In this example, the following three constraints are present: a 600-unit maximum sales demand for Product A, a 500-unit maximum sales demand for Product B, and a total of 1,000 available machine-hours. The optimal feasible solution represents all the possible combinations of Product A and Product B that can be manufactured and sold. The following mathematical symbols are used in linear programming equations:

$\geq$ equal to or greater than
$\leq$ equal to or less than
$=$ equal to

Linear programming requirements

To summarize, the following requirements must be present in a decision situation to employ linear programming:

1. The objective function and the limitations must be expressed as mathematical equations or inequalities, because the decision to be made is based on a determinate solution.

2. The objective function must be specified; it is either a profit-maximizing or cost-minimizing function.
3. Constraints must be specified and quantified because resources are limited. Constraints must also be consistent and define a feasible region for a solution. The constraints cannot be specified so that there is no solution for every value of the objective function.
4. The objective function and the constraints must be linear and continuous.
5. Both the objective function and the constraints must be independent and known with certainty.
6. The objective function and all constraints must be a function of a prespecified set of quantitative variables, and these variables must be interrelated. They generally represent resources that must be combined to produce one or more products.

Solution methods

The following solution methods are available for linear programming problems:

1. *Graphic method:* the easiest technique, but limited to simple problems. The basic rule is that the optimum solution lies at the extreme point of feasible combinations of products without going beyond the constraints.
2. *Simplex method:* this technique is most commonly used because it is very effective. The simplex method is a stepwise process which approaches an optimum solution. It is an algorithm to move from a possible solution to another solution which is at least as good; the optimum solution has been reached when a better solution cannot be found. Many computer facilities have a linear programming packages available which use the simplex algorithm to find the optimal solution.

GRAPHIC METHOD

When a linear programming problem involves only two variables, a two-dimensional graph can be used to determine the optional solution. The graphic method is illustrated in Exhibit 19–1 where the x-axis represents the number of Product A units and the y-axis represents the number of Product B units. The combination of Product A and B that results in the largest contribution margin attainable within the limits set by the constraints will maximize profits. In the example presented in Exhibit 19–1, this can be stated algebraically as:

$$CM = \$2.00A + \$1.50B$$

The constraints can also be expressed algebraically as follows:

EXHIBIT 19–1

Graphic solution depicting feasible combinations

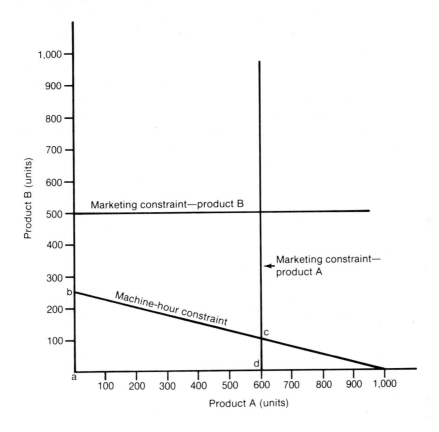

Sales demand for Product A:	$A \leq 600$
Sales demand for Product B:	$B \leq 500$
Machine-hours available:	$1A + 4B \leq 1{,}000$

In addition, the following obvious statements are needed so that negative quantities of products are not determined mathematically:

$$A \geq 0 \quad B \geq 0$$

The constraints are first plotted. If all 1,000 machine-hours are devoted to the production of A, 1,000 units of A can be produced, but there is no Product B manufactured. If, instead, all of the hours are devoted to manufacturing Product B, 250 units (1,000 hours/4 hours per Product B) of B can be produced, but there is no Product A manufactured. By connecting these points, the maximum limits of production possibilities are given. Along this line are all combinations of Products A and B that can be manufactured fully utilizing the machine-hours limitation of 1,000 hours. The marketing constraints, 600 sales demand for Product A and 500 units for Product B, are next plotted. However, in Exhibit 19–1, the marketing constraint that sales demand for Product B will not exceed 500 units is redundant since the production constraint indicates that only 250 units of Product B can be manufactured with the 1,000 machine-hours available. Connecting lines are not needed for the marketing constraints for Products A and B because they each involve only one product.

After plotting all constraints, the boundaries of the feasible area of combination are established. In Exhibit 19–1, this area is a polygon with four corners labeled *a, b, c,* and *d.* Within this feasible area, numerous combinations of Product A and B exist that can be manufactured and sold. For example, the following are a few of these combinations available:

Units of A	Units of B
0	250
200	200
400	150
600	100

Even though there are numerous combinations of Products A and B that satisfy the production and marketing constraints, there is one combination that maximizes the contribution margin. According to mathematical laws, the best feasible solution is at one of the four corner points. As a result, all corner point variables are tested to find the combination that maximizes profits.

Corner point	Combination		Contribution margin = $2.00A + $1.50B
	Units of A	Units of B	
a.	0	0	($2 × 0) + ($1.50 × 0) = $0
b	0	250	($2 × 0) + ($1.50 × 250) = $375
c	600	100	($2 × 600) + ($1.50 × 100) = $1,350*
d	600	0	($2 × 600) + ($1.50 × 0) = $1,200

*Optimum.
Profits are maximized at corner *c* representing 600 units of A and 100 units of B and giving a total contribution margin of $1,350.

OBJECTIVE FUNCTION LINES

Instead of the trial and error method of working with the coordinates of the corners of the polygon, objective function lines can be plotted as illustrated in Exhibit 19–2. The slope of the objective function line can be determined from the two products' contributions as follows using the total contribution margin equation:

$$CM = \$2.00A + \$1.50B$$

To find the slope, which reflects the rate of change of B for one additional A, divide by the coefficient of B and then transfer B to the left-hand side of the equation:

EXHIBIT 19–2

Objective function lines plotted for Products A and B

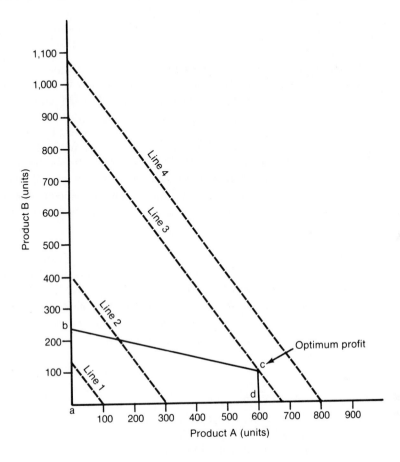

$$\frac{CM}{\$1.50} = \frac{\$2.00}{\$1.50} A + B$$

$$B = \frac{CM}{\$1.50} - \frac{\$2.00}{\$1.50} A$$

Thus, the slope of the objective function is a negative $2.00/1.50 or $-\frac{2}{3}$. In our example, Product A contributes $2 per unit and Product B contributes $1.50 per unit. Therefore, one unit of A equals one and one third units of Product B. If we connect any two quantities of Product A and B in the ratio of A, 1 and B, $\frac{4}{3}$ (or A, $\frac{3}{4}$; B, 1) many product combinations, each having the same marginal contribution, can be calculated. The following four lines have been drawn in Exhibit 19–2.

Line	Units of Product A ($2.00 CM/unit)	Units of Product B ($1.50 CM/unit)
1.	100	133
2.	300	400
3.	675	900
4.	800	1,066

Along Line 1, any combination of Product A and B yields a total contribution margin of $200; along Line 2, the total contribution is $600; along Line 3, a $1,350 contribution margin, and along Line 4, a $1,600 contribution margin. This illustrates that as the objective function lines move out from the point of origin, the total contribution margin increases. Realization of the optimum profit is achieved when no further lines can be drawn without going beyond the constraints. This occurs in Exhibit 19–2 at corner c. If the objective function is optimized at two corner points, any point on the line joining these two points is also optimal. Even though along line 4 the $1,600 contribution margin is greater than at corner c, the combinations of Products A and B along this line are outside the constraints.

Four constraints.   The previous example involving Products A and B is less complex than many business problems because the constraints were limited. For example, if a company's labor-hours per period are divided into two departments and each product requires varying amounts of time in each department, the solution is not as obvious. A linear programming model can be used to determine how many units of each product should be produced each period to obtain the maximum profit.

Consider a company that manufactures regular and super products in its mixing and finishing departments. There are 400 hours of mixing capacity and 240 hours of finishing capacity each day. Regular products require 2 hours of mixing and 0.8 hour of finishing per unit. If all production facilities are devoted to manufacturing regular products, the maximum daily output is 200 units (400/2 hours per regular product) in the mixing department and 300 units (240/0.8 hours per regular product) in the finishing department. Super products, however, require one and one-quarter hours of mixing and one-hour of finishing per unit. If, instead, all facilities are devoted to processing the super products, maximum daily output of super products in the mixing department is 320 units (400/1.25 hours per super product) and 240 units (240/1 hour per super product) in the finishing department. In addition to these constraints, there is such a critical shortage of material used in processing super products that production is limited to a maximum of 180 units per day. Management is concerned that this shortage exists because market demand is sufficient for the company to sell all it produces. (In effect, there is no marketing constraint for super products.) However, sales forecasts indicate a maximum of 150 units of regular products can be sold daily. The following summarizes these constraints and the contribution margin per unit:

	Regular products	Super products
Mixing—maximum daily output	200 units	320 units
Finishing—maximum daily output. . . .	300 units	240 units
Material shortage constraint.	—	180 units
Marketing constraint	150 units	—
Unit contribution margin	$5	$3

The objective is to find the combination of regular and super products that maximizes the following profit function:

Let R = number of units of regular product.
Let S = number of units of super product.
$$CM = \$5R + \$3S$$

These constraints are plotted in Exhibit 19–3:
Production hours constraints:

$$\text{Mixing:} \quad 2R + 1.25S \leq 400$$
$$\text{Finishing:} \ 0.8R + \quad 1S \ \leq 240$$

Material shortage constraint:

$$S \leq 180$$

EXHIBIT 19–3

Four constraints plotted

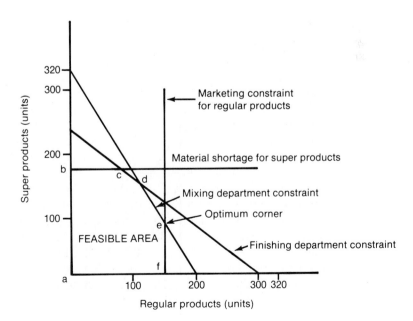

Marketing constraint:

$$R \leq 150$$

Additionally:

$$R \geq 0$$
$$S \geq 0$$

As shown in Exhibit 19–3, the area of feasible production combinations is a polygon with six corners denoted by a, b, c, d, e, and f. Contributions at each of these corners are as follows:

Corner point	Regular units	Super units	CM = $5R + $3S
a	–0–	–0–	$0
b	0	180	$540
c	80	180	$940
d	100	160	$980
e	150	80	$990*
f	150	0	$750

*Optimum.

If, instead, objective function lines are plotted, the slope is $-\frac{5}{3}$ indicating that 1 unit of regular product equals $1\frac{2}{3}$ units of super product. In Exhibit 19–4, the objective function lines are plotted for the regular and the super products. Along line 1, the contribution margin is $500; along line 2, $752; and along line

EXHIBIT 19–4

Objective function lines plotted for regular and super products

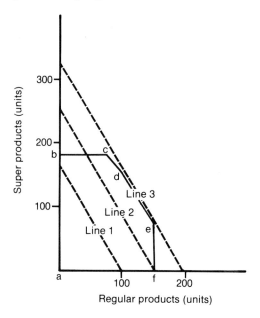

3, \$990, which is the largest margin that can be earned within production constraints. Note how close line 3 comes to corner *d* since the contribution margin at corner *d* is \$980, which is \$10 less than at corner *e*. It could be argued that either corner *d* or *e* is the optimum combination.

SIMPLEX METHOD

The graphic approach works best when there are only two products involved, therefore requiring only a two-dimensional treatment. The simplex method is used to solve more complex problems involving a large number of cost centers and products. Matrix algebra is used to reach an optimum solution. The equations which form the constraints are arranged in a matrix of coefficients and manipulated as a group with matrix algebra. Even though it is too detailed to describe extensively in this book, the simplex method basically involves solving sets of simultaneous equations where the number of unknowns in each set is equal to the number of constraints.

The following steps are taken before the method can be applied. (Note that the first two steps are identical to those used with the graphic method.)

1. Establish the relationships for the constraints or inequalities. The set of constraints for the super and regular product is:

$$\text{Mixing: } 2R + 1.25S \le 400$$
$$\text{Finishing: } 0.8R + 1S \le 240$$
$$\text{Material shortage: } S \le 180$$
$$\text{Marketing: } R \le 150$$

Both *R* and *S* must be zero or positive values:

$$R \ge 0; S \ge 0$$

2. Establish the objective function. A contribution of \$5 and \$3 is expected for each unit of regular product and super product respectively, thus:

$$CM = \$5R + \$3S$$

3. Change the set of inequalities into a set of equations by introducing slack variables. By adding an arbitrary variable to one side of the inequality, an equality results. This arbitrary variable is referred to as a *slack variable* since it takes up the slack in the inequality. The resulting equalities from the four inequalities introduced above are:

$$2R + 1.25S + s_1 = 400$$
$$0.8R + 1S + s_2 = 240$$
$$S + s_3 = 180$$
$$R + s_4 = 150$$

Maximize:

$$CM = \$5R + \$3S + 0s_1 + 0s_2$$

Slack variable s_1 represents unused mixing hours; s_2, unused finishing hours; s_3, unused material; and s_4, unused marketing demand. Because the slack variables do not contribute to profits, they are not added to the profit equation. In tabular format this is:

		S_1	S_2	S_3	S_4	R	S
Solution variable	Solution values	0	0	0	0	5	3
	400	1	0	0	0	2	1.25
	240	0	1	0	0	.8	1
	180	0	0	1	0	0	1
	150	0	0	0	1	1	0

$$\frac{Z}{C_j} - Z_j$$

The tableau results from rewriting the equations of the problem. Row 1 results from the first constraint written as:

$$400 = 2R + 1.25S + 1s_1 + 0s_2$$

Row 2 results from the second constraint written as:

$$240 = .8R + 1S + 0s_1 + 1s_2$$

After the tableau is manipulated using simplex algorithm, the final solution tableau is generated by a computer program:

C_j	Solution variable	Solution values	S_1	S_2	S_3	S_4	R	S	
			$C_j 0$	0	0	0	5	3	
0	S_2	40	−0.8	1	0	0.8	0	0	
0	S_3	100	−0.8	0	1	1.6	0	0	
3	S	80	0.8	0	0	−1.6	0	1	
5	R	150	0	0	0	1	1	0	Profit
		Z_j	2.4	0	0	0.2	5	3	990
		$C_j - Z_j$	−2.4	0	0	−0.2	0	0	

Reading the solution value, the optimal solution is 80 units of super product and 150 units of regular products with an optimal value of Z = 990, from:

$$Z = 5R + 3S + 0s_1 + 0s_2$$
$$Z = 5(150) + 3(80) = 990$$

SENSITIVITY ANALYSIS

This final tableau is the key to sensitivity analysis because the data in it can be used to calculate how much the contribution margin can vary, if at all, without changing the optimal solution. *Sensitivity analysis* is the term used to describe how sensitive the linear programming optimal solution is to a change in any one number. Sensitivity analysis is used to answer "what if" questions concerning the effect of changes in prices or variable costs; changes in value; addition or deletion of constraints, such as available machine-hours; and changes in industrial coefficients, such as the labor-hours required in manufacturing a specific unit. An exhaustive treatment of sensitivity analysis is beyond the scope or intent of this chapter; however, a discussion of shadow prices is appropriate.

Shadow price.   The output above produced with the linear programming computer package provides additional information of economic significance. In the last row of the table $(C_j - Z_j)$ is the amount of profit which will be added if one unit of the variable j is added to the solution. This measure of the contribution foregone by failing to have one more unit of scarce capacity in a specific incident is referred to as a *shadow price*.

Earlier, slack variables s_1 and s_2 were added to convert the constraints into equalities as follows:

$$\text{Mixing: } 2R + 1.25S + s_1 = 400$$
$$\text{Finishing: } 0.8R + 1S + s_2 = 240$$

The tableau indicates that increasing slack variables s_1 by 1 unit will make Z increase by $2.40 from $990 to $992.40. If we increase the right side of the constraint from 400 to 401, this is the same as adding a negative one unit of s_1 and will increase Z by + $2.40. This number, −2.4, is the shadow price or dual price of s_1 the slack variable in the first constraint. This represents the maximum amount we should pay for an additional unit of the resource described in the first constraint. Thus, shadow prices facilitate the calculation of the potential variation in contribution margin from expanding capacity and alleviating the constraint.

The value in the s_2 column, $C_j - Z_j$, raw, is −0 representing the shadow price of s_2, and the opposite of the amount Z increases with every additional unit of Finishing Department resource. Since in the solution, we already have enough finishing capacity to make 40 additional units, no gain would occur if we added more finishing resources.

Caution is needed in interpreting shadow prices because these variations in the right-hand side of the constraints produce the shadow price change in the objective function only within a certain range of their optimal values. Shadow prices are effective quantifications of opportunity cost only if the products and idle capacity do not change. In our example, if all regular products or all super products become the optimal solution, the shadow prices would change.

SUMMARY

As the emphasis in cost accounting shifts even more from providing costs for inventory valuation to determining relevant costs for decision making and internal planning, new techniques are needed. The information needed is not easily available using conventional cost accounting techniques. Thus, it is important that accountants be familar with such quantitative tools as linear programming. However, cost accountants seldom have full responsibility for the development and use of linear programming models. Instead, the primary concern of cost accountants is in determining objective function coefficients. In addition, the cost accountant's focus should be on recognizing situations in which linear programming may be applicable and then obtaining any needed operations research assistance in solving the problem. Certainly, linear programming is a powerful management tool, but it is complex and usually requires use of a computer.

IMPORTANT TERMS AND CONCEPTS

Linear programming
Objective functions
Constraints
Graphic method

Objective function lines
Simplex method
Sensitivity analysis
Shadow price

PROBLEM FOR SELF-STUDY

Michael Reynolds, Inc. manufactures Products A and B. The contribution margin for Product A is $2.25 and $1.25 for Product B. One unit of A requires two hours of machining time and one unit of B requires four hours. There is a limit of 20,000 hours of machining time and 18,000 hours of finishing time available. One unit of A requires 2.25 hours of finishing time; B requires 2 hours. In addition, both units require a direct material that is difficult to obtain. One unit of A requires 1.25 gallons and one unit of B requires 2 gallons. Company purchases of the material are limited to 15,000 gallons.

Required:

Use the graphic method to determine the optimal combination of A and B for the firm to maximize contribution margin.

Solution

Product	Machining	Finishing	Direct material	Contribution margin
A.......	2	2.25	1.25	$2.25
B.......	4	2	2	1.25
Constraints....	20,000	18,000	15,000	

Examine the constraints:

$$\begin{aligned}
\text{Machining:} & \quad 2A + 4B \le 20,000 \\
\text{Finishing:} & \quad 2.25A + 2B \le 18,000 \\
\text{Direct material:} & \quad 1.25A + 2B \le 15,000 \\
& CM = \$2.25A + \$1.25B
\end{aligned}$$

if B = 0:

$$
\begin{aligned}
\text{Machining:} \quad & 2A \le 20{,}000 \\
& A \le 10{,}000 \\
\text{Finishing:} \quad & 2.25A \le 18{,}000 \\
& A \le 8{,}000 \\
\text{Direct material:} \quad & 1.25A \le 15{,}000 \\
& A \le 12{,}000
\end{aligned}
$$

if A = 0:

$$
\begin{aligned}
\text{Machining:} \quad & 4B \le 20{,}000 \\
& B \le 5{,}000 \\
\text{Finishing:} \quad & 2B \le 18{,}000 \\
& B \le 9{,}000 \\
\text{Direct material:} \quad & 2B \le 15{,}000 \\
& B \le 7{,}500
\end{aligned}
$$

These values determine the limits of the constraint equations depicted on the graph.

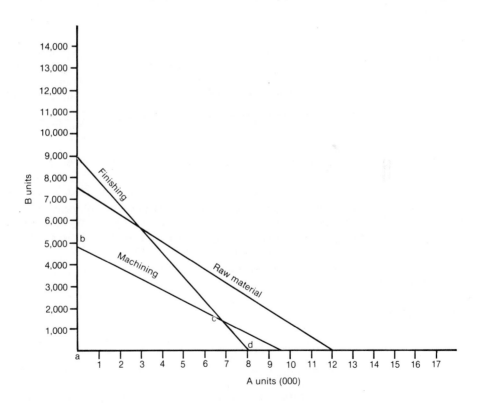

Determine the contribution margin for each corner point using the equation

$$CM = \$2.25A + \$1.25B$$

Table of corner point contribution margin values

Corner point	A value	B value	Contribution margin
a	–0–	–0–	–0–
b	–0–	5,000	$ 6,250.00
c	6,666	1,500	16,873.50
d	8,000	–0–	18,000.00*

*Optimal solution.

REVIEW QUESTIONS

1. What is the major benefit of using models to represent real-world situations?
2. Define linear programming.
3. How are resources regarded in a linear programming model?
4. Give three applications of linear programming.
5. Define the term "objective function" and give an example.
6. What are constraints in linear programming and how do they affect the decision?
7. Give three examples of constraints encountered in business problems.
8. Contrast the two solution methods used with linear programming.
9. Assume a company has 900 hours of skilled labor available and that one unit of A requires 1.5 hours of labor while one unit of B requires 2.25 hours. Marketing analysis reveals a maximum sales demand of 500 units of A and 800 of B. Algebraically express all the constraints involved in this situation.
10. In plotting the marketing and labor-hour constraints described in Question 9, indicate where the constraint lines would intercept the X and Y axis if A is plotted on the X-axis and B on the Y-axis.
11. In reference to Question 9, which marketing constraint deserves limited consideration? Why?
12. In reference to Question 9, indicate where connecting lines are needed. Why?
13. How is the area of feasible combinations determined? Where is the optimal solution located?
14. How is the slope of objective function lines determined and how is the optimum profit determined with their use?
15. Discuss the relationship between sensitivity analysis and shadow prices.

EXERCISES

E19–1.   Graphic solution

Management of Richard Hercher is analyzing the requirements for producing chemicals on idle machines during January and February. Based on past results, the production of 100 gallons of Calciux requires two hours of labor in January and two hours of labor, $70 in cash, and 2.5 hours of machine time in February. To produce 100 gallons of Potasiux, 4 hours of labor are required in January, 10 hours of labor, $50 in cash, and 5 hours of machine time in February. Available for the production of these chemicals are 200 labor-hours in January, 160 labor-hours, $2,100 cash, and 100 machine-hours in

February. The contribution margin is $1.50 per gallon of Calciux and $2.50 per gallon of Potasiux.

Required:

Using graphic techniques, determine how the company should divide its production between Calciux and Potasiux for the two-month period to maximize profits. Express the relationships in mathematical form and indicate the total contribution margin.

E19–2. Determining optimum combination (AICPA adapted)

The Hale Company manufactures Products A and B, each of which requires two processes, polishing and grinding. The contribution margin is $3 for Product A and $4 for Product B. The graph below shows the maximum number of units of each product that may be processed in the two departments.

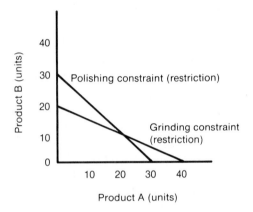

Required:

a. Algebraically express the objective function.
b. Considering the constraints (restrictions) on processing, which combination of Products A and B maximizes the total contribution margin?

E19–3. Production constraints and objective function (AICPA adapted)

Random Company manufactures two products, Zeta and Beta. Each product must pass through two processing operations. All materials are introduced at the start of Process 1. There are no work in process inventories. Random may produce either one product exclusively or various combinations of both products subject to the following constraints:

	Hours required to produce one unit		Contribution margin per unit
	Process 1	Process 2	
Zeta.	1	1	$4.00
Beta.	2	3	$5.25
Total capacity, hours per day	1,000	1,275	

A shortage of technical labor has limited Beta production to 400 units per day. There are no constraints on the production of Zeta other than the hour constraints in the above schedule. Assume that all relationships between capacity and production are linear, and that all the above data and relationships are deterministic rather than probabilistic.

Required:

a. Given the objective to maximize total contribution margin, what are the production constraints for Process 1 and Process 2?
b. Given the objective of maximizing total contribution margin, what is the labor constraint for production of Beta?
c. What is the objective function of the data presented?

E19–4. Analyzing simplex method (CIA adapted)

A company's top management is seeking ways to improve the profitability of one of its newer plants. The president asked the director of internal auditing to review that plant's product mix decisions to assist management in meeting its objective of improved profitability. The internal auditor assigned to the review developed the following.
Monthly profit data by product line:

	Product X_1	Product X_2	Product X_3	Total hours available
Sales................	$3,750	$3,000	$6,000	
Variable costs	$1,200	$1,350	$2,250	
Fixed costs	$2,625	$1,050	$3,675	
Operating profit	$ (75)	$ 600	$ 75	
Monthly production (units).............	150	50	150	
Unit selling price ...... $	25	$ 60	$ 40	
Unit variable cost...... $	8	$ 27	$ 15	
Net contribution per unit .... $	17	$ 33	$ 25	
Labor-hours per unit:				
Department 1	2	5	3	1,000
Department 2	3	1	4	1,360

Demand for each of the plant's three products is so great that the plant can easily sell whatever quantity of each product it produces. The internal auditor constructed the following linear programming model of the plant's operation:

$$\text{Maximize } Z = \$17 \, X_1 + \$33 \, X_2 + \$25 \, X_3$$

Subject to:
$$2 \, X_1 + 5 \, X_2 + 3 \, X_3 \leq 1,000$$
$$3 \, X_1 + 1 \, X_2 + 4 \, X_3 \leq 1,360$$
$$X_1 \geq 0$$
$$X_2 \geq 0$$
$$X_3 \geq 0$$

Slack variables X_4 and X_5 were added to constraints 1 and 2 respectively, and the following optimal tableau was generated by a computer program:

	$C_j - 0$		17	33	25	0	0
C_j		X_0	X_1	X_2	X_3	X_4	X_5
25	X_3	280 units	0	13	1	3	−2
17	X_1	80 units	1	−17	0	−4	3
$Z_j - C_j$		$8,360	$0	$3	$0	$7	$1

Required:

Analyze the information given and provide answers to the following questions:

a. How many units of X_1 and X_3 should be produced, and what would be their total contribution margin?
b. How many units of X_2 should be produced? Explain your answer.
c. Why is linear programming the appropriate technique to employ in the situation above?

PROBLEMS

P19–1. Linear programming techniques

The following information was furnished for the Ray Company's two products, tables and chairs:

| | Maximum daily capacities in units | | | |
	Shaping department	Sanding department	Sales price per unit	Variable cost per unit
Tables	300	250	$75	$45
Chairs	225	150	20	14

Any combination of tables and chairs can be produced as long as the maximum capacity of the department is not exceeded because the daily capacities of each department represent the maximum production for either product. Shortages of skilled labor prohibit the production of more than 200 tables per day. The production information above is used to develop the following graph:

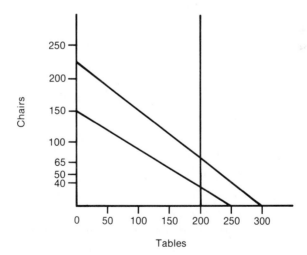

Required:

a. Comparing the information in the table with the graph, identify and list the graphic location (coordinates) of the:
   (1) Shaping department's capacity.

(2) Production limitation for tables because of the labor shortage.
(3) Area of feasible production combinations.

b. Determine the total contribution margin of each of the points of intersections of lines bounding the feasible production area, identifying the best production alternative.

P19–2. Formulating objective and constraint functions (CMA adapted)

Leastan Company manufactures a line of carpeting which includes a commercial carpet and a residential carpet. Two grades of fiber—heavy-duty and regular—are used in manufacturing both types of carpeting. The mix of the two grades differs in each type of carpeting, with the commercial grade using a greater amount of heavy-duty fiber.

Leastan will introduce a new line of carpeting in two months to replace the current line. The present fiber in stock will not be used in the new line. Management wants to exhaust the present stock of regular and heavy-duty fiber during the last month of production.

Data on the current line of commercial residential carpeting are presented below:

	Commercial	Residential
Selling price per roll.	$1,000	$800
Production specifications per roll of carpet:		
Heavy-duty fiber.	80 lb.	40 lb.
Regular fiber	20 lb.	40 lb.
Direct labor-hours.	15 hrs.	15 hrs.
Standard cost per roll of carpet:		
Heavy-duty fiber ($3 per pound)	$240	$120
Regular fiber ($2 per pound).	40	80
Direct labor-hours ($10 per hour)	150	150
Variable manufacturing overhead (60% of direct labor cost).	90	90
Fixed manufacturing overhead (120% of direct labor cost)	180	180
Total standard cost per roll	$700	$620

Leastan has 42,000 pounds of heavy-duty fiber and 24,000 pounds of regular fiber in stock. All fiber not used in the manufacture of the present types of carpeting during the last month of production can be sold as scrap at $0.25 a pound.

There is a maximum of 10,500 direct labor-hours available during the month. The labor force can work on either type of carpeting.

Sufficient demand exists for the present line of carpeting so that all quantities produced can be sold.

Required:

a. Calculate the number of rolls of commercial carpet and residential carpet Leastan Company must manufacture during the last month of production to completely exhaust the heavy-duty and regular fiber still in stock.

b. Can Leastan Company manufacture these quantities of commercial and residential carpeting during the last month of production? Explain your answer.

c. A member of Leastan Company's cost accounting staff has stated that linear programming should be used to determine the number of rolls of commercial and residential carpeting to manufacture during the last month of production.

(1)   Explain why linear programming should be used in this application.
(2)   Formulate the objective and constraint functions so that this application can be solved by linear programming.

P19–3.   Graphic solution with varying conditions

Dean Pipkin, Inc. manufactures two products, regular and super. Each product must be processed in each of three departments: fabricating, assembling, and finishing. The hours needed to produce one unit per department and the maximum possible hours per department follow:

	Production hours per unit		Maximum capacity hours
	Regular	Super	
Fabricating.	3	5.25	1,050
Assembling	6.4	4	1,600
Finishing	6	5	1,800
Other restrictions follow:			
	Regular ≥ 75		
	Super ≥ 50		

The objective is to maximize profits; unit contribution margin is $8—regular and $6—super.

Required:

a.   Given the objective and constraints, what is the most profitable number of units of regular products and super products to manufacture? Determine your answer by utilizing the graphic solution method.

b.   What would your answer be to *a* if there were no minimum restrictions on the products and the direct material cost for regular products has been reduced $2 per unit due to quantity buying?

P19–4.   Linear programming equations (CMA adapted)

The Elon Company manufactures two industrial products—X-10 which sells for $90 a unit, and Y-12 which sells for $85 a unit. Each product is processed through both of the company's manufacturing departments. The limited availability of labor, material, and equipment capacity has restricted the ability of the firm to meet the demand for its products. The Production Department believes that linear programming can be used to routinize the production schedule for the two products.

The data following are available to the Production Department.

	Amount required per unit	
	X-10	Y-12
Direct material: Weekly supply is limited to 1,800 pounds at $12 per pound	4 lbs.	2 lbs.
Direct labor:		
Department 1—weekly supply limited to 10 people at 40 hours each at an hourly cost of $6	⅔ hr.	1 hr.
Department 2—weekly supply limited to 15 people at 40 hours each at an hourly rate of $8	1¼ hrs.	1 hr.
Machine time:		
Department 1—weekly capacity limited to 250 hours	½ hr.	½ hr.
Department 2—weekly capacity limited to 300 hours	–0–	1 hr.

The overhead costs for Elon are accumulated on a plantwide basis. The overhead is assigned to products on the basis of the number of direct labor-hours required to manufacture the product. This base is appropriate for overhead assignment because most of the variable overhead costs vary as a function of labor time. The estimated overhead cost per direct labor-hour is:

Variable overhead cost.	$ 6
Fixed overhead cost.	6
Total overhead cost per direct labor-hour	$12

The production department formulated the following equations for the linear programming statement of the problem.

A = number of units of X-10 to be produced.
B = number of units of Y-12 to be produced.

Objective function to minimize costs:

$$\text{Minimize } Z = 85A + 62B$$

Constraints:

$$\text{Material:} \quad 4A + 28 \leq 1800 \text{ pounds}$$
$$\text{Department 1 labor:} \quad \tfrac{2}{3}A + 1B \leq 400 \text{ hours}$$
$$\text{Department 2 labor:} \quad 1\tfrac{1}{4}A + 1B \leq 600 \text{ hours}$$
$$\text{Non-negativity: } A \geq 0, B \geq 0.$$

Required:

a. The formulation of the linear programming equations as prepared by Elon Company's production department is incorrect. Explain what errors have been made in the formulation prepared.

b. Formulate and label the proper equations for the linear programming statement of Elon Company's production problem.

c. Explain how linear programming could help Elon Company determine how large a change in the price of direct materials would have to be to change the optimum production mix of X-10 and Y-12.

P19–5. Graphic linear programming

Barbara Johnston Corporation manufactures Products A and B. The daily production requirements are shown below:

Product	Contribution margin per unit	Hours required per unit per department		
		Machining	Plating	Finishing
A	$ 6	2	5.0	1.5
B	15	4	2.5	1.0
Total hours per day per department		16,000	20,000	15,000

Maximum daily demand is expected to be 13,000 units for A and 7,000 units for B.

Required:

a. Indicate the objective function in determining daily production of each unit.

b. Set linear equations for the constraints.

c. Determine the optimal solution using the graphic method.

P19–6. Formulating the objective function and constraints. (CMA adapted)

Excelsion Corporation manufactures and sells two kinds of container—paperboard and plastic. The company produced and sold 100,000 paperboard containers and 75,000 plastic containers during the month of April. A total of 4,000 and 6,000 direct labor-hours were used in producing the paperboard and plastic containers, respectively.

The company has not been able to maintain an inventory of either product, due to high demand; this situation is expected to continue in the future. Workers can be shifted from the production of paperboard to plastic containers and vice versa, but additional labor is not available in the community. In addition, there will be a shortage of plastic material used in the manufacture of the plastic container in the coming months due to a labor strike at the facilities of a key supplier. Management has estimated there will be only enough direct material to produce 60,000 plastic containers during June.

In the following income statement for Excelsion Corporation for the month of April, the costs presented are representative of prior periods and are expected to continue at the same rates or levels in the future.

EXCELSION CORPORATION
Income Statement
For the Month Ended April 30, 19—

	Paperboard containers	Plastic containers
Sales	$220,800	$222,900
Less:		
Return and allowances.	$ 6,360	$ 7,200
Discounts	2,440	3,450
Total	$ 8,800	$ 10,650
Net sales	$212,000	$212,250
Cost of sales:		
Direct material cost	$123,000	$120,750
Direct labor.	26,000	28,500
Indirect labor (variable with		
direct labor-hours)	4,000	4,500
Depreciation—machinery.	14,000	12,250
Depreciation—building.	10,000	10,000
Cost of sales.	$177,000	$176,000
Gross profit	$ 35,000	$ 36,250
Selling and general expenses:		
General expenses—variable.	$ 8,000	$ 7,500
General expenses—fixed	1,000	1,000
Commissions.	11,000	15,750
Total operating expenses	$ 20,000	$ 24,250
Income before tax.	$ 15,000	$ 12,000
Income taxes (40%)	6,000	4,800
Net income.	$ 9,000	$ 7,200

Required:

a. The management of Excelsion Corporation plans to use linear programming to determine the optimal mix of paperboard and plastic containers for the month of June to achieve maximum profits. Using data from the April income statement, formulate and label the:

(1) Objective function.

(2) Constraint functions.

b. Identify the underlying assumptions of linear programming.

c. What contribution would the management accountant normally make to a team established to develop the linear programming model and apply it to a decision problem?

P19–7. Formulating constraints and graphic analysis (CMA adapted)

The Marlan Metal Products Company has just established a department for the production of two new products—metal trays and storage devices. This department is ready to begin operation with five metal-forming machines and five metal-cutting machines which have been rented for $300 each per month from a local machine company. Both products require production time on both machines. Each of the machines is capable of 400 hours of production per month. No additional machines can be obtained.

	Machine-hours per unit		Total available machine-hours/month
	Trays	Storage devices	
Metal-cutting machines.	1	2	2,000
Metal-forming machines	2	2	2,000

The controller's department has summarized expected costs and revenues as follows:

	Trays	Storage devices
Selling price per unit . . .	$18	$27
Variable cost per unit. . .	14	20

Demand for the storage devices is unlimited, but Marlan believes that no more than 800 units of the trays can be sold per month.

Required:

a. Mathematically express the objective function and the constraints necessary to determine the optimal production mix of trays and storage devices. (Use S = storage trays and T = trays.)

b. Use graphic techniques to determine the optimal solution and the value of the objective function.

c. Determine the maximum amount Marlan should be willing to spend on advertising to increase the demand for trays to 1,000 units per month.

d. Determine Marlan's total profit per month if one metal-forming machine is returned to the rental agency and the rent can be avoided on the returned machine.

e. Marlan has just realized that a material needed for the production of both products is in short supply. The company can obtain enough of this material to produce 1,200 trays. Each tray requires two thirds as much of this material as a storage device. Develop the constraint necessary to incorporate this additional information into the formulation of the problem.

P19–8. Maximizing a production schedule (CMA adapted)

The Witchell Corporation manufactures and sells three grades, A, B, and C, of a single wood product. Each grade must be processed through three phases—cutting, fitting, and finishing—before it is sold.

The following unit information is provided:

	A	B	C
Selling price	$10.00	$15.00	$20.00
Direct labor	$ 5.00	$ 6.00	$ 9.00
Direct materials	$ .70	$ .70	$ 1.00
Variable overhead	$ 1.00	$ 1.20	$ 1.80
Fixed overhead	$ .60	$ .72	$ 1.08
Materials requirements in board feet	7	7	10
Labor requirements in hours:			
Cutting	$3/6$	$3/6$	$4/6$
Fitting	$1/6$	$1/6$	$2/6$
Finishing	$1/6$	$2/6$	$3/6$

Only 5,000 board feet per week can be obtained. Each week, the cutting department has 180 hours of labor available, and the fitting and finishing departments each have 120 hours of labor available. No overtime is allowed.

Contract commitments require the company to make 50 units of A per week. In addition, company policy is to produce at least 50 additional units of A and 50 units each of B and C every week to actively remain in each of the three markets. Because of competition, only 130 units of C can be sold each week.

Required:

a. Formulate and label the linear objective function and the constraint functions necessary to maximize the contribution margin.

b. The graph provided below presents the constraint functions for a chair manufacturing company whose production problem can be solved by linear programming. The company earns $8 for each kitchen chair sold and $5 for each office chair sold:

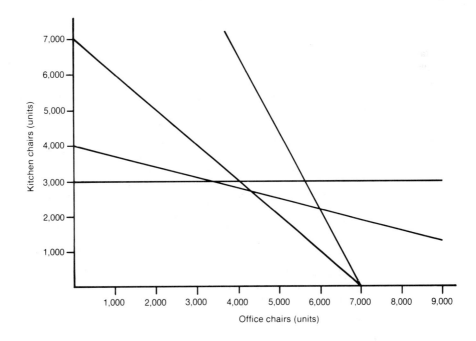

(1)   What is the profit maximizing production schedule?
(2)   How did you select this production schedule?

P19–9.   Multiple regression data in formulating linear programming models (CMA adapted)

The Tripro Company produces and sells three products, hereafter referred to as Products A, B, and C. The company is currently changing its short-range planning approach in an attempt to incorporate some of the newer planning techniques. The controller and some of the staff have been conferring with a consultant on the feasibility of using a linear programming model for determining the optimum product mix.

Information for short-range planning has been developed using the same format as in previous years. This information includes expected sales prices and expected direct labor and material costs for each product. In addition, variable and fixed overhead costs were assumed to be the same for each product because approximately equal quantities of the products were produced and sold.

| | Price and cost information (per unit) | | |
	A	B	C
Selling price	$25.00	$30.00	$40.00
Direct labor	7.50	10.00	12.50
Direct materials	9.00	6.00	10.50
Variable overhead	6.00	6.00	6.00
Fixed overhead	6.00	6.00	6.00

All three products use the same type of direct material which costs $1.50 per pound. Direct labor is paid at the rate of $5 per direct labor-hour. There are 2,000 direct labor-hours and 20,000 pounds of direct material available in a month.

Required:

a.   Formulate and label the linear programming objective function and constraint functions necessary to maximize Tripro's contribution margin. Use Q_A, Q_B, and Q_C, to represent units of the three products.

b.   What underlying assumption must be satisfied to justify the use of linear programming?

c.   The consultant, upon reviewing the data presented and the linear programming functions developed, performed further analysis of overhead cost behavior using a multiple linear regression model. The regression model incorporated observations of total overhead costs and the direct labor-hours for each product from the past 48 months. The following equation was the result:

$$Y = \$5{,}000 + \$2X_A + \$4X_B + \$3X_C$$

where

Y = monthly total overhead in dollars.
X_A = monthly direct labor-hours for Product A.
X_B = monthly direct labor-hours for Product B.
X_C = monthly direct labor-hours for Product C.

The total regression has been determined to be statistically significant as have each of the individual regression coefficients. Reformulate the objective function for Tripro Company using the results of this analysis.

P19–10. Maximizing daily profits (CMA adapted)

Girth, Inc. makes two kinds of men's suede leather belts. Belt A is high-quality, while Belt B is of somewhat lower quality. The company earns $7 for each unit of Belt A that is sold, and $2 for each unit sold of Belt B. Each unit (belt) of type A requires twice as much manufacturing time as required for a unit of type B. Further, if only Belt B is made, Girth has the capacity to manufacture 1,000 units per day. Suede leather is purchased by Girth under a long-term contract which makes available to Girth enough leather to make 800 belts per day (A and B combined). Belt A requires a fancy buckle, of which only 400 per day are available. Belt B requires a different (plain) buckle, of which 700 per day are available. The demand for the suede leather belts (A or B) is such that Girth can sell all that it produces.

The graph below displays the constraint functions based upon the facts presented above:

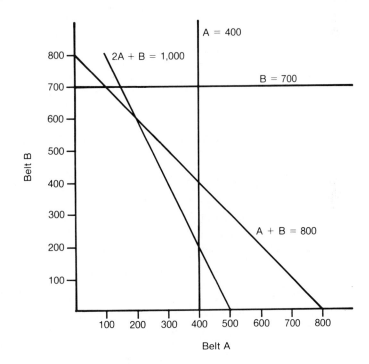

Required:

a. Using the graph, determine how many units of Belt A and Belt B should be produced to maximize daily profits.

b. Assume the same facts above except that the sole supplier of buckles for Belt A informs Girth, Inc. that it will be unable to supply more than 100 fancy buckles per day. How many units of each of the two belts should be produced each day to maximize profits?

c.   Assume the same facts as in *b* except that Texas Buckles, Inc. could supply Girth, Inc. with the additional fancy buckles it needs. The price would be $3.50 more than Girth, Inc. is paying for such buckles. How many, if any, fancy buckles should Girth, Inc. buy from Texas Buckles? Explain how you determined your answer.

P19–11.   Product mix and shadow prices (CMA)

Frey Company manufactures and sells two products—a toddler bike and a toy high chair. Linear programming is employed to determine the best production and sales mix of bikes and chairs. This approach also allows Frey to speculate on economic changes. For example, management is often interested in knowing how variations in selling prices, resource costs, resource availabilities, and marketing strategies would affect the company's performance.

The demand for bikes and chairs is relatively constant throughout the year. The following economic data pertain to the two products:

	Bike (B)	Chair (C)
Selling price per unit	$12	$10
Variable cost per unit	8	7
Contribution margin per unit	$ 4	$ 3
Raw materials required:		
Wood	1 board foot	2 board feet
Plastic	2 pounds	1 pound
Direct labor required	2 hours	2 hours

Estimates of the resource quantities available in a nonvacation month during the year are

Wood	10,000 board feet
Plastic	10,000 pounds
Direct labor	12,000 hours

The graphic formulation of the constraints of the linear programming model that Frey Company has developed for nonvacation months is presented below. The algebraic formulation of the model for the nonvacation months is as follows:

$$\text{Objective function: } Max\ Z = 4B + 3C$$

Constraints:

$$B + 2C \le 10{,}000 \text{ board feet}$$
$$2B + C \le 10{,}000 \text{ pounds}$$
$$2B + 2C \le 12{,}000 \text{ direct labor-hours}$$
$$B,\ C \ge 0$$

The results from the linear programming model, illustrated below, indicate that Frey Company can maximize its contribution margin (and thus profits) for a nonvacation month by producing and selling 4,000 toddler bikes and 2,000 toy highchairs. This sales mix will yield a total contribution margin of $22,000 in a month.

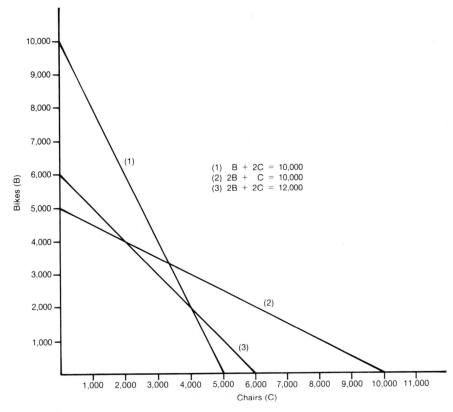

Required:

a. During the months of June, July, and August, the total direct labor-hours available are reduced from 12,000 to 10,000 hours per month due to vacations.

   (1) What would be the best product mix and maximum total contribution margin when only 10,000 direct labor-hours are available during a month?

   (2) The *shadow price* of a resource is defined as the marginal contribution of a resource or the rate at which profit would increase (decrease) if the amount of resource were increased (decreased). Based upon your solution for (1), what is the shadow price on direct labor-hours in the original model for a nonvacation month?

b. Competition in the toy market is very strong. Consequently, the prices of the two products tend to fluctuate. Can analysis of data from the linear programming model provide information to management which will indicate when price changes made to meet market conditions will alter the optimum product mix? Explain your answer.

PART VI

Performance evaluation and pricing analysis

20

Behavioral factors in accounting control

Certainly, both managers and accountants should recognize that since costs will rise if left unchecked, certain control techniques must be applied. However, too many accounting systems are built on the Theory X principles which emphasize unfavorable rather than favorable variances. The psychological result is often budget exaggeration and employee dishonesty. As a result, the traditional assumptions of employees' behavior in business are being questioned by many accountants. Since these behavioral assumptions are reflected in the methods used for internal reporting, they are important. The impact of measuring and reporting on people and companies is discussed in this chapter. Accountants should certainly be concerned about the effectiveness of such internal and external reporting.

Before considering the conditions which should be met in an effective responsibility accounting system, the network of formal and informal relationships should be studied. Within each company there is an organization which is a system of consciously coordinated human activity. For an effective organization to emerge, the people involved must be willing to work together toward a common objective, and there must be a communication flow between these individuals. The functions required of an organization determine its size and form. In turn, these functions are assigned to employees so that areas of responsibility and authority can be defined.

UNIVERSALITY OF MANAGEMENT

Before defining these areas of responsibility and authority, the designer of the responsibility accounting system should recognize the functions of manage-

755

ment. While these functions may be fulfilled in various manners by different people, they remain essentially the same for a small business or a big one, for a manufacturing company or a retail company. This is why a successful manager in one company can transfer to an entirely different industry and still be successful. For example, military officers often become successful managers in universities, industry, and other fields of endeavor. This is because the core of principles applied in management are universal. These principles are usable in all types of companies and by all levels of management.

Functions of management

Regardless of the exact names given to management functions, the following activities must be included: *planning, organizing, staffing, directing,* and *controlling.* It is not possible to state which of these functions is most important in general because one function may receive priority in certain situations while the emphasis may change later. In addition, the organization level involved determines which function is emphasized. For example, top management spends a larger percentage of time in strategic planning than does middle management or a first-line supervisor. However, the overall company is really only as strong as its weakest function. These functions are defined as follows: *Planning* involves selecting objectives and policies, and then choosing the programs and procedures for achieving them. Planning is a form of decision making since it involves choosing among alternatives. It is inaccurate to say that planning precedes the other functions, because this function is an ongoing activity and is continuously changing. *Organizing* involves the determination and enumeration of the activities required to achieve the objectives of the enterprise. These activities are then grouped into cost, profit, or investment centers headed by a manager who has been given the authority to carry out the assigned activities. *Staffing* is concerned with manning, and keeping manned, the positions provided for by the organization structure. This includes the selection and training of employees according to specified job requirements. Care should be taken in this selection, for the effectiveness of all the functions depends on the people involved. *Directing* involves keeping the operations in motion by guiding and supervising subordinates. How well subordinates are directed determines to a great extent how successful the company really is. The final function, control, is defined in more detail later in the chapter, because the cost accountant is more involved with this function than with other managerial activities. The control function is not to be thought of as following all the other functions, for it occurs continuously; in fact, all functions occur simultaneously and are interdependent.

Formal and informal organization

Designers of the responsibility accounting system should also recognize that within each company there is a network of both formal and informal relationships. The formal organization, which is displayed on the organization chart, establishes lines of authority and responsibility and is subject to managerial control. In contrast to informal relationships, the formal organization is larger and more stable; however, communication between lines and levels of the organization is not as frequent as in the informal organization and is usually written, not spoken. The informal organization is a network of personal and social relations which is not established or required by the formal organization and which cannot be rescinded by management. It arises from the social interaction of people, which means that it develops spontaneously as people associate with each other. Communications within an informal organization are more rapid and dynamic than those in formal relationships and consist mainly of oral messages. Informal organizations by their nature are unstable, subjective, and smaller. They often develop into formal relationships as they become larger, thereby giving rise to a new set of informal relationships. The emphasis within informal organizations is on people and their relationships, whereas formal organizations emphasize positions in terms of authority and functions. Informal authority, therefore, attaches to a person, while formal authority attaches to a position, and a person receives it only by virtue of his or her position.

Status within the informal organization may be more important to an individual than is that delegated by the formal organization, depending upon each individual's sense of values. Formal status refers to the relation of supervisor and subordinate as designated by the chain of command in any company. Informal status refers to the social rank which others accord to a person because of their feelings toward the person; it is the position which one has in a social system. Status is more clearly defined within the formal organization; it is generally received because of one's position within the company. Status within the informal organization is determined by such things as an individual's personality, age, seniority, technical competence, work location, and freedom to move about in his or her work area. While status is an intangible state of mind, it serves the following functions: furnishes an incentive for more effective operations, provides for ranking and comparison, supplies a framework for cooperation and communication, and gives people a sense of responsibility.

Management's attitude toward informal organization. Management should identify the leaders of the network of informal relationships within the company and obtain the support of these leaders. This process provides management an opportunity to communicate its operational goals to these leaders for the purpose of soliciting their support and ensuring that the leader's actions are consistent with the company's objectives. Without a doubt, a company should use its informal organization, but not to the detriment of the formal organization. This network of informal relationships is an excellent place for future formal leaders to develop status and satisfaction, and management should recognize that some needs and requirements are better met by informal groups. Rather than have the attitude that the informal organization is bad, management should take advantage of the opportunities the informal organization offers.

Functions of formal and informal organizations. Through plans and policies, the formal organization has the means to run the company; these involve the economic purpose of the total enterprise so that the continuity of the company is preserved and cooperation is obtained. On the other hand, the functions of the informal organization may vary to satisfy the wants and needs of its members. Not only does the informal organization serve as a means of communication, but it also represents a social control through which the behavior of others is influenced and regulated. For *overall* company activities, the formal organization should be the primary control, but certain single activities may be primarily controlled informally. For example, a manager may use the informal organization, more commonly referred to as the "grapevine," as a means of controlling the speech, conduct, or dress of employees. The wise manager sends the grapevine accurate information because it is a rapid means of communication.

Effective management requires an atmosphere in which both the formal organization and the informal organization can work together. If used properly, the informal organization can lighten the workload of the manager by filling in gaps in formal orders or in the manager's abilities. For example, in the formal lines of communication, a scandal would never be formally disclosed. However, if the manager realizes that the informal organization can be a powerful weapon, he or she usually plans and acts carefully. Informal groups further serve as a safety valve for frustrations and other emotional problems that group work involves. Employees often use the informal organization to maintain a specified standard of education or training. For example, if a department employs college graduates exclusively, they may unify and oppose the use of a nongraduate for some of their jobs.

Goal congruence

One of the most difficult, and yet most important, tasks of leaders is reconciling the values and goals of the group they lead—be it formal or informal—with the objectives of the company. Within each organization, a number of leaders will be found who act to hold the group together. However, for a leader to do this, a common basis of beliefs or objectives must be accepted by the group. In many companies, managers are evaluated based on the profits of their division. Near the end of an accounting period, managers may realize that some costs must be cut soon for a profit to be shown. They are, therefore, tempted to eliminate those costs that are totally under their control and do not require the approval of any other party. A manager may delay some needed machine repair and maintenance, for example, or avoid replacing needed personnel. Both of these actions are detrimental to the company's overall goals. Hiring and training new employees is necessary, and failing to make timely repairs may hamper production or even cause permanent damage to a machine.

The responsibility accounting system, in contrast, should encourage managers to pursue objectives which are in harmony with the overall goals of the company. This is referred to as *goal congruence;* that is, goals and subgoals are designed to encourage action consistent with top-management objectives. In addition, employees should participate in establishing goals and standards of performance that will help ensure attainment of company objectives. Care must be taken so that employees understand not only the reasons for the standards, but also how each will be affected by them; employee participation in selecting measures of goal achievement increases their acceptance of an evaluation program.

Regardless of the extent to which employees participate in setting performance standards, both management and employees should recognize that budgets and standards may require changes. For example, environmental conditions over which no one has control, such as an increase in material prices, may change. Employees need assurance that they will not be unfairly censured for infrequent failure to meet the budget or standard due to such changes. In addition, accountants should recognize the tendency of participants to over- or underestimate in setting goals. The information system should provide for monitoring this tendency so that goals and plans are contained within reasonable limits.

To judge a responsibility accounting system's effectiveness in achieving goal congruence, it should be remembered that an organization is comprised of individuals seeking to satisfy their own needs and goals which may not correlate with those of the company. This requires that management set the tone of the environment so subordinates are able to satisfy their needs at the same time that company objectives are being met. Subordinates need the security of knowing what is expected of them, and discipline must be consistent for a responsibility accounting system to be effective. Given this security, subordinates are more likely to assert their independence by participating in the group's activity and assuming responsibility for these activities.

BEHAVIORAL IMPLICATIONS OF PROFIT AND COST CENTERS

Some companies rely on the profit center as a motivational tool by giving specific levels of management a percentage of divisional profits. As Chapter 5 explained, a *profit center* is accountable for both revenues and costs, while a *cost center* is a segment responsible only for costs. The profit center concept recognizes that individual personal objectives may be dominant over corporate objectives because this concept allows the individual manager more flexibility in setting goals within his/her own area of responsibility. Operating within overall corporate policies is implicit within this concept; however, the manager is encouraged to be more innovative. This trend toward decentralization may lead to more individual-oriented goals. This may also be of especial importance as a company grows because employees may have less identity and feel that they are only an "employee number."

Some managers view profit centers as educational devices encouraging lower level management to think in terms of corporate objectives. Some behavioral scientists agree that the profit center can be used to educate employees and that, if it is used effectively, even arbitrary allocations of indirect costs can serve as motivators since profit can be defined as contribution in excess of some "arbitrarily" assigned cost factors. These behavioral scientists further argue that what to a lower level manager appears to be an arbitrary assignment at one level may appear to be a manipulable variable at another.

Managers of profit and cost centers should thus understand the accounting information with which they are presented. If the data are too complicated or considered unfair by managers, conflict will result. Managers should know which costs are allocated and why they are assigned to a given center. They should be encouraged to use the data received in their decision making. It is also important that the information managers receive be clear and simple and as close to the reality of the tasks these managers are working on as possible. There should be a consistency in the data used to report results to profit or cost centers. If there is not, managers will spend much time just arguing over the inconsistencies in the numbers before them.

Designers of the accounting system should also be certain that profit center managers are provided with data about the total performance of the organization; otherwise, suboptimization and narrow-mindedness will result. *Suboptimization* is a condition in which each segment benefits to the detriment of the overall company; this is just the opposite of goal congruence.

The use of larger computer facilities with their improved capabilities for centralized decision making may reverse a trend toward decentralization. Profit maximization may demand more centralized decision making. As a result, decentralized profit responsibility could be changed so that each center can be given responsibility for implementing a portion of a centrally derived profit decision. Thus, the profit goal for a segment may be much less than the maximum profit which the segment could make if left to itself. This holistic approach may continue even to the point that certain profit centers are expected to operate at a loss; as an example, management may decide that to satisfy the overall company goals, a center must supply other parts of the business with materials or products at marginal cost and allow the company to take all the profit on resale. Budgeted goals are thus substituted for goal maximization. Whether a manager will be as effectively motivated by a profit goal that is less than maximum is questionable. Motivating individuals to enhance someone else's performance, rather than one's own directly measurable performance, is difficult.

CONTROL ACTIVITIES

Since a responsibility accounting system relates expenses to the manager responsible for them, the effectiveness of the system often depends on control activities. Control activities are designed to compel events to conform to predetermined plans; thus, they involve the measurement and correction of activities of subordinates to ensure that plans are accomplished within the time specified. Control takes two forms—positive and negative: positive control is an attempt to ensure that the objectives of the company are reached; negative control is an attempt at preventing unwanted or undesirable activities. Control activities must thus involve both the forces that integrate company activities and the forces that disrupt. Effective managers emphasize the integrating forces and suppress and prevent the disrupting forces.

Responsibility accounting and control

Control involves seeing not only that a plan is carried out, but also that objectives are met with the resources committed. A plan cannot be considered under control if more resources are needed than were originally forecast. One of the objectives of responsibility accounting is to trace the costs incurred in such circumstances to the person responsible for the transaction. Responsibility accounting is based on the assumption that all costs are controllable; however, the degree of control depends on the time period in question as well as the level of management. Admittedly, some costs are more difficult to control than others, but all costs are controllable at some level at some time. For example, all costs are controllable by top management in the long run because management at this level has enough time to relieve itself of all commitments such as insurance, depreciation, and other costs of plant asset ownership. In addition, since a lower line supervisor does not have the necessary authority to determine which machine or building will be purchased or leased, this supervisor should not be held accountable for the depreciation or rent charge. Instead, higher levels of management are responsible for such costs.

Responsibility accounting should facilitate the decentralization of decision making so that the expertise of all managers is utilized. However, managers may hesitate to give up some of their authority and areas of control. It is very ego satisfying to have their own "empire of control." Managers must recognize that this is a natural tendency, but that this attitude is very dangerous because it places so great a burden on a few individuals that they are not able to carry out all the functions effectively. Often it is difficult in the early stages to detect a situation in which there are more tasks than there are minds and hands to adequately accomplish them. At this stage, management is caught up in the idea of success and believes that it is taking advantage of a great opportunity to keep expenses down by not expanding human resources. This is the time that a company can reap the benefits of a responsibility accounting system, because such a system requires that overall goals be defined and communicated to subunits as operational goals. Whether they can be accomplished should become apparent at this point.

An important aspect of the control function involves reporting on the progress of performance in meeting the objectives established. To do this, management should provide for effective communication of performance information to the person responsible for meeting such objectives. This communication may include routine and special reports, which may be in written, oral, or graphic form. Reporting also includes other means of communication such as staff meetings and conferences, through which information is also transmitted to a manager as a basis for control of action. The existence of control is also implied, even if no information is received, as in the case of management by exception, if the variance from objectives is insignificant and does not warrant a report calling for action. Management by exception is discussed more fully under "Theory X" on page 767.

Insufficient controls can become an ever-growing problem. Such lack of control, or randomness, is readily sensed by employees and can seriously undermine their performance. To compound the problem, often management realizes that control is insufficient, but may be unable to exactly determine what factors are actually out of control. Lack of control breeds randomness; for example, if the supervisor of the mixing department finds that any needed material can be secured without following the established procedures given in the company's manuals, the assembly department supervisor will soon follow this pattern, too.

Various types of information must be prepared by the accountant depending on which managerial function is being fulfilled. If the primary objective is an evaluation of past events, the accountant provides information that is relatively objective and descriptive. If, on the other hand, management is involved in choosing among several alternatives, the accountants should provide information that describes each option so that differences among the choices are highlighted. Differential analysis showing the forecasted consequences of each alternative is then needed. Because of the nature of this information, it tends to be subjective and reflect hypothetical future conditions. Information that is needed to fulfill the control function involves fixing the responsibility for performance by measuring operations against some standard or objective. This information must be objectively and consistently defined. Thus, accountants must be prepared to furnish sound information for each phase of the management process. They must also recognize that the character of the information is somewhat different for each of the management functions.

Guidelines for control reports

As accountants realize the importance of their role as communicators, they spend less time on the mechanical aspects of accounting and concentrate their attention on improving the clarity of their reports. For example, before management can be certain that control is being maintained, certain guidelines relating to the preparation of control reports should be established.

Since one of the most important guidelines is that the reports be available to managers on a timely basis, the plant's cost structure must be organized so that reports can be prepared periodically to keep management informed of progress relative to the standards. The plant reports of daily activities should, therefore, flow through the cost and accounting sections on a regular basis to keep the reports current.

Control is more effective if variances are detected as the work is in process rather than at the end of operations. These variances can be compiled in daily or weekly reports and expressed in physical terms, such as pounds or hours. Inspection at key production stages during operations can reveal spoilage and other losses. Generally, the closer it is to the event, the more useful a report is. In addition, the format of the reports should be consistent; if changes in report layout are warranted, they should be explained to recipients.

Not only should accountants be concerned that reports are available to managers on a timely basis, they must also relate the report to the user's needs and responsibilities. Reports should avoid areas over which the manager to whom they are directed has no control or authority. For example, a lower line supervisor usually has little voice in choosing what plant facilities are purchased or leased; as a result, the reports this person receives should not focus on the rent or depreciation expense the cost center incurred. Also, since the time that the report recipient is willing to spend in studying the information is limited, the report should be stated in the fewest possible words needed to convey the true picture. Explanations should be brief and to the point, and all unnecessary data should be omitted. The results should be laid out in a clear and concise pattern. In addition, the report should be geared to the personality of the person reviewing it: some managers want detailed analysis with tabulations of statistics; others want the facts in a simple form. Certainly, these reports need to be prepared in terms that management understands; regardless of whether the executive has a sales or a production background, he or she should be able to interpret the accounting terminology used.

Supportive comments.   While management may be aware that such factors as work stoppage, overtime, and extra help affect performance, they may not accurately know how efficient the operation is without supportive comments. Such comments, on both positive and negative performance, can be used as a guide for action to improve operations. Supportive comments should point out danger areas, for example, in a manner that the report users can understand. Reports which include comments that give direction on how to improve performance and/or reinforce successful performance are of more value to the recipient than those that do not. Reports containing supportive comments play an important role in coordinating goals and in combining the varied interests of management.

Regardless of how much attention accountants devote to the preparation of the reports, they waste much of the effort devoted to report preparation if no follow-up advice on inefficient performance is made. All too often, the variances determined are simply compiled in reports, the cycle ends, and another one begins. Management misses a very important phase of the control process in these circumstances by not specifying the *reasons* for the variances from standards so that corrective action can be taken. If employees see that management intends to do nothing about any variances, they tend to disregard the standards.

Accountants should realize that their responsibility for effective internal reporting also involves educating the report recipient. Recipients are more willing to study the data if the purpose of the information is explained. In addition, accountants should recognize an obligation to educate report recipients regarding how they can more effectively use the data prepared.

Highlight exceptions. While it is *management's* responsibility to take corrective action to eliminate the factors causing cost variances, it is the *accountant's* duty to report the facts in such a manner that the control of costs can be facilitated. The report should highlight areas requiring management action to improve performance. Evidence of good performance, as well as performance below acceptable levels, should be emphasized. For this reason, the reports should compare actual performance for a cost or profit center against that center's planned performance. Accountants run a risk if they compare one cost center's actual performance against the actual operations of another cost center, because the conditions under which these results were obtained are likely to differ considerably.

Determining which variances represent the "exceptions" that require management action can be complex. In distinguishing significant variances from insignificant variances, subjective judgment, hunches, and rules of thumb are used. In some instances, a small variance may deserve management's attention and follow-up. Obviously, a 6 percent variance in a $5 million cost item warrants more attention than a 30 percent variance in a $15,000 cost. As a result, many companies use a rule of thumb which incorporates both a dollar amount and a percentage; for example, investigate all variances exceeding $4,000 or 20 percent of standard cost, whichever is lower. Statistical tools are available which reduce the subjective element by separating those variances which are controllable from those that are the result of random events.

Cost-benefit analysis

Variance analysis is subject to the same cost-benefit analysis as other elements in the information system. Unfortunately, the interdependence of the sources of variances make such an analysis complex. For example, should a supervisor be held responsible for the spoilage of material caused by a machine malfunction? On the one hand, the supervisor may not have control over the machine's operation and thus should not be held accountable. However, if the machine malfunction is the result of improper usage or lack of repairs and maintenance, an argument exists for holding the supervisor responsible. In addition, the supervisor is responsible for reporting machine malfunction to the proper party. Interdependence also becomes a factor should the purchasing department order material which does not meet required specifications and must be cut or shaped by production workers before being used in the manufacturing process. This becomes an even larger issue if it is difficult to determine exactly how much extra labor is involved. Thus, the process, people, and techniques involved in variance analysis are often related.

This interdependence, in turn, makes it difficult to ascertain the cost and benefit associated with variance analysis. In making a decision about whether to investigate a variance for the purpose of discovering its cause, accountants must consider the time needed for analysis. The search may involve conferences with production supervisors or workers, or it may focus on engineering or scientific issues. This search may be both costly and time-consuming.

There will always be a trade-off in data gathering between the cost of acquiring additional data and the benefit of these data. A system becomes too expensive when it produces more reports than management can or will use. This also has a detrimental effect on the morale of the employees who have prepared the reports; they cannot feel pride in their work when they see that it is not fulfilling a purpose. The accountant should strive to strike an optimum balance between the cost of the information and the benefits of this information. Information users should also be consulted in evaluating these cost-benefit relationships, because they are aware of the internal and external constraints affecting their needs.

Accounting controls

For the responsibility accounting system to provide an objective measure of an individual's performance, certain accounting controls should be in effect; otherwise, there is no assurance that the performance feedback is valid and should be used as a basis for corrective action. Accounting controls involve methods and processes designed to protect assets and the reliability of financial records. A company normally has such control features as annual audits by independent accountants, fidelity bonds on their employees, electronic data processing equipment, organization charts detailing employee responsibility, and proofs and controls for documents and reports. Also included are procedures manuals, a system of budgets and standards, and an internal auditing staff. Chapters 10 & 11 introduce standard costing while Chapters 12 and 13 discuss budgeting. This chapter briefly discusses procedures manuals and internal auditing procedures.

Procedures manual.   An accounting procedures manual is of invaluable help, for it can provide information about initiating and approving changes in accounting methods as well as detailed instructions for individual accounting procedures. It can also include both the chart of accounts for the accounting systems, including a general description of the classifications, and methods for analyzing operating accounts. A schedule showing the departments responsible for specific report preparation, the report due dates, and the distribution dates is usually incorporated in a procedures manual. Including the summarizing procedures and closing schedules is helpful later for training new employees. Other information, such as the following, may also be included: cost determination for government contracts, standard form letters, conversion tables, table of equivalents, Financial Accounting Standards Board reporting requirements, and Securities and Exchange Commission and other government requirements concerning records and reports.

A procedures manual saves time because it means information and instructions do not have to be verbally repeated. And with written communication like this, there is less chance of misunderstanding instructions. Management can have increased assurance that instructions are correctly understood and interpreted. An additional advantage of procedures manuals is that they assist new employees by providing them with information and clearer knowledge of what is expected of them.

To have an effective procedures manual, the accounting department should make regular revisions, keeping the material current. Revisions should then be periodically distributed to all persons affected by the changes. Enthusiasm must also be generated so that personnel will follow the manual. A clearly written and prepared manual that personnel can comprehend is more likely to be accepted and followed. The internal auditing staff should conduct periodic audits to determine the degree of compliance with the procedures listed in the manual.

Internal auditing. A company may also have its own internal auditing department to review accounting, financial, and other operations as an independent appraisal activity. Since the internal auditing department is usually classified as performing a staff function, it has no operating responsibilities and usually reports to the controller or top management. Internal auditors make evaluations of the degree of compliance with managerial procedures, including whether accounting procedures, government regulations, and contractual obligations are being met. This evaluation of the effectiveness of control is supported by objective analyses, appraisals, and recommendations, and is furnished to members of management. But while the internal auditing department can make recommendations, only management can implement them. In addition, since internal auditors are employees, they do not have the external auditor's independence in fact and in appearance. External and internal auditors both appraise the effectiveness of internal control; however, the internal auditor's evaluations are not limited to accounting controls; he or she also studies administrative controls.

TRADITIONAL ACCOUNTING MODEL: THEORY X

The traditional accounting model and the controls it stresses embody *Theory X*, which considers workers to be motivated solely by economic forces, to be innately lazy, and to be interested in doing as little work as possible. Since this theory presents workers as ordinarily inefficient and wasteful, it assumes that tight budgets and controls are necessary, and it strongly emphasizes the use of accounting as an instrument to reduce and control costs. This model establishes the formal organization chart and the job title as the source of management authority.

These underlying ideas about human nature are reflected in the scientific management movement begun by Frederick W. Taylor and which considers the employee as an additional part of the machine. Taylor was interested in maximizing the productivity of the worker by increasing efficiency and reducing costs. After Taylor's famous work, *The Principles of Scientific Management*, was published in 1911, the scientific management movement flourished and rapidly became an important part of the business scene; many of Taylor's views are widely accepted today. Taylor and his successors studied factory costs in detail and stimulated the development of modern cost and management accounting. Their emphasis on control, segment responsibility, and accountability also affected cost accounting concepts. But the scientific management movement had several drawbacks.

For one thing, it allowed the creation of many repetitive, nonmotivating jobs. As a result, in many large industrial plants today, there is much inattention and sometimes even conscious motivation to do a bad job. Workers are often bored and may think of new, often destructive, ways to break the monotony. While persons with low intelligence and low creative ability usually find assembly-line work acceptable, many people in these jobs are over-qualified. Accountants have contributed to the assembly-line problem by overemphasizing short-run unit costs and by not determining the cost of boredom-induced absenteeism and turnover, which is instead allocated to and hidden in general overhead.

The scientific method also fails to avoid distorted reporting. If accountants agree that the major purpose of cost accounting is to provide various levels of administration with data that facilitate decision making, they must also be certain that performance measurement is not distorted by employees who can develop many ingenious ways of falsifying accounting reports to hide poor performance. Such falsification often occurs in an organizational climate of fear and distrust in which the employees feel they must protect themselves. Employees can justify, to themselves at least, this falsification of accounting records if they do not understand the reporting system or feel that it is too strict. As discussed later in the chapter, the behavioral science approach helps overcome some of these problems.

Spending spree.   A similar kind of distortion is often seen in the recurring government and business budget cycle, in which the measurement of performance against the budget influences the next budget. In cases where the expenditure is less than the amount budgeted, there is a tendency to revise the subsequent budget downward. In cases where the expenditure exceeds the budgeted amount, the manager is criticized and often penalized. It usually takes a manager only one cycle to recognize "the rules of this game." The manager will then engage in a spending spree the last few weeks of an appropriation year to avoid being cut down the next year. This cycle occurs because budgets often overemphasize specialized departments and not the total organization.

Another problem an accountant faces if he or she uses the scientific method is being caught between the demands of two people or groups who exert conflicting pressures to make a decision in favor of the action that each desires. Such incompatible expectations are frequent in the budgeting process. Production personnel, for example, usually feel that the accountant should not make the budget contain tight controls, while top management usually feels that the budget contains too much slack. Accountants recognize the conflicting position in which they are placed, and hence often become defensive about their work, reverting to technical accounting language to confuse one faction or the other.

The reporting of unfavorable variances sometimes causes further breakdowns in the communication chain, especially if the reasons for the unfavorable variances are not published along with the results. For instance, suppose the supervisor of Department A has used more material than the standard specifications allow because the purchasing department ordered a cheaper grade of material than the standard specified. The accountant will then show an unfavorable material quantity variance for Department A, and the supervisor is penalized when, in fact, the fault lies with the purchasing department. Such errors are avoided when the *causes* of unfavorable variances are made clear.

Emphasis on punishment.   The traditional practice in accounting and the scientific management approach is *management by exception,* which holds that control reports should only emphasize and highlight areas that vary significantly from the objective or standard. However, many times the exception is defined as studying only unfavorable variances rather than also investigating exceptionally high favorable variances. The emphasis is on punishment rather than a combination of reward and punishment, which is a combination that more effectively improves production. Workers who are striving for high performance may become quite anxious because management by exception highlights only their mistakes. They may find themselves preoccupied with the number of times they have unfavorable variances rather than with their performance level over the long run. Employees who are highly interested in their work may suffer unnecessarily when deficiencies in their cost centers are emphasized, especially if these are deficiencies over which they had no control.

As a result, they may doubt the validity of the standard or budget set by management and may soon ignore it.

As a result of these deficiencies in the traditional accounting model and scientific management approach, research studies have been conducted which analyze the behavior of employees in a work group. These studies have led to the behavioral science movement, which utilizes a human relations approach. This human relations approach is often referred to as the *Theory Y* concept, which assumes that the average person learns to accept and to seek responsibility. Workers are not viewed as being lazy; in fact, this concept stresses that the expenditure of physical and mental effort in work is as natural as play or rest. Using this approach, human beings are presumed to exercise self-direction and self-control in the service of objectives to which they are committed.

BEHAVIORAL SCIENCE APPROACH: THEORY Y

Behavioral scientists believe that authority is earned; good leaders get someone to follow them because they deserve respect. By proving their ability, these leaders command the respect of individuals below them. The traditional view of leadership, on the other hand, states that the source of authority is merely a person's position on the organization chart. The behavioral scientists attack the organization chart, however, saying that it does not reflect the way people really work together. They further believe that organization charts often unduly restrict or inhibit individual employees by forcing them into a preconceived mold.

The *behavioral science movement* was spurred on by the Hawthorne experiments of 1927–32 and an awakened interest in human relations in the 1930s and 1940s. The Hawthorne study revealed that the attitude of management toward employees affects efficiency and productivity more than do such material factors as rest periods, illumination, and money. The behavioral science approach is based on the thesis that management involves getting things done with and through people, and that managers should center their attention on interpersonal relations. The human aspect of management is emphasized in this approach along with the principle that when people work together to accomplish group objectives, they should understand each other. The focus of the behavioral science approach is on individuals and their motivations as sociopsychological beings.

In general, management has abandoned autocratic leadership for a human relations approach. Research in the social sciences has provided a better understanding of human behavior and acknowledges that people need to feel important and wanted. Even though employees do not always reveal their feelings in words, they do have a strong desire for psychological security, and they need a sense of belonging. The principal theories in behavioral science and their relationship to responsibility accounting are described in the following sections.

Hierarchy of needs

Abraham Maslow attempted to explain behavior in terms of individuals seeking satisfaction through a hierarchy of needs. According to his theory, humans have definite categories of needs that can be arranged in a natural hierarchy of urgency. Maslow's general thesis is that all needs do not emerge at the same time; when one level of needs has been satisfied, an individual may then engage in other forms of behavior to satisfy needs at the next level. Maslow presented the following five basic categories of needs, in order of fulfillment priority: (1) physiological—including the need for food, water, oxygen, rest, and sex; (2) safety—need for a predictable and organized world; (3) belongingness and love—desire for affectionate relations with others and a recognized place in a group; (4) esteem—self-respect and achievement; (5) self-actualization—needs of individuals to become what they are capable of being.

According to Maslow's theory, in a work context, once basic lower-order needs are satisfied, individuals are able to move from routine and boring jobs to ones that hold more potential for satisfying their higher-order needs. However, in evaluating Maslow's theory, one must ask whether a need must be completely satisfied before the next level need emerges. Maslow himself stated that needs are inseparable and interrelated. He also recognized that the hierarchy is not necessarily rigid; for example, a creative person may experience the self-actualization need long before the lower-level needs are even partially satisfied.

Herzberg's two-factor theory

An alternative theory was provided by Frederick Herzberg. According to Herzberg, factors in the work environment which provide job satisfaction are not necessarily the same as those that cause dissatisfaction. *Hygiene factors*, which include company personnel policies, salary, quality of working conditions, and technical supervision on the job, are characteristics of the work environment that cause dissatisfaction. Herzberg felt that employee dissatisfaction is likely when these factors are absent in the work situation; however, the presence of hygiene factors does not necessarily motivate employees—they only prevent dissatisfaction. *Motivators* are the job content factors which produce satisfaction; these include job achievement, recognition of achievement, and responsibility for achievement. According to Herzberg's theory, the absence of motivational factors in the work situation does not bring about dissatisfaction, but when present, motivators relate to a high level of job satisfaction. Motivators involve intrinsic factors or the actual content of a job, not just extrinsic factors of the job environment.

According to Herzberg's findings, the factors that make people unhappy on a job are not the same as those that contribute to lasting satisfaction. Responsibility, advancement, and the nature of the job are the most important job conditions contributing to lasting satisfaction. However, there is an overlap of motivators and hygiene factors, and what is a motivator for one person may be a hygiene factor for another. The Herzberg model does offer managers many things to consider because motivation may not necessarily be increased through the traditional methods of increasing wages and fringe benefits; instead, employees should be given the opportunity for individual accomplishment associated with work.

Reinforcement theory

Because managers are interested in improving job performance, they seek various models and theories to explain human behavior and to effectively motivate employees. In their search they may obtain some job improvement by making consequences contingent on job performance. A *contingency* is the link that connects job behavior with the consquences of that behavior. These contingencies are an important factor in reinforcement theory.

Reinforcement theory is the psychological theory that three elements—desired behavior, contingencies, and consequences—constitute a framework for motivating job performance. Thus, a manager can use contingencies and consequences to influence behavior. Even though reinforcement theory is sometimes seen as manipulative and unethical, contingencies of reinforcement do influence job behavior and performance. It is useful for managers to recognize these concepts in their efforts to create work environments in which people can "self-actualize." Reinforcement theory cannot force an employee to find a particular consequence reinforcing or rewarding. Instead, it requires that managers find behavior-contingency-consequence relationships that reinforce employee behavior.

Evaluation of human relations approach

The behavioral science thesis that management involves human behavior cannot be denied; clearly, good leadership is important in good management. However, to assert that the field of human relations is equivalent to management is quite another issue. Human relations should not be taken as an end in itself but rather as a means to improve productivity. Certainly, employees should be respected and treated as individuals, but management should not make a "production" out of it.

The danger with this approach is that insincerity often creeps in when a person consciously tries to practice human relations. It may reach the point where human relations is regarded as a "skill" or "amateur psychiatry." The human relations approach can lead to the manipulation of employees when an attempt is made to manage people's lives. Also, too much emphasis on human relations can make people feel sorry for themselves, and they can use their psychological problems as an excuse for poor performance. In addition, an overemphasis on behavioral science can distort individual responsibility and make it easy for people to slough off their duties. Rather than producing a good or service that is desired, a company may focus too much attention on individual employees and their relations.

CAS STANDARDS

In designing an information system, several standards issued by the Cost Accounting Standards Board (CASB) must be considered. For example, the information system must provide for the identification and exclusion of any costs determined to be unallowable. In addition, the fiscal year that a contractor can use is specified by the CASB.

CAS 401

One of the standards affecting the information system is Standard 401—*Consistency in Estimating, Accumulating, and Reporting Costs*—which was issued to ensure that each contractor's methods of estimating costs for a proposal are consistent with the cost accounting practices used by the contractor in accumulating and reporting costs. Consistency in the application of cost accounting practices is necessary so comparable transactions are treated alike. It was also felt that the consistent application of cost accounting practices would facilitate the preparation of reliable cost estimates in pricing a proposal and their comparison with the costs of performance of the resulting contract. Such comparisons provide one important basis for financial control over costs during contract performance and aid in establishing accountability for costs in the manner agreed to by both parties at the time of contracting. The comparisons also provide an improved basis for evaluating estimating capabilities.

CAS 401 also requires that a contractor's cost accounting practices in accumulating and reporting actual costs for a contract are consistent with the contractor's practices in estimating costs in pricing the related proposal. In addition, CAS 401 requires that the grouping of homogeneous costs in estimates prepared for proposal purposes shall not per se be deemed an inconsistent application of cost accounting practices under the preceding requirements.

CAS 405

Another standard which the designer of information systems must consider is CAS 405—*Accounting for Unallowable Costs*—the purpose of which is to facilitate the negotiation, audit, administration, and settlement of contracts by establishing guidelines covering (1) identification of costs specifically described as unallowable at the time such costs first are defined or authoritatively designated as unallowable; and (2) the cost accounting treatment of such identified unallowable costs to promote the consistent application of sound cost accounting principles covering all incurred costs. The standard is predicated on the proposition that costs incurred in carrying on the activities of an enterprise —regardless of whether such costs are allowed in government contracts—are allocable to the cost objectives with which they are identified on the basis of their beneficial or causal relationships.

One of the requirements of CAS 405 is that costs expressly unallowable or mutually agreed to be unallowable, including costs mutually agreed to be unallowable directly associated costs, are identified and excluded from any billing, claim, or proposal applicable to a government contract. CAS 405 also requires that costs which are specifically designated as unallowable as a result of a written decision furnished by a contracting officer pursuant to a contract dispute are identified if included in or used in the computation of any billing, claim, or proposal applicable to a government contract. Another requirement is that the costs of any work project not contractually authorized, whether or not related to performance of a proposed or existing contract, is accounted for, to the extent appropriate, in a manner which permits ready separation from the costs of authorized work projects. There are additional requirements in CAS 405.

CAS 406

Another standard is CAS 406—*Cost Accounting Period*—which provides criteria for the selection of the time periods used as cost accounting periods for contract cost estimating, accumulating, and reporting. It was felt that this standard would reduce the effects of variations in the flow of costs within each cost accounting period and also would enhance objectivity, consistency, and verifiability, and promote uniformity and comparability in contract cost measurements. CAS 406 indicates when a contractor cannot use his or her fiscal year as a cost accounting period.

SUMMARY

The basic management functions of planning, organizing, staffing, directing, and controlling are universal in the sense that they must be performed by anyone who administers any type of organized activity, regardless of whether the objective is profit making or not. In general, the manager's job is to create within the company an environment which facilitates the accomplishment of organization objectives. One of the manager's main responsibilities is to achieve coordination of company activities. Without the control function, all other management functions are ineffective.

Certainly, future managers will be required to take more risks and for greater lengths of time. This requires team building and the development of management replacement to meet the demands of the future. Because of these increased demands, management needs the support of a responsibility accounting system. This information system is beneficial because a company must define its overall goals and, in turn, communicate these objectives to each subunit in such a way that areas of responsibility are thoroughly understood. Responsibility accounting also permits effective utilization of the management by exception concept; however, the accountant should ensure that both favorable and unfavorable significant deviations are analyzed. Another important benefit of a responsibility accounting system is that an objective measure of an individual's performance is provided; this performance feedback then allows rapid corrective action to be taken.

Accounting reports should give greater emphasis to favorable performance. Management should not only be made aware of poor performance, but should also have the information available for rewarding efficient production. More thought should be given to the effects of failure on the company's participants so that accounting measurements do not pave the way for additional failure.

IMPORTANT TERMS AND CONCEPTS

Planning function

Organizing function

Staffing function

Directing function

Controlling function

Informal and formal organizations

Goal congruence

Profit centers

Cost centers

Suboptimization

Responsibility accounting

Cost-benefit analysis

Procedures manual

Internal auditing

Theory X

Theory Y

Bahavioral science movement

Maslow's hierarchy of needs

Herzberg's two-factor theory

Reinforcement theory

CAS 401, 405 and 406

REVIEW QUESTIONS

1. Are workers in a group so dissimilar that the same incentives cannot be used for all of them?
2. What is meant by the "universality" of management?
3. List the functions of management and discuss the objectives of each function.
4. Indicate the difference between a formal and an informal organization.
5. What is the effect of status on formal and informal organizations?
6. What should management's attitude be toward informal organizations?
7. Contrast the functions of formal and informal organizations.
8. Discuss the difficulties a leader has in achieving goal congruence.
9. What do you see as possible criticisms of the concept of the hierarchy of needs?

10. How are responsibility accounting and control related?

11. Before control can be effective, what steps must be taken?

12. Discuss the accountant's role in control functions.

13. Why must the accountant prepare various types of information depending upon the managerial function involved?

14. Discuss the criteria that a good report must meet.

15. Define accounting control and give several examples.

16. What is the purpose of a procedures manual? What steps must be taken to ensure that it is effective?

17. What are Herzberg's motivators and hygiene factors?

18. What dangers does a company face if it has insufficient control?

19. What are the underlying concepts of the traditional accounting model?

20. What impact did the scientific management movement have on cost accounting concepts?

21. Discuss the behavioral science approach to leadership. How does this differ from the traditional view of leadership?

22. What do you see as some advantages and disadvantages of the human relations approach?

EXERCISES

E20–1. Compliance with procedure manual

A series of authorizing signatures is required before a requisition will be accepted by the purchasing department of the Scott Company. Normally, the requisition moves through intracompany mail to each person whose signature is required, and then to the purchasing department, where a written order is placed with an outside vendor.

When supervisors need an item in a hurry, they expedite the procedure by carrying the requisition to each person whose signature is required. If a person whose authorizing approval is required cannot be reached, alternative signatures are required. In some cases, secretaries provide the signature, either using a signature stamp or signing their superior's name to the requisition.

After accumulating all the necessary authorizations, the supervisor may personally take the requisition to the purchasing department, at which time a plea for rapid handling of the order is made. If the purchasing agent is convinced of the urgency of the order, a verbal purchase order is placed with the vendor and additional time is saved.

The policy manual states that all requisitions must have supporting documents. If it is convenient for supervisors to attach these data, they do so. Otherwise, they either attach no supporting documents or some miscellaneous documents which contain little useful information. It is well known that often the authorized signer may approve the requisition after only superficial examination of the supporting documents.

Required:

a. Do the documents resulting from the short-cut procedure provide adequate evidence of compliance with the procedure manual? What changes should be made so rush orders can be handled?

b. Assume you are employed as the accounts payable clerk at the Scott Company and have received a copy of the policy manual which states that all purchase invoices must be supported by purchase requisitions in good form. What would you do if you continually receive purchase requisitions which do not have supporting documents or have supervisors' names signed by their secretaries?

E20–2. Credibility of top management

Elmo Fain has just returned from an executive training program that encouraged top managers to publicly praise the efforts of subordinates. As a result, he sends out the following memo to his division managers:

"It gives me great pleasure to review each of your operations and find that your efforts to cut costs have been most successful. I am confident that all of you will continue to put forth your best effort so that our company will have one of its best years ever."

Each of the five division managers is impressed with the memo when they first read it. However, four division managers begin thinking and reflecting on the memo's content. Each of these four managers know that the northern division's performance has been poor because costs have been considerably higher than ever before. These four managers begin talking among themselves and soon arrive at the conclusion that Elmo does not really know what is going on.

Required:

What caused Elmo Fain to damage his credibility?

E20–3. Conflict in communications

Clifton Key, president, remarked casually to the Data Processing Manager, Quiller Knight, that it would be helpful if he had the printouts concerning the capital expenditures being proposed by Friday to study them over the weekend before meeting with the equipment salespersons and board of directors the following week.

Quiller immediately called a halt to all programs being run so that his staff could concentrate on having these reports for the president. This meant that the monthly income statement with its detailed cost of production reports comparing actual costs to standard costs would be delayed for several days.

Quiller and his staff worked overtime and were pleased that they were able to produce the reports for the president by Friday. However, on the following Tuesday, the fifth working day after the end of the month, when the income statements and budget comparisons were normally delivered to the president, the statements were not complete. The data processing manager felt that the president would understand the delay and was quite upset when he received an angry phone call asking for an explanation of the missing reports.

Required:

What do you think has caused the problem? Could anything have prevented this situation from occurring?

E20–4. Application of control techniques

After much investigation, the Crews Company decided to use its own employees in adding another floor to their present building. A $400,000 budget was approved. It is estimated that the project will take two years for completion. Plans are made to transfer some employees from production of ZERXO, which is now experiencing depressed sales. Because there is no union labor, the company has this flexibility.

Sales of ZERXO became even more depressed after construction began. Market research, however, feels that this is only a temporary decline, and that production should not be halted on this line. After consultation, management decides to offer additional ZERXO workers the chance to transfer to building construction.

Periodically, top management inspects the building site so they will have a general idea of the stage of completion. The assistant plant manager assumed the position of building supervisor and furnishes top management with a review of operations only as they request it.

Because of these additional workers, construction is completed in one and one-half years, but at a cost of $440,000. The construction passes all building codes and also meets all the company's specifications.

Required:

Do you believe the control function was effectively applied? If not, what control techniques should have been used?

E20–5. Corporate and individual goals

The president of Ferony Company has spent several hours reviewing the previous year's financial statement. He is concerned that earnings declined last year. Ferony experienced steady growth and excellent profit margins in its first eight years of operations, but in the last two years, its share of the market has remained stable. In view of these developments, the president has called a meeting of the top management team which consists of the firm's four vice presidents. After studying historical data and predicting future sales, each member of the team was asked to present his or her strategy for profit improvement.

The vice president of marketing suggested that the advertising approach be changed so that sales promotion is directed toward additional markets. He also recommended that additional funds be applied toward advertising so that a national television campaign can be included. He believes that this strategy will improve earnings enough so that an increase in sales price will be unnecessary.

The vice president of finance disagrees with the vice president of marketing's approach. She believes an increase in sales price is justified since competitors' prices are already higher than Ferony's prices. In addition, she is skeptical about increasing the advertising budget, because she is doubtful about the short-run benefit. The financial vice president's concern is that the company's cash and short-term investment position will be jeopardized.

The vice president of marketing insists that even though many of the additional sales generated by the national television campaign would be credit sales, 95 percent of them would be collected within 90 days.

The vice president of engineering and research agrees that additional markets should be sought, but that product improvement is the answer. He suggests that the company conduct extensive tests for the purpose of making innovations in the company's product line. He believes that with these additional features, the company will be recognized as an industry leader.

The vice president of production is concerned about rising labor rates and believes that unless Ferony increases its labor rates, many of the skilled labor workers will look for work elsewhere. She agrees with the vice president of engineering and research that the product could be improved by incorporating new features and possibly by using a higher grade of material. In addition, she believes that time and motion studies would result in an improvement in the work flow.

The president has listened intently to each suggestion and agrees with many of these ideas, as he recognizes the need for increasing labor rates. However, he believes that company management should become more involved in civic activities; in fact, he has just been approached by the campaign manager for the United Fund Drive about volunteers. He believes additional study is required before a specific strategy is chosen.

Required:

State the implied corporate goals being expressed by each of the following and how these relate to their own personal goals:

a.   Vice president of marketing.
b.   Vice president of finance.
c.   Vice president of engineering and research.
d.   Vice president of production.
e.   President.

E20–6.   Responsibility for costs of idle capacity

After studying future market conditions, the management of Snowden Company built a modern, highly automated factory adjacent to its 30-year-old plant. Management believes that in the next four years, demand for the company's products will be sufficient that both factories will be operating at normal capacity. However, at present, only part of the new plant's capacity is needed. Within the last year, the new plant has only been used to 60 percent of capacity for two months during the peak season; the plant has been used at 30 percent capacity during the remaining months.

Snowden Company management considered building a smaller plant with possible additions later, but their architect advised the construction of the larger facility. The new plant differs considerably from the old plant because it is highly automated. In addition, the cost of the new plant facilities is several times greater than the cost when the old plant was built. Since the old plant was built at a much lower cost and a substantial portion of the plant and equipment are fully depreciated, the cost per unit processed is much lower in the old plant. Because of these conditions, when full capacity is not required in both plants, the old plant is used to capacity with the new plant absorbing any excess.

The company is decentralized with a superintendent responsible for each plant. Rather than apply factory overhead, actual factory overhead costing rates are determined by dividing actual costs for each factory by the units processed. Each superintendent is responsible for the plant's volume variance.

The superintendent in charge of the new plant does not believe that this procedure is fair. However, top management considers this the only policy to follow since each plant superintendent has authority for plant operations. The superintendent of the new plant believes that the old plant should bear all the cost of carrying idle space and equipment. However, the president contends that the two plants should be treated as two separate companies.

Required:

a.   Evaluate the problem and make suggestions for improving the situation.
b.   Indicate how you would determine and treat idle capacity.
c.   What effect (if any) would this idle capacity cost have on the product cost?

PROBLEMS

P20–1. Responsibility for variances

Dixie Company has adopted the following standards in the Fabricating Department for its product:

	Per unit
Direct material (4 pounds @ $5).	$20
Direct labor (2 hours @ $6)	12
Variable factory overhead (2 hours @ $2)	4
Fixed factory overhead (2 hours @ $3)	6

Normal capacity is 10,000 units per year.

Due to a slack in demand which management considers temporary, production was cut to 9,000 units. The following actual costs were incurred:

Material (40,000 pounds).	$180,000
Labor (18,500 hours).	115,625
Variable factory overhead	37,810
Fixed factory overhead	59,600

The purchasing department was unable to obtain the quality of material specified. As a result, a lower grade of material was purchased which was expected to require the use of 10 percent more pounds per unit. There were 41,000 pounds of material purchased at a total cost of $184,500; LIFO inventory costing is used.

The company's personnel department hires and trains all production personnel.

Required:

a. Calculate the variances for which you feel the supervisor of the Fabricating Department should be held responsible.

b. Indicate the variances for which you feel other individuals should be held accountable.

P20–2. Evaluating departmental reports

Flint has reason to reflect on the past 10 years with pride as his company has grown from a small operation to its present stage of being recognized as an industry leader. It is believed that much of this success is due to the supervision of Flint. As majority owner, he became familiar with all facets of operation. The rapport he developed with factory supervisors was so excellent that there was a constant interchange of ideas for product improvement.

As the company grew, more and more of Flint's time had to be devoted to planning and policymaking so that factory supervisors became responsible for operations. Flint regretted this situation because he believed it resulted in a breakdown in communications. In addition, not all of the problems in operations are being brought to Flint's attention.

As a result, Flint has asked a management consultant to prepare a system of monthly reports that would provide him with more information than he can gain from his limited direct observation.

After the management consultant spent many hours of study and discussion with Flint and his supervisors, she prepared the following sample of a departmental report. A copy of this report will be given to the supervisor in charge of each department with an additional copy given to Flint.

FLINT COMPANY
July 19X2

Supervisor   Harold Douglass   Department   Mixing

	July 19X2	June 19X2	Average for last 6 months	July 19X1
Direct material cost	$20,000	$18,800	$18,000	$15,000
Scrap as a percent of material cost	5%	5.5%	6%	5.8%
Direct labor cost	$24,000	$24,600	$23,000	$22,300
Sales value of production	82,000	80,000	76,000	72,000
Allocated administrative cost	6,000	5,800	5,400	5,000

Direct material cost represents a summary of the actual material used—obtained from material requisitions for each department.

Scrap as a percent of material cost represents the net cost of scrap (direct material cost less sales value of scrap recovered) expressed as a percentage of direct material cost.

Direct labor cost includes regular wages (regular hourly rate multiplied by actual hours worked) and overtime premiums. Individual supervisors are responsible for scheduling operations and are expected to keep overtime to a minimum.

Sales value of production represents the sales price of the production being processed through the department. Actual sales price has increased an average of 10 percent each year due to the effect of inflation.

Allocated administrative cost represents the department's share of such costs as top management salaries, rent and utilities for the administrative offices, administrative staff salaries, and so forth. Floor space occupied by each department is used as the basis for allocation.

Currently, monthly figures are compared to the previous month's results, the average for the last six months, and results for the same month in the preceding year. In addition, the accountant suggested that Flint compare individual departmental reports with those from other departments.

Required:

List any weaknesses in the departmental report suggested by the management consultant. Give any suggestions for improving the report.

P20–3.   Control features lacking

You have been called in as a consultant to advise Duncan Company regarding their branch manufacturing company. The president says, "I hate to think this, but I have 'feelings' that the branch manager is stealing some of the valuable raw material and selling it elsewhere." When you ask the president to explain, he says that the branch manager's wife has a new luxury car and he has heard rumors that she has a new mink coat. The president explains that on a salary of $15,000, the branch manager, who has three children, could not afford such luxuries.

The company informs you that all inventory records are maintained at the home office and that LIFO inventory costing is used. You examine the material ledger cards; a typical card is shown below:

Receipts	Material C28			Balance		
	Issued	Quantity	Amount	Quantity	Unit cost	Amount
June 1 Balance				20 10	$90.00 92.00	$1,800 920
	June 5	2	$184	20 8	$90.00 92.00	$1,800 736
	June 15	3	$300	20 5	$90.00 87.20	$1,800 436
	July 2	3	$315	20 2	$90.00 60.50	$1,800 121

Twice a month, the major supplier sends a price revision to the company. You find that the June 15 price was $100 and the June 30 price was $105.

All purchasing is done by the home office. Whenever the branch manager is running low on a material item, he calls the home office and they forward the material parts. The president points out that since it is really all one company, he sees no need for such transactions to require any document flow. Thus, the inventory records reflect the balance on hand at either the home office or the branch.

The branch manager feels that one of the reasons for the reduced profit last year was poor buying procedures. He is confident that he can secure better prices for the company through some contacts he has made in the civic work he does. However, the president refuses to listen to the branch manager's argument because he is confident that his Purchasing Department is getting good buys.

All personnel are hired at the home office, and transfers are made to the branch by the president according to the workload.

The president says they receive monthly certified net income statements. After investigating the arrangement the firm has with an outside CPA firm, you find that Duncan's bookkeeper forwards the journals and ledgers to the CPA firm for the preparation of the statements. Then, four weeks later, management is given a monthly net income statement. All work by the CPA firm is performed at their offices. The charge for the statement preparation constitutes a significant portion of the administrative expense budget.

Required:

What control features are lacking? Suggest ways improvements can be made.

P20–4. Improved analysis of variances

Kevin Ryan Company is engaged in the manufacture of motors. The following per unit standards have been set for material and labor in the assembly department:

Material (3 pounds @ $2.10 per pound)	$ 6.30
Labor (4 hours @ $3.50 per hour).	14.00
	$20.30

During the year, 5,500 motors were produced in the mixing department and the following variances were charged to the assembly department supervisor:

Actual material cost (18,000 pounds @ $2.10).	$37,800
Standard material cost	34,650
Unfavorable material variance.	$ 3,150
Actual labor cost (23,000 hours @ $3.60)	$82,800
Standard labor cost	77,000
Unfavorable labor variance.	$ 5,800

A plantwide variance report is prepared showing variances for all departments. This report is widely circulated at all plant management levels, causing the assembly department supervisor much embarrassment.

Later, this supervisor is called in by the vice president of manufacturing to explain such large unfavorable variances. The supervisor explains that the purchasing department made a mistake in ordering the material; as a result, direct labor workers had to cut the metal before it could enter the assembly line. Some mistakes were also made in cutting the metal, which destroyed its usefulness. The material could not be returned to the supplier.

A new labor contract was signed by the company in January of this year calling for a $0.10 per hour increase in wages. Since standards are only reviewed at year-end, this change was not reflected in the standard specifications.

Required:

If you feel that the supervisor's arguments have merit, prepare a better analysis of the variances which should be charged to the assembly department supervisor.

P20–5.   Responsibility accounting

Each division of the Raymond Lesikar Company receives a monthly report similar to the one below. Division performance is evaluated on the basis of income before taxes.

RAYMOND LESIKAR COMPANY
New Jersey Territory
For Month Ended December 31, 19–

Sales to outsiders		$100,000
Sales to New York Division (at market price).		20,000
		$120,000
Expenses:		
Material purchases from New York Territory (at full cost)	$ 30,000	
Direct labor.	20,000	
Factory overhead	35,000	
Employee training (allocated on new employees hired)	5,000	
General corporation public relations (allocated equally		
to all divisions).	5,000	
Marketing research staff (allocated on the time spent		
on projects requested by New Jersey manager)	9,000	
Home office administration staff costs (5% of sales)	6,000	
Total expenses.		$110,000
Income before taxes		$ 10,000

Required:

Indicate which of the amounts shown above are inconsistent with the "responsibility accounting" concept. Support each answer with a brief explanation.

P20–6. Improved analysis of variances

In the manufacture of batteries, Monroe Company has established the following per unit standards for material and labor in Department 22, based on 1,000 units normal capacity per period.

Material (4 pounds @ $0.50 per pound) $2.00
Labor (½ hour @ $8.40 per hour) $4.20

During the period, 1,200 batteries were produced in Department 22 and the following variances were charged to the supervisor of this department. Since the cost accountant is on sick leave, other personnel who are not thoroughly familiar with standard cost have had to prepare these variances.

Net material variance:
Actual material cost (5,160 pounds) $3,354
Standard material cost at normal capacity 2,000
Unfavorable material variance $1,354

Net labor variance:
Actual labor cost ($8.40 actual rate) $5,124
Standard labor cost at normal capacity 4,200
Unfavorable labor variance . . . . $ 924

Variance reports for each department are combined on a report and circulated to all plant management levels. The supervisor of Department 22 believes that he has unfairly had to bear the brunt of embarrassment caused by these significant unfavorable variances. When he asked the purchasing department about the increase in material cost, he was told that all suppliers were faced with a shortage of the material needed and had increased their prices. Due to this shortage, the purchasing department also had to order a lower quality that required an increase of 5 percent in the handling and processing Department 22 had to perform and an increase in waste of 10 percent.
The supervisor of Department 22 was also displeased with the labor workers that the personnel department had recently recruited, as these employees did not have the training necessary to immediately begin processing batteries. As a result, the supervisor had to spend 25 hours last period explaining the processing technique to these new recruits.

Required:

If you see any errors in the computations or the variances presented or if you believe a better analysis of variances should be presented, prepare a variance report for Department 22.

P20–7. Needed changes in the reporting system

McSparrin Company is a manufacturer of costume jewelry and employs a standard cost system. The ingredients for the "fake" stones are combined in the mixing department. From there, the mixture is sent in 500-gallon batches to the molding department, where various sizes of stones are molded. After the stones are removed from the molds and cleaned, they are forwarded to the assembly department, where the stones are mounted in rings, bracelets, and necklaces. The frames for these are purchased from an outside vendor.

McSparrin operates on a modified job order process system. For example, all operations use a mass-production, assembly-line approach; however, they do produce according to job order. A job order calling for 1,000 rings of a specified type may be received for inventory stock. After this order is completed, another job order is issued for the production of other types of jewelry. No jewelry is manufactured according to customer specification.

A standard cost system allows for some spoilage in the assembly department. However, the supervisor of the department has been complaining recently about the extra work for her employees in cutting the stones to fit the bracelets they are assembling.

If the stones are even $\frac{1}{64}$ of an inch too large, the assembler must cut and polish the stone so that it can be inserted in the bracelet frame and clasped down.

The plant supervisor has had conferences with the molding department supervisor, and together they have inspected the quality control program. All stones are examined and measured before being forwarded to the assembly department. However, slight variations in size are difficult to detect. The molding department supervisor feels that the bracelet frames supplied by the outside vendor are at fault; he claims that many of these are not consistent in size.

The assembly department supervisor claims that she should not be held accountable for any unfavorable labor quantity variance. She admits that the quantity standard was explained to her before operations began and that an allowance for some stone cutting was made in the standard.

Required:

Suggest ways that this matter should be settled. Make recommendations for any needed changes in the reporting system.

P20–8. Difference in management styles

As owner and general manager of the Bruceton Manufacturing Company, Guy Bruceton feels that he "runs a tight ship." Ever since he founded the company 20 years ago, he has insisted on tight budgets and has employed a number of cost control techniques. A standard cost system is in effect, and variances are reported weekly to his two production supervisors, Bob Smith and Jane Jones.

Bruceton is quite proud of Bob's insistence that the standards should be tight. He has often heard Bob remark, "Remember, our workers will not produce unless they see that they have to." Bob feels the company should install even tighter controls if they are to survive in the future. Bob spends very little time talking with the employees under him; however, he has told them that any time they have a problem relating to either their jobs or their personal lives, they should feel free to come to him. Bob is a rather quiet, reserved individual who has been heard to say that he didn't want to be "nosy" and interfere in his employees' lives. Bob prepares most of his cost center's budgets himself rather than further increasing the workload of each of his supervisors. When he is in doubt concerning an issue, he seeks their advice.

Jane, on the other hand, has been known to disagree with both Bruceton and Bob on a number of issues. In fact, Bruceton has called Jane in on a number of occasions to remind her of the image she should project to the employees under her. Bruceton feels all Jane's subordinates should call her "Ms. Jones" rather than "Jane," as this will remind the employees that she is their superior. Jane is an "outgoing" individual with a friendly personality. Bruceton has further reprimanded Jane several times for joking and laughing with subordinates. Jane is known to have an open-door policy, and employees are often seen in her office discussing on-the-job problems as well as personal matters.

Jane spends much time at the end of the year explaining the budgeting procedure to supervisors, who further briefly explain the process to employees under them. Each supervisor prepares a budget for their respective cost center which Jane reviews and revises before forwarding it to Bruceton. If Jane revises a budget, she explains to the supervisor the reason for the necessary change.

Despite the number of times Bruceton has "talked" with Jane, he cannot honestly say he is disappointed with the performance of any of Jane's cost centers. In fact, there is little difference between the level of efficiency of the cost centers that report to Jane and those that report to Bob.

Required:

Can you explain why there is little difference in the efficiency level of Jane's and Bob's cost centers?

CASES

C20-1. Recognizing employee's needs in training program

On Friday when Bob Smith, vice president of production, received a call from the personnel director concerning a new training program that was to begin next Monday, his comment was, "Training doesn't change all people. I told you that a month ago when you asked me which supervisors I would send to the program." However, the personnel director replied that the president had been asking who of Bob's people would attend. This prompted Bob to call in two of his supervisors, Mary Jones and George Brown.

In describing what he knew about the training program, he said, "Oh, it is about reinforcement theory—some psychologists are coming in to explain to you the theory and language that they derived from experiments using rats, monkeys, and pigeons. But," he continued, "you and I have no choice since the president keeps asking the personnel director whom I am sending." With that, he dismissed them to make plans for supervision of their department's operations while they were attending the week-long training program.

At the beginning of the training program, the lecturers were introduced. Both leaders were young assistant professors at a nearby university. Since these individuals had each just completed their dissertations in reinforcement theory, they were eager to impress the participants with their knowledge. While neither was very familiar with the auto industry, each had observed the production process in the chemical industry and had written a case for a doctoral class about it. After the first day, the professors became more acclimated to the environment and were better able to relate to the participants.

On Monday morning, Mary and George were surprised to see not only the president in attendance, but also several vice presidents. The vocabulary introduced—conditioning, escape learning, stimulus and response—was indeed new and strange to them. However, in open discussions, they observed that the personnel director and her department heads were not frustrated with the language.

As Mary and George learned more about reinforcement theory, they began to see that human behavior can often be indirectly explained in term of concepts derived from animal experiments. They began to understand that in supervision, contingencies of reinforcement do indeed influence job behavior and performance.

Upon returning to their jobs, Mary and George were brimming over with excitement with plans for implementing the new concepts they had learned in the training program. When they attempted to explain these ideas to Bob, he responded with "Yeah, I know you learned about some great ideas there, but now you must get the problems that developed last week straightened out. I'll talk with you about your 'school' some other time." Several weeks passed and nothing more was said about their plans. In fact, the only comment that George and Mary ever heard about the training program came from one co-supervisor who expressed some curiosity as to what they did during their "vacation" from the job.

Required:

Comment upon the training program and its failures.

C20–2. Conflicts in objectives and plans (CMA adapted)

R. J. Cupon is the founder and major stockholder in Cupon SuperMarkets, Inc. The supermarket chain grew from one small store in a southeastern state which opened in 1942 to its present size of 210 stores in 14 states with sales of $819 million. The growth has been accomplished largely by acquiring vacant stores from other grocery chains or independents. Six to nine months are required to open a store and have it reach its sales potential.

Cupon actively manages the company, although its growth and geographic distribution have led to creation of a fully developed management team with comprehensive accounting and budgeting systems. Cupon's management theme seems to be "bigger is better." On a number of occasions he has been heard to say, "I want to have the most stores and largest sales volume of any supermarket chain in the markets I choose to enter." He has customarily awarded bonuses and given recognition to store managers and district managers on the basis of the dollar sales volume and the number of stores opened in a district.

Each year, Cupon initiates the budget process by specifying the goals and objectives he wishes Cupon SuperMarkets, Inc. to achieve. The current year's objective was one of consolidation, and consequently, no new stores were opened. Cupon prepared a memorandum to be sent to all district and store managers identifying the following objectives to be used as the basis for next year's operating budget:

1. An increase in sales volume of 14 percent.
2. An increase in the number of stores to 230.
3. An increase in dollar profits of 17 percent.
4. An improvement in the return on investment from 12 to 13.5 percent.

Required:

a. Identify the communication channels through which R.J. Cupon's goals and objectives for the supermarket chain have been communicated. Explain your answer with reference to the facts presented.
b. Explain whether the messages being sent by R. J. Cupon:
    (1) Reinforce or conflict with each other.

   (2)   Are more likely to enlighten or confuse the receiver.

   (3)   Are likely to have positive, negative, or no effect on the achievement of the goals and objectives for the supermarket chain.

Use specific facts presented in the question to justify your explanation.

C20–3. Conflict concerning responsibility

When Mark Wells joined Ripley Enterprises as a supervisor, he was impressed with the company's emphasis on "responsibility" for they stressed this in their selection of all managers, regardless of the organizational level. All managers were proud of their responsibility because it set them apart from non-managers. As the corporation grew and Mark was promoted to production manager, he discovered there were various kinds of managers. While all were devoted to this concept of responsibility, Mark learned some managers were not the same type of manager he was.

The variety of manager that confused him most was the staff manager; many times, these managers acted as if they were responsible for the same assignments that Mark thought he was responsible for. Mark later discovered that the staff managers were also not as confident as they first appeared; he found they were confused as to their role. In talking with fellow line managers, he was relieved to find that they were equally puzzled; however, the confusion continued. Unkind words were said, and managers became angry. Staff managers hid behind their technical language under the cloak of professionalism. Production managers retaliated by failing to inform staff managers of important facts. Each side used various power tactics and organized its own empire to the extent that finally the president sensed that managers were growing restless.

After calling together the vice presidents for advice, the president discovered the same uneasiness among them. Each vice president was so confident that it was his or her responsibility to give the president the answer to the company problem that each failed to listen to what others in the meeting were saying. Before closing the meeting of vice presidents, the president announced that all line and staff managers were to begin a management development program. Further, he stated that he wanted all managers to work together as a team and to learn about the different types of responsibility.

Later in the week, Mark overheard the marketing manager say: "This management development program is really a waste of my time; the fundamental problem is that too few managers think in terms of increasing sales." As Mark was going over this remark in the quiet of his office, the controller dropped in. After discussing several factors related to the budget, the controller said, "The president is 'all wet' in thinking executive development is the answer when he should instead prevent managers from spending so much money." Mark was relieved that the controller was called away to a long-distance telephone call, and he did not have to make a comment. Mark had decided when the management development program was announced that the fundamental problem could be solved if the other managers would quit talking and get to work in helping him meet production deadlines.

University professors were called in to conduct the management development program. The president gave these professors little instruction concerning course content since he felt they were better qualified than he was to design the program. Although Mark did not like the development idea, he attended some of the meetings, especially those he thought the president was going to attend. Not only did Mark learn about Taylor's scientific management ideas concerning organization structure and management measurement techniques, but he listened to lectures on the delegation of responsibility and authority. He was heartened to hear one professor state emphatically that there could be one and only one boss in an efficiently run organization. In support of this contention, the professor asked the participants to think of the company's salary structure. The fact that executives are traditionally compensated in an ascending order relative to their proximity to the top of the organization supports the contention that enterprise success or failure rests with the highest ranking executive within the organization. Mark was also formally introduced to the concept of participative management and the advantages of improved employee communications. Mark was challenged to become more skilled in communications and counseling so that he could recognize the unexpressed needs of his employees. The professors convinced Mark and others attending the program that human relations were indeed their responsibility and that an effective manager knew that he or she must treat each employee as a unique individual with specific goals and needs.

While the development program did introduce new ideas, it did little to resolve the concern over responsibility that Mark and other managers had. In fact, it appeared to them that their area of responsibility had been broadened, for now they had to be counselor and psychologist in addition to fulfilling their managerial functions. As a result, Mark became confused as to which aspect of his job should be emphasized in confrontation with staff members.

Required:

Discuss the issues that led to the conflicts Mark Wells experienced.

C20–4. Recognition of employees' needs (CMA adapted)

Herbertson Company designs and manufactures teaching aids and teaching machines. The company forecasts a 3 percent growth in sales revenue for next year. The sales revenue growth rate has been declining for the past several years; four years ago, sales revenue growth rate was over 15 percent. The company does not expect the rate to change significantly from the current 3 percent level because school populations are leveling off and school systems are facing more restrictive budgets.

The reduced sales growth rate and a stagnant profit rate have caused Herbertson to cut back on new projects and research into teaching methods. The Teaching Aids Design Department (TADD) particularly has been affected by the cutbacks. The department has become smaller because employees who left have not been replaced. Further, the majority of work in TADD has been refining existing teaching aids and updating the content to correspond with revised editions of textbooks rather than designing new aids. Only three new, relatively small projects have been authorized in the past two years.

TADD currently employs 14 persons; nine have doctoral degrees in various education fields while the remaining five have lower degrees or technical certificates. TADD lost six people in the past two years; five held doctoral degrees and one had a technical certificate.

The Department Manager of TADD is quite concerned about the recent developments. The six people represented many years of experience in teaching aid design and innovation. Several other employees have expressed dissatisfaction with their current assignments. Measures of personnel behavior and production performance attest to the decreasing morale within the department. Employees have requested and taken significantly more sick days and personal days this year than in any previous year. Work thought to be complete has had to be redone because it contained errors. The errors included such things as incorrectly spelled words, improperly located lines, and illustrations whose details did not match precisely the corresponding item in a textbook.

Errors of this kind were virtually unknown in this department in previous years. Also, deadlines are more often missed than met.

Required:

a.   Focusing on employee needs, discuss the apparent reasons for the decline in employee morale and quality of work in the Teaching Aids Design Department.

b.   Recommend steps that management can take to improve the performance of the Teaching Aids Design Department.

C20–5.   Violation of organizational concepts

A policy of pay based on seniority is strictly enforced at the Frank Toombs Company. In fact, a survey revealed the salaries on the graph below are being paid. These salaries are indicated on a partial organization chart to provide an insight into the positions held:

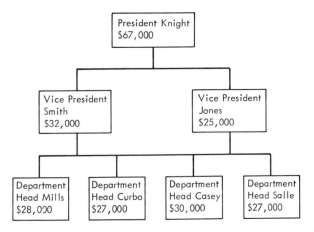

Vice president Jones is having great difficulty accepting the fact that even though his responsibilities are as great as those of vice president Smith, his salary is much lower. In addition, his two department heads each make more than he does. However, Jones has only been with the company 3 years and was promoted rapidly, while Casey and Smith each have 10 years of service with the company.

An additional problem that Jones finds difficult to accept is the salary paid to Salle. Salle had previous experience with a competitor but was brought in earning a starting salary that is more than Jones receives. It is well known that department heads within the company have fewer responsibilities than do vice presidents.

When Jones was promoted from department head to vice president, no increase in salary was given. However, his duties increased. When he asked the president about this, the president reminded him of the possibility that he might hold the top position in two years, when the president retires. It is not clear whether Smith, Jones, or an outsider will step into the president's position at retirement.

Jones also has another problem: Casey generally refers all important requests directly to the president. For the last several years, he reported directly to the president because of the nature of his job. It is well known that Casey expected to get the vice presidency position that was created for Jones.

Required:

Indicate the organizational concepts that were violated and recommend any necessary changes.

C20–6. Behavior perceptions (CMA)

Denny Daniels is production manager of the Alumalloy Division of WRT Inc. Alumalloy has limited contact with outside customers and has no sales staff. Most of its customers are other divisions of WRT. All sales to and purchases by outside customers are handled by other corporate divisions. Therefore, Alumalloy is treated as a cost center for reporting and evaluation purposes rather than as a revenue or profit center.

Daniels perceives the accounting department as a historical number generating process that provides little useful information for conducting his job. Consequently, the entire accounting process is perceived as a negative motivational device that does not reflect how hard or how effectively he works as a production manager. Daniels tried to discuss these perceptions and concerns with John Scott, the Controller for the Alumalloy Division. Daniels told Scott, "I think the cost report is misleading. I know I've had better production over a number of operating periods, but the cost report still says I have excessive costs. Look, I'm not an accountant, I'm a production manager. I know how to get a good quality product out. Over a number of years, I've even cut the raw materials used to do it. But the cost report doesn't show any of this. Basically, it's always negative, no matter what I do. There's no way you can win with accounting or the people at corporate who use those reports."

Scott gave Daniels little consolation. Scott stated that the accounting system and the cost reports generated by headquarters are just part of the corporate game and almost impossible for an individual to change. "Although these accounting reports are pretty much the basis for evaluating the efficiency of your division and the means corporate uses to determine whether you have done the job they want, you shouldn't worry too much. You haven't been fired yet! Besides, these cost reports have been used by WRT for the last 25 years."

Daniels perceived from talking to the production manager of the Zinc division that most of what Scott said was probably true. However, some minor cost reporting changes for Zinc had been agreed to by corporate headquarters. He also knew from the trade grapevine that the turnover of production managers was considered high at WRT, even though relatively few were fired. Most seemed to end up quitting, usually in disgust, because of beliefs that they were not being evaluated fairly. Typical comments of production managers who have left WRT are:

"Corporate headquarters doesn't really listen to us. All they consider are those misleading cost reports. They don't want them changed and they don't want any supplemental information."

"The accountants may be quick with numbers but they don't know anything about production. As it was, I either had to ignore the cost reports entirely or pretend they are important even though they didn't tell how good a job I had done. No matter what they say about not firing people, negative reports mean negative evaluations. I'm better off working for another company."

A recent copy of the cost report prepared by corporate headquarters for the Alumalloy division is shown below. Daniels does not like this report because he believes it fails to reflect the division's operations properly, thereby resulting in an unfair evaluation of performance.

ALLUMALLOY DIVISION
Cost Report
For the Month of April, 19X0
($000)

	Master budget	Actual cost	Excess cost
Aluminum...........	$ 400	$ 437	$37
Labor..............	560	540	(20)
Overhead..........	100	134	34
Total	$1,060	$1,111	$51

Required:

a. Comment on Denny Daniel's perception of:
    (1) John Scott, the Controller.
    (2) Corporate headquarters.
    (3) The cost report.
    (4) Himself as a production manager.
        Discuss how his perception affects his behavior and probable performance as production manager and an employee of WRT.
b. Identify and explain three changes that could be made in the cost information presented to the production managers that would make the information more meaningful and less threatening to them.

C20–7. Alternative compensation plans (CMA)

Pre-Fab Corporation, a relatively large company in the manufactured housing industry, is known for its aggressive sales promotion campaigns. Pre-Fab's innovative advertising and sales strategies have resulted in generally satisfactory performance in the last few years.

One of Pre-Fab's objectives is to increase sales revenue by at least 10 percent annually. This objective has been attained. Return on investment is considered good and had increased annually until last year when net income decreased for the first time in nine years. The latest economic recession could be the cause of the change, but other factors such as sales growth discount this reason.

A significant portion of Pre-Fab's administrative expenses are fixed, but the majority of the manufacturing expenses are variable. The increases in selling prices have been consistent with the 12 percent increase in manufacturing expenses. Pre-Fab has consistently been able to maintain a companywide manufacturing contribution margin of approximately 40 percent. However, the manufacturing contribution margin on individual product lines varies from 25 to 55 percent.

Sales commission expenses increased 30 percent over the past year. The prefabricated housing industry has always been sales oriented and Pre-Fab's management has believed in generously rewarding the efforts of its sales personnel. The sales force compensation plan consists of three segments:

A guaranteed annual salary which is increased by about 6 percent annually. The salary is below industry average.

A sales commission of 9 percent of total sales dollars. This is higher than the industry average.

A year-end bonus of 5 percent of total sales dollars to each sales person when total sales dollars exceed those of previous year by at least 12 percent.

The current compensation plan has resulted in an average annual income of $42,500 per sales employee, compared with an industry annual average of $30,000. The compensation plan has been effective in generating increased sales. Further, the sales department employees are satisfied with the plan. Management, however, is concerned about the financial implications of the current plan. They believe the plan has resulted in higher selling expenses and a lower net income relative to the sales revenue increase.

At the last staff meeting, the controller suggested that the sales compensation plan be modified so that sales employees could earn an annual average income of $37,500. The controller believed that such a plan still would be attractive to sales personnel and, at the same time, allow the company to earn a more satisfactory profit.

The Vice President for Sales voiced strong objections to altering the current compensation plan because employee morale and incentive would drop significantly if there were any change. Nevertheless, most of the staff believed that the area of sales compensation merited a review. The President stated that all phases of a company operation can benefit from a periodic review, no matter how successful they have been in the past.

Several compensation plans known to be used by other companies in the manufactured housing industry are:

Straight commission as a percentage of sales.

Straight salary.

Salary plus compensation based upon sales to new customers.

Salary plus compensation based upon contribution margin.

Salary plus compensation based upon sales unit volume.

Required:

a. Discuss the advantages and disadvantages of Pre-Fab Corporation's current sales compensation plan with respect to:
   (1) The financial aspects of the company.
   (2) The behavioral aspects of the sales personnel.

b. For each of the alternative compensation plans used by other companies in the manufactured housing industry, discuss whether the plan would be an improvement over the current plan in terms of:
   (1) The financial performance of the company.
   (2) The behavioral implications for sales personnel.

C20–8. Profit centers in the evaluation system

According to Jay Doran, president of Baltimore Company, one reason morale is so high among employees is that a stock option plan was adopted several years ago. Thus, key people can see the immediate impact of their personal efforts on company sales and earnings as well as on the stock price. He admits, however, that as the company has grown from 100 employees to 500, stock options have become less motivational.

Now the company relies more on the profit center concept as a motivational tool and pays a percentage of division profits to all employees from supervisors upward. With corporate objectives losing their importance as a motivational force, individual personal objectives are clearly becoming dominant. For instance, Doran explains, learning that the profits of a particular division exceeded the overall profitability of the total company is of more personal interest to its supervisor than is learning that the overall company profits were X percent during the previous quarter. In addition, Doran informs you that the profit center concept allows individuals to combat the feeling that as the company grows, they become smaller and smaller fish in a bigger and bigger pond. Doran further contends that employees favorably identify with profit centers psychologically—what their center is called does make a difference to the division managers.

The philosophy of Baltimore management is that profit centers are primarily educational devices to get lower level management to think in terms of corporate-level objectives. This method of training exposes supervisors to various environmental constraints, which they soon realize vary with management level. To illustrate his point, Doran presented the following partial organization chart:

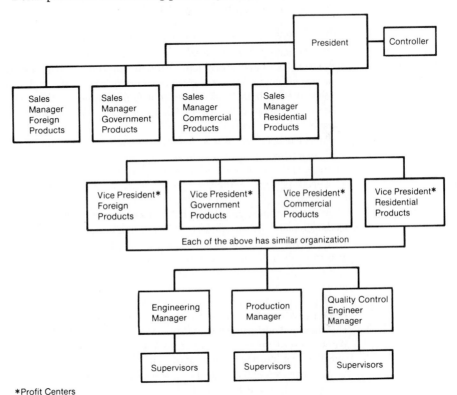

*Profit Centers

To reinforce this treatment of each product line serving as a profit center, prices are established for transfers of semifinished components between product lines. Where available, competitive outside market prices are used as the bases; otherwise, the sales managers impose a transfer price. When questioned as to how successful transfer pricing has been at Baltimore, Doran acknowledged that he has heard some grumbling from managers and vice presidents.

Even though Doran is the first to admit that he lacks accounting expertise, he believes that not enough changes have been made in the accounting system as the company has grown. For example, supervisors often have to wait a month after the quarter ends before receiving profit reports. Also, many of them do not understand how marketing and administrative costs are allocated to their departments or why in some quarters they have exceeded budget merely because the marketing and administrative expense allocations were larger than budgeted.

Annually, the president and the sales managers review the product lines and make sales projections and consider price levels. These individuals work closely with the controller in arriving at logical bases for allocating marketing and administrative expenses. From this analysis, profits for the product lines are forecasted.

Required:

a.   Discuss any existing factors that could lead to problems in the company's evaluation system. Give possible solutions to these problems.

b.   Suggest improvements in the design of the accounting information system.

C20–9.   Conflict in management philosophy

Jones Cannery is an intermediate-sized company located in a large, metropolitan city in the western United States. Jones has approximately $100 million worth of assets, after depreciation, and is in the business of canning vegetables and soups. Vegetables are purchased from both local sources and farms located in the southeast. The finished products are then delivered to wholesalers via rail and trucks. Jones has its own transport truck delivery department.

Jones has been in business for approximately 50 years and has grown from a small, local, independent cannery to an intermediate-sized one. Jones has its own marketing company and markets its products through approximately 300 retail chain outlets. It also markets its products to the U.S. government, various state and municipal governments, other final consumers, and wholesalers.

Both the cannery and its marketing company are subsidiaries of a large, diversified foods company with headquarters in the southern United States. Over the past few years, Jones, its marketing arm, and its parent company have all realized substantial growth in all facets of operations.

Evolution of management dilemma.   Along with Jones's growth, however, certain management difficulties have become apparent. Actually, the roots of these management problems originate in the company's development and history. Jones began its existence as a small cannery fighting for survival in a highly competitive atmosphere. The management philosophy of its early period was strictly the Puritan work ethic. Workers were viewed as having an inherent dislike of work, with relatively little ambition and wanting security above all.

The management philosophy of the early period reflected a solid commitment to external control and the threat of punishment. Top management in this period was composed of individuals who strictly enforced management policies and directives. The threat of being fired was ever present and stiff tongue lashings were quite common. The task of management was to drive employees to get their work done, and the employees' only concern was to work as hard as necessary and keep their mouths shut.

However, as Jones began to grow and was finally acquired by a larger company, individuals with a more behavioristic approach to management began to be hired. As these managers replaced the old managers, the company began to face a very difficult and stressful period in its growth. Often, the young managers found themselves subordinate to older managers who strongly disagreed with behavioral science methods, and there was tremendous tension as the older managers resisted change. This problem was compounded when people who were subordinate to the new managers but trained in the old ways also resisted change.

Some of the original managers who learned management techniques in the early, supervisor-dominated period are now top executives in the company. As Jones has grown and become a subsidiary of the large international foods company, however, new executive talent has been recruited to fill openings created by expansion and retirement. The new managers are young, and many possess advanced graduate degrees. They are generally more liberal and particularly more behavioristically oriented than are any of the older executives from the early period. The problem resulting from the clash between the old and the new has reached dilemma proportions in the finance and accounting department at Jones.

Problem in Accounting Department.   The finance and accounting function at Jones has grown from just a few clerks working in different functional areas to two junior accountants, six accounting supervisors in charge of the various functional areas, two accounting managers, an assistant controller, and a controller. Mary Miller had been the controller for many years until her promotion to Vice President for Finance. She has been responsible for the growth and development of the accounting and finance function from its bare beginning to what it is at present. Miller is a CPA and believes in a strict disciplinary approach to management. She believes employees should keep their mouths shut and work hard. Further, she contends that employees need the motivation that is provided by the constant threat of either a thorough tongue lashing or being fired. While Miller was controller, she developed two degreed accountants under her, James Key and Thelma Ezell, who became strong adherents of her method. Key, a non-CPA, believes that competence and hard work are all that count and that just because one has a CPA certificate does not mean that one is either competent or a hard worker. Of course, he feels that Miller is an exceptional CPA.

As assistant controller, Key strictly enforces deadlines and requires considerable overtime hours from his employees if deadlines are not met. His idea of management by exception is to inform employees when they are making mistakes and let them know mistakes will not be tolerated. Further, he believes that there is no reason to compliment or reward an employee for doing a good job. After all, that is what they get paid for.

Key's management by exception approach has been something of a disaster for the finance and accounting function. Workers who are striving for high performance often become quite anxious because this management by exception policy highlights only their mistakes. They find themselves preoccupied with the number of times they make mistakes rather than with their performance level over the long run. Over the years this policy was in effect, there was considerable turnover in the accounting department. As many as three different employees occupied a single position during one six-week period. Morale has been quite low and various employees have reported Key to the personnel director from time to time. This has resulted in practically no relief for the employees, however, since Miller, Key's mentor, has considerably more power at Jones Cannery than does the personnel director. Moreover, Key and Miller have traditionally, in an effort to impress top parent-company management, set high standards that are difficult for the accounting and finance function to fulfill. This has only served to increase anxiety and turnover and decrease morale. Miller's other disciple is Thelma Ezell, who is currently one of the two accounting managers; however, she is limited in her management function because of living in the shadow of Miller and Key. She is extremely devoted to them, believes in their methods, and feels the finance/accounting function could not survive without them.

When Miller was promoted to vice president a year ago, a major restructuring of the accounting department took place. Before the restructuring, the department was made up of a large number of clerks and a credit manager, all of whom reported to Key, then called the accounting manager. Miller was controller and Ezell worked for her. After the restructuring, the accounting department was organized into functional areas, and supervisors were both appointed from within the company and hired from without. Two accounting manager positions were created, and Ezell was appointed to one of them. The position of assistant controller was created for Key. However, the vacant position of controller was filled from outside the cannery. For this position, top management in the parent company wanted an intelligent, experienced individual who possessed both an MBA degree and a CPA certificate. Further, they wanted a person who was more in keeping with "modern" management techniques. Harold Douglas was hired to fill this position. He possessed an MBA degree, was a CPA, represented the epitome of diplomacy and tact, and was an adherent of the behavioral management school. Almost immediately, Key began to resent the fact that an outsider had been brought in to fill the position for which he felt he had worked so hard. However, Douglas charged ahead and began to introduce many new ideas relating to financial reports and the handling of employee discipline problems. He held management seminars for accounting supervisors and advanced management seminars for the managers and Key. He began to set realistic goals for the department and attempted to trim back overtime hours. Amidst all of this, Key continued to resist Douglas. He continually made uncomplimentary remarks, in the presence of Ezell and some of the supervisors, about Douglas and his methods. Ezell, still under the considerable influence of Key, began to develop a bad attitude toward Douglas. In Key's words, "Douglas is trying to turn us all into a bunch of psychiatrists. We're wasting so much time counseling employees that we're not getting any work done."

Key also began to work around Douglas by seeking out Miller for advice and counsel rather than following the chain of command and going to Douglas. Douglas, displeased with Key, countered by stepping around Key in relaying instruction rather than going through Key, and often countermanded instructions supervisors had received from Key. To make matters worse, a discipline problem arose one day concerning a female clerk who worked for one of the accounting supervisors. The supervisor counseled the clerk using Douglas' approach. Key, feeling that Douglas' approach was not severe enough and knowing that Douglas was out of town at the time, called in the clerk after the supervisor had talked with her and gave her a thorough tongue lashing. Key then informed Miller, who became infuriated with the clerk and also called her in and gave her another tongue lashing and threatened to fire her. News of the treatment of the clerk spread through the office and morale dropped considerably. Several employees complained to the initially involved supervisor. When Douglas returned, he found out about what had happened and relations between Douglas and Key were strained further. This clash of management philosophies has continued. Morale is at an all-time low in the accounting department, and several employees have resigned to seek employment elsewhere. Important progress toward greater automation of accounting systems has also been hindered.

Required:

a. Indicate the factors that have caused the management dilemma.
b. What is your reaction to Key's comment that Douglas is trying to turn the management team into psychiatrists?
c. Suggest solutions to alleviate the conflict.

OBJECTIVES OF CHAPTER 21

1. To describe the responsibility of cost accountants in applying cost analysis and control to marketing activities.

2. To illustrate the techniques used in establishing standards for marketing functions based on their units of variability.

3. To emphasize the care that is needed in interpreting the variances obtained using marketing standards.

21

Marketing cost analysis

Until recent years, relatively little attention has been given to the study of marketing cost; instead, accountants have concentrated their time and talents on solving the problems of production cost accounting, and the cost associated with inefficient marketing has simply been accepted as inevitable. Hence, accountants have failed to fulfill their responsibility to provide management with informed judgments on such important considerations as the financial consequences of new product introduction. To rectify this situation, every accountant should be familiar with the elements of marketing to be able to sensibly evaluate marketing performance.

MARKETING COSTS DEFINED

Broadly, marketing includes all activities involved in the flow of goods from production to consumption. These functions are the second stage in the life of every commercial product as goods are produced, marketed, and consumed. While there is no one accepted definition of marketing, it is generally considered to encompass the procedures that begin at the time the product is manufactured and end when goods reach the ultimate consumer. When the costs of these procedures are described, the term *distribution cost* is often used interchangeably with *marketing cost*.

Chapter 2 introduced three classes of costs: production, marketing, and administrative. Production costs, which include direct material, direct labor, and factory overhead, are incurred to process a product. Marketing costs are incurred so that an actual exchange between the company and an outside party may be effected. These costs include promotion and advertising, as well as physical distribution. Administrative costs are incurred in both production and marketing and include management salaries, financial accounting, and clerical costs, telephone and telegraph, rent, and legal fees. When administrative costs are considered in relation to the work with which they are so closely related, they are actual, though indirect, portions of production and marketing costs. In view of this, some companies feel that only the two classes of costs—production and marketing—need be recognized.

Significance of marketing cost

In recent years, production efficiency has been increased by the use of specialized machinery, labor, and materials. This change, however, has made marketing all the more complicated. To sell the large volume of goods that must be produced to offset the large investment in equipment requires skilled promotion and advertising technology. Since consumers must be persuaded that they need the goods before they will buy them, marketing executives must try, among other things, to create new demand for the product.

This expanded role for marketing has caused expenditures for advertising and sales promotion to increase. More companies are faced with competitive pressures that require extra effort to increase sales volume. This cost-price squeeze is forcing management to pay closer attention to operating costs. In fact, there is every evidence that—since such cost factors as labor, direct materials, and taxes are becoming more standard within industries and less under the control of management—in the future the best chance for a company to secure competitive advantages will be for it to reduce its marketing costs.

Marketing management concept

The growing importance of marketing cost has led to the marketing management concept. This places the marketing manager in the important position of assuming a role in production/marketing decisions and helping develop a companywide plan that involves all aspects of the operating cycle.

Clearly, the expanding role of marketing demands more of the accountant in developing tools for analysis. To this end, the accountant and the marketing manager must work together to develop improved methods of measuring marketing efficiency.

Marketing cost accounting

There is a close parallel, in the cost accountant's duties, between accounting for production costs and accounting for marketing costs. For example, in both cases, the person held responsible for incurring the cost must be indicated for cost control purposes. Marketing cost control, however, is more difficult in the long run because marketing activities, by their very nature, involve many factors which are beyond the control of the company. For example, while the company can use advertising to influence consumer demand, management cannot control demand. The many intangible cost elements inherent in marketing activities such as eye appeal, fads, and seasonal trends also help explain why accounting for marketing costs has lagged behind production cost accounting.

Another distinction between production costs and marketing cost is that while production costs are presented on a per product unit basis, more meaningful ways to present marketing cost exist. Production costs are collected by department or cost center so that a cost per unit can be calculated. Marketing costs, on the other hand, are related to specific marketing functions or distribution channels and are determined for such factors as territories, size of order, product line, or customer grouping.

There is yet another difference between manufacturing and marketing. In manufacturing, much attention is given to full utilization of capacity so that there will be additional units to absorb total fixed costs and so that production cost per unit will decrease as manufacturing volume increases. The effect on *marketing* of increased production volume is that more effort is required to find additional customers and to open new territories; hence, marketing cost per unit normally *increases* when the company attempts to expand sales volume, especially during periods of keen competition. Moreover, the accountant should be aware that increased sales volume should not be the sole measure of marketing efficiency, since increased sales volume does not necessarily mean increased income.

OBJECTIVES OF MARKETING COST ACCOUNTING

In general, there are two purposes of marketing cost accounting. First, marketing cost control and analysis is motivated by a company's desire for more effective planning which leads to better control over marketing cost. Second, marketing cost accounting is designed to justify courses of action to regulatory bodies concerned with marketing policies. To fulfill both of these objectives, marketing cost control and cost analysis are necessary.

Cost control and cost analysis

Different approaches involving divergent techniques are used in *cost control* and *cost analysis*. *Cost control* measures the actual performance of a function against a predetermined standard and investigates any differences between actual performance and the standard. Marketing cost control involves the application of the principles of budgeting and standards to functional costs; the efficient utilization of company assets is of primary concern in cost control. *Cost analysis*, on the other hand, is concerned with searching for better ways to perform marketing tasks. Marketing costs are assembled in meaningful classifications (such as functional categories, including advertising, warehousing, and transportation) so that the classifications can be compared with alternative expenditures and with related sales volumes and gross margins. Marketing cost analysis seeks to discover and eliminate the weak areas in the marketing policy and is concerned with efforts to discover the most promising aspects of the business. Both marketing cost control and marketing cost analysis are discussed in this chapter, with more attention given to marketing cost control.

The objective of marketing cost accounting is not necessarily cost reduction; instead, it is to ensure the most effective use of distribution expenditures to maximize profits. This approach differs in certain respects from production cost analysis, the objective of which is usually cost reduction. As a result of marketing cost analysis, distribution expenditures may, in fact, be increased so the company attracts a greater share of the market.

Government regulations

Since regulation of business necessarily affects distribution, no study of marketing should ignore the effects of the increasing intervention of government in private business. Federal legislation concerning marketing practices and price fixing has now made a knowledge of marketing costs a necessity. The Sherman Antitrust Act, the Federal Trade Commission Act, and the Clayton Act reflect the government's concern with marketing. The Sherman Act declared every contract, combination in the form of a trust, or conspiracy in restraint of trade to be illegal. The Federal Trade Commission has jurisdiction over a wide range of unfair competitive methods and practices; one provision of the Federal Trade Commission Act declares that unfair methods of competition are unlawful. The Clayton Act is designed to eliminate certain competitive methods considered to be potential weapons of monopoly. This act is directed at such practices as price discrimination, interlocking directorates, acquisition of stock in competing corporations, and tying contracts which force the buyer to purchase supplementary and possibly undesirable lines. The purpose of the Clayton Act is to prohibit discrimination only when it has a serious effect on competition generally.

Robinson-Patman Amendment.   In June 1936, the Robinson-Patman Act, which amended Section 2 of the Clayton Act, was passed. With the passage of this amendment, knowledge of marketing cost became a prerequisite for intelligent price determination. The amendment concerned price differentials which involve charging different customers in a single market different prices. The amendment does not imply either that price differentials are entirely prohibited or that price differentials must be granted; rather, it is concerned with the relationship between the prices different customers pay in a single market.

The purpose of the Robinson-Patman Amendment is to protect small business organizations from the advantages that a larger competitor can obtain because of size and buying power. The amendment declares that when different customers are charged different prices, the price differential may not exceed the difference between the costs of serving the different customers. For this purpose, the costs of manufacturing, selling, and delivery are included in the cost of serving customers. A company may be required to support any discounts granted with a cost justification study. The result of the Robinson-Patman Amendment has been an increase in pricing schedules which consider the differences in marketing costs so that consumers can receive the advantage of buying in quantities and by methods which result in savings to the seller.

Since discriminatory price setting can be avoided when complete cost information is available, the Robinson-Patman Amendment continues to be an important motivating force for improving marketing cost accounting methods. The cost accountant should be prepared to study the subject continuously so that unintentional price discrimination that may be in violation of the law is avoided. In addition, successful *enforcement* of such regulatory measures as the Robinson-Patman Amendment requires the development and improvement of marketing cost accounting techniques. What follows is a discussion of such techniques.

Segmentation

As you recall, standards covering *production* are discussed in Chapters 10 and 11. Such standards can also be used to help control and interpret marketing costs. However, the methods of establishing standards for marketing costs differ somewhat from the approach suggested for factory costs. In setting standards for marketing costs, an accountant should first determine how the costs are to be accumulated. For this purpose, there are various segments of the market which can be used, such as territories, products, salespersons, customers grouping, or any combination of these segments. Since Chapter 23 discusses segmental analysis, the discussion concerning segment reporting in this chapter is limited.

Natural expense classification

After the segments are chosen, the functions to be costed, such as by transportation, warehousing, or direct selling, are determined, and costs are accumulated by these functions. Most companies express costs in their records by the nature, or object, of the expenditure—for example, material, wages, and rent. This natural expense classification identifies the kind of service the company secures for its expenditure. But unless these costs are also charged to the function for which they are incurred, they are of little value in determining the cost of the various marketing functions. Therefore, for analysis purposes, the individual natural expense items must then be distributed among the various functions, such as credit and collection or sales promotion. Those costs which are direct require no basis allocation; however, indirect costs must be distributed to the functions on some basis. This requires the same process that is used in allocating indirect manufacturing overhead costs to producing and service departments.

Functionalization

Marketing functions are defined here as any separate and distinct marketing activities in which a company engages, such as direct selling. Consideration of cost responsibility and control should be made, since the responsibility of individuals within a company is generally assigned by function. For example, one individual may be held responsible for warehousing and handling while another employee is in charge of advertising. Marketing executives and accountants should jointly determine the functions to be costed, since the selection depends on the degree of cost control and cost responsibility desired. The size of the company and its method of operation also help determine the number of functions chosen. For instance, a larger company using several means of distribution should have a larger number of functions to cost than does a smaller company using a simple means of distribution. Representative functional classifications of marketing costs are difficult to establish because there are so many marketing procedures and practices in which companies may engage. To illustrate the procedures involved, this chapter uses the following functional classifications for the entire marketing effort: warehousing and handling, transportation, credit and collection, direct selling, advertising and sales promotion, and general marketing.

The weakness of allocating the entire cost of a function to segments is that some elements of the functional cost may be more accurately allocated on more than one basis. This is the reason that in the illustrations in this chapter a more precise method considering degree of functionalization is used to assign costs to functions. Degree of functionalization refers to the homogeneity of the marketing activities classified within categories; the extent of this homogeneity varies. For example, pricing and tagging finished products for storage and shipment is so different from soliciting sales orders by telephone that these two marketing activities should not be combined.

Assigning costs to functions is integrated in the accounts in some companies while it is made independent of the accounting records in others. The integration of functions can be accomplished through the use of digit codes. Digit codes can provide for analysis both by function and by segment, with charges coded at the source of the expenditure. For example, the company could use a 1 in the third digit of the account numbers to refer to the Northern Territory, a 2 for the Eastern Territory, and so forth. A 1 in the fourth digit could indicate the function, such as warehousing or direct selling, being costed. Each segment and function would be assigned a different number to facilitate the costing of each function. To the extent possible, the accounts should be designated so that as many costs as possible are charged to the function directly rather than through allocation.

Detailed functional classification.   Approaches that involve finely defined functional categories consider measures of variability. That is, the expenses included in a functional group are not only closely related, but also vary according to the same factor of measurement. For example, advertising and sales promotion may be further broken down into radio, television, direct mail, and other advertising media. Dividing major functions into small classifications of responsibility is intended to ensure that the work performed is homogenous. However, the benefit of a detailed functional classification must be considered in relation to the extra cost involved in accounting this way. It is not feasible, for instance, for a small company to detail all its functions; instead, it should establish a standard for the entire marketing function using the most appropriate unit of variability. Generally, however, the more precise functionalization is preferable, for a greater degree of control is usually obtained if the major marketing functions are broken down in detail.

Functional costs should be reviewed to determine whether the costs are direct or indirect charges to the segment. No allocation is required for the *direct functional cost;* however, *indirect costs* are applied to territories, customer groupings, or other market segments on a unit fractional cost basis using the factor of variability that appears most appropriate.

Units of variability

In manufacturing costs, the basis of cost control is the relationship between input and output. Standard input costs per unit of physical output are often used for direct material and direct labor. A broadly defined unit of activity is also generally used for factory overhead. To extend this concept to marketing cost, the factor which causes the marketing costs to vary must be identified. Such a measure is known as the *unit of variability, work unit,* or *service unit.* Since the standards are based on the unit of variability, great care must be exercised in deciding what that unit is to be. In selecting suitable units of variability, a company should be practical to the extent that the unit should be measurable and produce results which are reasonably accurate and yet are economical in application.

STANDARDS FOR MARKETING COSTS

There are several differences between the standard costing approach used for production operations and that used for marketing operations. For example, the direct relationship between effort and result in production costs is often lacking in marketing activities. Also, in the past, many companies have hesitated to set standards for marketing functions because they felt that there was so much variation between time periods that it was impossible to establish and use standard costs. However, many marketing activities are uniform enough so that standards can be set on a physical basis. A combination of past experience, industrial engineering studies, and judgment can be used to establish standards for each functional factor of variability.

A company must consider past, present, and forecasted conditions in the company itself and in the trade territories before setting marketing standards for territories, since the same standards may not be applicable in different geographical areas. The distance of the territory from the manufacturing plant, for example, must be considered in establishing standards; obviously, markets farther from the manufacturing plant have greater transportation expense per unit than markets located in the same territory as the plant.

Standard costs for advertising also vary according to the different zones advertising is to cover. One explanation for this is that different advertising media are used in selected territories because dissimilar types of consumers are found in the various territories. For example, an industrial goods manufacturer likely has only a few practical media alternatives, such as advertising in the one trade publication or direct mail. A consumer products manufacturer has more potential customers and several media from which to choose. A salesperson working in a highly populated area also has a lower standard cost per customer than does a salesperson traveling in a sparsely settled area. The nature of the coverage also affects the time and cost required to serve a territory. Salespersons in some locales may be required to stop weekly at each possible outlet, while other territories are covered less frequently. The nature of the competition in the different regions also affects the standard costs for advertising and direct selling.

Repetitive and nonrepetitive operations

One of the first steps in establishing marketing standards is to determine whether the marketing function is repetitive or nonrepetitive. This can be most easily accomplished by conducting a job audit or analysis in which the operations performed in each function are listed. Each operation is then studied to determine whether the necessary procedures are repetitive and routine so that they can be standardized. For example, in warehousing and handling, the procedures necessary to receive, price, mark, sort, and wrap goods are fairly routine and uniform. On the other hand, making a sales call or handling sales adjustments and returns varies considerably between customers and salespersons. It is thus more difficult to standardize the procedures involved with functions, such as direct selling, than it is for functions of a routine nature.

In such an analysis, time and motion studies offer an advantage over averages of past performance in determining the standard time for each marketing operation, since past performance may include unnecessary delays and may not reflect good performance. The standard should be adjusted for nonproductive time lost through unavoidable factors like fatigue, interruptions, and rest. Standard time may then be converted into standard unit costs by applying the costs expected during the period for which standards are set. When this standard time is related to the wage rate for the employees performing the tasks, the standard cost can be determined. This standard can be used for periodic comparison with the actual costs.

Marketing materials also require standards, and for this purpose the same principles used in establishing standards for production material are used. Work sampling, which involves recording how much material is being used or what people are doing at particular times, selected at random, may be used. In addition, the engineering department may conduct controlled tests in which a quantity of material is entered into the marketing process and the resulting rate of usage carefully studied. Marketing supervisors familiar with the material used in distribution operations should assist in this analysis. As a last resort, historical data on the material quantity used may become guides in setting the standard physical quantity of marketing materials needed. The purchasing department should then be asked to help price these standards.

Order-getting and order-filling costs

. Marketing costs can be broken down into two categories: *order-getting* and *order-filling*. *Order-getting* costs are incurred in direct selling, advertising, and sales promotion for the purpose of persuading the customer to buy. (Note that direct selling varies from the other order-getting costs because it is primarily concerned with personal presentation of the service or product to prospective buyers.) *Order-filling* activities relate to the other marketing costs necessary to complete the sales. For example, marketing costs to perform warehousing and handling, transportation, and credit and collection functions are necessary to complete the sale even after the customer has made a commitment to buy the product. These are referred to as order-filling costs. Standards are easier to establish for order-filling costs since many of the operations, such as the physical handling of goods and clerical operations, are repetitive. In contrast, order-getting activities are usually nonrepetitive. The unit of variability for order-getting activities usually measures effort expended rather than results obtained. For example, the standard for direct selling cost may be based on a unit of cost per customer or sales call, while the standard for advertising may be cost per item mailed or newspaper inch.

While most order-filling costs vary with sales volume, the individual cost units respond to different sales activities. For example, increases in warehousing costs are expected as the number of shipments made increases; however, the receiving function varies with the number of items shipped, while the cost of handling returns relates more to the number of returns handled. This relationship between the amount of each variable cost component and an appropriate measure of activity must be established. For example, when products are sold on consignment, the costs of transporting the product to the consignee are incurred in one month, and the sales of the product may not occur until much later.

Warehousing and handling. One important order-filling cost involves warehousing and handling, that is, receiving finished goods from the manufacturing process or from another business concern and storing them until they are delivered to customers. Because the nature of such operations is largely repetitive, standardization and cost control can be applied in a manner similar to that applied for manufacturing operations. If each territory or other segment used has its own warehousing and handling facilities and clerical employees for handling the orders, these costs become direct costs to the segment and do not require an allocation. However, if central facilities are used, a cost allocation must be made to the segments. To this end, the employees involved may be asked to record the time spent for each segment's orders.

Units of variability for warehousing and handling. The following units of variability for establishing cost standards for warehousing and handling are illustrated for each detailed function. The most appropriate of these units of variability should be chosen to determine standard and actual unit cost.

Function	*Units of variability*
Receiving	Dollar of merchandise purchased, shipment, weight or number of shipping units, or purchase invoice line
Pricing, tagging, and marking	Invoice line or warehouse unit handled
Sorting	Order, dollar of average inventory, or physical unit stored
Assembling stock for shipment	Sales transaction, shipment, item, order line, or order
Handling returns	Return
Packing and wrapping	Shipment, physical unit shipped, order line, or order
Taking physical inventory	Dollar of average inventory or warehouse unit
Clerical handling of shipping orders	Order line, sales transaction, shipment, item, or order
Total warehousing and handling	Physical unit of goods handled (product, weight, or weighted factor), item handled, order line, or shipment

Transportation. The transportation function, which follows handling and warehousing, consists of the shipping and delivery operations in getting the products to the customers. To set standard costs for this function, a company should establish economical traffic routings for the required distribution pattern. Again, if each territory or other segment used has its own delivery equipment, the transportation cost is a direct charge; otherwise, the cost of centralized facilities must be allocated to the territories. Since physical operations are used to fulfill most transportation functions, the techniques applied to manufacturing operations can also be used to develop transportation standards. Time and motion studies conducted for a broader operation than that used in production can be utilized. For example, rather than conduct time and motion studies for each procedure, as is done for production operations, time studies for marketing functions can be conducted for longer time periods involving several operations. Because the cost of operating each class of delivery equipment varies, a separate set of functional unit standard costs should be computed for each type of equipment used.

Units of variability for transportation. The actual and standard costs for the following units of variability may be developed for each detailed transportation cost:

Function	Units of variability
Planning and supervision	Unit shipped, ton-mile, customer served, route, or sales dollar
Clerical entries in shipping records	Delivery or shipment
Preparing shipping documents and recording shipment	Weighted unit of product shipped, unit or product shipped, or shipment
Transportation bills	Shipment or unit audited
Handling claims	Entry, shipment, or claim handled
Loading and unloading	Pounds loaded
Drivers' and helpers' wages	Cubic-foot space, truck-miles, or truck-hours of operation
Gasoline, oil, repair, and maintenance	Truck operating-hours or mile
Total transportation	Unit of classes of product, weighted unit of product, unit of product shipped as delivered, or dollar of shipments as delivered

Credit and collection.   Obviously, after a product is delivered, the customer must pay for it or the company must extend credit to the customer. Extending credit to customers for the purchase of goods and subsequently collecting the invoice varies considerably among companies. Industrial engineering methods may be applied to some of the office operations involved, such as preparing invoices, posting charges and credits to accounts receivable, and preparing customers' statements. These methods, such as time and motion studies, can be used because repetitive procedures are employed in much of the credit and collection procedure. For example, uniform procedures can be used in the typing of each letter and invoice, with length becoming the variable factor. A time study can be made to determine the standard variable cost per line in the body of the letter. In addition, standards can be developed for a large number of orders rather than for the number of minutes per line spent on an order.

Units of variability for credit and collection.   The following units of variability can be used for the credit and collection function:

Function	Units of variability
Credit investigation and approval	Credit sales transaction, account sold, or sales order
Credit correspondence, records and files	Item, sales order, account sold, or letter
Preparing invoice—heading	Invoice
Preparing invoices—line item	Invoice line or order line
Posting charges to accounts receivable	Shipment, invoice, or number of postings per hour
Posting credits to accounts receivable	Account sold, remittances, or number of postings per hour
Preparing customers' statements	Account sold or statement
Making street collections	Customer or dollar collected
Handling window collections	Collection
Total credit and collection	Account sold, credit sales transaction, or sales order

General marketing activities.   There are additional costs relating to marketing activities, such as clerical, office, and accounting costs, which vary in importance in different companies. In some companies, these activities are not significant enough to be treated as a separate function. On the whole, past experience and knowledge of the segment's activities are needed before a company can successfully establish standards for general marketing activities such as these. Analysis of invoices and charges, for example, can provide information that will enable a unit of variability to be established for such factors as supplies, telephone, and stationery. Clearly, more effective control over marketing supplies can be maintained if standards are established for each type of office supply used by each segment. Typically, a large number of the costs of general marketing activities are indirect costs of the segment and require allocations.

Units of variability for general marketing activities.   Units of variability which can be applied to general marketing activities are:

Function	Units of variability
General accounting including auditing fee, salaries of general bookkeeper, and accounting supplies	Invoice lines, customers' orders, or general ledger posting
Sales analyses and statistics	Order or invoice line
Financial expense	Ratio of inventory turnover, ratio of average distribution investment to sales, or ratio of total distribution cost to sales
Personnel expense	Number of employees or number of persons employed, discharged, and reclassified
Filing and maintaining order and letter files	Units filed, letter, or order
Mail handling	Number of pieces in and out
Vouchering	Number of vouchers
Sales auditing	Number of sales slips
Punching cards	Number of cards
Tabulating	Number of cards run
Cashiering	Number of transactions
Fixed administration and market research	Time spent

Standards for nonrepetitive operations.   Some marketing activities vary so much that it is most difficult to base standards on time and motion studies and material sampling. Since such marketing costs as advertising affect the total sales volume, the company must relate the advertising expenditure to the competitive conditions within the segment. Business executives usually have a definite plan underlying the performance of each nonrepetitive function such as advertising, and these plans can be modified to reflect general expansion or contraction of business activities. Standard cost for these functions can be estimated on the basis of such plans.

In some cases, on the other hand, standard functional unit costs for marketing can also be set by analyzing actual unit costs for a past period and eliminating any obvious excess costs from this unit cost. Past experience may also be used to select the best performance procedures. When using historical analysis, a company must be sure to consider effects on costs of both expected changes in external conditions and planned sales programs.

Standard per dollar of sale. Cost of advertising and sales promotion per dollar of sales can be a valuable basis for establishing standards when these costs are designed to stimulate immediate sales of specific goods. Comparison of standard and actual costs of advertising per dollar of sales may be supplemented by share-of-the-market statistics to measure the effect of general changes in market conditions. If, for example, the sales volume of all companies in the market is lower than expected, this condition, not poor advertising, may be the actual cause of an unfavorable variance. Management can evaluate advertising performance under the changed conditions by observing share-of-the-market statistics to determine whether the company has maintained or increased its share of the market.

Direct selling. The direct selling function, as opposed to advertising, is concerned with securing orders through personal contact, as we have noted. Since some of the detailed functions are of a repetitive nature, they can be rather easily standardized. But since other direct selling activities are nonrepetitive, their cost standards are more difficult to determine.

Despite individual differences among salespersons and sales situations, certain sales techniques, such as product presentation, which one might initially think to be nonrepetitive, can be standardized enough that a time for each sales call can be determined. The widespread use of sales training programs in industry is evidence of this trend toward uniformity.

To determine sales call standards, a time-study observer can accompany salespersons on calls to examine how they spend their working time. This approach, however, has some inherent weaknesses in that the presence of the observer may embarrass both the salesperson and the customer and cause atypical behavior of the salesperson. A more practical approach may be to obtain data from the salesperson's daily reports showing the time spent with each customer and the sales made. From this information a standard list of activities to be performed can be compiled for salespersons so that standards can be developed for the number of accounts per salesperson and calls per day. The type of assistance the salesperson is to render each customer, along with the number of individual products he or she is expected to sell, must also be considered in establishing the standards for sales calls per day. The standard number of calls can be increased if the salesperson can conduct calls by telephone rather than through personal contact.

An analysis of sales salaries can provide the basis for setting standard salary rates for each class of employee in each segment. In addition, accountants must study each segment before preparing the standards for salespersons' traveling expense, and the number of customer calls required to meet the sales quota must be estimated so that the calls to be made each day can be determined.

Since the products sold as well as the channel of distribution vary among company segments, the units of variability chosen will differ. Because direct selling expenses are significantly influenced by the segment's conditions, different standards may also be required for each segment.

Standards expressed as a percentage of sales. Rather than express direct selling standards as a percentage of gross margin or gross or net sales, an accountant can develop more reliable units of variability by studying the relationship of direct selling expense to miles traveled, number of sales calls, and other factors. For sales or gross margin to be appropriate units of variability, all products must be equally easy to sell and the markup on all goods must be uniform. These requirements are so limiting that rarely can sales be accurately used as a basis. However, if salespersons are given a commission or bonus based on sales, standards can be established as a percentage of net sales.

Units of variability for direct selling. The following units of variability can be used to develop standard and actual cost per direct selling function:

Function	Units of variability
Salespersons salaries	Salespersons' hour or sales call
Commissions and bonuses	Sales order, net sales dollar, sales transaction, product units sold, or sales call
Subsistence	Days
Entertainment	Customer
General sales office expense and supervision salaries	Sales transaction, salespersons, customer account, salespersons' hours, or sales order
Salespersons' traveling expense	Sales order, days traveled, customer, call, or miles traveled
Selling equipment	Sales call
Telephone solicitation	Order received or telephone call
Salespersons' training and education	Number of salespersons' calls or number of salespersons
Routing and scheduling of salespersons	Number of salespersons' calls or number of salespersons
Making quotations	Quotations made
Payroll insurance and taxes and supplemental labor costs	Payroll dollars
Handling sales adjustments and returns	Adjustments and returns handled
Total direct selling	Cost per customer served, cost per sales transaction, cost per sales order, or cost per unit of product sold

Advertising and sales promotion. The advertising and sales promotion function's purpose is to create demand for the company's products and services and to build and maintain goodwill toward the organization. The manner in which this is carried out varies from company to company. Some companies handle all their own advertising, even to the extent of producing their own advertising and sales promotion material. Other firms contract all their advertising to an outside firm. Because advertising and promotion activities vary so widely among companies, it is probably one of the most difficult of all marketing efforts for which to develop cost standards. For institutional advertising expenditures in which the objective is to establish favorable consumer attitudes toward the company or to build a more favorable reputation for the company, the cost measure must be general and applied to considerable periods of time. For example, since the prime objective of institutional advertising is not to increase sales in the short run, standard costs should not be expressed as a percentage of sales. More accurate cost standards can be developed for other advertising expenditures, such as product or service advertising which has the objective of increasing sales of a product or service, even though some of these standards may be quantity measurements only and not reflect the quality of the output. Historical data are used extensively since most companies must maintain some continuity in their advertising programs.

Some of the advertising programs in which a company engages are designed to reach more than one territory or other segment chosen as a basis of study. This requires an allocation of the cost on the basis of units of variability. For example, advertising cost can be allocated to territories based on the number of families in each segment who, on an average day or night, watch the television station used for advertising; newspaper advertising can be distributed based on the number of readers in each territory. Additional allocations may be necessary for the costs of dealers' aids, which include displays, store arrangement services, and demonstrations. A study of the amount of service each segment is to receive can be used as the basis here. The catalog cost to allocate to each segment can be based on the number of catalogs distributed in each territory or other segment used.

If advertising and sales promotion are designed to stimulate immediate sales of specific products, the standard may be expressed as a cost per dollar of sales. Comparisons of standard and actual costs of advertising per dollar of sales may be supplemented by *share-of-the-market statistics* to measure the effect of general changes in market conditions. If industry sales are down, for example, management will want to study the company's share of the market to see whether there has been an increase or decrease in its percentage share.

Standards as percentage of sales.   While it is recognized that over a few years the average cost of advertising and sales promotion shows a fairly constant percentage ratio to sales, a direct relationship between sales and advertising is often impossible to establish. For example, although the amount of sales orders received may depend on the amount of dollars spent for advertising and an increase in advertising and sales promotion may increase sales volume, sales may not increase at the same rate as advertising cost. This is one reason for not using sales as the unit of variability. Another reason is that there is an element of fixed costs in many advertising and sales promotion expenditures.

Units of variability for advertising and sales promotion.   Unit costs for advertising and sales promotion can be developed using any of the following units of variability.

Function	Units of variability
Direct media costs:	
Newspaper	Newspaper inches, sales transaction, or gross or net sales (where this is the chief medium used)
Outdoor billboards and signs	Billboard and other outdoor sign units
Radio and television	Number of set owners or minute of radio or television time
Letters, circulars, calendars, and other direct mail	Item mailed or distributed, inquiry received, or gross or net direct-mail sales
Demonstrations	Demonstration
Technical and professional publications	Unit space or inquiry received
Sample distribution	Number of samples distributed
Directories, house organs, and theater programs	Inquiry received or unit of space
Catalogs	Gross or net catalog sales when identifiable or page or standard space unit
Store and window displays	Day of window trimming and display
Advertising allowances to dealers	Net sales or unit of product cost
Dealers' aids	Customers or pieces or units
Entertainment of visitors at plants	Visitors
Advertising administration (salaries, supplies, rent, and miscellaneous administrative expenses)	Cost per dollar of all direct advertising and sales promotion costs or cost per dollar of net sales
Total advertising and sales promotion	Prospect secured, sales transaction, or product unit sold

Variable budgets

After marketing costs are assigned to functions and their variability is studied, a variable (flexible) budget can be prepared using the approaches suggested in Chapter 5. Levels of marketing activity appropriate to the levels of production output are most practical. After the company's sales objective is determined, the marketing requirements needed to achieve the sales goals should be estimated. These marketing efforts are then costed by applying the standards previously established. In addition, the degree of complexity introduced in the marketing cost budget should be tailored to the company's need.

VARIANCE ANALYSIS

As with production costing, the analysis of cost variances for marketing is the first step toward identifying the factors that caused the difference between the standard and actual costs so that any inefficiencies can be eliminated. To do this, each enterprise has to decide what specific variance analyses it wants to use. Often companies only compute a net variance for marketing costs and do not attempt to break the variance down into causal factors. This practice is not to be encouraged, however, since it tends to hide inefficiencies; instead, the variance must be further explained in terms of price and efficiency to be meaningful. Such price and quantity or efficiency variances can be computed for marketing activities. The computation for the price variance is the same as that shown for material and labor costs in Chapter 10. The computation for each of these variances is as follows:

Price Variance
(Standard price − Actual price) × Actual work units

Quantity or Efficiency Variance
(Budgeted work units − Actual work units) × Standard price

Expense variance report

Exhibit 21–1 illustrates a detailed expense variance report for the warehousing and handling function. The marketing function is analyzed by territories; the Southern Territory is shown in Exhibit 21–1. The warehousing and handling function, with its standards, are as follows:

	Total standard for direct and indirect costs (in dollars)
Variable costs:	
Receiving	$ 21 per shipment
Pricing, tagging, and marking.	6 per unit handled
Sorting	5 per order
Handling returns	10 per return
Taking physical inventory	0.50 per warehouse unit
Clerical handling of shipping orders	2 per item
Fixed costs:	
Rent	600 per month per territory
Depreciation	450 per month per territory

The following units of variability were budgeted and recorded for the month of January:

	Budgeted	*Actual*
Shipments.	400	420
Units handled	200	223
Orders	110	108
Returns.	70	71
Warehouse unit	1,600	1,630
Item	750	780

EXHIBIT 21–1

HILL COMPANY—SOUTHERN TERRITORY
Expense Variance Report—Warehousing and Handling
January 19X1

Detailed function: Units of variability	(1) Actual cost (actual units @ actual price)	(2) Actual units @ standard price	(3) Budgeted costs (budgeted units @ standard price)	(2–1) Price variance	(3–2) Efficiency variance	(3–1) Net variance
Receiving: *Shipment*						
Direct costs	$ 6,400					
Indirect costs	$\left(\dfrac{420}{500} \times \$2,500\right)$ 2,100					
Total	$ 8,500	$8,820 (420 × $21)	$8,400 (400 × $21)	$320F	$420U	$100U
Pricing, tagging, and marking: *Unit Handled*						
Direct costs	1,115	1,338 (223 × $6)	1,200 (200 × $6)	223F	138U	85F
Sorting: direct costs	Order.... 565	540 (108 × $5)	550 (110 × $5)	25U	10F	15U
Handling returns:						
direct costs	Return.... 680	710 (71 × $10)	700 (70 × $10)	30F	10U	20F
Warehouse unit....	880	815 (1,630 × $0.50)	800 (1,600 × $0.50)	65U	15U	80U
Clerical handling of shipping orders:						
Direct costs	item.... $ 500					
Indirect costs	$\left(\dfrac{780}{900} \times \$1,223\right)$ 1,060					
Total	1,560	1,560 (780 × $2)	1,500 (750 × $2)	0	60U	60U
Total variable expense	$13,300		$13,150	$483F	$633U	$150U
Fixed expense:						
Rent	650		600		50U	
Depreciation	445		450		5F	
Total warehousing and handling	$14,395		$14,200			$195U

F = favorable; U = unfavorable.

Southern Territory's actual direct costs for the month are as follows:

Receiving	$6,400
Pricing, tagging, and marking	1,115
Sorting	565
Handling returns	680
Taking physical inventory	880
Clerical handling of shipping orders	500
Rent	650
Depreciation	445

The company allocates the following actual indirect costs to its Southern and Northern Territories:

Receiving (allocated on actual shipments:	
Southern, 420; Northern, 80)	$2,500
Clerical handling of shipping orders	
(allocated on actual items:	
Southern, 780; Northern, 120)	1,223

Efficiency variance

Shipments received is the unit of variability chosen for the receiving function. There were a total of 420 shipments made, while only 400 shipments were budgeted. This results in an unfavorable efficiency variance because actual shipments exceeded those budgeted. (It should be noted here that care must be exercised in analyzing marketing cost variances because it is easy to misinterpret the results associated with marketing costs. Each marketing cost variance is considered favorable or unfavorable as far as that individual detailed function is concerned, not for its effect on the overall company.) The efficiency variance in this case is unfavorable because 20 more shipments were made than planned. Hence, orders of larger quantities should be encouraged to save costs in receiving.

Price variance

The actual unit cost of $20.238 ($8,500 total actual cost of receiving as shown in Exhibit 21–1, divided by 420 actual units) for each shipment received is less than the standard price of $21, which results in a favorable price variance. This difference in price is multiplied by the actual shipments to give a total favorable price variance of $320. It is not necessary to compute the actual cost per unit using the format illustrated in Exhibit 21-1, since the price variance can be determined by comparing total actual cost to the actual units at standard price shown in Column (2).

Efficiency and price variances are computed for variable costs only. A net variance only is computed for the two fixed expenses shown in Exhibit 21–1. This measures the difference between budgeted costs (budgeted units at standard price) and actual costs (actual units at actual price).

Incorporation of marketing standards

After the preliminary work has been done, the accounts needed for the system may be set up in the general ledger. Marketing standards may be incorporated in the ledger accounts by debiting the accounts for each function with the actual cost and crediting them with standard cost for the number of service units performed. Executives may take standards more seriously if standards and variances are incorporated in the accounting journals and ledgers; sometimes, however, as in certain aspects of production accounting, it is not practical to incorporate marketing standards in the accounting system because distribution costs are constantly fluctuating. Fortunately, incorporation is not as important here as for production cost standards because distribution costs are not usually charged to inventory.

The assumption made in this chapter is that the choice of the accounting method is of no great consequence as long as the actual marketing costs are subjected to proper measurements and control. Hence, while it is fundamental to cost control that marketing cost standards be established, their use in connection with a standard cost accounting system is not essential. In some companies it may be advisable to record actual costs in the accounts and compare these with budgets and statistical standards. In some concerns, the actual reflection of marketing standards in the accounts may be preferable.

If marketing cost standards are incorporated within the accounting records, the variances must be disposed of. To this end, marketing variances are usually considered to be a period cost rather than a cost of product because marketing costs are not usually charged to inventory. Under this approach the variances are charged or credited against the accounting period's revenues, and it is assumed that the variance represents an inefficiency or saving from standard.

Marginal contribution versus full cost.   Chapter 23 presents the marginal cost approach for segment reporting. If this approach is used, it is necessary to develop units of variability only for direct marketing costs. Advocates of the marginal contribution approach believe that an effort to allocate costs is confusing and misleading. With the opposing view, known as full costing, net income figures are studied in segment analysis. Advocates of full costing believe that each segment of the company should bear its share of the company's indirect cost in addition to its own direct costs. They make the argument that many indirect costs can be assigned to the segment or function being costed on the basis of demonstrable cost relationship and that even where a strong relationship does not exist, a reasonable basis of allocation can be discovered. Since these approaches are discussed in detail in Chapter 23, they are not illustrated in this chapter.

SUMMARY

Because the definition and measurement of marketing costs and functions have not advanced nearly as far as the definition and measurement of production costs, no one can make statements concerning marketing efficiency with the same degree of assurance. Hence, there are no widely accepted standards of performance for marketing costs.

Greater latitude must therefore be allowed in the establishment and interpretation of standards for marketing functions. However, the repetitive operations in marketing are fully as measurable as manufacturing activities. Because of this, the techniques used in setting production standards can be adapted and employed in establishing marketing cost standards. Less scientific approaches will have to be used for marketing activities that are not repetitive, and while it is preferable that standards be set only after rigorous engineering studies have been conducted, these less scientific standards can also provide for meaningful variance analysis. This allows management to examine the marketing function more thoroughly than it could if actual cost is compared only to historical data.

Cost accountants have an outstanding opportunity and also a definite responsibility for applying cost analysis to the field of marketing so that accurate and intelligent interpretation of the data can help marketing executives act with confidence and certainty. In addition, as management becomes aware of the cost of marketing functions and the importance of these functions to business, they can evaluate the effectiveness of people charged with performing these functions. It must be emphasized that marketing standards are not substitutes for executive leadership because, just like production standards, they are not self-enforcing. Effort is needed to analyze marketing cost variances.

IMPORTANT TERMS AND CONCEPTS

Marketing costs

Distribution costs

Administrative costs

Production costs

Marketing management concept

Cost analysis

Cost control

Functionalization

Detailed functional classification

Units of variability or work units

Work sampling

Order-filling costs

Order-getting costs

REVIEW QUESTIONS

1. Indicate the distinction between production, marketing, and administrative costs.
2. Why is it important for companies to evaluate the effectiveness of their marketing expenditures?

3. Define the marketing management concept.

4. Why have accountants traditionally devoted less attention to the study of marketing costs than to production costs?

5. Why are marketing costs presented on a "per production unit" basis not as meaningful as production costs presented on the same basis?

6. Discuss the objectives of marketing cost accounting.

7. Distinguish between cost control and cost analysis in marketing cost accounting.

8. Discuss the impact of the Sherman Act, the Federal Trade Commission Act, the Clayton Act, and the Robinson-Patman Amendment on marketing activities.

9. Discuss the various segments of the market which can be used to analyze marketing costs.

10. Define the degree of functionalization.

11. Why is the selection of the unit of variability so important?

12. What basic criteria should be considered in choosing an appropriate unit of variability?

13. Why have many companies been hesitant to establish standards for marketing costs?

14. Contrast order-getting and order-filling costs.

15. Should direct selling standards be expressed as a percentage of gross margin or as a percentage of gross sales?

16. Why are cost standards most difficult to develop for advertising and sales promotion?

17. What type of variance analyses can be used for variable and fixed marketing costs?

18. Why is the incorporation into the accounting records of marketing cost standards not as important as the incorporation of production cost standards?

EXERCISES

E21–1. Cost per order size

Presently, the Atkins Company lacks the personnel and funds to establish marketing cost standards. Management does believe that a cost study is justified because it may be accepting orders that are too small. As a result, they analyze the sizes of orders received last year and break their orders down by the simple categories of small (1 to 10 items), medium (11 to 50 items), and large (over 50 items).

The actual marketing costs incurred last year were as follows:

Marketing cost	Amount	Basis for distribution
Marketing personnel salaries	$52,000	Direct charge
Delivery	25,000	Weight shipped
Salespeople's commissions	23,000	Amount of sales
Advertising and direct selling	80,000	Amount of sales
Marketing manager's salary	34,000	Time spent
Credit and collection	24,000	Number of orders

An analysis of their records produced the following statistics:

| | Order sizes | | | |
	Small	Medium	Large	Total
Marketing personnel salaries	$14,000	$18,000	$20,000	$52,000
Weight shipped	5,100	2,000	2,900	10,000
Amount of sales	$362,500	$478,500	$609,000	$1,450,000
Time spent by marketing manager	40%	20%	40%	100%
Number of orders	400	300	100	800

Required:

Prepare a detailed schedule showing the marketing cost per order size and marketing cost as a percentage of total sales for each size order.

E21–2. Quantity and price variances for transportation

Kipp Company provides you with information concerning the standards established for the detailed transportation function. Actual data are also included in the following:

Function	Budgeted cost	Standard cost per unit	Actual cost	Actual cost per unit
Clerical work (per shipment)	$1,000	$2.00	$1,350	$2.25
Planning and supervision (per unit shipped)	8,000	0.50 + $4,000 per period	8,880	0.60 + $4,020 per period
Loading and unloading (per pound loaded)	975	0.65	1,131	0.78
Drivers' and helpers' wages (per truck-mile)	2,400	0.80	2,646	0.84

Required:

Calculate variances for each of the functions detailed.

E21–3. Price and quantity variances for direct selling

You extract the following data concerning the direct selling function from the Dale Lubbers Company for the period ending December 31, 19X1:

| | Northern territory | | Southern territory | |
	Cost per unit	Estimated units of variability	Cost per unit	Estimated units of variability
Budgeted data:				
Salespersons' salaries (per call)	$25.00	280	$35.00	200
Entertainment (per customer)	15.00	100	20.00	80
Salespersons' traveling expense (per day traveled)	30.00	15	35.00	12
Telephone solicitation (per telephone call)	0.40	1,000	0.20	900
Actual results:				
Salespersons' salaries	28.00	260	31.00	215
Entertainment	12.00	110	26.00	70
Salespersons' traveling expense	32.00	17	34.00	16
Telephone solicitation	0.35	1,040	0.30	930

Required:

a. Analyze each detailed function by computing two variances for each function.
b. What interpretation would you place on the quantity variances if the salespeople passed their sales quota by 25 percent?

E21–4. Expected monetary value (CMA adapted)

The Jon Company has just agreed to supply Arom Chemical, Inc. with a substance critical to one of Arom's manufacturing processes. Due to the critical nature of this substance, Jon Company has agreed to pay Arom $1,000 for any shipment that is not received by Arom on the day it is required.

Arom establishes a production schedule which enables it to notify Jon Company of the necessary quantity 15 days in advance of the required date. Jon can produce the substance in five days. However, capacity is not always readily available, which means that Jon may not be able to produce the substance for several days. Therefore, there may be occasions when there are only one or two days available to deliver the substance. When the substance is completed by Jon Company's manufacturing department and released to its shipping department, the number of days remaining before Arom Chemical, Inc. needs the substance will be known.

Jon Company has undertaken a review of delivery reliability and costs of alternative shipping methods. The results are presented in the following table:

Shipping method	Costs per shipment	Probability that the shipment will take _____ days					
		1	2	3	4	5	6
Motor freight......	$100	—	—	.10	.20	.40	.30
Air freight........	$200	—	.30	.60	.10	—	—
Air express.......	$400	.80	.20	—	—	—	—

Required:

Prepare a decision table which can be used by Jon Company's shipping clerk to decide which delivery alternative to select. Use the expected monetary value decision criteria as the basis for constructing the table.

E21–5. Variance analysis for customer groups

The controller for the Brown Company has helped establish the following standards for each detailed area of the advertising function broken down by customer group:

	Retailers		Wholesalers	
	Unit cost	Estimated units of variability	Unit cost	Estimated units of variability
Demonstrations (per demonstration)......	$ 50.00	150	$ 45.00	130
Dealers' aids (per customer)............	40.00	800	50.00	750
Store and window display (per day of window trimming).........	100.00	50	125.00	60
Letters, circulars (per item distributed).....................	1.00	1,000	1.15	900
Catalogs (per standard space unit).......	20.00	600	22.00	500

The following actual units of variability and actual costs were incurred for each customer grouping:

	Retailers		Wholesalers	
	Cost per unit of variability	Units of variability	Cost per unit of variability	Units of variability
Demonstrations	$ 52.00	155	$ 47.00	125
Dealers' help	42.50	750	46.40	785
Store and window display.	105.00	54	132.00	65
Letters, circulars	1.30	980	$1.35	960
Catalogs	24.15	615	24.16	438

Required:

Prepare a variance analysis for each customer group; a formal statement is not required.

E21–6. Price and quantity variances for direct selling

You extract the following data concerning the direct selling function from the Leonard MacEachern Company for the period ending December 31, 19X1:

	Eastern territory		Western territory	
Budgeted data:	Cost per unit	Estimated units of variability	Cost per unit	Estimated units of variability
Salespersons' salaries (per call).	$40.00	330	$38.00	220
Entertainment (per customer)	14.00	180	18.00	100
Salespersons' traveling expense (per sales call)	45.00	17	42.00	16
Telephone solicitation (per telephone call).	0.85	960	0.40	900
Actual results:				
Salespersons' salaries.	49.00	300	30.00	240
Entertainment.	8.00	200	21.00	90
Salespersons' traveling expense	49.00	20	36.00	18
Telephone solicitation	0.75	900	0.45	980

Required:

a. Analyze each detailed function by computing two variances for each.

b. What interpretation would you place on the quantity variances if the salespeople exceeded their sales quota by 25 percent?

PROBLEMS

P21–1. Cost of placing and storing order; EOQ and high-low methods

Mary Nelle Cook, Inc. is a manufacturer of electrical appliances; the company has decided to use the economic order quantity method to help determine the optimal quantities of motors to order from the different manufacturers. Annual demand for the motors totals 66,000; the purchase price of each motor is $40. Values for the cost of placing an order and the annual cost of storage will be developed using cost data from last year. There were 4,100 purchase orders placed last year; during the highest activity month of April, 600 orders were placed, while only 300 orders were placed during the slack period of November.

The purchasing department places all orders. The accounts payable division of the accounting department processes the purchase orders for payment. Another division of the accounting department, accounts receivable, processes all amounts due from customers. The warehousing department handles both receiving and shipping. The receiving clerks inspect all incoming shipment and store items received. The shipping clerks process all sales orders to customers.

Cost data from last year were as follows:

	Costs for April (600 orders)	Costs for November (300 orders)	Annual costs
Purchasing Department:			
Supervisor	$2,000	$2,000	$24,000
Agents	4,200	2,400	31,200
Supplies and other expenses.	600	300	6,800
Accounting Department:			
Accounts Payable			
Clerks	2,000	1,200	19,200
Supplies and other expenses	800	500	8,400
Accounts Receivable			
Clerks	2,000	1,000	18,000
Supplies and other expenses	600	400	6,100
Warehousing Department:			
Supervisor	1,800	1,800	21,600
Receiving clerks	2,600	1,500	24,000
Other receiving expenses	650	450	7,200
Shipping clerks.	2,500	1,580	27,600
Other shipping expenses.	700	420	7,200
	$20,450	$13,550	$201,300

Space is leased in a public warehouse on a rental fee per square foot occupied. This charge totaled $55,000 last year. Motors are stored in boxes of approximately the same size; consequently, each motor occupies about the same amount of storage space in the warehouse. Fire and theft insurance and property taxes on the motors stored amounted to $3,000 and $6,104, respectively. The company pays 12 percent annual interest charge on a short-term seasonal bank loan. Long-term capital investment is expected to earn 15 percent after taxes. The effective tax rate is 42 percent. Inventory balances tend to fluctuate during the year, depending upon the demand for motors. Selected data on inventory balances are shown below:

	Units	Cost
Beginning inventory.	5,000	$200,000
Ending inventory	4,800	192,000
April inventory balance	7,000	280,000
November inventory balance	3,200	128,000
Average monthly inventory.	5,500	220,000

Required:

a. Using last year's data determine estimated values for:
    (1) The cost of placing an order.
    (2) The annual cost of storing a unit.
b. Calculate the EOQ and the number of orders that will be made using the EOQ.
c. Explain why the company should or should not use the cost parameters developed solely from historical data in calculating EOQ.

P21–2. Allocating actual marketing costs

Even though management of the Scenic Toy Company plans to establish marketing standards in the near future, all they do now in analyzing marketing costs is to allocate actual costs at the end of the period to three major product lines: bicycles, tricycles, and wagons. The following direct and indirect actual marketing costs were incurred last year:

Marketing costs	Amount	Basis for distribution
Sales salaries	$90,000	Direct charge
Warehousing and handling	7,500	Item handled
Transportation.	6,000	Shipments
Credit and collection.	10,500	Amount of sales orders
Direct selling	18,000	Customers served
Advertising and sales promotion	7,500	Amount of sales order
General accounting	5,400	Customers served

Statistics extracted from the records of the company are as follows:

	Bicycle	Tricycle	Wagon
Sales salaries	$ 32,000	$ 40,000	$ 18,000
Items handled	40,000	25,600	14,400
Shipments	800	500	700
Sales orders	$300,000	$504,000	$396,000
Customers served	50	30	20

Required:

Distribute these actual marketing costs to the three product lines, and then compare marketing costs as a percentage of sales for each product line.

P21–3. Variance report—warehousing and handling

Standard costs are applied to marketing costs for the Capp Company. Management supplies you with the following budgeted unit cost and estimated units of variability for the warehousing and handling function:

Function	Budgeted unit cost	Estimated units of variability
Receiving	$ 0.10	2,000 purchase invoice lines
Sorting	15.00	500 orders
Handling returns	2.00	50 returns
Packing and shipping	18.00	450 shipments
Clerical handling of shipping orders	5.00	500 orders

At the end of the period, you determine that the following actual unit cost and actual units of variability were incurred:

Function	Actual unit cost	Estimated units of variability
Receiving	$ 0.12	1,890 purchase invoice lines
Sorting	14.75	480 orders
Handling returns	2.10	55 returns
Packing and shipping	20.00	460 shipments
Clerical handling of shipping orders	5.25	480 orders

Fixed cost of $1,000 was budgeted for depreciation and $1,500 for supervision. Actual costs were depreciation—$1,100 and supervision—$1,450.

Required:

Prepare an expense variance report showing price, quantity, and net variances for the detailed functions. Indicate the unit of variability on the report.

P21–4. Expense variance report—direct selling function

Norman Dorian Company has established the following standards for the direct selling function for each of its territories:

Detailed function	Total standard for direct and indirect	
	Southeastern territory	Northwestern territory
Variable expenses:		
Telephone solicitation (per telephone call)	$ 1.10	$ 1.25
Salespersons' training (per salesperson per month).	60.00	75.00
Handling sales adjustments (per adjustment).	2.00	1.80
Making quotations (per quotation)	5.00	6.00
Selling equipment (per sales call).	10.00	12.00
Fixed expenses:		
Sales supervision (per month)	1,500.00	1,200.00
Insurance (per month)	100.00	125.00

The following units of variability were budgeted and recorded:

	Southeastern territory		Northwestern territory	
	Budgeted	Actual	Budgeted	Actual
Telephone calls	1,000	1,100	1,500	1,400
Salespersons.	10	8	15	17
Adjustments	60	65	80	75
Quotations.	70	74	90	82
Sales calls.	150	160	120	115

Actual direct costs incurred were as follows:

	Southeastern territory	Northwestern territory
Telephone solicitation	$ 250	$ 400
Salespersons' training.	300	700
Handling sales adjustments	30	10
Making quotations	380	575
Selling equipment.	1,690	1,500
Sales supervision	1,750	1,420
Insurance.	180	90

Actual indirect costs incurred were as follows:

Telephone solicitation	$2,375
Salespersons' training	750
Handling sales adjustments	280

Required:

Prepare an expense variance report for each territory indicating price and efficiency variances for each detailed function. Indirect costs are allocated on actual units of variability.

P21–5. Price and efficiency variance; prices for different order sizes

Actual and standard distribution costs data for the month of March 19X1, for Ashley Martin, Inc. are as follows:

	Actual operations	Budget at standard cost
Sales—Net of cash discount............	$900,000	$900,000
Selling expenses	15,000	12,000
Warehousing costs:		
Packing and wrapping salaries	2,360	2,000
Shipping salaries	12,040	12,000
Order-filling costs.................	33,500	32,000

March shipping-hours data follow:

	Shipping hours
Budgeted...................	4,000
Standard operating level	3,800
Actual....................	4,300

All warehousing salaries are allocated on the basis of shipping-hours. Order-filling costs are allocated on the basis of sales and comprise freight, packing, and warehousing costs. An analysis of the amount of these standard costs by unit order size follows:

Unit-volume classifications	Order-filling standard costs classified by unit order size			
	1–10	11–30	Over 30	Total
Units Sold	18,000	32,000	20,000	70,000
Freight.......................	$2,700	$3,520	$1,600	$7,820
Packing	7,200	10,240	4,480	21,920
Warehousing	900	960	400	2,260
Total..................	$10,800	$14,720	$ 6,480	$32,000

Required:

a. Compute and analyze price and efficiency variances from standard cost for:
  (1) Packing and wrapping salaries.
  (2) Shipping salaries.
b. Presently, Martin Company is charging a constant price per unit sold; however, management is considering revising its unit sales prices upward or downward on the basis of quantity ordered in proportion to the allocated freight, packing, and warehousing standard cost since they believe that the distribution cost per unit decreases with an increase in the size of the order.
  (1) To help management in this pricing decision, prepare a schedule computing the standard cost per unit for each order-filling cost—freight, packing, and warehousing—for each unit volume classification.
  (2) Prepare a schedule computing the revised unit sales prices for each unit-

volume classification while at the same time maintaining total sales of $900,000.

P21–6.   Price and quantity variances

Management of the Greatman Company has assigned marketing costs to functions to establish standards for marketing cost analysis. With standard costing rates set for various functional costs, the difference between budgeted and actual results can be analyzed.

The following data are obtained from the company's controller:

	Planned results			
	Units handled	Truck miles	Credit orders	Sales orders
Wholesalers.	500	4,500	200	300
Retailers	600	6,000	250	350

Standards for marketing expenses:

Warehousing and handling:		
Wholesalers	$0.75	per unit
Retailers	$0.80	per unit
Transportation	$0.60	per truck mile + $1,000 per customer class
Credit and collection	$0.50	per credit order + $1,500 per customer class
Direct selling	$1.00	per sales order
Advertising	$0.75	per sales order

	Actual results for the period			
	Units handled	Truck miles	Credit orders	Sales orders
Wholesalers.	580	4,350	220	270
Retailers	590	5,800	189	390

	Expenses for the period			
	Wholesalers		Retailers	
	Fixed	Variable	Fixed	Variable
Warehousing handling	—	$ 522.00	—	$ 442.50
Transportation	$ 950	2,697.00	$1,040	3,190.00
Credit and collection	1,410	116.60	1,450	113.40
Direct selling	—	256.50	—	429.00
Advertising	—	213.30	—	312.00

Required:

Prepare an analysis of marketing expenses showing budgeted expenses contrasted with actual expenses and the resulting variances for each class of customers. (If appropriate, compute two variances. Otherwise, only one variance is needed for each expense component.)

P21–7.   Functional distribution of marketing costs and variance analysis

Piper Company manufactures a product which is sold in two territories: Eastern and Western. The data used in establishing the standards for the marketing administrative expense for each territory for the period ending December 31, 19X1 are given below:

Territory	Number of sales calls @ $12 per call	Number of orders @ $6 per order	Number of invoice lines @ $.08 per line	Hours spent @ $125 per hour
Eastern	3,000	1,600	8,100	180
Western. . . .	4,100	1,700	9,300	210

Actual indirect costs for the period ending December 31, 19X1 are:

Function	Costs	Unit of variability
Direct selling	$93,990	Eastern—3,180 sales calls Western—4,050 sales calls
Warehousing and handling	18,700	Eastern—1,650 orders Western—1,750 orders
Credit and collection	1,770	Eastern—7,900 invoice lines Western—9,800 invoice lines
General administration	47,946	Eastern—165 hours Western—228 hours

Management was pleased that actual sales for Eastern were 98 percent of the $300,000 budgeted, while Western's actual sales were 96 percent of the $350,000 budgeted sales. Actual cost of goods sold averaged 58 percent of sales, which represented a decrease of 2 percent under standard.

Required:

Prepare an income statement by territory with functional distribution of actual marketing expenses on the basis of actual units of variability. Compare actual revenue and expenses to budgeted revenues and expenses and compute two variances for each expense after expenses have been allocated to each territory. Determine a net variance for each territory's sales and cost of goods sold.

P21–8. Determining standards for direct selling

Gladys Williams Company applies standard costs to its marketing costs. Direct selling expense has been broken down into the following functional classifications. The monthly estimated costs and units of variability are also given.

	Product line AA	
	Estimated direct costs	Estimated units of variability
Salespersons' salaries	$6,000	300 sales calls
Entertainment	1,080	90 customers
General sales office expense and supervision salaries	640	4 salespersons
Salespersons' traveling expense	900	6,000 miles
Telephone solicitation	1,050	840 telephone calls

	Product line BB	
	Estimated direct costs	Estimated units of variability
Salespersons' salaries	$4,100	200 sales calls
Entertainment	1,560	120 customers
General sales office expense and supervision salaries	680	4 salespersons
Salespersons' traveling expense	924	6,600 miles
Telephone solicitation	949	730 telephone calls

At the end of January 19X1, you determine that the following actual units of variability and actual costs were incurred by the company's two product lines.

	Product line AA	
	Actual costs	Units of variability
Salespersons' salaries	$6,175	325
Entertainment	985	80
General sales office expense and supervision salaries	850	5
Salespersons' traveling expense.	987	6,160
Telephone solicitation	1,105	850

	Product line BB	
	Actual costs	Units of variability
Salespersons' salaries	$4,620	210
Entertainment	1,155	105
General sales office expense and supervision salaries	750	5
Salespersons' traveling expense.	990	6,570
Telephone solicitation	894	680

Required:

a. Determine the standard for each detailed function.
b. Calculate price, efficiency, and net variances for the detailed functions broken down by product line. Round to the nearest dollar.

CASES

C21–1.   Standard cost system for marketing costs

Paragon Luggage Company has established a reputation for producing attractive, high-quality luggage, handbags, and leather accessories. The leather goods are manufactured in three facilities located in the southeastern United States and are sold through company-owned retail stores located in the eastern United States. The home office is housed in one of the manufacturing facilities and is composed essentially of three departments—production, marketing, and administration. Each department is evaluated independently of the others.

The company recognizes the advantages of a standard cost system and has been using this in accounting for its manufacturing operations for several years. Attempts are being made to incorporate standards in accounting for marketing costs as well, but adequate effort has not been put into determining the units of variability, with the result that too many functions are simply based on a percentage of sales. For example, unsalable (stores) account, which is the account for irregular products, is related to sales, and the standard is expressed as a percentage of this unit.

Standards for packaging material were established through work sampling. Standards were set for boxes, tape, liners, and dividers. The individual boxes are packed in master shipping box cases. Since these box cases are reusable, an estimate was made of the expected life, based on actual experience, to arrive at a standard cost. This estimate has proved to be reliable, so it is unusual for a significant variance to occur.

Standards for packaging labor were established by an outside engineering firm, which used time and motion studies. A daily record is kept of the number of leather goods packaged and the packaging material and labor used. A packaging material quantity variance account and a packaging labor efficiency variance account are used to ascertain any difference between actual and standard usage. Packaging material standards were not studied in as great detail as were raw material standards, since the company found that packaging materials are easier to control than are leather materials.

The manufacturing facilities package the leather goods and transfer them to the Transportation Department; this department's expenses appear on the operating budgets for the manufacturing plants. The retail stores submit orders to the Transportation Department and are billed at standard cost. The leather goods are transported on company-owned trailer trucks. Most of the expense items are expressed as a standard cost per mile traveled, but some, such as gasoline, were established using historical data and are expressed as a percentage of sales. Time studies were used to establish transportation labor standards.

The standards for repair and maintenance are based on historical data and the age of the vehicles. A report is prepared listing each vehicle by age. The company revises the maintenance standard to increase the cost as the vehicle becomes older. Vehicle depreciation standards are based on what actual depreciation is expected to be.

The company revised its advertising standards three years ago to decrease the standard, which is expressed as a percentage of gross sales. Before that, the company employed an advertising agency to plan sales promotion, and standards were established by both company management and the agency based on what they thought was needed to accomplish the sales objective. But when Paragon decided to use its own marketing personnel for all advertising activities, advertising expenditures were reduced.

Percentage analysis is used extensively for control and planning, since management considers percentage analysis important in evaluating performance efficiency. A total operations standard is set for the seasoned retail stores that have been in operation for some length of time. This standard is expressed as a percentage of sales. A store is considered unprofitable if its expenses are more than 30 percent of gross sales, because then either sales volume is too low or expenses are too high. Generally, the seasoned stores operate with expenses that are below 30 percent of actual gross sales.

At the end of each four-week period, store variances are analyzed. If a variance is significant in the opinion of the regional sales manager, the accountant or the store manager begins an investigation to determine the cause. If an actual expense deviates from standard by a material amount, the standard and actual percentages of sales are evaluated to determine whether a trend can be detected. Management uses the information gained from variance analysis in revising standards for the next budget year.

Required:

Evaluate Paragon's standard cost system for marketing costs.

C21–2. Marketing cost analysis for department stores

Fink Department Store, Inc. has three department stores in the total organization. One of the stores is basically a soft goods store specializing in ladies' and men's ready-to-wear clothes and accessories; it is located in the downtown section of the city, which is suffering decaying economic conditions. Another store carries hard goods merchandise such as furniture, household appliances, radios, and television sets; it is located in the city's wealthy suburbs. The company also has a branch store in another state which performs some marketing functions independently.

Standards are not incorporated into the accounting system, but statistical standards are used for planning and control. Management of this company uses the statistics obtained through a publication of the Controllers' Congress, a division of the National Retail Merchants Association, in establishing marketing standards. Members of the National Retail Merchants Association may submit their sales and cost figures to this division, which compiles the data. All the standards are expressed as a percentage of net sales and are broken down into different sales volume classifications. Since the Fink Department Store falls in the $5 to $10 million sales volume range, management refers to the percentages for this classification. Even though department stores are not required to report their cost percentages, so many stores participate that management feels the figures are representative. The Controllers' Congress publishes these figures once a year.

Management of this company does not establish its standards entirely on these representative figures, however, since it believes the peculiarities of its operation should also be given some consideration. Thus, reference is also made to past experiences and future plans in establishing the standards.

Monthly income and expense statements are prepared for each store; these show dollar amounts and percentages for current operations, budgeted operations, and the previous year's operation for the same month. A statement is also prepared showing the actual and budgeted dollar amounts and percentages for the direct expenses of each store. Each store's performance is evaluated on its contribution to indirect expenses and profits. The treasurer and controller hold monthly conferences with each supervisor responsible for a cost center's performance to discuss the expense elements which have unfavorable variances.

Required:

Evaluate the store's system for establishing and analyzing standard costs for marketing expense.

C21–3. Marketing standards in a production operation

Glen Jones Aluminum and Chemical Corporation entered the aluminum industry in 1946, but since that time the company has grown and its interests have been diversified. It has used an engineered standard cost system since it began operations. This system is based on an engineered standard cost which is established through sound engineering and accounting studies. An integrated standard cost system is used in which the cost system is an integral part of the plant financial accounting system. Cost centers, general ledger accounts, and cost element codes are established for the purpose of identifying, classifying, and accumulating costs.

Standards are set on a reasonable basis that takes into account all known normal factors. There is no provision for abnormal losses. Standards are set tight enough to encourage high performance, yet they are not set so tight as to be detrimental to employee morale.

Standards are set for one year; at the end of each year a study is made to determine whether standard revision is required. The conditions under which the standards are operating may change during the year; for example, the shipping department may change from rail to barge transportation. In this case, the standard is updated at the time of the change.

After the industrial engineer completes the study and arrives at a standard for each cost center, the person responsible for the cost center's performance is asked to sign the standard. On this expense standard is spelled out in dollars the standard costs necessary to operate this cost center. There is a definite basis for the computation of each cost.

A total is made for all items, and the total is the standard cost for this particular cost center. If the supervisor of the cost center does not agree with the standard established by the industrial engineer, he or she must support the position. If any adjustments are necessary, they are made and the expense standard is forwarded to the controller for approval. The expense standard is then sent to the cost accounting department, where it is utilized in a computer program.

The shipping department's three major expense items are loadout operators, power, and repair and maintenance. Some loadout operators must be present continuously during the normal working day, even though actual loading may be performed for only four hours on some days. The base unit for this minimum work force is scheduled days, which is a standard work day, Monday through Friday. Scheduled days will vary with each month; the normal monthly quantity is 21.73 scheduled days.

Industrial engineers establish by time study the worker-hour requirements to load 70-ton and 100-ton railcars. Time-study analysis is essential; for example, shipping department employees can load a 100-ton car faster than a 70-ton car, as the 70-ton car has to be moved twice because of hopper locations. This is a variable expense determined by the number of cars loaded. Power expense also varies with the tons shipped.

Some personnel are assigned to the shipping department on a flexible basis. If the workers are not needed to load cars, they are used in the production process. The worker-hours in each cost center are determined through the use of time cards. The job ticket shows the expense distribution by hour to each cost center. This source document will report whether a shipping clerk is changed to a production cost center during the day.

The corporation computes two variances for its marketing costs: the price variance and the operations practice variance. The price variance reflects changes in wages or purchased materials. All labor is first isolated to determine whether there is any price variance before it is charged to the cost centers. The negotiation of labor cost changes is the responsibility of the industrial relations department. Material price variances are the responsibility of the purchasing department. These variances are not controllable by the cost center manager.

The operations practice variance indicates the use of alternate production methods, that is, situations in which the product was not manufactured or shipped in the manner planned. An example of this variance is the underloading of railcars. This would not necessarily be under the control of the cost center manager.

Required:

While recognizing that Jones Aluminum and Chemical Corporation has installed a fairly effective system for marketing cost standards, do you see any areas in which additional work is needed?

C21–4. Steps in establishing marketing cost standards

Verba Key Yarn Company is being organized to produce various types of yarn and threads. Ms. Key, the president and major stockholder, has spent several months studying the feasibility of entry into the thread industry. Most of the thread sold in the

United States is produced by three large companies. Each company is well established and has been in business for many years. Even though Key Yarn Company would be smaller, management feels that it would be able to concentrate on producing a fine quality of thread rather than diversifying operations by also producing needles, buttons, and zippers as do the three large producers.

The thread produced by all companies in the market is basically the same. Generally, the companies offer either a polyester or a cotton thread, with the polyester thread increasing in proportion to the cotton thread in the market. A consumer research study conducted by Key Yarn revealed several shortcomings in the polyester thread now being marketed. Consumers expressed a desire for fuzz-free thread and for a heavier spool which would be more stable when turning on a spindle.

The company plans national advertising on television to introduce its thread. Emphasis will be on the product's unique characteristics including the fact that it is fuzz-free and has a heavier spool. In addition, mailing lists will be purchased from several needlecraft magazine publishers. Subscribers to these magazines will be mailed a free sample of the smaller spools of thread. Cents-off coupons will also be attached to the package. Company salespersons will also call on wholesalers and vending companies. Management feels that a market for a limited variety of thread colors exists in grocery stores.

Key Company management has spent much time studying the work flow they plan to use. After the thread is processed and wound on spools, it is placed in boxes and sent to the finished goods warehouse. The boxes of thread remain there until they are assembled to fill a shipment. After an order is assembled for shipment, it is packed and wrapped.

However, before shipments are made, Key Yarn Company plans to have an employee in the credit and collection department investigate all credit sales transactions. Approval will be on the basis of the financial stability of the buying company. If credit is approved, an invoice is prepared by the credit and collection department. Other employees in this department will be responsible for posting charges and credits to accounts receivable.

The company has its own trucks which will deliver the orders to regional warehouses. Each truck will have a driver and a helper who will be paid an hourly wage. They will be furnished oil company credit cards with which they will purchase gasoline and oil.

Management plans to establish production standards for its manufacturing process and is keenly interested in measuring the efficiency of its marketing operation in this manner, as well. However, they are at a loss as to how they should proceed.

Required:

Assume that you are employed as a management consultant for the purpose of helping the company establish and use marketing standards. Outline the steps you would take in this process and suggest ways of establishing the standards.

Influence of various parties

Determinants of pricing

Competitive structures

Economic profits

Relationship among demand, supply, and cost

OBJECTIVES OF CHAPTER 22

1. To emphasize that an important purpose of full cost accounting is providing a basis for setting normal prices.

2. To discuss the variety of market conditions in which prices are determined, ranging from a monopolistic market, in which a company has some control over the prices charged, to a perfectly competitive market, in which a company accepts the sales price established by the market.

3. To discuss the role of cost in the final pricing decision.

4. To evaluate the various cost-based methods upon which prices can be established.

22

The use of costs in pricing decisions

The first nine chapters of this book are concerned with the collection of costs which influence determining sales price. While the accumulation of costs serves inventory valuation purposes, these data are also used in pricing decisions. This chapter discusses ways of establishing sales price according to various cost concepts and explains when each approach is most appropriate. For example, differential cost pricing may be appropriate for short-run, specialized situations, but it could be risky to use in the long run.

While it is recognized that a product's sales price is only one element of many that determines the product's success or failure, it certainly warrants much of the manager's time and consideration. A difficulty associated with price determination is that it cannot be separated from other elements in the marketing mix, such as advertising, product quality, and delivery terms. Management must also decide whether quantity discounts are to be offered and under what terms. The profitability of varying prices to stimulate sales in certain seasons of the year is also included in the pricing decision.

INFLUENCE OF VARIOUS PARTIES

Since the pricing policy established affects so many people both inside and outside the company, some conflict of interest among managers, salespersons, and customers is to be expected. To reflect each of these interests, a company may establish a pricing committee to study the market structure and data supplied. This committee should be aware of *suboptimization;* that is, departments that are not attempting to fulfill company-wide goals but instead have set their own departmental objectives. A company must also identify its interpretation of profit maximization, since this may be expressed as either a rate of return on capital or a specific dollar amount of net income; and a company's interpretation of profit maximization should be in harmony with the market share it is trying to gain. For example, it may have to be satisfied with a lower profit in the short run to improve its chance of profit maximization in the long run.

Among the possible conflicting interests which must be considered by a pricing committee are the following:

Salespersons generally prefer as low a sales price as possible so that their product is easier to sell. Because sales personnel must explain to prospective customers any differences from competitors' prices, the sales force should be given information enabling them to explain these differences.

Top management in the advertising department should be involved in the pricing procedure because the price quoted can be a form of sales promotion. For example, a $0.98 or $0.99 price sounds less expensive than $1.

Because customers help make up the market structure, the company should attempt to obtain a profile of their buying habits and the factors that motivate them. The needs, whether physical or social, that the customer satisfies when he or she purchases the product should be studied.

Consumer behavior.   The interpretation that customers place on the price of a product is most important in analyzing consumer behavior. Most customers justify buying something only if they feel they are getting it at a fair price; as a result, they may view a price cut as a reduction in quality or an attempt by the company to dispose of merchandise that few people desire or that has become outdated.

Often a lower price may not be the best answer if the customer is trying to satisfy a social need such as status or prestige. In fact, a price increase may be interpreted by customers as a quality improvement or as an increase in product demand, indicating that other customers feel that this is a good product. Additionally, some customers may feel that a price rise means that supply is limited and that they should purchase the product before the supply is exhausted.

As mentioned in connection with the Robinson-Patman Amendment, the government influences pricing policies by designating some competitive practices unfair. Even though local governments have some impact on pricing policies, state and federal governments have the largest effect. Certain industries, such as petroleum and agriculture, are subject to additional restrictions. While these restrictions cannot be ignored, other factors play a more important role in the pricing decision of most companies.

The sales price established must allow a fair return to all those handling the product; however, conflict may arise in trying to determine what return is fair and adequate. This can be done by estimating the optimum price range to charge customers and then working backward through the various distribution stages. The process obviously becomes more complex when a wide distribution through several intermediaries is used. While the manufacturer usually prefers that several intermediaries distribute the product, a distributor may prefer to sell the product on an exclusive basis, so the distribution channel should also be determined before the pricing decision is reached.

Because competitors help form the market structure in which the company operates, a study of the competitive situation helps determine which pricing strategy is most appropriate. Competitors do influence upper limits because, generally, it is not good pricing policy to set a price materially above that of a competitor unless a higher quality service or product is offered. When the supply and demand concept is introduced later in the chapter, the various market structures, such as perfect competition and monopoly, will be discussed.

DETERMINANTS OF PRICING

For a price to be successful, not only must it take into account the other elements in the marketing mix, but it must also satisfy certain external and internal constraints. External factors include the influence of supply and demand, fads and trends, competition, and other market conditions. Internal factors include the cost of the product or service and the company's objectives.

Most companies today recognize that profit maximization, while desirable, should not be the overriding objective because it is often difficult to achieve along with long-run survival. Certainly, this does not overshadow the fact that both long-run and short-run profitability are important considerations, because for a company to continue operations in the future, the product's price clearly must cover all costs and yield a reasonable rate of return to investors if the manufacturer is a profit-making company. The relationship between pricing theory and company objectives is a factor that most often overshadows other considerations.

External determinants of pricing. Accountants must consider the following external determinants of pricing before they begin an analysis of cost studies:

1. The environment in which the product is sold.
2. The product's characteristics compared with those of competing products so that the importance of brand loyalty and other factors affecting product demand can be studied. For example, if a product's characteristics are differentiated from those of competitors' products, sales promotion can emphasize these characteristics and a higher price can be charged for the product.

3.   The market structure, including the number of competitors as well as the number of customers.
4.   Customers' buying habits to better understand the significance of price in their decision to buy.
5.   The influence of such legislation as the Robinson-Patman Amendment.

Each of these external pricing determinants is discussed individually, with the exception of the Robinson-Patman Amendment, which was discussed in Chapter 21.

Demand and supply curves

Of all external price determinants, demand is one of the most important. The relationship between the market price of the good and the quantity demanded can be expressed in a demand curve. With all other variables constant *(ceteris paribus)*, the quantity demanded of an economic good varies inversely with the price of the good. Thus, the higher the price, the lower the quantity demanded. Demand curves are derived so that the characteristics of the individual consumer can be analyzed. Before production is begun, management must be assured that the price established will be accepted by enough consumers so that production is warranted. Tastes, income, and the price of other goods are treated as constants in determining the consumer's demand curve. A *change in the quantity demanded* refers to a movement along a given single demand curve, while a shift in a demand curve refers to a *change in demand.* This distinction is important to the pricing decision, because a change in quantity demanded is the result of a price change, while a change in demand refers to the effect of changes in variables other than the price on the quantity of the good demanded. For example, if consumers become willing and able to buy more of a particular good at each possible price because their income has increased, an increase in demand has occurred. If, on the other hand, consumers' taste for a product changes and they buy less of the product at each possible price, a decrease in demand is experienced and the demand curve shifts.

Price elasticity of demand

The relationship between customer behavior and price changes must be analyzed in any pricing decision; usually, this relationship is best expressed as the elasticity of demand. *Price elasticity of demand* indicates how total revenue changes when a price change causes a change in quantity demanded. The elasticity concept measures the degree of responsiveness of quantity demanded to changes in the market price. When a price decrease causes quantity demanded to increase so much that total revenue increases, demand is referred to as elastic, or greater than unity. However, if a price decrease causes no change in total revenue, unitary elasticity is assumed because the percentage cut in price is offset by a percentage rise in quantity. On the other hand, if the price decrease causes such a small increase in quantity demanded that total revenue decreases, demand is inelastic, or less than unity. When demand is referred to as "inelastic," it does not mean that consumers are unresponsive to price changes; only when demand is perfectly inelastic will there be no change in the quantity demanded with a price change. If quantity demanded is infinitely responsive to a change in price, demand is said to be perfectly elastic.

This relationship between customer behavior and price changes is best understood by determining exact numerical measurement through the use of the following formula, where Q represents quantity demanded and P represents the price of the goods:

$$\frac{(\Delta Q)/Q}{(\Delta P)/P}$$

For example, if the quantity demanded is very responsive to price changes, a given relative change in price causes a more than proportionate change in quantity demanded. If a small change in price results in a large change in the quantity demanded, the price elasticity of demand is high. If the formula results in an absolute value less than 1, or unity, the demand curve is inelastic, and total revenue increases when the price is raised. By analyzing elasticity of demand, management gains an insight into whether a price can be profitably raised or lowered.

Because sellers react to higher prices by increasing the quantity of goods supplied, the supply curve illustrated in Exhibit 22–1 is upward sloping. Conversely, since consumers demand less at higher prices, the demand curve is downward sloping. The price is determined in the market, as shown in Exhibit 22–1 for a perfectly competitive market and given the assumptions

EXHIBIT 22–1

Demand and supply curves

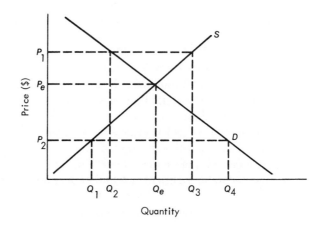

made earlier about consumers. If, initially, a price of P_1 is assumed and quantity demanded is only Q_2, sellers have excess inventory since they are willing to offer Q_3 at this price. To avoid having this excess inventory, the product's price is bid down. However, as is discussed later in the chapter, the cost of the product provides a floor below which the price usually will not fall. In a purely competitive market, price falls until market equilibrium occurs at the point where the quantities supplied and demanded are equal. Assume, instead, that initially the price is P_2 and the quantity that sellers are willing to supply is Q_1; this results in excess demand because consumers want to buy Q_4. The price is bid up to P_e because of the consumers' excess demand.

COMPETITIVE STRUCTURES

One of the important external factors affecting pricing is the market structure in which a company operates. An individual company's demand differs from the total market demand depending on the relationship of the sellers to each other. At one extreme is the monopolist whose company's demand is the same as the industry's because the monopolist is the only seller. At the other extreme is the pure, or perfect, competitor whose output does not affect the market price because there are so many competing companies and no one company sells a large enough portion of the industry output to significantly influence price. Therefore, a firm operating in perfect competition is totally a price taker, and the sales price is constant. In other markets, marginal revenue from each additional unit of sales declines resulting in a curvilinear total revenue function. In a perfectly competitive market, the price elasticities of the industry determine the degree of difference between a company's elasticity and the industry's. Thus, in perfect competition, the difference is infinite, while the difference is zero in a monopoly.

Monopoly

A market in which there is only one seller is referred to as a monopoly, which means that the company's demand is identical to the market demand for the products. However, for this to have any meaning, the monopolist must be assured that other companies will not enter the market regardless of the price of the monopolist's products. Even though there may be more than one seller, a monopoly can be said to exist if there are no close substitutes for the monopoly product.

As can be seen in Exhibit 22–2, the quantity sold of a monopolist's products varies inversely with the sales price. The change in the total revenue received from selling one more unit is referred to as *marginal revenue (MR)*. As shown in Exhibit 22–2, marginal revenue for any given quantity is less than the price or the average revenue because, to sell an additional unit, sales price must be reduced. In the first elastic range of the demand curve, total revenue rises with

EXHIBIT 22–2

Marginal cost and marginal revenue for a monopolist

Quantity	Average revenue or price	Total revenue	Total cost	Total profit	Marginal revenue (MR)		Marginal cost (MC)
1.........	$300	$ 300	$ 170	$130			
2.........	275	550	320	230	$250	>	$150
3.........	245	735	460	275	185	>	140
4.........	218	872	585	287	137	>	125
5.........	201	1,005	718	287	133	=	133
6.........	150	900	875	25	−105	<	157
7.........	125	875	1,075	−200	−25	<	200

quantity sold. When the quantity sold places the company in inelastic demand regions, total revenue reaches its maximum, which is five units in Exhibit 22–2.

The additional cost of producing one more unit, which is referred to as *marginal cost (MC)*, is also shown in Exhibit 22–2. Marginal cost initially declines due to increasing economies of scale resulting from greater efficiencies of production as more units are produced. Eventually the marginal costs will increase at an increasing rate due to diseconomies of scale because inputs become scarce or are limited. Maximum profit equilibrium for a monopolist is where marginal revenue equals marginal cost. In Exhibit 22–2, this is at a price of $201 which yields a total profit of $287, and where marginal revenue and marginal cost are both equal at $133.

Law of diminishing returns. At some point in operations, diminishing returns set in and output cannot be increased except by increasing the marginal cost. The *law of diminishing returns* states that beyond some point, decreasing amounts of additional output are obtained when equal extra units of a varying input are added to a fixed amount of some other input. Stated in another manner, if additional labor is applied to a fixed amount of plant and equipment, eventually output will rise less proportionately to the increase in the number of workers employed. In Exhibit 22–2, marginal cost decreases with each additional unit until it reaches four units of output. Hence, in this case, the point of diminishing returns is four units. In the short run, management must work with a fixed capacity; as a result, costs rise sharply beyond the point of diminishing returns or decreasing cost. In the long run, when management has enough time to adjust its production facilities, it can produce at a capacity at which the average cost is at the lowest point. Because of diminishing returns, producers usually require a higher price to make extra, higher-cost quantity.

Profit maximization in monopoly. As seen in Exhibit 22–2, profit maximization for a monopolist is where marginal revenue equals marginal cost. This is not at the highest price possible, which is $300 for the monopolist in Exhibit

EXHIBIT 22–3

Profit maximization under monopoly

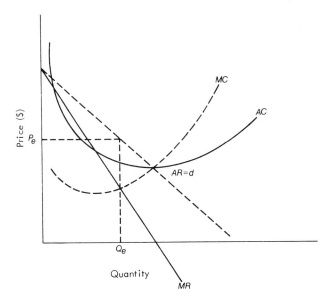

22–2. With a monopolist's downward sloping demand curve, as illustrated in Exhibit 22–3, marginal revenue (MR) is less than average revenue (AR) at any specific point. Maximum equilibrium occurs at the point where marginal cost intersects with marginal revenue. Equilibrium price (P_e) is determined by going up the demand curve; quantity Q_e would be sold at this point. As shown in Exhibit 22–3, average total cost is not used to arrive at the monopolist's maximum equilibrium point; however, total cost cannot be ignored because it must be covered for a company to remain in operation in the long run. Note that the behavior of variable and fixed costs affects the shape of the average cost curve; as volume increases, the point is reached at which added production is obtained only by increasing plant capacity, which increases fixed costs. Remember in Chapter 2 it was emphasized that accountants assume a particular firm is operating within a relevant range of output where the revenue and cost functions are approximately linear.

Monopolistic competition

The term *imperfect competition* refers to all market structures such as monopoly, monopolistic competition, and oligopoly, which deviate from the purely competitive market model; the next form of imperfect competition we will discuss is monopolistic competition. *Monopolistic competition* is a market condition in which a relatively large number of small producers are offering similar but not identical products. Even though monopolistic competition conditions do not involve as many companies as does perfect competition, there are enough firms so that each has little or no control over the market price because each firm has a relatively small percentage of the total market. Sellers use packaging, trade names, and other types of sales promotion to differentiate their products in the minds of buyers. This type of market structure assumes that companies can easily enter the industry, since there are no significant barriers. If a monopolistic competitor changes output or price, he or she need not fear retaliation from other companies in the industry. There is no mutual interdependence among the firms in the industry because of the large number of companies involved; as a result, each firm determines its policies without considering the possible reactions of rival firms. However, a company does not have much freedom to change prices because the goods that competitors are selling are close substitutes and the cross-elasticities of demand are high. For example with high cross-elasticities of demand, a change in price causes a relatively large change in quantity demanded because consumers often switch to another product. While product differentiation helps alleviate some of this switching from one product to another, the number of sales gained by any individual company is small, since there are so many companies in the industry. The result is that competition among companies in a monopolistically competitive market is more concerned with product differentiation than with price.

Profit maximization in monopolistic competition.   The demand curve for a monopolistic competitor, as shown in Exhibit 22–4, is more elastic at a given price than that of the entire industry. Profit maximization for a monopolistic

EXHIBIT 22–4

Profit maximization under monopolistic competition

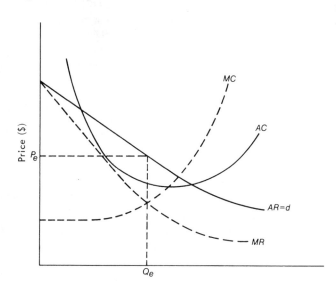

competitor occurs at a price where marginal revenue (MR) equals marginal cost $MC)$, as shown in Exhibit 22–4. In the short run, new companies are attracted to the industry if profits exist; this causes the demand for an individual company's output to fall and become more elastic. In the struggle to keep its customers, a company usually increases its sales promotion, causing total cost to increase. This generally results in no economic profits since the average cost (AC) curve would be tangent to the demand curve.

Oligopoly

An oligopoly exists if the number of companies in the industry is small and little product differentiation exists. Because of the availability of close substitutes, each company closely watches the pricing strategy of its competitors. For example, a company knows that if it cuts its prices, the price cut will be matched by its competitors, resulting in a less favorable condition for all companies. On the other hand, if an oligopolist raises prices, competitors probably will not follow and the oligopolist will lose its share of the market. When faced with these conditions, sellers of homogenous goods have a strong incentive to charge only the prevailing price. Generally, this price is above marginal cost and is higher than that established in a perfectly competitive market, which will be discussed later. In the past, oligopolistic companies have been accused of tacitly agreeing to price their products at a specified figure, which leads to administered pricing. Before antitrust laws were passed outlawing such a strategy, trusts, cartels, and mergers were formed that collusively set prices.

Profit maximization in oligopoly.   Rather than use pricing as a marketing strategy, most oligopolists use other techniques; however, even these techniques have short-term effects because competitors rapidly move to counteract them. These close interactions make it difficult to generalize regarding the appearance of the oligopolist's demand curve. Assuming tacit agreement between companies, the demand curve could appear as in Exhibit 22–5. Line DD represents the demand curve for all sellers when they move prices together and share a total market. Line dd, which is more elastic, represents one company's demand curve when it acts alone in changing its price, resulting in sales lost to competitors.

Any price cut below point X is matched by the company's rivals and the DD demand curve prevails; conversely, at any point above X, dd prevails, since competitors do not match the company's price cuts. Because two different demand curves exist, there are different MR curves, as shown by the dotted lines in Exhibit 22–5. Significant shifts in the marginal cost (MC) curve do not change the price charged because of the discontinuity in the MR curve, which is the reason oligopolists' prices are often described as sticky; they remain stable even with considerable cost changes.

EXHIBIT 22–5

Profit maximization under oligopoly

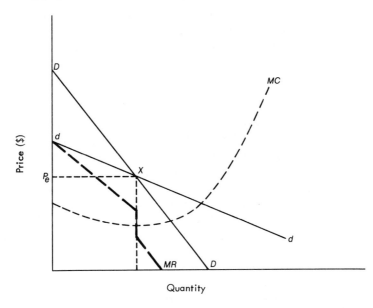

Perfect competition

The market structures described above involve imperfect competition. The companies must compete for their market share because an individual company's market share is always uncertain and it cannot sell as much as it desires. In addition, in imperfect competition, a company never is certain of the marketing strategy of its competitors if it changes its prices. However, these conditions do not exist for a perfect competitor because, in perfect competition, there are so many producers that no one individual company has any influence on the market price. There is little need for nonprice competition, such as sales promotion, because the products sold are homogenous and no consumer preference for a specific brand exists. While the monopolistic competitor uses packaging, trade names, and other means of sales promotion to differentiate its products in the buyers' minds, the perfect competitor does not. A perfect competitor accepts the price established in the market; however, sellers hoard products if the prices are too low and buyers do not buy if prices are too high.

In a perfectly competitive market, a random relationship exists between buyer and seller, as neither cares with whom he or she deals. This market structure is not found often in practice, although some metal products, agricultural stock exchanges, and commodities markets resemble perfectly competitive situations. Instead, most products are sold in situations in which the pricing decision is complex because product differentiation exists, even if only in the consumer's mind.

Exhibit 22–6 illustrates both the pure competitor's demand and the industry demand, which indicates that the pure competitor cannot influence the market

EXHIBIT 22–6

Pure or perfect competition

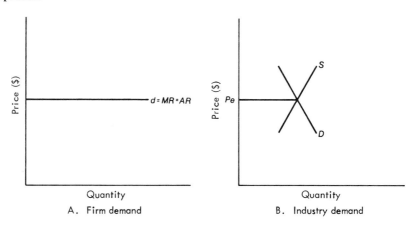

A. Firm demand

B. Industry demand

price by changing output. In fact, the company's demand is a horizontal line of infinite elasticity at equilibrium because the pure competitor must take the market price for each product sold. The company's average revenue *(AR)* equals the market price. In addition, because all units are sold at the same price, marginal revenue *(MR)* equals the equilibrium market price. The pricing decision that perfect competitors must make is not complex; they merely accept the price that competitors are offering because they do not control a large enough share of the market to influence prices.

Profit maximization in perfect competition.   Profit maximization for a perfect competitor is easy because all the competitor must do is find the output quantity that yields maximum profit and sell at that output with the given market price. As shown in Exhibit 22–7, the perfect competitor refers to its marginal cost curve *(MC)* because its point of profit maximization is where $P = MC = MR$, or point 1 above selling Q_1. However, the company would not operate if average revenue *(AR)* lies below average variable costs *(AVC)*, because then average revenue does not cover the differential cost per unit. The perfect competitor obtains its supply curve by referring to only that portion of its marginal cost curve which is above the lowest point of the company's average variable cost curve. If all the company's supply curves are added horizontally, the industry supply curve is determined.

As stated above, a company operating in a perfectly competitive market does not have the power to influence price and therefore must accept the prevailing one. However, this does not mean that the cost accountant in this company is of no value to management. On the contrary, the cost accountant should prepare budgets showing profitability at different operating levels based on total costs and revenues. Management can use these budgets to determine optimum operations.

EXHIBIT 22–7

Profit maximization in perfect competition

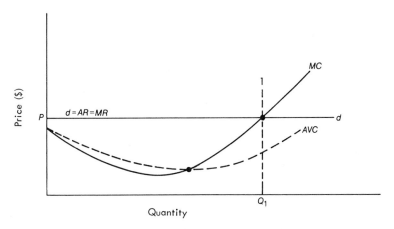

While the theory of the role of supply and demand in pricing is sound, often management may not know what the exact demand for its product is at each price offered because business conditions, the political environment, and the actions of competitors all affect demand. Since the executives responsible for the pricing decision do not know how consumers will react to these changing factors, a good pricing policy is difficult to establish. In addition, the economist's demand curve assumes that all consumers have the same characteristics when, in fact, different classes of consumers have varying characteristics. The relationship of customers to the pricing process is more complex than indicated by price elasticity and the law of demand, for each product has several demand curves representing different classes of potential customers. To best meet the needs of each class of customers, companies should consider offering different grades of each product.

ECONOMIC PROFITS

Economic profits, involve both implicit and explicit costs and differ from accounting income. *Explicit costs* consist of payments for resources bought or rented by the company. *Implicit costs* are costs of self-owned, self-employed resources which do not require an outlay of cash. Economic (pure) profit is the excess revenue remaining after all explicit costs and implicit costs have been absorbed. Implicit costs include charges for owners' capital and risk taking. Economic profit is a return over and above a normal profit. *Normal profit* is the imputed return to capital which is the minimum amount of profit to keep the firm in business in the long run; normal profit is considered by the economist to be part of total cost.

Accounting income, in contrast, is defined as revenue less explicit expenses and is based on actual transactions. The economist's concept of profit is less precise because expenses are defined in broader terms. Using the accountant's concept of profit, there is no distinction between normal profit and economic profit.

Residual income, which will be illustrated in Chapter 23 in the discussion of divisional performance measurement, is closely associated with economic profit. Residual income is divisional net income less the imputed interest on invested capital. Imputed interest is the cost of capital or the desired rate of return on divisional investment. This imputed interest charge is equivalent to the economist's normal profit.

RELATIONSHIP AMONG DEMAND, SUPPLY, AND COST

The discussion up to this point has been concerned with demand-based pricing theory; almost no mention has been made of the relationship between cost and price. This relationship is vividly displayed through examination of the familiar supply and demand curve. While economists believe that supply and demand determine price, costs, in turn, help determine the supply offered for sale. By matching supply, demand, price, and costs, the products that will be produced, who will produce them, and for which customers are determined. Generally, the supply side expressed in dollars is the cost of production and distribution, and the demand side is the revenue obtained from that production and distribution.

Pricing considers the interests of both buyers and sellers because if the selling price is reduced without corresponding reductions in cost, the supply of a given product will be reduced. The product's cost forces a company to resist lowering the selling price, both in the short run and the long run. Certainly, regardless of the cost concept used, companies strive to keep cost to a minimum by adopting the most efficient methods of production.

While the relationship between cost and price exists, there is little agreement regarding how close this relationship actually is in practice. Costs are generally considered to be simply a floor below which price cannot fall. The difficulty is that opinions differ regarding how this cost is to be measured. The long-run approach to pricing must take into consideration different costs because its objective is not the same as that of short-run pricing. The price established for long-run purposes must cover full costs as well as a satisfactory return on the assets invested, while a short-run price tries to maximize the utilization of existing facilities. As discussed in Chapter 17, differential costs are relevant in a short-run, accept-or-decline decision.

A principal objective of a business is to earn a satisfactory return on the assets used. To do this, a product or service must be provided at a price that consumers will accept. Earlier in the chapter, profit maximization for the different market structures was discussed. However, profit maximization often ignores long-run survival because if the return on investment is too high, new companies are drawn into the industry by the profits. This increase in the number of companies supplying the product drives the price down and, hence, lowers the return on investment. In addition, companies earning such high returns are subject to the criticism that they do not have the public interest at heart; this can lead to public, political, or legal pressure for price reduction. As a result, some companies cover only their variable costs in the short run, so no new entrant is attracted. Conversely, investors refuse to place additional assets in a company if the return is too low.

While it is recognized that a company's total revenue must exceed its total cost before a profit is generated, the pricing procedure becomes more complex when selling prices must be set separately for each product. A significant part of the complexity lies in deciding how much of indirect costs each product's price should cover. It is generally felt that in a normal pricing situation, the selling price of a product should be high enough to recover (a) the direct costs that are traceable to the product, (b) a fair share of indirect costs which must be allocated to each product line, and (c) a satisfactory profit. However, as will be discussed later, in a specialized pricing situation it may be more profitable for management to resort to other methods of price determination.

Social costs

The pricing method chosen may not consider the company's social costs; *social costs* are the outcome of an interaction of several complex economic, physical, biological, and meteorological systems. Air and water pollution, soil erosion, and emissions of residual waste products are examples of social costs. An externality arises whenever a firm's activities have a negative or positive impact on the environment for which the firm is not held accountable. If the activities of a company lead to depletion of social resources, the result is a social cost. If the activities lead to an increase in social resources, the result is a social benefit. These costs created by the production-related activities of a business enterprise are not used in variable or differential cost pricing because they are not measured directly in monetary units.

It is generally agreed that perfect competition in all markets leads to maximum social welfare. If markets are highly competitive and consumers and producers rationally attempt to reach a maximum level of satisfaction, available resources will be allocated in a way that maximizes social welfare. If private market prices are manipulated, then marginal social costs will not equal the marginal social benefit, and maximum social welfare will not be achieved. The indirect effects of this situation, referred to as external economies or dis-economies, are the social costs and social benefits not taken into account with the private marginal cost pricing rule.

Return on assets employed

The pricing strategy used by some companies is to base the selling price on a desired rate of *return on assets employed*. The following formula can be used in determining a percentage markup on cost in trying to generate a specified rate of return on assets employed. Assume that management wants to earn a 25 percent return on the $40 million assets employed and that annual costs total $16 million.

$$\text{Percentage markup on cost} = \frac{\text{Assets employed}}{\text{Total annual costs}} \times \frac{\text{Desired rate of return}}{\text{on capital employed}}$$

$$\text{Percentage markup on cost} = \frac{\$40,000,000}{\$16,000,000} \times 25 \text{ percent} = 62.5 \text{ percent}$$

$$\text{Sales volumes} = \text{Total annual costs} + \left(\text{Total annual costs} \times \text{Percentage markup on costs} \right)$$

$$\text{Sales volumes} = \$16,000,000 + (\$16,000,000 \times 62.5 \text{ percent})$$
$$= \$16,000,000 + \$10,000,000 = \$26,000,000$$

Rather than being expressed as a percentage markup on cost, the desired rate of return on assets employed can be multiplied by the capital employed (25 percent × $40,000,000 = $10,000,000) and added to the total annual costs as follows:

$$(\$10,000,000 + \$16,000,000) = \$26,000,000$$

The number of units expected to be sold is divided by the $26 million necessary sales volume to yield the unit sales price.

The above formula ignores many complexities in that the assets employed are assumed to be static; in reality, this is rarely true. As volume increases, the assets used, such as cash and inventory, usually increase. A change in the product's sales price or cost can also cause a change in assets employed; for example, with higher prices, accounts receivable are higher. Decreases in cost and sales price have the opposite effect. Despite these complexities, a consideration of the assets used does give management an insight into more valid pricing.

COST-PLUS PRICING METHODS

The measurement of cost is especially important when the buyer has agreed to pay a price based on cost, as in the case of cost plus an allowance for profit. Many federal government contracts, such as those for highway construction and defense projects, reimburse the provider for the cost plus an allowance for profits. The cost referred to in these projects is full cost; however, it is necessary to spell out in detail how the cost is to be computed to avoid misunderstandings later. This is one reason that Congress created the Cost Accounting Standards Board to develop better descriptions of how the cost of such contracts is to be measured.

As seen on page 852, cost does play a vital part in cost-plus, or backward-cost as they are sometimes called, pricing methods. With this approach, a desired percentage for profit is added to the full cost of the product; however, determination of the desired profit percentage is often difficult. As illustrated above, the profit percentage may be expressed as a percentage of the assets employed; yet the varying amount of assets required is a factor which must receive some attention.

Variable cost pricing

Variable cost pricing emphasizes the contribution margin by delineating the behavior of variable and fixed cost. One form of variable cost pricing involves adding a markup on variable costs to full costs. Cost-volume-profit relationships are carefully studied in determining variable cost formulas. Proponents of variable costing argue that this method allows management to determine prices for either the short run or the long run because the effect of different prices can be related to total fixed costs. However, there is a danger in focusing all attention on variable costs and contribution margin. Suppose a company has two products, A and B, for which monthly operating statements prepared on a variable costing basis show the following:

	Product A	Product B
Sales (1,000 units each)	$23,000	$16,000
Less variable expense	15,000	8,000
Contribution margin	$ 8,000	$ 8,000

Because Products A and B have identical contribution margins, there may be a temptation to treat them as equals in pricing. However, further study may be needed as an analysis of only contribution margin may lead to erroneous conclusions. If management is able to determine that these products require different effort and costs of marketing, executive analysis, and research and engineering, the cost should be arrived at by including these expenses. For example, assume that fixed manufacturing costs is $2,000 for each product, fixed marketing costs for the period is $3,000, engineering costs, $1,000 and executive analysis, $2,000. The marketing staff estimates that it spends 60 percent of its time on Product A and 40 percent on Product B because of the unstable market demand for Product A. In addition, Product A is packaged in a glass container. The engineering staff estimates that over the last several years it has spent 70 percent of its time in redesigning Product A's container. Despite these attempts to improve the container, there have been several lawsuits from customers for damages. Because management normally spend many hours in consultation with the firm's lawyers and in court trials, it believes 75 percent of its time has been spent with Product A. As a result of this information, the following analysis is made:

	Product A	Product B
Contribution margin	$8,000	$8,000
Fixed expenses:		
Manufacturing	2,000	2,000
Marketing	1,800 (60%)	1,200 (40%)
Engineering	700 (70%)	300 (30%)
Executive analysis	1,500 (75%)	500 (25%)
	$6,000	$4,000
Operating income	$2,000	$4,000
Cost per unit	$ 6	$ 4
Income per unit	2	4

This analysis shows that the products should not be treated as equals. Even though the allocations may not be precise, they do give management a better insight into the costs to use for pricing in this situation than do results obtained using a contribution approach. However, the allocations may change next period depending upon the attention given to either of the products.

Another problem with using contribution margin analysis in pricing is that fixed costs are labeled as irrelevant and omitted from consideration. Assume that the company has determined the span of control for a supervisor is five direct labor workers. At present, with 10 supervisors and 50 direct labor workers employed, the company has received several bids of $2,000 each for processing 100 additional units per month. Because the present work force cannot handle any increase in workload, one additional direct labor worker earning $900 monthly is required to handle each 100-unit order. Variable material and overhead amount to $8 per unit; supervisors earn $1,200 monthly.

As shown below, contribution margin analysis generally does not include a charge for the supervisor until the 55th worker is employed and the supervisor is added. However, an argument can be made that the supervisor's cost is really due to adding the 51st, 52d . . . 55th worker as well and the 56th and 57th worker in the future. Contribution marginal analysis might lead to rejection of profitable opportunities, as illustrated below:

Contribution margin approach

Worker number	Revenue	Cost	Contribution	Decision
51	$2,000	$1,700	$300	Accept
52	2,000	1,700	300	Accept
53	2,000	1,700	300	Accept
54	2,000	1,700	300	Accept
55	2,000	2,900	(900)	Reject

Alternative approach

Worker number	Revenue	Cost*	Profit	Decision
51	$2,000	$1,940	$60	Accept
52	2,000	1,940	60	Accept
53	2,000	1,940	60	Accept
54	2,000	1,940	60	Accept
55	2,000	1,940	60	Accept

*$900 per direct labor worker + $800 variable materials and overhead + $1,200/5 supervisor's cost.

Under these circumstances, differential cost pricing may be more appropriate.

Differential cost pricing

Differential cost pricing (also referred to as *marginal cost pricing*) focuses attention on the contribution to fixed costs and profit that an additional order generates; this method involves adding a markup on differential cost. The differential cost of an order is the increase in total costs resulting from the production of additional units. Differential cost pricing differs from variable cost pricing, in which a markup on variable costs is added to full cost, because both variable and fixed costs are included in the differential cost on which a markup is determined. Differential cost pricing is appropriate for some specific situations, especially those of a short-run nature. But it must be applied with caution and only after all related facts have been considered.

To illustrate differential cost pricing, assume the following product costs are gathered from accounting records:

	Product C	Product D
Direct material.	$ 5	$ 5
Direct labor.	6	2
Factory overhead:		
Variable.	4	1
Differential fixed.	3	2
Allocated fixed.	3	2
Total production cost	$21	$12

The differential cost of material, labor, and factory overhead for Product C is $18 and $10 for Product D. If a 25 percent markup on differential cost is used, the sales price becomes:

	Product C	Product D
Markup on differential costs	$ 4.50 (25% × $18)	$ 2.50 (25% × $10)
Full cost.	21.00	12.00
Sales price.	$25.50	$14.50

The differential cost and variable cost pricing theories can be appropriately used when the company is faced with difficult times and profits could be improved if some revenue above variable or differential cost is received rather than no revenue at all. Such revenue makes some contribution to the fixed costs for which the company has already made a commitment. Admittedly, contribution margin is helpful in short-run pricing and profit planning because the increase in cost resulting from a sale can be compared with the revenue increment to determine whether the order should be accepted.

With some even rarer short-run projects, it may be more profitable in the long run for the company to sell below variable costs. Generally, variable cost is the floor below which sales price cannot fall; however, this statement could be challenged in some situations. For example, if a company has a skilled labor force that is difficult to replace, management might accept an order in which sales price is below variable costs to receive some revenue to apply to existing wages and other costs. This approach might be more profitable in the long run than laying off the workers and running the risk of not being able to replace them.

Full-cost pricing

Instead of setting the sales price by adding a markup on differential costs, a markup on full cost can be used. This *full-cost pricing* involves determining not only the product's direct costs but also the indirect costs incurred by the overall company but which cannot be traced to one product line. The allocation methods described in Chapter 6 can be used; however, there is no way to prove that one method is more correct than another. Despite the fact that the full cost of any product involves cost allocations which are often based on judgment, opinion, and habit, the use of allocations which attempts to meet the criteria discussed in Chapter 6 provides that each product is bearing an equitable share of the production costs incurred by the company. If management establishes a sales price of $28 for Product C and of $16 for Product D, the gross margin is 25 percent of the selling price. The $7 gross margin for Product C and the $4 gross margin for Product D is a 33⅓ percent mark-on ($7/$21 of Product C's full cost and $4/$12 of Product D's full cost) to the production cost.

Conversion cost pricing

Use of *conversion cost pricing* allows no profits for the material used in the product; instead, attention is directed to the labor and factory overhead required, known as conversion cost. Conversion cost pricing is used mainly when the customer furnishes the material. The rationale behind this pricing theory is that greater profits can be realized if efforts are directed to the products requiring less labor and overhead because more units can be produced and sold. This applies when factory capacity is limited if the capacity constraint is labor and overhead cost.

In the example illustrated for full-cost pricing, Product D requires the same amount of material as Product C, but only $7 of direct labor and factory overhead, while Product C requires $16 direct labor and overhead. If a 25 percent markup on conversion cost is used, the sales price for each product becomes the following:

	Product C	Product D
Full cost	$21.00	$12.00
Markup on conversion cost	4.00 (25% × $16)	1.75 (25% × $7)
Sales price	$25.00	13.75

Using this pricing strategy, each product generates the same profit per unit of scarce resource.

Standard costs.   Standard costs can be used in the pricing decision regardless of whether the full cost or variable cost approach is adopted. Standard costs represent the costs that should be attained with efficient production methods at a normal capacity. If standard cost data are available, cost studies can be prepared more quickly. However, before standard costs are used as a basis for the pricing decision, care should be taken that the standards established reflect current conditions. An advantage of this approach is that standard costs are usually broken down into fixed and variable components, and this is critical in many pricing decisions.

Direct cost pricing

If the direct cost pricing theory is used, selling prices are established at a certain percentage above the direct, or traceable, costs incurred in manufacturing the product. This resembles the use of uniform gross profit percentages by merchandising companies. This pricing procedure has validity when the amount of indirect costs that should be equitably borne by each product line is essentially the same percentage of direct costs and when the assets employed by product lines are similar. Some managers feel that this method is more valid to apply in practice because it does not require prices to be based on indirect costs. They believe that since allocations of indirect costs cannot be achieved with a high degree of accuracy, they should not be used in the pricing decision.

Direct cost pricing can be illustrated as follows for Product E. With indirect costs of approximately 18 percent of direct costs and management wishing to earn a profit equal to 25 percent of total cost, the following calculation compares the direct cost pricing method with the full-cost pricing method.

	Product E	
	Direct cost pricing	Full cost pricing
Direct costs	$17	$17
Indirect costs		3
Total costs		$20
Mark-on [18% + 25% + (25% × 18%) = 47%]	8 ($17 × 47%)	5 ($20 × 25%)
Selling price	$25	$25

As shown above, total costs of $20 under the full-cost method are multiplied by the desired profit percentage to arrive at a markup of $5 and a resulting sales price of $25. If, instead, the direct cost pricing method is used, the mark-on percentage must cover indirect costs plus the desired 25 percent profit. A 47 percent mark-on is determined as follows: $[18\% + 25\% + (25\% \times 18\%)] = 47$ percent. After this 47 percent mark-on is applied to direct costs, a $25 selling price is determined, which is identical to that computed using the full-cost pricing method.

As stated earlier, direct cost pricing has validity if the cost characteristics of the various product lines are similar. Some managers might argue that even if their product lines do have different margins, the difference is offset because losses on one product line are counterbalanced by gains on other product lines. However, this reasoning is dangerous, for these differences will only be counterbalanced if the sales quantities of each product line are in the proportion originally assumed when the sales prices were set. For example, if a larger proportion of the high-cost products and a smaller proportion of the low-cost products are sold, overall company profits will be less than planned. In addition, the sales price of each product line may not be justified, since some products will be sold for a price lower than what their costs require, while other products will have a price that is higher than required by cost. In the latter case, the company runs the risk of losing sales to competitors.

Evaluation of all cost-based pricing methods.   There is little agreement about which costing theory is most appropriate for use in pricing, and all methods can be criticized. While the full-costing method does consider all production costs, it generally ignores marketing and administrative costs. The volume level at which unit fixed costs are calculated also significantly affects full costs, as emphasized in previous illustrations. There is also a danger in using only differential costs or variable costs in pricing, because all expenses, whether fixed or variable, must be covered for the company to earn a profit. The marketing staff might be misled or tempted to cut prices to the point where only variable costs are covered; this results in underpricing and ultimate disaster for the company.

Certainly, if the product can be sold for full cost plus a profit, the company should not base the sales price only on differential cost. Pricing includes much more than totaling the specific costs involved and adding a mark-on to these costs. Cost information merely provides an estimate of the sales price. In fact, many companies merely accept the existing market price without any involved pricing decision. They realize that customers will not pay more than this price and that there is no justification in charging less. While each of the costing theories presented is appropriate for specific pricing decisions, pricing strategy involves many considerations. Basing prices solely on one costing approach is dangerous; other factors must be considered.

Regardless of which costing concept is used, however, the relevant costs to consider are the ones incurred in the future, not necessarily those of the past. A change in plant equipment or facilities, for example, can affect the overhead cost of a product, and more efficient methods of production are constantly being developed, which may reduce costs. Similarly, a change in the level of activity affects costs. In addition, the product's specifications may change, resulting in a corresponding change in cost. Even if the product remains the same, its cost may change. For example, a supplier may charge a higher price for material, or a labor union contract may be signed which calls for increased wages.

Inflation is another factor which can cause future cost to vary from historical cost. Inflation seems to be a somewhat permanent condition in the United States and many other countries. As a result, historical cost must be adjusted to reflect different rates of inflation; in fact, if the different cost components are expected to increase by different percentages, more detailed calculations of future cost are necessary.

Even after it conducts sophisticated analyses of the market structure and cost studies to arrive at the optimum price for a product or service, management should give attention to the profitability of price revisions. This phase of the pricing problem is almost a continual process; management should be constantly studying the changing market environment in which the product or service is being offered for sale, for example, the effect of price changes in substitute and complementary products. More specifically, while golf balls and golf clubs are complementary products, they could be considered substitute goods for tennis balls and rackets. A company may find it profitable to lower its price of golf clubs to improve the market for golf balls. However, if the sporting goods dealer is not careful, this price reduction can cause some sporting enthusiast to switch from playing tennis to golf. Management thus should not assume that the optimum price will be static.

SUMMARY

Even though pricing is a complicated procedure which requires an understanding of several factors, many companies allow managers who have no special training or experience to set prices. A dangerous consequence is that these managers often rely strictly on intuition in pricing decisions rather than on careful cost studies. Certainly a trade-off exists between the pricing data management desires and the cost of gathering this data; however, the time spent in examining cost and the effect of price changes on demand is usually worthwhile.

As pointed out in this chapter, trial and error is not an adequate basis for developing a product's price. Sophisticated analysis of full cost, differential cost, and elasticity of supply and demand are needed—not just a slight consideration of the additional revenue and cost generated by a price change. While costs have a major influence on pricing decisions, competitors and customers cannot be disregarded. A company must consider the impact of a pricing decision on these influences, as well as on the profitability and survival of the company.

As stressed in the chapter, pricing is a complex subject that involves many people within the company, each believing that a particular pricing theory is the most appropriate. Admittedly, for instance, there is difficulty in using full costing because a unit's full cost depends on the volume of sales and production; however, the volume of sales is partially determined by the product's price. An additional complexity is caused by the numerous factors which must be considered, many of which are difficult to measure and quantify. The accountant has both the responsibility and the challenge of providing management with cost studies that can be used for guidance in this area.

IMPORTANT TERMS AND CONCEPTS

Suboptimization

Ceteris paribus

Change in quantity demanded

Change in demand

Price elasticity of demand

Demand and supply curves

Market equilibrium

Monopolist

Marginal revenue

Marginal cost

Law of diminishing returns

Imperfect competition

Monopolistic competition

Oligopoly

Perfect competition

Economic (pure) profit

Explicit and implicit Costs

Normal profit

Residual income

Social costs

Return on assets employed

Variable cost pricing

Differential cost pricing (marginal cost pricing)

Full-cost pricing

Conversion cost pricing

Direct cost pricing

REVIEW QUESTIONS

1. Discuss the role of cost in pricing decisions.
2. Define differential cost pricing and give an illustration of when it is in the company's best interest for management *not* to use this method.
3. Social costs are not considered in differential cost pricing. Define these costs.
4. Discuss the factors that can cause future costs to be different from historical costs.
5. Why is the determination of a product's price so difficult?
6. Discuss the influence of various parties on the pricing decision.
7. Name some external and internal factors that influence the pricing decision.
8. Indicate the difference between a change in quantity demanded and a change in demand.
9. Define and give the formula for the price elasticity of demand.
10. At what point does market equilibrium occur?

11. Define the terms *marginal revenue* and *marginal cost.*

12. How does the law of diminishing returns play a role in the pricing decision?

13. At what point does profit maximization occur in a monopoly?

14. Discuss the conditions of monopolistic competition.

15. How is profit maximization achieved in a monopolistic competitive market structure?

16. Give the characteristics of an oligopoly and indicate why it is difficult for an oligopolist to offer a product for sale at a price that is different from that of his or her competitors.

17. With what market conditions is perfect competition in effect?

18. How is profit maximization achieved in perfect competition? Of what use is cost information to a perfect competitor?

19. Discuss the relationship between demand, supply, and cost.

20. Describe several cost-plus pricing methods.

21. When would a company establish its sales price below variable cost?

EXERCISES

E22–1.   Determining volume and sales price to achieve objectives

Management of Morgan Jennings Company wishes to earn a 20 percent return on the $77 million of assets employed in manufacturing a new product. Annual costs total $35 million, and management expects to sell 210,000 units.

Required:

Determine the necessary total sales volume and unit sales price to achieve these objectives.

E22–2.   Direct cost pricing and full-cost pricing

Robert Roan Company has determined that the indirect cost of all its products is 60 percent of direct costs. Management wishes to earn a profit equal to 15 percent of total costs.

Required:

Compare the direct cost pricing method to the full-cost pricing method if the direct costs of a product are $10.

E22–3.   Contribution margin and pricing

The marketing personnel of Feaver Company conducted numerous market surveys in an attempt to determine the most profitable price for its product. Based on these surveys, the following sales volumes at the various prices are projected:

27,500 units at $74 per unit
25,400 units at $75.40 per unit
21,000 units at $80.90 per unit
18,750 units at $89 per unit

Fixed costs of $450,000 would remain unchanged over the range of production capacities predicted for these prices, while variable expense is forecasted to be $42.25 per unit.

Required:

Determine the selling price that would maximize company income.

E22–4.   Profit maximization in a mononopolistic market

South Company has developed a new product that is enjoying a monopolistic market. Due to the complex technological changes the product involves, South Company expects to maintain this market position for some time in the future. The following data show the quantity demanded at various prices, along with total cost:

Quantity (000)	Unit price	Total cost (000)
1	$125.00	$121
2	115.00	223
3	108.33	310
4	102.50	395
5	95.00	490
6	90.00	600

Required:

Determine the price at which profits are maximized.

E22–5.   Accept-decline special offer

Butterfly Company builds greenhouses for residential homes. The company has two sizes of greenhouses, which are known as the Green Thumb and Deluxe Green Thumb.

Estimates of the cost of each line are as follows:

	Green Thumb per unit	Deluxe Green Thumb per unit
Direct material	$200	$ 450
Direct labor	325	375
Overhead	65	75
Total cost	$590	$ 900
Sales price	$870	$1,160

Overhead is allocated on the basis of 20 percent of direct labor costs. Total manufacturing, marketing, and administrative overhead is $130,000; 55 percent is variable in direct proportion to direct labor costs. The company has excess capacity.

Required:

a.   A customer outside the present market region offers to buy 1,000 Green Thumb greenhouses for $580 and 200 Deluxe Green Thumb greenhouses for $860. Show the difference in income if only the Green Thumb offer is accepted.

b.   Show the difference in income if only the Deluxe Green Thumb offer is accepted.

c.   Identify the weaknesses in the pricing analysis you used in answering *a* and *b*.

E22–6. Economic profit (CMA adapted)

The assumptions, concepts, and terminology used by economists and accountants often differ and seem to conflict. For instance, the economist normally assumes that the functions for total revenue, variable (marginal) cost, and total cost are curvilinear, while the accountant traditionally assumes that these same functions are linear. The concept of profit also differs. The economist refers to two terms to describe profits—normal profit and economic (or pure) profit.

Required:

a. Explain the concept behind the economist's assumption of curvilinear functions for:
    (1) Total revenue.
    (2) Variable (marginal) cost.
    (3) Total cost.
b. Explain why the accountant's assumption of linear functions need not invalidate accounting analyses.
c. Economists use the terms normal profit and economic (pure) profit.
    (1) Explain what is meant by the terms.
    (2) Contrast the accountant's concept of profit with the economist's concepts of normal and economic profit.
    (3) Contrast the economic concepts of normal and economic profit with the accountant's notion of residual income as used in measuring the performance of divisions.

PROBLEMS

P22–1. Desired sales; Return on capital

The following information is available from Stallings Company

Assets

Cash	$ 75,000
Accounts receivable	111,000
Inventory	231,000
Property.	408,000
	$825,000

Liabilities and Owners' Equity

Current liabilities.	$380,000
Owners' equity	445,000
	$825,000

Fixed expenses	$73,250
Variable expenses	$7.75 per unit
Estimated volume for next year	13,000 units sold

Required:

a. What sales must the company have if management wants a 12 percent return on its investment in total assets? What sales price must be set?
b. What is the budgeted capital turnover?

c. What is the budgeted margin?
d. If the company sells 15,000 units instead of 13,000, what will be the return on capital?

P22–2.   Sales and cash breakeven point

Mason Rental Service operates 16 carpet cleaners which are rented for both residential and industrial cleaning. Each cleaner rents for $7.50 per hour. Detergent costs $3 per hour; repairs and maintenance, $2 per hour; and commission, $1 per hour. Other expenses per machine per year are insurance, $60, and depreciation, $125. Utilities for the office space and building maintenance amount to $180 per month; rent on this space is $250 and insurance is $80 per month. Salaries are $300 per month.

Mason, the owner, considers 60 hours per month per cleaner to be the maximum usage for this area. Each cleaner costs $600, and all but four have been paid for. Mason plans to pay for these in monthly installments within the next year.

Required:

a. Determine the sales breakeven point and cash breakeven point in hours per month per cleaner (without considering the payment on the cleaners).
b. Determine the average hours per month the company must sell this year to meet all cash outlays required, including the payments on the four cleaners.

P22–3.   Determining sales price to achieve objectives

Sills Company produces valves and motors for industrial use. The company expects to sell 5,000 valves and 7,000 motors next year. Unit costs have been estimated as follows:

	Cost per unit	
	Valves	Motors
Cost of goods sold	$ 8	$18
Direct marketing and administrative costs	2	10
Total direct costs	$10	$28
Indirect costs	4	6
Total costs	$14	$34

Management estimates that $500,000 of assets are employed annually in the production of valves, while $560,000 in assets are employed annually in the production of motors. The president feels that a 10 percent return on assets employed can be achieved. Income taxes are to be disregarded.

Required:

a. Using the sales estimates given, how much total profit per product line and profit per motor and valve must the company earn to yield a 10 percent return on assets employed?
b. At what uniform percentage above total costs for both products should the selling prices be established to earn the total profit required?
c. If, instead, management establishes a sales price so as to earn a 10 percent return on the assets employed on each product, what should the sales prices be?
d. If, instead, management establishes the sales price based on direct cost, what

uniform percentage above direct cost should be used? What should the sales price be?

e.   If, during the year, total sales were 12,000 units as estimated, but the sales mix was 4,000 valves and 8,000 motors, calculate the return on assets employed using the sales prices computed in *b* through *d.*

P22–4.   Calculating the overhead rate and its uses (CMA adapted)

Tastee-Treat Company prepares, packages and distributes six frozen vegetables in two different sized containers. The different vegetables and different sizes are prepared in large batches. The company employs an actual cost job order costing system. Manufacturing overhead is assigned to batches at a predetermined rate on the basis of direct labor-hours. The manufacturing overhead costs incurred by the company during two recent years (adjusted for changes using current prices and wage rates) are presented below.

	Year 1	Year 2
Direct labor-hours worked	2,760,000	2,160,000
Manufacturing overhead costs incurred *:		
Indirect labor	$11,040,000	$ 8,640,000
Employee benefits	4,140,000	3,240,000
Supplies.	2,760,000	2,160,000
Power	2,208,000	1,728,000
Heat and light.	552,000	552,000
Supervision	2,865,000	2,625,000
Depreciation.	7,930,000	7,930,000
Property taxes and		
insurance	3,005,000	3,005,000
Total overhead costs	$34,500,000	$29,880,000

*Adjusted for changes in current prices and wage rates.

Required:

a.   Tastee-Treat Company expects to operate at a 2,300,000 direct labor-hour level of activity next year. Using the data from two recent years, calculate the rate Tastee-Treat should employ to assign manufacturing overhead to its products.

b.   Explain how the company can use the information it developed for calculating the overhead rate for:

(1)   Evaluation of product pricing decisions.

(2)   Cost control evaluation.

(3)   Development of budgets.

P22–5.   Price decreases and volume

After studying the following income statement for its product, management of Ott Company feels that a reduction in sales price may be justified.

Year Ending December 31, 19X1

Sales (100,000 units)		$500,000
Variable costs	$200,000	
Fixed costs	210,000	410,000
Income before taxes		$ 90,000

Required:

a. How much extra volume must be sold in 19X2 to yield an income equal to that earned in 19X1 if decreases of 8 percent, 12 percent, and 20 percent in selling prices become necessary?

b. Why do successive price decreases of equal amounts require progressively larger increases in volume to equalize profits?

c. With the limited information given, discuss the factors you would advise management to study further before reducing the sales price.

P22–6.   Estimating gross margin with sales price increase

Sales of Charles Alworth Company's principal product totaled $600,000 in 19X1. Cost of goods sold was as follows:

Direct material used	$180,000
Direct labor	60,000
Variable factory overhead	30,000
Fixed factory overhead	90,000

One of the company's suppliers changed prices so that material prices will average 10 percent higher in 19X2. A labor contract has just been signed calling for an 8 percent wage increase. Variable factory overhead is applied on the basis of direct labor dollars. To earn the same gross margin as in 19X1, the sales price will be increased. This sales price increase will result in a 6 percent decrease in the number of units sold.

Required:

Determine what 19X2 total sales must be to earn the same gross margin as in 19X1.

P22–7.   Determining optimal pricing alternative

William Grasty Investment Corporation completed the construction of a $2 million building last year. The building is located on the outskirts of a major western city on an important highway leading into the city. The building was designed to appeal to a professional clientele such as doctors, dentists, lawyers, and accountants.

Even though tenants have different rates depending on the lease period and the options involved, the average price of the space has been set as follows, based upon floor location:

Floor style	Average rate per square foot per year	Square feet available
A.	$8.00	71,000
B.	7.50	100,000
C.	6.50	80,000

The prices are higher than those of the competition, but management believes that its price is justified by product differentiation. The building offers its tenants free use of a health club so that they can exercise during lunch hours. A plush restaurant and bar is also located on top of the building and is open to the public for both lunch and dinner. Management believes that the convenience of a nice restaurant for business entertaining is an added attraction.

Even though the building is located 10 miles from the nearest hospital, management believes that this should not be a great hindrance to the medical profession. In comparison to the office space located nearer the hospital, Grasty Investment's building is more plush. As its advertisements emphasize, occupants of the building avoid heavy downtown traffic. The building is located in a higher income suburb where more of its proposed tenants live; management believes this is an added attraction.

Management has, however, been concerned with the average tenant roll for the first 12 months of operation. The projected overall occupancy rate for this period of time was 85 percent, although the actual rates never reached expectations. The actual average percentage of occupancy by floor style for the year was Style A, 70 percent; Style B, 75 percent; and Style C, 78 percent.

Management had hoped that by the second year of operations the occupancy rate would be approximately 95 percent; however, since the rate of increase of tenants moving into the building has been much slower than anticipated, the company believes that it must carefully study the problem. Management believes that the low occupancy rate may stem from several causes. One may be that the rates charged are not justified; the "extras" perceived by management may not be viewed as such by the clientele and do not warrant the higher rates. In addition, the selected target market may be too small. Members of the medical profession may so prefer the convenience of office space near the hospital with which they are affiliated that the plush surroundings are not inducement enough.

In addition, the company is faced with rising utility costs. Variable costs per square foot occupied for each floor style are expected to increase to $3.50, including utilities and newspaper advertising, for the second year. Fixed annual costs are expected to be $680,000 for the second year.

Management is also faced with the possibility that some of the present tenants may break their leasing agreement and leave the building. These tenants include a snack bar, pharmacy, and hairstyling salon; their marketing plan is geared to having many people in the building. These three major tenants are upset because business is not as profitable as expected since the building has not been occupied faster. Each of the three has seriously threatened to move if the occupancy rate does not improve immediately. The hairstyling salon rents 1,500 square feet of Floor Style B; the snack bar and the pharmacy, 2,000 square feet, and 3,000 square feet, of Floor Style C, respectively.

Thus far, management has been able to postpone the move of these three tenants because of negotiation with a large government agency to lease one entire floor. This agency has offered to rent 10,000 square feet of Floor Style A at a $6.20 rate per square foot per year. In addition, the agency is asking for additional janitorial service amounting to $2 per square foot because of extra traffic. Management recognizes that the probability of the government agency leasing the building for a long period of time is much greater than for other clients. Variable costs of $3.50 per square foot are also expected for the space occupied by the government agency. In addition, if the government agency becomes a tenant, management expects an increased occupancy of 6 percent of total square footage of Floor Space A and 5 percent each in Floor Spaces B and C. These leases will be signed at the existing rates.

The vice president of finance argues that the company cannot afford a reduction in rate for the government agency. He believes even if the three tenants leasing the snack bar, pharmacy, and hairstyling salon do leave because the government agency does not sign a lease, he will be able to lease, at existing rates, 60 percent of the space that would be occupied by the government agency and 70 percent of the space lost if the three tenants move. To accomplish this, he plans to use an agency to personally contact physicians and lawyers and explain the benefits of the building. The agency will charge a flat fee of $5,000 plus 10 percent of the first year's rental fees for space that they sell.

The vice president of marketing has been trying for months to convince top management that the present promotion policy of only using newspaper advertising is inadequate. She agrees with using the services of the vice president of finance's agency to increase occupancy, but suggests the company also conduct a television advertising campaign involving 50 minutes of local television time which will cost $260 per minute. Data from a market survey conducted last month show that if both these promotion services are added, 80 percent of the space under consideration by the government agency and 78 percent of the space lost if the three tenants move would be occupied at existing rates. (Assume the increase in occupancy over the vice president of finance's proposal is the result of the television advertising campaign.)

The president of Grasty Company disagrees with both vice presidents and with the rate reduction necessary for the government agency to move in. Instead, he proposes the following change in price for all tenants effective at the beginning of the second year.

Room style	Average rate per square foot per year
A	$7.00
B	6.50
C	5.50

The president's forecast shows that this will result in the following average rates of occupancy for the second year: Style A, 82 percent; Style B, 90 percent; Style C, 95 percent. This additional volume would also increase the already profitable restaurant and bar.

Other members of the management team disagree with all plans thus far proposed and believe that a time lag between opening the offices and the desired occupancy levels should be expected for a building of this size. They argue that no change in rates should be made; instead, the company should wait and allow potential occupants to become more aware of the benefits this office building offers. These executives believe that if no change in the promotion policy or the price rates is made, the following rates of occupancy will be in effect: Style A, 70 percent; Style B, 76 percent; Style C, 80 percent.

Required:

a. Determine income before taxes from leasing activities using the following alternatives:
   (1) The government agency offer is accepted.
   (2) Vice president of finance's recommendation.
   (3) Vice president of marketing's recommendation.
   (4) President's recommendation for rate reduction.
   (5) Rate schedule stays same allowing for a time lag.
b. What additional factors should be considered before a decision is made?

P22–8.   Net present value of investment opportunities

Clark Automotive Parts is entering its 12th year of operations. The agenda for its upcoming monthly meeting of company executives includes consideration of several investment decisions. Those attending are provided a summary of the possibilities and are instructed to be prepared to discuss and defend their positions. The list appears as follows:

1.   Determination of the sales price for a new automotive part needs to be finalized. The following estimated probabilities of annual sales at previously suggested prices have been furnished by the sales manager. The part has a variable cost per unit of $12.

	Selling price			
Sales in units	$12	$13	$14	$15
40,000	—	—	5%	90%
50,000	—	40%	10	10
60,000	40%	20	45	—
70,000	60	40	40	—

2.   Evaluation of two mutually exclusive plans for improving operating results:

   Plan A—Double volume through an intensive promotional effort. This will lower the profit margin to 3 percent of sales and require an additional investment of $100,000.

   Plan B—Eliminate some unprofitable products and improve efficiency by adding $350,000 in capital equipment. This will decrease sales volume by 5 percent but improve the profit margin to 6 percent.

   The current profit margin is 4 percent on net annual sales of $2,500,000. An investment of $400,000 is needed to finance these sales. The company uses return on investment to measure operating results.

3.   Consideration of requests for short-term financing from three franchised dealers. The dealers have agreed to repay the loans within three years and to pay 6 percent of net income for the three-year period for the use of the funds. The following table summarizes by dealer the financing requested and the total remittances (principal plus 6 percent of net income) expected at the end of each year:

	Adams	Brock	Crane
Financing requested	$100,000	$ 70,000	$ 40,000
Remittances expected at end of			
Year 1	$ 30,000	$ 40,000	$ 30,000
Year 2	40,000	30,000	20,000
Year 3	60,000	20,000	10,000
	$130,000	$ 90,000	$ 60,000

The financing will be made available only if the annual beforetax return to Clark exceeds the required rate of 22 percent on investment. Discount factors (rounded) which will provide this rate of return are:

Year 1	.8
Year 2	.7
Year 3	.6

Required:

a.   Prepare a schedule computing the expected incremental income for each of the sales prices proposed for the new automotive part in 1 above. Include the expected sales in units (weighted according to the sales manager's estimated probabilities), the expected total monetary sales, expected total variable costs, and expected incremental income.

b. Prepare schedules comparing Clark's current rate of return on investment to the anticipated rates of return for each of the two plans in 2 above.

c. Prepare a schedule to compute the net present value of the investment opportunities of financing Adams, Brock, and Crane. The schedule should determine whether the discounted cash flows expected from each dealer are more or less than Clark's investment in loans to each.

P22–9.   Determining sales price to achieve objectives

Ms. Kimberly Wells plans to establish a drapery company specializing in the manufacture of custom-made draperies and bedspreads, as well as purchased hardware parts, exclusively for the residential market of Butler County. The company will have manufacturing, display, and office space in a light industrial area occupied by similar businesses. Management expects very little walk-in trade; thus, location is important only from a general geographic standpoint.

After extensive research, the following forecasted data were obtained to estimate sales and costs for the first year.

Total market—United States (millions)

Drapery hardware	$ 334
Draperies	935
Bedspreads	534
Curtains	334
Total expected sales	$2,137
U.S. population	203,300,000
Butler County population	722,017

Management is confident that their company can capture 10 percent of the Butler County custom market, recognizing that custom drapes represent 20 percent of all drapery sales. From previous experience in this field, management expects that 10 percent of total hardware sales are for custom drapes. In addition, it is expected that 1 percent of all bedspread sales are for the custom market. No curtains are custom-made.

Drapery shops typically base the quoted price of their product on the amount of estimated material and estimated labor used to manufacture the product. Butler Drapery Shop has taken the following typical product and estimated its material and labor cost. Material and labor for custom bedspreads bear the same relationship to sales price as do drapery costs.

Manufactured items (typical product 48″ × 84″ lined drapery made of satin)

Direct material cost	$13.52
Labor cost	9.36
	$22.88
Markup	29.12
Sales price	$52.00

Less markup is realized on drapery hardware parts that are purchased since the material cost constitutes 50 percent of the sales price, while direct labor on such parts remains at 18 percent of sales price.

Management expects all other costs to total $19,100 for the year.

Required:

a. Develop a market forecast which provides (1) the expected Butler County expenditures for drapery and curtain hardware, draperies, bedspreads, and curtains; (2) the portion of these expenditures which represents the custom-made market; and (3) Butler Drapery Shop's projected sales and expenses for the year.

b. By what percentage must sales price increase if management wishes to earn a 25 percent return on the $125,000 in assets employed in the company?

CASES

C22–1.   Use of contribution margin in pricing decisions

As a consultant strongly supportive of the contribution reporting concept, you are surprised to find that contribution reporting is not employed to a great extent at Spritt, Inc. Instead, you find that marketing, engineering, and administrative expenses are allocated in detail. When you ask Ann Brown, Director of Financial Planning at Spritt, why contribution reporting is not employed more extensively, she indicates that while the concept is employed to some degree, management also believes that the profit after allocating marketing, administrative, and engineering expenses is very important. Management also believes an analysis of only contribution margin may lead a company to false conclusions, especially in pricing decisions.

When you press Brown for an explanation, she gives you the following monthly data for two of the firm's products:

	Totals
Sales—Product A (500 units)	$100,000
Sales—Product B (700 units)	210,000
Variable manufacturing cost—Product A	35,000
Variable manufacturing cost—Product B	87,500
Variable marketing and administrative—Product A	15,000
Variable marketing and administrative—Product B	52,500
Fixed manufacturing cost	40,000
Marketing (fixed)	20,000
Executive analysis (fixed)	42,000
Research and patents (fixed)	10,000

All four products processed use approximately the same amount of floor space and supervision. However, of the hours spent in promoting these two products, the marketing staff estimates that 45 percent of their time is spent on Product A, 20 percent on Product B, and the remainder equally on the other two company products. A customer claims physical damage from using Product A. Consequently, management has spent many hours in consultation with their lawyers. In estimating the time spent on each product, managment believes an allocation of 30 percent to Product A and 20 percent to Product B is appropriate. Because the customer claims Product A's glass container is defective, management is concerned there may be additional lawsuits unless changes are made. The engineering staff has been working on a new design for the container that managment hopes to patent soon. However, the explosive nature of Product A will always present additional hazards, and it is doubtful that a container can be designed which is completely free of potential problems. Time sheets for the research department show 70 percent of their hours were spent in analyzing and testing

Product A, while the remainder of the time was divided equally among the other three products.

Brown further believes that while marginal analysis is a very useful tool, its benefits are overemphasized. One reason for this, she says, is that too many costs are omitted because they are labeled as fixed and irrelevant. She describes the following situation which occurred recently in the fabricating department. Management had determined that a ratio of one supervisor to eight direct labor workers is maximum. When the fabricating department was employing two supervisors and 16 direct labor workers, several orders were received for processing 100 additional units per month. The revenue from each 100-unit order would amount to $1,000 monthly. Since the work force could not handle any increase in workload, one additional direct labor worker was required to handle each 100-unit increase. Direct labor workers and supervisors earn $700 and $1,248 per month, respectively. Variable materials and overhead amount to $1 per finished unit.

Brown claims that the use of marginal analysis in this situation would have been a costly mistake. Instead, a total cost approach was used, further supporting her contention that fixed costs and allocated costs are indispensable in the operation of a business and that they should not be omitted from the accountant's analysis in pricing decisions.

Required:

a.   Do you agree with Brown's contention that contribution reporting can lead to false conclusions? Support your position with financial analyses of Products A and B.

b.   Prepare marginal and total cost analyses for use in making a decision as to whether to accept any one of eight additional 100-unit orders.

C22–2.   Optimum price volume alternatives (CMA adapted)

Stac Industries is a multiproduct company with several manufacturing plants. The Clinton Plant manufactures and distributes two household cleaning and polishing compounds, regular and heavy-duty, under the Cleen-Brite label. Forecasted operating results for the first six months of 19X1, when 100,000 cases of each compound are expected to be manufactured and sold, are presented in the following statement.

CLEEN-BRITE COMPOUNDS—Clinton Plant
Forecasted Results of Operations
Six-month Period Ending June 30, 19X1
($000)

	Regular	Heavy-duty	Total
Sales.	$2,000	$3,000	$5,000
Cost of sales	1,600	1,900	3,500
Gross profit	400	1,100	1,500
Selling and administrative expenses			
Variable	400	700	1,100
Fixed*	240	360	600
Total selling and administrative			
expenses	$ 640	$1,060	$1,700
Income (loss) before taxes	$ (240)	$ 40	$ (200)

*The fixed selling and administrative expenses are allocated to the two products on the basis of dollar sales volume on the internal reports.

The regular compound sells for $20 a case and the heavy-duty for $30 a case during the first six months of 19X1. The manufacturing costs by case of product are presented below. Each product is manufactured on a separate production line. Annual normal manufacturing capacity is 200,000 cases of each product. However, the plant is capable of producing 250,000 cases of regular compound and 350,000 cases of heavy-duty compound annually.

	Cost per case	
	Regular	Heavy-duty
Raw materials.	$ 7.00	$ 8.00
Direct labor	4.00	4.00
Variable manufacturing overhead.	1.00	2.00
Fixed manufacturing overhead*.	4.00	5.00
Total manufacturing cost	$16.00	$19.00
Variable selling and administrative costs	$ 4.00	$ 7.00

*Depreciation charges are 50 percent of the fixed manufacturing overhead of each line.

The schedule below reflects the consensus of top management regarding the price/volume alternatives for the Cleen-Brite products for the last six months of 19X1. These are essentially the same alternatives management had during the first six months of 19X1.

Regular compound		Heavy-duty compound	
Price (per case)	Sales volume (in cases)	Price (per case)	Sales volume (in cases)
$18	120,000	$25	175,000
20	100,000	27	140,000
21	90,000	30	100,000
22	80,000	32	55,000
23	50,000	35	35,000

Top management believes the loss for the first six months reflects a tight profit margin caused by intense competition. Management also believes that many companies will be forced out of this market by next year and profits should improve.

Required:

a. What unit selling price should Stac Industries select for each of the Cleen-Brite compounds (regular and heavy-duty) for the remaining six months of 19X1? Support your selection with appropriate calculations.

b. Without prejudice to your answer to a, assume the optimum price/volume alternatives for the last six months were a selling price of $23 and a volume level of 50,000 cases for the regular compound and a selling price of $35 and a volume of 35,000 cases for the heavy-duty compound.

   (1) Should Stac Industries consider closing down its operations until 19X2 to minimize its losses? Support your answer with appropriate calculations.

   (2) Identify and discuss the qualitative factors which should be considered in deciding whether the Clinton Plant should close down during the last six months of 19X1.

C22–3. Professional ethics (CMA adapted)

Jay Shoner, Corporate Controller for Wuster Company, was concerned because there was no code of professional ethics for the management accountants in his company. Based upon some reading he had done, he believed a series of steps should be followed culminating in a code of professional ethics for the management accountants at Wuster Company. The steps he intended to follow in the development of such a code are:

1. Review the role of the management accounting function within the company.
2. Determine the objectives of such a code and what it would accomplish.
3. Establish general ethical standards classified according to the nature of the obligations of management accounting.
4. Review specific situations to develop guidelines which would enable management accountants to interpret and apply ethical standards.

Required:

a. Formulate a statement of objectives for a code of professional ethics, including an identification of expected company benefits from such a code, which Jay Shoner would be likely to present to justify the establishment of such a code.

b. Three activities considered a normal part of management accounting responsibility are:
   (1) Preparation of quarterly financial statements for distribution to external parties (i.e., stockholders, lending institutions, etc.).
   (2) Approval for payment of corporate employees' expense reimbursements.
   (3) Accumulation and reporting of cost data for a nonrecurring decision such as a special order of raw materials.

c. For each of the three activities presented above:
   (1) Describe a specific ethical situation which might arise in relation to the activity.
   (2) Identify and prepare a specific provision which would appear in a code of professional ethics for management accountants.

C22–4.   Management philosophy and its effect on pricing

Ben Boston Printing Press is constantly faced with a shortage of cash. The owners-managers are Mae Boston, her two sons, Ben and Tom, and their wives. Mae Boston supervises the bookbinders; Ben is the sales manager; Tom, the production manager; Ben's wife, the payroll clerk-bookkeeper; and Tom's wife, the supervisor of the layout operation. There are 12 people, excluding the family, employed full-time. In addition, there are several skilled people available to work part-time, if needed. The 12 employees operate the company's various pieces of equipment.

Management is faced with pressing working capital needs. They feel part of their problem may be inadequate costing procedures. Management feels very strongly that they should never turn down business. Much of their work is custom orders which vary considerably in use of equipment and time. Ben, the sales manager, claims that he has no trouble getting orders; in fact, he says when he sees that volume will be down next week because of lack of orders, he "hustles" more orders in.

None of the owners has had formal business training; however, they feel that the practical experience that they have had in the business is quite adequate. In fact, all family members see themselves in a supervisory role and only if necessary will they assume a direct labor position.

The cash flow in and out is very erratic. The company is behind several months on equipment payments. When there is a strong fear that the equipment may be repossessed, the owners "hurry around" and find enough cash to quiet the creditors temporarily. Often this means that when deliveries are made, the Ben Boston customer is given a chance to deduct 5 percent from the bill if he or she can immediately make a cash payment.

The company claims that it cannot use a cost-based pricing system because it must meet competition. In addition, no cost figures are available. Their pricing strategy consists of referring to an eight-year-old industry price schedule classified by standard jobs. Then an additional fee is added to reflect whatever inflation they feel is necessary. After this total figure is determined, management asks itself whether that is the maximum the customer will bear. If it is not, the bid price is increased. If they feel that they have priced themselves out of a job, they automatically reduce the bid price without reference to any other factor.

After the family contacts you concerning their needs, you visit the plant still undecided whether you will be able to help them or agree to perform the consulting work needed. Then, early one morning, Tom calls you to plead for assistance. When you are able to calm Tom down, you find that he and Ben have had a big fuss. It seems that Ben purchased a large hospitalization insurance policy for the company. This was purchased the day following his wife's visit to a neurosurgeon who had scheduled back surgery for her in two weeks. Ben claims that the insurance agent assured him that the neurosurgery would be covered under their policy. When the facts are actually uncovered, you determine that the real reason Tom got so upset was because he had just received a call from one of his equipment creditors threatening to repossess one of his printing presses.

While drinking your morning coffee, you remember that the company's income statement from last month had such expenses as the following, arranged in alphabetical order:

Accountant's fee	Miscellaneous expense
Advertising	Payroll taxes
Casual labor	Property insurance
Delivery expense	Rent expense
Depreciation expense	Repair expense
Employees' salaries	Supplies expense
Freight expense	Telephone expense
Interest expense (on current and past-due notes)	Utility expense

All of these were in addition to the salaries each family member draws. You feel that one of your first steps is to calculate the approximate cost of operating each machine per hour. This will become the basis for their pricing strategy. You gather the following data for two pieces of the company's total equipment, each requiring one machine operator:

Printing press cost—$7,770.00 (7-year life)

Monthly rent expense	$121.00
Monthly repairs.........................	30.00
Machine operator	5.51 per hour
Payroll taxes, 9%	
Occupies 10% of floor space	
Present volume, 86 hours per month	

Folder cost—$1,500 (6-year life)

Machine operator	$ 5.51 per hour
Payroll taxes, 9%	
Monthly repairs	10.00
Occupies 12.5% of floor space	
Present volume, 22 hours per month	

The total monthly indirect overhead amounts to $3,472 based on a normal volume.

Required:

a.   Do you see anything wrong with the management philosophy of the company?
b.   Are there any inherent problems that will be difficult to solve with the existing structure?
c.   In view of the hospitalization insurance crisis, do you think the company needs a schedule showing the order in which monthly payments should be made? If so, prepare one.
d.   Determine the hourly cost of operating the printing press and the folder.

C22–5.   Price quotes (CMA adapted)

Jenco, Inc. manufactures a combination fertilizer/weed killer under the name Fertikil. This is the only product Jenco produces at the present time. Fertikil is sold nationwide through normal marketing channels to retail nurseries and garden stores.

Taylor Nursery plans to sell a similar fertilizer/weed killer through its regional nursery chain under its own private label. Taylor has asked Jenco to submit a bid for a 25,000-pound order of the private brand compound. While the chemical composition of the Taylor compound differs from Fertikil, the manufacturing process is very similar.

The Taylor compound would be produced in 1,000-pound lots. Each lot would require 60 direct labor-hours and the following chemicals:

Chemicals	Quantity in pounds
CW-3	400
JX-6	300
MZ-8	200
BE-7	100

The first three chemicals (CW-3, JX-6, and MZ-8) are all used in the production of Fertikil. BE-7 was used in a compound that Jenco has discontinued. This chemical was not sold or discarded because it does not deteriorate and storage facilities were adequate. Jenco could sell BE-7 at the prevailing market price less $0.10 per pound selling/handling expenses.

Jenco also has on hand a chemical called CN-5 which was manufactured for use in another product which is no longer produced. CN-5, which cannot be used in Fertikil, can be substituted for CW-3 on a one-for-one basis without affecting the quality of the Taylor compound. The quantity of CN-5 in inventory has a salvage value of $500.

Inventory and cost data for the chemicals which can be used to produce the Taylor compound are as shown:

Raw material	Pounds in inventory	Actual price per pound when purchased	Current market price per pound
CW-3	22,000	$ .80	$ .90
JX-6	5,000	.55	.60
MZ-8	8,000	1.40	1.60
BE-7	4,000	.60	.65
CN-5	5,500	.75	(salvage)

The current direct labor rate is $7 per hour. The manufacturing overhead rate is established at the beginning of the year and is applied consistently throughout the year, using direct labor-hours (DLH) as the base. The predetermined overhead rate for the current year, based on a two-shift capacity of 400,000 total DLH with no overtime, is as follows:

	Cost per direct labor-hour
Variable manufacturing overhead	$2.25
Fixed manufacturing overhead	3.75
Combined rate	$6.00

Jenco's production manager reports that the present equipment and facilities are adequate to manufacture the Taylor compound. However, Jenco is within 800 hours of its two-shift capacity this month, after which it must schedule overtime. If need be, the Taylor compound could be produced on regular time by shifting a portion of Fertikil production to overtime. Jenco's rate for overtime is one-and-one-half times the regular pay rate or $10.50 per hour. There is no allowance for any overtime premium in the manufacturing overhead rate.

Jenco's standard markup policy for new products is 25 percent of full manufacturing cost.

Required:

a. Assume Jenco, Inc. has decided to submit a bid for a 25,000-pound order of Taylor's new compound. The order must be delivered by the end of the current month. Taylor has indicated that this is a one-time order which will not be repeated. Calculate the lowest price Jenco should bid for the order and not reduce its net income.

b. Without prejudice to your answer to *a*, assume that Taylor Nursery plans to place regular orders for 25,000 pound lots of the new compound during the coming year. Jenco expects the demand for Fertikil to remain strong in the coming year. Therefore, the recurring orders from Taylor will put Jenco over its two-shift capacity. However, production can be scheduled so that 60 percent of each Taylor order can be completed during regular hours or Fertikil production could be shifted temporarily to overtime so that the Taylor orders can be produced on regular time. Jenco's production manager has estimated that the prices of all chemicals will stabilize at the current market rates for the coming year and that all other manufacturing costs are expected to be maintained at the same rates or amounts. Calculate the price Jenco, Inc. should quote Taylor Nursery for each 25,000-

pound lot of the new compound, assuming that there will be recurring orders during the coming year.

C22–6. Price guidelines (CMA adapted)

Berco Company manufactures and wholesales hardward supplies. One of its product lines is composed of drill bit sets and router bit sets. The company employs a calendar year for reporting purposes.

The company is subject to voluntary wage and price guidelines. Berco's management is attempting to determine how much latitude it has for wage and price increases in the drill/router bit product line and still be in compliance with the voluntary guidelines.

Certain key dates and time periods are specified in the guidelines and are defined below.

Base quarter. Last complete fiscal quarter prior to October 2, 19X4. For Berco Company, this quarter runs from July 1, 19X4 through September 30, 19X4.

Program year. Twelve-month period immediately following the base quarter. The program year for Berco extends from October 1, 19X4 through September 30, 19X5.

Base period. Two-year period measured from the end of the last calendar or complete fiscal quarter of 19X1 through the corresponding quarter of 19X3. The base period for Berco extends from December 31, 19X1 through December 31, 19X3.

Base year. The 12-month period prior to the program year, or October 1, 19X3 through September 30, 19X4 for Berco Company.

The guidelines specify standards for wages and prices, but the standards for each are not interrelated. The price standard is really a deceleration standard; i.e., the rate of the price increase allowed in the program year must be less than the price increase instituted in the base period. The standards with which Berco must comply are defined as follows:

Wage standard. Increases in the hourly wage rate in the program year cannot be more than 7 percent of the average hourly pay rate in effect in the base quarter (July 1 through September 30, 19X4).

Price standard. The rate of increase for a product line in the program year must be the lesser of (1) one-half of 1 percent (0.5 percent) less than the average rate of price increase for a product line for the base period stated as an annual percentage, or (2) no more than 9.5 percent annually.

The regulations which accompany the standards define the average rate of price increase for a product line for the base period as the weighted average of the price increase rates of each individual product line during the base period (12/31/19X1 to 12/31/19X3), stated as an annual rate. The regulations specify that the average rate is to be calculated as follows. The price increase rate for the base period of each individual product in the line is to be weighted by the ratio of actual sales revenue of each individual product in the line to the actual total sales revenue of the product line as measured at the beginning of the base period. The weighted average price increase rates for the base period for all products in the product line are summed and then divided by two (the base period is a two-year period) to get the average annual rate of price increase for a product line for the base period.

Once the allowable rate of price increase for a product line for the base period is determined (i.e., the amount calculated above, less 0.5 percent or the maximum of 9.5 percent), the rate of price increase is divided among all products in the line by the ratio of actual sales revenue of each product in the line to the total sales revenue of the product line, as measured at the end of the base quarter (September 30, 19X4).

Historical data on wages and prices for the drill/router bit product line are given in the following schedule:

		Price data				
	Drill bit sets			Router bit sets		
Quarter ending	Unit price	Units sold (millions)	Revenue (millions)	Unit price	Units sold (millions)	Revenue (millions)
12/31/X1	$3.00	5.00	$15.00	$12.00	3.75	$45.00
12/31/X3	3.75	5.80	21.75	13.80	4.25	58.65
9/30/X4	4.20	6.00	25.20	15.00	4.32	64.80

	Wage data		
Quarter ending	Total revenue (millions)	Labor-hours (millions)	Labor costs (millions)
12/31/X1	$60.0	2.20	$16.50
12/31/X3	80.4	2.40	21.12
9/30/X4	90.0	2.60	23.92

Required:

a. Calculate the maximum hourly wage rate for the drill/router bit product line in the program year that will allow Berco Company to still be in compliance with the wage standard of the voluntary wage and price guidelines.

b. Calculate the maximum rate of price increase Berco Company is allowed for the drill/router bit product line in the program year and still be in compliance with the price standard of the voluntary wage and price guidelines.

c. Without prejudice to your answer for *b*, assume that Berco Company is allowed the maximum rate of price increase of 9.5 percent for its drill/router bit product line. Further, Berco Company plans to increase the price of its router bit sets to $16.20 during the program year. Calculate the maximum price the company can charge for the drill bit sets in the program year and still be in compliance with the price standard of the voluntary guidelines.

d. The voluntary wage and price guidelines exclude the following product groups from compliance with the price standard:

    (1) Commodities traded in open exchange markets.

    (2) Exported goods and services.

    (3) New products introduced during or after the base year.

    (4) Products delivered during the program year under a contract signed prior to the start of the program year.

    (5) Products exchanged in other than arms-length transactions, e.g., intra-company sales.

For any three of these product groups, discuss why the product group was probably excluded from the guidelines.

OBJECTIVES OF CHAPTER 23

1. To discuss the various degrees of decentralization and centralization and the advantages and disadvantages of each.

2. To study the factors which determine whether products or services are related and should be grouped into segments.

3. To illustrate various performance measurements that can be used in evaluating segments.

23

Segmental analysis

Recently, many companies have expanded their activities into different markets, foreign countries, and various industries. The resulting size and complexity of these companies make it imperative that their operations be decentralized. This creation of various company segments in turn requires that the accountant provide some measure of each segment's level of efficiency. The different methods available for evaluating segments are discussed and illustrated in this chapter. The method that a company chooses varies depending on its organizational structure and the type of segment involved.

Chapter 20 discussed the impact of responsibility accounting on improving the measurement of management performance. Even though responsibility accounting was first applied to cost centers, the concept was later used in evaluating the effectiveness of profit and investment centers as well. As defined in Chapter 5, a *cost center* is the smallest area of responsibility for which costs are accumulated, while a *profit center* is a segment or division responsible for both revenue and expenses. In addition, income is related to invested capital for investment centers; however, the term, "profit center," may also be used in referring to these company divisions which are assigned responsibility for invested capital.

DEGREE OF DECENTRALIZATION

As companies grow not only larger but also more diverse, they are generally divided into several segments or divisions. Each segment becomes a separately identifiable center of operating activity and managerial responsibility. The degree of autonomy enjoyed by these segments varies because some companies issue tightly defined policies to segment managers, while other companies give their segment managers much flexibility and hold them responsible only for the broad task of operating efficiently and profitably. This degree of autonomy reflects the extent to which a company is decentralized: the more autonomous each segment, the more decentralized is the company as a whole.

A company's human relations philosophy also influences its decentralization. If a behavioral science approach is adopted, the company is likely to decentralize operations. As discussed in Chapter 20, the behavioral science approach is based on the thesis that management involves getting things done with and through people. To accomplish this, autocratic leadership is abandoned and individuals are given the opportunity to prove their ability. At one extreme is *total decentralization*, in which managers operate under minimum constraints and have maximum freedom because there is a lack of central authority. At the other extreme is *total centralization*, in which division managers have limited authority because top management maintains tight constraints. Few companies use either of these extremes. Absolute centralization is rarely economical because it is difficult to administer a large volume of decisions at the top management level; and absolute decentralization is rarely practical because with this approach each division operates as a separate business and makes no attempt to contribute to the success of the overall company. While the profit center concept implies that decentralization is maximized, not all divisions called profit centers, in fact, have the freedom to make most of their decisions; in some companies, managers of cost centers may have great latitude in making decisions which affect their division.

Advantages of decentralization.   Since there are varying degrees of decentralization, management should determine the advantages offered and the costs involved. The optimum solution is one that results in the most benefits with the least cost. Decentralization offers the following advantages:

1.   Frees top management from daily operating problems so that they can direct attention to strategic planning.
2.   Allows decision making as near as possible to the scene of action. This permits true teamwork among all executives, each skilled in his or her own area.
3.   Results in more accurate, timely decisions since segment managers are more familiar with local conditions than is top management.
4.   Recognizes the value of people who provide brainpower for a company.
5.   Provides training in decision making for segment managers so that they are better prepared to advance in the organizational hierarchy.
6.   Offers stimulus for more efficient performance because managers are given authority to match their responsibility.
7.   Eliminates unprofitable activities more rapidly since, for example, managers may be given authority to purchase direct materials from outside

parties rather than being forced to buy from one of the company's segments. If the market price is lower than the price of an intracompany transfer, attention should be directed to investigating the situation. (Chapter 24 discusses transfer pricing in detail.)

8. Provides a stimulus for segment managers to look for outside markets for their finished goods.

Disadvantages of decentralization. While the above advantages should lead to profits greater than those in a more heavily centralized organization, the costs associated with decentralization cannot be ignored. One of decentralization's greatest threats comes from the barriers it presents to goal congruence. The goals of the individual segments of a decentralized company may not be in harmony with overall company goals. Since decentralization encourages segment managers to focus attention on local operating conditions, the contribution that each segment should make to the profitability of the overall company may not be emphasized enough. In addition, because decision making is decentralized, there may be little communication among segment managers. As a result, decentralization may require a more elaborate and effective information system, which can be expensive. Furthermore, as will be discussed in Chapter 24, transfer prices must be established resulting in negotiation, friction, and additional cost studies. As a result, decentralization is least costly when the segments are independent of each other; that is, they do not supply each other with goods, compete with each other for the same market, or buy goods from the same sources.

SEGMENT PERFORMANCE

Regardless of the degree of decentralization, top management desires a dependable method of measuring segment performance. The term *segment* is defined in various ways, but generally it refers to any logical subcomponent of a company, usually identified with the responsibility for profit in supplying a product or service. Some segments which are distinct organization subcomponents are formally designated as divisions, for example, the Truck and Coach Division of General Motors Corporation. A segment may also be designated as, among other things, a territory, department, branch office, or service center. In analyzing marketing operations, one encounters other types of segments, such as a product line, class of customer, or channel of distribution, but these are not separate organizational entities. The important characteristic of a segment is that its operating performance is separately identifiable and measurable.

Management should study a number of factors in determining whether products or services are related and should be grouped into one segment, or are unrelated, and financial data should be gathered for each segment. The characteristics of the product is one such consideration since related products or services normally have similar rates of profitability, similar degrees of risk, and similar opportunities for growth. The production process for related products requires similar types of material, labor, and manufacturing facilities. If production facilities or labor forces or skills are shared, or if similar basic raw materials are used, the products or services probably are related. Likewise, if similar marketing methods are used, a relationship among the products or services is indicated.

METHODS OF EVALUATING SEGMENTS

Several means of evaluating segment performance were discussed in previous chapters: Chapter 21 discussed the establishment of standards for marketing activities, and Chapter 14 discussed the use of cash payback, return on investment, and present value in connection with capital expenditures. Some of these methods have inherent weaknesses either because of the dissimilarity of segments involved or the difficulty of establishing objective measurements. However, despite these weaknesses, they are helpful in pinpointing areas where additional investigation is needed.

Return on investment

Often managers become preoccupied with sales or income dollars rather than with the actual return generated on the investment in the segment; in fact, the relationship of income to invested capital is a better measure of profitability. *Return on investment (ROI)* focuses attention on the optimum asset investment because it enables management to determine whether the activity is profitable enough to support the amount of resources devoted to it. In addition, return on investment analyses can identify segments to which top management should direct attention. For example, if a segment's ROI is lower than planned or lower than that earned by other segments, corrective action may be possible so that performance is improved; on the other hand, management may also be able to capitalize on a situation in which the ROI is higher than expected. ROI analysis emphasizes that long-run profits will be maximized if the optimum level of investment in each asset is achieved.

Companies use both return on investment and *return on assets committed* (R.O.A.C.) to refer to the same performance measurement. While R.O.A.C. is more descriptive because it emphasizes that the return is calculated on the assets committed, either term is appropriate. The important factor is that only those assets used exclusively by the segment should be included. Assets that are controlled by the overall company and used for the general benefit of all segments should not be included. Some companies calculate a return on the assets employed by excluding standby equipment and other assets available but not used. This has the obvious result of increasing the rate of return, because idle assets are assumed to generate no income; however, it fails to measure how efficiently assets are used. The presence of idle assets suggests inefficient utilization of resources, and this should be reflected in the rate of return.

Valuing segment assets.   Determining the appropriate measurement of a segment's assets to compute the R.O.A.C. is most difficult. While the most readily available measure is usually the book value of the assets, which is found in the company's accounts, this measure may be least useful. If a significant portion of a segment's assets are depreciable, using the book value of assets committed tends to cause the rate of return to increase as the assets become older and increasingly depreciated. The rate of return rises as long as the segment's margin does not decline as rapidly as the book value of the assets identifiable with the segment. Using the gross value of depreciable assets without a deduction for depreciation eliminates such a meaningless increase in the rate of return. However, this basis still does not reflect the current economic value of the assets. Use of the current replacement cost of the assets committed is generally considered a more appropriate basis on which to measure the segment's performance. While replacement cost is not reflected in the ledger accounts, it can be obtained fairly readily. Quoted market prices can be used for inventories and equipment for which an actual market exists, and appraisals can be made of building, land, and other assets. Reliable replacement costs for intangible assets and special equipment are more difficult to obtain, but if no other current value estimate is possible, the original cost of the asset can be adjusted for a change in the general price level.

Measuring segment income also poses a number of difficulties. Just as companies use different terms in referring to the rate of return calculated, various profit figures can also be used. For example, if assets are based on replacement cost, depreciation expense should also be calculated on this basis in determining segment income. In addition, the rate of return computed for an overall company generally uses income after tax. Since a segment by itself pays no tax, an inconsistency arises if the segment rate of return is compared with the company's aftertax rate. While it is possible to apply the tax rate to segment income, this is rarely done in practice. The better approach is not to apply the tax rate to segment income, but to compare the rate of return for individual segments with that of other segments and/or with the budgeted rate determined by management in advance of actual operations.

An even more critical problem in determining the rate of return for a division is deciding whether segment net income or segment margin should be used. Average net income can be used, as shown in the following relationship outlining ROI:

$$\frac{\text{Sales}}{\text{Invested capital}} \times \frac{\text{Net income}}{\text{Sales}} = \frac{\text{Net income}}{\text{Invested capital}}$$

The formula can also be expressed as follows:

Margin percentage on sales × Capital turnover = Return on investment

Contribution reporting

Segments may also be evaluated on the basis of *contribution margin*, which is calculated by deducting only segment variable costs from segment revenue.

An even better evaluation method is to determine segment margin, which reflects each segment's contribution to indirect expenses. *Segment margin* is the revenue a segment earns less the variable and fixed expenses that can be traced directly to the segment. These traceable, or direct, expenses are those that would be eliminated if the segment were discontinued.

Traceable expenses include both fixed and variable expenses, with the larger part composed of variable expenses. Examples of traceable variable costs include salaries earned by employees whose effort is devoted strictly to the segment and material and supplies used for the segment. Depreciation, rent, and insurance on plant assets used by the individual territories and salespeople are included in the nonvariable costs traceable to the segment. The *nontraceable costs* which benefit more than one segment are not allocated.

Segment margin

Using contribution reporting, the profitability analysis of two territories is presented in a condensed statement in Exhibit 23–1. (In practice, the expenses are listed in more detail.) Two salespersons are assumed to be used in each territory. No nontraceable, or indirect, costs of the overall company are allocated to the territories. As can be seen in Exhibit 23–1, the Northeast Territory has a much more favorable operating performance, which results in a larger segment margin. The segment margin generated by Mr. A and Ms. D also is greater than the performance of the other two salespersons.

As can be seen in Exhibit 23–1, the *segment margin* represents what remains after both the direct, or traceable, variable and fixed costs are subtracted from each segment's revenue. Segment margin is what may be applied to cover the nontraceable, indirect, or common costs and finally to the income of the company as a whole. The segment margin is thus the best gauge of the long-run profitability of a segment. As a result, it is useful when decisions must be made regarding long-run capacity and the allocation of resources to each segment. For example, suppose Douglass Company is considering adding another salesperson to the Northwest Territory. The best estimates of the accounting and marketing staff reveal that the following revenue and costs would be generated by the fifth salesperson:

Sales.		$90,000
Less:		
Variable production expense	$40,000	
Variable marketing and administrative		
expenses	10,000	50,000
Contribution margin		$40,000
Less:		
Fixed costs traceable to segment		45,000
Segment margin.		$(5,000)

Fixed costs amounting to $45,000 would be incurred by the fifth salesperson because additional office space and equipment must be rented, which results in a negative segment margin. Even though a $40,000 contribution margin is

EXHIBIT 23–1

DOUGLASS COMPANY
Contribution Analysis for Territories and Salespeople
For Period Ending —

	Company totals	Territory		Northeast Territory		Northwest Territory	
		Northeast	Northwest	Mr. A	Ms. B	Mr. C	Ms. D
Revenue	$500,000	$300,000	$200,000	$175,000	$125,000	$70,000	$130,000
Less:							
Variable production expense	200,000	140,000	60,000	80,000	60,000	25,000	35,000
Variable marketing and administrative expenses	80,000	25,000	55,000	14,500	10,500	23,000	32,000
Total variable expenses	280,000	165,000	115,000	94,500	70,500	48,000	67,000
Contribution margin	$220,000	$135,000	$ 85,000	$ 80,500	$ 54,500	$22,000	$ 63,000
Percent of sales	44%	45%	42.5%	46%	43.6%	31.4%	48.5%
Less:							
Fixed costs traceable to segments	130,000	69,000	61,000	33,500	35,500	18,000	43,000
Segment margin	$ 90,000	$ 66,000	$ 24,000	$ 47,000	$ 19,000	$ 4,000	$ 20,000
Percent of sales	18%	22%	12%	26.9%	15.2%	5.7%	15.4%
Nontraceable costs	20,000						
Income before taxes	$ 70,000						
Percent of sales	14%						

projected for this segment, the segment margin should form the basis for the decision, because long-run capacity is involved. While contribution margin is most useful for short-run decisions such as the pricing of special orders, segment margin is most useful in evaluating long-run segment performance.

Nontraceable costs.   Allocations of indirect or nontraceable costs may reduce the usefulness of data for segment evaluation purposes, especially if these allocations are arbitrary. Arbitrary allocations distort the costs over which a segment manager has control; as a result, for internal appraisal of the manager's performance, nontraceable costs should not usually be included. Arbitrary allocations of nontraceable costs may indicate that a specific segment is unprofitable when, in fact, there is a positive segment margin which is contributing to overall indirect costs and any income. Generally, a segment should be retained as long as its segment margin is positive, unless a more profitable investment alternative is available.

While Exhibit 23–1 indicates that the Northeast Territory is more profitable than the Northwest Territory and that Mr. A is most profitable, a danger exists in the use of segment margin expressed as a percentage of sales. The Northeast Territory and Mr. A are not necessarily the most profitable if they require more resources. If a large difference in the resources committed to each segment exists, segment margin should be expressed as a return on the assets employed.

Rather than use income to reflect a rate of return, segment margin may be divided by the assets employed to give the *return on assets committed (R.O.A.C.)*. Assets employed can include working capital and the current value of long-term assets or, less desirably, their gross value. For example, assume the assets of the Northwest Territory are as follows, resulting in a 15 percent R.O.A.C.:

Assets Employed by Northwest Territory
For Period Ending 19—

Working capital	$ 40,000
Current replacement cost of long term assets	120,000
Net assets	$160,000
Segment margin (from Exhibit 23–1)	$ 24,000
Return on assets committed $24,000/$160,000	15%

Assets employed.   Certainly, if the assets employed vary as significantly, as they do in Exhibit 23–2, R.O.A.C. evaluation is necessary. The segment margin for each division is divided by the assets employed to determine how profitably the resources are being utilized. The return generated by Mr. C in Exhibit 23–2 is highest despite the fact that his segment contribution margin is lowest. A similar situation arises when product lines are being evaluated if the hours to complete a unit vary considerably. In this case, segment margin per hour required to complete the product is a better means of evaluating the segments than is total segment contribution.

EXHIBIT 23–2

DOUGLASS COMPANY
Segment Margin as a Percentage of Assets Employed
For Period Ending 19—

	Territory		Northeast Territory		Northwest Territory	
	Northeast	Northwest	Mr. A	Ms. B	Mr. C	Ms. D
Segment margin	$ 66,000	$ 24,000	$ 47,000	$ 19,000	$ 4,000	$ 20,000
Assets employed	660,000	160,000	335,714	324,286	20,000	140,000
Segment margin as percentage of assets employed	10.0%	15.0%	14.0%	5.9%	20.0%	14.3%

Improving ROI or R.O.A.C. By evaluating the segments through ROI, managerial attention can be focused on the factors that increase ROI by either increasing sales or reducing invested capital or expenses. Likewise, an improvement in capital turnover or the gross margin percentage without a change in the other factors increases ROI or R.O.A.C.

Limitations of R.O.A.C. or ROI. Some managers say that the use of R.O.A.C. for divisional performance evaluation is misleading as it requires that both tangible and intangible assets be assigned a value, which is often difficult to do. For example, the development of customer loyalty, recruiting costs, and research expenditures have a value beyond the current accounting period, and these are not usually capitalized as assets. In addition, historical cost and current economic value may have no direct relationship since some assets depreciate in value while others appreciate. Historical cost is the result of decisions made several years ago, while current economic usefulness depends upon the current market, technology, and other facts. Both the numerator and the denominator in R.O.A.C. and ROI are the result of and/or subject to wide ranges of arbitrary decisions which make them somewhat unreliable.

R.O.A.C. is therefore a useful index of performance only if reasonable criteria for comparison are available, such as R.O.A.C. for the same segment in previous periods, the ratio in other segments, the rate in another company, or some desired rate of return. However, considerable danger exists in comparing the R.O.A.C. of one company with that earned by another company, even if they are approximately the same size and are in the same industry, because a segment must rely on overall company management for many services which a separate company must provide for itself. In addition, a segment is considered to be more profitable per sales dollar volume than is a separate company; otherwise, there is little advantage to having a large company with many operating segments.

By evaluating segment managers on the basis of R.O.A.C., a company may be trying to maximize the ratio rather than the overall company's performance. For example, assume a segment manager uses assets valued at $200,000 and earns a segment margin of $50,000, with a resulting 25 percent R.O.A.C. Then assume that the manager has the opportunity to purchase an asset for $50,000 that would increase the segment's margin by $10,000, and that the overall company has excess cash of $50,000 that may otherwise be invested in marketable securities yielding 10 percent. The company's cost of capital is 12 percent. The new asset earns a 20 percent R.O.A.C. ($10,000/$50,000), which is higher than the cost of capital. However, if the purchase is made, the segment manager's R.O.A.C. would be reduced to 24 percent ($60,000/$250,000). If the company evaluates the segment manager strictly on the basis of the rate of return rather than also giving some attention to the dollar amount of segment margin generated, the segment manager may forego the purchase. With this evaluation method, the segment manager may be tempted to dispose of any asset that is not earning a 25 percent R.O.A.C. For example, if the manager holds an asset valued at $100,000 that can be disposed of with a resulting reduction in segment margin of less than $25,000, the manager's R.O.A.C. increases in the short run if he or she disposes of the asset. But in the long run this decision may weaken the company.

To avoid situations of this nature, companies should evaluate segment performance using several different measures. Return on investment helps meet this purpose, if the segments are completely independent of each other. However, if the segments are closely interrelated and purchase goods from each other, a valid return on investment is more difficult to determine. As will be discussed in Chapter 24, a company must calculate transfer prices to place a value on these purchases, and sometimes these transfer prices result from arbitrary decisions. As a result, ROI or R.O.A.C. can be most effectively applied to evaluate the operations of segments that are somewhat independent of each other and with output that can be objectively valued.

But ROI also has its weaknesses. Often companies make a monthly estimate for income and expense adjustments, such as depreciation, interest, and amortization, and wait until year-end to determine more exact figures. Since ROI uses both net income and sales, an inaccurate ratio may be determined if estimated monthly revenues and expenses are used. On the other hand, waiting until year-end to calculate ROI is limiting, since management needs current information concerning operations. An additional limitation is that some investments may have more than one rate of return; for example, there may be periods of positive proceeds followed by periods of negative cash flows. The return on investment ratio cannot be adjusted for this factor. Because of these limitations, performance measurements other than ROI must also be used.

Breakeven point analysis

Another means of evaluating segments is to apply the breakeven point analysis presented in Chapter 15. The breakeven point is the level of sales at which the segment recovers all expenses and shows neither income nor loss. However, breakeven point analysis has limitations when applied to segments, since fixed costs must be considered in determining the breakeven point, and allocating fixed costs may be difficult and involve some arbitrary allocations. Additional limitations of breakeven analysis are discussed in Chapter 15.

Full costing and segment analysis

While full costing is necessary for reporting segment performance to the SEC, it has limited usefulness in segment analysis. As discussed in Chapter 17, full costing cannot be used to test alternatives because some of the cost allocated is not affected by the alternative. For example, if a territory reports a net loss, the entire loss reported cannot be avoided by eliminating the territory because the indirect costs allocated to the territory are nonescapable.

If instead of using contribution reporting, full costing were applied to the data in Exhibit 23–1, the performance picture would be quite different. In arriving at a full-costing income, the $20,000 nontraceable cost would be allocated to the territories and salespersons. This is likely to cause the performance of Mr. C in the Northwest Territory to reflect a net loss using full-cost reporting. An evaluation of profitability is especially important when management is faced with the decision of whether to eliminate a segment or not. A segment is considered profitable if its revenue exceeds its traceable costs, regardless of whether or not it covers what someone has determined is its fair share of the nontraceable costs. A segment should be retained as long as it yields a positive contribution and the resources of the segment cannot be put to better use.

While this discussion of contribution reporting and full costing emphasize traceable and nontraceable costs, controllable and noncontrollable costs should not be ignored. Regardless of whether full costing or contribution reporting is used, controllable costs should be separated from noncontrollable costs. Advocates of contribution reporting argue that the separation of controllable from noncontrollable cost is not adequate for segment performance evaluation; they feel that noncontrollable costs should not be shown in segment reports at all. On the other hand, full-costing proponents feel that segment managers should be aware of the total costs associated with their division and, in turn, be more supportive of cost control. In addition, if noncontrollable costs are reported, segment managers are made aware of the services they receive from other parts of the company. However, those segment managers should be assured that even though their controllable costs are small in relation to noncontrollable costs, it is imperative that they direct full attention to those areas over which they have authority.

Since it is unfair to hold segment managers responsible for costs over which they have no control, the full-costing approach may be used in segment reporting, but should not be used in segment *evaluation*. However, this does not imply that each segment should not be expected to contribute toward these indirect costs. Only the overall company can earn income; all that each segment can do is to contribute to that income. It should be emphasized to segment managers that companywide income is maximized only when the marginal contribution of each segment is maximized. Thus, it is important for management to receive contribution margin analyses for each segment when evaluating the individual divisions of a company.

Residual income

Instead of using R.O.A.C., segment margin, or any of the other methods mentioned to evaluate a segment, a company might use residual income, which is the operating income of the investment center after the imputed interest on the assets used by the center has been deducted. Residual income eliminates some of the problems associated with expressing a rate of return because it is not expressed as a ratio. The interest rate used for this computation is normally the company's average cost of capital. Chapter 14 discussed the computation of cost of capital, which is the cost of debt capital added to the cost of equity capital, each weighted by its proportion of the company's total capital structure. This cost of capital rate should not be uniform if the different segments involved are earning various rates; in that case, the better approach is to use different rates for each segment.

Some authorities argue that rather than compute imputed interest on the segment's *invested capital*, only interest on the segment's *controllable investment* should be considered. They believe that segment managers cannot currently control much of the segment's plant and equipment because it remains unchanged for long periods. As a result, these authorities stress that segment managers should be evaluated on the investment in working capital, especially receivables and inventories. Their argument is that segment managers can control the receivable investment through their credit and collection policy. Likewise, the reordering levels chosen affect inventory investment. Usually, a segment's accounts payable and accrual balances are subtracted from its receivables and inventories to arrive at the controllable investment.

Residual income is calculated using the illustration presented earlier in which a segment earns a $50,000 segment margin while employing $200,000 of assets. With a cost of capital 12 percent, its residual income is calculated thus:

Segment margin	$50,000
Less imputed interest on invested capital (12% × $200,000)	24,000
Residual income	$26,000

If attention is focused on residual income, a segment manager would be encouraged to purchase a new asset for $50,000, which would generate a segment margin of $10,000, even though the asset purchased does not earn as high a return as the segment is now earning. Yet, as illustrated in the R.O.A.C. discussion, before the purchase, the segment earned a 25 percent ($50,000/$200,000) R.O.A.C.; however the new assets earn only a 20 percent ($10,000/$50,000) R.O.A.C. Residual income increases as follows:

Segment margin	$60,000
Less imputed interest on invested capital (12% × $250,000)	30,000
Residual income	$30,000

A similar format would be adopted if controllable segment investments are used instead of investment capital. By using residual income as a performance measure, a company encourages segment managers to concentrate on maximizing dollars of residual income rather than on maximizing a percentage return.

Evaluation of residual income.   Residual income is not as widely applied in segment evaluations as is the rate of return. Yet, some of the limitations and dangers inherent in the rate of return methods are overcome through the use of the residual income performance measurement. For example, by using controllable capital rather than invested capital, the segment manager is not held responsible for plant and equipment decisions which are generally made at the top management level. In addition, projects that result in an increase in segment margin may be rejected simply because the rate of return is not as high for these projects as that presently earned. Residual income analysis, on the other hand, emphasizes the increase in profits generated by these projects. It should, however, be recognized that the residual income approach can also be misused. Either measure is useful to management if correctly used and properly interpreted. Reliance on one single measure for evaluation should be avoided; rather, several different performance measurements should be used.

Ratios

A limitless number of ratios can be computed for each segment operation, ranging from current ratio, which compares current assets to current liabilities, to ratios of various expenses to sales. Many trade associations collect and make available to their members information in ratio form for comparative purposes. However, because of the wide variation in classifying items such as marketing and distribution expenses, these comparisons may have little meaning. For example, one company may employ account titles identical to those used by the rest of the industry, but charge different cost items to the titles. In addition, different management concepts within the same industry militate against valid intercompany cost comparisons. Industry figures are representative of an average firm with characteristics that may differ significantly from those of any given company making the comparison. Thus, the value of this analysis depends on the analysts' ability to interpret differences between a given company and the industry average.

Nonfinancial evaluations

The methods presented in this chapter for evaluating segments all involve financial data. While this type of evaluation is usually the one assigned to the accountant, some useful measures of performance can be made which do not involve financial data. For example, a segment may be analyzed on the basis of employee attitudes, delivery schedules, customer relations, and plant asset maintenance. While all these factors affect the financial performance of a segment, the direct measurement itself involves nonfinancial data. Even though none of these nonfinancial evaluations are detailed in this chapter, they can be useful to management.

Rather than rely on some written form of segment evaluation, some companies use only personal observation. Visits to the territory are made to observe performance, and sales managers make calls with salespeople to observe methods of presenting the products. While the advantages of personal observations are the time saved in communication and the firsthand appraisal of such intangibles as employee morale, customer reaction, and personnel development, it does have definite disadvantages. Personal observation is often an inconsistent measure of segment performance, and it often takes a good deal of time to explain and report these evaluations. For example, the personality of the territory manager may bias the evaluation of actual performance. In addition, there are no permanent records if only oral evaluations are made. The advantage of permanent records is that they can be reviewed at a later date. Companies should consider using both oral and written evaluations, not just one or the other, to gain a better insight into a segment's level of operating efficiency.

In any case, management should only request information from segment managers that will actually be used. In requesting information from salespeople, the marketing manager must consider the trade-off between the time a salesperson spends preparing the report and the time spent making sales in actual contact with customers. Salespeople are less resentful of the time required in record-keeping if they are assured that the reports are being used by management, and in a way that is beneficial. An added advantage of such record-keeping to salespeople is that it helps them plan and direct their work, since they must be aware of their daily accomplishments if they are to make their quotas.

GOAL CONGRUENCE AND SUBOPTIMIZATION

The approach to profitability analysis suggested in this chapter has a wide range of applicability regardless of whether the company is profit oriented. For example, in hospitals the segments could be patient floors, therapy services, X-ray, and pharmacy. In a university, the segments could be various graduate and undergraduate programs in the different colleges. In a continuing education division, each course offering, such as CPA Review, CMA Review, Art Appreciation, or Quilt Making could be considered a separate segment. The tuition generated by each course can be compared with the instructor's salary and other traceable costs to determine whether the course can pay for itself. However, in both hospitals and universities, it may not be advisable to drop a segment merely because of a negative segment margin. Both of these institutions have other objectives which may assume priority over profitability. Nevertheless, segment analysis is helpful in arriving at the most appropriate decision, since it compares costs with the revenue received.

Regardless of the method used in measuring and evaluating segment performance, top management should design the performance measurement in such a way that segment managers in seeking to achieve their own goals are also simultaneously working toward the overall company's goals. Such *goal congruence* is most difficult to achieve. Certainly, segment managers attempt to make their own segment look good, especially if there is a bonus system from which they can gain personally by profitable performance. While such behavior is perfectly normal and can be expected, company management must guard against *suboptimization* with which each segment benefits to the detriment of the overall company; this is just the opposite of goal congruence. For example, segment managers may universally reduce or defer such discretionary expenditures as preventive maintenance solely for the purpose of increasing short-run segment margin. It will take several months before costly breakdowns and repairs occur that offset the apparent savings from deferring such maintenance.

CAS 403

Not only must accountants be concerned with the SEC and FASB requirements in segment reporting for external purposes, they may also be required to allocate expenses as specified by the Cost Accounting Standards Board (CASB). CAS 403 establishes criteria for allocating the expenses of a home office to the segments of a company based on the beneficial or causal relationship between such expenses and the receiving segments. The standard provides for identification of expenses for direct allocation to segments to the maximum extent practical. Significant indirectly allocated expenses are to be accumulated in logical and relatively homogenous pools to be allocated on bases reflecting the relationship of the expenses to the segments concerned. Even though the appropriate implementation of Standard 403 limits the amount of the home office expenses classified as residual, these remaining home office expenses are allocated to all segments.

Cost Accounting Standard 403 provides criteria for the allocation of groups of home office expenses into such pools as centralized service functions, central payments or accruals, and independent research and bidding and proposal costs. The number of expense groupings will depend primarily on the variety and significance of service and management functions performed by a particular home office. Typical pools with illustrative allocation bases are also given in the standard. A few of these are listed below:

Home office expense or function	Illustrative allocation bases
Centralized service functions:	
Personnel administration	Number of personnel, labor-hours, payroll, number of persons hired.
Data processing services.	Machine time, number of reports.
Staff management of specific activities:	
Material/purchasing policies	Number of purchase orders, value of purchases.
Marketing policies	Sales, segment marketing costs.
Central payments or accruals:	
Pension expenses	Payroll or other factor on which total payment is based.
State and local income taxes and franchise taxes	Any base or method which results in an allocation that equals or approximates a segment's proportionate share of the tax imposed by the jurisdiction in which the segment does business, as measured by the same factors used to determine taxable income for that jurisdiction.

SUMMARY

A segment is a division, department, or other subdivision of a company. There are various types of segments, including territories, product lines, salespeople, projects, channels of distribution, and market tests. Several performance measurements can be used to evaluate segment performance, including segment margin, breakeven analysis, and the computation of ROI or R.O.A.C. or residual income. Many complexities are encountered in arriving at the ROI or R.O.A.C. because various income figures can be compared with different measures of the assets employed. Rather than use the net book value of long-term assets to determine these, the current value of long-term assets may be used to get a more valid R.O.A.C. A danger is inherent in calculating R.O.A.C., however, because if the asset figure is incomplete or inaccurate, the rate of return calculated is misleading.

Regardless of the approach used to evaluate the different segments of a company, a danger exists in encouraging managers to concentrate on maximizing the segment's performance to the detriment of the overall company. Projects that are profitable to the overall company but are not as favorable to a specific segment as alternative projects should not be rejected. Management needs to be aware of when a segment is not fulfilling expectations. Certainly, if short-term market evaluations are to be meaningful, they must be accompanied by an understanding of the consequences of the costs being incurred.

IMPORTANT TERMS AND CONCEPTS

Profit center   Contribution margin

Cost center   Nontraceable costs

Total decentralization   Segment margin

Total centralization   Full costing

Segment   Residual income

ROI or R.O.A.C.   Goal congruence

Contribution reporting   Suboptimization

REVIEW QUESTIONS

1. Contrast total decentralization with total centralization. Are examples of these two extremes found often in practice? Why or why not?
2. Give some advantages and disadvantages of decentralization.
3. Define a segment and explain what factors should be studied in grouping segments.

4. What misleading inferences can be made if segment margin is expressed as a percentage of sales?

5. When should segment margin be expressed as a percentage of assets employed or on a per hour basis?

6. Discuss some limitations of R.O.A.C. and ROI. What criteria should be adopted in using these ratios in comparison analysis?

7. How could the use of R.O.A.C. encourage unprofitable behavior?

8. Do you feel that full costing has limited usefulness in evaluations of segments? Support your answer.

9. Define residual income and discuss its use as a performance measurement.

10. Do you feel that idle assets should be included in the asset base when calculating ROI or R.O.A.C.? Why or why not?

11. Discuss several ways that a segment's assets may be measured. Which of these do you consider most appropriate?

12. What complexities arise in measuring segment income for use in ROI analysis?

13. If you were evaluating the performance of a segment, would you consider nontraceable costs in your analysis? Why or why not?

14. In choosing which segment performance measurements to use, why should management be concerned about suboptimization?

EXERCISES

E23–1. Disclosure of segment information

Luther, Inc.'s controller advocates segment reporting, arguing the merits of management identifying and reporting significant aspects of the organization's operations. Other members of the management team are not convinced that the effort involved is worth it.

Required:

a. Present arguments against the disclosure of segment information.
b. Present arguments in support of the disclosure of segment information.

E23–2. Profitability of product lines

Dulcie Douglass, Inc. produces three different products and wishes to evaluate the profitability of each product line. The firm supplies you with the following data for the year ended September 30, 19X2:

Sales—Product A (2,000 units)	$200,000
Sales—Product B (4,000 units)	500,000
Sales—Product C (6,000 units)	180,000
Direct cost—Product A	80,000
Direct cost—Product B	360,000
Direct cost—Product C	90,000
Indirect costs—allocated on per unit basis	240,000

Each unit of Product A requires six hours to produce; of Product B, four hours; of Product C, five hours.

Required:

Evaluate the profitability of each product line.

E23–3.   Minimum order size

Louis Wells, salesperson for Ann Martin Manufacturing, was upset about the amount of time he felt he was wasting with customers that made only small orders. He discussed his complaint with Harold Douglass, sales manager. Harold informed him that other salespersons had raised the same question.

Together, they approached the controller to prepare an analysis by sales order so that top management would be better able to set guidelines for the salespeople.

A cost clerk prepares the following average processing cost per order, based on 2,000 orders per period:

Receiving.	$0.40
Warehousing and handling	0.50
Preparing invoice	0.25
Posting charges and credits to Accounts Receivable.	0.35
Credit investigation.	0.30
Total cost per order	$1.80

A markup of 25 percent over production cost is planned.

Required:

a. What is the minimum order size in dollars that the company should accept using the $1.80 unit processing cost per order?

b. Evaluate any weaknesses that you see in the above approach for deciding on minimum order sizes.

E23–4.   Contribution margin, segment margin, and residual income

Humphreys Key Company manufactures several product lines, one of which is the Nesti line. Management is concerned about the profitability of this line and requests your help in preparing a segment analysis. The following data are supplied:

Units sold.	13,000
Unit sales price	$ 50
Unit variable production expense	20
Unit variable marketing and administrative expense	15
Traceable fixed costs	60,000

A total of $600,000 of capital has been invested in this product line.

Required:

Determine contribution margin, segment margin, and residual income for this product line, assuming a 12 percent cost of capital.

E23–5.   Residual income

Data for the Settle Company are extracted from their records as follows:

	Products			
	A	B	C	D
Units sold.	8,000	6,000	6,200	5,800
Unit sales price . . . . $	30	$ 55	$ 40	$ 44
Unit cost of goods sold:				
Direct material. . . . . $	6	$ 14	$ 13	$ 12
Direct labor.	4	6	9	8
Variable factory				
overhead	8	3	4	6
Fixed factory				
overhead	3	2	5	4
Unit variable marketing and				
administrative expense	2	2	6	3
Other traceable fixed				
costs	8,000	17,500	2,080	6,010

Various types of machinery are required to manufacture each product, depending upon the features involved. In addition, the plant facilities housing each production process differ. As a result, the invested capital for each product line is as follows: A, $200,000; B, $800,000; C, $100,000; D, $350,000. A recent study indicates the company's cost of capital is 12 percent.

Required:

Prepare a profit report for use in appraising product line performance. Use the residual income approach.

E23–6. Divisional breakeven and rate of return

Management of Walter, Inc. wishes to earn a 20 percent return on assets employed by all segments. Assets employed by the Ace product line amount to $400,000, while fixed costs directly attributable to this product line amount to $50,000. The accountant for this territory informs you that the variable cost per unit is $8.

Required:

a. To earn the desired rate of return, how many units must be sold if the sales price is $12 per unit?
b. Determine breakeven sales in units for this division.
c. What rate of return would be earned if 25,000 units were sold at an $11.50 sales price?
d. Calculate the segment's residual income assuming an interest rate of 10 percent, if 30,000 units are sold at a $12 unit sales price.

E23–7. Profitability of product lines

Top management of the Park Company is concerned about the profitability of its three product lines, A, B, and C. The following data are obtained from its financial statements.

Sales (2,500 units of A, 1,200 units of B, and 3,000 units of C)	$216,200
Cost of goods sold	156,600
Salespeople's commissions	8,772
Direct selling	25,000
Sales manager's salary	9,000
Administrative salaries and other expenses	36,000

Each unit of A sells for $20; of B, $26; and of C, $45. The cost per unit is composed of 25 percent direct material, 30 percent direct labor, and 5 percent variable factory overhead. The full cost per unit is $12 for A, $18 for B, and $35 for C.

Salespeople are paid a commission equal to 3 percent of sales of A, 6 percent of sales of B, and 4 percent of sales of C. The provision for bad debt is estimated to be 5 percent of sales. The marketing manager informs you that 20 percent of direct selling is devoted to Product A, 25 percent to B, and the remainder to C. Top management estimates that the entire administrative staff spends 25 percent of its effort on A, 30 percent on B, and the remainder on C.

Required:

Prepare a segment analysis of the profitability of each product.

E23–8.   Contribution analysis and R.O.A.C.

Annette Cox, controller, provides you with the following monthly data regarding two product lines, A and B:

	Product A	Product B
Units manufactured and sold	30,000	10,000
Unit sales price	$10.00	$ 8.00
Unit standard production cost:		
Direct material	2.00	3.00
Direct labor	1.00	1.00
Factory overhead	4.00	2.00
Sales commission per unit	0.40	0.70
Sales discounts and allowances	4,500	1,000
Advertising and sales promotion—fixed	6,000	1,500

Variable overhead costs comprise 60 percent of the standard factory overhead. Marketing expenses of $20,000 and administrative expenses of $10,000 were incurred by the central office. These are to be allocated to the product lines based on units sold.

Production cost variances not traceable to either product line are as follows:

Material price variance.	$ 5,000	favorable
Material quantity variance	10,000	favorable
Labor rate variance	16,000	unfavorable
Labor efficiency variance	8,000	unfavorable
Overhead controllable variance	800	favorable
Overhead volume variance.	1,800	unfavorable

These variances are distributed between the two product lines on the basis of relative total standard direct labor and factory overhead per period.

Required:

a.   Prepare a contribution analysis for each product line in total and on a per unit basis and for the overall company, including the allocation of nontraceable expenses so that income before taxes can be determined for each product line.

b.   Management desires a 22 percent return on assets employed. Assets employed by Product A total $260,000 and $87,500 for Product B. In view of this, would you recommend discontinuation of either product line? Support your answer.

PROBLEMS

P23–1. Economic advantage of interdivisional sales

Richards, Inc. management has recently incorporated a companywide policy for their 20 divisions which states that a selling division must always sell to a buying division at current market price. The Seattle Division was asked to submit bids to the Boston Division on 2,500 standard parts representing 15 percent of its normal capacity for the year. Seattle Division quoted a price of $40, but was forced by company policy to fill the order at $32, the price an outside supplier quoted. At a price of $40, Seattle Division could have earned a contribution margin of $36,000.

Required:

a. How much is the total contribution margin of Seattle Division decreased by selling at the price of $32?

b. What is the impact on total income of Richards, Inc. of requiring Boston Division to buy internally?

c. Assume further that by selling to Boston Division, Seattle Division must forego an order to an outside company for 2,200 units of special design. These specially designed parts could be sold for $45 each; the variable cost per unit is $28. Seattle is unable to process both Boston's standard parts and the outside order because of volume limitations. By requiring Boston to buy inside, how will the income of Seattle Division and overall income be affected? What would you suggest as a solution?

P23–2. Segment analysis

Jeffrey Thaler, Inc. manufactures two products, A and B, and employs Ms. Brown and Mr. Smith to sell Product A and Mr. Jones and Ms. Black to sell Product B. For the year ending December 31, 19X1, the following data were extracted from the records:

	Product A		Product B	
	Ms. Brown	Mr. Smith	Mr. Jones	Ms. Black
Revenue	$400,000	$180,000	$500,000	$300,000
Variable production expense	60%	38%	55%	42%
Variable marketing and adminis-				
trative expense.	12%	10%	7%	8%
Traceable fixed costs	$ 75,000	$ 48,400	$ 39,800	$ 40,500

Nontraceable costs totaled $42,180.

Required:

Round all percentages to two decimal places.

a. Prepare a segment analysis for each product line and for each of the salespersons by determining contribution margin and segment margin. Express each of these and income for the overall company as a percentage of sales.

b. Prepare any additional analysis you believe is necessary if the assets employed are as follows: Product A—Ms. Brown, $281,250; Product A—Mr. Smith, $180,000; Product B—Mr. Jones, $768,750; and Product B—Ms. Black, $450,000.

P23–3.   Contribution margin and segment margin

Dorothy Griest Corporation manufactures and sells three products, A, B, C, in western and eastern markets. At the end of the first quarter of 19X3, the following income statement has been prepared:

	Western	Eastern	Total
Sales	$200,000	$1,200,000	$1,400,000
Cost of goods sold	140,000	780,000	920,000
Gross margin	60,000	420,000	480,000
Marketing expenses	45,000	100,000	145,000
Administrative expense	31,000	40,000	71,000
Income before taxes	$(16,000)	$ 280,000	$ 264,000

Griest Company is concerned about the poor performance of the Western Territory. They have tried a number of advertising campaigns, but the expected improvements have not materialized.

In making their decision regarding the elimination of the western market, the following information has been gathered:

	Products		
	A	B	C
Sales	$575,000	$500,000	$325,000
Variable production expenses as a percentage of sales	50%	65%	70%
Variable marketing expenses as a percentage of sales	3%	3%	2%

	Sales by markets	
Product	Western	Eastern
A	$ 75,000	$500,000
B	100,000	400,000
C	25,000	300,000

All administrative expenses and fixed production expenses are indirect to the two markets and three products. Fixed marketing expenses are separable by market. All fixed expenses are based upon a prorated yearly amount.

Required:

a.   Prepare a segment analysis for each market.
b.   Assuming there are no alternatives for present capacity, would you recommend dropping the western market? Why or why not?
c.   Prepare an analysis for each product indicating its profitability.
d.   Marketing research is investigating a new product that can be produced by converting equipment presently used in producing Product B. This conversion will increase fixed costs by $20,000 per quarter. What must the minimum contribution margin per quarter be for the new product to make the changeover financially feasible?

P23–4.   Territorial contribution margin and segment margin

Kosha Jones Company analyzes its Eastern and Western Territories by product line as well as by total territory performance. The Eastern Territory manufactures and sells

Products A and B, while the Western Territory manufactures and sells Products C and D. For the quarter ending March 31, 19X1, you extract the following data from the records.

	Products			
	A	B	C	D
Units sold	1,500	2,600	3,000	3,800
Unit sales price . . . . $	5	$ 8	$ 10	$ 6
Unit variable production expense	2	4	7	3
Unit variable marketing and				
administrative expense	1	2	1	2
Traceable fixed costs	1,000	1,800	4,200	1,200

Costs that could not be traced to a segment totaled $5,400.

Required:

a. Prepare a contribution margin and segment margin for the two territories and the four product lines. Express both of these measures and income for the overall company as a percent of sales.

b. Prepare additional analysis for the territories and product lines if the hours to complete each unit are as follows: Product A, two hours; Product B, one hour; Product C, one-half hour; and Product D, one and one-half hours.

P23–5.   Segment analysis for product lines

The following data are available from the John Griest Company for use in segment analysis:

	Northern Territory		Southern Territory	
	Product A	Product B	Product A	Product C
Sales	$40,000	$12,000	$80,000	$100,000
Contribution margin	30%	60%	30%	40%
Traceable fixed expenses	$ 4,000	$ 1,000	$ 9,000	$ 15,000

Nondirect fixed costs total $12,000 for the company.

Required:

a. Prepare segment analyses by product line and determine income before taxes for the overall company.

b. The company's research and development department has found ways that improvements can be made in Products B and C. However, company funds are limited so that only $5,000 can be spent to complete the improvements to either Product B or Product C. This improvement would increase the sale of Product B by 40 percent and Product C by 25 percent. On which product line should the company spend the funds?

c. A proposed advertising campaign for Product A costing $6,000 in the Northern Territory is expected to increase sales by $27,500. Would you advise management to go through with the campaign?

d. Assume that after you present your segment statements computed in *a* to the president, he asks you to explain why segment statements prepared by another accountant on a territorial basis only showed traceable fixed costs of $7,000 for the Northern Territory and $28,000 for the Southern Territory. What would you tell him?

P23–6.   Segment margin and R.O.A.C.

Robert Dufour Company manufactures two products, LL and MM, and employs Mr. A and Ms. B to sell Product LL and Mr. C and Ms. D to sell Product MM. For the year ending December 31, 19X1, the following data were extracted from the records.

	Product LL		Product MM	
	Mr. A	Ms. B	Mr. C	Ms. D
Revenue	$480,000	$360,000	$300,000	$500,000
Variable production expense	55%	45%	62%	60%
Variable marketing and				
administrative expense	12%	10%	8%	14%
Traceable fixed costs	$ 80,000	$ 67,600	$ 27,800	$ 85,100

Nontraceable costs totaled $96,470.

Required:

a.   Prepare segment analyses for each product line and for each of the salespersons by determining contribution margin and segment margin. Express each of these and income for the overall company as a percentage of sales.

b.   Prepare any additional analysis you believe is necessary if the assets employed are as follows: Product LL—Mr. A, $560,000; Product LL—Ms. B, $377,600; Product MM—Mr. C, $777,500; Product MM—Ms. D, $224,500.

P23–7.   ROI performance measures (CMA adapted)

The Notewon Corporation is a highly diversified company which grants its divisional executives a significant amount of authority in operating the divisions. Each division is responsible for its own sales, pricing, production, costs of operations, and the management of accounts receivable, inventories, accounts payable, and use of existing facilities. Cash is managed by corporate headquarters; all cash in excess of normal operating needs of the divisions is transferred periodically to corporate headquarters for redistribution or investment.

The divisional executives are responsible for presenting requests to corporate management for investment projects. The proposals are analyzed and documented at corporate headquarters. The final decision to commit funds to acquire equipment, to expand existing facilities, or for other investment purposes rests with corporate management. This procedure for investment projects is necessitated by Notewon's capital allocation policy.

The corporation evaluates the performance of division executives using return on investment (ROI). The asset base is composed of fixed assets employed plus working capital exclusive of cash.

The ROI performance of a divisional executive is the most important appraisal factor for salary changes. In addition, an annual performance bonus is based on the ROI results with increases in ROI having a significant impact on the amount of the bonus.

The Notewon Corporation adopted the ROI performance measure and related compensation procedures about 10 years ago. The corporation did so to increase the awareness of divisional management of the importance of the profit/asset relationship and to provide additional incentive for divisional executives to seek investment opportunities.

The corporation seems to have benefited from the program. The ROI for the corporation as a whole increased during the first years of the program. Although the ROI has continued to grow in each division, the corporate ROI has declined in recent years. The corporation has accumulated a sizable amount of cash and short-term marketable securities in the past three years.

Corporation management is concerned about the increase in the short-term marketable securities. A recent article in a financial publication suggested that the use of ROI was overemphasized by some companies with results similar to those of Notewon.

Required:

a. Describe the specific actions division managers might have taken to cause the ROI to grow in each division but decline for the corporation. Illustrate your explanation with appropriate examples.

b. Explain, using the concepts of goal congruence and motivation of divisional executives, how Notewon Corporation's overemphasis on the use of the ROI measure might result in the recent decline in the corporation's return on investment and increase in cash and short-term marketable securities.

c. What changes could be made in Notewon Corporation's compensation policy to avoid this problem? Explain your answer.

P23–8. Segment margin and R.O.A.C. for product lines

McAuley Company manufactures tables and chairs in contemporary design. During 19X1, the costs, revenues, and capital employed by the company in the production of these two items were:

	Chairs	Tables
Sales (units)	200,000	60,000
Sales (dollars)	$4,000,000	$3,000,000
Material costs	1,600,000	480,000
Labor	1,300,000	720,000
Variable factory overhead	150,000	450,000
Variable marketing expense	185,000	285,000
Fixed factory overhead	260,000	285,000
Fixed marketing and administrative expense	320,000	195,000
Variable capital committed	10% of sales	15% of sales
Fixed capital committed	$ 756,250	$2,375,000

Nontraceable costs of the company amount to $600,000.

After management analyzes market forecasts, it believes that the sale of chairs can be expanded 25 percent with a change in design. The change will involve production equipment that is presently being used by the Table Division. A transfer of $40,000 of fixed factory overhead and $800,000 of fixed capital would be made for this equipment.

The transfer of this equipment would mean limiting the production of tables to 40,000. These tables could either be sold at a sales price increase of $5 with an increase of $22,000 in fixed advertising expense or sold at the same sales price with an $80,000 reduction in fixed advertising expense.

Required:

a. Calculate the segment margin and return on assets committed (R.O.A.C.) for each product line for 19X1.

b.   Calculate the segment margin and R.O.A.C. for each product line and income for the company using each alternative presented.

P23–9.   Income statements for territories

Management of the Carlton Company believes that it should be analyzing its marketing costs in more detail. The company has learned that its competitors are classifying their marketing costs into variable and fixed order-getting and order-filling categories. The company serves three territories: Mississippi, Kentucky, and Tennessee.

Costs incurred by the home office are as follows:

Regional warehousing	$11,000
Regional advertising	30,000
Regional administration	27,000

Regional warehousing is allocated to the three territories on the basis of pounds shipped; regional advertising, on the basis of sales; and regional administration equally to all territories.

The salespeople receive a base salary plus 3 percent of all items sold within their territories.

Each territory has responsibility for its own advertising in addition to the fixed yearly retainer fee contracted by the entire organization for regional advertising. Each territory manager has signed a contract with an advertising agency in which they pay a fee equal to .5 percent of sales.

Travel expense is incurred by the salesperson calling on the customer. Territorial salespeople each have a budget for customer entertainment. Freight-out averages $0.30 per pound shipped for each territory warehouse. Warehouse supplies average $0.05 per pound shipped. Warehouse salaries are considered fixed costs.

Standards are set for the manufacturing process. The standard specification per unit is:

Direct material	$3.00
Direct labor	2.83
Variable factory overhead	1.27
Fixed factory overhead	0.78
	$7.88

Partial results of operations for the year ended April 30, 19X1, are as follows:

	Mississippi	Kentucky	Tennessee	Total
Sales	$200,000	$600,000	$400,000	$1,200,000
Territory office expense	6,100	6,900	5,810	18,810
Territory manager salary	24,000	27,000	23,600	74,600
Salespersons' salaries (excluding commissions)	20,000	24,000	21,000	65,000
Advertising retainer fee	25,000	15,000	20,000	60,000
Travel	4,000	4,800	3,900	12,700
Warehouse salaries	10,050	11,800	9,900	31,750
Warehouse insurance	960	1,170	2,310	4,440
Warehouse depreciation	1,810	1,990	1,508	5,308
Pounds shipped	18,000	19,500	17,500	55,000
Units sold	5,100	18,000	9,700	32,800

Required:

a. Prepare an income statement for each territory in which costs are separated into their variable and fixed components in the following categories: cost of sales, marketing—order-getting, marketing—order-filling, and administrative.

b. If you feel that another format is more appropriate for evaluating each territory, prepare this statement.

P23–10. Product-line operating results (CMA adapted)

Valmar Products is a plumbing supply distributing company which carries the products of several manufacturers. Valmar sells its products to retail plumbing stores and to contractors over the counter. In addition, Valmar places orders for plumbing supplies and related materials for specific building and plumbing contractors directly with the manufacturers' factories. These special orders are sent directly to the contractors from the factories. Valmar bills the contractors for the direct orders and pays the manufacturer after the contractor has paid for the order. All customer orders except the direct shipment orders are filled from Valmar's inventories in its warehouse.

The income statement shown below presents the operating results for the past two fiscal years: In addition, the operating results by product line for the most recent fiscal year are presented. For internal reporting purposes, the selling expenses, warehouse costs, and other operating expenses are allocated to the product lines on the basis of sales.

VALMAR PRODUCTS
Income Statement
For the Fiscal Year Ended May 31
($000 omitted)

	19X1	19X2
Revenue from sales	$12,000	$10,000
Cost of goods sold	9,810	8,300
Gross margin	2,190	1,700
Operating expenses:		
Selling expenses	250	200
Warehouse costs	150	150
Other operating expenses	100	100
Total operating expenses	500	450
Net income from operations	1,690	1,250
Interest expense	250	300
Income before taxes	1,440	950
Income taxes (40%)	576	380
Net income	$ 864	$ 570

Jeremy Lypor, president of Valmar, is concerned because the current year's operating results are not up to expectations and have deteriorated from the previous year's results. The operating results by product line indicate that the cash counter sales are marginally profitable and the direct shipment business may not be worth the effort. However, Lypor does not have adequate information with which to make decisions concerning the separate product lines, nor does he have enough information to enable him to decide which lines should be promoted to improve the total results.

Statistics regarding the number of orders handled and the average book value of inventory carried in the warehouse were developed at the request of Lypor and are presented in the schedule shown on page 908.

	Number of orders handled		Average value of inventory	
	Quantity	Percent	($000)	Percent
Trims and accessories	1,008	12	$ 160	10
Valve and pipe fittings	6,048	72	1,248	78
Fixtures	756	9	160	10
Cash counter sales	—	—	32	2
Direct shipments	588	7	—	—
Totals.	8,400	100%	$1,600	100%

In addition, the following information has been developed regarding Valmar's operations.

Fifty percent of the selling expenses are commissions paid to salespeople on the basis of a flat percentage of sales billed; this same percentage is also paid on all cash counter sales.

The other operating expenses and the balance of the selling expenses are related directly to the number of orders handled.

Warehouse expenses are related to the value of inventory in the warehouse.

Money is borrowed to carry inventory in the warehouse.

Valmar Products
Product-Line Operating Results
For the Fiscal Year Ended May 31, 19X2
($000 omitted)

	Trims and accessories	Valve and pipe fittings	Fixtures	Cash counter sales	Direct shipments	Total
Sales.	$2,000	$3,000	$1,000	$1,000	$3,000	$10,000
Cost of sales	1,480	2,445	705	865	2,805	8,300
Gross margin.	$ 520	$ 555	$ 295	$ 135	$ 195	$ 1,700
Allocated operating expenses. . .	90	135	45	45	135	450
Operating income	$ 430	$ 420	$ 250	$ 90	$ 60	$ 1,250
Return on sales	21.5%	14.0%	25.0%	9.0%	2.0%	12.5

Required:

a. President Lypor has requested that the present product-line statement be reviewed to determine if it can be revised to make it more useful in managing Valmar's business. Prepare a revised product-line statement for Valmar Products and explain all changes that were made in the revised statement.

b. Based upon your revised product-line statement for Valmar Products and the other facts presented in the problem, what advice wuld you give to President Lypor regarding:

1. the direct shipment business?
2. the cash counter sales business?
3. the other three product lines?

Explain your response in each case.

P23–11. CVP analysis of segments

Margaret Crawford Company takes baking ingredients and assembles these into dry mixes for three product lines—cakes, muffins, and cookies. Since the company experiences a stable market, inventories do not vary significantly from period to period. All mixes are packaged in 16-ounce boxes. The income statement for last year, prepared on an absorption costing basis, is represented below:

MARGARET CRAWFORD COMPANY
Income Statement
For the Year Ended May 31, 19–
($000 omitted)

	Cake	Muffin	Cookie	Total
Sales	$600	$400	$800	$1,800
Cost of sales:				
Direct material	100	60	200	360
Direct labor	210	150	300	660
Factory overhead (a)	168	120	240	528
Total cost of sales	478	330	740	1,548
Gross margin	122	70	60	252
Operating expenses:				
Marketing expenses:				
Salaries (b)	10	12	15	37
Commissions (c)	48	32	80	160
Advertising (d)	6	3	2	11
Rent (e)	2	4	3	9
Total marketing expenses	66	51	100	217
Administrative expenses:				
Salaries (b)	5	3	2	10
Rent (e)	3	6	4	13
Patents (f)	4	2	3	9
Total administrative expenses	12	11	9	32
Total operating expenses	78	62	109	249
Operating income before taxes	$ 44	$ 8	$ (49)	$ 3

Notes to income statement:
(a) Factory overhead is applied on the basis of 80 percent of direct labor cost. At year-end there was no overapplied or underapplied overhead. Analysis of factory overhead reveals the following:

Rent	$ 73,000
Depreciation—straight-line	50,000
Plant supervisory salaries	141,000
Variable indirect labor and benefits	164,000
Variable supplies and miscellaneous expense	100,000
	$528,000

(b) Marketing and administrative personnel devote effort to all product lines; allocation of their salaries is based on management's estimates of time spent on each product line.
(c) Commissions are paid to the marketing personnel at the rate of 8 percent on the cakes and muffins, and 10 percent on the cookies.
(d) Analysis of past financial data reveals no direct causal relationship between sales and advertising expenses. However, management is convinced each product should continue to be advertised independently.
(e) Rent is allocated on the basis of square footage occupied by each division.
(f) Patents are required to protect the ingredient mix of each line; these are renewed annually.

Required:

a. An outside consultant suggests that the company use cost-volume-profit (CVP) analysis for a better evaluation of its product lines. Discuss the advantages to Margaret Crawford management if CVP analysis were used.

b. Discuss the dangers and difficulties management could experience in using CVP analysis.

c. Prepare a statement utilizing CVP analysis which shows the profit contribution of each product line and the net income before taxes for the company as a whole.

d. If inventories had increased 20 percent over the previous year's, what would be the effect on net income before taxes if:
   (1) Absorption costing were used.
   (2) Variable costing were used.

CASES

C23–1.   Evaluating divisional performance (CMA adapted)

The Jackson Corporation is a large, divisional manufacturing company. Each division is viewed as an investment center and has virtually complete autonomy for product development, marketing, and production.

Performance of division managers is evaluated periodically by senior corporate management. Divisional return on investment is the sole criterion used in performance evaluation under current corporate policy. Corporate management believes return on investment is an adequate measure because it incorporates quantitative information from the divisional income statement and balance sheet in the analysis.

Some division managers complained that a single criterion for performance evaluation is insufficient and ineffective. These managers have compiled a list of criteria which they believe should be used in evaluating division managers' performance. The criteria include profitability, market position, productivity, product leadership, personnel development, employee attitudes, public responsibility, and balance between short-range and long-range goals.

Required:

a. Jackson management believes that return on investment is an adequate criterion for evaluating division management performance. Discuss the shortcomings or possible inconsistencies of using return on investment as the sole criterion to evaluate divisional management performance.

b. Discuss the advantages of using multiple criteria versus a single criterion to evaluate divisional management performance.

c. Describe the problems or disadvantages which can be associated with the implementation of the multiple performance criteria measurement system suggested to Jackson Corporation by its division managers.

C23–2.   Divisional budgets—procedures and behavior problems (CMA adapted)

Rouge Corporation is a medium-sized company in the steel fabrication industry with six divisions located in different geographical sectors of the United States. Considerable autonomy in operational management is permitted in the divisions due, in part, to the distance between corporate headquarters in St. Louis and five of the six divisions. Corporate management establishes divisional budgets using previous year's data adjusted for industry and economic changes expected for the coming year. Budgets are prepared by year and by quarter, with top management attempting to recognize problems unique to each division in the divisional budget-setting process. Once the year's divisional budgets are set by corporate management, they cannot be modified by division management.

The budget for calendar year 19– projects total corporate net income before taxes of $3,750,000 for the year, including $937,500 for the first quarter. Results of first-quarter operations presented to corporate management in early April showed corporate net income of $865,000, which was $72,500 below the projected net income for the quarter. The St. Louis Division operated at 4.5 percent above its projected divisional net income, while the other five divisions showed net incomes with variances ranging from 1.5 to 22 percent below budgeted net income.

Corporate management is concerned with the first quarter results because they believe strongly that differences between divisions had been recognized. An entire day in late November of last year had been spent presenting and explaining the corporate and divisional budgets to the division managers and their division controllers. A mid-April meeting of corporate and division management has generated unusual candor. All five out-of-state division managers cited reasons that first quarter results in their respective divisions represented effective management and were the best that could be expected. Corporate management has remained unconvinced and informs division managers that "results will be brought into line with the budget by the end of the second quarter."

Required:

a.   Identify and explain the major disadvantages in the procedures employed by Rouge Corporation's corporate management in preparing and implementing the divisional budgets.

b.   Discuss the behavioral problems that may arise by requiring Rouge Corporation's division managers to meet the quarterly budgeted net income figures as well as the annual budgeted net income.

C23–3.   Centralized and decentralized management (CMA adapted)

Edwin Hall, Chairman of the Board and President of Arrow Works Products Company, founded the company in the mid-1950's. He is a talented and creative engineer. Arrow Works was started with one of his inventions, an intricate die-cast item which required a minimum of finish work. The item was manufactured for Arrow Works by a Gary, Indiana foundry. The product sold well in a wide market.

The company issued common stock in 1962 to finance the purchase of the Gary foundry. Additional shares were issued in 1965 when Arrow purchased a fabricating plant in Cleveland to meet the capacity requirement of a defense contract.

The company now consists of five divisions. Each division is headed by a manager who reports to Hall. The Chicago Division contains the product development and engineering department and the finishing (assembly) operation for the basic products. The Gary and Cleveland plants are the other two divisions engaged in manufacturing operations. All products manufactured are sold through two selling divisions. The

Eastern Sales Division is located in Pittsburgh and covers the country from Chicago to the east coast. The Western Sales Division, which covers the rest of the country, is located in Denver. The Western Sales Division is the newest operation and was established just eight months ago.

Hall, who still owns 53 percent of the outstanding stock, actively participates in the management of the company. He travels frequently and regularly to all of the company's plants and offices. He says "Having a business with locations in five different cities spread over half the country requires all my time." Despite his regular and frequent visits, he believes the company is decentralized with the managers having complete autonomy. "They make all the decisions and run their own shops. Of course they don't understand the total business as I do, so I have to straighten them out once in a while. My managers are all good people, but they can't be expected to handle everything alone. I try to help all I can."

The last two months have been a period of considerable stress for Hall. During this period, John Staple, manager of the fabricating plant, was advised by his physician to request a six-month sick leave to relieve the work pressures that had made him nervous and tense. This request came three days after a phone call in which Hall had directly and bluntly blamed Staple for the lagging production output and increased rework and scrap of the fabricating plant. Hall made no allowances for the pressures created by the operation of the plant at volumes in excess of normal and close to its maximum capacity for the previous nine months.

Hall thought he and Staple had had a long and good relationship prior to this event. Hall attributed his loss of temper in this case to his frustration with several other management problems that had arisen in the past two months. The Sales Manager of the Denver office had resigned shortly after a visit from Hall. The letter of resignation stated he was seeking a position with greater responsibility. The sales manager in Pittsburgh asked to be reassigned to a sales position in the field; he did not feel he could cope with the pressure of management.

Required:

a. Explain the difference between centralized and decentralized management.

b. Is Arrow Works Products Company decentralized as Edwin Hall believes? Explain your answer.

c. On the basis of the facts presented in the problem, could the events that occurred over the past two months in Arrow Works Products Company have been expected? Explain your answer.

C23–4. Divisional performance evaluation (CMA adapted)

Bio-grade Products is a multiproduct company manufacturing animal feeds and feed supplements. The need for a widely based manufacturing and distribution system has led to a highly decentralized management structure. Each divisional manager is responsible for production and distribution of corporate products in one of eight geographical areas of the country.

Residual income is used to evaluate divisional managers. The residual income for each division equals each division's contribution to corporate profits before taxes less a 20 percent investment charge on a division's investment base. The investment base for each division is the sum of its year-end balances of accounts receivable, inventories, and net plant fixed assets (cost less accumulated depreciation). Corporate policies dictate that divisions minimize their investments in receivables and inventories. Investments in plant fixed assets are a joint division/corporate decision based on proposals made by divisional plant managers, available corporate funds, and general corporate policy.

Alex Williams, Divisional Manager for the Southeastern Sector, prepared the 19X2 and preliminary 19X3 budget for his division in late 19X1. Final approval of the 19X3 budget took place in late 19X2 after adjustments for trends and other information developed during 19X2. Preliminary work on the 19X4 budget also took place at that time. In early October of 19X3, Williams asked the division controller to prepare a report which presents performance for the first nine months of 19X3. The report is reproduced below:

BIO-GRADE PRODUCTS
Southeastern Sector
($000)

	19X3			19X2	
	Annual budget	Nine month budget*	Nine month actual	Annual budget	Actual results
Sales	$2,800	$2,100	$2,200	$2,500	$2,430
Divisional cost and expenses:					
Direct materials and labor	1,064	798	995	900	890
Supplies	44	33	35	35	43
Maintenance and repairs	200	150	60	175	160
Plant depreciation	120	90	90	110	110
Administration	120	90	90	90	100
Total divisional costs and expenses	1,548	1,161	1,270	1,310	1,303
Divisional margin	1,252	939	930	1,190	1,127
Allocated corporate fixed costs	360	270	240	340	320
Divisional contribution to corporate profits	892	669	690	850	807
Imputed interest on divisional investment (20%)	420	321†	300†	370	365
Divisional residual income	$ 472	$ 348	$ 390	$ 480	$ 442

	Budgeted balance 12/31/X3	Budgeted balance 9/30/X3	Actual balance 9/30/X3	Budgeted balance 12/31/X2	Actual balance 12/31/X2
Division investment:					
Accounts receivable	$ 280	$ 290	$ 250	$ 250	$ 250
Inventories	500	500	650	450	475
Plant fixed assets (net)	1,320	1,350	1,100	1,150	1,100
Total	$2,100	$2,140	$2,000	$1,850	$1,825
Imputed interest (20%)	$ 420	$ 321†	$ 300†	$ 370	$ 365

*Bio-grade's sales occur uniformly throughout the year.
†Imputed interest is calculated at 15 percent to reflect that only nine months or three fourths of the fiscal year elapsed.

Required:

a. Evaluate the performance of Alex Williams for the nine months ending September 19X3. Support your evaluation with pertinent facts from the problem.

b. Identify the features of Bio-grade Products division performance measurement reporting and evaluating system which need to be revised if it is to reflect effectively the responsibilities of the division managers.

C23–5.   Measuring divisional performance (CMA adapted)

Divisional managers of SIU, Inc. have been expressing growing dissatisfaction with the current methods used to measure division performance. Division operations are evaluated every quarter in comparison to the static budget prepared during the previous year. Divisional managers claim that many factors are completely out of their control but are included in this comparison. This results in an unfair and misleading performance evaluation.

The managers have been particularly critical of the process used to establish standards and budgets. The annual budget, stated by quarters, is prepared six months prior to the beginning of the operating year. Pressure by top management to reflect increased earnings has often caused division managers to overstate revenues and/or understate expenses. In addition, once the budget had been established, divisions are required to "live with the budget." Frequently external factors such as the state of economy, changes in consumer preferences, and actions of competitors have not been adequately recognized in the budget parameters that top management supplied to the divisions. The credibility of the performance review is impaired when the budget can not be adjusted to incorporate these changes.

Top management, recognizing the current problems, has agreed to establish a committee to review the situation and to make recommendations for a new performance evaluation system. The committee consists of each division manager, the Corporate Controller, and the Executive Vice President who serves as the chairman. At the first meeting, one division manager outlined an Achievement of Objectives System (AOS). In this performance evaluation system, divisional managers would be evaluated according to three criteria:

Doing better than last year—Various measures would be compared to the same measures for the previous year.

Planning realistically—Actual performance for the current year would be compared to realistic plans and/or goals.

Managing current assets—various measures would be used to evaluate division management's achievements and reactions to changing business and economic conditions.

The division manager believes this system would overcome many of the inconsistencies of the current system because divisions could be evaluated from three different viewpoints. In addition, managers would have the opportunity to show how they would react and account for changes in uncontrollable external factors.

A second division manager was also in favor of the proposed AOS. However, he cautioned that the success of a new performance evaluation system would be limited unless it had the complete support of top management. Further, this support should be visible within all divisions. He believes that the committee should recommend some procedures which would enhance the motivational and competitive spirit of the divisions.

Required:

a. Explain whether or not the proposed AOS would be an improvement over the measure of division performance now used by SIU Incorporated.

b. Develop specific performance measures for each of the three criteria in the proposed AOS which could be used to evaluate division managers.

c. Discuss the motivational and behavioral aspects of the proposed performance system. Also, recommend specific programs which could be instituted to promote morale and give incentives to divisional management.

Transfer pricing bases

Dual transfer pricing

Suboptimization

Recording internal transfers

1. To discuss the relationship between the degrees of interdependence and the necessity of establishing transfer prices.

2. To present the criteria that should be used in choosing a transfer price.

3. To describe the two methods that become the basis for transfer prices.

4. To discuss the advantages of a dual pricing system for transfers and to explain where this system is appropriate.

5. To illustrate how suboptimization can occur in decentralized segments.

Transfer pricing in multidivisional companies

Traditionally, companies have transferred products and services from one cost center to another at accumulated cost. In a centralized company, cost responsibility is generally used in measuring managerial performance, since income responsibility is centralized. However, in the past two or three decades, industry has grown from the small one-man-one-plant operation to giant conglomerates and multi-interest businesses. With the growth of enterprises and a trend towards decentralization of management within these companies, a cost-based transfer price may not be either sufficient or satisfactory.

Those companies divided into independent operating units which are free to transact business outside the company as well as inside must establish transfer prices. One department's transfer of goods and services to a second department is thus part of its sales yielding income. That same transfer is the second department's purchase of service or cost of materials. Such transfers create the problem of determining the best procedure or procedures for calculating the proper transfer prices of products being sent for further production before ultimate consumption.

The increasing need for diversified firms to issue segment reports, as discussed in Chapter 23, is evident. These reports should show the contribution to income of the company's various segments. Transfer prices should be used not only as a guide for segment managers in decision making, but also as a partial basis for the evaluation of division performance. As long as the

917

manager's unit is not entirely independent and separable, goods and services are generally transferred from one unit to another so that the finished or semifinished product from one segment often becomes the raw material of another division in a decentralized organization; all this makes it difficult to appraise managerial performance. The prices at which these goods and services are transferred have an important effect on the income of both the supplying and receiving segments. Thus, transfer pricing policies must be carefully established so that divisions do not purchase outside when there are high-fixed-cost internal facilities that can *provide* the product. Keeping these facilities idle can harm the overall company.

Transfer pricing in this chapter refers to the unit price assigned to goods that are transferred among segments. It is used for purposes other than inventory costing. Regardless of the transfer price in effect, consolidated financial statements still show the unit production cost computed in accordance with generally accepted accounting principles, and transactions between segments are eliminated so that inventories on hand are reduced to cost.

Degrees of interdependence

Usually, the greater the degree of interdependence among major segments, the more significant is the transfer pricing problem. The type of diversification also affects the degree of interdependence; few or no transfer pricing problems exist in a company that diversifies into different basic industries. For example, a pharmaceutical company which also engages in furniture manufacturing and coal mining has few, if any, transfers among these divisions. However, in a vertically integrated firm there is a large volume of intracompany transfers, as in a paper supply company which owns timberlands and manufactures paper, which it cuts to customer specification.

Decentralized divisions may be operated as either *cost centers* or *profit centers*. The profit center allows divisional managers the authority to trade with whom they please and permits them to establish prices they are willing to accept or pay. Transfer prices are essential for profit center analysis and are generally associated with this concept because profit centers are segments of an organization which are assigned both revenues and costs. Managers of cost centers are responsible for costs only. It is normally true that as central management increases its control, a profit center loses efficiency; however, profit centers can exist in highly centralized organizations. In this case, managers of profit centers may have little authority in decision making, they may have to seek approval for every capital expenditure over a small amount, and they may not be able to buy or sell outside the company. Managers of cost centers in decentralized companies may have much leeway in where they purchase goods and services and in establishing capital expenditure policies. To summarize, profit centers and cost centers are not indications of degree of decentralization.

Purposes of transfer prices

Before deciding on a transfer price, management should determine how the information generated by transfer prices will be used. For example, a company may record transfers from foreign countries, where the wage level and/or tax rate is low, at a domestic market price rather than on a cost basis because foreign economic conditions are so different than domestic conditions. Transfer prices can also be established to maximize profit by motivating segment managers or to measure segment profit and evaluate the efficiency of segment managers' performance. Thus, before choosing which transfer pricing basis to adopt, management must decide what use it plans to make of transfer pricing. Yet, it must be recognized that the entire area of transfer pricing is also complicated by human relations problems such as the desire of division managers to improve the performance of their segments even at the expense of the overall company, especially if they receive a bonus based on segment profits. Certainly, it is most difficult to determine a transfer price that meets all needs.

Transfer pricing guides segment managers toward decisions that lead to an economic allocation of resources. In a free economy, competition among independent economic entities determines where resources are allocated. Normally, production is directed to those companies which most efficiently use the resources, since the company that uses the resources most efficiently is able to pay a higher price for them. This competitive process is typically influenced by various degrees of government intervention. For example, various laws exist, such as the Robinson-Patman Amendment, which protect small businesses even though they may be less efficient than their larger competitors.

TRANSFER PRICING BASES

The transfer price which is derived internally replaces the independent market transaction as a means of directing the allocation of economic resources. The appropriate price at which goods and services are transferred from one organizational segment to another is doubly important since it affects the reported income of both the selling segment and the buying segment. A particular transfer pricing basis may also be an excellent management tool for motivating division managers, for establishing and maintaining cost control systems, and for internal performance measurements. However, this basis may not be applicable for financial reporting. The differences between internal and external aspects of transfer pricing will become more apparent when the available bases are discussed below.

There are two basic methods for establishing transfer prices. The first involves some form of cost derived from the company books or from financial analysis. Included are full cost, full cost plus a markup for a reasonable profit, variable cost, and opportunity, differential, or marginal cost. The second method includes market price, negotiated price, or some variation of the two. After these methods are all discussed, the applicability of different transfer prices will be illustrated.

Full-cost transfer pricing

Using full cost as a transfer price is probably the oldest transfer-pricing method. Full cost includes actual manufacturing cost plus portions of marketing and administrative costs. In centralized companies, the principle of full cost has been firmly established since almost all companies use full cost to value inventory for external reporting.

Full cost is commonly used primarily because it is convenient to apply. In fact, probably the greatest single advantage of any cost-based pricing method is its simplicity; full-costing data are already available and can be obtained at very low expense and a tremendous savings of time. Another prime advantage of the full-cost transfer price is that it leaves no intracompany profits in inventory to eliminate when consolidated statements are prepared. If intracompany transfers are recorded below cost, inventories must be increased to cost before the inventory accounts can be consolidated. If intracompany transfers are recorded at prices above cost, all profits in ending inventories must be eliminated before the inventory accounts can be consolidated. A transferred cost may also be readily used to measure production efficiency if it is compared with budgeted costs. This method allows simple and adequate end-product costing for profit analysis by product lines.

Such cost-based pricing methods are endorsed by the government. These cost methods have been accepted by the Internal Revenue Service (IRS) if a firm has been accused of using pricing methods to take advantage of preferential tax treatment; for example, when, to reduce taxes, a corporate group attempts to transfer most of its income to a subsidiary which has a tax advantage over other members of the corporate group. When this occurs, the IRS enters the picture and attempts to refute the corporate group's actions.

However, despite these advantages, full cost is not suitable for companies with decentralized structure which requires that the profitability of autonomous units be measured. Full-cost transfer pricing has little worth for evaluating performance, since use of full cost does not permit an income to be shown on interdivisional sales. This, in turn, leads to another criticism of all cost-based pricing methods—they do not create incentives for segment managers to control or reduce costs. All cost-based transfer prices reflect the accumulated efficiency level of the supplying division; as a result, accumulated inefficiencies from divisions which previously handled the product affect the reported income of the division in question.

Adding an arbitrary markup results in meaningless data and may even mislead management into believing that a division is profitable when it is not.

Full cost does not provide management with a divisional profit figure for the selling division; therefore, decentralized companies which need to measure the profitability of autonomous units do not find cost-based transfer prices appropriate. In addition, there is a tendency for segments to become complacent and less concerned about controlling costs if they know that their costs are merely passed along to the next segment.

Another justifiable criticism of the full-cost method is that it departs from goal congruence. The use of full-cost transfer prices can lead to decisions which are not goal congruent if the supplying division is not operating at capacity. For example, a division may decide to purchase outside the company at an apparent savings. However, on closer examination, it may be seen that a reduction of the full-cost transfer price to the market price would recover all variable costs and a portion of fixed costs. These fixed costs are not covered because of the decision to purchase outside. To avoid such suboptimization, top management must order the lowering of transfer prices or require internal purchasing, but both of these solutions dilute the authority of the division.

Standard full cost. The use of standard full cost rather than historical average cost eliminates the negative effect of fluctuations in production efficiency in one division on the reported income of another division. Standard full cost also permits division managers to know in advance what price they will receive or what price they will pay for transferred goods; this eliminates one source of delay in processing transfers. Spending variances from standard, which are primarily due to variable costs, should be absorbed by the supplying division. Volume or capacity variances from standard, which reflect the effect of fixed costs, should be jointly allocated to both the supplying and receiving divisions. Standard costs have the same limitations as actual costs when used as a transfer price in external reports, however.

Using either actual or standard full cost weakens the earnings statement as a performance measure because their objectives are not the long-range profitability of the firm. The local unit lacks the incentive to control or reduce cost when cost recovery is assured. A full-cost transfer price does not provide an accurate guide for decision making since it offers no sound basis on which management can delegate decision-making authority to segment managers. For this reason, full-cost transfer prices should be restricted to situations in which this authority is not granted.

Variable cost transfer pricing

While variable cost transfer pricing does not eliminate many of the weaknesses of full-cost transfer pricing, it may have the advantage of ensuring, in the short run, the best utilization of total corporate facilities. Because total fixed costs do not change in the short run, by using variable cost pricing, a company focuses attention on the contribution margin a transfer generates and on how it increases short-run profitability. A danger of this approach, however, is that all costs must be covered before a profit is yielded, and fixed costs cannot be ignored. As a result, a variable cost transfer price might be profitable in the short run, but not in the long run. An additional weakness of a variable cost transfer price is that it allows one segment manager to make a profit at the expense of another segment manager, because all profit is loaded onto the receiving segment.

Opportunity cost and differential cost

As discussed above, it is difficult to find a transfer price that not only provides an incentive to management, but also encourages goal congruence. However, the addition of opportunity cost and the differential cost incurred to the point of transfer may provide a general basis for the minimum transfer price. *Differential cost* is found by determining how much total company cost increases if the contemplated alternative is added to the present volume of activities. Differential cost may be approximated by variable cost in many situations. *Opportunity cost* is defined, for transfer pricing purposes, as the maximum contribution to profit lost if the goods are not sold outside the company but are transferred internally. While differential costs are shown in the accounting records, since they represent outlay cost, opportunity costs are not. The buying segment's opportunity cost is the lower of either its net marginal revenue or the price at which it could obtain the intermediate product in the open market.

If, for the intermediate product, there is a perfectly competitive market in which the maximum available output may be sold at unchanging prices, the opportunity cost to the selling segment is the market price less the differential costs incurred for the product. The reason is that in refusing to accept outside business and instead making an internal transfer, the selling segment has foregone income that could have been earned on this business. If there is no intermediate market, the opportunity costs are zero, and the most appropriate transfer price is the differential cost.

The use of opportunity cost and differential cost gives an immediate indication of the proper decision about selling the product inside or outside the company if a perfectly competitive market for the intermediate product exists. However, where there is imperfect competition in the intermediate market, the manager of either the buying or selling division can decrease the overall income of the company by attempting to maximize his or her own income. This might result in improved performance for the segment, but it does not result in goal congruence because the income of the company as a whole is less than optimum. For example, if the selling division is operating at capacity and can sell all its products at $5, but the buying division must operate at 70 percent capacity because it cannot secure enough products, should management force the selling division to transfer products at $4 if the selling division's unit differential cost is $3?

For the selling segment to maximize income, it should continue to sell outside the company, yet this strategy hurts overall company income. Assume the buying division's cost of the finished product is as follows:

Part (being manufactured by selling division)	$ 4
Other variable cost	6
Allocated expenses	7
	$17

Assuming the allocated expenses represent expenses that the company incurs regardless, the overall company income would be $6 ($7 allocated expenses minus $1 difference in outside sales price and inside transfer price) higher per unit if the transfer occurs internally. In the short run, there is an advantage to the internal transfer even though this action is counter to the purposes of decentralized decision making. Since it requires top management to overrule the selling management's decision if this action occurs on a regular basis, this situation would not be viable in a divisional organizational structure.

Differential cost and revenue schedules. The determination of differential cost and revenue schedules that change with volume is expensive. Very few companies have a sophisticated enough cost system for determining anything but marginal or differential cost using a constant cost assumption. In addition, transfer prices based on differential costs diminish the decision-making autonomy of the profit center. If differential cost increases with volume, the segment is dependent on the total demands of the buying division and the supplying division's external customers. This means that neither segment can make its output decisions independently.

Market-based transfer prices

The use of market prices as transfer prices is essentially an opportunity cost approach, because company segments are charged the same price that outside customers have to pay; however, some companies have a discount for any economies of intracompany transfers. Each individual segment is regarded as a completely separate company, because if the profit centers were independent businesses, any transfer of intermediate products would require a market transaction for which a market price could be recorded. In addition, market prices are established objectively rather than by parties who have an interest in the results. Products might be transferred at a price lower than market price, because market prices can be legitimately adjusted for selling costs and trade discounts in the case of large purchases. In addition, a discount may also be subtracted from the market price to reflect the economies obtained by intracompany transfers. Even though profit centers are not independent businesses and these transactions do not go through the market, it may be possible to maintain the self-regulatory conditions of the market by pricing these internal transfers at market prices.

Market price is used as a basis for transfer pricing when the product is actively traded on the open market. The principal argument for use of market price is that it represents the opportunity cost of the intermediate product. The price the buying unit is paying is the same as if the unit were forced to buy from an outside source. The use of the market price creates a fair and equal chance for both the buying and selling departments to make the most profit they can. Market-based pricing also places segment operations on a competitive basis, results in charging all internal and external customers the same price, and reflects product profitability at various stages of production.

Another argument for the use of market price is that if a segment or company cannot improve on the product sufficiently to recover both the acquisition cost of the product on the open market and the production cost of the department, then the segment or company should not be in operation. For example, if a segment cannot afford to pay market prices, it should not be permitted to buy internally at less than market. Conversely, if it can sell outside at market, it should not be required to sell internally for less. However, this argument can be rebutted in the short run by the fact that this is a customer service and through this customer service a larger piece of the market can be acquired and the segment can be made profitable.

The use of market prices as transfer prices is especially appropriate when evaluating performance of segments since segment income is determined by how well the division functions in a competitive market given that intermediate products are transferred from one segment to another at market price. The income determined in this way also shows how effectively the segment can perform in an outside independent market. In appraising efficiency, this type of income measurement has stronger appeal than the arbitrary income which results when variable cost or full-cost transfer pricing is used.

A serious disadvantage to market-based transfer pricing, however, is that it requires the existence of a well-developed outside competitive market. Transfers based on market prices work quite well in a decentralized organization if there is a perfectly competitive intermediate market and the supply and demand of segments are practically independent of one another. However, there is no market price for some products; this is most likely to occur when all companies in the industry are fully integrated and each division produces only for internal consumption. For example, a department may produce a unit that is not sold to outsiders, as when parts are secretly designed. Also, if the transfer is nonrepetitive, there may not be a large enough market for the product to give a valid market price, since market prices based on a very small number of market transactions are not usually valid.

Negotiated transfer prices

To overcome these difficulties, very often a compromise transfer price is used which gives weight to competition and a fair return to the supplying division. Such a price can be negotiated between the supplying and receiving departments, with top management serving as arbitrator to avoid time-consuming and inflammatory negotiations.

A negotiated price is an attempt to simulate an arm's length transaction between supplying and buying segments; it is generally used in the absence of a competitive outside market price. In theory, a strong case can be made for market-based negotiated prices, since all market prices are based on negotiation between buyer and seller. It follows then that if segment managers are given autonomous authority to buy and sell as they deem necessary and if they bargain in good faith, the result of this bargaining is the equivalent of a market price.

An additional advantage of pricing through negotiation is that usually sales of intracompany products are in such large volume that the use of any market price is meaningless because the quoted market price is based on smaller, normal order sizes. For example, suppose that the selling division has excess capacity and the buying division can use more of the product. In this case, a negotiated price somewhere between the market price and the seller's differential cost increases the profits of both segments and is advantageous to the company as a whole.

However, negotiation may be very time-consuming and require frequent reexamination and revision of prices. For this method to work, the subunits must be allowed to go to the outside markets if negotiation fails. In addition, negotiated prices eliminate the objectivity necessary to ensure that profits for the company as a whole are maximized. As a result, the negotiated price may distort segment financial statements and mislead top management in its attempts to evaluate performance and make decisions.

The primary problem with this method arises when there is no established market price and the segment managers cannot reach agreement. Top management must then intervene to establish an arbitrary transfer price. This central control must exist to ensure against suboptimization of company profits by division managers in the event that the purchasing division can buy more cheaply outside than it can within the company. If the segment managers can not agree on the transfer price and the purchasing manager has the option of purchasing in the outside market without the approval of top management, overall profit may be reduced.

If arbitration between subunits becomes necessary, then divisional authority is breached and the purpose of decentralization and profit centers is subverted; in fact, if arbitration is frequent, the purpose of decentralization is nullified completely. Certainly, arbitrary pricing severely hampers the profit incentive of segment managers. However, the policy of decentralization cannot be carried to the point where all profits are ignored for the sake of allowing local management to have full control of purchasing when the product is available within the company.

Transfer pricing illustrated

The application of several transfer prices will be considered in the following example. Assume the Transistor Division of a company supplies transistors to outside customers at a price of $3.50 each. The company has just acquired a radio assembly company, and the president believes that this newly acquired Radio Division should purchase transistors from the company's own Transistor Division, because the division has excess capacity.

Until the acquisition, the radio assembly company had purchased transistors for $3.50 less a 10 percent discount.

The Transistor Division's cost per unit is presented below:

```
Direct material . . . . . . . . . . . . . . . . . . . . . . . . . . . . $1.00
Direct labor . . . . . . . . . . . . . . . . . . . . . . . . . . . . . .   1.15
Variable overhead . . . . . . . . . . . . . . . . . . . . . . . . . .    0.50
Fixed overhead (now operating at 1,000,000
    units activity level) . . . . . . . . . . . . . . . . . . . . . . .    0.30
Total cost. . . . . . . . . . . . . . . . . . . . . . . . . . . . . . . $2.95
```

Various members of management have proposed the following transfer prices:

1. *Prime cost*—$2.15. This price would not be appropriate because it does not cover all the variable costs of the Transistor Division.
2. *Variable cost*—$2.65. This is an appropriate transfer price for guiding top management in deciding whether there should be transfers between the two divisions as long as the total variable costs are less than the outside purchase price of the buying division. This transfer price would be appropriate only if the selling division had excess capacity. All benefits of using variable costs as the basis for the transfer price accrue to the buying division.
3. *Full cost*—$2.95. This transfer price would be appropriate if both divisions were treated as cost centers rather than as independent, autonomous profit centers. If this transfer price is used, the profits from the Transistor Division will all be reflected in profits of the Radio Division.
4. *Market price*—$3.15. This transfer price represents the price that the Radio Division would pay an independent, outside supplier and is appropriate if both divisions are treated as independent units.
5. *Negotiated price*—$2.90. A negotiated price of $2.90 would be appropriate if both divisions are treated as profit centers and both divisions share in the benefits. The $0.50 ($3.15 − $2.65) difference between the Transistor Division's variable cost and the net outside purchase price is divided between the two divisions.
6. *Full cost plus markup*—$3.50. This price is not appropriate because it exceeds the price that the Radio Division would have to pay an outside supplier. In addition, the Transistor Division has excess capacity, and its opportunity costs are zero. However, if the Transistor Division receives more outside orders than it can fill, $3.50 would be an appropriate transfer price because it represents the Transistor Division's opportunity cost. Because this represents a higher price than the price at which the Radio Division can purchase transistors outside the company, on the other hand, the buying division should not be charged $3.50.

As can be seen above, the transfer price selected should depend on the capacity level at which the selling division is operating, as well as on other factors unique to the situation.

DUAL TRANSFER PRICING

In discussing transfer pricing, this chapter has emphasized the advantage of each method over the other methods available, and attempted to show that all of the bases are reasonable under specific circumstances. In practice, however, one transfer pricing method should not be accepted as the one and only, because it is unlikely that only one fulfills all the needs of management. Instead, guidelines should be given so that management recognizes that it is not necessary to have just one transfer price. Different transfer prices should be used depending on the purposes for which they are needed.

Dual pricing allows each segment to use the transfer price which provides the optimum decision for the segment and still remains within the goals of the overall company. This dual pricing is applied primarily to evaluate performance, while still allowing goal congruence and autonomy. Obviously, dual pricing does not fit into the neat balancing act of accounting; company profit does not equal the sum of division profits. Some of the segment profits have to be eliminated.

For example, suppose that Segment A can sell its product in the market for $20 but its variable cost is only $14, and that this product can be further refined in Segment B. However, the manager of Segment B does not feel he should pay the same price as an outsider, especially since top management is forcing him to buy from Segment A. If management wishes to evaluate the performance of Segment A, it should consider using the market price as the transfer price since there is no reason for Segment A to transfer at a lower price. This gives Segment A credit for the opportunity it loses in the market by making the sale to another segment of the company. If this market price is, in turn, imposed on the buying division which does not have the complete authority to choose whether to buy from Segment A or not, a conflict can arise because the manager of Segment B probably resents Segment A's making a profit at the segment's expense when the manager does not have the authority to buy elsewhere. The better procedure in this circumstance is to charge the buying division with variable or differential cost. The interdependence of the subunits is then recognized. This solution does not allow one segment manager to make a profit at the expense of another segment manager.

Nevertheless, dual pricing has not been widely adopted in practice because of a major inherent weakness—all segment managers may win, but the overall company may lose, because the buying segment purchases at a low price while the supplying segment sells at a high price. As a result, the incentive to control cost is missing and inefficiencies may develop.

However, it is dangerous to assume with dual pricing that market price is always used as the selling segment's transfer price, and that a cost-based transfer price is always used for the buying division. For example, suppose the full cost or differential cost of a product from Segment A is $10 and this product is further refined in Segment B. However, assume also that Segment B could purchase this elsewhere for $9. The solution using dual pricing should here involve Segment A's selling the product to the home office for $10 and, in turn, Segment B's buying it for $9 from the home office. In this case, the home office has created a fictitious loss which is eliminated when the overall company profit is determined.

SUBOPTIMIZATION

If this approach is not taken, the manager of Segment B will try to buy from the outside, which results in a $1 savings per unit to his segment. But this lower external price could be the result of temporary excess capacity in a competitor's plant. If management fails to investigate the situation and eliminates Segment A because it feels that it can buy all the products it needs on the outside for $9, the company may be hurt financially when the outside party sells its excess supply and raises prices above $10. A company must guard against such suboptimization. Suboptimization can occur if the external purchase price is lower than a related segment's differential cost. Transfer pricing should be carefully established so that segments do not purchase outside when there are high-fixed-cost internal facilities that would thereby be kept idle.

Suboptimization often occurs when the total full cost at the transfer point is greater than the outside purchase price available to the purchasing division. To maximize division income, a manager will buy from the outside source. Assuming the supplying division has excess capacity, the total profit of the company is decreased because the purchasing division bought outside. This decrease occurs if the difference between the full-cost transfer price and the outside purchase price is less than the difference between the incremental cost in the selling division and the full-cost transfer price. Stated differently, suboptimization can arise if the outside purchase price is greater than the variable or differential cost in the supplying division.

The following example illustrates suboptimization:

	Cost per unit
Material	$ 20
Labor (4 hours)	30
Overhead 40% fixed ($25 overhead rate per direct labor-hour)	100
Full-cost transfer price of product in Division A	$150
Outside purchase price available to Division B for product identical in quality, delivered.	$130

Given these conditions, the Division B manager has an incentive to purchase the product outside, which results in a $20 savings to the division. Yet, Division

A may argue that its full cost should be covered. The differential costs in this division amount to $110 (material, $20; labor, $30; and variable overhead, $60). If Division B accepts the competitor's bid, the entire company loses a contribution to fixed cost of $40 per unit, and the loss in company total income is $20 per unit, as shown below. Thus:

Addition to total company cost to purchase externally	$130
Addition to total company cost if produced by Division A	110
Decrease in total company income	$ 20

In this case, even though full-cost transfers usually foster healthy competition, the policy of completely decentralized decision making should not be adhered to. At the same time, management should be cautious in establishing policies requiring that divisions always purchase internally.

In summary, suboptimization can occur if the external purchase price is lower than a related division's differential cost. A temporary excess capacity in a competitor's plant can result in a. lower external price, but this price may ultimately be raised when the surplus is sold.

While the ideal transfer pricing system should motivate segment managers to most effectively fulfill overall company objectives, this is virtually impossible because of the nature of division performance evaluation. Division managers are usually evaluated on the basis of the profit the segment earns; but if one segment charges another segment too much, the overall company is hurt. The interests of both the buyer and the seller must therefore be considered when transfer prices are set, because an advantage given to one of these parties is a disadvantage to the other. The problem becomes even more crucial if the segment manager is given a bonus based on the segment's performance and if the manager therefore tries all the harder to get maximum beneficial prices from the other segments. Under these circumstances, the segment manager has good reason to argue that the transfer price of goods sold to another segment be kept high and the price of those bought from another segment be kept low. The transfer price thus chosen is likely to lead to a lack of goal congruence for the overall company.

A bonus system actually encourages segment managers to make decisions that may be good for their segments but are detrimental to the company as a whole. For instance, using the previous example illustrating suboptimization, if segment managers receive a bonus based on their division's income, the Division B manager will be more eager to accept the outside offer which results in a $20 savings per unit because this increases the segment's income which, in turn, increases the manager's bonus.

The problem described above can be solved, with complete goal congruence, by reducing the transfer price to $130 at which both the individual segments and the overall company benefit. Another solution is a transfer price that divides the difference between Division A's variable cost and the outside purchase price. For example, the $20 ($130 − $110) difference can be divided equally, resulting in a transfer price of $120 [$110 variable cost + $10 difference

($20/2)]. While transfer pricing should be a tool for motivating segment managers, it should also lead to segment action which benefits the company as a whole.

Internal competition

Competition between segments of a company, referred to as internal competition, is often very healthy. Division managers may feel assured of a market for their production if the company does not allow buying segments the freedom to purchase externally. This assurance on the part of the supplying divisions is not conducive to effective cost control, because if one has a captive source of sales, it is less likely to be aggressive in the development of more efficient methods and lower costs than if it must meet competition on each sale. Internal competition is, therefore, one means of preventing division managers from becoming complacent and failing to incorporate current technological developments.

Division performance should also be compared to that of outside companies. An outdated, unprofitable division in the organization might be overlooked if it is not compared with like companies outside the organization. In determining transfer prices, a company should focus attention on uneconomical activities which otherwise might go undetected and should force managers to check outside markets and supplies more carefully.

External procurement

Management should establish a policy concerning outside purchases of products and services. When the company's own product is superior to or equal in quality and performance to that from outside sources, assuming an acceptable delivery schedule can be met, the product should be procured internally. If the internal source of supply is not competitive, however, management may agree to outside procurement as long as the receiving division can justify its action. It is reasonable to allow division managers the freedom to purchase externally if the external price is lower and the quality comparable. In justifying outside purchasing, the division should supply evidence that a reasonable effort was made to bring the internal supplier's terms into competition with those of the outside source.

Some companies have a policy of splitting purchases between external and internal supplying divisions. This policy is appropriate only when management considers it important to have alternative sources available or when internal facilities are not adequate.

By not imposing the strict requirement that all possible purchases be made from other segments and, in turn, allowing segment managers some leeway in purchasing from outsiders, segment managers may be motivated to find out whether the intermediate product should be sold as it is in its present form or processed further; they are encouraged to seek each others' advice in regard to the best plant layout and work flow. Furthermore, if a segment manager sees that a competitor's price is cheaper, he or she should be stimulated to find out the reasons for this. This approach thereby emphasizes each segment manager's contribution to the overall company.

Although some conflict of interest is usually unavoidable no matter how well developed the transfer pricing system, a workable system can be designed that resolves much of this conflict, if management keeps certain facts in mind. For example, management should avoid creating situations which hold division managers responsible for their segment's performance yet restrict their purchasing function. If managers have income responsibility, they must have the authority to purchase material that best meets their requirements. It is, therefore, important that the system provide measures of division income that are objectively determined and are as free from administrative bias as possible. The objective should be to prevent the transfer price from becoming an alibi for poor income performance.

RECORDING INTERNAL TRANSFERS

Regardless of the basis used for transfer prices, the accounting system must provide a means of adjusting internal company data to a cost basis for external financial reporting. If the transfer price is less than inventory cost—that is, if variable costing is used as a basis—a portion of the fixed cost usually should be applied to goods remaining in inventory. Conversely, if the transfer price is above inventory cost, as with market or negotiated prices, the excess must be subtracted from inventory and profit accounts in consolidation.

Intradivisional sales must be eliminated from the income statement in consolidated financial statements, even if transfers are made at standard full cost. A distinction must be made between external and internal purchases to assist management in consolidating financial data and to provide information concerning the relative importance of intracompany transactions.

With this approach, an accountant should use the following entries to record a shipment from one segment to another at a 20 percent markup on sales. On the supplying division's books:

Accounts Receivable—Purchasing Division	1,000	
Intracompany Sales		1,000
Cost of Goods Sold—Intracompany	800	
Inventory		800

On the purchasing division's books:

Inventory—from Supplying Division	1,000	
Accounts Payable—Supplying Division		1,000

Assume that one fourth of these goods are sold by the Purchasing Division to an external customer for $500. The entries on the Purchasing Division's books are as follows:

| Accounts Receivable—External Customer................. | 500 | |
| Sales .... | | 500 |

| Cost of Goods Sold—External Customer................ | 250 | |
| Inventory—from Supplying Division .... | | 250 |

Assuming intracompany sales are handled in this manner, the accountant makes the following adjusting entry at the end of the period:

Intracompany Sales..................................	1,000	
Cost of Goods Sold—Intracompany		800
Cost of Goods Sold—External Customer (20% × $250).........		50
Inventory Adjustment Allowance (20% × $750).............		150

The Inventory Adjustment Allowance account credited in the journal entry above is a contra account to inventory for external financial reporting. This allows for intracompany transactions in which inventories are sold at prices above cost to be eliminated from both the overall company balance sheet and the income statements. Segment income is computed from the segment books, unadjusted.

SUMMARY

The shift from centralized to decentralized organizations has increased the role of transfer pricing as portions of the revenue from one income center become portions of the costs of another. Many transfer pricing alternatives, such as full cost, variable cost, market price, or negotiated price, are available to top management. Before deciding on a transfer pricing method, management should establish its purpose for such a system. There is no single best pricing method from an absolute point of view, but there may be a best method for a particular set of circumstances. Product type, degree of decentralization, and managerial skills are some of the factors which should be considered by top management in reaching a decision on the method of transfer pricing. In any case, this chapter does not advocate extreme decentralization, in which there is complete freedom to make local decisions in the best interests of the segment alone, and not of the company in general.

It should be understood that transfer pricing and divisional income measurement are intended to serve several purposes: to guide division managers in decision making; to help evaluate divisional performance; and to aid top management in allocating resources and in long-range planning. While the traditional emphasis has been on the selection of one transfer price, this chapter argues that there should be periodic evaluations to see whether there are cost overruns in the plant and whether the company's costs are out of line with those of the competition. If a supplying division is always assured of a market for its products, it may lapse into inefficiencies which are difficult and expensive to discover and correct. In the process of establishing transfer prices, segment managers should be encouraged not only to communicate with each other, but also to study and eliminate uneconomical activities within their divisions.

Companies must guard against suboptimization, which often occurs when the total full cost at the transfer point is greater than the outside purchase price available to the purchasing division. Suboptimization can also arise if the outside purchase price is greater than the variable or differential cost in the supplying division. Transfer pricing policies must be carefully established so that divisions do not purchase outside when there are high-fixed-cost internal facilities that are thereby kept idle, thus hurting the overall company.

One definitely undesirable alternative available to management is to eliminate transfer pricing completely. This undoubtedly causes more problems than it eliminates. Without transfer pricing, top management is simply forced to establish a different plan to motivate the segment managers and is unable to evaluate each segment's profitability or effectiveness at minimizing costs.

IMPORTANT TERMS AND CONCEPTS

Transfer pricing

Decentralization

Transfer Pricing Methods

    Full cost

    Variable cost

    Opportunity and differential

      cost

Market price

Negotiated price

Dual pricing

Suboptimization

Inventory adjustment allowance

    account

PROBLEM FOR SELF-STUDY

Segment margin using various transfer prices

The Motor Division of Haggs-Scranton manufactures 3-horsepower gasoline motors for both go-carts and lawn mowers. Sales are made to the Go-cart Division of Haggs-Scranton as well as to outsiders. Motors are sold for $75 to outsiders. Go-carts are sold for $300 to wholesale distributors. Operating results of the divisions for 19X1 are given below:

	Motor Division	Go-cart Division
Intracompany sales	6,000 units	–0–
Sales—outsiders	8,000 units	5,500 units
Direct material	$280,000	$100,000
Direct labor	420,000	180,000
Variable factory overhead	40,000	30,000
Fixed factory overhead	127,000	145,000
Traceable fixed home office expense	14,000	132,000
Marketing and administrative—variable	30,000	86,000
Marketing and administrative—fixed	13,000	128,000

If either of the divisions were discontinued, two thirds of the traceable home office expense could be eliminated.

Required:

Prepare statements of segment margin for each division under each of the following conditions:

a.   Intracompany sales are made at average segment cost.
b.   Intracompany sales are made at market price.
c.   Intracompany sales are made at variable cost.

Solution

HAGGS-SCRANTON
Segment Margin for Motor and Go-cart Divisions
For Year 19X1

a.

	Motor Division	Go-cart Division
Revenue:		
Sales—outsiders	$ 600,000 (8,000 × $75)	$1,650,000 (5,500 × $300)
Sales—Go-cart Division	396,000 (6,000 × $66)*	–0–
	996,000	1,650,000
Less variable costs:		
Cost from Motor Division		396,000
Direct material.	280,000	100,000
Direct labor.	420,000	180,000
Variable factory overhead	40,000	30,000
Marketing and administrative		
variable	30,000	86,000
Total variable expenses	770,000	792,000
Contribution margin.	226,000	858,000
Less traceable fixed expenses:		
Fixed factory overhead	127,000	145,000
Home office expenses	14,000	132,000
Marketing and administrative	13,000	128,000
Total traceable fixed expenses	154,000	405,000
Segment margin	$ 72,000	$ 453,000

*$770,000 total variable expenses + $154,000 traceable fixed = $924,000 ÷ 14,000 units = $66.

b.

	Motor Division	Go-cart Division
Sales—Outsiders.	$ 600,000	$1,650,000
Sales—Go-cart Division	450,000 (6,000 × $75)	
	1,050,000	1,650,000
Less variable costs:		
Cost from Motor Division		450,000
Direct material.	280,000	100,000
Direct labor.	420,000	180,000
Variable factory overhead	40,000	30,000
Marketing and administrative—		
variable	30,000	86,000
Total variable expenses	770,000	846,000
Contribution margin.	280,000	804,000
Total traceable fixed expenses		
(as shown above)	154,000	405,000
Segment margin	$ 126,000	$ 399,000

c.

	Motor Division	Go-cart Division
Sales—Outsiders.............	$ 600,000	$1,650,000
Sales—Go-cart Division...........	330,000 (6,000 × $55)†	
	930,000	1,650,000
Less variable costs:		
Cost from Motor Division..........		330,000
Direct material.................	280,000	100,000
Direct labor...................	420,000	180,000
Variable factory overhead..........	40,000	30,000
Marketing and administrative—		
variable.................	30,000	86,000
Total variable expenses.........	770,000	726,000
Contribution margin..............	160,000	924,000
Traceable fixed expenses...........	154,000	405,000
Segment margin.................	$ 6,000	$ 519,000

$$\dagger \frac{\$770,000}{14,000} = \$55.$$

REVIEW QUESTIONS

1. Define *transfer pricing* and indicate when it is necessary to establish transfer prices.
2. Are transfer prices necessarily shown on consolidated financial statements? How are inventories on such statements shown?
3. Indicate the relationship between the degree of interdependence and diversification among company segments and the significance of the transfer pricing problem.
4. What effect does the use of transfer pricing information have upon the pricing basis that is chosen?
5. With regard to both the segment and the overall company, how should the transfer pricing system motivate segment managers?
6. Discuss the dangers of establishing a bonus system for segment managers based on segment profit.
7. What advantages do you see to allowing internal competition to exist among segment managers?
8. When would you allow segment managers to purchase outside the company?
9. List the two bases on which transfer prices can be established, and state some variations of these two methods.
10. Discuss some advantages and limitations of using full cost as the transfer price.
11. What advantages does standard full cost have over historical average cost as a transfer price?
12. How can opportunity cost be used as the basis on which transfer prices are established?
13. Discuss several arguments which support the use of market transfer pricing.
14. What important requirement is necessary for market transfer pricing to be successfully applied?
15. State two advantages of negotiated transfer prices.

16. Why may dual pricing be the optimum solution for establishing transfer prices?

17. What happens to any fictitious profit that is developed using dual pricing?

18. Why is some conflict of interest inherent in almost any transfer pricing system?

19. In preparing consolidated financial statements, how are intradivisional sales treated?

20. Of what use is an Inventory Adjustment account? Does this account affect the division income for each segment?

EXERCISES

E24–1. Transfer pricing to provide normal return

Division A of the Diamond Company manufactures motors which are used by other divisions of the company and which are also sold to outside customers. Division B of Diamond Company has requested that Division A supply a certain style of motor, and Division A has computed a proposed transfer price on this motor, as follows:

	Per 800 motors
Variable cost	$35
Fixed cost	25
	$60
Mark-on on full cost to provide a normal return	6
Transfer price	$66

Management of Division B believes this transfer price is too high because it knows that this style of motor is sold to outside customers for $62 per 800 motors. Management of Division A indicates that it is forced to lower the price below $66 to meet competition. Even though it cannot earn a normal return from outside customers, it feels that Division B should pay for this return.

Required:

Explain what you believe the transfer price should be.

E24–2. Conditions conducive to transfers

The Motor Division of French Company produces components that the Fabricating Division incorporates into a final product. Components from the Motor Division can also be sold to outsiders. Each division has been established as a separate profit center. Data gathered from records of both segments reveal the following:

Market price—final product	$600
Market price—components	300
Motor Division—variable cost	170
Fabricating Division—variable completion cost	375

Required:

a. Under what conditions should transfers be made to the Fabricating Division? Support your answer with a quantitative analysis.

b. Assuming the conditions that you suggested in *a* exist, at what price do you think transfers should be made?

E24–3. Rejection of outside order

At practical capacity, the Fabricating Division of Crossville Company has facilities to produce 8,000 units per month. Each unit requires five direct labor-hours. The Assembly Division of the company has forwarded a requisition for 8,000 units to the Fabricating Division. Since Crossville Company uses a market-based transfer pricing system, contribution margin using a $50 market price would be $168,000. The receipt of this requisition from the Assembly Division upset the Fabricating Division manager as he had just been approached by an outside buyer with a rush order for 5,000 units at a $56 unit sale price.

Top management's initial reaction to the conflict is that the outside order should be rejected so that the Assembly Division's order can be filled.

Required:

a. Determine how the income of the Fabricating Division and Crossville Company will be affected if the outside order is rejected.
b. List four additional factors that should be known before a final decision is made.

E24–4. Sales to company division

Owens Company is a producer of various kinds of pumps. After recently acquiring a home appliance assembly company, management wonders whether they should establish two autonomous divisions. Presently, the appliance company is purchasing 1,500 pumps a month at $40 per pump from an outsider, who gives the company a 10 percent quantity discount.

The Pump Division supplies you with the following costs per pump:

Direct materials	$16
Direct labor	10
Variable factory overhead	2
Fixed factory overhead, based on 3,600	
pumps (normal capacity) per month	4
	$32

The Pump Division presently sells 2,100 pumps of this line with a 25 percent markup on cost. No quantity discount is given by the Pump Division.

Required:

a. Would you advise the Pump Division to sell to the Appliance Division? If so, at what transfer price?
b. Assume, instead, that the Pump Division presently sells 3,600 pumps to outsiders. Under these conditions, should the Pump Division sell to the Appliance Division? If so, at what transfer price?
c. Disregard your answers above and assume that presently the Pump Division sells 2,100 pumps to outsiders and the Appliance Division manager offers to purchase 1,500 pumps a month for $30 each. What decision should each make? Why?

E24–5. Transfer prices and desired R.O.A.C.

The cost accountant for the Mischke Company provides you with the following data for the Tire Division:

Division assets
Cash . . . . $ 100,000
Inventories   250,000
Plant assets, net   1,150,000
                                                                          $1,500,000

                                                                                 Per
                                                                                unit
Variable costs $10
Fixed costs (based on normal volume
   of 40,000 tires)   5

She also informs you that 5,000 of the 40,000 tires are usually sold to the Motorcycle Division of the company. Currently, the two division managers cannot agree on the price at which these tires should be transferred. The Motorcycle Division manager has offered to pay $14, claiming he can purchase these tires from another company at that price. The Tire Division manager feels that the Motorcycle Division should pay the same price as the other customers, $18.

Analysis shows that the Tire Division can eliminate $5,000 of inventories, $10,000 in plant assets, and $20,000 in cash fixed costs if the manager does not sell to the Motorcycle Division. The assets can be converted into cash.

Required:

a. Should the Tire Division sell to the Motorcycle Division at a transfer price of $14?
b. Assuming that top management decides that the tires will be sold to the Motorcycle Division at a $14 transfer price, at what price must the 35,000 tires be sold to outsiders to achieve a 15 percent desired return on assets employed?

E24–6.   Short-run economic advantage of interdivisional sales

The Northern Division of Kremer Company requests that the Southern Division supply it with B62 motors. Southern Division presently operates at capacity and sells motors to outside customers at $15 each. The variable costs of these motors produced by the Southern Division is $9.

Northern Division, operating at 70 percent of capacity because it cannot secure enough motors, is willing to pay $12 for each one. The cost of the finished product as it is being built by the Northern Division is as follows, based on normal capacity:

Motor $12.00
Other purchased parts 1.00
Other variable costs 4.80
Fixed factory overhead, marketing, and
   administrative expense 7.00
            Total $24.80

Kremer Company uses dollar net income and return on investment in measuring division performance.

Required:

a. Ignoring income tax, should the Northern Division be supplied motors by the Southern Division?
b. Ignoring income tax, discuss the short-run economic advantage per unit for the Kremer Company if the Southern Division supplies motors at $12 each to the Northern Division.

c.   In view of the present organizational structure and long-run economic profits, what recommendation would you make to Kremer top management regarding the transfer?

E24–7.   Choice of transfer price (CIA adapted)

A large, diversified corporation operates its divisions on a decentralized basis. Division A makes Product X, which can be sold either to Division B or to outside customers.

At current levels of production, the variable cost of making Product X is $1.50 per unit, the fixed cost is $0.30, and the market price is $2.75 per unit.

Division B processes Product X into Product Y. The additional variable cost of producing Product Y is $1 per unit.

Top management is developing a corporate transfer pricing policy. The following bases for setting transfer prices are being reviewed: full cost; variable cost; and market price.

Required:

a.   To avoid waste and maximize efficiency up to the transfer point, which of the transfer price bases being reviewed should be used and why?
b.   Which of the transfer price bases in the short run would tend to encourage the best utilization of the corporation's productive capacity? Why would this not be true in the long run?
c.   Identify *two* possible advantages which Division B might expect if it purchased Product X from Division A at the current market price.
d.   What possible disadvantage might accrue to Division A if it was committed to sell all of its production of X to Division B at the current market price?

E24–8.   Differential cost per unit and desired R.O.A.C.

A division of Neale Equipment Company manufactures motors exclusively for the Assembly Division. Annual sales and production volume is 5,000 units, which represents normal capacity. All unit fixed costs are based on normal capacity. Analysis of the records revealed the following unit cost.

	Per motor
Direct material	$10
Direct labor	5
Variable overhead	7
Traceable fixed overhead	12
Allocated fixed overhead	4
Variable marketing expense	6
	$44
Assets committed	$300,000

If the Motor Division were discontinued, $10,000 of the annual traceable fixed costs could be eliminated.

Required:

a.   Determine the differential cost per motor.
b.   Assuming that 2,000 motors are transferred to the Assembly Division at a transfer price based on the differential cost determined in *a*, at what price must the other

3,000 motors be sold to outsiders to earn a 10 percent desired return on assets employed?

PROBLEMS

P24–1. Recommendations regarding transfer prices

Outland Division's budget for next year for a special wheel based on a volume of 40,000 units is as follows:

Direct material.	$ 134,400
Direct labor.	112,000
Factory overhead—variable	56,000
Factory overhead—fixed	210,000
Marketing expense	38,000
Administrative expense	82,000
	$ 632,400

Of the fixed factory overhead, $60,000 represents allocated joint costs. Management's analysis shows that shipping and handling expense, which is included in the marketing expense, amounts to $0.65 per unit; the remainder is division fixed expense. The division manager's salary of $30,000 is included in administrative expenses. This represents the only expense that could be eliminated, since the other components are allocated home office expense.

Required:

a. What is the segment cost per unit?
b. If Outland Division has no market for its wheels except for inside sales to other divisions and is not operating at normal capacity, what should the transfer price be?
c. If buying divisions within the company are able to purchase wheels at a price of $17.50 less an 8 percent discount from outside suppliers, what transfer price should be used?
d. Assuming instead that Outland Division can sell all its production to outsiders for $18, what transfer price would you recommend?

P24–2. Segment margin for divisions

Lula Gray Grogan Cosmetics Company manufactures pressed powder in compacts. The manufacturing process is a series of mixing operations with various coloring ingredients added to obtain specified shades. The powder is then pressed in a company-produced compact and packed in cases containing 24 compacts.

Grogan Cosmetics feels that the sale of its product is heavily influenced by the highly decorated compact which contains the powder. Much advertising has stressed the uniqueness of the compact's decorative style.

The company has organized its process into two divisions: the powder process and compact production. Each division is supervised by a plant superintendent, with supervisors of the various cost centers reporting to the plant superintendent. All compact production has been used by the powder division. Little interchange of management ideas or personnel takes place between the two divisions, which is unfortunate because this has been a factor causing intense rivalry to develop between the divisions. Top management feels that their decision several years ago to establish each division as a profit center may have also contributed to the rivalry. Each plant superintendent receives a commission based on the net income generated by the division.

You have just been asked to determine a proper transfer price for the compact division to use in charging the powder profit center. The compact plant superintendent informs you that cost studies have determined variable costs are $11 per case, while total annual fixed costs are $1 million. An outside compact production company has contacted the company president and supplied the following price quotations:

Volume (in cases)	Price per case
250,000	$18
500,000	16
750,000	13

Top management has reviewed the reliability of the outside supplier and is confident that a compact identical in quality to that of the Compact Division can be supplied.

In addition to the compact costs, the Powder Division has the following costs. The sales price for the finished product is also given below, which reflects the price-demand relationship.

Volume (in cases)	Powder cost per case	Sales price per case
250,000	$19	$60
500,000	18	54
750,000	16	48

The current market value is presently used as the transfer price.

Required:

a. Determine the segment margin for each division and income for the overall company at a volume of 500,000 cases.
b. Determine the volume that would be most profitable for each division and the overall company.
c. What conditions should exist for a division to be established as a profit center?
d. Should the Compact and Powder Divisions be organized as profit centers?
e. Indicate two other transfer pricing methods that could be used, and show what the price would be at the various volume levels.

P24–3. Evaluating various transfer prices

The Battery Division of the Herndon Company supplies batteries to outside customers at a price of $100 per 100 batteries. The company has just acquired a flashlight company and the president believes the newly acquired Flashlight Division should purchase batteries from the company's own Battery Division, even though the latter now has all the outside orders it can process.

Until the acquisition, the flashlight company had purchased batteries for $95 per 100 batteries.

The Battery Division's cost per lot of 100 batteries is presented below:

```
Direct material . . . . . . . . . . . . . . . . . . . . . . . . . . . . . . . . . . . . . . . . . . . . . $30
Direct labor . . . . . . . . . . . . . . . . . . . . . . . . . . . . . . . . . . . . . . . . . . . . . . .   18
Variable overhead. . . . . . . . . . . . . . . . . . . . . . . . . . . . . . . . . . . . . . . . . .      17
Fixed overhead (now operating at a 1 million
    battery lots level). . . . . . . . . . . . . . . . . . . . . . . . . . . . . . . . . . . . . . . . .    10
            Total cost . . . . . . . . . . . . . . . . . . . . . . . . . . . . . . . . . . . . . . . . . . $75
```

Herndon Company management is undecided as to the transfer price for sales between the two divisions.

Required:

a. Explain why each of the following transfer prices would or would not be appropriate to charge the Flashlight Division on the intracompany sales:
   (1) $60   (4) $80
   (2) $65   (5) $95
   (3) $75   (6) $100

b. Assume, instead, that the Battery Division has excess capacity. In view of this changed condition, explain why or why not each of the transfer prices in *a* would be appropriate to charge the Flashlight Division.

P24–4.   Profitable volume for decentralized organization

Emma's Deodorant Company was organized several years ago as a manufacturer of both men's and women's deodorant. When the company was first organized, the deodorant was sold as a paste in a "Plain Jane" jar. When one of the supervisors developed a roll-on bottle, sales skyrocketed. It was so successful that Emma's management decided to set up two divisions: a Manufacturing Division and a division to make bottles. Competition between the two divisions has become quite intense, because each of the division managers receives a bonus based on the center's contribution margin.

The president is quite concerned that the transfer price used is not fair and has called you in as a consultant to evaluate the circumstances. One of your first projects is to determine the costs of each division in addition to the prices charged by competitive bottle companies. Your findings are as follows:

Quantity	Bottle division's cost per case	Average competitor's sales price per case
1,000,000 cases	$10.00	$12.00
4,000,000 cases	9.50	11.00
8,000,000 cases	9.10	10.50

The Manufacturing Division's costs of ingredients are as follows:

Quantity	Cost per case	Sales price per case for finished product packaged
1,000,000 cases	$25.00	$45.00
4,000,000 cases	23.40	43.60
8,000,000 cases	22.60	41.80

Required:

a. Evaulate the success of decentralizing the divisions.
b. If the market price is used as the transfer price, calculate the income for each division and for the overall organization using a volume of 1 million cases, 4 million cases, and 8 million cases.
c. What is the most profitable volume for each of the divisions and for the overall company?

P24–5. Cost plus markup transfer price and variance analysis

Warship Company has two decentralized divisions known simply as the Buying and Selling Divisions. Each division is treated as a profit center, even though products of the Selling Division are presently only sold internally. A change in the transfer pricing method is being considered, with the price determined by adding a 15 percent markup to the standard cost per unit. Budgets for various outputs of the Selling Division are as follows:

Hours.	80,000	85,000	90,000	95,000
Units	40,000	42,500	45,000	47,500
Direct material	$224,000	$238,000	$252,000	$266,000
Direct labor	448,000	476,000	504,000	532,000
Overhead:				
Indirect labor	150,000	152,100	153,600	154,800
Utilities	153,250	158,000	160,800	163,000
Supplies	11,500	12,500	13,500	14,500
Rent	110,100	110,100	110,100	110,100
	$1,096,850	$1,146,700	$1,194,000	$1,240,400

Required:

a. Calculate the transfer price per unit under the proposed plan.
b. Determine overhead variances using the four-variance method, assuming actual variable overhead is $105,720 and fixed overhead is $332,000 at an output of 42,400 units and 86,000 hours. Indicate who should be held responsible for each of these variances.
c. With actual direct material of $230,000 and actual direct labor of $475,000, compute the Selling Division's income using the information given in *b*. Should the Selling Division's performance be evaluated on this income?

P24–6. Comparison of gross margin using different transfer prices

The Cathode Ray Tube Division of Emmett Company sells various styles of tubes to outsiders. Recently, an engineer for Emmett Company's newly acquired toy company has developed a unique idea for a television game employing a cathode ray tube.

The Tube Division presently produces and sells 120,000 tubes of this style for $140. The plant has an annual capacity of 150,000 tubes with a variable cost of $80. Fixed cost related to this style amount to $3.6 million per year.

The Toy Division plans to sell the television game for $350 and has received offers from outside companies to supply the tubes needed for $125. Total variable cost per game amounts to $155. Fixed costs for 30,000 games assembled per year amount to $3 million.

The Tube Division offers to supply the Toy Division with the style of tubes needed for $140; however, the Toy Division manager wants to refuse the offer. Top management asks for your recommendations.

Required:

Compare the gross margin for both divisions and the total company if tubes are purchased outside with a pricing system based on cost, assuming a production level of 150,000 tubes.

P24–7.   Decentralization in a CPA firm

The firm of Myrtle Douglass, CPA has prepared the following budgets for its three groups. The firm has recently been organized into three independent groups, with each group providing services to outside clients as well as to other groups within the firm. The fees budgeted are representative of those of other CPA firms in the geographical area.

	Tax group	Auditing group	Management services group
Budgeted consulting hours	10,000	16,000	12,000
Fees.	$450,000	$960,000	$780,000
Variable cost.	280,000	720,000	456,000
Fixed cost	50,000	96,000	60,000

The firm asks your advice in evaluating each group as if it were an autonomous company.

Required:

a.   Assume that the auditing group has need for tax consulting services. The tax accountants are busy preparing tax returns to meet approaching deadlines. What transfer price should be charged the auditing group?

b.   Use the conditions given in *a* but assume that the services are needed during the summer months when the tax accountants are less rushed and have fewer deadlines to meet. If the tax accountants did not perform this work, they would be spending time catching up on their professional reading. What transfer price should now be charged to the auditing group?

c.   Assume that a former employee of the firm started her own tax practice and, to acquire clients, charges $35 per hour. The auditing group needs some tax analysis that would become part of the audit. Since the company's own tax group has adequate opportunity to use its time with outside clients, would you advise the auditing group to go outside the firm? What nonfinancial factors must be considered?

d.   In view of the characteristics of this firm and its employees, do you think the three groups should be established as autonomous companies?

P24–8.   Evaluating the merits of transfer pricing positions

The Kentucky Division of the Kenneth Grogan Company manufactures and distributes a wide range of industrial pumps. This division sells pumps at $10 to the Texas Division of the company, which uses the pumps in the manufacture of washing machines. Pumps of this type are also sold for $12 to outside customers.

The Texas Division manager complained that pumps similar to the ones being purchased from the Kentucky Division can be bought from an outside supplier for $9. As a result, the Texas Division manager argues that the maximum he should pay is $9.

When the Kentucky Division manager is confronted with the issue, she refuses to meet this price on the basis that it is less than costs. She provides the Texas Division with the following previous year's actual product line income statement in support of the position that a $9 transfer price would be lower than her cost of $10.50.

Sales—outside (50,000 × $12)	$600,000
Sales—Texas Division (10,000 @ $10)	100,000
Total sales	700,000
Direct materials	180,000
Direct labor	90,000
Variable factory overhead	120,000
Fixed factory overhead	180,000
	570,000
Segment margin	130,000
Allocated indirect fixed costs	60,000
Net profit before taxes	$ 70,000

$$\text{Cost per pump: } \frac{\$630,000}{60,000} = \$10.50$$

Required:

a. As controller of the Texas Division, you are asked to draft a letter to the top management of Kenneth Grogan Company explaining your position in support of the proposed $9 price.

b. As top management, evaluate the merits of the arguments supplied by the controller.

P24–9.   Transfer price reduction (CMA adapted)

National Industries is a diversified corporation with separate and distinct operating divisions. Each divisions' performance is evaluated on the basis of total dollar profits and return on division investment.

The WindAir Division manufactures and sells air conditioner units. The coming year's budgeted income statement, based upon a sales volume of 15,000 units, appears below.

WINDAIR DIVISION
Budgeted Income Statement
For the Next Fiscal Year

	Per unit	Total (000)
Sales revenue	$400	$6,000
Manufacturing costs:		
Compressor	70	1,050
Other direct materials	37	555
Direct labor	30	450
Variable overhead	45	675
Fixed overhead	32	480
Total manufacturing costs	$214	$3,210
Gross margin	$186	$2,790
Operating expenses:		
Variable selling	18	270
Fixed selling	19	285
Fixed administrative	38	570
Total operating expenses	75	1,125
Net income before taxes	$111	$1,665

WindAir's division manager believes sales can be increased if the unit selling price of the air conditioners is reduced. A market research study conducted by an independent firm at the request of the manager indicates that a 5 percent reduction in the selling price ($20) would increase sales volume 16 percent or 2,400 units. WindAir has sufficient production capacity to manage this increased volume with no increase in fixed costs.

At the present time, WindAir uses a compressor in its units which it purchases from an outside supplier at a cost of $70 per compressor. The division manager of WindAir has approached the manager of the Compressor Division regarding the sale of a compressor unit to WindAir. The Compressor Division currently manufactures and sells exclusively to outside firms a unit which is similar to the unit used by WindAir. The specifications of the WindAir compressor are slightly different, which would reduce the Compressor Division's direct material cost by $1.50 per unit. In addition, the Compressor Division would not incur any variable selling costs in the units sold to WindAir. The manager of WindAir wants all of the compressors it uses to come from one supplier and has offered to pay $50 for each compressor unit.

The Compressor Division has the capacity to produce 75,000 units. The coming year's budgeted income statement for the Compressor Division is shown below and is based upon a sales volume of 64,000 units without considering WindAir's proposal.

COMPRESSOR DIVISION
Budgeted Income Statement
For the Next Fiscal Year

	Per unit	Total (000)
Sales revenue.	$100	$6,400
Manufacturing costs:		
Direct materials	12	768
Direct labor	8	512
Variable overhead	10	640
Fixed overhead	11	704
Total manufacturing costs	$ 41	$2,624
Gross margin	$ 59	$3,776
Operating expenses:		
Variable selling	6	384
Fixed selling	4	256
Fixed administrative	7	448
Total operating expenses.	17	1,088
Net income before taxes	$ 42	$2,688

Required:

a. Should WindAir Division institute the 5 percent price reduction on its air conditioner units even if it cannot acquire the compressors internally for $50 each? Support your conclusion with appropriate calculations.

b. Without prejudice to your answer in *a*, assume WindAir needs 17,400 units. Should the Compressor Division be willing to supply the compressor units for $50 each? Support your conclusions with appropriate calculations.

c. Without prejudice to your answer in *a*, assume WindAir needs 17,400 units. Would it be in the best interest of National Industries for the Compressor Division to supply the compressor units at $50 each to the WindAir Division? Support your conclusions with appropriate calculations.

CASES

C24–1. Conflict in pricing quotes

Robert Bingham, Inc. manufactures force pumps for water wells and fire engines. Force pumps resemble lift pumps which are the simplest type of reciprocating pump and are used to pump water from wells. However, force pumps discharge water at high pressure instead of merely lifting the water out. Force pumps are generally run by mechanical power rather than by hand.

Bingham has three divisions, each specializing in various components of the pump. Sales of these components are also made to outsiders. The Southern Division produces the piston and valve; the Northern Division, the pump handles that attach to the piston, and the Western Division, the cylinder and outside container.

Bingham, Inc. is highly decentralized, with each division being judged independently as a profit center. Profit and return on investment are used to evaluate each division manager. Top management believes that in the past five years while this decentralized policy has been in force, profits have improved. Each division manager is normally free to buy from whichever supplier he or she desires. For sales within the company, divisions are expected to meet the current market price.

Mr. Weston, the Western Division manager, has completed the design of a special water well for leisure-home owners. Such wells are smaller than those for residential homes and are less expensive. After requesting bids for 1,000 completed pistons valves, the following bids per completed unit were received: Southern Division—$500; Outboard Company—$400; Exxel Company—$425. The Southern Division had received an agreement from the Northern Division to supply pump handles at the present market price of $100 per unit. The Northern Division presently is operating at full capacity and does not have excess inventory; however, the Northern Division has agreed to sell the needed handles to Southern rather than to outside customers. The differential cost of pump handles is $65.

Ms. Smith, the division manager of the Southern Division, indicates that she cannot quote a unit price lower than $500 because she must cover full cost as well as give her division some profit for their efforts. She provides further support for her position by arguing that her salespeople have been told they must cover full costs in all price quotes. An analysis of the accounting records reveals that the differential cost of each completed piston and valve is $375. Of this amount, 30 percent represents the cost of the pump handles.

In the Exxel Company bid, there was an agreement to buy certain unassembled parts from both the Southern and Northern Divisions. The price agreed to with Southern for a portion of the valve is $50 each part. Exxel agreed to purchase 1,000 hand grips parts from the Northern Division for $70 each. The unit differential cost of Southern's valve is $20, and it is $30 for Northern's hand-grip part.

Weston is quite annoyed that Southern's price quote is so much higher than the competitors' quotes. He calls the controller at corporate headquarters for advice. Weston indicates that unless told otherwise, he plans to accept the lowest bid.

The controller is concerned that Smith has submitted such a high bid in view of the recent slack in work experienced by her division. However, the controller also knows that intervention by top management must be carefully handled because a precedent may be established that could raise similar problems later.

Required:

You may find it useful to diagram the alternatives with the respective prices and differential costs.

a. Regarding this order, provide support indicating the most profitable action for:
   (1) The Western Division.
   (2) Bingham, Inc.
b. Should the controller instruct Western to buy from Southern? If so, at what price?
c. If the controller intervenes in this situation, what will the effect be on:
   (1) The division profit measurement system?
   (2) Outside firms?
d. Should the controller ask Northern to lower its bid of $100 to Southern? Why or why not?
e. If Southern had idle capacity for several months, how would your answer be affected?
f. Discuss the impact on the situation if division managers receive a bonus based on division profits.

C24–2. Solving a transfer pricing problem (CMA adapted)

MBR, Inc. consists of three divisions which formerly were three independent manufacturing companies. Bader Corporation and Roach Company merged in 19X1 and the merged corporation acquired Mitchell Company in 19X2. The name of the corporation was subsequently changed to MBR, Inc., and each company became a separate division retaining its former name.

The three divisions have operated as if they were still independent companies. Each division has its own sales force and production facilities. Each division's management is responsible for sales, cost of operations, acquisition and financing of divisional assets, and working capital management. The corporate management of MBR evaluates the performance of the divisions and division managements on the basis of return on investment.

Mitchell Division has just been awarded a contract for a product which uses a component that is manufactured by the Roach Division as well as by outside suppliers. Mitchell used a cost figure of $3.80 for the component manufactured by Roach in preparing its bid for the new product. This cost figure was supplied by Roach in response to Mitchell's request for the average variable cost of the component and represents the standard variable manufacturing cost and variable selling and distribution expense.

Roach has an active sales force that is continually contacting new prospects. Roach's regular selling price for the component Mitchell needs for the new product is $6.50. Sales of this component are expected to increase. However, Roach management has indicated that it could supply Mitchell with the required quantities of the component at the regular selling price less variable selling and distribution expenses. Mitchell's management has responded by offering to pay standard variable manufacturing cost plus 20 percent.

The two divisions have been unable to agree on a transfer price. Corporate management has never established a transfer price policy because interdivisional transactions have never occurred. As a compromise, the corporate Vice President of Finance has suggested a price equal to the standard full manufacturing cost (i.e., no selling and distribution expenses) plus a 15 percent markup. This price has also been rejected by the two division managers, because each considered it grossly unfair.

The unit cost structure for the Roach component and the three suggested prices are shown below.

Regular selling price.	$6.50
Standard variable manufacturing cost	$3.20
Standard fixed manufacturing cost	1.20
Variable selling and distribution expenses	.60
	$5.00
Regular selling price less variable selling	
and distribution expenses ($6.50 − .60).	$5.90
Variable manufacturing plus 20%	
($3.20 × 1.20)	$3.84
Standard full manufacturing cost	
plus 15% ($4.40 × 1.15)	$5.06

Required:

a.   Discuss the effect each of the three proposed prices might have on the Roach division management's attitude toward intracompany business.

b.   Is the negotiation of a price between the Mitchell and Roach Divisions a satisfactory method of solving the transfer price problem? Explain your answer.

c.   Should the corporate management of MBR, Inc. become involved in this transfer price controversy? Explain your answer.

C24–3.   Internal competition and transfer pricing

Determining a transfer price to charge the production department for packaging is a recurring problem at Bonner Paper Supplies. Bonner is a leading producer of paper products which are packaged in varying numbers of sheets. Some of the products require the insertion of holes for use in notebooks. The packaging department is required to perform this hole cutting.

Being firmly convinced of the advantages of a standard cost system, the company had established, through the engineering department, detailed standards for each of its manufacturing operations. A standard cost system was introduced and department heads were given the responsibility of earning income for their own departments, as each cost center constituted a separate business within the company.

To further the department managers' interest and create internal competition, an income sharing plan was adopted in which department managers receive a percent of their segments' net income. The production department was allowed to place orders with competing firms should the company's own packaging department fail to meet competitive costs. Due to the company's location, there are a number of local competitors which have facilities to do the required packaging.

Management feels that internal competition is healthy, since department managers will be too certain of a market for their production if the company does not allow external purchases. They feel this certainty is not conducive to effective cost control.

Management has established the policy that internal procurement is expected when the company's product is superior or equal in quality and performance to the competition's, assuming an acceptable delivery schedule can be met. If the internal source of supply is not competitive, management has the policy that outside purchases may be made as long as the receiving department can justify its action. In justifying purchasing outside, the department should supply evidence that a reasonable effort was made to bring the internal supplier's terms into competition with those of the outside source.

The company has received and is filling a special order. When the first roll of paper was produced, the company's own Packaging Department was requested to cut the paper to a customer's specification and insert the required holes. The sheets were then bundled 500 sheets to a package. The cost of packaging by the company's own department was $160, as shown below:

Packaging Department—Cost Estimates
(10,000 packages)

	Standard cost per 100 packages
Packaging material	$ 20.00
Packaging labor (4 hours)	30.00
Overhead—40% fixed ($25 burden rate per direct labor-hour)	100.00
Income to packaging department.	10.00
	$160.00

The supervisor of the production department felt that this cost was excessive and began contacting competitors for bids when the customer forwarded a second order for 10,000 packages. One competitor, Brown Paper Products, offered to package the paper and perform the necessary hole cutting and paper cutting at $130 per 100 packages, delivered. Given these conditions, the production manager has an incentive to have the packaging performed outside, which will result in what he believes will be a $30 savings.

Required:

a. What do you think about the desirability of an income sharing bonus to encourage internal competition?
b. Can you see any advantage to keeping the work within the company?
c. Should the company's own packaging department receive any departmental income?
d. What price do you think the packaging department should quote for the packaging job?
e. What is the minimum amount the company's own packaging department should be paid?
f. If you were the supervisor of the production department, what action would you take?

After investigating the correct transfer pricing method to use, accountants determine the following:

The selling price per 100 packages, cut to customer's specifications with the required holes punched	$170
The selling price of the paper, not cut, but processed in rolls.	100
The cost of the paper processing:	
Material.	$ 20
Labor	10
Overhead (40% fixed)	10
	$ 40

g. Why would the packaging department supervisor suggest that the paper be packaged by the company? What contribution to income does the manager see if the transfer price is based on variable cost?

h. Do you agree? What would you suggest that the company do?

C24–4. Alternative transfer price system (CMA adapted)

PortCo Products is a furniture manufacturer with autonomous divisions, each responsible for sales, costs of operations, working capital management, and equipment acquisition. Each division serves a different market in the furniture industry. Because the markets and products of the divisions are so different, there have never been any transfers between divisions.

The Commercial Division manufactures equipment and furniture that is purchased by the restaurant industry. The division plans to introduce a new line of counter and chair units which feature a cushioned seat for the counter chairs. John Kline, the Division Manager, has discussed the manufacturing of the cushioned seat with Judy Fiegel of the Office Division. They both believe a cushioned seat currently made by the Office Division for use on its deluxe office stool could be modified for use on the new counter chair. Consequently, Kline has asked Fiegel for a price for 100-unit lots of the cushioned seat. The following is a conversation about the price to be charged for the cushioned seats:

Fiegel: John, we can make the necessary modifications to the cushioned seat easily. The raw materials used in your seat are slightly different and should cost about 10 percent more than those used in our deluxe office stool. However, the labor time should be the same because the seat fabrication operation basically is the same. I would price the seat at our regular rate—full cost plus 30 percent markup.

Kline: That's higher than I expected, Judy. I was thinking that a good price would be your variable manufacturing costs. After all, your capacity costs will be incurred regardless of this job.

Fiegel: John, I'm at capacity. By making the cushion seats for you, I'll have to cut my production of deluxe office stools. Of course, I can increase my production of economy office stools. The labor time freed by not having to fabricate the frame or assemble the deluxe stool can be shifted to the frame fabrication and assembly of the economy office stool. Fortunately, I can switch my labor force between these two models of stools without any loss of efficiency. As you know, overtime is not a feasible alternative in our community. I'd like to sell it to you at variable cost, but I have excess demand for both products. I don't mind changing my product mix to the economy model if I get a good return on the seats I make for you. Here are my standard costs for the two stools and a schedule of my manufacturing overhead. [See page 952 for standard costs and for overhead schedule]

Kline: I guess I see your point, Judy, but I don't want to price myself out of the market. Maybe we should talk to corporate to see if they can give us any guidance.

OFFICE DIVISION
Standard Costs and Prices

	Deluxe office stool		Economy office stool	
Direct materials:				
Framing.	$ 8.15			$ 9.76
Cushioned seat:				
Padding.	2.40			—
Vinyl	4.00			—
Molded seat				
(purchased).	—			6.00
Direct labor:				
Frame fabrication (.5 × $7.50/DLH)*	3.75	(.5 × $7.50/DLH)*		3.75
Cushion fabrication (.5 × $7.50/DLH)*	3.75			—
Assembly† (.5 × $7.50/DLH)*	3.75	(.3 × $7.50/DLH)*		2.25
Manufacturing overhead				
(1.5DLH × $12.80/DLH)	19.20	(.8DLH × $12.80/DLH)		10.24
Total standard cost	$45.00			$32.00
Selling price				
(30% markup).	$58.50			$41.60

*DLH = direct labor-hours.
†Attaching seats to frames and attaching rubber feet.

OFFICE DIVISION
Manufacturing Overhead Budget

Overhead item	Nature	Amount
Supplies	Variable—at current market prices	$ 420,000
Indirect labor	Variable	375,000
Supervision.	Nonvariable	250,000
Power.	Use varies with activity: rates are fixed	180,000
Heat and light	Nonvariable—light is fixed regardless of production while heat/ air conditioning varies with fuel charges	140,000
Property taxes and insurance taxes	Nonvariable—any change in amounts/ rates is independent of production	200,000
Depreciation	Fixed dollar total	1,700,000
Employee benefits.	20% of supervision, direct and indirect labor	575,000
	Total overhead	$3,840,000
	Capacity in direct labor-hours	300,000
	Overhead rate/ direct labor-hours	$12.80

Required:

Using the information in the table, determine the following:

a. John Kline and Judy Fiegel did ask PortCo corporate management for guidance on an appropriate transfer price. Corporate management suggested they consider using a transfer price based on variable manufacturing cost plus opportunity cost. Calculate a transfer price for the cushioned seat based upon variable manufacturing cost plus opportunity cost.

b. Which alternative transfer price system—full cost, variable manufacturing cost, or variable manufacturing cost plus opportunity cost—would be better as the underlying concept for an intracompany transfer price policy? Explain your answer.

APPENDIXES

APPENDIX A: PRESENT VALUE TABLES

Table A: Present value of $1

Years Hence	1%	2%	4%	6%	8%	10%	12%	14%	15%	16%	18%	20%	22%	24%	25%	26%	28%	30%	35%	40%	45%	50%
1	0.990	0.980	0.962	0.943	0.926	0.909	0.893	0.877	0.870	0.862	0.847	0.833	0.820	0.806	0.800	0.794	0.781	0.769	0.741	0.714	0.690	0.667
2	0.980	0.961	0.925	0.890	0.857	0.826	0.797	0.769	0.756	0.743	0.718	0.694	0.672	0.650	0.640	0.630	0.610	0.592	0.549	0.510	0.476	0.444
3	0.971	0.942	0.889	0.840	0.794	0.751	0.712	0.675	0.658	0.641	0.609	0.579	0.551	0.524	0.512	0.500	0.477	0.455	0.406	0.364	0.328	0.296
4	0.961	0.924	0.855	0.792	0.735	0.683	0.636	0.592	0.572	0.552	0.516	0.482	0.451	0.423	0.410	0.397	0.373	0.350	0.301	0.260	0.226	0.198
5	0.951	0.906	0.822	0.747	0.681	0.621	0.567	0.519	0.497	0.476	0.437	0.402	0.370	0.341	0.328	0.315	0.291	0.269	0.223	0.186	0.156	0.132
6	0.942	0.888	0.790	0.705	0.630	0.564	0.507	0.456	0.432	0.410	0.370	0.335	0.303	0.275	0.262	0.250	0.227	0.207	0.165	0.133	0.108	0.088
7	0.933	0.871	0.760	0.665	0.583	0.513	0.452	0.400	0.376	0.354	0.314	0.279	0.249	0.222	0.210	0.198	0.178	0.159	0.122	0.095	0.074	0.059
8	0.923	0.853	0.731	0.627	0.540	0.467	0.404	0.351	0.327	0.305	0.266	0.233	0.204	0.179	0.168	0.157	0.139	0.123	0.091	0.068	0.051	0.039
9	0.914	0.837	0.703	0.592	0.500	0.424	0.361	0.308	0.284	0.263	0.225	0.194	0.167	0.144	0.134	0.125	0.108	0.094	0.067	0.048	0.035	0.026
10	0.905	0.820	0.676	0.558	0.463	0.386	0.322	0.270	0.247	0.227	0.191	0.162	0.137	0.116	0.107	0.099	0.085	0.073	0.050	0.035	0.024	0.017
11	0.896	0.804	0.650	0.527	0.429	0.350	0.287	0.237	0.215	0.195	0.162	0.135	0.112	0.094	0.086	0.079	0.066	0.056	0.037	0.025	0.017	0.012
12	0.887	0.788	0.625	0.497	0.397	0.319	0.257	0.208	0.187	0.168	0.137	0.112	0.092	0.076	0.069	0.062	0.052	0.043	0.027	0.018	0.012	0.008
13	0.879	0.773	0.601	0.469	0.368	0.290	0.229	0.182	0.163	0.145	0.116	0.093	0.075	0.061	0.055	0.050	0.040	0.033	0.020	0.013	0.008	0.005
14	0.870	0.758	0.577	0.442	0.340	0.263	0.205	0.160	0.141	0.125	0.099	0.078	0.062	0.049	0.044	0.039	0.032	0.025	0.015	0.009	0.006	0.003
15	0.861	0.743	0.555	0.417	0.315	0.239	0.183	0.140	0.123	0.108	0.084	0.065	0.051	0.040	0.035	0.031	0.025	0.020	0.011	0.006	0.004	0.002
16	0.853	0.728	0.534	0.394	0.292	0.218	0.163	0.123	0.107	0.093	0.071	0.054	0.042	0.032	0.028	0.025	0.019	0.015	0.008	0.005	0.003	0.002
17	0.844	0.714	0.513	0.371	0.270	0.198	0.146	0.108	0.093	0.080	0.060	0.045	0.034	0.026	0.023	0.020	0.015	0.012	0.006	0.003	0.002	0.001
18	0.836	0.700	0.494	0.350	0.250	0.180	0.130	0.095	0.081	0.069	0.051	0.038	0.028	0.021	0.018	0.016	0.012	0.009	0.005	0.002	0.001	0.001
19	0.828	0.686	0.475	0.331	0.232	0.164	0.116	0.083	0.070	0.060	0.043	0.031	0.023	0.017	0.014	0.012	0.009	0.007	0.003	0.002	0.001	
20	0.820	0.673	0.456	0.312	0.215	0.149	0.104	0.073	0.061	0.051	0.037	0.026	0.019	0.014	0.012	0.010	0.007	0.005	0.002	0.001	0.001	
21	0.811	0.660	0.439	0.294	0.199	0.135	0.093	0.064	0.053	0.044	0.031	0.022	0.015	0.011	0.009	0.008	0.006	0.004	0.002	0.001		
22	0.803	0.647	0.422	0.278	0.184	0.123	0.083	0.056	0.046	0.038	0.026	0.018	0.013	0.009	0.007	0.006	0.004	0.003	0.001	0.001		
23	0.795	0.634	0.406	0.262	0.170	0.112	0.074	0.049	0.040	0.033	0.022	0.015	0.010	0.007	0.006	0.005	0.003	0.002	0.001			
24	0.788	0.622	0.390	0.247	0.158	0.102	0.066	0.043	0.035	0.028	0.019	0.013	0.008	0.006	0.005	0.004	0.003	0.002	0.001			
25	0.780	0.610	0.375	0.233	0.146	0.092	0.059	0.038	0.030	0.024	0.016	0.010	0.007	0.005	0.004	0.003	0.002	0.001	0.001			
26	0.772	0.598	0.361	0.220	0.135	0.084	0.053	0.033	0.026	0.021	0.014	0.009	0.006	0.004	0.003	0.002	0.002	0.001				
27	0.764	0.586	0.347	0.207	0.125	0.076	0.047	0.029	0.023	0.018	0.011	0.007	0.005	0.003	0.002	0.002	0.001	0.001				
28	0.757	0.574	0.333	0.196	0.116	0.069	0.042	0.026	0.020	0.016	0.010	0.006	0.004	0.002	0.002	0.002	0.001	0.001				
29	0.749	0.563	0.321	0.185	0.107	0.063	0.037	0.022	0.017	0.014	0.008	0.005	0.003	0.002	0.002	0.001	0.001	0.001				
30	0.742	0.552	0.308	0.174	0.099	0.057	0.033	0.020	0.015	0.012	0.007	0.004	0.003	0.002	0.001	0.001	0.001	0.001				
40	0.672	0.453	0.208	0.097	0.046	0.022	0.011	0.005	0.004	0.003	0.001	0.001										
50	0.608	0.372	0.141	0.054	0.021	0.009	0.003	0.001	0.001	0.001												

APPENDIX A: PRESENT VALUE TABLES

Table B: Present value of $1 received annually for N years

Years (N)	1%	2%	4%	6%	8%	10%	12%	14%	15%	16%	18%	20%	22%	24%	25%	26%	28%	30%	35%	40%	45%	50%
1	0.990	0.980	0.962	0.943	0.926	0.909	0.893	0.877	0.870	0.862	0.847	0.833	0.820	0.806	0.800	0.794	0.781	0.769	0.741	0.714	0.690	0.667
2	1.970	1.942	1.886	1.833	1.783	1.736	1.690	1.647	1.626	1.605	1.566	1.528	1.492	1.457	1.440	1.424	1.392	1.361	1.289	1.224	1.165	1.111
3	2.941	2.884	2.775	2.673	2.577	2.487	2.402	2.322	2.283	2.246	2.174	2.106	2.042	1.981	1.952	1.923	1.868	1.816	1.696	1.589	1.493	1.407
4	3.902	3.808	3.630	3.465	3.312	3.170	3.037	2.914	2.855	2.798	2.690	2.589	2.494	2.404	2.362	2.320	2.241	2.166	1.997	1.849	1.720	1.605
5	4.853	4.713	4.452	4.212	3.993	3.791	3.605	3.433	3.352	3.274	3.127	2.991	2.864	2.745	2.689	2.635	2.532	2.436	2.220	2.035	1.876	1.737
6	5.795	5.601	5.242	4.917	4.623	4.355	4.111	3.889	3.784	3.685	3.498	3.326	3.167	3.020	2.951	2.885	2.759	2.643	2.385	2.168	1.983	1.824
7	6.728	6.472	6.002	5.582	5.206	4.868	4.564	4.288	4.160	4.039	3.812	3.605	3.416	3.242	3.161	3.083	2.937	2.802	2.508	2.263	2.057	1.883
8	7.652	7.325	6.733	6.210	5.747	5.335	4.968	4.639	4.487	4.344	4.078	3.837	3.619	3.421	3.329	3.241	3.076	2.925	2.598	2.331	2.108	1.922
9	8.566	8.162	7.435	6.802	6.247	5.759	5.328	4.946	4.772	4.607	4.303	4.031	3.786	3.566	3.463	3.366	3.184	3.019	2.665	2.379	2.144	1.948
10	9.471	8.983	8.111	7.360	6.710	6.145	5.650	5.216	5.019	4.833	4.494	4.192	3.923	3.682	3.571	3.465	3.269	3.092	2.715	2.414	2.168	1.965
11	10.368	9.787	8.760	7.887	7.139	6.495	5.937	5.453	5.234	5.029	4.656	4.327	4.035	3.776	3.656	3.544	3.335	3.147	2.757	2.438	2.185	1.977
12	11.255	10.575	9.385	8.384	7.536	6.814	6.194	5.660	5.421	5.197	4.793	4.439	4.127	3.851	3.725	3.606	3.387	3.190	2.779	2.456	2.196	1.985
13	12.114	11.343	9.986	8.853	7.904	7.103	6.424	5.842	5.583	5.342	4.910	4.533	4.203	3.912	3.780	3.656	3.427	3.223	2.799	2.468	2.204	1.990
14	13.004	12.106	10.563	9.295	8.244	7.367	6.628	6.002	5.724	5.468	5.008	4.611	4.265	3.962	3.824	3.695	3.459	3.249	2.814	2.477	2.210	1.993
15	13.865	12.849	11.118	9.712	8.559	7.606	6.811	6.142	5.847	5.575	5.092	4.675	4.315	4.001	3.859	3.726	3.483	3.268	2.825	2.484	2.214	1.995
16	14.718	13.578	11.652	10.106	8.851	7.824	6.974	6.265	5.954	5.669	5.162	4.730	4.357	4.033	3.887	3.751	3.503	3.283	2.834	2.489	2.216	1.997
17	15.562	14.292	12.166	10.477	9.122	8.022	7.120	6.373	6.047	5.749	5.222	4.775	4.391	4.059	3.910	3.771	3.518	3.295	2.840	2.492	2.218	1.998
18	16.398	14.992	12.659	10.828	9.372	8.201	7.250	6.467	6.128	5.818	5.273	4.812	4.419	4.080	3.928	3.786	3.529	3.304	2.844	2.494	2.219	1.999
19	17.226	15.678	13.134	11.158	9.604	8.365	7.366	6.550	6.198	5.877	5.316	4.844	4.442	4.097	3.942	3.799	3.539	3.311	2.848	2.496	2.220	1.999
20	18.046	16.351	13.590	11.470	9.818	8.514	7.469	6.623	6.259	5.929	5.353	4.870	4.460	4.110	3.954	3.808	3.546	3.316	2.850	2.497	2.221	1.999
21	18.857	17.011	14.029	11.764	10.017	8.649	7.562	6.687	6.312	5.973	5.384	4.891	4.476	4.121	3.963	3.816	3.551	3.320	2.852	2.498	2.221	2.000
22	19.660	17.658	14.451	12.042	10.201	8.772	7.645	6.743	6.359	6.011	5.410	4.909	4.488	4.130	3.970	3.822	3.556	3.323	2.853	2.498	2.222	2.000
23	20.456	18.292	14.857	12.303	10.371	8.883	7.718	6.792	6.399	6.044	5.432	4.925	4.499	4.137	3.976	3.827	3.559	3.325	2.854	2.499	2.222	2.000
24	21.243	18.914	15.247	12.550	10.529	8.985	7.784	6.835	6.434	6.073	5.451	4.937	4.507	4.143	3.981	3.831	3.562	3.327	2.855	2.499	2.222	2.000
25	22.023	19.523	15.622	12.783	10.675	9.077	7.843	6.873	6.464	6.097	5.467	4.948	4.514	4.147	3.985	3.834	3.564	3.329	2.856	2.499	2.222	2.000
26	22.795	20.121	15.983	13.003	10.810	9.161	7.896	6.906	6.491	6.118	5.480	4.956	4.520	4.151	3.988	3.837	3.566	3.330	2.856	2.500	2.222	2.000
27	23.560	20.707	16.330	13.211	10.935	9.237	7.943	6.935	6.514	6.136	5.492	4.964	4.524	4.154	3.990	3.839	3.567	3.331	2.856	2.500	2.222	2.000
28	24.316	21.281	16.663	13.406	11.051	9.307	7.984	6.961	6.534	6.152	5.502	4.970	4.528	4.157	3.992	3.840	3.568	3.331	2.857	2.500	2.222	2.000
29	25.066	21.844	16.984	13.591	11.158	9.370	8.022	6.983	6.551	6.166	5.510	4.975	4.531	4.159	3.994	3.841	3.569	3.332	2.857	2.500	2.222	2.000
30	25.808	22.396	17.292	13.765	11.258	9.427	8.055	7.003	6.566	6.177	5.517	4.979	4.534	4.160	3.995	3.842	3.569	3.332	2.857	2.500	2.222	2.000
40	32.835	27.355	19.793	15.046	11.925	9.779	8.244	7.105	6.642	6.234	5.548	4.997	4.544	4.166	3.999	3.846	3.571	3.333	2.857	2.500	2.222	2.000
50	39.196	31.424	21.482	15.762	12.234	9.915	8.304	7.133	6.661	6.246	5.554	4.999	4.545	4.167	4.000	3.846	3.571	3.333	2.857	2.500	2.222	2.000

APPENDIX B: COST ACCOUNTING STANDARDS BOARD

The following are the currently released Cost Accounting Standards. The standards begin with number 400.

400. Definitions of key terms used in Cost Accounting Standards.

401. Consistency in Estimating, Accumulating, and Reporting Costs—Requires that a contractor's practices in estimating costs for a proposal are consistent with the cost accounting practices used in accumulating and reporting costs for the contract. (Discussed in more detail on page 772.)

402. Consistency in Allocating Costs Incurred for the Same Purpose—Requires that each type of cost be allocated only once and on only one basis to any contract or other cost objective. (Discussed in more detail on page 230.)

403. Allocation of Home Office Expenses to Segment—Establishes criteria for allocation of the expenses of a home office to the segments of the organization based on the beneficial or casual relationship between such expenses and the receiving segments. (Discussed in more detail on page 895.)

404. Capitalization of Tangible Assets—Requires that contractors establish and adhere to policies with respect to capitalization of tangible assets. (Discussed in more detail on page 552–53.)

405. Accounting for Unallowable Costs—Establishes guidelines covering costs identified as unallowable and the cost accounting treatment to be accorded these costs. Costs expressly unallowable or mutually agreed to be unallowable, including costs mutually agreed to be unallowable directly associated costs, shall be identified and excluded from any billing, claim, or proposal applicable to a government contract. (Discussed in more detail on page 772–73.)

406. Cost Accounting Period—Provides criteria for the selection of the time periods to be used as cost

accounting periods for contract cost estimating, accumulating, and reporting. The contractor must use the fiscal year as the cost accounting period unless otherwise agreed. (Discussed in more detail on page 773.)

407. Use of Standard Costs for Direct Material and Direct Labor—Provides criteria for these costs and for the accumulation and disposition of variances from standard costs. (Discussed in more detail on page 392–93.)

408. Accounting for Costs of Compensated Personal Absence—Provides principles for the measurement of costs of vacation, sick leave, holidays, and other compensated personal absence, and for the allocation of these costs to cost objectives. (Discussed in more detail on page 156.)

409. Depreciation of Tangible Capital Assets—Provides criteria for assigning costs of tangible capital assets to cost accounting periods and for allocating such costs to cost objectives within such periods in an objective and consistent manner. (Discussed in more detail on page 553.)

410. Allocation of Business Unit General and Administrative Expenses to Final Cost Objectives—Provides principles for the allocation of business unit general and administrative expenses to final cost objectives. (Discussed in more detail on page 230–31.)

411. Accounting for Acquisition Costs of Material—Provides criteria for the accounting of acquisition costs of materials and describes allowable inventory costing methods. (Discussed in more detail on page 106–7.)

412. Cost Accounting Standards for Composition and Measurement of Pension Cost—Provides principles for determining and measuring the pension costs applicable to cost objectives. (Discussed in more detail on page 156–57.)

413. Adjustment and Allocation of Pension Cost—Indicates that actuarial gains and losses should be calculated annually and gives criteria for assigning pension expense to cost accounting periods and for valuing and allocating pension fund assets to business segments. (Discussed in more detail on page 157.)

414. Cost of Money as an Element of the Cost of Facilities Capital—Allows as a contract cost a cost of facilities capital charge determined using an interest rate determined by the Secretary of the Treasury applied to the net book value of tangible capital assets and intangible assets subject to amortization. (Discussed in more detail on page 553–54.)

415. Accounting for the Cost of Deferred Compensation—Provides principles for the measurement of the cost of deferred compensation and the assignment of such cost to cost accounting periods. (Discussed in more detail on page 157.)

416. Accounting for Insurance Costs—Provides criteria for the measurement of insurance costs, the assignment of such costs to cost accounting periods, and their allocation to cost objectives. (Discussed in more detail on page 231.)

417. Cost of Money as an Element of the Cost of Capital Assets Under Construction—Establishes criteria for the measurement of the cost of money attributable to capital assets under construction, fabrication, or development as an element of the cost of those assets. (Discussed in more detail on page 554.)

418.   Allocation of Direct and Indirect Costs—Provides for consistent determination of direct and indirect costs; provides criteria for the accumulation of indirect costs, including service center and overhead costs, in indirect cost pools, and provides guidance in the selection of allocation measures based on the beneficial or causal relationship between an indirect cost pool and cost objectives. (Discussed in more detail on page 231.)

419.   Withdrawn.

420.   Accounting for Independent Research and Development Costs and Bid and Proposal Costs—Provides criteria for the accumulation of independent research and development costs and bid and proposal costs and for the allocation of such costs to cost objectives based on the beneficial or causal relationship between such costs and cost objectives. (Discussed in more detail on page 232.)

Index

This book has been set on the Linotron 606 in 10 and 9 point Caledonia leaded two points. Part and Chapter numbers are in 24 point Caledonia Bold. Part titles are 20 point Caledonia Bold, and Chapter titles are 18 point Caledonia Bold. The trim size is 7½" by 9¼", and the maximum type page area is 34 picas by 47 picas.